FEMINISM IN LITERATURE

A Gale Critical Companion

FEMINISM IN LITERATURE

A Gale Critical Companion

Volume 4: 20th Century, Topics

Foreword by *Amy Hudock, Ph.D.*
University of South Carolina

Jessica Bomarito, Jeffrey W. Hunter, Project Editors

THOMSON
GALE

Detroit • New York • San Francisco • San Diego • New Haven, Conn. • Waterville, Maine • London • Munich

THOMSON
GALE

Feminism in Literature, Vol. 4

Project Editors
Jessica Bomarito, Jeffrey W. Hunter

Editorial
Tom Burns, Jenny Cromie, Kathy D. Darrow, Michelle Kazensky, Jelena O. Krstović, Michael L. LaBlanc, Julie Landelius, Michelle Lee, Allison McClintic Marion, Ellen McGeagh, Joseph Palmisano, Linda Pavlovski, James E. Person Jr., Thomas J. Schoenberg, Marie Toft, Lawrence J. Trudeau, Russel Whitaker

Indexing Services
Synapse, the Knowledge Link Corporation

Permissions
Emma Hull, Lori Hines, Shalice Shah-Caldwell

Imaging and Multimedia
Lezlie Light, Daniel Newell, Kelly A. Quin

Product Design
Michael Logusz, Pamela Galbreath

Composition and Electronic Capture
Carolyn Roney

Manufacturing
Rhonda Williams

Product Manager
Janet Witalec

This publication is a creative work fully protected by all applicable copyright laws, as well as by misappropriation, trade secret, unfair competition, and other applicable laws. The authors and editors of this work have added value to the underlying factual material herein through one or more of the following: unique and original selection, coordination, expression, arrangement, and classification of the information.

For permission to use material from the product, submit your request via the Web at http://www.gale-edit.com/permissions, or you may download our Permissions Request form and submit your request by fax or mail to:

Permisssions Department
Thomson Gale
27500 Drake Rd.
Farmington Hills, MI 48331-3535
Permissions Hotline:
248-699-8006 or 800-877-4253, ext. 8006
Fax 248-699-8074 or 800-762-4058

Cover photograph reproduced by permission of Corbis (portrait of Charlotte Perkins Gilman).

Since this page cannot legibly accommodate all copyright notices, the acknowledgments constitute an extension of the copyright notice.

While every effort has been made to secure permission to reprint material and to ensure the reliability of the information presented in this publication, Thomson Gale neither guarantees the accuracy of the data contained herein nor assumes any responsibility for errors, omissions or discrepancies. Thomson Gale accepts no payment for listing; and inclusion in the publication of any organization, agency, institution, publication, service, or individual does not imply endorsement of the editors or publisher. Errors brought to the attention of the publisher and verified to the satisfaction of the publisher will be corrected in future editions.

LIBRARY OF CONGRESS CATALOGING-IN-PUBLICATION DATA

Feminism in literature : a Gale critical companion / foreword by Amy Hudock ; Jessica Bomarito, project editor, Jeffrey W. Hunter, project editor.
      p. cm. -- (Gale critical companion collection)
   Includes bibliographical references and index.
   ISBN 0-7876-7573-3 (set hardcover : alk. paper) -- ISBN 0-7876-7574-1 (vol 1) -- ISBN 0-7876-7575-X (vol 2) -- ISBN 0-7876-7576-8 (vol 3) -- ISBN 0-7876-9115-1 (vol 4) -- ISBN 0-7876-9116-X (vol 5) -- ISBN 0-7876-9065-1 (vol 6)
   1. Literature--Women authors--History and criticism. 2. Women authors--Biography. 3. Women--History. I. Bomarito, Jessica, 1975- II. Hunter, Jeffrey W., 1966- III. Series.
   PN471.F43 2005
   809'.89287--dc22
                                                                    2004017989

Printed in the United States of America
10 9 8 7 6 5 4 3 2

CONTENTS

v

VOLUME 2

Louisa May Alcott 1832-1888
American novelist, short story writer, and
playwright

Jane Austen 1775-1817
English novelist

Charlotte Brontë 1816-1855
English novelist and poet

Emily Brontë 1818-1848
English novelist and poet

Elizabeth Barrett Browning 1806-1861
English poet and translator

Fanny Burney 1752-1840
English novelist, playwright, and diarist

VOLUME 3

VOLUME 4

VOLUME 5

Anna Akhmatova 1889-1966
Russian poet, essayist, and translator

Isabel Allende 1942-
Chilean novelist, essayist, journalist, short
story writer, memoirist, playwright, and
juvenile fiction writer

VOLUME 6

Virginia Woolf 1882-1941
English novelist, critic, essayist, short story
writer, diarist, autobiographer, and
biographer

When I was a girl, I would go to the library with my class, and all the girls would run to the Nancy Drew books, while the boys would head toward the Hardy Boys books—each group drawn to heroes that resembled themselves. Yet, when I entered formal literary studies in high school and college, I was told that I should not read so much in the girls' section any more, that the boys' section held books that were more literary, more universal, and more valuable. Teachers and professors told me this in such seemingly objective language that I never questioned it. At the time, the literary canon was built on a model of scarcity that claimed that only a few literary works could attain "greatness"—defined according to a supposed objective set of aesthetic criteria that more often than not excluded women authors. New Criticism, a way of reading texts that focuses on a poem, short story, or novel as an autonomous artistic production without connections to the historical and social conditions out of which it came, ruled my classrooms, making the author's gender ostensibly irrelevant. Masculine experience was coded as universal, while women's experience was particular. Overall, I had no reason to question the values I had been taught, until I encountered feminism.

Feminism, sometimes put in the plural *feminisms*, is a loose confederation of social, political, spiritual, and intellectual movements that places women and gender at the center of inquiry with the goal of social justice. When people in the United States speak of feminism, they are often referring to the mainstream liberal feminism that grew out of the relationship between grassroots civil rights movements of the 1960s and 1970s and these movements' entrance into the academy through the creation of Women's Studies as an interdisciplinary program of study in many colleges and universities. Mainstream liberal feminism helped many women achieve more equity in pay and access to a wider range of careers while it also transformed many academic disciplines to reflect women's achievements. However, liberal feminism quickly came under attack as largely a movement of white, heterosexual, university-educated, middle-class women who were simply trying to gain access to the same privileges that white, middle-class men enjoyed, and who assumed their experiences were the norm for a mythical universal "woman." Liberal feminists have also been critiqued for echoing the patriarchal devaluation of traditional women's nurturing work in their efforts to encourage women to pursue traditional men's work, for creating a false opposition between work and home, and for creating the superwoman stereotype that can cause women to believe they have failed if they do not achieve the perfect balance of work and home lives. Other feminisms developed representing other women and other modes of thought: Marxist, psychoanalytic, social/radical, lesbian, trans- and bi-sexual, black womanist, first nations, chicana, nonwestern, postcolonial, and approaches that even question the use of "woman" as a unifying signifier in the first place. As Women's Studies and these many feminims gained power and credibility in the academy, their presence forced the literary establishment to question its methodology, definitions, structures, philosophies, aesthetics, and visions as well at to alter the curriculum to reflect women's achievements.

Once I learned from Women's Studies that women mattered in the academy, I began exploring women in my own field of literary studies. Since male-authored texts were often the only works taught in my classes, I began to explore the images of women as constructed by male authors. Many other women writers also began their critique of women's place in society studying similar sites of representation. Mary Wollstonecraft's *A Vindication of the Rights of Women* (1792), Margaret Fuller's *Woman in the Nineteenth Century* (1845), Simone de Beauvoir's *The Second Sex* (1949), and Kate Millet's *Sexual Politics* (1969) explored how published images of women can serve as a means of social manipulation and control—a type of gender propaganda.

However, I began to find, as did others, that looking at women largely through male eyes did not do enough to reclaim women's voices and did not recognize women's agency in creating images of themselves. In *Sexual/Textual Politics* (1985), Toril Moi further questioned the limited natures of these early critical readings, even when including both male and female authors. She argued that reading literature for the accuracy of images of women led critics into assuming their own sense of reality as universal: "If the women in the book feel real to me, then the book is good." This kind of criticism never develops or changes, she argued, because it looks for the same elements repetitively, just in new texts. Also, she was disturbed by its focus on content rather than on how the text is written—the form, language, and literary elements. Moi and others argued for the development of new feminist critical methods.

However, examination of images of women over time has been fruitful. It has shown us that representation of women changes as historical forces change, that we must examine the historical influences on the creators of literary texts to understand the images they manufacture, and that we cannot assume that these images of women are universal and somehow separate from political and culture forces. These early explorations of woman as image also led to discussions of

femininity as image, not biologically but culturally defined, thus allowing analysis of the feminine ideal as separate from real women. This separation of biological sex and socially constructed gender laid the foundation for the later work of Judith Butler in *Gender Trouble: Feminism and the Subversion of Identity* (1990) and Marjorie Garber's *Vested Interests: Cross Dressing and Cultural Anxiety* (1992) in questioning what IS this thing we call "woman." These critics argued that gender is a social construct, a performance that can be learned by people who are biologically male, female, or transgendered, and therefore should not be used as the only essential connecting element in feminist studies. The study of woman and gender as image then has contributed much to feminist literary studies.

Tired of reading almost exclusively texts by men and a small emerging canon of women writers, I wanted to expand my understanding of writing by women. As a new Ph. D. student at the University of South Carolina in 1989, I walked up the stairs into the Women's Studies program and asked the first person I saw one question: were there any nineteenth-century American women writers who are worth reading? I had recently been told there were not, but I was no longer satisfied with this answer. And I found I was right to be skeptical. The woman I met at the top of those stairs handed me a thick book and said, "Go home and read this. Then you tell me if there were any nineteenth-century American women writers who are worth reading." So, I did. The book was the *Norton Anthology of Literature by Women* (1985), and once I had read it, I came back to the office at the top of the stairs and asked, "What more do you have?" My search for literary women began here, and this journey into new terrain parallels the development of the relationship between western feminism and literary studies.

In *A Room of Her Own* (1929), Virginia Woolf asks the same questions. She sits, looking at her bookshelves, thinking about the women writers who are there, and the ones who are not, and she calls for a reclaiming and celebrating of lost women artists. Other writers answered her call. Patricia Meyer Spacks's *The Female Imagination: A Literary and Psychological Investigation of Women's Writing* (1972), Ellen Moers's *Literary Women: The Great Writers* (1976), Elaine Showalter's *A Literature of Their Own: British Women Novelists from Brontë to Lessing* (1977), and Sandra Gilbert and Susan Gubar's *The Madwoman in the Attic* (1979) are a few of the early critical studies that explored the possibility of a tradition in women's literature.

While each of these influential and important books has different goals, methods, and theories, they share the attempt to establish a tradition in women's literature, a vital means through which marginalized groups establish a community identity and move from invisibility to visibility. These literary scholars and others worked to republish and reclaim women authors, expanding the number and types of women-authored texts available to readers, students, and scholars.

Yet, I began to notice that tradition formation presented some problems. As Marjorie Stone pointed out in her essay "The Search for a Lost Atlantis" (2003), the search for women's traditions in language and literature has been envisioned as the quest for a lost continent, a mythical motherland, similar to the lost but hopefully recoverable Atlantis. Such a quest tends to search for similarities among writers to attempt to prove the tradition existed, but this can sometimes obscure the differences among women writers. Looking to establish a tradition can also shape what is actually "found": only texts that fit that tradition. Traditions are defined by what is left in and what is left out, and the grand narratives of tradition formation as constructed in the early phases of feminist literary criticism inadvertently mirrored the exclusionary structures of the canon they were revising.

Some critics began discussing a women's tradition, a lost motherland of language, in not only what was written but also how it was written: in a female language or *ecriture feminine*. Feminist thinkers writing in France such as Hélène Cixous, Julia Kristeva, and Luce Irigaray argued that gender shapes language and that language shapes gender. Basing their ideas on those of psychoanalyst Jacques Lacan, they argued that pre-oedipal language—the original mother language—was lost when the law and language of the fathers asserted itself. While each of these writers explored this language differently, they all rewrote and revisioned how we might talk about literature, thus offering us new models for scholarship. However, as Alicia Ostriker argued in her essay, "Notes on 'Listen'" (2003), for the most part, women teach children language at home and at school. So, she questioned, is language really male and the "the language of the father," or is it the formal discourse of the academy that is male? Ostriker and others question the primacy of the father as the main social/language influence in these discussions. Other critics attacked what came to be known as "French Feminism" for its ahistorical, essentializing approach to finding a women's

tradition in language. Despite its problems, it offered much to the general understanding of gender and language and helped us imagine new possible forms for scholarship.

The idea that language might be gendered itself raised questions about how aesthetic judgement, defined in language, might also be gendered. Problems with how to judge what is "good" literature also arose, and feminist literary critics were accused of imposing a limited standard because much of what was being recovered looked the same in form as the traditional male canon, only written by women. Early recovered texts tended to highlight women in opposition to family, holding more modern liberal political views, and living nontraditional lives. If a text was "feminist" enough, it was included. Often times, this approach valued content over form, and the forms that were included did not differ much from the canon they were reacting against. These critics were still using the model of scarcity with a similar set of critical lens through which to judge texts worthy of inclusion. However, because later scholars started creating different critical lenses through which to view texts does not mean we need to perceive difference as inequality. Rather, texts that differ greatly began to be valued equally for different reasons. In order to do this, critics had to forfeit their tendency to place literary forms on a hierarchical model that allows only one at the apex. Instead, they exchanged the structure of value from one pyramid with a few writers at the apex for one with multiple high points, a model which celebrates a diversity of voices, styles, and forms. The model functioning in many past critical dialogues allowed for little diversity, privileging one type of literature—western, male, linear, logical, structured according to an accepted formula—over others—created by women and men who fail to fit the formula, and, thus, are judged not worthy. Creating hierarchies of value which privilege one discourse, predominantly Anglo male, over another, largely female, non-Anglo, and nonwestern undermines the supposed "impartiality" of critical standards. Breaking down the structure of canon formation that looks for the "great men" and "great women" of literature and instead studies what was actually written, then judging it on its own terms, has the potential for less bias. Challenging the existence of the canon itself allows more writers to be read and heard; perhaps we can base our understanding of literature not on a model of scarcity where only a few great ones are allowed at the top of the one peak, but where there are multiple peaks.

Another problem is that the tradition that was being recovered tended to look most like the critics who were establishing it. Barbara Smith's essay "Toward a Black Feminist Criticism" (1977) and bell hooks's *Ain't I a Woman? Black Women and Feminism* (1981) argued that academic feminism focused on the lives, conditions, histories, and texts of white, middle-class, educated women. Such writers revealed how the same methods of canon formation that excluded women were now being used by white feminists to exclude women of color. They also highlighted the silencing of black women by white women through the assumption that white womanhood was the norm. These writers and others changed the quest for one lost Atlantis to a quest for many lost continents as anthologies of African American, Chicana, Native American, Asian, Jewish, lesbian, mothers, and many more women writers grouped together by identity began to emerge. *This Bridge Called My Back: Writings by Radical Women of Color* (1981), edited by Ana Castillo and Cherríe Moraga, is one such collection. Yet, while these and other writers looked for new traditions of women's writing by the identity politics of the 1980s and 1990s, they were still imposing the same structures of tradition formation on new groups of women writers, still looking for the lost Atlantis.

Western feminist critics also began looking for the lost Atlantis on a global scale. Critiques from non-western critics and writers about their exclusion from feminist literary histories that claimed to represent world feminisms is bringing about the same pattern of starting with an exploration of image, moving to recovery of writers and traditions, then a questioning of recovery efforts that we have seen before. Now, however, all these stages are occurring at the once. For example, American feminist critics are still attempting to make global primary texts available in English so they can be studied and included at the same time they are being critiqued for doing so. Chandra Talpade Mohanty in "Under Western Eyes: Feminist Scholarship and Colonial Discourses" (1991) argues that systems of oppression do not affect us all equally, and to isolate gender as the primary source of oppression ignores the differing and complex webs of oppressions non-western women face. Western tendencies to view non-western women as suffering from a totalizing and undifferentiated oppression similar to their own "universal" female oppression cause feminist literary critics to impose structures of meaning onto non-western texts that fail to reflect the actual cultures and experiences of the writers. Therefore, to simply add the women from non-western literary traditions into existing western timelines, categories, and periodizations may not fully reflect the complexity of non-western writing. In fact, critics such as Gayatri Chakravorty Spivak, Ann DuCille, and Teresa Ebert argue post-colonial and transnational critics have created yet another master narrative that must be challenged. Yet, before the westernness of this new, transnational narrative can be addressed, critics need to be able read, discuss, and share the global texts that are now being translated and published before we can do anything else; therefore, this reclaiming and celebration of a global women's tradition is a necessary step in the process of transforming the very foundations of western feminist literary criticism. But it is only an early step in the continual speak, react, revise pattern of feminist scholarship.

Some critics argue that the ultimate goal of feminist literary history should be to move beyond using gender as the central, essential criteria—to give up looking for only a woman's isolated traditions and to examine gender as one of many elements. In that way, we could better examine female-authored texts in relationship with male-authored texts, and, thus, end the tendency to examine texts by women as either in opposition to the dominant discourse or as co-opted by it. As Kathryn R. King argues in her essay "Cowley Among the Women; or, Poetry in the Contact Zone" (2003), women writers, like male writers, did not write in a vacuum or only in relationship to other women writers. King argues for a more complex method of examining literary influence, and she holds up Mary Louise Pratt's discussion of the contact zone in *Imperial Eyes: Travel Writing and Transculturation* (1992) as a potential model for exploring the web of textual relationships that influence women writers. Pratt argues that the relationship between the colonized and the colonizer, though inflected by unequal power, often creates influence that works both ways (the contact zone). Using Pratt's idea of mutual influence and cultural hybridity allows, King argues, women's literary history to be better grounded in social, historical, philosophical, and religious traditions that influenced the texts of women writers.

So, what has feminism taught me about literary studies? That it is not "artistic value" or "universal themes" that keeps authors' works alive. Professors decide which authors and themes are going to "count" by teaching them, writing scholarly books and articles on them, and by making sure they appear in dictionaries of literary biography, bibliographies, and in the grand narratives of literary history. Reviewers decide who gets attention by reviewing them. Editors and publishers decide who gets read by keeping them in print. And librarians decide what books to buy and to keep on the shelves. Like the ancient storytellers who passed on the tribes' history from generation to generation, these groups keep our cultural memory. Therefore, we gatekeepers, who are biased humans living in and shaped by the intellectual, cultural, and aesthetic paradigms of an actual historical period must constantly reassess our methods, theories, and techniques, continually examining how our own ethnicities, classes, genders, nationalities, and sexualities mold our critical judgements.

What has literary studies taught me about feminism? That being gendered is a text that can be read, interpreted, manipulated, and altered. That feminisms themselves are texts written by real people in actual historical situations, and that feminists, too, must always recognize our own biases, and let others recognize them. That feminism is forever growing and changing and reinventing itself in a continual cycle of statement, reaction, and revision. As the definitions and goals of feminisms change before my eyes, I have learned that feminism is a process, its meaning constantly deferred.

—*Amy Hudock, Ph.D.*
University of South Carolina

The Gale Critical Companion Collection

In response to a growing demand for relevant criticism and interpretation of perennial topics and important literary movements throughout history, the Gale Critical Companion Collection (GCCC) was designed to meet the research needs of upper high school and undergraduate students. Each edition of GCCC focuses on a different literary movement or topic of broad interest to students of literature, history, multicultural studies, humanities, foreign language studies, and other subject areas. Topics covered are based on feedback from a standing advisory board consisting of reference librarians and subject specialists from public, academic, and school library systems.

The GCCC is designed to complement Gale's existing Literary Criticism Series (LCS) , which includes such award-winning and distinguished titles as *Nineteenth-Century Literature Criticism* (*NCLC*), *Twentieth-Century Literary Criticism* (*TCLC*), and *Contemporary Literary Criticism* (*CLC*). Like the LCS titles, the GCCC editions provide selected reprinted essays that offer an inclusive range of critical and scholarly response to authors and topics widely studied in high school and undergraduate classes; however, the GCCC also includes primary source documents, chronologies, sidebars, supplemental photographs, and other material not included in the LCS products. The graphic and supplemental material is designed to extend the usefulness of the critical essays and

provide students with historical and cultural context on a topic or author's work. GCCC titles will benefit larger institutions with ongoing subscriptions to Gale's LCS products as well as smaller libraries and school systems with less extensive reference collections. Each edition of the GCCC is created as a stand-alone set providing a wealth of information on the topic or movement. Importantly, the overlap between the GCCC and LCS titles is 15% or less, ensuring that LCS subscribers will not duplicate resources in their collection.

Editions within the GCCC are either single-volume or multi-volume sets, depending on the nature and scope of the topic being covered. Topic entries and author entries are treated separately, with entries on related topics appearing first, followed by author entries in an A-Z arrangement. Each volume is approximately 500 pages in length and includes approximately 50 images and sidebar graphics. These sidebars include summaries of important historical events, newspaper clippings, brief biographies of important figures, complete poems or passages of fiction written by the author, descriptions of events in the related arts (music, visual arts, and dance), and so on.

The reprinted essays in each GCCC edition explicate the major themes and literary techniques of the authors and literary works. It is important to note that approximately 85% of the essays reprinted in GCCC editions are full-text, meaning that they are reprinted in their entirety, including footnotes and lists of abbreviations. Essays are selected based on their coverage of the seminal works and themes of an author, and based on the importance of those essays to an appreciation of the author's contribution to the movement and to literature in general. Gale's editors select those essays of most value to upper high school and undergraduate students, avoiding narrow and highly pedantic interpretations of individual works or of an author's canon.

Scope of Feminism in Literature

Feminism in Literature, the third set in the Gale Critical Companion Collection, consists of six volumes. Each volume includes a detailed table of contents, a foreword on the subject of feminism in literature written by noted scholar Amy Hudock, and a descriptive chronology of key events throughout the history of women's writing. Volume 1 focuses on feminism in literature from antiquity through the 18th century. It consists of three topic entries, including Women and Women's Writings from Classical Antiquity through the Middle Ages, and seven author entries on such women writers from this time period as Christine de Pizan, Sappho, and Mary Wollstonecraft. Volumes 2 and 3 focus on the 19th century. Volume 2 includes such topic entries as United States Women's Suffrage Movement in the 19th Century, as well as author entries on Jane Austen, Charlotte Brontë, and Elizabeth Barrett Browning. Volume 3 contains additional author entries on figures of the 19th century, including such notables as Kate Chopin, Emily Dickinson, and Harriet Beecher Stowe. Volumes 4, 5, and 6 focus on the 20th century to the present day; volume 4 includes coverage of topics relevant to feminism in literature during the 20th century and early 21st century, including the Feminist Movement, and volumes 5 and 6 include author entries on such figures as Margaret Atwood, Charlotte Perkins Gilman, Sylvia Plath, and Virginia Woolf.

Organization of Feminism in Literature

A *Feminism in Literature* topic entry consists of the following elements:

- The **Introduction** defines the subject of the entry and provides social and historical information important to understanding the criticism.

- The list of **Representative Works** identifies writings and works by authors and figures associated with the subject. The list is divided into alphabetical sections by name; works listed under each name appear in chronologi-

cal order. The genre and publication date of each work is given. Unless otherwise indicated, dramas are dated by first performance, not first publication.

- Entries generally begin with a section of **Primary Sources**, which includes essays, speeches, social history, newspaper accounts and other materials that were produced during the time covered.

- Reprinted **Criticism** in topic entries is arranged thematically. Topic entries commonly begin with general surveys of the subject or essays providing historical or background information, followed by essays that develop particular aspects of the topic. Each section has a separate title heading and is identified with a page number in the table of contents. The critic's name and the date of composition or publication of the critical work are given at the beginning of each piece of criticism. Unsigned criticism is preceded by the title of the source in which it appeared. Footnotes are reprinted at the end of each essay or excerpt. In the case of excerpted criticism, only those footnotes that pertain to the excerpted texts are included.

- A complete **Bibliographical Citation** of the original essay or book precedes each piece of criticism.

- Critical essays are prefaced by brief **Annotations** explicating each piece. Unless the descriptor "excerpt" is used in the annotation, the essay is being reprinted in its entirety.

- An annotated bibliography of **Further Reading** appears at the end of each entry and suggests resources for additional study. In some cases, significant essays for which the editors could not obtain reprint rights are included here.

A *Feminism in Literature* author entry consists of the following elements:

- The **Author Heading** cites the name under which the author most commonly wrote, followed by birth and death dates. Also located here are any name variations under which an author wrote. If the author wrote consistently under a pseudonym, the pseudonym will be listed in the author heading and the author's actual name given in parentheses on the first line of the biographical and critical information. Uncertain birth or death dates are indicated by question marks.

- A **Portrait of the Author** is included when available.

- The **Introduction** contains background information that introduces the reader to the author that is the subject of the entry.

- The list of **Principal Works** is ordered chronologically by date of first publication and lists the most important works by the author. The genre and publication date of each work is given. Unless otherwise indicated, dramas are dated by first performance, not first publication.

- Author entries are arranged into three sections: **Primary Sources, General Commentary,** and **Title Commentary.** The Primary Sources section includes letters, poems, short stories, journal entries, novel excerpts, and essays written by the featured author. General Commentary includes overviews of the author's career and general studies; Title Commentary includes in-depth analyses of seminal works by the author. Within the Title Commentary section, the reprinted criticism is further organized by title, then by date of publication. The critic's name and the date of composition or publication of the critical work are given at the beginning of each piece of criticism. Unsigned criticism is preceded by the title of the source in which it appeared. All titles by the author featured in the text are printed in boldface type. However, not all boldfaced titles are included in the author and subject indexes; only substantial discussions of works are indexed. Footnotes are reprinted at the end of each essay or excerpt. In the case of excerpted criticism, only those footnotes that pertain to the excerpted texts are included.

- A complete **Bibliographical Citation** of the original essay or book precedes each piece of criticism.

- Critical essays are prefaced by brief **Annotations** explicating each piece. Unless the descriptor "excerpt" is used in the annotation, the essay is being reprinted in its entirety.

- An annotated bibliography of **Further Reading** appears at the end of each entry and suggests resources for additional study. In some cases, significant essays for which the editors could not obtain reprint rights are included here. A list of **Other Sources from Gale** follows the further reading section and provides references to other biographical and critical sources on the author in series published by Gale.

Indexes

The **Author Index** lists all of the authors featured in the *Feminism in Literature* set, with references to the main author entries in volumes 1, 2, 3, 5, and 6 as well as commentary on the featured author in other author entries and in the topic volumes. Page references to substantial discussions of the authors appear in boldface. The Author Index also includes birth and death dates and cross references between pseudonyms and actual names, and cross references to other Gale series in which the authors have appeared. A complete list of these sources is found facing the first page of the Author Index.

The **Title Index** alphabetically lists the titles of works written by the authors featured in volumes 1 through 6 and provides page numbers or page ranges where commentary on these titles can be found. Page references to substantial discussions of the titles appear in boldface. English translations of foreign titles and variations of titles are cross-referenced to the title under which a work was originally published. Titles of novels, dramas, nonfiction books, films, and poetry, short story, or essay collections are printed in italics, while individual poems, short stories, and essays are printed in roman type within quotation marks.

The **Subject Index** includes the authors and titles that appear in the Author Index and the Title Index as well as the names of other authors and figures that are discussed in the set, including those covered in sidebars. The Subject Index also lists hundreds of literary terms and topics covered in the criticism. The index provides page numbers or page ranges where subjects are discussed and is fully cross referenced.

Citing Feminism in Literature

When writing papers, students who quote directly from the *FL* set may use the following general format to footnote reprinted criticism. The first example pertains to material drawn from periodicals, the second to material reprinted from books.

Bloom, Harold. " Feminism as the Love of Reading," *Raritan* 14, no. 2 (fall 1994): 29-42; reprinted in *Feminism in Literature: A Gale Critical Companion*, vol. 6, eds. Jessica Bomarito and Jeffrey W. Hunter (Farmington Hills, Mich: Thomson Gale, 2004), 29-42.

Coole, Diana H. "The Origin of Western Thought and the Birth of Misogyny," in *Women in Political Theory: From Ancient Misogyny to Contemporary Feminism* (Brighton, Sussex: Wheatsheaf Books, 1988), 10-28; reprinted in *Feminism in Literature: A Gale Critical Companion*, vol. 1, eds. Jessica Bomarito and Jeffrey W. Hunter (Farmington Hills, Mich: Thomson Gale, 2004), 15-25.

Feminism in Literature *Advisory Board*

The members of the *Feminism in Literature* Advisory Board—reference librarians and subject specialists from public, academic, and school library systems—offered a variety of informed perspectives on both the presentation and content of the *Feminism in Literature* set. Advisory board members assessed and defined such quality issues as the relevance, currency, and usefulness of the author coverage, critical content, and topics included in our product; evaluated the layout, presentation, and general quality of our product; provided feedback on the criteria used for selecting authors and topics covered in our product; identified any gaps in our coverage of authors or topics, recommending authors or topics for inclusion; and analyzed the appropriateness of our content and presentation for various user audiences, such as high school students, undergraduates, graduate students, librarians, and educators.

We wish to thank the advisors for their advice during the development of *Feminism in Literature*.

Suggestions are Welcome

Readers who wish to suggest new features, topics, or authors to appear in future volumes of the Gale Critical Companion Collection, or who have other suggestions or comments are cordially invited to call, write, or fax the Product Manager.

Product Manager, Gale Critical Companion
    Collection
Thomson Gale
27500 Drake Road
Farmington Hills, MI 48331-3535
1-800-347-4253 (GALE)
Fax: 248-699-8054

The editors wish to thank the copyright holders of the excerpted criticism included in this volume and the permissions managers of many book and magazine publishing companies for assisting us in securing reproduction rights. We are also grateful to the staffs of the Detroit Public Library, the Library of Congress, the University of Detroit Mercy Library, Wayne State University Purdy/ Kresge Library Complex, and the University of Michigan Libraries for making their resources available to us. Following is a list of the copyright holders who have granted us permission to reproduce material in this edition of *Feminism in Literature*. Every effort has been made to trace copyright, but if omissions have been made, please let us know.

Copyrighted material in Feminism in Literature *was reproduced from the following periodicals:*

African American Review, v. 35, winter, 2001 for "'The Porch Couldn't Talk for Looking': Voice and Vision in *Their Eyes Were Watching God*" by Deborah Clarke; v. 36, 2002 for "Phillis Wheatley's Construction of Otherness and the Rhetoric of Performed Ideology" by Mary McAleer Balkun. Copyright © 2001, 2002 by the respective authors. Both reproduced by permission of the respective authors.—*Agora: An Online Graduate Journal*, v. 1, fall, 2002 for "Virgin Territory: Murasaki Shiki-bu's Ôigimi Resists the Male" by Valerie Henitiuk. Copyright © 2001-2002 Maximiliaan van Woudenberg. All rights reserved. Reproduced by permission of the author.—*American Literary History*, v. 1, winter, 1989 for "Bio-Political Resistance in Domestic Ideology and *Uncle Tom's Cabin*" by Lora Romero. Copyright © 1989 by Oxford University Press. Reproduced by permission of the publisher and the author.—*American Literature*, v. 53, January, 1982. Copyright © 1982, by Duke University Press. Reproduced by permission.—*The American Scholar*, v. 44, spring, 1975. Copyright © 1975 by the United Chapters of Phi Beta Kappa. Reproduced by permission of Curtis Brown Ltd.—*The Antioch Review*, v. 32, 1973. Copyright © 1973 by the Antioch Review Inc. Reproduced by permission of the Editors.—*Ariel: A Review of International English Literature*, v. 21, January, 1990 for "Female Sexuality in Willa Cather's *O Pioneers!* and the Era of Scientific Sexology: A Dialogue between Frontiers" by C. Susan Wiesenthal; v. 22, October, 1991 for "Margaret Atwood's *Cat's Eye*: Re-Viewing Women in a Postmodern World" by Earl G. Ingersoll. Copyright © 1990, 1991 The Board of Governors, The University of Calgary. Both reproduced by permission of the publisher and the author.—*Atlantis: A Women's Studies Journal*, v. 9, fall, 1983. Copyright © 1983 by *Atlantis*. Reproduced by permission.—*Black American Literature Forum*, v. 24, summer, 1990 for "Singing the Black Mother: Maya Angelou and Autobiographical Continuity" by Mary Jane Lupton. Copyright © 1990 by the author. Reproduced by permission of the author.—*The Book Collector*, v. 31, spring, 1982. Reproduced by permission.—*The CEA Critic,* v. 56, spring/summer, 1994 for "Feminism and Children's Literature: Fitting *Little Women* into the American Literary Canon" by Jill P. May. Copyright © 1994 by the College English Association, Inc. Reproduced by permission of the publisher and the author.—*The Centennial Review,* v. xxix, spring, 1985 for "'An Order of Constancy': Notes on Brooks and the Feminine" by Hortense J. Spillers. Michigan State University Press. Copyright © 1985 by *The Centennial Review.* Reproduced by permission of the publisher.—*Chaucer Review,* v. 37, 2003. Copyright © 2003 by The Pennsylvania State University. All rights reserved. Reproduced by permission.—*Christianity and Literature,* v. 51, spring, 2002. Copyright © 2002 by the Conference on Christianity and Literature. Reproduced by permission.—*CLA Journal,* v. XXXIX, March, 1996. Copyright © 1966 by The College Language Association. Used by permission of The College Language Association.—*Classical Quarterly,* v. 31, 1981 for "Spartan Wives: Liberation or Licence?" by Paul Cartledge. Copyright © 1981 The Classical Association. Reproduced by permission of Oxford University Press and the author.—*Colby Library Quarterly,* v. 21, March, 1986. Reproduced by permission.—*Colby Quarterly,* v. XXVI, September 1990; v. XXXIV, June, 1998. Both reproduced by permission.—*College English,* v. 36, March, 1975 for "Who Buried H. D.?: A Poet, Her Critics, and Her Place in 'The Literary Tradition'" by Susan Friedman. Copyright © 1975 by the National Council of Teachers of English. Reproduced by permission of the publisher and the author.—*Connotations,* v. 5, 1995-96. Copyright © Waxmann Verlag GmbH, Munster/New York 1996. Reproduced by permission.—*Contemporary Literature,* v. 34, winter, 1993. Copyright © 1993 by University of Wisconsin Press. Reproduced by permission.—*Critical Quarterly,* v. 14, autumn, 1972; v. 27, spring, 1985. Copyright © 1972, 1985 by Manchester University Press. Both reproduced by permission of Blackwell Publishers.—*Critical Survey,* v. 14, January, 2002. Copyright © 2002 Berghahn Books, Inc. Reproduced by permission.—*Critique: Studies in Modern Fiction,* v. XV, 1973. Copyright © by *Critique,* 1973. Copyright © 1973 by Helen Dwight Reid Educational Foundation. Reproduced with permission of the Helen Dwight Reid Educational Foundation, published by Heldref Publications, 1319 18th Street, NW, Washington, DC 20036-1802.—*Cultural Critique,* v. 32, winter, 1995-96. Copyright © 1996 by *Cultural Critique.* All rights reserved. Reproduced by permission.—*Denver Quarterly,* v. 18, winter, 1984 for "Becoming Anne Sexton" by Diane Middlebrook. Copyright © 1994 by Diane Middlebrook. Reproduced by permission of Georges Bou-

chardt, Inc. for the author.—*Dissent,* summer, 1987. Copyright © 1987, by Dissent Publishing Corporation. Reproduced by permission.—*The Eighteenth Century,* v. 43, spring, 2002. Copyright © 2002 by Texas Tech University Press. Reproduced by permission.—*Eighteenth-Century Fiction,* v. 3, July, 1991. Copyright © McMaster University 1991. Reproduced by permission.—*Emily Dickinson Journal,* v. 10, 2000. Copyright © 2000 by The Johns Hopkins University Press for the Emily Dickinson International Society. All rights reserved. Reproduced by permission.—*The Emporia State Research Studies,* v. 24, winter, 1976. Reproduced by permission.—*Essays and Studies,* 2002. Copyright © 2002 Boydell & Brewer Inc. Reproduced by permission.—*Essays in Literature,* v. 12, fall, 1985. Copyright © 1985 Western Illinois University. Reproduced by permission.—*Feminist Studies,* v. 6, summer, 1980; v. 25, fall, 1999. Copyright © 1980, 1999 by *Feminist Studies.* Both reproduced by permission of Feminist Studies, Inc., Department of Women's Studies, University of Maryland, College Park, MD 20724.—*French Studies,* v. XLVIII, April, 1994; v. LII, April, 1998. Copyright © 1994, 1998 by The Society for French Studies. Reproduced by permission.—*Frontiers,* v. IX, 1987; v. XIV, 1994. Copyright © The University of Nebraska Press 1987, 1994. Both reproduced by permission.—*Glamour,* v. 88, November 1990 for "Only Daughter" by Sandra Cisneros. Copyright © 1996 by Wendy Martin. All rights reserved. Reproduced by permission of Susan Bergholz Literary Services, New York.—*Harper's Magazine,* for "Women's Work" by Louise Erdrich. Copyright © 1995 by *Harper's Magazine.* All rights reserved. Reproduced from the May edition by special permission.—*History Today,* v. 50, October, 2000; v. 51, November, 2001. Copyright © 2000, 2001 by The H. W. Wilson Company. All rights reserved. Reproduced by permission.—*The Hudson Review,* v. XXXVI, summer, 1983. Copyright © 1983 by The Hudson Review, Inc. Reproduced by permission.—*Hypatia,* v. 5, summer, 1990 for "Is There a Feminist Aesthetic?" by Marilyn French. Copyright by Marilyn French. Reproduced by permission.—*International Fiction Review,* v. 29, 2002. Copyright © 2002. International Fiction Association. Reproduced by permission.—*Irish Studies Review,* spring, 1996 from "History, Gender and the Colonial Movement: Castle Rackrent" by Colin Graham. Reproduced by permission of Taylor & Francis and the author.—*Journal of Evolutionary Psychology,* v. 7, August, 1986. Reproduced by permission.—*Journal of the Midwest Modern Language Association,* v. 35, 2002 for "The Gospel According to Jane Eyre: The Suttee and the Seraglio" by Maryanne C. Ward. Copyright © 2002 by The Midwest Modern Language Association. Reproduced by permission of the publisher and the author.—*Journal of the Short Story in English,* autumn, 2002. Copyright © Université d'Angers, 2002. Reproduced by permission.—*Keats-Shelley Journal,* v. XLVI, 1997. Reproduced by permission.—*Legacy,* v. 6, fall, 1989. Copyright © The University of Nebraska Press 1989. Reproduced by permission.—*The Massachusetts Review,* v. 27, summer, 1986. Reproduced from *The Massachusetts Review,* The Massachusetts Review, Inc. by permission.—*Meanjin,* v. 38, 1979 for "The Liberated Heroine: New Varieties of Defeat?" by Amanda Lohrey. Copyright © 1979 by *Meanjin.* Reproduced by permission of the author.—*MELUS,* v. 7, fall, 1980; v. 12, fall, 1985; v.18, fall, 1993. Copyright © MELUS: The Society for the Study of Multi-Ethnic Literature of the United States, 1980, 1985, 1993. Reproduced by permission.—*Modern Drama,* v. 21, September, 1978. Copyright © 1978 by the University of Toronto, Graduate Centre for Study of Drama. Reproduced by permission.—*Modern Language Studies,* v. 24, spring, 1994 for "Jewett's Unspeakable Unspoken: Retracing the Female Body Through *The Country of the Pointed Firs*" by George Smith. Copyright © Northeast Modern Language Association 1990. Reproduced by permission of the publisher and author.—*Mosaic,* v. 23, summer, 1990; v. 35, 2002. Copyright © 1990, 2002 by *Mosaic.* All rights reserved. Acknowledgment of previous publication is herewith made.—*Ms.,* v. II, July, 1973 for "Visionary Anger" by Erica Mann Jong; June 1988 for "Changing My Mind About Andrea Dworkin" by Erica Jong. Copyright © 1973, 1988. Both reproduced by permission of the author.—*New Directions for Women,* September-October, 1987 for "Dworkin Critiques Relations Between the Sexes" by Joanne Glasgow. Copyright © 1987 New Directions for Women, Inc., 25 West Fairview Ave., Dover, NJ 07801-3417. Reproduced by permission of the author.—*The New Yorker,* 1978 for "Girl" by Jamaica Kincaid. Copyright © 1979 by Jamaica Kinkaid. All rights reserved. Reproduced by permission of the Wylie Agency; v. 73, February 17, 1997 for "A Society of One: Zora Neal Hurston, American Contrarian" by Claudia Roth Pierpont. Copyright © 1997 by The New Yorker Magazine, Inc. All rights reserved. Reproduced by permission of the author.—*Nineteenth-Century Feminisms,* v. 2, spring-summer, 2000. Reproduced by permission.—*Nineteenth-Century French Studies,* v. 25, spring-summer, 1997. Copyright © 1977 by *Nineteenth-Century French Studies.* Reproduced by permission.—*Novel,* v. 34, spring, 2001. Copyright © NOVEL Corp. 2001. Reproduced with permission.—*Oxford Literary Review,* v. 13, 1991. Copyright © 1991 the *Oxford Literary Review.* All rights reserved. Reproduced by permission.—*P. N. Review,* v. 18, January/February, 1992. Reproduced by permission of Carcanet Press Ltd.—*Papers on Language & Literature,* v. 5, winter, 1969. Copyright © 1969 by The Board of Trustees, Southern Illinois University at Edwardsville. Reproduced by permission.—*Parnassus,* v. 12, fall-winter, 1985 for "Throwing the Scarecrows from the Garden" by Tess Gallagher; v. 12-13, 1985 for "Adrienne Rich and Lesbian/Feminist Poetry" by Catharine Stimpson. Copyright © 1985, 1986 by Poetry in Review Foundation. Both reproduced by permission of the publisher and the respective authors.—*Philological Papers,* v. 38, 1992. Copyright © 1992 by *Philological Papers.* Reproduced by permission.—*Philological Quarterly,* v. 79, winter, 2000. Copyright © 2001 by the University of Iowa. Reproduced by permission.—*Quadrant,* v. 46, November, 2002 for "The Mirror of Honour and Love: A Woman's View of Chivalry" by Sophie Masson. Copyright © 2002 Quadrant Magazine Company, Inc. Reproduced by permission of the publisher and the author.—*Raritan,* v. 14, fall, 1994. Copyright © 1994 by *Raritan: A Quarterly Review.* Reproduced by permission.—*Resources for American Literary Study,* v. 22, 1996. Copyright © 1996 by The Pennsylvania State University. Reproduced by permission of The Pennsylvania State University Press.—*Revista Hispánica Moderna,* v. 47, June, 1994. Copyright © 1994 by Hispanic Institute, Columbia University. Reproduced by permission.—*Rhetoric Society Quarterly,* v. 32, winter, 2002. Reproduced by permission of the publisher, conveyed through the Copyright Clearance Center.—*Romanic Review,* v. 79, 1988. Copyright © 1988 by The Trustees of Columbia University in the City of New York. Reproduced by permission.—*The Russian Review,* v. 57, April, 1998. Copyright © 1998 *The Russian Review.* Reproduced by permission of Blackwell Publishers.—*San Jose Studies,* v. VIII, spring, 1982 for "Dea, Awakening: A Reading of H. D.'s *Trilogy*" by Joyce Lorraine Beck. Copyright © 1982 by Trustees of the San Jose State University Foundation. Reproduced by permission of the publisher and the author.—*South Atlantic Review,* v. 66, winter, 2001. Copyright © 2001 by the South Atlantic Modern Language Association. Reproduced by permission.—*Southern Humanities Review,* v. xxii, summer, 1988. Copyright © 1988 by Auburn University. Reproduced by permission.—*The Southern Quarterly,* v. 35, spring, 1997; v. 37, spring-summer, 1999. Copyright © 1997, 1999 by the University of Southern Mississippi. Both reproduced by permission.—*Southern Review,* v. 18, for "Hilda in Egypt" by Albert Gelpi. Reproduced by permission of the author.—*Soviet Literature,* v. 6, June, 1989. Reproduced by permission of FTM Agency Ltd.—*Studies in American Fiction,* v. 9, autumn, 1981. Copyright © 1981 Northeastern University. Reproduced by permission.—*Studies in American Humor,* v. 3, 1994. Copyright © 1994 American Humor Studies Association. Reproduced by permission.—*Studies in the Humanities,* v. 19, December, 1992. Copyright © 1992 by Indiana University Press of Pennsylvania. Reproduced by permission.—*Studies in the Novel,* v. 31, fall 1999; v. 35, spring, 2003. Copyright © 1999, 2003 by North Texas State University. Reproduced by permission.—*Textual Practice,* v. 13, 1999 for "Speaking Un-likeness: The Double Text in Christina Rossetti's 'After Death' and 'Remember'" by Margaret Reynolds. Copyright © 1999 Routledge. Reproduced by permission of the publisher and the author.—*The Threepenny Review,* 1990 for "Mother Tongue" by Amy Tan. Reproduced by permission.—*Transactions of the American Philological Association,* v. 128, 1998. Copyright © 1998 American Philological Association. Reproduced by permission of The Johns Hopkins University Press.—*Tulsa Studies in Women's Literature,* v. 6, fall, 1987 for "Revolutionary Women" by Betsy Erkkila. Copyright © 1987, The University of Tulsa. All rights reserved. Reproduced by permission of the publisher and the author.—*The Victorian Newsletter,* v. 82, fall, 1992 for "Revisionist Mythmaking in Christina Rossetti's 'Goblin Market': Eve's Apple and Other Questions" by Sylvia Bailey Shurbutt; v. 92, fall, 1997 for "The Poet and the Bible: Christina Rossetti's Feminist Hermeneutics" by Lynda Palazzo; spring, 1998 for "'No Sorrow I Have Thought More About': The Tragic Failure of George Eliot's St. Theresa" by June Skye Szirotny. All reproduced by permission of The Victorian Newsletter and the author.—*Victorians Institute Journal,* v. 13, 1985. Copyright © Victorians Institute Journal 1985. Reproduced by permission.—*Women: A Cultural Review,* v. 10, winter, 1999 from "Consorting with Angels: Anne Sexton and the Art of Confession" by Deryn Rees-Jones. Copyright © 1999, by Taylor & Francis Ltd. Reproduced by permission of the publisher and the author. (http://www.tandf.co.uk/journals).—*Women and Language,* v. 13, March 31, 1995; v. 19, fall, 1996. Copyright © 1995, 1996 by Communication Department at George Mason University. Reproduced by permission of the publisher.—*Women's Studies: An Interdisciplinary Journal,* v. 3, 1975; v. 4, 1976; v. 17, 1990; v. 18, 1990; v. 23, September, 1994; v. 30, 2001. Copyright © 1975, 1976, 1990, 1994, 2001 Gordon and Breach Science Publishers S.A. Reproduced by permission.—*Women's Studies in Communication,* v. 24, spring, 2001. Reproduced by permission.—*Women's Writing,* v. 3, June, 1996. Reproduced by permission of the publisher; v. 4, 1997 for "(Female) Philosophy in the Bedroom: Mary Wollstonecraft and Female Sexuality" by Gary Kelly. Copyright © Triangle Journals Ltd, 1997. All rights reserved. Reproduced by permission of the publisher and the author.—*World & I,* v. 18, March, 2003. Copyright © 2003 News World Communications, Inc. Reproduced by permission.—*World Literature Today,* v. 73, spring, 1999. Copyright © 1999 by the University of Oklahoma Press. Reprinted by permission of the publisher.—*World Literature Written in English,* v. 15, November, 1976 for "Doris Lessing's Feminist Plays" by Agate Nesaule Krouse. Copyright © 1976 by WLWE. Reproduced by permission of the publisher and the author.

Copyrighted material in Feminism in Literature *was reproduced from the following books:*

Acocella, Joan. From *Willa Cather and the Politics of Criticism.* University of Nebraska Press, 2000. Copyright © 2000, by Joan Acocella. All rights reserved. Reproduced by permission.—Aimone, Joseph. From "Millay's Big Book, or the Feminist Formalist as Modern," in *Unmanning Modernism: Gendered Re-Readings.* Edited by Elizabeth Jane Harrison and Shirley Peterson. University of Tennessee Press, 1997. Copyright © 1997 by The University of Tennessee Press. All rights reserved. Reproduced by permission of The University of Tennessee Press.—Allende, Isabel. From "Writing as an Act of Hope," in *Paths of Resistance: The Art and Craft of the Political Novel.* Edited by William Zinsser. Houghton Mifflin Company, 1989. Copyright © 1989 Isabel Allende. Reproduced by permission of the author.—Angelou, Maya. From *And Still I Rise.* Random House, 1978. Copyright © 1978 by Maya Angelou. Reproduced by permission of Random House, Inc. and Time Warner Books UK.—Arenal, Electa. From "The Convent as Catalyst for Autonomy: Two Hispanic Nuns of the Seventeenth Century," in *Women in Hispanic Literature.* Edited by Beth Kurti Miller. University of California Press, 1983. Copyright © 1983 by The Regents of the University of California. Reproduced by permission of the publisher and the author.—Arndt, Walter. From "Introduction: I The Akhmatova Phenomenon and II Rendering the Whole Poem," in *Anna Akhmatova: Selected Poems.* Edited and translated by Walter Arndt. Ardis, 1976. Reproduced by permission.—Atwood, Margaret. From *Second Words.* Anansi Press Limited, 1982. Copyright © 1982, by O. W. Toad Limited. All rights reserved. Reproduced by permission of the author.—Baker, Deborah Lesko. From "Memory, Love, and Inaccessibility in *Hiroshima mon amour,*" in *Marguerite*

Duras Lives On. Edited by Janine Ricouart. University Press of America, 1998. Copyright © 1998 University Press of America, Inc. All rights reserved. Reproduced by permission.—Barlow, Judith E. From "Into the Foxhole: Feminism, Realism, and Lillian Hellman," in *Realism and the American Dramatic Tradition.* Edited by William W. Demastes. University of Alabama Press, 1996. Copyright © 1996, The University of Alabama Press. Reproduced by permission.—Barratt, Alexandra. From *Women's Writing in Middle English.* Edited by Alexandra Barratt. Longman Group UK Limited, 1992. Copyright © Longman Group UK Limited 1992. Reproduced by permission.—Barrett Browning, Elizabeth. From "A Letter to Mary Russell Mitford, September 18, 1846," in *Women of Letters: Selected Letters of Elizabeth Barrett Browning and Mary Russell Mitford.* Edited by Meredith B. Raymond and Mary Rose Sullivan. Twayne Publishers, 1987. Reproduced by permission of The Gale Group.—Barrett Browning, Elizabeth. From "Glimpses into My Own Life and Literary Character," in *The Brownings' Correspondence,* Vol. 1. Edited by Phillip Kelley and Ronald Hudson. Wedgestone Press, 1984. All rights reserved. Reproduced by permission of Eton College.—Bassard, Katherine Clay. From *Spiritual Interrogations: Culture, Gender, and Community in Early African American Women's Writing.* Princeton University Press, 1999. Copyright © 1999 by Katherine Clay Bassard. Reproduced by permission of Princeton University Press.—Beauvoir, Simone de. From "The Independent Woman," in *The Second Sex.* Translated by H. M. Parshley. Alfred A. Knopf, Inc., 1952. Copyright © 1952, renewed 1980 by Alfred A. Knopf, Inc. All rights reserved. Reproduced by permission of Alfred A. Knopf, Inc., a division of Random House, Inc. and The Random House Group.—Behrendt, Stephen. From "Mary Shelley, Frankenstein, and the Woman Writer's Fate," in *Romantic Women Writers: Voices and Countervoices.* Edited by Paula R. Feldman and Theresa M. Kelley. University Press of New England, 1995. Copyright © 1995 by University Press of New England. All rights reserved. Reproduced by permission.—Bell, Barbara Currier and Carol Ohmann. From "Virginia Woolf's Criticism: A Polemical Preface," in *Feminist Literary Criticism: Explorations in Theory.* Edited by Josephine Donovan. The University Press of Kentucky, 1989. Copyright © 1975, 1989 by The University Press of Kentucky. Reproduced by permission of The University Press of Kentucky.—Berry, Mary Frances. From *Why ERA Failed: Politics, Women's Rights, and the Amending Process of the Constitution.* Indiana University Press, 1986. Copyright © 1986 by Mary Frances Berry. All rights reserved. Reproduced by permission.—Birgitta of Sweden. From *Life and Selected Revelations.* Edited with a preface by Marguerite Tjader Harris, translation and notes by Albert Ryle Kezel, introduction by Tore Nyberg from *The Classics of Western Spirituality.* Paulist Press, 1990. Copyright © 1990 by the Order of St. Birgitte, Rome. Translation, notes and Foreword copyright © 1990 by Albert Ryle Kezel, New York/Mahwah, NJ. Reproduced by permission of Paulist Press. www.paulistpress.com.—Blundell, Sue. From *Women in Ancient Greece.* British Museum Press, 1995. Copyright © 1995 Sue Blundell. Reproduced by permission of the author.—Bogan, Louise. From *The Blue Estuaries: Poems 1923-1968.* Farrar, Straus & Giroux, Inc., 1968. Copyright © 1968 by Louise Bogan. Copyright renewed 1996 by Ruth Limmer. All rights reserved. Reproduced by permission of Farrar, Straus and Giroux, LLC.—Booth, Alison. From "Not All Men Are Selfish and Cruel," in *Greatness Engendered: George Eliot and Virginia Woolf.* Cornell University Press, 1992. Copyright © 1992 by Cornell University Press. Reproduced by permission of the publisher, Cornell University Press.—Brammer, Leila R. From *Excluded from Suffrage History: Matilda Joslyn Gage, Nineteenth-Century American Feminist.* Greenwood Press, 2000. Copyright © by Leila R. Brammer. All rights reserved. Reproduced by permission of Greenwood Publishing Group, Inc., Westport, CT.—Britzolakis, Christina. From *Sylvia Plath and the Theatre of Mourning.* Oxford at the Clarendon Press, 1999. Copyright © 1999 by Christina Britzolakis. All rights reserved. Reproduced by permission of Oxford University Press.—Broe, Mary Lynn. From "Bohemia Bumps into Calvin: The Deception of Passivity in Lillian Hellman's Drama," in *Critical Essays on Lillian Hellman.* Edited by Mark W. Estrin. G. K. Hall, 1989. Copyright © 1989 by Mark W. Estrin. All rights reserved. Reproduced by permission of The Gale Group.—Brontë, Charlotte. From "Caroline Vernon," in *Legends of Angria: Compiled from The Early Writings of Charlotte Brontë.* Edited by Fannie E. Ratchford. Yale University Press, 1933. Copyright © 1933 by Yale University Press. Renewed 1961 by Fannit Ratchford. Reproduced by permission.—Brooks, Gwendolyn. From *Blacks.* The David Company, 1987. Copyright © 1945, 1949, 1953, 1960, 1963, 1968, 1969, 1970, 1971, 1975, 1981, 1986 by Gwendolyn Brooks Blakely. All rights reserved. Reproduced by consent of Brooks Permissions.—Brown-Grant, Rosalind. From "Christine de Pizan: Feminist Linguist Avant la Lettre?," in *Christine de Pizan 2000: Studies on Christine de Pizan in Honour of Angus J. Kennedy.* Edited by John Campbell and Nadia Margolis. Rodopi, 2000. Copyright © Editions Rodopi B. Reproduced by permission.—Brownmiller,

ACKNOWLEDGMENTS

From *The Sixties: From Memory to History.* Edited by David R. Farber. University of North Carolina Press, 1994. Copyright © 1994 by the University of North Carolina Press. Used by permission of the Publisher.—Ehrenreich, Barbara and Deirdre English. From *For Her Own Good: 150 Years of the Experts' Advice to Women.* Anchor Books/Doubleday, 1978. Copyright © 1978 by Barbara Ehrenreich and Deirdre English. All rights reserved. Used by permission of Doubleday, a division of Random House.—Elbert, Sarah. From *A Hunger for Home: Louisa May Alcott and Little Women.* Temple University Press, 1984. Copyright © 1984 by Temple University. All rights reserved. Reproduced by permission of the author.—Emecheta, Buchi. From "Feminism with a Small 'f'!," in *Criticism and Ideology: Second African Writers' Conference.* Edited by Kirsten Holst Petersen. Scandinavian Institute of African Studies, 1988. Copyright © 1988 by Scandinavian Institute of African Studies. All rights reserved. Reproduced by permission of Nordic Africa Institute.—Ensler, Eve. From *The Vagina Monologues: The V-Day Edition.* Villard, 2001. Copyright © 1998, 2001 by Eve Ensler. All rights reserved. Reproduced by permission of Villard Books, a division of Random House, Inc.—Enstad, Nan. From *Ladies of Labor, Girls of Adventure: Working Women, Popular Culture, and Labor Politics at the Turn of the Twentieth Century.* Columbia University Press, 1999. Copyright © 1999 Columbia University Press, New York. All rights reserved. Republished with permission of the Columbia University Press, 61 W. 62nd St., New York, NY 10023.—Ezell, Margaret J. M. From "Women and Writing," in *A Companion to Early Modern Women's Writing.* Edited by Anita Pacheco. Blackwell Publishing Ltd, 2002. Copyright © 2002 by Blackwell Publishers Ltd. Reproduced by permission of Blackwell Publishers.—Fallaize, Elizabeth. From "Resisting Romance: Simone de Beauvoir, *The Woman Destroyed* and the Romance Script," in *Contemporary French Fiction by Women: Feminist Perspectives.* Edited by Margaret Atack and Phil Powrie. Manchester University Press, 1990. Reproduced by permission of the author.—Feng, Pin-chia. From *The Female Bildungsroman by Toni Morrison and Maxine Hong Kingston: A Postmodern Reading.* Peter Lang, 1998. Copyright © 1988 Peter Lang Publishing, Inc. All rights reserved. Reproduced by permission.—Ferree, Myra Marx and Beth B. Hess. From *Controversy and Coalition: The New Feminist Movement across Three Decades of Change.* Twayne Publishers, 1994. Copyright © 1994 by Twayne Publishers. All rights reserved. Reproduced by permission of The Gale Group.—Fishkin, Shelley Fisher. From an interview with Maxine Hong Kingston, in *Conversations with Maxine Hong Kingston.* Edited by Paul Skenazy and Tera Martin. University Press of Mississippi, 1998. Copyright © 1998 by University Press of Mississippi. All rights reserved. Reproduced by permission of the author.—Fishkin, Shelley Fisher. From "Reading Gilman in the Twenty-First Century," in *The Mixed Legacy of Charlotte Perkins Gilman.* Edited by Catherine J. Golden and Joanna Schneider Zangrando. University of Delaware Press, 2000. Copyright © 2000 by Associated University Press. Reproduced by permission.—Fleischmann, Fritz. From "Margaret Fuller, the Eternal Feminine, and the 'Liberties of the Republic'," in *Women's Studies and Literature.* Edited by Fritz Fleischmann and Deborah Lucas Schneider. Palm & Enke, 1987. Reproduced by permission.—Foster, M. Marie Booth. From "Voice, Mind, Self: Mother-Daughter Relationships in Amy Tan's *The Joy Luck Club* and *The Kitchen God's Wife*," in *Women of Color: Mother-Daughter Relationships in 20th-Century Literature.* Edited by Elizabeth Brown-Guillory. University of Texas Press, 1996. Copyright © 1996 by the University of Texas Press. All rights reserved. Reproduced by permission.—Fowler, Robert Booth. From *Carrie Catt: Feminist Politician.* Northeastern University Press, 1986. Copyright © 1986 by R. B. Fowler. All rights reserved. Reproduced by permission.—Fraiman, Susan. From "The Humiliation of Elizabeth Bennett," in *Refiguring the Father: New Feminist Readings of Patriarchy.* Edited by Patricia Yaeger and Beth Kowaleski-Wallace. Southern Illinois University Press, 1989. Copyright © 1989 by the Board of Trustees, Southern Illinois University. All rights reserved. Reproduced by permission.—Francis, Emma. From "Is Emily Brontë a Woman?: Femininity, Feminism, and the Paranoid Critical Subject," in *Subjectivity and Literature from the Romantics to the Present Day.* Edited by Philip Shaw and Peter Stockwell. Pinter, 1991. Copyright © Emma Francis. All rights reserved. Reproduced by permission of the author.—Freedman, Estelle B. and Erna Olafson Hellerstein. From an introduction to *Victorian Women: A Documentary Account of Women's Lives in Nineteenth-Century England, France, and the United States.* Edited by Erna Olafson Hellerstein, Leslie Parker Hume, and Karen M. Offen. Stanford University Press, 1981. Copyright © 1981 by the Board of Trustees of Leland Stanford Junior University. Reproduced with permission of Stanford University Press, www.sup.org.—Frenk, Susan. From "The Wandering Text: Situating the Narratives of Isabel Allende," in *Latin American Women's Writing: Feminist Readings in Theory and Crisis.* Edited by Anny Brooksbank Jones and Catherine Davies. Oxford at the Clarendon Press, 1996. Copyright © 1996 by Anny Brooksbank Jones and Catherine Davies. All rights reserved. Reproduced by permission of Oxford University Press.—From *Victorian Women: A Documentary Account of Women's Lives in Nineteenth-Century England, France, and the United States.* Edited by Erna Olafson Hellerstein, Leslie Parker Hume, and Karen M. Offen. Stanford University Press, 1981. Copyright © 1981 by the Board of Trustees of Leland Stanford Junior University. Reproduced with permission of Stanford University Press, www.sup.org.—Galvin, Mary E. From *Queer Poetics: Five Modernist Women Writers.* Praeger, 1999. Copyright © 1999 by Mary E. Galvin. All rights reserved. Reproduced by permission.—Garner, Shirley Nelson. From "Constructing the Mother: Contemporary Psychoanalytic Theorists and Women Autobiographers," in *Narrating Mother: Theorizing Maternal Subjectivities.* Edited by Brenda O. Daly and Maureen T. Reddy. University of Tennessee Press, 1991. Copyright © 1991 by The University of Tennessee Press. Reproduced by permission of the publisher.—Ghymn, Esther Mikyung. From an introduction to *Images of Asian American Women by Asian American Women Writers.* Peter Lang, 1995. Copyright © 1995, by Esther Mikyung Ghymn. All rights reserved. Reproduced by permission.—Gilbert, Sandra M. and Gubar, Susan. From "Charred Skirts and Deathmask: World War II and the Blitz on Women," in *No Man's Land: The Place of the Woman Writer in the Twentieth Century, Volume 3: Letters from the Front.* Yale University Press, 1994. Copyright © 1994, by Sandra M. Gilbert and Susan Gubar. All rights reserved. Reproduced by permission.—Gilbert, Sandra M. and Susan Gubar. From "The Battle of the Sexes: The Men's Case," in *No Man's Land: The Place of the Woman Writer in the Twentieth Century, Volume 1: The War of the Words.* Yale University Press, 1988. Copyright © 1988, by Yale University Press, All rights reserved. Reproduced by permission.—Gilbert, Sandra M., and Susan Gubar. From "The Second Coming of Aphrodite: Kate Chopin's Fantasy of Desire," in *No Man's Land: The Place of the Woman Writer in the Twentieth Century.* Yale University Press, 1989. Copyright © 1989 by Yale University. Copyright © 1984 by Sandra M. Gilbert and Susan Gubar. All rights reserved. Reproduced by permission.—Gilbert, Susan M., and Susan Gubar. From *The Madwoman in the Attic: The Woman Writer and the Nineteenth-Century Literary Imagination.* Yale University Press, 1979. Copyright © 1979 by Yale University. All rights reserved. Reproduced by permission.—Gleadle, Kathryn. From an introduction to *The Early Feminists: Radical Unitarians and the Emergence of The Women's Rights Movement, 1831-51.* Macmillan Press Ltd., 1995.

Copyright © Kathryn Gleadle 1995. All rights reserved. Reproduced by permission of Palgrave Macmillan.—Golden, Catherine. From "One Hundred Years of Reading 'The Yellow Wallpaper'," in *The Captive Imagination: A Casebook on "The Yellow Wallpaper."* Edited by Catherine Golden. The Feminist Press at the City University of New York, 1992. Copyright © 1992 by Catherine Golden. All rights reserved. Reproduced by permission.—Gorsky, Susan Rubinow. From *Femininity to Feminism: Women and Literature in the Nineteenth Century.* Twayne Publishers, 1992. Copyright © 1992 by Twayne Publishers. All rights reserved. Reproduced by permission of The Gale Group.—Greer, Germaine. From *The Madwoman's Underclothes: Essays and Occasional Writings.* The Atlantic Monthly Press, 1986. Copyright © 1970, 1986, by Germaine Greer. All rights reserved. Reproduced by permission.—Grewal, Gurleen. From *Circles of Sorrow, Lines of Struggle: The Novels of Toni Morrison.* Louisiana State University Press, 1998. Copyright © 1998 by Louisiana State University Press. All rights reserved. Reproduced by permission.—Griffin, Alice and Geraldine Thorsten. From *Understanding Lillian Hellman.* University of South Carolina Press, 1999. Copyright © 1999 University of South Carolina. Reproduced by permission.—Griffin, Susan E. From "Resistance and Reinvention in Sandra Cisneros' *Woman Hollering Creek*," in *Ethnicity and the American Short Story.* Edited by Julie Brown. Garland Publishing, Inc., 1997. Copyright © 1997 by Julie Brown. All rights reserved. Reproduced by permission of the publisher and the author.—Grogan, Susan K. From an introduction to *French Socialism and Sexual Difference: Women and the New Society, 1803-44.* St. Martin's Press, 1992. Copyright © Susan K. Grogan 1992. All rights reserved. Reprinted by permission of Palgrave Macmillan.—Grössinger, Christa. From *Picturing Women in Late Medieval and Renaissance Art.* Manchester University Press, 1997. Copyright © Christa Grössinger 1997. Reproduced by permission.—Grubbs, Judith Evans. From *Women and the Law in the Roman Empire: A Sourcebook on Marriage, Divorce and Widowhood.* Routledge, 2002. Reproduced by permission of the publisher.—Grundy, Isobel. From "(Re)discovering Women's Texts," in *Women and Literature in Britain 1700-1800.* Edited by Vivien Jones. Cambridge University Press, 2000. Copyright © 2000 by Cambridge University Press. Reproduced by permission of Cambridge University Press.—Gubar, Susan. From "Feminist Misogyny: Mary Wollstonecraft and the Paradox of 'It Takes One to Know One'," in *Feminism Beside Itself.* Edited by Diane Elam and Robyn Wiegman. Routledge, 1995. Copyright © 1995 by Routledge.

All rights reserved. Reproduced by permission of Routledge/Taylor & Francis and the author.—Gubar, Susan. From "Sapphistries," in *Re-reading Sappho: Reception and Transmission.* Edited by Ellen Greene. University of California Press, 1996. Copyright © 1996 by The Regents of The University of California. Reproduced by permission of the publisher and the author.—Gunther-Canada, Wendy. From *Rebel Writer: Mary Wollstonecraft and Enlightenment Politics.* Northern Illinois University Press, 2001. Copyright © 2001 by Northern Illinois University Press. All rights reserved. Reproduced by permission.—Hagen, Lyman B. From *Heart of a Woman, Mind of a Writer, and Soul of a Poet: A Critical Analysis of the Writings of Maya Angelou.* University Press of America, 1997. Copyright © 1997 by University Press of America. All rights reserved. Reproduced by permission.—Hallett, Judith From "The Role of Women in Roman Elegy: Counter-Cultural Feminism," in *Women in the Ancient World: The Arethusa Papers.* Edited by John Peradotto and J. Sullivan. State University of New York Press, 1984. Reproduced by permission of the State University of New York Press.—Hansberry, Lorraine. From *A Raisin in the Sun.* Modern Library, 1995. Copyright © 1958, 1986 by Robert Nemiroff, as an unpublished work. Copyright © 1959, 1966, 1984, 1987, 1988 by Robert Nemiroff. All rights reserved. Reproduced by permission of Random House, Inc., Jewell Gresham-Nemiroff and Methuen Publishing Ltd.—Harris, Susan K. From "'But is it any good?' Evaluating Nineteenth-Century American Women's Fiction," in *The (Other) American Traditions: Nineteenth-Century Women Writers.* Edited by Joyce W. Warren. Rutgers University Press, 1993. Copyright © 1993 by Rutgers University Press. All rights reserved. Reproduced by permission of the author.—Head, Bessie. From "Despite Broken Bondage, Botswana Women Are Still Unloved," in *A Woman Alone: Autobiographical Writings.* Selected and edited by Craig MacKenzie. Heinemann, 1990. Copyright © 1990, by The Estate of Bessie Head. Reproduced by permission of Johnson & Alcock.—Head, Bessie. From "The Woman from America," in *A Woman Alone: Autobiographical Writings.* Selected and edited by Craig MacKenzie. Heinemann, 1990. Copyright © 1990, by The Estate of Bessie Head. Reproduced by permission of Johnson & Alcock.—Hellerstein, Erna, Leslie Parker Hume and Karen M. Offen from an introduction to *Victorian Women: A Documentary Account of Women's Lives in Nineteenth-Century England, France, and the United States.* Edited by Erna Olafson Hellerstein, Leslie Parker Hume, and Karen M. Offen. Stanford University Press, 1981. Copyright © 1981 by the Board of Trustees of the Leland Stanford Junior University. Reproduced with permission of Stanford University Press, www.sup.org.—Henderson, Bruce. From *Images of the Self as Female: The Achievement of Women Artists in Re-envisioning Feminine Identity.* Edited by Kathryn N. Benzel and Lauren Pringle De La Vars. The Edwin Mellen Press, 1992. Copyright © 1992 by Kathryn N. Benzel and Lauren Pringle De La Vars. All rights reserved. Reproduced by permission.—Hill, Mary A. From "Charlotte Perkins Gilman: A Feminist's Struggle with Womanhood," in *Charlotte Perkins Gilman: The Woman and Her Work.* Edited by Sheryl L. Meyering. UMI Research Press, 1989. Copyright © 1989 by Sheryl L. Meyering. All rights reserved. Reproduced by permission of Boydell & Brewer, Inc.—Hobby, Elaine. From *Virtue of Necessity: English Women's Writing 1649-88.* The University of Michigan Press, 1989. Copyright © 1988 by Elaine Hobby. All rights reserved. Reproduced by permission of the author.—Hoffert, Sylvia D. From an introduction to *When Hens Crow: The Woman's Rights Movement in Antebellum America.* Indiana University Press, 1995. Copyright © 1995 by Sylvia D. Hoffert. All rights reserved. Reproduced by permission.—Hurston, Zora Neale. From *Their Eyes Were Watching God.* Perennial Library, 1990. Copyright © 1937 by Harper & Row, Publishers, Inc. Renewed 1965 by John C. Hurston and Joel Hurston. Reproduced by permission of Time Warner Books UK. In North America by HarperCollins Publishers Inc.—James, Adeola. From "Bessie Head's Perspectives on Women," in *Black Women Writers across Cultures.* Edited by Valentine Udoh James, James S. Etim, Melanie Marshall James, and Ambe J. Njoh. International Scholars Publications, 2000. Copyright © 2000, by International Scholars Publications. All rights reserved. Reproduced by permission.—Jardine, Alice A. From an interview with Marguerite Duras, translated by Katherine Ann Jensen, in *Shifting Scenes: Interviews on Women, Writing, and Politics in Post-68 France.* Edited by Alice A. Jardine and Anne M. Menke. Columbia University Press, 1991. Copyright © 1991 Columbia University Press, New York. All rights reserved. Reprinted with the permission of the publisher.—Jelinek, Estelle C. From "The Paradox and Success of Elizabeth Cady Stanton," in *Women's Autobiography: Essays in Criticism.* Edited by Estelle C. Jelinek. Indiana University Press, 1980. Copyright © Estelle C. Jelinek. Reproduced by permission of the author.—Juhasz, Suzanne. From "Maxine Hong Kingston: Narrative Technique & Female Identity," in *Contemporary American Women Writers: Narrative Strategies.* Edited by Catherine Rainwater and William J. Scheik. The University Press of Kentucky, 1985. Copyright © 1985 by The University Press of

Kentucky. Reproduced by permission.—Kaminer, Wendy. From "Feminism's Identity Crisis," in *Public Women, Public Words: A Documentary History of American Feminism.* Edited by Dawn Keetley and John Pettegrew. First published in *The Atlantic.* Reproduced by permission of the author.—Kaplan, Cora. From "Pandora's Box: Subjectivity, Class and Sexuality in Socialist Feminist Criticism," in *Making a Difference: Feminist Literary Criticism.* Edited by Gayle Greene and Coppélia Kahn. Methuen & Co., 1985. Copyright © 1985 Gayle Greene and Coppélia Kahn. All rights reserved. Reproduced by permission of Routledge and the author.—Keetley, Dawn and John Pettegrew. From "Identities through Adversity," in *Public Women, Public Words: A Documentary History of American Feminism.* Edited by Dawn Keetley and John Pettegrew. Madison House Publishers, Inc., 1997. Copyright © 1997 by Madison House Publisher, Inc. All rights reserved. Reproduced by permission.—Kelly, Gary. From *Revolutionary Feminism: The Mind and Career of Mary Wollstonecraft.* St. Martin's Press, 1996. Copyright © 1996 by Gary Kelly. All rights reserved. Reproduced by permission of Palgrave Macmillan.—Kempe, Margery. From "Margery Kempe's Visit to Julian of Norwich," in *The Shewings of Julian Norwich.* Edited by Georgia Ronan Crampton. Medieval Publishing Institute, 1994. Reproduced by permission.—Kempe, Margery. From *The Book of Margery Kempe.* Translated by B. A. Windeatt. Penguin, 1985. Copyright © B. A. Windeatt, 1985. All rights reserved. Reproduced by permission.—Kirkham, Margaret. From *Jane Austen, Feminism, and Fiction.* Harvester Press Limited, 1983. Copyright © Margaret Kirkham, 1983. All rights reserved. Reproduced by permission.—Klemans, Patricia A. From "'Being Born a Woman': A New Look at Edna St. Vincent Millay," in *Critical Essays on Edna St. Vincent Millay.* Edited by William B. Thesing. G. K. Hall, 1993. Copyright © by 1993 by William B. Thesing. All rights reserved. Reproduced by permission of The Gale Group.—Knapp, Bettina L. From *Gertrude Stein.* Continuum, 1990. Copyright © 1990 by Bettina L. Knapp. All rights reserved. Reproduced by permission.—Kolodny, Annette. From "Dancing Through the Minefield: Some Observations on the Theory, Practice, and Politics of a Feminist Literary Criticism," originally published in *Feminist Studies,* 1980. Copyright © 1980 by Annette Kolodny. All rights reserved. Reproduced by permission of the author.—Kumin, Maxine. From "How It Was," in *The Complete Poems: Anne Sexton.* Houghton Mifflin Company, 1981. Copyright © 1981, by Maxine Kumin. All rights reserved. Reproduced by permission of Houghton Mifflin and The Anderson Literary Agency.—Lam-

onica, Drew. From *We Are Three Sisters: Self and Family in the Writing of the Brontës.* University of Missouri Press, 2003. Copyright © 2003 by The Curators of the University of Missouri. All rights reserved. Reproduced by permission.—Larsen, Jeanne. From "Lowell, Teasdale, Wylie, Millay, and Bogan," in *The Columbia History of American Poetry.* Edited by Jay Parini. Columbia University Press, 1993. Copyright © 1993 Columbia University Press, New York. All rights reserved. Reprinted with permission of the publisher.—Lascelles, Mary. From *Jane Austen and Her Art.* Oxford University Press, 1939. Reproduced by permission of Oxford University Press.—Lavezzo, Kathy. From "Sobs and Sighs Between Women: The Homoerotics of Compassion in *The Book of Margery Kempe,*" in *Premodern Sexualities.* Edited by Louise Fradenburg and Carla Freccero. Routledge, 1996. Copyright © 1996 by Routledge. All rights reserved. Reproduced by permission of Routledge/Taylor & Francis and the author.—Lessing, Doris. From a preface to *The Golden Notebook* in *A Small Personal Voice.* Edited by Paul Schleuter. Alfred A. Knopf, Inc., 1974. Copyright © 1974 by Doris Lessing. All rights reserved. Reproduced by permission of Jonathan Clowes, Ltd.—Levertov, Denise. From *Poems, 1960-67.* New Directions, 1966. Copyright © 1967, by Denise Levertov. All rights reserved. Reproduced by permission of New Directions Publishing Corporation and in the UK by Pollinger Limited and the proprietor.—Logan, Shirley Wilson. From *"We are Coming": The Persuasive Discourse of Nineteenth-Century Black Women.* Southern Illinois University Press, 1999. Copyright © 1999 by the Board of Trustees, Southern Illinois University. All rights reserved. Reproduced by permission of Southern Illinois University Press and the University of South Carolina Press.—Lorde, Audre. From *The Black Unicorn.* Norton, 1978. Copyright © 1978, by Audre Lorde. All rights reserved. Reproduced by permission of W. W. Norton & Company and Charlotte Sheedy Literary Agency.—Lumsden, Linda J. From *Rampant Women: Suffragists and the Right of Assembly.* The University of Tennessee Press, 1997. Copyright © 1997 by The University of Tennessee Press. Reproduced by permission of The University of Tennessee Press.—Lunardini, Christine A. *From Equal Suffrage to Equal Rights: Alice Paul and the National Women's Party, 1910-1928.* New York University Press, 1986. Copyright © 1986 by New York University. All rights reserved. Reproduced by permission of the author.—Madsen, Deborah L. From "Sandra Cisneros," in *Understanding Contemporary Chicana Literature.* Edited by Matthew J. Bruccoli. University of South Carolina Press, 2000. Copyright © 2000 by University of South Carolina. Reproduced by permis-

Studies in Literature, History, and the Arts in Nineteenth-Century France: Selected Proceedings of the Sixteenth Colloquium in Nineteenth-Century French Studies, The University of Oklahoma-Norman, October 11th-13th, 1990. Edited by Keith Busby. Rodopi, 1992. Copyright © Editions Rodopi B. V. Reproduced by permission.—Motard-Noar, Martine. From "From Persephone to Demeter: A Feminist Experience in Cixous's Fiction," in *Images of Persephone: Feminist Readings in Western Literature.* Edited by Elizabeth T. Hayes. University Press of Florida, 1994. Copyright © 1994 by Board of Regents of the State of Florida. All rights reserved. Reproduced with the permission of the University Press of Florida.—Mukherjee, Bharati. From *The Middleman and Other Stories.* Viking, 1988. Copyright © 1988, by Bharati Mukherjee. All rights reserved. Reprinted by permission of Penguin Group Canada and the author.—Mumford, Marilyn R. From "A Feminist Prolegomenon for the Study of Hildegard of Bingen," in *Gender, Culture, and the Arts: Women, the Arts, and Society.* Edited by Ronald Dotterer and Susan Bowers. Associated University Presses, 1993. Copyright © 1993 by Associated University Presses.—Oates, Joyce Carol. From *Where I've Been, and Where I'm Going.* Plume, 1999. Copyright © The Ontario Review, 1999. All rights reserved. Reproduced by permission of Plume, an imprint of Penguin Putnam Inc. In the United Kingdom by John Hawkins & Associates, Inc.—Okely, Judith. From "Re-reading The Second Sex," in *Simone de Beauvoir: A Re-Reading.* Virago, 1986. Reproduced by permission of the author.—Ovid. From "Sappho to Phaon," in *The Sappho Companion.* Edited by Margaret Reynolds. Chatto and Windus, 2000. Copyright © Margaret Reynolds 2000. Reproduced by permission of the editor.—Pan Chao. From *Pan Chao: Foremost Woman Scholar of China.* Edited by Nancy Lee Swann. University of Michigan Center for Chinese Studies, 1932. Copyright © The East Asian Library and the Gest Collection, Princeton University. Reproduced by permission.—Parks, Sheri. From "In My Mother's House: Black Feminist Aesthetics, Television, and *A Raisin in the Sun,*" in *Theatre and Feminist Aesthetics.* Edited by Karen Laughlin and Catherine Schuler. Farleigh Dickinson University Press, 1995. Copyright © 1995 by Associated University Presses. All rights reserved. Reproduced by permission.—Paul, Alice. From *Party Papers: 1913-1974.* Microfilming Corporation of America, 1978. Reproduced by permission of Sewall-Belmont House and Museum.—Paz, Octavio. From "The Response," in *Sor Juana or, The Traps of Faith.* Translated by Margaret Sayers Peden. Cambridge, Mass.: The Belknap Press of Harvard University Press, 1988. Copyright © 1988 by the President and Fellows of Harvard College. All rights reserved. Reproduced by permission.—Perkins, Annie. From "The Poetry of Gwendolyn Brooks (1970s-1980s)," in *Women Making Art: Women in the Visual, Literary, and Performing Arts Since 1960.* Edited by Deborah Johnson and Wendy Oliver. Peter Lang, 2001. Copyright © 2001 Peter Lang Publishing, Inc., New York. Reproduced by permission.—Pierpont, Claudia Roth. From *Passionate Minds: Women Rewriting the World.* Alfred A. Knopf, 2000. Copyright © 2000 by Claudia Roth Piepont. All rights reserved. Reproduced by permission of Alfred A. Knopf, Inc., a division of Random House, Inc.—Plath, Sylvia. From *The Bell Jar.* Faber & Faber, 1966; Harper & Row, 1971. Copyright © 1971 by Harper & Row, Publishers, Inc. Reproduced by permission Faber & Faber Ltd. In the United States by HarperCollins Publishers Inc.—Pryse, Marjorie. From "Origins of American Literary Regionalism: Gender in Irving, Stowe, and Longstreet," in *Breaking Boundaries: New Perspectives on Women's Regional Writing.* Edited by Sherrie A. Inness and Diana Royer. University of Iowa Press, 1997. Copyright © 1997 by the University of Iowa Press. All rights reserved. Reproduced by permission.—Radice, Betty. From an introduction to *The Letters of Abelard and Heloise.* Translated by Betty Radice. Penguin Books, 1974. Copyright © Betty Radice, 1974. Reproduced by permission of Penguin Books, a division of Penguin Putnam Inc.—Rendall, Jane. From an introduction to *The Origins of Modern Feminism: Women in Britain, France and the United States 1780-1860.* Macmillan, 1985. Copyright © Jane Rendall 1985. All rights reserved. Reproduced by permission of Palgrave Macmillan.—Rich, Adrienne. From "Vesuvius at Home: The Power of Emily Dickinson," in *On Lies, Secrets, and Silence: Selected Prose 1966-1978.* W. W. Norton & Company, Inc., 1979. Copyright © 1979 by W. W. Norton & Company, Inc. Reproduced by permission of the author and W. W. Norton & Company, Inc.—Rich, Adrienne. From "When We Dead Awaken: Writing as Re-Vision," in *Arts of the Possible: Essays and Conversations.* W. W. Norton & Company, Inc., 2001. Copyright © 2001 by Adrienne Rich. Reproduced by permission of the publisher and the author.—Richmond, M. A. From *Bid the Vassal Soar: Essays on the Life and Poetry of Phillis Wheatley and George Moses Horton.* Howard University Press, 1974. All rights reserved. Copyright © 1974 by Merle A. Richmond. Reproduced by permission.—Risjord, Norman K. From *Representative Americans: The Colonists.* Second Edition. Rowman & Littlefield Publishers, Inc., 2001. Copyright © 2001 by Rowman & Littlefield Publishers, Inc. All rights reserved. Reproduced by permission.—Robbins,

Johanna M. From "'Cooped Up': Feminine Domesticity in *Frankenstein*," in **Case Studies in Contemporary Criticism: Mary Shelley's** **Frankenstein**. Edited by Johanna M. Smith. St. Martin's Press, 1992. Copyright © 1992 by Bedford Books of St. Martin's Press. All rights reserved. Reproduced by permission.—Smith, Sidonie. From "Resisting the Gaze of Embodiment: Women's Autobiography in the Nineteenth Century," in **American Women's Autobiography: Fea(s)ts of Memory**. Edited by Margo Culley. University of Wisconsin University Press, 1992. Copyright © 1992 The Board of Regents of the University of Wisconsin System. All rights reserved. Reproduced by permission.—Smith, Sidonie. From **Where I'm Bound: Patterns of Slavery and Freedom in Black American Autobiography**. Greenwood Press, 1974. Copyright © 1974 by Sidonie Smith. All rights reserved. Reproduced by permission of Greenwood Publishing Group, Inc., Westport, CT.—Snyder, Jane McIntosh. From **The Woman and the Lyre: Women Writers in Classical Greece and Rome**. Southern Illinois University Press, 1989. Copyright © 1989 by the Board of Trustees, Southern Illinois University. All rights reserved. Reproduced by permission.—Sor Juana Ines de la Cruz. From **The Answer = La respuesta**. Edited by Electa Arenal and Amanda Powell. The Feminist Press, 1994. Copyright © 1994 by Electa Arenal and Amanda Powell. All rights reserved. Reproduced by permission of The Feminist Press at the City University of New York. www.feministpress.org.—Spender, Dale. From "Introduction: A Vindication of the Writing Woman," in **Living by the Pen: Early British Women Writers**. Edited by Dale Spender. Teachers College Press, 1992. Copyright © 1992 by Teachers College. All rights reserved. Reproduced by permission.—Staley, Lynn. From **Margery Kempe's Dissenting Fictions**. Pennsylvania State University Press, 1994. Copyright © 1994 The Pennsylvania State University. All rights reserved. Reproduced by permission.—Stehle, Eva. From **Performance and Gender in Ancient Greece: Nondramatic Poetry in Its Setting**. Princeton University Press, 1997. Copyright © 1997 by Princeton University Press. All rights reserved. Reproduced by permission of Princeton University Press.—Stein, Gertrude. From "Degeneration in American Women," in **Sister Brother: Gertrude and Leo Stein**. Edited by Brenda Wineapple. G. Putnam's Sons, 1996. Copyright © 1996 by Brenda Wineapple. All rights reserved. Used by permission of G. Putnam's Sons, a division of Penguin Group (USA) Inc. and Bloomsbury Publishing Plc.—Stott, Rebecca. From **Elizabeth Barrett Browning**. Pearson Education Limited, 2003. Copyright © Pearson Educated Limited 2003. All rights reserved. Reproduced by permission.—Straub, Kristina. From **Divided Fic-** **tions: Fanny Burney and Feminine Strategy**. University Press of Kentucky, 1987. Copyright © 1987 by the University Press of Kentucky. Reproduced by permission.—Swann, Nancy Lee. From **Pan Chao: Foremost Woman Scholar of China**. Russell & Russell, 1968. Copyright © The East Asian Library and the Gest Collection, Princeton University. Reproduced by permission.—Tanner, Laura E. From **Intimate Violence: Reading Rape and Torture in Twentieth-Century Fiction**. Indiana University Press, 1994. Copyright © 1994, by Laura E. Tanner. All rights reserved. Reproduced by permission.—Terborg-Penn, Rosalyn. From **African American Women in the Struggle for the Vote, 1850-1920**. Indiana University Press, 1998. Reproduced by permission.—Tharp, Julie. From "Women's Community and Survival in the Novels of Louise Erdrich," in **Communication and Women's Friendships: Parallels and Intersections in Literature and Life**. Edited by Janet Doubler Ward and JoAnna Stephens Mink. Bowling Green State University Popular Press, 1993. Copyright © 1993 by Bowling Green State University Popular Press. Reproduced by permission of the University of Wisconsin Press.—Trilling, Lionel. From "Emma and the Legend of Jane Austen," in **Beyond Culture: Essays on Literature and Learning**. Harcourt Brace Jovanovich, 1965. Copyright © 1965 by Lionel Trilling. All rights reserved. Reproduced by permission of the Wylie Agency, Inc.—Turner, Katherine S. H. From "From Classical to Imperial: Changing Visions of Turkey in the Eighteenth Century," in **Travel Writing and Empire: Postcolonial Theory in Transit**. Edited by Steve Clark. Zed Books, 1999. Copyright © Katherine S. H. Turner. Reproduced by permission.—Van Dyke, Annette. From "Of Vision Quests and Spirit Guardians: Female Power in the Novels of Louise Erdrich," in **The Chippewa Landscape of Louise Erdrich**. Edited by Allan Chavkin. The University of Alabama Press, 1999. Copyright © 1999, by The University of Alabama Press. Copyright © 1999. All rights reserved. Reproduced by permission.—Waelti-Waters, Jennifer and Steven C. Hause. From an introduction to **Feminisms of the Belle Époque: A Historical and Literary Anthology**. Edited by Jennifer Waelti-Waters and Steven C. Hause. University of Nebraska Press, 1994. Copyright © The University of Nebraska Press, 1994. All rights reserved. Reproduced by permission.—Wagner-Martin, Linda. From "Panoramic, Unpredictable, and Human: Joyce Carol Oates' Recent Novels," in **Traditions, Voices, and Dreams: The American Novel since the 1960s**. Edited by Melvin J. Friedman and Ben Siegel. University of Delaware Press, 1995. Copyright © 1995 by Associated University Presses, Inc. Reproduced by permission.—Wagner-Martin, Linda. From **Sylvia Plath: A Literary Life**.

ACKNOWLEDGMENTS

St. Martin's Press, 1999. Copyright © 1999 by Linda Wagner-Martin. All rights reserved. Reproduced by permission of Palgrave Macmillan.—Walker, Alice. From *Revolutionary Petunias & Other Poems.* Harcourt Brace Jovanovich, 1971. Copyright © 1970, 1971, 1972, 1973, renewed 1998 by Alice Walker. All right reserved. Reproduced by permission of Harcourt Inc. In the British Commonwealth by David Higham Associates.—Watts, Linda S. From *Rapture Untold: Gender, Mysticism, and the 'Moment of Recognition' in Works by Gertrude Stein.* Peter Lang, 1996. Copyright © 1996 Peter Lang Publishing, Inc., New York. All rights reserved. Reproduced by permission.—Weatherford, Doris. From *A History of the American Suffragist Movement.* ABC-CLIO, 1998. Copyright © 1998 by The Moschovitis Group, Inc. Reproduced by permission of Moschovitis Group, Inc.—Weeton, Nellie. From "The Trials of an English Governess: Nelly Weeton Stock," originally published in *Miss Weeton: Journal of a Governess.* Edited by Edward Hall. Oxford University Press (London), H. Milford, 1936-39. Reproduced by permission of Oxford University Press.—Weston, Ruth D. From "Who Touches This Touches a Woman," in *Critical Essays on Alice Walker.* Edited by Ikenna Dieke. Greenwood Press 1999. Reproduced by permission of Greenwood Publishing Group, Inc., Westport, CT.—Wheeler, Marjorie Spruill. From an introduction to *One Woman, One Vote: Rediscovering the Woman Suffrage Movement.* Edited by Marjorie Spruill Wheeler. NewSage Press, 1995. Copyright © 1995 by NewSage Press and Educational Film Company. All rights reserved. Reproduced by permission.—Willard, Charity Cannon. From *Christine de Pizan: Her Life and Works.* Persea Books, 1984. Copyright © 1984 by Charity Cannon Willard. Reproduced by permission.—Willis, Sharon A. From "Staging Sexual Difference: Reading, Recitation, and Repetition in Duras' *Malady of Death*," in *Feminine Focus: The New Women Playwrights.* Edited by Enoch Brater. Oxford University Press, 1989. Copyright © 1989 by Oxford University Press, Inc. Reproduced by permission of Oxford University Press.—Winter, Kate H. From *Marietta Holley: Life with "Josiah Allen's Wife."* Syracuse University Press, 1984. Copyright © 1984 by Syracuse University Press. All rights reserved. Reproduced by permission.—Woolf, Virginia. From "George Eliot," in *The Common Reader,* Harcourt, Brace & Company, 1925, L. & V. Woolf, 1925. Copyright 1925 by Harcourt Brace & Company. Renewed 1953 by Leonard Woolf. Reprinted by permission of Harcourt, Brace & Company and The Society of Authors.—Wynne-Davies, Marion. From an introduction to *Women Poets of the Renaissance.* Edited by Marion Wynne-Davies.

Routledge, 1999. Reprint. Copyright © 1998 by J. M. Dent. All rights reserved. Reproduced by permission of Routledge/Taylor & Francis and the author—Yalom, Marilyn. From "Toward a History of Female Adolescence: The Contribution of George Sand," in *George Sand: Collected Essays.* Edited by Janis Glasgow. The Whitson Publishing Company, 1985. Reproduced by permission of the author.—Yu Xuanji. From "Joining Somebody's Mourning and Three Beautiful Sisters, Orphaned Young," in *The Clouds Float North: The Complete Poems of Yu Xuanji.* Translated by David Young and Jiann I. Lin. Wesleyan University Press, 1998. Copyright © 1998 by David Young and Jiann I. Lin. All rights reserved. Reproduced by permission.

Photographs and Illustrations in Feminism in Literature *were received from the following sources:*

16th century men and women wearing fashionable clothing, ca. 1565 engraving. Hulton/Archive.—A lay sister preparing medicine as shown on the cover of *The Book of Margery Kempe,* photograph. MS. Royal 15 D 1, British Library, London.—Akhmatova, Anna, photograph. Archive Photos, Inc./Express Newspaper.—Alcott, Louisa May, drawing. The Granger Collection, New York.—Alcott, Louisa May, photograph. Archive Photos, Inc.—Allen, Joan, Joanne Camp, Anne Lange, and Cynthia Nixon, in a scene from the play "The Heidi Chronicles," photograph. Time Life Pictures/Getty Images.—Allende, Isabelle, photograph. Getty Images.—An estimated 5,000 people march outside the Minnesota Capitol Building in protest to the January 22, 1973 Supreme Court ruling on abortion as a result of the "Roe vs. Wade" case, photograph. AP/Wide World Photos.—Angelou, Maya, photograph. AP/Wide World Photos.—Anthony, Susan B., Frances Willard, and other members of the International Council of Women, photograph. Copyright © Corbis.—Atwood, Margaret, photograph by Jerry Bauer. Copyright © Jerry Bauer.—Autographed manuscript of Phillis Weatley's poem "To the University of Cambridge." The Granger Collection, New York.—Beller, Kathleen as Kate in the 1980 film version of Margaret Atwood's novel, *Surfacing,* photograph. Kobal Collection/Surfacing Film.—Blackshear, Thomas, illustrator. From a cover of *The Bluest Eye,* written by Toni Morrison. Plume, 1994. Reproduced by permission of Plume, a division of Penguin USA.—Broadside published by the National American Woman Suffrage Association, featuring "Why Women Want to Vote." The Library of Congress.—Brontë, Anne, Emily and Charlotte, painting by Patrick Branwell Brontë, located at the National Portrait Gallery,

1939, photograph. Copyright © Corbis-Bettmann.—Brontë, Charlotte, painting. Archive Photos.—Brooks, Gwendolyn, holding a copy of *The World of Gwendolyn Brooks,* photograph. AP/Wide World Photos.—Brown, John Mason (right) talking to National Book Award winners Marianne Moore, James Jones, and Rachel Carson, in New York City, NY, 1952, photograph. AP/Wide World Photos.—Brown, Rita Mae, photograph. AP/Wide World Photos.—Browning, Elizabeth Barret, 1848, illustration. Copyright © Corbis-Bettmann.—Burney, Fanny, engraving. Archive Photos, Inc.—Carter, Angela, photograph by Jerry Bauer. Copyright © Jerry Bauer.—Cather, Willa, photograph. AP/Wide World Photos.—Catherine the Great, illustration. Copyright © Archivo Iconografico, S.A./Corbis.—Catt, Carrie Chapman, photograph. The Library of Congress.—Cavendish, Margaret Lucas, engraving. Mary Evans Picture Library.—Child, Lydia Maria, photograph. The Library of Congress.—Childress, Alice, photograph by Jerry Bauer. Copyright © Jerry Bauer.—Chin, Tsai and Tamlyn Tomita in the 1993 film production of Amy Tan's *The Joy Luck Club.* Buena Vista/Hollywood/The Kobal Collection.—Chopin, Kate, photograph. The Library of Congress.—Cisneros, Sandra, 1991, photograph by Dana Tynan. AP/Wide World Photos.—Cixous, Hélène, photograph. Copyright © Bassouls Sophie/Corbis Sygma.—Class on a field trip to Library of Congress, photograph by Frances Benjamin Johnston. Copyright © Corbis.—Cleopatra VII, illustration. The Library of Congress.—Cyanotype by Frances Benjamin Johnson, ca. 1899, of girls and a teacher in a high school cooking class, photograph. Copyright © Corbis.—de la Cruz, Juana Inez, painting. Copyright © Philadelphia Museum of Art/Corbis-Bettmann.—de Pizan, Christine, writing in her study, photograph. MS. Harley 4431, f.4R. British Library, London.—Dickinson, Emily, photograph of a painting. The Library of Congress.—Doolittle, Hilda, 1949, photograph. AP/Wide World Photos.—Duras, Marguerite, photograph. AP/Wide World Photos.—Dworkin, Andrea, 1986, photograph. AP/Wide World Photos.—Edgeworth, Maria, engraving. The Library of Congress.—Eliot, George, photograph. Copyright © The Bettman Archive.—Emecheta, Buchi, photograph by Jerry Bauer. Copyright © Jerry Bauer.—Emily Dickinson Homestead in Amherst, Massachusetts, photograph. Copyright © James Marshall/Corbis.—Erdrich, Louise, photograph by Eric Miller. AP/Wide World Photos.—French, Marilyn, photograph by Jerry Bauer. Copyright © Jerry Bauer.—Friedan, Betty, president of the National Organization for Women, and other feminists march in New York City, photograph. Copyright © JP Laffont/Sygma/Corbis.—Friedan, Betty, with

Yoko Ono, photograph. Copyright © Bettmann/Corbis.—Frontpiece and title page from *Poems on Various Subjects, Religious and Moral,* written by Phillis Wheatley. Copyright © The Pierpont Morgan Library/Art Resource, NY.—Fuller, Margaret, painting by John Plumbe. The Library of Congress.—Gandhi, Indira, photograph. Copyright © Corbis-Bettmann.—Garrison, William Lloyd, (bottom right), with the Pennsylvania Abolition Society, photograph. National Portrait Gallery.—Gilman, Charlotte Perkins, cover photograph. Copyright © Corbis.—Gilman, Charlotte P., photograph. Copyright © Corbis-Bettmann.—Godwin, Mary Wollstonecraft, illustration. Copyright © Corbis-Bettmann.—Hansberry, Lorraine, photograph by David Attie. AP/Wide World Photos.—Head, Bessie, photograph. Reproduced by the kind permission of the Estate of Bessie Head.—"Head of Medusa," marble sculpture by Gianlorenzo Bernini. Copyright © Araldo de Luca/Corbis.—Hellman, Lillian, photograph. AP/Wide World Photos.—Hurston, Zora Neale looking at "American Stuff," at the *New York Times* book fair, photograph. The Library of Congress.—Hurston, Zora Neale, photograph by Carl Van Vechten. The Carl Van Vechten Trust.—Hypatia, conte crayon drawing. Copyright © Corbis-Bettmann.—Illustration depicting a woman's body being the subject of political and social conflict, photograph. Barbara Kruger/Mary Boone Gallery.—Jolie, Angelina (right), and unidentified person, in the film *Foxfire,* photograph by Jane O'Neal. The Kobal Collection/O'Neal, Jane.—Karloff, Boris, in movie *Frankenstein;* 1935, photograph. The Kobal Collection.—Kingston, Maxine Hong, photograph by Jerry Bauer. Copyright © Jerry Bauer.—"La Temptation," depicting Adam and Eve in the Garden of Paradise. The Library of Congress.—Lessing, Doris, photograph by Jerry Bauer. Copyright © Jerry Bauer.—Luce, Clare Booth, portrait. Copyright © UPI/Bettmann Archive.—Manuscript page from *The Book of Ladies,* by Christine de Pizan. Bibliotheque Nationale de France.—Manuscript page of *Vieyra Impugnado,* written by Sor Margarita Ignacia and translated to Spanish by Inigo Rosende. Madrid: Antonio Sanz, 1731. The Special Collections Library, University of Michigan.—Martineau, Harriet, engraving. The Library of Congress.—Migrant mother with child huddled on either shoulder, Nipomo, California, 1936, photograph by Dorothea Lange. The Library of Congress.—Millay, Edna St. Vincent, photograph. AP/Wide World Photos.—Montagu, Lady Mary Wortley, engraving. Archive Photos, Inc.—Moore, Marianne, photograph by Jerry Bauer. Copyright © Jerry Bauer.—Morrison, Toni, 1993, photograph. AP/Wide World Photos.—Murasaki, Lady, looking out from the veranda of a monastery, illustration

ACKNOWLEDGMENTS

from *Tale of Genji.* Copyright © Asian Art Archaeology, Inc./Corbis.—National League of Women Voters' Headquarters, photograph. Copyright © Corbis-Bettmann.—National Women's Suffrage Association (NWSA), during a political convention in Chicago, Illinois, photograph. Copyright © Bettmann/Corbis.—Naylor, Gloria, photograph. Marion Ettlinger/AP/Wide World Photos.—Oates, Joyce Carol, 1991, photograph. AP/Wide World Photos.—October 15, 1913 publication of the early feminist periodical, *The New Freewoman,* photograph. McFarlin Library, Department of Special Collections, The University of Tulsa.—Paul, Alice (second from right), standing with five other suffragettes, photograph. AP/Wide World Photos.—Pfeiffer, Michelle, and Daniel Day-Lewis, in the film *The Age of Innocence,* 1993, photograph by Phillip Caruso. The Kobal Collection.—Plath, Sylvia, photograph. AP/Wide World Photos.—Poster advertising *Uncle Tom's Cabin,* by Harriet Beecher Stowe, "The Greatest Book of the Age," photograph. Copyright © Bettmann/Corbis.—Rich, Adrienne, holding certificate of poetry award, Chicago, Illinois, 1986, photograph. AP/Wide World Photos.—Rossetti, Christina, 1863, photograph by Lewis Carroll. Copyright © UPI/Bettmann.—Russell, Rosalind and Joan Crawford in the 1939 movie *The Women,* written by Clare Boothe Luce, photograph. MGM/The Kobal Collection.—Salem Witch Trial, lithograph by George H. Walker. Copyright © Bettmann/Corbis.—Sand, George, illustration. Copyright © Leonard de Selva/Corbis.—Sand, George, photograph. The Library of Congress.—Sanger, Margaret, Miss Clara Louise Rowe, and Mrs. Anne Kennedy, arranging the first American Birth Control Conference, photograph. Copyright © Underwood and Underwood/Corbis.—Sappho, bronze sculpture. The Library of Congress.—Sappho, illustration. The Library of Congress.—Sappho performing outdoors, illustration. The Library of Congress.—"Sara in a Green Bonnet," painting by Mary Cassatt, c. 1901. National Museum of American Art, Smithsonian Institution, Washington, DC, U.S.A.—Scene from the film *Mill on the Floss,* by George Eliot, engraving. Hulton Archive/Getty Images.—Segwick, Catherine Maria, slide. Archive Photos, Inc.—Sexton, Anne, photograph. Copyright © Bettmann/Corbis.—Sexton, Anne, with her daughters Joy and Linda, photograph. Time Life Pictures/Getty Images.—Shelley, Mary Wollstonecraft, painting by Samuel John Stump. Copyright © Corbis-Bettmann.—Stael, Madame de, color lithograph. Archive Photos, Inc.—Stanton, Elizabeth Cady, illustration. Copyright © Bettmann/Corbis.—Stanton, Elizabeth Cady, photograph. AP/Wide World Photos.—Stein, Gertrude (left), arriving in New York aboard the S. S. Champlain with her secretary and companion Alice B. Toklas, photograph. AP/Wide World Photos.—Stein, Gertrude, photograph by Carl Van Vechten. The Estate of Carl Van Vechten.—Steinem, Gloria, photograph. AP/Wide World Photos.—Stowe, Harriet Beecher, photograph. Copyright © Bettmann/Corbis.—Suffrage parade in New York, New York, October 15, 1915, photograph. The Library of Congress.—Supporters of the Equal Rights Amendment carry a banner down Pennsylvania Avenue, Washington, DC, photograph. AP/Wide World Photos.—Sur la Falaise aux Petites Dalles, 1873. Painting by Berthe Morisot. Copyright © Francis G. Mayer/Corbis.—Tan, Amy, 1993, photograph. AP/Wide World Photos.—*Time,* cover of Kate Millett, from August 31, 1970. Time Life Pictures/Stringer/Getty Images.—Title page of *A Vindication of the Rights of Woman: With Strictures on Political and Moral Subjects,* written by Mary Wollstonecraft. William L. Clements Library, University of Michigan.—Title page of *Adam Bede,* written by George Eliot. Edinburgh & London: Blackwood, 1859, Volume 1, New York: Harper, 1859. The Graduate Library, University of Michigan.—Title page from *De L'influence des Passions sur le Bonheur des Individus et des Nations,* (A Treatise on the Influence of the Passions upon the Happiness of Individuals and of Nations), written by Stael de Holstein, photograph. The Special Collections Library, University of Michigan.—Title page from *Evelina,* written by Fanny Burney, photograph. The Special Collections Library, University of Michigan.—Title page from *Mansfield Park,* written by Jane Austen. The Special Collections Library, University of Michigan.—Title page of *Mary, A Fiction,* written by Mary Wollstonecraft.—Title page from *Youth and the Bright Medusa,* written by Willa Cather. New York, Alfred A Knopf. The Special Collections Library, University of Michigan.—Title page of *A New-England Tale,* written by Catharine Maria Sedgewick. New York: E. Bliss and E. White, 1822. The Special Collections Library, University of Michigan.—Title page of *Aurora Leigh,* written by Elizabeth Barrett Browning. New York, Boston: C. S. Francis and Co., 1857. The Special Collections Library, University of Michigan.—Title page of *Mrs. Dalloway,* written by Virginia Woolf. London: Hogarth Press, 1925. The Special Collections Library, University of Michigan.—Title page of *The Dial: A Magazine for Literature, Philosophy, and Religion.* Boston. Weeks, Jordan and Company (etc.); London, Wiley and Putnam (etc.). Volume 1. The Special Collections Library, University of Michigan.—Title page of *The House of Mirth,* written by Edith Wharton. New York: C. Scribner's Sons, 1905. The Special Collections Library, University of Michigan.—Title page of *The Little Review,*

March 1916. The Purdy/Kresge Library, Wayne State University.—Title page of *Woman in the Nineteenth Century,* written by Sarah Margaret Fuller. New York, Greeley and McElrath. 1845. The Special Collections Library, University of Michigan.—Title page of *Wuthering Heights,* written by Emily Brontë. New York: Harper and Brothers. 1848. The Special Collections Library, University of Michigan.—Truth, Sojourner, photograph. Archive Photos, Inc.—Tubman, Harriet, photograph. The Library of Congress.—Victoria, Queen of England, illustration. The Library of Congress.—Walker, Alice, 1989, photograph. AP/Wide World Photos.—Welles, Orson, as Edward Rochester, with Joan Fontaine as Jane Eyre, in the film *Jane Eyre,* photograph. The Kobal Collection.—Wharton, Edith, photograph. AP/Wide World Photos.—Wheatley, Phillis, photograph. Copyright © The Bettman Archive.—Winfrey, Oprah, as Celie and Danny Glover as Albert with baby in scene from the film *The Color Purple,* written by Alice Walker, directed by Steven Spielberg, photograph. The Kobal Collection.—Women in French Revolution, invade assembly, demanding death penalty for members of the aristocracy, Woodcut. Copyright © Bettmann/Corbis.—Women workers in a shoe factory in Lynn, Massachusetts, photograph. Copyright © Corbis.—Woodhull, Victoria, reading statement before House Committee, drawing. The Library of Congress.—Woolf, Virginia, photograph. AP/Wide World Photos.—Woolson, Constance Fenimore, engraving. Archive Photos.

● = historical event

■ = literary event

1570 B.C.

● Queen Ahmose Nefertari, sister and principal wife of King Ahmose, rules as "god's wife," in a new position created by a law enacted by the King.

C. 1490 B.C.

● Queen Hatshepsut rules as pharaoh, several years after the death of her husband, King Thutmose II.

C. 1360 B.C.

● Queen Nefertiti rules Egypt alongside her husband, pharaoh Akhenaten.

C. 620 B.C.

● Sappho is born on the Isle of Lesbos, Greece.

C. 600 B.C.

■ Sappho organizes and operates a *thiasos,* an academy for young, unmarried Greek women.

● Spartan women are the most independent women in the world, and are able to own property, pursue an education, and participate in athletics.

C. 550 B.C.

● Sappho dies on the Isle of Lesbos.

C. 100 B.C.

● Roman laws allow a husband: to kill his wife if she is found in the act of adultery, to determine the amount of money his wife is owed in the event of divorce, and to claim his children as property.

69 B.C.

● Cleopatra VII Philopator is born in Egypt.

36 B.C.

● Marriage of Antony and Cleopatra.

C. 30 B.C.

● Cleopatra VII Philopator commits suicide in Egypt.

18

● Emperor Augustus decrees the *Lex Julia,* which penalizes childless Roman citizens, adulterers, and those who marry outside of their social rank or status.

C. 370

- Hypatia is born in Alexandria, Egypt.

415

- Hypatia is murdered in Alexandria, Egypt.

C. 500

- Salians (Germanic Franks living in Gaul) issue a code of laws which prohibit women from inheriting land; the law is used for centuries to prevent women from ruling in France.

592

- Empress Suiko (554-628) becomes the first woman sovereign of Japan.

C. 690

- Wu Zetian (624-705) becomes the only female emperor of Imperial China.

C. 700

- Japanese legal code specifies that in law, ceremony, and practice, Japanese men can be polygamous—having first wives and an unlimited number of "second wives" or concubines—, but women cannot.

877

- Lady Ise, Japanese court lady, is born. She is considered one of the most accomplished poets of her time and her poems are widely anthologized.

935

- Hrotsvitha (also Hrotsvit or Roswitha), considered the first German woman poet, is born.

940

- Lady Ise dies.

950

- Publication of the *Kagero Nikki* (*The Gossamer Years*), a diary written by an anonymous Japanese courtesan. The realism and confessional quality of the work influence the works of later court diarists.

C. 960

- Japanese poet Izumi Shikibu, known for her expression of erotic and Buddhist themes, is born. Her body of work includes more than 1,500 *waka* (31-syllable poems).

C. 1002

- Sei Shonagon, Japanese court lady, writes *Makura no Soshi* (*The Pillow Book*), considered a classic of Japanese literature and the originator of the genre known as *zuihitsu* ("to follow the brush") that employs a stream-of-consciousness literary style.

C. 1008

- Murasaki Shikibu writes *Genji Monogatari* (*The Tale of Genji*), considered a masterpiece of classical prose literature in Japan.

C. 1030

- Izumi Shikibu dies.

1098

- Hildegard von Bingen is born in Bermersheim, Germany.

C. 1100

- Twenty women troubadours—aristocratic poet-composers who write songs dealing with love—write popular love songs in France. About twenty-four of their songs survive, including four written by the famous female troubadour known as the Countess of Dia, or Beatrix.

1122

- Eleanor of Aquitaine is born in Aquitaine, France. Her unconventional life is chronicled for centuries in books and dramatic works.

C. 1150

- Sometime in the twelfth century (some sources say 1122), Marie de France, the earliest known female French writer and author of *lais*, a collection of twelve verse tales written in octosyllabic rhyming couplets, flourished. She is thought to be the originator of the *lay* as a poetic form.

C. 1170

■ Marie of Champagne (1145-1198), daughter of King Louis VII of France and Eleanor of Aquitaine, cosponsors "courts of love" to debate points on the proper conduct of knights toward their ladies. Marie encourages Chrétien de Troyes to write *Lancelot,* and Andreas Capellanus to write *The Art of Courtly Love.*

1179

● Hildegard von Bingen dies in Disibodenberg, Germany.

C. 1200

■ Women shirabyoshi performances are a part of Japanese court and Buddhist temple festivities. In their songs and dances, women performers dress in white, male attire which includes fans, court caps, and swords. This form of traditional dance plays an important role in the development of classical Japanese noh drama.

1204

● Eleanor of Aquitaine dies on 1 April.

C. 1275

■ Japanese poet and court lady Abutsu Ni (1222?-1283) writes her poetic travel diary, *Izayoi Nikki* (*Diary of the Waning Moon*) on the occasion of her travel to Kyoto to seek inheritance rights for herself and her children.

C. 1328

● The French cite the Salic Law, which was promulgated in the early medieval period and prohibits women from inheriting land, as the authority for denying the crown of France to anyone—man or woman—whose descent from a French king can be traced only through the female line.

1346

● Famous mystic St. Birgitta of Sweden (c.1303-1373) founds the Roman Catholic Order of St. Saviour, whose members are called the Brigittines. She authors *Revelations,* an account of her supernatural visions.

1347

● Caterina Benincasa (later St. Catherine of Siena) is born on 25 March in Siena, Italy.

C. 1365

● Christine de Pizan is born in Venice, Italy.

C. 1373

● Margery Kempe is born in King's Lynn (now known as Lynn), in Norfolk, England.

1380

● St. Catherine of Siena dies on 29 April in Rome, Italy.

C. 1393

■ Julian of Norwich (1342?-1416?), the most famous of all the medieval recluses in England, writes *Revelations of Divine Love,* expounding on the idea of Christ as mother.

1399

■ Christine de Pizan writes the long poem "Letter to the God of Love," which marks the beginning of the *querelle des femmes* (debate on women). This attack on misogyny in medieval literature triggers a lively exchange of letters among the foremost French scholars of the day, and the *querelle* is continued by various European literary scholars for centuries.

1429

● Joan of Arc (1412-1431)—in support of Charles I, who is prevented by the English from assuming his rightful place as King of France—leads liberation forces to victory in Orléans.

1431

● Joan of Arc is burned at the stake as a heretic by the English on 30 May. She is acquitted of heresy by another church court in 1456 and proclaimed a saint in 1920.

C. 1431

● Christine de Pizan dies in France.

C. 1440

● Margery Kempe dies in England.

1451

● Isabella of Castile, future Queen of Spain, is born. She succeeds her brother in 1474 and rules jointly with her husband, Ferdinand of Aragon, from 1479.

1465

● Cassandra Fedele, who becomes the most famous woman scholar in Italy, is born in Venice.

1469

● Laura Cereta, outspoken feminist and humanist scholar, is born in Brescia, Italy.

1485

● Veronica Gambara is born in Italy. Her court becomes an important center of the Italian Renaissance, and Gambara earns distinction as an author of Petrarchan sonnets as well as for her patronage of the artist Corregio.

1486

■ *Malleus Maleficarum* (*The Hammer of Witches*), an encyclopedia of contemporary knowledge about witches and methods of investigating the crime of witchcraft, is published in Europe. The volume details numerous justifications for women's greater susceptibility to evil, and contributes to the almost universal European persecution of women as witches that reaches its height between 1580 and 1660 and makes its way to Salem, Massachusetts in 1692.

1492

● Marguerite de Navarre is born on 11 April in France.

1499

● Laura Cereta dies in Brescia, Italy.

C. 1512

● Catherine Parr is born in England.

1515

● Teresa de Alhumadawas (later St. Teresa de Ávila) is born on 28 March in Gotarrendura, Spain.

1524

● Courtesan Gaspara Stampa, widely regarded as the greatest woman poet of the Renaissance, is born in Padua, Italy.

1533

● Queen Elizabeth I is born on 7 September in Greenwich, England, the daughter of King Henry VIII and his second wife, Anne Boleyn.

1536

● King Henry VIII of England beheads his second wife, Anne Boleyn, on 19 May. Boleyn is convicted of infidelity and treason after she fails to produce the desired male heir.

1538

■ Vittoria Colonna (1492-1547), an influential woman in Renaissance Italy, achieves distinction as a poet with the publication of her first book of poetry.

1548

● Catherine Parr dies in England.

1549

● Marguerite de Navarre dies in France.

1550

● Veronica Gambara dies in Italy.

1554

● Gaspara Stampa dies on 23 April in Venice, Italy.

1555

● Moderata Fonte (pseudonym of Modesta Pozzo) is born in Venice, Italy.

1558

● Elizabeth I assumes the throne of England and presides over a period of peace and prosperity known as the Elizabethan Age.

- Cassandra Fedele dies in Venice. She is honored with a state funeral.

1559

- Marguerite de Navarre completes her *L'Heptaméron des Nouvelles* (the *Heptameron*), a series of stories primarily concerned with the themes of love and spirituality.

1561

- Mary Sidney, noted English literary patron, is born in England. She is the sister of poet Sir Philip Sidney, whose poems she edits and publishes after his death in 1586, and whose English translation of the Psalms she completes.

1565

- French scholar Marie de Gournay is born on 6 October in Paris. Known as the French "Minerva" (a woman of great wisdom or learning), she is a financial success as a writer of treatises on various subjects, including *Equality of Men and Women* (1622) and *Complaint of Ladies* (1626), which demand better education for women.

1582

- St. Teresa de Avila dies on 4 October in Alba.

1592

- Moderata Fonte (pseudonym of Modesta Pozzo) dies in Venice, Italy.

C. 1600

- Catherine de Vivonne (c. 1588-1665), Madame de Rambouillet, inaugurates and then presides over salon society in Paris, in which hostesses hold receptions in their salons or drawing rooms for the purpose of intellectual conversation. Salon society flourishes in the seventeenth and eighteenth centuries, and stimulates scholarly and literary development in France and England.

- Geisha (female artists and entertainers) and prostitutes are licensed by the Japanese government to work in the pleasure quarters of major cities in Japan.

1603

- Queen Elizabeth I dies on 24 March in Surrey, England.

- Izumo no Okuni is believed to originate kabuki, the combination of dance, drama, and music which dominates Japanese theater throughout the Tokugawa period (1600-1868).

1607

- Madeleine de Scudéry, one of the best-known and most influential writers of romance tales in seventeeth-century Europe, is born on 15 November in Le Havre, France.

C. 1612

- American poet Anne Bradstreet is born in Northampton, England.

1614

- Margaret Askew Fell, who helps establish the Society of Friends, or Quakers, and becomes known as the "mother of Quakerism," is born in Lancashire, England. Quakers give women unusual freedom in religious life. An impassioned advocate of the right of women to preach, Fell publishes the tract *Women's Speaking Justified, Proved and Allowed of by the Scriptures* in 1666.

1621

- Mary Sidney dies in England.

C. 1623

- Margaret Lucas Cavendish, later Duchess of Newcastle, is born in England. She authors fourteen volumes of works, including scientific treatises, poems, and plays, and her autobiography *The True Relation of My Birth, Breeding and Life* (1656).

1631

- Katherine Phillips (1631-1664), who writes poetry under the pseudonym "Orinda," is born. She is the founder of a London literary salon called the Society of Friendship that includes such luminaries as Jeremy Taylor and Henry Vaughn.

C. 1640

● Aphra Behn is born.

C. 1645

● Deborah Moody (c. 1580-c. 1659) becomes the first woman to receive a land grant in colonial America when she is given the title to land in Kings County (now Brooklyn), New York. She is also the first colonial woman to vote.

C. 1646

● Glückel of Hameln, who records her life as a Jewish merchant in Germany in her memoirs, is born in Hamburg.

1651

● Juana Ramírez de Asbaje (later known as Sor Juana Inés de la Cruz) is born on 12 November on a small farm called San Miguel de Nepantla in New Spain (now Mexico).

1670

▨ Aphra Behn becomes the first professional woman writer in England when her first play *The Forced Marriage; or, The Jealous Bridegroom,* is performed in London.

1672

● Anne Bradstreet dies on 16 September in Andover, Massachusetts.

C. 1673

▨ Francois Poulain de la Barre publishes *The Equality of the Sexes,* in which he supports the idea that women have intellectual powers equal to those of men. His work stimulates the betterment of women's education in succeeding centuries.

1673

● Margaret Lucas Cavendish, Duchess of Newcastle, dies in England.

1676

▨ After being captured and then released by Wampanaoag Indians, Puritan settler Mary White Rowlandson (1636-1678) writes what becomes a famous account of her captivity.

1689

● Mary Pierrpont (later Lady Mary Wortley Montagu) is born on 26 May in London, England.

● Aphra Behn dies on 16 April and is buried in the cloisters at Westminster Abbey.

1692

● The Salem, Massachusetts, witch hysteria begins in February, and eventually leads to the execution of eighteen women convicted of witchcraft in the infamous Salem Witchcraft Trials (1692-1693).

C. 1694

▨ Mary Astell (1666-1731) publishes the treatise *A Serious Proposal to the Ladies* in two volumes (1694-1697). In the work, Astell calls for the establishment of private institutions where single women live together for a time and receive quality education.

1695

● Sor Juana Inés de la Cruz dies on 17 April at the Convent of St. Jerome in Mexico.

1701

● Madeleine de Scudéry dies on 2 June in Paris, France.

C. 1704

▨ Sarah Kemble Knight (1666-1727), a Puritan author, records her arduous journey from Boston to New York to settle the estate of her cousin.

C. 1713

▨ Anne Kingsmill Finch (1661-1720) writes many poems dealing with the injustices suffered by women of the aristocratic class to which she belonged. As Countess of Winchilsea, she becomes the center of a literary circle at her husband's estate in Eastwell, England.

1728

● Mercy Otis Warren is born on 14 September in Barnstable, Massachusetts.

1729

- Catherine the Great is born on 2 May in Germany as Sophia Friederica Augusta.

1744

- Abigail Adams is born Abigail Smith on 11 November in Weymouth, Massachusetts.

1748

- Olympe de Gouges, French Revolutionary feminist, is born Olympe Gouze in Montauban, France. She plays an active role in the French Revolution, demanding equal rights for women in the new French Republic.

1752

- Frances "Fanny" Burney is born on 13 June in England.

C. 1753

- Phillis Wheatley is born in Africa.

1759

- Mary Wollstonecraft is born on 27 April in England.

1762

- Lady Mary Wortley Montagu dies on 21 August in London, England.
- Catherine the Great becomes Empress of Russia.

1766

- Germaine Necker (later Madame de Staël) is born on 22 April in Paris, France.

1768

- Maria Edgeworth is born on 1 January at Black Bourton in Oxfordshire, England.

1774

- Clementina Rind (1740-1774) is appointed publisher of the *Virginia Gazette* by the House of Burgesses in Virginia.

1775

- Jane Austen is born on 16 December at Steventon Rectory, Hampshire, England.

1776

- Men and women who hold property worth over 50 pounds are granted suffrage in New Jersey.

C. 1780

- Madame Roland (1754-1793), formerly Marie Philppon, hosts an important salon where revolutionary politicians and thinkers debate during the French Revolution. An outspoken feminist, she presses for women's political and social rights.

1784

- Hannah Adams (1758-1831) becomes the first American woman author to support herself with money earned from writing, with the publication of her first book, *View of Religions* (later *Dictionary of Religions*).
- Phillis Wheatley dies on 5 December in Boston, Massachusetts.

1787

- Catherine Sawbridge Macaulay publishes *Letters on Education*, an appeal for better education of women.
- Mary Wollstonecraft's *Thoughts on the Education of Daughters: With Reflections on Female Conduct, in the More Important Duties of Life* is published by J. Johnson.

1789

- Catharine Maria Sedgwick is born on 28 December in Stockbridge, Massachusetts.
- Olympe de Gouges writes *The Declaration of the Rights of Women and Citizen*, a 17-point document demanding the recognition of women as political, civil, and legal equals of men, and including a sample marriage contract that emphasizes free will and equality in marriage.

1792

- Sarah Moore Grimké is born on 26 November in Charleston, South Carolina.

■ Mary Wollstonecraft's *A Vindication of the Rights of Woman, with Strictures on Political and Moral Subjects* is published by J. Johnson.

1793

● Lucretia Coffin Mott is born on 3 January in Nantucket, Massachusetts.

● Olympe de Gouges is executed by guillotine for treason on 3 November.

● Madame Roland is executed in November, ostensibly for treason, but actually because the Jacobins want to suppress feminist elements in the French Revolution.

1796

● Catherine the Great dies following a stroke on 6 November in Russia.

1797

● Mary Wollstonecraft Shelley is born on 30 August, in London, England.

● Mary Wollstonecraft dies on 10 September in London, England, from complications following childbirth.

● Sojourner Truth is born Isabella Bomefree in Ulster County, New York.

1799

■ Mary Wollstonecraft's *Maria; or, The Wrongs of Woman: A Posthumous Fragment* is published by James Carey.

1801

● Caroline M. (Stansbury) Kirkland is born on 11 January in New York City.

1802

● Lydia Maria Child is born on 11 February in Medford, Massachusetts.

1804

● George Sand (pseudonym of Armandine Aurore Lucille Dupin) is born on 1 July in Paris, France.

● The Napoleonic Code is established in France under Napoleon I, and makes women legally subordinate to men. The code requires women to be obedient to their husbands, bars women from voting, sitting on juries, serving as legal witnesses, or sitting on chambers of commerce or boards of trade.

1805

● Angelina Emily Grimké is born on 20 February in Charleston, South Carolina.

1806

● Elizabeth Barrett Browning is born on 6 March in Coxhoe Hall, Durham, England.

1807

■ Germaine de Staël's *Corinne, ou l'Italie* (*Corinne, or Italy*) is published by Nicolle.

● Suffrage in New Jersey is limited to "white male citizens."

1808

● Caroline Sheridan Norton is born on 22 March in England.

1810

● (Sarah) Margaret Fuller is born on 23 May in Cambridgeport, Massachusetts.

● Elizabeth Cleghorn Gaskell is born on 29 September in London, England.

1811

● Harriet Beecher Stowe is born on 14 June in Litchfield, Connecticut.

■ Jane Austen's *Sense and Sensibility* is published by T. Egerton.

1813

● Harriet A. Jacobs is born in North Carolina.

■ Jane Austen's *Pride and Prejudice* is published by T. Egerton.

1814

● Mercy Otis Warren dies on 19 October in Plymouth, Massachusetts.

1815

- Elizabeth Cady Stanton is born on 12 November in Johnstown, New York.
- King Louis XVIII of France outlaws divorce.

1816

- Charlotte Brontë is born on 21 April in Thornton, Yorkshire, England.
- Jane Austen's *Emma* is published by M. Carey.

1817

- Madame Germaine de Staël dies on 14 July in Paris, France.
- Jane Austen dies on 18 July in Winchester, Hampshire, England.

1818

- Emily Brontë is born on 30 July in Thornton, Yorkshire, England.
- Lucy Stone is born on 13 August near West Brookfield, Massachusetts.
- Abigail Adams dies on 28 October in Quincy, Massachusetts.
- Jane Austen's *Northanger Abbey and Persuasion* is published by John Murray.
- Educator Emma Hart Willard's *A Plan for Improving Female Education* is published by Middlebury College.
- Mary Wollstonecraft Shelley's *Frankenstein; or, The Modern Prometheus* is published by Lackington, Hughes, Harding, Mavor & Jones.

1819

- Julia Ward Howe is born on 27 May in New York City.
- George Eliot (pseudonym of Mary Ann Evans) is born on 22 November in Arbury, Warwickshire, England.

1820

- Susan B. Anthony is born on 15 February in Adams, Massachusetts.

1821

- Emma Hart Willard establishes the Troy Female Seminary in Troy, New York.

1822

- Frances Power Cobbe is born on 4 December in Dublin, Ireland.

1823

- Charlotte Yonge is born 11 August in Otterbourne, Hampshire, England.

1825

- Frances Ellen Watkins Harper is born on 24 September in Baltimore, Maryland.

1826

- Matilda Joslyn Gage is born on 24 March in Cicero, New York.

1830

- Christina Rossetti is born on 5 December in London, England.
- Emily Dickinson is born on 10 December in Amherst, Massachusetts.
- *Godey's Lady's Book*—the first American women's magazine—is founded by Louis Antoine Godey and edited by Sarah Josepha Hale (1788-1879).

1832

- Louisa May Alcott is born on 29 November in Germantown, Pennsylvania.
- George Sand's *Indiana* is published by Roret et Dupuy.

1833

- Oberlin Collegiate Institute—the first coeducational institution of higher learning— is established in Oberlin, Ohio.

1836

- Marietta Holley is born on 16 July near Adams, New York.

1837

- Mt. Holyoke College—the first college for women—is founded by Mary Lyon in South Hadley, Massachusetts.

- Alexandria Victoria (1819-1901) becomes Queen Victoria at the age of eighteen. Her reign lasts for 63 years, the longest reign of any British monarch.

1838

- Victoria Woodhull is born on 23 September in Homer, Ohio.
- Sarah Moore Grimké's *Letters on the Equality of the Sexes, and the Condition of Woman* is published by I. Knapp.

1840

- Frances "Fanny" Burney dies on 6 January in London, England.
- Ernestine Rose (1810-1892) writes the petition for what will become the Married Woman's Property Law (1848).

C. 1844

- Sarah Winnemucca is born on Paiute land near Humboldt Lake in what is now Nevada.

1845

- Margaret Fuller's *Woman in the Nineteenth Century* is published by Greeley & McElrath.

1847

- Charlotte Brontë's *Jane Eyre* is published by Smith, Elder.
- Emily Brontë's *Wuthering Heights* is published by T. C. Newby.

1848

- The first women's rights convention is called by Lucretia Coffin Mott and Elizabeth Cady Stanton on 19 July and is held in Seneca Falls, New York on 20 July.
- Emily Brontë dies on 19 December in Haworth, Yorkshire, England.
- New York State Legislature passes the Married Woman's Property Law, granting women the right to retain possession of property they owned prior to marriage.

1849

- Maria Edgeworth dies on 22 May in Edgeworthstown, her family's estate in Ireland.

- Sarah Orne Jewett is born on 3 September in South Berwick, Maine.
- Amelia Bloomer publishes the first issue of her Seneca Falls newspaper *The Lily*, which provides a forum for both temperance and women's rights reformers.
- The first state constitution of California extends property rights to women in their own name.

1850

- Margaret Fuller drowns—along with her husband and son—on 19 July in a shipwreck off of Fire Island, New York.
- The first National Woman's Rights Convention, planned by Lucy Stone and Lucretia Mott, is attended by over one thousand women on 23 and 24 October in Worcester, Massachusetts.
- Elizabeth Barrett Browning's *Poems*, containing her *Sonnets from the Portuguese*, is published by Chapman & Hall.
- *The Narrative of Sojourner Truth*, transcribed by Olive Gilbert, is published in the Boston periodical, the *Liberator*.

1851

- Mary Wollstonecraft Shelley dies on 1 February in Bournemouth, England.
- Kate Chopin is born on 8 February in St. Louis, Missouri.
- Sojourner Truth delivers her "A'n't I a Woman?" speech at the Women's Rights Convention on 29 May in Akron, Ohio.

1852

- Harriet Beecher Stowe's *Uncle Tom's Cabin; or, Life among the Lowly* is published by Jewett, Proctor & Worthington.
- Susan B. Anthony founds The Women's Temperance Society, the first temperance organization in the United States.

1853

- Charlotte Brontë's *Villette* is published by Smith, Elder.
- Paulina Kellogg Wright Davis (1813-1876) edits and publishes *Una*, the first newspaper of the women's rights movement.

1854

▪ Margaret Oliphant's *A Brief Summary in Plain Language of the Most Important Laws Concerning Women,* a pamphlet explaining the unfair laws concerning women and exposing the need for reform, is published in London.

1855

● Charlotte Brontë dies on 31 March in Haworth, Yorkshire, England.

● Elizabeth Cady Stanton, speaking in favor of expanding the Married Woman's Property Law, becomes the first woman to appear before the New York State Legislature.

1856

● Harriot Eaton Stanton Blatch is born on 20 January in Seneca Falls, New York.

1857

▪ Elizabeth Barrett Browning's *Aurora Leigh* is published by Chapman & Hall.

1858

● Emmeline Pankhurst is born on 4 July in Manchester, England.

● Anna Julia Haywood Cooper is born on 10 August in Raleigh, North Carolina.

1859

● Carrie Chapman Catt is born on 9 January in Ripon, Wisconsin.

1860

● Charlotte Perkins Gilman is born on 3 July in Hartford, Connecticut.

● Jane Addams is born on 6 September in Cedarville, Illinois.

1861

● Victoria Earle Matthews is born on 27 May in Fort Valley, Georgia.

● Elizabeth Barrett Browning dies on 29 June in Florence, Italy.

▪ Harriet Jacobs's *Incidents in the Life of a Slave Girl, Written by Herself,* edited by Lydia Maria Child, is published in Boston.

1862

● Edith Wharton is born on 24 January in New York City.

● Ida B. Wells-Barnett is born on 16 July in Holly Springs, Mississippi.

▪ Julia Ward Howe's "The Battle Hymn of the Republic" is published in the *Atlantic Monthly.*

1864

● Caroline M. (Stansbury) Kirkland dies of a stroke on 6 April in New York City.

1865

● Elizabeth Cleghorn Gaskell dies on 12 November in Holybourne, Hampshire, England.

1866

● The American Equal Rights Association—dedicated to winning suffrage for African American men and for women of all colors—is founded by Susan B. Anthony and Elizabeth Cady Stanton on 1 May. Lucretia Coffin Mott is elected as the group's president.

● Elizabeth Cady Stanton runs for Congress as an independent; she receives 24 of 12,000 votes cast.

1867

● Catharine Maria Sedgwick dies on 31 July in Boston, Massachusetts.

1868

▪ Susan B. Anthony and Elizabeth Cady Stanton found the New York-based weekly newspaper, *The Revolution,* with the motto: "The true republic—men, their rights and nothing more; women, their rights and nothing less," in January.

● Julia Ward Howe founds the New England Woman Suffrage Association and the New England Women's Club.

▪ Louisa May Alcott's *Little Women; or, Meg, Jo, Beth, and Amy* (2 vols., 1868-69) is published by Roberts Brothers.

1869

▪ John Stuart Mill's treatise in support of women's suffrage, *The Subjection of Women,* is published in London.

- Emma Goldman is born on 27 June in Kovno, Lithuania.

- Louisa May Alcott's *Hospital Sketches and Camp and Fireside Stories* is published by Roberts Brothers.

- Women are granted full and equal suffrage and are permitted to hold office within the territory of Wyoming.

- The National Woman Suffrage Association is founded by Elizabeth Cady Stanton and Susan B. Anthony in May in New York City.

- The American Woman Suffrage Association is founded by Lucy Stone, Julia Ward Howe, and others in November in Boston, Massachusetts.

1870

- *The Woman's Journal,* edited by Lucy Stone, Henry Blackwell, and Mary Livermore, begins publication on 8 January.

- Victoria Woodhull and Tennessee Claflin publish the first issue of their controversial New York weekly newspaper, *Woodhull and Claflin's Weekly.*

1871

- Women are granted full and equal suffrage in the territory of Utah. Their rights are revoked in 1887 and restored in 1896.

- Victoria Woodhull presents her views on women's rights in a passionate speech to the House Judiciary Committee, marking the first personal appearance before such a high congressional committee by a woman.

- Wives of many prominent U. S. politicians, military officers, and businessmen found the Anti-Suffrage party to fight against women's suffrage.

1872

- Victoria Woodhull, as a member of the Equal Rights Party (or National Radical Reform Party), becomes the first woman candidate for the office of U.S. President. Her running mate is Frederick Douglass.

- Susan B. Anthony and 15 other women attempt to cast their votes in Rochester, New York, in the presidential election. Anthony is arrested and fined $100, which she refuses to pay.

- Sojourner Truth attempts to cast her vote in Grand Rapids, Michigan in the presidential election but is denied a ballot.

1873

- Colette is born on 28 January in Burgundy, France.

- Maria Mitchell (1818-1889), astronomer and faculty member at Vassar College, establishes the Association of the Advancement of Women.

- Willa Cather is born on 7 December in Back Creek Valley, Virginia.

- Sarah Moore Grimké dies on 23 December in Hyde Park, Massachusetts.

- Louisa May Alcott's *Work: A Story of Experience* is published by Roberts Brothers.

1874

- Gertrude Stein is born on 3 February in Allegheny, Pennsylvania.

- Amy Lowell is born on 9 February in Brookline, Massachusetts.

1876

- George Sand dies on 9 June in Nohant, France.

- Susan Glaspell is born on 1 July (some sources say 1882) in Davenport, Iowa.

1877

- Caroline Sheridan Norton dies on 15 June in England.

1878

- Passage of the Matrimonial Causes Act in England enables abused wives to obtain separation orders to keep their husbands away from them.

- The "Susan B. Anthony Amendment," which will extend suffrage to women in the United States, is first proposed in Congress by Senator A. A. Sargent.

1879

- Margaret Sanger is born on 14 September in Corning, New York.

- Angelina Emily Grimké dies on 26 October in Hyde Park, Massachusetts.

1880

- Christabel Pankhurst is born on 22 September in Manchester, England.

- Lydia Maria Child dies on 20 October in Wayland, Massachusetts.

- Lucretia Coffin Mott dies on 11 November in Philadelphia, Pennsylvania.

- George Eliot (pseudonym of Mary Ann Evans) dies on 22 December in London, England.

1881

- Hubertine Auclert founds *La Citoyenne* (*The Citizen*), a newspaper dedicated to female suffrage.

- The first volume of *A History of Woman Suffrage* (Vols. 1-3, 1881-1888; Vol. 4, 1903), edited and compiled by Susan B. Anthony, Elizabeth Cady Stanton, Ida Harper Husted, and Matilda Joslyn Gage, is published by Fowler & Welles.

1882

- Virginia Woolf is born on 25 January in London, England.

- Sylvia Pankhurst is born on 5 May in Manchester, England.

- Aletta Jacobs (1854-1929), the first woman doctor in Holland, opens the first birth control clinic in Europe.

1883

- Sojourner Truth dies on 26 November in Battle Creek, Michigan.

- Olive Schreiner's *The Story of an African Farm* is published by Chapman & Hall.

1884

- Eleanor Roosevelt is born on 11 October in New York City.

1885

- Alice Paul is born on 11 January in Moorestown, New Jersey.

- Isak Dinesen is born Karen Christentze Dinesen on 17 April in Rungsted, Denmark.

1886

- Emily Dickinson dies on 15 May in Amherst, Massachusetts.

- H. D. (Hilda Doolittle) is born on 10 September in Bethlehem, Pennsylvania.

1887

- Marianne Moore is born on 15 November in Kirkwood, Missouri.

- Article five of the Peace Preservation Law in Japan prohibits women and minors from joining political organizations and attending meetings where political speeches are given, and from engaging in academic studies of political subjects.

1888

- Louisa May Alcott dies on 6 March in Boston, Massachusetts, and is buried in Sleepy Hollow Cemetery in Concord, Massachusetts.

- Susan B. Anthony organizes the International Council of Women with representatives from 48 countries.

- Louisa Lawson (1848-1920) founds Australia's first feminist newspaper, *The Dawn*.

- The National Council of Women in the United States is formed to promote the advancement of women in society. The group also serves as a clearinghouse for various women's organizations.

1889

- Anna Akhmatova is born Anna Adreyevna Gorenko on 23 June in Bolshoy Fontan, Russia.

1890

- The National American Woman Suffrage Association (NAWSA) is formed by the merging of the American Woman Suffrage Assocation and the National Woman Suffrage Association. Elizabeth Cady Stanton is the NAWSA's first president; she is succeeded by Susan B. Anthony in 1892.

1891

- Zora Neale Hurston is born on 15 (some sources say 7) January in Nostasulga, Alabama. (Some sources cite birth year as c. 1901 or 1903, and birth place as Eatonville, Florida).

- Sarah Winnemucca dies on 16 October in Monida, Montana.

1892

- Edna St. Vincent Millay is born on 22 February in Rockland, Maine.

- Djuna Barnes is born on 12 June in Cornwall on Hudson, New York.

- Rebecca West (pseudonym of Cicily Isabel Fairfield) is born on 21 December in County Kerry, Ireland.

- Charlotte Perkins Gilman's *The Yellow Wallpaper* is published in *New England Magazine.*

- Frances E. W. Harper's *Iola Leroy; or, Shadows Uplifted* is published by Garrigues Bros.

- Olympia Brown (1835-1926), first woman ordained minister in the United States, founds the Federal Suffrage Association to campaign for women's suffrage.

- Ida Wells-Barnett's *Southern Horrors. Lynch Law in All its Phases* is published by Donohue and Henneberry.

1893

- Lucy Stone dies on 18 October in Dorchester, Massachusetts.

- The National Council of Women of Canada is founded by Lady Aberdeen.

- Suffrage is granted to women in Colorado.

- New Zealand becomes the first nation to grant women the vote.

1894

- Christina Rossetti dies on 29 December in London, England.

1895

- The first volume of Elizabeth Cady Stanton's *The Woman's Bible* (3 vols., 1895-1898) is published by European Publishing Company.

1896

- Harriet Beecher Stowe dies on 1 July in Hartford, Connecticut.

- Idaho grants women the right to vote.

- The National Assocation of Colored Women's Clubs is founded in Washington, D.C.

1897

- Harriet A. Jacobs dies on 7 March in Cambridge, Massachusetts.

1898

- Matilda Joslyn Gage dies on 18 March in Chicago, Illinois.

- Charlotte Perkins Gilman's *Women and Economics* is published by Small Maynard.

- The Meiji Civil Law Code, the law of the Japanese nation state, makes the patriarchal family, rather than the individual, the legally recognized entity.

1899

- Elizabeth Bowen is born on 7 June in Dublin, Ireland.

- Kate Chopin's *The Awakening* is published by Herbert S. Stone.

1900

- Colette's *Claudine a l'ecole* (*Claudine at School,* 1930) is published by Ollendorf.

- Carrie Chapman Catt succeeds Susan B. Anthony as president of the NAWSA.

1901

- Charlotte Yonge dies of bronchitis and pneumonia on 24 March in Elderfield, England.

1902

- Elizabeth Cady Stanton dies on 26 October in New York City.

- Women of European descent gain suffrage in Australia.

1903

- The Women's Social and Political Union, led by suffragists Emmeline and Christabel Pankhurst, stage demonstrations in Hyde Park in London, England.

1904

- Frances Power Cobbe dies on 5 April.

- Kate Chopin dies following a cerebral hemorrhage on 22 August in St. Louis, Missouri.

Susan B. Anthony establishes the International Woman Suffrage Alliance in Berlin, Germany.

C. 1905

Lillian Hellman is born on 20 June in New Orleans, Louisiana.

1905

Austrian activist and novelist Bertha von Suttner (1843-1914) receives the Nobel Peace Prize.

1906

Susan B. Anthony dies on 13 March in Rochester, New York.

Finnish women gain suffrage and the right to be elected to public office.

1907

Victoria Earle Matthews dies of tuberculosis on 10 March in New York City.

Mary Edwards Walker, M.D.'s pamphlet on women's suffrage, "Crowning Constitutional Argument," is published.

Harriot Stanton Blatch founds the Equality League of Self-Supporting Women, later called the Women's Political Union.

1908

Simone de Beauvoir is born on 9 January in Paris, France.

Julia Ward Howe becomes the first woman to be elected to the American Academy of Arts and Letters.

1909

Sarah Orne Jewett dies on 24 June in South Berwick, Maine.

Swedish author Selma Lagerlöf (1858-1940) becomes the first woman to receive the Nobel Prize for Literature.

"The Uprising of the 20,000" grows from one local to a general strike against several shirtwaist factories in New York City. Over 700 women and girls are arrested, and 19 receive

workhouse sentences. The strike is called off on 15 February 1910. Over 300 shops settle with the union, and workers achieve the terms demanded.

Jeanne-Elisabeth Archer Schmahl (1846-1915) founds the French Union for Woman Suffrage.

1910

Julia Ward Howe dies of pneumonia on 17 October in Newport, Rhode Island.

The Women' Political Union holds the first large suffrage parade in New York City.

Suffrage is granted to women in Washington State.

Jane Addams's *Twenty Years at Hull House* is published by Macmillan.

1911

Frances Ellen Watkins Harper dies on 22 February in Philadelphia, Pennsylvania.

A fire at the Triangle Shirtwaist Factory in New York City on 25 March claims the lives of 146 factory workers, 133 of them women. Public outrage over the fire leads to reforms in labor laws and improvement in working conditions.

Suffrage is granted to women in California.

Edith Wharton's *Ethan Frome* is published by Scribner.

1912

Suffrage is granted to women in Arizona, Kansas, and Oregon.

A parade in support of women's suffrage is held in New York City and draws 20,000 participants and half a million onlookers.

1913

Muriel Rukeyser is born on 15 December in New York City.

Willa Cather's *O Pioneers!* is published by Houghton.

Ida Wells-Barnett founds the Alpha Suffrage Club in Chicago.

Suffrage is granted to women in Alaska.

The Congressional Union is founded by Alice Paul and Lucy Burns.

1914

- Marguerite Duras is born on 4 April in Gia Dinh, Indochina (now Vietnam).

- The National Federation of Women's Clubs, which includes over two million white women and women of color, formally endorses the campaign for women's suffrage.

- Suffrage is granted to women in Montana and Nevada.

- Margaret Sanger begins publication of her controversial monthly newsletter *The Woman Rebel,* which is banned as obscene literature.

1915

- Charlotte Perkins Gilman's *Herland* is published in the journal *Forerunner.*

- *Woman's Work in Municipalities,* by American suffragist and historian Mary Ritter Beard (1876-1958), is published by Appleton.

- Icelandic women who are age 40 or older gain suffrage.

- Members of the NAWSA from across the United States hold a large parade in New York city.

- Most Danish women over age 25 gain suffrage.

1916

- Ardent suffragist and pacifist Jeannette Pickering Rankin (1880-1973) of Montana becomes the first woman elected to the U. S. House of Representatives. She later votes against U. S. involvement in both World Wars.

- The Congressional Union becomes the National Women's Party, led by Alice Paul and Lucy Burns.

- NAWSA president Carrie Chapman Catt unveils her "Winning Plan" for American women's suffrage at a convention held in Atlantic City, New Jersey.

- Suffrage is granted to women in Alberta, Manitoba, and Saskatchewan, Canada.

- Margaret Sanger opens the first U. S. birth-control clinic in Brooklyn, New York. The clinic is shut down 10 days after it opens and Sanger is arrested.

- Margaret Sanger's *What Every Mother Should Know; or, How Six Little Children were Taught the Truth* is published by M. N. Maisel.

1917

- Gwendolyn Brooks is born on 7 June in Topeka, Kansas.

- The National Women's Party becomes the first group in U.S. history to picket in front of the White House. Picketers are arrested and incarcerated; during their incarceration, Alice Paul leads them in a hunger strike. Many of the imprisoned suffragists are brutally force-fed, including Paul. The suffragettes' mistreatment is published in newspapers, the White House bows to public pressure, and they are released.

- White women in Arkansas are granted partial suffrage; they are able to vote in primary, but not general, elections.

- Suffrage is granted to women in New York.

- Suffrage is granted to women in Estonia, Latvia, and Lithuania.

- Women in Ontario and British Columbia, Canada, gain suffrage.

- Suffragists and members of the NAWSA, led by president Carrie Chapman Catt, march in a parade in New York City.

- Margaret Sanger founds and edits *The Birth Control Review,* the first scientific journal devoted to the subject of birth control.

1918

- Willa Cather's *My Antonia* is published by Houghton.

- Suffrage is granted to women in Michigan, Oklahoma, and South Dakota; women in Texas gain suffrage for primary elections only.

- President Woodrow Wilson issues a statement in support of a federal constitutional amendment granting full suffrage to American women.

- A resolution to amend the U.S. constitution to ensure that the voting rights of U.S. citizens cannot "be denied or abridged by the United States or any state on account of sex" passes in the House of Representatives.

- President Wilson urges the Senate to support the 19th amendment, but fails to win the two-thirds majority necessary for passage.

- Women in the United Kingdom who are married, own property, or are college graduates over the age of 30, are granted suffrage.

- Women in Austria, Czechoslovakia, Germany, Luxembourg, and Poland gain suffrage.

- Women in New Brunswick and Nova Scotia, Canada, gain suffrage. Canadian women of British or French heritage gain voting rights in Federal elections.

- Marie Stopes's *Married Love* and *Wise Parenthood* are published by A. C. Fifield.

- Harriot Stanton Blatch's *Mobilizing Woman-Power,* with a foreword by Theodore Roosevelt, is published by The Womans Press.

1919

- Women in the Netherlands, Rhodesia, and Sweden gain suffrage.

- Doris Lessing is born on 22 October in Kermanshah, Persia (now Iran).

- The "Susan B. Anthony Amendment," also known as the 19th Amendment to the U. S. Constitution, after it is defeated twice in the Senate, passes in both houses of Congress. The amendment is sent to states for ratification.

1920

- The 19th Amendment to the U.S. Constitution is ratified by the necessary two-thirds of states and American women are guaranteed suffrage on 26 August when Secretary of State Bainbridge Colby signs the amendment into law.

- The NAWSA is reorganized as the National League of Women Voters and elects Maud Wood Park as its first president.

- Bella Abzug is born on 24 July in New York City.

- Icelandic women gain full suffrage.

- Edith Wharton's *The Age of Innocence* is published by Meredith.

- Colette's *Cheri* is published by Fayard.

1921

- Betty Friedan is born on 4 February in Peoria, Illinois.

- Edith Wharton receives the Pulitzer Prize for fiction for *The Age of Innocence.*

- Margaret Sanger organizes the first American Conference on Birth Control in New York City.

1922

- Irish women gain full suffrage.

- Grace Paley is born on 11 December in New York City.

- Edna St. Vincent Millay's *The Ballad of the Harp-Weaver* is published by F. Shay.

1923

- Edna St. Vincent Millay receives the Pulitzer Prize for Poetry for *The Ballad of the Harp-Weaver.*

- Margaret Sanger opens the Birth Control Clinical Research Bureau in New York to dispense contraceptives to women under the supervision of a licensed physician and to study the effect of contraception upon women's health.

- Margaret Sanger founds the American Birth Control League.

- The Equal Rights Amendment (ERA), written by Alice Paul, is introduced in Congress for the first time in December.

1924

- Phyllis Schlafly is born on 15 August in St. Louis, Missouri.

- Shirley Chisolm is born on 30 November in Brooklyn, New York.

1925

- Amy Lowell dies on 12 May in Brookline, Massachusetts.

- *Collected Poems of H.D.* is published by Boni & Liveright.

- Virginia Woolf's *Mrs. Dalloway* is published by Harcourt.

1926

- Marietta Holley dies on 1 March near Adams, New York.

- Marianne Moore becomes the first woman editor of *The Dial* in New York City, a post she holds until 1929.

- Carrie Chapman Catt and Nettie Rogers Schuler's *Woman Suffrage and Politics; the Inner Story of the Suffrage Movement* is published by Charles Scribner's Sons.

- Grazia Deledda receives the Nobel Prize in Literature.

1927

- Victoria Woodhull dies on 10 June in Norton Park, England.

- Virginia Woolf's *To the Lighthouse* is published by Harcourt.

1928

- Maya Angelou is born Marguerite Johnson on 4 April in St. Louis, Missouri.

- Emmeline Pankhurst dies on 14 June in London, England.

- Anne Sexton is born on 9 November in Newton, Massachusetts.

- Virginia Woolf's *Orlando* is published by Crosby Gaige.

- Women are granted full suffrage in Great Britain.

- Gertrude Stein's *Useful Knowledge* is published by Payson & Clarke.

- Sigrid Undset receives the Nobel Prize in Literature.

1929

- Adrienne Rich is born on 16 May in Baltimore, Maryland.

- Marilyn French is born on 21 November in New York City.

- While Arthur M. Schlesinger Sr. reads her speech for her, Margaret Sanger appears in a gag on a stage in Boston where she has been prevented from speaking.

- Virginia Woolf's *A Room of One's Own* is published by Harcourt.

1930

- Lorraine Hansberry is born on 19 May in Chicago, Illinois.

- Cairine Wilson is appointed the first woman senator in Canada.

1931

- Jane Addams receives the Nobel Peace Prize.

- Toni Morrison is born Chloe Anthony Wofford on 18 February in Lorain, Ohio.

- Ida B. Wells-Barnett dies on 25 March in Chicago, Illinois.

1932

- Sylvia Plath is born on 27 October in Boston, Massachusetts.

1933

- Gertrude Stein's *The Autobiography of Alice B. Toklas* is published by Harcourt.

- Frances Perkins (1882-1965) is appointed Secretary of Labor by President Franklin D. Roosevelt, and becomes the first female cabinet member in the United States.

1934

- Gloria Steinem is born on 25 March in Toledo, Ohio.

- Kate Millett is born on 14 September in St. Paul, Minnesota.

- Lillian Hellman's *The Children's Hour* debuts on 20 November at Maxine Elliot's Theatre in New York City.

1935

- Jane Addams dies of cancer on 21 May in Chicago, Illinois.

- Charlotte Perkins Gilman commits suicide on 17 August in Pasadena, California.

- The National Council of Negro Women is founded by Mary McLeod Bethune (1875-1955).

1936

- First lady Eleanor Roosevelt begins writing a daily syndicated newspaper column, "My Day."

- Margaret Mitchell's *Gone with the Wind* is published by Macmillan.

1937

- Hélène Cixous is born on 5 June in Oran, Algeria.

- Bessie Head is born on 6 July in Pietermaritzburg, South Africa.

- Edith Wharton dies on 11 August in St. Brice-sous-Foret, France.

- Zora Neale Hurston's *Their Eyes Were Watching God* is published by Lippincott.

- Margaret Mitchell (1900-1949) receives the Pulitzer Prize in Letters & Drama for novel for *Gone with the Wind*.

- Anne O'Hare McCormick becomes the first woman to receive the Pulitzer Prize in Journalism, which she is given for distinguished correspondence for her international reporting on the rise of Italian Fascism in the *New York Times*.

1938

- Joyce Carol Oates is born on 16 June in Lockport, New York.

- Pearl Buck receives the Nobel Prize in Literature.

1939

- Germaine Greer is born on 29 January near Melbourne, Australia.

- Lillian Hellman's *The Little Foxes* debuts on 15 February at National Theatre in New York City.

- Margaret Atwood is born on 18 November in Ottawa, Ontario, Canada.

- Paula Gunn Allen is born in Cubero, New Mexico.

- French physician Madeleine Pelletier (1874-1939) is arrested for performing abortions in Paris, France; she dies later the same year. Throughout her medical career, Pelletier advocated women's rights to birth control and abortion, and founded her own journal, *La Suffragist*.

1940

- Emma Goldman dies on 14 May in Toronto, Ontario, Canada.

- Maxine Hong Kingston is born on 27 October in Stockton, California.

- Harriot Eaton Stanton Blatch dies on 20 November in Greenwich, Connecticut.

1941

- Virginia Woolf commits suicide on 28 March in Lewes, Sussex, England.

1942

- Erica Jong is born on 26 March in New York City.

- Isabel Allende is born on 2 August in Lima, Peru.

- Ellen Glasgow (1873-1945) receives the Pulitzer Prize for her novel *In This Our Life*.

- Margaret Walker (1915-1998) becomes the first African American to receive the Yale Series of Young Poets Award for her collection *For My People*.

1944

- Alice Walker is born on 9 February in Eatonton, Georgia.

- Martha Gellhorn (1908-1998) is the only woman journalist to go ashore with Allied troops during the D-Day invasion of Normandy, France in June.

- Buchi Emecheta is born on 21 July in Yaba, Lagos, Nigeria.

- Rita Mae Brown is born on 28 November in Hanover, Pennsylvania.

- Women are granted suffrage in France and Jamaica.

1945

- Eleanor Roosevelt becomes the first person to represent the U. S. at the United Nations. She serves until 1951, is reappointed in 1961, and serves until her death in 1962.

- Gabriela Mistral receives the Nobel Prize in Literature.

- Louise Bogan is named U. S. Poet Laureate.

1946

- Gertrude Stein dies of cancer on 27 July in Neuilly-sur-Seine, France.

- Andrea Dworkin is born on 26 September in Camden, New Jersey.

- Mary Ritter Beard's *Woman as a Force in History: A Study in Traditions and Realities* is published by Macmillan.

- Eleanor Roosevelt becomes chair of the United Nations Human Rights Commission. She remains chair until 1951.

1947

- Carrie Chapman Catt dies on 9 March in New Rochelle, New York.

- Willa Cather dies on 24 April in New York City.

- Dorothy Fuldheim, a newscaster in Cleveland, Ohio, becomes the first female television news anchor at WEWS-TV.

1948

- Susan Glaspell dies on 27 July in Provincetown, Massachusetts.

- Ntozake Shange is born Paulette Linda Williams on 18 October in Trenton, New Jersey.

- Leonie Adams is named U. S. Poet Laureate.

1949

- Simone de Beauvoir's *Le deuxième sexe* (*The Second Sex*, H. M. Parshley, translator: Knopf, 1953) is published by Gallimard.

- Elizabeth Bishop is named U. S. Poet Laureate.

- Gwendolyn Brooks's *Annie Allen* is published by Harper.

1950

- Gloria Naylor is born on 25 January in New York City.

- Edna St. Vincent Millay dies of a heart attack on 19 October at Steepletop, Austerlitz, New York.

- Gwendolyn Brooks receives the Pulitzer Prize for poetry for *Annie Allen.*

1951

- Marianne Moore's *Collected Poems* is published by Macmillan.

- Marguerite Higgins (1920-1960) receives the Pulitzer Prize for Journalism in overseas reporting for her account of the battle at Inchon, Korea in September, 1950.

1952

- Amy Tan is born on 19 February in Oakland, California.

- Rita Dove is born on 28 August in Akron, Ohio.

- bell hooks is born Gloria Jean Watkins on 25 September in Hopkinsville, Kentucky.

- Marianne Moore receives the National Book Critics Circle award for poetry and the Pulitzer Prize for poetry for *Collected Poems.*

1953

- *A Writer's Diary: Being Extracts from the Diary of Virigina Woolf,* edited by Leonard Woolf, is published by Hogarth.

- The International Planned Parenthood Federation is founded by Margaret Sanger, who serves as the organization's first president.

- Women are granted suffrage in Mexico.

1954

- Louise Erdrich is born on 7 June in Little Falls, Minnesota.

- Colette dies on 3 August in Paris, France.

- Sandra Cisneros is born on 20 December in Chicago, Illinois.

1955

- On 1 December American civil rights activist Rosa Parks (1913-) refuses to move from her seat for a white passenger on a Montgomery, Alabama bus and is arrested.

1956

- The Anti-Prostitution Act, written and campaigned for by Kamichika Ichiko, makes prostitution illegal in Japan.

1958

- Christabel Pankhurst dies on 13 February in Los Angeles, California.

1959

- Susan Faludi is born on 18 April in New York City.

- Lorraine Hansberry's *A Raisin in the Sun* debuts in March at the Ethel Barrymore Theatre in New York City.

- Lorraine Hansberry becomes the youngest woman and first black artist to receive a New York Drama Critics Circle Award for best American play for *A Raisin in the Sun.*

1960

- Zora Neale Hurston dies on 28 January in Fort Pierce, Florida.

- Sylvia Pankhurst dies on 27 September in Addis Ababa, Ethiopia.

- The U.S. Food and Drug Administration approves the first oral contraceptive for distribution to consumers in May.

- Harper Lee's *To Kill a Mockingbird* is published by Lippincott.

1961

- H. D. (Hilda Doolittle) dies on 27 September in Zurich, Switzerland.

- Harper Lee receives the Pulitzer Prize for the novel for *To Kill a Mockingbird.*

- President John F. Kennedy establishes the President's Commission on the Status of Women on 14 December and appoints Eleanor Roosevelt as head of the commission.

1962

- Isak Dinesen dies on 7 September in Rungsted Kyst, Denmark.

- Eleanor Roosevelt dies on 7 November in New York City.

- Naomi Wolf is born on 12 November in San Francisco, California.

- Doris Lessing's *The Golden Notebook* is published by Simon & Schuster.

1963

- Betty Friedan's *The Feminine Mystique* is published by Norton and becomes a bestseller.

- Sylvia Plath's *The Bell Jar* is published under the pseudonym Victoria Lucas by Heinemann.

- Sylvia Plath commits suicide on 11 February in London, England.

- Barbara Wertheim Tuchman (1912-1989) becomes the first woman to receive the Pulitzer Prize for general nonfiction for *The Guns of August.*

- The Equal Pay Act is passed by the U.S. Congress on 28 May. It is the first federal law requiring equal compensation for men and women in federal jobs.

- Entitled *American Women,* the report issued by the President's Commission on the Status of Women documents sex discrimination in nearly all corners of American society, and urges the U.S. Supreme Court to clarify legal status of women under the U.S. Constitution.

1964

- Anna Julia Haywood Cooper dies on 27 February in Washington, DC.

1965

- Lorraine Hansberry dies of cancer on 12 January in New York City.

- Women are granted suffrage in Afghanistan.

1966

- Anna Akhmatova dies on 6 March in Russia.

- Margaret Sanger dies on 6 September in Tucson, Arizona.

- National Organization for Women (NOW) is founded on 29 June by Betty Friedan and 27 other founding members. NOW is dedicated to promoting full participation in society for women and advocates for adequate child care for working mothers, reproductive rights, and the Equal Rights Amendment to the U.S. Constitution.

- Anne Sexton's *Live or Die* is published by Houghton.

- Nelly Sachs (1891-1970) receives the Nobel Prize in Literature, which she shares with Shmuel Yosef Agnon.

1967

- Anne Sexton receives the Pulitzer Prize for poetry for *Live or Die.*

- Senator Eugene McCarthy, with 37 co-sponsors, introduces the Equal Rights Amendment in the U.S. Senate.

1968

- Audre Lorde's *The First Cities* is published by Poets Press.

1969

- Joyce Carol Oates's *them* is published by Vanguard Press.

- Shirley Chisolm becomes the first African American woman elected to Congress when she takes her seat in the U.S. House of Representatives on 3 January.

- Golda Meir (1898-1978) becomes the fourth Prime Minister of Israel on 17 March.

- California adopts the nation's first "no fault" divorce law, allowing divorce by mutual consent.

1970

- Toni Morrison's *The Bluest Eye* is published by Holt.

- Germaine Greer's *The Female Eunuch* is published by MacGibbon & Kee.

- Maya Angelou's *I Know Why the Caged Bird Sings* is published by Random House.

- Kate Millett's *Sexual Politics* is published by Doubleday and becomes a bestseller.

- Joyce Carol Oates receives the National Book Award for fiction for *them*.

- The Equal Rights Amendment passes in the U.S. House of Representatives by a vote of 350 to 15 on 10 August.

- Bella Abzug is elected to the U.S. House of Representatives on 3 November.

- The Feminist Press is founded at the City University of New York.

- *Off Our Backs: A Women's News Journal* is founded in Washington, D.C.

- *The Women's Rights Law Reporter* is founded in Newark, New Jersey.

1971

- Josephine Jacobsen is named U. S. Poet Laureate.

1972

- Marianne Moore dies on 5 February in New York City.

- *Ms.* magazine is founded; Gloria Steinem serves as editor of *Ms.* until 1987. The 300,000 copy print run of the first issue of *Ms.* magazine sells out within a week of its release in January.

- Shirley Chisolm becomes the first African American woman to seek the presidential nomination of a major political party, although her bid for the Democratic Party nomination is unsuccessful.

- The Equal Rights Amendment is passed by both houses of the U.S. Congress and is signed by President Richard M. Nixon. The amend-ment expires in 1982, without being ratified by the required two-thirds of the states; it is three states short of full ratification.

- President Nixon signs into law Title IX of the Higher Education Act banning sex bias in athletics and other activities at all educational institutions receiving federal assistance.

- Women's Press is established in Canada.

1973

- The U.S. Supreme Court, in their decision handed down on 21 January in *Roe v. Wade*, decides that in the first trimester of pregnancy women have the right to choose an abortion.

- Elizabeth Bowen dies of lung cancer on 22 February in London, England.

- Rita Mae Brown's *Rubyfruit Jungle* is published by Daughters, Inc.

- Erica Jong's *Fear of Flying* is published by Holt and becomes a bestseller.

- Alice Walker's *In Love and Trouble: Stories of Black Women* is published by Harcourt.

- The Boston Women's Health Book Collective's *Our Bodies, Ourselves: A Book By and For Women* is published by Simon and Schuster.

1974

- Andrea Dworkin's *Women Hating* is published by Dutton.

- Adrienne Rich receives the National Book Award for *Diving into the Wreck: Poems, 1971-1972*.

- Anne Sexton commits suicide on 4 October in Weston, Massachusetts.

- Katharine Graham (1917-2001), publisher of the *Washington Post,* becomes the first woman member of the board of the Associated Press.

1975

- Paula Gunn Allen' essay "The Sacred Hoop: A Contemporary Indian Perspective on American Indian Literature" appears in *Literature of the American Indian: Views and Interpretations,* edited by Abraham Chapman and published by New American Library.

- Hélène Cixous and Catherine Clement's *La Jeune nee* (*The Newly Born Woman*, University of Minnesota Press, 1986) is published by Union Generale.

- Margaret Thatcher is elected leader of the Conservative Party and becomes the first woman to head a major party in Great Britain.

- Susan Brownmiller's *Against our Will: Men, Women, and Rape* is published by Simon and Schuster.

1976

- Andrea Dworkin's *Our Blood: Prophecies and Discourses on Sexual Politics* is published by Harper.

- Maxine Hong Kingston's *The Woman Warrior: Memoirs of a Girlhood among Ghosts* is published by Knopf.

- Maxine Hong Kingston's receives the National Book Critics Circle award for general nonfiction for *The Woman Warrior*.

- Barbara Walters (1931-) becomes the first female network television news anchorwoman when she joins Harry Reasoner as coanchor of the *ABC Evening News*.

- Shere Hite's *The Hite Report: A Nationwide Study of Female Sexuality* is published by Macmillan.

1977

- Alice Paul dies on 9 July in Moorestown, New Jersey.

- Marilyn French's *The Women's Room* is published by Summit.

- Toni Morrison's *Song of Solomon* is published by Knopf.

- Toni Morrison receives the National Book Critics Circle Award for fiction for *Song of Solomon*.

- Labor organizer Barbara Mayer Wertheimer's *We Were There: The Story of Working Women in America* is published by Pantheon.

- Women's Press is established in Great Britain.

1978

- The Pregnancy Discrimination Act bans employment discrimination against pregnant women.

- Tillie Olsen's *Silences* is published by Delcorte Press/Seymour Lawrence.

1979

- Margaret Thatcher becomes the first woman prime minister of Great Britain. She serves until her resignation in 1990, marking the longest term of any twentieth-century prime minister.

- Barbara Wertheim Tuchman becomes the first woman elected president of the American Academy and Institute of Arts and Letters.

- Mother Teresa (1910-1997) receives the Nobel Peace Prize.

- Sandra M. Gilbert and Susan Gubar's *The Madwoman in the Attic: The Woman Writer and the Nineteenth-Century Imagination* is published by Yale University Press.

1980

- Muriel Rukeyser dies on 12 February in New York City.

- Adrienne Rich's essay "Compulsory Heterosexuality and Lesbian Experience" is published in *Signs: Journal of Women in Culture and Society*.

1981

- bell hooks's *Ain't I a Woman: Black Women and Feminism* is published by South End Press.

- Sylvia Plath's *Collected Poems*, edited by Ted Hughes, is published by Harper.

- Sandra Day O'Connor (1930-) becomes the first woman Justice of the U.S. Supreme Court, after being nominated by President Ronald Reagan and sworn in on 25 September.

- Women of Color Press is founded in Albany, New York by Barbara Smith.

- Cleis Press is established in Pittsburgh, Pennsylvania, and San Francisco, California.

- *This Bridge Called My Back: Writings by Radical Women of Color*, edited by Cherríe Moraga and Gloria Anzaldúa, is published by Persephone Press.

- Maxine Kumin is named U. S. Poet Laureate.

1982

- Djuna Barnes dies on 19 June in New York City.

- Sylvia Plath is posthumously awarded the Pulitzer Prize in poetry for *Collected Poems*.

- Alice Walker's *The Color Purple* is published by Harcourt.

- Carol Gilligan's *In a Different Voice: Psychological Theory and Women's Development* is published by Harvard University Press.

1983

- Rebecca West dies on 15 March in London, England.

- Gloria Steinem's *Outrageous Acts and Everyday Rebellions* is published by Holt.

1984

- Sandra Cisneros's *The House on Mango Street* is published by Arte Publico.

- Lillian Hellman dies on 30 June in Martha's Vineyard, Massachusetts.

- Geraldine Ferraro (1935-) becomes the first woman to win the Vice-Presidential nomination and runs unsuccessfully for office with Democratic Presidential candidate Walter Mondale.

- Firebrand Books, publisher of feminist and lesbian literature, is established in Ann Arbor, Michigan.

- bell hooks's *Feminist Theory: From Margin to Center* is published by South End Press.

1985

- Margaret Atwood's *The Handmaid's Tale* is published by McClelland & Stewart.

- Wilma P. Mankiller is sworn in as the first woman tribal chief of the Cherokee nation. She serves until 1994.

- Gwendolyn Brooks is named U. S. Poet Laureate.

1986

- Simone de Beauvoir dies on 14 April in Paris, France.

- Bessie Head dies on 17 April in Botswana.

- Rita Dove's *Thomas and Beulah* is published by Carnegie-Mellon University Press.

- Sylvia Ann Hewlett's *A Lesser Life: The Myth of Women's Liberation in America* is published by Morrow.

1987

- Toni Morrison's *Beloved* is published by Knopf.

- Rita Dove receives the Pulitzer Prize for poetry for *Thomas and Beulah.*

1988

- Toni Morrison receives the Pulitzer Prize for fiction for *Beloved.*

- *The War of the Words,* Volume 1 of Sandra M. Gilbert and Susan Gubar's *No Man's Land: The Place of the Woman Writer in the Twentieth Century,* is published by Yale University Press.

1989

- Amy Tan's *The Joy Luck Club* is published by Putnam.

1990

- Naomi Wolf's *The Beauty Myth: How Images of Beauty Are Used against Women* is published by Chatto & Windus.

- The Norplant contraceptive is approved by the FDA on 10 December.

- Camille Paglia's *Sexual Personae: Art and Decadence from Nefertiti to Emily Dickinson* is published by Yale University Press.

- Wendy Kaminer's *A Fearful Freedom: Women's Flight from Equality* is published by Addison-Wesley.

- Laurel Thatcher Ulrich's *A Midwife's Tale: The Life of Martha Ballard, Based on Her Diary, 1785-1812* is published by Knopf.

- Judith Butler's *Gender Trouble: Feminism and the Subversion of Identity* is published by Routledge.

1991

- Susan Faludi's *Backlash: The Undeclared War Against American Women* is published by Crown.

- Antonia Novello (1944-) is appointed by President George H.W. Bush and becomes the first woman and first person of Hispanic descent to serve as U. S. Surgeon General.

- Bernadine Healy, M.D. (1944-) is appointed by President George H.W. Bush and becomes the first woman to head the National Institutes of Health.

- Suzanne Gordon's *Prisoners of Men's Dreams: Striking Out for a New Feminine Future* is published by Little, Brown.

- Laurel Thatcher Ulrich receives the Pulitzer Prize for history for *A Midwife's Tale: The Life of Martha Ballard, Based on Her Diary, 1785-1812.*

1992

- Carol Elizabeth Moseley Braun (1947-) becomes the first African American woman elected to the U. S. Senate on 3 November.

- Carolyne Larrington's *The Feminist Companion to Mythology* is published by Pandora.

- Marilyn French's *The War against Women* is published by Summit.

- Clarissa Pinkola Estes's *Women Who Run with the Wolves: Myths and Stories of the Wild Woman Archetype* is published by Ballantine.

- Naomi Wolf's *Fire with Fire: The New Female Power and How It Will Change the Twenty-first Century* is published by Random House.

- Mona Van Duyn is named U. S. Poet Laureate.

1993

- Appointed by President Bill Clinton, Janet Reno (1938-) becomes the first woman U.S. Attorney General when she is sworn in on 12 March.

- Toni Morrison receives the Nobel Prize in Literature.

- Toni Morrison receives the Elizabeth Cady Stanton Award from the National Organization for Women.

- Canada's Progressive Conservative party votes on 13 June to make Defense Minister Kim Campbell the nation's first woman prime minister. Canadian voters oust the Conservative party in elections on 25 October as recession continues; Liberal leader Jean Chrétien becomes prime minister.

- On 1 October Rita Dove becomes the youngest person and the first African American to be named U. S. Poet Laureate.

- Faye Myenne Ng's *Bone* is published by Hyperion.

1994

- The Violence Against Women Act tightens federal penalties for sex offenders, funds services for victims of rape and domestic violence, and provides funds for special training for police officers in domestic violence and rape cases.

- Mary Pipher's *Reviving Ophelia: Saving the Selves of Adolescent Girls* is published by Putnam.

1995

- Ireland's electorate votes by a narrow margin in November to end the nation's ban on divorce (no other European country has such a ban), but only after 4 years' legal separation.

1996

- Marguerite Duras dies on 3 March in Paris, France.

- Hillary Rodham Clinton's *It Takes a Village, and Other Lessons Children Teach Us* is published by Simon and Schuster.

1998

- Bella Abzug dies on 31 March in New York City.

- Drucilla Cornell's *At the Heart of Freedom: Feminism, Sex, and Equality* is published by Princeton University Press.

1999

- Susan Brownmiller's *In Our Time: Memoir of a Revolution* is published by Dial Press.

- Gwendolyn Mink's *Welfare's End* is published by Cornell University Press.

- Martha C. Nussbaum's *Sex and Social Justice* is published by Oxford University Press.

2000

- Gwendolyn Brooks dies on 3 December in Chicago, Illinois.

- Patricia Hill Collins's *Black Feminist Thought: Knowledge, Consciousness, and the Politics of Empowerment* is published by Routledge.

- Jennifer Baumgardner and Amy Richards's *Manifesta: Young Women, Feminism, and the Future* is published by Farrar, Straus, and Giroux.

2002

- Estelle B. Freedman's *No Turning Back: The History of Feminism and the Future of Women* is published by Ballantine.

- *Colonize This! Young Women of Color on Today's Feminism,* edited by Daisy Hernandez and Bushra Rehman, is published by Seal Press.

2003

- Iranian feminist and human rights activist Shirin Ebadi (1947-) receives the Nobel Peace Prize.

- Louise Glück is named U. S. Poet Laureate.

- *Catching a Wave: Reclaiming Feminism for the 21st Century,* edited by Rory Cooke Dicker and Alison Piepmeier, is published by Northeastern University Press.

2004

- The FDA approves the contraceptive mifepristone, following a 16-year struggle by reproductive rights activists to have the abortion drug approved. Opponents made repeated efforts to prevent approval and distribution of mifepristone.

- *The Fire This Time: Young Activists and the New Feminism,* edited by Vivien Labaton and Dawn Lundy Martin, is published by Anchor Books.

- *The Future of Women's Rights: Global Visions and Strategies,* edited by Joanna Kerr, Ellen Sprenger, and Alison Symington, is published by ZED Books and Palgrave Macmillan.

WOMEN IN THE EARLY TO MID-20TH CENTURY (1900-1960): AN OVERVIEW

The dawn of the twentieth century witnessed changes in almost every aspect of the day-to-day lives of women, from the domestic sphere to the public. The women's movement, with its emphasis on advocacy of equal rights, newly formed women's organizations, and the rise of a new generation of female artists, photographers, and professionals, transformed the traditional patriarchal social structure across the globe. Followed closely by the advent of World War I, these social shifts, which had been set in motion at the beginning of the century, developed further as women were propelled into the workforce, exposing them to previously male-dominated professional and political situations. By the midpoint of the twentieth century, women's activities and concerns had been recognized as a significant element of the literary, scientific, and cultural landscape of several countries, marking a revolutionary change in the social and domestic roles of women.

The end of the nineteenth century saw tremendous growth in the suffrage movement in England and the United States, with women struggling to attain political equality. The suffragists—who were often militant in their expressions of protest—presented a sometimes stark contrast to the feminine ideal of the era, which portrayed women as delicate, demure, and silent, confined to a domestic world that cocooned them from the harsh realities of the world. Despite many challenges English and American women eventually won the right to vote, in part due to the changed perception of women's abilities following World War I. As men were called to war, companies that had previously limited employment in better-paying jobs to white males found themselves opening their doors to white women and women and men of color. Racial and gender tensions escalated during this time, and many jobs were in fact permanently redefined as "women's work," including teaching, nursing, secretarial work, and telephone operations. As well as functioning in the workforce, women actively participated in the political and cultural life of England and the United States. The early decades of the twentieth century, often referred to as the Progressive Era, saw the emergence of a new image of women in society which had undergone a marked transformation from the demure, frail, female stereotype of the late Victorian Era. The women of the Progressive Era, according to Sarah Jane Deutsch, were portrayed as "women with short hair and short skirts . . . kicking up their legs and kicking off a century of social restrictions." Progressive women smoked, danced in public, held jobs, and generally did most things that nineteenth-century women were barred from doing. However, Deutsch asserts that this image of the 1920s "flapper" was restricted to certain portions of the population, namely white, young, and middle-class communities. Women elsewhere, particularly women from other ethnic backgrounds, such as African-Americans, Asian-Americans, and Hispanics, lived much differently, struggling in their new roles as mothers and professionals. The number of women who worked outside the home in the 1920s rose almost 50 percent throughout the decade. While women still constituted a small number of the professional population, they were slowly increasing their participation in more significant occupations, including law, social work, engineering, and medicine.

The presence of a large class of young working women after World War I was reflected in what had become a major cultural force—the film industry. Nevertheless, films of the era continued to reinforce outdated stereotypes about women's place in society. While early cinematic storylines often featured poor women finding success and contentment through marriage to rich men, the films of the 1920s depicted young, feisty working women who, like their predecessors, could attain true happiness only by marrying their bosses. Such plotlines helped many to cope with the growing fear that the domestic and family structure of society was being eroded by the emergence of the new, independent woman. Rarely did depictions of women in mass media, including film, radio, and theater, convey the true circumstances of working women. Instead, audiences were presented with images of flappers or visions of glorified motherhood and marriage.

Women in the early twentieth century were perhaps most active and influential as writers and artists. The advent of the new century did witness a change in the style and content of women's writing, as well as an increase in the depiction of feminine images and themes in literature. Male authors such as D. H. Lawrence and W. D. Howells explored issues pertaining to sexuality and the newly redefined sexual politics between men and women. Women authors such as Dorothy Richardson, May Sinclair, and Katherine Mansfield focused on topics pertinent to women, bringing attention to the myriad difficulties they faced redefining their identities in a changing world. Other major women writers of the period included Gertrude Stein, Virginia Woolf, Charlotte Perkins Gilman, and Edith Wharton. In the arena of art, the early twentieth century provided growing opportunities for women to exhibit their work. In 1914, for example, the National Academy of Design first allowed women to attend anatomy lectures, thus providing them with a chance to study draftsmanship and develop drawing skills in a formal setting. Such artists as Emerson Baum

and photographers like Alfred Steiglitz helped promote exhibitions of women's art, including the works of Imogen Cunningham and Georgia O'Keefe. Many female artists—among them Dorothea Lange and Claire Leighton—used their talents to highlight the social realities of their times, and some of the most powerful images of this period, including stirring portrayals of coal miners and farmers, were produced by these women.

By the mid-twentieth century, women throughout the Western world had completely redefined their roles in almost every social, political, and cultural sphere. While the fight for equal rights and recognition for women would continue into the 1950s and beyond, the first major steps towards such changes began at the advent of the twentieth century, with women writers, photographers, artists, activists, and workers blazing a new trail for generations of women to follow.

REPRESENTATIVE WORKS

Jane Addams
Democracy and Social Ethics (nonfiction) 1902

Twenty Years at Hull House, with Autobiographical Notes (essays) 1910

The Long Road of Woman's Memory (nonfiction) 1916

Peace and Bread in Time of War (nonfiction) 1922

Margaret Bourke-White
*Fort Peck Dam (photograph) 1936

You Have Seen Their Faces (photographs) 1937

Imogen Cunningham
The Dream (photograph) 1910

Magnolia Blossom (photograph) 1925

Isadora Duncan
Der Tanz der Zukunft [*The Dance*] (nonfiction) 1903

The Art of the Dance (nonfiction) 1928

My Life (autobiography) 1928

Crystal Eastman
Crystal Eastman on Women and Revolution [edited by Blanche Wiesen Cook] (essays) 1978

Charlotte Perkins Gilman
"The Yellow Wallpaper" (novella) 1892

Women and Economics (nonfiction) 1898

Concerning Children (nonfiction) 1900

The Home: Its Work and Influence (nonfiction) 1903

Human Work (nonfiction) 1904

The Man-Made World; or, Our Androcentric Culture (nonfiction) 1911

Emma Goldman
Anarchism and Other Essays (essays) 1910

Living My Life (autobiography) 1931

Red Emma Speaks [compiled and edited by Alix Kates Shulman] (essays) 1972

Frida Kahlo
Self Portrait (painting) 1926

Fruits of the Earth (painting) 1938

Dorothea Lange
Cotton Picker (photograph) 1930

White Angel Bread Line (photograph) 1932

Claire Leighton
Lapful of Windfalls (woodcut) 1932

Margaret Mead
Coming of Age in Samoa (nonfiction) 1928

Georgia O'Keeffe
Tent Door at Night (painting) 1913

Oriental Poppies (painting) 1928

Cow's Skull: Red, White, and Blue (painting) 1931

Eleanor Roosevelt
This Is My Story (autobiography) 1937

The American Mothers' Declaration (nonfiction) 1939

Ladies of Courage [with Lorena A. Hickok] (essays) 1954

On My Own (autobiography) 1958

Margaret Sanger
Woman Rebel (periodical) 1914

What Every Mother Should Know; or, How Six Little Children Were Taught the Truth (nonfiction) 1916

Woman and the New Race (nonfiction) 1920

Motherhood in Bondage (nonfiction) 1928

My Fight for Birth Control (nonfiction) 1931

Olive Schreiner
The Story of An African Farm [as Ralph Iron] (novel) 1883

Woman and Labour (nonfiction) 1911

Gertrude Stein
Useful Knowledge (nonfiction) 1928

The Autobiography of Alice B. Toklas (memoir) 1933

Lectures in America (lectures) 1935

Marie Stopes
Married Love (nonfiction) 1918

Wise Parenthood (nonfiction) 1918

Rebecca West
The Return of the Soldier (novel) 1918

Harriet Hume (novel) 1929

Black Lamb and Grey Falcon. 2 vols. (nonfiction) 1942

Edith Wharton
The House of Mirth (novel) 1905

The Fruit of the Tree (novel) 1907

The Age of Innocence (novel) 1920

---

*   This photograph was used on the first cover of *Life*, 23 November 1936.

PRIMARY SOURCES

CHARLOTTE PERKINS GILMAN (ESSAY DATE 1898)

SOURCE: Gilman, Charlotte Perkins. "Chapter XIV." In *Women and Economics: A Study of the Economic Relation Between Men and Women as a Factor in Social Evolution.* Berkeley, Calif.: University of California Press, 1998.

In the following excerpt from her book Women and Economics, *originally published in 1898, Gilman reflects on the changing relationship between men and women.*

The changes in our conception and expression of home life, so rapidly and steadily going on about us, involve many far-reaching effects, all helpful to human advancement. Not the least of these is the improvement in our machinery of social intercourse.

This necessity of civilization was unknown in those primitive ages when family intercourse was sufficient for all, and when any further contact between individuals meant war. Trade and its travel, the specialization of labor and the distribution of its products, with their ensuing development, have produced a wider, freer, and more frequent movement and interchange among the innumerable individuals whose interaction makes society. Only recently, and as yet but partially, have women as individuals come to their share of this fluent social intercourse which is the essential condition of civilization. It is not merely a pleasure or an indulgence: it is the human necessity.

For women as individuals to meet men and other women as individuals, with no regard whatever to the family relation, is a growing demand of our time. As a social necessity, it is perforce being met in some fashion; but its right development is greatly impeded by the clinging folds of domestic and social customs derived from the sexuo-economic relation. The demand for a wider and freer social intercourse between the sexes rests, primarily, on the needs of their respective natures, but is developed in modern life to a far subtler and higher range of emotion than existed in the primitive state, where they had but one need and but one way of meeting it; and this demand, too, calls for a better arrangement of our machinery of living.

Always in social evolution, as in other evolution, the external form suited to earlier needs is but slowly outgrown; and the period of transition, while the new functions are fumbling through the old organs, and slowly forcing mechanical expression for themselves, is necessarily painful. So far in our development, acting on a deep-seated conviction that the world consisted only of families and the necessary business arrangements involved in providing for those families, we have conscientiously striven to build and plan for family advantage, and either unconsciously or grudgingly have been forced to make transient provision for individuals. Whatever did not tend to promote family life, and did tend to provide for the needs of individuals not at the time in family relation, we have deprecated in principle, though reluctantly forced to admit it in practice.

To this day articles are written, seriously and humorously, protesting against the increasing luxury and comfort of bachelor apartments for men, as well as against the pecuniary independence of women, on the ground that these conditions militate against marriage and family life. Most men, even now, pass through a period of perhaps ten years, when they are individuals, business calling them away from their parental family, and business not allowing them to start new families of their own. Women, also, more and more each year, are entering upon a similar period of individual life. And there is a certain permanent percentage of individuals, "odd numbers" and "broken sets," who fall short of family life or who are left over from it; and these need to live.

The residence hotel, the boarding-house, club, lodging-house, and restaurant are our present provision for this large and constantly increasing class. It is not a travelling class. These are people who want to live somewhere for years at a time, but who are not married or otherwise provided with a family. Home life being in our minds inextricably connected with married life, a home being held to imply a family, and a family implying a head, these detached persons are unable to achieve any home life, and are thereby subjected to the inconvenience, deprivation, and expense, the often unhygienic, and sometimes immoral influences, of our makeshift substitutes.

What the human race requires is permanent provision for the needs of individuals, disconnected from the sex-relation. Our assumption that only married people and their immediate relatives have any right to live in comfort and health is erroneous. Every human being needs a home,—bachelor, husband, or widower, girl, wife, or widow, young or old. They need it from the cradle to the grave, and without regard to sex-connections. We should so build and arrange for the shelter and comfort of humanity as not to interfere with marriage, and yet not to make that comfort dependent upon marriage. With the industries of home life managed professionally, with rooms and suites of rooms and houses obtainable by any person or persons desiring them, we could live singly without losing home comfort and general companionship, we could meet bereavement without being robbed of the common conveniences of living as well as of the heart's love, and we could marry in ease and freedom without involving any change in the economic base of either party concerned.

Married people will always prefer a home together, and can have it; but groups of women or groups of men can also have a home together if they like, or contiguous rooms. And individuals even could have a house to themselves, without having, also, the business of a home upon their shoulders.

Take the kitchens out of the houses, and you leave rooms which are open to any form of arrangement and extension; and the occupancy of them does not mean "housekeeping." In such living, personal character and taste would flower as never before; the home of each individual would be at last a true personal expression; and the union of individuals in marriage would not compel the jumbling together of all the external machinery of their lives,—a process in which much of the delicacy and freshness of love, to say nothing of the power of mutual rest and refreshment, is constantly lost. The sense of lifelong freedom and self-respect and of the peace and permanence of one's own home will do much to purify and uplift the personal relations of life, and more to strengthen and extend the social relations. The individual will learn to feel himself an integral part of the social structure, in close, direct, permanent connection with the needs and uses of society.

This is especially needed for women, who are generally considered, and who consider themselves, mere fractions of families, and incapable of any wholesome life of their own. The knowledge that peace and comfort may be theirs for life, even if they do not marry,—and may be still theirs for life, even if they do,—will develope a serenity and strength in women most beneficial to them and to the world. It is a glaring proof of the insufficient and irritating character of our existing form of marriage that women must be forced to it by the need of food and clothes, and men by the need of cooks and housekeepers. We are absurdly afraid that, if men or women can meet these needs of life by other means, they will cheerfully renounce the marriage relation. And yet we sing adoringly of the power of love!

In reality, we may hope that the most valuable effect of this change in the basis of living will be the cleansing of love and marriage from this base admixture of pecuniary interest and creature comfort, and that men and women, eternally drawn together by the deepest force in nature, will be able at last to meet on a plane of pure and perfect love. We shame our own ideals, our deepest instincts, our highest knowledge, by this gross assumption that the noblest race on earth will not mate, or, at least, not mate monogamously, unless bought and bribed through the common animal necessities of food and shelter, and chained by law and custom.

REBECCA WEST (ESSAY DATE 26 NOVEMBER 1912)

SOURCE: West, Rebecca. "The Woman as Workmate: Her Claim to Equal Rates of Pay for Equal Quality of Work." *Manchester Daily Dispatch* (26 November 1912).

In the following excerpt, West responds to an article by George Edgar denouncing women's participation in the workplace, and makes a case for equal pay for equal work.

Every man likes to think of himself as a kind of Whiteley's—a universal provider. The patriarchal system is the ideal for which he longs. He

likes to dream of himself sitting on the verandah after dinner, with his wife beside him and the children in the garden, while his unmarried sisters play duets in the drawing-room and his maiden aunts hand round the coffee. This maintenance of helpless, penniless, subservient womanhood is the nearest he can get in England to the spiritual delights of the harem.

So when womanhood declares that she is no longer helpless, dislikes being penniless and refuses to be subservient the men become indignant and inarticulate. An example of this was to be seen in Mr George Edgar's recent article, 'Why Men Do Not Marry', in the *Daily Dispatch*. Mr Edgar's thesis is difficult to criticise because it consists of two mutually destructive conclusions. He stated, first, that it is absurd for women to ask for equal wages with men because they are inferior workers and have no dependants; and then he vehemently denounces women for ousting men from their work by accepting lower wages. This is the kind of argument one rarely hears except from cross-talk comedians on the halls. What makes it still more elusive is that both his conclusions are incorrect.

Mr Edgar takes the usual masculinist standpoint of regarding women as incompetent weaklings except for their maternal functions which God bestowed on them, and for which, therefore, they deserve no credit.

> It is not necessary for me to discuss the question whether a woman is the equal of a man in the performance of a day's work. In the past our practice has assumed that she is not. . . . In actual terms of wages, where in the past women have elected to work in competition with men, commerce has decided that her day's work is less valuable than a man's, and has given her less wages.

This engaging contempt for the value of the women's work is an error which comes of considering only the economic conditions of England since the industrial revolution. It is as though a Chinese mandarin were to spend a short weekend in Whitechapel and then return to Peking proclaiming that all Englishmen got drunk every night and beat their wives. This degradation of women is simply the accident of a new social order that has not yet righted itself.

Why does a man support his wife? It is not only because the mother needs to be relieved from the stress of earning her own livelihood. That is a principle that has never been universally adopted even in our own country in our own time: the Lancashire cotton-operative continues to work after she has children. The maintenance of wives is a survival of the time when England was an agricultural country. It was then recognised that the work of women in the home was so valuable that the husband and wife were regarded as equal partners of a firm, and shared the profits. The wife had then to grind the corn, bake the bread, brew, do all the dairy work and tend much of the livestock, doctor her household, spin the wool and weave the cloth, make her family's clothes and cobble their shoes, and prepare all the food stuffs, such as hams and preserves. And she did it very well indeed. On the rare occasions when she did go out to work beside men she seems—so far as we can judge from documents such as the pay-sheets of agricultural labourers in the fifteenth century—to have been paid the same wages.

And England went very well then. It was certainly a happier and—many economists agree—a more prosperous country than it is today. Then came the industrial revolution which snatched these occupations out of the women's hands and gave them to men, leaving women only the dish-washing and floor-scrubbing, which is now regarded as peculiarly feminine work, but which had previously been done mainly by boys. The ugliness and economic embarrassment of England since then ought to cause searchings of heart among masculinists such as Mr Edgar.

So much for Mr Edgar's historical researches. Now for his theory that women have no dependants. It is true that the wife does not contribute directly to the family income (men having left her no work to do) and that her maintenance and that of her children has to be borne entirely by her husband. But there are the old as well as the young. It is the woman's place to support the old. Many working-class parents will tell one that a daughter is a better investment than a son, for the son marries and keeps a family, while the daughter will probably remain single so that she can work and provide for her parents. So one cannot advocate the restriction of a woman's wage to the sum sufficient for the support of herself alone, unless one upholds the Tierra del Fuego theory that the aged are useless, dangerous, and ought to be abolished, by exposure if possible, by a club if necessary.

Moreover, I grant that men are efficient and godlike, but they sometimes die. They then leave widows and orphans, who have to be supported. And it also happens occasionally that husbands prove more ornamental than useful, 'dainty rogues in porcelain', unable to wrestle with the rough world, and then their wives have to work for them and the children.

Mr Edgar's fear that if wages were equalised they would tend to drop to the women's level is unsupported by logical proof, and is contradicted by fact. The England of the fifteenth century, which paid its women agricultural labourers as it paid its men, was the paradise of the worker. Never since have they enjoyed similar prosperity. The Lancashire cotton-operatives, who are paid without distinction of sex, are the most well-to-do workers of today. The women are not merely asking for prestige, they are fighting for hard cash. It is not the equality, but the increase in wages they want. Of course, if men insist on women getting lower wages they may create an army of blacklegs to their own undoing.

The second conclusion, that women are ousting men out of the labour world, is a popular and curiously persistent error. In the investigations made twenty years ago by Beatrice and Sidney Webb it was stated that it was very rare for men and women to compete in the same occupation, and Mary Macarthur agrees with them today. When it appears that some industry has shifted from men to women it will usually be found that some new mechanical process has been introduced which demands the manual dexterity and attention to detail characteristic of women. In the few occupations where men and women compete equal wages will benefit men by ridding employers of the temptation to employ women as blacklegs. But, as a rule, the cry for 'equal pay for equal work' does not mean equal pay for the *same* work, but equal pay for work which exacts the same time, skill and energy.

Or, to put it differently, it is a declaration on the woman's part that she is not going to live by bread alone. She wants butter, and cake if possible; pocket money for an occasional theatre and holiday; and the ability to obey the Fifth Commandment and keep her parents out of the workhouse.

The effect on the marriage-rate of the competition between men and women must be quite insignificant. There are much more forcible reasons which prevent marriage. Important among these is the isolation of modern city life. It is possible for men and women to come up to London and live there for years without making a friend. How different from the small communities of our forefathers, when every child was born 'into society' and grew up among a circle of young men and women of the same class! And another deterrent to marriage is the raising of the standard of comfort. Few men and women are prepared to risk bringing up a family on the small means that would have sufficed for their grandparents. And this disinclination to bring children into a poverty-stricken home is not altogether contemptible. City life, with the accompanying miseries of dear food and rent, holds cruel torments for child life.

And if there is to be any romance in marriage women must be given every chance to earn a decent living at other occupations. Otherwise no man can be sure that he is loved for himself alone, and that his wife did not come to the Registry Office because she had had no luck at the Labour Exchange. Only the materialist can fear that a fair day's wage for a fair day's work will kill the wife and mother in women. The trinity of the man, the woman and the child is as indestructible as the trinity of the sun, the moon and the stars.

But one admires the humility of men who think otherwise, and hold that only by the fear of starvation are women coerced into having husbands.

EMMA GOLDMAN (ESSAY DATE C. 1913)

SOURCE: Goldman, Emma. "Victims of Morality." In *Red Emma Speaks,* Alix Kates Shulman, pp. 126-32. New York: Random House, 1972.

In the following excerpt, originally written circa 1913, Goldman responds to the Comstock Law of 1873, which made it difficult for women and men to obtain contraceptives, denouncing its imposition of a narrow version of morality on the lives of men and women.

Not so very long ago I attended a meeting addressed by Anthony Comstock, who has for forty years been the guardian of American morals. A more incoherent, ignorant ramble I have never heard from any platform.

The question that presented itself to me, listening to the commonplace, bigoted talk of the man, was, How could anyone so limited and unintelligent wield the power of censor and dictator over a supposedly democratic nation? True, Comstock has the law to back him. Forty years ago, when puritanism was even more rampant than to-day, completely shutting out the light of reason and progress, Comstock succeeded, through shady machination and political wire pulling, to introduce a bill which gave him complete control over the Post Office Department—a control which has proved disastrous to the freedom of the press, as well as the right of privacy of the American citizen.

Since then, Comstock has broken into the private chambers of people, has confiscated per-sonal correspondence, as well as works of art, and has established a system of espionage and graft which would put Russia to shame. Yet the law does not explain the power of Anthony Comstock. There is something else, more terrible than the law. It is the narrow puritanic spirit, as represented in the sterile minds of the Young-Men-and-Old-Maid's Christian Union, Temperance Union, Sabbath Union, Purity League, etc. A spirit which is absolutely blind to the simplest manifestations of life; hence stands for stagnation and decay. As in antebellum days, these old fossils lament the terrible immorality of our time. Science, art, literature, the drama, are at the mercy of bigoted censorship and legal procedure, with the result that America, with all her boastful claims to progress and liberty is still steeped in the densest provincialism. . . .

Unfortunately, the Lie of Morality still stalks about in fine feathers, since no one dares to come within hailing distance of that holy of holies. Yet [it] is safe to say that no other superstition is so detrimental to growth, so enervating and paralyzing to the minds and hearts of the people, as the superstition of Morality. . . .

However, it is with the effect of Morality upon women that I am here mostly concerned. So disastrous, so paralyzing has this effect been, that some even of the most advanced among my sisters never thoroughly outgrow it.

It is Morality which condemns woman to the position of a celibate, a prostitute, or a reckless, incessant breeder of hapless children.

First, as to the celibate, the famished and withered human plant. When still a young, beautiful flower, she falls in love with a respectable young man. But Morality decrees that unless he can marry the girl, she must never know the raptures of love, the ecstasy of passion, which reaches its culminating expression in the sex embrace. The respectable young man is willing to marry, but the Property Morality, the Family and Social Moralities decree that he must first make his pile, must save up enough to establish a home and be able to provide for a family. The young people must wait, often many long, weary years.

Meanwhile the respectable young man, excited through the daily association and contact with his sweetheart, seeks an outlet for his nature in return for money [given to a prostitute]. In ninety-nine cases out of a hundred, he will be infected [with a sexually transmitted disease], and when he is materially able to marry, he will infect his wife and possible offspring. And the young flower, with every fiber aglow with the fire of life, with all her being crying out for love and passion? She has no outlet. She develops headaches, insomnia, hysteria; grows embittered, quarrelsome, and soon becomes a faded, withered, joyless being, a nuisance to herself and everyone else. . . .

Now, as to the prostitute. In spite of laws, ordinances, persecution, and prisons; in spite of segregation, registration, vice crusades, and other similar devices, the prostitute is the real specter of our age. She sweeps across the plains like a fire burning into every nook of life, devastating, destroying.

After all, she is paying back, in a very small measure, the curse and horrors society has strewn in her path. She . . . is yet the Nemesis of modern times, the avenging angel, ruthlessly wielding the sword of fire. For has she not the man in her power? And, through him, the home, the child, the race. Thus she slays, and is herself the most brutally slain. . . .

The prostitute is victimized by still other forces, foremost among them the Property Morality, which compels woman to sell herself as a sex commodity for a dollar per, out of wedlock, or for fifteen dollars a week, in the sacred fold of matrimony. The latter is no doubt safer, more respected, more recognized, but of the two forms of prostitution the girl of the street is the least hypocritical, the least debased, since her trade lacks the pious mask of hypocrisy; and yet she is hounded, fleeced, outraged, and shunned, by the very powers that have made her: the financier, the priest, the moralist, the judge, the jailor, and the detective, not to forget her sheltered, respectably virtuous sister, who is the most relentless and brutal in her persecution of the prostitute.

Morality and its victim, the mother—what a terrible picture! Is there indeed anything more terrible, more criminal, than our glorified sacred function of motherhood? The woman, physically and mentally unfit to be a mother, yet condemned to breed; the woman, economically taxed to the very last spark of energy, yet forced to breed; . . . the woman, worn and used-up from the process of procreation, yet coerced to breed, more, ever more. What a hideous thing, this much-lauded motherhood! No wonder thousands of women risk mutilation, and prefer even death to this curse of the cruel imposition of the spook of Morality. Five thousand are yearly sacrificed upon the altar of this monster, that will not stand for prevention but would cure by abortion. Five thousand soldiers in the battle for their physical and spiritual freedom, and as many thousands more who are crippled and mutilated rather than bring forth life in a society based on decay and destruction.

Is it because the modern woman wants to shirk responsibilities, or that she lacks love for her offspring, that she is driven to the most drastic and dangerous means to avoid bearing children? Only shallow, bigoted minds can bring such an accusation. Else they would know that the modern woman has become race-conscious, sensitive to the needs and rights of the child, as the unit of the race, and that therefore the modern woman has a sense of responsibility and humanity, which was quite foreign to her grandmother.

With the economic war raging all around her, with strife, misery, crime, disease, and insanity staring her in the face, with numberless little children ground into gold dust, how can the self- and race-conscious woman become a mother? Morality can not answer this question. It can only dictate, coerce, or condemn—and how many women are strong enough to face this condemnation, to defy the moral dicta? Few, indeed. Hence they fill the factories, the reformatories, the homes for feeble minded, the prisons, the insane asylums, or they die in the attempt to prevent child-birth. Oh, Motherhood, what crimes are committed in thy name! What hosts are laid at your feet, Morality, destroyer of life!

Fortunately, the Dawn is emerging from the chaos and darkness. Woman is awakening, she is throwing off the nightmare of Morality; she will no longer be bound. In her love for the man, she is not concerned in the contents of his pocketbook, but in the wealth of his nature, which alone is the fountain of life and joy. Nor does she need the sanction of the State. Her love is sanction enough for her. Thus she can abandon herself to the man of her choice, as the flowers abandon themselves to dew and light, in freedom, beauty, and ecstasy.

Through her re-born consciousness as a unit, a personality, a race builder, she will become a mother only if she desires the child, and if she can give to the child, even before its birth, all that her nature and intellect can yield: harmony, health, comfort, beauty, and, above all, understanding, reverence, and love, which is the only fertile soil for new life, a new being.

Morality has no terrors for her who has risen beyond good and evil. And though Morality may continue to devour its victims, it is utterly power-

ON THE SUBJECT OF...

EMMA GOLDMAN (1869-1940)

Popularly known as "Red Emma," Emma Goldman became one of the most vilified women in America for her socialist and anarchist politics and activism. Born in 1869 in what was then part of the Russian empire, Goldman escaped an arranged marriage by emigrating to the United States. Goldman attracted large audiences as she advocated birth control, elevated the position of working women, and criticized the social and economic inequities that, she believed, forced many young women into prostitution. While in the United States she was arrested for agitation, accused of involvement in President William McKinley's assassination, forced underground, and deported. Goldman expressed her anarchist viewpoints in *Mother Earth,* a journal she founded in 1903 and edited with her lover, anarchist Alexander Berkman. Publication ended in 1917 when she and Berkman were arrested and deported to Russia for opposing the conscription of young men during World War I. Anarchy without violence and the drive to achieve individual rights for women were related ideologies, according to Goldman, who pursued both vigorously. In *Anarchism and Other Essays* (1910) Goldman stressed this theme, describing the constant victimization that women endured. Skilled as both a nurse and midwife, Goldman knew how women's health was endangered by frequent pregnancies. She was jailed for distributing contraception information alongside birth-control advocate Margaret Sanger in 1915 and also contributed articles to Sanger's magazine, *Woman Rebel.* Goldman held that a correlation existed between a woman's substandard wages and her need to exchange her sexual favors for money. In fact, she argued, economic necessity was not only the motive behind prostitution; it was the basis of marriage. Goldman argued that even with the power to vote, women would still be bound to oppression and the home. Goldman's published works include *What I Believe* (1908), *The Psychology of Political Violence* (1911), and *Living My Life,* her 1931 autobiography.

less in the face of the modern spirit, that shines in all its glory upon the brow of man and woman, liberated and unafraid.

CRYSTAL EASTMAN (ESSAY DATE 1918)

SOURCE: Eastman, Crystal. "Birth Control in the Feminist Program." In *Crystal Eastman on Women and Revolution,* Blanche Wiesen Cook, pp. 46-9. New York: Oxford University Press, 1978.

In the following article, originally published in the Birth Control Review *in 1918, Eastman contends that birth control is a fundamental right for women and must be available as an alternative if they are to participate fully in the modern world.*

Feminism means different things to different people, I suppose. To women with a taste for politics and reform it means the right to vote and hold office. To women physically strong and adventuresome it means freedom to enter all kinds of athletic contests and games, to compete with men in aviation, to drive racing cars, . . . to enter dangerous trades, etc. To many it means social and sex freedom, doing away with exclusively feminine virtues. To most of all it means economic freedom,—not the ideal economic freedom dreamed of by revolutionary socialism, but such economic freedom as it is possible for a human being to achieve under the existing system of competitive production and distribution,—in short such freedom to choose one's way of making a living as men now enjoy, and definite economic rewards for one's work when it happens to be "home-making." This is to me the central fact of feminism. Until women learn to want economic independence, i.e., the ability to earn their own living independently of husbands, fathers, brothers or lovers,—and until they work out a way to get this independence without denying themselves the joys of love and motherhood, it seems to me feminism has no roots. Its manifestations are often delightful and stimulating but they are sporadic, they effect no lasting change in the attitude of men to women, or of women to themselves.

Whether other feminists would agree with me that the economic is the fundamental aspect of feminism, I don't know. But on this we are surely agreed, that Birth Control is an elementary essential in all aspects of feminism. Whether we are the special followers of Alice Paul [founder of the National Woman's Party] or Ruth Law, or Ellen Key, or Olive Schreiner [South African author known for her pro-women's rights and pacifist writings], we must all be followers of Margaret

ON THE SUBJECT OF...

MARGARET SANGER (1879-1966)

"Because I believe that woman is enslaved by the world machine, by sex conventions, by mother-hood and its present necessary child-rearing, by wage-slavery, by middle-class morality, by customs, laws, and superstitions.

Because I believe that women's freedom depends upon awakening that spirit of revolt within her against these things which enslave her."

Sanger, Margaret. "Why the Woman Rebel?" In *The Woman Rebel* 1, no. 1 (March 1914): 7.

Born September 14, 1879, in Corning, New York, Margaret Sanger is known as the leader of the birth control movement in the United States. In 1912, Sanger launched a long struggle against the ignorance, prejudice, religious tenets, and laws that prevented or opposed the practice of birth control. As a maternity nurse working in New York City's Lower East Side, she confronted the over-whelmingly high mortality rates, chronic ill-ness, and social and political powerlessness that plagued poverty-stricken, pregnant women. Disillusioned by the suffering she saw and her own inability to help and advise, she renounced her nursing career forever and resolved to campaign for the collection and dissemination of birth control literature and devices. In 1914 she founded the National Birth Control League and published *Woman Rebel* magazine. Sanger's crusade was met with persecution, court trials, and imprison-ment: she was indicted in 1915 for sending pleas for birth control through the mails, and in 1916 she was arrested for operating a birth control clinic in Brooklyn, N.Y. While still in prison, she founded and edited the *Birth Control Review*. After organizing national and international conferences, founding the Birth Control Clinical Research Bureau, and writing and speaking on behalf of her cause, Sanger finally won the needed legislative changes that would allow doctors to prescribe contra-ceptives and educate the public. Sanger was the author of numerous books on birth control and sex education, including *What Every Mother Should Know* (1914), *The Case for Birth Control* (1917), and *Motherhood in Bondage*. (1928).

Sanger [pioneer in the birth control movement]. Feminists are not nuns. That should be estab-lished. We want to love and to be loved, and most of us want children, one or two at least. But we want our love to be joyous and free—not clouded with ignorance and fear. And we want our children to be deliberately, eagerly called into being, when we are at our best, not crowded upon us in times of poverty and weakness. We want this precious sex knowledge not just for ourselves, the conscious feminists; we want it for all the millions of unconscious feminists that swarm the earth,—we want it for all women.

Life is a big battle for the complete feminist even when she can regulate the size of her family. Women who are creative, or who have administra-tive gifts, or business ability, and who are ambi-tious to achieve and fulfill themselves in these lines, if they also have the normal desire to be mothers, must make up their minds to be a sort of supermen, I think. They must develop greater powers of concentration, a stronger will to "keep at it," a more determined ambition than men of equal gifts, in order to make up for the time and energy and thought and devotion that child-bearing, even in the most "advanced" families, seems inexorably to demand of the mother. But if we add to this handicap complete uncertainty as to when children may come, how often they come or how many there shall be, the thing becomes impossible. I would almost say that the whole structure of the feminist's dream of society rests upon the rapid extension of scientific knowl-edge about birth control.

This seems so obvious to me that I was aston-ished the other day to come upon a group of distinguished feminists who discussed for an hour what could be done with the woman's vote in New York State and did not once mention birth control.

As the readers of this magazine well know, the laws of this state, instead of establishing free clin-ics as necessary centers of information for the facts about sex hygiene and birth control, actually make it a crime, even on the part of a doctor, to tell grown men and women how to limit the size of their families. What could be a more pressing demand on the released energies of all these valiant suffrage workers than to repeal the law?

This work should especially commend itself, now in wartime when so many kinds of reform are outlawed. There is nothing about Birth Control agitation to embarrass the President or obstruct the prosecution of the war. . . . It is a reform absolutely vital to the progress of woman and one which the war does not interfere with. While American men are fighting to rid the old world of autocracy let American women set to and rid the new world of this intolerable old burden of sex ignorance. It should not be a difficult task.

I don't believe there is one woman within the confines of this state who does not believe in birth control. I never met one. That is, I never met one who thought that *she* should be kept in ignorance of contraceptive methods. Many I have met . . . valued the knowledge they possessed, but thought there were certain other classes who would be better kept in ignorance. The old would protect the young. The rich would keep the poor in ignorance. The good would keep their knowledge from the bad, the strong from the weak, and so on. But never in all my travels have I come on one married woman who, possessed of this knowledge would willingly part with it, or who not yet informed, was not eager for knowledge. It is only hypocrisy, and here and there a little hard-faced puritanism we have to overcome. No genuine human interest will be against the repeal of this law. Of course capitalism thrives on an oversupplied labor market, but with our usual enormous immigration to be counted on as soon as the war [World War I] is over, it is not likely that an organized economic opposition to birth control will develop.

In short, if feminism, conscious and bold and intelligent, leads the demand, it will be supported by the secret eagerness of all women to control the size of their families, and a suffrage state should make short work of repealing these old laws that stand in the way of birth control.

ELISE JOHNSON MCDOUGALD
(ESSAY DATE 1 MARCH 1925)

SOURCE: McDougald, Elise Johnson. "The Double Task: The Struggle of Negro Women for Sex and Race Emancipation." *The Survey* 53, no. 11 (1 March 1925): 689-91.

In the following article, McDougald reflects on the struggle confronting young African American women in their efforts to obtain employment in areas hitherto denied to them.

Throughout the long years of history, woman has been the weather-vane, the indicator, showing in which direction the wind of destiny blows. Her status and development have augured now calm and stability, now swift currents of progress. What then is to be said of the Negro woman today?

In Harlem, more than anywhere else, the Negro woman is free from the cruder handicaps of primitive household hardships and the grosser forms of sex and race subjugation. Here she has considerable opportunity to measure her powers in the intellectual and industrial fields of the great city. Here the questions naturally arise: "What are her problems?" and "How is she solving them?"

To answer these questions, one must have in mind not any one Negro woman, but rather a colorful pageant of individuals, each differently endowed. Like the red and yellow of the tiger-lily, the skin of one is brilliant against the star-lit darkness of a racial sister. From grace to strength, they vary in infinite degree, with traces of the race's history left in physical and mental outline on each. With a discerning mind, one catches the multiform charm, beauty and character of Negro women; and grasps the fact that their problem cannot be thought of in mass.

Because only a few have caught this vision, the attitude of mind of most New Yorkers causes the Negro woman serious difficulty. She is conscious that what is left of chivalry is not directed toward her. She realizes that the ideals of beauty, built up in the fine arts, exclude her almost entirely. Instead, the grotesque Aunt Jemimas of the street-car advertisements proclaim only an ability to serve, without grace or loveliness. Nor does the drama catch her finest spirit. She is most often used to provoke the mirthless laugh of ridicule; or to portray feminine viciousness or vulgarity not peculiar to Negroes. This is the shadow over her. To a race naturally sunny comes the twilight of self-doubt and a sense of personal inferiority. It cannot be denied that these are potent and detrimental influences, though not generally recognized because they are in the realm of the mental and spiritual. More apparent are the economic handicaps which follow her recent entrance into industry. It is conceded that she has special difficulties because of the poor working conditions and low wages of her men. It is not surprising that only the determined women forge ahead to results other than mere survival. The few who do prove their mettle stimulate one to a closer study of how this achievement is won in Harlem.

Better to visualize the Negro woman at her job, our vision of a host of individuals must once more resolve itself into groups on the basis of activity. First, comes a very small leisure group— the wives and daughters of men who are in business, in the professions and in a few well-paid personal service occupations. Second, a most active and progressive group, the women in business and the professions. Third, the many women in the trades and industry. Fourth, a group weighty in numbers struggling on in domestic service, with an even less fortunate fringe of casual workers, fluctuating with the economic temper of the times.

The first is a pleasing group to see. It is picked for outward beauty by Negro men with much the same feeling as other Americans of the same economic class. Keeping their women free to preside over the family, these women are affected by the problems of every wife and mother, but touched only faintly by their race's hardships. They do share acutely in the prevailing difficulty of finding competent household help. Negro wives find Negro maids unwilling generally to work in their own neighborhoods, for various reasons. They do not wish to work where there is a possibility of acquaintances coming into contact with them while they serve and they still harbor the misconception that Negroes of any station are unable to pay as much as persons of the other race. It is in these homes of comparative ease that we find the polite activities of social exclusiveness. The luxuries of well-appointed homes, modest motors, tennis, golf and country clubs, trips to Europe and California, make for social standing. The problem confronting the refined Negro family is to know others of the same achievement. The search for kindred spirits gradually grows less difficult; in the past it led to the custom of visiting all the large cities in order to know similar groups of cultured Negro people.

A spirit of stress and struggle characterizes the second two groups. These women of business, profession and trade are the hub of the wheel of progress. Their burden is two-fold. Many are wives and mothers whose husbands are insufficiently paid, or who have succumbed to social maladjustment and have abandoned their families. An appalling number are widows. They face the great problem of leaving home each day and at the same time trying to rear children in their spare time—this too in neighborhoods where rents are large, standards of dress and recreation high and costly, and social danger on the increase.

The great commercial life of New York City is only slightly touched by the Negro woman of our second group. Negro business men offer most of their work, but their number is limited. Outside of this field, custom is once more against her and competition is keen for all. However, Negro girls

are training and some are holding exceptional jobs. One of the professors in a New York college has had a young colored woman as secretary for the past three years. Another holds the head clerical position in an organization where reliable handling of detail and a sense of business ethics are essential. For four years she has steadily advanced. Quietly these women prove their worth, so that when vacancy exists and there is a call, it is difficult to find even one competent colored secretary who is not employed. As a result of opportunity in clerical work in the educational system of New York City a number have qualified for such positions, one being appointed within the year to the office work of a high school. In other departments the civil service in New York City is no longer free from discrimination. The casual personal interview, that tenacious and retrogressive practice introduced in the Federal administration during the World War has spread and often nullifies the Negro woman's success in written tests. The successful woman just cited above was three times "turned down" as undesirable on the basis of the personal interview. In the great mercantile houses, the many young Negro girls who might be well suited to salesmanship are barred from all but the menial positions. Even so, one Negro woman, beginning as a uniformed maid, has pulled herself up to the position of "head of stock."

Again, the telephone and insurance companies which receive considerable patronage from Negroes deny them proportionate employment. Fortunately, this is an era of changing customs. There is hope that a less selfish racial attitude will prevail. It is a heartening fact that there is an increasing number of Americans who will lend a hand in the game fight of the worthy.

In the less crowded professional vocations, the outlook is more cheerful. In these fields, the Negro woman is dependent largely upon herself and her own race for work. In the legal, dental, medical and nursing professions, successful women practitioners have usually worked their way through college and are "managing" on the small fees that can be received from an underpaid public. Social conditions in America are hardest upon the Negro because he is lowest in the economic scale. This gives rise to demand for trained college women in the profession of social work. It has met with a response from young college women, anxious to devote their education and lives to the needs of the submerged classes. In New York City, some fifty-odd women are engaged in social work, other than nursing. In the latter profession there are over two hundred and fifty. Much of the social work has been pioneer[ing] in nature: the pay has been small with little possibility of advancement. For even in work among Negroes, the better paying positions are reserved for whites. The Negro college woman is doing her bit in this field at a sacrifice, along such lines as these: in the correctional departments of the city, as probation officers, investigators, and police women; as Big Sisters attached to the Children's Court; as field workers and visitors and for relief organizations and missions; as secretaries for travelers-aid and mission societies; as visiting teachers and vocational guides for the schools of the city; and, in the many branches of public health nursing, in schools, organizations devoted to preventive and educational medicine, in hospitals and in private nursing.

In New York City, nearly three hundred Negro women share the good conditions in the teaching profession. They measure up to the high pedagogical requirements of the city and state law and are, increasingly, leaders in the community. Here too the Negro woman finds evidence of the white workers' fear of competition. The need for teachers is still so strong that little friction exists. When it does seem to be imminent, it is smothered away, as it recently was at a meeting of school principals. From the floor, a discussion began with: "What are we going to do about this problem of the increasing number of Negro teachers coming into our schools?" It ended promptly through the suggestion of another principal: "Send all you get and don't want over to my school. I have two now and I'll match their work to any two of your best whom you name." One might go on to such interesting and more unusual professions as journalism, chiropody, bacteriology, pharmacy, etc., and find that, though the number in any one may be small, the Negro woman is creditably represented in practically every one. According to individual ability she is meeting with success.

Closing the door on the home anxieties, the woman engaged in trades and in industry faces equally serious difficulty in competition in the open working field. Custom is against her in all but a few trade and industrial occupations. She has, however, been established long in the dressmaking trade among the helpers and finishers, and more recently among the drapers and fitters in some of the best establishments. Several Negro women are themselves proprietors of shops in the country's greatest fashion district. Each of them has, against great odds, convinced skeptical employers of her business value: and, at the same time, has educated fellow workers of other races, doing much to show the oneness of interest of all workers. In millinery, power sewing machine operating on cloth, straw and leather, there are few Negro women. The laissez-faire attitude of practically all trade unions makes the Negro woman an unwilling menace to the cause of labor.

In trade cookery, the Negro woman's talent and past experience is recognized. Her problem here is to find employers who will let her work her way to managerial positions, in tea rooms, candy shops and institutions. One such employer became convinced that the managing cook, a young colored graduate of Pratt Institute, would continue to build up a business that had been failing. She offered her a partnership. As in the cases of a number of such women her barrier was lack of capital. No matter how highly trained, now how much speed and business acumen has been acquired, the Negro's credit is held in doubt. An exception in this matter of capital will serve to prove the rule. Thirty years ago, a young Negro girl began learning all branches of the fur trade. She is now in business for herself, employing three women of her race and one Jewish man. She has made fur experts of still another half-dozen colored girls. Such instances as these justify the prediction that the foot hold gained in the trade world will, year by year, become more secure.

Because of the limited fields for workers in this group many of the unsuccessful drift into the fourth social grade: the domestic and casual workers. These drifters increase the difficulties of the Negro woman suited to housework. New standards of household management are forming and the problem of the Negro woman is to meet these new business-like ideals. The constant influx of workers unfamiliar with household conditions in New York keeps the situation one of turmoil. The Negro woman, moreover, is revolting against essential domestic service. It is a last stand in her fight to maintain a semblance of family life. For that reason, principally, the number of day or casual workers is on the increase. Happiness is almost impossible under the strain of these conditions. Health and morale suffer, but how else can her children, loose all afternoon, be gathered together at night-fall? Through her drudgery, the women of other groups find leisure time for progress. This is one of her contributions to America.

OVERVIEWS

SARAH JANE DEUTSCH (ESSAY DATE 2000)

SOURCE: Deutsch, Sarah Jane. "From Ballots to Breadlines: 1920-1940." In *No Small Courage: A History of Women in the United States,* edited by Nancy F. Cott, pp. 413-72. New York: Oxford University Press, 2000.

In the following essay, Deutsch provides an overview of the social, economic, cultural, and political status of American women in the early part of the twentieth century, focusing on their growing role in the public sphere, the changes in their domestic world, and their entry into the workforce.

Our images of the 1920s, when we have images, are filled with young women with short hair and short skirts. They are kicking up their legs and kicking off a century of social restrictions. They smoke. They dance. They read racy literature. And they do it all in public. They have "advanced" ideas about sex, too. They have taken the socially outrageous, bohemian behavior of the previous generation's Greenwich Village set, and, to the horror of their parents, have brought it to Main Street.

What was going on with women in the 1920s and 1930s was, of course, more complicated than these images of "flappers," which tend to be of young, white, middle-class women. African Americans, Chicanas, Asian Americans, and other women aspired to be or were flappers, too, but most women of any race or ethnicity lived quite differently. Their lives, like our visions of the past, were affected by these images, but they did not mirror them. Although the 1920s did abound with flappers and would-be flappers, the decade also hosted mothers, professionals, women struggling in poverty, and women asserting new power.

Above all, in the 1920s, there was a pervasive sense of newness. To many it seemed that the world was made new after the massive destruction of World War I ended in 1918—and that women were made new too. What was the "new" woman, this creature who, by 1920, could legally vote in national elections on the same basis as men everywhere in the United States? She was the result of competing desires, visions, and needs from a variety of sources. She looked different to different eyes.

When historians discuss such transformations, they like to talk about the way we, as a society, construct ideas about what a woman is. It is perhaps easiest to understand what historians mean by the social construction of womanhood by looking at the literal construction of woman. Both of the figures on the next page [Figure A is a line drawing of "hourglass" shape; Figure B is two vertical parallel lines] were literal constructions of women. People created fashions that demanded a certain "look" from women, then designed clothing to create that look by shaping women's bodies in certain ways. Neither Figure A nor Figure B looks very much like women's own bodies. The first one, the nineteenth-century hourglass figure, took twenty-five pounds of pressure per square inch, in the form of tightly laced whalebone corsets, to create. The second one, the figure of the 1920s new woman, required breast binders and girdles, which were more comfortable, perhaps, but no more natural.

Why would anyone do this to women? The woman in Figure A could not breathe well with all that pressure and could not move freely without fainting. But women were not supposed to. That figure represented the ideal of nineteenth-century womanhood—a homebound, domestic creature unfit (thanks in part to corsets) for the rough world outside the home. She was a creature for a private world and a sign that her husband or father was making enough money to spare her any need to put forth physical effort.

Women without such providers had to do a substantial amount of physical labor themselves. They could not wear tight, confining corsets and were not seen by the upper classes as being "real" women; they were too free with their actions, too free with their bodies, too free altogether.

On the other hand, in the 1920s the new woman, represented by those two straight lines in Figure B, was clearly not a domestic woman. Like men of the day, she was a public figure, so her public figure would be like men's. But the reconstruction of the concept of "woman," of what it meant to be female, even in the ideal, was not as easy as the reconstruction of fashion.

Images and Lives

World War I had wrought dramatic changes in the United States, changes with vital implications for the lives of women. In its year and a half of active participation in the war, the government vastly increased its armed forces, took over the running of the railroads and telephones, began some basic health services in remote rural areas, controlled prices for food and other commodities, negotiated with representatives of business and workers over working conditions and pay, created new government departments to look after the interests of women workers, and generally entered into the daily economic, social, and political lives of its citizens in newly intimate ways.

For many workers, the government was a far better boss than the private individuals who had been in charge of their lives. It paid better, set better hours, and was more responsive to their complaints. These and other workers faced the post-war world with increased expectations. They had worked hard. They had sacrificed for the war. They had been told they were fighting to save democracy. Now they expected a better world.

The war had also moved people around from place to place and job to job. As men of all races were called up to fight, companies that had previously hired only white men for well-paying jobs found themselves short of labor. For the first time, they began to hire white women and black men. Such jobs as streetcar conducting and railroad work paid more than these women had earned before. For black men, this was often their first chance to move from day labor or agricultural work into steadier, better-paying factory jobs. Some black women managed to break into these newly available jobs, particularly on the railroad, but most of the jobs they found available were the ones white women had left. Even these jobs, even domestic service, in the North tended to pay better and offer better conditions than the ones southern African Americans could find at home. Since before the Civil War a steady stream of black men and women had left the South for the North. Now that stream became a torrent. At the same time, the United States made special arrangements with Mexico to bring Mexican workers across the border to work on railroads, in construction, and in harvesting. What began as wartime migrations continued throughout the 1920s.

All this movement brought new groups of people together and gave them new ways to think about their roles in society. There were racial tensions and sudden strikes by whites protesting the employment of blacks and by blacks protesting discrimination. Black women, whom whites were used to thinking of as quiet and obedient, threw down their tools and quit when foremen cursed at them for protesting conditions or when companies hired white women to supervise them. And white women and men also struggled over what their new working positions would mean after the war. The men of the Amalgamated Association of Street and Electric Railway Employees in New York City were so worried about the changes that they wrote a poem:

> We wonder where we are drifting, where is the
>   freedom of the stripes
>   and stars
> If for the sake of greed and profit we put women
>   conductors on the cars
> When our dear brothers left us, shouldered their
>   guns and went to war,
> Little did we think street railway kings would use
>   women like a squaw.
> Woman is God's most tender flower, made to
>   blossom and to bear
> She was made by God the weaker, like a vine on
>   man to lean
> She was meant to work like her nature, tender
>   sweet and clean. . . .
> We pray God to protect and keep women off the
>   cars.

Many women had a different notion of their "nature," however. As if in answer to the men's poem, women machine tool workers retorted:

> The simple, tender, clinging vine,
> That once around the oak did twine
> Is something of the past;
> We stand now by your side
> And surmount obstacles with pride,
> We're equal, free at last
> And I would rather polish steel,
> Than get you up a tasty meal.

Changes had occurred during the war, and life would not be the same again. In the two years after the war ended, the United States witnessed perhaps its greatest upheaval. In 1919 alone, 4 million workers, or one out of every five workers, went out on strike, and there were major race riots in twenty-five towns and cities, including Charleston, South Carolina; Washington, D.C.; and Chicago. In Chicago, five hundred people were wounded, and twenty-three blacks and fifteen whites were killed. The number of lynchings of black citizens, many of the victims still wearing their army uniforms, skyrocketed.

In April 1919, the women of the New England Union of Telephone Operators went on strike. Postmaster General Albert Burleson, who still retained his temporary wartime control over the telephone industry, refused to negotiate. He hired company spies to infiltrate the strikers' ranks and used armed force. What had started as a struggle over wages became a fight to defend the right to bargain collectively. The women presented a solid front, and the male phone workers joined them. When Burleson threatened to replace them with soldiers, one hundred women picketers, accompanied by male relatives in uniform carrying military service flags, blocked their way. The disgusted soldiers said they had not expected to come home from the war to fight women. Nor would the Boston police arrest the strikers. Women doctors gave the strikers free medical care, and restaurant owners kept them fed. Burleson brought in scabs from out of town, but no one would serve them or work with them. The solidarity of the workers and community support brought the strikers victory in only five days.

Few other strikes enjoyed similar success. When a general strike in Seattle peacefully shut down the city, the mayor called in the troops. In the steel industry, where more than half the common laborers were immigrants, employers played up an image of the strikers as foreign agitators. In the wake of the 1917 Russian Revolution and the creation of an international Communist party in 1919, the employers labeled the strikers radical revolutionaries.

To much of the public witnessing the strikes and riots, it did seem as though the United States was verging on revolution. Steel-plant employers succeeded in convincing federal agents to round up and deport thousands of immigrant strikers with no proof of wrongdoing, and the general public did not protest. This anti-Communist fever, known as the Red Scare, raged in 1919 and 1920. Americans watched in near silence as government agents invaded private homes and raided not just union offices but also the offices of dissenting political organizations, arrested and deported members, and destroyed records. They held people on false charges and denied them lawyers in the name of restoring order. No one who had ever raised a voice in protest was safe. By the end of 1920, all was quiet. Yet no one could know what the future would hold. It was into this uneasy peace that the new woman would emerge.

Inventing a Public Woman

When the Tennessee state legislature ratified the national woman suffrage amendment in August 1920, American suffragists had won a seventy-year battle. Suddenly, it was over. What had the victory meant? By the end of the 1920s, the united power of American womanhood that had fought the battle seemed scarcely visible. The promises of unity would not be met in succeeding decades. During the 1920s, the country moved from an era of intense, collective action by women on behalf of women to an era when women's groups had little visibility and limited validity in the eyes of most people. It was not clear whether

gaining the vote had liberated women or whether liberation had changed its meaning.

Americans had high expectations of woman suffrage. The world, they were convinced, would be a different place once women had the vote. After 1920, politicians began to respond more carefully to women's grievances. For a time, it seemed safest to do so. Yoncalla, Oregon, woke up after the election of 1920 to a "feminist revolution," according to one journalist. In this town of 323 residents, men outnumbered women by almost two to one, but the *Literary Digest* reported that the women had "risen in their wrath, stirred by the alleged inefficiency of the municipal officials, and swept every masculine office-holder out of his job." The women of the town had worked in absolute secrecy, not even telling their brothers and husbands. Only the town's women were in on the secret, and they prevailed at the polls. Mrs. Mary Burt, a university graduate, was the new mayor. She had lived in Yoncalla for forty years and had long been active in the community. Also elected to the town government was Mrs. Laswell, wife of the ousted mayor. The only thing Mr. Laswell and his assistants could find to tell the press was that they were "much surprised."

At the other end of the country, in Washington, D.C., a spate of legislative and other victories also greeted women. The women's peace movement succeeded in getting the United States to host and participate in an international disarmament conference in 1921. In the same year, the Sheppard-Towner Act allotted the first federal money for health care. Also called the Maternity and Infancy Act, it provided federal matching funds to states to improve prenatal care and infant health. (The program lapsed in 1929.) The Cable Act of 1922 gave married women independent citizenship; no longer would women who married foreigners lose their United States citizenship. And the Women's Bureau of the federal government, created during the war to look after the interests of women workers, became a permanent part of the Department of Labor in 1920.

Women streamed into public office in the 1920s, the largest single increase in women's officeholding to that date, leveling off only after 1930. The Democrats and Republicans began to mandate equal representation of men and women on party committees. Altogether, these achievements covering peace, politics, labor, health care, and the home seemed to indicate a wide acceptance of women's significance in the public arena.

Yet by 1924 popular magazines were running articles (written by men) with such titles as "Is Woman Suffrage a Failure?" and "Women's Ineffective Use of the Vote." There were signs, even early on, that not all was going according to plan. The only woman in Congress in 1921, Alice Robertson, was an anti-suffragist. Women vastly increased their numbers in office, but the meaning of that increase must be set in a wider context. In 1924, there were eighty-four women legislators in thirty states. Five years later there were two hundred, an increase of almost 250 percent. But while there were two hundred women in office, there were ten thousand men. The numbers were similar at other levels of government. In New Jersey, for example, only 19 of 788 county officeholders were women. At the federal level, there were just ten women in Congress in 1926; that year only two women were reelected to Congress in their own right, and only one was elected without the benefit of having completed a dead family member's term. The gains women sought could obviously not rely on strength at the top.

Political parties were reluctant to nominate women for offices that mattered. After arguing for so long that they were above politics, that they were interested in human welfare, not part of self-serving party political machines, women would have to prove to the men controlling political parties that they knew how to play the game. They had to prove that they could be loyal to the party and not just to principles. They had to prove that they represented a separate constituency, a group of voters they could mobilize to support them.

But women did not vote as a bloc; the fragments that had come together for the suffrage fight once more went their separate ways. As the 1920s wore on, an increasing number of delegations of women came to party conventions, only to have the party leaders pay less and less attention to them. The 1924 Democratic convention had 180 women delegates and 239 women alternates. Eleanor Roosevelt, long active in politics and social welfare, headed a subcommittee to gather suggestions from women's organizations for planks on social welfare. But, as she recalled in her autobiography, *This Is My Story,* at the convention itself the women "stood outside the door of all important meetings and waited." Their turn never seemed to come.

Some activist women had long foreseen that the right to vote would not be a miracle cure for social ills, including the inferior status of women. Rose Schneiderman, an activist for the rights of working women, declared of the vote, "Men had

it all these years and nothing of great importance had happened." The population in general, men as well as women, seemed to echo her disillusionment. Smaller and smaller percentages of those eligible to vote did so. The number had been declining since 1896, when it had peaked at 79 percent. In 1912, before the passage of the woman suffrage amendment, only 59 percent of all people eligible to vote did so. By 1920, the number had sunk to 49 percent.

At the same time, government officials and most of those who elected them were retreating from a vision of government as an instrument to change society. They looked instead to a government that would restore law and order and protect business. They cared more about assisting employers than protecting the welfare of employees and the unemployed. The Republicans held the Presidency throughout the 1920s. Calvin Coolidge, who became President when Warren Harding died in 1923, believed in business and in businessmen. He stocked his cabinet with businessmen and made them at home in the Republican party. As their money poured into Republican coffers, protective tariffs on industrial goods rose and the courts made it harder for workers to strike. The *Wall Street Journal* happily announced, "Never before, here or anywhere else, has a government been so completely fused with business."

The new attitudes were reflected in the rulings of the courts, as they consistently overturned two decades of reform legislation aimed at regulating business, such as laws setting maximum hours or minimum wages for women. There was no federal minimum-wage or maximum-hour law; workers simply struck the best bargain they could with their employers. Often they worked twelve-hour days, six or seven days a week, and earned only enough to provide them with food and shelter. Workers who belonged to strong unions could get better conditions. Most unions, however, organized only skilled workers, and even among those unions, few organized women workers. Most women lacked the resources, education, or skills to have strong bargaining positions on their own.

Reformers looked to the government for a remedy, recognizing that only the government could set uniform minimum standards that would cover working women. The courts had always struck down such protective legislation for men, on the grounds that it interfered with men's freedom to make their own bargains. But in 1908, the Supreme Court, in *Muller* v. *Oregon,* decided to distinguish between men and women. In part, the Supreme Court argued that women were potential mothers of future citizens, so the government had a special interest in their well-being. The *Muller* ruling opened the way for legislation that would protect women's working conditions.

By 1923, forty states regulated the hours of women's work, and fifteen states as well as the District of Columbia regulated their wages. But two years earlier, an unemployed female worker had petitioned the federal district court for the District of Columbia to keep the minimum wage board of Washington, D.C., from enforcing its decisions on wages for women. She claimed that such enforcement had cost her a job. The Children's Hospital also brought action to prevent the minimum wage board and the board's chairman, Jesse C. Adkins, from forcing the hospital to pay higher wages. The case went to the Supreme Court on appeal. When it decided the case, *Adkins* v. *Children's Hospital,* in 1923, the Supreme Court struck down the Washington, D.C., minimum wage law for women, threatening all the protective legislation that progressive politicians and citizens had fought for and won in the previous twenty years.

The Supreme Court ruled that minimum wage boards were an arbitrary government interference in private affairs, infringing on freedom of contract. Justice George Sutherland, writing for the majority of the justices, struck over and over at what he considered false distinctions between women and men. Women, he declared, "are legally as capable of contracting for themselves as men." Giving women the vote had, according to Sutherland, eradicated differences in the civil status of men and women. With that in mind, he concluded that the law was unfair to the employer, "compelling him to pay not less than a certain sum . . . irrespective of the ability of his business to sustain the burden." Sutherland's claim regarding women's equality with men was ironic given the vast number of inequalities that remained embedded in the laws of the states and in the practices of governments as well as private corporations. Among other restraints, women found certain jobs legally closed to them, companies legally paid them less than men for the same work, some states barred them from serving on juries, and most states denied them equal access to credit.

To some triumphant suffragists the next logical step was an equal rights amendment, which would sweep away all remaining forms of discrimination at once. Activist Alice Paul spearheaded the drive for the Equal Rights Amendment (ERA). She presided over the National Women's Party

(NWP) when in November 1923, the seventy-fifth anniversary of the convention at Seneca Falls, it announced the text of the ERA: "Men and women shall have equal rights throughout the United States and every place subject to its jurisdiction." A month later the amendment was introduced into Congress. To Paul, it was logical that the ERA should succeed suffrage as the focus of the NWP. Like suffrage, the ERA was only part of the feminist agenda, but it would give women power, which they could then use as they pleased.

Instead of becoming the new mass women's movement, however, the NWP dwindled. It emerged from the suffrage fight in 1920 with 35,000 members; by the end of the decade, it had 1,000. The problem lay partly in the tactics of the party, which neglected the local precinct-by-precinct organizing that had helped suffrage succeed and instead recruited highly visible celebrities, such as the artist Georgia O'Keeffe, the writer Edna St. Vincent Millay, and the aviator Amelia Earhart. Symbolic of women's advances rather than representative of most women's lives, these women could not help broaden the base for a mass movement.

There were other problems as well. Crystal Eastman supported the Equal Rights Amendment but found it too narrow. A labor lawyer, social investigator, and the first female member of New York's Employer's Liability Commission, Eastman had written in 1918, "Life is a big battle for the complete feminist." For someone like Eastman, the ERA was not the ultimate solution to women's inequality. It touched only on legal issues, not on social relations. It neither affected such concerns as birth control nor required a change in the social roles of men and women in the family. Referring to the NWP convention that had adopted the ERA, Eastman wrote, "If some such [broader] program could have been exhaustively discussed at that convention we might be congratulating ourselves that the feminist movement had begun in America. As it is all we can say is that the suffrage movement is ended."

The ERA's narrowness was particularly evident in regard to race. Alice Paul tried to ensure that the NWP, unlike some other suffrage groups, did not discriminate on the grounds of race. In 1921, the party encouraged black women to attend its national convention as delegates and speak there. But when Addie Hunton, a field secretary for the National Association for the Advancement of Colored People (NAACP), led a delegation of sixty black women from fourteen states asking Paul to throw the party's energy into fighting against southern regulations and terrorism that kept black women as well as men from voting, Paul refused. That, she insisted, was a racial issue, not a women's issue. Paul drew a distinction between racial and gender-based injustice that African-American women could not make in their daily lives.

Increasingly impatient with organizations, from the NWP to the Young Women's Christian Association (YWCA), that insisted they patiently wait until the nation was ready for further progress, black women turned to their own organizing. Lugenia Hope had led Atlanta's Neighborhood Union during World War I when it had teamed up with the newly formed Atlanta Colored Women's War Council to further the war effort. The Neighborhood Union organized each neighborhood to work for community betterment in education, morals, food conservation, employment, health, housing, and entertainment. By 1922, its campaigns had resulted in streets being paved, sewers installed, houses repaired, and classes given on health, wages, and citizenship. Two years earlier, Hope had written Eva Bowles at the national YWCA board, demanding that "full recognition of leadership be given Negro women."

In September 1922, Mrs. Robert M. Patterson, a black socialist candidate for Pennsylvania's General Assembly, declared in the newspaper *Women's Voice:* "Never was there a time in which there was greater need for sane and sober thought on the part of Negro women. . . . We need women who will not sell their rights for a mess of pottage. . . . We must not permit the fight for equal civil rights to cease until it will be possible for every citizen, without regard to race, to have complete civil rights granted to him or her."

Yet white women quarreled among themselves over what civil rights for women meant. At the very moment when social reformer and activist Florence Kelley was marshaling her forces to try to avert the overturn of protective legislation in the *Adkins* case, the NWP submitted a brief on the other side. It was, after all, an unemployed woman who was co-petitioner against the minimum wage for women. In the NWP, Paul and Eastman both had worked closely with working women. They now believed that protective legislation—not just for the minimum wage but also laws against women working at night—prevented women from getting the most lucrative jobs and justified persistent inequalities. On the other hand, Kelley had as allies the Women's Trade Union League, an organization partly made up of and led by wage-earning women. To them, protective legislation acknowledged the realities of unequal social and economic power; the ERA did not. If woman suffrage could produce the kind of damage evident in Justice Sutherland's argument, the ERA seemed to them even more potentially damaging in his hands. Caught by the reality of women's diverse social and economic situations and needs, women divided instead of uniting over the ERA and protective legislation.

Divisions among women were not all caused by the women themselves. For one thing, the raids and prosecutions of the Red Scare had a chilling effect on women's groups. Facing possible jail terms or deportation simply for associating with radical women, some women turned a cold shoulder to former friends. In an era in which organizing at all was suspect, women in the 1920s could either organize together for equality and rights and be labeled "red" and fired, or they could try to go it alone.

Unsurprisingly, women in their twenties and thirties who wanted to succeed in the public world of business or politics believed the most important thing to leave behind was "sex-consciousness," their sense of themselves as women who shared interests with other women. They abandoned any organized quest for general social reform and opted instead for individualism. "Breaking into the human race," as they put it, and individual success in the world as it was became their goals. In 1927, journalist Dorothy Dunbar Bromley wrote in "Feminist—New Style," in *Harper's:* "The pioneer feminists were hard-hitting individuals, and the modern young woman admires them for their courage, even while she judges them for their zealotry and their inartistic methods. . . . They fought her battle, but *she* does not want to wear their mantle." These women wanted to emancipate themselves from each other, from their families, and from the assumption that women were more virtuous than men and more responsible for social welfare. For them, individuality became a way to allow for diversity among women, and it would lead to models of individual accomplishment. It would not, however, lead to the betterment of the group.

The rejection of an older style of feminism and virtuous womanhood came at a time when there was not yet an alternative with which to replace it. In opting to make it in a man's world without changing that world, these women had to try to become like men. Feminists had not yet succeeded in creating a third category, though they desired it, of the "human" sex. Even when

ON THE SUBJECT OF...

THE TRIANGLE SHIRTWAIST FACTORY FIRE (25 MARCH 1911)

The Triangle Shirtwaist Factory in New York City was the site of the 1909 "Uprising of the 20,000," one of the first demonstrations of the International Ladies Garment Workers Union (ILGWU) and the Women's Trade Union League (WTUL). Factory owners Max Blanck and Issac Harris thwarted workers' attempts to unionize, and began locking the factory doors to prevent union organizers from entering. In February, 1911, a U.S. Labor Department inspection of the factory cited several hazardous conditions: the locked exits; a perilously narrow, 18-inch-wide stairwell leading to the street; doorways that swung inward, making them difficult to open in a crowded situation; oily rags and piles of flammable fabric strewn about the work areas, which also contained cutting machines fueled by gasoline and work tables marred with cigarette burns. No action was taken to address these safety violations. On Saturday, 25 March 1911, the day of the fire, about five hundred workers were in the factory. Workers were trampled and crushed as they rushed to escape through the narrow stairwells and open the inward-swinging doors. People were jammed into the elevator, some attempting to ride on top of the car; bodies soon blocked the shafts so that the elevator could no longer be used. Those trapped in the workroom threw themselves out of the eighth-story windows and were dashed to death on the pavement. Others tried to use the flimsy fire escape, which quickly melted in the heat. Firefighters were unable to save the workers who did not manage to escape via the elevator, stairs, or fire escape. The nets and blankets they spread to catch the workers tore, and their ladder wasn't long enough to reach the workroom. The death toll was 146: 133 women and 13 men. The Triangle fire provoked enough public outrage to establish stricter fire codes and inspire new and inexperienced labor organizations to press for supportive legislation. This was part of the beginning of a long struggle for fair labor practices for all workers, equal treatment of women, and safe working conditions.

coalitions of women formed to support the ERA, they did it, they claimed, so that they could be treated "just like men."

Despite antagonism toward feminist groups, the 1920s found activist women not so much absent as scattered. No longer were they the "woman movement," as they had been in the nineteenth century; now they were women. They still organized, but in a multitude of smaller groups that often opposed each other. Every woman seemed to belong to at least one group, and often to several. There were church groups, parents' associations, self-improvement clubs, and civic leagues. Many women returned to the causes that had most concerned them before the peak of the suffrage movement. Some threw all their efforts into the peace movement. Others returned to such issues as social reform, hours and wages for women, clean city streets and water, adequate schooling and playgrounds, and safe factory conditions, for example. In the South, new interracial efforts against lynching occupied some women. In the Southwest, some Hispanic women worked for bilingual education.

Still other women lobbied for their professional interests. The members of Business and Professional Women, founded in 1918, had originally promoted a broad program to make marriage and divorce laws the same in all states, to gain higher status for home economics in federal aid to state education, and to pass laws regulating the use of child labor. In the 1920s, they increasingly focused on their own interests as professional women and office workers. All this activity, though scattered, was still movement.

Women's Work

In 1921, a Chicago telephone operator reported the inside scoop on her job to the Women's Trade Union League paper, *Life and Labor*. She found the phone company to be not just an employer but a nosy and demanding parent. When she had applied to the company, she had had to undergo a medical examination and take psychological tests and answer such questions as whether she lived with her husband and whether he objected to her working. She spent three weeks in training, during which gum chewing was strictly forbidden. The classes taught more than how to handle telephone equipment; they also instructed operators how to talk. She learned to reply to callers with a particular singsong set of phrases. Unshakably polite, musical tones were required.

When not in classes, and later, on their breaks, the telephone operators could enjoy the company's recreation room, with comfortable couches and chairs, reading lamps, magazines, a piano, and a record player. It also had spotlessly clean, spacious bathrooms with lots of large mirrors and all the modern conveniences. Moreover, the company provided free lunches, free medical service, and reduced prices for theater tickets and groceries. It did not pay wages as high as work that required less education and less expensive clothing and placed fewer restrictions on language and behavior, but the operator wrote that few of the girls would complain. They did not seem to share her opinion that "those of us who retain any sense of independence and self-respect would prefer to have our salaries large enough so that we could pay for our own lunches and medical service."

This description encapsulates much about women's paid work in the 1920s. As a married woman, this particular operator had plenty of company; the percentage of wives working for pay soared in the decade, especially among those aged twenty to thirty-five. But this shift was not matched by a change in attitudes toward women. One national advice columnist claimed that the question she was asked most frequently was, "Should a woman work outside the home after marriage?" despite the fact that increasing numbers of women were already doing so. By 1930, 40 percent of white and black working women were wives, one-third with children under age thirteen, but they still constituted only 11.7 percent of all wives. Several states still banned married women from holding government jobs. Though the percentage of married women teachers doubled, the majority of school boards refused to hire them.

When they worried about wives working outside the home, most people were thinking of *white* married women. Black married women had long been forced by economic necessity to work for wages, and among agricultural worker families, 60 percent of Chicanas with children worked in the fields. Japanese immigrant women had been partners in their husbands' businesses, domestic servants in other people's homes, and agricultural laborers ever since their arrival in large numbers between 1907 and 1921. Married Puerto Rican women in New York City contracted with textile manufacturers to make garments, fine lace, and other goods in their homes. The press and policymakers had never worried about what those women's work would do to their families. Only

when white married women began to work outside the home in larger numbers did the issue become a public one.

The work that married or marriageable white women did had to be seen as compatible with older notions of proper womanly behavior. A telephone operator had to have her husband's permission to work. She had to dress with decorum and maintain a sweet temperament. Indeed, the telephone company used the very assumption that women were by nature sweet and submissive to justify hiring women as operators. The company then converted this assumption into fact by training its employees to sound sweet and submissive on the phone and firing those who did not.

The telephone industry formed just one part of an expanding service sector in the 1920s. New forms of communication and new business technologies, such as typing and stenography, vastly increased the number of clerical jobs available. As such jobs became dead-end, fewer men and more women wound up in clerical positions. Clerical work thus became a larger and larger proportion of the posts women held, outdistancing domestic service, teaching, and industrial jobs. By 1930, 2 million women, or one-fifth of the female labor force, were office workers.

As more women came to hold these positions, the jobs became redefined. The secretary was no longer the man on the rise, but the office wife, radiating sunshine and sympathy. Women uneasy about becoming mannish by being on male terrain helped along the redefinition. They wore unbusinesslike clothes—soft and stylish dresses, for example. For the men in management, redefining clerical workers made women less threatening by clearly distinguishing their separate roles. Clerical work, previously a man's job, became "women's work," something requiring a "woman's touch."

There were still tensions in the workplace. As women increasingly dominated clerical positions, businesses were enlarging. Women got stuck in low-paying office jobs, but men could now get stuck in middle management, without much freedom to do the job as they wished. Men felt hemmed in and blamed their new office wives. For their part, secretaries found men they worked for moody, difficult, and irrational. Grace Robinson, a former secretary, complained to the readers of *Liberty* in 1928 that "the man one works for has, more than likely, a healthy, well nourished temper that all its life has been permitted to cavort about naked, untrammeled, and undisciplined." Male bosses began to prefer their female office workers to have only a high school, not a college, degree and to be young enough that the term *girl* could become just another word for *clerical worker*. Youth and education would make the hierarchy in the office clearer. By the decade's end, this equation was so thoroughly cemented that no matter how old the secretary was, she was still a girl to her boss.

It was not only in the "girlishness" of telephone operators that they typified some aspects of the 1920s. Part of the appeal of telephone work undoubtedly lay in the well-appointed lounge. At the turn of the century, young working women had most often lived at home or as boarders with other families. Now, between school and marriage they lived in their own apartments, which they often shared with other young working women. Having their own apartments gave them a sense of autonomy, of young adulthood, of being unsupervised and unrestrained. It gave their parents a lot of worry.

At the same time, young working women hardly lived in the lap of luxury. At fifteen dollars a week, their wages supported only tiny, often ill-lit apartments with sparse furnishings. For women doing dull work and living in dingy, dark apartments on boring, cheap food, the phone company's lounge and benefits gave them as close a glimpse as they might ever have of the middle-class world many wanted. Whenever they sought more from life, to take in the new movies or go to amusement parks, or have a decent dinner, they had to find a better-paid man to treat them. Young working women had started dating men to whom they had not been introduced, without supervision, almost a generation earlier. By the 1920s, this practice was widespread.

Lounges, theater tickets, and lunches formed part of the new strategies by which large corporations had responded to strikes in 1919. Many adopted something called the American Plan of corporate welfare. Instead of paying higher wages, companies provided increased benefits to workers, perhaps subsidized housing or loans. Such benefits made it harder for workers to leave the company, no matter what the conditions of the work itself, and they were less likely to risk losing their benefits by striking. Only large companies could afford such programs, and most women who worked in industry worked for smaller firms. Women of color, in particular, rarely found such enlightened employers.

During World War I, half a million black southerners moved to northern cities. More fol-

lowed them after the war. They thought they were heading toward the Promised Land, where they could work as well as vote on equal terms with whites. Mothers labored outside the home so that their daughters could stay in high school long enough to qualify for clerical work. Yet they found, in the North as in the South, that few white people would hire them as anything but domestic servants or manual laborers. As African-American neighborhoods in northern cities expanded, some black women found opportunities as teachers, but the few black-owned businesses large enough to employ clerical workers often hired male office workers, as educated black men found their job options just as tightly restricted. The only place large numbers of black women office workers found employment was Montgomery Ward in Chicago, which employed 1,050 in 1920. Because it was a mail-order business, customers had no direct contact with and never had to know they were served by black clerical workers.

In the 1920s, large numbers of Puerto Ricans also came to the urban North seeking economic opportunity. By 1930, there were fifty thousand Puerto Ricans on the mainland, 81 percent of whom lived in New York City. Almost half were women. The Puerto Rican women, like African-American women, found their opportunities curtailed. Honorina Irizarry left her job as a secretary in Puerto Rico to join her brother in Brooklyn, New York, where she became a bilingual secretary and a Democratic activist. But she was exceptional. In 1925, only 3.4 percent of all Puerto Rican women in New York, and about 15 percent of the women who worked outside the home held clerical positions. Language formed one barrier, but race also played a part.

Despite the tendency to redefine jobs women entered into as "women's work," and despite the prevalent racism, women of all races and ethnic groups did make some headway in the professions in the 1920s. Although the percentage of women workers in the professions grew only from 11.9 percent to 14.2 percent, that rise represented an increase of 50 percent in the number of women professionals. By far most were teachers; the next largest number were nurses, but there were also lawyers, social workers, engineers, and professors. Only the percentage of female medical doctors fell; medical schools imposed a quota on women of no more than 5 percent of a class from 1925 to 1945, and few hospitals accepted female interns.

Professional women came largely from the ranks of college graduates. By the 1920s more than 40 percent of college students were women. They were still the privileged few, however. The proportion of college-age women in the United States who entered college rose from 3.8 percent in 1910 to 7.6 percent in 1920 but would increase to only 10.5 percent by 1930. Not all women had an equal chance of entering college, even if they could afford it. Many colleges carefully controlled the number of Jewish students on campus, and only at Oberlin did black students constitute even 4 percent of the student body. Black women found black colleges more receptive; by 1929, women formed the majority at some coeducational black colleges. Catholic women also found their options enlarged by special schools. The number of Catholic women's colleges rose from 14 in 1915 to 37 in 1925.

Many women faced cultural as well as gender and racial battles. After years of schooling in Kansas and Los Angeles, Polingaysi Qoyawayma, a Hopi Indian, returned to her reservation in Arizona in the late 1920s to become a teacher and missionary. These jobs gave her a chance to have what she had always dreamed of building, her own house, but they also brought tensions. Told she could not speak the Hopi language to her Hopi first graders, Qoyawayma decided at least to use Hopi legends to teach them to read. In her autobiography, *No Turning Back*, she confessed that she was not sure the missionaries would like the burrowing owls song, which began, "We are little burrowing owls, children of Germinating God." It was hostility from Hopi parents, however, that caught her by surprise. They complained, "What are you teaching our children? . . . We send them to school to learn the white man's way, not Hopi. They can learn the Hopi way at home."

Many professional and businesswomen faced tensions regarding marriage and career. Sue Shelton White, a lawyer born in 1887, had led the southern wing of the National Women's Party and was a Democratic party politician. Poverty and discrimination had kept her from getting her law degree until she was thirty-six. Her mother, she wrote for a special series on modern women in the *Nation* in 1926, "drew few distinctions between her boys and girls. I have seen my brothers sweep, wipe dishes, and even cook." When her brothers left home, it was Sue who had to carry the water from the well and cut the kindling. By 1926, however, she considered marriage and a career a difficult combination: "Marriage is too much of a compromise; it lops off a woman's life as an individual. Yet the renunciation too is a lopping off. We choose between the frying-pan and the fire—both very uncomfortable."

Though many professional women continued to find satisfaction in lifelong support from other women, a growing minority of professional women married in the 1920s. In 1910, only 12.2 percent of professional women were married. In 1920, 19.3 percent were; in 1930, 24.7 percent. Psychologist Phyllis Blanchard earned her doctorate from Clark University, where she met a graduate student in chemistry, Walter Lucasse. When the couple married in 1925, Blanchard kept her own name and continued her career as a child guidance counselor. "He respects my work as much as I do his," she told the *Nation*'s readers. "If he does not feel quite so keenly as I the need of economic independence after marriage, he is more eager that I have leisure for creative work than I am myself." Blanchard was typical of the new generation of women professionals. In the 1920s, most were not active in social reform, which had gone from being a task of amateur middle-class women to a new profession, social work, with its own college courses and degrees. Many professional women still wanted to increase women's economic status, improve women's sense of their own worth, reorient family life, and redefine sex roles, but they did so only as individuals.

Although clerical workers and businesswomen were newly conspicuous among women workers in the 1920s, most women workers remained in domestic service, agricultural labor, and certain manufacturing jobs. For them, wage labor was a matter of necessity. In the 1920s, 71 percent of U.S. workers earned less than the wage required to support what the government defined as the minimum acceptable standard of living for their families. As a result, in low-income families, 25 percent of all married women worked for wages.

In 1920 five times more married black women than women of any other racial or ethnic group worked outside the home. More than 50 percent of adult black women earned wages. In rural areas most performed back-breaking labor in the fields. In the cities most performed domestic service or laundering. Only 5.5 percent were able to gain employment in manufacturing, a better-paid sector, by 1930. As the total number of servants declined, black women became a larger and larger share of those remaining. Between one-fifth and one-half of the domestics in New York, Chicago, Philadelphia, and other cities were black women. Almost two-thirds of all gainfully employed black women in the North worked as servants or laundresses. In Pittsburgh, for example, 90 percent of black women earned their way as day workers, washerwomen, or live-in servants.

In service, as in other areas of black life, the growth of black enclaves in the North and the greater degree of freedom there than in the South encouraged a new generation of black female northerners to be more assertive in their relations with whites, to join civil rights groups, such as the National Association for the Advancement of Colored People, and to make their relations with their employers more professional. But by the end of the decade, black women still earned only 20 cents, and white women 61 cents, for every dollar that white men earned.

Domestic service meant something different for the fourteen hundred Japanese immigrant women who worked in such positions during the 1920s, making up slightly more than one-fourth of the gainfully employed among them. As with black women and other domestic servants, Japanese women found that sometimes employers became like additional family members, visiting them when they were sick, teaching them English, and giving them gifts. Other employers spied on them constantly, suspecting them of stealing or laziness. For the Japanese, however, domestic work was something new and seen as strictly temporary. Mrs. Uematsu told an interviewer, "My husband didn't bring in enough money, so I went out to work. I didn't even think twice about it." Though the husbands of Japanese immigrant women expected them to contribute to the family income, domestic service, unlike helping in the family business or doing farm work with the family, gave these women an independent wage and time away from their families.

For many black women, on the other hand, domestic service was not a new opportunity to work away from the watchful eye of a husband and to earn an independent income. Rather, it was all that had been available to them for generations. It meant stealing time from their own families and giving it to the families of the very people who foreclosed other opportunities.

In the Southwest, Chicana employment patterns tended to mirror those of black women in the East, except that a larger percentage were employed in industrial work, particularly in food processing and garment making. The situation for them varied more than for black women. In San Antonio, Texas, Mexican women worked in pecan shelling and clothing factories while black women could get only domestic service jobs. In Colorado, however, the situation was virtually reversed. Chicana migrant farm workers faced broken-down shacks for housing, long hours in the fields, and wages that would not keep the family warm and fed and the children clothed decently enough to stay in school through the winter. As a result, they tried to earn money in the winter as domestic servants or laundresses if they could not get work in the canneries, which they preferred.

When black and white women, or Anglo and Chicana women, mingled in factories, the outcome was sometimes predictable but sometimes surprising. In the tobacco factories of Durham, North Carolina, the white women workers arrived from a countryside where whites had gone to great lengths to ensure that blacks held only menial jobs. Their own status depended on being different from the black women who worked in the same factory. In an interview, one worker recalled that black women had to "press hard to hold [themselves] up" against the harassment of white bosses and coworkers, even at the risk of losing a job. "You're over here doing all the nasty dirty work," another recalled of the blacks' assignment, the gritty work of stripping the stems off tobacco leaves. "And over there on the cigarette side . . . The white women over there wear white uniforms." On the other hand, in the canneries of southern California some Anglo women and Chicana workers developed friendships at work. "I had a Jewish friend," Maria Rodriguez told an interviewer. "She was my work buddy. . . . I never saw her outside the cannery but we were friends at work. . . . We broke the ice by talking about Clark Gable. We were crazy about him."

The 1920s was a hard time to be a factory worker, even without racial tensions. The corporations, courts, and government had made it harder to strike or to protest conditions. Efforts to organize women met with hostility not only from the employers but from male union organizers. Ann Washington Craton, a union organizer herself, reported to the *Nation* in 1927 what happened when one woman organizer got arrested in the course of her job. A small flood of working girls rushed into the union office, demanding that the union pay her bail. But the union men took the news cheerfully. The official in charge told them, "Let her stay in jail. . . . She's all right. Let her stay until we can have a nice, quiet little executive board meeting without her. Then we will get her out. Ladies should stay at home. If ladies won't stay at home, let them stay in jail." When Craton and a coworker wanted to organize women in Newark, New Jersey, a union official complained, "Why don't you forget all this business and leave the labor movement to men? It's too rough for women. Why don't you get married?" Craton and her colleague responded, "Perhaps we are married. . . . We still want to organize women into trade unions in Newark."

Despite all the difficulties, there were strikes of women workers in the 1920s, emerging from the desperation of white as well as black women. In March 1929, the women in the inspection room of an Elizabethton, North Carolina, textile mill walked off the job. All but 17 of the 360 walked out, and the next morning they gathered at the factory gate. When the plant manager did not arrive to negotiate, they rushed through the plant and persuaded their coworkers, women and men, to join them.

The young women of Elizabethton wanted more from life than an endless round of low pay; they wanted more than their mothers had. On the picket lines they were feisty, bold, assertive, saucy, firm, and, above all, funny. Trixie Perry and Texas Bill were ringleaders and friends on the picket line. Both women were brought to court when they were accused of taunting the National Guard and blocking the way to the mills for new, replacement workers; women had marched in front of the National Guard draped in the American flag, forcing the guardsmen to present arms each time they passed. In court, Trixie Perry wore a cap made out of the U.S. flag. When the prosecuting attorney questioned her, she replied, "I was born under it, guess I have a right." When asked if she had blocked the road, she retorted, "A little thing like me block a big road?" Texas Bill was equally unshakable. Asked what she was doing on the road in the early morning, she responded with great dignity, "I take a walk every morning before breakfast for my health." The guards had threatened the picketing women with guns, used tear gas on them, and arrested them, and the women answered them with laughter.

Like the new generation of black domestic workers and the frustrated union organizers, Trixie Perry and Texas Bill represented a new, more aggressive woman worker. They wanted part of what the 1920s had to offer—not just movies and fine clothes, but independence and the wherewithal to buy those goods for themselves.

Fun, Fads, Family

It wasn't just the Trixie Perrys in North Carolina or the cannery workers in California who wanted more from life and dreamed of movie stars. In remote Hispanic New Mexican villages,

young women had abandoned their sandals and shawls for high heels and elaborate hats. They learned the new, fast, provocative dance steps of the shimmy and the Charleston, and in villages where there were cars, they even went on dates. Before World War I, flappers had started to appear in certain city neighborhoods; now they were everywhere.

Flappers were women who lived—and lived it up—in public. They wore short skirts that exposed their legs and made them freer than prewar styles had allowed. They bobbed their hair, shearing off the long Victorian tresses that had distinguished them from men and taken so much time to maintain. They wore makeup and flesh-colored stockings. It was still close enough to a time when "painted women" had been actresses and harlots to make wearing makeup seem daring, sexually aware, and definitely modern. These women even smoked in public. In recognition of the new womanhood, in 1925 Bryn Mawr College for women lifted its ban on smoking.

Not everyone agreed on the new rules for America's young women. That same year another women's college, Vassar, instituted a ban on smoking. The editor of the student paper of the University of Illinois called the shimmy "that insult to our whole moral code." But these critics were waging a losing battle. Young women and men were redefining what was proper and seemed to assume that the older systems of order, control, and communication had been destroyed by the war.

Young working women modeled their behavior and their dreams on the movies. In the 1920s, polls showed that movie stars had replaced political, business, and artistic leaders as role models for young people. Ironically, the movies had in turn picked up their themes from the lives of the young working women who made up a large proportion of their audience and had simply glamorized them. The film stories were often created by such women writers as Anita Loos, who wrote *Gentlemen Prefer Blondes* (1925). Fan magazines let their readers know that stars had come from their own ranks: Joan Crawford began as a shop girl in Kansas City, Janet Gaynor as a clerk in a shoe store.

Like the lounge at the telephone company, the new picture palaces gave working women a few hours in opulence. In that luxurious atmosphere they watched films like *Ankles Preferred* (1926), in which a bored Madge Bellamy waited on customers in a department store. In *Soft Living* (1928), secretaries labored over long columns of numbers. It was not the life of the working girl that the movies glamorized; it was the chance for escape; in *Soft Living,* Bellamy, who portrays a secretary for a divorce lawyer, hunts for a millionaire and lands one. Office workers and department store clerks, the films showed, worked amid wealthier male bosses and customers. Through spunk and cleverness, according to the movies, they could use their positions to escape the boring monotony of their work. In *Ankles Preferred,* Bellamy becomes successful in the retail trade in her own right and rejects her wealthy suitors, who are interested only in her body. Instead she turns to a trustworthy young man from a lower-class boardinghouse. But the themes of the two films were the same; they echoed the enormously popular novels that Horatio Alger had written fifty years earlier about poor young men who, through luck, pluck, and virtue, became rich. Usually, their success was assured in part by marrying the boss's daughter. In the 1920s, it was working women who embodied this spirit of entrepreneurial drive. But instead of being the passive maidens rescued by Alger's heroes, now they were in charge of their own futures. Success for them meant marrying the boss, not the boss's daughter.

Reassuringly, the movies tended to end with marriage. Many Americans had begun to fear that the family was being destroyed. If women were free to vote and to live in apartments on their own, and if wives were working outside the home in increasing numbers, then who would keep the home fires burning? The mass media responded by making actual working mothers virtually invisible. Instead, at the same time as the flapper flounced into view, a new glorification of motherhood and marriage emerged. It seemed that after a period of youthful independence and indiscretion, women were to go back home.

It would be a different home, one with fewer children and more machines. Manufacturers found housewives eager for new household technology. With immigration on the decline in the 1920s, fewer white women were available for domestic service. The black, Asian, and Mexican women who took their places did not quite fill the gap. They, too, wanted their independence. They were less willing to be full-time help and live in the homes of their employers. They preferred day work. In response, fewer homes had servants' quarters, and more women became their own maids.

Many of these women worked for wages outside the home as well as doing housewifery within it. Working-class and middle-class women

justified going out to work in terms of their families' needs. Their work tended to be intermittent. It most often hinged on their husbands becoming unemployed, a frequent occurrence in the 1920s. Others worked themselves, rather than withdrawing their children from school to work. "It takes the work of two to keep a family these days," claimed one Muncie, Indiana, woman in *Middletown,* Robert and Helen Lynd's pioneering 1929 study of a "typical" American town. Whereas in earlier decades the two workers would have been a father and a child, it would now be a husband and a wife, because more jobs required a high school education.

For many of the families the Lynds interviewed, however, family needs now meant more than just putting food on the table. "An electric washing machine, electric iron, and vacuum sweeper" also had become necessities for working mothers. "I don't even have to ask my husband any more," revealed another Muncie wife, "because I buy these things with my own money. I bought an ice box last year. . . . We own a twelve-hundred-dollar Studebaker [car] with a nice California top, semi-enclosed. . . . The two boys want to go to college, and I want them to. I graduated from high school myself, but I feel if I can't give my boys a little more all my work will have been useless." To many women, being a good mother increasingly meant earning an income to provide purchasing power for the family.

Yet despite all the new technology, the women surveyed by the Lynds claimed that they spent more, not less, time on housework in the 1920s than before. Indeed, the time had almost doubled, from 44.3 to 87.5 hours a week. Standards, it seemed, had risen. At the very moment technology could have freed women from much household drudgery, suddenly their wash had to be whiter than white. Advertisers played on women's guilt. "What do the neighbors think of *her* children?" read one 1928 detergent's ad copy in the *Ladies' Home Journal.*

Advertising reached new levels of psychological sophistication. Because women made most consumer decisions, advertisers took aim at them, giving housework a new, exalted meaning. Suddenly, washing clothes was not simply laundering, as it had always been, but an expression of love. Getting the gray out of a man's collar was not simply an issue of cleanliness; it was saving the American home. Cooking, cleaning, and other housework all fell into the same category. By 1931, *American Home* could declare that "the careful housekeeper . . . will know that prime rib roast, like peach ice cream, is a wonderful stimulant to family loyalty."

These advertisements also indicated the increasing degree to which mothering was seen as a full-time job. More household technology could have given women more time to spend outside the house. So could the declining birth rate. In 1900, white women had given birth to an average of 3.56 children each; in 1929, 2.4. Birth control was still controversial, even illegal in many states, but middle-class women were able to get birth control devices from their private physicians, and in large cities some clinics opened to serve working-class women. This left many working-class women without birth control. Even when they could get birth control information, they often found their husbands uncooperative. Yet, even though they continued to have more children than middle-class women, birth rates among the working class also declined. No sooner were there fewer children in the home, however, than experts began to agree that mothers should pay more attention to each one. As advertisements for a laundromat in Muncie asked, "Isn't Bobby more important than his clothes?" And one ad selling electricity declared of the "successful mother" that "she puts first things first. She does not give to sweeping the time that belongs to her children. . . . The wise woman delegates to electricity all that electricity can do."

Women involved in charitable work, social and political service, and even wage work—despite the fact that most working mothers took paying jobs only out of dire need—were attacked as selfish, as taking jobs away from men who needed them to support families, and as undermining the stability of the home. It was argued that having a woman in the home would keep a child off the streets. "I accommodate my entire life to my little girl," one middle-class woman boasted to the Lynds. With these new ideas, it was hard for working women to feel that they were also successful mothers, particularly when they lived in homes without electricity—like almost half the homes in the country in 1925.

These new ideas of what women should be sharpened social divisions in the United States. One indication of these divisions was the rapid development of ethnically and economically homogeneous suburbs in the 1920s. The new suburbs were linked to choices about technology and policy that affected women's lives and options. New household technology could have been used, for example, to enhance urban apartment life, which had been on the rise in the previous decades. It could have helped create communal day care facilities and laundries that would have left women freer for other activities. In their zeal to save the family from absent mothers, however, policy makers focused on the private home. Each family was to have its own home, and each home its own mother taking care of her own children, using her own kitchen and laundry.

Increasingly, such individual homes were in suburbs. From 1920 to 1930 the population of New York City rose 21 percent; in the same period the population of one of its suburbs, Scarsdale, soared 176 percent. The allure of suburbs lay in their very sameness. Suburban developers promised buyers spacious houses with children's playrooms and private lawns. They promised to remove and protect women and children from the dirt and tensions of the city. The suburbs also created another social division: masculine cities and feminine suburbs. Men would leave home for work all day, and women would remain home to tend the children. In the newly ubiquitous automobiles, women spent their time driving their children from store to store or to school, all of which had been within walking distance in the city.

Despite the confining aspects of marriage and suburbia, most college women surveyed claimed they aspired above all else to the role of wife. The percentage of women who never married had risen throughout the nineteenth century to a high of 20 percent; now it dropped to 5 percent. The women's average age at marriage also fell.

The 1920s saw the popularization of Sigmund Freud's brand of psychology, particularly its emphasis on the pivotal role of sex in mental health and its depiction of women as incomplete and envious of men. Moreover, at the very moment when women no longer seemed to need marriage on economic or political grounds, people began to define "normal" sexuality in new, narrower terms and to give it increased attention. Despite evidence from a 1926 study that more than one-fourth of adult college-educated women had enjoyed intense emotional relations with other women after puberty, including overt sexual practices, women who never married began to be defined as unfulfilled and neurotic. In an economy built around gratification rather than thrift, women's activism outside the home was taken as a sign of an unfulfilled life.

Women did not cease, of course, to rely on other women for support and intimacy. As with

Margaret Sanger, Miss Clara Louise Rowe and Mrs. Anne Kennedy arranging the first American Birth Control Conference.

politics, however, the range of tolerated behavior shrank, and what had been acceptable before the war now was questionable. Some young women even feared to share apartments with each other lest they be suspected of homosexuality. And, in the same way that new fears of radicalism split women's political organizations in the 1920s, new fears of homosexuality made it harder for women to form women's groups whose purpose was women's equality and independence.

Women's focus was not supposed to be other women. According to the advertisers and the new psychologists, their emphasis was supposed to be on how to attract men. Women could find fulfillment, the argument went, only through marriage. In the nineteenth century, marriage had been expected to involve women's self-denial and self-sacrifice; now, particularly for the highly educated middle class, it was supposed to provide sexual satisfaction and self realization. Marriage was supposed to be the gateway to a fuller life, not just for women with low-paying, monotonous jobs but also for college-educated women. Sexual fulfillment in marriage, not a career, was depicted as the ultimate fulfillment for women.

Increasingly, businesses used sex and the desire for sexual attraction and passion in their advertisements. Women's appearance, rather than women's virtue, would secure their husbands' fidelity. Cosmetic companies began to sponsor the first beauty contests. "The first duty of woman is to attract," ran one advertisement. Women had been liberated from the corset only to be entrapped by breast binders, dieting, and makeup. They were told that by purchasing the right goods they could create the proper effect. "Your masterpiece—yourself," another advertisement promised its readers. Men as well as women were affected by these trends. Advertisers insisted that the proper collar and the right deodorant would gain a man the desired job, but while men were to use goods to re-create themselves in order to gain jobs, promotions, and public esteem, women were to use goods to re-create themselves in order to get men.

It was in part this focus on sexuality that increased the pressure to legalize birth control. Sex was no longer simply about creating children. With the popularization of psychology, it was about necessary release and pleasure and self-determination. The original birth control activists had aimed to put control of reproduction into the hands of those who had to bear the children—women. By the 1920s, however, the movement had attracted strange bedfellows. Doctors who wanted to legalize birth control tended to want to control it themselves. Other activists, many of them racist, favored it to keep the "unfit" from reproducing. On the other side, William Henry Cardinal O'Connell of the Catholic church in Boston called a bill to legalize birth control a "direct threat . . . towards increasing impurity and unchastity not only in our married life but . . . among our unmarried people."

Yet, as the decade progressed, more and more birth control clinics opened. In Chicago a judge ruled in 1924 that the health commissioner could not deny a license to a clinic, because to do so amounted to enforcing religious doctrines, an illegal joining of church and state. In 1929, when Margaret Sanger's New York City birth control clinic was raided by the police for illegally dispensing birth control devices, the case was thrown out of court, and the plainclothes policewoman who had first entrapped the clinic returned later, in her off-duty hours, to seek treatment. Middle-class women could get birth control devices from their private physicians, but only the clinics gave the poor access to contraceptives. By 1930, fifty-five birth control clinics served the public in twenty-three cities in twelve states.

In the early 20th century, teaching became defined as a woman's profession. Here, a teacher and her class visit the Library of Congress.

Despite the increasing availability of birth control, a new focus on sexuality, and a redefined concept of housework, marriage had a hard time living up to its reputation. Not all women found it a way to a fuller life. Tensions arose around consumption. Raising children became more and more expensive, and working-class women continued to have less access to money and birth control. Fears of conceiving another child they could ill afford affected these women's sexual pleasure. And expectations of a way of life that did not materialize led to disappointment. In a 1920s study that asked working-class women what gave them the courage to go on in life when they had become thoroughly discouraged, not one mentioned her husband. In difficult times, husbands became not so much individuals as the focus of their wives' problems and fears about jobs and conception.

The divorce rate rose steeply. From 1870 to 1920, the number of divorces in the United States increased by a factor of fifteen. In 1924, one marriage in seven ended in divorce. More wives than ever before had done paid work during marriage and knew they had options other than staying in an unsatisfactory marriage. Life was not easy for divorced women, but no longer was divorce the disgrace it had been in the previous century.

The rise in divorce prompted attacks on women's education, particularly colleges, for not preparing women for their proper vocation: motherhood and wifehood. A few rebels replied by creating institutes like the one Ethel Howe headed at Smith College, the Institute to Coordinate Women's Interests. It aimed to enable college-educated wives to have professional careers by helping to found cooperative nurseries, laundries, shopping groups, and kitchens. Most women's colleges, however, seemed eager to offer some sop to their critics. In 1924, Vassar's board of trustees created a whole interdisciplinary school of "Euthenics" focused on the development and care of the family, including such courses as "Husband and Wife," "Motherhood," and "The Family as an Economic Unit." At the University of Chicago, Dean of Women Marion Talbot pioneered a graduate program in home economics.

The trajectory from flappers to home economics epitomized an essential dilemma in the 1920s. If women could support themselves and represent themselves politically, why should they bother getting married? In the 1920s, prompted by the mass media and advertising, the family had had to change its meaning. No longer would it be portrayed as a necessary economic unit, though it often still was, or as a microcosm of the social and political structure. Now family was about self-fulfillment, consumption, and nurturing the newly discovered psyche of the child. Writing on women and the state in the mid-1920s, journalist Suzanne LaFollette saw marriage as an economic trap that stifled the independence of both men and women. But marriage did not end in the 1920s. Individual "new women" might get divorced, but marriage as an institution changed its rationale and endured.

Rebels

While her husband went to Europe in 1925, anthropologist Margaret Mead set off for Samoa to study adolescent girls; she published her results in *Coming of Age in Samoa* (1928), a best-seller. In her autobiography, Mead offered this advice: "Women must learn to give up pandering to male sensitivities, something at which they succeeded so well as long as it was a woman's primary role, as a wife, to keep her family intact, or, as a mistress, to comfort her lover." Modern women, Mead implied, had a larger role, and men would have to look after their own sensitivities.

Mead was not alone in her rebellion against the 1920s formula of man-centered woman. When New York lawyer Crystal Eastman and her husband had to move out of their apartment because the building was to be torn down, they moved into two places instead of one. It was Eastman's idea. "You're breaking up our home," her husband had said. But according to an article she wrote for *Cosmopolitan* in 1923, she had replied staunchly, "No I'm not. I'm trying to hold it together." She took a small apartment for herself and her children, and her husband moved to a rooming house near his office. "Every morning," she told her readers, "like lovers, we telephone to exchange the day's greetings and make plans for the evenings. . . . It is wonderful sometimes to be alone in the night and just know that someone loves you. In other moods you must have that lover in your arms. Marriage under two roofs makes room for moods." In a decade when the country had decided that marriage was about sex and romance but that life was about the struggle for individuality, Eastman's solution seemed fitting, if unorthodox.

Other rebellions also took into account 1920s sensibilities and options. Tennis champion Helen Wills personified vigorous, rather than delicate, womanliness. Wills at least had the support of her family in shaping her career. Her father, a physician, had taught her all he knew of tennis, and when she could beat him he set her up with coaches who helped her, at age seventeen, win the 1923 National Women's Championship. Zelda Fitzgerald, on the other hand, was a southern belle, trained to be beautiful, decorative, and amusing. Her husband, the novelist F. Scott Fitzgerald, expected a companionate marriage; he wanted her to amuse herself quietly when he worked and to play when he played. Her sense of emptiness in this life, however, led her into an affair and then to ballet and writing. Even though he wrote novels that chronicled the new morals of the 1920s, her husband objected to her writing in traditional terms: "I am the highest paid short story writer in the world. . . . That is all my material. None of it is your material. . . . I would like you to think of my interests. That is your primary concern, because I am the one to steer the course, the pilot. . . . I want you to stop writing fiction."

Many women did not stop writing fiction in the 1920s, no matter who told them to, and many of the writers were black women who joined Harlem's literary circles. Harlem had only recently ceased to be a Jewish immigrant enclave, becoming a large black community within New York City. For both blacks and whites it was a symbol of African-American aspirations and possibilities, the one place an African American could be anything. College-educated black men and women flocked to Harlem from all over the nation. Most other towns had room for perhaps one black doctor or lawyer, who would then serve primarily—and sometimes only—the black community. In Harlem, the largest black community in the country, blacks owned businesses and real estate, were librarians and teachers, and ran literary magazines and cultural gatherings.

In the Harlem of the 1920s, the women and men writers of the Harlem Renaissance also worked to create a new image of blackness. They were a varied lot. Louise Thompson's family had moved to the Far West as domestic help. She grew up in Oregon and California with few other blacks, and often was taken for white or, sometimes, Mexican. When "passing" for white she could not recognize her black friends in public. She began to long for a stronger race identity. While Thompson was studying at the University of California, she heard a speech by W. E. B. Du

Bois, a black equal rights activist and scholar who had been instrumental in founding the National Association for the Advancement of Colored People (NAACP); it was the first time she had seen a black man appear in public without self-effacement. After earning a degree in business administration, Thompson taught at Hampton Institute, a black college in Virginia founded by white philanthropists after the Civil War. She supported a student strike against the school's paternalism, and then headed for Harlem.

Another Harlem writer, Jessie Fauset, came from an old Philadelphia family and graduated Phi Beta Kappa from Cornell. She served as literary editor of *The Crisis,* the NAACP's journal and the most common outlet for Harlem writers. She also wrote four novels, as well as poems and stories. Fauset's novels portrayed middle-class African Americans in middle-class professions striving for middle-class goals, emphasizing similarities between blacks and whites. In her foreword to *Chinaberry Tree* (1931), she declared that the black man "started out as a slave but he rarely thinks of that. To himself he is a citizen of the United States whose ancestors came over not along with the emigrants in the *Mayflower,* it is true, but merely a little earlier in the good year, 1619. . . . And he has a wholesome respect for family and education and labor and the fruits of labor." Although Fauset criticized white society in her novels, she refused to go beyond a mild rebuke.

Others took the rebellion further. Harlem was no paradise. The death rate for blacks in New York City was almost twice that for whites; 60 percent of the black working women in New York City worked as laundresses or servants. Although blacks in New York appeared in 316 of the 321 possible occupations in the 1920 census, they could not be served in many of the Harlem theaters where they performed.

Yet some whites flocked from their homes in Manhattan to Harlem's nightlife. Tired of and alienated from the modern industrial world—especially after witnessing the carnage of World War I—some whites were on the prowl for something fresh, for a less complicated existence, more in harmony with nature and each other. Aided by popularized anthropology and psychology, many looked to the poorer Harlemites for their spiritual salvation. They dipped into Harlem for an evening, making up audiences that, as Walter White, then head of the NAACP, put it, "receive [blacks] as artists but refuse to accept them as men."

The Harlem Renaissance writers rejected the white image of blacks as primitive, one-dimensional, and uncomplicated. "For generations in the mind of America," wrote Rhodes scholar and Harvard graduate Alain Locke in his essay "The New Negro," "the Negro has been more of a formula than a human being." For poet Langston Hughes, the literary movement was a declaration of independence, a chance for black people to create their own images. In 1926 he wrote, "if white people are pleased we are glad. If they are not, it doesn't matter. We know we are beautiful. And ugly too. . . . If colored people are pleased we are glad. If they are not, their displeasure doesn't matter either. We build our temples for tomorrow, strong as we know how, and we stand on the top of the mountain free from within ourselves."

Reality was more complicated than Hughes's declaration. Writers needed money to survive. For a time, Hughes, Thompson, and Zora Neale Hurston shared the same patron, a wealthy, white Park Avenue matron named Mrs. Rufus Osgood Mason, who was both generous and controlling. Mason tried to ensure that her protégées stuck to the image of the simple, emotional primitive, and Hurston had to tread a fine line to write what she wanted. Like Margaret Mead, Hurston had studied anthropology at Columbia University. Unlike Mead, she returned to her own roots, an all-black town in Florida, to collect folklore, funded by Mason. Hurston's novels were not filled with middle-class blacks striving for acceptance in the white world. Instead they depicted, often in dialect, a black world with little direct interaction between blacks and whites. Her characters filled many Harlem Renaissance writers with dismay. As one critic complained, "Her darkies always smiled through their tears, sang spirituals on the slightest provocation, and performed buck dances when they should have been working."

This criticism missed the essential point. Hurston's stories were radical both in their blackness and in their feminism. Indeed, that combination may have been one source of her friction with Harlem's black intellectual elite. As Hurston depicted the world, the competition among blacks and black men's subordination of women stemmed from their relations with white society. Her novels showed African Americans left to themselves, in towns like the one in which she had been born, developing an alternative to white society, a communal culture of social equality. If Hurston's characters spoke in dialect, they were not mindless primitives. Her characters and their thoughts were complex, but it was not a white world that she described. Nor was it a man's world. The men in Hurston's stories had a noticeable tendency to die off, while women survived. Hurston's struggle, like that of Langston Hughes, was for autonomy, but it seemed that she could not conceive of a way for women to achieve full growth and become fully human without writing off the men who, in her stories, kept trying to define them.

Other women sought refuge and self-definition in Harlem, which in the 1920s hosted a lesbian subculture. Lesbian communities also existed in Salt Lake City, Greenwich Village in New York City, San Francisco, and other cities, but Harlem's was the largest. For the first time, in the 1920s, love between women was assumed to be sexual, even when it was not, and "homosexual" was becoming an identity. At this stage, the popular fascination with Freud had two opposing effects. On the one hand, it made people more comfortable with sexual experimentation; in this view, bisexuality became an adventure. On the other hand, popular Freudian psychology defined exclusive homosexuality as a disease. The writer Edna St. Vincent Millay, resisting pressure to add men to the women she loved, referred to Freud's ideas as an "attempt to lock women up in the home and restore them to cooking and baby-tending."

Harlem, already identified with primitivism in the minds of many whites, seemed the ideal place to give in to sexual desires. Although blacks in general shared the mixed feelings of whites toward homosexuality, a series of bars catering particularly to homosexuals opened their doors to all comers.

Both white and black women enjoyed the lesbian subculture, in which many black blues stars participated. Blues had reached its first great popularity in the 1920s, and blues singer Bessie Smith was among the most highly paid women entertainers. She and Ma Rainey, another blues singer, both of whom were married, found a way to keep their lesbian affairs in Harlem from harming their popularity with their audiences. Ma Rainey recorded "Prove It on Me Blues," about a woman who preferred women, but she carefully cultivated an image of herself as being interested in men too. Bisexuality could simply seem twice as sexy.

Concern with individualism and sexuality dominated the decade. Even the rebellions of the 1920s took their shape from those impulses, yet the decade did not resolve the dilemma its open-ing years had raised. With Zora Neale Hurston able to have women achieve fulfillment only by killing off men, with "New Style" feminists thinking they had to be like men, with no legitimacy granted to organized feminism, with no good fit between ideology and reality, women had only a fragile foothold in the brave new world. Despite having the vote, despite having broken into the human race, they would be ill-equipped to face challenges that the 1930s depression would bring.

Making Do with Disaster

In the mid-1930s, scholar Margaret Jarman Hagood drove deep into rural North Carolina to talk with more than 250 white farm tenant families for her book *Mothers of the South* (1939). In it she described the life of a typical woman named Mollie, from when she was ten years old until Hagood met her at age thirty-seven. Mollie was pregnant again and wishing, she told Hagood, that "doctors would tell you what to do when they say, 'Now you shouldn't have any more children.'"

As a child, Mollie had stayed home from school on wash days to help her mother scrub her father's and brothers' overalls and the baby's diapers in a huge wash pot on top of a wood fire her brothers kindled before school. She worked in a dress worn and outgrown, saving the year's two new dresses for school and church. In 1920, when Mollie was sixteen, she heard about a neighboring girl who had moved to a town to work in a tobacco factory, about the money she made, and the things she could buy. Telling no one, Mollie made a bundle of her clothes and left one morning. For four months she boarded with a relative of her father and made twenty dollars a week. She bought a coat for fifteen dollars, high-top shoes for eleven dollars, and a hat for eight dollars and spent the rest on all the small items denied her on the farm. She reveled in this taste of "urban" culture and the freedom to buy what she chose. She ate store-bought food for the first time and shared meals and good times with the five other women boarding in the same house.

But then her father called her back home and forbade her to return to the factory. She married before the age of twenty, and by the time she was twenty-three she was pregnant for the third time. Her husband, Jim, bought her one Sunday dress each year, when he could afford it. At the time she talked with Hagood, she and Jim lived in a three-room log cabin, and Mollie sold eggs to bring in some extra money. She was determined that her little girl would go to school regularly and get a wage-earning job, far from farming.

Life had changed little for Mollie over twenty years. For many rural women, the drastic economic downturn of the Great Depression started long before the stock market crashed in 1929. Tenant farmers in particular had experienced hard times ever since the Civil War, and farmers in the rural West had never recovered the prosperity they had enjoyed during World War I. Black families fared particularly badly. In Macon County, Georgia, for example, most black farm families lived in houses with dirt floors. Only one-fifth of these homes had indoor water, and three-fourths had no sewage disposal. Black income in Macon County averaged less than a dollar per day.

Young women like Mollie were part of a family economy in which their labor helped the family survive but gained them no cash. Young men could work for pay in the fields of more prosperous farmers, but if women wanted to earn money—and be able to spend it—they had to head for town. Hopeful rural migrants who arrived in the cities after 1929, however, confronted an urban America reeling from an economic collapse that touched every sector of the economy. Factories closed. Businesses failed. When one-fifth of the country's banks failed, 9 million families lost their savings. As many as one-third of all workers were either unemployed or on short hours and reduced wages. In some places and for certain groups, the numbers were even higher. By the end of 1930, 70 percent of the African Americans in Charleston, South Carolina, and 75 percent of those in Memphis, Tennessee, were jobless. So were more than half the black women in Chicago and three-fourths of them in Detroit. Only eight states offered workers any form of unemployment insurance. There was no federal unemployment program. Workers' families lost the furniture and cars they had bought on installment plans because they could not meet the payments. Many also lost their homes. By 1934, in Indianapolis, Indiana, and Birmingham, Alabama, more than half the home owners had defaulted on their loans. So had 40 percent of home owners in twenty other cities.

If the 1920s had been a time of optimism and energy for many people in the United States, the 1930s began with fear and desperation. The basic assumptions of the previous decade—that technology was the answer to all problems, that businessmen knew best how to run the country, and that women's and men's greatest duty to society was to seek their own personal satisfaction—tottered.

As for the new women of the 1920s, what had looked like vigorous independence and strong-mindedness in the flapper now seemed careless, selfish, and superficial. A whole generation was tempted by an older, comforting vision of mom as a plump, slightly frazzled woman who could be relied on to sacrifice herself to nurture others and make it all better. That shift, along with the economic realities of the depression, created a different set of possibilities and limits for women.

Families coped with economic disaster in different ways. Helen Hong Wong had come to the United States in 1928 from Hong Kong dreaming of luxury. Instead she found herself, as she told an interviewer, working "like a slave" in her husband's restaurant and laundry. "I was not prepared for such a hard time," she recalled. "I found no streets paved with gold." Despite all the potatoes she peeled and the vegetables she chopped, the couple lost their restaurant in Fort Wayne, Indiana, during the depression. "People couldn't afford to eat," she concluded. Helen and her husband moved to Chicago but could find no work and could not collect welfare. Finally, her husband went to Chinatown and borrowed money from gamblers.

Other families also relied on ethnic connections. Many Americans were only a generation away, if that, from immigration. They still lived in neighborhoods where the shopkeepers and the customers alike spoke Polish, Italian, Spanish, or Yiddish. In Chicago, Mary Rupcinski and her husband had taken in tenants for years. During the depression, they let them stay on for months, even though the tenants could not pay their rent because they had lost their jobs. Neighborhood grocers often carried people on credit as long as they could, and neighborhood banks sometimes held off foreclosing on homes. Relatives doubled up, moving their families together into a single apartment or house. People shared.

Women often had a strong role in keeping such relationships alive. They visited, watched each other's children, and shared recipes. Women needed such networks because they could not make as much money as men could, but the depression proved the fragility of these networks. Without the rent from their tenants, the Rupcinskis ultimately could not make their mortgage payments, and they lost their house. Neighborhood banks closed. Ethnic organizations went bankrupt. When their neighborhood networks failed, women turned to other avenues for help. They cashed in insurance policies, and they visited welfare agencies.

It was hardest for single women to get food, shelter, work, or money from welfare agencies. Policymakers assumed that these women all had families somewhere that would care for them. In New York City, the $8 million government work-relief program focused on helping male heads of families. It took the private effort of well-known women to raise $350,000 to provide work for what they called the unemployed "army of women clerical workers." Men could sleep in flophouses, places charging twenty-five cents a night to sleep on a mattress in a large common room, but there were no flophouses for women. In 1930 the mayor of Minneapolis offered them the city jail.

Women continued to come to the city seeking work, but there was little to be had. In January 1930, one agency in Minneapolis could place only seventy of the three hundred women who applied. Women factory workers, teachers, and clerical workers who had lost their jobs turned to domestic service. Some women, in desperation, turned to prostitution.

At the unemployment bureaus, women waited for hours, day after day. Journalist Meridel Le Sueur wrote of one woman who "went crazy yesterday at the YW[CA]." She had had no work for eight months. As she kept saying, "You've got to give me something," the woman in charge of the agency began scolding the girl for her scuffed shoes. According to Le Sueur, "they were facing each other in a rage both helpless, helpless."

The Great Depression reached into every corner of the country, but it did not affect all people equally. For many middle-class women of all races, the depression required certain changes in spending patterns: buying cheaper cuts of meat, feeding the homeless men who stopped at the back door, and doing without new clothes. Some of these women continued to do community volunteer work, raising money for the unemployed. They saw the food lines, but they did not have to join them.

Among women workers, race played an important role. The fierce competition for jobs fueled racial resentments. Mexican-American and African-American women were the first to lose their jobs and the last to get relief from welfare agencies. Often, they were already living on the margin of survival. Before 1933, when the Prohibition amendment making the manufacture or sale of alcoholic beverages illegal was repealed, many of these women turned to bootlegging, making their own beer or liquor and selling it.

Other women struggled to survive within the bounds of the law. On street corners in the congested neighborhoods of the Bronx in New York City, black women, old and young, dressed as neatly as they could and stood ready to sell their cleaning services for an hour or two, or even for the whole day, for as little as fifteen cents an hour in an arrangement called the Bronx Slave Market. The two black women who investigated the Market for the NAACP's *Crisis* in 1935 found that these low rates had produced a new set of employers. Women of the lower middle-class who could not have dreamed of affording a servant during the 1920s could afford one now.

The number of married women in the labor force increased by 52 percent during the 1930s. By 1940, although the percentage of single women who worked for wages had dropped slightly, 15.6 percent of married women worked for pay. Most of the increase consisted of white native-born women, who provided only 43 percent of the total female labor force in 1930 but 70 percent in 1940. Of these white working women, the fastest-growing group was that between the ages of twenty-five and forty-five, the group most likely to have children at home. Their ability to hire African-American and Mexican-American women for extremely low wages made it easier for them to leave the home.

Not all married women coped with hard times by leaving the home. Many women took in home work. In Durham, North Carolina, women who had worked in tobacco factories now tagged tobacco sacks at home. In Rhode Island, women who had lost their jobs in the textile mill took home worsted wool to mend. Home work networks relied on ethnic neighborhood ties. In West Warwick, Rhode Island, the lace makers for American Textile were Portuguese women; the lace pullers who worked at home for Rhode Island Lace were Italian women; and the lace pullers who worked for Richmond Lace in the rural southwestern part of Rhode Island were descended from English, Scots, or Irish immigrants. There were advantages to home work for women. It allowed them to tend their own children, gather in chatty groups with other home workers, and barter among themselves, using their receipts for work completed as a kind of currency.

Home work had disadvantages, however. In San Antonio, Texas, the presence of thousands of temporarily unemployed families, largely Mexican-American, attracted home work industries from as far away as New York. Garment makers fleeing New York's higher labor costs joined the local pecan-shelling companies that were providing home work in San Antonio. As in Rhode Island and New York, where Puerto Ricans worked in the garment industry, the sewing required was hand work, in this case including embroidery. As the depression took hold, prices dropped continually. Between 1929 and the mid-1930s, employers cut the rates by 50 percent. For Chicanas, as for other home workers, the lack of alternatives kept them on the job. In 1936 the Women's Bureau of the U.S. Department of Labor interviewed home workers in San Antonio and Laredo, Texas. It found that many of the workers lived in one- or two-room shacks without plumbing or electricity. In one home/workshop there was no light source and the renter had to cook all her meals outside and share water and toilet facilities with fifteen other families. Moreover, home work encouraged competition among women. Factory women complained that home workers undercut their wages and their working conditions. Competition between cities also affected women, as garment manufacturers pitted Puerto Rican home workers in the East against Chicanas in the Southwest.

Despite all the rural women fleeing the farms, a Hispanic woman who lived in northern Colorado during the depression told an interviewer, "People on the farm were better off than downtown; we had our gardens." Even relatively prosperous farm women—owners, not tenants—in general produced as much as 70 percent of what their families consumed in clothing, toys, and food. They not only gardened but raised poultry. During the depression, women increased the size of their gardens and the number of their hens. They made more butter from their dairy cows and sold it. They cut up the sacks that held large amounts of flour and sewed them into underwear. In the previous decade, they had proudly begun to participate in a culture of store-bought goods. Now they began to can food again. Government agents dragged huge canning kettles across the mountains of northern New Mexico and eastern Tennessee so that women in remote farming villages could preserve their food.

Even with all this work, rural children suffered from malnutrition, and rural women faced childbirth without a doctor or midwife because they could afford neither the medical fees nor the gasoline for transportation. The women resented their declining standards of living, particularly whose who owned their own farms and had, during the 1920s, aspired to participate in the new domestic technology of indoor bathrooms, mod-

ern stoves and heating, and supercleanliness. Through national women's magazines and the Sears Roebuck catalogs, these women had internalized the 1920s message that women's duty was to create a beautiful home and a beautiful self. The women writing the advice columns in farm magazines held each other to city standards of tidiness. Women without toilets or sinks, without running water in their homes, who nevertheless preserved fifteen hundred quarts of food a year, were advised to try wearing powder and rouge to please their husbands.

In the 1920s, people had worried about how to keep the family together when faced with women's increasing independence. Now they worried about how to keep men in the family as it became clear that many women still depended on the income of men, after all, and many men were now unemployed. Powder and rouge were not enough. Divorce rates dropped in the 1930s, more because people could not afford the costs of an official divorce than because families were staying together. Desertion ran rampant. Men went out to look for work and never returned, leaving their wives to try to convince increasingly suspicious and underfunded charity agents and city officials that they were virtuous enough to be worthy of aid. Families that stayed together tried not to add new members. The birthrate, which had been declining steadily for a century, hit its lowest point in 1933, when only 75.7 of every 1,000 women of childbearing age gave birth.

In 1936 a federal appeals court overruled an earlier law that had classified birth control information as obscene and thus illegal to dispense, although the decision left state laws intact. The number of birth control clinics nationwide rose from fifty-five in 1930 to three hundred by 1938, but in some states and in many rural areas women still had no access to birth control. In 1937 North Carolina became the first state to provide contraceptives with tax dollars, and six others soon followed. Ironically, North Carolina's reasoning was not that birth control was a human right but that birth control would reduce the black population. Despite statistics showing that black women had fewer babies than white women with similar incomes and living situations, many white southern officials in states with large black populations feared a black population explosion. In 1939 the Birth Control Federation of America responded to eager southern state governments by developing "The Negro Project," a program to disseminate birth control information, which they carefully staffed with local black community leaders.

Whatever the logic, one quarter of all women in the United States in their twenties during the depression never bore children—the highest rate of childlessness for any decade. Many people simply decided not to get married, and marriage rates fell.

With men unable to fulfill their traditional roles as providers and many deserting their homes, women were increasingly left to run the family, with little money and few opportunities. Many people worried that chaos would follow. To them, orderly society depended on a family organized around a strong, dominant father. A few people did suggest that the solution might lie in providing more opportunities for the women left running the family, but most focused on men's unemployment and on how to keep the family together. They tended to decide that the real culprits were married working women, stealing jobs from married men.

The media, which had made married working women invisible in the 1920s, now often vilified them. During the 1920s, married women had experienced discrimination at the local level, particularly as teachers. By the early 1930s, public officials such as New York Assemblyman Arthur Swartz were calling them "undeserving parasites." Several cities ordered the dismissal of wives whose husbands earned what they defined as "living wages." In 1931 legislators in Massachusetts, New York, and California introduced bills to limit government employment of married women. The federal government's 1932 Economy Act required that when personnel reductions took place in the executive branch, married persons be the first discharged if their spouse also worked for the government. Women earned less than men, even for the same job, so given the choice, a family would logically retain the higher-salaried man's job and let the wife go unemployed.

Many women's groups rallied in opposition to this legislation. The leaders of the Business and Professional Women's Clubs declared in their journal, *Independent Woman,* "Such legislation is not only a blow to married women, but through implication to all women workers and to marriage itself." Women in government work had to choose between a job and a husband.

Despite mounting protests, the controversial clause of the Economy Act was not repealed until 1937. In 1936 George Gallup, witnessing the results of his new public opinion polls, in which 82 percent of the respondents agreed that wives should not work if their husbands were employed,

observed that he had "discovered an issue on which voters are about as solidly united as on any subject imaginable—including sin and hay fever."

Local governments followed the lead of the federal government. During the 1920s, the proportion of female teachers who were married had almost doubled, reaching more than 150,000 by 1930. The depression saw communities cut back on school funds, reduce the number of teachers, and slash their salaries. They also reduced the number of married teachers. By 1940 only 13 percent of communities would hire wives as teachers, and only 30 percent would retain women teachers who got married. The percentage of male teachers rose from 19 percent to 24.3 percent of teachers during the 1930s. Married women teachers, however, did not disappear. Indeed, over the same period they increased from 17.9 percent to 22 percent of all female teachers, but the absolute number of women teachers had dropped by 81,000.

On the other hand, women retained their hold on clerical positions, which steadily increased in number in the 1930s. Advocates of women's employment found themselves making a virtue out of the fact that women were by and large limited to certain jobs. The number of women in male-dominated professions, including science and college teaching, decreased in the 1930s. Because all women's jobs were threatened, women who were trying to salvage these jobs reinforced the notion that some occupations were particularly suited to women. Running beauty salons, of which there were forty thousand by 1930, or working as dental hygienists and occupational therapists all offered women increased opportunities and had the added advantage of placing women where they would not compete with men. The proportion of women working outside the home rose only slightly from 1930 to 1940, from 24.4 percent to 25.4 percent, a far smaller rise than in previous decades.

Women seemed to receive mixed messages from the mass media. On the one hand, in 1930, the *Ladies' Home Journal* featured a former career woman confessing, "I know now without any hesitation . . . that [my husband's job] must come first." In 1931 the popular magazine *Outlook and Independent* quoted the dean of Barnard College, a women's college in New York City, telling her students that "perhaps the greatest service that you can render to the community . . . is to have the courage to refuse to work for gain." And on its front page in 1935, the *New York Times* reported that women "suffering from masculine psychological states" and an "aversion to marriage" were being "cured" by the removal of their adrenal gland. In this atmosphere, not only were women workers under fire, but women who centered their lives on women rather than on men came under attack. Lesbianism was no longer chic. Lesbian bars almost disappeared. Homosexuality was now seen by many people as just one more threat to the family.

On the other hand, movie houses showed zany screwball comedies with more complicated lessons. Often, deliciously ditsy, incompetent women were rescued by sensible, capable men—yet men were also frequently portrayed as bumbling or slower-witted than the women. Sometimes the men needed joy and whimsy restored to their lives, not an unexpected theme for a nation in the throes of an economic depression.

In other movies, women were by no means incompetent. The women portrayed by Katharine Hepburn, Bette Davis, and Joan Crawford in the 1930s were often intelligent but needed men to tame and soften them. At the other end of the spectrum, in the dancing movies of Ginger Rogers and Fred Astaire, Rogers often played the responsible, capable, working partner while Astaire's devil-may-care ways needed reforming. Their movies usually ended not with blissful domestic life for her but with successful professional partnership for them both.

How were women to understand their roles through these films? Were they to go from the free but irresponsible flapper to the submissive, nurturing wife who could lighten the burden of dark days but stay safely in her place? Or was there another model still available? It was, after all, in the 1930s that Babe Didrikson emerged as a sports hero, winning two gold medals at the 1932 Olympics, in javelin and hurdles, and a silver in the high jump, and eschewing all feminine wiles. What society demanded of women in the 1930s was complex and contradictory, but it did not completely erode the image of confident, competent, public womanhood created in the 1920s.

Women and the New Deal

In 1931 Emily Newell Blair, a former national vice-chairman of the Democratic party, wrote an article entitled "Why I Am Discouraged about Women in Politics." "Now at the end of ten years of suffrage," she confessed, "I find politics still a male monopoly. It is hardly easier for women to get themselves elected to office than it was before the Equal Suffrage Amendment was passed.

Women still have little part in framing political policies and determining party tactics." Indeed, Blair claimed that women had less of a voice in party leadership than they had in 1920, when, as an unknown quantity, they had been courted by male politicians.

In the 1930s, few women held elected office. Of the dozen women who served in Congress at some point during the decade, only two were active on women's issues. Blair lamented, "Unfortunately for feminism, it was agreed to drop the sex line in politics. And it was dropped by the women. Even those who ran for office forgot that they were women." Yet the 1930s saw a dramatic increase in women's political influence through appointed, rather than elected, offices. It came as the fruit of Franklin Delano Roosevelt's program, the New Deal that he promised Americans when they elected him President in 1932. The increase in influence was also the result of his wife Eleanor's strong and deeply rooted networks among women reformers and her political abilities as a shaper of New Deal policy.

By early 1933, when Roosevelt took office, the depression was four years old. Herbert Hoover, elected President in 1928, had hesitated to intervene drastically in the economy. Hoover had created public works projects that erected large dams but employed few workers. He had provided some support for banks and had said many encouraging things, but the economy went from bad to worse.

Faced with declining opportunities and increased racial hostility, ten thousand Puerto Ricans headed for home, and many Chinese returned to China. Unable to create jobs or to meet the needs of the unemployed, officials in the Southwest closed ranks against Mexicans and Mexican Americans, accusing them of stealing jobs and using up relief dollars. In 1932, officials in Los Angeles rounded up all the Mexicans they could find, put them and their American-born children in boxcars, and sent them to Mexico. In all, across the United States, these deportations affected approximately 400,000 Mexicans. They solved nothing. Indeed, many "Mexicans" on relief roles were, in fact, U.S. citizens, born and raised on this side of the border. To the officials responsible, however, they all looked alike.

Many Chicanos made their way to the cities in search of opportunities or help. They were joined by 400,000 African Americans migrating from the South to the North for the same reason. And farmers who had lost their homes, along with

ON THE SUBJECT OF...

ELEANOR ROOSEVELT (1884-1962)

Eleanor Roosevelt, wife of President Franklin Delano Roosevelt, was an especially active and visible First Lady. Her innumerable trips across the country, visiting Americans from all socioeconomic, political, and cultural backgrounds, proved invaluable in gaining support for her husband and his administration and in advancing the causes of poor and disenfranchised Americans. Roosevelt's syndicated column, "My Day," was read by millions of Americans, who also regularly tuned in to her 15-minute radio broadcasts. She was deeply committed to social service projects, particularly to ensuring that those projects ushered in by her husband's New Deal program served *all* Americans, including women, people of color, youths, and tenant farmers. During World War II, Roosevelt's personal visits with American and Allied troops, during which she spoke to soldiers at front-line installations, army camps, and field hospitals in Great Britain, Australia, the South Pacific, and the United States, were received with universal enthusiasm. As popular as she was, however, Roosevelt was also widely criticized for her support of the allegedly Communist-dominated American Youth Congress, American Newspaper Guild, and the Works Progress Administration. She also received negative attention for her outspoken support of birth control and equal opportunities for women, her opposition to censorship, and her actions in support of human and civil rights. Nevertheless, she remained unwavering in her dedication to these groups and causes. After her husband's death in 1945, Roosevelt was appointed by President Truman to the U.S. delegation to the United Nations. She was also elected chair of the Commission on Human Rights. She received numerous awards, including the first annual Franklin Delano Roosevelt Brotherhood Award in 1946 and the Four Freedoms award. In addition to her syndicated column, Roosevelt authored numerous magazine articles and several books, including *When You Grow Up to Vote* (1932) and *It's Up to the Women* (1933).

tenant farmers unable to get leases, rolled west, as one observer noted, "like a parade." Whole counties hit the road.

The cities offered no respite from the hard times. In 1933 half the workers in Cleveland were unemployed, as were 80 percent of those in Toledo. Average family income plummeted from $2,300 in 1929 to $1,500 in 1933. In 1932 28 percent of U.S. households had no employed worker at all. Even those who had work suffered. Stenographers in New York who had made forty dollars a week in 1929 were making only sixteen dollars four years later. Most working women in Chicago earned less than twenty-five cents an hour. Unable to pay their teachers, school districts cut school to three days a week, to two months a year, or simply closed them altogether, depriving a third of a million children of school in 1932.

People looked to Roosevelt's administration to make order of the chaos, to reopen the banks and schools, and to put people back to work. In the process of accomplishing these tasks, the Roosevelts and their allies changed the relationship between individuals and the government. With her long history of work in social welfare, Eleanor Roosevelt stood at the center of that change.

Anna Eleanor Roosevelt had been born into an old, wealthy, and distinguished New York family. By the time Eleanor was ten, both her parents had died—her mother after an operation and her father from alcoholism. She spent the rest of her childhood with relatives. When she reached fifteen, she was sent to a London boarding school. When Roosevelt returned to New York to enter high society, she plunged into social service activities. At the age of eighteen, she worked at the Rivington Street Settlement House, teaching calisthenics and dancing to the impoverished neighbors. She also joined the National Consumers' League, which used the power of consumers to try to better the conditions of workers, particularly women. Employers who met the Consumers' League standards could use the League label, and consumers could buy the goods they produced knowing they had been produced under decent conditions. Roosevelt visited the clothing factories and sweatshops that the League targeted and never forgot what she saw.

Roosevelt married her cousin, Franklin Roosevelt, an ambitious young Harvard graduate, in March 1905. For the next ten years Eleanor was either pregnant or recovering from pregnancy. She helped Franklin's early political career by organizing and hosting social and political gatherings. Then, in 1917, she discovered that her husband was having an affair with her trusted friend, Lucy Mercer. Devastated, she offered him a divorce, but a divorce would have ruined his political career and deprived him of a valued friend and partner. The couple reconciled, and both plunged into politics.

Even the setback of Franklin's lifelong paralysis from a polio attack in 1921 could not stop the Roosevelts. During the 1920s, Franklin played an ever-increasing role in the Democratic party, and Eleanor joined reform organizations, including the Women's Trade Union League. She discovered in the women reformers a warm, supportive network of friends and an astute set of politicians. This warmth sustained her in the rough and tumble political world. In particular, her intimate relationship with journalist Lorena Hickok provided the essential emotional support she could no longer get from her husband. In turn, as early as 1924, women reformers saw Eleanor Roosevelt as a major leader. By 1928 she expressed her frustration that these women politicians met with so few rewards. She would carry this sense of politics and reform—and this network of women—with her into the White House in 1933.

The women who would join Eleanor Roosevelt in Washington were not new to politics. In overlapping networks, they had been building connections and careers throughout the 1910s and 1920s. For example, Mary W. Dewson started her career in Massachusetts reform and suffrage circles. In the 1920s in New York, she served as the civic secretary of the Women's City Club and the research secretary of the National Consumers' League. By 1929 Dewson knew all the leading women reformers in the city. With these connections in mind, Eleanor Roosevelt recruited her into Democratic politics. By 1937 Dewson was vice chairman of the Democratic National Committee and on a number of government advisory boards. Dewson wanted to use political appointments both to get nonpartisan women reformers into the government and to reward loyal Democratic women. For his part, Franklin Roosevelt wanted to be the first President to appoint a woman to the cabinet. In Frances Perkins he found an ideal candidate with connections to both political and reform networks.

Perkins had graduated from Mount Holyoke College in 1902, worked in settlement houses in Chicago, and then studied and conducted research for her master's degree in sociology and economics at Columbia University. She had worked for the Consumers' League as a lobbyist. In 1918 Governor Al Smith appointed her to the New York State Industrial Commission. In 1928 the new governor, Franklin Roosevelt, appointed Perkins Industrial Commissioner, a promotion. After he was elected President, Roosevelt agreed to nominate Perkins as secretary of labor, and Dewson launched a nationwide campaign in her support.

Other women received posts in every agency from the diplomatic corps and the U.S. Mint to the Consumers' Advisory Board of the National Recovery Administration (NRA), an economic agency that was part of the New Deal program. Under Roosevelt, a higher percentage of women received government appointments than ever before, except during World War I.

Women fared best in new agencies. In the seven newest New Deal agencies, including the Social Security Board, the Works Progress Administration, and the Home Owners' Loan Corporation, women made up 44.4 percent of the employees in 1939. The ten executive departments were another story. In the Departments of Labor, State, and Interior, women constituted more than one-third of the employees, but in the Departments of War, Navy, Commerce, and the Post Office, they ranged from 15.2 percent to only 5.5 percent of employees.

Some women had built up political networks over the previous decades whose networks touched, rather than overlapped, those of Eleanor Roosevelt and Mary Dewson. Mary McLeod Bethune was one such woman. Born in South Carolina in the 1870s, the fifteenth of seventeen children, she was the one chosen to attend school and teach the others. A determined mother and scholarships helped Bethune, who was proud of her African heritage, attend a seminary, a bible school, and a number of mission schools in pursuit of her desire to be a missionary in Africa. During her training, Bethune married and had a child. As her efforts to go to Africa failed, she realized that her true mission was in the United States and founded a school for girls in Daytona, Florida; in 1929, it became Bethune-Cookman College.

But Bethune's activities ranged far beyond her school. A vital force in women's clubs, in 1924 she was elected president of the National Association of Colored Women (NACW). Like all Bethune's organizations, it had a large vision, working to secure a federal antilynching bill, helping rural women and women in industry, training clerks and typists, and raising the status of women in the Philippines, Puerto Rico, Haiti, and Africa.

Bethune knew that the number of black women graduating from college was increasing but that the status of black working women had declined in depression conditions. She wanted to mobilize the power of college women on behalf of the others. She felt frustrated with the lack of progress, the conservatism of the NACW, and the difficulties of working in mixed-race organizations such as the Association of Southern Women for the Prevention of Lynching, whose white members had refused to support a federal antilynching law, claiming it violated states' rights. Though Bethune remained more friendly to such groups than did many black women leaders, she decided to found her own organization. On December 5, 1935, she held the founding meeting of the National Council of Negro Women at the Harlem branch of the YWCA.

Bethune's stature had led to her involvement in national-level politics. In 1928, she had participated in the White House Conference on Child Welfare. Yet the New Deal was slow to call on her. As late as 1929, Franklin Roosevelt had boasted that he had never lunched with an African American. He ignored NAACP requests to support a civil rights platform. African Americans supported Roosevelt only because of his job creation and welfare programs. Then, in 1934, Eleanor Roosevelt began taking public stands on racial issues. Unlike her husband, she lent her public support to the antilynching bill. Finally, in 1936, when 76 percent of the black vote returned Roosevelt to office, despite the defection of white Southern Democrats, Roosevelt responded with black political appointments.

The press called the new appointees the "Black Cabinet." Bethune was among them. She directed the Negro Division of the National Youth Administration (NYA), whose mandate was to find jobs for people between the ages of sixteen and twenty-four. Bethune soon made her mark. Seeing the Black Cabinet divided by internal disputes, she organized its members into the Federal Council of Negro Affairs to achieve consensus on policy issues. She also made certain that black universities benefited from the NYA, implementing a small, special scholarship fund for African-American college students because of their greater need. In the 1930s, 48 percent of the fathers of black college students worked in unskilled, low-paying jobs; only 4.7 percent of white students' fathers did.

Many black southern women with fewer connections, less education, and less power than Bethune, surrounded by the terrorist, racist activities of the Ku Klux Klan, felt they had no choice but to repress their anger and resentment in order to keep their jobs and provide for their families. Bethune would have to express their feelings for them. She did not hesitate. In a typical moment, she wrote to Secretary of War Henry L. Stimson on learning that the War Department had failed to invite black women to a 1941 conference on organizing women for the war effort, "We are not humiliated. We are incensed."

Together these women, black and white, tried to ensure that other women benefited from New Deal programs. They were consummate lobbyists. Eleanor Roosevelt had unprecedented access to policymakers, addressing committees of the House of Representatives, conferring with committee chairmen, and sending members of Congress letters demanding the appointment of a coordinator of child care—all the while claiming to act only as a private citizen.

With public charities running dry and states going bankrupt, the federal government swept in like a benign wind. The New Deal created massive temporary job programs and provided relief payments, first through the Federal Relief Administration (FERA), created in March 1933 with $500 million, and the Public Works Administration (PWA), which funded major construction projects with $3.3 billion. Then, in the desperate winter of 1933-34, the Civil Works Administration (CWA) was established; it hired 2.6 million people within a month. At its peak in January 1934, the CWA employed more than 4 million people with wages averaging about fifteen dollars per week, twice the usual FERA rate. When the depression lingered, at Roosevelt's request Congress passed the Emergency Relief Act, under which Roosevelt created the Works Progress Administration (WPA) with the largest single appropriation to that date, $4.88 billion, in order to create jobs.

The New Deal also attempted a more permanent restructuring of the economy. In 1933 the Agricultural Adjustment Act (AAA) and the National Industrial Recovery Act (NIRA), which created the National Recovery Administration (NRA), tried to stabilize production on farms and in factories. These agencies tried to ensure decent working conditions by bringing consumers, employers, and workers together to create codes for the industries and prices and quotas for the farmers. They also made it harder for employers to discriminate against workers for joining a union. These measures were so popular that when the Supreme Court declared the laws unconstitutional in 1935 and 1936, new, more carefully drafted laws swiftly replaced the major provisions of the

AAA and the provisions of the NIRA that protected workers' rights. Industrial codes were abandoned, but in 1938 the Fair Labor Standards Act legislated minimum wages and maximum hours, and this time the Supreme Court let the act stand.

The federal government also entered more permanently and more broadly into social welfare. Finally, the United States, like most European countries, had unemployment insurance, old age insurance (Social Security), and aid to dependent children. The last was a provision of the 1935 Social Security Act drafted by the reformers Grace Abbott and Katherine Lenroot, who headed the Children's Bureau. For the first time, the U.S. government became a major guarantor of family welfare.

Some of these programs greatly benefited women; others had mixed and often unexpected consequences. New Deal programs employed countless numbers of women. They also kept many women in college; 45 percent of the college students helped by the NYA in 1936-37 were women. The number of women in college rose almost as fast as the number of men, from 480,000 in 1930 to 601,000 in 1940. For many women, New Deal programs made the difference between starvation and survival, or between despair and self-respect. Stella Boone and Ethel Stringer took time out from their new jobs as WPA Adult Education teachers at a Hispanic secondary school in San Antonio to write to Eleanor Roosevelt in 1936. "Many of us were desperate," they explained, "the unhappy victims of circumstances over which we had no control. . . . It is unalterably true that shabbiness and hunger are the foes of self-respect. With our homes broken, our children scattered, our souls torn with anguish and desperation . . . Some of us had lost our homes which were nearly paid for, had sold our furniture, piece by piece, our jewelry, and even most of our clothes. . . . Just when all seemed lost and maddened by grief and fear we were ready for anything, this Adult Educational Program came, providing us with a means of livelihood, a ladder up which we could climb again to patriotism and self-respect."

In such programs, Hispanic and Anglo women in San Antonio studied business and clerical subjects in the hope of obtaining white-collar employment. With its vast bureaucracy, the New Deal did provide many clerical and professional jobs throughout the government. At the state level, women ran the WPA's Division of Women's Work. They also participated in the WPA's writing, music, and theater projects. Zora Neale Hurston collected folklore from African Americans in Florida for the WPA Writers Project. Photographers Dorothea Lange and Marion Post Wolcott took pictures for the Farm Security Administration. Other women worked in government-funded positions in hospitals, nursery schools, and cafeterias or cleaned public buildings and organized city records.

Most women's work projects consisted, however, of sewing rooms, where workers made garments for relief recipients; food processing, such as canning factories; health care; and domestic-service training programs. In San Antonio, for example, by early 1936, the WPA employed 1,280 women and just over twice that many men in professional projects. On the other hand, a single sewing room in that city employed 2,300 people. In the country as a whole, 56 percent of the women employed by the WPA worked in sewing rooms.

New Deal policies focused on promoting domestic roles for women; administrators tended to see women as temporary workers who were helping out in an emergency and would return to the home after the depression. Why teach them nondomestic skills they would never use again? Operating procedures in the WPA mandated that job preference be given to male family heads or, if none existed, to adult male children in the household. Only if a husband were absent or disabled and no adult sons lived at home could women receive a high priority at the agency. Even in the National Youth Administration, men received preference over women in job placement. The WPA limited the proportion of jobs it opened to women to between 12 and 16 percent.

There were other limits to the New Deal programs. Social Security excluded domestic servants and agricultural workers, and by doing so excluded most black female and Chicana workers; in the 1930s, 90 percent of black women worked in agricultural labor or domestic service. No code and, later, no minimum wage or maximum hours law covered these workers. Nor was government relief evenly distributed. It went disproportionately to whites. Black women in the South and Chicanas in the Southwest found themselves ousted from work relief programs and had to take poorly paid domestic work or labor in the cotton or vegetable and fruit fields. In addition, the New Deal's crop reduction policies, geared toward increasing agricultural prices by reducing supply, led landowners to evict large numbers of black women who had raised crops on their land as tenants or sharecroppers.

The administrators of government programs were overwhelmingly white. They had little interest in creating jobs programs that would pull women of color away from domestic service, and they were thoroughly imbued with the racial attitudes that dominated their regions. In 1935 *Opportunity*, the journal of the Urban League, quoted a Georgia black woman who complained, "When I go to them for help they talk to me like I was a dog." Some government officials simply refused relief to black or Chicano clients. Mosel Brinson of Georgia wrote to the U.S. Department of Agriculture in 1935, "I am a widow woman with seven head of children, and I live on my place with a plenty of help. All are good workers and I wants to farm. I has no mule, no wagon, no feed, no grocery, and these women and men that is controlling the Civil Work for the Government won't help me." She added a telling postscript: "P.S. These poor white people that lives around me wants the colored people to work for them for nothing and if you won't do that they goes down to the relief office and tell the women,—'don't help the colored people, we will give them plenty of work to do, but they won't work.'"

Yet white program directors continued to create programs that channeled women of color into domestic service. Mary Katherine Dickson, who administered federal relief programs in San Antonio in 1937, complained that "the majority of housewives in San Antonio have a very real servant problem on their hands and, at present, no means of solving it satisfactorily." She offered her proposal for training black adults in domestic service as the best solution to their unemployment and white housewives' needs, because "between 75% and 85% of persons employed in household service are black." She condemned the public school system for providing the same curriculum and the same expectations for black and white students.

In Denver, officials found they could not fill the classes they had created to train Chicanas in domestic service. Chicanas and black women found almost any other kind of work preferable. Some of these women benefited from New Deal-sponsored classes in clerical skills, but most avoided domestic work by finding jobs in WPA sewing rooms, and even some sewing rooms discriminated. In Fayetteville, North Carolina, officials closed the sewing project and opened a cleaning project for black women. And, unlike white women, black women in the WPA were often assigned to heavy outdoor labor. A physician in Florence, South Carolina, complained to

the WPA in 1936 of a "beautification" project where "women are worked in 'gangs' in connection with the City's dump pile, incinerator and ditch piles."

Some programs not particularly aimed at women had unexpected results. The Indian Reorganization Act of 1934 aimed to give Native American tribes increased autonomy by creating tribal governments built around newly written constitutions. Although the underlying sentiment of the act was a new respect for tribal cultures, the new constitutions tended to be built on white models. In tribes where women had been excluded from formal political participation, they gained new voting power, and new women leaders emerged. In other tribes, women lost economic rights and political power. Among the Navajo, for example, New Deal policies of reducing stock in the name of conserving overgrazed land lessened the economic power of women, who were the traditional tribal stock owners. At the same time, jobs programs favoring men made the Navajo men less dependent economically on the clan's women and less willing to contribute their income to the extended family.

Even industrial codes aimed at improving work conditions could backfire. Wages increased rapidly. Between July 1933 and August 1934, southern women textile workers doubled their hourly wages, a more rapid increase than the men's. Even so, however, the twelve dollars a week they now received would scarcely make ends meet. Besides, most received only three-fourths of that amount because, to meet code requirements regarding the number of work hours per week, many mills closed every fourth week. Short hours and production cuts undermined women's wage advances. Increased demands for productivity, on the other hand, made a mockery of the reduction to an eight-hour day. Higher wages could also lead to mechanization and layoffs as machines became cheaper than human workers. In 1935 a black woman worker told an NRA investigator, "They laid off one-fourth of the people in my room after the last raise we got."

Secretary of Labor Frances Perkins may not have been entirely satisfied with the treatment women got from the New Deal. In her papers at the National Archives there is an unsigned, unattributed, undated "Resolution on Unemployment and Working Women." According to that document, "They have been thrown out of jobs as married women, refused relief as single women, discriminated against by the N.R.A. and ignored by the C.W.A." Pondering these issues in 1935, writer and editor Genevieve Parkhurst wondered in *Harper's* magazine whether feminism was dead. After all, almost one-fourth of the NRA codes established wage rates for women that were 14 percent to 30 percent lower than those for men, and southern codes for laundries established earnings for black laundresses below precode levels.

The emphasis throughout the Roosevelt administration, including that of Eleanor Roosevelt and Frances Perkins, remained on providing male workers with jobs and supporting families. Single women earners were invisible; married women workers existed only as mothers or wives. WPA rules prohibited the agency from providing work for women eligible for aid from the Aid to Dependent Children program as well as for most married women. Such policies aimed at curbing the seeming trend of women becoming the family breadwinner; if there was no man to do so, the role would be assumed by the state.

With the tremendous anxiety over social stability and fears for the family as the core of social order, few spoke for the woman workers, and feminist individualism was rarely seen. In 1935 the *New York Herald Tribune* reported that the president of the national League of Women Voters, the organizational heir to the suffrage movement, was defining "a 1935 new-style feminism." This new feminism, she insisted, did not demand that women disappear into their kitchens. Instead, it required "women making good in positions of responsibility, other women backing them up, and all preparing themselves for similar service," as they did in Roosevelt's administration. Yet the new focus was less on personal achievement than it had been in the 1920s. Women social reformers had achieved high visibility and power with the New Deal, and those focusing instead on equal rights for women were in disarray.

The social reformers saw themselves as bettering the world for women, helping women and children fend off economic disaster, fostering the success of women in government positions, and safeguarding the welfare of working women. But in Frances Perkins's Department of Labor, the Children's Bureau expanded rapidly, while the Women's Bureau remained small. That policy decision left childless women stranded and left little room for a notion of women's rights that did not depend on their family roles. Despite its powerful women, the New Deal did not revolutionize the position of women in relation to men or the family.

For all its contradictions, however, the New Deal had drastically changed the relationship of women to the state. By providing Social Security, however limited, unemployment insurance, jobs, NRA hearings where workers could air their grievances directly to federal officials, wage and hour legislation, and other programs, the New Deal altered what people believed they could expect and took new responsibility for the welfare of families and workers. These heightened expectations, particularly among working-class women, led them to take matters into their own hands.

Taking Matters into Their Own Hands

Throughout the 1930s, impoverished and unemployed people found that those from whom they sought help—charity agents, local, state, and federal officials, and employers—all sought to define their needs, aims, and the limits of their aspirations. Some women resisted such definitions and insisted on defining their own needs, desires, and identities. Many went beyond writing letters. They joined together, sometimes with men, sometimes without them, to protest as a community.

Eviction protests offer an example. In journalist Caroline Bird's memoir of the Great Depression, *The Invisible Scar,* she recalled, "Eviction was so common that children in a Philadelphia daycare center made a game of it. They would pile all the doll furniture up first in one corner and then in another." Rents dropped precipitously during the 1930s, but however low they fell, unemployed workers could not afford to pay them. Tired of moving, desperate for housing and self-respect, they began to fight the evictions. Women played a central role in eviction protests. They had built up neighborhood networks over the years, visiting, sharing work with and caring for neighbors, gossiping, distributing home work, and taking in boarders. Now these women's neighborhood networks were matched by newer networks of unemployed men. With the help of the Communist party, they united into Unemployed Councils. These councils organized the bulk of the eviction protests, but it was the neighborhood networks that made them successful. In cities as different as New York, Baltimore, and Sioux City, Iowa, women and men would gather up the neighborhood and march to a site where a city official, on behalf of a landlord, had just thrown a family into the street. Vastly outnumbered, the city official could only leave or watch helplessly as the crowd took the tenant's belongings back into the apartment. Eviction proceedings took two or three months, which gave unemployed tenants valuable breathing space before the city marshal would again appear to evict them.

In such community protests men made most of the street-corner speeches, but women maintained the picket lines. They did so even when, as the Communist paper the *Daily Worker* reported in 1933 about a Brownsville, New York, rent protest, "day after day thugs and police beat women and children who picketed in front of the house." Black women organized neighborhood Housewives Leagues over jobs as well as housing. Discrimination ran rampant in the job market, and many employers refused to hire African Americans. In Chicago, Baltimore, Detroit, Harlem, and Cleveland, Housewives Leagues used their power as consumers to launch "Don't Buy Where You Can't Work" campaigns. Stores in black neighborhoods would either have to employ black workers or lose black business. These boycotts resulted in as many as 75,000 new jobs for blacks during the 1930s.

Women also took the power of their neighborhood networks beyond their own streets. As members of women's auxiliaries to largely male unions, they played a vital role in supporting the major men's labor strikes of the decade, including the Minneapolis general strike and the Flint, Michigan, sit-down strike at General Motors. But the women also organized on their own behalf, as workers.

In 1933 in St. Louis, Missouri, nine hundred black women pecan workers walked out of seven factories owned by the same man. They demanded higher pay and better working conditions—pay and conditions equal to those of white women workers. Connie Smith, a middle-aged black woman, led the protest, and she secured widespread cooperation, including that of the Unemployed Councils. When the factory owner tried to pit whites against blacks by offering white women a wage increase if they would return to work, a group of fifteen hundred black and white women marched together to City Hall to refuse the offer. Faced with solidarity between black and white women, the owner surrendered on all counts—equal treatment, higher wages, and better conditions.

Determined to take advantage of the ferment, in 1934 William Green, head of the American Federation of Labor (AFL), announced a campaign to bring women into the unions. Yet just bringing them in as members did not guarantee them a voice in policy-making. At Philco, the nation's leading radio maker and Philadelphia's largest single employer, even with the union, women and men had different assignments and were subject to different wage rates. Although women made up about half of Philco's six to seven thousand employees and half the union members of the United Electrical, Radio and Machine Workers of America, men held the offices, including those in departments with large female majorities.

Few women protested the distribution of labor. As former worker Catherine McGill told an interviewer, "At that time, you were glad to have a job." And most of Philco's women workers believed that some jobs were more appropriate to women and others to men. They accepted that those jobs labeled "women's jobs" had lower wages. Ironically, at Philco this acceptance of jobs and wages defined by sex, which had started as a way to keep women from competing for "men's jobs," resulted in men losing jobs to women after all. An unsuccessful strike by the union at the end of 1937 led to a reclassification of fifteen hundred positions from "men's jobs" to "women's jobs" at correspondingly lower pay, and women became the majority of workers at the plant.

In the same year that Green announced his policy shift, the International Ladies' Garment Workers Union (ILGWU) began organizing women workers in San Antonio. They struggled to unite Anglo and Mexican-American women factory workers with the largely Chicana hand sewers and embroiderers who worked at home, but high unemployment made it easy for employers to fire or otherwise harass union members and replace them. No lasting success was achieved until 1935, when New Deal legislation made company harassment of union members illegal. From 1936 to 1938, the union helped garment factory workers make steady gains in San Antonio.

The changes in labor legislation fostered dramatic growth in union membership and the formation of a new Committee on Industrial Organization of the American Federation of Labor. It soon split off, amid bitter disputes, to become the Congress of Industrial Organizations (CIO). The CIO proved more hospitable to women workers because it organized by industry rather than by skills, many of which had excluded women. Of course, this shift did not change the prevalent ideas about men's and women's work overnight, and even CIO unions approved settlements with employers that allowed lower wages for women than for men in the same jobs. Stella Nowicki, an organizer in Chicago meat-packing plants at the time, recalled, "Women had an awfully tough time in the union because the men brought their prejudices there." Moreover, after a day's work many women still had to care for children, make meals, and clean the house. "The union didn't encourage women to come to meetings," Nowicki said. "They didn't actually want to take up the problems that women had." And most women workers remained in fields that were hardly touched by union organization.

Yet over the decade women's union membership tripled, reaching 800,000 by 1940. Two hundred thousand of them were in the ILGWU, but women also organized in a wide variety of occupations and industries, from domestic work to clerical work, canning to radio manufacturing. Often women were hungry for unions. United, they had a chance to take some control over the conditions of their work and livelihoods. Instead of depending solely on their employers, they could depend on each other and bargain with their employers.

Despite continued wage inequities, the unions, new legislation, and federal attempts at regulating the workplace gave women workers an expanded vision of their rights and a sense that their government would hear them and act. In NRA hearings, for example, women complained again and again about sexual harassment. In textile mills, men used profane and vulgar language, which the women found humiliating and degrading. Worse yet, bosses pressured young women workers into sexual relations and fired them if they did not comply. Mothers who tried to protect their daughters were turned away and told it was none of their business. These issues still lay outside the formal codes and contracts affecting workers. Women used these new forums to make this hidden abuse, this particularly female problem, visible and to demand remedies.

Sexual harassment was one of the shared experiences that bound cannery workers at the California Sanitary Canning Company (Cal San) together. In 1939, during a record-breaking heat wave, nearly all 430 women workers, most of them Mexican Americans, walked off their fruit-canning jobs. The tremendous solidarity of this union local was built on ethnic, kinship, and neighborhood as well as gender lines. Sometimes three generations of women worked in the plant. They shared the experience of slippery floors, itchy peach fuzz, and the ever-swifter pace of production, in addition to sexual harassment. Those workers who were not Chicanas, the Russian Jews, lived in Boyle Heights in East Los

Angeles. The two ethnic groups lived on separate blocks but met at the same streetcar stops in the early morning.

Twenty-four-year-old Dorothy Ray Healey, an international vice president of the United Cannery, Agricultural, Packing and Allied Workers of America (UCA-PAWA) and a cannery worker organizer since the age of sixteen, led the campaign. The strikers established a twenty-four-hour picket line to demand that the company recognize their union and that all workers be union members. Although the workers had walked out at the height of the peach-canning season, the factory owners, the Shapiros, refused to negotiate. Neighborhood grocers donated food to sustain the strikers. Many grocers refused to stock Cal San products. The National Labor Relations Board reprimanded the Shapiros for refusing to bargain, but the stalemate continued. After two and a half months, one morning the Shapiros awoke in their comfortable house to an unusual sight. A small group of children in orderly picket lines on the Shapiros' well-manicured lawn carried signs saying "Shapiro is starving my Mama" and "I'm underfed because my Mama is underpaid." Surprised and moved, many of the Shapiros' neighbors brought the young picketers food, and several members of the Shapiros' synagogue reproached them. Finally the Shapiros agreed to meet with the union representatives. The cannery workers' success had hinged on a strategy of incorporating women workers as parts of entire kinship and friendship networks, rather than as isolated individuals. In that way, the union represented these women's own sense of themselves as whole people. Unlike many relief and welfare policies, it did not force them to choose between being workers or wives, daughters or mothers.

For women textile workers too, the boundary between "mother" and "worker" was fuzzy. By 1940 72 percent of the women workers in North Carolina's textile mills were married, up from less than half ten years earlier. To these women, having a working husband was no guarantee of security. Even if a man neither drank nor gambled away his earnings he could fall ill, and in this delicately balanced economy every cent was essential. One unemployed widow told the editor of the Greenville, North Carolina, *News* that she valued the security that came from knowing she herself was a good mill hand. What she and other women wanted was not a handout, but "a chance to earn our bread." Laid off for their inability to match the speedup of machinery or by reduced mill hours, these women wanted work, not welfare or charity.

In the South and West, some new unions attempted to organize across racial lines. Sometimes they tried more than they succeeded. When the Tobacco Workers International Union (TWIU) won a major strike in Durham, North Carolina, against Liggett & Myers in 1939, the union readily sacrificed black women workers to secure their contract. They allowed the company to mechanize the stemming department swiftly and to fire the large number of black women who worked there.

But some unions went in the other direction. The ILGWU had excluded black women from its Boston union as recently as 1933, and a victorious strike there had put black presser Mary Sweet out of work. However, a coalition of unions in New York City had created the Negro Labor Committee to advance the condition of black workers, and in 1934 the ILGWU asked Sweet to help them organize black women into the union. By the end of the year, ILGWU locals—not only in Boston but in New York, Chicago, and Philadelphia—included black women, and some had black officers. The union wage scale made some black garment workers among the best-paid women in Harlem, earning forty-five to fifty dollars for a thirty-five-hour week.

Still, the cavalier treatment of black women by many organizations dominated by white men and women contributed to the special allure of the Communist party for black women and men in the 1930s. The Communist party (CP), more than any other organization in the decade, outspokenly supported black civil rights. Even the NAACP recognized by mid-decade that it was losing its role as primary civil rights advocate to the CP. The CP also paid at least lip service to equality between men and women. In the South, it created organizations where whites and blacks worked together.

Members of the CP came from a variety of backgrounds. Mary Leonard, the widow of an Alabama druggist, had a solidly working-class background, but through her speaking abilities and her base of support among poor white housewives she became a party leader. Jane Speed was more demure in appearance than Leonard. Born into a wealthy southern family and educated in Austria, where she and her mother picked up left-wing sympathies, she appeared refined and unthreatening. Among the African-American women in the party, Estelle Milner, daughter of an Ala-

bama sharecropper, played a vital part as a young schoolteacher in linking black farmers to Communist leaders in Birmingham, Alabama. And Eula Gray, who at age nineteen in 1931 held together the Communist-aided interracial Sharecroppers' Union and spurred the organization of twenty-eight locals and twelve women's auxiliaries, came from a long line of black Alabama militants. Her great-grandfather had been a state legislator shortly after the Civil War. Her uncle Ralph, an independent farmer, was assassinated by white officials in 1931 for his role in organizing sharecroppers, and her father continued to risk his life for the same cause.

The women's auxiliaries met separately from the men in the Sharecroppers Union, both so that one parent could always stay home with the children and to divert the suspicions of local white authorities, who were hostile to this attempt on the part of sharecroppers to drive a better bargain. But the women involved themselves as intimately as the men in the main business of the union. They read the Communist newspapers and kept up a correspondence that linked them to the national and international Communist movement. Like many neighborhood women who organized in the 1930s, they emphasized their need to feed and care for their families and their inability to do so under current conditions.

Perhaps the most telling protests of the decade, the ones that brought together the threads of women's roles, the New Deal, and worker relations, were the protests by WPA sewing project workers in 1939. In that year, Congress passed a relief appropriations act that cut WPA programs in half by revising eligibility requirements for WPA employment. Among other groups, the act barred workers who could receive Aid to Dependent Children (ADC). In Minneapolis, WPA officials dismissed nine hundred women workers in early 1939, assuming they were eligible for ADC. Even if these women had been eligible, they would first have had to have ADC interviews and then await processing before they would receive any money, and the process was delayed because other people had recently been transferred into the system. Moreover, even if these women had ultimately gotten ADC, after weeks or months of no income, ADC still paid less than the WPA's work relief.

Many of the remaining women working in the sewing project, who were the chief support of their families, viewed themselves as the prime targets of the policy. WPA cuts continued into the spring. In May, fifteen hundred WPA workers voted to take a one-day holiday to protest the cuts.

They formulated demands for the reinstatement of laid-off workers and an increase in relief work budgets, and they planned a march for June 2. On that day, more than five thousand workers gathered in front of the Minneapolis WPA office. Yet on July 5 there were more layoffs and wage cuts. Workers on the Minneapolis state fairgrounds put down their tools and drove from one WPA project to the next, urging a general WPA strike. The next day, eight thousand Minneapolis workers stayed away from work, nearly closing all of the city's projects, and joining almost 125,000 relief workers on strike across the country.

After three days, the mayor of Minneapolis ordered police to go to the north Minneapolis sewing project, where fights began between women strikers and those women who continued to work. Despite a police escort through the strikers' lines, striking women harassed the non-strikers. Minnie Kohn organized a squad of women strikers who rushed the entering women workers and tore their clothes off. As one witness told the press, "It was quite a sight. The strike-breakers naked amidst the jeers of the strikers."

Even this tactic failed. On July 21 the WPA workers agreed to end the strike, having made no gains. Strikers who had missed more than five days of work were fired. At least 160 people, about one-third of them women, were brought to trial on felony charges of conspiracy to intimidate relief clients. Most of them had worked on the WPA project and were more than fifty years old. Some were self-supporting single women, and many others had families dependent on their WPA wage. Normally, they would have fit perfectly the image of crusading motherhood, as defenders of hearth and home. Instead, by taking matters into their own hands they threatened the New Deal image of women as helpless victims needing assistance.

At the trial, the attorneys and the press portrayed Kohn and her allies either as self-seeking individuals who had misled their followers (the prosecution's view) or as the victims not of job cuts but of jealous coworkers (the defense view). In neither case were they presented as working women defending their right to jobs because of their need to feed themselves and others. Minnie Kohn was sentenced to forty-five days in the workhouse. The self-expressions of militant women workers had not succeeded in altering the dominant stereotypes of women or the policies based on them.

The women who took part in these protests had refused to accept invisibility as their fate. They had taken matters into their own hands, including the matter of what it meant to be a woman struggling to survive in the 1930s. They rejected New Deal distinctions between women as workers and women as mothers, and they drew support from networks that related instead of separated neighborhood and workplace. These women met with many defeats, but they did enjoy some successes. Evictions were postponed. Wages were raised. And perhaps most important of all, women workers had made themselves seen and heard.

Histories of the Era 1920-1940

Agee, James, and Walker Evans. *Let Us Now Praise Famous Men.* Boston: Houghton Mifflin, 1941.

Cohen, Lizabeth. *Making a New Deal: Industrial Workers in Chicago, 1919-1939.* New York: Cambridge University Press, 1990.

Kelley, Robin D. G. *Hammer and Hoe: Alabama Communists During the Great Depression.* Chapel Hill: University of North Carolina Press, 1990.

Leuchtenburg, William. *The Perils of Prosperity: 1914-1932.* Chicago: University of Chicago Press, 1958.

Lynd, Robert, and Helen Lynd. *Middletown.* 1929. New York: Harcourt, Brace, 1959.

McElvaine, Robert. *The Great Depression, America, 1929-1941.* New York: Times Books, 1984.

Terkel, Studs. *Hard Times: An Oral History of the Great Depression in America.* New York: Pantheon, 1986.

Histories of Women

Acosta-Belen, Edna, ed. *The Puerto Rican Woman: Perspectives on Culture, History and Society.* New York: Praeger, 1986.

Blackwelder, Julia Kirk. *Women of the Depression: Caste and Culture in San Antonio, 1929-1939.* College Station: Texas A&M Press, 1984.

Chafe, William H. *The Paradox of Change: American Women in the Twentieth Century.* New York: Oxford University Press, 1992.

Cook, Blanche Wiesen. *Eleanor Roosevelt.* Vol. 1, 2. New York: Viking, 1992, 1999.

Cott, Nancy F. *The Grounding of Modern Feminism.* New Haven: Yale University Press, 1987.

Faderman, Lillian. *Odd Girls and Twilight Lovers: A History of Lesbian Life in Twentieth-Century America.* New York: Viking Penguin, 1992.

Hagood, Margaret. *Mothers of the South: Portraiture of the White Tenant Farm Woman.* New York: Norton, 1977.

Hall, Jacquelyn Dowd. *Revolt Against Chivalry: Jessie Daniel Ames and the Women's Campaign Against Lynching.* New York: Columbia University Press, 1979.

———, et. al. *Like a Family: The Making of a Southern Cotton Mill World.* Chapel Hill: University of North Carolina Press, 1987.

Hine, Darlene Clark. *Black Women in White: Racial Conflict and Cooperation in the Nursing Profession, 1890-1950.* Bloomington: Indiana University Press, 1989.

Low, Marie Ann. *Dust Bowl Diary.* Lincoln: University of Nebraska Press, 1984.

Mead, Margaret. *Blackberry Winter.* Magnolia, Mass.: Peter Smith, 1989.

O'Connor, Carol. *A Sort of Utopia: Scarsdale, 1891-1981.* Albany, N.Y.: SUNY Press, 1983.

Qoyawayma, Polingaysi. *No Turning Back: A True Account of a Hopi Indian's Struggle to Bridge the Gap Between the World of Her People and the World of the White Man.* Albuquerque: University of New Mexico Press, 1964.

Roosevelt, Eleanor. *The Autobiography of Eleanor Roosevelt.* 1961. New York: Da Capo Press, 1992.

Ruiz, Vicki. *Cannery Women/Cannery Lives: Mexican Women, Unionization, and the California Food Processing Industry, 1930-1950.* Albuquerque: University of New Mexico Press, 1987.

Sanchez, George J. *Becoming Mexican American: Ethnicity, Culture, and Identity in Chicano Los Angeles, 1900-1945.* New York: Oxford University Press, 1993.

Scharf, Lois. *To Work and to Wed: Female Employment, Feminism, and the Great Depression.* Westport, Conn.: Greenwood, 1980.

Shaw, Stephanie J. *What a Woman ought to Be and to Do: Black Professional Women Workers During the Jim Crow Era.* Chicago: University of Chicago Press, 1996.

Showalter, Elaine, ed. *These Modern Women: Autobiographical Essays from the Twenties.* Old Westbury, N.Y.: Feminist Press, 1978.

Wall, Cheryl A. *Women of the Harlem Renaissance.* Bloomington: Indiana University Press, 1995.

Ware, Susan. *Beyond Suffrage: Women in the New Deal.* Cambridge: Harvard University Press, 1981.

———. *Partner and I: Molly Dewson, Feminism, and New Deal Politics.* New Haven: Yale University Press, 1987.

SOCIAL AND ECONOMIC CONDITIONS

WILLIAM H. CHAFE (ESSAY DATE 1990)

SOURCE: Chafe, William H. "World War II as a Pivotal Experience for American Women." In *Women and War: The Changing Status of American Women from the 1930s to the 1940s,* edited by Maria Diedrich and Dorothea Fischer-Hornung, pp. 21-34. New York: Berg, 1990.

In the following essay, Chafe provides an overview of the changes in the social and economic roles played by women during and immediately following the end of World War II.

Few areas of American life demonstrated such rapid and dramatic change during World War II as the social and economic roles of women. Just a few months before Pearl Harbor, more than 80 percent of American men and women declared that it was wrong for wives to work outside the home if their husbands were employed. School systems throughout the country refused to hire women teachers if they were married, and fired them if they got married after being employed. Secretary of Labor Frances Perkins had denounced women as "pin money" workers for taking jobs away from needy men (the charge had no basis in fact), and the federal government itself prohibited by law the employment of two members of the same family in the civil service. Now, suddenly, all that changed. Women workers became the secret weapons of democracy's arsenal, "Womanpower," the key to victory against fascism. Those who had been told just a few years earlier that they were threatening the nation's survival by taking jobs were now enjoined to rush to the workplace as part of their sacred patriotic duty.

As it turned out, of course, much of that dramatic change disappeared with the war's end. Rosie the Riveter went back home when the soldiers returned, or at least moved to a less well-paying, less rewarding job. Some have argued that in the long run of history, especially in a subsequent era featured by the Baby Boom and the "feminine mystique," the war signified very little substantive change for women's lives. Others, including myself, have contended that despite the absence of progress toward sexual equality during the war, the behavioral changes that did occur played an important role in breaking previous patterns and setting in motion long-term, important shifts in employment patterns and sex role expectations. This essay will seek to address the issue of what changes did and did not occur in women's lives as a result of World War II. It begins by surveying briefly some of the highlights of the wartime experience and then examines three specific problem areas: (a) why there was no feminist protest when women were forced to leave their wartime jobs; (b) why child care centers never became a well-entrenched and widely accepted feature of wartime society; and (c) how to explain the paradox of women's growing employment in the postwar years in light of the Baby Boom, the "feminine mystique," and continued barriers to sexual equality.

Employment statistics convey some of the radical up and down quality of women's wartime experience in the labor force. At the beginning of the war there were only 143 women employees in seven airplane factories surveyed by the Women's

Bureau of the Department of Labor; eighteen months later the same plants employed 65,000 women. At the end of 1939 only thirty-six women were involved in the construction of ships. Three years later the figure was 160,000. As men were called to war, women took their places on assembly lines and in offices. Between 1941 and 1945 the female labor force increased by more than six million, or approximately 55 percent. Wages increased substantially, the number of women in unions grew fourfold, and women suddenly found themselves doing jobs hitherto strictly defined as men's work. In Gary, Indiana, women operated giant overhead cranes and cleaned blast furnaces, while in the state of Washington, women took the place of men lumberjacks cutting down huge redwoods.

The about-face of government propaganda on women's "proper place" suggested the dramatic changes that occurred, at least temporarily. "Getting these women into industry is a tremendous sales proposition," the head of the War Manpower Commission declared. As a result, public relations campaigns were mounted to persuade women to enter the work force. "Men are needed at the battlefront," one Office of War Information filmstrip noted; "women are needed at the home front. Men are needed with minds clear and steady. Women are needed with attention for their work undivided." Magazines were enlisted to celebrate the heroism of women war workers, and hardly a week went by without some newsreel or national publication singing the praises of women pilots, steelmakers, or taxi drivers. The impact of such messages could be seen in public opinion polls. In 1942, 60 percent of the American people declared that wives should be employed in war industries and 71 percent believed there was a need for more married women to take jobs—a striking contrast to the four out of five Americans who four years earlier had said that married women should not hold jobs if their husbands were employed.

Naturally, the most startling changes occurred in areas where defense industries were concentrated. The female labor force doubled in San Francisco, growing from 138,000 to 276,000, while in Detroit, center of the automobile industry now converted to wartime production, the increase was from 182,000 to 387,000. Overall, the number of women serving as operatives in heavy industry climbed 109 percent. Yet, other areas also showed considerable change. More than 900,000 women, for example, went to work for Uncle Sam, most of them doing clerical work with the War

Department and other agencies. By the end of the war, women comprised almost 38 percent of all federal workers, more than double the percentage in 1940. Indeed, gains in clerical fields turned out to be among the most permanent from the war years, with the ranks of women clerical workers 65 percent greater in 1948 than in 1940.

Significantly, millions of women took advantage of the war emergency to improve their economic situation. More than 700,000 war workers, for example, moved from other occupations, so that an assembly line at a typical aircraft plant consisted of former saleswomen, waitresses, stenographers, and seamstresses, as well as factory employees who had shifted from textiles to airplanes. One Women's Bureau survey showed that two-thirds of women who had previously held jobs in eating and drinking establishments moved to other jobs during the war. Nor was the reason hard to find. In addition to the rhetoric of patriotism that existed everywhere, wages and benefits were a critical incentive. Employees in defense industries received 40 percent more than those in non-defense factories. A woman shipbuilder in Mobile, Alabama took home $37 a week, a saleswoman $21, and a waitress $14. It was not surprising, then, that more than half the women employed in Mobile in 1944 had changed jobs since 1940.

The most important change produced by the war, however, had less to do with the jobs women held and more to do with the identity of the women who went to work. Throughout the history of women's gainful employment, young, single, and poor women had dominated the work force. It had become a sign of men reaching middle-class status if they could afford to support their families solely through their own work. If married women held jobs, they were seen as acting in an unseemly fashion—violating their primary and natural responsibility to their home and children. Women who wished to pursue careers ordinarily faced the necessity of foregoing marriage, since the majority of people saw the two as incompatible. It was true that most women worked at some point in their lives, but usually for just a few years, in their late teens or early twenties, before getting married.

Now, however, the primary source of recruitment for employers consisted of women who were married and middle-aged, and who often came from middle-class backgrounds. By the end of the war, it was just as likely for a wife over forty to be employed as for a single woman under twenty-five. During the war, nearly three out of four of the new women workers were married. Sixty percent were over thirty-five. By 1945, married women, for the first time, comprised almost a majority of the female labor force. Nearly 4 million of the 6.5 million women who joined the labor force listed themselves as former housewives. They may have worked at an earlier point in their lives, but given the deep prejudice in society against married women working, especially in light of the intensification of that prejudice during the Depression, it seems highly unlikely that they would ever have gone back to work had it not been for the war.

Despite such changes, there was little, if any, progress made on issues of sexual equality during World War II. Women may have done a thousand new jobs, but rarely, if ever, were they given supervisory responsibility or placed in executive positions. Women were also excluded from policy-making positions in the government, even on questions directly related to women workers. Although a Women's Advisory Commission was appointed as an adjunct to the War Manpower Commission, all the decisions were made in a group composed entirely of men, causing one woman to comment: "You can only make yourself felt . . . if you are where a thing happens, and they apparently don't happen here [in the advisory committee]." Women who served in the armed forces frequently were objects of derision, rarely receiving the credit or the autonomy they deserved. Women in the nurses corps fared better, but the army refused even to commission women doctors until 1943.

In the workplace, meanwhile, conditions often failed to measure up to the government's rhetoric of democracy and equality. Although the National War Labor Board announced a policy of equal pay for equal work in 1942, the policy was rarely implemented. Employers could simply change the label attached to a job, substituting the categories "heavy" and "light" for "male" and "female" in order to keep women's wages lower than men's. The government itself ruled that the equal-pay policy did not apply to jobs that were "historically" women's, which meant that wherever they constituted a significant majority of the work force, women would be treated less well than men. Job segregation remained the primary source of poor wages for women, and notwithstanding some breakthroughs, job segregation actually increased overall during the war, as Ruth Milkman has shown. A number of employers did significantly improve the safety features in factories, creating, as well, better recreational and rest

room facilities, which helped the morale of all employees. Still, there were too few women counselors and personnel directors to help with the problems women workers encountered—problems ranging from sexual harassment on the job to difficulties in coordinating one's work schedule with time needed for shopping, laundry, and cooking.

It was in this last area—broadly defined as community services—that absence of progress was most noticeable—and most harmful to the war effort. Virtually all women workers were being asked to do two full-time jobs simultaneously, working a forty-eight to sixty hour week in an office or factory while also managing a home. Central kitchens, take-away hot meals, communal laundries, easily accessible child care centers—all these were essential both to promote the war effort and to provide a greater possibility of securing sexual equality for women workers. A 1943 survey of defense plants showed that 40 percent of all women who left work cited marital, household, and associated difficulties as reasons; another study by the National Industrial Conference Board indicated that, after illness, family needs ranked as the cause most often given for women's absenteeism.

Yet little was done to address these problems. Some private employers, such as Kaiser in Portland, Oregon, worked to develop high-quality day-care facilities and to provide such additional services as hot take-home meals. But these were the exception rather than the rule. Although the government estimated that two million youngsters needed some form of assistance, it was not until the end of the war that federal efforts to build and run child care centers went into high gear.

The experience of women workers during the war thus seemed uneven. Some observers, noting the dramatic increase in women's economic contributions, predicted continuing change. "Women must get it out of their heads [that they belong in the home]," one prominent woman leader declared. "We are in the throes of a stupendous social revolution. Because of their work in the war, [women have] come to feel that they are socially useful. They will want to continue that feeling of independence." Certainly, the testimony of women war workers lent credence to such predictions. More than 75 percent of women in war jobs indicated that they intended to keep their positions when the war ended. As one worker said: "War jobs have uncovered unsuspected abilities in American women. Why lose all these abilities because of a belief that 'a woman's place is the home'? For some it is, for others it is not." On the other side, however, the persistence of a double standard of wages, the absence of executive opportunities, the inadequacy of community services, and the continued prevalence of traditional notions of sex roles, all suggested a more restrained, cautionary stance. What came after the war would ultimately say the most about what had been accomplished during the war itself.

On that issue, however, the results were also ambiguous. Certainly in the immediate months after the war came to an end, demobilization proved disastrous for women workers who had wanted to continue in their war jobs. Layoff rates for women workers averaged 75 percent higher than those for men. Over 800,000 workers were terminated in the aircraft industry, most of them women. Under federal legislation, returning veterans had first claim on their old jobs, which by itself put women at a disadvantage. Their problems were compounded even further by the fact that unions had kept separate seniority lists for women, thus denying female employees the accumulated benefits of their tenure vis-à-vis male union members. With the wartime crisis over, some companies even reinstituted age requirements which threw women over forty-five out of work, or reimposed earlier restrictions against hiring married women.

There was also a strong campaign by leaders in business, labor, and the mass media to reinforce traditional definitions of women's place. Congress, one Southern senator declared, should "force wives and mothers back to the kitchen" in order to assure jobs for returning veterans. Ironically, even some of the wartime propaganda to recruit women workers fed into the new campaign. In one ad, used at the end of the war, a daughter asks her working mother, dressed in overalls, "Mother, when will you stay home again?" The answer was clear. "Some jubilant day," the mother responded, "mother *will stay home again,* doing the job she likes best—making a home for you and Daddy, when he gets back." As Leila Rupp has shown, such propaganda appealed to a concept of "extended motherhood," with women war workers taking jobs in order to serve their men while away, but by implication, eager to resume their traditional way of serving loved ones after the emergency had passed.

Within a few months, what Betty Friedan later dubbed "the feminine mystique" had come to dominate American popular culture. According to this constellation of values, women could only be happy if they devoted full time to the roles of housewife and mother. College newspapers described young coeds as distraught if they were not engaged by their senior year, and young women told pollsters that they looked forward to four or more children. According to *Modern Woman: The Lost Sex,* a popular best seller, the independent woman was a "contradiction in terms." Women had to unearth the old arts of canning, preserving, and interior decorating, making household work into a creative adventure. Any woman who wanted a career must be "masculinized," neurotic, rejecting the path of "normal femininity." What modern woman needs to recapture, one magazine writer declared, "is that just being a woman is her central task and greatest honor. . . . Women must boldly announce that no job is more exacting, more necessary, or more rewarding than that of housewife and mother." The fact that such sentiments were expressed at exactly the same time as the marriage rate skyrocketed, the Baby Boom was in full swing, and the mass migration to suburbia began, all suggest that the years after the war represented a headlong return to the "good old days" of gender relationships, not some radical new departure fueled by women's wartime experiences.

But on closer examination, the story is more complicated. Despite the seemingly frantic embrace of traditional values, many women seemed dissatisfied with their role in society. "Choose any set of criteria you like," Margaret Mead wrote, "and the answer is the same: women—and men— are confused, uncertain, and discontented with the present definition of women's place in America." When a 1946 *Fortune* magazine poll asked women whether they would prefer to be born again as women or as men, a startling 25 percent declared that they would prefer to be born as men. A later poll of the 1934 graduates of the best women's colleges indicated that fully one third felt frustrated and unfulfilled.

Employment statistics, meanwhile, belied the notion that all women had returned permanently to the home after their wartime experience. Many women went back to work after the immediate impact of demobilization. Although the total number of women in manufacturing jobs declined by nearly a million between spring 1945 and winter 1946, there were still one million more women workers in the nation's factories shortly after the war than in 1940. By the end of the decade the proportion of women at work had increased to 32 percent as opposed to 27 percent a decade earlier. The change was greater than that for the entire preceding thirty years. The proportion of married women workers had increased 50 percent. Moreover, the greatest change—77 percent—occurred among women forty-five to fifty-four years old, the group most committed to retaining wartime jobs.

None of this suggested progress toward equality. Those who came back to work generally were forced to take jobs that were lower paying and less intrinsically rewarding than those they had held during the war. Although wartime clerical employees had for the most part stayed on the job, many munitions and durable good workers had now taken jobs as waitresses, saleswomen or service workers. One survey of Baltimore's women war workers showed that their average weekly wage fell from $50 to $37 by 1948. For women in manufacturing, median earnings fell from 66 percent of men's pay in 1945 to just 53 percent in 1950. Discrimination continued in professional positions as well. The number of women doctors and lawyers continued to decline.

Still, millions of women were continuing to take jobs; in ever increasing numbers, they were middle-class and married. By 1960 twice as many women were employed as in 1940, and the proportion of wives holding jobs had doubled from 15 percent in 1940 to 30 percent in 1960. The employment rate for women in the 1950s increased four times faster than that for men. Significantly, the greatest changes occurred among women who before World War II had not usually been employed. The number of married workers grew from 7.5 million in 1947 to 10.4 million in 1952. The number of mothers at work leapt 400 percent, from 1.5 million to 6.6 million. And the percentage of wives who were employed in households where the husband earned between $7,000 to 10,000 a year (clearly a middle-class salary in the 1950s) increased from 7 percent in 1950 to 25 percent in 1960. By the early 1960s, more than half of all women college graduates were at work compared with only 36 percent of those with just a high school diploma. Almost none of these women were holding jobs that were in competition with men. Most were trapped in dead-end sales and clerical positions, with little chance of promotion or increased wages. Yet they were doing jobs that women in their class and position had not previously held. In many cases, these were the same women whom Betty Friedan described as totally controlled by the feminine mystique. By the 1970s and 1980s, of course, these changes seemed moderate. The female labor force continued to swell, often dramatically, so that by the

end of the 1970s, a majority of married women were employed. Sixty percent of mothers of children aged six to seventeen were in the labor force, as were more than half of mothers with children under six. The shape of women's lifelong participation in the work force came to resemble much more the shape of men's participation, with just a few years taken out for childbearing and early child rearing.

What then are we to make of this puzzling picture? One way to proceed is to examine more closely the three questions mentioned earlier. Why was there no feminist protest when women were forced back into the home after the war ended? How did the United States manage to avoid widespread reliance on day-care centers during the war (unlike her Allies)? And what is the explanation for the continued growth of the female labor force after 1947, during a period of seeming conservatism in cultural values and an unprecedented twentieth-century birthrate? Although these questions may not seem intrinsically related, the answers, I think, help make sense of what did and did not happen to American women as a result of World War II and may offer a framework for assessing the larger question of how much change occurred.

The absence of feminist protest at the end of World War II has many explanations, but one of the most salient is the fact that feminism per se lacked substantial standing and credibility in the culture. In the years after suffrage for women was won, the feminist movement split into multiple factions, with one group in particular—the National Women's Party—claiming for itself the authority to be called "feminist." Yet this particular group was often viewed as extremist, even narrow and reactionary, because of its insistence that women be treated as identical with men, and thus denied the right to protective legislation. The National Women's Party devoted itself totally to support of the Equal Rights Amendment, but in those years, the ERA was seen by many "liberal" women as a right-wing measure. Hence, the Women's Bureau of the Department of Labor denounced ERA supporters as a "small but militant group of leisure class women [venting] their resentment at not having been born men." Thus, the feminist label was associated with a fringe group. Most other women's organizations did not unite around a common program to support the interests of women workers, and there was no viable, coherent, politically effective point of reference around which aggrieved women could organize. If we accept the contention that social protest movements require some leadership with a coherent point of view, then the absence of such leadership in 1945 offers one reason for the failure of women workers to join a feminist protest of their treatment.

A second, equally important reason for the lack of protest was the way in which the layoffs took place, the context in which they occurred, and the resources which women did or did not have to respond. By the very nature of the demobilization process, layoffs took place over time. Not every worker received her pink slip the same day. Moreover, most workers accepted the necessity of some period for reconversion. It was a time of joy and anticipation. The Allies had won. Understandably, then, there would be ambivalence and confusion over how to respond when layoffs occurred. Many were overjoyed that husbands and brothers were coming home, welcomed the opportunity to have some time off, and did not necessarily see, in immediate terms, that a pink slip meant that their jobs, or jobs like them, would never be available again. After all, wasn't protest and recrimination out of place in the midst of victory celebrations?

Finally, it was significant that those who were concerned lacked a place in which to gather to express their concern. Although women had become union members in record numbers during the war, the unions themselves had not demonstrated much concern with women's issues and had not made any substantial effort to involve women in the day-to-day policy-making or activity of the unions. With most women having to rush home after a twelve-hour day to do laundry and housework, there was little prior experience of meeting together at a union hall to discuss common grievances. In short, women did not have the benefit of a common space, or common institutions through which to express their solidarity and concern. Thus, in the moment of transition, they lacked the political organisms through which they might formulate and express their concerns.

In many ways the same lack of an alternative political and cultural perspective also helps to explain the failure of America's experiment with child care centers. Here, there was an interesting process of mutual reinforcement between popular cultural values and government policies. Although military and business leaders pressed for building day-care centers in order to assure a more reliable work force not tied to the home by family problems, politicians were reluctant to act. The idea of child care centers violated conventional notions that mothers should take care of their own children. Most policymakers appeared to agree with the Children's Bureau when it said: "A mother's primary duty is to her home and children. This duty is one that she cannot lay aside, no matter what the emergency." Reflecting the same approach, the Women's Bureau noted that "in this time of crisis . . . mothers of young children can make no finer contribution to the strength of the nation than to assure their children the security of the home, individual care and affection."

The operative words here were "individual care and affection." Child care centers were seen as impersonal, institutional, and thus a threat to the primacy of the nuclear family. Yet, as D'Ann Campbell has shown, most women retained their commitment to the nuclear family and were devoted to the idea of providing personal, family care for their children. Thus, when the government finally did commit itself to building a substantial number of day-care centers, most women workers chose not to use them, preferring instead to work out alternative, *private* arrangements for child care by enlisting either other family members or friends as caretakers. On this issue, then, devotion to traditional values of family and maternal care, together with the absence of a sanctioned, alternative set of values, helped to insure that a significant prerequisite to gender equality was not implemented. The absence of a fully-developed social and political program committed to feminism was significant, helping to explain the persistence of relatively traditional attitudes and values.

This same persistence of traditional values provides a key to understanding how women's work-force participation could continue to accelerate at the same time that the Baby Boom and the feminine mystique dominated social and cultural life. The women who went back to work after the war, and continued to take jobs during the 1950s and 1960s, were not acting from "feminist motivations." They were not competing for men's jobs, nor demanding equal pay or promotion. Rather, they were seeking jobs to "help the family," thus acting in a manner totally consistent with their traditional role as "helpmates," even as they found the only way open to them in the culture for creating a wider range of options. In short, the persistence of traditional attitudes may well have been a prerequisite for the expansion of the female labor force rather than an impediment.

It is also imperative to recognize how indispensable women's economic activity was to the development of America's postwar, consumer society. In the 1960s, Census Bureau officials noted that the number of households earning $15,000 or more would be cut in half if women's incomes were excluded. Many members of the "new middle class," in fact, could never have afforded a new home or new appliances without the wife's second income. The extent to which this second income did not involve a direct challenge to the other values of the consumer culture, including the values of the feminine mystique, simply made easier the triumph of the "affluent society." A woman could live in suburbia, have children, take care of them in their preschool years, then return to work without challenging, or even thinking about challenging, traditional gender role values.

How, then, does all this fit into the debate over the permanent impact of World War II on American women's lives? Arguably, it could support the contention that the war brought little long-range change. As Lynn Weiner and Karen Anderson have pointed out, the increase in employment among married women had already begun during the 1930s, and although virulent prejudice accompanied this increase, it still existed as an economic fact. Furthermore, the movement of women into clerical and sales positions had a long prior history. Thus, it could be argued that subsequent increases in married women's employment during the 1950s were part of a longitudinal trend that was affected little, if at all, by the Second World War experience. Furthermore, the absence of any progress on feminist issues during these years suggests a persistence, rather than an alteration, of social customs involving women.

I would still argue, however, that the war did make a significant difference, albeit in a paradoxical fashion. First, it sanctioned, and made possible, the employment of married women who were middle-aged and middle-class. Regardless of the increase in the number of married women in the work force during the 1930s, the female work force still consisted primarily of younger and poorer women, and it was still viewed as socially inappropriate for older, more well-off married women to work. Now, with the war, it was these middle-class women who took jobs *with the approval* of the dominant culture.

Second, it was these same women who went back to work after demobilization and helped to make possible the growth of the female labor force—and of a burgeoning middle class—during the 1950s and 1960s. Indeed, there was a clear, cultural logic to the changes in the female labor force after World War II. During the period 1945 to 1960, most new women workers were married women whose children were already in school. Then during the 1960s and 1970s, women in their primary childbearing age led the increase among women workers, culminating in the explosive growth of employment among young mothers in more recent times. I would argue that this cultural logic had its starting point with the sanctioned participation of middle-aged, married women during the war, and that ironically, the very absence of agitation about feminist issues during and after the war helped to facilitate acceptance of the growth in the female labor force.

Finally, I would like to propose that these changes, indirectly at least, had the paradoxical effect of facilitating the development of feminist protest during the 1960s and 1970s. The employment changes that began with the war did not cause the feminist challenge of recent decades. But by creating a basis in social reality for the idea that a woman's "place" is not in the home, and by creating an audience of women who knew firsthand how unequal their treatment in the work force was, these changes helped to provide a crucial precondition for the emergence of a coherent political movement that challenged traditional values regarding women's and men's proper roles. It was precisely such a movement that did not exist at the conclusion of World War II, and which, in the end, may have been possible only as a result of changes set in motion during World War II. Thus, paradoxically, the war did not create a revolution in women's lives. But it may eventually have helped to create a context in which another generation could attempt a revolution.

Select Bibliography

Anderson, Karen. *Wartime Women: Sex Roles, Family Relations, and the Status of Women during World War II.* Westport: Greenwood, 1982.

Campbell, D'Ann. *Women at War with America: Private Lives in a Patriotic Era.* Cambridge, Mass.: Harvard University Press, 1984.

Chafe, William H. *The American Woman: Her Changing Social, Economic, and Political Roles, 1920-1970.* London: Oxford University Press, 1972.

Clive, Alan. "Women Workers in World War II: Michigan as a Test Case." *Labor History* 20 (Winter 1979).

Hartmann, Susan M. *The Home Front and Beyond: American Women in the 1940s.* Boston: Twayne, 1982.

Honey, Maureen. *Creating Rosie the Riveter: Class, Gender, and Propaganda during World War II.* Amherst: University of Massachusetts Press, 1984.

Kessler-Harris, Alice. *Out to Work: A History of Wage Earning Women in the United States.* London: Oxford University Press, 1982.

Milkman, Ruth. "Redefining 'Women's Work': The Sexual Division of Labor in the Auto Industry during World War II." *Feminist Studies* 8, no. 2 (Summer 1982).

Rupp, Leila. *Mobilizing Women for War: German and American Propaganda, 1939-1945.* Princeton: Princeton University Press, 1978.

Skold, Karen. "The Job He Left Behind: Women and Shipyard Workers in Portland, Oregon during World War II." In Carol R. Berkin and Clara M. Lovett, eds., *Women, War, and Revolution.* New York: Holmes & Meier, 1980.

Weiner, Lynn. *From Working Girl to Working Mother: The Female Labor Force in the United States, 1820-1980.* Chapel Hill: University of North Carolina Press, 1986.

ELLEN CHESLER (ESSAY DATE 1992)

SOURCE: Chesler, Ellen. "Organizing for Birth Control." In *Woman of Valor: Margaret Sanger and the Birth Control Movement in America,* pp. 223-42. New York, N.Y.: Anchor Books, Doubleday, 1992.

In the essay below, Chesler documents and discusses Sanger's efforts to promote birth control legislation in the United States, emphasizing the democratic aspect of the movement.

If the dreamer in Margaret survived through the 1920s, it was hidden from all but an intimate few. What had been an outsider's begrudging accommodation to the role of elites in accomplishing change became an insider's willful determination to manipulate the system on her own terms.

In 1922, after considerable lobbying of dubious New York State officials, Margaret incorporated the American Birth Control League in accordance with the laws governing not-for-profit charitable institutions and set out an ambitious and far-reaching declaration of intentions that included public education, legislative reform, medical research in contraception, and the actual provision of services. The league was to be a national voluntary organization headquartered in New York. It would spawn affiliates at the state and local level throughout the country, while also acting as a vehicle for Margaret's leadership aspirations on an international scale.

To manage the new enterprise, she simply expanded the board of directors and staff that she already had in place to publish the *Birth Control Review.* She took charge with the assistance of her personally loyal, if not always professionally seasoned, entourage of women, some comfortably middle-class, and others who were very well-to-do, including Juliet Rublee as vice president of the board, Frances Ackerman, a long-standing Manhattan volunteer, as treasurer, and Anne Kennedy as a paid, full-time executive director. Margaret took no salary for herself, but lived off expense money, book and lecture fees, and eventually, most of all, the generosity of her wealthy second husband, Noah Slee.

Kennedy, a capable but somewhat eccentric and emotionally erratic woman, found her way into the birth control movement after a messy divorce. Margaret's sense of mission gave renewed meaning to her life, and her devotion in return was especially intense. In their first year, Kennedy and a handful of volunteers distributed an estimated 75,000 pamphlets, more than 300,000 letters, and twelve different books about birth control, including Margaret's own. Somewhere from 15,000 to 30,000 copies of the *Birth Control Review* were printed at the highest point of its circulation, with paid subscriptions augmented by newsstand distribution and by Kitty Marion's indefatigable street sales in New York. This outreach, in turn, produced 18,000 paid memberships and an additional 132,000 inquiries by letter and phone. The budget grew to more than $38,000, and a plan of expansion was adopted that nearly doubled that amount the following year. In 1925 alone, the league's Motherhood Department answered almost 30,000 letters from women who wrote for practical advice on contraception, infertility, and a whole host of sexual problems, referring them to sympathetic local doctors where possible, or just offering words of understanding, since the mailing of practical instruction remained illegal. In some instances, volunteers, including Margaret herself, also took letters home and answered them privately, removing the organization from legal liability.[1]

The mail was Margaret's link to popular American culture. Thousands of the letters she received were destroyed, but surviving examples bear witness to the often tragic circumstances of women from Maine to California who were unable to find reliable contraceptive guidance. They wrote of strict and falsely modest mothers who had told them nothing of sex or birth control, of callous physicians who claimed ignorance of reliable methods, of husbands who abandoned them when they chose continence over the risk of another pregnancy, of illegal abortionists who cost them their fertility. They wrote with a sisterly affection and intimacy made possible by distance and anonymity, often not even asking about contraception but instead confessing sexual anxieties or transgressions. A nineteen-year-old woman from Tarrant, Alabama, confided in 1924:

> Dear Friend. What I am going to tell you this afternoon has never been breathed to a single soul

but the one who was the cause of it. . . . What I am fixing to tell you is a hidden chapter in my life, and the reason I choose you to "bare my heart to" was because you are far away and you do not know me and because I have to have some advice and I believe you will tell me what to do and tell me the right thing.

The overwrought letter went on to report a family history of poverty and parental abuse followed by a brief love affair with a young man named Tom whom the correspondent had met at work. He had made her pregnant, secured her an illegal abortion, and then abandoned her. The dilemma she posed for Margaret was this: should she tell a new boyfriend who wanted to marry her about this complicated—perhaps, some would say, sordid—past? Margaret wrote back immediately with enormous and respectful compassion:

> You must not think of yourself or your relations with Tom, whom you have loved, in the wrong light. If you loved him and he loved you, any relations between you were just as holy and as pure in the sight of God as if a marriage certificate had been given you. You must not look upon this relationship as if you were a bad girl.

Assuring the girl that no physical evidence of her prior relations was likely to be detected, she also encouraged her not to say anything if the knowledge would upset her new beau. "Keep your head high and your heart light," the letter cautioned.

The sheer volume of this confessional correspondence testified to Margaret's continued notoriety and the extent to which her personal magnetism helped sustain the birth control cause. Just how well-known she became is impossible to measure with precision, but the mail at least confirms that substantial numbers of poor women on farms and in small towns came to identify her with their concerns. "If I could only be one part as sporty as you have been, I'd be so happy," wrote the wife of a cotton-mill worker in Weaver, Alabama.[2]

In this respect, the birth control movement had a democratic impact, which its own paid constituency surely did not reflect. The typical league member was an upper-middle-class, thirty-five-year-old housewife still in her childbearing years—white, native-born, Protestant, and identified as politically "independent"—though about one fourth reported foreign-born parents. And when willing to list party affiliation, just over half said they were Republicans, while 8 percent identified themselves as Socialists, reflecting the movement's, and Margaret's own, idiosyncratic histories. Nevertheless, the *typical* female member was

also married to a college graduate who earned $3,000 per year, or well above the national average, and the vast majority of the men who belonged to the organization independent of their wives (about 17 percent of the total) were identified as professionals or academics.

At first, membership accounted for up to a third of the league's total budget, and an ambitious expansion was anticipated, but the various objectives of the organization quickly came into conflict. Along with advocacy, Margaret's goal was to mobilize local groups to provide clinical birth control services throughout the country. To this end, a field operation was immediately put into place to revive dormant interest in the nine states where it had existed prior to the end of World War I. As state and local leagues flourished, however, they drained energy and money from the parent organization. Over the years, various formulas would be adopted requiring them to share a portion of their membership receipts with New York, but the tension was never fully resolved. To offset its losses in 1925, the American Birth Control League tried assembling a national council of wealthy and professionally prominent individuals. Of some 250 members, almost half were listed in *Who's Who in America,* or had spouses with that distinction, but this did not automatically translate into funding, and the national operation's growth quickly leveled off and then declined, as did that of the *Birth Control Review.*[3]

Organized birth control, in fact, advanced only tentatively through the 1920s with the formation of state affiliates and local clinics as its major achievement. The most substantial impact by far was made in New York City, where Margaret concentrated her personal energies and resources on the Birth Control Clinical Research Bureau she founded in 1923, in an office next door to the league's. This pioneering medical facility later moved to independent space and became enormously successful, a story to which we shall return. Meanwhile, birth control organizations were, in fact, revived or begun anew outside New York through the efforts of women and social welfare activists.

In 1923 in Chicago, Rachelle Yarros, a physician and reformer who lived at Hull House and had long publicly advocated contraception, reactivated the Illinois Birth Control League, which had formed briefly after Margaret's speech at the Stockyards seven years earlier. Motivated by the extremely high incidence of illegal abortion she discovered among women in the city's Jewish immigrant neighborhoods, Dr. Yarros then opened a clinic modeled after the work of Marie Stopes in London. Her backers included a staid University of Chicago demographer by the name of James Field, and Harold and Anna Ickes, the prominent local attorney who would subsequently serve in the Roosevelt administration, and his first wife. At first they publicly disavowed Margaret, casting their lot instead with Mary Ware Dennett's organization, but after Margaret came to Chicago later that year, they changed their minds and sponsored a conference under the auspices of the American Birth Control League. This conclave was specifically targeted to social welfare groups concerned with "practical and feasible methods of decreasing dependency and delinquency." Its stated purpose was "to seek the reduction of the burden of charities and taxation resultant from the support of the dependent and the defective classes." Its clear intent was to distance Margaret from her former radical associations in order to make her more acceptable to new audiences like theirs.

The approach worked. Within a decade, five additional birth control facilities were operating in Chicago under Yarros's aegis, one of them at Hull House itself, and close to 22,000 indigent women had been served. All were affiliated with the American Birth Control League. The city's Jewish social service agency also opened a clinic, which gained national recognition with a program that sent visiting nurses into the homes of clients to instruct them in the use of diaphragms and other matters of sexual hygiene. By 1941, ten local facilities joined in a voluntary family planning confederation, for a brief time calling themselves Margaret Sanger Centers, to honor the woman who had in the interim gained international acclaim, and whose name was by then thought to have substantial publicity value with the larger public.[4]

Similarly, birth control agitation in Los Angeles, where a local league and the nation's third clinic were founded in 1925, traced its roots to Margaret's first appearance there before the war and to the subsequent organization of a local Committee of 100 in response to the national publicity generated by Ethel Byrne's hunger strike. With the war's interference, no further birth control activity occurred for nine years, until the Los Angeles Mothers' Clinic was formed with the cooperation of the city and county boards of health, the Bureau of Charities, several medical societies and philanthropic organizations. In the still progressive political atmosphere of the west, no effective political or religious opposition

materialized, and the clinic's future was secured further by a substantial endowment from a local benefactress. Even so, it still only serviced about 1,500 clients a year.

No legacy survived of Margaret's prewar activity in San Francisco, where IWW activity and anarchist agitation had been particularly virulent, but a birth control league was founded there in 1924, in response to a visit by native daughter Anne Kennedy. Efforts to start a clinic failed until 1929, when several women doctors, working at the local Children's Hospital, encouraged a group of volunteer aides to join them in offering birth control services off the premises. Their first Maternal Health Center opened in a baby clinic sponsored by the local chapter of the American Association of University Women, which, regrettably, then reneged on its offer of space in the face of protest by Catholic members. The operation moved nearby, however, and a second one was also opened in an Oakland cottage belonging to the Children's Home Society.[5]

The pattern was similar elsewhere. Margaret had addressed a crowded audience of about 1,000 supporters in Detroit in 1916, but the only postwar emissary of her efforts there was a local dowager named Mrs. William McGraw, who used to return from vacations in New York carrying diaphragms from the birth control offices on lower Fifth Avenue, which she then distributed to needy women from her room in an elegant local residence hotel. In this manner, she evaded federal Comstock laws prohibiting shipment by mail. Mrs. McGraw was willing to finance a clinic but was unable to find any organizational support apart from a few members of the International Ladies Garment Workers Union. In 1926 several women active in Jewish philanthropy then raised $1,000 privately and prevailed on the local Jewish Welfare Board for an additional $3,000 to open the first birth control clinic between New York and Chicago. Several small clinics were also annexed to Detroit's two major maternity hospitals. A state group, calling itself the Michigan Maternal Health League in order to avoid some of the controversy associated with the name "birth control," organized in 1930 and expanded in response to heavy unemployment in the automobile and steel industries during the Depression. Still, inadequate funding, timidity in the face of opposition, and difficulty in getting supplies meant that fewer than 10,000 women were reached by Michigan's affiliated birth control agencies in their first decade of operation.

In nearby Cleveland, Margaret had been the guest of Eastern European Jewish radicals when she spoke before the war. Frederick Blossom then managed to mobilize an active local birth control constituency, including establishment reformers. This coalition fell apart, however, when anarchist Ben Reitman was arrested and jailed in Cleveland in 1916 for distributing birth control fliers, and when a visit the following year by the locally bred Socialist, Rose Pastor Stokes, again stirred controversy. The intense publicity left the progressive elite quite wary of the issue, and it was not until 1923 that several young women from the local Junior League again demonstrated interest, ostensibly propelled to action by the reported suicide of an indigent mother who drowned herself in Lake Erie, rather than face another pregnancy. The Junior Leaguers then formed a deliberately cautious Maternal Health League, and five years later, after a subsequent visit to Cleveland by Margaret, they also started a clinic. Operating with referrals from the Associated Charities of Cleveland, the facility served about 1,000 women per year.[6]

The Baltimore experience was unique. In 1927, the staid physicians of Johns Hopkins University, not yet convinced that Margaret Sanger was doing good work, agreed to sponsor a five-year experiment among their dispensary patients who exhibited clear medical indications for contraception. Their proposal was advertised to every physician, hospital, and social agency in the state of Maryland. But with a handful of women doctors working only part-time and devoting up to an hour for each patient visit, even this well-connected effort wound up handling little more than 1,000 cases in total.

Elsewhere, the American Birth Control League in New York sent its own organizers into the field. In 1925, Margaret hired James Cooper, M.D., a former instructor at Boston University's medical school, who had recently returned from medical missionary work in China. Cooper acted as her emissary to professional medical societies, which would never have deigned to listen to a lay woman propagandist. Until his resignation in 1929, he traveled to virtually every state in the nation and reached thousands of physicians through individual contacts and lectures, his reputation considerably enhanced by the publication of his *Technique of Contraception,* the first well-regarded technical text on the subject. In journeys of more than 40,000 miles, he also mobilized social workers, nurses, volunteers, and businessmen to support birth control affiliates. Another field secretary by the name of Henriette Hart explained in a memo summarizing her activities for 1927 that it had been necessary to hold a total of twenty-seven separate meetings in eleven different communities in order to get a state league going in New Jersey, which then raised several thousand dollars to open a single birth control clinic in downtown Newark.

By 1930, there were also small facilities advertising themselves as birth control clinics in Cincinnati, Atlanta, Denver, and San Antonio. A sociologist surveying the movement's progress identified thirty clinics nationwide, though her figure was deceptive, because it incorporated some negligible operations annexed to private practices or hospitals. Indeed, in 1930, Margaret's own Birth Control Clinical Research Bureau in New York alone serviced almost twice as many patients as all of the rest of the clinics in the country combined.[7]

The law prohibited contraception outright in Massachusetts and Connecticut, and for almost a decade Catholic threats there effectively quieted local activists. Then in 1928, Dr. Antoinette Konikow was arrested in Boston for distributing a handbill advertising a lecture on birth control and sex hygiene. The incident propelled the imperious Blanche Ames back into action to reform the state obscenity statute. Ames brought Margaret up to speak, but a birth control bill introduced in the state legislature never made it beyond committee, and several small clinics that opened around the state during the Depression were closed down by police raids in 1937—raids launched on the authority of the Commonwealth's original Comstock provisions of 1879. A case was brought on behalf of the clinic in Salem, but the statute was sustained in the lower courts and by the Massachusetts Supreme Court, which refused to make any exceptions to the ban on distributing contraception, even for licensed physicians. In neighboring Connecticut, clinics were opened in New Haven, Danbury, Greenwich, and Waterbury. The closing of the Waterbury facility in 1939 also provoked a legal challenge, but as in Massachusetts, state courts sustained the action, and all the clinics shut down after a final appeal was lost in 1940. Connecticut had no organized birth control services until 1961, when services were made available through Planned Parenthood in New Haven. The forced closing of this operation provided the test case that wound its way to the United States Supreme Court four years later and resulted in the historic ruling in *Griswold v. Connecticut,* when the Supreme Court finally accepted jurisdiction and declared contraception a constitutional right of married Americans.[8]

Yet even where birth control was legal, the cautious interpretation of provisions governing the transport of supplies and the eligibility of patients also acted as impediments to growth of the movement overall. Progress rested largely on the voluntary efforts of women whose financial and organizational resources never kept pace with their dedication to the cause, and whose sense of propriety in some cases actually compromised their effectiveness. Increasingly conservative by temperament, many of the new generation of activists outside New York shied away from publicity for fear of provoking controversy, and this made it especially hard for needy clients to find them. Many clinics, shunned by established social welfare networks that feared reprisals from Catholic voluntary agencies, were cut off from professional referrals. What is more, medical indications for birth control were often construed narrowly to conform to the letter of laws defining medical eligibility, while, at the same time, economic criteria for clinic service were also established, so as not to offend private physicians who were quick to voice their dismay about middle-class women receiving a subsidy. Finally, doubts were raised about the efficacy and cost of the recommended diaphragm procedure. All in all, there seem to have been almost as many constraints on expansion as there were incentives for growth.

Even so, numerous small clinics sprouted up, in response to increased attention and demand brought on by the Depression. By the mid-1930s birth control leagues existed in more than half the states, and there were at one point as many as 300 clinics. Still, it was unreasonable to expect that the essentially voluntary efforts of women could possibly result in comprehensive service delivery. Until the marketing of the pill and the provision of federal funding in the 1960s, the growth of birth control clinics stalled.

However, halting, the slow progress of this clinic organization was still more substantial than the league's legislative accomplishments. Despite her bleak view of politicians, Margaret grew convinced that birth control would never win full acceptance as a social and medical practice while the onus of illegality still hung over it. In 1923 she persuaded Samuel Rosenman, then a well-connected young legislator from Manhattan, but soon to become senior speech writer and adviser to Franklin Roosevelt, to sponsor a new birth control bill in the New York State Assembly. The measure affirmatively licensed physicians to prescribe contraception for reasons of health, in accordance with the judicial ruling she had achieved earlier. The support of a mainstream Democrat was noteworthy, and the bill was also widely endorsed by grass-roots women's organizations, including, for the first time, the 10,000 member New York State League of Women Voters. Several leading Manhattan physicians also testified in its behalf, along with the same cast of liberal clergymen, university professors, and society women who had been to Albany to lobby for birth control in years past. To restore the effort's credibility as an issue for working people, Margaret also recruited Norman Thomas, then head of a Socialist Labor organization called the League for Industrial Democracy. Thomas gave a rousing speech to those who convened in the state capital to push the bill, but his appearance, however well-intended, did little to further its prospects.

When Margaret herself was scheduled to address this lobby, the mayor of the substantially Catholic town of Albany arbitrarily revoked the permit licensing the hotel meeting room where she was to speak. Her appearance was canceled and then moved to a private home. Once again, the intervention provoked a militant confrontation and created a rash of newspaper publicity, furthering the educational objectives of the movement but, at the same time, entrenching the opposition and effectively killing any hope of victory. In a sarcastic editorial in the *Birth Control Review,* Margaret then attacked the integrity of the elected officials who stood by in the face of this "despotism" and refused to grant her a respectful hearing. She suggested facetiously that "intelligence tests"—then still the rage of eugenicists and psychologists—be required for all legislators. The Rosenman bill never made it out of the Assembly Codes Committee, but the virtue of pursuing a strategy of legal reform at the state level was nonetheless affirmed, either because of Margaret's persuasiveness, or perhaps because the strategy replicated the prior efforts of suffragists, who had spent years in the states before focusing on Washington.

The weight of Margaret's argument for a doctor's preference also prevailed, even over Mary Ware Dennett's efforts in Washington. Dennett had strongly opposed Margaret's decision to pursue a legislative campaign in Albany. Earlier she had promised to support Margaret's efforts to establish clinics, if Margaret in turn stayed out of politics, a compromise Margaret saw no reason to make. In December of 1923, on her sixteenth request, Dennett finally enlisted Sen. Albert B. Cummins of Iowa, then president pro tempore of the Senate, to introduce her legislation, but this time she made a concession to Margaret by inserting a provision requiring five physicians to certify the reliability of any contraceptive product protected by law. Hearings were held by a joint subcommittee of the judiciary committees of the House and Senate, but the Cummins-Vaile bill (identified by the names of its Senate and House sponsors, the latter, Colorado Congressman William N. Vaile) then stalled and never got to the floor of either chamber. Support eroded for Dennett's goal of trying to repeal the federal Comstock statutes altogether, and within a year her Voluntary Parenthood League closed down, leaving Margaret's hegemony over the birth control movement uncontested. Dennett more or less retired to writing and subsequently attacked Margaret publicly in a book entitled *Birth Control Laws,* which made a final plea for the repeal of the federal Comstock statutes. "The poor sick woman has failed in her work and in order to explain her failure, she throws the blame on me and my work and early views, most of them very good but *radical,*" Margaret confided in a private letter. To Juliet, she described it as "devilish and cruel," but she refrained from public comment.[9]

However much she scorned Dennett in private, Margaret saw an opening for herself in this legislative setback on Capitol Hill. During the 1924 Presidential campaign, she quietly made an effort to put birth control on the national political agenda by enlisting Oswald Garrison Villard, the eminent publisher of *The Nation,* to talk to Progressive Presidential candidate Robert LaFollette about it. Predictably, however, LaFollette resisted embracing a contentious issue that would inevitably detract from the major domestic issues of his campaign. Delegates to the major party conventions were also lobbied on birth control that year, but to no avail.

After two years without any birth control activity in Washington, Margaret then decided to try to fill the vacuum by attempting some lobbying of her own devising. In 1926, she sent Anne Kennedy to Washington to test the waters for a "physicians' bill," but after surveying the scene, Kennedy left without even drafting legislation, convinced any effort would probably be futile, and that money was better expended elsewhere for the time being. Told by Senator Cummins that he had never been able to get his bill taken seriously—by others that it was "the laughing stock of the cloakroom"—Kennedy encouraged Margaret to invest in more public education.[10]

While in Washington, Kennedy also went to interview a National Catholic Welfare Conference public relations deputy by the name of Patrick J. Ward, whom she understood to be the official spokesman of the organization. Kennedy subsequently transcribed the interview, had Ward sign off on its contents, and then quoted him in an American Birth Control League circular saying that the NCWC was organizing a special committee to fight birth control openly and to legislate for Catholics and non-Catholics alike, according to the dictates of the church. When Kennedy made the contents of the interview public, however, Father John Burke, general secretary of the NCWC, first angrily denied that Ward had any authority to speak at all for the organization and then subsequently challenged the authenticity of Kennedy's account. Predictably annoyed, Margaret published a scathing attack in *The New Republic.*

She also intensified her public excoriation of the Catholic Church. In a particularly extreme example from 1928, the *Birth Control Review* carried an article by the journalist Floyd Dell called "The Anti-Birth Control Neurosis." A popularizer of Freudian theory, Dell boldly charged that Catholic clerics who opposed birth control were really just counteracting their own impotency anxiety. This kind of material was certainly not calculated to win support from Catholics—or from any politicians for that matter.

Having all but given up on partisan politics for the moment, Margaret attacked the Democrats for nominating New York's Catholic Governor, Al Smith, as their candidate for President and voted for Herbert Hoover, just to be safe. Nevertheless, she continued to file legislation in Albany to repeal the state's birth control laws, as she had been doing each year since 1923, only to have it repeatedly stalled in committee. By 1929, an opposition led by Catholic interests had rallied in force, and public lobbies for and against birth control met head to head in the Capitol chambers.[11]

The frustrations of continued setbacks and political defeats weighed heavily upon her, and Margaret blamed them for the periodic bouts of depression that began to plague her again in mid-decade. This recurrent malaise may also have been occasioned by the loss of her revered older sister, Mary, who died in 1926 from the complications of a ruptured appendix. Always the compliant domestic servant, Mary simply refused to tell anyone she wasn't feeling well before it was too late. In this respect and all others, the two sisters could not have been more different, or followed more divergent paths. They saw each other infrequently, if at all. Yet when Mary was operated on in 1925 in Buffalo, where for almost thirty years she had worked for the same family, Margaret at long last went up to visit. She returned soon thereafter for the funeral and noted in her journal that Mary had been "the stable sympathetic member of a large family. Her passing loosens up the foundations." With a small bequest from Mary, she built a rose arbor in her memory.

A still feisty Michael Higgins survived his oldest daughter, and Margaret also observed the irony of this situation, but within weeks of Mary's death, he suffered a severe stroke at the cottage in Truro, where he was living. He spent the following year as an invalid. When he then died at the ripe age of eighty-eight, most of his children did not even bother to attend the funeral. Margaret, however, did make the trip to Corning and took Grant along with her, who many years later recalled his horror that Michael had been buried apart from his wife at the cemetery's edge. Yet no observation of these events appears in Margaret's journals or correspondence, just as there is no record of any response by her father to her work. He would emerge as a far larger presence in her autobiographies than in these less self-conscious materials.[12]

Though scarcely mentioned, the deaths may nonetheless have been deeply felt. Margaret wrote frequently during this period to such intimate friends as Juliet and Hugh, confiding the wish that she might abandon America altogether for the more tolerant and happy atmosphere of Europe. Pampered and undisciplined, Juliet had long since tired of birth control and was preoccupied with archaeology and filmmaking, her two newest passions. En route to Italy in 1925, where she was about to descend to the ocean floor in a cylinder to look for ruins, she scribbled back to Margaret: "Darling—we must hurry—hurry—hurry—to pass B.C. on to others so that we can work for this other, super, bigger thing which will make men and women into Gods and Goddesses. B.C. was a necessary step, but useless unless we can also create finer human beings spiritually and mentally. . . . The desire and will to Freedom & free imagination & aspiration—Realization of all the Beauties & joys they have dreamed of, must be stirred and awakened in women just as you have succeeded in stirring & awakening them to a desire to control their own bodies."

Such romantic excess was characteristic of the letters the two women often exchanged. Juliet would tempt Margaret to slip away and indulge in the loftier personal and intellectual pursuits to which they had been introduced by the Wantley circle. This was no simple invitation to sexual promiscuity, but an honestly perceived commitment to the development of a higher and more spiritually attuned life—an idealized existence set apart from the turmoil of the real world. Invariably, Margaret would agree, promising to let go and allow others to carry on the more mundane matters of birth control, but then she would find an excuse to recant, usually arguing that she could find no one with comparable vision to succeed her.[13]

In fact, her international stature had grown substantially as a result of Dennett's decline and in the wake of the American Birth Control League's sponsorship in New York in 1925 of the Sixth International Neo-Malthusian Conference and Birth Control. Neo-Malthusian sympathizers of various European nationalities had been meeting together since 1900, when a first conclave was held in Paris, which Emma Goldman attended. Delegates gathered again in Belgium in 1905, in the Netherlands in 1910, and in Germany a year later. Little came of these prewar sessions other than spirited debate about the relevance of Malthusian doctrine to Marxism. But the fifth session, in London in 1922, which Margaret attended, had attracted the attention of mainstream economists, demographers, social theorists and physicians, including such notable figures as John Maynard Keynes and H. G. Wells. As birthrates in the West declined, interest began to develop, albeit slowly, in the problems of unrestrained population growth in the developing nations.

The 1925 gathering in New York then drew more than 1,000 delegates, produced four volumes of papers, was covered extensively by the press and made a significant impression on professional, scholarly, and political audiences. Among the participants from Europe was Aletta Jacobs, M.D., and from the United States, the Freudian A. A. Brill, the Socialist Norman Thomas, and the flamboyant feminist and pacifist Rosika Schwimmer, who would be denied United States citizenship in 1929 in a historic Supreme Court case challenging her refusal to promise to bear arms in defense of her country. Also attending were numbers of professionals from medicine and the social sciences who were less controversial but perhaps more influential. Having hosted this event and been left with the responsibility of perpetuating international contacts and cooperation, Margaret was enjoying new prominence in what was becoming a movement of worldwide interest.[14]

The conference hardly provided an excuse to retreat from her public responsibilities as Juliet beckoned, but it did present an opportunity to indulge the fantasy of spending more time in Europe, where the demands of international leadership could more comfortably accommodate intellectual, aesthetic, and no doubt romantic opportunities, as well. With the business of clinic organization at home proceeding slowly, and with legislative reform in Albany and Washington stalled, Margaret decided to grant herself a sabbatical from her obligations in the United States and once again go abroad.

In June of 1926, she announced to the New York newspapers that she would be taking a leave of absence from the American league to study and prepare for another international conference scheduled the following year in Geneva, home of the League of Nations, whose delegates she sought to impress with the importance of population doctrine to world peace and prosperity. She did not resign from the organization, but instead named as acting president a formidable younger woman named Eleanor Dwight Jones, who had risen out of the ranks of birth control volunteers.

Mrs. F. Robertson Jones, as she liked to be known, was the wife of an establishment New York lawyer, and her many concessions to social convention may have deceived Margaret into believing that she had chosen a deferential stand-in. Instead, Jones emerged as a determined, independent presence, and with Margaret no longer around to interfere, she quickly instituted more professional standards of management for the organization. She regularized what had been fairly lax administrative practices, streamlined fund-raising, established formal accounting procedures, and instituted changes in governance, which diffused powers the president had previously exercised unilaterally.[15]

Margaret was not initially averse to these changes. She recognized the need to introduce formal procedures to an operation that had expanded substantially from its beginnings as a largely volunteer cause, whose leaders were emotionally driven. Indeed, she returned to the United States briefly in 1927 and agreed to a series of Jones's proposals, including her desire to remove Anne Kennedy, an original recruit and a close personal friend of Margaret's, from the organization altogether. Margaret apparently promised to

find Anne a position in private business but then went back to Europe and did nothing about it. Later that year, Mrs. Jones then fired Kennedy outright, ostensibly because she had neglected to file daily expense sheets in connection with her field activities, though staff and board members who wrote confidentially to Margaret about the incident said that overall insubordination to Jones underlay the action. Recognizing the unhappy truth that the old-timers were accustomed to more or less making up rules as they went along and would probably never be able to accommodate to professional standards of accountability, Margaret brought Anne over to Europe temporarily to assist with the Geneva conference. She then sent her off to Cleveland, where she helped organize the clinic there, and then for an entire year drove herself by car through the midwestern states and as far away as Texas, in some cases literally knocking on the doors of strangers, to introduce herself and the birth control cause. Later, Margaret helped secure a permanent position for her with a company manufacturing diaphragms. Margaret complained that Jones had been clumsy in handling the departure but went along with it nonetheless. Indeed, of her own accord and in an identical spirit of committing herself to a higher level of professionalism, she also found a position outside the movement for Anna Lifschiz, her devoted secretary of more than thirteen years, who had been with her since the days of the Brownsville Clinic.[16]

Margaret may have been willing to sacrifice some of her most loyal associates, but she was not prepared to allow the league's new administrative regulations and procedures to interfere with her own work. In 1928, when she returned to New York permanently and resumed the presidency of the organization, she found herself in the untenable position of being a supplicant to a board of directors, whose views did not always reflect her own. Like most self-styled pioneers in social causes, she did not always move gracefully among a second generation of reformers who brought a corporate mentality to an endeavor in which they had far less of a personal stake. A deep emotional investment in her work and a temperamental disdain for the give-and-take of bureaucracy made her testy toward newcomers who thought they knew better than she did. On the other hand, she was happy to have them carry on independently when she wasn't prepared to pay attention, as this same group of women had done reasonably well during the eighteen months she spent in Europe.

On her return, minor disputes arose over the most trivial of expenditures, and in June of 1928, telling Juliet that she could not do her best work in an atmosphere that had sacrificed "spirit, love and trust" to "rules and regulations," Margaret submitted her resignation as president. She tried to name her own successor by engineering the election of Charlotte Delafield, a current vice president and director of the organization who had been loyal in the past, but when that maneuver failed, she acquiesced to the permanent election of Eleanor Jones. Her official letter of resignation acknowledged a growing interest in birth control research and clinical service, along with a recognition that the league had reached a new stage of "maturity and organization" and was moving forward in its educational and legislative objectives without her. She could afford to be gracious, because the league board had worked out an agreement allowing her to remain as a director and also retain her title as editor-in-chief of the *Birth Control Review*. She thought she could continue to exercise control where she wanted it, without being president.[17]

But within months, this carefully constructed détente proved unworkable. Margaret had initially incorporated and always administered the Birth Control Clinical Research Bureau as an autonomous legal and financial entity, wholly independent of the league, and she insisted it should remain so. Mrs. Jones argued instead that the parent organization had made important policy decisions with respect to the clinic and should continue in an advisory role. Cordial relations quickly deteriorated between the two women, and the resolution of legitimate differences became impossible. Margaret convinced herself that Jones was, on the one hand, a timid soul who only did what her lawyer-husband advised her to do, and on the other, a personally ambitious woman whose foremost interest was self-aggrandizement. In Margaret's view, Jones displayed an impertinent disregard for her own judgment and years of prior experience. The final break came when Jones, having lost the battle over the clinic, tried to reclaim control of the *Review* by appointing an editorial advisory board. Margaret then angrily resigned altogether, leaving the magazine behind, but taking the clinic with her.

"Politics, jealousies, selfishness, desire for glory and power kill the spirit always," she wrote to Hugh in a confession that may have described her own behavior as accurately as her adversary's. And yet she hardly seemed all that concerned over the entire matter, adding: "the movement grows and blossoms & I am getting happier everyday over it." She told the press that the controversy represented the maturing of the movement, which, like a growing cell, got to a certain point and then divided. "We are still the same body, however," she hastened to add.

Both women seem to have behaved badly, yet whatever character weaknesses they revealed, their personal dispute, much like those that had embroiled Margaret in the past, also reflected substantive differences in leadership style and in basic ideology. The schism was probably inevitable because Jones and the board members she controlled were intent on building an institution quietly and methodically by slowly compiling a record of endorsements, affiliations, and clinic openings. Margaret had little patience for this incremental approach and was, instead, eager to take risks and extend the organization beyond conventional and prudent tactics. Busy building institutions in the United States and in Europe, she had also been out of the press and the public eye for several years. As soon as she returned from Europe, she began to talk about throwing caution to the winds and mounting another major legislative campaign in Washington. She did not necessarily count on political victory but saw no other means except renewed lobbying to educate and arouse an increasingly apathetic public. She was willing to let Senators tell her what to do only for so long.[18]

Still defending her position to a wary ABCL leadership in 1932, she would admit that whether the Comstock laws actually still meant much or were enforced was not important to her. "There is no better way of educating public opinion than by changing the laws," she explained. "Such agitation arouses interest, awakens forces that have been sleeping or apathetic and creates a new attitude not only toward government, but toward our part in bringing about constructive changes in obsolete and vicious laws. In my estimation the agitation for legislation is the means, and precedes the knowledge and the awakening of interest in the establishment of clinics." Eleanor Jones, however, believed that lobbying would only divert energy and money from the practical, constructive work of bringing contraceptive services to the poor. As the Depression took hold, Jones also decided that propaganda was having a negative effect by encouraging a middle-class birthrate that was already too low. She could see no instrumental value in public relations arising from legal issues.[19]

While Margaret joined ranks with women of the establishment, she was also never completely comfortable with any but the most independent-minded—some might say the most eccentric—among them. She convinced herself that Jones, like Mary Ware Dennett before her, was simply not a compatible spirit, if for no other reason than that she looked down upon Margaret's social background and schooling. "I wonder if Mrs. J. thinks the *N.R.* asks 'uneducated' people to write for its columns," she wrote caustically to Juliet Rublee early in 1929, when *The New Republic* published a piece Margaret had prepared about her New York clinic. Her ego must still have been bruised a year later when Havelock Ellis responded to one of her letters in consolation: "The BC movement was magnificent in its day and it is splendid that you should be its St. Margaret," he responded, "but it is no longer a visionary movement, no longer an adventure, but, though always important, quite dull and commonplace and best left to dull and commonplace people."[20]

There was, indeed, a disturbing change of emphasis in the league under Jones's direction. For almost a decade, Margaret had pandered to a eugenically minded audience, but she was always careful to qualify her definition of hereditary fitness to exclude outright prejudice on the basis of race, ethnicity, or class. By contrast, Jones was unabashedly elitist and undemocratic. "Couples who cannot endow their children with health, vigor, and intelligence should have fewer children than those who can," she told the National Conference of Social Work in 1929. "In order that people of inferior stock shall have fewer children, all we need to do is to remove the obstacles put in the way of their getting birth control advice." The following year Jones applied to the Rockefeller family-supported Bureau of Social Hygiene and to other foundations for funding to underwrite a "systematic campaign against the present dysgenic multiplication of the unfit." She explained her intentions this way: "The public is beginning to realize that scientific, constructive philanthropy does not merely care for the diseased, the poor, and the degenerate, but takes steps to prevent the birth of babies destined to be paupers, invalids, degenerates, or all three."

A tactful Lawrence Dunham, director of the Social Hygiene Bureau's staff, counseled his board that the application "assumed as facts statements which were in reality highly debatable opinions." Elsewhere he added: "The [birth control] movement has the support of many of the best and most intelligent people in the world and it also has the support of some persons whose mental balance is not the best. In between these two classes, we find the people who hold debatable opinions, the most capable group being the Eugenists [sic], some of whom make claims which many eminent scientists in the field of biology and other related sciences contend are utterly false, or at least unproven."

Dunham did not recommend support for the league's application. He instead took the advice of another member of his staff—to await the results of research on birth control being conducted under the auspices of Margaret Sanger's Birth Control Clinical Research Bureau. The American Birth Control League was given $10,000 to continue educational work among physicians, but its funding from the Rockefellers did not grow beyond that level so long as Eleanor Jones—"a martinet," as she was described in another Bureau of Social Hygiene memorandum—remained in charge.[21]

By contrast, Margaret's own reputation, however controversial she remained in many quarters, transcended the identity of the group she had founded. Freed of bureaucratic constraints and infighting, and fiercely determined to best her detractors, she moved forward on her own, expanding the Birth Control Clinical Research Bureau in New York, while also launching her proposed educational and lobbying campaign for birth control in Washington. Indeed, she fortuitously located the headquarters of this effort in the nation's capital just as that city found itself the center of the country's New Deal reform energies, and, in so doing, she valiantly attempted to ally the birth control cause with affirmative social welfare and planning initiatives in response to the economic crisis.

By leaving the league, Margaret deprived it of her firebrand temperament. She also took much of its fund-raising capability, as the Bureau of Social Hygiene records clearly confirm. Eroding the confidence of the Rockefellers was no small matter, but they did inevitably fund both the league and many of Margaret's new requests, as well, at least in small amounts. The far more significant loss proved to be a stately, monocled, self-made millionaire by the name of James Henry Noah Slee, who had become the birth control movement's principal benefactor by way of marrying Margaret Sanger. Having secured this one man's devotion and his checkbook, she was, for the time being at least, substantially able to pay her own way.

Notes

1. The incorporation controversy is in "Birth Control Wins Charter Fight," *The New York Times*, Apr. 14, 1922, 36:2, and Apr. 23, 1922, Pt.1, 2:3. On Anne Kennedy, see M. S. to Juliet Rublee, "Juliet darling, Your special letter with enclosure came yesterday . . . ," n.d. (1924) MS-DC, and *Autobiography*, p. 261. On the organization of the ABCL, see "Report of the American Birth Control League Activities," 1922, and "Minutes of the American Birth Control League for 1922," in PPFA-SS. The goals were announced in an editorial in the *Birth Control Review* 5:11 (Nov. 1921), pp. 4-5. Also see Francis McLennon Vreeland, "The Process of Reform with Especial Reference to Reform Groups in the Field of Population," doctoral dissertation, University of Michigan, 1929, p. 135. The league actually claimed distribution of 600,000 pamphlets in 1923, but I use Vreeland's estimate, pp. 146, 240, and he maintains that these early figures may have been inflated, accounting for some falloff when he himself kept more accurate records while working in the ABCL offices in 1926-27, as part of the research for his study. On the Motherhood Department, see Bertha Potter Smith's report for Jan. 12, 1926, PPFA-SS, and Helena Huntington Smith, "Profiles, They Were Eleven," *The New Yorker*, 1930, clipping in MS-SS.

2. For published examples of the early correspondence, see "The Doctor Only Laughed," *Birth Control Review* 7:6 (June 1923); "Prevention or Abortion—Which?" *BCR* 7:7 (July 1923); "Is Continence the Solution?" *BCR* 7:9 (Sept. 1923). The quotes are from Bobby Walls to M. S., Mar. 2, 1924, a twenty-four-page handwritten letter; M. S. to Bobby Walls, Mar. 7, 1924; and Mrs. M. M. Gardner to M. S., June 21, 1935, all in MS-LC. As we shall see, Margaret collected and published less controversial letters in *Motherhood in Bondage* (New York: 1928).

3. This statistical profile of the membership is taken from Vreeland, "Process of Reform," pp. 153, 164-67, 171, 192, 208, 210-11, of contributors, p. 252, of the budget, p. 327, and of the National Council, pp. 428-29. On *Birth Control Review* distribution, also see M. S. to Francis Fitzgerald, Aug. 11, 1924, MS-LC. (Fitzgerald was the librarian at Creighton University, a Jesuit school, and although a free subscription had been donated to the library by an alumnus, he refused to accept it.) ABCL memos dated Jan. 13, 1927, and Jan. 20, 1932, in PPFA-SS discuss a reduction of affiliate contributions from 25 percent to 10 percent of annual membership receipts.

4. M. S., form letter, July 15, 1923, asking support for the Chicago conference. Also see, Clara L. Rowe (the conference organizer) to Prof. Michael Frederick Guyer, July 6, 1923, both in the American Birth Control League Papers, 1923-28, Houghton Library, Harvard University, hereinafter, ABCL-Houghton. On the high incidence of abortion among Jewish immigrant women in Chicago, see Harry L. Lurie, "The Sex Hygiene of Family Life," *Jewish Social Service Quarterly* (Dec. 1926), cited in Caroline Hadley Robinson, *Seventy Birth Control Clinics: A Survey and Analysis Including the General Effects of Control on Size and Quality of Population* (Philadelphia: 1930), p. 66. Also see Bernice Guthmann, *The Planned Parenthood Movement in Illinois, 1923-1965*, a 1965 pamphlet published by the PPFA, Chicago Area, pp. 3-6; Rachelle Yarros, M.D., "Illinois Looks Ahead," *Birth Control Review* 2:4 (Jan.

1935), p. 2; and Vreeland, "Process of Reform," p. 367. On Yarros, see Christopher Lasch, "Rachelle Slobodinsky Yarros," in *Notable American Women, 1607-1950: A Biographical Dictionary* (Cambridge, Mass.: 1971), edited by Edward and Janet James, pp. 693-94.

5. On the organization of the L.A. clinic, see Vreeland, "Process of Reform," pp. 365-68, and on the endowment of $180,000, see Robinson, *Seventy Clinics*, p. 33. Patient data is in Robinson and in *The Los Angeles Mothers' Clinic Association Annual Report*, 1930, copy in MS-LC. On San Francisco, see *Alameda County Birth Control League and Mothers' Health Clinic*, 1929 pamphlet in MS-SS; and Planned Parenthood League of Alameda County and Planned Parenthood Association of San Francisco, *Joint Annual Report, 1969*, pp. 5-7, a pamphlet also collected by the author.

6. On Detroit, see Eloise K. Sulzberger, "Instant Birth Control," and Betsy Graves Reyneau, "Nobody Came," in "Our M. S.," Sanger Seventy-Fifth Birthday Reminiscences, pp. 264-67 and 230-32, MS-SS; Anne Kennedy to Mrs. Willard Pope, Jan. 5, 1944, MS-SS; and "Birth Control League of Michigan," *Birth Control Review* 16:1 (Jan. 1932), p. 23. On Cleveland, see Vreeland, "Process of Reform," pp. 401-409; *The Maternal Health Association of Cleveland*, 1937 pamphlet summarizing the history of their clinic program in MS-SS; Dorothy Brush, "Impressions of Margaret Sanger," in "Our M. S.," MS-SS; and finally, Nancy Peacock, "Everything You Wanted to Know About Noblesse Oblige But Were Afraid to Ask," *Cleveland* (May 1988). My thanks to my mother, Celia Chesler of Cleveland, for this last citation.

7. On Baltimore, see "The Baltimore Birth Control Clinic," *Birth Control Review* 13:5 (May 1929), p. 137, and Bessie L. Moses, M.D., *Contraception as a Therapeutic Measure* (Baltimore: 1936), esp. introduction and pp. 3-7, 14, summary. Moses' primary purpose was to test and compare the efficacy of the diaphragm against Sanger's New York statistics, which are discussed in Chapter 13. On Cooper, see M. S. to J. Noah. H. Slee, Feb. 22, 1925, with a handwritten notation by Sanger's secretary, Florence Rose, that Cooper spoke to 248 groups in practically every state, and M. S. to James Cooper, Feb. 5, 1925, both in MS-LC. Schedules and reports for Cooper's tours are in ABCL-Houghton, along with some early correspondence, including J. C. to M. S., Sept. 14, 1923, and J. C. to Clara L. Rowe, July 19, 1923. Miscellaneous reports from Cooper in the field including "Report on St. Louis, Mo. October, 15, 16, 17, 1925"; and "Report on North Jersey Medical Society (colored), Tioga County Medical Meeting and Indianapolis, Indiana," October 1925, are in MS-LC. Monthly reports from 1926-28 are in James Cooper, M.D., "Clinical Report File," uncataloged papers, Margaret Sanger Center, N.Y.C.; and a summary of 1928 activities is in MS-LC. Also see James F. Cooper, M.D., *Motherhood and Birth Control*, and *Some Reasons for the Popularity of the Birth Control Movement*, pamphlets in BA-SS. Biographical material in S. Adolphus Knopf, M.D., "In Memoriam: James F. Cooper," reprint from *The Medical Journal and Record*, May 20, 1931, in MS-SS and clipping from a *New York Herald Tribune* obituary, Mar. 28, 1931, in MS-LC. On New Jersey, see "Report of ABCL Executive Secretary Penelope B. Huse," Mar. 8, 1927; and Henriette Hart, "Report of the New Jersey Field Work," Apr. 12-May 8, 1927, both in PPFA-SS. Also see "News Notes," *BCR*

12:1 (Jan. 1928), p. 25. Aggregate data for 1930 is in Robinson, *Seventy Clinics,* passim. Robinson's outlook about the future of the clinic movement was optimistic, and her statistics were inflated by the inclusion of case data from facilities in Europe, as well as the United States. When one actually looks beyond the Sanger clinic in New York, however, her conclusion seems unfounded. For more on the Sanger clinic, see Chaps. 13 and 14.

8. On Massachusetts, see Lucile Lord-Heinstein, M.D., "An Account of the Salem Raid and Trial," July 28, 1937, PPLM-MS; "Massachusetts Clinic Case," an account of the Massachusetts Supreme Court ruling of May 26, 1938, n.d. (1938), MS-SS; and Ruth Smith, ed., *PPLM Reports* 24 (Spring 1974), copy in PPLM-SS. My thanks to David Garrow for summarizing the situation in Connecticut.

9. On the Albany lobbying effort, see "Despotic Government at Albany," *Birth Control Review* 7:2 (Feb. 23, 1923), p. 47; "To All Our Friends," *BCR* 7:3 (Mar. 23, 1923) p. 71; "Intelligence Tests for Legislators," and "The Hearing at Albany," *BCR* 7:5 (May 1925) pp. 107-108 and 111-12. Also see "Albany Mayor Fails to Halt Birth Control Meeting," *The New York Times,* Feb. 21, 1923, and assorted clippings from local Albany papers in MS-LC. The denouement of Dennett's efforts is chronicled in the Stopes correspondence, MS-BM. The Sanger quotations are in M. S. to J. N. H. S., Mar. 2, 1927, MS-SS, and M. S. to J. R., n.d. (from Geneva), MS-DC. Also see U.S. Congress. Joint Subcommittees of the Committees on the Judiciary. *Joint Hearings on the Cummins-Vaile Bill.* 68th Cong., 1st sess., Apr. 8 and May 9, 1924.

10. Anne Kennedy, report on "Federal Work," n.d. (1926), and Anne Kennedy to the Board of Directors and National Council of the ABCL, "Facts You Should Know," Jan. 19, 1926, both in MS-LC. The quotations are from Anne Kennedy, "Short Synopsis of Interviews with Senators," a sixty-page document. She quoted Vaile and George W. Norris, among many others, see esp. pp. 1 and 4.

11. On the 1924 campaign, see Oswald G. Villard to M. S., Sept. 3, 1924, MS-LC and "Summary of Events for 1924," PPFA-SS. The 1926 events are in Anne Kennedy, "Report of an Interview with Father Ward of the National Catholic Welfare Conference, Washington D.C., Also Father Ryan of the Publicity Department," n.d. (1926); Mrs. Anne Kennedy, "Report of an Interview with Mr. P. J. Ward of the NCWC, Washington, D.C.," Mar. 2, 1926, copies in MS-SS and MS-LC; Patrick J. Ward to Clarence C. Little, president of the University of Michigan, Mar. 18, 1926; Rev. John J. Burke, general secretary of the NCWC, to M. S., Apr. 21, 1926; M. S. to John J. Burke, May 13, 1926, and June 24; Burke to M. S., June 12 and July 28; Patrick J. Ward to the editor, *The New Republic,* Oct. 29, 1928, all in MS-LC. From 1928, see Floyd S. Dell, "The Anti-Birth Control Neurosis," *Birth Control Review* 12:9 (Sept. 1928), pp. 252-54, and "Mrs. Sanger Calls Catholics Bigots . . . Attacks Smith Candidacy," *The New York Times,* Apr. 25, 1928, 14:2-3; and on the Hoover vote, M. S. to Juliet Rublee, n.d. (Nov. 1928), MS-DC. Finally, on New York lobbying efforts, "Legislators Wake to a Vital Problem," *BCR* 9:5 (May 1925), pp. 143-55. A copy of Assembly Bill 684, dated Feb. 1, 1927, is in MS-LC. A summary of the progress made on a subsequent bill introduced in 1929 is in "Doctors and Birth Control," American Birth Control League, Report of the executive secretary for 1929, PPFA-SS.

12. Grant Sanger, Schlesinger Library interview, p. 54; interview with the author, Dec. 18, 1987. Olive Byrne Richard, Jacqueline Van Voris interview, Smith College, p. 17. Margaret Sanger Marston, Jacqueline Van Voris interview, Smith College, p. 44.

13. Sanger Journal, Mar. 7, 1925, Jan. 11, 1926, MS-SS. M. S. to "Juliet Dearest," n.d. (possibly as early as 1921) and M. S. to J. R., "Aug. 20," n.d. (sometime in the 1920s) on Mount Royal Hotel letterhead, MS-DC. The quote is from J. R. to M. S., Sept. 11, 1925, MS-SS, also see letters dated Sept. 11, Oct. 7, and Oct. 12, 1925.

14. Margaret Sanger, ed. *The Sixth International Neo-Malthusian and Birth Control Conference,* 4 vols. (New York, 1925-26), copy in MS-SS. The conference was held at the McAlpin Hotel, March 25-31, 1925. Also see, news releases and other materials from the event in ABCL-Houghton. *The New York Times* coverage began with "Birth Control Conference; Noted Advocates from Abroad to Attend Sessions Opening Tomorrow," Mar. 25, 1925, 12:2, and continued for a week. See *NYT,* Mar. 27, 1925, 8:1-2; Mar. 28, 9:1; Mar. 29, Sec. 1, 9:1; Mar. 30, 10:3; Mar. 31, 7:1; Apr. 1, 15:1; Apr. 2, 17:2. Also, "Neo-Malthusians," *The Nation* 120:15 (Apr. 15, 1925), p. 401; John Langdon-Davies, "Race-Suicide No Murder," *The New Republic* 42: 541 (Apr. 15, 1925), pp. 209-11. On the participation of Rosika Schwimmer, see R. S. to M. S., Mar. 17 and Dec. 4, 1924, Jan. 30, 1925, and M. S. to R. S., Mar. 26 and Dec. 9, 1924, Jan. 17 and Apr. 6, 1925, all in the Schwimmer-Lloyd (Lola Maverick Lloyd) Collection, New York Public Library.

15. "Margaret Sanger Begins to Study Birth Control; Leaving League She Created 'to Catch Up With Subject,'" *New York World,* June 6, 1926, clipping in MS-LC. *Autobiography,* p. 393, and David Kennedy, *Birth Control in America: The Career of Margaret Sanger,* (New Haven: 1970), p. 103.

16. Sanger's positive assessment of Anne Kennedy and the league's progress is in Journal, "Notes during the Geneva Conference, 1928," MS-SS. The events surrounding the Kennedy firing are chronicled in the following correspondence: Eleanor Jones to M. S., "Friday, July 8," n.d. (1927); M. S. to E. J., Dec. 20, 1927; M. S. to A. K., Dec. 22, 1927, and A. K. to M. S., Jan. 10, 1928, and "Geneva, Sat. the 5th," (n.d.) (1927 or 1928); P. B. Huse to M. S., Nov. 3, 1927; Annie G. Porritt to M. S., Dec. 29, 1927; Frances Ackerman, Nov. 3-13, 1927, and Dec. 3, 1927; and Charlotte Delafield to M. S., Nov. 29, 1927, all in MS-LC. On Lifschiz, see Anna Lifschiz to Margaret Sanger, Aug. 15, 1930, MS-SS. Without apparent rancor, Lifschiz went to the western office of Holland-Rantos, manufacturer of diaphragms, in Los Angeles, saying to M. S., "There are no words to express how I cherish my contact with you."

17. M. S. to Juliet Rublee, May 17, 1928, MS-DC. M. S. to "The Board of Directors," the American Birth Control League, Inc. June 8, 1928, MS-SS. Charlotte Delafield to M. S., Apr. 16, 1928, indicates her refusal to serve as a replacement President.

18. "Minutes of Special Meeting, Sept. 20, 1928," MS-LC, discuss the dispute over the autonomy of the clinic. M. S. to Juliet Rublee, Sept. 14 and Sept. 23, 1928, and "Juliet dear" on 39 Fifth Ave. letterhead (n.d.), reveal her view of the dispute as it was developing, all in MS-DC. M. S. to "the Secretary of the A.B.C.L., Inc. January 31, 1929," communicates her formal resignation as editor and director, and M. S. to Mrs. F. Robertson Jones, Feb. 11, 1929, and Eleanor Dwight Jones to J.

N. H. S., testily explain the differences between the two women, all in the ABCL papers, MS-SS. The direct quotes are respectively from M. S. to H. de S., Feb. 19, 1929, MS-LC; and from a story in the *Brooklyn Eagle*, Dec. 28, 1930, clipping in MS-LC. Also see, "Mrs. Sanger Quits Birth Control Post," *The New York Times*, Sept. 12, 1928, 11:1-3 and "Mrs. F. Robertson Jones Becomes Head of Birth Control League," *NYT*, Sept. 13, 29:8. Kennedy, *Birth Control*, pp. 103-104, attributes the break to Sanger's emotionalism and her "autocratic and often chaotic leadership," without giving her any benefit of doubt and without fully examining the particulars of the controversy that led up to it.

19. M. S. to Dr. Alice Boughton, executive director, ABCL, in 1932 ABCL correspondence, MS-LC. Also M. S. to Annie G. Porritt, secretary of the ABCL board, Jan. 20, 1930, MS-LC.

20. M. S. to Juliet Rublee in Mexico, "Willowlake, Friday 26, Darling Juliet," n.d. (1929) MS-DC, and H. E. to M. S., Nov. 3, 1930, MS-LC. For the article, see Margaret Sanger, "The Birth Control Raid," *The New Republic* (May 1, 1929), pp. 305-306, clipping in MS-LC.

21. The first quotes are from Eleanor Dwight Jones, "Birth Control: First Aid in Social Work," speech reprinted in *Birth Control Review* 13:8 (Aug. 1929), p. 218. The next two are from Eleanor Dwight (Mrs. F. Robertson) Jones to Lawrence B. Dunham, Nov. 3, 1930, Bureau of Social Hygiene Papers, Rockefeller Archive, Record Group 2, Pocantico Hills, New York, hereinafter Rocky, followed by the appropriate record group number. My thanks to Joan Dunlop for helping to facilitate my use of the Rockefeller archives by putting me in touch with Peter Johnson, the Rockefeller family archivist whose preliminary search helped me locate these papers, which, to my knowledge, have not been previously examined. For the Bureau of Social Hygiene Response, see memorandum: "To Mr. Dunham from Dr. Sellin," Nov. 17, 1930; and Lawrence Dunham to Thomas M. Debevoise, Mar. 5, 1931, and R. (Ruth) Topping to Mr. Dunham, "ABCL-Comments on Report of Activities for 1931," Jan. 5, 1932, and RT (Ruth Topping), "File Memorandum re: ABCL," Dec. 2, 1932, in which she quotes Robert Dickinson, M.D., calling Jones a "martinet," all in Rocky-RG2. When the Bureau of Social Hygiene closed down, Topping ironically took a job with the league, but by that time, it was supporting Sanger.

WOMEN AND THE ARTS

ELAINE SHOWALTER (ESSAY DATE 1977)

SOURCE: Showalter, Elaine. "The Female Aesthetic." In *A Literature of Their Own: British Women Novelists from Brontë to Lessing*, pp. 240-62. Princeton, N.J.: Princeton University Press, 1977.

In the following essay, Showalter contends that many women writers of the early twentieth century reacted to the violence of the First World War and the almost-masculine nature of the feminist movement by attempting to create a new kind of writing that offered a retreat from the real world rather than an expression of it.

The last generation of Victorian women novelists began to publish during the suffrage campaigns and the First World War. Suffragette writers had taken up John Stuart Mill's challenge to transmute the moral issues of Victorian feminism into an aesthetic philosophy. After the war, women novelists, half-inspired by the promise of a purely female art, half-frightened by the spectacle of how closely feminist militance resembled its masculine form, began to develop a fiction that celebrated a new consciousness. The female aesthetic applied feminist ideology to language as well as to literature, to words and sentences as well as to perceptions and values. Perhaps the war, coming at the height of suffrage militance, inflicted a sense of collective guilt upon activist women; certainly members of the W.S.P.U. transferred their energies from the vote to the war with suspicious alacrity. Women writers responded to the war by turning within; yet they renounced the demands of the individual narrative self. The world seemed dominated by the violence of ego; women writers wanted no part of it. Thus the fiction of this generation seems oddly impersonal and renunciatory at the same time that it is openly and insistently female. The female aesthetic was to become another form of self-annihilation for women writers, rather than a way of self-realization. One detects in this generation clear and disturbing signs of retreat: retreat from the ego, retreat from the physical experience of women, retreat from the material world, retreat into separate rooms and separate cities. Under the banner of the female aesthetic marched the army of the secession.

At the time, however, female aestheticism looked like a step forward. Some women novelists and critics felt that, as Mill had predicted, the literature of women had finally emancipated itself from its cultural subjection to a male tradition, and that its historical moment had arrived. It is true that James Joyce and Dorothy Richardson were pursuing some of the same experiments, and that Virginia Woolf and D. H. Lawrence had similar visions of sexual polarity. Yet no reader would mistake one for the other, mainly because their verbal territories scarcely overlap, but also, as women writers liked to repeat, because women were holding to their own experience, values, and grievances. Virginia Woolf felt altogether pleased with what she saw of women's fiction in 1929: "It is courageous; it is sincere, it keeps closely to what women feel. It is not bitter. It does not insist upon its femininity. But at the same time, a woman's book is not written as a man would write it."[1]

In 1920 a critical study called *Some Contemporary Novelists (Women)* by R. Brimley Johnson attempted to define the collective nature of women's fiction and to explain what was meant by the female version of realism: "The new woman, the female novelist of the twentieth century, has abandoned the old realism. She does not accept *observed* revelation. She is seeking, with passionate determination, for that Reality which is behind the material, the things that matter, spiritual things, ultimate Truth. And here she finds man an outsider, wilfully blind, purposely indifferent."[2] Johnson romanticized this quest in relating it to the war, which he thought had brought "a new spirituality" to a disillusioned generation. But he also thought it stemmed from feminist ideology.

In terms of subject matter and approach, the novels that Johnson discussed have a number of common traits that come from their feminism. They reverse the orthodox argument that women have limited experience by defining reality as subjective. In *The Creators* (1910) May Sinclair wrote that experience "spoils you. It ties you hand and foot. It perverts you, twists you, blinds you to everything but yourself. I know women—artists— who have never got over their experience, women who'll never do anything because of it." When she read Dorothy Richardson's novels, Sinclair was charmed by the total obliteration of structured experience: "Nothing happens. It just goes on and on."[3] Several of the novels were attacks on the Victorian nuclear family; Eleanor Mordaunt's *The Family* (1915) and Rose Macaulay's *Potterism* (1920) were especially biting; Ivy Compton-Burnett's austere sensationalism was based on an exposure of the murderous psychic combat of parents and children.

Early twentieth-century novels were also anti-male, both in the sense that they attacked "male" technology, law, and politics, and that they belittled masculine morality. We can hear the muted clash of swords in the 1909 correspondence between Clive Bell and Virginia Woolf over the first drafts of *The Voyage Out*. Bell began diplomatically but quickly became less tactful: "Our views about men & women are doubtless quite different, and the difference doesn't matter much; but to draw such sharp & marked contrasts between the subtle, sensitive, tactful, gracious, delicately perceptive, & perspicacious women, & the obtuse, vulgar, blind, florid, rude, tactless, emphatic, indelicate, vain, tyrannical, stupid men, is not only rather absurd, but rather bad art, I think." Woolf responded with even more devastating courtesy, depersonalizing the disagreement, but putting Bell in his place: "Possibly, for psychological reasons which seem to me very interesting, a man, in the present state of the world, is not a very good judge of his sex; and a 'creation' may seem to him 'didactic.'"[4]

It is by "their tiresome restlessness," wrote Amber Reeves, "their curiosity, their disregard for security, for seemliness, even for life itself, that men have mastered the world, and filled it with the wealth of civilization . . . that they have armed the race with science, dignified it with art."[5] Civilization and the illusion of progress was a by-product of the masculine way of being, which women writers now came to see as sterile, egocentric, and self-deluding. Coming to terms with the paradox of male culture required an ironic inversion of some of the most cherished Victorian notions of male and female codes of living. Women were claiming that men's allegiance to external "objective" standards of knowledge and behavior cut them off from the "real reality" of subjective understanding. Just as the Victorians had maintained that women were too emotionally involved and anarchic to judge personality, let alone history, women now sweetly hinted that men were too caught up in the preservation of a system to comprehend its meaning.

Yet for all their new awareness, the heroines of this fiction remain victims; indeed they are victimized by their awareness. Whereas the heroines of Victorian fiction often did not perceive that they had choices, and in fact had only a selection of bad options, these heroines are confronted with choices and lack the nerve to seize their time. F. M. Mayor's *The Rector's Daughter* (1924) describes the plight of Mary Jocelyn, who deliberately abandons all hope of fulfillment or self-expression out of devotion to her father. Similarly Radclyffe Hall, in *The Unlit Lamp* (1924), makes her heroine Joan a self-destructive martyr to duty. In the end Joan's lover cries, "How long is it to go on, . . . this incredibly wicked thing that tradition sanctifies? You were so splendid. How fine you were! You had everything in you that was needed to have put life within your grasp, and you had a right to life, to a life of your own; everyone has. You might have been a brilliant woman, a woman that counted for a great deal, and yet what are you now?"[6] Men resisted the tyranny of the family and broke away into silence, exile, and cunning; women succumbed. The female *Künstlerroman* of this period is a saga of defeat. Women novelists punish and blame their heroines for their weakness, their laziness, and their lack of purpose, for the manuscript yellowing in the desk, for the risk abjured. There is indeed a new interest in the creative psychology of women, but it is full of self-recrimination.

Part of the problem was tension between the novelists' lives as women and their commitment to literature. Members of a generation of women in rebellion against the traditional feminine domestic roles, they tried free love, only to find themselves exploited; if they then chose marriage, they often felt trapped. Storm Jameson, who admitted that her ideas about childbearing had come primarily from *Anna Karenina,* found herself near madness from the monotonous drudgery of her marriage: "I cannot explain my pathological hatred of domestic life and my frantic need to be free."[7] D. H. Lawrence could maintain that the secret of artistic stability was to love a wife.[8] Women, however, found themselves pulled apart by the conflicting claims of love and art. Those who fared best were emotional tycoons like Katherine Mansfield and Vita Sackville-West, who made their own terms with men and also retained title to the adoration and the services of less-demanding women friends. Other women—Stella Benson was one—insisted vehemently "on being a writer first and a wife second; a man would insist and I insist. A hundred years hence it will seem absurd that a woman should have to say this, just as it would seem absurd now if we should hear that Mr. William Blake's wife wanted him to take up breeding pigs to help her and he obstinately preferred writing poetry."[9] But it came to nothing in the end. When the crises came, women went bitterly with their husbands, as they had always done.

Self-sacrifice generates bitterness and makes, as Yeats said, a stone of the heart. But beyond the outspoken contempt for male selfishness in this fiction is a much more intense self-hatred. Women gave in and despised themselves for giving in. Insofar as it is recorded in the novels, the concept of female autonomy is frighteningly undercut by theories of post-Darwinian determinism and retributive systems of almost theological rigidity. In Rebecca West's powerful novel *The Judge* (1922), for example, male egoism is portrayed in Richard Haverland, a twentieth-century Rochester whose romantic action is shown to be empty and escapist. Two women, Haverland's mother, Marion, and his lover, Ellen Melville, have to pay the price for his impulsiveness, his emotionalism, and his immaturity. Marion, who had sacrificed the potential of her own life to protect her son—she had agreed to a sexless marriage with a man she despised in order to make Richard legitimate—learns that one sacrifice leads inevitably to others. Her husband rapes her and she must bear a despised legitimate son. Richard kills his brother and flees with Ellen, who is pregnant with his illegitimate child. At the end, only Marion's suicide seems adequate to the situation. The story of Ellen Melville, a socialist and a suffragette, is equally futile; her dream of female equality is seen to have been a snare and a delusion. West's epigraph for the novel reflects on the political hierarchies that lead to diminishing returns of affection and hope: "Every mother is a judge who sentences the children for the sins of the fathers."

Men are the sinners, but women are both the judges and the convicts. One feels overwhelmingly that the women are punished in this novel, punished for their innocence, for their self-betrayal, for their willingness to become victims. The collapse of the long love affair between West and H. G. Wells, which took place about this time, probably accounts for some of the bitterness of the book. As "their relationship deteriorated rapidly, with Rebecca increasingly anxious to break free and Wells increasingly determined not to let her go,"[10] the tensions between West and Wells as artists became more pronounced. Ellen Melville, the suffragette who seems fated to relive an earlier generation's pattern of womanly suffering and self-sacrifice, is clearly related to West's disillusionment with the compromises she had made with Wells. He disliked *The Judge* very much and told her so; he called it "an ill conceived sprawl of a book with a faked climax, an aimless waste of your powers."[11] The book is flawed, but it is not aimless. Many of West's subsequent books, both fiction and reportage, dealt with the same questions of betrayal and judgment.

In the short stories of Katherine Mansfield, the moment of self-awareness is also the moment of self-betrayal. Typically, a woman in her fiction who steps across the threshold into a new understanding of womanhood is humiliated, or destroyed. Mansfield's fiction is cautionary and punitive; women are lured out onto the limbs of consciousness, which are then lopped off by the author. In "Bliss," for example, Bertha's recognition that the feeling she calls "bliss," the "fire in her bosom," is sexual ardor, is quickly followed by her discovery of her husband's adultery.

Virginia Woolf was disgusted with "Bliss," which she read in the *English Review* in 1918. Woolf confided to her diary: "She is content with superficial smartness; and the whole conception is poor, cheap, not the vision, however imperfect, of an interesting mind. She writes badly too. And the effect was, as I say, to give me an impression of her callousness and hardness as a human being. I shall read it again, but I don't suppose I shall change."[12] Yet in Mansfield's brutality, Woolf recognized herself, her own hardness and her own vulnerability. Mansfield insisted that Woolf recognize the bond: "We have got the same job, Virginia," she wrote after their first meeting, "and it is really very curious and thrilling that we should both . . . be after so nearly the same thing. We are, you know. There's no denying it."[13] A 1924 short story by Woolf, "The New Dress," echoes the theme and even the language of "Bliss." *Mrs. Dalloway* is closest of all to Mansfield's style and subject matter; Woolf merely substitutes revery for epiphany. Both Woolf and Mansfield see women as artists whose creative energy has gone chiefly into the maintenance of myths about themselves and about those they love. To become aware of the creation of a myth is to lose faith in it. Mansfield's characters are seen repeatedly at this moment of realization and collapse, but Mrs. Dalloway manages to escape by projecting her anxieties onto someone else. There is something instructive and chilling in the survival tactics of this fiction. Writing about one of Mansfield's most famous stories, "Miss Brill" (in which a lonely woman's marginally sustaining fantasy of self is wrecked when she overhears two lovers making fun of her in a park), Margaret Drabble recalled that she had been horrified by its cruelty: "I couldn't get it out of my mind: I think it changed something in me forever . . . one would not like to have written it oneself, however fine the achievement."[14] As Septimus Smith becomes the scapegoat for Mrs. Dalloway's failures, so the heroines of Katherine Mansfield's stories become the scapegoats for hers.

The most consistent representative of female aestheticism was Dorothy M. Richardson, who might have been the Gertrude Stein of the English novel if she had been more self-promoting and more affluent. Edward Garnett, accepting the first volume of *Pilgrimage* for the firm of Duckworth in 1915, christened Richardson's work "feminine impressionism" and saw its connections with the work of other women novelists (Garnett had recommended Olive Schreiner's *Women and Labour* to Fisher Unwin, and he had also accepted Woolf's *The Voyage Out*). Richardson's later admirers linked her with Proust and Joyce; but her real tradition was female, and her subject was female consciousness. In considering her career and her art, we can see how her narrative techniques and her aesthetic theories grew out of a struggle to de-

personalize and control a female identity that was potent with the promise of self-destruction.

Richardson had the professional life of a Mary Wollstonecraft or a George Eliot: she began as a teacher, then worked as a translator and journalist; she had affairs with selfish and unscrupulous men, and made contact with both the solid center and the louche fringes of London intellectual society. She was nearly forty years old when she began to write *Pointed Roofs,* the first volume of her twelve-volume, thirty-year study of "Miriam Henderson," a heroine whose life paralleled her own up to the point of authorship. In its diffuse way, *Pilgrimage* is a portrait of the young woman on the way to becoming an artist, and it is in this convolution—the novel ends when the heroine is ready to write it—that Richardson most resembles Proust and Joyce.

Like Olive Schreiner, Sarah Grand, and many other women writers, Dorothy Richardson was the child of a forceful but unreliable father and a passive, depressed mother. In a family of girls, she became the surrogate son, a role that her sister-in-law later attributed to her "wilful and at times unmanageable nature."[15] In times of financial difficulty—unhappily frequent in the Richardson home—Dorothy was spared the domestic routines that her sisters had to take on. On the other hand, she was expected to be her father's companion at meetings of the British Association for the Advancement of Science, an organization he devotedly supported. Her father's scientific rationalism and the "deadness" of the association oppressed her, and later she came to identify "the dark veil under which I grew up"[16] as the shadow of male scientific philosophy. Her own pseudo-maleness within the family became a source of uneasiness, particularly when she found herself identifying with her mother. Unlike her resilient, socially ambitious father, Dorothy felt threatened by the precariousness of their financial position and deeply humiliated in times of hardship. When Charles Richardson was finally declared bankrupt in 1893, his wife's invalidism was complicated by deep depression. Dorothy, herself feeling "trapped and helpless,"[17] had to respond to, and care for, her mother; in November 1895 they went on a desperate holiday together to Hastings. But Mrs. Richardson was by then too despondent and alienated to be helped, and Dorothy returned one afternoon from a walk to find her mother dead in their room, having cut her throat with a carving knife.

In many ways this traumatic episode was the turning point in Dorothy's life; it freed her from the emotional demands of her family and allowed her to move to an independent life in London. As women writers always did, however, she paid dearly for her freedom. Her mother's suicide was first of all a warning, a hereditary hint that no daughter of an ardent Darwinian could ignore. More basically, it established a terrible precedent, a terrible contrast between the impregnable materialism and rationalism of men, secure with their built-in defenses, and the intuitive, involuntary, fatal sensitivity of women like her mother, defenseless against the deadly atmosphere of an indifferent culture. One sees this contrast stated most explicitly in *The Tunnel* (1919), the volume of *Pilgrimage* that describes Miriam Henderson's first years in London. Miriam's epiphany comes when she reads an insulting entry on "Woman" in an encyclopedia, and rebels against the futility of women's lives in an age controlled by science.[18]

At this moment of despair in the novel, Miriam, convinced that "life is poisoned for women, at the very source," can only recommend that, in protest, "all women ought to agree to commit suicide."[19] Suicide becomes a grotesquely fantasized female weapon, a way of cheating men out of dominance. Martyrdom and self-immolation are viewed as aggressive, as a way of inflicting punishment on the guilty survivors. This passage, with its suggestion that Richardson saw her own mother's suicide as a protest against her father, is extremely significant; it is a direct advocacy of the art of self-annihilation that is the hallmark of female aestheticism. At times Richardson recognized that suicide was just another form of power politics: "If women commit suicide in becoming partisan, what is the use of their entering party politics?" she wrote in her journal.[20] She would not choose the martyrdom of commitment because that was masculine. Instead she chose to live at the perilous borders of egolessness, in the female country of multiple receptivity. She risked self-destruction through psychic overload, ego death from the state of pure receptive sensibility that George Eliot had described as the roar on the other side of silence.[21]

Richardson saw this openness to psychological stimuli—we could also call it a form of negative capability—as the natural result of woman's position in the world, as "the human demand, besieging her wherever she is, for an inclusive awareness, from which men, for good or evil, are exempt."[22] One gets a clue in this passage to the sources of her lifelong sense of being embattled. Women's responsiveness to human demands had always kept them from becoming great artists, but

Richardson thought she could see a way to turn this liability into an asset. Women had always been accused of a chameleon-like susceptibility to the ideas of their lovers. From her perspective, this openness merely demonstrated women's greater range, their comprehension of the timeless oneness beyond the ideological flux. "Views and opinions are masculine things," she wrote in *Revolving Lights*. "Women are indifferent to them really. . . . Women can hold all opinions at once, or any, or none. It's because they see the relations of things which don't change, more than things which are always changing."[23]

Richardson's view helped her make sense of her own fragmented life in London at the turn of the century. During the day she worked as a dentist's assistant; at night she immersed herself in books and radical societies. She attended meetings of the Fabian Society, contacted Anarchists, and met with suffragettes, Quakers, and Zionists. In 1906 the publisher Charles Daniel asked her to write reviews for his new periodical, *Crank*. Among the cranks on Daniel's staff, Mary Everest Boole most impressed Richardson. She was the wife of the mathematician George Boole and mother of the novelist Ethel Voynich; she wrote with cabalistic intensity of epistemology and spiritualism and rated women's intuition high on the scale of human faculties. Richardson remained aloof in terms of committing herself to any of these groups or ideologies. Noncommitment itself became one of her ideals; she saw it as a characteristic attribute of feminine genius. Partisan politics, organized religion, and even personal relationships imposed false patterns on pure reality; women unsexed themselves by declaring any allegiance. The feminine mind, she wrote, "is capable of being all over the place and in all camps at once."[24] Her refusal as a novelist to structure consciousness came from this same refusal to impose any pattern or system on being.

But just as any novel *must* structure consciousness, whatever its pretensions to be pure, so Richardson's independence was a pose. She was much more easily swayed than she could ever bear to admit; the collective influence of London radicalism certainly affected her at this time. In the early 1900s she was particularly swayed by Fabian ideas. Much later she made fun of the doctrines of the Fabian Nursery, especially those of free love and the destruction of the nuclear family: "I recall a solemn discussion at a meeting of young women, on the desirability of selecting a suitable male, producing an infant, and going on the rates."[25] But in 1906, when she discovered that she was pregnant with H. G. Wells's child, she was determined to follow the Fabian gospel by raising the child completely on her own. Unhappily—for she had an intense maternal drive—she had a miscarriage in 1907, around Easter, shortly after visiting suffragette prisoners in Holloway. The whole affair brought her close to breakdown.

Wells, of course, cast his seed far and wide; in the recent biography of him by Norman and Jeanne Mackenzie, Dorothy Richardson is scarcely mentioned. She is simply part of the chorus, another Fabian groupie. In her biography, however, the Wells affair was a major event, both in personal and artistic terms. In the aftermath of this experience (Wells had moved on to Amber Reeves), she began to struggle with the first volume of her novel. I think we can assume that when she said that the novel came from her effort to "produce a feminine equivalent of the current masculine realism" it was chiefly Wells's realism she had in mind.[26] Richardson's first literary efforts to define the female artistic identity took the form of a dialectic; eventually she wrote the anti-Wellsian novel.

There were historical as well as personal reasons why Richardson should have had to define herself in opposition to Wells. Although they were almost the same age, they came from different literary generations. In the year that Richardson began serious work on *Pilgrimage,* Wells published his twenty-seventh book, *The New Machiavelli.* He was an Edwardian with Bennett and Galsworthy; she was a Georgian with Forster and Woolf. Thus Richardson's repudiation of Wells was also a repudiation of the Edwardian novel of external realism and accumulated detail. It is also clear that to Richardson and Woolf the Edwardians represented a male literary culture. And though male artists too have had to struggle against the influence of famous predecessors, only in rare cases have those celebrities been their lovers.

In fact it had been Wells who had first encouraged Richardson to write. Some idea of how she recalled his cheerful and businesslike egoism, and her own unyielding epistemology, may be gleaned from the dialogues in *Dawn's Early Light*:

> "Perhaps the novel's not your form. Women ought to be good novelists. But they write best about their own experiences. Love-affairs and so forth. They lack imagination."
>
> "Ah, imagination. Lies."
>
> "Try a novel of ideas. Philosophical. There's George Eliot."

> "Writes like a man."
>
> "Just so. Lewes. Be a feminine George Eliot. Try your hand."[27]

Even though Richardson admired Wells and had been educated by him, she came to see him as an opponent, the quintessential male artist. Her name for him in *Pilgrimage* is "Hypo Wilson": Hypo (with its innuendos of hippoes and hypocrisy) actually means "less than, or subordinated to"; Wilson echoes "Wilkins," the name Wells used for himself as public figure in his own novels. Her Hypo is the public man, the figurehead, larger than life and slightly absurd.

Horace Gregory has commented on the debt that Richardson owed to Wells as a teacher; from him she learned conversational style, realistic observation, mimicry, and use of the novel as a medium for advanced ideas. Gregory also finds "undertones of Wellsian prophecy" in Richardson's feminism.[28] The debt is there, in the sense that any antinovel pays tribute to its antagonist. But the antagonism, the dialectic, is much more important. Wells was concerned with the visionary and the Utopian; Richardson opted for the prosaic continual present. He chose a novel of ideas; she chose a novel of consciousness. He was politically engaged (and serially monogamous in his politics); she disdained any ideological or temporal division of the all-embracing female psyche. Wells constantly changed, shifted, developed, and exchanged old ideas for new; Richardson worked at *Pilgrimage* for thirty years without any significant modification of her style, approach, technique, or ideas. In her serene lack of development, she was like the cello player in the joke who never moves his finger because he has found the note for which all the other cellists are searching.

On the personal level too, Richardson needed to free herself from the influence of Wells, whose exuberance and inventiveness had come close to taking over her personality. For Wells, possession was a challenge; he confided to a friend that "the more marked the individuality, the more difficult it is to discover a complete reciprocity."[29] Richardson cannot have been too difficult a conquest; Wells was only the most dominant figure in a series of male mentors, beginning with her father. Her efforts at psychological liberation came in middle age, and perhaps that is why they have something of the fanaticism of late converts to obscure religions. In her novels, if not in her statements to friends, she was able to analyze with considerable delicacy the process by which she discovered that Wells had transformed her into an extension of himself. Miriam becomes aware that she is seeing her own experience with Hypo's eyes and then betraying its integrity and complexity in an effort to entertain him. To reverse this process, which she understands as a feminist problem, the unconscious expression of her training in female subordination, she must deliberately and persistently oppose him. At the same time, she recognizes how round and firm and fully packed his personality is, and how wispy, tentative, and embryonic her own looks next to it. Defining an authentic self necessarily takes the form of "wide opposition" and negation for her; and, in this sense, she is still dependent: "The joy of making statements not drawn from things heard or read but plumbed directly from the unconscious accumulations of her own experience was fermented by the surprise of his increased attention, and the pride of getting him occasionally to accept an idea or to modify a point of view. It beamed compensation for what she was losing in sacrificing, whenever expression was urgent in her, his unmatchable monologue to her own shapeless outpourings. But she laboured, now and then successfully, to hold this emotion in subjection to the urgency of the things she longed to express."[30] Even honesty can become merely a tactic for pleasing a man; as long as Richardson worried about holding Wells's attention, the ideas themselves were secondary. As with the Fabian Society, it went against Richardson's grain to admit that she had been annexed, and she had to rationalize her own susceptibility by arguing that women remain basically themselves, despite shifting their allegiances with their men.

She also rationalized the problem of her "shapeless outpourings" by working out a theory that saw shapelessness as the natural expression of female empathy, and pattern as the sign of male one-sidedness. If a novel had symbolic form, that was because a man's truncated vision was responsible for it. Men could be tidy in their fiction because they saw so little. Richardson's battle with Wells became more than a battle of the books, or even a sexual skirmish. She was claiming that the entire tradition of the English novel had misrepresented feminine reality. In her letters to the poet and essayist Henry Savage, especially during the 1950s, when she was able to put it most positively, Richardson returned obsessively to her theories of the female novel: "Monstrously, when I began, I felt that all masculine novels to date, despite their various fascinations, were somehow irrelevant, and the feminine ones far too much infl. [sic] by

magic traditions, and too much set upon exploiting the sex motif as hitherto seen and depicted by men."[31]

In pursuing a distinctively female consciousness, rather than attempting to explore female experience, Richardson was applying the ideas of the feminists, especially those of the social evolutionists and the spiritualists. She was fascinated by idealist theories of language and by the mystic's claims to being superior to the artist. Spiritualism in its highest and lowest forms she found irresistible; sixty years after the event she still loved to tell friends about a female palmist who had read her hand at a garden party and whispered "Begin to write." The faculty of prophecy, she wrote solemnly to Savage, seems to be a female trait, "save in those countries, notably Tibet, where men specialize in esoteric research."[32] Women had a monopoly on the essences of being; men had a monopoly on the metaphors of being.

The distinction between consciousness and experience was an important determinant of the direction modernist women's writing took. The Victorian world had been sexually polarized by experience; the normal lives of men and women had scarcely overlapped. By 1910, however, advanced women like Dorothy Richardson could move freely in social atmospheres previously closed to them; they could enjoy a masculine range of sexual and professional experiences. But the possession of quantitatively more experience did not lead to picaresque or even naturalistic fiction. Instead women writers found the world sexually polarized in psychological terms. They had fought to have a share in male knowledge; getting it, they decided that there were other ways of knowing. And by "other" they meant "better"; the tone of the female aesthetic usually wavered between the defiant and the superior.

Women, Richardson thought, were wise in their ancient maternal suffering. If they were to keep their advantage, therefore, they must continue to monopolize suffering and refuse to benefit by the social changes that would permit them to share masculine consciousness. Conversely, men had to remain emotionally childish, or women would lose their power. Socialists had observed with distress that, in the political realm, Mrs. Pankhurst's initial motives, which had included personal ambition, gradually merged with a mystical self-destructive identification with the Cause. Similarly, the quest for the female consciousness, basically a liberating and fulfilling pilgrimage, could become a self-defeating rejection of all male culture, an end in itself, a journey to nowhere. In the case of Dorothy Richardson, I think, female consciousness became a closed and sterile world; thus she was an innovator who did not attract disciples.

When we try to get down to some hard definitions of female realism as Richardson understood it, we are faced with a difficult task. For one thing, her own antipathy to definitions and schools was an obstacle to, and an evasion of, any personal effort to sort out her ideas. In addition, her most enthusiastic critics and interpreters have tended to circle around her theories. The most troublesome problem has been isolating the qualities, if there are any, that make the writing female in an absolute sense. It is one thing to show that fiction before 1910 differed from fiction after 1910, and to label the differences metaphorically "male" and "female" (or "masculine" and "androgynous" or "bisexual"). It is another thing altogether to talk about female style when you mean female content. And it is the hardest of all to prove that there are inherent sexual qualities to prose apart from its content, which was the crucial point Richardson wished to make.

Like Joyce, Richardson had philosophical objections to the inadequacy of language; unlike Joyce, she regarded language as a male construct. Richardson maintained that men and women used two different languages, or rather, the same language with different meanings. As might an Englishman and an American, "by every word they use men and women mean different things." Typically, she never gives an example of these differences, and sometimes she seems to imply that women have a separate dialect, which they speak to each other.[33] Generally, she implies that women communicate on a higher level; in using the language—the "words," as she says—of men, they limit themselves the way an intergalactic race of telepathics would limit itself in using speech. Thus in all social interactions dependent on "words" women are disadvantaged—not as a deprived subculture forced to use the dominant tongue, but as a superior race forced to operate on a lower level. "In speech with a man," she wrote in *The Tunnel,* "a woman is at a disadvantage—because they speak different languages. She may understand his. Hers he will never speak or understand. In pity, or from some other motives, she must therefore, stammeringly, speak his. He listens and is flattered and thinks he has her mental measure when he has not touched even the fringe of her consciousness."[34] Similarly in law, art, systems of thought, religions, and even writing, women were merely participating in men's games. Arid intel-

lect and egoism were the sources of all these foolish efforts; by becoming "women of letters," women risked spiritual sterility.

Such a philosophy would seem to preclude any successful competition with men in the fields of art, but Richardson argued that women's art was both qualitatively different and superior. It was the invisible art of creating atmosphere. Like mediums at the seance, women exhausted themselves in animating the inanimate, in creating harmony out of clashing personalities. Their preeminence in this art was the true source of emancipation. "It's as big an art as any other," Miriam assures Hypo in *Revolving Lights.* "Most women work at it the whole of the time. Not one man in a million is aware of it. It's like air within the air. It may be deadly. Cramping and awful, or simply destructive, so that no life is possible without it. So is the bad art of men. At its best it is absolutely life-giving. And not soft. Very hard and stern and austere in its beauty. And like mountain air. A woman's way of 'being' can be discovered in the way she pours out tea. . . . I feel the atmosphere created by the lady of the house as soon as I get on to the door step."[35]

This whole approach to the female consciousness had affinities to spiritualism. Men might invent religions, but women were in touch with the Beyond. The utter paradox of this theory, however, was that, as Richardson ruefully admitted, "it would be easier to make all this clear to a man than to a woman. The very words expressing it have been made by men."[36]

The stream-of-consciousness technique (a term, incidentally, that Richardson deplored, and parodied as the "Shroud of Consciousness") was an effort to transcend the dilemma by presenting the multiplicity and variety of associations held simultaneously in the female mode of perception. Henri Bergson's hypothesis that the intensity of an emotion depended on the number of memories and associations awakened by an event was relevant to this undertaking, but in Richardson's version all events evoke the same number of associations and thus have the same intensity.[37]

Dorothy Richardson did not want to suggest intensity. As many critics pointed out, her lack of punctuation, use of ellipsis, and fragmented sentences, worked against the structural potential of the sentence in terms of wit and climax, and main and subordinate ideas. Virginia Woolf was sufficiently impressed by this technique to call it "the psychological sentence of the feminine gender, a sentence of a more elastic fibre than the old, capable of stretching to the extreme, of suspending the frailest particles, of enveloping the vaguest shapes. Other writers of the opposite sex have used sentences of this description and stretched them to the extreme. But there is a difference. Miss Richardson has fashioned her sentence consciously, in order that it may descend to the depths and investigate the crannies of Miriam Henderson's consciousness. It is a woman's sentence, but only in the sense that it is used to describe a woman's mind by a writer who is neither proud nor afraid of anything she may discover in the psychology of her sex."[38]

Richardson may indeed have fashioned the woman's sentence, or at least the chosen sentence of the female aesthetic. But Woolf is seriously mistaken in calling it unafraid. It is afraid of the unique, the intimate, the physical. By placing the center of reality in the subjective consciousness, and then making consciousness a prism that divides sensation into its equally meaningful single colors, Richardson avoids any discussion of sensation itself, especially as a unified and powerful force. Just as she would not commit herself to ideologies, she would not discriminate among her experiences.

Most of all, Richardson's art is afraid of an ending. Looked at from one point of view, her inability to finish is a statement in itself, a response to the apocalyptic vision of Wells and Lawrence. If men were so obsessed by their sense of an ending that they could not understand the present moment, women were outside of time and epoch, and within eternity. But as Richardson grew older, her relationship to *Pilgrimage* became more obviously possessive and anxious. The book was an extension of herself; to complete it was to die. When Dent published an edition of *Pilgrimage* in 1938, Richardson was deeply upset to read that critics thought this was the whole book. From 1939 to 1951 she worked on a final section of *Pilgrimage;* after her death the manuscript (published as *March Moonlight*) was discovered among her papers; presumably, it was still unfinished. Her conception of the book as a continuous process was the myth that enabled her to publish at all; without such a sustaining illusion, Olive Schreiner, a novelist of very similar temperament, found herself endlessly writing and rewriting the same unfinished book. It is significant that in *March Moonlight* Richardson finally identified her obsession with the process of her own life as guilt: "If one could fully forgive oneself, the energy it takes to screen off the memory of the past would be set free."[39]

Pilgrimage can be read as the artistic equivalent of a screen, a way of hiding and containing and disarming the raw energy of a rampaging past. Richardson devised an aesthetic strategy that protected her enough from the confrontation with her own violence, rage, grief, and sexuality that she could work. The female aesthetic was meant for survival, and one cannot deny that Richardson was able to produce an enormous novel, or that Virginia Woolf wrote several, under its shelter. But ultimately, how much better it would have been if they could have forgiven themselves, if they could have faced the anger instead of denying it, could have translated the consciousness of their own darkness into confrontation instead of struggling to transcend it. For when the books were finished, the darkness was still with them, as dangerous and as inviting as it had always been, and they were helpless to fight it.

Notes

1. "Women and Fiction," *Collected Essays,* II, London, 1966, p. 147.

2. *Some Contemporary Novelists (Women)*, London, 1920, pp. xiv-xv.

3. May Sinclair, *The Creators*, quoted in Johnson, *Some Contemporary Novelists*, p. 37; and "The Novels of Dorothy Richardson," *Little Review,* IV (April 1918), quoted in Johnson, *Some Contemporary Novelists*, p. 135.

4. Quentin Bell, *Virginia Woolf: A Biography,* I, London, 1972, pp. 209, 211.

5. Quoted in Johnson, *Some Contemporary Novelists*, p. xiv.

6. Radclyffe Hall, *The Unlit Lamp,* New York, 1929, pp. 358-359. See also May Sinclair, *Mary Olivier: A Life,* London, 1919, for an elaborate study of female role-conflict and renunciation.

7. *Journey from the North,* I, London, 1969, p. 88.

8. D. H. Lawrence to Thomas Dacre Dunlap, 7 July 1914, *Selected Letters of D. H. Lawrence,* ed. Diana Trilling, New York, 1961, p. 83.

9. R. Ellis Roberts, *Portrait of Stella Benson,* London, 1939, p. 215.

10. Gordon N. Ray, *H. G. Wells and Rebecca West,* New Haven, 1974, p. xv.

11. Ray, p. 123. See also Norman and Jeanne Mackenzie, *The Time Traveller,* London, 1973, p. 339.

12. *A Writer's Diary,* ed. Leonard Woolf, New York, 1968, p. 14.

13. *The Letters of Katherine Mansfield,* I, ed. J. Middleton Murry, New York, 1929, p. 71.

14. "Katherine Mansfield: Fifty Years On," *Harpers & Queen* (July 1973): 107.

15. Rose Odle, "Some Memories of Dorothy M. Richardson and Alan Odle," November 18, 1957; unpublished ms., Dorothy Richardson Collection, Beinecke Library, Yale University.

16. John Rosenberg, *Dorothy Richardson: The Genius They Forgot*, London, 1973, p. 8.

17. Ibid., p. 17.

18. *The Tunnel, Pilgrimage*, II, New York, 1967, p. 220. There is a very similar passage in *A Room of One's Own*, in which the narrator, doing research on women in the British Museum Reading Room, imagines a definitive male treatise on female inferiority. Virginia Woolf reviewed *The Tunnel* for the *Times Literary Supplement* (February 13, 1919): 81.

19. *The Tunnel*, p. 221.

20. Dorothy Richardson Collection, Beinecke Library, Yale University.

21. *Middlemarch*, ed. Gordon S. Haight, Cambridge, Mass., 1956, bk. II, ch. 20, p. 144.

22. "Women in the Arts," *Vanity Fair,* May 1925.

23. *Revolving Lights, Pilgrimage*, III, New York, 1967, p. 259.

24. Quoted in Sydney Kaplan, "Featureless Freedom or Ironic Submission," *College English* (May 1971): 917.

25. Letter to Curtis Brown, January 16, 1950, Dorothy Richardson Collection, Beinecke Library, Yale University.

26. Foreword to *Pilgrimage*, New York, 1938. See also Caesar Blake, *Dorothy Richardson*, Ann Arbor, 1960, pp. 181-182.

27. *Dawn's Left Hand, Pilgrimage*, IV, New York, 1967, pp. 239-240.

28. Horace Gregory, *Dorothy Richardson: An Adventure in Self-Discovery*, New York, 1967, p. 113.

29. Vincent Brome, *H. G. Wells*, New York, 1951, p. 127.

30. *Revolving Lights*, p. 255.

31. Quoted in Gregory, *Dorothy Richardson*, p. 12.

32. Ibid.

33. *Oberland, Pilgrimage*, IV, New York, 1967, p. 93.

34. *The Tunnel*, p. 210.

35. *Revolving Lights*, p. 257.

36. *Revolving Lights*, p. 79.

37. See Henri Bergson, *Time and Free Will*, New York, 1960. Katherine Mansfield had no sympathy with this refusal to take hold. "Everything being of equal importance," she wrote of *Interim*, "it is impossible that everything should not be of equal unimportance" (*Novels and Novelists*, New York, 1930, p. 137).

38. Virginia Woolf, "Romance and the Heart," *Nation and Athenaeum* (May 19, 1923): 229.

39. *March Moonlight*, p. 607.

SANDRA M. GILBERT AND SUSAN GUBAR (ESSAY DATE 1988)

SOURCE: Gilbert, Sandra M., and Susan Gubar. "The Battle of the Sexes: The Men's Case." In *No Man's Land: The Place of the Woman Writer in the Twentieth Century*, pp. 3-62. New Haven, Conn.: Yale University Press, 1988.

In the following excerpt, Gilbert and Gubar detail the views of early twentieth-century male authors regarding the burgeoning women's movement.

In 1913, one Walter Heape, M.A., F.R.S.—a reader in zoology at Cambridge—produced a book entitled *Sex Antagonism* in which he summarized the increasing fervor with which the battle of the sexes was being waged as the suffrage campaign intensified during the first two decades of the twentieth century. Reviewing many of the same social transformations that, say, Henry Adams summarized, he cogently described the escalated hostilities to which those transformations led:

> To most of us a sex war appears to be an entirely new experience. For fifty years we may have noted the gradual growth of opinions which have led to a more or less indefinite alteration in the tone of the sexes to each other; for the last twenty-five years we may have recognized just cause for that alteration and some of the advantages to be derived from it; but of late we have been face to face with strife as selfish, as brutal, as bitter, and as unrestrained as that shown in any class war between men alone, and man's opinion of woman has been definitely modified—his attitude toward her as an integral component of society can never be the same again.[1]

Later in the book, Heape elaborated and clarified this point, declaring that "the present woman's movement has its origin in sex antagonism" and that regardless of its avowed goals the movement's "driving force is engendered by desire to alter the laws which regulate the relations, and therefore the relative power, of the sexes" (205).

Heape's view of the matter was one shared by many contemporary literary men, though relatively few of them spoke so plainly about the connection between the suffrage battle and sex antagonism. In the same year that Heape's book appeared, for instance, Ford Madox Ford began to write his classic, *The Good Soldier: A Tale of Passion* (1915). Though this book is usually read as an epistemological analysis of a moral maze in which its unreliable narrator is hopelessly trapped, it is significant that this moral maze is a labyrinth of sex antagonisms and that its author's characterizations of women seem to controvert his own frequently expressed feminist leanings.[2] Leonora, the anti-heroine who is married to Edward Ashburnham, the "good soldier" of the book's ironic title, fights "a long, silent duel with invisible weapons" against her husband because she sees "Life as a perpetual sex-battle between husbands who desire to be unfaithful to their wives, and wives who desire to recapture their husbands in the end."[3] As for the woman Edward desires, propelled by what the narrator defines as "the sex instinct that makes women be intolerably cruel to the beloved person" (245), she joins with Leonora to give him an unimaginable hell. Those two women pursued that poor devil and flayed the skin off him as if they had done it with whips. I tell you his mind bled almost visibly. I seem to see him stand, naked to the waist, his forearms shielding his eyes, and flesh hanging from him in rags. I tell you that is no exaggeration of what I feel. It was as if Leonora and Nancy banded themselves together to do execution, for the sake of humanity, upon the body of a man who was at their disposal. They were like a couple of Sioux who had got hold of an Apache and had him well tied to a stake. I tell you there was no end to the tortures they inflicted upon him.[4]

That the "finest French novel in the English language" (xx), as Ford liked to report his book had been characterized, dramatizes moral and epistemological problems through a sex antagonism that is infiltrated by Swinburnean (and Flaubertian) imagery of flagellation suggests the ways in which the "brutal," "bitter" strife Walter Heape describes became crucial in even the most apparently rarefied modernist aesthetic experiments. More openly than Ford, for instance, such figures as T. S. Eliot and D. H. Lawrence often concentrate with virtually sadistic fervor on the war between the sexes, a war that they frequently imagine as being waged with Swinburnean eroticism. Like Quintus's Achilles or Kleist's Penthesilea, their protagonists fetishize dead bodies with necrophiliac intensity or savor sadistic bites as if they were kisses. But where the mythic Amazons of earlier texts were allegorized as private sexual threats to a public social order that was perceived as ultimately changeless, the modernists' Amazonian New Women represented a female sexual autonomy that was a sign of radical social change, a kind of social change that only partially surfaced in Swinburne's work but whose implications Walter Heape has analyzed and protested.

To be sure, Eliot's early unpublished "The Love Song of St. Sebastian" seems to be entirely under the sado-masochistic influence of Swinburne in its depiction of the battle between men and women, and this text may seem shocking, coming as it does from the classical, royalist, Anglican Nobel prizewinner who produced such orthodox works as "Ash Wednesday" and *Murder in the Cathedral*. Yet in a sense the poem simply dramatizes the most "brutal" implications of sexual hostilities that are also embedded in other texts by Eliot, including the far more subdued "Love Song of J. Alfred Prufrock." Swearing deadly loyalty to his mistress, the self-flagellating speaker of "St. Sebastian" openly associates desire with destruction, sex with violence, for he promises first to flog himself in order to demonstrate his erotic passion

and then to strangle and disfigure his beloved so that she will no longer be beautiful to anyone but him.[5] Indeed, the rhetoric of this extraordinary "Love Song" virtually replicates a passage in Swinburne's *Lesbia Brandon* (written ca. 1864-70; published 1952) about one of the novel's men in love, a character who seems to represent many of Swinburne's enamoured personae when he fantasizes about his beloved that

> Deeply he desired to die by her, if that could be; and more deeply, if this could be, to destroy her: scourge her with swooning and absorb the blood with kisses; caress and lacerate her loveliness, alleviate and heighten her pains; to feel her foot upon his throat, and wound her own with his teeth; submit his body and soul for a little to her lightest will, and satiate upon hers the desperate caprice of his immeasurable desire; to inflict careful torture on limbs too tender to embrace, suck the tears off her laden eyelids, bite through her sweet and shuddering lips.[6]

It is significant that, beyond its Swinburnean overtones, "St. Sebastian" points to a consciousness of sex warfare that permeates much of Eliot's work because several other texts written in the same period specifically associate such struggle with the demands of the New Woman. "Petit Epître," a Laforguian verse in French from the same manuscript in which "St. Sebastian" appears, mockingly takes a stand against votes for women, while "Cousin Nancy" (1917) frankly satirizes the specious modernity of the liberated Miss Nancy Ellicott, who not only "smoked / And danced all the modern dances" but also, as if to destroy the earth itself, "Strode across the hills and *broke* them" (emphasis ours).[7] Even the poem's allusive conclusion implicitly censures this aggressive protoflapper:

> Upon the glazen shelves kept watch
> Matthew and Waldo, guardians of the faith,
> The army of unalterable law.
>
> [22]

Though Eliot presents Matthew (Arnold) and Waldo (Emerson) ironically, as fragile "guardians of the faith," the fact that they are identified with the "army of unalterable law" which defeats "Prince Lucifer" in Meredith's "Lucifer in Starlight" suggests that Eliot sees the rebellious Nancy as a diabolical upstart whose breaking of nature (the hills) also threatens to break the grounds of culture.

But if Nancy Ellicott is characterized through metaphor and allusion as a problematic figure, the unnatural culture she epitomizes is more graphically explored in "Prufrock Among the Women," a draft of "The Love Song of J. Alfred

Prufrock" (1917) in which Eliot's famously balding, modern anti-Hamlet wanders woefully through what is clearly a red-light district, a sinister city of women that is even sleazier than the city of women from which James's Ransom rescues his Verena in *The Bostonians*.[8] And the published text of "Prufrock" also emphasizes the ways in which the absurdly self-conscious modern male intellectual is rendered impotent by, and in, the company of women. Pinned to the wall by "eyes that fix you in a formulated phrase" (5) and that make it impossible for him to formulate his own phrases, Prufrock becomes a helpless object of the deadly female gaze. Yet his escapist encounters with "seagirls wreathed with seaweed red and brown" (7) are equally fatal. Nature, contaminated by female sexuality, drowns the male subject while culture, polluted by women who "come and go / Talking of Michelangelo" (3), denies or derides him.

Oddly enough, Prufrock's obsession with the fact that women *could* freely come and go, not only "talking of" but also gazing at and metaphorically possessing the paintings and sculptures of Michelangelo, foreshadows a reference to the Renaissance artist in a later, and very dissimilar, poem by another modernist writer, and a conflation of the two texts illuminates twentieth-century men's heightened anxiety about women's invasion of culture. Yeats's "Under Ben Bulben," praising "measurement," notes that

> Michael Angelo left a proof
> On the Sistine Chapel roof,
> Where but half-awakened Adam
> Can disturb globe-trotting Madam
> Till her bowels are in heat. . . .[9]

Both the travels and the sexuality of Yeats's heated, "globe-trotting Madam" help reveal the problems of Eliot and his contemporaries, problems that Yeats, like Eliot, probably at least at first associated with the suffrage movement. Just as Eliot indicated his opposition to votes for women in "Petit Epître," Yeats had expressed in "In Memory of Eva Gore-Booth and Con Markiewicz" his antagonism toward feminism, noting of the suffrage partisan Gore-Booth that she "dreams— / Some vague Utopia—and she seems, / When withered old and skeleton-gaunt, / An image of such politics" (229).

But Madam's travels and her sexuality also symbolize a modernist transformation of the turn-of-the-century world inhabited by Princess Ida that was as drastic as the change reflected in the shift from Tennyson's text to Gilbert and Sullivan's operetta. Where fin-de-siècle lady travelers

explored the globe, early twentieth-century women began to colonize it, creating not only intellectual communities—colleges and professional societies—where women might "come and go / Talking of Michelangelo," but also artistic circles and avant-garde salons where they might, and did, experiment with new aesthetic as well as erotic styles. As Winifred Holtby observed in the first major study of Virginia Woolf (1932).

> When she wrote of women, [Virginia Woolf] wrote of a generation as adventurous in its exploration of experience as the Elizabethan men had been in their exploration of the globe. The women whom Mrs. Woolf knew were exploring the professional world, the political world, the world of business, discovering that they themselves had legs as well as wombs, brains as well as nerves, reason as well as sensibility; their Americas lay within themselves, and altered the map as profoundly as any added by Cabot or Columbus. Like Raleigh, they founded their new colonies; like Drake, they combined national service with privateering.[10]

What Holtby intuited has, of course, long since been statistically documented. According to the historian William Chafe, the first two decades of the twentieth century witnessed, in America, a "1000 per cent" increase of women's enrollment in public colleges and a "482 per cent" increase of female enrollment in private schools; if the figures for England were not quite so striking, they were almost equally impressive to contemporary observers, so much so that an advertisement for Abdulla cigarettes, which appeared in Oxford's *Isis* magazine, comically articulated the defensive bravado with which male undergraduates greeted their female classmates:

> Pretty Phyllis with a vote
> And a Varsity degree,
> Greek and Latin you may quote
> But you can't bamboozle me!
> Brilliant, up-to-date and smart,
> You're a savage squaw at heart. . . .
>
> Phyllis, when I come to woo,
> Disregarding sneer and snub
> I shall act as cave-men do—
> Knock you senseless with a club!
> Courtships of a higher grade
> Simply bore a savage maid.[11]

Besides educational advances, the years between 1914 and 1918 saw the entrance of massive numbers of women into the work force, an event necessitated by the exigencies of World War I; as we shall demonstrate in our next volume, when formerly male-occupied places in industry were taken by women, men often felt as assaulted on the home front as they were on the military front itself. Finally, the end of the second decade of the century witnessed what seemed at the time the ultimate female victory: the winning of the vote by English and American women like *Isis*'s "pretty Phyllis" after almost a century-long battle.

But the crisis caused by male dispossession and female self-possession would also have been intensified by the dramatic achievements of a growing number of notable women. From the spiritualists Madame Blavatsky and Annie Besant, founders of the Theosophical Society, and the anthropologists Jane Harrison, Jessie Weston, Ruth Benedict, Margaret Mead, and Zora Neale Hurston to such dancers, painters, and musicians as Isadora Duncan, Martha Graham, Mary Cassatt, and Ethel Smyth, such birth-control advocates as Margaret Sanger and Marie Stopes, and such psychologists as Helene Deutsch, Karen Horney, and Melanie Klein, women established themselves in positions of increasing intellectual centrality. In addition, from Renée Vivien and Natalie Barney to Vita Sackville-West, Gertrude Stein, Edna St. Vincent Millay, and Elinor Wylie, female writers flouted Victorian conventions as they flaunted their sexuality through well-publicized lesbian affairs or equally well-publicized heterosexual promiscuity.

Clearly the new liberation of these literary women, like the awakened desire of Yeats's "globetrotting Madam," reflected a radical alteration in the very conception of female sexuality, an alteration that began with the proselytizings of Free Love advocates like Victoria Woodhull and Emma Goldman and was further implemented by the obviously influential works of the sexologists Edward Carpenter and Havelock Ellis and, even more obviously, by the writings of Sigmund Freud. Though Freud in particular may have had—and may have meant to have—a negative impact on feminism because, among other things, of his theory that woman had to accept the "fact" of her "castration," the general effect of his studies and others was a reimagining of female desire.[12] Where most Victorian theorists had hypothesized an essential and appropriate female "passionlessness," modernist thinkers assumed an essential and somewhat alarming female passion.[13] They knew, too, that women were now freer than ever before to act on that passion, for the dissemination of birth-control information and equipment in the 1910s and 1920s disengaged reproduction from sexuality, removing one major impediment to female erotic freedom.[14]

Inevitably, then, such a feminist theorist as Dora Russell supported Yeats's suspicion about his Madam's "bowels" by claiming in her 1925 *Hypatia* that, for women, "sex, even without children and without marriage is . . . a thing of dignity, beauty, and delight."[15] Perhaps just as inevitably, male thinkers were daunted by women's newfound libidinous energy, and literary men tended to reenvision the battle of the sexes as an erotically charged sexual struggle. Where both *The Princess* and *Princess Ida* had set masses of women, represented by male champions, against platoons of men in a publicly enacted military contest, modernist texts describe explicitly sexual duels between characters who tend to incarnate female voracity and male impotence. "A feature of modern life," mused Dora Russell in *Hypatia*, "is that matrimonial quarrels, like modern war, are carried on on a large scale, involving not individuals, nor even small groups of individuals, but both sexes and whole classes of society" (1). That Russell's female contemporaries felt they would win that modern war is evident from the title of their polemical journal, *Time and Tide*, with its allusion to a feminist victory which will "wait for no man."[16]

But that men feared they were losing such contests is plain even in a number of texts which do not explicitly deal with sexual battles. Images of impotence recur with unnerving frequency in the most canonical male modernist novels and poems. Of course, a number of Victorian literary men also deal with threats to masculine authority. As early as 1852, for example, Charles Dickens created a character whose name, Nemo, as much as his enthrallment to the sinister Lady Deadlock, implied that a no man lingers and sickens at the heart of *Bleak House*, while Tennyson presented both his King Arthur and his Prince Hilarion as feminized and, in the case of Arthur, cuckolded.[17] But from the betrayed and passive narrator of Ford's *Good Soldier* to cuckolded Leopold Bloom in Joyce's *Ulysses* and the wounded Fisher King in Eliot's *The Waste Land* to the eunuch Jake Barnes in Hemingway's *The Sun Also Rises*, the paralyzed Clifford Chatterley in Lawrence's *Lady Chatterley's Lover*, and the gelded Benjy in Faulkner's *The Sound and the Fury* as well as the castrated Joe Christmas in *Light in August*, maimed, unmanned, victimized characters are obsessively created by early twentieth-century literary men.[18] Because until recently the texts in which these characters appear have been privileged as documents in a history of cultural crises, the sexual anxieties they articulate have been seen mainly as metaphors of metaphysical angst. But though they do, of course, express angst, it is significant that these modernist

ON THE SUBJECT OF...

KATE MILLETT (1934-)

Millett's 1970 book *Sexual Politics*, widely perceived as an impetus for second-wave feminism, examines what Millett calls "male supremacy" from an historical, anthropological, sociological, and literary perspective. In the book, which began as Millett's 1969 doctoral thesis, she asserts that "all historical civilizations are patriarchies," and defines patriarchy as "the ideology of male supremacy socialized through temperament, role, and status," providing extensive historical examples to support her assertions, including an analysis of the misogyny present in Freudian theory and of the degradation of women characters in the works of such authors as D. H. Lawrence and Henry Miller. While viewed as provocative and polemical, *Sexual Politics* was enormously popular, selling 80,000 copies within months of its release. Millett became a well-known media figure. During the mid-1960s Millett was active in the women's movement, serving as a charter member of the National Organization for Women (NOW), as well as in the antiwar and civil rights movements. Her role as a central figure in the political and social controversy surrounding the 1970s women's movement was difficult for Millett, who received harsh criticism for her work as well as for her lifestyle, when her lesbianism was revealed in the mainstream media. Millett chronicles her experiences following the publication of *Sexual Politics* in her 1974 book, *Flying*. Millett was born in St. Paul, Minnesota and is an accomplished educator, literary scholar, and artist as well as an author. She has taught English at such institutions as the University of North Carolina at Chapel Hill, Wasada University in Japan, and Barnard College. Her later works include 1981's *Going to Iran*, in which she relates her journey to Iran, where she addressed Iranian feminists on International Women's Day in 1979, and *The Politics of Cruelty: An Essay on the Literature of Political Imprisonment* (1994).

Millett, Kate. In *Sexual Politics: The Classic Analysis of the Interplay Between Men, Women and Culture*. 3rd ed., p. 26. New York: Touchstone, 1990.

formulations of societal breakdown consistently employed imagery of male impotence and female potency.

Not only in letters but in life, moreover, a number of modernist authors record, if not their own, their contemporaries' sexual anxiety. William Carlos Williams, for instance, recalls in his *Autobiography* that a member of the French Chamber of Deputies, during a visit to Natalie Barney's Paris salon, had responded to the sight of women "dancing gaily together on all sides" by undoing "his pants buttons, [taking] out his tool and, shaking it right and left, yell[ing] out in a rage, 'Have you never seen one of these?'"[19] Similarly, Hemingway remembers in *A Moveable Feast* how, in his role as "Papa," he had allayed F. Scott Fitzgerald's fears about penile inadequacy not only by explaining that "It is not basically the size in repose . . . It is the size that it becomes. It is also a question of angle" but also by taking the author of *The Great Gatsby* to the Louvre—which they viewed as a veritable penile colony—where the anxious Fitzgerald could compare his own equipment with that attached to Greek statues.[20]

Given such nightmarish intimations of no-manhood, the virulence with which many of these writers struck out against the women whom they saw as both the sources and the witnesses of their emasculation was perhaps understandable. Again, the author of *Sex Antagonism* describes the situation, recording the link between male discontent and masculinist backlash. "Perhaps the most remarkable fact in connection with the modern woman's revolt is not the activity of the dissatisfied woman so much as the complacency of the dissatisfied man," Walter Heape observes, but he then goes on to warn that the oppressed man will "act with all the more force when the proper time comes for action" (214). As if to illustrate his point, modernist men of letters sought to define appropriately virile reactions. Whether they imagined male characters defeating or defeated in the sexual combats and marital quarrels which Dora Russell associated with a world embroiled in gender warfare, their side of the war of the words was motivated by murderous intensity.

Even T. S. Eliot, his theories about the "extinction of personality" in poetry notwithstanding, responded to the threats posed by women who "come and go / Talking of Michelangelo" with fantasies of femicide. In life, the creator of Prufrock was fascinated by—and once attended a party costumed as—the wife-murderer Dr. Crippen.[21] And in the fragmentary drama *Sweeney Agonistes* (1927), a work whose title obviously alludes to Milton's *Samson Agonistes,* Eliot's protagonist, who may well be modeled on murderous Sweeney Todd, "the demon barber of Fleet Street," first threatens the floozy Doris by promising to take her to a "cannibal isle" and convert her into "a nice little, white little, missionary stew" and then tells the sinister story of a man who "once did a girl in," explaining that

Any man might do a girl in
Any man has to, needs to, wants to
Once in a lifetime, do a girl in.

[122]

In *The Family Reunion* (1939), moreover, Eliot dramatized the tale of a man who may have killed (and certainly believes he has killed) a hard-drinking, New Womanly, Delilahesque wife of whom his mother remarks that "She never wanted to fit herself to Harry, / But only to bring Harry down to her own level" because she was no more than "A restless shievering painted shadow."[22] That in reality the author of *The Family Reunion* had abandoned his own wife a few years before his composition of this play suggests the subjective intensity that shaped the "objective correlative" he constructed here.[23]

As many critics have observed, such intensity also permeates the work of D. H. Lawrence, the male contemporary whom Eliot so savagely attacked in his 1934 *After Strange Gods.* Expatriates in different directions, D. H. Lawrence and T. S. Eliot would seem to have been diametrically opposed both in class allegiances and in theological theories. Yet even while the philosophical quarrels that characterized their careers made them into aesthetic opposites, their sexual anxieties made them into mirror images of each other—indeed, to use one of Lawrence's favorite terms, into blood brothers. Lawrence's short story "Samson and Delilah," for instance, alludes, as did *Sweeney Agonistes,* to the Biblical and Miltonic account of *Samson Agonistes* but imagines female defeat by male sexuality rather than by male murderousness. The tale begins by describing an Amazonian woman who, with the help of some soldiers, inflicts bondage and discipline on her estranged husband while questioning and ridiculing his manhood ("Do you call yourself a *man?*"), but it concludes with his insistence on his sexual authority: as "his hand insinuate[s] itself between her breasts," he blandly remarks that "a bit of a fight for a how-de-do pleases me, that it do. But that doesn't mean that you're going to deny as you're my missis."[24]

Elsewhere, lamenting a world occupied by "cocksure women" and "hensure men," Lawrence finds it harder to envision male victory.[25] In the poem "Figs," for instance, he brings to the surface the sexual tensions that haunt Eliotian texts from "The Love Song of St. Sebastian" to "The Love Song of J. Alfred Prufrock" and *Sweeney Agonistes,* complaining that "the year of our women has fallen overripe"; for, demanding an equal place in the sun, "our women" have horrifyingly "bursten into self-assertion."[26] But nowhere is the *Blütbruderschaft* of that odd couple Eliot and Lawrence more vividly revealed than in Lawrence's ironically titled *Women in Love* (1920). Although this novel, like its precursor *The Rainbow,* frequently adopts a female perspective in order both to celebrate the sensitivity and receptivity of one of its heroines—Ursula Brangwen—and, in the case of *Women in Love,* to critique the priggish "Salvator Mundi" quality of its hero, Rupert Birkin, the book also records the corrosiveness of female desire in order to repudiate "'Cybele—curse her! the accursed Syria Dea!'"[27]

With varying degrees of intensity, three couples in this work engage in metaphysical and physical struggles for primacy which seem to replicate the Swinburnean struggles Eliot records and to dramatize the implications of the more superficially civilized struggles enacted in *The Bostonians, The Blithedale Romance, Princess Ida,* and *The Princess.* In the chapter called "Breadalby," for instance, Birkin's sometime mistress Hermione experiences "a terrible voluptuous thrill" (78) in her arms as she approaches the moment of "perfect, unutterable consummation" (78) when she will smash a ball of lapis lazuli on her lover's head. Her arms tingling with what seems like Zenobia's "terrible inflexibility" and with what Lawrence describes as "never-ending hostility," she knows that "It was coming!" (78)—a consummation of agonistic desire not unlike the sexual fury Eliot and Swinburne transcribe. Again, in the chapter called "Water Party," a woman assaults a man. Gerald's sister Diana is not content to drown alone the way Zenobia does; having fallen overboard from a miniature steamer like the one that plies the squire's lake at the opening of *The Princess,* this young girl, who is tellingly nicknamed "Di," dies with "her arms tight round the neck" of the young doctor who tried to save her; and "'She killed him,' said Gerald" (181). But finally, of course, the most radical combat in the book is between Gerald and Gudrun, two characters whose profoundly sexual struggle is central to *Women in Love.*

Modeled in part on Katherine Mansfield, Gudrun is an archetypal New Woman whose feelings for Gerald are even more ambivalent than those of Hermione for Birkin. But while the famous "Rabbit" chapter reveals the perverse sadism she and her lover share, their struggle in the snow at the end of the novel epitomizes the sexual hostility which engendered so much literary violence in the modernist period. High in the glittering Alps, after the relationship between the pair has begun seriously to disintegrate, Gerald feels a sudden desire to murder Gudrun: "He thought, what a perfect voluptuous fulfillment it would be to kill her . . . to strangle her, to strangle every spark of life out of her, till she lay completely inert, soft, relaxed for ever, a soft heap lying dead between his hands, utterly dead. Then he would have had her finally and for ever; there would be such a perfect voluptuous finality" (452). As if he were reworking Robert Browning's "Porphyria's Lover" with little of Browning's distance, Lawrence transcribes Gerald's femicidal desire without irony. Yet what happens on the slopes is that Gudrun, unlike the seductively passive Porphyria, raises "her clenched hand high, and [brings] it down, with a great downward stroke on to the face and on to the breast of Gerald" (463), and it is only at this point that he decides to "take the apple of his desire" and, like Eliot's Saint Sebastian, strangle his mistress. "What bliss! Oh what bliss, at last, what satisfaction, at last!" he thinks while—as if echoing Hawthorne's Coverdale—he observes the horror of her "swollen face" and notices "How ugly she was!" (463) When his own murderous desire fails, however, and he climbs an icy ridge, lit by "a small bright moon" (464)—a moon reminiscent of "the accursed Syria Dea" Birkin tries to shatter—her deadly will at least figuratively triumphs, for he understands, as he ascends toward death, that "Somebody was going to murder him" (465).

Not insignificantly, the triumph of Gudrun's New Womanly determination at the end of *Women in Love* is facilitated by the intervention of a New Man, the terrifying no-man named (after Wagner's Loge) Loerke, a dwarfish and, says Birkin, probably Jewish industrial artist whose arrogance and cynicism utterly undermine the plans of the Siegfried-like hero that Gerald ought to have been. Discussing him earlier, Gerald and Birkin have mused on his inexplicable attractiveness to women. In response to Gerald's quasi-Freudian query "What *do* women want, at the bottom?," Birkin has speculated that it is "Some satisfaction in basic repulsion, it seems to me. They seem to creep down some ghastly tunnel of darkness, and will never be satisfied till they've come to the end. . . . They want to explore the sewers, and

[Loerke] is the wizard rat that swims ahead" (418-19). It is therefore fitting that during the battle in the snow Loerke's intervention arrests Gerald's murderous will to throttle Gudrun. "Monsieur," says the little sculptor sardonically in a French which represents the sinister country that had threatened Tennyson's college men, "Quand vous aurez fini—" (464), and it is this phrase which inspires in Gerald "a decay of strength . . . a fearful weakness" that causes him to abandon his femicidal project and "drift" up the mountainside toward annihilation. In a world inhabited by murderous women who seek "satisfaction in basic repulsion," Gerald must die because there are "no more *men*, there [are] only creatures, little, ultimate *creatures* like Loerke" (443).[28]

Such a no man's land of mad women and unmanned or maddened men appears with striking frequency throughout the works of a number of Lawrence's and Eliot's contemporaries. Booth Tarkington, Ernest Hemingway, William Faulkner, and Nathanael West, for instance, record their horror at a battle they fear men are losing. In Tarkington's fantasy "The Veiled Feminists of Atlantis" (1926), women's rebellion against male rule takes the form of wanting not just equality but superiority, and specifically a superiority which depends on their gaining access to the educational mysteries once solely known to men even while they retain the erotic mystery conferred by the female veil. Because the men "had accepted equality" but "they could not accept the new inequality" which placed them at a "disadvantage," the two sexes go to war, using "mountain ranges and thunder and lightning as familiar weapons," until "the ocean came over the land in waves thousands of feet tall" and both sexes perish in the fabled sinking of Atlantis.[29] Less apocalyptically but just as catastrophically, in "The Short Happy Life of Francis Macomber" (1936) Hemingway describes a married couple, the Macombers, on safari with their white hunter, Robert Wilson; Wilson's belief that Mrs. Macomber is "simply enamelled in that American female cruelty" is corroborated, first, when she responds to her husband's cowardice on a lion hunt by sleeping with Wilson and then when she reacts to her husband's courageous confrontation with a buffalo by accidentally-on-purpose shooting him, while ostensibly firing at the wounded beast. "Why didn't you poison him? That's what they do in England," Wilson scathingly remarks, for, though Wilson may be in some ways a problematic character, Hemingway's tale implies that Macomber is trapped in a dire double bind: whether he is cowardly or courageous, unmanned or manly, his wife is determined to betray him.[30]

Even more disturbing depictions of female sexuality and aggression occur in Faulkner's *Light in August* (1932) and West's *Miss Lonelyhearts* (1933). Joanna Burden, the mannish spinster of *Light in August,* is shown to want and to deserve the phallic retribution exacted by her black lover Joe Christmas, who first despoils her virginity, then arouses her desire, and finally murders her after a long sexual struggle. Perhaps because she is unnatural—she has the "strength and fortitude of a man" and "man-trained muscles and . . . man-trained habit[s] of thinking"—Joe experiences intercourse with her as combat, musing that "It was as if he struggled physically with another man." Yet when she is erotically unmanned, Joanna becomes even more unnatural: yielding to nymphomania, she reveals a "rotten richness ready to flow into putrefaction at a touch, like something growing in a swamp."[31] Finally, therefore, her unnatural toxicity leads to Joe's own unmanning, for after he murders her he is castrated and killed by a vengeful white man. And as Joyce Carol Oates observes, "the dead woman at the center of the novel is judged [by Faulkner] as rightly dead, and her murderer is 'innocently' guilty in the service of a complex of passions that dramatize the tragic relations between white and black *men.*"[32]

Similarly, although all the characters in West's *Miss Lonelyhearts* are grotesque, the final unmanning of the man called "Miss Lonelyhearts" is a direct result of his sexual victimization by, and struggle against, the monstrous Mrs. Doyle. Looking "like a police captain," with "legs like Indian clubs" and "massive hams . . . like two enormous grindstones,"[33] this insatiable lady seduces the columnist at their first meeting, then a few days later sends her crippled husband to invite him to dinner. The meal is bizarrely marked by her skirmishes with both men: as Miss Lonelyhearts enters her house, she "goose[s] him and laugh[s]" (47); then she "roll[s] a newspaper into a club and [strikes] her husband on the mouth with it." At this Doyle unaccountably tears open Miss Lonelyhearts' fly as the gigantic woman kicks the cripple.

Finally, after her mate has left to buy some gin, Mrs. Doyle tries again to seduce Miss Lonelyhearts in what becomes virtually a rape scene. Although he tries to fend her off,

> she opened the neck of her dress and tried to force his head between her breasts [and] he parted his knees with a quick jerk that slipped her to the floor. She tried to pull him down on top of her. He struck out blindly and hit her in the face. She screamed and he hit her again and again. He kept hitting her until she stopped trying to hold him, then he ran out of the house.
>
> [50]

When at the end of the novel Miss Lonelyhearts rushes downstairs to greet the crippled Mr. Doyle in a Christlike effort to restore him to wholeness, the explosion of Doyle's gun functions at least covertly as an assertion of Mrs. Doyle's will (not unlike Loerke's assertion of Gudrun's will in *Women in Love*). Thus when the columnist dies, locked in the deadly embrace of a dwarfish noman, West implies that, like so many other male characters created by modernist men of letters, he is not only a prisoner of sex but a prisoner of the female sex.

Notes

1. Heape, *Sex Antagonism* (London: Constable, 1913), pp. 2-3. Further references will be to this edition, and page numbers will appear in the text.

2. Ford articulated his feminist sympathies in an early suffrage pamphlet, *This Monstrous Regiment of Women* (London: Women's Freedom League, n.d.) as well as in "Women and Men," but in a later volume we will also discuss the sex antagonism that he dramatizes in the four books of *Parades End* (1924, 1925, 1926, 1928).

3. Ford, *The Good Soldier: A Tale of Passion* (1927; New York: Vintage, 1955), pp. 123 and 186. Further references will be to this edition and will appear in the text.

4. Interestingly, this description of Edward Ashburnham as a sacrifice, flayed alive, echoes the denouement of Flaubert's *Salammbo* (1862), in which Matho, the lover of the femme fatale Salammbo, is ritually flayed alive.

5. A manuscript of "The Love Song of St. Sebastian" is held in the Berg Collection of the New York Public Library; for fuller discussions of this text, see Lyndall Gordon, *Eliot's Early Years* (New York: Oxford University Press, 1977), pp. 55-62; Ronald Bush, *T. S. Eliot: A Study in Character and Style* (New York: Oxford University Press, 1983), pp. 19, 58; and Peter Ackroyd, *T. S. Eliot: A Life* (New York: Simon & Schuster, 1984), p. 52.

6. Swinburne, *The Novels of A. C. Swinburne* (New York: Farrar, 1962), p. 225.

7. The manuscript of "Petit Epître" is held in the Berg Collection of the New York Public Library; for "Cousin Nancy," see Eliot's *Collected Poems, 1909-1962* (New York: Harcourt, 1963), p. 22; further references to the poetry of T. S. Eliot will be to this edition, and page numbers will appear in the text.

8. A manuscript of "Prufrock Among the Women" is held in the Berg collection of the New York Public Library.

9. Yeats, *Collected Poems of W. B. Yeats* (New York: Macmillan, 1956), p. 342; further references to the poetry of Yeats will be to this edition, and page numbers will appear in the text.

10. Holtby, *Virginia Woolf: A Critical Memoir* (1932; Chicago: Academy, 1978), pp. 90-91.

11. Chafe, *The American Woman: Her Changing Social, Economic, and Political Roles, 1920-1970* (New York: Oxford University Press, 1972), p. 89. In Britain, the numbers of women in higher education were comparatively small—only thirteen-thousand women in universities by 1930—but they were so troublesome to authorities that in 1926 Oxford imposed strict limits on the admissions of female students. Far more dramatic was the more than nine-fold gain (up to one-hundred-eighty-five thousand) in female secondary school enrollment in England during the first two decades of the twentieth century. See Ernest Barker, *Universities in Great Britain: Their Position and Their Problems* (London: Student Christian Movement Press, 1931), p. 59; S. J. Curtis, *Higher Education in Britain Since 1900* (1952; Westport, Conn.: Greenwood, 1970), pp. 184-85; Josephine Kamm, *Hope Deferred: Girls' Education in English History* (London: Methuen, 1965), p. 233. The Abdullah cigarette advertisement appeared in the March 30, 1920, issue of *Isis,* and we are grateful to Susan Leonardi for bringing it to our attention.

12. See, for instance, Freud, "Female Sexuality" (1931) in *Freud, Sexuality and the Psychology of Love,* ed. Philip Rieff (New York: Collier, 1963); further references to this important essay will be to this edition. For a fuller discussion of this essay, see chapter 4 of the present volume.

13. On passionlessness, see Nancy Cott, "Passionlessness: A Reinterpretation of Victorian Sexual Ideology, 1790-1850," *Signs* 4 (1978): 219-36. This point has recently been challenged by Peter Gay in volume 1, *Education of the Senses,* of *The Bourgeois Experience: Victoria to Freud* (New York: Oxford University Press, 1984); see esp. "Sweet Bourgeois Communions," pp. 109-68.

14. Linda Gordon discusses the history of birth control in *Woman's Body, Woman's Right: A Social History of Birth Control in America* (New York: Penguin, 1977). See especially pp. 186-300.

15. Russell, *Hypatia* (New York: Dutton, 1925), p. 33. Further references to this volume will appear in the text.

16. A selection of articles from the first fifteen years of that journal is available in *Time and Tide Wait for No Man,* ed. Dale Spender (London: Pandora, 1984).

17. On Arthur's situation in The Idylls of the King, see Elliot L. Gilbert, "The Female King: Tennyson's Arthurian Apocalypse," *PMLA* 98 (1983): 863-78.

18. For a study which examines such figures from a somewhat different perspective, see Peter Hays, *The Limping Hero: Grotesques in Literature* (New York: New York University Press, 1971).

19. Williams, *Autobiography* (New York: New Directions, 1967), p. 229.

20. Hemingway, *A Moveable Feast* (New York: Scribner's 1964), p. 191.

21. See Ackroyd, pp. 143, 246.

22. Eliot, *The Family Reunion,* in *The Complete Plays of T. S. Eliot* (New York: Harcourt, 1967), p. 62 (act 1, scene 1).

23. For Eliot's relationship with Vivien Haigh-Wood Eliot, see Gordon, pp. 72-80, and Ackroyd, passim.

24. Lawrence, "Samson and Delilah," *Complete Short Stories,* 3 vols. (New York: Viking, 1977) 2: 424, 426.

25. See Lawrence, "Women are So Cocksure," in *Phoenix: The Posthumous Papers of D. H. Lawrence,* ed. Edward D. McDonald (New York: Viking, 1936), pp. 167-69. In the same collection, "The Real Thing" describes woman's struggle for freedom as a fight in which "man has fallen" (196). See also "Cocksure Women and Hensure Men," in *Phoenix II: Uncollected, Unpublished and Other Prose Works by D. H. Lawrence,* ed. Warren Roberts and Harry T. Moore (New York: Viking, 1968), pp. 553-55.

26. Lawrence, "Figs," *Complete Poems,* ed. Vivian de Sola Pinto and Warren Roberts, 2 vols. (New York: Viking, 1964), 1: 284.

27. Lawrence, *Women in Love* (New York: Penguin, 1976), p. 238. Further references will be to this edition, and page numbers will appear in the text. For discussions, from various perspectives, of Lawrence's identification with women, his sense of male secondariness, and what seem to some critics to be his intermittent feminist sympathies, see Carol Dix, *D. H. Lawrence and Women* (Totowa, New Jersey: Rowman and Littlefield, 1980); Judith Ruderman, *D. H. Lawrence and the Devouring Mother: The search for a patriarchal ideal of leadership* (Durham: Duke University Press, 1984); and Sandra M. Gilbert, "Potent Griselda: D. H. Lawrence and the Great Mother," in Peter Balbert and Phillip Marcus, ed., *Centenary Essays on D. H. Lawrence* (Ithaca: Cornell University Press, 1985).

28. Comparable enactments of male-female combat characterize Lawrence's short stories "Tickets, Please" (in which a streetcar inspector with the Lawrentian name *John Thomas* has to ward off the erotic and aggressive assaults of a band of wartime female tram conductors) and "The Princess" (whose virginal heroine shoots her Spanish guide, Romero, after he has sexually assaulted her high in the mountains of New Mexico). See D. H. Lawrence, *The Complete Short Stories,* vol. 2.

29. Tarkington's story is included in *The World Does Move: The Works of Booth Tarkington* 26 vols. (Garden City, New York: Doubleday, 1922-32) 23: 266-79. It is briefly discussed by Joanna Russ in "Amor Vincit Foeminam: The Battle of the Sexes in Science Fiction," *Science Fiction Studies* 7 (1980) 2-15; rpt. in *Gender Studies: New Directions in Feminist Criticism,* ed. Judith Spector (Bowling Green, Ohio: Bowling Green State University Popular Press, 1986), pp. 60-69. We are grateful to William Collins for calling this story to our attention. Collins has also refereed us to Owen M. Johnson's *The Coming of the Amazons* (New York: Longmans, Green, 1931), a work by the author of Stover at Yale in which a man who has been frozen in 1929 awakens in 2075 to find that, in Collins's words, "Seven-foot, blonde giantesses rule the world. A woman scientist had invented a death ray which decimated much of the earth . . . Women seized power, and the remaining men are second-class citizens . . . The thawed hero organizes the men and wins equality when they use a reversal of the Lysistrata ploy." (William Collins, personal letter.)

30. Hemingway, "The Short Happy Life of Francis Macomber," *The Snows of Kilimanjaro and other Stories* (New York: Scribner's, 1970), pp. 127, 154.

31. Faulkner, *Light in August* (New York: Random House, 1959) pp. 221-22, pp. 247-48.

32. Oates, "'At Least I Have Made a Woman of Her': Images of Women in Yeats, Lawrence, Faulkner," *The Profane Art: Essays and Reviews* (New York: Dutton, 1983), pp. 61-62.

33. West, *Miss Lonelyhearts & The Day of the Locust* (New York: New Directions, 1969), pp. 27-28. Further references will be to this edition, and page numbers will be included in the text.

WHITNEY CHADWICK (ESSAY DATE 1990)

SOURCE: Chadwick, Whitney. "The Independents." In *Women, Art, and Society*, pp. 265-96. London: Thames and Hudson, 1990.

In the following excerpt, Chadwick presents an overview of female artists and sculptors of the early-twentieth century, including Suzanne Valadon, Emily Karr, Georgia O'Keeffe, Paula Modersohn-Becker, Gwen John, Frida Kahlo, and Germain Richier.

Referring to women artists as "independents" is already an arbitrary and misleading designation for no artist is independent of the complex of economic, social, and cultural practices through which art is produced. Nor can lumping together a diverse group of women be intellectually or theoretically justified when it produces alliances reducible only to gender. Yet at the same time, many women artists working in the late nineteenth and early twentieth centuries had an ambiguous relationship with the developing mythology of the vanguard modern artist.

The view of the modern artist as a heroic (male) individualist finds its fullest expression in the literature of post-Second World War art. The emergence of a self-conscious set of practices and characteristics through which the modern in art is understood, and the closely related notion of an "avant-garde" as the dominant ideology of artistic production and scholarship, coincides with the emergence of a first generation of women artists with more or less equal access to artistic training.

Vanguard ideology marginalizes the woman artist as surely as did the guilds in the fifteenth century, and the academies in the seventeenth and eighteenth. There is no female Bohemia against which to measure the exploits of a Suzanne Valadon, no psychoanalytic equating of artistic creativity and female sexuality, no Romantic legacy of the woman artist as an intense, gifted, and spiritual being. If Expressionism, as feminist art historians have argued, stands as a revolt of "sons" against "fathers," the relationship of Paula Modersohn-Becker, Käthe Kollwitz, and other women artists to German Expressionism is difficult to elucidate. In eliding representation by

women with the social production of middle-class femininity, the work of Suzanne Valadon is left in a representational void, subject only to the creation of a new myth of the woman artist as "undiscovered." Valorizing stylistic innovation and monumental size leaves little room for the modest, stylistically consistent paintings of Gwen John and Florine Stettheimer. Identifying woman with nature and imaging femininity in its instinctive, enigmatic, sexual, and destructive aspects places major female practitioners of landscape painting like Georgia O'Keeffe and Emily Carr in an impossible double-bind in which femininity and art become self-cancelling phrases. Admitting women artists to canonical art history only retrospectively, and basing evaluations of their work on what Anne Wagner has called a "heroics of survival," removes artists from the social contexts which, in fact, made possible their work. Constructing woman as a signifier for male creativity banishes to the margins of the avant-garde a group of gifted women Surrealists.

Another aspect of the early Modernist myth which is receiving increasing attention from feminist art historians and critics concerns the extent to which the major paintings—and sometimes sculptures—associated with the development of modern art wrest their formal and stylistic innovations from an erotically based assault on female form: Manet's and Picasso's prostitutes, Gauguin's "primitives," Matisse's nudes, Surrealism's objects. Modern artists from Renoir ("I paint with my prick") to Picasso ("Painting, that is actual lovemaking") have collaborated in fusing the sexual and the artistic by equating artistic creation with male sexual energy, presenting women as powerless and sexually subjugated.

In her article, "Domination and Virility in Vanguard Painting," Carol Duncan traces the further sexualizing of creativity in the work of the Fauves, the Cubists, and the German Expressionists. She concludes that the vanguard myth of individual artistic freedom is built on maintaining sexual and social inequalities: "The socially radical claims of a Vlaminck, a Van Dongen or a Kirchner are thus contradicted. According to their paintings, the liberation of the artist means the domination of others; his freedom requires their unfreedom. Far from contesting the established social order, the male-female relationship that these paintings imply—the drastic reduction of women to objects of specialized male interests—embodies on a sexual level the basic class relationships of capitalist society."

Suzanne Valadon and Paula Modersohn-Becker were two of the first women artists to work extensively with the nude female form and their paintings both collude with, and challenge, such configurations. Confronted with the powerful presence of Valadon's nudes, critics were unable to sever the nude from its status as a signifier for male creativity; instead, they severed Valadon (who was not a "respectable" middle-class woman) from her femininity and allowed her to circulate as a pseudo-male, complete with "masculine power" and "virility." "And perhaps in this disregard for logic," wrote Bernard Dorival, "in this inconsistency and indifference to contradiction, lies the only feminine trait in the art of Suzanne Valadon—that most virile—and greatest—of all the women in painting."

Dorival's critical position is similar to that taken by many twentieth-century critics who, having jettisoned one half of the ideology of separate spheres bequeathed them by nineteenth-century critics, have confidently asserted that "art has no sex," and at the same time admitted to the canon only work by women artists which might be contained by the term "virile." Nevertheless, Valadon's status in the eyes of Dorival and other contemporary critics was not sufficient to insure her place in histories of modern art. Although she exhibited at the Société Nationale des Beaux-Arts, the Indépendants, and at private galleries like Berthe Weil and Bernheim-Jeune, and although Ambroise Vollard published and sold her engravings in 1897, by the 1920s her work was all but ignored.

The illegitimate daughter of a laundress, Valadon (1867-1938) became an artist's model in the early 1880s after working as a cricus performer. Posing for Puvis de Chavannes, Toulouse-Lautrec, Renoir, and other artists, she was part of the sexually free bohemian life of early twentieth-century Paris. Her entrée to the world of art came not through education, for she was largely self-taught, but through her identification with a class of sexually available artist's models, an association which liberated her from any lingering expectations about respectability and allowed her to enter into the sort of easy relationship with other artists and with her patrons which we seldom see in the careers of middle-class women artists of those years.

The subject of the nude in art brings together discourses of representation, morality, and female sexuality, but the persistent presentation of the nude female body as a site of male viewing pleasure, a commodified image of exchange, and a fetishized defense against the fear of castration leaves little place for explorations of female subjectivity, knowledge, and experience. The difficulty of distinguishing between overtly sexualized (i.e., voyeurism, fetishism, and scopophilia) and other forms of looking, and the fact that the male relationship of power and control over the female image would seem to allow women only a vicarious pleasure in looking, has prompted a significant body of feminist literature on issues of spectatorship.

Valadon's female nudes fuse observation with a knowledge of the female body based on her experience as a model. Rejecting the static and timeless presentation of the monumental nude that dominates Western art, she emphasizes context, specific moment and physical action. Instead of presenting the female body as a lush surface isolated and controlled by the male gaze, she emphasizes the awkward gestures of figures apparently in control of their own movements. Valadon often placed her figures in specific domestic settings, surrounding them with images of domesticity and community, as in *Grandmother and Young Girl Stepping into the Bath* (c. 1908), a striking departure from the practises of her contemporaries, like Renoir, who referred to *his* models as "beautiful fruit."

Like Degas, who recognized and encouraged her talent, Valadon often turned her bathers away from the viewer and depicted them absorbed in their own activities. But in her emphasis on the tension of the body as it executes specific movements there is little or no attempt to establish the closely framed single point of visual connection between viewer and model that is the hallmark of Degas's many pastels of bathers. The nakedness of Valadon's figures is specific to the act of bathing. Her nudes are full-bodied, weighty, and sturdy. Although sensuous, they stand in opposition to the archetypal and fertile female figures so prevalent in the avant-garde circles of Gauguin and the Fauves.

The shift from the imagery of seductive and devouring femininity produced by Symbolist painters and poets to an ideology of "natural womanhood" which identified the female body with biological nature was part of a reaction against feminism and the neo-Malthusians. Modest gains made by women in education and employment in France at the end of the nineteenth century provoked an intense anti-feminist backlash. It culminated in the battle over control of reproductive rights in France. Indignation among demographers over declining birth rates at the end of the nineteenth century was taken up by literary figures such as Zola, whose novel *La Fé-condité* (1899) gave fictional form to a growing cult of fertility; "There is no more glorious blossoming, no more sacred symbol of living eternity than an infant at its mother's breast." The cry was taken up by artists, including Gauguin, whose colonization of the "natural" female Tahitian body reinforced early Modernism's exaltation of the "natural" female body always subject to the literal and metaphoric control of man.

Among the work of women artists associated with Expressionism, that of Paula Modersohn-Becker and Käthe Kollwitz most clearly reveals the clash between Modernist ideology and social reality. Caught between the artistic and social conservatism of the Worpswede nature painters and the influence of French Modernism, Modersohn-Becker struggled to produce images that embodied both poles of experience. Kollwitz (1867-1945) was committed to an art of radical social content unrivalled in her day, and her choice of graphic realism as a style, her exclusive use of printmaking media, and her production of posters and humanitarian leaflets, all contributed to later devaluations of her work and its dismissal by art historians as "illustration" and "propaganda."

Born in Dresden in 1876, Modersohn-Becker was the child of comfortably middle-class parents who encouraged her artistic interests until she showed signs of serious professional ambition. She made her first visit to the Worpswede artists' community in northern Germany in the Summer of 1897 where she began to study with Fritz Makensen. Encouraged by Julius Langbehn's eccentric book *Rembrandt as a Teacher* (1890), and by their interest in Nietzsche, Zola, Rembrandt, and Dürer, the Worpswede painters embraced nature, the primitive simplicity of peasant life, and the purity of youth. Langbehn's book became the textbook of the "Volkish" movement, a utopian reaction against industrialization which celebrated the rural values of the peasantry. Although she settled more or less permanently in the village after completing her studies in 1898, later marrying the painter Otto Modersohn, Modersohn-Becker did not share the group's disdain for academic training; the flattened and simplified forms that mark her mature style derive from the influence of French painters, particularly Cézanne and Gauguin, whose work she saw during four visits to Paris between 1899 and 1906, the year before her premature death.

Modersohn-Becker's interest in her models as personifications of nature developed in the context of the Worpswede artists' cultivation of the

"earth mother," but it was not until after her first trip to Paris in 1899 that it entered her work as a major theme. One of Fritz Makensen's first Worpswede canvases was a life-sized *Madonna of the Moors* (1892) and as early as 1898 Modersohn-Becker recorded her impression of a peasant woman suckling a child in her diary; "Frau Meyer, a voluptuous blonde. . . . This time with her little boy at her breast. I had to draw her as a mother. That is her single true purpose." Linda Nochlin has also pointed to sources for Modersohn-Becker's cultivation of the imagery of fecund maternity in J. J. Bachofen's *Mutterecht* (1861), which was reissued in 1897 and widely circulated among artists and writers. Surrounding her figures with a tapestry of flowers and foliage, Modersohn-Becker ignored conventional perspective and anecdotal detail to produce monumental images of idealized motherhood; "I kneel before it [motherhood] in humility," she wrote.

Her diary records an ambivalence toward marriage, motherhood, and art. Modeled on the diaries of Marie Bashkirtseff, Modersohn-Becker, unlike the former, had little sympathy for the growing women's movement. Although Karl Scheffler's misogynist *Die Fraue und die Kunst* (Woman and Art) was not published until 1908, the year after her death, its sentiments were commonly accepted throughout the period of Modersohn-Becker's development as an artist. Scheffler emphasized woman's inability to participate in the production of culture because of her ties to nature and her lack of spiritual insight. Modersohn-Becker's own ambivalence on these points is recorded in an allegorical prose poem in which she acknowledges her artistic ambitions as "masculine" and remarks on the mutual exclusivity of female sexual love and artistic success.

Modersohn-Becker participated in the second Worpswede group exhibition in the Bremen Kunsthalle in 1899, despite attempts by the director of the Kunsthalle to dissuade her. Negative critical response focused mainly on the work of the women artists in the colony and Modersohn-Becker left almost immediately for Paris. There she entered the Académie Colarossi and visited galleries showing the work of Puvis de Chavannes, the Barbizon painters, Courbet, and Monet. Gradually rejecting the Worpswede artists' commitment to a crude naturalism, her work began to record influences from Rodin, Japanese art, Daumier, Millet, and other French painters. By 1906, back in Germany, she had requested a copy of Gauguin's autobiography, *Noa Noa,* from her sister in Paris and had thrown off her husband's artistic influence.

Viewing Gauguin's retrospective exhibition in Paris in 1906 helped move Modersohn-Becker's figurative works in the direction of a primordial power sought through nature. Her nude self-portraits may be the first such paintings in oil by a woman artist, but as such, they are strangely ambiguous. Rejecting Gauguin's romantic nostalgia, she carries the simplification of form to an extreme which blunts the sensuality normally assigned female flesh in the history of art. The immobility, monumentality, and gravelly surfaces of these self-portrait nudes universalize the images, but the careful scrutiny of the female body and the frank confrontation between the woman and the artist fuse the issues of femaleness and creativity in new ways.

Modersohn-Becker's archetypal fertility images of 1906 and 1907, *Mother and Child Lying Nude* and *Mother and Child* are closely related to Gauguin paintings like the *Kneeling Day of the God,* but they clothe the subject of fertility and nurture with dignity, while at the same time collaborating with a late nineteenth-century ideology of timeless, unvarying "natural" womanhood. The subtext of violence and control that accompanies Gauguin's representations of Tahitian women is missing from Modersohn-Becker's paintings with their lowered viewpoint and direct gaze. Gauguin's many paintings of Tahitian women replay the unequal relationship of the male artist and the female model in the inequities of the white male artist's relationship to native women in a colonialized society. His paintings bind women to nature through repetitions of colors, patterns, and contours; crouching female figures are placed in a submissive relationship to the downward gaze of the male artist and the women's blank gazes offer little insight into the specifics of their lives.

Modersohn-Becker's death shortly after giving birth provides an ironic commentary on the gulf between idealized motherhood and the biological realities of fecundity. Nochlin has pointed out this disjunction, observing that it is Käthe Kollwitz's depictions of women and children that insert motherhood "into the bitterly concrete context of class and history."

Kollwitz replaces the archetypal imagery of female abundance with the realities of a poverty which often prevents women from nourishing their children or enjoying their motherhood; in *Portraits of Misery III,* a lithograph, and in many

other works, pregnancy without material support is cause for grief rather than rejoicing. Kollwitz, the first woman elected to the Prussian Academy of the Arts (1919) and the foremost graphic artist of the first half of the twentieth century, was encouraged to draw as a child by her father. Studies in Berlin and Munich followed a period of training in Königsberg (now Kaliningrad) under the engraver Rudolph Maurer. In 1891, she married Dr. Karl Kollwitz and settled in Berlin where she came in contact with the industrial workers of Berlin through his practice. A socialist, feminist (founder of the Frauen Kunstverband [Women's Arts Union] in Berlin in 1913), and pacifist, the themes of war, hatred, poverty, love, grief, death, and struggle dominate her mature work.

Influenced by Max Klinger's engravings, by Zola's realism, and by the memory of her father reciting Thomas Hood's "The Song of the Shirt" with its passionate appeal on behalf of working women, she turned to themes of social conditions and to the expressive mediums of engraving and lithography. Kollwitz's first major success came with a cycle of three engravings and three lithographs titled *The Weavers' Uprising* (1895-97). Based on Gerhart Hauptmann's play, *The Weavers,* about the revolt of the Silesian weavers in 1844, the cycle moves from the sufferings, including death, of the weavers to their decision to take collective action. Somber grays and blacks and sharp lines relieved by strong lights powerfully evoke the weavers' tragic revolt against inhumane working conditions.

As a result of the success of *The Weavers' Uprising* (which proved so politically effective when exhibited in 1898 that the Kaiser refused to award Kollwitz the gold medal she had won), Kollwitz was appointed to teach graphics and nude studies at the Berlin Künstlerinnenschule. Her subsequent concentration on the mother and child theme developed hand in hand with a series of personal tragedies which included the death of a son in the First World War and the loss of a grandson in the Second. Documenting the suffering that results from war and poverty led Kollwitz away from the expressions of individual torment that mark the work of her contemporaries Edvard Munch and James Ensor and that would soon dominate German Expressionism. Although her work shares the graphic expressiveness of the prints by members of the Brücke and Blaue Reiter groups, she increasingly came to see Expressionism as a rarefied art of the studio, divorced from social reality. "I am convinced," she wrote in her diary dating from 1908, "that there must be an understanding between the artist and the people such as there always used to be in the best periods in history."

Kollwitz's insistence on the social function of art divorced her work from the Modernist cultivation of individual artistic freedom. Vanguard mythologies have proved equally difficult to sustain in the face of work which refuses the scope, and often the scale, of Modernist ambitions.

Despite regular exhibitions, Gwen John (1876-1939), like Valadon, was until recently most often presented as an "unknown," to be regularly "rediscovered" by subsequent generations of curators and critics, always in relation to her brother Augustus John, whose work bears little similarity to hers; her lover, the sculptor Auguste Rodin; and her patron, the American collector John Quinn.

Though she knew Picasso, Braque, Matisse, Rodin, and many other contemporary artists, and read widely, John had little interest in the theoretical aspects of artistic movements. Nor was she a joiner. Born and raised in Wales, and educated at the Slade School in London under Whistler's influence, John went to France at the age of twenty-seven and remained there for the rest of her life. Her work contains superficial affinities with that of Rodin, Puvis de Chavannes, Vuillard, Bonnard, Modigliani, and Rouault, but its dry surfaces, restrained color and patterned brushwork are closer to the paintings produced by the Camden Town Group in London than to the French Modernists. Her reliance on intimate subject-matter was shaped by her early experiences at the Slade and her paintings, subdued in tone, and formal in arrangement, evoke powerful emotional responses.

John first exhibited in 1900 at the New English Art Club, returning to Paris after that exhibition partly to escape Augustus John's influence over her life. She supported herself by posing as an artist's model, often for English women artists, and by the Summer of 1904 she was posing for Rodin. John's relationship with Rodin belongs to the difficult history of women who, lacking familial and social support for their endeavors, have annexed their talent to that of male mentors and seen their own work suffer as a result. But it is art historians who have extracted her life from the historical circumstances in which she lived, and from the lives of the hundreds of other women painters working in London and Paris in the same years. Like many other women artists, she has been "rediscovered" as an exception and represented as unique.

Rodin defined his own artistic genius in sexual terms and his critics followed suit; "The period when Rodin was caught up in the grand passion of his life coincided with the creation of his most impassioned works," notes one twentieth-century critic. "Such was his innate vigor, even in decline, that everything which flowed from his hands with such dangerous facility bore the imprint of genius. . . ." John, like the sculptor Camille Claudel (1856-1920), who entered Rodin's studio as an assistant in 1883 and remained to become model, lover, collaborator, and artist in her own right, saw her creative life merged with that of Rodin in the eyes of others. Claudel's assistance in Rodin's studio helped insure his myth of superhuman productivity during the 1880s and early 1890s, and much of her creative output remains to be disengaged from his work of these years. John's relationship with Rodin, while equally intense, was not played out through their commitment to a shared medium. Describing herself as "une petite morceau de souffrance et de désir," and expressing a growing coldness toward painting, she nevertheless continued to paint, executing numerous drawings and at least a dozen paintings during her first decade in Paris.

Distinctive themes emerged in John's work during this period: simple interiors bathed in soft light and isolated female figures set against textured walls. Formally constructed, these works capture specific moments filled with light and atmosphere. The repetition of compositions is characteristic of her mature work and provided a means for the formal investigations which were her primary concern as a painter.

John's reflective, dedicated life allowed her to live largely independent of the social obligations placed on most women of her time, but critics continue to search for the "essentially feminine" in her work. The term "feminine" has also been used to build contexts within which to view the work of other women who moved in avant-garde circles, but whose personal and idiosyncratic styles have no place in vanguard mythology. Marie Laurencin's work was promoted by the poet Guillaume Apollinaire, who introduced her to the Cubist painters; Florine Stettheimer's social relationships with the New York avant-garde before and after the First World War proved more binding than her artistic ties to them. Both artists embraced the decorative and the fanciful in their work, and both fashioned a myth of the feminine that allowed them to be heard, but that insured they would never be taken as seriously as their male colleagues.

Educated at the Lycée Lamartine and at the Académie Humbert, where she met the Cubist painter Georges Braque, Laurencin (1885-1956) had a long, stormy affair with Apollinaire, which placed her in the group of artists who gathered around Picasso in the studio at the Bateau Lavoir, a run-down former wash house in Montmartre. Her painting *Group of Artists* (1908) includes Apollinaire, Picasso, herself, and Picasso's companion, Fernande Olivier, but the presence of herself and Olivier in the painting signals friendship rather than art.

In his 1913 treatise, *Les Peintres Cubistes: Méditations esthétiques,* Apollinaire called her a "scientific Cubist," but in fact her work has little to do with Cubism's conceptual and formal investigations. Instead it was her "femininity" which became the artistic yardstick against which her work was measured. She brought "feminine art to major status," claimed Apollinaire, but it was as his muse that she entered the Modernist mainstream and it was this construction which provided the Surrealists with a new image of the creative couple. Henri Rousseau's painting of Apollinaire and Laurencin, *The Muse Inspiring the Poet* (1909), presents her as a nature goddess. Apollinaire designated her "a little sun—a feminine version of myself," thereby removing her entirely from the creative ferment that propelled his male friends. "Though she has masculine defects," he wrote, "she has every conceivable feminine quality. The greatest error of most women artists is that they try to surpass men, losing in the process their taste and charm. Laurencin is very different. She is aware of the deep differences that separate men from women—essential, ideal differences. Mademoiselle Laurencin's personality is vibrant and joyful. Purity is her very element." Laurencin exhibited alongside the Cubists in 1907, and from 1909 to 1913, while Florine Stettheimer had only a single solo exhibition during her lifetime. After 1916, she exhibited only at the Independent Society of Arts Annuals, using her wealth and social position as a defense against art world intrusion and elaborating a notion of the "feminine" until her life and her art became largely indistinguishable.

Born in Rochester, New York, in 1871, Florine Stettheimer was the youngest of five children in a prosperous family. She studied at the Art Students' League in New York from 1892 to 1895 and then travelled in Europe with two of her sisters, taking painting lessons in Germany and visiting museums. The outbreak of war in 1914 forced the Stettheimer sisters to return to New York where the family home soon became famous as the social center of a group of avant-garde art dealers, dancers, musicians, artists, and writers. Stettheimer's paintings of this period are bright, calligraphic sketches full of personal symbolism, amusing anecdote, and social satire. Her unique personal style evolved out of a rigorous academic training, but her paintings focus almost exclusively on the social milieu in which she lived. The *Studio Party* (1917), like many of her other works, includes her social and artistic circle: Maurice Sterne, Gaston and Isabelle Lachaise, Albert Gleizes, Leo Stein, her sisters.

Stettheimer produced paintings as part of a self-consciously cultivated lifestyle which drew few, if any, distinctions between making art and living well. Protected by her wealth from having to exhibit or sell, she further insulated herself from the professional art world through her demand that any gallery wishing to exhibit her works be redecorated like her home. Stettheimer's exaggerated "femininity" was a way of establishing a role for herself as a woman and an artist; her contemporary, Georgia O'Keeffe, on the other hand, spent much of her life trying to escape attempts by critics and a well-meaning public to read her life in her work.

O'Keeffe's place in the history of American modern art, while far more secure than that of Stettheimer, remains circumscribed by critical attempts to create a special category for her. Her career, the critic Hilton Kramer later wrote, "is unlike almost any other in the history of modern art in America," for it embraced its whole history, from the founding of Alfred Stieglitz's gallery with its shocking displays of European Modernism to the eventual acceptance of modern art in America. And it anticipated by some years the color field paintings of Clyfford Still, Helen Frankenthaler, Ellsworth Kelly, Barnett Newman, and others. The "rediscovery" that began her recent meteoric rise to the forefront of American art came only with her retrospective exhibition at the Whitney Museum, New York, in 1970 when a new generation of viewers were drawn to the uncompromising example of her life and the quiet integrity of her work.

Her relationship to her colleagues in the circle around Stieglitz, with whom she began living in 1919—the painters Marsden Hartley, Charles Demuth, Arthur Dove, and the photographer Paul Strand—was often equivocal. Referring to them as "the boys," she later commented that, "The men liked to put me down as the best woman painter. I think I'm one of the best painters." O'Keefe chose to live much of her life away from New York, developing her paintings in relation to the vast, austere landscape of the southwestern United States, particularly the area around Abiqui, New Mexico, where she moved permanently after Stieglitz's death in 1946.

Born in 1887, O'Keeffe studied anatomical drawing with John Vanderpoel at the Art Institute of Chicago in 1905; two years later she was in New York studying painting at the Art Students' League. Quickly losing interest in academic styles derived from European models, she left to work as a commercial artist in Chicago. After attending a course on the principles of abstract design taught by Alan Bement—a follower of the art educator Arthur Wesley Dow—she taught Dow's principles in schools in Virginia, South Carolina, and Texas. She met Stieglitz after she sent a batch of abstract charcoal drawings based on personal feelings and sensations to Anita Politzer, a friend in New York who subsequently took them to Stieglitz.

In 1916, Stieglitz was one of the organizers of "The Forum Exhibition of Modern American Painters." The only woman included among the seventeen leading American Modernists was Marguerite Zorach, a California artist who helped introduce Fauve painting into the United States, but who is better known for her brilliant abstract tapestries. Thus, O'Keeffe was not the only woman shown by Stieglitz at his avant-garde 291 Gallery, but her situation there was unique.

O'Keeffe's paintings of the 1920s—from the planar precisionist studies of New York's buildings and skyline to the New Mexico landscapes with their distilled forms and intense colors, and the many paintings of single flowers—are intensely personal statements expressed in the reductive language of early Modernism. Her emergence during the early 1920s as an artist of great promise coincided with what appeared to be more liberal attitudes toward women including their increased attendance in art schools. Between 1912 and 1918, a number of women students at the Art Students' League, among them Cornelia Barnes, Alice Beach Winter, and Josephine Verstille Nivison, contributed drawings and illustrations to the radical Socialist magazine, *The Masses,* which promoted women's causes from suffrage to birth control. Other women produced paintings addressing current social realities, like Theresa Bernstein's *Suffragette Parade* (1916) and *Waiting Room—Employment Office* (1917), which depicts a group of weary women waiting for jobs.

Throughout the 1920s, the complex associations between O'Keeffe's paintings of natural forms and the female body elicited readings which the artist herself recognized as ideological constructions. Responding to the widespread popularizing of Freud's ideas in America, Henry McBride noted; "Georgia O'Keeffe is probably what they will be calling in a few years a B.F. (before Freud) since all her inhibitions seem to have been removed before the Freudian recommendations were preached upon this side of the Atlantic. She became free without the aid of Freud. But she had aid. There was another who took the place of Freud. . . . It is of course Alfred Stieglitz. . . ."

The ideology of femininity, which presented O'Keeffe as Stieglitz's protégée, that constructed her considerable talent as "essentially feminine" legitimized male authority and male succession. "Alfred Stieglitz presents" read the announcement for O'Keeffe's 1923 exhibition at his gallery; the following year he declared, "Women can only create babies, say the scientists, but I say they can produce art—and Georgia O'Keeffe is the proof of it."

In a decade of declining birth rates women were confronted by a barrage of literature urging them to stay home where, as mothers and homemakers, they became perfect marketing targets for a new peacetime economy based on household consumption. Throughout the 1920s, O'Keeffe was forced to watch her work constantly appropriated to an ideology of sexual difference built on the emotional differences between the sexes which supported this social reorganization. Men were "rational," manipulating the environment for the good of their families; women were "intuitive" and "expressive," dominated by their feelings and their biological roles. She was shocked when, in 1920, Marsden Hartley wrote an article casting her abstractions in Freudian terms and discussing "feminine perceptions and feminine powers of expression" in her work and that of Delaunay and Laurencin. "No man could feel as Georgia O'Keeffe," noted the Modernist critic Paul Rosenfeld in 1924, "and utter himself in precisely such curves and colors; for in those curves and spots and prismatic color there is the woman referring the universe to her own frame, her own balance; and rendering in her picture of things her body's subconscious knowledge of itself."

Criticisms such as these constructed a specific category for O'Keeffe. Hailed as the epitome of emancipated womanhood, she was accorded star status, but only at the top of a female class. The biological fact of her femininity took precedence over serious critical evaluations of her work. At the time when radical feminists were advocating "androgyny," and designers like Coco Chanel were "masculinizing" women's fashions, the art world countered by presenting a woman who was "emancipated" but "feminine," and in a class by herself. While Edmund Wilson lauded her "particularly feminine intensity," and the *New York Times* critic declared that, "she reveals woman as an elementary being, closer to the earth than men, suffering pain with passionate ecstasy and enjoying love with beyond-good-and-evil delight," O'Keeffe threatened to quit painting if Freudian interpretations continued to be made. Complaining that Hartley's and Demuth's flower paintings were not interpreted erotically she struggled against a cultural identification of the female with the biological nature of the body that has long been used to assign woman a negative role in the production of culture. It is hardly surprising that she responded with so little sympathy to attempts by feminist artists and critics during the 1970s to annex her formal language to the renewed search for a "female" imagery.

O'Keeffe met the Canadian painter Emily Carr (1871-1945) at Stieglitz's gallery in 1930. Although no details remain of the brief meeting, these two major figures in North American landscape painting were evidently sympathetic. If O'Keeffe finally found the art world's insistent refusal to allow her painting to stand in relation to that of her contemporaries a burden and a barrier to her development as a painter, Carr's isolation in British Columbia saved her from most such intrusions. After studying painting in San Francisco, London, and Paris for short periods between 1890 and 1910, Carr's strong, brooding paintings of the Pacific northwest and its Indians went almost completely unnoticed until the 1920s, when she met Mark Tobey and the painters of Canada's Group of Seven. Although never formally a member of the group, she exhibited with them beginning in 1927 in an exhibition called "Canadian West Coast Art: Native and Modern." Like O'Keeffe, Carr built an intensely personal style from a range of influences, and she distilled essential forms from a monumental and imposing nature and presented them without sentiment, moralizing, or anecdote. The breadth of these painters' visions, and the muscularity of their forms, should provoke new investigations into the contributions made by women artists to the traditions of modernist landscape painting. The

success of such investigations will, however, rest on our ability to redraw the boundaries between woman, nature, and art.

During the 1930s, the sculptors Germaine Richier and Barbara Hepworth also elaborated the connections between nature's cycles of generation and erosion. Hepworth (1903-75), one of England's leading sculptors, studied at the Leed's School of Art and at the Royal College of Art in London where she and Henry Moore became fascinated by the interplay of mass and negative space. Visits to the studios of Constantin Brancusi and Jean Arp in Paris in 1931 encouraged Hepworth to explore biomorphism within an increasingly abstract vocabulary. Living with the painter Ben Nicholson in the 1930s, she was an active participant in the development of abstraction in England. She worked steadily, even after the birth of triplets in 1934 slowed her sculptural production, and gradually evolved a totally abstract, geometric vocabulary.

Adrian Stokes, the painter and essayist, was a member of the group in England—with the painter Paul Nash and the physicist J. D. Bernal—who helped define this formal vocabulary. Writing in *The Spectator* in 1933 after Hepworth's exhibition at Reid and Lefevre, he noted; "These stones are inhabited with feeling, even if, in common with the majority of 'advanced' carvers, Miss Hepworth has felt not only the block, but also its potential fruit, to be always feminine. . . ."

This generative metaphor was deeply internalized by artists working under the influence of Surrealism. In a poem written in the early 1930s and dedicated to Max Ernst, the English poet David Gascoyne celebrated "the great bursting womb of desire." Jean Arp also chose procreation as a metaphor for artistic generation, writing in 1948 that "art is a fruit that grows in man, like a fruit on a plant or like a child in its mother's womb." The reasons for this particular trope lie outside the present work, but its effects proved nowhere more conflicting than for women artists in the Surrealist movement.

No artistic movement since the nineteenth century has celebrated the idea of woman and her creativity as passionately as did Surrealism during the 1920s and 1930s. None has had as many female practitioners, and none has evolved a more complex role for the woman artist in a modern movement. André Breton's romantic vision of perfect union with the loved woman as the source for an art of convulsive disorientation that would resolve polarized states of experience and awareness into a new, revolutionary surreality was formulated in response to a culture shaken by war. He advanced his image of the spontaneous, instinctive woman in a social context in which women were demanding the right to work and to vote, and the French government was promoting pronatalism as a strategy for repopulating the war-ravaged country. "The fate of France, its existence, depends on the family," declared a slogan of 1919, the same year that Breton, recently demobilized, returned to Paris. The following year a law was passed forbidding the mere advocacy of abortion or birth control; by 1924, when the First Surrealist Manifesto appeared, Breton had dedicated himself to liberating woman from such "bourgeois" considerations.

The image of ethereal and disruptive womanhood which enters Breton's poetry of the 1920s owes much to Apollinaire's imbrication of erotic and poetic emotion, his reliance on Symbolist polarities to express the duality of female nature, and his presentation of Laurencin as muse and eternal child. But the Surrealist woman was also born out of Freud's ambivalent and dualistic positioning of woman at the center of the creative and the subversive powers of the love instinct, in her incompatible roles as mother and bearer of life, and destroyer of man.

During the 1930s, women artists came to Surrealism in large numbers, attracted by the movement's anti-academic stance and by its sanctioning of an art in which personal reality dominates. But they found themselves struggling toward artistic maturity in the context of a movement that defined them as confirming and completing a male creative cycle and that metaphorically obliterated subject/object polarities through violent assaults on the female image. Not surprisingly, most women ended by asserting their independence from Surrealism.

Almost without exception, women artists saw themselves as outside the inner circle of poets and painters which produced Surrealist manifestos and formulated Surrealist theory. Most of them were young women just embarking on artistic careers when they came to Paris; many of them did their mature work only after leaving the Surrealist circle. Often they came to Surrealism through personal relationships with men in the group rather than shared political or theoretical goals. Yet they made significant contributions to the language of Surrealism, replacing the male Sur-

realists' love of hallucination and erotic violence with an art of magical fantasy and narrative flow.

Surrealism's multiple and ambivalent visions of woman converge in its identification of her with the mysterious forces and regenerative powers of nature. Women artists were quick to draw on this identification, but they did it with an analytic mind and an ironic stance. Artists like Leonora Carrington (b. 1917), Leonor Fini (b. 1918), the American painters Kay Sage (1898-1963) and Dorothea Tanning (b. 1912), and the Spanish-Mexican artist Remedios Varo (b. 1908) received varying degrees of formal training. Yet they meticulously built up tight surfaces with layers of small and carefully modulated brushstrokes. However fantastic their imagery, they often worked with the precision and care of illustrators, as if their creative model was scientific investigation rather than Surrealist explosiveness. Fini's many paintings of bones and rotting vegetation—like *Sphinx Regina* (1946)—and Varo's carefully crafted scientific fantasies—like *Harmony* (1956) and *Unsubmissive Plant* (1961)—resituate the woman artist in the worlds of science and art.

Women artists dismissed male romanticizing of nature as female and nurturing (or female and destructive) and replaced it with a more austere and ironic vision. Bizarre and unusual natural forms attracted the photographic eye of Eileen Agar (b. 1899) and Lee Miller (1908-77), while the Czech painter Marie Čerminova, called Toyen (1902-80), in a series of paintings and drawings executed during and after the Second World War presents nature as a potent metaphor for inhumanity.

Toyen's use of nature as a metaphor for political reality finds an echo in the work of Kay Sage, who met the Surrealists in Paris in 1937 and who spent the War years in New York with the Surrealist painter Yves Tanguy. Her paintings are among the most abstract produced within a Surrealism that embraced symbolic figuration as the key to the language of the dream and the unconscious. A predilection for sharp, spiny forms, slaty surfaces, and subdued melancholy light infuses her landscapes with an air of emptiness and abandonment; she herself identified strongly with these barren vistas stripped of human habitation.

Alienated from Surrealist theorizing about women, and from the search for a female muse, women turned instead to their own reality. Surrealism constructed women as magic objects and sites on which to project male erotic desire. They recreated themselves as beguiling personalities, poised uneasily between the worlds of artifice (art) and nature, or the instinctual life. The duality of the Mexican Frida Kahlo's life (1907-54)—an exterior persona constantly reinvented with costume and ornament, and an interior image nourished on the pain of a body crippled in a trolley-bus accident when she was an adolescent—invests her painting with a haunting complexity and a narrative quality which disturbs in its ambiguity. This is also characteristic of much of the work of another contemporary Mexican artist, Maria Izquierdo (1902-55).

Like Kahlo's *Broken Column* (1944), Leonora Carrington's *Self-Portrait* (1938) reinforces the woman artist's use of the mirror to assert the duality of being, the self as observer and observed. In *The Second Sex,* Simone de Beauvoir holds up the image of the mirror as the key to the feminine condition. Women concern themselves with their own images, she asserts, men with the enlarged self-images provided by their reflection in a woman. Kahlo used painting as a means of exploring the reality of her own body and her consciousness of that reality; in many cases the reality dissolves into a duality, exterior reality versus interior perception of that reality. The self-image in the work of women artists in the Surrealist movement becomes the focus for a dialogue between the constructed social being and the powerful forces of the instinctual life, which Surrealism celebrated as the revolutionary tool that would overthrow the control exerted by the conscious mind.

When it came to taking a position vis-à-vis Surrealism's inflammatory erotic language, women artists vacillated. More often than not they approached the issue of eroticism obliquely, focusing attention on aspects of the erotic other than woman's sexual desires. Carrington rejected Freud and turned to alchemy and magic for subjects; Tanning transferred sexuality from the world of adults to that of children. Paintings like *Palaestra* (1947) and *Children's Games* (1942) reveal nubile young girls caught in moments of ecstatic transformation. Their bodies respond to unseen forces which sweep through the room, animating drapery and whipping the children's hair and garments into the air.

Unmoved by Surrealist theorizing on the subject of erotic desire, and by Freud's writings, women appear to have found little theoretical support for the more liberated understanding of sexuality which Surrealism pursued so avidly. Turning to their own sexual reality as source and subject, they were unable to escape the conflicts engendered by their flight from conventional female roles. The imagery of the sexually mature, sometimes maternal, woman has almost no place in the work of women Surrealists. Their conflicts about this aspect of female sexuality reflect the difficult choices forced upon women of their generation who attempted to reconcile traditional female roles with lives as artists in a movement that prized the innocence of the child-woman and violently attacked the institutions of marriage and the family.

Less than positive views of maternity carry over into their work. The most disturbing images of maternal reality in twentieth-century art are to be found in Tanning's *Maternity* (1946), Varo's *Celestial Pablum* (1958), and Kahlo's *My Birth* (1932), *Henry Ford Hospital* (1932), and other paintings on this theme. In Varo's *Celestial Pablum,* an isolated woman sits in a lonely tower, a blank expression on her exhausted face, and mechanically grinds up stars which she feeds to an insatiable moon. The somber palette and matt surface cast their own pall over the work. These paintings are remarkable for their powerful imaging of the conflicts inherent in maternity: the physical changes initiated by pregnancy and lactation, the mother's exhaustion and feared loss of autonomy. The element of erotic violence so prevalent in the work of male Surrealist artists makes its first appearance here in the works of Tanning, Meret Oppenheim (b.1913), and Kahlo that deal with childbirth and motherhood. Now it is violence directed against the self, not projected onto another, violence inseparable from the physiological reality of woman's sexuality and the social construction of her feminine role.

For Kahlo, as for other women artists associated with the Surrealists, painting became a means of sustaining a dialogue with inner reality. Surrealism sanctioned personal exploration for both men and women; in doing so, it legitimized a path familiar to many women and gave new artistic form to some of the conflicts confronting women in early twentieth-century artistic movements.

NAN ENSTAD (ESSAY DATE 1999)

SOURCE: Enstad, Nan. "Movie-Struck Girls: Motion Pictures and Consumer Subjectivities." In *Ladies of Labor, Girls of Adventure: Working Women, Popular Culture, and Labor Politics at the Turn of the Twentieth Century,* pp. 161-200. New York: Columbia University Press, 1999.

In the following excerpt, Enstad explores the relationship between women and the film industry in the early twentieth century.

[Working women walking on Eighth Avenue see] the flashing, gaudy, poster-lined entrances of Hickman's and of the Galaxy. These supply the girls with a "craze," the same that sends those with a more liberal allowance to the [stage] matinees. Their pictures spread out adventure and melodrama which are soul-satisfying.
—Ruth True, *The Neglected Girl* (1914)[1]

Mary's eyes were smoldering that day with the fire of strange yearnings. She moved about her work as one walking in a dream—burning with a life that was not the life around her.
—opening lines, print version of *What Happened to Mary* (1912)[2]

During the same years that working women went on strike in unprecedented numbers, they were creating a motion picture "craze." Working women attended movies by 1905, but only formed a distinctive "fan" relationship with them after 1908. As reformer Ruth True noted, women's fascination with the movies exceeded the experience of the films themselves. Young working women gazed at the "flashing, gaudy" posters that lined the entrances to nickelodeon theaters, daydreamed about stars and about becoming stars themselves, and attended motion pictures regularly to socialize and to imaginatively step into the visual fantasies of the silver screen. When these women consumed motion pictures, they created new urban experiences and occupied the public spaces of streets and theaters in new ways. They built particular and distinctive social practices around motion picture consumption and incorporated the movies into their established consumer practices around dime novels and fashion, weaving motion pictures into their identities as ladies. Like the strikes of the 1910s, the movies signaled a new relationship of working women to public life. Of course, the motion picture industry did not promote the democratic participation in economic decisions that unions had sought. But for working women, the movies became a parallel site of social change in the public realm.

Neighborhood theaters, called nickelodeons, boomed after 1905. In the scramble for more narratives to satisfy eager audiences, producers translated a plethora of print fiction genres into film form, including dime novel romances. Working women saw elements of the dime novel romance formula in a variety of short melodramas after 1908, as producers presented working heroines who encountered adventures, gained inheritances, or married millionaires. In July 1912, the Edison Company and *The Ladies' World,* a popular magazine, collaborated to produce the sensationally popular serial story *What Happened to Mary.*

Edison released the story about a New York working woman in twelve twenty-minute film episodes to coincide with publication of the segments in print form in *The Ladies' World.* This successful collaboration would be the first in a long line of motion picture serials featuring female heroines. Mary and her successors excelled in their work, triumphed over personal danger, heroically saved others, and gained promotion and respect. Romance took a back seat to adventure in these narratives; the working heroines captured robbers, raced through burning buildings, and leapt from moving freight trains. They did not, however, go on strike.

The motion picture theaters constituted a new public space in the early twentieth century, uniquely open to working-class women of all ethnicities.[3] As historian Kathy Peiss notes, when movies moved from the arcade kinetoscopes to nickelodeons after 1905, women's attendance soared.[4] There were at least six hundred nickelodeons in greater New York City by 1910, showing movies to 1.5 million people, or a quarter of the city's population, each week. Most of this early audience was working class. Historian Steven Ross notes that 72 percent of those attending were blue collar workers, 25 percent were clerical workers, and only 3 percent belonged to the "leisure" class. Women's attendance was greater for this amusement than for any other in the city: they comprised 40 percent of the working-class audience in 1910.[5] Whereas many working-class parents believed that other places of public amusement, such as dance halls or amusement parks, were not appropriate for unchaperoned daughters, they thought the nickelodeons were safe and respectable. The motion picture theaters thus constituted a new public sphere. Film historian Miriam Hansen argues that while the movies certainly did not operate like Habermas's ideal of democratic exchange, they did serve as a new "public space, part of a social horizon of experience" for a new kind of collective, the audience.[6] Motion pictures, then, offered both new urban experiences and new kinds of commodities to working women.

Working women's public mobility allowed them to enact public subjectivities within consumer culture. As part of these new subjectivities, working women claimed an active gaze in the streets and in the local theaters. This gaze was a consumer gaze—that is, it was tied to and justified by a consumer activity—but it was not merely acquisitive. Rather, it was interwoven with complex narratives and fantasies. When working women gazed at posters, dreamed of stars, and attended shows, they enacted subjectivities in a new public arena and engaged contradictions that they experienced as immigrant women workers, just as they did in their consumption of fashion and dime novel products. The motion picture serials directly catered to working women with visual fantasies related to their established practices of ladyhood. The serials solicited an identification with heroines who desired—and achieved—lavish social recognition both as workers and as women, in jobs that delivered adventure. This is not to say that motion pictures were an arena of freedom for working women; theaters and the range and content of films themselves regularly replicated hierarchies working women found elsewhere in society. Nevertheless, women's social practices of motion picture consumption generated new resources for the creation of public identities.

This chapter explores working women's relationship to the movies with the methods used to examine their experiences with fiction and fashion in chapters 1 and 2. First, I analyze motion picture production, particularly how the industry shaped and limited the range and content of the products available for women's consumption. I will trace the emergence of the serials compared to other types of film narratives, and the film industry's production of early "fan" products. I turn next to working women's consumption of motion pictures, focusing on the social practices they made in relation to the movies. As in chapter 2, I will distinguish between the acts of consumption—buying tickets, looking at posters, attending theaters—and the imaginative experiences of the films themselves. All of these aspects of consumption worked together as women imbued "the movies" with significance.

Studying working women's experiences with motion pictures presents a unique problem: identifying which specific films to study. While working women's consumption of all types of popular culture was varied, many read an identifiable set of dime novels and dressed in particular and distinctive styles. However, they saw *all* types of motion pictures. Nickelodeons typically showed four or five short films on the same bill, interspersed with singers or vaudeville acts. Exhibitors demanded that distributors provide a mixed bill of different types of narratives. Working women saw them all: social problem films, Westerns, melodramas, comedies, labor-capital films, travel films, railroad dramas, adventure serials, and military films. The problem of assessing women's relationship to the movies is thus complex. Historian Kathy Peiss has focused on comedies

produced before 1910, citing a 1907 source indicating that comedies were the most popular with early movie audiences. Peiss's results are important and pathbreaking, but largely predate 1908, the era when more complex dramatic narratives developed and working women formed more specific fan practices. Historian Elizabeth Ewen has looked at popular stars and the types of stories that they played in. This too stands as an important beginning, but is focused primarily on the feature film era, 1915 and after.[7]

Here I focus on the adventure serials, in particular *What Happened to Mary* and the long-lived *Hazards of Helen* (Kalem, 1914), because they had roots in dime novel formulas and were aimed at working women as well as a broader audience. The market for motion pictures was relatively undifferentiated; that is, everyone attended all the time rather than dividing into particular market segments according to different interests. However, by 1909, producers standardized and differentiated fictional film products into types of narratives that they knew would be more appealing to some segments of the audience than others. Like the early story papers of the 1840s, the mixed bill of nickelodeon theaters operated on the principal of "something for everyone." Working-class women constituted a significant portion of the motion picture audience; it was in producers' interests to maintain their loyalty while ensuring that films would entice the widest possible audience approval. The adventure serials, beginning with *What Happened to Mary,* grew directly out of dime novel romance conventions and tapped a female reading public through their connection with *The Ladies' World,* a "low-brow" women's magazine. More than any other type of narrative, they emerged from, and intended to reproduce, established fiction consumption practices of working women. Thus, the serials are the best place to start examining specific film texts in relationship to working women's social practices of film consumption during the formative years of 1909 to 1916.

The motion picture industry struggled to become big business in the early 1900s, and that struggle profoundly shaped the films that working women could see by 1909. Leading producers pursued three related goals in their efforts to organize the early film industry and maximize their profits. First, they attempted to control the production, distribution, and exhibition of films. Second, they increased the pace and volume of production, and third, they standardized the film product to make it as predictable and interchangeable as possible, while maintaining audience enthusiasm. These forces shaped and limited the narratives, but they did not eliminate creativity. Rather, scenario writers, directors, actors, and producers applied their creative energies at once to economic and aesthetic challenges in this rapidly developing form of visual storytelling. As with dime novels and fashion products, the relations of production conferred both limits and possibilities on the products. When those commodities entered social circulation, working women wound them into their own social practices and imbued them with their own meanings.

Some film and social historians have celebrated the relative lack of organization of the young film industry before Hollywood, seeing it as providing a particular possibility for working-class expression. They note the predominantly working-class immigrant audience for movies before World War I, the preponderance of narratives representing working-class life, and the large number of immigrants among the independent film producers, particularly after 1912. The silent movies, according to these historians, were largely produced by, represented, and were viewed by the working class. These historians celebrate the silent era as a time of relative freedom of expression for film makers.[8] In contrast, they see the Hollywood era as the time when movies became a big business and drove out working-class interests.

The relationship between working-class audiences and the developing popular culture industry of film is more complex than this view suggests. As a number of other film historians have pointed out, the industry wooed a middle-class audience as early as 1908. This is not, however, to claim that the movies were "middle class" rather than "working class." Indeed, to ascribe a class designation to a set of products deflects attention from how the capitalist marketplace shapes cultural products for all classes. The view that Hollywood signaled the decline of free expression because of the rise of rationalized production misconstrues the early industry and seems to assume that meaningful film can only be produced outside of the capitalist marketplace. Ironically, critics of the later, Hollywood era unwittingly maintain the bourgeois myth that some cultural artifacts under capitalism are free of market interests. However, as chapter 1 argued, this myth operated principally to maintain class distinction through commodities while denying that it was doing so. When some film and social historians celebrate the early movies as free or working-class expression, they underestimate the ways that the young industry's

strenuous attempts to rationalize and organize production profoundly shaped its products by 1909, including those that overtly represented class conflict.

The emergence of the adventure serials was itself a result of economic interests and requires a more nuanced analysis. The serials engaged central issues of gender and class, but were standardized products of the *most* rationalized arm of the film industry. They offered powerful representations of women as heroic workers but, like the dime novel romances, did not represent working-class women's strikes or overt political action. Indeed, with very few exceptions, the motion picture industry did not make films that represented groups of women on strike. While this omission was consistent with the dime novel formula, it seems odd in the context of the dramatic strikes of the 1910s, especially considering the fact that movies about male strikers were rather common. As Steven Ross has pointed out, motion picture producers created a genre they called the "labor-capital film," which represented strike scenes from a variety of perspectives and served as a medium for social debate about the role of labor unionism in U.S. society.[9] But labor-capital films only very rarely represented groups of women strikers. As a public realm of debate, the motion pictures replicated and even accentuated exclusions that existed elsewhere in public life. These exclusions did not occur naturally; they were effects of producers' efforts to standardize film production between 1908 and 1912.

Before 1908, many producers perceived the young U.S. film industry to be in a crisis. The simultaneous emergence of the fictional story film and the growth of nickelodeons around 1905 drew an ever-expanding audience with a voracious appetite for new motion pictures. As film historian Eileen Bowser notes, the French company Pathé-Frères filled most of the spectacular demand for films in the United States. Companies based in the United States felt hampered by the depression of 1907 and by the distribution and exhibition system, and were reluctant or unable to increase the capital investment necessary to expand production. The system of distribution and exhibition in the U.S. was entirely unregulated; films could be rented out repeatedly, providing increased profits to distributors and exhibitors but limiting producers' sales.[10]

The Edison Company led the move to gain control over production, distribution, and exhibition by founding the Motion Picture Patents Company (MPPC) in December of 1908 with a group of eight other large producers, a distributor, and Eastman Kodak, the principal manufacturer of film stock. The MPPC consisted of many companies, such as Edison, that held patents for technology used in production and projection of motion pictures. By limiting rights to use of such technology to its members and licensees, the MPPC gained control of the industry, including the distribution system. Independent companies could and did exist, but they faced shortages of good materials and equipment, limited access to distributors, and regular lawsuits for patent infringement. Once the MPPC ensured that licensed producers would make tidy profits on their capital investments, the rate and scale of film production increased rapidly. The MPPC held the reins of the industry until 1912, when independent producers, and eventually the U.S. government, successfully challenged its monopolistic practices in court. During those four years, however, the film industry stabilized and underwent dramatic and irreversible changes.[11]

The crisis in the film industry was not only economic but also aesthetic. As producers created more, and more complex, narratives to please clamoring audiences, they found viewers could not follow the silent stories. After the formation of the MPPC, producers responded by changing the mode of narration to utilize visual cues that could be widely understood across differences in class or national origin, including an increased number of camera cuts, closer shots, and new styles of acting.[12] Bowser argues that the changes in American film production originating in 1908 and 1909 were as radical as those at any other time in film history, and profoundly altered the relationship between spectator and film narrative. Before 1905, motion picture producers supplied a variety of narratives to the new theaters, including "actuality" films, comedies or jokes rooted in vaudeville traditions, lantern-slide shows, and comic strips. Directors shot these early narratives in presentational style; that is, the camera viewed the action as though it were on a stage, mimicking the live theater experience. Such techniques did not work well with more complex fictional narratives. In response to this problem, producers layered an increased number of camera shots to create depth and point of view, effectively bringing the spectator's view into the frame of action. Spectators now viewed scenes as invisible participants rather than as a removed audience. Closer shots accentuated this sense of intimacy, as spectators could see subtle shifts in emotion in actors' faces and postures. As a result, acting styles moved away from the large gestures and pantomime that worked to convey emotion on the stage. All of these techniques made possible a more distinctive and elaborate imaginative relationship between film viewers and motion pictures, particularly viewers' closer identification with film stars, and led to the birth of the star system.

Once producers reformed the system of distribution so that it granted them more control and profit, they rationalized production in order to increase their rate and volume of film output. A principal change involved modifying the role of the director. Previously, directors typically came up with stories, conveyed their intentions to actors, and worked the photoplays out in short rehearsals before shooting. As producers sought to increase the number and complexity of fictional narratives this system became impractical. First, it was too slow. Second, it worked better with shorter, less complicated narratives than it did with the longer films in which directors layered shots in more complex ways. Increasingly, companies hired scenario writers to craft visual stories according to the emerging types or genres of film narratives. Producers incorporated editorial practices from the cheap fiction industry, or "the fiction factory," as writer William Wallace Cook called it, and hired many writers who also wrote for that industry. The *New York Times* in 1913 noted that scenario writers were valued most for their ability to write according to specific instructions: "Many of [the scenario writers] work on order. A company suddenly requires a play about a certain actor, a certain locality, or possibly an animal it has purchased. Immediately, the company communicates with one of its writers, tells its needs and asks for a script, 'within a day or so.' . . . Companies are always desirous of finding new authors in this by-order method." The *Times* asserted that story ideas themselves were a dime a dozen. Companies paid scenario writers to explain "in short, jerky clauses, the direction for every movement on the part of each actor." Bannister Merwin and James Oppenheim, both of whom wrote scenarios for *What Happened to Mary*, were two of the six successful writers that the *Times* named as making scenario writing a "lucrative profession" because they were willing and able to provide what producers wanted.[13]

In some cases, scenario writing was even more rationalized. While writers like Merwin, Oppenheim, and Cook supplied fully developed visual narratives in scenario form, others simply sent plot ideas to editors who then assigned them to staff writers to develop into movie scenarios. For the freelance writers or amateurs supplying ideas, scenario writing was not particularly lucrative. As in dime novel fiction writing, much of the financial risk and unpredictability of the business was borne by the writers rather than by the producers. In 1909, Cook answered a Vitagraph advertisement he saw in the newspaper that claimed "We pay $10 to $100 for Picture Plays." Cook sent in an idea, and was shocked to receive a $10 check in return. Upon querying Vitagraph, Cook received a letter from the editor explaining that "The manuscript has to be revised in almost every instance in order to put it in practical shape for the directors. . . . The members of our staff, who are obliged to write practical working scenarios, appreciate the above facts because they know what it means to perfect a scenario with the synopsis of the story, the properties, settings, etc., etc." But mastering the art of "short, jerky clauses" would not raise Cook's rate appreciably: "The editor merely surmises, or so we think, that a thoroughly original manuscript in practical shape would be worth at least $25, but we seldom get one of that kind." Cook eventually did master the art of scenario writing, and in 1910 wrote a "good many" scenarios for an unnamed company that paid him $35 each. Cook complained that scenario writers were paid poorly, endured slow responses on scripts from movie companies, and were not listed as authors in the film credits. From his experiences in both dime novel and scenario writing, Cook considered, "Possibly the film manufacturers borrow their ideas of equitable treatment for the writer from some of the publishing houses."[14]

Such editorial control over scenario writing went hand-in-hand with creating a standardized product, which would make the industry more predictable and profit margins more stable. Films before 1909 ranged from 200 feet to 1000 feet in length; setting a standard length made it possible to set a single price for films, making them more interchangeable from a marketing perspective. In addition, producers sought to create customer loyalty by promoting films through company brand names as well as by genre. A distributor could put a Biograph drama in a package with an Kalem adventure serial episode and a Vitagraph comedy, for example, and exhibitors and audiences would have an approximate idea of what they would receive. Bowser notes that Biograph films were the most popular with U.S. audiences by 1910. As early as 1909, then, standardization meant that the creative energy of motion picture makers would be channeled into particular "lines"

of roughly predictable products. Finally, the shift in film techniques was also part of the effort to standardize film products. Producers needed the widely understood visual cues to ensure audience involvement with the films. The new use of camera cuts and close shots invited strong emotional responses to the film.[15]

Ultimately, the purpose of a standardized product was to standardize audience attendance and emotional response to the films as much as possible. Producers wished not only to make *movies* but also to create a pleasurable movie-going *experience* that could be replicated on a weekly or even nightly basis. This involved shaping both industry structures and audiences' desires into a workable system of motion picture production and reception. Perhaps the most challenging element of this was capturing audience members' imaginations and desires in predictable and reproducible ways. Thus, it was at this point in film history (1908-1915) that producers began speaking of "spectators" conceived as individuals responding emotionally to a screen fantasy, as often as they used the older term "audience," which positioned viewers as a group.[16] It would prove very difficult to control the various meanings that viewers took from films, but quite possible to create enough of a satisfying emotional response to ensure increasing popularity and success for the newly structured industry.

The final ingredient necessary to make motion pictures big business was a wider audience at the theaters. Because the industry had developed with a predominantly working-class audience, this meant reaching out to the middle class. Some exhibitors did so by building new, large theaters in theater districts to remove motion pictures from their association with the immigrant, working-class neighborhood nickelodeons.[17] In addition, producers like Edison adopted a Progressive tone, arguing that films could be a tool of uplift for working and middle class alike. Like vaudeville producers two decades earlier, producers tailored films to please the desired middle class and even agreed to self-censorship to convince the public of their respectability.[18] But producers could not ignore their working-class customers altogether. Bowser notes that they tried to create "educational" films, but working-class audiences rejected them so exhibitors refused to rent them.[19] Nevertheless, the middle class had an effect on motion pictures long before its members attended movies in great numbers. Indeed, the need to please a middle-class audience, real or only wished-for, played a large role in determining which representations of working women would become standard in the movies.

According to Steven Ross, "social problem" films regularly featured groups of women workers, while labor-capital films almost never did. Social problem films emerged as part of the Progressive mission of some producers and focused on current social issues, including the exploitation of so-called "dependent" workers—women, children, and the elderly. While they regularly exposed the dark side of industrial capitalism, they represented women workers as victims, not as politically empowered strikers. Indeed, Ross notes that in social problem films, "working women were portrayed less as workers than as women in need of constant protection by well-intentioned males." Labor-capital films, however, represented male—not female—workers on strike. According to Ross, who counts 274 labor-capital films produced between 1905 and 1917, this genre conveyed a variety of political perspectives on strikes. But I have found only one film that definitely represented a group of women on strike. Young working-class female characters did appear in labor-capital films, sometimes in heroic roles, but usually as daughters of strikers, not workers or strikers themselves: their loyalty and heroism were defined by their family relationships. In addition, labor-capital films typically represented a single working-class heroine rather than groups of women.[20]

As chapter 3 noted, many middle-class people were accustomed to and comfortable with representations of working women as victims rather than as strikers. This may explain why film producers largely avoided the women's strikes as starting points for labor-capital films. A narrative that positioned working women as strikers would challenge both unregulated industrial capitalism and the prevalent masculine definition of political actors. Ross, however, praises the labor-capital film for "concentrat[ing] on a more controversial sector of the working class. Instead of focusing on unorganized women, children, and elderly wage earners, their plots dealt with adult male workers who labored in the nation's most contentious and highly organized industries." Such male workers, he notes, could not be construed as victims.[21] Ross fails to consider that the controversial element of a film sprang not from the sector of the working class it pictured, but from the modes of representation and narration it utilized. As vulnerable victims, immigrant women workers on the screen could solicit pity from audiences. But as political actors, young immigrant women were far more controversial than skilled white men who worked in the highly organized industries of the early twentieth century. Indeed, as chapter 3 showed, some middle-class commentators who *supported* the shirtwaist strike persisted in representing striking women as victims asking for charity even in the context of overt, dramatic, and often militant political action. Labor-capital films usually focused on the workers most favored by the AFL and those closest to attaining political legitimacy in the eyes of the middle class, particularly Progressives. Both social problem and labor-capital films bore the imprint of producers' goal to please—or minimally offend—a middle-class audience.

The one film that I have found that represented a group of women on strike, *The Girl Strike Leader* (Thanhouser, 1910), relied as much on the dime novel formula as on labor-capital film conventions to tell its story. Thanhouser released *The Girl Strike Leader* only five months after the New York shirtwaist strike. In this film, producers did not represent working women merely as victims. Rather, the heroines take action by striking successfully to better their working conditions. At the end, the girl strike leader marries the factory owner, which validated her adventures as a striker and extricated her from labor altogether.[22] This film placed the strike in the position of adventures in the dime novel formula, treating women viewers to a familiar ending, but one quite different from the actual conclusion of the shirtwaist strike. Film historians have interpreted the marriage to the factory owner as undercutting the representation of class conflict, but for working women well-versed in dime novel romance conventions, the story could profoundly validate their actions as strikers by rewarding the heroine for brave adventures.[23]

The Girl Strike Leader fit into a developing genre of female adventure films, popular between 1908 and 1912, as much as into the labor-capital genre. Female adventure films drew on a variety of cheap fiction formulas and formed the basis for later adventure serials. A film "series" was a set of shorts featuring the same characters, such as the Keystone Cops, but unconnected by plot and released on no particular schedule. A "serial," however, tied episodes together by some element of an ongoing plot and was released regularly, usually weekly. Eileen Bowser notes that in 1909 the Kalem Company produced a series about a female spy working for the South in the Civil War that was an important precursor to the serials. The independent Yankee Film Company started a female detective series in 1910 in which a male detective's daughter takes over his job after he is killed.[24] Railroad dramas also regularly featured heroic women workers. *The Lonedale Operator* (Biograph, 1911, d. D. W. Griffith) shows a girl telegraph operator capturing robbers in a scene that at once anticipates both *Hazards of Helen* and an episode of *What Happened to Mary*. Indeed, Kalem's popular *Hazards of Helen* serial reused a railroad drama produced years earlier in order to avoid lags in the production schedule. *The Grit of the Girl Telegrapher* first appeared in the theaters as a regular short in 1912, and appeared again under the title *The Girl Telegrapher's Nerve* in March 1916 as episode number 69 of *Hazards of Helen*. Thus, the serials emerged from a group of films that were already popular with motion picture audiences and drew on popular fiction conventions for female adventures.[25] These films largely avoided representing women as victims or as overtly political actors.

The Edison Company joined forces with the magazine *The Ladies' World* to create the first female adventure serial, *What Happened to Mary*, in 1912. Edison was the leader in rationalizing film production, and *What Happened to Mary* was largely a product of producers' attempts to standardize production and reception even further. Edison and *The Ladies' World* released the twelve-episode story monthly in both film and print formats. The two producers sought a story with elements proven popular with fiction and film audiences. They hired seasoned scenario writer Bannister Merwin to writer the first scenarios and texts for both the film and print versions of the story. Later, James Oppenheim took over the scenarios while Frank Blighton continued the print episodes. The Edison Company used both Merwin and Oppenheim on a regular basis and could be confident that they would supply stories "on order."[26] The film company and the magazine publisher overtly aimed to share audiences: the magazine printed photographs from the movie set as illustrations, urged readers to see the film version at the close of each segment, and supplemented the story with articles on how films were made. Film episodes closed with a title urging viewers to read about Mary in *The Ladies' World*. The continuity of the story helped the Edison Company create a sustained interest in a set of related film products and linked film directly to women's established reading practices.

With *What Happened to Mary, The Ladies' World* gained motion picture fans as readers and associated itself with the glamour and modernity of the movies. *The Ladies' World* already had an estab-
lished audience of working-class and lower middle-class female readers. It had begun as a "mail order journal," that is, it made money from mail-order advertisements printed throughout the magazine rather than from subscriptions. Hundreds of such journals existed at the turn of the century. They were highly accessible: producers mass-mailed the journals to homes free of charge. They typically printed "low-brow" fiction to draw consumers to look at the advertisements. Though considered a step down from the "legitimate" women's journals, such as *Ladies' Home Journal* or *Woman's Home Companion,* mail-order journals distributed a great deal of fiction to working people. In 1907, the post office withdrew mail-order journals' second-class mailing privileges unless they produced legitimate subscription lists, paid in advance. This drove many journals out of business immediately, and by 1912 the future of *The Ladies' World,* whose subscription rate was fifty cents per year, was in question. But within less than a year, after five episodes of *What Happened to Mary,* the editor credited the serial for the bulk of 100,000 new subscriptions.[27]

The Edison Company and *The Ladies' World* heavily promoted the film and print story through the new star system and together shaped a fan culture. Before 1909, producers did not divulge the names of film actors. Rather, they operated with a stock system in which they steadily employed a group of actors whom they assigned to play parts as needed. By 1909, audiences were clamoring to know the names of the actors with whom they emotionally identified. Producers soon realized that this avid interest among the new fans, many of whom were working women, could be very lucrative, and began advertising motion pictures with the stars' names and photographs.[28] The Edison Company hired the popular Mary Fuller to play the leading role and launched an aggressive promotional campaign. Fuller had starred in female adventure shorts already and was a proven hit with audiences. One reviewer remarked on the Edison Company's "striking advertising campaign," which made him confident that all of his readers knew Fuller was the film's star even before the motion picture opened. In addition, *The Ladies' World* included photographs of and articles about Mary Fuller.[29] As part of the promotion of Mary, *The Ladies' World* and the Edison Company offered some of the film industry's first fan products. *The Ladies' World* encouraged admirers to buy "the Mary hat," modeled in the advertisement by Mary Fuller, a "What Happened to Mary Board Game," and a "What Happened to

Mary Jigsaw Puzzle." The producers invited additional suggestions from readers: "It would seem only logical that we should have 'Mary' hats and gowns—perhaps a 'Mary' color for the women who are her admirers. . . . Perhaps there are other entertaining or utilitarian purposes to which the character of 'Mary' may be applied; and perhaps there are readers . . . who can originate ideas that have not occurred to the originators of 'Mary.' If so, let us have them."[30] Serial producers navigated uncharted territory in the consumer culture industry by requesting the guidance of working-class and lower-middle-class women.

Producers also relied on consumers to guide them in creating the plot of *What Happened to Mary*. Through promotional contests, producers encouraged fans' imaginative engagement with Mary and gained audience response from women readers. Each month *The Ladies' World* staged a contest that awarded $100 for the essay that best answered the question "What Happened to Mary Next?" The magazine reported that it received 2,000 entries in the first month of the contest and that by the fifth month the numbers approached 10,000. Three or four contest winners were published each month. On two occasions the winning essays for the contest did indeed outline the plot for the story that month.[31] The ongoing contest informed the producers of audience desires that they could then utilize in shaping the unfolding narrative. In addition, the contest encouraged readers to create an imaginative fantasy world around *What Happened to Mary*. Such participation in the narrative could promote loyal purchases of movie tickets and magazines.

Other film producers soon tried to replicate *What Happened to Mary*'s great success with serials of their own. The Selig Company joined with the *Chicago Tribune* to produce *The Adventures of Kathlyn* in 1913, and dozens of others followed. While *What Happened to Mary* was released on a monthly basis, later serials appeared weekly. The adventure serials quickly became a new and noted genre in silent film. By April 1914 *Variety* magazine declared that, "The serial thing in movies has come to stay. There's hardly a big concern now that isn't getting out a melodramatic series in which a young woman is the heroine and the camera has her having hair breadth escapes by the score."[32] Many of the serials featured wage-earning women and some were detective stories, but all centered on adventure. As a group, the serials were products of producers' well-planned efforts to capture and sustain audience interest. For working women, though they contained no depictions of collective action, they constituted an exciting type of film product with roots in familiar fiction formulas.

Despite producers' self-conscious efforts to rationalize production and shape consumption, the movies took on new meaning once in social circulation. Producers could not fully control how working women wove motion pictures into the social fabric of their daily lives. Indeed, the cultural impact of the movies was far greater than the visual experience of the films themselves. Like dime novels and fashion, the meanings of motion pictures emerged in part from the social practices of the working women who consumed them. When working women bought tickets, viewed posters, dreamed of stars, and attended theaters, they made motion pictures part of their collective culture, including their workplace culture.

The ways working women acquired their movie tickets greatly influenced the kind of experience they had at neighborhood theaters. As working-class communities incorporated motion pictures into their daily routines, they blended family and ethnically based leisure customs with women's new patterns of consumption. Working women attended motion pictures with family groups, dates, and alone. Motion pictures became a new ethnic community event that everyone could attend, like picnics in the park, religious holiday celebrations, and weddings. One observer noted that motion picture theaters were practically the only place, along with public parks, where "whole families can together enjoy any kind of recreation." Another remarked in 1907, "Father and mother, the baby, the older children, the grandparents—all were there."[33] Depending on how family economies were managed, the price of a working daughter's ticket might come from the family purse or from her own wages after the bulk had been turned over to the mother. Either way, women's wages contributed to ticket purchases, but their position as dependent daughters would be reinforced if their tickets were paid out of family funds. Many girls and young women probably had their first experiences at the movies with their families, reinforcing their family-based identities in the new public arena.

Even as motion picture theaters fit into established neighborhood leisure practices, they fostered new forms of dating that were free of direct supervision and also considered respectable. Working women often attended motion pictures with young men who paid for their tickets. Reformer Ruth True noted that many workers did not hurry home after work but would "linger with a boy companion making 'dates' for a 'movie.'" This way of getting through the nickelodeon door set in motion a quite different set of social relations than when women attended with families. At motion picture theaters, working women had unprecedented opportunities for social intimacy with men. Jane Addams noted that the "very darkness of the room, necessary for an exhibition of the films, is an added attraction to many young people, for whom the space is filled with the glamour of love making." Such glamour must have been intensified by the occasional larger-than-life representations of romance on the silver screen. Many middle-class reformers found this attraction alarming and warned regularly against the "danger of undue familiarity made possible by dim lights."[34] Nevertheless, working-class parents continued to see the space as safe and respectable, perhaps because there were so many families there. Young working women and men thus made the movies a site of romantic and sexual experimentation and change.

When women gained access to motion picture theaters through dates with men, they participated in a developing sexual economy in which their appearance carried high value. The purchase of the movie ticket was only one item in a series of exchanges. According to middle-class reformers, men regularly expected "payment" for their movie tickets in the form of sexual relations: "They do not treat for nothing," warned one. Reformer Mary Simkhovitch noted that when a young woman went weekly with a man to the movies, he expected in return that she would "go with no one else and . . . [would] give him the privileges of engagement." Simkhovitch noted that this could lead to trouble: "Sometimes a passion for the theater will lead a girl to go with a man with whom she is unwilling to keep company and yet who expects his payment." The movies thus fit into the sexual economy of "treating" described by Kathy Peiss, in which payment for dates carried a tacit expectation for reciprocal payment of engagement or sexual favors.[35]

From many working women's perspectives, however, they had already paid up front. In this sexual economy, the first step often was women's cultivation of an attractive appearance, which solicited the men's purchase. Fashion was necessary to achieve visibility. Jane Addams recorded that one young woman stole a "mass of artificial flowers with which to trim a hat," because she believed that "a girl has to be dressy if she expects to be seen." The woman was reportedly afraid of losing the attention of a man who had taken her to the nickelodeon. "If he failed her," Addams

explained, "she was sure that she would never go again, and she sobbed out incoherently that she 'couldn't live at all without it.'" As chapter 2 noted, in a context in which women were systematically paid less than men, clothing could be seen as an investment in the future if it helped women make a good match. Dates to the movies were smaller prizes, but functioned as part of the same system. Reformer Clara Laughlin observed two women who "limited their indulgence in nickel shows" for several weeks in order to save money to buy very dressy clothes on the installment plan. Their clothes, in turn, won them dates that led to weeks' worth of regular movie tickets.[36] Though successful, the two women found themselves doubly in debt: to the store that sold them the clothes, and to the men whom they "owed" for the movie tickets, and who did not recognize their initial payment. Thus, women's love of the movies could socialize them simultaneously in the new practices of heterosexuality and in U.S. values of capitalist investment, and potentially also teach them the pitfalls of both for those in economically disadvantaged positions. Even when women attended the movies with dates for the "glamour of love making," they could find themselves enmeshed in new gendered hierarchies.

The newest pattern of leisure at the motion picture theaters was working women attending alone or with female friends. They bought their own tickets with their wages and often met groups of other young people once at the theater. While some working women also went to dance halls and amusement parks with female friends, the cheapness and respectability of the movies made them especially accessible. Louise Odencrantz notes that though young Italian women rarely socialized without a chaperon, many "were allowed to go out without their parents [to] moving-picture shows." Filomena Ognibene, an Italian woman garment maker, recalled that "the one place I was allowed to go by myself was the movies. I went to the movies for fun. My parents wouldn't let me go out anywhere else, even when I was twenty-four." Reformers noted that many working women attended the movies at least once a week, some with even greater frequency. Ognibene went to the movies two or three times each week.[37] When women used their wages for their own evening amusements, they laid claim to the practices and privileges of male wage-earners, just as they did when they bought clothing and dime novels. In addition, in these cases they occupied the public space of motion picture theaters outside of family or dating relationships.

Women's social practices of attending theaters and engaging in related fan activities also inflected the motion picture experience with specific meanings. For working women, the films themselves were not the only, and sometimes not the principal, draw. The nickelodeon served as a "general social center and club house," in Jane Addams' words, for people of all ages. For one woman worker who lived in a New York boarding house, having a place to talk in mixed-gender groups was the primary reason to go to the movies. She and a group of friends talked one night in her hallway "as it was too wet and cold to walk around the streets. After shifting from one foot to the other several times and being very tired of standing, some one suggested that we either go to a moving picture theater or to a cafe to have a drink." Likewise, a study of Progressive-run organized "homes" for working women showed that "in houses where there was only one reception room, the girls usually preferred to go to the movies or places giving an opportunity for intimate conversation."[38] Women who lived in tenements also lacked space for socializing. Movie audiences often talked through the films, interacting with the characters or ignoring the screen to continue a conversation.[39] The film itself was certainly important, but such testimony demonstrates how women used motion picture theaters to create a new public site for themselves. They imbued the movies with a sense of unprecedented freedom of mobility—a new and exciting public identity—quite apart from the content of specific films.

Working women's emerging fan practices claimed access to public space through the assertion of an active consumer gaze. Women's consumption of new fan products—particularly the posters at theater entrances and the photographs of stars that exhibitors often handed out free of charge—shaped a distinctive "fan culture" that far exceeded the event of motion picture attendance. Their fan practices also became part of workplace culture as women discussed motion picture stars and plots, much as they talked about dime novels, at the shops. In this way, women imbued both their night life and their daytime life with the glamour of the movies. Fan paraphernalia certainly was not working women's own cultural creation, but the product of producers' promotional efforts. Nevertheless, when fans wove the posters and photos into their own lives, they created what historian Kathryn Fuller called "a truly popular culture of film."[40]

Specifically, posters functioned like shop windows to legitimate women's presence in the urban landscape and their active gaze at products and images that filled the modern city. Walter Benjamin notes that the rationalization of industry and the reverence for "reason" that characterized modern life did not drain the urban landscape of myth and magic. On the contrary, capitalist industry caused a re-enchantment of modern life within the urban consumer spaces of arcades and amusement parks, in the city streets plastered with theater and movie posters, and in the cinema itself.[41] Stores created window displays to beckon and entice; department stores used glass and mirrors to focus shoppers' gazes upon products newly packaged to capture attention and promise delight. While shop windows and nickelodeon exteriors covered with posters existed primarily to sell products, they also became women's spaces. Historian William Leach notes that department stores became important spaces for middle-class women,[42] but the degree to which working-class women participated in a similar space of visual spectacle and consumer desire on the streets is less acknowledged. Many had an established practice of window shopping on their way home from the factory, laundry, or sweatshop. One reformer noted that for working women "the shop windows . . . were one of the chief sources of entertainment and delight."[43] Gazing at the posters that lined nickelodeon entrances connected closely to this practice. When working women made the nickelodeon exteriors a site for their public subjectivities they made the enchantment of the city part of their own subcultural landscape, and made an active and desiring gaze a part of their public identities. Like the use of fashion, the social practice of motion picture consumption negotiated a modern culture that privileged looking in the construction of meaning.

Young working women created somewhat different patterns of consumption of movie posters in the evening than during the day. At evening, poster-lined nickelodeon entrances became sites where both men and women could meet and socialize. Jane Addams recorded that one group of women refused her efforts to interest them in a sponsored day in the country, "because the return on a late train would compel them to miss one evening's performance. They found it impossible to tear themselves away not only from the excitements of the theater itself but from the gaiety of the crowd of young men and girls invariably gathered outside discussing the sensational posters." Social workers Robert Wood and Albert Kennedy found this phenomenon threatening to young women, noting that "the crowds outside the door [of the motion picture theater], the lurid and sensational advertisements, and the absence of all chaperonage, are sources of danger."[44] Posters allowed working women to linger on the street in mixed-gender groups that were not composed primarily of dating couples.

During the day, working women looked at motion picture posters on their way to and from work, much as they gazed in shop windows at the latest fashions. Louise de Koven Bowen noted that two workers at a candy factory combined window shopping and gazing at posters: "On their way to and from the factory Hilda and Freda would often stop and gaze longingly in the shop windows . . . or they would read the fascinating posters which described the delights of the theatre they had no money to enter."[45] Some working women also looked at posters while on their lunch breaks. The brief time allowed—usually only thirty to forty minutes—and inclement weather often kept women inside the factories. But on occasion they took the opportunity to leave and linger on the streets. Reformer Harriet McDonald Daniels worried that the short lunch periods could lead the working woman astray. "On every side the picture shows flaunt their lurid posters before her eyes and on every corner and before every entrance groups of young men congregate to 'treat.'" The lunch break was usually too short for women to actually attend the movies, but like reading a dime novel, gazing at a poster could interrupt the tedium of the workday with a splash of color and a romantic image. Workers gazed at stars whose fame represented a counterpoint to their own devalued labor. Daniels believed Italian women to be particularly susceptible to such pleasures, precisely because their parents otherwise limited their freedom of movement in public. Some Italian women did not even walk to work without escort, but were accompanied to the factory door by brothers. Daniels wrote, "During working hours she is under the watchful eye of the boss, out of working hours she is under the strict surveillance of her parents; during this one little hour she is free and it would be strange indeed if in many cases she were not led astray."[46] Thus, although Italian women generally had less mobility in public than Jewish women, their social practices of moviegoing, including viewing posters, did allow them to occupy new public settings.

When working women looked at shop windows and movie posters they legitimated their public presence through a consumer gaze. But this gaze was not simply acquisitive. Rather, it connected to a complex realm of fantasy, imagina-

tion, and desire. In particular, posters prompted the imagination by presenting single images from larger narratives. Commentators noted the power of these large, colorful, and dramatic displays to capture attention. Reformer Michael Davis called the motion picture poster "a psychological blow in the face." He explained that "the poster is to catch the eye of the street passenger; it must hold him up," and described how a poster could suggest a sensational story with a single image:

> The poster takes some feature or even suggestion of the performance having an elemental appeal, and exaggerates this to a point sometimes passing all resemblance to the actual show. Thus, a black-whiskered villain stands flourishing a revolver; Slouch-hat Charlie smites the swell with a bludgeon, while pals make off with the lady; by the side of the bleeding father, the pale hero utters a fully printed oath of revenge; a short-skirted female dances upon a globe of the world, supported by three gilded youths gazing upward! These are but four recollections of reality.[47]

Working women's social practice of gazing at posters connected to a larger imaginative world, just as looking at shop windows connected to working ladyhood. Crucially, working women had great latitude to make their own meanings from the posters, both individually and in conversation with each other.

The significance of this active and imaginative gaze in public spaces has often been dismissed as acquisitive consumerism. But in important ways, this gaze created a possibility for women's desires, and not only desires for *stuff*.[48] The consumer gaze legitimated women's presence in public spaces on a daily, informal basis, altering entrenched gendered patterns of mobility. In addition, in U.S. society, conventions of looking have long operated as a way to signal dominance or deference. Custom allowed propertied white men to look directly at everyone, while women in public had to avert their eyes if they wished to avoid appearing "brazen" or sexually available. While white men became autonomous subjects in part through looking, people of color and all women were properly the objects of that look. When working women gazed at posters in public, they did not overturn established practices, but they did open up a new site of desire that could exceed the expectations of producers. I am not making a liberal pluralist argument that women gained freedom because they now could do what men had done; women's consumer gaze was certainly imbued with new hierarchies. Indeed, the capitalist marketplace repeatedly promised women a "modern" freedom from patriarchal constraints, even as it promoted subjectivities oriented to consumption and reconfigured gendered power relations. Just as the clothing that working women wore was not in itself "democratic," the new gaze was not inherently liberating. However, in both cases producers could not fully control the desires women would develop in relation to consumer culture.

In a context of unrelenting labor and inadequate compensation, the pleasure and power of participating in the new, modern public could be a way to maintain dignity and even a sense of hope, as one striking woman's story about the death of a co-worker indicates. During the Chicago garment strike of 1910, one young woman died after becoming ill while selling union newspapers. A striker described her grief to a reporter for *American Magazine:* "When I hear for sure thing a girl striker is dead, I lay on the bed crying' like everything. And then Anna, my chum, she lays on the bed cryin', and we both cry together so, on the bed. I don't know the girl, but I was feel so sorry that I must to cry. Oh, she was a poor girl, poorer'n we . . . and when I think on how it is with poor girls, I can't help from cryin.'" This young woman cried for herself and her poverty as well as for her co-worker. Strike leaders feared the despondency that could overcome workers who saw little in their futures but toil and poverty. The Chicago striker explained how she resisted giving in to her fear and despair:

> Then suddenly I stop cryin' and I say to Anna: 'For why do we cry? Ain't she better off'n we! She ain't cold; she don't have to buy no winter underwears; she don't have to worry for the eats; she won't never go scabbin.' She's lucky, lucky more as we.' And Anna says 'Sure she is.' And then we both say ain't it a foolishness for to cry for someone as is luckier'n we. So we get dressed and we goes out on Halsted Street and we looks on nickel picture shows and mill'n'ry windows. Honest, I ain't been to a nickel show in nine weeks and I'm forgettin' how they looks![49]

These young strikers' trip to look at shop windows and films could be termed an "escape" from their troubles, but this would simplify a complex survival mechanism. The two women certainly did not deny their connection to the dead striker and her oppression—indeed, they declared themselves in a *worse* condition. Still, they sought out public activities that granted them a modicum of mobility, an active gaze, and a sense of possibility. The next day, they were back at their strike duties.

The quality of some women's desires in relation to motion pictures can be discerned in what

contemporaries termed the "movie-struck" fantasy, that is, the dream of a job in motion pictures. As Jane Addams noted, the motion pictures and the evenings at the nickelodeon became "the sole topic of conversation" for working women through the week, "forming the ground pattern of their social life."[50] A central part of this was discussion of stars and the potential pathways to stardom. Indeed, many working women even applied at the motion picture studios in hopes of gaining more lucrative and rewarding jobs. This reflected close identification with female film heroines, and deep-seated desires for jobs that paid well and valued workers rather than exploiting and discarding them. The movie-struck fantasy was a dream of lavish recognition much like that showered on the working-girl heroines in dime novel romances. It imaginatively combined women's workplace struggles with their rewarding consumer culture experiences and pleasures. Through this collective fantasy, working women wove the movies into the established fantasies of romance, adventure, and sudden changes in fortune that characterized working ladyhood.

Working women became movie-struck after 1908, when the shift in film techniques to closer shots and more cuts fostered a closer identification with players. Audiences clamored for information about and names of particular stars, and in response producers slowly shifted from a stock to a star system. Some neighborhoods, impatient for information from producers, named the stars themselves. *The Survey* noted in 1909 that "One little girl who plays a prominent part in the pictures of a certain New York manufacturer has been named Annette by her admirers on the East Side. Her appearance on the screen [always] brings a round of applause."[51] Posters aided the imaginative process of identifying with or following particular stars, and producers supplied exhibitors with free photographs of stars to hand out as promotional tools. Working women could fuel their fascination with motion pictures and stars through the penny papers, which regularly carried articles about the movies; trade and fan magazines; and gossip. One observer noted that whatever their means of information, "the children of New York are sophisticated and . . . know quite as much about motion picture stars and the latest productions."[52]

Many young people still fantasize about being in the movies, but such dreams were considerably less abstract during the nickelodeon era in New York City. Movies were literally being made on the streets all around working women. Most of the studios still were based in New York, including Biograph and Kalem, and journalists remarked that "a crowd always gathers" to see movies being shot at popular locations like Grand Central Station, a street lined with pushcarts on the Lower East Side, Midtown, or Brooklyn. It was well known that most of the studios hired "extras" or "supers" at the rate of three to five dollars per day, though extras seldom got work on a daily basis.[53] This was an enormous sum of money for a factory worker used to making six dollars per week, and the work seemed exciting and easy. In addition, working as an extra was known to be one route to a position as a stock player for a company. Applying for a motion picture position was little different than applying for a factory position, until assigned to a role, as one journalist described: "[The applicant] will have to report every day at eight o'clock, stand in line before the directors as their assistants pick out the 'types,' and then, if she is picked, she will have to make up as a Spanish girl, a factory girl, a 'society lady' wearing a borrowed evening gown, or anything else the director may suggest." The Biograph Company studio at 11 East Fourteenth Street was especially accessible to workers on the Lower East Side, many of whom worked in factories within easy walking distance. Kathryn Fuller noted that the Biograph studio was daily besieged by movie-struck young women hoping to win jobs, and some stars like Lillian and Dorothy Gish actually got their start in this manner.[54]

The ways that producers promoted the earliest stars may have encouraged working women to dream of motion pictures as a possible employment option. Before 1908, commentary on the films focused on technology and explained how the films were made and projected. By 1907 to 1908, the shift in filming techniques and acting styles directed more attention to the actors themselves. Articles about stars in popular and trade papers and magazines from 1909 to 1914 focused on the *work* of acting in motion pictures, rather than on stars' private lives, as they would by 1915. As film historian Richard de Cordova notes, promotional material created a discourse on acting that participated in the larger effort to assert the respectability and "art" of the cinema, and thus draw a middle-class audience. Nevertheless, the early articles clearly represented the stars as workers whose main task was to express emotions with facial expressions, "gesture," and "motion." Articles regularly explained the action of a picture from the point of view of an actor who endeavored to communicate a particular emotion or

perform a stunt. De Cordova rightly argues that this should not be viewed as a demystification of the means of production, but as a creation of a certain kind of knowledge about film.[55] Indeed, trade papers, newspapers, and magazines portrayed acting both as paid labor and as involving real adventures: "at times the moving picture woman is subjected to dangers. Her horse may throw her when she is doing fast riding, or the wolf dogs may become unmanageable and bite." Articles about Mary Fuller described her work routine of real-life dangers, including sliding down a rope from a seventh-floor window, driving a motor boat, and riding a bucking bronco.[56] For working women reading the penny press or cheap magazines, this knowledge encouraged fantasies of new, exciting jobs and provided tips on how to act. A *Ladies' World* article entitled "The Photoplay: An Entertainment and an Occupation" reported that a successful motion picture actress must "be so inspired with her theme, and really feel the part so thoroughly, that she can go through it at a moment's notice. Her facial expressions and movements carry the whole idea to the audience. Then, too, she must learn to move very slowly and deliberately or the actions on the screen will be blurred."[57] Such press coverage could fan the flames of fantasy by collapsing the distance between paid labor and familiar narratives of adventure. Whereas in the dime novel romances, heroines encountered adventures after losing their jobs, in the movie-struck fantasy stars got paid for adventures in the course of their work.

The movie-struck fantasy is significant not because working women really got jobs in motion pictures—certainly few did. The encouragement women received through promotional material intended to capitalize on movie-struck women's intense loyalty as consumers. Nevertheless, the fantasy provides clues to the imaginative element of movie consumption. In many ways, the movie craze dovetailed with the practices of ladyhood. The latter was a signifying practice, a shifting identity that built upon the exclusions working women faced and the possibilities that consumer culture provided for appropriation of cultural codes. The imaginative self-construction of ladyhood could prepare women to embrace the movie-struck fantasy. Many working ladies would be confident of their ability to fulfill the requirements Mary Pickford claimed qualified one for motion pictures: "A girl cannot take the part of a lady unless she is one—she can not fake poise, grace, repose, the courteous gesture and air of good breeding unless she has the instincts of a lady and the necessary training in manners."[58] Like the dime novels, the movie-struck fantasy figured a magical transformation that served to confirm one's true inner qualities. Film historian Charles Musser has argued that immigrant audiences constructed fantasies around early stars of silent films, and also enjoyed the ways that the same star could take on dramatically new identities week after week, including diverse ethnic roles. Musser has suggested that immigrants' daily practices of constructing themselves as Americans, with new dress, mannerisms, and patterns of speech, could make them identify with, and enjoy watching, stars do the same thing in the movies. The way that such rapid change was accepted in the movies made them appealing as a counterpoint to the oppressions that immigrants faced. As Musser said, "the movies provided [immigrants] with an alternative to the alienation and struggle experienced while constructing a new world during the course of their everyday lives."[59] For working women who enacted identities as ladies, the movies provided fantasies and models of magical transformation.

Women's social practices of film consumption thus created a collective culture connected to their consumption of other commodities, such as dime novels and fashion. Film became more than an object or a narrative in women's lives; it became part of their imaginative landscape—or collective dreamworld—and as such was integral to their enacted identities. This collective culture framed women's viewing of specific films, though as with dime novels and fashion, individual idiosyncrasies and multiple possibilities for interpretation ensured that working women made a variety of meanings from those films. We cannot know how different women responded to the content of the posters or the serials. Nevertheless, a close look at how the serials *What Happened to Mary* and *Hazards of Helen* solicited audiences' identification and offered them visual fantasies can reveal more about the contours of working women's collective culture of film.[60]

The specific process and mechanism of identification with a fictional character and scenario in print or film has been the subject of great debate in film and literary theory. It is generally accepted that the identifications people make with fictional characters can be very important in how people develop their own identities. Film critics argue that identity emerges not as the sum of the content of images with which people are presented, but from a *process* of identification rooted in the affective experience of the film. When a spectator comes to identify with a character, she or he takes up residence in a fictional world. The story that the spectator participates in is not real, but his or her responses to it certainly are, and can be formative in the construction of the self. Individuals bring different identities, perspectives, and histories of interpellation to the viewing experience and inevitably make a variety of meanings as they interpret the films for themselves. It is crucial, then, to work with a sophisticated notion of identification that can accommodate the complexity and variability of individual responses.

Film critic Elizabeth Cowie argues that identification occurs not when we see or read about someone who is "like" us, but when we see a character who has a similar "structural relation of desire" to our own. That is, when we can come to *desire with* a character, we can identify with them, even if the character is of a different gender, class, or race, or is in a story about a different time or culture. According to Cowie, "The pleasure in identification lies not only in what is signified—a meaning—in that traditional realist sense, that is, a coming to know; it also lies in a coming to desire made possible by the scenario of desire which I come to participate in as I watch a film, view an image, or read a text."[61] The protagonist's "characteristics" are less important to the process of identification than her desires and how spectators are invited to participate in them. Following Cowie, I will examine *What Happened to Mary* and *Hazards of Helen* for the structural relations of desire of the working-girl heroine, and the ways an identification with her is solicited through print and visual narrative devices. The serials offered working women an identification with a heroine who desired and received dramatic social recognition as a worker and a woman.

What Happened to Mary, like the majority of silent films, no longer exists in film format. However, the print version of the story from *The Ladies' World* has survived. Comparison of scenario plot descriptions and the print episodes reveals that the film and fiction versions of *What Happened to Mary* followed the same plot line, although they necessarily used different devices to solicit the identification of viewers and readers. While the film relied on visual cues and conventions, the print version could narrate characters' thoughts and emotions. This created inevitable differences in storytelling. For example, the first film episode began with Mary as an abandoned baby found in a basket on Moseses Island by Billy Peart. A *Bioscope* review reported that "Mary rapidly grows up, as is the way in films" and the film story continues when she is eighteen. By centering on Mary and her rapid growth, the film signaled to viewers that she, not Billy Peart, would be the protagonist of the story. Through the new techniques of film cuts, the viewer would be a silent observer of the basket being left, and of Mary quickly growing to young womanhood. The print version, in contrast, begins with a description of Mary's appearance as a young woman. Readers learn that she was left on Moseses Island in a basket in a later scene, told as Billy Peart's memory.[62]

Despite these differences, the print version of *What Happened to Mary* was remarkable for print fiction in that it solicited readers' identification in large part by portraying looking relations. Bannister Merwin, who wrote both the print and film versions of the early episodes, appears to have structured the magazine story to describe the scenes in the film. *The Ladies' World* encouraged readers to approach the story as a narration of the motion picture, and provided articles describing how particular central film scenes were made.[63] Indeed, the print narrative is almost completely devoid of dialogue; it consists predominantly of visual description. Along with the photographs from the movie set as illustrations, the print version sought to parallel the film experience and allow fans to "read" the movie. Of course, the print version is not the same as the film version and cannot stand in for it. However, a close look at the print version reveals something of the overall experience of the serials. In addition, it reveals a solicitation of identification, through looking and a particular set of desires in the working-class heroine, that would be common to other serials.

The print version of *What Happened to Mary* designates Mary as the protagonist and solicits identification with her not by consistently narrating from Mary's point of view, but by setting up a suspenseful series of looking relations that encourages an emotional response on her behalf. The opening lines of the story describe an open-ended desire in Mary, a longing for something she cannot name: "Mary's eyes were smoldering that day with the fire of strange yearnings. She moved about at her work as one walking in a dream— burning with a life that was not the life around her." While the story gives an intimate if vague portrayal of Mary's emotional state, like the film it also invites the reader to position herself as part of the scene, observing Mary as one of the villagers: "If you who had known her long had asked her suddenly, 'What is different with you, Mary?' she would have looked at you with startled query

. . . for she did not know that anything was different. Her new yearnings had not yet burst into flames." Readers knew that Mary was the protagonist because it was her desire that they follow and watch. But what did Mary desire? Suddenly, readers discover that Mary is at the harbor, looking at a yacht that has just landed. Four wealthy people get off a launch from the yacht: two older people who are rudely "aloof to her," and a young man and woman. "And the girl's eyes had met Mary's, and something subtle had passed between them— the secret unspoken password of maidenhood."[64] This scene figures class distinction and the alienation and longing that can go with it for the working class.

Scenes 2 and 3 invite an emotional identification by prompting anxiety and indignation on Mary's behalf. Readers see Mary enter the store owned by her adoptive stepfather, Billy Peart. She does not look at him as she heads to the ice cream parlor in the rear, but readers see him watching her: "Billy glanced at her in his quick, hard, speculative way, and clamped his lips together in a fashion even more frog-like than usual . . . and shifted his weight from foot to foot." Thus readers are cued that Billy is not a person to be trusted: he's speculative, shifty, and nervous. The fact that readers see Peart but Mary is not watching inaugurates a device common to the *What Happened to Mary* story and later serials: readers know something the protagonist does not. The scene might mildly prompt readers to be wary of Billy for Mary's sake. In scene 3, readers witness Mrs. Peart yelling at and physically threatening Mary for being away from the shop for too long. Mary, however, does not answer, but "smiled faintly at the two children, who were tasting [ice cream]." This scene demonstrates that Mary is oppressed in her household, and that she is good and kind to children in spite of it. These two scenes solicit an identification imbued with feelings of indignance or anxiety for Mary, so good yet treated so badly. Readers may have wanted to defend her.

Scene 4 of the first episode sets up the soon-to-be-familiar pattern of suspense, in which the audience knows more about the heroine's danger than she initially does. Readers and film viewers learn that when Peart found Mary in the basket, he also found a note promising him $1,000 if he marries her to a local man before she turns twenty-one years old. Mary, however, is unaware of her adoptive status or Peart's financial interest in her marrying. Readers see Mary in town, approached by a young local man. They then learn that this whole scene has been witnessed by Billy

Peart. The print version has to narrate Billy's gaze sequentially, but the film version could have placed Peart in the background through much of the encounter, letting the viewer know that this scene was of interest to him. The print version notes, "Billy stopped in his tracks, his bulging eyes fixed on the young couple with an astonishment that quickly gave place to satisfaction."[65] While Mary casts an active, desiring gaze toward the yacht and the rich girl, she is often unwitting of, and therefore vulnerable to, the gaze of others. This scene solicits anxiety for Mary, distrust of Billy, and perhaps a desire for her liberation. Through a set of accidents and incidental kindnesses of strangers, by the end of the first episode Mary learns of Billy Peart's plot and that her parentage is a mystery, and acquires a bit of money to escape the island. Readers identifying with Mary would feel relief and exhilaration at the denouement of the first episode. The whole audience is invited to identify with the freedom of a young woman alone, newly released from patriarchal authority and her established social identity.

The narrative strategy of letting the audience know more than the protagonist is common in suspense thrillers. Suspense arises not simply because we do not know what will happen, but because readers or viewers know *something* will happen, but not exactly what. Knowing more about the situation than the characters prompts anxiety on their behalf. Cowie cites Alfred Hitchcock's distinction between surprise and suspense: a bomb going off is a surprise; the audience seeing a bomb planted under a table where people are sitting is suspense. Hitchcock notes that in suspense "the public is participating in the scene. The audience is longing to warn the characters on the screen."[66] In *What Happened to Mary,* the suspenseful scene is not as dramatic as a bomb under a table (though subsequent episodes and later serials did utilize such extreme devices), but readers do know about a plot of which she is entirely unaware and are invited to desire her escape and liberation, that is, to come to desire *with* Mary.

The process of an intensely pleasurable identification hinges on readers participating in Mary's predicament. The story's mechanisms invite readers to take up her cause and align their desires with hers. They will then become implicated in a dramatic moment, full of an intensity of feeling, even though some of it, like anxiety, might seem unpleasant. In the suspense plot of *What Happened to Mary,* readers could come to desire *more* than

Mary did. While Mary's desires and her sense of danger are vague, readers know the details of her predicament and can wish for her liberation all the more. By Cowie's model, when readers identify, they align their own loss, lack, or desire to the character's, so that they are feeling on behalf of the character, and indirectly on their own behalf as well. Thus, the apparently unpleasant aspect of the identification process may be imperative for an emotionally intense and satisfying experience. Of course, such identification is not inevitable. Readers can resist narrative cues or impose other emotional tones upon them. But if readers long with Mary in some way during the episode, they can feel an intense thrill when she escapes the island and achieves liberation.

At the close of the first episode, Mary arrives at a status familiar to dime novel enthusiasts: she is an orphan. As chapter 4 demonstrated, the metaphor of the orphan as free from patriarchal control was one that some working women had already incorporated into their own imaginative resources from the dime novels, and they used it to express a desire for freedom from sexual harassment. Like the dime novels, *What Happened to Mary* follows a melodramatic structure in which a heroine loses her established social identity, encounters a number of challenges and adventures, gains new social recognition for her adventures, and finally receives a reward. The first episode of the Mary serial merely initiates this larger plot formula. A good part of Mary's enigma has not been resolved. What more does she really want? Who were her parents? And how will Mary make it alone in the world? Indeed, even as readers might find the ending to the first episode satisfying, they may feel a curiosity and perhaps an anxiety about Mary's future.

Homeless and penniless, Mary is freed from her established social identity; the next several episodes portray her adventures in finding and performing work and confer new social recognition on her as both a worker and a woman. Mary's job is full of challenge and danger, but she ultimately receives fabulous rewards and recognition from co-workers, bosses, clients, and audiences. Later episodes maintain a similar emphasis on visual description and methods of soliciting identification with Mary by first prompting anxiety or indignance on her behalf.[67] Mary inevitably faces some adventure or challenge in which others oppose her unjustly or secretly plot against her. In episode 3, Mary gets a job as a chorus girl in a play. When the lead falls ill on opening night, Mary performs in her place, and like one dime novel heroine, is a smash hit. Readers might cheer her success particularly because she has been unjustly ridiculed by the other chorus girls. Unlike the dime novel heroine, Mary is a paid stage worker when she performs, which links work and adventure more closely.

Mary's adventures, like those of the dime novel heroine, revolve around her status as a woman worker. The constructed categories of honorable "worker" and honorable "woman" both largely excluded working women. Dime novel and serial narratives centered on the contradictions at the juncture of those exclusions. For example, *What Happened to Mary* raises the question of whether Mary can succeed in her workplace *despite* being female. Though Mary excells at her job, a competitive co-worker, a covert embezzler, regularly spoils it purposely to make her look bad. Mary proves her status as a worker, and gains revenge, by lying in wait in the office for him one evening, catching him stealing from the safe, and holding him [. . .] at gunpoint for several tense moments. Finally, the co-worker lunges at Mary, knocks the gun from her hand, and wrestles with her until the boss arrives with the police. When they ask Mary how she held a male rival with "superior masculine strength" for so long, Mary shows them the gun. Then the boss reveals that the gun, which Mary found in his desk, is not loaded. Lacking maleness—or a loaded gun—Mary achieves social recognition as a worker even as the episode reaffirms her femininity by marking her "natural" weakness—she is more vulnerable than a male hero would be. In recognition of Mary's proficiency, her boss gives her a promotion.

The plot of *What Happened to Mary* significantly revised the dime novel formula of social recognition and reward for adventure: Mary's reward hinged on recognition for her work rather than marriage to a rich hero. Her final reward in the last episode of the story was to gain her inheritance, while the dime novel heroine received her inheritance about half way through the narrative, in what Peter Brooks calls the "recognition" in the melodrama. Readers and viewers of *What Happened to Mary* learned that Mary was a "missing heiress" by episode 5, but dastardly villains and adventures kept her from collecting the cash for seven more episodes. Literary critic Rachel Brownstein argues that the traditional novel ending of marriage, for example in Samuel Richardson's *Pamela,* offered the female protagonist not just a husband but a realized feminine identity. Others' recognition of the protagonist's new status was as important, she

argues, as the marriage itself.[68] In dime novel romances, marriage essentially affirmed the working heroine's adventures and her feminine worth, so that she could visit her former co-workers as an honorable working woman. *What Happened to Mary* omitted this narrative tradition of signaling female social recognition, reconfiguring the affirmation of femininity within the praise she won from coworkers and bosses for her adventures.

The Ladies' World and the Edison Company drastically broke from formula by *not* ending the serial with the heroine's wedding. While Mary had occasional romantic episodes, romance did not structure the plot. This innovation was probably a fluke. Producers fully expected their female and male audience to be anxiously awaiting Mary's romantic fate, and encouraged that expectation with the regular appearance of admirers. A male reviewer for the *Bioscope* complained about this aspect of the serial, revealing the importance to him of a recontainment of Mary's power—and her cash. "One regrets the absence of any real 'love interest.' At one moment in her career, Mary seems about to succumb to the tender passion, but a new adventure crops up, and the eligible young man is forgotten. We must confess that we should have liked to see him brought in again at the end, to share Mary's dollars, which we feel sure are far too many to be safe in the keeping of a lonely spinster, even though she is so capable a manageress as our heroine." Producers' prime motivation in subverting audience expectations was additional profit: they had already planned a sequel, *Who Will Marry Mary,* based entirely on romance. However, the sequel never approached the popularity of *What Happened to Mary* and was terminated after six months. *Who Will Marry Mary* lacked the adventure and the struggle in work that readers and viewers found exciting. Serials that followed kept romance marginal. Despite the popular culture industry's initial assumption that women always cared most about romance, it recognized that this profit-motivated accident revealed audience desires.

Later serials learned from the mistake of *Who Will Marry Mary*: they emphasized adventure over romance and accentuated suspense and sensationalism. One reviewer even criticized *What Happened to Mary* for being too mild: "One fancies that the author, or the producer, might have 'taken his gloves off' more effectually to one or two of the more sensational passages. One doesn't desire horrors, but it is possible to be realistic without incurring the censor's displeasure."[69] Perhaps Edison held back in order to please a cross-class audience.

But later serials chocked their episodes full of hair-raising feats of daring, car chases, fires, and the capture or death of numerous villains.

Hazards of Helen, which began in 1914, combined the workplace-based adventures of *What Happened to Mary* and popular fascination with the powers and dangers of technology. *Hazards of Helen* featured a female telegraph operator who weekly encountered life-imperiling mishap or villainy in the course of her job. Helen was constantly running atop trains to prevent them from crashing. Viewers were invited to identify with the working woman in a setting that typically connoted masculinity, modernity, and the paradoxes of industrialization for working-class audiences. "Railroading," as historian Walter Licht says, "held out the lure of adventure, travel and escape." The world of railroading was the world of men: the homosocial space of railroad work and the regular absences from family and community created a camaraderie around labor that became the source of many popular stories.[70] Women were just beginning to work in the railroad industry in 1914. Their numbers would climb during World War I, but when *Hazards of Helen* ran, Helen was particularly modern—she worked at a kind of job long celebrated as epitomizing the honorable *male* worker.[71]

Railroads themselves were distinctly modern and epitomized the power and danger of the machine. Although railroads had transformed the U.S. economy and social life, the industry had a particularly high accident rate. Trains signaled workers' heroic achievements in production as well as their significant vulnerabilities.[72] *Hazards of Helen* played on people's fascination with this potential danger. While Helen usually prevented a crash, occasionally the audience got to see trains collide. Such catastrophes had cross-class appeal, but had become particularly common in "low-brow" cultural forms and in working-class spectator events. Some cheap stage melodramas at the turn of the century featured train wrecks. Additionally, in 1907, nearly 250,000 New Yorkers turned out at Brighton Beach to see two locomotives in a staged head-on collision at sixty miles per hour, an event repeated at the 1909 Chicago Labor Day celebration. The *Union Labor Advocate* noted that "thousands of railroad operating employees will be on the ground to study the 'disaster.'" Labor-capital films often included such sensationalism as well. For example, an advertisement for *The Wage Earners* (Atlas, 1912) read, "Everyone will want to see this great picture of Labor and Capital. Many thrilling and exciting

scenes, such as the big train wreck, auto wreck, the wild ride on the handcar, the flying leap onto a moving train, the big walkout, the mob scene and many others."[73] A female heroine, traditionally seen as particularly physically vulnerable, could epitomize the dichotomy between the power of machinery and the vulnerability of humans for both male and female audiences. Through cunning and bravery, as well as strength, Helen always prevailed. Thus, the railroad serial maintained *What Happened to Mary*'s focus on the female character's desire for social recognition as a worker and a woman, while linking this theme to a working-class cultural motif that had an established history with a male audience.

Close analysis of episode 58, "The Wrong Order," demonstrates that the serial solicited an identification with Helen through suspense and offered a fantasy of recognition and admiration. This episode opens with an intertitle that reads: "Helen, a telegraph operator, returns from her vacation." Audiences then see Helen walking into the telegraph office and greeting her male co-workers. The camera positions viewers as an invisible part of the staff, visually following Helen as she greets each man heartily. The men are clearly delighted to see her, and shake her hand in a demonstration of camaraderie. Part of the group goes out to the yard, where an express train awaits. An intertitle signals the action to come: "The observation car is a better place for you to ride than this dirty engine." The camera views the group from the back as Helen starts to climb onto the engine car. One of the men stops her and mouths the line of the intertitle, and Helen shrugs and agrees. This sets up one question of the short: Should Helen be treated differently because she's a woman? Does she need to keep her clothes clean? The audience then sees Helen and her boyfriend on the observation car, the last car on the express. Medium-close shots allow an intimate view of Helen and her easy manner with her boyfriend. Camera cuts to the engine car show that there is a mechanical problem, while Helen and her boyfriend grow impatient. The boyfriend goes to investigate, leaving Helen alone on the back of the car reading an issue of *Collier's*. Cross-cutting between the engine and observation cars serves to accentuate Helen's isolation from the work of the men. The train leaves twenty minutes late.

The episode next sets up a suspenseful situation and an identification with Helen as the only person who can save the day. The camera shows the engineer abandoning the train to tend his injured wife, leaving the express, now late and running out of control, on a collision course with a freight train. The audience learns about the problem, but Helen is unaware. The camera, in medium shots, shows the last station before the collision point receive a wire with instructions to stop the express, but it is too late—the express has just sped by. But the audience, viewing the action via a long shot from Helen's point of view on the back of the train, sees a man running out of the station waving his arms. Helen is thus notified of the problem. This point-of-view shot reinforces audience identification with Helen partly because only she, from her "feminine" position on the observation car, realizes the danger. The audience sees a medium-close shot of Helen's face as she registers the horror of the situation and then springs to action. The doors from the observation balcony to the train itself, however, are locked. Always resourceful, Helen immediately climbs up onto the top of the speeding train and runs along it to the engine car. An intertitle explains the action to come: "Unable to enter the steam filled cab, Helen makes a desperate attempt to stop the train." In medium-close shots the audience watches Helen climb on top of the engine and then slide down on one side to reach the hand-brake at the front. Pulling hard on the brake, Helen slows the express enough that, as the camera cuts to a long shot, the freight has time to change tracks at the switch before the express train speeds past it. A medium shot shows Helen leaping from her precarious perch into the ditch when the express is almost stopped. Immediately, Helen is surrounded by railroad men, who help her up and congratulate her. The final scene parallels the opening scene: Helen is back in the office at a new desk, signaling a promotion. A medium-close shot shows her proudly admiring the desk. The final shot shows Helen standing while the men help her brush the dirt off her skirt.[74]

Hazards of Helen thus solicited an emotional identification from viewers. If they became indignant for Helen when she was excluded from the male workers' activities, or anxious when she was unaware of her danger, they would also feel a vicarious thrill at her physical bravery and hero-ism. Helen faces a limit because of her femininity, placed on the observation car in order to keep her clothes clean, and she literally goes over the top to demonstrate her ability to be a good worker. In the process, she gets her clothes dirty, indicating that the imposed limits on her were, in fact, rather silly. Helen is affirmed in her job with a new desk and a promotion, but she is also affirmed as a

woman when the men help her brush off her skirt. The male camaraderie of the workplace is extended to Helen, and is charged with a special intimacy or mild eroticism. Like the dime novel heroines who proved their ladyhood in part through physically aggressive adventures, Helen proved her worth through physically demanding work that did not abrogate her femininity.

Helen could represent the disadvantaged overcoming social restraint in spectacles similar to those staged by the Jewish immigrant Houdini. Helen was often placed in a position of vulner-ability and peril to the nearly ubiquitous train robbers. Trapped, tied, gagged, locked away, Helen routinely performed Houdini-like tricks of evasion and escape. Though the villains were always armed, Helen, like Mary, rarely had access to a loaded gun. When she did require one, she used her creativity to procure it. In the thirty-first episode, villains lock Helen into a cattle car on a freight train that, unbeknownst to the conductor, is on a collision course with a passenger train. As the bad guys fight the good guys on the platform outside Helen's cell, one drops his gun. Helen makes a fishing line out of a hairpin and a strip of her dress, drags the gun to her in the cattle car, and shoots and severs the wire holding the sema-phore arm so it swings to DANGER, prompting the conductor to stop the train [. . .]. Here Helen uses her feminine accoutrements to make up for her initial lack of a gun and emerges, again, the hero.[75]

Hazards of Helen played on the space of contra-diction inhabited by women workers and provided fantasies of power and belonging. Her reward was neither an inheritance nor marriage but simply warm recognition at the end of every episode. (Indeed, the *refusal* of a marriage proposal appears to have become a common narrative device.) Helen was fired from her position and had to prove herself to her bosses in at least two episodes. In episode 42, Helen is discharged because man-agement believes she failed to turn a copy of an order over to a conductor, resulting in a near train collision. In fact, she did so, but cannot prove it because a spiteful coworker has destroyed the order. Through an array of spectacular adventures, Helen captures both the conductor, who has gone insane, and the spiteful employee, who plotted to dynamite the train. Helen is exonerated and restored to her duty with special recognition. In episode 13, Helen loses her job after being robbed by two crooks. Later, she sees the culprits flee on a freight. Hot in pursuit, Helen drops off a bridge onto the moving train, fighting until she falls off the train with one of the robbers and lands in the water. The thieves are thus captured and Helen is given her job back, with honor.[76]

The serials were products of the most rationalized arm of the film industry, and bore the limiting effects of industry priorities. Most notably, they did not represent strikes as a kind of female adventure like the labor-capital films did with male strikers, nor did they represent heroines as overtly political. But the serials' sensationalism and melodrama were not meaningless or trite. Like the dime novels, adventure serials engaged contradictions that working women faced on a daily basis and offered them gratifying fantasies of social recognition as women and workers. Of course, the movies invariably ended and working women went back to their daily lives of devalued labor and social contradiction. But while the serials did not directly change women's material conditions, they did, in Cowie's words, make possible "the scene of the wish." That is, like labor unions, motion pictures provided a legitimate place for women to imagine recognition and value as workers.

The meanings of the movies emerged from an array of social practices that working women created around their motion picture consumption. Motion picture theaters were new kinds of social spaces in which women could enact public identities. Looking at posters, dreaming of stars, and viewing the films all privileged looking and appearance in the construction of meaning and the self. Women's participation in this certainly implicated them in new gendered hierarchies. But working women's consumer gaze was more than simply superficial or acquisitive. It entailed complex fantasies of worth connected to their workday; to their status as workers, women, and immigrants; and to their established practices of ladyhood. The films themselves were far from simply emancipatory for working women. However, working women made them into resources for the ongoing tasks of maintaining dignity and creating identities. Just as they embraced the shirtwaist strike and its utopian promises, working women could make motion pictures a site for new public identities and new dreams of being valued.

Notes

1. Ruth True, *The Neglected Girl* (New York: Russell Sage, 1914), 67.

2. "What Happened to Mary," *The Ladies World* (Aug. 1912): 3.

3. I am indebted to Miriam Hansen's brilliant work on cinema as a public sphere. See Hansen, *Babel and Babylon,* 1-19, 90-126. Roy Rosenzweig also talks about the

importance of the early motion picture theaters as a public space in *Eight Hours for What We Will.* See also Peiss, *Cheap Amusements.*

4. Ibid., 148.

5. Michael M. Davis, *The Exploitation of Pleasure: A Study of Commercial Recreations in New York City* (New York: Sage, 1911), 21; Steven J. Ross, *Working-Class Hollywood: Silent Film and the Shaping of Class in America* (Princeton: Princeton University Press, 1997), 19; Peiss, *Cheap Amusements,* 146, 148.

6. Hansen, *Babel and Babylon,* 14.

7. Peiss, *Cheap Amusements,* 226n53; 154-58; Elizabeth Ewen, "City Lights: Immigrant Women and the Rise of the Movies," *Signs* 5 (3) Supplement (Spring 1980): S45-S66. Comedies were the most numerous of the motion pictures before 1908, but with the advent of new filming techniques and more complex narratives, they became less central. See Eileen Bowser's superb *History of the American Cinema, vol. 2: The Transformation of Cinema, 1907-1915* (New York: Charles Scribner's Sons, 1990), 56.

8. The scholar most associated with this view is Lewis Jacobs, *The Rise of the American Film* (New York: Teachers College Press, 1939). See also Garth Jowett, *Film: the Democratic Art* (Boston: Little, Brown, 1976). The most recent application of this perspective is Ross, *Working-Class Hollywood.* See Hansen's excellent critique of this view in *Babel and Babylon,* 68-70.

9. Ross, *Working-Class Hollywood,* 56-85.

10. My understanding of early film history relies principally on Bowser, *History of the American Cinema, vol. 2.* See especially 28-32 for a discussion of the early crisis in the industry. I also draw on Charles Musser, *The Emergence of Cinema: The American Screen to 1907* (New York: Scribner, 1990); David Bordwell, *On the History of Film Style* (Cambridge: Harvard University Press, 1997); Robert Sklar, *Movie-made America: A Cultural History of American Movies* (New York: Vintage, 1994).

11. Bowser, *History of the American Cinema, vol. 2,* 28-32, 217.

12. See ibid., 19, 53-54; Hansen, *Babel and Babylon,* 16, 23.

13. Cook, *The Fiction Factory;* "Writing the Movies: A New and Well-Paid Business," *New York Times,* August 3, 1913 (printed in Gene Brown, ed., *New York Times Encyclopedia of Film 1896-1979* [New York: Times Books, 1983]).

14. Cook, *The Fiction Factory,* 155-56, 167.

15. Bowser, *History of the American Cinema, vol. 2,* 54, 167-68.

16. Hansen, *Babel and Babylon,* 84.

17. Lary May, *Screening Out the Past: The Birth of Mass Culture and the Motion Picture Industry* (New York: Oxford University Press, 1980).

18. Snyder, *The Voice of the City.* For a discussion of regulation of the early cinema, see Janet Staiger, *Bad Women: Regulating Sexuality in Early American Cinema* (Minneapolis: University of Minnesota Press, 1995).

19. Bowser, *History of the American Cinema, vol. 2,* 44.

20. Ross, *Working-Class Hollywood,* 48, 57, 74. See also Kay Sloan, *The Loud Silents: Origins of the Social Problem Film* (Urbana: University of Illinois Press, 1988), 62-69.

Sloan claims, "After the long shirtwaist strike in New York in 1909 and 1910, films starring courageous, beautiful women strike leaders inundated theaters" (64). I have been unable to substantiate this claim. There were a number of films, such as *The Struggle* (Kalem, 1913) in which the daughter of a striker played a significant role among a group of male strikers, but even in these movies the female character did not play a role as a recognized leader. Sloan claims that *The Long Strike* (Essanay, 1911) "featured a labor leader who courted the boss' son to win the demands of the women strikers." However, the *Moving Picture World* review that Sloan cites as her only evidence does not indicate a strike of women workers. Indeed, the heroine meets the boss's son when on her way to the factory at the noon hour, carrying her father's lunch pail. She is the daughter of a striker, not a striker herself. See "The Struggle," *Moving Picture World* 16 (June 7, 1913): 1009; "The Long Strike," *Moving Picture World* 10 (December 23, 1911): 989.

21. Ross, *Working-Class Hollywood*, 57.

22. "The Girl Strike Leader," *Moving Picture World* 7 (July 23, 1910): 193.

23. Ross, *Working-Class Hollywood*, 74; Sloan, *The Loud Silents*, 64-66.

24. Bowser, *History of the American Cinema*, vol. 2, 178, 185. The episodes of *What Happened to Mary* could be understood if viewed separately, as each traced a particular adventure that was resolved within the time of the short. This has caused some not to classify *What Happened to Mary* as a serial. See Bowser 206. However, themes of Mary's mysterious origin, her struggle in the work world, and romance all were pursued across different segments and tied the stories together. Indeed, *What Happened to Mary* had far more narrative continuity than *Hazards of Helen*, which is always classed as a serial. In *Hazards of Helen*, a romance between Helen and another worker provides a very loose continuity between rather interchangeable episodes of adventure. However, by the time *Hazards of Helen* began in 1914, serials were an established genre, and the film fit the bill in terms of its sensational content and its release schedule.

25. Some of these films drew quite directly on the "Laura Jean Libbey" dime novel formula, while others drew on other cheap fiction conventions, including the dime novel romances featuring wealthy heroines that were read by working women. As chapter 1 argued, even these characters usually figured class inequities in some way. Female characters could also be found in Westerns and other dime novels targeting a primarily male audience. The film industry creatively mixed a number of dime novel conventions in creating the female adventure short.

26. "What Happened to Mary," *Bioscope* (July 31, 1913): 368-69; Rothvin Wallace, "The Activities of Mary," *The Ladies' World* (Mar. 1913): 11.

27. Frank Luther Mott, *A History of American Magazines* (Cambridge: Harvard University Press, 1957), 4:360-68. *The Ladies World* was bought by McClure Publications, Inc., in February of 1912. Charles Dwyer discussed the impact of *What Happened to Mary* on subscription rates in "The Editor and the Reader," *The Ladies World* 33 (12) (Dec. 1912): 1. 42.

28. Lewis E. Palmer, "The World in Motion," *The Survey* 22 (June 5, 1909): 356; Bowser, *History of the American Cinema*, vol. 2, 93, 106-19; Kathryn Fuller, *At the Picture Show: Small-Town Audiences and the Creation of Movie Fan Culture* (Washington, D.C.: Smithsonian Institution Press, 1996), 115-33; Richard de Cordova, *Picture Personalities: The Emergence of the Star System in America* (Urbana: University of Illinois Press, 1990).

29. Mary Fuller with Bailey Millard, "My Adventures as a Motion-Picture Heroine," *Collier's* 48 (15) (Dec. 30, 1911): 16-17; "What Happened to Mary," *Bioscope* (July 31, 1913): 369. (*Bioscope* was a British film magazine; *What Happened to Mary* opened in England in 1913.)

30. "Miss Mary Fuller Wearing the 'Mary' Hat," *The Ladies World* (June 1913): 4; Wallace, "The Activities of Mary," 11.

31. *The Ladies World* 33 (8) (Aug. 1912): 4; 33 (9) (Sept. 1912): 1. For winners that matched plot developments, see 33 (11) (Nov. 1912): 40; 34 (1) (Jan. 1913). Later serials overtly promised that winners would determine the upcoming plot. See "The Perils of Pauline: Today's Prize Offer," *Atlanta Georgian*, June 14, 1914. See also Kathryn Fuller's description of a Thanhousser contest for an ending to the serial *A Million Dollar Mystery* (1913) in *At the Picture Show*, 128.

32. Buck Rainey, *Those Fabulous Serial Heroines: Their Lives and Films* (Metuchen, N.J.: Scarecrow Press, 1990), 459; Ben Singer, "Female Power in the Serial-Queen Melodrama: The Etiology of an Anomaly," *Camera Obscura* 22 (Jan. 1990): 91-129; "Perils of Pauline," *Variety* (April 10, 1914); see also "The Trey O'Hearts," *Variety* (August 7, 1914).

33. Simkhovitch, *The City Worker's World in America*, 124; Sherman C. Kingsley, "The Penny Arcade and the Cheap Theatre," *Charities and the Commons* 18 (Jan. 1907): 295. For discussions of the role of theaters in ethnic working-class neighborhoods during the silent era see Peiss, *Cheap Amusements*, on New York, 139-53; and on Chicago in the 1920s see Cohen, *Making a New Deal*, 120-29.

34. True, *The Neglected Girl*, 116; Jane Addams, *The Spirit of Youth and the City Streets* (New York: Macmillan, 1909), 86; Robert A. Woods and Albert J. Kennedy, *Young Working Girls: A Summary of Evidence from Two Thousand Social Workers* (Boston: Houghton Mifflin, 1913), 114. See also Louise de Koven Bowen, *Five and Ten Cent Theaters* (Juvenile Protection Association of Chicago, 1909, 1911). Addams and de Koven Bowen were both talking about Chicago. Patterns of motion picture projection and attendance were very specific to each city at this time. I have only used Chicago sources when I also have a source from New York City that corroborates its basic point.

35. Harriet McDoual Daniels, *The Girl and Her Chance* (New York: Fleming H. Revell, 1914), 73; Simkhovitch, *The City Worker's World in America*, 131. See also Peiss, *Cheap Amusements*, 53-55, 110-13.

36. Addams, *The Spirit of Youth and the City Streets*, 80-81; Hasanovitz, *One of Them*, 247; Laughlin, *The Work-a-day Girl*, 147.

37. Odencrantz, *Italian Women in Industry*, 204, 235. Filomena Ognibene quoted in Ewen, "City Lights," S58. Laughlin reported that working women typically attended motion picture theaters more than twice per week. Laughlin, *The Work-a-day Girl*, 143.

38. Esther Packard, *A Study of Living Conditions of Self-Supporting Women in New York City* (New York: Metropolitan Board of the YWCA, 1915), 51, 86.

39. Mary Heaton Vorse, "Some Picture Show Audiences," *Outlook* 98 (June 24, 1911): 443, 446.

40. Fuller, *At the Picture Show*, 115.

41. Buck-Morss, *The Dialectics of Seeing*, 253-55; see also McRobbie, "The *Passagenwerk* and the Place of Walter Benjamin in Cultural Studies," 96-120; and Leo Charney and Vanessa R. Schwartz, eds., *Cinema and the Invention of Modern Life* (Berkeley: University of California Press, 1995) for discussions about the connections among modernity, the city, and motion pictures. In particular, see Marcus Verhagen, "The Poster in *Fin-de-Siècle* Paris: 'That Mobile and Degenerate Art'," 103-29.

42. William R. Leach, "Transformations in a Culture of Consumption: Women and Department Stores, 1890-1925," *Journal of American History* 71 (2) (Sept. 1984): 319-42.

43. Laughlin, *The Work-a-day Girl*, 142.

44. Addams, *The Spirit of Youth and the City Streets*, 91; Woods and Kennedy, *Young Working Girls*, 114.

45. Louise de Koven Bowen, *Safeguards for City Youth at Work and at Play* (New York: Macmillan, 1914), 19.

46. Daniels, *The Girl and Her Chance*, 73. Some white-collar workers did attend motion pictures on their lunch hours. In addition, the Strand theater on Broadway opened an inexpensive lunchroom for "working girls" within the massive theater structure. Many factory workers, however, would not have had time to walk there to have lunch. See "A Theater with Four Million Patrons a Year," *Photoplay Magazine* 7 (Apr. 1915): 84.

47. Davis, *The Exploitation of Pleasure*, 54.

48. See Lauren Rabinowitz, *For the Love of Pleasure: Women, Movies, and Culture in Turn-of-the-Century Chicago* (New Brunswick, N.J.: Rutgers University Press, 1998), 22-26, 82-97, for discussions of the meaning of the female gaze in public and in cinema.

49. Quoted in Mary Field, "'On Strike' A Collection of True Stories," *American Magazine* (Oct. 1911): 736. In the Women's Trade Union League Papers, Tamiment Library.

50. Addams, *The Spirit of Youth and the City Streets*, 86.

51. Palmer, "The World in Motion," 356.

52. Quoted in Peiss, *Cheap Amusements*, 153.

53. Sarah Helen Starr, "The Photoplay: An Entertainment, An Occupation," *The Ladies' World* 33 (6) (June 1912): 9; Ernest A. Dench, "Our Brooklyn Jungle," *Illustrated World* 26 (Oct. 1916): 222-23; William A. Page, "The Movie-Struck Girl," *Woman's Home Companion* 45 (June 1918): 18. See also Fuller, *At the Picture Show*, 129.

54. Page, "The Movie-Struck Girl," 18; Bowser, *History of the American Cinema*, vol. 2, 24; Fuller, *At the Picture Show*, 130.

55. Richard de Cordova, "The Emergence of the Star System in America," in Christine Gledhill, ed., *Stardom: Industry of Desire* (London: Routledge, 1991), 17-29.

56. "Acting for the 'Movies'" *Literary Digest* 48 (Feb. 28, 1914). This first-person article about Mary Fuller was reprinted from the newspaper the *Indianapolis Star*.

57. Starr, "The Photoplay," 9.

58. "Mary Pickford Has a Word to Say" *Harper's Bazaar* (Apr. 1917): 55.

59. Charles Musser, "Ethnicity, Role-playing, and American Film Comedy: From *Chinese Laundry Scene* to *Whoopee* (1894-1930)" in Lester D. Friedman, ed., *Unspeakable Images: Ethnicity and the American Cinema* (Urbana: University of Illinois Press, 1991), 54.

60. I have chosen to look closely in this chapter at only two of the serials, but my analysis of these two is informed by a broader examination of the genre. I viewed a number of serial episodes at the Library of Congress, Motion Picture Division, including episodes from *Lucille Love, Girl of Mystery, The Ventures of Marguerite, Hazards of Helen, Girl and the Game, Pearl of the Army, The Lightening Raider, The Purple Mask,* and *A Woman in Grey*. I read print versions of *What Happened to Mary, Who Will Marry Mary, Plunder, The Adventures of Kathlyn,* and *The Perils of Pauline*.

61. Cowie, *Representing the Woman*, 4.

62. Advertisement for *What Happened to Mary*, Edison Archives; "What Happened to Mary," *Bioscope* (July 31, 1913): 368-69; "'Mary' and the Movies," *The Ladies' World* 33 (10) (Sept. 1912): 1.

63. Ibid.

64. "What Happened to Mary: The Remarkable Story of a Remarkable Girl," *The Ladies' World* 33 (8) (Aug. 1912): 3.

65. Ibid.

66. Quoted in Cowie, *Representing the Woman*, 51.

67. For example, in episode 2 Mary buys some new clothes to replace her clothes from the island. (For immigrant women whose purchases of new clothes were among their first acts in the new country this scene could have particular appeal.) The female shopkeeper, however, treats her rudely because she is so plainly dressed. When Mary picks out the loveliest clothes in the shop, she repeats the common dime novel convention of the working girl instinctively dressing herself impeccably once she becomes an heiress. The presence of the storekeeper who degrades Mary because of her plain dress invokes class distinction, and invites indignation on Mary's behalf and enjoyment of Mary's purchases as a vindication of her ill treatment. "What Happened to Mary in the City," *The Ladies World* 33 (10) (Sept. 1912): 12.

68. Rachel M. Brownstein, *Becoming a Heroine* (New York: Viking Press, 1984), xxi. See also Cowie, *Representing the Woman*, 6-7.

69. "What Happened to Mary," *Bioscope* (July 31, 1913): 369. Note that for this reviewer, sensationalism was necessary to achieve a "realistic" effect.

70. Walter Licht, *Working for the Railroad: The Organization of Work in the Nineteenth Century* (Princeton: Princeton University Press, 1983), 163, 160.

71. The producer's decision to make Helen a telegraph operator for a railroad dovetailed men's heroic stories of labor with formulas based on female heroines.

Women did work in the railroad industry at this time; however, their positions were redefined to exclude them from men's promotional track. In 1918, only 2.6 percent of all women railroad workers were telegraph operators. Helen served, like Mary, not as a representation of the "real" working opportunities or experiences of working-class women, but as a fantasy of women in the (masculine) workplace, privy to masculine adventures and amenities. See Maureen Weiner Greenwald, "Women Workers and World War One: The American Railroad Industry, A Case Study," *Journal of Social History* 9 (Winter 1975): 154-77.

72. Film critic Ben Singer argues that this combination of power and vulnerability undergirded a desire for sensationalist films and images by the turn of the century; sensationalist images particularly focused on new and dangerous forms of transportation such as the train, the streetcar, and the automobile. Singer, "Modernity, Hyperstimulus, and the Rise of Popular Sensationalism" in Charney and Schwartz, eds., *Cinema and the Invention of Modern Life*, 72-99. See also Singer's discussion of the *Hazards of Helen* serial in "Female Power in the Serial-Queen Melodrama," 102-3.

73. The stage melodrama version of "Bertha, the Sewing Machine Girl" when revived in early 1900s, for example, featured a "realistic" train collision. "Labor's Grandest Demonstration," *Union Labor Advocate* (Sept. 1909): 15; advertisement, *Moving Picture World* 14 (3) (Oct. 1912): 262.

74. Episode 58, "The Wrong Order" is at the Motion Picture Division, Library of Congress.

75. A number of reviews and synopses of episode 31 can be found in the Helen Holmes clipping file, New York Public Library for Performing Arts.

76. Information on episodes gained from promotional material found in the *Hazards of Helen* clipping file, New York Public Library for Performing Arts. In *The Girl and the Game*, a railroad series starring Helen Holmes, the heroine refuses a proposal in the first episode. The camera cuts between two romantic close-ups: the man proposing, and Helen smiling slightly, shaking her head, "no." The romantic film techniques, all the more startling because true close-ups were rare at this time, served to highlight the narrative innovation of the refusal. For information on episode 13, see Bowser, *History of the American Cinema*, vol. 2, 187.

MARTIN W. SANDLER (ESSAY DATE 2002)

SOURCE: Sandler, Martin W. "For the Printed Page." In *Against the Odds: Women Pioneers in the First Hundred Years of Photography*, pp. 140-67. New York: Rizzoli International Publications, 2002.

In the following essay, Sandler recounts the lives of such female photographers as Jesse Tarbox Beals, Consuelo Kanaga, Margaret Bourke-White, Marjory Collins, and Louise Dahl-Wolf, remarking on their pioneering efforts and far-reaching influence on every aspect of the medium.

At the turn of the century Eva Watson-Schütze stated, "There is one open field yet very little touched by the camera, and that is illustrations, and I look for great things in that direction in the future." Little more than a decade later, *Collier's* magazine would proclaim, "It is the photographer who writes history these days. The journalist only labels the characters."

Actually, photographs had been used as the basis for illustration as early as the 1850s, when wood engravings copied from photographs adorned the pages of many newspapers and magazines. It was the introduction of the halftone plate in the 1880s that made the reproduction of actual photographs in publications possible. The key to the halftone printing process was the use of a screen of fine lines on glass that broke a photographic image into thousands of dots. The pattern of dots was transferred photographically onto a chemically treated printing plate. All of the tones—blacks, whites, grays—could be reproduced.

Of all the countless advancements in the history of the medium none had a more profound impact on emblazoning photography in the public's consciousness than did the halftone plate. By the late 1920s, photographs printed in newspapers became one of the chief means by which people received their news. Out of this development grew the news photographer, a new type of cameraperson with the ability to anticipate when a newsworthy event was about to take place, the talent to snap the shutter at the most telling moment during the event, and the stamina to travel from assignment to assignment.

By the 1930s, the success of photographs in newspapers led to the establishment of photographic magazines. Destined to become extraordinarily popular, the picture magazine spawned the photo essay and created yet another new type of photographer, the photojournalist.

New types of photographic styles would emerge as well. The ability to put pictures into print would lead to the development of advertising, fashion, and industrial photography as vital and distinct avenues of photographic expression. As in news photography and photojournalism, women would play a pioneering role in all these approaches.

A woman, in fact, was among the earliest photographers to have their pictures appear on the printed page as news photographers. Jesse Tarbox Beals, born Jesse Tarbox in 1879, received her first camera at the age of eighteen when, while teaching in a one-room schoolhouse in Williamsburg, Massachusetts, she responded to an advertisement in *Youth's Companion* offering a free camera, plates, and instructions to new subscribers. After taking some pictures, she found that she could make more money taking portraits than she could teaching school.

In 1897, she married machinist Alfred Beals and taught him photography. Three years later the couple went into business together as itinerant photographers. In 1902, Beals was hired by the *Buffalo Courier* to head its fledgling photographic department. She approached her new position with extraordinary energy and ingenuity. In 1903, she achieved what may well have been the nation's first newspaper "scoop" when, at a murder trial where no cameras were allowed, she captured images of the proceedings by photographing through a transom above a door. The amazing number of pictures that she produced for the newspaper on a variety of subjects soon captured national attention. "She levels her camera lens," stated a magazine, "on nearly everything that creeps, walks, swims, or crawls within the boundaries of the United States and Canada."

Her determination to photograph every newsworthy event within her reach often placed her in real danger. When her editor at the newspaper informed her of a major fire in Rochester, New York, and told her she had fifteen minutes to catch a train to the site, Beals hastily gathered up her bulky equipment, finished dressing on the trolley to the station, and made the train. Of her experience in recording the fire she later wrote, "I had never seen anything that so reminded me of Dante's Inferno as the smoking areas of burned-over blocks at the fire. But I plunged in and did all that I could, and when I came out of that fire place I would not have known myself. Icicles were frozen over all my wraps and it took literally hours to get thawed out so I could finish up my negatives."

Some of Beals' most moving photographs were those she took of the appalling conditions under which immigrant families were forced to live in New York City's tenement districts. Her photographs of life in these tenements and alleys, like the work of fellow photographer Jacob Riis, helped make the nation aware of this social ill and influenced the reform that was eventually achieved.

While Beals focused exclusively on news photography, Frances Benjamin Johnston, like many of her colleagues, captured both newsworthy images for newspapers and compiled photographic stories for some of the earliest picture magazines. As early as 1886, Johnston distributed posters describing herself as "making a business of photographic illustration and the writing of descriptions for magazines, illustrated weeklies, and newspapers." An astute businesswoman, she revealed her personal and professional approach to her work by stating, "I have not been able to lose sight of the pecuniary side, though for the sake of money or anything else I would not publish a photograph that fell below the standard I set for myself."

As in the documentary photographs she captured at Tuskegee and Hampton Institutes, the pictures Johnston took for various publications revealed her concern for humanity, particularly the status of women. The series of pictures she took of women working in a Lynn, Massachusetts, shoe factory, for example, are marked by a sensitivity to the dignity of these workers who labored long hours for three to five dollars a week.

One of Johnston's most dramatic accomplishments as a press photographer came about in 1899 through her friendship with then Assistant Secretary of the Navy Theodore Roosevelt. Vacationing in Europe, she was made aware that Commodore George Dewey, the hero of Manila Bay, was making several European stops before returning to a triumphant homecoming in America. At Johnston's request, Roosevelt contacted Dewey and got the commodore's permission for Johnston to board his flagship *Olympia* in Naples and take the first photographs of America's newest hero and of life aboard the celebrated vessel.

The scores of photographs that Johnston took of Dewey and of the members of the *Olympia*'s crew at work and at leisure represented a real coup. Dozens of photographers had been attempting to get such pictures. That this early photographic scoop had been accomplished by a woman was, no doubt, particularly galling to many of her male competitors.

Consuelo Kanaga also earned her living by pursuing a variety of photographic genres. She entered the world of news photography in 1919 as a photographer-reporter for the *San Francisco Daily News*. In the early 1920s, she photographed for the *San Francisco Chronicle*. For the better part of the next forty years she would intermittently carry out news assignments for a variety of publications.

Kanaga brought to her press photography all those special talents that distinguished her work in other areas of the medium. As author Barbara Millstein has written, where Kanaga differed from her fellow press photographers "was in her choice of subject matter, in her deliberate composition, in her meticulous printing, and finally, in her heart."

Kanaga's talent at composition is clearly apparent in the photograph she titled *Fire.* Photographing at close range, Kanaga waited until the main figure in the center revealed her deepest anguish. She framed this woman with two other figures, capturing the solemn expression of the woman to her right and the hint of curiosity on the face of the woman to her left. Given that this was all accomplished under the constraints of a spontaneous news photograph, it was a masterful achievement.

By the beginning of the 1930s, pictures in newspapers and early picture magazines had established the photograph as a primary means of communication. Early picture-dominated magazines such as *Fortune, Collier's,* and *National Geographic* in particular had captured the nation's attention through their photographic coverage of people and conditions throughout the world. It would be one picture magazine above all, however, that would have the greatest impact.

In 1936, Henry Luce, the founder of *Fortune,* launched a new picture magazine called *Life.* The prospectus described the publication as different from even the most ambitious of its predecessors: "Pictures are taken haphazardly. Pictures are published haphazardly," the prospectus proclaimed. "Naturally therefore they are looked at haphazardly . . . almost nowhere is there any attempt to edit pictures into a coherent story. . . . The mind-guided camera . . . can reveal to us far more explicitly the nature of the dynamic social world in which we live."

On November 19, 1936, the first issue of *Life* hit the newsstands with an impact equaled only by the advent of television some two decades later. Optimistic estimates predicted an initial circulation of about 250,000. Within four hours, all 466,000 copies of the first issue had been sold. The "mind-guided camera" had touched a vital nerve.

Over the years countless photographers, many of them famous or destined to become so, would join *Life* or contribute images to the magazine. They were aided in great measure by technical advancements, particularly advantageous to photojournalists and news photographers. These advancements included the introduction of the Leica and other small 35mm cameras that permitted a photographer to shoot quickly and repeat-

ON THE SUBJECT OF...

CLARE BOOTHE LUCE (1903-1987)
A socialite, politician, diplomat, editor, and author, Clare Boothe Luce was celebrated for her wit, charm, and wide-ranging talents. After divorcing millionaire George Tuttle Brokaw in 1929 she took a position at fellow socialite Conde Nast's magazine *Vanity Fair,* where she became managing editor until 1934. She next turned to writing for the stage, but her first play proved a failure. Two days after production commenced, however, she wedded millionaire publisher Henry R. Luce, whose publications included *Time* and *Fortune.* A subsequent play, *The Women,* scored enormously on Broadway, and two more plays also earned acclaim. Critics praised the book version of *The Women,* calling it "exceedingly clever, original, and ingenious." Luce also brought her husband greater success, for his magazine *Life* had been created at her suggestion and had become immensely popular with American readers.

In the 1940s Luce became increasingly active in American politics. She was elected to the House of Representatives in 1943 and re-elected the following year. During the administration of President Dwight D. Eisenhower she was appointed ambassador to Italy. A subsequent appointment to the ambassadorship of Brazil proved controversial, however, and in 1959 Luce left the world of politics to work for *McCall's.* Throughout her life Luce served several organizations, including the World Wildlife Fund, the Oceanic Foundation, and the Hawaii Foundation for American Freedoms. Her published works include *Stuffed Shirts* (1933), a collection of satirical sketches about New York City society, and *Europe in the Spring* (1940), an account of her travels in Europe at the onset of World War II. Additionally, she wrote the plays *Kiss the Boys Goodbye* (1938), and *Margin for Error* (1939), and edited the volume *Saints for Now* (1952), a collection of biographies of saints.

Clare Boothe Luce (1903-1987).

edly at eye level, rolled "fast" film that allowed for the taking of sequences of pictures in thousandths of a second, and the flashbulb, which replaced cumbersome, often ineffective, flash powder. Armed with these new tools, *Life*'s photographers captured images that would remain in the public memory. Of all these photographers, none was more important or more vital to the magazine's early success than Margaret Bourke-White. Destined to become the world's best-known photojournalist, she would shoot more press photographs than any other photographer in history. She traveled the globe, captured images of people and places rarely seen, and set the standard for generations of photojournalists to follow.

She was born in New York City in 1904 and raised in Bound Brook, New Jersey. Both of her parents were connected to the publishing industry—her father a printing engineer, her mother working on publications for the blind. In 1921, Bourke-White studied photography with Clarence White. She went on to college, but was far from a committed student and attended seven colleges before finally earning a bachelor's degree at Cornell. It was while taking photographs for the yearbook at the University of Michigan that she determined what her life's work must be. "We all find something," she later wrote, "that is just right for us, and after I found the camera I never really felt a whole person again unless I was planning pictures or taking them. . . ."

Bourke-White began her professional career as an architectural photographer in Cleveland, Ohio. She then undertook advertising work before accepting a commission to photograph a Cleveland steel company. These industrial images so impressed Henry Luce that, in 1929, he offered her a job as a staff photographer on his new magazine, *Fortune.* Her photography was so instrumental in *Fortune*'s success that when Luce launched *Life,* he immediately hired her as one of the publication's first photographers.

Bourke-White's photograph of the newly built Fort Peck Dam in Montana adorned the cover of *Life*'s premier issue. The main story in the magazine was her long photo-essay on the workers who were building the dam and the local townspeople, and for this she received *Life*'s first photo credit.

For the next twenty-one years, Bourke-White was *Life*'s most prolific and important photographer. She took tens of thousands of pictures recording people and places at home and in almost every corner of the globe. She photographed miners in South Africa, field-workers in Slovakia, aristocrats in Hungary, and emigrants in Pakistan. She took memorable photographs of Mahatma Gandhi just six hours before he was assassinated and recorded the first German air raids on Moscow. She was the first photojournalist to enter Russia after its revolution and sent back the first views of this almost unknown society that Americans had ever seen. In 1943 she became the first woman to fly on a United States combat mission. Two years later, she was among the press corps that encountered the barbarism at Buchenwald and other concentration camps.

Bourke-White was the consummate photojournalist. She would let nothing deter her from getting the pictures or the story she pursued. "Sometimes," she said, "I could murder someone who gets in my way when I am taking a picture. I become irrational. There is only one moment when a picture is there, and an instant later it is gone—gone forever. My memory is full of those pictures that were lost."

Aside from her photographs themselves, one of the most important contributions Bourke-White made to photography was pioneering the photo essay. Two other women photographers, although they were not photo-journalists, also provided early evidence of the effectiveness and appeal of stories told through a series of pictures.

They accomplished this through two special assignments they carried out while members of the FSA photographic corps.

One of these picture stories, titled "Cross Country Bus Tour," was taken by Esther Bubley. Born in 1921, she was raised in Superior, Wisconsin, and attended Superior State Teacher's College for two years before studying art at the Minneapolis School of Art and Design. In 1940, she moved to Washington, D.C., and a year later became a microfilmer at the National Archives. Some months later she was hired by the FSA as a darkroom technician. In 1942, she was promoted to join the ranks of the agency's photographers.

Bubley's assignment in compiling "Cross Country Bus Tour" was to capture images of a specific aspect of the American home front in World War II. Her task was to photograph soldiers, and other wartime travelers, on a Greyhound bus route that went from Washington to Pittsburgh and then on to Chicago, Louisville, Memphis, Chattanooga, Knoxville, and then back to Washington. Bubley boarded a bus and traveled the entire route capturing images of passengers waiting in the bus terminals, boarding the bus, traveling aboard the vehicle, and pausing between stops. She displayed a particular talent for depicting passengers in relaxed and poignant moments, elevating the series beyond that of a mere visual chronicle. She also accompanied each of her pictures with detailed notes. The photographs that the FSA photographers took were made available free of charge to commercial publications. Editors of several magazines and newspapers selected images from Bubley's series and created their own "Cross Country Bus Tour" picture stories.

Marjory Collins's major contribution to the FSA files was also a photographic series designed to portray the American home front during World War II. Collins was born in 1912 and spent her childhood in Scarsdale, New York. After studying photography with Ralph Steiner in the 1930s, she worked as a photographer in New York City before being hired by the FSA.

One of her early assignments was to portray small-town life in wartime. Specifically, it was to capture images of people engaged in civil defense activities, planting victory gardens, and immersing themselves in other patriotic wartime efforts. "Make people appear as if they really believed in the U.S.," read her shooting script.

Collins selected Lititz, Pennsylvania, as the appropriate setting for the series she titled "Small Town in Wartime." There she took many pictures of such home front activities as scrap drives and draft board meetings—but she went much deeper. As one studies the photographs in the series, it becomes apparent that her main goal was to portray the special nature of everyday life in a small town even during a time of national stress. Like Bubley's "Cross Country Bus Tour" images, select photographs from "Small Town in Wartime" were acquired by national publications that presented their own picture stories based on the Collins series.

Aside from providing photographers the opportunity to produce images for magazines and newspapers, the ability to reproduce photographs on the printed page created another vital outlet for photographic expression. Once the halftone process was fully developed, photographs began to appear in all types of books. One of the most significant of these books was *An American Exodus,* compiled by Dorothea Lange and her husband, Paul Taylor, published in 1939. A pioneering effort to combine words and photographs in book form, Lange and Taylor used conversations by Lange's subjects as the basis for the book's narrative. A different narrative technique was used in their book, *Land of the Free.* In this book, the photographs were accompanied by a "sound track," a lyrical poem written by Archibald MacLeish. So impressed was MacLeish by the images that he later explained, "The original purpose had been to write some sort of text to which the photographs might serve as commentary. But so great was the power . . . of these vivid American documents that the result was a reversal of that plan."

One of the images with which MacLeish was so taken was a Great Depression-era picture destined to become the most widely reproduced photograph in history. It took Dorothea Lange all of ten minutes to produce the immortal image that she titled *Migrant Mother.* Passing by a sign that read PEA PICKERS CAMP, she turned her car around and entered the wet, soggy place where she almost immediately encountered a woman and her two children. As Lange later described it, "I saw and approached the hungry and desperate mother, as if drawn by a magnet. I do not remember how I explained my presence or my camera to her, but I do remember she asked me no questions. . . . She told me her age, that she was thirty-two. She said that they had been living on frozen vegetables from the surrounding fields, and birds that the children killed. She had just sold the tires from her car to buy food. There she sat in the lean-to tent with her children huddled around

Migrant Mother, (1936), photograph by Dorothea Lange.

her, and seemed to know that my pictures might help her, and so she helped me. There was a sort of equality about it." Beginning with its publication in *Land of the Free, Migrant Mother* became such an icon of an era that throughout the rest of her career Lange would complain that it threatened to make her known for nothing but having taken that image.

An American Exodus and *Land of the Free* were but two of the many books that appeared in the 1930s and 1940s featuring FSA photographs. Of all these volumes, one that found the largest readership was *In This Proud Land,* with text by Roy Stryker and Nancy Woods. Works by Marion Post Wolcott and Marjory Collins were all featured in the book, including Lange's memorable photograph of a woman at a revival meeting and Wolcott's compelling image of a judge at a Virginia horse show.

It was through books such as *American Exodus, Land of the Free,* and *In This Proud Land* that Dorothea Lange's photographs in particular received their widest distribution. In the decades following their publication, other women photographers such as Laura Gilpin, Barbara Morgan, Imogen Cunningham, Nell Dorr, and Margaret Bourke-White would all present many of their images to the world in book form.

The halftone printing process was introduced at a time when the United States was rapidly becoming the world's industrial leader. In a nation of people who had long been captivated by pictures of the "largest" or the "most recent," images of machines and industrial structures held a particular fascination. The ability to reproduce photographs in newspapers and magazines came also at a time when, more than ever before, the camera was becoming regarded as a faithful recorder of those symbols that defined an era. As the nation entered a new century, there was no greater symbol of all that America had achieved and of the widely held belief in the inevitability of continued progress than the machine. By the late 1920s, the pages of the nation's magazines and major newspapers were filled with photographs of the latest machines and industrial structures and with images of those who worked above, beneath, and around them. Within a decade, museums throughout the nation were proudly displaying photographs as well as paintings depicting all the various aspects of industrialism.

Out of this burgeoning industrial photography emerged photographers who would not only record the evidence of industrial progress but would bring their own interpretations to their images. Of these photographers Margaret Bourke-White most significantly expanded the horizons of photographing the industrial world.

Many of the earliest Bourke-White industrial images were taken on assignment for *Fortune.* Dedicated to presenting industrial life in words and pictures, *Fortune* became American industry's greatest champion. And Bourke-White was the magazine's most important photographer—not only in terms of the photographs she contributed but in the manner in which she helped make the pictures as important as the words in the publication's approach.

To Bourke-White, it was the aesthetic qualities found in otherwise utilitarian industrial objects that defined their importance to photography. "Any important art coming out of the industrial age," she wrote, "will draw inspiration from industry, because industry is alive and vital. The beauty of industry lies in its truth and simplicity: every line is essential and therefore beautiful." It was this focus on simplicity and detail, even in the largest objects, as well as the emotion she conveyed through these images that characterized her industrial photographs.

One of the greatest icons of the industrial age was New York's George Washington Bridge. The building of the bridge was a monumental achievement to which Bourke-White paid homage. Of the many pictures she took of the structure, the most compelling is the one in which the viewer is drawn into the photograph by the two enormous pipes in the foreground of the image. The long spans of cable, the gigantic superstructure, even the huge bolts anchoring the pipes are revealed, testimony to Bourke-White's special ability to portray size and detail while simultaneously conveying the special type of beauty that she continually found in the industrial world.

Just as *Fortune* and other publications played a pivotal early role in advancing the development of industrial photography, so too did one of America's largest corporations, Standard Oil of New Jersey. In 1941, a Roper poll revealed that Standard Oil was the least respected company in the nation. In response, the corporation hired a public relations firm to better its public image. After a period of study, the public relations people sent back a report stating that the image problems Standard Oil was having were due in large measure to the fact that the company, despite many good things it was doing, was not controlling the publicity that surrounded the corporation and its work. Among the recommendations was that Standard Oil hire a team of photographers to take pictures showing as many aspects as possible of the work that company employees were doing and the many benefits that the nation's citizens were deriving from these activities. The report went on to point out that these photographs should not only be published regularly in the company's trade journal, *The Lamp,* but even more importantly, funneled to the large-circulation magazines.

Standard Oil's management seized upon the report, particularly the idea of disseminating photographs that would enhance the company's image. Using the FSA's photographic accomplishments as a model, they created the Standard Oil of New Jersey Photographic Project. Convinced that they could replicate the FSA's success, they hired Roy Stryker away from his government work and instructed him to hire the best photographers with a bent toward industrial photography he could find. Among those Stryker brought aboard were Todd Webb, Edwin Rosskam, and Esther Bubley. Such FSA luminaries as Russell Lee, John Vachon, and Gordon Parks also agreed to take on special assignments.

The photographers who worked for what came to be known as the SONJ project were given great latitude. They were allowed to apply the broadest of interpretations to their mandate of extolling the virtues of Standard Oil. Esther Bubley, for example, produced a photo story on cross-country bus travelers similar to the one she had compiled for the FSA.

Many other images that Bubley captured for the SONJ project were industrial photographs in the truest sense of the term, and although she never attained the status of a Bourke-White, they are images that rival the best of the genre. One theme that developed within the world of industrial photography, for example, was in direct contrast to the notion of the all-powerful machine, espousing instead that regardless of the awe-inspiring feats of modern machinery brought to everyday life were, human beings still controlled them. Bubley's photograph of a worker standing atop an enormous structure at the Tomball, Texas, gasoline plant is a powerful presentation of this theme.

The SONJ project photographers produced more than eight thousand images. Ironically, despite their quality, the photographs never achieved the results that Standard Oil desired. While due to the images *The Lamp* became the most effectively illustrated of all trade journals, their use by national magazines was extremely limited, probably because they were regarded by many editors as an extreme example of Standard Oil "blowing its own horn." Today we can appreciate the role the project played in giving industrial photographers the chance to experiment within certain parameters and how it revealed that corporate sponsorship, like government support, could provide photographic opportunities.

The development of the halftone had also given rise to the proliferation of the photograph in mass media and perhaps nowhere more effectively than in advertising. Those with products to sell could now enhance their ads with photographs of their goods rather than with drawings. As early as 1902, Kodak featured photographs by Nancy Ford Cones in its newspaper and magazine advertisements. In the 1920s, Ruth Bernard, Clara Sipprell, and other female photographers enhanced their careers with advertising work, and two women, Margaret Watkins and Wynn Richards, became leaders in the field.

No area of commerce benefited more from the ability to include photographs on the printed page than did the fashion industry. For designers and merchants, the photograph became an indispensable means of conveying trends and selling merchandise. For photographers, the world of fashion presented broad new vistas accompanied by significant new challenges.

By the late 1930s, increasingly successful magazines such as *Vogue, Harper's Bazaar,* and *Woman's Home Companion* were bringing the latest styles into homes throughout America and abroad. With millions of dollars at stake in potential sales and with designers' reputations continually on the line, fashion photography became the most competitive undertaking women photographers had ever faced. Even more than the world of advertising, it was a field dominated by men, one in which significant barriers against women photographers, consciously and subconsciously, had been established from the beginning.

Some women, however, did break through. Two sisters, Kathryn Abbe and Frances McLaughlin-Gill, along with Genevieve Naylor and Kay Bell Ragnall were among those women who were able to secure significant freelance work. And two women, Toni Frissell and Louise Dahl-Wolfe, not only succeeded but became true pioneers of the high-fashion image.

Toni Frissell first gained widespread recognition for her fashion work when she became a staff photographer for *Vogue* in 1931, a position she held for eleven years. Just prior to that, *Town and Country* had published her first series of fashion photographs, titled *Beauties at Newport.*

Frissell brought both energy and daring to her work. She let nothing deter her from getting exactly the picture she sought: "[T]he other photographers were all men," she would recall, "but I didn't think much about it. I used to be absolutely unself-conscious. For example, when I was very, very pregnant and photographing from an odd angle from the floor I saw next to me a beautifully creased pair of pants and perfectly polished shoes. I looked up and there was Condé Nast himself looking down at me. He said, 'What are you doing down there?' and I answered, 'Well, I'm interested in the way it looks from down here. I see things in my own way.'"

Frissell's pictures are marked by her understanding that a great fashion photograph is as much an image of a woman as it is of an article of clothing. "Instead of using studio lights," she later wrote, "I took my models outside to natural settings, even though they were dressed in furs and evening gowns. I wanted them to look like human beings, with the wind blowing their hair and clothes. As a photographer I was most successful when I did things naturally."

Frissell was the first fashion photographer to take models away from the confines of the studio. In conducting her "shoots" in exotic places around the world, she set a pattern followed by fashion photographers to this day. As her greatest contribution to the field, it was an innovation that in great measure paved the way for a fashion photograph to be judged not simply for its content but for its photographic attributes. Along with the images she captured for *Vogue* and *Harper's Bazaar,* Frissell also photographed extensively for Garfinkel's department stores in Washington, D.C., images which were distinguished by the inclusion of treasured national landmarks.

In the 1930s, another woman photographer, Louise Dahl-Wolfe, began a career in fashion photography that would eventually bring her to the top of the field. Born Louise Dahl in San Francisco in 1895, she attended the California School of Design and studied painting with artist Frank Van Sloan. In 1921, a friend invited her to the studio of Anne W. Brigman, a visit that changed her life: "I was floored by the beauty of the Brigman photographs," she later wrote, "and entranced by the prospects of what the camera could do."

In order to make ends meet while developing her photographic skills she took a job designing electric signs in New York, and then returned to San Francisco to work for a decorator. Her career took another positive turn when she was introduced to Consuelo Kanaga, who became a lifelong friend. In 1927, the two traveled together to Italy and Morocco where Dahl-Wolfe carefully observed Kanaga's photographic techniques.

In 1928, Dahl met and married sculptor Mike Wolfe. Four years later the couple moved to a mountain cabin in the Great Smoky Mountains of Tennessee. It was there that Dahl-Wolfe began to photograph seriously. She captured scores of images of mountain people, which were eventually published in *Vanity Fair.* In 1933, she and her husband returned to New York and a year later she acquired her first advertising account. Encouraged by her success, she set herself up as a freelancer and obtained photographic commissions from *Woman's Home Companion* and from department stores, including Bonwit Teller and Saks Fifth Avenue. In 1936, she became a staff photographer for *Harper's Bazaar,* a position she held for twenty-two years, and one through which she produced her finest work.

A leader in the photographic presentation of high fashion, *Harper's Bazaar,* following the lead set by Toni Frissell, sent Dahl-Wolfe throughout the world to capture images of the world's top models, elegantly clothed in exotic surroundings. Her fashion assignments took her to South America, Africa, Hawaii, the Caribbean, and many other locales. At a time when most fashion photographers worked in black and white, Dahl-Wolfe became known for her mastery of color. "One has to have a sense of putting color together in harmonious arrangements," she said, "planning backgrounds carefully, with an eye responsive to color." Her photographs were marked also by the dramatic manner in which she positioned each of her models within the framework of the page upon which the image would be published. She had a special ability to include arresting scenes within her photographs without diminishing the viewer's focus on the clothing the model was wearing. These groundbreaking techniques combined to establish Louise-Dahl Wolfe as one of the most influential photographers to bring the world of fashion to the printed page.

FURTHER READING

Criticism

Ammons, Elizabeth. "Men of Color, Women, and Uppity Art at the Turn of the Century." *American Literary Realism, 1870-1910* 23, no. 3 (spring 1991): 14-24.

Analyzes turn-of-century American literature as being distinguished by its concern for topical issues and experimentation, with women and black authors forming the majority of the most important authors at this time.

Byles, Joan Montgomery. "Women's Experience of World War II: Britain and Germany." In *War, Women, and Poetry, 1914-1945: British and German Writers and Activists,* pp. 23-42. Newark, N.J.: University of Delaware Press, 1995.

Literary and historical overview of the role of women in German and British social history during World War II.

Campbell, D'Ann. *Women at War with America: Private Lives in a Patriotic Era.* Cambridge, Mass.: Harvard University Press, 1984, 320 p.

Collection of essays detailing various aspects of women's lives in the first half of the twentieth century, including data on wages and labor statistics.

Carpenter, Lynette. "Deadly Letters, Sexual Politics, and the Dilemma of the Woman Writer: Edith Wharton's 'The House of the Dead Hand.'" *American Literary Realism, 1870-1910* 24, no. 2 (winter 1992): 55-69.

Examines Wharton's short story as a work that focuses on significant issues regarding the role of women in literature.

Daugherty, Sarah B. "The Ideology of Gender in Howell's Early Novels." *American Literary Realism, 1870-1910* 25, no. 1 (fall 1992): 2-19.

States that Howell's early fiction shows that the author limited his development of feminist themes in his work more because of his concern with male themes than because of his sexual chauvinism.

Dupree, Ellen. "The New Woman, Progressivism, and the Woman Writer in Edith Wharton's *The Fruit of the Tree.*" *American Literary Realism, 1870-1910* 31, no. 2 (winter 1999): 44-62.

Disagrees with many critics who have dismissed Wharton's The Fruit of the Tree *as unfocused, arguing that the work's unity becomes apparent when the reader understands that in this novel Wharton was "trying to replicate the Progressive problem novel."*

Ehrenreich, Barbara and Deirdre English. "Microbes and the Manufacture of Housework." In *For Her Own Good: 150 Years of the Experts' Advice to Women,* pp. 141-82. New York: Doubleday, 1978.

Reviews the emergence of the idea of the active housewife at the turn of the century, which resulted in the newly created sciences of housekeeping, childrearing, and domestic process.

Gordon, Marsha. "Onward Kitchen Soldiers: Mobilizing the Domestic During World War I." *Canadian Review of American Studies* 29, no. 2 (1999): 61-87.

Studies how the home became the nexus of women's participation in the First World War.

Habegger, Alfred. "Portrait of a Lady." In *Gender, Fantasy, and Realism in American Literature,* pp. 66-79. New York: Columbia University Press, 1982.

Analysis of Henry James's novel as one of the first books of the late nineteenth-century that highlighted the suffocating nature of some marriages.

Hanson, Philip. "The Feminine Image in Films of the Great Depression." *The Cambridge Quarterly* 32, no. 2 (2003): 113-41.

Presents an overview of female characters in films made during the early 1900s.

Honey, Maureen, ed. *Bitter Fruit: African American Women in World War II.* Columbia: University of Missouri Press, 1999, 424 p.

Collection of photos, essays, fiction, and poetry by and about African American women who contributed to the war effort.

Kerber, Linda K., Alice Kessler-Harris, and Kathryn Kish Sklar, eds. *U.S. History as Women's History: New Feminist Essays.* Chapel Hill: University of North Carolina Press, 1995.

Contains several essays on women's participation in political and social changes at the turn of the century.

Latham, Angela J. "The Right to Bare: Containing and Encoding American Women in the Popular Theater." In *Posing a Threat: Flappers, Chorus Girls, and Other Brazen Performers of the American 1920s,* pp. 99-121. Hanover, N.H.: Wesleyan University Press, 2000.

Examines the role of women performers on the American stage during the 1920s, placing their lives in context of contemporary censorship laws and cultural norms and theorizing that female performers often used the stage as a means of contesting, affirming, and even revolutionizing "female self-presentation and self-stylization."

Martin, David E. "Pioneer Women Photographers." *American Art Review* xiv, no. 6 (November-December 2002): 100-05.

Brief perspectives on pioneer women photographers such as Myra Albert Wiggins, Imogen Cunningham, and Ella McBride.

Oates, Joyce Carol. "'At Least I Have Made a Woman of Her': Images of Women in Twentieth Century Literature." *Georgia Review* xxxvii, no. 1 (spring 1983): 7-30.

Surveys literary representations of feminine images in twentieth century literature.

Rosenblum, Naomi. *A History of Women Photographers*. New York: Abbeville Press Publishers, 1994.

Collection of essays tracing the development of women photographers from the late 1800s to the 1990s, including overview essays on the feminist vision in photography.

Schneider, Dorothy and Carl J. Schneider. "Dawning of an Age of Hope and Glory." In *American Women in the Progressive Era, 1900-1920*, pp. 1-22. New York: Facts on File, 1993.

Discussion of the transition women underwent from the end of the nineteenth century to the beginning of the twentieth.

SUFFRAGE IN THE 20TH CENTURY

Before suffragists began arguing for legislation that would guarantee women the right to vote, governments assumed that women's interests should be and were represented by their husbands, fathers, or brothers. In the last decades of the nineteenth century the movement for women's right to vote gathered momentum. Led by such charismatic figures as Susan B. Anthony, Elizabeth Cady Stanton, and Christabel, Emmeline, and Sylvia Pankhurst, many women organized into groups, the largest of which were the National American Women Suffrage Association (NAWSA), the Women's Social and Political Union (WSPU), and the Women's Christian Temperance Union (WCTU). Such groups participated in public demonstrations, parades, marches, and meetings, and circulated literature designed to call attention to their cause and demand equal treatment under the law. Despite strong opposition from those opposed to suffrage and the suffragists's own wide-ranging differences in interests, beliefs, methodology, and ideology, women around the world were successful in increasing awareness of and support for equal treatment of women under the law, as well as for labor reform and other social issues.

Because of the efforts of members of the WCTU, women of European descent in Australia gained suffrage in 1902. Susan B. Anthony established the International Woman Suffrage Alliance in Berlin, Germany, in 1904, and Finnish women gained suffrage and the right to hold public office in 1906. Between 1900 and the beginning of World War I in 1914, British suffrage groups such as the WSPU, led by Christabel and Emmeline Pankhurst, engaged in militant tactics to enact social and legislative change. They interrupted political meetings, held public demonstrations, and subjected themselves to hunger strikes, arrest, and imprisonment. The British movement was divided mainly along class lines, with some suffragists calling for support of working-class issues and others focusing on the issue of suffrage alone, but there were also disagreements over politics (particularly socialism), and peaceful, lawful protests versus militant, sometimes violent protests. These divisions deepened as Great Britain entered World War I. Members of the WSPU and other groups left to form other special-interest groups, such as the Women's Peace Army, founded by Sylvia Pankhurst and Charlotte Despard, while the WSPU focused its efforts primarily on supporting the war, rather than on women's suffrage. Women in the United Kingdom were granted suffrage in 1918.

The American suffrage movement was also somewhat fragmented: women of color, women trade workers, and women advocating temperance pushed for more activism in support of racial equality, temperance, and labor reforms in addition to pursuing suffrage, and suffragists disagreed over both ideology and overall strategy. The right to suffrage was divided along geographic lines as well, as women in the western United States gained suffrage much earlier than women in other parts of the country. In 1913, Alice Paul and Lucy Burns, who had been active in militant protests with British suffragists and who disagreed with NAWSA leadership over the most effective course of action, formed the Congressional Union of Woman Suffrage, a branch of NAWSA that became an independent organization the following year. Paul and Burns led many protests, including one in front of the White House, and a well-publicized hunger strike that brought widespread public attention to the suffragists's cause. They formed the National Women's Party in 1916, the same year that NAWSA President Carrie Chapman Catt delivered a speech entitled "The Crisis," in which she revealed what she called her "winning plan" to focus the group's efforts on a national campaign (versus separate, state-wide campaigns) for a Constitutional amendment guaranteeing women the right to vote. In 1918 President Wilson delivered a speech pleading for the passage of women's vote legislation as an emergency measure, arguing that the full support of women's groups was an essential component of the anti-war effort. Victory came in 1920 with the ratification of the nineteenth amendment to the Constitution guaranteeing women the right to vote nationwide in all elections. After the amendment was signed into law, the NAWSA was reorganized and named the League of Women Voters.

The suffrage movement generated critical commentary beginning in the late nineteenth century, and continues to receive widespread scholarly attention. One recent trend has centered on exploring the global dimensions of the suffrage movement, especially the formal and informal international coalitions formed by suffragists. Scholars analyze the suffrage movement in the context of Progressive Era politics in general, identifying how it influenced and was, in turn, influenced by other events of that time period. Modern scholarship also focuses on the role of women of color and working-class women in the movement, and biographical research has led to revisionist biographies of some of the key figures of the suffrage movement. Historians continue to explore the effect of the movement on later labor and social legislation. Literary scholars examine both written responses to suffrage issues, the representation of women's issues in literature, and suffragist authors's use of imagery and symbolism as a means of influencing public sentiment in favor of their cause.

REPRESENTATIVE WORKS

Mary Ritter Beard
A Short History of the American Labor Movement (history) 1920

On Understanding Women (nonfiction) 1931

Harriot Stanton Blatch
Mobilizing Woman-Power (nonfiction) 1918

A Woman's Point of View: Some Roads to Peace (nonfiction) 1920

Challenging Years [with Alma Lutz] (memoir) 1940

Carrie Chapman Catt
Woman Suffrage and Politics: The Inner Story of the Suffrage Movement [with Nettie Rogers Shuler] (nonfiction) 1923

Why Wars Must Cease [with Eleanor Roosevelt, Jane Addams, and others] (nonfiction) 1935

Charlotte Despard and Mabel Collins
Outlawed: A Novel on the Woman Suffrage Question (novel) 1908

G. Colmore
Suffragette Sally (novel) 1911

Cicely Hamilton
How the Vote Was Won (play) 1909

Inez Hayes Irwin
The Story of the Woman's Party (nonfiction) 1921

Christabel Pankhurst
The Great Scourge and How to End It (nonfiction) 1913

Elizabeth Robins
The Convert (novel) 1907

Evelyn Sharp
Rebel Women (short stories) 1910

Anna Howard Shaw
The Story of a Pioneer (nonfiction) 1915

May Sinclair
The Tree of Heaven (novel) 1917

Mrs. Humphry Ward
Delia Blanchflower (novel) 1914

Ida B. Wells-Barnett
Southern Horrors (nonfiction) 1892

Lynch Law in Georgia (pamphlet) 1899

Crusade for Justice (autobiography) 1970

PRIMARY SOURCES

CARRIE CHAPMAN CATT, ANNA HOWARD SHAW, ALICE STONE BLACKWELL, AND IDA HUSTED HARPER (ESSAY DATE 1904)

SOURCE: Catt, Carrie Chapman, Anna Howard Shaw, Alice Stone Blackwell, and Ida Husted Harper. "NAWSA Declaration of Principles." In *History of Woman Suffrage*, Ida Husted Harper, pp. 742-43. New York: J. J. Little and Ives, 1922.

The following is an excerpt from the 1904 declaration of principles by the National American Woman Suffrage Association (NAWSA).

When our forefathers gained the victory in a seven years' war to establish the principle that representation should go hand in hand with taxation, they marked a new epoch in the history of man; but though our foremothers bore an equal part in that long conflict its triumph brought to them no added rights and through all the following century and a quarter, taxation without representation has been continuously imposed on women by as great tyranny as King George exercised over the American colonists.

So long as no married woman was permitted to own property and all women were barred from the money-making occupations this discrimination did not seem so invidious; but to-day the situation is without a parallel. The women of the United States now pay taxes on real and personal estate valued at billions of dollars. In a number of individual States their holdings amount to many millions. Everywhere they are accumulating property. In hundreds of places they form one-third of the taxpayers, with the number constantly increasing, and yet they are absolutely without representation in the affairs of the nation, of the State, even of the community in which they live and pay taxes. We enter our protest against this injustice and we demand that the immortal principles established by the War of the Revolution shall be applied equally to women and men citizens.

As our new republic passed into a higher stage of development the gross inequality became apparent of giving representation to capital and denying it to labor; therefore the right of suffrage was extended to the workingman. Now we demand for the 4,000,000 wage-earning women of our country the same protection of the ballot as is possessed by the wage-earning men. . . .

VIRGINIA B. LE ROY (ESSAY DATE 15 OCTOBER 1908)

SOURCE: Le Roy, Virginia B. "A Woman's Argument against Woman's Suffrage." *The World To-Day* (15 October 1908): pp.

In the following excerpt, Le Roy argues against suffrage, stating that social change and public responsibility are values that dig deeper than mere voting rights, and that women have been active participants in those activities for generations, with or without voting rights.

This age is developing an acute consciousness of the symptoms of our social disorders. Masterly and brilliant are the arraignments of our public corruptions; the pitiless searchlight of publicity illumines our most subtle perversities. We are, through the exercise of this awakened social consciousness, becoming experts in the diagnosis of our social diseases, and in our new-found zeal are prone to overlook the fact that this capacity, however valuable for some purposes, does not of itself qualify us as social healers, or inspire us with knowledge of adequate remedies. It is one thing to recognize the symptoms described on the label of a bottle of patent medicine, and quite another to confide in the contents of the bottle as a cure for the disease. There is no necessary connection between the diagnosis and the proposed remedy, but many social reformers make the mistake of assuming such to be the case.

The Fallacy of Abstract Rights

All social reform movements to-day seem to focus on some conception of "rights." Somewhere, somehow, there seem to be things out there that we call "rights," and we feel that if we could once grasp them and hold tight, their possession would insure our social machinery a smoother running. These "rights" seem to be independent and preëxistent principles, foreordained fiats, absolute verities, which to discover and possess promise us a short cut to an earthly paradise.

For example, there are the "rights of labor" ever seeming to taunt us with their challenge: if

JUSTICE   EQUALITY

Why Women Want to Vote.

WOMEN ARE CITIZENS,

AND WISH TO DO THEIR CIVIC DUTY.

WORKING WOMEN need the ballot to regulate conditions under which they work.
Do working men think they can protect themselves without the right to vote?

HOUSEKEEPERS need the ballot to regulate the sanitary conditions under which
they and their families must live.
Do MEN think they can get what is needed for their district unless they can
vote for the men that will get it for them?

MOTHERS need the ballot to regulate the moral conditions under which their
children must be brought up.
Do MEN think they can fight against vicious conditions that are threatening their
children unless they can vote for the men that run the district?

TEACHERS need the ballot to secure just wages and to influence the management
of the public schools.
Do MEN think they could secure better school conditions without a vote to elect
the Mayor who nominates the Board of Education ?

BUSINESS WOMEN need the ballot to secure for themselves a fair opportunity
in their business.
Do business MEN think they could protect themselves against adverse legislation
without the right to vote?

TAX PAYING WOMEN need the ballot to protect their property.
Do not MEN know that "Taxation without representation" is tyranny ?

ALL WOMEN need the ballot, because they are concerned equally with men in
good and bad government; and equally responsible for civic righteousness.

ALL MEN need women's help to build a better and juster government, and

WOMEN need MEN to help them secure their right to fulfil their civic duties.

National American Woman Suffrage Association

Headquarters: 505 FIFTH AVENUE, NEW YORK

Broadside published by the National American Woman Suffrage Associaton in 1910.

all men had their bellies full of food and the right kind of rags to cover them, democracy, that other glorious right and privilege, would be attained. Then there are those "inalienable rights of freedom," which can not be downed, but come frothing and sizzling from the word-intoxicated orator as he hypnotizes his emotionally receptive audience. These "rights" we have always with us. Our children begin to imbibe them with Patrick Henry, and we continue to absorb them till the last campaign gun is fired. True, they are becoming somewhat overworked, but under the wiles of the spellbinder they are often potent to galvanize into spasmodic semblance of activity the sluggish wills of the people.

Then there are those blessed rights called "woman's rights," that sound the clarion call to the recently emancipated industrial slave who fondly fancies because she has relegated the making of soap to the factories and the world's medicine to the chemist, she may with profit employ her leisure in legislating world politics. This is perhaps the most interesting, as it is the most recent, example of the "rights" fallacy.

Women's Reasons for Woman's Rights

I have interviewed many prominent women, putting to them the question: "Why do you want to vote?"

Most of them replied: "It is our right. We have been deprived of our rights by man long enough. We must assert ourselves and demand the ballot." It requires no prophet's eye to see that these pseudo-individualists urged into politics by their personal longings for political prerogatives would speedily come to grief in the maelstrom of party politics, where the male politicians have the first innings in the game.

Again, a large number of women make the reply: "We have property interests to protect, and if we pay taxes we should vote on municipal questions. Our property rights are violated."

"Taxation without representation" is another one of those embalmed traditions, to gainsay which is to the average American like shaking the proverbial red rag at a bull.

An Interview with Susan B. Anthony

I well remember one winter's afternoon several years ago, sitting with Susan B. Anthony in her cozy study in Rochester. Outdoors the frozen snow gleamed like crystal, the wind howled through the specter-like elms, but inside round the big fireplace the huge logs slowly smoldering sent out intermittently rose-colored flames, dispelling at rare intervals the twilight shadows, and softly lighting up the noble face of one great woman. As we sat there in the comfort and cheer of the firelight, reminiscing on "the woman question," the little maid brought in the evening paper. Instantly the quiet atmosphere was disturbed and the spell broken. The lights were turned on, and in indignant voice the priestess of woman suffrage read a certain city ordinance just passed which would mean the payment of a considerable tax by her.

"Now are you convinced?" she asked with confident directness. "Here am I obliged to pay this money, and I am allowed no voice in the direction of these civic affairs. Isn't this a rank injustice? Am I not deprived of my legitimate rights as a property-holder and taxpayer?"

I could fully understand her indignation but I could not assent to the inferences she drew, so I replied:

"But, Miss Anthony, do you think the suffrage should depend on property? If so, how much property? And should it vote if held by minors, imbeciles, or aliens? And if property is to be the test, should not the one who owns most vote most? In which case, wouldn't you be worse off than you are now? Isn't it rather doubtful after all whether representation should not depend on something other than taxation?"

A caller interrupted, and I never got Miss Anthony's response.

Hobbes and Rousseau Still Rule us

The fallacy of absolute and *a priori* "rights" seems to vitiate the reasoning of most of our reformers and especially of our suffrage reformers, who accept it with a child-like naiveté that is touching. As it appears fundamental to the discussion I would like to turn the calcium on this whole question of "rights." I want to show that the idea itself is a mere verbal abstraction concocted in the intellectual laboratories of medieval Europe; that it is a sawdust idol fit to-day only for the circus ring, bloodless, lifeless, hopelessly grotesque and inadequate to form the backbone of any practical social purpose.

Our modern brand of "rights" runs way back to the sixteenth century when Hobbes manufactured the first batch of them to serve as a mediator between the leaders of the Long Parliament and the King. Hobbes declared the state was like a large man in whom was vested supreme rights, and that as the King personified the state, his sovereignty could not be impugned. Later came Rousseau, who let out a whole brood of rights, called "natural rights." The French Revolution scattered these rights as burning brands over the then civilized world, until every state smoldered with sympathetic conflagrations. This country, already aflame, gave generous recognition to them, supplemented the list with several varieties of its own, until to-day it is difficult to keep tab on all the different kinds of rights, more or less inalienable and independent.

The Pragmatist Declaration of Independence

The old-world doctrine of abstract rights has so permeated the structure of our social thinking that hardly a step can be taken in our reasoning processes without stumbling over its catch phrases. It holds us so tight that nothing short of a new declaration of independence can free us—and a few of the bolder spirits have already celebrated their new Fourth of July. These radicals are asking the old doctrinaires to make good, to turn their abstract "rights" into cash values, to test them by

their power to do work. What will these "rights" do for us? Will they bake bread? Will they build schoolhouses? No. Then away with them, for they hinder the coming of ideas that are dynamic, that have the power to turn the wheels of social progress.

To the modern radical your communist, socialist, or anarchist, who prates about the rights of man and rants loudly about the principles of liberty, fraternity and equality, is as hopelessly conservative and reactionary as the most hidebound Tory. For to the real radical all social rights are man-made. They are made by him for his own purposes, and can be unmade when his purposes change. To him all the rights of the individual are rights which he holds not as a unit apart from, but as an integral element in the social organism. These rights are not foreordained, not preëxistent, not independent, not things in themselves. They are called into being through the harmonious intercourse of rational beings, are man-wrought transformations in the social process, facilitating the interchange of human relations, elastic in their nature, their values relative and immediate.

New Test for Suffrage Wanted

Now it is evident that this new conception of human rights must have an important bearing on the question of suffrage. If the ballot is not a natural or abstract right but simply a question of social expediency, an instrument to effect a desired end, the whole question may be considered from a new viewpoint.

The fact that we made the mistake of thinking in our callow youth that giving the ballot was giving equality and freedom is no reason for continuing the mistake now that we have arrived at the years of discretion. Because we gave the ballot to hundreds of thousands who are unfit; because to-day we are suffering the full penalty of our mistaken zeal for freedom, and are trying to unbungle the whole miserable business by illegally disfranchising as many as possible, will it further the solution of our problem to add several million more votes from generally ignorant and unqualified voters?

If, following this reasoning, we are to discard the old criteria of suffrage, we ought to be able to apply some more adequate test before we can intelligently discuss the question. What should the test be? It does not fall within my purpose to define it, but it is at any rate clear that it should not be based on an abstraction. It should result in some concrete good to the voter, to the state, or to society at large, and it is up to the proponents of woman's suffrage to show that it will work practical good in some tangible way. If they can prove it can accomplish useful social results, as a good pragmatist I am bound to be with them. Up to the present time the arguments have not been forthcoming.

How would Suffrage Affect Woman?

What, for example, will the influence of suffrage be on woman herself? This is an old question, and it has been treated in a too trifling, too supercilious tone by men. I do not intend to rehash the old bosh about the defeminization of women, or the lowering of the sanctities of the home, etc. That sort of talk is puerile. Participation in public work need not of itself make a woman unwomanly, and I score no point on that ground. What damage, then, is to come to woman from voting? How are we to forecast the effect of suffrage on woman nature?

Obviously, by examining the influence of political activities on those who have had the suffrage—on the men. . . .

. . . What do men fight for to-day in the political arena? The most casual observer must be struck with the juggling of our political machinery which is making it possible for this huge organized political appetite to devour the public spoils. Men are playing the game for material prizes, not for principles. They join forces, play off great issues, toss the destinies of the nations lightly to and fro, all for the glittering bait of political advancement. The political conscience has become so atrophied, the public standard of morality so low, the premium on undiscovered chicanery so high, that the best brains of the century can find no more inspiring task than to haul over the political grab-bag and fight for such baubles as it may contain.

Would women play the game more wisely? There is nothing in my experience as a twentieth-century club woman that would warrant me in supposing them superior to the spoils of office or political preferment. The promise of a "merry-widow hat" or a "directoire gown" might as easily turn a nation's destiny as any form of a more masculine graft. . . .

. . . The point I here emphasize is that the suffrage would divert woman from her real social purpose. As between the two sexes today woman has practically a monopoly of the social spirit. Were she to become a competitor for political prizes on the same terms as men, there is little

reason for believing she could preserve her social spirit any better than men have done. Her motives would tend to become personal and selfish instead of public and patriotic, and society can not afford to lose her as a generator of pure social spirit unpolluted by lust of political gain.

I am more and more convinced that women are particularly fortunate in being exempt from the temptations of political activity. Just because woman may not participate in the political scramble, just because she is free, unhampered to let her generous impulses have full sway, just because she, and she alone, has heart-to-heart contact with the great ideals and problems of human destiny, unbiased by political expediencies, is she the potent power to-day in the direction of the great spiritual forces that are slowly but surely undermining the crass materialism of our sordid age. She it is to-day who is really influencing great public issues, accomplishing great humanitarian reforms, devising expedient measures of public sanitation, becoming in a word a great municipal housekeeper. She it is who is royally diffusing maternal tenderness for all motherless children, who is battling for a militant idealism that shall rescue us from the gross complacency of our idols of clay and reveal to us the shining gods of beauty, order and love.

DOROTHY DIX (ESSAY DATE 1908)

SOURCE: Dix, Dorothy. "Dorothy Dix on Women's Suffrage." In *Women in America,* edited by Elizabeth Meriwether Gilmer. N.p., 1908.

In the following excerpt, Dix (a pseudonym for Elizabeth Meriwether Gilmer) makes a case for women's suffrage, listing reasons why women should have the right to vote.

Women Ought to Vote, Because—

Taxation without representation is tyranny, whether the individual who pays the taxes wears trousers or petticoats, and because all just government must rest upon the consent of the governed.

Women form one half of the population, and as long as they have no voice in the government, they are held in serfdom. It is not just that, merely by reason of sex, one half of the people of the country should rule the other half.

It is folly to say that women are represented by the votes of the men of their family. No man is willing to sacrifice his suffrage and let his father or brother vote for him.

Women Should Vote because they are unlike men, because they have different aspirations, different needs, a different point of view, a different way of reaching conclusions. Feminine talents, which are invaluable everywhere else in life, should be equally useful in politics.

Women Should Vote because every question of politics affects the home, and particularly affects the woman in the home. Out of the woman's housekeeping allowance, which has not increased, come the increased profits of the beef trust, and the milk trust, and the sugar trust, and the canned goods trust. If women had a say-so in making the laws, they would have long ago clipped the wings of the predatory combinations that have increased the cost of living so greatly.

Women Should Vote because their vote would supplement man's, and, while he looked after the big things, they would look after the little things. The man might interest himself in making his country a world power, the woman voter would see that the street-cleaner did his duty so that her children might not be killed by diphtheria.

Women Should Vote because they would look just as much at the candidate as they did the platform upon which he stood. It is practically impossible to put the party yoke on women. This has been proven in the States in which women have suffrage. When a clean man was put up on either the Democratic or the Republican ticket and a corrupt man named on the other ticket, the woman vote invariably has flopped over to the good man. It was the women of Denver, irrespective of party, who kept Judge Lindsay in office after the party committees had turned him down, and thus enabled him to continue his great work of child-saving.

Women Should Vote, if for no other reason than because women, if they had a chance would be just as potent a factor in politics as they are in religion. They would compel men's interest in the subject.

CARRIE CHAPMAN CATT (ESSAY DATE 16 SEPTEMBER 1916)

SOURCE: Catt, Carrie Chapman. "The Crisis." *Rhetoric Society Quarterly* 28, no. 3 (spring 1998): 52.

The following is an excerpt from Catt's famous 1916 presidential address to the National American Woman Suffrage Association. This excerpt is taken from a complete text compiled in Rhetoric Society Quarterly *that combines versions of the address that were printed in* The Women's Journal *on September 16, 1916; the Catt papers in the New York Public Library; the Catt papers at the Library of Congress; and an article in the* New York Times *dated September 8, 1916.*

The Crisis

I have taken for my subject, "The Crisis" because I believe that a crisis has come in our movement which, if recognized and the opportunity seized with vigor, enthusiasm and will, means the final victory of our great cause in the very near future. I am aware that some suffragists do not share this belief; they see no signs nor symptoms today which were not present yesterday; no manifestations in the year 1916 which differ significantly from those in the year 1910. To them, the movement has been a steady, normal growth from the beginning and must so continue until the end. I can only defend my claim with the plea that it is better to imagine a crisis where none exists than to fail to recognize one when it comes; for a crisis is a culmination of events which calls for new considerations and new decisions. A failure to answer the call may mean an opportunity lost, a possible victory postponed.

The object of the life of an organized movement is to secure its aim. Necessarily, it must obey the law of evolution and pass through the stages of agitation and education and finally through the stage of realization. As one has put it: "A new idea floats in the air over the heads of the people and for a long, indefinite period evades their understanding but, by and by, when through familiarity, human vision grows clearer, it is caught out of the clouds and crystallized into law." Such a period comes to every movement and is its crisis. In my judgement, that crucial moment, bidding us to renewed consecration and redoubled activity has come to our cause. I believe our victory hangs within our grasp, inviting us to pluck it out of the clouds and establish it among the good things of the world.

If this be true, the time is past when we should say: "Men and women of America, look upon that wonderful idea up there; see, one day it will come down." Instead, the time has come to shout aloud in every city, village and hamlet, and in tones so clear and jubilant that they will reverberate from every mountain peak and echo from shore to shore: "The Woman's Hour has struck." Suppose suffragists as a whole do not believe a crisis has come and do not extend their hands to grasp the victory, what will happen? Why, we shall all continue to work and our cause will continue to hang, waiting for those who possess a clearer vision and more daring enterprise. On the other hand, suppose we reach out with united earnest-

ON THE SUBJECT OF...

CARRIE CHAPMAN CATT (1859-1947)

Carrie Chapman Catt entered Iowa State University in 1877, despite the objections of her father. In 1881 she began serving as principal of the high school in Mason City, Iowa, and was named superintendent of schools two years later. Catt left her position when she married Leo Chapman in 1885, and became an assistant editor of the Mason City *Republican,* the paper her husband edited. After her husband's death in 1886, Catt spent a year working on a newspaper in San Francisco. Catt returned to Iowa in 1887; she joined the Iowa Woman Suffrage Association while embarking on a new career as a lecturer. She married George Catt in 1890 and served as a member of the Iowa delegation to the NAWSA's annual convention that same year. Catt rose rapidly through the leadership ranks of the NAWSA, and in 1900 Susan B. Anthony supported Catt as her successor when she stepped down from the presidency of the NAWSA. Catt proved an able fund-raiser and secured a stable financial foundation for the NAWSA. In 1904, she resigned as president to care for George Catt, who died a year later. Catt then headed the suffrage effort in New York state and devoted herself to the newly formed International Woman Suffrage Alliance (IWSA). Divided by the defection of Alice Paul and her followers and lacking any overall strategy for winning the vote, the NAWSA again turned to Catt for leadership in 1915. At an emergency meeting in 1916, she presented what became known as the "Winning Plan." To win the vote, Catt argued, the NAWSA must become a single-issue group, pursuing suffrage to the exclusion of all other reforms. Catt's "Winning Plan" succeeded; by June 1919 Congress had passed the Anthony amendment. Her goal of 30 years accomplished, Catt resigned from the NAWSA presidency in 1920. She continued her work on an international level with the IWSA, serving as president until 1923.

ness and determination to grasp our victory while it still hangs a bit too high? Has any harm been done? None!

Therefore, fellow suffragists, I invite your attention to the signs which point of a crisis and your consideration of plans for turning the crisis into victory. . . .

WOODROW WILSON (SPEECH DATE 30 SEPTEMBER 1918)

SOURCE: Wilson, Woodrow. "Appeal to the U.S. Senate to Submit the Federal Amendment for Woman Suffrage." 1918.

The following is an excerpt from President Woodrow Wilson's speech to the U.S. Senate on September 30, 1918, to grant the federal amendment for women's Suffrage.

This is a people's war and the people's thinking constitutes its atmosphere and morale, not the predilections of the drawing room or the political considerations of the caucus. If we be indeed democrats and wish to lead the world to democracy, we can ask other peoples to accept in proof of our sincerity and our ability to lead them whither they wish to be led, nothing less persuasive and convincing than our actions.

Our professions will not suffice. Verification must be forthcoming when verification is asked for. And in this case verification is asked for— asked for in this particular matter. You ask by whom? Not through diplomatic channels; not by foreign ministers; not by the intimations of parliaments. It is asked for by the anxious, expectant, suffering peoples with whom we are dealing and who are willing to put their destinies in some measure in our hands, if they are sure that we wish the same things that they do.

I do not speak by conjecture. It is not alone that the voices of statesmen and of newspapers reach me, and that the voices of foolish and intemperate agitators do not reach me at all. Through many, many channels I have been made aware what the plain, struggling, workaday folk are thinking, upon whom the chief terror and suffering of this tragic war fall. They are looking to the great, powerful, famous democracy of the West to lead them to the new day for which they have so long waited; and they think, in their logical simplicity, that democracy means that women shall play their part in affairs alongside men and upon an equal footing with them.

If we reject measures like this, in ignorant defiance of what a new age has brought forth, of what they have seen but we have not, they will cease to believe in us; they will cease to follow or to trust us. They have seen their own governments accept this interpretation of democracy—seen old governments like that of Great Britain, which did not profess to be democratic, promise readily and as of course this justice to women, though they had before refused it; the strange revelations of this war having made many things new and plain to governments as well as to peoples.

Are we alone to refuse to learn the lesson? Are we alone to ask and take the utmost that our women can give—service and sacrifice of every kind—and still say we do not see what title that gives them to stand by our side in the guidance of the affairs of their nation and ours? We have made partners of the women in this war. Shall we admit them only to a partnership of suffering and sacrifice and toil and not to a partnership of privilege and right? This war could not have been fought, either by the other nations engaged or by America, if it had not been for the services of the women—services rendered in every sphere—not merely in the fields of efforts in which we have been accustomed to see them work but wherever men have worked and upon the very skirts and edges of the battle itself.

We shall not only be distrusted, but shall deserve to be distrusted if we do not enfranchise women with the fullest possible enfranchisement, as it is now certain that the other great free nations will enfranchise them. We cannot isolate our thought or action in such a matter from the thought of the rest of the world. We must either conform or deliberately reject what they approve and resign the leadership of liberal minds to others.

The women of America are too intelligent and too devoted to be slackers whether you give or withhold this thing that is mere justice; but I know the magic it will work in their thoughts and spirits if you give it to them. I propose it as I would propose to admit soldiers to the suffrage—the men fighting in the field of our liberties of the world—were they excluded.

The tasks of the women lie at the very heart of the war and I know how much stronger that heart will beat if you do this just thing and show our women that you trust them as much as you in fact and of necessity depend upon them. . . .

ALICE PAUL (ESSAY DATE 1924)

SOURCE: Paul, Alice. "The Woman's Party and the Minimum Wage for Women." In *Party Papers: 1913-1974*. Glen Rock: Microfilming Corporation of America, 1978.

In the following excerpt, Paul clarifies the Woman's Party position on minimum wage laws as applied to women.

The Woman's Party takes no stand upon minimum wage legislation, except that it stands for the principle that wage legislation, if enacted, should be upon a non-sex basis, as is already the case in various foreign countries.

The Woman's Party opposes a sex basis for a minimum wage law, because it believes that establishing minimum wage laws which apply to women but not to men, gives recognition to the idea that women are a class apart in industry who can only enter the industrial field by permission of the government and under various restrictions laid down by the government.

The Woman's Party contends that there is no more reason for a minimum wage law applying to women only, than for a minimum wage law applying to one particular race or one particularly creed.

That this point of view is gradually coming to be accepted is evidenced by the latest opinion of the United States Supreme Court on this subject. The Supreme Court, in discussing the minimum wage law for women in the District of Columbia, said in 1923:

> We can not accept the doctrine that women of mature age, sui juris, require or may be subjected to restrictions upon their liberty of contract which could not lawfully be imposed in the case of men under similar circumstances. To do so would be to ignore all the implications to be drawn from the present-day trend of legislation, as well as that of common thought and usage, by which woman is accorded emancipation, from the old doctrine that she must be given special protection or be subjected to special restraint in her contractual and civil relationship.
>
> (*Adkins v. The Children's Hospital*, 261, U.S. 525, 1923)

The courts are among the last places to reflect changes in popular opinion. When one finds the Supreme Court stating that women should be "accorded emancipation from the old doctrine that she must be given special [protection] or be subjected to special restraint in her contractual and civil relationship," one feels that the demand of the modern woman for Equal Rights with men in industry is at last beginning to be heard.

ON THE SUBJECT OF...

ALICE PAUL (1885-1977)

Alice Paul was born in 1885 in Moorstown, New Jersey, into a Quaker family that ardently believed in women's suffrage. Paul earned a B.S. at Swarthmore College in 1905, and an M.A. at the University of Pennsylvania in 1907. She traveled to England on a fellowship, became involved in the British suffrage movement, and met fellow American suffragist Lucy Burns, with whom she worked throughout the 1910s. Like many British suffragettes, Burns and Paul were arrested numerous times and participated in several hunger strikes in England. Paul returned to the United States in 1910, completed her Ph.D. at the University of Pennsylvania in 1912, and began her work for National American Woman Suffrage Association (NAWSA). After a disagreement on strategy with NAWSA leaders, Paul and Burns founded the Congressional Union of the NAWSA in 1913, which became an independent organization the following year. Paul founded the National Woman's Party (NWP) in 1916. In 1917 the NWP became the first group in U.S. history to picket in front of the White House; the picketers were arrested and incarcerated. Paul led the women in a hunger strike; many were brutally force-fed, including Paul. When news of the suffragists' mistreatment was published in newspapers, the White House bowed to public pressure, and they were released.

Paul wrote the Equal Rights Amendment (ERA) in 1923 and saw it introduced in Congress for the first time in December of that year. In the 1930s, Paul chaired the nationality committee of the Inter-American Commission of Women, served on the executive committee of Equal Rights International, and was chair of the World Women's Party in Geneva. She returned to the United States in 1941. Paul was a visible and vocal activist for women's equality and against the Vietnam War during the 1960s, and was instrumental in the placement of a passage on gender equality in the preamble of the United Nations Charter. She continued to lobby for the ERA until disabled by a stroke in 1974.

The modern woman wants "Equal Rights" with her male competitor in earning her living. She wants nothing more and nothing less.

OVERVIEWS

ELAINE SHOWALTER (ESSAY DATE 1977)

SOURCE: Showalter, Elaine. "Women Writers and the Suffrage Movement." In *A Literature of Their Own: British Women Novelists from Brontë to Lessing*, pp. 216-39. Princeton, N.J.: Princeton University Press, 1977.

In the following essay, Showalter explores the response of British women writers to the suffrage movement, noting that the struggle for votes did not seem to have a generally positive influence on writers, stimulating guilt, hostility, and class-based criticism instead.

The lyrical and diffuse feminist protest literature of the 1890s became political in the hands of the suffragettes. Most Victorian women novelists had dissociated themselves from the women's suffrage movement, which had its theoretical origins as far back as Mary Wollstonecraft's *Vindication of the Rights of Women* (1792) and its formal English organization in Manchester in 1865. The strategy of public anti-feminism came partly from women writers' reluctance to take on the extra burden of this huge battle and partly from their own sense of being superior and exceptional. In an early article on "The Enfranchisement of Women" (1851), Harriet Taylor had attacked women novelists for being "anxious to earn pardon and toleration" from men by pretending to be content with their lot: "The literary class of women, especially in England, are ostentatious in disdaining the desire for equality or citizenship, and proclaiming their complete satisfaction with the place which society assigns to them."[1] Charlotte Brontë, who thought it sensible not to brood on evils beyond repair, and Mrs. Gaskell, who believed that women should fight for others but not for themselves, were offended by Taylor's innuendoes. George Eliot and Elizabeth Barrett Browning approved of feminism in theory, but did not think that Victorian women were ready to assume the responsibilities of political equality. Browning believed that, "considering men and women in the mass, there *is* an *inequality* of intellect."[2] Charlotte Yonge, Elizabeth Linton, Dinah Craik, Christina Rossetti, and Margaret Oliphant, among the feminine writers, were vehemently opposed to what Oliphant called "the mad notion of the franchise for women."[3]

There were women writers who supported the suffrage idea from the first. In 1866 a petition requesting the franchise was signed by 1,500 women; John Stuart Mill presented it in their behalf to the House of Commons. Barbara Bodichon, Jessie Boucherett, Rosamond Hill, and Elizabeth Garrett were the authors of the petition, and the women writers who signed it included Amelia Edwards, Matilda Bethem-Edwards, Harriet Martineau, Annie Keary, and Anna Swanwick. The names of the greatest women of the day—George Eliot and Florence Nightingale—were conspicuously absent. Both had refused to participate, Eliot on the grounds that woman's harder lot should be "the basis for a sublimer resignation in woman and a more regenerating tenderness in men,"[4] Nightingale on the grounds that "there are evils which press more hardly on women than the want of the suffrage."[5]

In 1889 a number of prominent women and wives of prominent men, alarmed at the radicalism of the feminists, signed "An Appeal Against Female Suffrage," which was published in the *Nineteenth Century*. Mrs. Leslie Stephen, Mrs. Walter Bagehot, Mrs. Matthew Arnold, Mrs. Humphry Ward, Christina Rossetti, Elizabeth Linton, and Beatrice Potter joined in asserting that the limits of the emancipation process had been reached. Later Beatrice Potter—who had become Mrs. Webb—recanted; her explanation of her earlier motives probably speaks for other women as well: "At the root of my anti-feminism lay the fact that I had never myself suffered the disabilities assumed to arise from my sex."[6]

From about 1905 to 1914 a new militancy in the suffrage movement created a climate in which excuses of the sublimity of suffering, the existence of other problems, or the class privileges of a female elite no longer sufficed. Women writers could not continue to ignore the issues or to remain neutral. Under the charismatic leadership of the Pankhursts, the suffrage campaign became an integral part of the female consciousness. On both sides of the issue, women produced an enormous quantity of writing, from political pamphlets to novels. Relatively little of this work is distinguished as fiction, but it is of immense interest historically; it provided the link between the ambivalent altruism of the feminists and the self-contained theories of the postwar female aesthetic.

Elizabeth Robins became the president of the Women Writers Suffrage League in 1908. In Robins the suffragettes had one of their most versatile and vigorous crusaders. Like Olive Schreiner and Sarah Grand, she had a dazzling personality that attracted disciples, men as well as women.[7] Under the pseudonym of "C. E. Raimond" she had written several novels, including *George Mandeville's Husband* (1894); one novel, *The Magnetic North* (1894), became a best seller. Robins' play, *Votes for Women* (1907), which she later made into a novel, was the most influential piece of literary propaganda to come out of the suffrage movement.

The Women Writers Suffrage League was the brainchild of two young journalists, Cecily Hamilton and Bessie Hatton; they founded it in 1908 as an auxiliary of the National Union of Women's Suffrage Societies, with the object of obtaining "the Parliamentary Franchise for women on the same terms as it is, or may be, granted to men." In this endeavor the talents of writers were of particular use. Other auxiliaries committed their specific skills to the goals of the campaign; the actresses' league, for example, came to make up and disguise the W.S.P.U. leadership in their hideouts from the police.[8] The W.W.S.L. prospectus stated that:

> Its methods are the methods proper to writers—the use of the pen. The qualification for membership is the publication or production of a book, article, story, poem, or play, for which the author has received payment, and a subscription of 2s6d to be paid annually. . . . Women writers are urged to join the League. A body of writers working for a common cause cannot fail to influence public opinion.[9]

League members were expected to send frequent letters to newspapers, to contribute to suffrage periodicals, and to write essays, stories, and plays dramatizing the demand for the vote. On the whole they did not engage in militant confrontations, but Elizabeth Robins and Beatrice Harraden, close advisors of the Pankhursts, frequently attended planning and fund-raising meetings. Another enthusiastic member, Violet Hunt, recalled selling tracts on Kensington High Street with May Sinclair and futilely attempting to get Henry James to sign a suffrage petition. Like most of the women writers, Violet Hunt was less than eager to participate in the large protest marches that led to jail terms, hunger strikes, and the horrors of forcible feeding. She was excused by the Pankhursts on the grounds that she had to support an invalid mother, that staple furniture of the woman writer's home: "So my nose remains its own shape, not squashed against the flank of a horse—voted by Miss Evelyn Sharp as the safest place of all when the mounted police were turned out to disperse us."[10]

Nonetheless, the women writers were a conspicuous part of the campaign. In the great

ON THE SUBJECT OF...

THE PANKHURSTS

Emmeline Pankhurst was born in Manchester in 1858 and attended suffrage meetings with her mother from the age of fourteen. In 1878 she met Richard Pankhurst; they married in 1879 and had five children, including daughters Christabel (born in 1880) and Sylvia (born in 1882). The family moved to London in 1885, and their home became a social center for Fabians, anarchists, and free-thinkers. The Pankhursts returned to Manchester and joined the Independent Labour Party (ILP) in 1893; Richard Pankhurst died in 1898. Sylvia studied art in Venice, while Christabel became involved in the National Union of Women's Suffrage Societies. On returning home from Venice, Sylvia was asked to decorate an ILP hall in memory of her father. When the newly decorated hall opened, the Pankhursts were shocked to learn that women were to be denied admission. In 1903 Emmeline and Christabel founded the Women's Social and Political Union (WSPU); in 1905 Christabel and a fellow suffragette disrupted Winston Churchill's speech at Manchester's Free Trade Hall to ask whether the Liberal Party, if it came to power, would support women's suffrage. The two women were ejected from the meeting and arrested outside when Christabel attempted to make a pro-suffrage speech. Such militant tactics intensified from 1908 until 1912, when they escalated to attacks on property and arson and the leaders of the WSPU were arrested on charges of conspiracy. Christabel escaped arrest by fleeing to Paris, continuing to direct the WSPU campaign and editing *The Suffragette* for the next two years. Sylvia became estranged from her mother and sister when her support of socialist and working-class concerns clashed with Emmeline and Christabel's belief that supporting such causes would impede progress toward women's suffrage. In 1914, the year the WSPU directed all of its energies toward the war effort, Sylvia broke with the WSPU, cofounded the Women's Peace Army with Charlotte Despard, and attended the International Congress of Women for Peace at the Hague. Emmeline died in 1928; the last time that Christabel and Sylvia met was at their mother's grave.

demonstration of June 1910, over a hundred women writers marched behind the "scrivener's banner" with Olive Schreiner, Sarah Grand, Gertrude Warden, Alice Meynell, May Sinclair, Flora Annie Steel, Mrs. Israel Zangwill, Mrs. Havelock Ellis, and Evelyn Sharp. For several years they, and their counterparts in the Men's Suffrage League and the Fabian Society, kept up a steady stream of commentary on the question of the vote and the subjection of women. There were fervent novels, like G. Colmore's *Suffragette Sally* (c. 1911) and Charlotte Despard's and Mabel Collins's *Outlawed: A Novel on the Woman Suffrage Question* (1908); short stories, like Evelyn Sharp's "Rebel Women" (c. 1912); and collections of poems, like Elizabeth Gibson's *From the Wilderness* (1910). Plays with a suffrage theme became popular, not only at regional and London meetings of the societies, but also in the West End. Cicely Hamilton wrote several such plays; her comedy about a women's general strike, *How the Vote Was Won,* had its debut April 13, 1909, at the Royalty Theatre; *A Pageant of Great Women,* a capsule history of artists, rulers, saints, and warriors that starred Ellen Terry, opened at the Scala Theatre in November 1909. Beatrice Harraden's skit *Lady Geraldine's Speech* and Bessie Hatton's more emotional *Before Sunrise,* on the familiar feminist theme of the girl forced to marry a syphilitic roué, were other well-known W.W.S.L. productions.

Of all the suffrage plays, Elizabeth Robins' *Votes for Women* (re-titled *The Convert* as a novel) excited the most comment. Its plot, which was the same in the play and the novel, was melodramatic but enthralling. Against a detailed and realistic background of suffragette activism, Robins presented the struggle between a militant woman, Vida Levering, and her former lover, Geoffrey Stoner, now an M. P. In the past the heroine had been forced to have an abortion because her lover dared not face marrying her. When he falls in love with a more aristocratic young girl, his magnetic and persuasive ex-mistress blackmails him into backing the suffrage bill with the threat of seducing his eager fiancée into the woman's movement. These motives and tactics were not those of the W.S.P.U., but in representing the struggle for the vote as a sexual combat between two individuals Robins was expressing the underlying anxieties and emotions of many of her contemporaries. Samuel Hynes, one of the few scholars to write about Elizabeth Robins, says that the tone of *Votes for Women,* "is not that of a debate but of a bitter, deep-felt, intimate quarrel, like a husband and wife on the brink of divorce. When the standard cases of suffering women are brought up—the ruined maids, the Piccadilly whores, the tramp women, the starving working mothers—they are involved in order that their sufferings may be laid to one cause, the sexual viciousness of men. The sex war has begun, and the play is a dispatch from the front, fiercely partisan and militant."[11]

The play and the novel also give a very clear and reliable account of what it felt like to be a suffragette. Involved in the campaigns almost from the start, Robins made a special effort with her documentation for this work. In November 1906, she accompanied Christabel Pankhurst and Mary Gawthorpe to Huddersfield for the by-election, "to get the atmosphere," as she told Hannah Mitchell, a socialist suffragette.[12] Mrs. Mitchell later recognized bits of her own interviews with Robins in the novel. At this point Robins had completed a draft of the play, which she wrote "at white heat" in the fall of 1906; but, as she wrote to Millicent Fawcett, it seemed too controversial and partisan to be produced: "Instead of wearying out my soul by battering at their doors, I shall set to and turn the thing into a book as fast as ever I can. No trouble to get *that* accepted, however much a firebrand!"[13]

As it turned out, theater managers were more willing to risk controversy of this sort than she had suspected, and the play was produced at the Court Theatre in April 1907 with C. Aubrey Smith and Edmund Gwenn. Critics particularly admired the Trafalgar Square suffrage meeting that took up most of the second act. The *Morning Post* called it "a marvel of realism. It may advance the cause of female suffrage more than any number of meetings in Trafalgar Square could do."[14] The novel was published in October 1907. It was the first thing that Robins had written "under the pressure of a strong moral conviction,"[15] and it displayed a histrionic intensity not wholly artistic. *The Convert*, however, is a worthy contribution to the literature of the suffrage movement, particularly in its willingness to face the spectre of sex-antagonism, and it should be read in conjunction with H. G. Wells' *Ann Veronica*. Robins repeatedly suggests that the handling of the suffragettes had brutally sexual significance, a fact that should have been obvious but was repressed in contemporary historical accounts. In the later years of the suffrage campaign, forcible feeding by tubes inserted through the nostrils or down the throat became the standard procedure for treating hunger-striking suffragettes in the prisons; like the Lock Hospital examinations of the Contagious Diseases Act, the whole struggle took on the quality of a rape.

Mary Leigh described her ordeal to her solicitor in 1909: "The sensation is most painful. . . . I have to lie on the bed, pinned down by wardresses; one doctor stands up on a chair holding the funnel end at arms' length, so as to have the funnel end above the level, and then the other doctor, who is behind, forces the other end up the nostrils."[16] Although this practice disgusted most citizens, it also appealed to sadistic fantasies; one account of the suffráge campaign mentions that a rumor in the pubs was that the imprisoned suffragettes were being forcibly fed through the rectum.[17]

Without being in the least explicit, Robins' novel manages to create an atmosphere of sexual tension and anxiety. There are veiled allusions to the sexual humiliation of the suffragettes by the police: "They punish us by underhand maltreatment—of the kind most intolerable to a decent woman."[18] Among themselves, the women decide who should volunteer to endure such abuse: "The older women saw they ought to save the younger ones from having to face that sort of thing. That was how we got some of the wives and mothers."[19] Robins herself used the term "sex-antagonism"; she saw the suffrage campaign as reflecting a deep hostility between men and women that finds its characteristic expression in sexual intercourse. Because they are able to acknowledge the existence of sex-antagonism, the suffragettes are free to act; other women deplete their energy in efforts to deny their own hostilities and revulsions. When a dowager protests that she deplores the sex-antagonism of the campaign, a suffragette replies, "You're so conscious it's here you're afraid to have it mentioned."[20]

Although her main purpose was political, Robins was also interested in a new direction for women's literature. Like George Egerton, she wanted to explore the *terra incognita* of the female psyche, both for its own sake and for the sake of confounding male complacency about human nature. She referred to male complacency in a speech to the W.W.S.L. in 1907: "If I were a man, and cared to know the world I lived in, I almost think it would make me a shade uneasy—the weight of that long silence of one-half the world."[21]

Robins further understood that the suffrage campaign needed a new literature of female psychology to raise the middle-class woman's consciousness about her life. Why had such a phenomenon failed to occur previously? In *Woman's Secret* Robins linked the woman writer with other members of a dependent working class that must turn out the products demanded by the market:

> Let us remember it is only yesterday that women in any number began to write for the public prints. But in taking up the pen, what did this new recruit conceive to be her task? To proclaim her own or other women's actual thoughts and feelings? Far from it. Her task, as she naturally and even inevitably conceived it, was to imitate as nearly as possible the method, but above all the point of view, of men.

> The realization that she had access to a rich and as yet unrifled storehouse may have crossed her mind, but there were cogent reasons for concealing her knowledge. With that wariness of ages, which has come to be instinct, she contented herself with echoing the old fables, presenting to a man-governed world puppets as nearly as possible like those that had from the beginning found such favour in men's sight.

> Contrary to the popular impression, to say in print what she thinks is the last thing the woman-novelist or journalist is so rash as to attempt. Here even more than elsewhere (unless she is reckless) she must wear the aspect that shall have the best chance of pleasing her brothers. Her publishers are not women.[22]

Cicely Hamilton suggested in a fascinating feminist polemic called *Marriage as a Trade* that women's psychological conditioning and experience were so specialized that, while superficially imitative, they were actually rebelling against their training by writing at all: "Any woman who has attained to even a small measure of success in literature or art has done so by discarding, consciously or unconsciously, the traditions in which she was reared, by turning her back upon the conventional ideas of dependence that were held up for her admiration in her youth." Hamilton also explored the theory that women writers viewed "romance" from an economic perspective, so that their love stories were not frivolous fantasies, but accounts of female survival: "To a woman, a woman in love is not only a woman swayed by emotion, but a human being engaged in carving for herself a career or securing for herself a means of livelihood. Her interest in a love story is, therefore, much more complex than a man's interest therein, and the appreciation which she brings to it is of a very different quality."[23] Hamilton's ideas were on the brink of a feminist criticism, but she bogged down in her efforts to connect women's literature to the specific goal of the vote.

Meanwhile the members of the Anti-Suffrage League, called Antis, were busily proclaiming their view of the world; they also had writers on their side. It was true, as Janet Courtney ruefully admitted afterward, that the Antis inevitably attracted "all the ultra-feminine and the ladylike incompetents,"[24] so that their propaganda was not as efficiently circulated, or as persuasively written, as that of the suffragettes. Some women writers, like "John Oliver Hobbes" (Mrs. Craigie), emulated George Eliot's majestic reserve and continued to see themselves as exceptions to the general inferiority of women: "I have no confidence in the honour of the average woman or her brains. The really distinguished women have been trained and influenced by men, and a man-hater I distrust and detest—she has the worst qualities of both sexes invariably. The great women Saints, the great Queens . . . the women writers,—Eliot, Sand, Brontë, Mrs. Browning, Christina Rossetti,—were all trained by men: they all liked men and preferred them infinitely before women."[25] Marie Corelli, who had made a career of portraying *femmes fatales,* saw in grace and beauty, and wiles and seduction, a truer and more lasting source of power than the vote. In her 1906 pamphlet for the Antis, "Woman, or—Suffragette?" she described her own macabre version of female activism: "The clever woman sits at home, and like a meadow spider spreads a pretty web of rose and gold, spangled with diamond dew. Flies—or men—fumble in by scores,—and she holds them all prisoners at her pleasure with a silken strand fine as a hair." The decorative imagery of gold, diamonds, and silk does little to conceal the very unpleasant central metaphor of the female spider. In fact, Marie Corelli had a profound New Womanish faith in female dominance, and saw the proper relation of the sexes as that of goddess and worshiper. In 1905 she declared that "Woman must learn the chief lesson of successful progress, which is not to copy Man, but to carefully preserve her beautiful Unlikeness to him in every possible way so that, while asserting and gaining intellectual equality with him, she shall gradually arrive at such ascendancy as to prove herself ever the finer and the nobler Creature."[26]

It can reasonably be argued that the Antis cherished a more romantic fantasy of the evolutionary advantages of femininity than did the suffragettes, and, despite their political differences, shared the intellectual tradition of the feminists. One has to wonder how genuinely Mrs. Craigie despised man-haters, when she felt it "impossible not to notice the inferiority of the English males in nearly every class. I am struck by it as I watch the Bank Holiday crowds. Pretty-looking, refined girls with common, sickly, feeble men. If the men were strong, one could stand their roughness. But they are inane."[27]

Mrs. Humphry Ward, who had worked for women's higher education and for social reform, was appalled by what seemed the selfish individualism of the new campaign, and she became the first president of the Anti-Suffrage League in 1908. In the tradition of Mrs. Gaskell, "she felt it to be the duty of all educated women to work themselves to the bone for the uplifting of women and children less fortunate than themselves, and so to repay their debt to the community; but clamour for their own rights was a different thing; ugly in itself, and likely to lead, in her opinion, to a sex-war of very dubious outcome."[28] Ward's self-sacrificing "feminine" position, which was appropriate in women novelists of Gaskell's generation, was awkwardly outdated in the twentieth century. Ward was sixteen years older than Elizabeth Robins, and as her insistence on writing under her married name suggests, her strongest identification came from her role as wife and mother. She was appalled by the demands of the suffragettes for the personal freedom that the vote symbolized:

> So women everywhere—many women at any rate—were turning undiscriminately against the old bonds, the old yokes, affections, servitudes, demanding "self-realization," freedom for the individuality and personal will; rebelling against motherhood and lifelong marriage; clamouring for easy divorce and denouncing their own fathers, brothers, and husbands as either tyrants or fools; casting away the old props and veils; determined, apparently, to know everything, however ugly, and to say everything, however outrageous.[29]

Ward herself was a regal woman who "played the public personage to perfection; it came quite naturally to her."[30] Other women writers reacted vehemently against her pretensions and her arrogance. In 1887, the Irish novelist May Hartley wrote angrily to Macmillan to complain about Mrs. Ward's having reviewed one of her books: "She condescends to allow jealousy and spite *according to my informants* to bias her judgments of other *women* writers." The same informants had told Mrs. Hartley that Mrs. Ward's consistent unfairness to women writers had caused her name to be struck from the reviewers list of the *Times*.[31] Whether or not this rumor was true, Mrs. Ward was a difficult and intimidating person, whose own warmth and feminine sympathy were held in careful check.

Yet Ward had absorbed many of the attitudes and prejudices of the feminists. Even in her anti-suffrage novel *Delia Blanchflower* (1914), her concern for women makes itself felt. One of her male observers meditates on his "profound pity" for women's "sorrows and burdens," for "their physical weakness, for their passive role in life." Ward did not favor passivity; herself an indefatigable public servant, she shared with women of an older generation, like Florence Nightingale and Dinah Craik, a desire to see women's maternal energies directed outward, and she believed in the beneficent effects of altruistic sisterhood. Painfully and personally aware of the deficiencies of women's education, she devoted the early years of her marriage to raising funds for a women's college at Oxford. These were the acceptable "feminist" activities of a "feminine" woman writer.

More significantly, the relationships between women in her books, "the tender and adoring friendship of women for women," reflect the intense bonds of the female subculture. Vineta Colby insists that these intimate friendships, which "modern readers would immediately designate as lesbian," are intended by Ward as "decorous outlets for her characters' passions . . . not only proper, but even poetic and elevating."[32] It is foolish to see the female friendships as perverted or unnatural, but they are also more than decorative. Ward's most powerful feelings are expressed in them. Bonds of loyalty, empathy, charity, and love between women are her answer to female oppression. Ward was also capable of a fierce response to any overtly sexual slurs. In 1913, when Dr. Almroth Wright published a notorious letter in the *Times* pronouncing suffrage militance a disease related to menopause and digressing on the ever-present danger of female "physiological emergencies," Ward (who was sixty-two) was as outraged as any suffragette. In her reply, she repudiated "for myself, and, I have no doubt whatever, for thousands of men and women who feel with me on the suffrage controversy, all connection with the bitter and unseemly violence which that letter displays."[33]

Ward shared with the suffragettes, and particularly with Mrs. Pankhurst, a sense that women were united by the terrible and holy suffering of childbirth. This shared experience obliterated class distinctions and brought all women down to the lowest common denominator of the body. Mrs. Pankhurst had been radicalized by her early experiences as Registrar of Births and Deaths in Manchester; Ward was profoundly stirred and disturbed by the pain of her own three pregnan-

ON THE SUBJECT OF...

REBECCA WEST (1892-1983)

Rebecca West was the pseudonym of Cicily Isabel Fairfield, born in London in 1892. As a student Royal Academy of Dramatic Art in London, Fairfield played the role of Rebecca West in Ibsen's *Romersholm,* and published her first article under this pen-name in *The Freewoman,* a feminist weekly, in February, 1912. West continued writing for *The Free-woman,* and attracted the attention of a number of prominent writers, among them H. G. Wells, who was struck by her 1912 review of his novel *Marriage.* This marked the beginning of a ten-year relationship between Wells and West—an affair that has tended to eclipse West's own success. It was as a book reviewer and journalist that she initially established her reputation, writing for a growing number of publications, including *The Freewoman, The New Freewoman, Clarion,* and *New Statesman* in Britain, and the *New York Herald Tribune* and *Vanity Fair* in the United States. Many of West's early articles were written in support of the women's suffrage movement. In addition to her journalistic output, West authored several works of fiction, including *The Return of the Soldier* (1918), which treats World War I from the perspective of the women awaiting the return of their loved ones. West received praise and wide attention for *Black Lamb and Grey Falcon* (1942), a 2-volume nonfiction work on Serbia and Yugoslavia that West had begun in the mid-1930s as a travel book assignment. West was present at the Nuremberg trials following World War II, and her reports on the proceedings, originally published in the *New Yorker,* were collected, along with West's accounts of other post-war trials in *The Meaning of Treason* (1949) and *A Train of Powder* (1955).

cies and deliveries. Clara Duff, after her first child was born, confessed to Ward: "I was so terribly upset by the horrors I had gone through I never could bear to see a woman in the street who was going to have a baby. I used to go home and cry!

Mrs. Humphry Ward's eyes filled with tears and she took hold of my hand and said, 'Oh, my dear, did you feel like that? I did too, and I thought it was morbid and no one else would ever understand.'"[34]

Rather than confronting the sources and the causes of women's suffering in the political and sexual systems, as the feminists did, Ward chose to channel her feelings into the feminine networks of charitable agencies and settlement houses. Impelled by acute sympathy for women in their maternal role, she published a pamphlet on infant-feeding to distribute in the Oxford slums. In her novels, moments of feminist illumination are inevitably connected to the physical pain of childbirth or disease, and the rebellious energy that such moments inspire is rapidly reinvested in feminine altruism. Ward and her privileged heroines found in social work both an outlet for, and a sublimation of, their own inner conflicts about womanhood.

In her most famous novel, *Robert Elsmere* (1888), Ward gave a cautious but sensitive account of a postpartum depression. Catherine Elsmere confides to her husband that childbirth has been so cruelly traumatic, has brought her so abruptly to a confrontation with mortality, that she has begun to question the fundamental institutions of her life. The pain of labor

> seems to take the joy even out of our love—and the child. I feel ashamed almost that mere physical pain should have laid such hold on me—and yet I can't get away from it. It's not for myself. . . . Comparatively I had so little to bear! But I know now for the first time what physical pain may mean—and I never knew before! I lie thinking, Robert, about all creatures in pain—workmen crushed by machinery, or soldiers, or poor things in hospitals—above all of women! Oh, when I get well, how I will take care of the women here! What women must suffer even here in out-of-the way cottages—no doctor, no kind nursing, all that agony and struggle![35]

The pain of workmen and soldiers might be blamed on bosses and generals; women's "agony and struggle" too might be attributed to an oppressive system: to inadequate medical care, to religious resistance to anaesthesia, to the lack of contraception, to the sexual demands of husbands, and ultimately to God's curse on Eve. But Ward's heroine quickly modulates the enunciation of her suffering; she denies it as a personal problem and rededicates her life to good works. Her outburst is nonetheless a brief moment of authenticity in an intellectual novel of abstruse theological argument.

Published the 1st and 15th of each month.

THE NEW
FREEWOMAN

AN INDIVIDUALIST REVIEW.

No. 9   Vol. I.   WEDNESDAY, OCTOBER 15th, 1913.   Sixpence.

CONTENTS.

Editor :
DORA MARSDEN, B.A.

Title page from October 13, 1913 publication of *The New Freewoman*, a prominent women's journal.

However hostile they may be to the methods and the theories of the suffragettes, Ward's heroines are helplessly susceptible to the poverty and the pain of other women. In *The Testing of Diana Mallory* (1908), the aristocratic Diana can resist the suffragette debates of her socialist friend Marion, but not the spectacle of Marion's fatal illness, the squalor of the slums, or the sound of "the wailing of babes":

One day, after a discussion on votes for women which had taken place beside Marion's sofa, Diana, when the talkers were gone, had thrown herself on her friend.

"Dear, you can't wish it!—you can't believe it! To brutalize—unsex us!"

Marion raised herself on her elbow, and looked down the narrow cross street beneath the windows of her lodging. It was a stifling evening. The street was strewn with refuse, the odors from it filled the room. Ragged children with smeared faces were sitting or playing listlessly in the gutters. The public-house at the corner was full of animation, and women were passing in and out. Through the roar of traffic from the main street beyond a nearer sound persisted: a note of wailing—the wailing of babes.

"There are the unsexed!" said Marion panting. "Is their brutalization the price we pay for our refinement?" Then as she sank back: "Try anything—everything—to change that."[36]

While the Antis opposed militance from the right, another group of women opposed it from the left. These were the anarchistic socialists, friends of the Fabian Society, contributors to the *New Age* magazine in London and to *Liberty* in New York. The chief organ of this group was a periodical that went through three phases: the *Freewoman,* the *New Freewoman,* and the *Egoist.* All of these papers were financed by Harriet Shaw Weaver and edited by Dora Marsden, a graduate of Manchester University who had gone to jail with the W.S.P.U. in 1910. As Storm Jameson described her, Dora Marsden was "a small delicately-boned woman . . . with a subtle and powerful mind and a passion for philosophy, I believe, her only passion."[37] She was working on a book ("apparently endless," wrote Robert McAlmon) of feminist metaphysics, and her essays on Bergson, Hegel, and Nietzsche helped break the provincialism of English literary philosophy. According to McAlmon, Harriet Weaver began publishing a paper in order to circulate Miss Marsden's work.[38]

In its initial format, the *Freewoman* (1911-1913) attacked the suffragists' obsession with the vote as the means to emancipate women, and developed its own philosophy of free love and individualism. Dora Marsden wrote lengthy and increasingly theoretical editorials defining a humanist philosophy and an aesthetic credo equally applicable to men and women; from the beginning male writers were involved in the paper.

The second incarnation, the *New Freewoman,* was born on June 15, 1913, with a minimized allegiance to feminism and a more general concern for other new ideas. In her first editorial, Marsden dissociated the periodical from the suffrage campaign: "For fear of being guilty of supporting the power of another 'empty concept' we hasten to add that the term 'Woman Movement' is one which deserves to go the way of all such—freedom, liberty, and the rest—to destruction."[39] As subsequent issues made clear, the *New Freewoman* was "not for the advancement of Woman, but for the empowering of individuals, men and women."[40] As the year wore on, the writers of the *New Freewoman* indicated more and more disgust with the fanaticism of the suffragettes.

An immediate source of irritation and alienation was the publication of Christabel Pankhurst's notorious *The Great Scourge and How to End It* (1913). The great scourge was venereal disease. Pankhurst estimated that 75 to 80 percent of all men were infected by gonorrhea; but, more basically, she argued that male lust lay at the root of female oppression:

> One of the chief objects of the book is to enlighten women as to the true reason where there is opposition to giving them the vote. That reason is sexual vice.
>
> The opponents of votes for women know that women, when they are politically free, and economically strong, will not be purchasable for the base uses of vice.[41]

In *The Great Scourge,* Pankhurst was simply restating feminist ideas that had been popularized in the 1890s by Sarah Grand and George Egerton. Her estimates of the extent of male vice were grotesquely exaggerated, but popular health manuals and medical texts at the turn of the century were equally frightening.[42] The timing of her pamphlet, however, was wrong. Coming in 1913, it seemed maidenly and hysterical to a generation that had seen the postimpressionists and read *The Way of All Flesh.*

Rebecca West, then a daring young journalist at the beginning of her career, responded with indignation at Pankhurst's prudery, seeing it as a step backward: "There was a long and desperate struggle before it became possible for women to write candidly on subjects such as these. That this power should be used to express views that would be old-fashioned . . . in the pastor of a Little Bethel is a matter for scalding tears."[43] Most suffragettes, however, could not imagine that sexual revolution would take the form of female license rather than male chastity. In this the *New Freewoman* was exceptional. In its single year of existence, it published some of the frankest material on sexuality to appear for several decades. In specific response to the prudery of the militant suffragists, Dora Marsden ran a series of articles suggesting a prostitutes' guild, like a labor union; she also published an extraordinary piece on female frigidity, which she believed to be an acquired characteristic of repression and economic dependence.

> If women are not under-sexed, their sexual apathy is beautifully simulated. It is conceivable that this simulation may exist up to the point of yielding to man, but can it exist through the sexual act? Proof must, necessarily, be largely in regard of personal experiences, and such a record might not, in good taste, be produced; but what else can be inferred when widely experienced male sexual varietists almost unanimously concur in the statement that only a small proportion of the women with whom they have been associated (not prostitutes) experience a normal sexual orgasm, and that the sphincter of the vagina is rarely active?[44]

Obviously Dora Marsden was not undersexed, and, although she offered space in the periodical for the discussion of such trendy subjects as free love, Neo-Malthusianism, vegetarianism, and spiritualism, she continued to consider these questions primarily from a feminist viewpoint, albeit a very radical one. For example, Edward Carpenter, as typical a progressive cult figure as could be found, wrote an article on "The Status of Women in Early Greek Times" (August 1) in which he argued that homosexuals, or Uranians, as he called them, were more egalitarian to women than heterosexual men. The next month Marsden coolly refuted him: "There is an undeniable tendency in many homosexuals to look upon woman as an inferior. . . . It is hardly to be presumed . . . that the men who entertain this instinctive aversion to women are absolutely uninfluenced by it when summoned by women to support their demand for independence."[45]

Over the year, however, impatience with the suffragettes, and pressure from such male contributors as Ezra Pound and John Gould Fletcher to print imagist poetry and translations from French and Japanese writers, took the *New Freewoman* farther and farther away from feminist questions. In the issue of December 15, Marsden announced that henceforth the paper would be called the *Egoist*. A letter from five men suggesting that the old title led to confusion with "organs devoted solely to the advocacy of an unimportant reform in an obsolete political institution," and Marsden's own feeling that the time for rhetoric was past, forced the decision. "The time has arrived," she wrote "when mentally-honest women feel that they have no use for the springing-board of large promises of powers redeemable in a distant future. . . . They know that their works can give evidence now of whatever quality they are capable of giving them."

Egoism and feminism, however, were strange bedfellows. In the *Egoist*'s five years of publication (1914-1919), male writers, including Pound, Eliot, and Ford Madox Ford, dominated its pages. In June 1914 Dora Marsden resigned her editorship to Harriet Weaver, who made the journal famous by publishing *Portrait of the Artist as a Young Man* and extracts from *Ulysses*. While the literary value of the *Egoist* appreciated over the years, its feminist potential declined. Leonard and Virginia Woolf both recorded their shock upon making the acquaintance of Miss Weaver, "a very mild blue-eyed advanced spinster," not at all what the "editress of the *Egoist* ought to be. . . . Her neat mauve suit fitted both body and soul; her grey gloves laid straight by her plate symbolised domestic rectitude; her table manners were those of a well-bred hen."[46]

On balance, the suffrage movement was not a happy stimulus to women writers. If they participated in its militant phase, they did get some sense of effective solidarity, but not as writers. Despite Elizabeth Robins' remarks, no real manifesto of female literature was produced; the Women Writers Suffrage League remained a political and, in many ways, a social organization. Alice Meynell, who opposed militance, nonetheless enjoyed her Women Writers dinners and the bustle of the marches. Several of the most committed activists felt frightened by the demanding fanaticism of the Pankhursts and by the dimension of the sacrifices they were asked to make for the Cause. Evelyn Sharp meant to pay the suffragettes a compliment when she had a male character in one of her short stories describe them as soldiers: "'This is the kind of thing you get on a bigger scale in war,' he said, in a half-jesting tone, as if afraid of seeming serious. 'Same mud and slush, same grit, same cowardice, same stupidity and beastliness all around. . . . The women here are fighting for something big; that's the only difference.'"[47] Sharp does not make clear who is being stupid and beastly, but the warlike qualities

of the W.S.P.U. were morally ambiguous. The Pankhursts maintained an internal military discipline, as well as a battle with the government; they awarded medals for valor and demanded unquestioning obedience.

Women writers respected the militants for their courage, but at the same time they expressed a combination of guilt and hostility toward the Pankhursts, simultaneously confessing their own lack of commitment and attacking the Pankhursts as being bullies and neurotics. Beatrice Harraden confided to Elizabeth Robins that she was glad when Mrs. Pankhurst thought kindly of her: "I always feel I've failed her by not giving up absolutely everything for the cause."[48] Stella Benson, herself a suffragette, caricatured movement despotism as

> The Chief Militant Suffragette, who believed that she held feminism in the hollow of her hand. . . . She was familiar with the knack of wringing sacrifices from other people. She was a little lady in a minor key, pale and plaintive, with short hair like spun sand. She dressed as nearly as possible like a man, and affected an eyeglass. She probably thought that in doing this she had sacrificed enough for the cause of women. She had safely found a husband before she cut her hair. I suppose she had sent more women to prison than any one magistrate in London, but she had never been in prison herself.[49]

Virginia Woolf, who once addressed some envelopes for the Adult Suffrage League, always depicted suffragists as incomplete and marginal people, seeking in the process and violence of the movement a passion that was lacking in their own lives. She described such a personality least sympathetically in Miss Kilman, the repressed governess in *Mrs. Dalloway,* and most sympathetically in Mary Datchet, the feminist in *Night and Day* who fully comprehends the compensatory nature of her life's work:

> She had entered in the army, and was a volunteer no longer. She had renounced something, and was now—how could she express it?—not quite "in the running" for life. She had always known that Mr. Clacton and Miss Seal were not in the running, and across the gulf that separated them she had seen them in the guise of shadow people, flitting in and out of the ranks of the living—eccentrics, undeveloped human beings, from whose substance some essential part had been cut away.[50]

There was also a strong class-element in the response of women writers to the suffrage movement, as Virginia Woolf's writing makes salient. Besides having other unfortunate qualities, Miss Kilman perspires and wears unsuitable clothing and obtrudes her poverty. In joining the movement, women writers had to abandon class distinctions, the privileges of being ladies. In Mrs. Humphry Ward's description of a suffrage society called "The Daughters of Revolt," a dressmaker and a farmer's daughter are included; the prospective companionship of the vulgar and the uncouth could frighten women back to their drawing-rooms.

In short, women writers found themselves confronted through the suffrage movement by a number of challenges and threats: by the spectre of violence, by the ruthlessness of female authoritarianism, by the elimination of class boundaries, by a politics of action rather than influence, by collectivism, and by the loss of the secure privacy in which they had been cultivating their "special moral qualities." The shift was too abrupt to be liberating, and in a reaction against it many women writers of this generation seem to have retreated from social involvement into a leisurely examination of the sensibility, into the cultivation of a beautiful womanly Unlikeness.

In *The Tree of Heaven* (1917), May Sinclair takes her heroine from a suffrage demonstration, to Holloway Gaol, and finally to a welcoming banquet for released prisoners, at which the Women's Marseillaise is sung: "The singing had threatened her when it began; so that she felt again her old terror of the collective soul. Its massed emotion threatened her. She longed for her white-washed prison cell, for its hardness, its nakedness, its quiet, its visionary peace."[51] Inside that cell, women could preserve the illusion of specialness, of being different. Outside it, they encountered the complexity of being merely human. It is no wonder that they sometimes yearned to go back.

Notes

1. *Westminster Review* LV: 310.

2. Alethea Hayter, *Mrs. Browning*, New York, 1963, p. 183.

3. *Autobiography and Letters of Mrs. M. O. W. Oliphant*, ed. Mrs. Harry Cogshill, New York, 1899, p. 211.

4. Gordon S. Haight, *George Eliot: A Biography*, New York, 1968, p. 396.

5. Cecil Woodham-Smith, *Florence Nightingale*, New York, 1951, p. 311.

6. *My Apprenticeship*, London, 1971, p. 354.

7. For an account of her charm in her old age, see "Profile of Leon Edel," *New Yorker* (March 13, 1971): 54.

8. See Antonia Raeburn, *The Militant Suffragettes*, London, 1973, for an account of the W.S.P.U. auxiliaries, and Andrew Rosen, *Rise Up, Women!* London, 1974, for a general history of the W.S.P.U.

9. Elizabeth Robins, *Way Stations*, London, 1913, p. 107.

10. *I Have This To Say: The Story of My Flurried Years*, New York, 1926, p. 7. When she asked James to sign a petition in 1909, he replied, "No, I confess, I am not eager for the *avenement* of a multitudinous and overwhelming female electorate—and don't see how any man in his senses *can* be!" (p. 52).

11. *The Edwardian Turn of Mind*, Princeton, 1968, p. 202.

12. Hannah Mitchell, *The Hard Way Up*, ed. Geoffrey Mitchell, London, 1968, p. 163.

13. Letter of November 1, 1906, in the Fawcett Library, London.

14. April 8, 1907. For other reviews see Scrapbook 10A of Newspaper Clippings 1907 at the Fawcett Library.

15. Letter to Millicent Garrett Fawcett, November 1, 1906.

16. Statement of Mary Leigh, September 22, 1909, quoted in *Shoulder to Shoulder*, ed. Midge Mackenzie, New York, 1975, pp. 128-129. See also statements by Sylvia Pankhurst (Acc. 57.70/13) and Janie Terrero ("Prison Experiences," 1912, Acc. 58.87.62) in the Museum of London.

17. Sir Harry Johnston, *Mrs. Warren's Daughter: A Story of the Woman's Movement*, New York, 1920, p. 246. Janet Arthur, a Scottish suffragette, "was subjected to the final indignity of rectal feeding" (George Dangerfield, *The Strange Death of Liberal England*, New York, 1961, p. 387). In large demonstrations suffragettes were "indecently assaulted" by plainclothes police (Raeburn, *Militant Suffragettes*, pp. 154-155).

18. Elizabeth Robins, *The Convert*, London, 1907, p. 158.

19. Ibid., p. 163.

20. Ibid., p. 238.

21. Elizabeth Robins, *Woman's Secret*, W.S.P.U. pamphlet in the collection of the Museum of London, p. 6.

22. Ibid., pp. 8-9.

23. *Marriage as a Trade*, New York, 1909, pp. 183, 196.

24. Janet Courtney, *The Women of My Time*, London, 1934, p. 174.

25. John Morgan Richards, *The Life of John Oliver Hobbes*, London, 1911, p. 326.

26. Marie Corelli, "The Advance of Women," *Free Opinions*, London, 1905, p. 184.

27. Richards, *Life of John Oliver Hobbes*, p. 325.

28. Janet Penrose Trevelyan, *The Life of Mrs. Humphry Ward*, London, 1923, p. 225.

29. *Delia Blanchflower*, quoted in Vineta Colby, *The Singular Anomaly: Women Novelists of the Nineteenth Century*, New York, 1970, p. 158.

30. Courtney, *Women of My Time*, p. 20.

31. Add. Mss. 54970, Macmillan Papers, British Museum.

32. Colby, *Singular Anomaly*, p. 122.

33. See Roger Fulford, *Votes for Women*, London, 1968, pp. 229-230.

34. Anne Fremantle, *Three-Cornered Hat*, London, 1971, p. 67.

35. *Robert Elsmere,* ed. Claude deL. Ryals, Lincoln, Nebraska, 1967, p. 265.

36. *The Testing of Diana Mallory,* New York, 1908, p. 381.

37. *Journey From the North,* I, London, 1969, p. 77.

38. See Robert McAlmon and Kay Boyle, *Being Geniuses Together,* New York, 1968, p. 82. McAlmon writes of Harriet Weaver: "When she was nineteen she was caught reading George Eliot's *Mill on the Floss* and was publicly reprimanded from the pulpit by the village minister."

39. *New Freewoman* (June 15, 1913): 5.

40. July 1, 1913, p. 25. For an account of the history of the periodical, hostile to its feminist phase, see Louis K. MacKendrick, "The *New Freewoman:* A Short Story of Literary Journalism," *English Literature in Transition* (1972): 180-188.

41. *The Great Scourge,* London, 1913, IX.

42. In their work in Manchester the Pankhursts had seen the effects of venereal disease on women. In 1914 Mrs. Pankhurst said, "The main motive behind the suffragette campaign had been her horror at the prevalence of filthy sexual disease and moral squalor" (quoted in David Mitchell, *The Fighting Pankhursts,* New York, p. 141).

43. Roger Fulford, *Votes for Women,* p. 256. Christabel Pankhurst, born in 1880, was twelve years older than Rebecca West.

44. September 15, 1913: 174.

45. September 1, 1915: 115.

46. Quoted from diaries of April 14, 1918, in Leonard Woolf, *Beginning Again,* London, 1964, p. 246. The "spinster" is Leonard's, the "editress," Virginia's.

47. "The Women at the Gate," in *Rebel Women,* London, c. 1912, p. 13.

48. Letter of September 14, 1912, in the Fales Collection, New York University Library.

49. R. Ellis Roberts, *A Portrait of Stella Benson,* London, 1939, p. 40.

50. *Night and Day,* London, 1971, ch. 20, p. 246.

51. *The Tree of Heaven,* New York, 1917, p. 225.

ELLEN CAROL DUBOIS (ESSAY DATE 1994)

SOURCE: DuBois, Ellen Carol. "Woman Suffrage around the World: Three Phases of Suffragist Internationalism." In *Suffrage and beyond: International Feminist Perspectives,* edited by Caroline Daley and Melanie Nolan, pp. 252-74. New York: New York University Press, 1994.

In the following essay, DuBois examines the international dimensions of the women's suffrage movement, commenting on the influence of the temperance movement, the development of socialism, and the rise of women's conventions, respectively.

Why Have Woman Suffrage Movements So Little History?

Even with the revival of modern feminism and women's history, woman suffrage movements have been a curiously understudied phenomenon. There are two related explanations for this lack of scholarly attention. One is the assumption that, with the exception of a few very well-known and highly dramatic cases such as England and the United States, women have been 'granted' the vote by friendly (or calculating) governments, rather than because of their own organised demand for it. Nowhere does this pre-emptive scholarly dismissal seem more pronounced than in the cases of New Zealand and Australia. Here, the movement's first historian, New Zealand progressive William Pember Reeves, observed, scarcely before the first women had returned from the polls in 1893, that chivalrous politicians granted women the vote without their having to mobilise significantly on its behalf.[1]

The claim that woman did not fight for their own political equality is closely related to another dismissive evaluation of women's enfranchisement and an even greater barrier to interested scholars. This is the very commonly made claim that the enfranchisement of women has been, on balance, a conservative development, both with respect to the forces responsible for achieving votes for women and the ultimate impact that women's votes have had on political life. This is unsubstantiated by empirical research, which has had remarkably little to contribute to our understanding of the impact of gender on voting behaviour, since men's and women's votes are only rarely counted separately. Whether or not women vote differently from men, and whether that difference is titled to the right or the left seems to vary a great deal, and to reflect not only the general political environment within which voters act but whether or not there are political factors working on women and not on men, especially when there is an active and widespread feminist movement at work.[2]

Perhaps the most remarkable thing about the claim of conservatism with respect to woman suffrage movements is that it predates, not only the actual enfranchisement of women, but even the heyday of the woman suffrage movement. The charge that women would vote more conservatively than men was an important element in the debate itself, coming both from conservatives in support of woman suffrage, and from leftists, as an argument against votes for women. During the 1875 debate over whether to include woman suffrage in the founding documents of the German Social Democratic party, opponents cited the allegedly reactionary political tendencies of women, especially their ties to the church. William Leibnicht responded that 'opponents of female suf-frage often maintain that women have no politi-cal education but there are plenty of men in the same position, and by this reasoning they ought not to be allowed to vote either. The "herd of vot-ers" which has figures at all elections did not consist of women.'[3] William Pember Reeves's curi-ous dismissal of woman suffrage activism in New Zealand and Australia might make sense in this context, reflecting some embarrassment on the part of this secular liberal over the evangelical forces behind the woman suffrage campaign and a wish to distance organised liberal women from what he regarded as the taint of its conservatism.

The general consensus as to the movement's conservatism is very widespread. Consider, for example, Richard Evans's classic survey, *The Femi-nists.*[4] Evans argues that while the demand for woman suffrage has its origins in classical liberal-ism, its achievement in the late nineteenth and early twentieth century coincided with and par-took of the decline and contraction of that tradi-tion. Led by elite and conservative 'ladies', Evans argued, the turn-of-the-century movement aban-doned its roots in universal suffrage traditions, and struck a Faustian bargain in which it accepted property restrictions in order to get the vote for privileged women. Particularly in Germany, he argues, 'The enfranchisement of women was seen both by politicians and by the suffragists them-selves, as a means of controlling society in the interests of the "table" part of the population, the middle classes.'[5]

For a while at the beginning of the women's history revival even feminists seemed to embrace their own version of the tendency to dismiss woman suffrage as a conservative development, especially with respect to issues of women's sexual and social freedom. From this perspective, the campaign for political equality appeared to be the least interesting and most narrow aspect of wom-en's efforts for self-liberation. Here the argument was that votes for women substitutes formal, legal equality for other, more radical aspects of the women's movement, for instance challenges to conservative sexual morality. Among United States historians, both Aileen Kraditor and William O'Neill set the tone for this type of argument.[6] Feminists such as Kollontai and Goldman are invoked as alternative heroines of women's eman-cipation to bourgeois suffrage leaders. Turning again to Australia and New Zealand, Pember Reeves's categorical dismissal of the role of any or-ganised women's movement in winning votes for women was replaced with a second set of interpre-

tations which focused on the woman suffrage leadership taken by the Women's Christian Tem-perance Union (WCTU) throughout New Zealand and many of the states of Australia. However, the WCTU's suffrage activism was not seen as a posi-tive force for women's emancipation, but rather as a reinforcement of the confining notions of separate spheres and women's responsibilities for morality, notions that are conservative both in terms of women's roles and larger social relations of class and power. This approach restores wom-en's agency to the suffrage story but pays the price of conceding the movement's fundamental con-servatism.[7] Is this price necessary?

I would like to offer an alternative, revisionist overview of woman suffrage movements around the world, in which I intend to stress two aspects. One is the internationalism of these movements, the co-operation among women of various na-tions, the influence that actions of women in one country have had on those in another, and the way that women's international co-operation gave them resources to combat their marginalisation in the politics of their own nations. Woman suffrage can be usefully conceptualised as an international protest movement, or perhaps more accurately several such movements. My own tendency has been to study suffragism in the context of a single country, in my case the United States, in order to demonstrate how much women's drive for politi-cal equality was shaped by, indeed part and parcel of, a particular national political history, that it cannot be understood without reference to that history.[8] Yet a national focus alone underplays the rich, international circulation of ideas, personali-ties, organisations and inspiration that sustained woman suffragism over its very long history and that in many cases has been a crucial element in the actual achievement of women's enfranchise-ment. Ian Tyrrell suggests instead a more interna-tional history (he uses the term 'transnational' so as not to suggest global harmony and equality) which takes into account, without taking for granted, the national framework of the political life from which women were excluded and which they wished to enter.[9]

The other and related aspect of my approach is to challenge the conservative hypothesis, to argue instead that woman suffrage has been, on balance, a progressive development, drawing on and adding to left-wing political forces, albeit frequently in an embattled fashion. This is an argument I have been putting forth ever since my first piece on suffragism in the US, entitled 'The radicalism of the woman suffrage movement', but here I want to reframe this claim in international terms.[10]

Most obviously, in the years of international woman suffragism's greatest strength, from 1890 through to World War I, it was influenced and spread by women associated with the Second Socialist International. However, especially inasmuch as this development took place against a substantial anti-feminist and anti-suffrage counter-tradition within international socialism, this argument need not be limited to women working within the framework of organised socialist parties. On either side (chronologically speaking) of the suffragism of the Second International, we can find the impact of the World's Women's Christian Temperance Union and the international character of the independent militant suffragettes, who had their beginnings in Britain. Such a reconceptualisation and a global survey can, not incidentally, help to expand our definition of progressive politics in this period to incorporate more women operating outside of formal (and male-dominated) left-wing environments.

This review takes place from a deliberately and self-consciously socialist-feminist perspective. A corollary to the conservative thesis is the insistence that there has historically been a fundamental antagonism between socialism and feminism. By contrast, modern socialist-feminists try to tolerate the tension between the two movements and to make of it a creative and powerful progressive politics. Describing United States women's theoretical and scholarly efforts in the 1970s to reconcile the two traditions, or at least put them on speaking terms with each other, Mary Bailey characterised the hyphen that separates the two sides of socialist-feminism as a metaphor for the unresolved tension, the creative conflicts that this wing of the modern feminist movement strives to tolerate, explore and advance. Movingly, Bailey writes, 'What intervenes in this relationship of two terms is desire, on every level. Hyphen as wish. We have heard its whisperings.'[11]

While modern socialist-feminism is uniquely self-aware, it is possible to trace such politics back into the nineteenth century, and to argue that they have consistently been a radicalising force in the movement for women's emancipation. This chapter can be read, therefore, as a contribution to the reconstruction of the socialist-feminist tradition, as part of a contest over the meaning and political direction of the contemporary women's movement. This argument can—and has—been directed to either side of the hyphen:

to the feminist audience, the emphasis is on the importance of socialist influences in our tradition; to the socialists, the message is the existence of a rich women's emancipatory vein to our history.

Women's Temperance and Woman Suffrage: The First Internationalism

The first international woman suffrage movement, much overlooked, was the World's Women's Christian Temperance Union. The WCTU, formed in the United States in 1874, began as a conventional Protestant women's organisation with a narrow moral reform focus, but soon became an amazingly ambitious, politically aggressive women's organisation. The leading figure in this transformation was Frances Willard, and one of the distinctive marks of her leadership was her brilliant work at enlisting the organisation in the fight for woman suffrage.

Willard profoundly expanded the WCTU by introducing what she called her 'do everything policy', a complex structure in which separate issues were pursued within semi autonomous 'departments', each under the authority of its own 'superintendent'. Within this framework, and fuelled by Willard's deeply political sensibilities, woman suffragism flourished. By convincing WCTU women that temperance itself was a political issue, she led her constituency to advocate woman suffrage, which had previously been taken up only by small and politically isolated advanced groups of women. Indeed, it is not too much to say that the WCTU under Willard's leadership was one of the first environments within which woman suffrage was made comprehensible and compelling to substantial numbers of women.[12]

In 1884, Willard, in conjunction with her companion Lady Henry Somerset, declared the formation of the World's Women's Christian Temperance Union, an international companion organisation to the American WCTU. The temperance movement had long been transatlantic, following British lines of international influence, and the formation of the World's WCTU had a great deal to do with Willard's deepening bonds with British temperance women. Still, what is striking about the World's WCTU is its movement in western and southern, rather than eastern and northern directions. WCTU organisers in the western United States, who were working to 'uplift' Asian women immigrants there from prostitution and opium addiction, began to see that if populations, workers and vices migrated from nation to nation, perhaps virtue and organised movements of upstanding women could do the same.[13]

The World's WCTU was spread by American organiser/missionaries. Two of the most intrepid of these missionaries to the world's women were Jessie Ackerman and Mary Leavitt, who planted the World's WCTU's first truly successful seeds in Australia and New Zealand. Leavitt's WCTU career had begun as suffrage superintendent in Massachusetts. WCTUs already existed in South Australia and New Zealand before Leavitt arrived, but what she brought with her was the broader, 'do everything' vision of the organisation that Willard had developed, and particularly the commitment to securing political equality for women. In her pioneering examination of the New Zealand woman suffrage movement, Patricia Grimshaw argues that the international links of WCTU suffragists in that country gave them considerable cachet, as well as access to the whole range of Anglo-American suffrage thought, including the advanced ideas of John Stuart Mill. In the far-flung outposts of Western civilisation, affiliation with the international women's temperance movement was a way to combat the sense of isolation on the periphery. Kate Sheppard touted the case of Wyoming, the sole American suffrage state, in her first New Zealand propaganda.[14]

One final comment about the internationalism of the woman suffrage movement in this early stage: it did not all go in one direction, carrying political authority and innovation only from the centre to the periphery. Early victories in Australia and New Zealand sent sophisticated women activists back to England and the United States, where they helped to move suffrage movements into new directions. Dora Montefiore, the mother of New South Wales suffragism, moved from Australia to England, where Sylvia Pankhurst credits her with encouraging her in the early 1900s to make her first outdoor suffrage speech.[15] Australian suffragism sent Alice Henry to the United States, where her biographer, Diane Kirkby, argues that she was one of the earliest to insist that wage-earning women must be made the centre of an expansive, modern woman suffrage movement.[16]

As suggested above, historians' recognition of the role of the WCTU in the early enfranchisement of women in Australia and New Zealand was at first accompanied by a consensus that this temperance/suffrage movement was basically conservative in thrust, in Tyrrell's words, intended to 'advance the women's culture of evangelical domesticity' rather than to move women into politics or politics in a progressive direction.[17] This judgement has begun to give way in two directions. One strategy has been to learn more and more about the diversity of women's suffrage activism in this early period. Audrey Oldfield, in her detailed study of Australian suffragism state by state, emphasises the substantial number of suffrage leaders who were secularists, not WCTU evangelicals; associated with the beginnings of the Australian Labor Party; and linked to groups of wage-earning women.[18] The emphasis here shifts from the WCTU to the larger political environment within which it was situated; woman suffragism in Australia and New Zealand flourished as part of a larger political context of expanding reform ambitions, maturing working-class and socialist movements, and new links between liberalism and state activism, in other words the emergence of what would soon be called progressivism in the US.

Alongside of this, there is another analytic strategy, which involves re-examining the political and ideological content of the WCTU itself. As Tyrrell argues, the WCTU's evangelical roots lent it a quite critical perspective on the commercial and material preoccupations of advancing capitalism. In England, temperance/suffragists and leaders of the World's WCTU were women like Margaret Bright Lucas and Hannah Whithall Smith, from families long at the cutting edge of British liberalism. In the western United States, where the WCTU was an extremely important and progressive locale for women's activism in the late 1880s, the union was a substantial source for the political upsurge of Populism. Willard herself played a significant role in the early stages of the People's party and state WCTU leaders included fiery Populist radicals like Mary Lease of Kansas, who urged her followers to 'raise less corn and more hell'. In the US, these political links were crucial to (although not always credited with) the first successes of woman suffrage. The first genuinely popular political victories of woman suffrage, in the 1890s, were in states where insurgent Populist parties were strong—Colorado, Idaho, and California, where suffrage was narrowly defeated in 1896. Colorado was the first state (as opposed to territory) in which voters authorised woman suffrage in a popular referendum; this took place the same year as women won the vote in New Zealand. The second successful voter referendum was in Idaho, the next year. There were important campaigns in Kansas (1894) and California (1896) which also reflected Populist support.

While the WCTU's class and economic politics demonstrate a significant left-leaning bent, its moralistic approach to the family and to sexuality was far more conservative. This aspect of the WCTU's moral reformism has been widely studied and needs even more examination, but here I want to observe that this sexual and familial conservatism equally characterised the socialist parties of the period. Indeed, in the United States, Mari Jo Buhle has demonstrated that the Protestant evangelical moralism of populist politics of the 1880s was crucial to the translation of socialism, which had been marginalised in German-American communities, into a genuinely American idiom; for US women, she demonstrates that the WCTU was virtually a conduit into socialism.[19] To take just one example, Ella Reeve Bloor, legendary founder of the Communist Party in the US, got her political start in the WCTU. In Australia, the WCTU had close relations with trade unionists and labour parties. Here and elsewhere, the Victorian, traditionalist perspective of moral reform movements on sex roles and the family was welcomed by socialists as a way to reinforce domestic peace in the working-class family and may have eased the way for working-class feminism.

Similar arguments can be made with respect to the issue of race. With the notable exception of New Zealand, where the woman suffrage campaign (relative to other countries) included indigenous Maori women in its scope, the WCTU's record on women of colour is mixed, to say the least. Over and over, the alleged inclusiveness of the WCTU's vision of a worldwide reform movement of politically empowered women gave way to claims or challenges about the barbarism or political incapacity of non-white peoples. On tour around England to raise international awareness of the plight of her people in the US, African American suffragist Ida B. Wells charged Frances Willard with aiding and abetting the epidemic of lynchings in the southern states by her readiness to accept the portrait of black people as fundamentally immoral.[20] In Australia, as Oldfield describes it, a superficial racial universalism quickly gave way to refusals to include Aboriginal women in the 1902 act of enfranchisement. But again, these same limitations were equally true of working-class, socialist and left-leaning political forces in the period, of which the WCTU suffragists were a part. Queensland, where the racialism of the suffragists was the most explicit and aggressive, also boasted exceptionally close ties between suffragists and the Labor Party.[21]

Cheryll Walker's work on South Africa is most revealing of this pattern. Woman suffragism, which was first brought to the Cape Colony in 1895 by the World's WCTU, was aided and supported by the rise of a South African labour party. For several decades, woman suffragists negotiated the treacherous waters of South African racial politics by taking the position that women should vote according to the same rules as men; in the Cape, this would have included Coloureds and Africans. Finally, in the 1920s, when the Labour Party enrolled in the campaign to remove Cape Africans from the voting rolls, woman suffragists easily gave in on principle and acceded to this exclusion, earning the aid of the ascendant National Party and the rapid resolution of their demands. Given what she judges to be the ultimate conservatism of these developments, Walker nonetheless comments on the fact that the movement's 'early sponsorship was from the left'.[22] Ian Tyrrell has thoughtfully explored the contradictions between the WCTU's decided commitment to Anglo-Saxon superiority and the fact that its deepest criticisms were reserved for the moral failings of British and American society. But here too, this constitutes a similarity to rather than a difference from socialism in the age of empire.

Woman Suffrage in the Second Socialist International

In the early twentieth century and overlapping with the World's WCTU, an even more openly and aggressively feminist movement began to develop within international socialism, with political equality one of its most consistent demands. The largest socialist women's movements were in Germany, the United States and Austria but there was also activity in Italy, France, Russia, all of Scandinavia, the Netherlands, Australia, Ireland, South Africa, Central and Eastern Europe, the Southern Cone of Latin America, and undoubtedly elsewhere.[23]

The figure most identified with this international socialist women's effusion was Clara Zetkin. Through the 1890s, Zetkin forged a socialist women's programme and practice within the German Social Democratic party which became the prototype for women in socialist parties around the world. There is, to take just one example, evidence of a socialist women's organisation in Argentina, the Feminist Centre, working from 1906 through to 1912 with Socialist deputy Alfredo Palacios, advocating the Second International feminist platform, including woman suffrage and special labour legislation for women.[24]

From 1907 though to 1915, the size and vigour of this worldwide socialist women's network constituted a sort of informal women's International, with annual conferences. International Women's Day, which is celebrated around the world, and Women's History Week, which American feminists now celebrate in March, are the lineal descendants of the International Proletarian Women's Day first authorised by the 1910 international socialist women's conference.

Socialist Women's Day seems to have begun in the United States in 1909, as part of the International-authorised socialist campaign for woman suffrage.[25] Zetkin picked it up within the International in 1910. The holiday was carried through the Comintern and became a solely Communist observance, until the American women's liberation movement, itself inspired by Communist women activists in the 1960s, reimported the celebration to the United States. By the late 1970s, liberal Democrats took the holiday through one more political transformation, and it became the federally mandated Women's History Week.[26]

Most accounts of these embattled socialist-feminists emphasise either their struggles with the sexism of male socialists or their challenge to middle-class women's movements, but it was really the balance they struck, always fragile and often upset, between these two political forces that determined their political environment.[27] In several of the leading parties, the tension between socialism and feminism led to open conflict between socialist women leaders themselves. Among German socialist women, for instance, Zetkin's loyalty to international socialism was counterpoised to (and balanced by) Lily Braun's greater inclination to the independent women's movement. There were similar sororal antagonisms in the French party between Elizabeth Renaud and Louise Saumoneau, and in Italy between Annas Kulisckoff and Mozzoni.[28] But backing off a bit from the continuing temptation to choose sides or to designate one position alone as correct, one can read the fierce battles between them as an expression of the dialectical situation of social feminism, the shifting and unstable but distinct and authentic political territory it occupied.

The issue of woman suffrage was at the very centre—the virtual expression of—the balance socialist women struck between the non-socialist women's movement and the male-dominated socialist left. Had they not forced their perspective forward within their parties, woman suffrage would have languished as a principle tainted by socialism but not really sustained by it. On the other hand, it is not too much to say that had it not been for the degree of autonomy socialist women were able to sustain within their parties from the mid 1890s on, and for the new classes of women to whom they brought the issue, the demand for woman suffrage probably would not have been revived and placed at the centre of a militant, mass, modern women's movement.

Zetkin first succeeded in getting the German Social Democratic Party (SPD) to adopt the explicit endorsement of political rights 'without distinction of sex' in 1891. For decades, socialist men had been thwarting suffrage petitioners by objecting that women were too reactionary to risk enfranchising. This time, Zetkin responded that the vote 'was a means to assemble the masses, to organise and educate them', and that it was precisely political organising, including working for the vote, that would 'educate' women out of whatever relative 'backwardness' they suffered.[29] Within the International, the first pro-woman suffrage resolution was passed in 1900, but particular nation parties continued to set aside demands for woman suffrage to concentrate on universal manhood suffrage. The campaign led by Zetkin, to strengthen organised socialism's commitment to woman suffrage, coincided with the first all-women international socialist conference, at Stuttgart in 1907. There the International accepted the principle that political equality for women was a non-contingent, fundamental demand which socialist parties must pursue 'strenuously'. A plank was adopted to the party's platform which insisted that 'the socialist parties of all countries have a duty to struggle energetically for the introduction of universal suffrage for women'.[30]

Women working from within socialist parties liked to argue that the bourgeois case for woman suffrage was a defence of property and individual privilege, while they demanded the vote as a weapon of working-class power and on the basis of fundamentally different presumptions. While full discussion of this issue cannot be included here, two points should be noted: first, that property qualifications on women's voting had at least as much to do with marital as class status; and that many of the leading non-socialist suffragists called for universal woman suffrage, without property restrictions.

What really distinguished socialist women's suffragism from the bourgeois variant was the link they made between women workers and political equality. The distinctively socialist argument for woman suffrage rested on the recognition that the increasingly public character of women's labour had to be matched with an equally public political role. The decidedly non-socialist Charlotte Perkins Gilman, whose historical account of women's evolution toward emancipation is indistinguishable from Engels's, was a major force in popularising the socialist approach to women's equality throughout the non-socialist women's movement in America.[31] 'The demand for woman suffrage results from the economic and social revolutions provoked by the capitalist mode of production', resolved a socialist women's conference in 1904, 'but in particular from the revolutionary change in labour and the status and consciousness of women.'[32] In the United States, England and elsewhere, such economic arguments came to be widely accepted among non-socialist suffragists, which is an indication of the degree to which socialist women led the larger suffrage movement into new territories.

Substantive support for woman suffrage within socialism thus required overcoming the powerful heritage of socialist and trade union hostility to wage-earning women. Previously female wage-earning had generally been decried as an index of working-class degradation; in the socialist utopia, adult women would be relieved of the necessity of wage-earning. After the 1890s, this was much less the case. The tradition of 'proletarian sexism' left its mark, however, in the policy of special regulation of women workers, offered as protection for the most vulnerable in the labour market, but actually functioning to keep women in a separate and unequal sector of the labour force.[33]

Through the 1880s, laws to regulate the wage relation only for women workers were advocated in male-dominated trade unions and socialist movements, but women activists, including those who concentrated on organising wage earners and who accepted the desirability of state regulation of the wage relation, opposed such selective legislation for women only. In England, the conflict between these two positions occurred early in the history of the Fabian Society, over the 1896 Factory Act. Socialist feminists, among them Elizabeth Cady Stanton's daughter Harriot Stanton Blatch, criticised the limitation of hours among women workers, while Beatrice Webb, representing the classic trade union position and the leading faction within the Fabians, argued (successfully) for laws against the exploitation of women workers.[34] In the complex interactions on behalf of suffragism within the Second International, support for sex-based labour legislation seems to have been the price extracted from women for substantive support from socialist men for woman suffrage. Zetkin, who had attacked special restrictions on working women at Stuttgart in 1889, changed her position in 1893, now faithfully advocating special labour legislation for women.

Organisationally, the intermediate position of socialist suffragists led to the twin principles of autonomy for women's organising in socialist parties and antagonism to collaboration with non-socialist suffragists. Of these, hostility to bourgeois women's efforts was the more intensely expressed, perhaps because they represented such serious competition. The initial impulse for the international socialist movement to organise working women in the 1890s, after decades of inactivity, was the necessity of countering the organisational inroads that non-socialist women were making among female wage earners. Barbara Clements argues that the great Russian socialist, Aleksandria Kollantai, was drawn to the organising of working women and to feminist issues by the fear that the bourgeois women's movement was becoming too influential among working-class women.[35]

In 1896, Zetkin made hostility to the non-socialist women's movement a fundamental principle of socialist women's organising in Germany. Despite the fact that their programmes were largely the same, Zetkin argued fiercely against any collaboration between women in the 'proletarian' and 'bourgeois' movements and struggled constantly (if futilely) to draw the line between the two. In 1907 at Stuttgart, Zetkin overcame strong opposition from Austrians and Americans to establish non-co-operation with bourgeois suffragists as the official policy for socialist women around the world. Like the concessions that Zetkin and other socialist women made to sex-based labour legislation, anti-collaborationism helped to offset the innovation that strong support for woman suffrage from a socialist platform represented. Anti-collaborationism was more important rhetorically than organisationally, and was honoured as frequently in the breach as in the observance. In the US socialist women kept their sectarian distance from their 'enemy sisters' only in New York City; everywhere else, there was considerable co-operation throughout the 1910s, especially around votes for women.[36]

Although Zetkin's rhetorical challenges were directed at bourgeois suffragists, she also fought to keep socialist women from being overwhelmed organisationally by men within socialism. In structural terms, this commitment to autonomy within socialism was expressed by organising women separately from men within the party, a corollary to the practice of organising them separately from the non-socialist women's movement. The most vigorous and powerful of the national socialist women's movements—United States, Austria, Scandinavia—followed the lead of the Germans and organised women separately from men. In the US, socialist women had their own organisation, the Socialist Women's National Union, even before Debs formed the American Party in 1902; in 1908 it metamorphised into the Women's National Committee of the Socialist Party, USA. To be sure, in Germany this strategy was dictated by laws which prohibited women from engaging in political activities.[37] (By definition, an all-women's organisation could not be political.) But the separate organisation of women within socialism served an enormously important positive function as well, making it possible to set up the infrastructure of a semi-autonomous women's movement, and to nurture an entire generation of socialist women leaders. Indeed when, in 1908, the repeal of the German anti-association laws led the leaders of the SPD to abolish separate women's organisations, Zetkin fought furiously against this action, which she felt would lead to women's eventual disempowerment within German socialism. However, she lost, and her own power within the SPD declined.

Such semi-autonomous socialist women's organisations never developed in France or Italy, which may be one of the reasons why woman suffrage did not come to either country after World War I. Despite the fact that the socialist parties in both countries formally supported woman suffrage as a parliamentary measure, and that, at least in France, there was a non-socialist woman suffrage movement of some size, the absence of the link between the two may well have been crucial. Finland serves as a fitting counter-example. There the SPD was unusually hospitable to feminists within the party, and a large socialist women's network developed, which played a major role in the first victory for woman suffrage in Europe, in 1906.

Feminist Internationalism: Militant Suffragism around the World

The emergence of a newly militant suffragism, influenced by the upsurge of socialist politics after 1890 but ideologically and organisationally independent of it, is the third source for the great growth of the woman suffrage movement interna-

tionally. While WCTU suffragists translated the goal of political equality into a familiar, female-friendly idiom, and suffragists within socialist parties prepared the way for a wage-earners' suffragism, these independent militant suffragists made their contribution to the revival of suffragism by linking it to a fundamental challenge to gender definitions and relations, and adding a whole new level of tactical radicalism to suffrage agitation. This independent militancy was decidedly internationalist, both in spirit and in substance. Its roots were in England, but its branches reached out, not only through Western Europe and North America, but also to China, South America, Central Europe and elsewhere.

This phenomenon of independent militant suffragism is related to, though not exactly the same as, the activity of those disruptive suffrage radicals who surfaced in England about 1906, and who were dismissed by the press as 'suffragettes', a term of opprobrium that the women themselves embraced and inverted. The British suffragettes are one of the few aspects of the international woman suffrage movement that have entered general historical consciousness, but study of them has, until recently, been limited largely to the complex and contradictory Pankhurst family, whose turn to Tory jingoism during the war has added considerable fuel to the thesis of suffragism's ultimate conservatism. However a new generation of women's historians is offering a revisionist interpretation of the history of suffrage militance in England which better allows us to appreciate its links with the left. They emphasise that the radicalisation of the suffrage movement in Britain reached far beyond the Pankhurst family; that its roots lay in the organisation of working-class women and the dedication of activists inspired by, but independent of, organised socialism; and that the mainstream of British suffragism eventually maintained the political alliance with Labour they initiated.[38]

The militant revival of British suffragism predates the involvement of the Pankhursts and can be traced to a working-class-based suffrage movement of Lancashire textile workers in the 1890s. Middle-class suffragists with socialist inclinations turned to organisations of working-class women, notably the female textile workers' unions, to generate a working women's suffrage movement. The tactics of this new kind of suffragism were borrowed from trade unionism, and emphasised 'open-air campaigning, factory-gate meetings and street corner speaking'.[39] Politically its goal was to pressure the fledgling Labour Party to provide a parliamentary route for woman suffrage. The Pankhursts, a family closely associated with Labour, began their suffrage work within this framework. In 1903, they organised the Women's Social and Political Union (WSPU), which initially emphasised public agitation, working-class organisation and Labour Party political links.

In 1906, the WSPU moved its operations from Manchester to London and at first concentrated on organising mass public demonstrations, the likes of which had never been seen in any women-led movement.[40] Soon other British suffrage societies, including the once conventional National Union of Women's Suffrage Societies (NUWSS), were organising 'monster demonstrations' for suffrage. By 1911, militant modern tactics under various organisational labels dominated the British suffrage movement.

As the WSPU moved away from Manchester and from its working-class origins, it developed its own highly influential form of civil disobedience, borrowed from the 'political law breaking' tradition of Irish nationalism.[41] Christabel Pankhurst, referring in 1908 to the 'Fenian outrages in Manchester and the blowing up of Clerkenwell Gaol', wondered 'how anybody after that can say that militant methods are not effectual'.[42] This civil disobedience strain took on an increasingly violent air, culminating in fire bombs and martyrdom on the part of the suffragettes and punitive forced feeding on the part of the state. Sandra Holton argues that the shift from mass to illegal tactics alienated many working-class women, who expressed their suffragism at giant demonstrations rather than in prison. Nonetheless, the political theatre of arrests and forced feedings intensified women's militance around the world.

These independent suffrage militants, labelled by the British press as 'suffragettes', came to stand for a modern, post-Victorian approach to building a mass woman-suffrage movement. The term 'suffragette' conjured up radical challenges to dominant definitions of womanhood. Until this point, bourgeois femininity—in Europe, North America, and their cultural outlands—was marked by a devotion to the separation of the domestic and private world of women and the public and political world of men. Suffragette militance literally took women out of the parlour and into the streets. Parades, outdoor demonstrations, street corner meetings - these were the marks of modern suffrage agitation. Inasmuch as wage-earning women provided the female army that first breached the walls around the public realm, suffragette militance was initially 'viewed as a specifically working class initiative'. But the challenge to cloistered femininity that it expressed eventually drew passion from women of all classes.[43] Indeed, the more upper class the woman who made the challenges to traditional sex-roles were, the more effective the challenges were.

In the same way as they had pioneered mass suffrage demonstrations, the Pankhursts inaugurated and then abandoned to other British suffragists the strategy of pressuring the Labour Party to support woman suffrage. This meant countering the Independent Labour Party's insistence that so long as votes for men were bound by property limitation, it could not support the suffragists' position of votes for women on the same terms as men; it would only endorse expansion of the suffrage to all adults of both sexes. About the same time as the WSPU shifted from Manchester to London, from mass demonstrations to civil disobedience, and from a working-class base to elite cadres, the WSPU repudiated Labour as a lost cause and started to move to the right, a shift which has weighed heavily in virtually all histories of British militance until recently. But Sandra Holton has shown that the NUWSS took up the paths that the Pankhursts had pioneered, that of hammering away at Labour's objections to woman suffrage. In 1911, this persistence was rewarded by Labour's agreement to support a compromise bill, which set the level of female enfranchisement at an intermediate position, between propertied and adult. The bill failed when the Liberals deserted it, but the détente between suffrage and Labour held firm.

The example of the British suffragettes had tremendous international influence, attributable to the extensive worldwide publicity they worked so hard to get. The International Woman Suffrage Association (IWSA), established between 1899 and 1902, also provided a conduit for their influence, much as the Second International did for the socialist suffragism of Zetkin and Kollontai. The IWSA had been designed to meet every five years, but it soon found itself meeting much more frequently infused with the spirit of suffragette militance.[44] In 1906, the IWSA met in Copenhagen, and delegates brought back the news of the British militants to Hungary, Russia, and elsewhere.[45] In 1909, it met in London, and delegates were treated to various demonstrations of militant tactics—mass marches, civil disobedience, hunger strikes. In 1913, in conjunction with IWSA meetings in Budapest, Sylvia Pankhurst toured Central Europe to talk about her working-class-based version of militance.[46]

ON THE SUBJECT OF...

HARRIOT STANTON BLATCH (1856-1940)

"Women fight for a place in the sun for those who hold right above might."

Stanton, Harriot Stanton. "Our Foe." In *Mobilizing Woman-Power*, p. 21. New York: The Womans Press, 1918.

Harriot Stanton Blatch was born in Seneca Falls, New York, in 1856, the daughter of prominent abolitionists and women's rights activists Henry Brewster and Elizabeth Cady Stanton. Blatch graduated with honors from Vassar College in 1878, attended the Boston School of Oratory in 1879, and then traveled in Europe. In 1882 she contributed a chapter on the American Woman Suffrage Association to the four-volume *History of Woman Suffrage* edited by her mother, Susan B. Anthony, and Matilda Joslyn Gage. She married English businessman William Henry Blatch in 1882 and lived in England for twenty years, serving on the executive committees of the Women's Local Government Society, the Women's Liberal Federation, and the Fabian Society, and actively involved in the woman suffrage movement. Blatch moved with her family to the United States in 1902 and became active in the Women's Trade Union League and the National American Woman Suffrage Association. In 1907 she formed the Equality League of Self-Supporting Women in New York City; the Equality League held the first open-air meetings, stationed women watchers at the polls, and in 1910, when its name was changed to the Women's Political Union, held its first woman suffrage parade down Fifth Avenue. In 1916 the Women's Political Union merged with the Congressional Union (later the National Woman's Party), led by Alice Paul. During World War I, Blatch served as director of the Woman's Land Army, and in her *Mobilizing Woman Power* (1918; foreword by Theodore Roosevelt) she urged American women to political activism and described the contributions of French and English women to the European war effort.

Socialist women of the Second International, who had helped to inspire the formation of the IWSA by their example, were in turn much influenced by the feminist militance it spread. Despite their oft-repeated opposition to 'collaboration' with 'bourgeois suffragists', they could not resist the energy of the suffragette example: Richard Evans believes that the mass demonstrations of International Proletarian Women's Day from 1911 through to 1913 were imitations of the 'monster parades' organised by British militants.[47]

American suffragists were especially quick to pick up the inspiration of the British militants. Many of them were influenced by and sympathetic to socialism, although not party members. Harriot Stanton Blatch, herself a veteran of British Fabianism in the 1890s, returned to the US to organise a working-class-based, tactically militant, independent women's suffrage insurgency. (After American women won the vote, Blatch became an active member of the Socialist Party and ran for office on its ticket.) In San Francisco, trade union activist Maud Younger ('the millionaire waitress') organised the Working Women's Suffrage Society.[48] By 1913, tens of thousands of women were marching in New York City and the example of suffrage parades was spreading across the country. Despite the dictums of the Second International, American socialist women cooperated closely with these independent militants. In California in 1911, in Wisconsin in 1912, even in New York, it was often difficult to distinguish the two groups or to predict which feminists would show up inside the party, which outside. In 1913, this suffrage revival culminated with a mass suffrage parade in Washington DC and the creation of a national suffragette society.[49]

The suffragette example also shaped the Irish woman suffrage movement, which was only fitting, given the role that Irish constitutional nationalists played in holding up a final parliamentary solution to votes for women in England. The Catholicism of France and Italy is often cited as an explanation for their outrageously delayed enfranchisement of women, but the influence of Catholicism proved no serious barrier to the flourishing of militant suffragism in Ireland. The leading figure here was Hanna Sheehy-Skeffington, a socialist, friend of Irish labour and militant suffragist. Inspired by the Pankhursts, she organised the Irish Women's Franchise League, which heckled politicians, held demonstrations and engaged in that signature suffragette activity—breaking windows with stones. In their struggle to influence the shape of the coming Irish nation, the suffragists eventually gained the support of the Irish Labour Party. In 1922, in their new republic, Irish women got the vote on equal terms with men, six years before the British.[50]

Nor was it only Europeans and North Americans who responded to the feminist excitement of the British suffragettes. In 1912 in Nanking, China, the Woman Suffrage Alliance, an independent socialist feminist group, petitioned the provisional parliament to 'enact equality of the sexes and recognize women's right to vote'. Convinced that the men would not take their demand seriously, they armed themselves with pistols, stormed the parliament building three days in a row and had to be dragged off by guards. In imitation of the WSPU, they broke windows, 'drenching their hands in fresh blood'. Around the world, suffragette sisters celebrated their dedication. The WSPU itself sent a message of support, and in New York, the president of the National American suffrage organisation paraded under a sign declaring 'Catching Up with China'.[51] Argentinian suffragists, exasperated with a ridiculously limited municipal suffrage, organised the *Partido Feminista Nacional,* in imitation of the British WSPU.[52]

World War I and Votes for Women: Moving into a New Era

The women of most European and North American countries won the formal right to vote in the years during and immediately after World War I. But to grant the war itself agency in enfranchising women is, in the words of French suffrage historians Steven Hause and Anne Kenney, a way of denying the 'generations of feminist labor that made enfranchisement possible'.[53] Nor is the correlation quite so precise. Combatant countries—France, Italy and Belgium—did not enfranchise women, while neutral nations—the Netherlands and Scandinavia—were among the first to do so. In some countries, for instance Denmark and Iceland, the war held up the enfranchisement of women, which was already in place by 1914. In England and the United States, the war provided time (and a supra-partisan environment) for the political forces necessary to enfranchise women to mature. In Germany and Austria, where defeat and revolution brought in Socialist governments which enfranchised women, a more direct causal role can be attributed to the war.

Indeed, a case can be also made that the war had a negative impact on existing woman suffrage movements. In France, according to Hause and

Kenney, the war was actually 'a setback for the woman suffrage movement'.[54] The war split national suffrage movements in two, just as it did socialist parties, and these were overwhelming setbacks. The majority of suffragists in combatant countries advocated preparedness, war work, and service to the state. In Germany, socialist and non-socialist suffrage women both formally embraced the war. In England, Christabel and Emmeline Pankhurst became intensely pro-war, renaming their *Suffragette* magazine *Britannia.* Extremely conservative political forces were set in motion which dominated European politics for the next twenty-five years and in which reaction against the gains made with respect to sexual equality was a significant component. In Italy, Mussolini briefly played the pro-suffrage card, instituting municipal suffrage for women just as local elections were being undermined. By 1930, woman suffrage and Italian feminism in general had collapsed.[55] In Italy and France, women had to wait until the end of a second world war to gain the vote.

While most suffragists became pro-war enthusiasts, a minority were determinedly anti-war. In England, Sylvia Pankhurst broke with her mother and sister to become a leading anti-war feminist. Outside of England, independent militants tended to the anti-war camp. In the US, the National Woman's Party resisted pro-war jingoism, being the first American organisation to run afoul of anti-sedition laws, even before the Industrial Workers of the World. In Ireland, Hanna Sheehy-Skeffington became a militant pacifist. The international feminist pacifist network formed by these women, most of them suffrage activists, named itself the Women's International League for Peace and Freedom, and constitutes one of the most important legacies of the pre-war suffrage movement.[56] Among women leaders within organised socialism, Clara Zetkin, who had long since been driven from the SDP's leadership, was notable for her opposition to the war.

In the 1920s and 1930s, the dynamic of international suffragism shifted away from Europe and North America, towards Latin America, the Middle East and Asia. These post-1920 movements for women's enfranchisement continued to develop in connection with larger working-class movements. Despite the fact that Communists disdained the parliamentary struggles which had allowed pre-war socialist suffragists to argue their case, left-wing advocates of political equality for women were still able to make some gains in the era of the Comintern; in Indochina and throughout Latin America, for instance, political equality for women was advocated in conjunction with working-class militancy beginning in the 1920s.[57] International networks established before World War I also continued to provide a medium for the ideas and history of women's enfranchisement to move between nations, notably the International Woman Suffrage Association, renamed the International Alliance of Women.

However, it was a new political force, anticolonial nationalist movements, which provided the major crucible for organised efforts for women's enfranchisement after World War I. Important preliminary work has been done in this area by Kumari Jayawardena with respect to Asia, and by Asunción Lavrin and Francesca Miller with respect to Latin America.[58] They have convincingly demonstrated that revolutionary nationalism incubated women's ambitions for political equality in this new period and within this expanded global territory; Asian, Latin American and Middle Eastern women political activists were both inspired and frustrated by the rising expectations of native-born, male-dominated elites, who sought to challenge imperial power and to cultivate political and cultural renewal in their new nations. More research is needed to build on this pioneering scholarship.

Moving the history of woman suffrage movements into the age of revolutionary nationalism would seem to pose a major challenge to the international framework I am advocating, but even here I think we will find that there is much to be gained by tracing the circulation of ideas, individuals, resources and inspirations between and among nations. New transnational women's organisations were formed, pan-American and pan-Pacific women's networks linking advocates of women's political equality; the League of Nations and the United Nations also facilitated the international spread of ideas of women's political equality. Finally, it is significant to recall the impact that images of fighting women activists from Asia and Latin America, women guerrillas carrying babies on one side and rifles on the other, had not so long ago on American and European women, who had become alienated from their own traditions of political activism and of struggles for sexual equality. It was as if these historical traditions, set in motion long ago in one part of the globe, returned to their origins, several epochs later, able to reinspire and reeducate anew.

Notes

1. Oldfield, *Woman Suffrage in Australia*, 212-14; Grimshaw, *Women's Suffrage in New Zealand*; and Katie Spearitt, 'New Dawns: First Wave Feminisms 1880-1914', in Kay Saunders & Raymond Evans, eds, *Gender Relations in Australia: Domination and Negotiations*, Harcourt, Brace, San Diego, 1992. Dr Caroline Daley of Auckland University has suggested that the focus on New Zealand woman suffrage as a gift rather than a political achievement comes from American and British interpretations, rather than New Zealand historians themselves, who turned away from Reeves's analysis to study the suffrage campaign in terms of political struggle.

2. Oldfield, *Woman Suffrage in Australia*, 221.

3. Quoted in Werner Thonnesson, *The Emancipation of Women: The Rise and Decline of the Women's Movement in German Social Democracy, 1863-1993*, Pluto Press, Bristol, 1969, 32.

4. Evans, *The Feminists*.

5. Ibid., 217. See also Ross Evans Paulson, *Women's Suffrage and Prohibition: A Comparative Study of Equality and Social Control*, Scott, Foresman, Glenview, Ill., 1973, for a similar evaluation of woman suffrage, which applauds rather than criticises its alleged conservatism.

6. Kraditor, *Ideas of the Woman Suffrage Movement;* and William O'Neill, *Everyone was Brave: The Rise and Fall of Feminism in America.* Ian Tyrrell re-examines Kraditor's influential thesis that over time suffragists shifted from 'justice' to 'expediency' claims in the vote, *Woman's World, Woman's Empire*.

7. Bunkle, 'The Origins of the Women's Movement in New Zealand'.

8. DuBois, *Feminism and Suffrage*.

9. Ian Tyrrell, 'American Exceptionalism in an Age of International History', *American Historical Review (AHR)*, 1991, 1031-55.

10. Ellen C. DuBois, 'The Radicalism of the Woman Suffrage Movement: Notes Toward the Reconstruction of American Feminism', *Feminist Studies (FS)*, 3, 1975, 63-71.

11. Rosalyn Petchevsky, 'Dissolving the Hyphen: A Report on Marxist-Feminist Groups', in Zillah Eisenstein, ed, *Capitalist Patriarchy and the Case for Socialist Feminism*, Monthly Review Press, New York, 1979, 375.

12. Ruth Bordin, *Women and Temperance: The Quest for Power and Liberty, 1873-1900*, Temple Univ. Press, Philadelphia, 1981.

13. Tyrrell, *Woman's World*, 19.

14. Patricia Grimshaw, *Women's Suffrage In New Zealand*, 37.

15. Sylvia Pankhurst, *The Suffragette Movement*, Virago, London, 1977, first published in 1931, 178.

16. Diane Kirkby, *Alice Henry: The Power of Pen and Voice*, Cambridge Univ. Press, Melbourne, 1991.

17. Tyrrell, *Woman's World*, 221.

18. Oldfield, *Woman Suffrage in Australia*, 21. This was made most clear to me in Diane Kirkby's excellent biography of Alice Henry, which begins with a portrait of the Australian suffrage movement.

19. Mari Jo Buhle, *Women and American Socialism, 1870-1920*, Univ. of Illinois Press, Urbana, 1981.

20. Vron Ware, *Beyond the Pale White Women: Racism and History*, Verso, London & New York, 1991, ch. 2.

21. Oldfield, *Woman Suffrage in Australia*, 63.

22. Cheryll Walker, *The Women's Suffrage Movement in South Africa*, Univ. of Cape Town, 1979, 26.

23. Marilyn J. Boxer & Jean H. Quataert, *Socialist Women: European Socialist Feminism in the Nineteenth and Early Twentieth Centuries*, Evans, *The Feminists* and *Comrades and Sisters: Feminism, Socialism and Pacifism in Europe, 1870-1945*; Charles Sowerwine, 'The Socialist Women's Movement from 1850 to 1940', in Renate Bridenthal, Claudia Koontz & Susan Stuard, eds, *Becoming Visible: Women in European History*, 2nd ed., Houghton Mifflin, Boston, 1987; Jane Slaughter & Robert Kern, eds, *European Women on the Left: Socialist, Feminism and the Problems Faced by Political Women, 1880-Present*, Greenwood, Westport, Conn., 1981.

24. Cynthia Little, 'Education, Philanthropy, and Feminism: Components of Argentine Womanhood, 1860-1926', in Asunción Lavrin, ed., *Latin American Women: Historic Perspectives*, Greenwood, Westport, Conn., 1978. On Second International feminism in South Africa, see Cheryll Walker, *The Women's Suffrage Movement in South Africa*. This was, of course, an all white-movement. On Galicia, see Martha Boyachevsky-Chomiak, 'Socialism and Feminism: The First Stages of Women's Organizations in the Eastern Part of the Austrian Empire', in Tova Yedlin, ed, *Women in Eastern Europe and the Soviet Union*, Carleton Univ. Press, Ottawa, 1975.

25. Meredith Tax, *Rising of the Women: Feminist Solidarity and Class Conflict, 1880-1917*, Monthly Review Press, New York, 1980, 188.

26. Temma Kaplan, 'On the Socialist Origins of International Women's Day', *FS*, 11, 1985.

27. Mari Jo Buhle, 'Women and the Socialist Party, 1901-1914', *Radical America (RA)*, 4, 1970; Boxer & Quataert, *Socialist Women*.

28. Sowerwine, 'The Socialist Women's Movement from 1850 to 1940', 409.

29. Quataert, *Reluctant Feminists in German Social Democracy, 1885-1917*, Princeton Univ. Press, Princeton, 1979, 94.

30. Sowerwine, 'The Socialist Women's Movement From 1850 to 1940', 416.

31. Buhle, *Women in American Socialism*, ch. 2.

32. Thonnesson, *The Emancipation of Women*, 63.

33. Alice Kessler Harris, *Out to Work: A History of Wage-Earning Women in the United States*, Oxford Univ. Press, New York, 1982, ch. 7. In her later work, Kessler Harris has backed away from this assessment to some degree; see Alice Kessler Harris, *A Woman's Wage: Historical Meanings and Social Consequences*, Univ. of Kentucky Press, Lexington, Kentucky, 1989.

34. Polly Beals, 'Fabian Feminism: Gender, Politics and Culture in London, 1880-1930', unpublished Ph.D thesis, Rutgers University, 1989.

35. Barbara Clements, *Bolshevik Feminist: The Life of Aleksandria Kollontai*, Indiana Univ. Press, Bloomington, 1979, 59. Similarly, Linda Edmonson argues that 'such was the abhorrence felt by Orthodox Marxists toward the idea of separate women's organisations that the potential value of the female proletariat went almost unnoticed' until the non-bourgeois women's movement forced it upon socialists' attention; see Linda Edmonson, *Feminism in Russia, 1900-1917*, Stanford Univ. Press, Stanford, CA., 1984, 171.

36. John D. Buenker, 'The Politics of Mutual Frustration: Socialists and Suffragists in New York and Wisconsin', in Sally Miller, ed, *Flawed Liberation: Socialism and Feminism*, Greenwood, Westport, Conn., 1981.

37. Kollontai's biographer says that when she discovered that the separate organising of socialist women, to which she was passionately committed in Russia, was the child of German necessity, she was astonished; Clements, *Bolshevik Feminist*, 64.

38. Holton, *Feminism and Democracy*: Jill Liddington & Jill Norris, *One Hand Tied Behind Us: The Rise of the Women's Suffrage Movement*; Lisa Tickner, *The Spectacle of Women: Imagery of the Suffrage Campaign, 1907-1914*, Chatto & Windus, London, 1987. In addition, there is another group of contemporary feminist historians of British suffragism who have emphasised instead the sexual politics—as anticipating modern anti-pornography feminism—especially in Christabel Pankhurst's leadership. See Susan Kinsley Kent, *Sex and Suffrage in Britain 1860-1914*, Princeton Univ. Press, Princeton, 1987 and Sheila Jeffreys, *The Spinster and Her Enemies: Feminism and Sexuality, 1880-1930*, Pandora Press, London, 1985.

39. Holton, 33.

40. Sylvia Pankhurst, *The Suffragette Movement*, 195.

41. Rosemary Cullen Owens, *Smashing Times: A History of the Irish Woman Suffrage Movement, 1889-1922*, Attic Press, Dublin, 1984, 40.

42. Quoted in Jane Marcus, ed, *Suffrage and the Pankhursts*, Routledge & Kegan Paul, London, 1987, 48.

43. Holton, *Feminism and Democracy*, 35; Ellen Carol DuBois, 'Working Women, Class Relations and Suffrage Militance: Harriot Stanton Blatch and the New York Woman Suffrage Movement, 1894-1907', *JAH*, 74/1, 1987, 34-58.

44. Evans, *The Feminists*, 248-53; Edith F. Hurwitz, 'The International Sisterhood', in Renate Bridenthal & Claudia Koontz, eds, *Becoming Visible: Women in European History*, Houghton Mifflin, Boston, 1977.

45. International Council of Women, *Women in a Changing World: The Dynamic Story of the International Council of Women since 1888*, Routledge & Kegan Paul, London, 1966.

46. Sylvia Pankhurst, *The Suffragette Movement*, 535.

47. Evans, *Comrades and Sisters*, 68-75.

48. Susan L. Englander, *Class Conflict and Coalition in the California Woman Suffrage Movement, 1907-1917*, Mellen Univ. Press, Lewiston, New York, 1992; DuBois, 'Working Women'.

49. Buhle, *Women in American Socialism*; Meredith Tax, *Rising of the Women*; Christine Lunardini, *From Equal Suffrage to Equal Rights: Alice Paul and the National Woman's Party, 1910-1928*, New York Univ. Press, New York, 1986.

50. Leah Levenson & Jerry H. Natterstad, *Hanna Sheehy-Skeffington: Irish Feminist*, Syracuse Univ. Press, Syracuse, New York, 1986, 37.

51. Ono Kazuko, *Chinese Women in a Century of Revolution, 1850-1950*, Stanford Univ. Press, Stanford, California, 1989, 80-92.

52. Ann Poscaletto, *Power and Pawn: The Female in Iberian Families, Societies and Cultures*, Greenwood Press, Westport, Conn., 1976, 191.

53. Hause & Kenney, *Women's Suffrage and Social Politics in the French Third Republic*, 202.

54. Hause & Kenney, *Women's Suffrage and Social Politics;* Evans, *The Feminists*, 223.

55. Donald Meyer, *Sex and Power: The Rise of Women in America, Russia, Sweden and Italy,* Wesleyan Univ. Press, Middletown, Conn., 1987, 37.

56. Gertrude Bussey & Margaret Tims, *Pioneers for Peace: Women's International League for Peace and Freedom 1915-1965,* Alden Press, Oxford, 1980, first published in 1967.

57. Sonia Kruks, Rayna Rapp & Marilyn Young, eds, *Promissory Notes: Women in the Transition to Socialism,* Monthly Review Press, New York, 1987.

58. The English-language scholarship on post-1920 suffrage movements is just beginning to be accumulated. Kumari Jayawardena, *Feminism and Nationalism in the Third World,* Zed Books, London, 1986; Francesca Miller, *Latin American Women and the Search for Social Justice,* Stanford Univ. Press, Stanford, CA., 1992; Asunción Lavrin, ed, *Latin American Women: Historic Perspectives.*

LINDA J. LUMSDEN (ESSAY DATE 1997)

SOURCE: Lumsden, Linda J. "The Right of Association: Mass Meetings, Delegations, and Conventions." In *Rampant Women: Suffragists and the Right of Assembly,* pp. 1-22. Knoxville: The University of Tennessee Press, 1997.

In the essay below, Lumsden presents a survey of the various ways in which suffragettes exercised their right to association through participation in mass meetings, delegations, and conventions.

The right of association lay at the heart of the woman suffrage movement, as it does with all political and social movements. Individuals who gather to achieve common aims exercise the right of association, which encompasses the right to belong. Almost every aspect of the suffrage movement employed the right: When a woman paid dues to her local suffrage association, swapped stories at a suffrage tea, signed a petition, gathered listeners at her soapbox, marched down Fifth Avenue, voted for new officers at a national convention, joined the White House picket line, or helped form a political party, she exercised her right of association.

The right of association evolved from but is broader than the right of assembly, with which it is inextricably entwined. Alexis de Tocqueville observed during his travels across America in the early 1800s that the right of association formed the foundation of American society: "The most natural privilege of man, next to the right of acting for himself, is that of combining his exertions with those of his fellow-creatures, and of acting in

common with them. I am therefore led to conclude, that the right of association is almost as inalienable as the right of personal liberty."[1]

Although America was founded on the right of religious association, the Bill of Rights ignored other associational rights, perhaps because the right was so basic it seemed self-evident.[2] As a result, the United States was slow to develop formal recognition of associational rights, even though these rights were deeply rooted in the American and British experience. Voluntary associations got their earliest legal recognition in the common-law right of contract. Later, tradesmen were free to associate for socializing or for education, but the advocacy function of the modern labor union remained unlawful until the mid-nineteenth century. Courts rigidly circumscribed union activities, applying criminal conspiracy laws to union efforts to compel members to unite for better wages or working conditions. No law guaranteed workers the right to organize in associations until the National Industrial Recovery Act of 1933.[3] The United States Supreme Court finally ruled in 1958 that freedom to associate for "political, economic, religious or cultural matters" was a constitutional right protected by the First Amendment.[4] Like other facets of freedom of expression, however, the limits of its protections continue to be subject to legal tugs of war.[5]

Although suffragists faced no legal challenges to their right to organize, authorities infringed upon suffragists' rights of association when those authorities refused the women meeting permits or hall rentals. Only rarely did violence disrupt women's conventions, as when rowdies shut down the 1853 woman's rights convention in New York. Women at the 1913 Tennessee state suffrage convention evacuated the proceedings, however, when someone tossed a container of vile-smelling chemicals into the meeting hall. Women faced considerable censure from family, employers, the media, and men on the street when they participated in the suffrage campaign.

Suffrage was both a part and a product of the urge to join that infected women throughout the nineteenth century, first in charities, then in reform associations, most notably the abolition movement. In the late nineteenth century, women had other options for associating. Women's colleges, by then proliferating, fostered female autonomy, self-esteem, and sorority. Settlement houses in poor urban neighborhoods gave many of these idealistic, intelligent young women a home and a career.[6] The Woman's Christian

Temperance Union helped stir a feminist consciousness. Historian Susan Dye Lee noted the power of association that surfaced in the temperance movement: "It brought thousands of women out of their homes and into the community. It gave many their first opportunity to speak publicly, to lead groups, to formulate plans, and to execute goals. Unity in a cause women could identify with gave the crusaders a chance to express shared feelings of sisterhood. And, having learned the power of association, they began to organize beyond the local level."[7]

All of these voluntary associations bridged private and public life, culminating by the end of the nineteenth century in the massive women's club movement. Hundreds of thousands of women joined the thousands of clubs united under the auspices of the General Federation of Women's Clubs and the National Association of Colored Women (NACW). Women's clubs served as training grounds for the activist, articulate reformers who steered the suffrage movement in the 1910s.[8] "Women saw [clubs] as vehicles for training themselves about public issues and for making an impact on the world," according to historian Glenna Matthews.[9] Suffrage study groups numbered among the clubs' many reforming activities. Club women applied the experience they had gained in organizing and legislative work to suffrage in the 1910s.[10] By then, suffrage finally had evolved into a mass movement, probably the first of the twentieth century.[11]

Women found many ways to associate with the suffrage movement. At the most basic level, they exercised the right of association simply by joining the National American Woman Suffrage Association or any of its hundreds of local affiliates. The rise in NAWSA membership in the 1910s indicated the snowballing strength of the movement: it increased from one hundred thousand women in 1915 to about two million in 1917, in contrast to some forty-five thousand members in 1907.[12]

The creation of a Denver suffrage league illustrates the reach of women's informal associational ties. While campaigning in South Dakota to remove the word "male" from the state constitution, Matilda Hindman traveled to Denver to raise funds. She persuaded local friends to form the Colorado Equal Suffrage Association Education Committee. Louise Tyler, recently moved from Boston to the territory, encouraged the group to formalize itself with a constitution, bylaws, and regular meetings. She also brought the local group an invitation to affiliate with NAWSA. Thus a

nineteenth-century prototype of networking expanded the suffrage movement.[13]

As suffragists banded together, they discovered the power of association, a power that becomes apparent when large numbers of people share a common purposeful identity. In the suffrage movement, the power of association first became visible in the three earliest forms of suffrage assemblies: mass meetings, delegations, and conventions.

Mass Meetings

Mass meetings were the least formal and most easily organized political assembly, with a long heritage in American politics. American men had traditionally gathered en masse in political parties or in trade unions, in halls or in the streets. Polemics and inspiration characterized the numerous speeches that were the hallmark of mass meetings. A popular strategy for citizens to protest unpopular legislation, mass meetings were sometimes called "indignation meetings" by suffragists. When rowdies disrupted a 1913 suffrage parade in Washington, D.C., for example, leaders that evening called an indignation meeting, where they called for—and won—a congressional investigation.[14]

The sight of hundreds and then thousands of women assembled to espouse suffrage made mass meetings an effective visual technique for women to show the public the extent of interest in their cause. Women in Utah Territory won the vote in 1870, for instance, partly because Mormon women's mass meetings across the state won legislators' attention and sympathy.[15] The Mormon women's gatherings predated even the widespread mass prayer meetings of the WCTU later in the decade. The site of many Mormon mass meetings was the temple, which provided a safe, respectable venue for women venturing into politics. African American women also turned to the church when they used mass meetings as a mobilization tactic. When the Maryland legislature proposed an amendment in 1909 that would exclude black men from the polls, black women organized a mass meeting at a Baltimore church. The amendment died.[16]

As suffrage sentiment expanded in the East in the twentieth century, mass meetings grew larger and more frequent. Popular indoor venues such as Cooper Union and Carnegie Hall began overflowing with suffrage crowds by the 1910s, so that eventually only the Metropolitan Opera House could house major assemblies of suffragists in New York City.[17]

Delegations

After assembling together, the next step for woman's rights activists was to place their demands before legislators. Suffrage speakers and delegations ventured at risk beyond the portals of male political power. They had as their role model Angelina Grimké, the first woman to address any legislature. Grimké spoke in 1838 before the Massachusetts legislature on behalf of antislavery petitions presented by women. The disapproval of most New England abolitionists exacerbated her "fear and trembling," yet politicians and the press roundly praised Grimké's speech.[18]

Elizabeth Cady Stanton delivered the first speech on woman's rights to a legislature in 1855, addressing the Joint Judiciary Committee of both legislative houses of New York on women's legal disabilities; in 1860, her speech to the legislature specifically centered on suffrage.[19] The legislators failed to act on her proposals, but Stanton's appearance paved the way for what by the 1910s would be a flood of women's delegations to governors' homes, state houses, the United States Congress, and the White House.

In Wyoming Territory in 1869, for instance, a small group of suffragists appeared at Governor John Campbell's home, making it clear they would stay until he signed a suffrage bill. He did.[20] Nearly half a century later, the Women's Political Union (WPU) in New York also marched on legislators' homes, where they serenaded them with suffrage songs.[21]

Beginning in 1868, suffragists attended every national political convention.[22] More important, the National Woman Suffrage Association annually convened in Washington, D.C., so suffragists could present suffrage arguments to congressional committees. African American activist Mary Ann Shadd Carey, for instance, addressed the House Judiciary Committee on suffrage in 1871.[23] Zerelda Wallace of Indiana told the Senate Judicial Committee in 1880, "We are no seditious women, clamoring for any peculiar rights," before she invoked women's responsibility for home life as a reason to give them the vote. "We find ourselves hedged in at every effort we make as mothers for the amelioration of society."[24]

Even women from the South, where sentiment against suffrage flowed strongest, chanced social censure back home by asking the Senate for the vote. "Voting will never lessen maternal love," Helen Morris Lewis of North Carolina promised the Senate Committee on Woman Suffrage in 1896. A South Carolina woman advanced the white supremacist argument that formed the foundation of the southern suffrage movement: southern white women voters with property and educational requirements would outnumber African American voters. The speaker argued suffrage would curb rapacious blacks and stop lynchings by whites.[25]

Suffragists also visited state legislatures, for much of the early suffrage movement focused on persuading individual states to let women vote. Texas women converged on a state legislative committee weighing a suffrage amendment to the state constitution in 1907.[26] The Equality League of Self Supporting Women in New York jolted legislators awake at the annual suffrage hearing in Albany that same year by introducing two working-class speakers whose moving personal accounts debunked the homily that woman's place was in the home.[27] The effect was so invigorating that by 1909 the league arranged for special trains to carry whole carloads of speakers to enliven the annual hearing. Hundreds of women packed the hearing room, crowding out the legislators during the four-hour debate.[28] Suffragists started to camp out at suffrage hearings in other states, such as Pennsylvania and Maryland.[29]

These group appearances were among the earliest demonstrations of the new assertive, public nature that would characterize suffrage assemblies in the 1910s. In 1909, two hundred women in Chicago boarded a special suffrage train that whisked them to Springfield. Twenty-five speakers, including Jane Addams, lectured the legislature for seven hours. The suffrage newspaper *Woman's Journal* became giddy over the female presence: "All day long the State House was in possession of the fair visitors. There corridors were a-flutter with spring millinery and gay frocks, the air was filled with soft laughter and dulcet-keyed arguments."[30]

The *Journal's* overwrought tone cloaked the radical, unfeminine nature of the women's ventures. Despite the *Journal's* frilly prose, women's appearance in previously all-male sanctums threatened men. The headline of an account by the *Boston Herald* of a similar demonstration conveyed their unease with the suffragists' demonstrations. "Women Suffragists 2,000 Strong Stormed the State House Today," announced the paper in 1909 after women marched from Beacon Hill to a legislative hearing.[31] The crowd spilled out from the meeting rooms onto the State House steps and sidewalks, where the women conducted "great, orderly, inspiring" meetings. "Never was there such a demonstration," boasted *Progress,* the NAWSA journal.[32]

Such displays empowered and inspired participants. "I realized solemnly that we had embarked on a new phase of our movement," said one woman after witnessing the Boston demonstration.[33] That new phase was characterized by an unapologetic recognition by women that they possessed the right to stand up and speak up in American politics. Marches upon state houses bordered on the militant and demonstrated a new confidence among suffragists in public. They were less fearful of being labeled unwomanly and more assured about taking their places in the corridors of male power, which had seemed so foreign and intimidating. The appearance of large numbers of women worked no overnight miracle on male legislators, but women's persistence began to get men's attention.

Women's presence also occasionally raised men's ire. In 1910, fifty automobiles deposited at the Senate hundreds of women carrying a mammoth national petition for a constitutional amendment solicited by NAWSA.[34] Women filled the Senate to hear their representatives present suffrage petitions from their districts. The women clapped and laughed during the proceedings, sparking a confrontation that indicated male discomfort when a bold group of women challenged their authority: When the women ignored his gavel for order, Senator Kean of New Jersey warned them that Senate rules prohibited any displays of emotion. But after Senator Robert LaFollette of Wisconsin delivered a particularly potent appeal, the women laughed again, and Senator Kean slammed down his gavel, threatening to clear the galleries. Silence ensued. "Dare to Laugh in Senate," said the *New York Times* subhead.[35]

The spirit of confrontation escalated following the creation in 1913 of the scrappy Congressional Union for Woman Suffrage (CU) headed by Alice Paul. A hint of the flamboyant CU protests to come occurred when the CU's Mabel Vernon sneaked a big yellow suffrage banner into the Senate gallery during Wilson's address to Congress in 1916. Vernon unfurled the banner, pages grabbed it, and police escorted her out.[36] In a more serious vein, the CU sent numerous delegations to President Woodrow Wilson beginning in 1913. The presence of women assembled in the White House to make political demands signified a new daring and seriousness in the movement. Dozens of CU deputations to Wilson over four years represented a broad cross-section of American women that included delegations of working women, college women, CU members, New Jersey women (Wilson's home state), and women from all of the states.[37] In June of 1914, for instance, five hundred members of the General Federation of Women's Clubs marched to the White House, where spokeswoman Rheta Childe Dorr futilely pressed Wilson to support the federal suffrage amendment.[38]

These deputations were treated as rude and bothersome by both the president and the press.[39] "The President of the United States is not to be bothered or made a defendant," the *New York Times* wrote of Dorr's defiant tone.[40] "From [the headlines] it might have been supposed that an Army of Amazons was going to brandish a hatchet over his head," the *Woman's Journal* reported of newspaper coverage about a 1913 deputation.[41] The press seemed annoyed simply by the women's belief that they were entitled to a hearing from the president. Even when a group of Pennsylvania women waited in vain for days to see Wilson in 1915, the press blasted them for "heckling" him.[42] Such rebuffs began edging Alice Paul closer to more confrontational tactics, which culminated in the picketing of the White House in 1917.

Yet highly visible assemblies of women worked some effect upon Washington. One sign of the growing influence of NAWSA was an unprecedented appearance by three members of the Cabinet at a prosuffrage reception hosted by Senator LaFollette in 1913.[43] And in 1915, Wilson and his daughter hosted a White House reception for suffragists during the 1915 NAWSA convention. "You ladies have a pretty strong clasp," he said upon shaking hands with Anna Howard Shaw. "Yes," she replied. "We hang on."[44] Wilson went to Atlantic City the following September to address the NAWSA convention.[45] A visit from the president of the United States to a female convention signaled a significant shift in suffrage sentiment. Wilson's appearance also underscored the centrality of conventions to the suffrage movement.

Conventions

Suffrage conventions formed the heart of the movement and epitomized the power of association. Suffrage conventions helped women discover a shared ideology and work toward social change to reflect that ideology. Conventions imbued the suffrage movement with a group identity that affected both participants and observers and created the "spark of life" deemed the key ingredient by sociologist Jo Freeman in the making of a social movement.[46]

The first spark was ignited in 1848 at the Woman's Rights Convention at Seneca Falls, where the radical Declaration of Sentiments contained the first formal call for woman suffrage. National woman's rights conventions held annually from 1850 to 1861 (except 1857) continued in that radical vein. Delegates cheered Lucy Stone when she exhorted members of the 1851 convention, "Instead of asking, 'Give us this, or give us that,' let us just get up and take it." The next year she urged convention delegates to refuse to pay taxes: "One such resistance, by the agitation that would grow out of it, will do more to settle this question of rights, than all the Conventions in the world." Woman's rights conventions helped legitimize the movement and the demand for the vote, because suffrage resolutions became routine calls at these gatherings that were dutifully (if derisively) reported by the press. Conventions thus provided an important forum for articulating suffrage demands. When conventions resumed after the Civil War in 1866, the annual suffrage resolution for the first time demanded a federal constitutional amendment granting women the vote because "it is the crowning right of citizenship; it is dignity, protection and power; it is civil and political life."[47]

Conventions fulfilled several key functions for suffragists that demonstrated the instrumentality of the right to associate. They were the forum at which suffragists could gain confidence and skills as they hammered out policy, devised strategies, approved resolutions, gained publicity, raised funds, and elected officers. Less tangible but vital services included exposing members to new ideas, reaffirming old ideals, and lending the movement a sense of sorority, history, continuity, and progress. One attendee of NAWSA's 1916 convention remarked upon how the gatherings linked women: "The union of generations is shown by second, third, sometimes fourth generations of women seeing each other with new sight and new friendship because they are all working together for what they believe to be good and beautiful and to be greatly desired."[48]

Suffragists blossomed as they became more practiced in the art of the large public meeting. Conventioneers in the 1910s exuded a confidence in the public sphere practically unheard of in the previous century as a result of women's immense strides into traditional male turf, which included

universities, factories, offices, and the professions as well as the streets.[49] Suffrage conventions contributed to and benefited from the trend of women moving into the public sphere. The *Woman's Journal* praised the "psychological impression" as "victors and conquerors" that suffragists made when groups of conventioneers wearing yellow badges bustled along Manhattan streets during the 1911 NAWSA convention.[50] The newspaper's choice of language indicated how suffragists were shedding their passivity.

By the mid-1910s, women began to feel absolutely cocky about their potential. One self-congratulatory NAWSA delegate said of the Atlantic City convention in 1916: "The great assembly represented the best of American womanhood: women of ability, women of education, women of achievement were gathered together in a spirit of consecration and determination." The contrast between that spirited gathering in 1916 and NAWSA conventions just a decade earlier prompted one veteran to exclaim, "How times have changed!"[51] Signs that more change lay ahead arose the next year, when the first female member of Congress, suffragist Jeannette Rankin of Montana, addressed the convention.

Conventions nurtured the political skills responsible for that progress. "Not Used to Voting?" is how a newspaper headlined a report that confusion clouded the election of NAWSA officers in Minneapolis at the turn of the century.[52] But by 1916, NAWSA women wielded considerable prowess in parliamentary procedure, staging a three-cornered debate after which they approved a major policy shift to focus on a federal amendment.[53] The press in the 1910s praised both the efficiency and idealism of women's conventions. "Their meeting was positively the most intelligent gathering in Chicago," the *New Republic* wrote after the formation of the Woman's Party of Western Voters in 1916.[54] The *New York Post* said NAWSA managed its Atlantic City convention in 1916 twice as well as the major political parties and pointed to how suffrage conventions in themselves molded good citizens: "[Suffrage conventioneers] have gained poise, a knowledge of public speaking, experience in Parliamentary procedure, and training in executive management, besides demonstrating their ability to debate clearly, logically and right to the point."[55]

Such analyses were in stark contrast to the sexist stereotypes that had dominated press reports a decade earlier. A press notice of the 1905 convention noted of the week-long proceedings, "It must be borne in mind that it is a woman's affair, and there will be much talking."[56] Women complained to editors in 1906 that what the press termed an "argument" by men became a "plain fuss" when indulged in by women.[57] By the 1910s, more women journalists were covering suffrage and the tone of coverage changed. "In questions of dull procedure they are petty," said an article in *McClure's Magazine* coauthored by a suffragist. "In manners of humanity they are enormously big."[58] Suffragists were dependent upon such magazines and newspapers to cast their movement in a positive light.

Newspapers played a key role in disseminating suffrage convention news, and they began to accord more respect to suffrage conventions as the century progressed. The *Woman's Journal* noted that the press gave the 1908 convention in Buffalo "full and unusually respectful reports."[59] By 1918, newspapers in forty-four states had covered the annual NAWSA convention. The *Woman Citizen* estimated coverage added up to more than half a million words.[60] Speeches and resolutions made news, and convention planners scheduled special events to get even more publicity.[61] Suffragists recognized that publicity was their lifeline.

Suffragists became adept at orchestrating their gatherings to coincide with the major political party conventions or other events where press and public would already be on hand. The gavel for the first Woman Voters Convention sponsored by the Congressional Union, for instance, sounded with the opening of the Panama Pacific Exposition in San Francisco in 1915. "It is doubtful if any assembly of women called together in this country ever reached such a high intellectual level in its personnel," the *Washington Post* editorialized. "[It] marks an epoch in the history of the country of more than passing importance."[62]

Suffragists became more attentive to the press and sophisticated about currying its favor. As early as 1906 NAWSA conventions urged local suffrage clubs to work more closely with the mainstream press, and a 1913 session discussed the importance of publicity.[63] A 1917 convention resolution even thanked the press.[64] Both NAWSA and the National Woman's Party, founded in 1917, operated large press departments that were leaders in the emerging field of public relations. By 1919, NAWSA's National Woman Suffrage Publishing Company had produced fifty million pieces of literature in the five years of its existence.[65]

Suffrage organizations also kept members apprised of convention proceedings through their own newspapers. Innumerable accounts in the *Woman's Journal* found conventions conducted weekly in every corner of the nation, and they appeared to be the main, if not sole, undertaking of many organizations.[66] The suffrage newspapers themselves promoted associational ties by keeping suffragists informed of each other's activities and heartening readers that women elsewhere shared the same values.

Resolutions proved to be an easily digestible item for the press, and passing resolutions proved the most tangible way conventioneers could deliver their message to the public. The scope of convention resolutions over the years showed that the suffragists' agenda extended beyond merely obtaining the vote. In 1913, NAWSA's resolutions included a call for world peace, denunciation of white slavery, excoriation of child labor, and commendation of political economics studies by the General Federation of Women's Clubs.[67] But suffrage resolutions predominated. In 1915, the Congressional Union staged simultaneous conventions in 212 congressional districts that churned out hundreds of resolutions backing the federal amendment that the women then delivered to their representatives.[68]

Besides passing resolutions, conventions expended much energy upon conducting most of the particular organizations' business. Mundane chores such as the election of officers or revising the group's constitution took up some time.[69] More important, members debated policies that often were decided far from them but that carried serious consequences for local work. At the NWP's 1917 convention, for instance, a discussion on the controversial White House picketing concluded that it had achieved its intended effect of drawing attention to the federal amendment.[70]

Fund raising was another crucial piece of convention business. Associations raised most of their annual budget by pledges made at conventions. In 1913, NAWSA started its own invaluable publishing company by selling more than eleven thousand dollars in shares at ten dollars apiece in less than four minutes during its New York convention.[71] The NWP collected fifty-one thousand dollars at its inaugural convention.[72] Convention fervor so inspired at least one teacher at NAWSA's 1914 convention in Nashville that she wrote a novel in her spare time, published it at her own expense, traveled and sold it while giving speeches in the South, and gave the proceeds to NAWSA.[73]

State groups also raised considerable sums at conventions, such as the $8,693 that the New York State Suffrage Association collected in 1913.[74] Because all of its members were under one roof and usually flushed with the success of the movement's progress, real or imaginary, conventions proved invaluable for organizations to solicit funds to carry out their suffrage work during the remainder of the year.

The most important business NAWSA leaders ever conducted occurred after Carrie Chapman Catt unveiled her secret "winning plan" in 1916 at a preconvention meeting of state association leaders. The plan was pivotal because it called for dropping the states' rights approach to the amendment.[75] After agreeing to switch to campaigning for a federal amendment, NAWSA delegates immediately pledged $818,000 toward its $1-million goal for the new campaign.[76] Conventioneers who approved the plan cheered Catt's most famous speech, "The Crisis," which ended on a militant note: "WILL to be free. Demand the vote. WOMEN ARISE!"[77]

Conventions helped instill this sense of female destiny by making space on every program for celebrations of suffrage history. Celebrating a common history created a group identity. "The Spirit of 1848" was the topic of a convention speech in Buffalo in 1908, and eighty-two-year-old Eugenia Farmer read a paper titled "A Voice from the Civil War" at Minnesota's 1917 convention.[78] New Hampshire's state convention in 1913 feted the sole survivor of its first meeting of sixty women forty-five years earlier, and the oldest speaker at a 1913 "Octogenarian Suffrage Meeting" in Oregon was ninety-seven years old.[79] NAWSA, in fact, moved its conventions from winter to early fall beginning in 1908 so that older members could avoid travel in winter (another reason was so that conventions would not interfere with spring housecleaning).[80] The presence of these suffrage relics seemed not to remind the women of the apparent futility of their cause. Fittingly, a lunch honoring the pioneers at NAWSA's 1920 victory convention in Chicago enabled them to finally celebrate the fruits of their lives' work.[81] Both NAWSA and the NWP scheduled their 1920 conventions celebrating passage of the suffrage amendment in 1919 on the centennial of Anthony's birth on 15 February 1820, suffragists' favorite holiday.[82] Annual Anthony birthday celebrations ranged from teas to a special Susan B. Anthony Day on the White House suffrage picket line featuring banners that quoted her. Suffragists'

reverence for their history satisfied more than nostalgia; it placed their current actions in the context of making history. Possessing a history helped them envision the possibility of a future. Conventions helped them work toward that future by offering a forum for new ideas and techniques.

Conventions sowed, spread, and tested new ideas and campaign techniques. Newly enfranchised women voters from Idaho in 1897 told NAWSA conventioneers how to organize in precincts to conduct door-to-door canvasses to educate voters, a technique to which many later attributed the success of the 1917 suffrage referendum in New York state.[83] Kentuckian Laura Clay introduced her highly successful idea of recruiting through parlor meetings at the 1904 convention.[84] The 1908 NAWSA convention vetoed conducting a controversial open-air, or soapbox, meeting, but 1910 conventioneers hit the Washington, D.C., streets after a how-to workshop on soapbox speaking.[85]

A look at the 1911 NAWSA convention program shows the explosion of new campaign ideas. Susan FitzGerald illustrated the new open-air propaganda techniques with one of the latest advances in technology, a lantern slide show.[86] "Three of the most renowned women in the world"—NAWSA president Anna Howard Shaw, Hull House founder Jane Addams, and Emmeline Pankhurst, leader of Britain's militant suffragettes—shared a dais.[87] Talks in 1911 included "The Working Woman's Interest in the Ballot," "What Woman Suffrage Means to College Women," and "The Effect of Suffrage Work Upon Women Themselves."[88]

NAWSA's rank and file heard a variety of important speakers. Subjects included a 1912 address on the evils of white slavery and a critique of child labor in cotton mills in 1914.[89] Russian-born Socialist Rose Winslow spoke in 1913 along with laundry worker Margaret Hinchey, whose working-class experience was far removed from that of NAWSA's mostly middle-class membership. "They bring vital, vivid arguments that carry weight and conviction," the *Journal* reported.[90] Elizabeth Robbins, president of the Women's Trade Union League (WTUL), in 1916 was among four experts in the social sciences who argued suffrage would help mothers, child laborers, working women, and public morality.[91] A 1917 panel featured French and British women discussing their war work, and a debate by Americans that same year asked, "Should We Work for Woman

Alice Paul (second from right) with five other suffragists in Chicago, 1920.

Suffrage in Wartime?"[92] Booths stacked with pamphlets and books provided much more information on suffrage campaigning.[93]

Ideas were disseminated not only at NAWSA's annual meeting but also at hundreds of smaller conventions organized by the many state and city suffrage leagues. Attendees of Pennsylvania suffragists' forty-fifth annual gathering in 1913 came away full of new ideas, such as raising money by setting up suffrage stores or selling suffrage stamps. They even inspected a model of a county fair suffrage booth.[94] Conventions were the "most spectacular function" of Tennessee's suffrage association, according to historian A. Elizabeth Taylor. "New converts were won at conventions, and confirmed suffragists returned home with renewed enthusiasm."[95]

Exposure to new speakers and ideas expanded suffragists' horizons while validating their own work and beliefs. The exposure showed women the progress being made in other parts of the nation and helped them develop campaigns in their communities. The dissemination of ideas and beliefs accelerated after Kentucky suffrage leader Laura Clay in 1895 persuaded NAWSA to convene outside of Washington. NAWSA met in seventeen other cities, from Portland, Oregon, to Atlanta, Georgia.[96]

Perhaps the most critical feature of conventions was the sorority they provided suffragists. Meeting in large numbers fortified women who often fought lonely battles in small towns, where they were isolated and perhaps considered eccentric. Dinners and receptions always followed floor business. Songs and skits held a place on every program. In 1911, Inez Milholland enacted a sketch called "If Women Voted," and two other women delivered suffrage monologues.[97] Inez's sister Vida Milholland sang a "Women's Marseillaise" at the NWP's inaugural meeting in Chicago in 1917.[98] The "Susan B. Anthony" pageant debuted during the CU's convention in Washington in 1915.[99] Special events such as Men's Night and College Night lent the proceedings thematic unity.[100]

One of the most sentimental convention tributes occurred when Catt succeeded Shaw as NAWSA president in December 1915. Each of the more than five hundred delegates passed by and threw a rose on the platform where Shaw sat before presenting her with a gift of thirty thousand dollars and a wreath of gold leaves. "Men say we are too emotional to vote," said Shaw, visibly moved, "but I am very sure that when we compare our emotions in political conventions with the kind they show in theirs, I prefer ours."[101]

Despite this sense of sorority, NAWSA conventions were no sea of tranquillity. Another important convention function was debating policy and strategy, and it sometimes seemed as many suffrage factions existed as there were suffragists. Suffrage conventions often were fractious gatherings that mirrored the many ideological and regional factions within the movement. "The Convention was chaotic from the start," wrote Maud Wood Park in 1912, complaining about several disputes over policy and personnel at the Philadelphia gathering.[102] The perennially upbeat *Woman's Journal* saw a silver lining in discord: "Even the marked differences of opinion in the Convention were encouraging," it stated in 1913, "as they showed that the delegates thought for themselves and had convictions of their own."[103]

Discord also had a dark side. Conventions became the battlefield for key decisions regarding racial issues. As suffrage historian Aileen Kraditor observed, white suffragists equated the capacity to exercise political liberty with Anglo-Saxon ancestry.[104] White suffragists' relations with black suffragists were fraught with contradictions and the racism that pervaded the era. The ostracism African American women experienced was one manifestation of the role privilege played in the suffrage movement. The mostly white, middle-class suffrage movement often did not work for equality for all women. A look at the record shows twentieth-century movement leaders invariably placed race loyalty above gender solidarity.[105] "Even the more radical suffragists appealed to racist attitudes to win support for woman suffrage," said historian Kay Sloan.[106] Northern white suffragists found it easier to practice racial tolerance in the abstract.[107] Susan B. Anthony, for instance, declined in the name of "expediency" to help African American women form a local branch of NAWSA in Atlanta.[108] Historian Paula Giddings has characterized white suffragists' attitude toward their African American counterparts as one of "patronizing arrogance."[109]

Black women generally were excluded from the decision-making body of NAWSA and were not recognized as a group to be included in general deliberations.[110] Adella Hunt Logan, a former assistant principal of the Tuskegee Institute and lifelong member of NAWSA, for instance, was not allowed to attend suffrage conventions in the South.[111] Suffrage newspapers advised southern readers on how white supremacy could be maintained despite woman suffrage.[112] To appease the South and its powerful politicians, NAWSA officially embarked upon a policy of racial discrimi-

nation at the 1903 NAWSA convention, when members implicitly endorsed white supremacy by passing a resolution endorsing a states' rights approach.[113] In addition to sanctioning racism, the states' rights policy derailed the movement by axing the more expeditious campaign for a federal constitutional amendment. Even long after ditching the states' rights approach, NAWSA president Carrie Chapman Catt in 1919 asked Mary Church Terrell, president of the National Association of Colored Women, to encourage the black National Association of the Northeastern Federation of Women's Clubs to withdraw its application for admission to NAWSA because she feared the pending federal amendment would lose southern support if NAWSA accepted the black clubs. "White women simply were willing to let black women go down the proverbial drain to get the vote for themselves," observed Giddings.[114]

Ironically, NAWSA welcomed prominent African American speakers even as it rejected African American members. Terrell addressed several NAWSA conventions beginning in 1898 and delivered a tribute to Frederick Douglass at the sixtieth anniversary of the Seneca Falls convention in 1908.[115] *Crisis* editor W. E. B. Du Bois also addressed NAWSA conventions several times.[116] More typical was the condescending snub Anthony handed Hunt Logan when the Atlanta University graduate asked to address the 1897 NAWSA convention. Anthony replied that an appearance by an "inferior speaker" would hurt both Logan's race and the suffrage movement.[117]

Despite such rebuffs from white groups, African Americans worked for woman suffrage because they saw the vote as integral to racial uplift.[118] Perhaps because their heritage of slavery and segregation made them especially sensitive to the need for political power, southern women led the black suffrage movement. The most influential black suffrage leaders—Terrell, Hunt Logan, Mary Ann Shadd Carey, Ida Wells-Barnett, and Frances Harper—all were natives of the South. Long before most of their white southern peers worked for the vote, southern black women worked for suffrage in nineteenth-century organizations such as the Phillis Wheatley Club of New Orleans. As late at 1908, the *Woman's Journal*'s only subscribers in Alabama were African American women or organizations.[119]

Many of the myriad African American women's organizations in every corner of the nation supported suffrage—temperance unions, church organizations, fraternal societies, and women's clubs.[120] Many African American suffragists found

ON THE SUBJECT OF...

IDA B. WELLS-BARNETT (1862-1931)

Ida B. Wells-Barnett was born to slaves in Holly Springs, Missouri, on July 16, 1862, six months before the passage of the Emancipation Proclamation. She attended Shaw University (later renamed Rust College), a school established for freedmen after the Civil War. As the eldest child, Wells-Barnett assumed the care of her younger siblings following the death of their parents in the 1878 yellow fever epidemic. She taught school for a time in Holly Springs, and later moved to Memphis, Tennessee. In 1884, she sued the Chesapeake, Ohio, and Southwestern Railroad after she was physically removed from a train for refusing to move from the whites-only "ladies" car (for which she had purchased a ticket) to the segregated, blacks-only coach. Wells-Barnett wrote about deplorable conditions in local black schools in a Memphis newspaper, and was subsequently fired from her teaching job. After the office of her employer, *Free Speech,* was destroyed following her stories on the evils of lynching, fear for her safety forced Wells-Barnett to leave Memphis. She moved to New York City. In her two published accounts of lynching practices, *Southern Horrors: Lynch Law in All Its Phases* (1892) and *A Red Record: Tabulated Statistics and Alleged Causes of Lynching in the United States, 1892-1893-1894* (1895), she indicts the hypocrisy of American whites who used any pretext, such as trumped-up rape charges and miscegenation laws, to justify the murder of American blacks. She also lectured in Europe, raising international awareness of lynching practices in the American South. She married Ferdinand L. Barnett in 1895, and devoted several years to motherhood. She later returned to her equal rights activism, and founded the first women's suffrage club for black women. Toward the end of the 1920s she began her autobiography, which her daughter, Alfreda Duster, published posthumously in 1970 as *Crusade for Justice: The Autobiography of Ida B. Wells.* An edited version of *The Memphis Diary of Ida B. Wells* was published in 1995.

sorority in the largest and most influential African American women's club, the forty-thousand-member NACW, which included a large suffrage department.[121] Shadd Carey had organized the first African American organization devoted solely to woman suffrage, the Colored Woman's Progressive Franchise Association in Washington, D.C., in 1880. In the twentieth century, African American journalist Ida Wells-Barnett formed the Alpha Suffrage Club in Chicago in 1913, and at least twenty black women suffrage organizations or groups existed by the mid-1910s.[122]

Other Suffrage Assemblies

Conventions, delegations, and mass meetings were integral to giving shape and form to the suffrage movement. They all, however, mirrored traditionally male forms of political assembly. As the movement began to coalesce, a wide range of innovative suffrage assemblies surfaced in new shapes. What set them apart from the initial suffrage assemblies was that they usually bore a distinctively feminine touch, indicating a burgeoning sense of self and confidence in their sponsors. A "banner meeting" of the New York Woman Suffrage Party to celebrate its new headquarters included singing, recitations, and a social half-hour.[123] New York suffragists sponsored a "Hopping for Suffrage" contest.[124] The Women's Political Union sponsored a "Votes for Women" ball at which women from the United Garment Workers Union mingled with society matrons.[125] Suffrage swimming races and potato sack races enlivened an open-air campaign across Long Island.[126] Determined to win recruits, suffragists in the 1910s went all out to imbue their assemblies with conviviality. Some suffragists touted their social political style as evidence of women's political superiority. "We began to dance about our cause at great balls," said suffrage leader Harriot Stanton Blatch of the New York campaign. "Men's idea was different. They could not ask for the vote for village constables without getting into a brawl over it. Their democracy grew by riots, revolutions, wars. Women conquered in peace and quiet, with some fun."[127]

Suffrage assemblies also attempted to meet the special needs of women. A baby rest tent at a Tennessee chatauqua provided free baby care. "In this way the first impression of our cause received by many a tired mother was that it meant to help her," noted one of the organizers. Suffrage baby shows in upstate New York attracted mothers to talks about children's health care. In Nashville, suffragists operated a sewing room in winter for unemployed women.[128] These assemblies seemed more earnest than simply an attempt by suffragists to prove citizenship and domesticity were not mutually exclusive. Even as critics heaped criticism upon suffragists for their "unwomanliness," suffragists celebrated feminine skills.

The work of the New York Woman Suffrage Party in the 1910s demonstrated the breadth of assemblies sponsored by suffrage organizations. The "What is Going On" column in the *Woman Voter* newsletter listed twenty-three suffrage activities in the boroughs in a month. The East Side Equal Rights League, for instance, offered programs for its numerous immigrant residents every day of the week: on Tuesday, a social gathering; Wednesday, a suffrage history lecture; Thursday, physical culture and dancing; Friday, a class for young women; Saturday, a discussion of current events; and Sunday, a concert and dance.[129] The hallmarks of suffrage gatherings were their creativity and sensitivity to the need or desire to imbue them with a sense of community.

Suffragists frequently found community in the traditionally feminine venue of preparing and sharing food. Sharing meals gave women emotional sustenance. While canvassing for petition signatures in 1913, Syracuse women eased that lonely, frustrating task with a picnic supper at a solicitor's home at the start of their evening, returning at nine o'clock to compare notes.[130] Tennessee suffragists added a regional flair by sponsoring suffrage barbecues.[131] A suffrage banquet proved the highlight of the anniversary celebration of the Woman's Era Club, an African American woman's club in Boston.[132] The Massachusetts Woman Suffrage Association suffrage store lured visitors with colorful window displays; once inside, they found petition forms and literature alongside the tea and cakes, and speakers discussed suffrage daily at noon.[133] Later, the "Sunflower Lunch" room of the Boston Equal Suffrage Association for Good Government served up suffrage sorority along with sandwiches, as did the "Grated Door" at the NWP's headquarters in Washington, D.C.[134]

Teatime proved a congenial assembly for marshaling ideas or recruiting members, partly because the parlor was a safe, familiar gathering place for women just beginning to consider joining the movement. At age 104, suffragist Sylvie Thegson reminisced about conducting parlor meetings: "You had these little afternoon gatherings of women, maybe six or eight women. You had a cup of tea. A little social gathering. While we were drinking tea, I gave a little talk and they

asked questions about what was going on. . . . It was a lot better, I thought at the time, than to have a lecture. Because a lot of them wouldn't go to a lecture."[135]

The militant NWP probably sponsored more teas than pickets as well as a Christmas card party, dance, and ball.[136] New York City suffragists and the female reporters who covered them became close after gathering daily for years to trade news over tea at suffrage headquarters.[137] No matter what form they took, suffrage assemblies always included opportunity for restorative sorority.

Suffrage Novelties

One way women showed their association with suffrage even when alone was to buy, display, or wear the many novelties spawned by the movement. Pins, sashes, and other regalia served as icons that expressed more powerfully than words a woman's support for suffrage. "Wearing the Suffrage badge implies courage and enthusiasm when the cause is unpopular," wrote Alice Park of California, who collected 178 pins. "It is one of the easy ways to advertise votes for women among strangers."[138] Souvenir seekers could find many more whimsical items that announced their support for votes for women at suffrage stores that opened their doors in cities. Novelties included suffrage soap, crackers, pin cushions, umbrellas, notepaper, gold-edged china stamped with "Votes for Women," jugs, and a doll wearing a suffrage-yellow sash and hat.[139] The *Woman Suffrage Cook-Book* featured seven hundred recipes; the College Suffrage Calendar contained a suffrage quote for every day of the year; a Chicago club's postcard displayed a girl clad in yellow; a suffrage jigsaw puzzle targeted children, and the Women's Political Union's purple, green, and white playing cards cost twenty-five cents. "A good suffragist will hardly play bridge without her own cards," said the *New York Times*.[140] NAWSA sold music sheets for the many suffrage songs that also united women, such as "For Women," sung to the tune of "Dixie," and the "Suffrage Song" to the tune of "America."[141] A Pennsylvania woman showed her colors by planting a suffrage garden filled, of course, with yellow flowers.[142]

The feminine cast of many suffrage articles and activities masked the revolutionary nature of the social movement that spawned them. The suffrage movement threatened many men and women who feared women's entrance into politics would upend the social order. Suffrage baby tents and suffrage cookbooks could help divert opposi-

Image depicting a suffrage parade in New York City, October 15, 1915.

tion by their link to mothering and the home, but less domestically endowed assemblies provoked outright antagonism.

The Woman's Party

Shock waves reverberated through the male political establishment when the Woman's Party of Western Voters organized in 1916. The Woman's Party convention marked the first time women organized their own political party, one of the most powerful forms of the right of association. By 1916, women were voting in thirteen states. Almost immediately, Republican and Progressive men also convening in Chicago came to curry the women's political favor, a "refreshing sight" in the view of the *New Republic*.[143]

Yet the specter of women forming their own political party sent chills up many men's spines. The *New York Times* castigated "the influence of sex for political blackmail." It feared the Woman's Party would rip apart the social fabric of the nation. "The Woman's Party has lighted a firebrand," an editorial warned.[144] Indeed, the WP immediately began campaigning against all Democratic candidates in the Western states where women voted to protest the Democratic administration's

failure to act on suffrage. Although relatively unsuccessful, the campaign enraged politicians as well as many suffragists, principally the leaders of NAWSA, who believed it counterproductive.[145]

Male fear of assemblies of independent women spiraled to near-hysterical heights when a prominent suffragist called upon New York City women to strike for one day in 1915 to show how essential women had become in the public sphere. Her theory was the city would grind to a halt if women abandoned their jobs in offices and factories or as teachers, nurses, servants, telephone operators, sales clerks, and settlement workers.[146] Although representatives of the Woman's Trade Union League, social clubs, suffrage organizations, and settlement houses met to discuss the plan, it was abandoned because it drew so much ire. "A promise by everybody never to say again that woman's place is home would be a small price to pay for the escape from the effects of such a strike," the *Times* wrote.[147] The over-reaction to the suggested strike revealed fear that chaos would occur if women rebelled against their assigned supportive roles in American society. It also acknowledged the potential power of women in association.

It is inconceivable that the woman's suffrage movement could have coalesced into any kind of political or social force without the right of association, the basic building block of a social or political movement. Until at least two people join forces to promote an idea, any effort to convert others to that idea or to effect change is no more than agitation by an individual. The more individuals who associate for a cause, the more significant the social movement, until it achieves critical mass. The associational ties that develop among followers as a movement grows increase individuals' devotion to a cause and their sense of possibilities for it. Associating with other women who shared their belief that they should vote reinforced suffragists' sense that they had been wronged by federal and state governments and that they had a right to demand a role in their government.

Suffrage associations in clubs, mass meetings, delegations, and conventions bore some fruit in the nineteenth century. A joint resolution for a federal suffrage amendment was introduced in Congress in 1878 and voted upon in 1887 in the Senate, where it fizzled, sixteen to thirty-four. By 1896, however, women were voting in Colorado, Idaho, Utah, and Wyoming.[148]

Then suffrage hit a wall. The problem was that conventions preached only to the converted, so that contrary to their rebellious roots, conventions by the turn of the century had become staid, insular affairs populated by white-haired women and neglected by the press. Radcliffe College student Maud Wood Park was appalled when she discovered that the 1900 NAWSA convention consisted of roughly one hundred older women meeting in the basement of a church. The first speaker presented a state report in rhyme.[149]

Procedural minutiae dominated convention agendas. Prayers, welcoming speeches, and the reading of letters, for instance, filled most of the first night of the 1906 NAWSA convention in Baltimore, Maryland. The greeting from the state association president set the tone: "Conservative—what a sweet-sounding word—what an ark for the timid soul!"[150] Reports from the states, a round of pleasant club receptions, and a "lively discussion" on whether to use the NAWSA label on its stationery nearly completed the program.[151] The insular atmosphere of conventions ensured that they made a rather limited impact upon politicians and the public. Before conventions could resume their role as dynamic fulcrums for suffrage activism, suffragists had to discover the power of taking their message to the streets.

Near the end of the first decade of the new century, a new breed of suffragist emerged willing to take the movement from the safety of convention halls to the unpredictable streets. It was time to test a new facet of the right of assembly, a facet that planted suffragists in the rollicking public sphere.

Notes

1. Alexis de Tocqueville, *Democracy in America,* 4th ed. (New York: Henry G. Langley, 1845), 1:209.

2. Melvin Rishe, Note, "Freedom of Assembly," *DePaul Law Review* 15 (1966): 339.

3. Abernathy, *Right of Assembly,* 173, 180, 187. The turning point came in *Commonwealth v. Hunt,* in which the Massachusetts Supreme Court said it was not a conspiracy for workers to associate or use their association's strength to agitate for better working conditions. Ibid., 182.

4. *NAACP v. Alabama,* 357 U.S. 449, 461 (1958). The U.S. Supreme Court implied freedom of assembly extended beyond a physical assemblage in *DeJonge v. Oregon,* 299 U.S. 353 (1937). It found political associations protected under the First Amendment in *Sweezy v. New Hampshire,* 354 U.S. 237 (1957).

5. The most raucous debates about rights of association have predictably involved controversial organizations such as the Ku Klux Klan, the Communist Party, and the National Association for the Advancement of Colored People at the dawn of the civil rights movement. Rights of association generally end where criminal conspiracy begins, although the acceptability of a group's ideology has affected United States Supreme Court rulings. The Communist Party has fared particularly poorly in court battles over its members' rights of association. See *Albertson v. Subversive Activities Control Board,* 382 U.S. 70 (1965); *Barenblatt v. United States,* 360 U.S. 109 (1959); *Yates v. United States,* 354 U.S. 298 (1957); and *Dennis v. United States,* 341 U.S. 464 (1951). In contrast, the U.S. Supreme Court has been quite protective of the right of civil rights supporters to freely associate. See *NAACP v. Alabama,* 357 U.S. 449 (1958) (membership lists need not be publicized). The Court continued to allow states to compel disclosure of KKK membership lists because it was a terroristic organization, as established in *Bryant v. Zimmerman,* 278 U.S. 63 (1928).

6. See Nancy Woloch, *Women and the American Experience* (New York: Alfred A. Knopf, 1984), 276-83, 299-303.

7. Lee, "Trampling Out the Vintage," 24.

8. Meredith Tax, *The Rising of the Women: Feminist Solidarity and Class Conflict, 1880-1917* (New York: Monthly Review Press, 1980), 32. For discussions of the women's club movement, see Karen Blair, *The Clubwoman as Feminist: True Womanhood Redefined, 1868-1914* (New York: Holmes and Meier, 1980); Paula Giddings, "'To Be a Woman Sublime': The Ideas of the National Black Women's Club Movement (to 1917)," in *When and Where I Enter . . . The Impact of Black Women on Race and Sex in America,* by Giddings (New York: William Morrow, 1984), 95-118; Gerda Lerner, "Early Community Work of Black Clubwomen," *Journal of*

Negro History 59 (Apr. 1974): 158-67; Scott, *Natural Allies;* and Anne Firor Scott, "Most Invisible of All: Black Women's Voluntary Associations," *Journal of Southern History* 56 (Feb. 1990): 3-22.

9. Matthews, *Rise of Public Woman,* 159.

10. "Women's Clubs and Suffrage," *Woman's Journal,* 18 Oct. 1913, 332.

11. Cott, *Grounding of Modern Feminism,* 30; and Ellen Carol DuBois, "Working Women, Class Relations, and Suffrage Militance: Harriot Stanton Blatch and the New York Woman Suffrage Movement, 1894-1909," *Journal of American History* 74 (1987): 35.

12. Kraditor, *Ideas of the Woman Suffrage Movement,* 7. In comparison, 13,150 women belonged in 1893. Ibid.

13. Beeton, *Women Vote in the West,* 110.

14. "Parade Protest Arouses Senate," *New York Times,* 5 Mar. 1912, 8.

15. Beeton, *Women Vote in the West,* 32. Mormon women employed the technique again (unsuccessfully) in 1886 to protest Congress' plans to repeal woman suffrage as part of its antipolygamy campaign. Ibid., 76.

16. Cynthia Neverdon-Morton, *Afro-American Women of the South and the Advancement of the Race, 1895-1925* (Knoxville: Univ. of Tennessee Press, 1989), 177.

17. Katzenstein, *Lifting the Curtain,* 83; "Votes for Women at the Home Stretch," Reel 58, NAWSA Papers; and "New York's Victory Convention," *Woman Citizen,* 1 Dec. 1917, 12.

18. Lerner, *Grimké Sisters,* 218, 222.

19. Flexner, *Century of Struggle,* 86.

20. Beeton, *Women Vote in the West,* 4.

21. "One Hundred Earnest Suffragets [sic] March Streets to Home of State Senator Walters," *Syracuse Journal,* n.d., n.p., Reel 1, microfilm edition, Papers of Harriot Stanton Blatch, Manuscript Division, Library of Congress (hereafter cited as HSB Papers).

22. Grimes, *Puritan Ethic,* 80.

23. Sterling, *We Are Your Sisters,* 412.

24. Anne Firor Scott and Andrew Scott, *One Half the People: the Fight for Woman Suffrage,* (Philadelphia: J. B. Lippincott, 1975), 97.

25. Ibid., 103, 105.

26. A. Elizabeth Taylor, *Citizens at Last: The Woman Suffrage Movement in Texas,* (Austin: Ellen C. Temple, 1987), 119.

27. "Two Speeches by Independent Women," Reel 1, HSB Papers.

28. "Women in Albany in Ballot Battle," *Progress,* 25 Feb. 1909, 1. The WPU later sent women to watch the polls, which involved considerable bravery because it could involve challenging the credentials of some of the city's "burliest citizens," as one newspaper put it. Several observers were arrested in Hell's Kitchen in 1910, but charges of obstructing the election were dropped. "College Girl Challenges Bowery Voters," unidentified newspaper clipping; and "Magistrates Uphold Women Watchers," *New York Evening Sun,* 14 Sept. 1910, n.p., both in Reel 1, HSB Papers.

29. "On to the Capitol, Suffragists Cry," unidentified newspaper clipping, Reel 64, NAWSA Papers; and "Pilgrimage to the Opening of the Maryland Legislature" *Suffragist,* 10 Jan. 1914, 7.

30. "Record Broken in Illinois," *Woman's Journal,* 25 Apr. 1909, 65.

31. Qtd. in "Broke All Records," *Woman's Journal,* 27 Jan. 1909, 34. Other newspapers also used war imagery to describe suffragist visits to legislatures. See "Suffrage Army Takes State Capitol in Silent Attack," *New York Evening Mail;* and "Women Storm Albany," *New York Daily Tribune,* both in Reel 1, HSB Papers.

32. "Woman Suffrage Demonstration in Boston," *Progress,* Mar. 1909, 4.

33. "The Great Boston Meeting," *Progress,* Apr. 1909, 1.

34. "Woman Suffragists Storm Congress with Petitions for Votes, Filling Galleries and Overwhelming Proceedings with Applause," *New York Herald,* 19 Apr. 1910, 4.

35. "Suffragists Storm National Capitol," *New York Times,* 19 Apr. 1910, 1.

36. Mabel Vernon, "Speaker for Suffrage and Petitioner for Peace," interview by Amelia Fry, Suffragists Oral History Collection, Univ. of California, Berkeley, microfiche edition (Sanford, N.C.: Microfilm Corp. of America, 1980) (hereafter cited as Vernon interview), 68-69; and Inez Haynes Irwin, *The Story of the Woman's Party,* (New York: Harcourt, Brace, 1921), 183-86.

37. Report of the Congressional Union, May 1913, Reel 87, National Woman's Party Papers: The Suffrage Years 1913-1920, microfilm edition, ed. Thomas Pardo. (Sanford, N.C.: Microfilm Corp. of America, 1979) (hereafter cited as NWP Papers: The Suffrage Years).

38. "President Refuses Aid to Deputation," *Suffragist,* 27 June 1914, 3.

39. "Heckling the President," *Suffragist,* 11 June 1914, 2.

40. Qtd. in Irwin, *Story of the Woman's Party,* 64.

41. "Polite to the President," *Woman's Journal,* 13 Dec. 1913, 396; and "President Will Favor Committee," *Woman's Journal,* 13 Dec. 1913, 393. The CU also sponsored mass meetings, lectures, receptions, tableaux, benefits, and teas. Irwin, *Story of the Woman's Party,* 46-47.

42. "Heckling the President," *Suffragist,* 22 May 1915, 4.

43. "President Will Favor Committee," *Woman's Journal,* 12 Dec. 1913, 393.

44. "Mrs. Catt Elected National President," *Woman's Journal,* 25 Dec. 1915, 407. Wilson's daughter Margaret supported suffrage. "Margaret Wilson Out for Woman Suffrage," *New York Tribune,* 29 Apr. 1913, n.p., Reel 3, HSB Papers.

45. "Speech of President Wilson at the 48th annual convention of the National American Woman Suffrage Association," 8 Sept. 1916, Reel 59, NAWSA Papers.

46. Freeman, *Social Movements of the Sixties and Seventies,* 8.

47. *Proceedings of the Eleventh National Woman's Rights Convention,* Church of the Puritans, New York City, 10 May 1866, 5, Reel 57, NAWSA Papers.

48. "Convention Gave Spirit of Union," *Woman's Journal*, 1 Jan. 1916, 2.

49. For discussions about women's progress in these sectors of the public sphere, see Susan Porter Benson, *Counter Cultures: Saleswomen, Managers, and Customers in American Department Stores, 1890-1940* (Urbana: Univ. of Illinois Press, 1986); Blair, *Clubwoman as Feminist*; Estelle Freedman, "Separatism as Strategy: Female Institution Building and American Feminism, 1870-1930," *Feminist Studies* 5 (Fall 1979): 512-49; Martin, *Sound of Our Own Voices*; Kathy Preiss, *Cheap Amusements: Working Women and Leisure in Turn-of-the-Century New York* (Philadelphia: Temple Univ. Press, 1986); Kathleen Kish Sklar, "Hull House in the 1890s: A Community of Women Reformers," *Signs* 10 (Summer 1985): 658-77; and Barbara Miller Solomon, *In the Company of Educated Women* (New Haven, Conn.: Yale Univ. Press, 1985).

50. "Convention Comes to a Successful Close," *Woman's Journal*, 28 Oct. 1911, 337.

51. "The National Convention," *Woman Voter*, Oct. 1916, 21.

52. "Not Used to Voting?" unidentified newspaper clipping, Ida Porter Boyer Scrapbooks, Reel 63, NAWSA Papers.

53. "The National Convention," *Woman's Journal*, 16 Sept. 1916, 300; and "Program of the National Convention," *Woman's Journal*, 26 Aug. 1916, 278.

54. Untitled, *New Republic* 7 (17 June 1916): 155.

55. "Convention Was Argument Itself," *Woman's Journal*, 23 Sept. 1916, 306.

56. "Suffragists in the Rose City," *Morning (Portland) Oregonian*, 28 June 1905, n.p., Ida Porter Boyer Scrapbooks, Reel 63, NAWSA Papers.

57. "Editors Grilled by Suffragists," unidentified newspaper clipping, 10 Feb. 1906, Reel 59, NAWSA Papers.

58. Wallace Irwin and Inez Milholland, "Two Million Women Vote," *McClure's Magazine*, Jan. 1913, 246-47. The authors repeated an exchange overheard at the convention to illustrate how the tenor of female conventions differed from male conventions: "The Chair: 'Do you mean to say the rule should apply to your State only?' The Delegate: 'My dear! I didn't say any such thing.'" Ibid., 251.

59. "Buffalo Convention," *Woman's Journal*, 24 Oct. 1908, 169.

60. "A Corner in Publicity," *Woman Citizen*, 2 Feb. 1918, 190.

61. See "The State Convention," *Woman Voter*, Nov. 1913, 17.

62. Program, Woman Voters' Convention, 14-16 Sept. 1915, Reel 140, National Woman's Party Papers, 1913-1974, microfilm edition (Glen Rock, N.J.: Microfilm Corp. of America, 1977-78) (hereafter cited as NWP Papers); and qtd. in "Assemble in Convention," *Suffragist*, 2 Oct. 1915, 6.

63. "Parties Greet State Meeting," *Woman's Journal*, 8 Nov. 1913, 358; and "The National Convention," *Woman's Journal*, 16 Feb. 1906, 25.

64. "What the 49th Annual Convention of the NAWSA Accomplished," *Woman Citizen*, 22 Dec. 1917, 68-69.

65. "A Boon in Suffrage Literature," *Woman Citizen*, 12 Apr. 1919, 961. The NWP Press Department also sent news stories, feature articles and photographs to hundreds of newspapers across the nation. "The Woman's Party and the Press," *Suffragist*, 13 Sept. 1919, 7.

66. See "Hold Convention in West Virginia," *Woman's Journal*, 8 Nov. 1913, 358; "Plan Convention for Wisconsin," *Woman's Journal*, 8 Nov. 1913, 358; "Hold Convention in Granite State," *Woman's Journal*, 20 Dec. 1913, 403; "Delegates Meet in Connecticut," *Woman's Journal*, 25 Oct. 1913, 342; "Twenty-three States Map Out Campaign," *Woman's Journal*, 13 Mar. 1915, 79; "Many States Hold Important Conventions," *Woman's Journal*, 20 Nov. 1915, 371; "Suffrage Work in the States," *Woman's Journal*, 16 Jan. 1915, 21; and "Across Country with Conventions," *Woman Citizen*, 1 Dec. 1917, 15.

67. "The National Convention," *Woman Voter*, Jan. 1913, 17.

68. "Will Petition Doubtful Congressmen," *Woman's Journal*, 18 Sept. 1915, 297.

69. "Convention Broadens Suffrage Policies," *Woman's Journal*, 20 Nov. 1912, 377.

70. "Conventions of the Woman's Party and Congressional Union," *Suffragist*, 10 Mar. 1917, 4-5.

71. "Delegates Pledged to Fill Money Chest," *Woman's Journal*, 13 Dec. 1913, 394; and "President Will Favor Committee," *Woman's Journal*, 13 Dec. 1913, 393.

72. "Conventions of the Woman's Party and Congressional Union," *Suffragist*, 10 Mar. 1917, 4-5.

73. A. Elizabeth Taylor, *The Woman Suffrage Movement in Tennessee* (New York: Bookman Associates, 1957), 59.

74. "New York Has Big Convention," *Woman's Journal*, 25 Oct. 1913, 342.

75. Minutes of the Meeting of the Executive Council of the National American Woman Suffrage Association at the Marlborough-Blenheim Hotel, Reel 59, NAWSA Papers. Catt's "winning plan" called for mobilizing committees in each of the states to lobby for a federal amendment; it also selected a few key states where it was feasible to win suffrage before Congress passed a federal amendment. Flexner, *Century of Struggle*, 280-81.

76. "Woman's Hour Strikes at Big National Convention," *Woman's Journal*, 16 Sept. 1916, 297.

77. "Platform Adopted at the Forty-eighth Annual Convention," Reel 59, NAWSA Papers; "The Crisis," manuscript, 16, Reel 59, NAWSA Papers; and "The Crisis," *Woman's Journal*, 16 Sept. 1916, 299, 303.

78. "Buffalo Convention," *Woman's Journal*, 24 Oct. 1908, 169; and "Across Country with the Conventions," *Woman Citizen*, 1 Dec. 1917, 15.

79. "Hold Convention in Granite State," *Woman's Journal*, 20 Dec. 1913, 403; and undated press release, Reel 49, NAWSA Papers.

80. "Suffragists Pick National Leaders," *Chicago Evening Post*, 18 Feb. 1907, n.p., in Ida Porter Boyer Scrapbooks, Reel 63, NAWSA Papers.

81. Carrie Chapman Catt and Nettie Rogers Shuler, *Woman Suffrage and Politics: The Inner Story of the Suffrage Movement* (New York: Charles Scribner's Sons, 1923), 381.

82. "Crowd at Suffrage Tea," *New York Times*, 10 Feb. 1915, 8; Doris Stevens, *Jailed for Freedom* (New York: Boni & Liveright, 1920), 72; "Special Convention Number," *Woman Citizen*, 14 Feb. 1920; and "Convention Issue," *Suffragist*, Jan.-Feb. 1920. After Congress approved the Nineteenth Amendment, the NWP raised funds to commission busts in the Capitol of Anthony, Stanton, and Lucretia Mott, who helped Stanton organize the Seneca Falls convention. "A Women's National Memorial," *Suffragist*, Dec. 1920, 303.

83. Beeton, *Women Vote in the West*, 133.

84. Paul Fuller, *Laura Clay and the Woman's Rights Movement* (Lexington: Univ. Press of Kentucky, 1975), 84.

85. "Convention News," *Progress*, Nov. 1908, 2; and "The National Convention," *Progress*, May 1910, 4.

86. Program of forty-third annual NAWSA convention, Louisville, Kentucky, Reel 58, NAWSA Papers.

87. "Convention Comes to a Successful Close," *Woman's Journal*, 28 Oct. 1911, 337.

88. Program of forty-third annual NAWSA convention, Louisville, Kentucky, 1911, Reel 58, NAWSA Papers.

89. Program of forty-fourth annual NAWSA convention, Philadelphia, 1912; and Taylor, *Woman Suffrage Movement in Tennessee*, 66.

90. Program of the forty-fifth annual NAWSA convention, Washington, D.C., 1913, Reel 58, NAWSA Papers; and "National Convention Strikes New Note," *Woman's Journal*, 6 Dec. 1913, 32.

91. "A Remarkable Evening," *Woman's Journal*, 16 Sept. 1916, 300.

92. "What the 49th Annual Convention of the NAWSA Accomplished," *Woman Citizen*, 22 Dec. 1917, 68-69.

93. Program of forty-fourth annual NAWSA convention, Philadelphia, 1912, Reel 59, NAWSA Papers; and "A Boon in Suffrage Literature," *Woman Citizen*, 12 Apr. 1919, 961.

94. "Parties Greet State Meeting," *Woman's Journal*, 8 Nov. 1913, 358.

95. Taylor, *Woman Suffrage Movement in Tennessee*, 58, 59.

96. Fuller, *Laura Clay*, 74.

97. Program of forty-third annual NAWSA convention, Louisville, Kentucky, 1911, Reel 58, NAWSA Papers; and "Rejoicing Suffragists Meet in National Convention," *Woman's Journal*, 21 Oct. 1911, 330.

98. "Conventions of the Woman's Party and Congressional Union," *Suffragist*, 10 Mar. 1917, 4-5.

99. Catt and Shuler, *Woman Suffrage and Politics*, 381; and "Pageant Closes Union Meeting," *Woman's Journal*, 18 Dec. 1915, 400.

100. Program of the forty-fourth annual NAWSA convention, Philadelphia, 1912, Reel 59, NAWSA Papers.

101. "Mrs. Catt Elected National President," *Woman's Journal*, 25 Dec. 1915, 408.

102. Program of forty-fourth annual NAWSA convention, Philadelphia, 1912, Reel 59, NAWSA Papers.

103. "After the Convention," *Woman's Journal*, 13 Dec. 1913, 397.

104. Kraditor, *Ideas of the Woman Suffrage Movement*, 254.

105. For a discussion of questions posed by the role privilege played in the suffrage movement, see Catherine Mitchell, "Historiography on the Woman's Rights Press," in *Outsiders in 19th-Century Press History: Multicultural Perspectives*, ed. Frankie Hutton and Barbara Straus Reed (Bowling Green, Ohio: Bowling Green Univ. Popular Press, 1995), 159-68.

106. Kay Sloan, "Sexual Warfare in the Silent Cinema: Comedies and Melodramas of Woman Suffragism," *American Quarterly* 33 (1981): 429. A silent film produced by the Women's Political Union (successor to Blatch's Equality League of Self-Supporting Women), for instance, contained a scene in which a man asked, "My butler and my bootblack vote—why not my wife and daughter?" Ibid., 425.

107. *Suffragist* newspaper, for instance, championed African Americans after the race riots in East St. Louis and described blacks and suffragists as comrades in their quest for equal rights. "Negro Unrest," *Suffragist*, 25 Aug. 1917, 3.

108. Adele Logan Alexander, "How I Discovered My Grandmother . . . ," *Ms.* 12 (Nov. 1983): 34.

109. Giddings, *When and Where I Enter*, 162. For other discussions on racial discrimination in the suffrage movement, see also "Anti-Black Woman Suffrage Efforts," in Rosalyn Terborg-Penn, "Afro-Americans in the Struggle for Woman Suffrage" (Ph.D. diss., Howard Univ., 1977), 277-311; Rosalyn Terborg-Penn, "Discrimination Against Afro-American Women in the Woman's Movement, 1830-1920," in *The Afro-American Woman: Struggles and Images*, ed. Sharon Harley and Rosalyn Terborg-Penn (Port Washington, N.Y.: Kennikat Press, 1978), 17-27; Beverly Guy-Sheftall, "Books, Brooms, Bibles, and Ballots: Black Women and the Public Sphere," in Guy-Sheftall, *Daughters of Sorrow*, 91-158; Aileen Kraditor, "The 'Southern Question,'" in Kraditor, *Ideas of the Woman Suffrage Movement*, 162-218; and Marjorie Spruill Wheeler, "Southern Suffragists and 'the Negro Problem,'" in *New Women of the New South: The Leaders of the Woman Suffrage Movement in the Southern States*, by Wheeler (New York: Oxford Univ. Press, 1993), 100-132.

White suffragists also treated Native American women contradictorily. On the one hand, they held up the example of matriarchy in Indian culture as an alternative to American patriarchy, but they resented being classified with "savages" in their disfranchised state. See Gail Landsman, "The 'Other' as Political Symbol: Images of Indians in the Woman Suffrage Movement," *Ethnohistory* 39 (Summer 1992): 247-84.

110. Neverdon-Morton, *Afro-American Women of the South*, 203.

111. Wheeler, *New Women of the New South*, 111.

112. Southern suffragists maintained the white woman's vote would offset the large "undesirable" vote in the South. "Southern Suffragists Roused Over Slacker Vote," *Woman Citizen*, 12 Jan. 1918, 132. The National Woman's Party argued that poll taxes and literacy tests

would continue to weed out undesirable voters of both races. "National Suffrage and the Race Problem," *Suffragist,* 14 Nov. 1914, 3.

113. Terborg-Penn, "Discrimination Against Afro-American Women," 27.

114. Giddings, *When and Where I Enter,* 161-63.

115. Mary Church Terrell, *A Colored Woman in a White World* (Washington, D.C.: Ransdell, 1940; reprint, Salem, N.H.: Ayer, 1992), 145-46; and "Programme, Anniversary Celebration of the 1848 Woman's Rights Convention," Reel 1, HSB Papers; Wilson Jeremiah Moses, "Domestic Female Conservatism, Sex Roles, and Black Women's Clubs 1893-1896," in *Black Women in American History: The Twentieth Century,* vol. 3, ed. Darlene Clark Hine, et al. (Brooklyn: Carlson Publishing, 1990), 968.

116. Guy-Sheftall, *Daughters of Sorrow,* 117. Du Bois dedicated several issues of the *Crisis* to woman suffrage. See issues for Sept. 1912, Aug. 1915, and Nov. 1917.

117. Alexander, "How I Discovered My Grandmother," 36.

118. Cott, *Grounding of Modern Feminism,* 31; and Terborg-Penn, "Afro-Americans in the Struggle," 287.

119. Terborg-Penn, "Afro-Americans in the Struggle," 109, 126; and Alexander, "How I Discovered My Grandmother," 30.

120. Terborg-Penn, "Afro-Americans in the Struggle," 184.

121. Giddings, *When and Where I Enter,* 129.

122. Alfreda Duster, ed., *Crusade for Justice: The Autobiography of Ida B. Wells* (Chicago: Univ. of Chicago Press, 1970), xxviii; and Rosalyn Terborg-Penn, "Discontented Black Feminists: Prelude and Postscript to the Passage of the Nineteenth Amendment," in *Black Women in American History: The Twentieth Century,* vol. 4, ed. Darlene Clark Hine (Brooklyn: Carlson Publishing, 1990), 1160.

123. *Woman Voter,* Mar. 1917, 24.

124. "Hopping for Suffrage," *Woman Voter and Suffrage News,* June 1915, 21.

125. "Society Mingles with Girl Toilers at Suffrage Ball," *New York American,* 12 Jan. 1913, n.p., Reel 2, HSB Papers.

126. "'Sunshade Race' and Other Novel Feats Attract Many Recruits at Shoreham," *New York American,* 20 July 1913, n.p.; and "Fair New York Girl Star of Suffrage Picnic," *New York Tribune,* 27 July 1913, n.p.; both in Reel 3, HSB Papers.

127. Harriot Stanton Blatch and Alma Lutz, *Challenging Years: The Memoirs of Harriot Stanton Blatch* (New York: G. P. Putnam's Sons, 1940), 192.

128. Taylor, *Woman Suffrage Movement in Tennessee,* 54, 55; and "Suffragist Baby Shows," *New York Times,* 16 Oct. 1913, 1.

129. "What Is Going On," *Woman Voter,* Apr. 1910, 6. See also the *Woman Voter* for Feb. 1901, 7; Mar. 1911, 3; Apr. 1912, 27; July 1913, 28; June 1914, 25; and Aug. 1915, 21.

130. "The Humors of Canvassing," *Woman Voter,* Aug. 1913, 12.

131. Taylor, *Woman Suffrage Movement in Tennessee,* 52.

132. Terborg-Penn, "Afro-Americans in the Struggle," 133.

133. "The Suffrage Store," *Woman's Journal,* 29 May 1909, 86.

134. "The Sunflower Lunch," *Woman Citizen,* 31 Aug. 1918, 272; and "An Impression of a Suffrage Tea Room," *Suffragist,* 21 Sept. 1918, 6.

135. Sherna Gluck, ed., *From Parlor to Prison: Five American Suffragists Talk About Their Lives, an Oral History* (New York: Vintage Books, 1976), 45.

136. "Parlor Meetings," Official Program, Woman Suffrage Procession, Washington, D.C., 3 Mar. 1913, Reel 49, NAWSA Papers; "Hospitality to Prevail in Old Cameron House," *Washington Star,* 27 Dec. 1916, n.p., in Reel 49, NAWSA Papers; and Invitation to Suffrage Ball, 21 Apr. 1914, Reel 149, NWP Papers.

137. Journalists so missed the ritual that they created the New York Newspaper Women's Club to fill the void in the 1920s. Ishbel Ross, *Ladies of the Press: The Story of Women in Journalism by an Insider* (New York: Harper & Brothers 1936), 126.

138. Alice Park, "Show Your Colors," Reel 49, NAWSA Papers.

139. "Trinkets and Songs of the Suffragists," *New York Times,* 28 June 1914, sec. 5, p. 8; and "The Suffrage Doll," *Woman's Journal,* 9 Sept. 1911, 286.

140. "Woman Suffrage Cook-Book," *Woman's Journal,* 24 July 1909, 1; "College Suffrage Calendar," *Woman's Journal,* 6 Nov. 1909, 177; "New Suffrage Post-Card," *Woman's Journal,* 9 Jan. 1909, 5; "Suffrage Game," *Suffragist,* 27 Dec. 1913, and "Trinkets and Songs of the Suffragists," *New York Times,* 28 June 1914, sec. 5, p. 8.

141. Reel 95, NWP Papers: The Suffrage Years.

142. "Suffrage Garden Grows Popular," *Woman's Journal,* 27 Mar. 1915, 102.

143. Untitled, *New Republic,* 17 June 1916, 155.

144. *New York Times,* 14 July 1916, 10.

145. See "The Election Policy of the Congressional Union for Woman Suffrage," Reel 149, NWP Papers; Anna Howard Shaw to Cora Lewis, 23 Sept. 1914, Reel 33, NAWSA Papers; and Mary Ware Dennett to Ruth McCormick, 6 Jan. 1914, Reel 33, NAWSA Papers.

146. "Novel Suffrage Stunts as Publicity Makers," *New York Sun,* 16 Feb. 1918, n.p., Reel 95, NWP Papers: The Suffrage Years.

147. "City Tie-Up Gets New Backing," *New York Times,* 19 Aug. 1915, 9; and "An Appalling Strike Is Threatened," *New York Times,* 20 Aug. 1915, 10.

148. For discussions of these state campaigns, see Beeton, *Women Vote in the West;* Eleanor Flexner, "First Victories in the West," in Flexner, *Century of Struggle,* 156-65; and Grimes, *Puritan Ethic.*

149. Sharon Hartman Strom, "Leadership and Tactics in the American Woman Suffrage Movement: A New Perspective from Massachusetts," *Journal of American History* 62 (1975): 302. Maud Wood Park then founded the College Equal Suffrage League and went on to head the NAWSA Congressional Committee from

1917 through 1920. Ibid. See also Park's memoir, *Front Door Lobby* (Boston: Beacon Press, 1960).

150. "The National Convention," *Woman's Journal,* 16 Feb. 1906, 25.

151. *Progress,* Mar. 1906, 1-2.

MAJOR FIGURES AND ORGANIZATIONS

ROBERT BOOTH FOWLER (ESSAY DATE 1986)

SOURCE: Fowler, Robert Booth. "The Case for Suffrage: Catt's Ideal for Women." In *Carrie Catt: Feminist Politician,* pp. 61-76. Boston, Mass.: Northeastern University Press, 1986.

In the following essay, Fowler identifies and analyzes the personal and social values that informed Catt's political position regarding suffrage.

Carrie Catt was not a great political philosopher or even an important contributor to political theory within the modest tradition of American political thought. She neither claimed to be nor wanted to be. Yet, outside her ideas, Catt cannot really be understood as a feminist politician. While they may not have soared much beyond her time and place, her ideas were integral to her definition of what she was doing and to how she was doing it.

Aileen Kraditor argues that the "woman suffrage movement had no official ideology," and Kraditor is undoubtedly correct.[1] This was true not only because there were many different strands in the arguments made for suffrage, but also because it was a Progressive Era movement, not inclined to think in abstract or philosophical terms. Nor did leaders such as Catt attempt to impose a single ideological unity on their movement. They took any allies they could find and did not ask for the reasons behind their support. Moreover, Catt herself was disposed to be eclectic in arguing for woman suffrage. She was not sure how to approach suffrage for women: as a right, as a duty, or as a privilege. What mattered to her was its achievement.

Yet Catt's arguments over time do have a unity that consists of much more than the eclectic grab bag that she sometimes suggested they were. She articulated certain approaches and themes faithfully that provide insight into her basic political values and goals beyond suffrage.

Aileen Kraditor and Janet Zollinger Giele pioneered in the study of the thought of the suffragists.[2] Kraditor's analysis stresses that suffragists supported the enfranchisement of women on two pillars, one drawing from natural-right arguments, the other emphasizing the social benefits that suffragists contended voting women would produce for society. Kraditor terms the latter arguments "expediency" claims, suggesting they were proposed in good part as a means for building support by whatever means worked. Giele notes in particular that the social-benefit approach made suffrage more attractive to men—and to women—because it appeared more "feminine."[3]

Undoubtedly this strategic consideration was important in the partial shift of suffragist arguments during the Progressive Era toward an "expediency" or public-welfare emphasis. But accenting expediency over social benefit can be misleading. Most suffragists were deeply convinced that wide-ranging public benefits would come from the Anthony amendment and sincerely sought most of these gains as public goods. In the Progressive Era most suffragist leaders naturally justified reforms in terms of their larger good.

Kraditor's general analysis does apply to Catt. She consistently invoked both general-benefit and natural-rights arguments for woman suffrage. At the same time, however, Catt employed another argument. Over and over she argued for suffrage as a means to end the *humiliation* of women, to restore their dignity as human beings equal to men. Though this view did not conflict with the standard arguments, it was not the same. And it mattered more to Catt than any other.

Public Benefit

The language of social benefit did routinely suffuse Catt's argument for woman suffrage. Even though women opponents insisted that where suffrage for women existed there were no discernible social gains, Catt thought differently. And she took for granted that woman suffrage could be and should be justified in this fashion, and that it represented an effective argument to do so. For her the vote was "a tool with which to build a better nation," and suffrage therefore could pass the supreme test for public policy—"to provide for the common welfare"—and the one test for Catt's personal morality—"To help humanity upward."[4] Her arguments here are familiar ones to those who know anything about the popular pro-suffrage case of her day. In particular, suffrage would aid society, Catt thought, because it would assist the weak, curtail vice, improve the home, and, especially, improve the chances tor peace abroad and for democratic government at home.

She was never very clear why votes for women would help the weak, though she seems to have thought women, or "the best women," would want to and could do so if they had the vote. Mostly she was content to affirm in vague terms that woman suffrage would benefit "all the weak and erring . . . all the homeless and unloved."[5] Or she would make a denunciation of "men who draw vast dividends from very underpaid labor" or proclaim that "posterity assuredly will pronounce child labor in our generation a disgrace."[6] But she never really made clear why woman suffrage could or would do much about these things.

Catt was specifically concerned with the possibility that women's enfranchisement would help socially vulnerable women—divorced and single women and those who had to work for a living— and their children. Catt expected that voting women would make a difference because women were sensitive to the plight of the vulnerable, children especially. She believed that developments in the 1920s, after women's enfranchisement, showed her to be right. The passage of the Sheppard-Towner Act and the success of the Child Labor Amendment in Congress suggested to her that voting women could make politicians assist the vulnerable, though much more needed to be done. The result, she was sure, would be a better nation.[7]

Ironically, her antisuffragist critics both disagreed and agreed with her. Before the adoption of the Anthony amendment they insisted that all it would produce was a formal equality which would not help the weak at all in the real world. Amendments and laws would change little and instead they would open the door to a covert exploitation that would be worse.[8] After 1920 and the appearance of the first protective legislation, especially for children, they turned around and charged that women's enfranchisement was producing dangerous social experiments that threatened the basic economic and social order of the United States.[9]

Fighting "vice" appealed to Catt at least as a reason for woman suffrage. She had in mind particularly the vice of alcohol, but the exploitation of women through prostitution was another topic she frequently addressed. For her to attack "vice" was really to strike back at the opponents of a proper democracy (and woman suffrage— since to her they were intimately linked) rather than to satisfy her personal puritanical urges. For example, she felt alcohol's political effects every day she campaigned for women's enfranchisement. Alcohol and those in the liquor business constantly corrupted American democracy by "buying" voters and politicians in an effort to defeat woman suffrage, which they feared would lead to Prohibition. So did all the forces of vice. "Have you ever known of a white slaver, a professional gambler, a political briber . . . who was not an anti-suffragist? I never have."[10]

When the public benefit that suffrage could bring was to promote a better home, Catt had somewhat less to say. Her perspective was different from Jane Addams's, who believed that every woman's heart was in the home. For Addams this meant that public action by women was a natural extension of the home into society, the addressing of family problems in public life.[11] Catt did at times affirm that "home means more to a woman than it ever can to a man," but she was not exactly family-oriented. She was only rarely a homemaker and she had no children. Nor did Catt think about women primarily as guardians of home and family. According to her analysis, things were rapidly changing. By then, many women worked and technological developments no longer required women to be in the home all the time even if they did not have to work. If Catt had any favorite unifying image of women it was as citizens rather than homemakers. Addams was very much a Progressive in her similar devotion to public citizenship, but she fused the role of homemaker and citizen for women in a way that Catt did not.[12]

There was, however, one dimension of the gain that Catt thought could come to the home after women voted that she deeply believed in and advocated. This was her belief that it could end ("destroy" was her word) "obedience of women in the home."[13] Indeed, she held the radical view that this was what the women's movement was all about "at home." She did not doubt that this change would enhance the life of the country as a whole, but that was *not* the context in which she presented it. It was, rather, part (an explosive part) of her argument for enfranchisement to abolish women's humiliation—regardless of its social costs.

Catt recognized that her views on family relations were too radical to advance as a popular argument—with men *or* women. She addressed the issue when critics pushed her to, but mostly she did not discuss family life.

Again and again antisuffragists asserted that women belonged in the home, where they served so well. They feared for home and motherhood itself. They worried that the "sanctity of . . . womanhood and her home" would disappear in a suffrage-stimulated social revolution that would involve "easy" divorce and "free love" and the death of monogomy and of love itself.[14]

There is no question that this charge was the core of the antisuffragist anxiety over women's enfranchisement. For them suffrage challenged "the link of woman to the home that underlay the entire ideology" of opposition to votes for women. To put it another way, what was at issue was different images of women, and the idea that women in particular were the defenders of a family-oriented society.[15]

Catt did not take lightly the charge that the enfranchisement of women would undermine the home and through it all society. Its potential to hurt her cause, especially with traditional women, was much too great for her to ignore the charge. Her responses were revealing. She deftly side-stepped her own goals and chose instead to insist that votes for women would not promote "free love" or "easy divorce." She did not see how they could and she hoped, in fact, that they would not. She also denied that such notions were attractive to most of her fellow workers: "Free love is not and never has been a tenet of suffragists."[16] There were a few public opponents of "family" and marriage within the women's movement, but Catt knew and insisted they were a tiny minority. And in a famous clash with the head of the Man Suffrage Association in 1915, she identified "red light district(s)" as places where defenseless and vote-less women were exploited, and as more significant strongholds of those in favor of divorce and permissive sexual behavior than was the suffragist movement.[17]

Such statements can naturally lead one to the mistaken belief that Catt fits in nicely with Ellen DuBois's perceptive suggestion that suffragists of Catt's generation were not at all radical in their conceptions of women in the home.[18] As we know, this was hardly the case for Catt, who thought "destroying obedience" was a real goal of the feminism she endorsed, and whose own marriages were far from traditional. But the public Catt did not go out of her way to let her larger audience know that her sexual conservatism was not a good guide to how much, in fact, she hoped that antisuffragist fears for the fate of patriarchal family would come true.

She was inclined simply to laugh at a related argument of the antisuffragists that suggested that women could not handle any life except the secure life of patriarchal domesticity. Opponents' contentions that a larger life for women would create too much stress, exhaust their limited psychological resources, and even promote the spread of "insanity" among women were not uncommon.[19] But Catt thought it was obvious that this was a myth propagated by rich Eastern women who knew little about most women in American life, and even less of history. "The objection that the 'nervous system' of women is not sufficiently stable to endure the strain of political responsibility, an objection heard disgustingly often in the East, is naturally not heard [in the West]. A 'Nervous System' which has sufficient caliber to face rattlesnakes . . . cyclones, and to 'Prove us' a claim, will hardly be charged here with too much delicacy."[20]

Perhaps it was her own experience as a woman married to two men who were from all accounts emotionally healthy and independent that explains why Catt did not rise to antisuffragist suggestions that proper, homebody women would lose contact with "real" men as the result of the revolution suffrage would instigate. Men would become effeminate, it was said, and there were public calls for "men" to stand up and be men and repulse the suffragists' attempt to destroy them.[21]

But another, greater reason was that Catt did not think primarily in family or gender terms. Always she searched for equal citizens united to serve the public good. It was in this spirit that she argued most strongly for the potential social gains of women's enfranchisement in terms of advancing democracy and world peace. Indeed, it was with these specific social benefits in mind that she spoke and wrote for woman suffrage with heart and soul.

I will discuss Catt's conceptions of democracy in some detail later. Here it is sufficient to note that Catt thought American democracy needed to be cleaned up and directed toward social rather than selfish ends. She was sure women could make a difference by eliminating corrupt officials, promoting honest elections, and negating selfish interest groups. Women could apply the only remedy available: "The remedy . . . lies in the integrity and courage of American citizens to rise . . . and declare that the time must speedily come when we shall have purity in government."[22]

But, the antisuffragists' question was, Why would voting women make such a difference? Why were they so special? They thought Catt and her legion of reformers were blinded by their enthusiasm. No one could alter the dirty and enduring realm of politics. Moreover, they thought women were innocent of politics, on the whole, and therefore particularly ill equipped to accomplish this unlikely mission.[23]

But Catt thought—or hoped—that women could improve American democracy. She never claimed that women were purer or nobler than men and thus would naturally defeat evil; Catt never celebrated women over men. Nor did she contend that women were more politically astute than men. Her view, rather, was that women *could* do the job *if* they entered politics and brought to bear their *potential* as human beings because they, unlike men, were free of the history, culture, and current practice of modern politics. The nature of women provided no guarantee, but their very innocence from the ways of politics and their relatively "pure" values because of this innocence provided the opportunity—*if* they were properly trained and led.[24]

Catt also took it for granted that democracy improved as more citizens gained incorporation into the political system. It became more alive and more authentic, and elite rule suffered. "With the enfranchisement of women the ruling class will disappear forever. Popular government, with no privileged class based on religion, wealth, race or sex . . . will become an established fact."[25] It was in light of this faith that she unhesitatingly affirmed that "The enfranchisement of women will be the crowning glory of democratic government."[26]

Such uplifting sentiments did not sit well, however with Catt's opponents. While Catt celebrated women's enfranchisement and democracy together, they insisted Catt and the N.A.W.S.A. were hypocrites. How, they demanded, could the leader of the suffragists and the "small but noisy" minority of women aligned with her claim to be serious democrats? Antisuffragists charged that suffragists were actually trying to "impose upon the majority of women . . . what they do not want and have never asked for": woman suffrage. Suffragists were flagrantly undertaking "to override the fundamental principle of democracy—the rule of the majority."[27]

For antisuffragists the proof of this hypocrisy lay in suffrage crusaders' affinity for pressing their cause through state legislatures and Congress rather than by using referenda or even initiatives in the many states when they were available. Antisuffragists urged that women be allowed to vote on women's enfranchisement (a proposal that had its own irony, of course). Short of that, even letting all men vote would have demonstrated some commitment to democracy by suffragists who, these critics often suspected, rejected the idea because they liked operating in the dark corridors with political machines and hidden elites whom they so ostentatiously denounced in public. They were not democrats but machine politicians par excellance.[28]

There was a good deal of truth to these charges where Catt is concerned. She was akin to a *machine* politician, at least insofar as she was prepared to match her opponents with all the skills of organization and wiles of strategy that she felt were so necessary to thread one's way through the American political process. And along the way Catt did not, in fact, show any enthusiasm for pursuing means that her critics believed to be more democratic, such as referenda by men—or women. Catt simply knew the facts, that suffrage referenda often lost as a majority of male voters voted "no," while referenda by women in nonsuffrage states simply were not going to happen. To be sure, Catt and her allies sometimes used existent referenda procedures and, in time, often won. But her decision by 1916 to push for a constitutional amendment rather than fighting only state-by-state and often referenda-by-referenda did represent a choice to reach for a victory in national legislative halls. Of course, even a constitutional amendment required three-quarters of the states to approve it. But Catt realized that the issue would be decided in state legislatures, not by public referenda. More to the point, perhaps, Catt's strategic choice to work for passage of the Nineteenth Amendment did not seem to her a denial of her commitment to democracy. It was only a practical calculation to advance her cause, not a significant statement of her philosophy of ideal government. Ideal government would be an inclusive, politically egalitarian, and uncorrupted democracy, which Catt was convinced woman suffrage would facilitate as nothing else could. This ideal was proof of Catt's commitment to democracy, she believed, and she was more than content to let the matter rest there.

However, she did rely on her limited faith in democracy when she thought it would serve her immediate goal of suffrage for women, during World War I in particular. It was then that she pounded home her conviction that a commitment to democracy in principle required the granting of suffrage to women. After all, was not America involved in the war to defend and promote democracy? If so, then how could Congress avoid making democracy real at home, especially in light of the fact that women could vote in Germany? Congress had no choice. It had to vote a constitutional amendment for woman suffrage to avoid rendering America's participation in the war a fraud.[29]

Catt's strategic purpose here was, obviously, not subtle. In part she was merely mobilizing proclaimed American war objectives to her advantage. Yet there was another, quite authentic side to her appeal. War could make sense to her only if it was fought for a cause, even a cause such as democracy. Granting women suffrage could make the war truly legitimate; U.S. war aims would be less hollow and no American woman would need be skeptical about the war.

As important in the long run for Catt was the potential enfranchising women had for her almost sacred goal: world peace. "For thousands of years," Catt argued, "men have begun all the wars," and their attempts to clean up the mess left behind merely led on to the next war.[30] While in later, postsuffrage years, Catt appreciated that in light of this sad record it would "take a long time to get the fighting habit out of them,"[31] her hopes were higher before 1920. To be sure, she granted that both sexes had great capacity for what she called hysterical, nonrational behavior. The difference was that men expressed theirs by fighting. Women did so in other ways and therefore voting women would inevitably check men's affinity for war. Catt was less clear as to why men expressed their "hysteria" in war and women did not. The explanation she usually favored was cultural. Catt also thought women's role in society placed them in a position to favor life and reject war, which was too often over matters such as "oil or coal or trade." She always claimed that, had women been able to be active citizens before World War I, there would have been no war.[32]

While her confidence here was in those days real, its plausibility was tissue-thin. Opponents ridiculed the idea that women could end war. They did not see women as quite the peace lovers Catt thought them to be. And the pacifists tended to encourage the warlike, as pacifists always did, even if unintentionally. While Catt thought differently both before and after the Great War, she implicitly agreed with her critics during the war. After all, her claim then was that enfranchised women would be strongly committed to the war

and to the fighting patriotism of that day. Then votes for women, were in Catt's phrase, "an imperative war measure." This was not merely Catt the strategist at work; she was perfectly sincere. And it never seems to have occurred to her that she could not have it both ways; if woman suffrage was socially beneficial because it would advance peace, how could it also be good because it would help win wars?[33]

Natural Rights

The first language of the women's movement in the United States was the language of rights. The Declaration of Rights and Sentiments spoke in these terms. So did the pioneers of the movement, such as Elizabeth Cady Stanton.[34] So did Catt, even though her arguments were complicated by her simultaneous claims for the social benefits of suffrage.

Her often repeated view was straightforward: Women had a right to vote as human beings who could not be governed without their consent and their participation. Catt often called on this tenet of Western liberalism with a special American twist, stressing the issue of taxation without representation. But mostly she—with others—invoked the familiar right of consent of the governed to press her suffrage claims and left it at that. For she knew that the language of rights, especially the right of consent, was so pervasive in American experience and culture that her appeal could not be ignored.[35]

Catt was unlike most others who invoked such a rights claim for women in that she did have at least some sense of what she meant when she made this kind of claim. While the ordinary "arguments" on this score consisted of little more than assertions that women had a vague thing known as equal right and thus should be allowed to vote, Catt spoke from her Spencerian naturalism, grounding her notion of rights in a view of human nature in which all people had an equal right to liberty and consent. However, Catt normally followed the popular path of announcing this right rather than developing its ontological, analytical, and epistemological meanings and implications.[36]

It is no surprise that most of Catt's attention went to stressing equality regarding the right to vote. She agreed with John Stuart Mill that the right was universal and, unlike Mill, she really meant it. That led her to an angry set of comparisons, time and again, with women's status as citizens vis-à-vis the males who had the right to

Carrie Chapman Catt (1859-1947).

vote in the United States and in some cases had no trouble obtaining it, despite the absence of any demonstrated record of merit. To her this was obviously absurd. Her message was that women and everyone else should have the equal right.

This was the kind of argument of which she was a master because it allowed her to bring rights down from an abstract philosophical realm in which she was neither comfortable nor particularly competent to show what was at stake in practical life. And by exposing in concrete terms what she took to be laughable inconsistencies in the application of human rights, she assumed people would be left with no choice. They would have to agree with her that women should receive the vote.[37]

The serious problem with Catt's rights argument was that she never explored how it fit or didn't fit with her social-benefit argument. She had no interest in examining questions such as how compatible the individualism of a rights approach was with the implicit social utilitarianism of her social-benefit claims or, in more practical terms, how likely a woman focused on her rights would be to care intensely about social evils and vice versa. The two arguments were lumped together, and that was that.

Only in one instance, carefully brought up after the Anthony suffrage amendment was law, did Catt suggest there might be a difficulty, specifically regarding mothers and their children. In the 1920s she thought she saw signs that some "liberated" women were pursuing lifestyles opened up by acknowledgment of their rights as persons that occasionally damaged the social good. She worried that some women were ignoring their children (as men also could and did), which no society could tolerate. It is significant, though, that Catt tried to have it both ways. Her complaint spoke in unmistakable terms of concern with social benefit, but she phrased it in the language of rights. What was at dispute, she thought, was a clash between the rights of children and those of their parents.[38]

Her inability to address the inevitable tension between social-benefit arguments and rights claims brings us to the interesting fact that Catt's (and others') natural-rights case for votes for women drew relatively little blood. It created only modest controversy among opponents of woman suffrage. Instead, antisuffragists engaged her taxation without representation theme, suggesting that the point was irrelevant. Taxation and representation were not linked in the United States in the first place. Moreover, for a democratic country suffrage should not be tied to taxation.[39]

On the whole, however, Catt received little response when she called for equal rights. The reason was that the antisuffragists did not propose to enter this realm. Catt spoke of the rights of women, while they spoke of the duty of women. Catt tried to balance rights and social-benefit arguments, or at least spoke in terms of both, while the antisuffragists consistently argued exclusively in terms of social benefit (disagreeing with Catt, of course, on what its nature was).

Kraditor suggests that we may conclude that Catt and her friends had a very different idea of women from that of the antisuffragists. Catt's image was of a free, independent, rights-bearing person. Theirs was of a duty-oriented, family-oriented, serving person.[40] This is a crucial point. But it is an incomplete one unless one also notes Catt's optimistic assumption that women could simultaneously be rights-oriented individuals concerned with their self-development *and* devoted to the service of the larger community.

Catt's characteristically American faith that enhanced individualism and expanded liberty would work for the betterment of all depended on her unspoken assumption that people could also be good Progressives. Her opponents thought this was naive and proposed simply to escape the danger of the triumph of selfishness among women (at least) by denying them any individual rights whatsoever. They refused to honor women as individuals, just as Catt refused to recognize that encouraging both individualism and community at the same time could not be accomplished merely by invoking Progressive optimism.[41]

Dignity

Much more than traditional accounts of Catt's arguments for woman suffrage suggest, anger motivated her. She was angry at the way women were treated and her anger went beyond arguments that held such treatment was wrong because it denied their rights or did not contribute to the communal good. Catt was furious because she thought women were daily humiliated and thus denied human dignity. She was insistent that they should rise up and refuse ever again to be "slave, or servant, or dependent, or plaything."[42] This would, she appreciated, require an enormous change in society and in many women. But it was what she wanted. And it was why, above all, she wanted suffrage. It was to be a means of leverage to force men to give ground, whether as a right or as a means to improve society overall. Here is what we may call the unknown Catt.

Catt tended to discuss the suffrage issue in a cool, rational fashion, a style we know she greatly admired in others and consciously strove to follow herself. Yet Catt could abandon that practice on occasion and her talk could turn fiery. This almost always happened when she reviewed the condition of women. More than any other topic and more than any other aspect of the suffrage question, the condition of women angered her and drove her to express her anger. Then she stopped being moderate and started attacking her country's record on women, deploring its "ghastly and inexcusable failures." Then she bitterly deplored the "hideous wrongs" women had experienced over time and the reality of their practical "martyrdom" in the United States.[43] Her anger was even greater when she looked at the experiences of women in other parts of the world. South America was a particular subject for her rage. There, as far as she was concerned, women had "a role little better than that of sexual slaves."[44]

We know that this anger was something that developed in Catt in her youth and her young adulthood. But her adult experiences in the American and international suffrage campaigns continued to fire and expand her feelings. In this she followed the pattern of the pioneers of the women's rights effort. For her as for them it was something intensely personal, developed not just from intellectual sentiments but from very real personal experience.[45]

When Catt did express her anger, she followed it up with ominous warnings that sex wars would develop if something were not done, usually if women did not get their opportunity through the vote. Of course, she always added that she was not threatening anybody, just stating a basic fact of psychology: keeping women down was bound to have disastrous consequences for the relations among the sexes. And one senses that Carrie Catt thought this was only reasonable. For from her perspective anger was entirely appropriate given the way women were treated in the United States (and in the world). She did not feel she could be expected to be "moderate" about the situation any longer.

Her frustration was that so many people just did not understand. "The humiliation which proud spirited American women feel . . . is deeper than I believe any man living can understand."[46] Catt meant that and she also meant her outrage at those who dared to say that most women liked the old, patriarchal order. "We are told these subjected earlier women were content. No doubt, content like the imprisoned bird which sings in its cage in forgetfulness of the freedom which is its birthright. But how quickly these imprisoned ones learn to lift their wings and to fly when the bars are no longer there!"[47]

Nothing made the appalling humiliation clearer to Catt than men's resistance to woman suffrage, their resistance denying women their legitimate dignity as equal citizens. "The truth is," she said, during the suffrage campaign and afterwards, "there never was but one objection to women suffrage on the part of men, and that was the 'superiority complex of the male.' There never was but one objection to their own enfranchisement on the part of women, and that was the 'inferiority complex of the female.'" At its heart Catt's suffrage work was an attempt to challenge such patriarchal ideas among men and, she thought sadly, among some women too. The "struggle for the vote was not what it appeared on the surface. Rather, it was an effort to bring men to feel less superior and women to feel less inferior."[48]

Thus while some suffragists may be criticized for not really challenging the image of women in their time as passive, weak, and unable to be independent, Catt may not. Her goal was to destroy not only the image, but the far too prevalent reality from which the image was formed.[49] Her opponents understood Catt's purposes very well. Again and again they attacked Catt and the suffrage movement on just these grounds, fearful of what the consequences would be in terms of women. They said that true womanhood would be destroyed and women would become like men and in the process acquire all the bad traits and habits of men. They would be "besmirched" by political activity; they would become competitive and antagonistic (especially towards men); they would no longer trust men—their fathers, brothers, husbands, and sons. They would lose their special "spiritual" side, as the obviously "nerve sick" suffragist women proved.[50]

Catt did not share these anxieties. Women would not lose all their positive traits, she thought, above all their concern for others. But they might well lose traits that Catt believed were unfortunate. They might become less naively trusting of men, or anyone, and this was all to the good. Trusting to others to decide one's fate was foolish, not admirable. Shrinking from competition was often a handicap in life, and women needed no additional handicaps. And a "spiritual" side of women, when it meant a fluttery dependence on men, would hardly be a loss.

Nor did Catt think exercising power was beyond women: they could and should exercise it. Indeed, she was bent on creating organizations that would allow them to do just that. As for the possible dangers to women in the dimension of politics involving force, Catt did not deny the dangers, whoever employed it. But if the antisuffragists feared the effects of force they should look first at men's behavior and condemn male use of force at home, in society, and among nations. To reduce its sway women should work to train women to discard this sad male record and adopt the political tools, such as suffrage, that would speed the end of this pernicious reality. Women would have to do it themselves, but they could. The outcome could not be guaranteed, but Catt was typically optimistic: "If these women have the power to put their hopes into the ballot they are going to mold a better future."[51]

To obtain a fitting, self-governing dignity, of course, women would have to be free. No one without extensive choice in life had dignity. The road to freedom involved rebelling at "the idea that obedience is necessary to women" so that they would obtain "such self-respect that they would not grant obedience."[52] Suffrage was, once again, crucial in the process. It would provide objective freedom in politics and could give them the means to expand liberty in other realms. Women who had the vote, in short, had the chance to become free individuals. As she said when the last state had ratified the suffrage amendment: "Let us remember we are no longer petitioners. We are not wards of the nation, but free and equal citizens. Let us practice the dignity of sovereigns." Or, as she put it on another occasion, "The woman with a vote can stand straight and look Godward. She is no longer a part of life's furniture established in this place or in that at the will of another."[53]

Yet we should not overemphasize Catt as a proponent of freedom as an end in itself. It was important to her, and certainly she believed women's enfranchisement would be a major step forward, but she was seeking something that to her was ultimately greater. She was after self-respect and the respect of others for women—she was after dignity. And she was convinced that choice was integral to this goal: it enabled women to control their lives.[54] In the voting booth and elsewhere freedom would propel women towards becoming masters of their fate. She wanted women to join men and obtain human dignity in a world without slaves—and for that end above all Catt fought for women suffrage.[55]

Perhaps Catt's stress on mastery was a bit unrealistic in her age of growing organization in America. But she contended it simply was not true that organization need limit human mastery. Indeed, she was confident, perhaps too confident, that efficient organization could only increase mastery. All her years and work in the N.A.W.S.A. were predicated on this assumption. Women had scant dignity and scant mastery in part because they were unorganized and faced enemies who knew and practiced the mysteries of organization. She sought to beat their enemies at their own game, and she was supremely confident that there was no other way to do so.

We can see Catt's commitment to self-mastery for women in a concrete fashion in her attitude towards the problem of "white slavery." The abuse of young women by men who forced them across state lines and into prostitution, and the male state's failure to eliminate the practice, deeply upset her. From her wide international experience, Catt knew that white slavery was a horrible reality that existed all over the world, wherever women lacked independence and the power to maintain it. White slavery was an ugly symbol of women's status, whether women were white, yellow, brown, or whatever. It existed because women were dependent, not by nature but by social condition. Unable to control their own lives, they were prey for others. They would inevitably remain so until they acquired a rebellious consciousness and the political resources to alter their condition. Suffrage for women would give them the leverage to assert their natural dignity and defeat its antithesis, in this case, white slavery.

To be sure, here as elsewhere Catt did not contend that enfranchisement of women was a magic solution. It would not eliminate white slavery, but it would provide the circumstances under which it could be gravely wounded. White slavery's ultimate extinction would require a change in the economic situation of poor women, better pay, more economic opportunity. All of which were also necessary for women if they were to obtain self-mastery. The broader point is, however, that for Catt white slavery was not unlike sexual assault for Brownmiller and other current feminists. It was the extreme example that revealed the ultimate reality of women's place in the patriarchal social order.[56]

The new, dignified woman that Catt sought, a person who was an independent citizen, free and equal with all other citizens, would escape such treatment. Humiliation would not be her fate. Nor should men expect that or any other negative consequences. The truth was that "every right gained has made women freer, more self-reliant, more respected by men. Every one of them has made women happier and far better comrades to men."[57]

Catt felt that time would work to her advantage. Again and again she invoked the inevitability of change for women, their enfranchisement in particular, and asserted it as a powerful reason for adopting votes for women. The basis for Catt's faith here was her evolutionary naturalism. Somehow the world was progressing and in her mind that ensured victory for woman suffrage. Conservatives, "the flotsam and jetsam of civilization," could not stop it: "They do not know the meaning of the word "progress," they have never heard of evolution."[58] They did not see the signs that were unmistakable. Women had demonstrated they were ready for suffrage. They were increasingly educated. They eagerly voted where they had the opportunity. Society was progressing in its natural way. Women were ready to take an equal part in American politics. Who were venal politicans and the masses of men to waste time denying what was good—and inevitable?[59]

Exactly why Catt thought inevitability was such a powerful argument for the enfranchisement of women is not always self-evident. But she was on to something, as evidenced by her opponents' equal insistence that woman suffrage was no certainty at all and should not be treated as such. Catt used the arguments as a morale builder for the faithful, often exhorting her followers forward with promises of victories to come. Mostly, though, her objective seems to have been different. Her aim was to express what she took to be a fact—the inevitability of suffrage—and thereby disarm her opponents' will. Why bother to fight us, she seemed to say. We are going to win and so you might as well give in now and, as she put it, we can go back to being friends again.[60]

Reassured by the direction of natural evolution, confident of women's natural rights, hopeful of the social benefits of women's enfranchisement, Catt spent half a lifetime promoting woman suffrage. The heart of her case, though, remained her belief in the ideal of women's self-mastery, that suffrage would be a step toward their self-realization as dignified, free beings in command (as much as possible) of their own lives. This is why Catt could and did *demand* suffrage and encouraged other women to do the same. For in demanding it they were affirming themselves as real people and acquiring a means to continue their march forward. "Women Arise: Demand the Vote . . . Demand to vote. Women, Arise." In the end, that was Catt's goal and dream. It was what she was all about: "Women arise."[61]

Notes

1. Kraditor, *Ideas*, p. vii.

2. Kraditor, *Ideas;* Janet Zollinger Giele, "Social Change in the Feminine Role: A Comparison of Woman's Suffrage and Woman's Temperance: 1870-1920" (Ph.D. dissertation, Harvard University, 1961) especially pp. 109-146 and 210-233; also see the controversial view in William O'Neill, *Everyone Was Brave: The Rise and Fall of Feminism in America* (Chicago: University of Chicago, 1969).

3. Kraditor, *Ideas*, chapter 3; Giele "Social Change," pp. 178-179, 185, and 224-233.

4. C. C. C., "The Nation Calls," *Woman Citizen* 3 (March 29, 1919): 917-921; C. C. C., speech, Chicago School of Citizenship (1920), LC 10; C. C. C., speech, Woman's Centennial Congress (November 25, 1940), LC P80-5456; Eliza D. Armstrong, "What Are The Very Latest Suffrage Arguments?" *Woman's Protest* 6 (April 1915): 4; "How Has It Worked Where They Vote?" *Woman's Protest* 7 (May 1915): 9-10.

5. C. C. C., "Why New York Women Want to Vote," *Woman Voter* 6 (January 1915): 5.

6. C. C. C. to Everett P. Wheeler (October 26, 1915), LC 9; Camhi, "Women Against Women," chapter 3.

7. "Mrs. Catt Believes Women Should Continue in Chosen Career, Although Married," *Wichita Eagle* (November 29, 1933), LC 14.

8. Some of the innumerable critical comments here: Brooklyn Auxiliary New York State Association Opposed to the Extension of Suffrage to Women, "Copy of Preamble and Protest," in *Why Women Do Not Want The Ballot* (Massachusetts Association Opposed to Further Extension of Suffrage to Women, 1903); Grace D. Goodwin, *Anti-Suffrage: Ten Good Reasons* (New York: Duffield and Co., 1912), chapters 5, 7, and 10; "Equal Suffrage and Equal Obligation," *Woman's Protest* 1 (July 1912): 4; Minnie Bronson, "How Suffrage States Compare with Non-Suffrage," *Woman's Protest* 4 (January 1914): 7-9; Lucy J. Price, "Why Wage Earning Women Oppose Suffrage," *Woman's Protest* 2 (January 1913): 7; "Laws of Suffrage and Non-Suffrage States Compared," *Woman's Protest* 1 (June 1912): 3.

9. For some sample critiques: "Petition Against the Child Labor Amendment," *Woman Patriot* 5 (May 15, 1921): 1-5; "Origin of the Children's Bureau," *Woman Patriot* 5 (August 15, 1921, and September 1, 1921); *Woman Patriot* 5 (October 15, 1921), entire issue devoted to denunciation of Sheppard-Towner Act.

10. C. C. C., "The Further Extension," *Woman Voter* 4 (May 1913): 17 and 20; C. C. C. to Everett P. Wheeler (October 24, 1915), LC 9; Mary G. Peck, "The Secretary Has Signed the Proclamation," in *Victory: How Women Won It*, p. 149.

11. See Jane Addams, "Women and Public Housekeeping," "Suffrage: U.S." Collection, Box 6, folder 121, SSL.

12. For an able, recent discussion of Jane Addams, see Anne Firor Scott, *Making the Invisible Woman Visible* (Urbana: University of Illinois Press, 1984), pp. 107-141; C. C. C., speech, Harrisburg, Pa. (March 7, 1916), pp. 16-17, Box 1, folder 2, SSL.

13. C. C. C., "Annual Address," N.A.W.S.A. (1902), Catt Collection, Box 1, folder 13, SSL.

14. For instance, Metta Folger Townsend, "Good Reasons for Opposition," *Woman's Protest* 3 (June 1913): 3; "Statement of the Illinois Association Opposed To The Extension Of Suffrage To Women," Brooklyn Auxiliary, "Copy of Preamble and Protest," Frances M. Scott, "Extension of the Suffrage to Women," and Priscilla Leonard, "A Help or A Hindrance?" all in *Why Women Do Not Want The Ballot*; Mrs. Simeon H. Guilford, "Woman's 'Emancipation'—From What?" *Woman's Protest* 7 (July 1915): 5; Helen Kendrick Johnson, "The End of Suffrage: A Social Revolution," *Woman's Protest* 7 (June 1915): 10-11; "Up-to-Date," *Woman Patriot* 1 (May 25, 1918): 4; "The Suffragist's Ideal of Womanhood," *Woman Patriot* 3 (August 23, 1919): 4-5.

15. Kraditor, *Ideas*, pp. 15, 24, and 41-42.

16. C. C. C. "Feminism and Suffrage" (1917), leaflet, Catt Collection, Box 1, folder 9, SSL.

17. C. C. C., "By Way of a New Beginning," *Woman Citizen* 5 (August 28, 1920): 329; C. C. C., "The Home and the Higher Education," *Woman's Journal* 33 (July 26, 1902): 234-235; C. C. C., "Woman's Place," *New York Herald Tribune* (August 22, 1914), in LC 14; C. C. C. to Everett P. Wheeler (October 24, 1915), LC 9; Anthony

and Harper, *History*. vol. 4, p. 371; Lillian E. Taaffe, "Man's Superiority Complex Called Bar to Equal Rights," *Minneapolis Tribune* (November 8, 1923), LC 14.

18. Ellen DuBois, "The Radicalism of the Woman Suffrage Movement: Notes Toward the Reconstruction of Nineteenth-Century Feminism," *Feminist Studies* 3 (Fall 1975): 63-70.

19. For example, "Feminism and Insanity," *Woman Patriot* 3 (October 18, 1919): 8.

20. C. C. C., Oklahoma Report #2 (November 4, 1898), Catt Collection, RL.

21. Mrs. John B. Heron, "Feminism a Return to Barbarism," *Woman's Protest* 6 (April 1915): 5-6; "Men Becoming Effeminate," *Woman Patriot* 3-4 (March 20, 1920): 6; "God Give Us Men," *Woman Patriot* 3-4 (April 10, 1920): 3.

22. "Mrs. Catt's Address," *Woman's Journal* 30 (June 10, 1899): 178; "Mrs. Catt's Address," *Woman's Journal* 35 (February 20, 1904): 57-59, 61, and 64; C. C. C., speech (1903), LC P80-5456; C. C. C., *Woman Suffrage by Federal Constitutional Amendment*, pp. 89-91.

23. Mary A. J. M'Intire, "Of What Benefit To Woman?" in *Why Women Do Not Want The Ballot*; "Woman Suffrage, the Enemy of Good Government," *Woman Patriot* 3 (May 10, 1919): 8.

24. Catt was an environmentalist through and through; see, for example, "Annual Address," N.A.W.S.A. (1902), Catt Collection, Box 1, folder 12, SSL.

25. C. C. C., "God and the People" (1915), p. 2, LC 12.

26. C. C. C., "Our New Responsibilities," *Woman's Journal* 29 (October 1, 1898): 317.

27. "Giving Or Forcing?" *Remonstrance* (January 1914): 1; "Their Fundamental Error," *Woman's Protest* 8 (April 1916): 8-9; Marjorie Dorman, "Suffragists Traitors To Democracy," *Woman's Protest* 8 (December 1915); C. C. C., "Will of the People," *Forum* 43 (1910): 599; Goodwin, *Anti-Suffrage*, chapter 2.

28. For example, see Mrs. John B. Heron, "Why Suffragists Prefer to Face Legislatures Rather Than Voters-At-The-Polls," *Woman's Protest* 6 (January 1915): 8-9; "A Referendum To Women," *Woman's Protest* 10 (January 1917): 4, one of many calls for a vote by women.

29. C. C. C., "Two Systems," *Woman Citizen* 3 (June 29, 1918): 85; "Two Letters and Sunday Senators," *Woman Citizen* 2 (May 4, 1918): 445-446; C. C. C., "Forward March!" *Woman Citizen* 1 (September 22, 1917): 305-306; C. C. C., speech (1918), LC P80-5455; C. C. C., speech, "Woman Suffrage As A War Measure" (1918), LC 10; C. C. C., *War Aims*, pp. 1-16.

30. C. C. C. to Margery Corbett Ashby (April 9, 1945), Catt Collection, Box 4, folder 29, SSL.

31. C. C. C. to Katharine Blake (June 1, 1937), Catt Collection, Box 1, folder 29, SSL.

32. For example, C. C. C. "Surplus Women," *Woman Citizen* 6 (October 22, 1921): 12; "Mrs. Catt Tells View on War," *Woman's Journal* 45 (August 15, 1914): 234.

33. Mrs. J. T. Waterman, "Women and War," *Woman's Protest* 5 (September 1914): 5-6; C. C. C., speech, "Woman Suffrage Now Will Stimulate Patriotism," LC 10; C. C. C., speech, "Woman Suffrage As A War Measure" (1918); C. C. C., *Home Defense*, pp. 1-16.

34. For example, Elizabeth Cady Stanton to E. B. H., Dillon Collection, Box 2, folder 27, RL.

35. On Catt and rights, for example, see C. C. C., speech, "An Appeal for Liberty" (1915), LC 10; Harper, *History,* vol. 5, pp. 144-145; Clevenger, "Invention and Arrangement," p. 86; C. C. C., "Why Women Want to Vote," *Woman's Journal* 46 (January 9, 1915): 11; C. C. C., "Why New York Women Want to Vote," *Woman Voter* 6 (January 1915): 5.

36. Walker, "Speeches," pp. 282-286.

37. Harper, *History,* vol. 5, pp. 745-746; Anthony and Harper, *History,* vol. 4, p. 213; Clevenger, "Invention and Arrangement," p. 95.

38. C. C. C., "Too Many Rights," pp. 31 and 168.

39. C. H. Kent, "Arguments For Suffrage Weighed and Found Wanting in Logic and Justice," *Woman's Protest* 2 (February 1913): 3, 5, and 6; "No 'Natural Right' to Vote," *Woman Patriot* 1-2 (October 26, 1918): 7-8; Mrs. George P. White, "Taxation Without Representation—Misapplied," *Woman's Protest* 6 (February 1915): 8-9; Mrs. H. A. Foster, "Taxation and Representation," in *Why Women Do Not Want The Ballot.*

40. Kraditor, *Ideas,* chapter 2.

41. See Carl Degler, *At Odds: Women and the Family in America* (New York: Oxford University Press, 1980), pp. 352-361, for an interesting, alternative view on this issue; for a discussion in present day terms, see Jean Elshtain, "The New Porn Wars," *New Republic* 190 (June 25, 1984): 15-20.

42. C. C. C., "Feminism and Suffrage," leaflet (1917), Catt Collection, Box 1, folder 9, SSL.

43. For example, C. C. C., "Why New York Women Want to Vote," *Woman Voter* 6 (January 1915): 5, and "Mrs. Catt's Address," *Woman's Journal* 42 (July 15, 1911): 217, 219, and 239; C. C. C., *An Address to the Legislature of the United States* (New York: National American Woman Suffrage Publishing, 1919), pp. 1-23.

44. C. C. C., "Anti-Feminism in South America," *Current History Magazine* 18 (September 1923): 1034.

45. For example, regarding Lucy Stone, see Gurko, *Ladies of Seneca Falls,* p. 128.

46. C. C. C. to Hon. Gilbert Hitchcock (January 24, 1919), Catt Collection, Box 4, folder 37, SSL.

47. C. C. C., "Annual Address," N.A.W.S.A. (1902), Catt Collection, Box 1, folder 13, p. 9, SSL.

48. C. C. C., "The Cave Man Complex vs. Woman Suffrage," *Woman Citizen* 8 (April 5, 1924): 16-17.

49. Jill Conway, "Women Reformers and American Culture: 1870-1930," *Journal of Social History* 5 (Winter 1971-1972): 166-167.

50. Leonard, "A Help or A Hindrance?" in *Why Women Do Not Want The Ballot;* Goodwin, *Anti-Suffrage,* pp. 23 and 91-92; "Another Danger Demonstrated," *Women's Protest* 10 (November 1916): 8-9; Paul Morris, "The Feminine Viewpoint," *Woman Patriot* 3 (April 26, 1919): 8; "Women Competing With Men," *Woman Patriot* 3 (May 31, 1919): 4; Mary A. J. M'Intire, "Of What Benefit to Woman?," Frances M. Scott, "Extension of the Suffrage to Women," and Frances J. Dyer, "A Remonstrance," all in *Why Women Do Not Want The Ballot;* Mrs. George P. White, "Taxation Without Representation—Misapplied," *Woman's Protest* 6 (February 1915): 8; also see Camhi, "Women Against Women," pp. 25-47.

51. C. C. C., speech at National Executive Council, National American Woman Suffrage Association (December 19, 1915), LCB 36.

52. C. C. C., "Annual Address" (1902), p. 11.

53. C. C. C., "Bringing the Victors Home," *Woman Citizen* 5 (September 4, 1920): 362-363; C. C. C., speech, "What the Vote Will Do For the Woman" (1917), LC 13.

54. For example, C. C. C., "What the N.A.W.S.A. Has Done," *Woman Citizen* 3 (November 9, 1918): 487; "Mrs. Catt's Norwegian Maid," *Woman's Journal* 38 (June 22, 1907): 98; Anthony and Harper, *History,* vol. 4, p. 369.

55. "Mrs. Catt vs. Mrs. Meyer," *Woman's Journal* 39 (March 21, 1908): 48; Clevenger, "Invention and Arrangement," p. 224.

56. C. C. C., "A True Story," *Woman's Journal* 44 (January 25, 1913): 26; "Mrs. Catt Tells of Slave Traffic," *Woman's Journal* 44 (January 11, 1913): 16; "Mrs. Catt on Woman Traffic," *Woman's Journal* 44 (January 25, 1913): 32; "Mrs. Catt Tells of White Slaves," *Woman's Journal* 44 (February 1, 1913): 40; C. C. C., speech, "The Traffic in Women" (1899), LC 10; C. C. C., "The Traffic in Women," *Women Voter* 4 (March 1913): 14-15; "Mrs. Catt and Mrs. Barry," *Woman's Journal* 41 (November 12, 1910): 204.

57. C. C. C., "Too Many Rights," p. 31; C. C. C., "Will of the People," p. 601.

58. C. C. C., speech, Harrisburg, Pa. (March 7, 1916), p. 10, Catt Collection, Box 1, folder 2, SSL.

59. C. C. C., *An Address to the Legislature of the United States* (1919), pp. 1-5 and 20; C. C. C., *An Address to the Congress of the United States* (New York: National American Woman Suffrage Publishing, 1917), pp. 1-7 and 19-21.

60. C. C. C., "An Address to the Congress of the United States" (December 13, 1917), in Walker, "Speeches," pp. 331-347; C. C. C., *Home Defense,* p. 14; "Mrs. Catt Scents State Victory," *Woman's Journal* 47 (September 9, 1916): 289; C. C. C., *An Address to the Legislature of the United States,* pp. 1-23; C. C. C., "Will of the People," pp. 595-599; "By No Means 'Sure To Come,'" *Remonstrance* (April 1914): 1; C. C. C. to Margaret Roberts (August 16, 1915), Margaret Roberts Collection, Box 4, folder 4, RL.

61. C. C. C., "The Crisis," *Woman's Journal* 47 (September 16, 1916): 299 and 301-303.

CHRISTINE A. LUNARDINI (ESSAY DATE 1986)

SOURCE: Lunardini, Christine A. "The Founding of the National Woman's Party and the Campaign of 1916." In *From Equal Suffrage to Equal Rights: Alice Paul and the National Women's Party, 1910-1928,* pp. 85-103. New York: New York University Press, 1986.

In the following essay, Lunardini describes the role of Alice Paul and the National Woman's party in the electoral campaign of 1916.

With a successful year of organizing ended, and buoyed by the prospects for the ensuing year, Alice Paul revealed her plans for the months ahead. The Executive Committee called a meeting of the Advisory Council and the state and national officers on April 8 and 9, 1916. The meeting was held at Cameron House, the [Congressional] Union's new headquarters. Cameron House, commonly referred to as the Little White House, and located across Pennsylvania Avenue from the real White House, had become the headquarters for the Congressional Union in January 1916. By April, it was well-settled into by the organization. While not as grand or imposing as Marble House, where Paul had announced the anti-Democratic campaign of 1914, Cameron House nevertheless served a similar purpose, as the members of the Advisory Council gathered to hear about the next step in Paul's plans.

Paul proposed to organize a woman's political party which, she believed, would serve as the balance of power in the national election which promised to be closely contended. "The state of Nevada was won by only forty votes in the last Senatorial election," Paul pointed out.[1] "In Utah, it was a week before the campaign was decided. In Colorado, the same. Going back over a period of twenty years, it would have been necessary to have changed only nine per cent of the total vote in the Presidential elections in order to have thrown the election to the other Party. This gives a position of wonderful power, a position that we have never held before and that we cannot hold again for at least four years, and which we may not hold then."[2] The delegates at the conference in April 1916 needed little convincing to give their blessing to the new program.

The Congressional Union lobby in Washington, directed by Nevada's Anne Martin and assisted by Maud Younger, the "Millionaire Waitress" from San Francisco, had labored furiously for three months in an attempt to persuade the House Judiciary Committee to report out the suffrage amendment. Alice Paul could not have asked for two more dedicated workers. Martin's experience as a NAWSA coordinator in Nevada during the referendum there was invaluable for her new task. Maud Younger earned her nickname when she single-handedly organized the Waitress's Union in San Francisco. Like many progressives of her time, Younger did not let her family wealth and status blind her to the plight of the poor and disadvantaged. She gradually focused her concern on working women and, in 1911, was influential in getting California's eight-hour workday law for

women passed. Although she was always a suffrage advocate, Maud did not get involved in the movement until 1914. Thereafter she devoted almost all of her time to suffrage and worked with the Congressional Union and then the National Woman's Party. By 1915, Maud Younger was Alice Paul's key Washington lobbyist, and she had amassed a card index file which provided an instant reference on every congressman and senator in Congress, as well as prominent administration figures. Maud Younger's card index became legendary in Congressional Union—and congressional—circles.[3]

Despite the efforts of Martin and Younger, the Democrats remained adamant about refusing to consider an amendment until the following December—after the national elections. The committee chairman did promise Martin and Younger that his committee would meet to consider the suffrage issue if the lobbyists could assemble a majority of the committee. With such an incentive, and after much cajoling, corraling, and steam-rolling, the lobbyists succeeded in persuading a majority of the committee to meet at an agreed upon day and time. All of Martin and Younger's hard work came to naught when the committee met. In a closed meeting, pro-amendment congressmen were stymied when a motion was immediately made to shelve *all* constitutional amendment proposals for an indefinite period of time. This master stroke at once created chaos within the committee, as members were forced to either accept or reject a whole range of pending amendments on such issues as marriage, divorce, and prohibition. This, as the authors of the scheme well knew, was impossible. The committee adjourned, after an angry two hours, with no action taken on anything. Once again, the Democrats, who controlled the committee, had delayed dealing with the suffrage amendment and, in the process, had convinced the Congressional Union members that the Democratic party was contemptuous of the issue.[4] When, therefore, Alice Paul called for a convention of women voters to meet at the Blackstone Theatre in Chicago on June 5, 6 and 7, 1916, for the purpose of organizing the National Woman's Party (NWP), the delegates gave their unstinting support.

Membership in the NWP was to be limited to enfranchised women, and its sole purpose would be to promote the federal amendment.[5] In preparation for the Chicago convention, Paul sent a delegation of twenty-three organizers to tour the western states on a train dubbed the *Suffrage Spe-*

cial. The timing of the western swing and the convention were important, as Lucy Burns explained, because the Union was in its "strongest position before a national election & ought to put on the pressure now—no wait till Congress has adjourned."[6]

Plans for the western trip had been under way for several weeks prior to the April 9 departure, with the groundwork for the emissaries' visits laid down by the state chapter members. By now, the Union expected some efforts to undermine their activities by NAWSA, regardless of circumstance, and they were not disappointed in this instance. "With two representatives of 'the National' in Laramie County throwing all the cold water they possibly can, we are keeping the newspapers in the quiet little town of Cheyenne busy," Wyoming organizer Margery Ross reported back to Washington. The conflict served Alice Paul's purposes well, however, for as Ross noted, "Incidentally, we are awakening these Cheyenne women who have, to be frank with you, gone to sleep."[7]

The *Suffrage Special* left Washington amidst a flurry of pageantry and publicity. For more than a month, the emissaries from the East lived and worked in the train, in cramped quarters, but with sustained good humor. "If you Washington ladies could peep into the Suffrage Special at any hour of any day when nine typewriters are pounding away and Press reports and resolutions are being written and literature being folded and counted and membership cards listed and the Business Manager receiving money . . . you would realize that this is no place for the graceful letter writer!" Ella Reigel wrote in response to pleas for the news from California.[8] Several days later, in Sacramento, Reigel noted, "My charges are busy and happy—not too much coddled—and so far no broken heads!"[9] The four-week tour met with enthusiastic response from women voters and a great deal of attendant publicity as well.[10]

As a consequence of the successful western tour, more than 1,500 women delegates from the suffrage states arrived at the Blackstone Theatre on June 6, eager to participate in the historic event. They believed success was within their grasp in the 1916 election since, they reasoned, less than nine per cent of the total vote in the suffrage states would be enough to deflect the election away from the Democrats.[11] The delegates quickly established a set of rules to govern the NWP. First, the party nucleus would be composed of Congressional Union members. Second, the party would remain independent and would not align itself, officially or unofficially, with any exist-

ing political party. Third, the only plank in the party's platform would be a resolution calling for immediate passage of the Anthony amendment. Fourth, the party would be organized along the same lines as the Congressional Union, with a chairwoman, two vice-chairwomen, and an Executive Committee composed of the officers, state chairwomen, and the chairwoman of the Congressional Union. Fifth, all state chairwomen would automatically become members of the Executive Committee of the Congressional Union.[12] It was as simply organized and—theoretically—as much as a single-issue political party as its founders could conceive. The convention delegates, therefore, quickly disposed of the major business at hand, voted to accept the proposal to establish the National Woman's Party, and elected Anne Martin chairwoman, and Alice Paul one of the two vice-chairwomen.[13]

The three-day convention received maximum press coverage, in part because Chicago was already flooded with reporters who were assigned to the Republican and Progressive party conventions. Indeed, as Inez Haynes Irwin said, the NWP convention was a "god-send" since the press was relieved of the chore of ferreting out preconvention stories that would keep both their editors and their readers satisfied. The NWP delegates were only too happy to help out their friends in the press with detailed information of the proceedings.

Alice Paul extended invitations to representatives of all the major parties, to address the NWP convention. Even this served as grist for the media's mill. Ida Tarbell, the famous muckraking journalist who had exposed the Standard Oil monopoly in the pages of *McClure's Magazine,* covered the convention for the *New York World.* Tarbell described with amusement the dispatch with which the women handled the male politicians. She reported:

> 'We do not ask you here to tell us what we can do for your Parties, but what your Parties can do for us,' Miss Martin told the speakers in a tone of exultant sweetness which sent a cheer from shore to shore of the human sea which filled the house. Another thing the gentlemen must have noticed— used as they are to the same game—and that was, that no amount of eloquence made the faintest scratch on the rock-ribbed determination of the women. The one and only thing they wanted to know . . . was whether or not they proposed to support the amendment, . . . Was it, yes or no?[14]

The NWP convention closed on the day that the Republican and Progressive party conventions convened with a "Suffrage First" luncheon, which turned into a standing-room-only affair. The speakers at the luncheon, who included Crystal Eastman, Rheta Childe Dorr, and Helen Keller, were only slightly less exuberant than their audiences. In spite of the lack of elbow room, the audience managed to cheer and clap wildly, so caught up were they by the feeling of solidarity that pervaded the room.[15]

In the months ahead, the NWP became almost a casebook example of Charles A. Beard's description of the purpose and function of third parties in a two-party system: "By agitation and by the use of marginal votes in close campaigns, minorities are able to force the gradual acceptance of some or all of their leading doctrines by one or the other of the great parties, and through inevitable competition between these parties, to educate the whole nation into accepting ideas that were once abhorrent."[16] In the meantime, the NWP would immediately have an opportunity to agitate the major parties.

Members of the NWP appeared before the resolutions committees of each of the parties in an effort to persuade them to support federal suffragism. For the first time, both major parties included suffrage planks in their party platforms, although neither one endorsed a federal amendment. The Republican delegates accepted their committee's resolution with little argument, probably because they were only too happy to cooperate with potential allies against their November adversaries. When the Democrats opened their convention in St. Louis on June 14, the NWP advised the resolutions committee that unless the Democrats, as the party in power, supported the Anthony amendment, the NWP intended to campaign against them in the West.[17] Not only were the Democrats unwilling to endorse federal suffragism, some of them did not wish to endorse suffrage at all. The suffrage plank, consequently, was brought to a floor fight—the only issue so debated at the convention.[18] The minority favored no plank at all and preferred that the states be left to their own devices regarding suffrage. Senator Thomas James Walsh of Montana, speaking on behalf of the states' rights plank, noted the advisability of including a suffrage plank of some sort since women voters had the power to defeat the President and to give the Senate majority to the Republicans.[19] In its follow-up analysis, the *New York Times* concurred with Walsh: "Whatever the more conservative suffragists think or say . . . the radical wing which calls itself the Woman's Party . . . offer[s] facts and figures to prove that they have an organized vote which can be swung in

any direction they want . . . Whether the hand that ruled the Democratic convention today, rocks the cradle in its hours of recreation . . . it can certainly add up a column of figures in a convincing manner."[20] The minority plank was subsequently defeated and the Democrats, too, included a suffrage plank based on state rights in their party platform, which, observers agreed, had been largely written by Woodrow Wilson. And, while the Republicans and Democrats could bring themselves only to endorse suffrage while refusing to support a federal amendment, the Progressive, Socialists, and Prohibitionist parties all came out unequivocally for a federal woman suffrage amendment.[21]

NAWSA could not have been happier at the turn of events since it had lobbied simply for recognition of the principle of woman suffrage and not for support of a federal amendment.[22] In NAWSA's eyes, the NWP had suffered a defeat. The NWP, although it was disappointed, certainly did not consider itself defeated. For one thing, it had received enormous amounts of publicity. There were few areas in the country where people remained unaware of the new political party composed entirely of women. Thus it had succeeded in large measure in making the "National Woman's Party convention in Chicago dominate the suffrage world, so that it seem[ed] to the public and to the politicians assembled there that the whole agitation [was] really on behalf of the national amendment."[23] The NWP also managed to secure support from quarters that previously had questioned its effectiveness. The *New Republic,* for example, had, in 1914, jailed NAWSA's "rational" and "thoughtful" approach as the best hope for success.[24] Now, the journal believed, "the time has undoubtedly come for NAWSA to revive their tactics. . . . The political power of the woman voter must be brought to bear on Washington now. . . . If the National Association cannot see its way to harvest this field, they should leave the field clear for the Congressional Union [i.e., NWP]."[25] Finally, Charles A. Beard, in a letter to Carrie Chapman Catt, expressed the view of many who believed that "all that was got at Chicago and St. Louis was got only because the politicians were afraid of the impending danger created by the Congressional Union and the Woman's Party, namely that western women would not be nonpartisan when the freedom of their sisters was at stake."[26]

Immediately following the conventions, the NWP began to put pressure on Republican nominee Charles Evans Hughes. Earlier that year, in

May 1916, Paul and Harriot Stanton Blatch had secured Theodore Roosevelt's support for the federal amendment.[27] Now, Paul sought to enlist Roosevelt's assistance to help persuade Hughes to come out for the amendment. Discussions with Roosevelt at Oyster Bay confirmed Paul's impression of Hughes' state of mind: the former President believed Hughes was ready to commit himself to the federal amendment. It was simply a matter of the proper timing.[28] Paul inaugurated a campaign calculated to help convince Hughes that the time was now. State NWP and Union officials were encouraged not only to write letters but to "flood Hughes with telegrams from every possible source."[29] In addition, Paul dispatched Anne Martin and Abby Scott Baker to track down Hughes on the campaign trail in order to make a personal appeal.[30]

The lobbying effort paid off handsomely. On August 1, Hughes, departing from his party's campaign platform, endorsed the federal amendment. His reasons for doing so, as he himself admitted, were to many people more eyebrow-raising than the fact that he was supporting federal suffragism at all. Hughes readily conceded that women should have the vote. That, he felt, was no longer at issue. What was at issue was the impact that suffrage agitation of the sort engaged in by the NWP would have on national politics. "Facts should be squarely met. We shall have a constantly intensified effort and a distinct feminist movement constantly perfecting its organization to the subversion of normal political issues. We shall have a struggle increase in bitterness . . . inimical to our welfare. . . . It seems to me that in the interest of the public life of this country, the contest should be ended promptly."[31]

Hughes' endorsement of the federal amendment was an important victory for suffragists. For the first time, a major party's presidential candidate had publicly stood up for federal suffragism. On such a momentous occasion, Paul debated whether or not to break policy and endorse Hughes straight out. She decided against such a step in order to retain her organization's independence. Besides, publicly allying herself and the NWP with the Republicans would give the Democrats an opportunity to turn the issue into a partisan one. The NWP, therefore, would not endorse Hughes' candidacy, but it applauded vigorously his endorsement.[32] Not only did they have Hughes' support, but the Republican's action would almost certainly require some response from the Democrats. But if Paul hoped that Wilson would follow Hughes' lead, those hopes

were short-lived. Carrie Chapman Catt, who apparently had the same thought, approached Wilson about announcing in favor of federal suffragism, particularly since his opponent now had the clear edge on the issue. Wilson declined. "If I should change my personal attitude now I should seem to the country like nothing better than an angler for votes."[33]

With Wilson obviously committed to the states' rights principle, in accordance with his party platform—his standard excuse for refusing to take up federal suffragism—Alice Paul called a meeting for August 10, 11, and 12, to take place in Colorado Springs. She had in mind to map out the role the NWP would play in the upcoming elections. The decision of the conference would be greatly influenced, Paul noted, by the record of the Democratic party when the women met on the tenth of August.[34] With her usual eye toward maximum publicity, Paul chose August 10 to convene the meeting because of the automobile races, scheduled for that time, celebrating the opening of the new road up Pike's Peak. "There will probably be large numbers of people there at the time," Paul explained.[35]

There were few delegates, if any, who arrived at the Antlers Hotel in Colorado Springs who were seriously in doubt as to the outcome of the conference. The Democrats had done next to nothing in recent months to suggest that their position on suffrage would change. The conference, then, was not concerned with whether the NWP ought to be involved. Discussions revolved instead around organizations, tactics, and issues. Wilson, of course, would be the primary target. As the leader of his party, Wilson symbolized the control which the Democrats exercised over all political and legislative matters. The issue of states' rights was to be handled in as straightforward a manner as possible, pointing out that since thirty-six states had to ratify a federal amendment, each state legislature could indeed be responsive to the needs and desires of its constituents by ratifying or failing to ratify when the time came. A federal amendment, secured under the terms of the Constitution, could in no way be construed as an infringement of states' rights.[36]

With state leaders thus armed with guidelines and instructions, the NWP inaugurated its campaign of 1916. In many ways it was a replay of 1914, with two organizers again assigned to each suffrage state, with essentially the same responsibilities as the organizers had in 1914. Alice Paul dispatched her most effective organizers—women who have proven their skills as managers, fundraisers, and especially as public speakers with "crowd pleaser" reputations. Doris Stevens, Sara Bard Field, Maud Younger, Elsie Hill, Anne Martin, and Mabel Vernon, all agreed to spend another fall enduring the rigors of the campaign trail.[37]

Longtime members who had not organized in 1914, but who demonstrated valuable organizing and speaking skills, were also enlisted. Perhaps the most noticeable of this group was Inez Milholland Boissevain, a lawyer and feminist who had graduated from Vassar and New York University. It was Inez who had led the suffrage parade, in flowing white robes and riding a white horse, in Washington in 1913. Her photograph, taken during the parade, became one of the memorable images that people associated with the event. It was not unusual to see her name accompanied by adjectives such as "brilliant" and "beautiful," for she was both. Inez' political beliefs led her to champion a number of feminist and radical causes. She was, for a time, part of the bohemian-radical group that dominated Greenwich Village in the early twentieth century—a group that included Crystal Eastman and her brother Max. Inez and Max Eastman, the editor of *The Masses,* had a short-lived romance that ended when she married Eugen Jan Boissevain, a Dutch entrepreneur. Following her marriage, Inez traveled to Europe with Guglielmo Marconi, another longtime admirer, in order to report on the war in Europe. Her pacifist articles earned Inez an invitation to leave Italy, where she was based, tendered by the Italian government. Within months, she was back in Europe, this time on Henry Ford's Peace Ship. On her return to the United States, Inez became more actively involved in suffrage, offering her services as a speaker throughout the West. So great was her reputation, that the success of political rallies sometimes hinged entirely on Inez' agreement to be the featured speaker.[38]

In addition to Inez Milholland, Alice Paul enlisted other promising and enthusiastic young women, a "second generation" of organizers to round out the contingent of seasoned organizers sent to the West.[39] Included in the second generation organizers, were Iris Calderhead, the daughter of a Kansas congressman; Hazel Hunkins Hallinan, the Vassar alumna who had taken the daring airplane ride over San Francisco; Lucy Branham, a Johns Hopkins graduate who had won a Carnegie medal for heroism after saving a man and woman from drowning in Florida; and Rebecca Hourwich Rehyer, who managed to squeeze in suffrage activities between her studies, first at Columbia and then at the University of Chicago, her marriage, and the birth of her first child.[40] This second generation of organizers tended to be younger than the first. In age, background, and education, the new organizers were very representative of the new members coming into the NWP. The NWP still attracted only a small percentage of the women joining suffrage organizations in 1916. But Paul needed all the volunteers she could get. The increase in membership permitted the NWP to engage not only in the political campaign in the suffrage states, but in increasingly active lobbying in Washington.[41]

Although the structure of the campaign of 1916 resembled that of 1914, there were new problems for Paul and the NWP. For one thing, 1916 was the organization's second political campaign effort. Democrats and antisuffragists were better prepared this time around. For another thing, 1914 was an off-year election featuring races for the Senate, the House, and state offices. In 1916, the Presidency was at stake. Local Democratic machines were even less willing to tolerate the organizers than they had been two years earlier. After distributing literature in Denver, for example, Elsie Hill was arrested and taken by "paddy wagon" to the local police station. In Colorado Springs, a banner whose legend demanded passage of the federal amendment was confiscated and held by the police authorities overnight, to the amusement of the suffragists who reported that their banner had been arrested and detained in a jail cell. In Chicago, 100 women stationed outside an auditorium where Wilson was scheduled to speak, were attacked by a mob. Their banners were torn down and the suffragists were pushed and shoved aside, with minor injuries sustained by some of the women in the process.[42] Iris Calderhead reported the increasing hostility of the Democrats in Arizona. Calderhead explained that the municipalities were largely controlled by the Democrats who could, and did, prohibit street meetings, advertising, poster and billboard notices, and most other forms of activity and advertising that the NWP engaged in.[43]

At the same time, the relationship between the NWP and the Republican party had to be carefully monitored. Paul did not want the NWP linked to the Republican party in an overt or official way. Yet, it was clearly in the best interest of suffrage and the NWP, to promote votes for the GOP. "Our interest is in . . . the amendment and not in.. Hughes, but it is vital to the success of the amendment . . . that we secure the defeat of Wilson," Paul noted. Nevertheless, she cautioned her lieutenants that it was paramount that the

NWP remain distinct from all other political parties in order to maintain its integrity among the voters. Furthermore, Paul believed that it was tactically more effective to conduct a campaign of opposition *against* Democrats rather than one of support *for* Republicans. Paul did not want the burden of having to defend Republican policy.[44]

The Republicans, for their part, viewed the NWP as a useful ally in the campaign, but they also maintained a patronizing attitude toward the women. W. Y. Morgan, the director of the Republican National Committee's publicity bureau, advised Kansas Republicans that the NWP could be "helped without any injury to the Republican Party."[45] In any event, the Republicans, while willing to make use of the NWP, did not particularly feel comfortable with the idea of an independent woman's political party. Offers of economic support from the Republicans to the NWP, which were declined in every instance, often came with conditions attached. "The truth is that they are unwilling to give us some money unless we will give up our independence and become an annex of the GOP," reported Abby Scott Baker in disgust. "When I am with the GOP's, I'd rather die than be one," she declared. But, she added ruefully, "I feel the same way when I am with the Democrats, so I think I'll go into a convent."[46] Rumors that the NWP was on the Republican payroll did not help their cause either. "Every indication that has ever been brought to my notice advances the theory of the oft-repeated statement that the National Woman's Party is merely an ally of the National Republican Committee," wrote the editor of the *Nevada State Herald* to Mabel Vernon.[47]

Moreover, the Republicans were unwilling to take seriously the overall campaign analysis provided by the NWP regarding the jeopardy in which Republican candidates stood in the suffrage states. Doris Stevens reported to Alice Paul from California that the Republicans were trailing Wilson in that state. Stevens believed that the GOP's difficulties had arisen in large part because the Hughes' people managed to alienate governor Hiram W. Johnson, the powerful Progressive candidate for the United States Senate, whose support Hughes badly needed.[48] "I have taken your various letters with regard to the situation in California to the Republican headquarters," Paul told Stevens. "But I have seemed unable to even suggest to them that there is any possibility that California may not go to Hughes."[49] In Nevada, the political situation seemed more hopeful on the local level, but it was still bad for Hughes. "The great trouble is that the Republican state campaign committee is not putting up an active fight—not as active as the Democratic campaign committee," Anne Martin observed. She added that the Republicans were not even as active as the NWP.[50] Martin also reported to Paul on the state of affairs in Utah. "Utah is in a very critical state. The Democrats have never stood such a good chance of carrying the state. . . . The Republican organization rely on the fact that the Mormon Church is Republican. They tell me to rest easy. . . . Perhaps there is some mystic word that can be sent out but I think they had better get busy and send it out pretty quickly because the situation looks alarming to me."[51] Martin's exasperation over the seemingly casual attitude of the Republican party to its own plight was only too obvious. In the face of such fumbling on the part of the GOP, it was no wonder that NWP campaigners became frustrated. "The Republican Party is really so stupid," complained Abby Scott Baker. "Sometimes I despair of pulling them through."[52]

To be sure, the lackadaisical campaigning of the Republican party during the first weeks of the campaign was not the major stumbling block for the NWP. The major campaign issue in 1916 was the peace issue. As the war in Europe raged on, with the growing threat of United States involvement in the conflict, hardly a voter in the country remained neutral about the peace issue. The NWP attempted to counter the Democratic slogan, "He Kept Us Out Of War," with its own slogan, "He Kept Us Out Of Suffrage."[53] The two appeals placed women voters in a quandary of conscience. Where did their allegiance lie? Ought they to place their desire for equality first, or their desire for peace? Even the members of the NWP felt torn by the dilemma. Some, like pacifist Crystal Eastman, decided that she could not support an anti-Democratic campaign at such a crucial juncture in the nation's wellbeing. A Hughes Presidency, Eastman believed, would surely mean United States entry into the war. Eastman chose to campaign for Wilson and peace, rather than for suffrage.[54] As the campaign progressed, it became more and more apparent that most voters agreed with Eastman's sentiments. And, although suffrage was considered by most observers the main local and domestic issue in the suffrage states, peace was the overriding national foreign-policy issue.[55] While the NWP almost always attracted audiences sympathetic to suffrage, their audiences frequently had to admit that they could not and would not support Hughes' position on preparedness and the implications of that policy.[56]

The campaign for the NWP was, to say the least, an uphill battle and was so reflected by the pessimistic note struck in many of the organizers' reports. "The opposition is so strong that no matter how much we try or how many people we interview, we seem to make little progress," wrote Helen Heffernon, the Goldfield, Nevada organizer.[57] "Nothing but luck will carry the Republicans through [in Nevada]," concurred Abby Scott Baker.[58] "There is no doubt that the women in this state [Oregon] are strong for Wilson," concluded Margaret Whittemore.[59] In Montana, organizer Clara Louise Rowe, who had been organizing the state since early spring, lamented then that, "It's very uphill here in Montana. I sometimes wonder if it is worth all the money & effort, but Miss Burns [Lucy] said it was . . . so I suppose it is."[60] Her task did not grow any easier as time went on.

In the circumstances, Paul was asked to reconsider the campaign which the NWP had embarked upon with such high hopes. Despite the pessimistic predictions from the field, Paul refused to even consider withdrawing from the campaign in order to cut NWP losses. "No," she insisted, "if we withdraw the speakers from the campaign, we withdraw the issue from the campaign. We must make this such an important thing in national elections that the Democrats will not want to meet it again."[61]

For the organizers and speakers, the campaign was physically taxing as well as psychologically difficult. Although the NWP now paid its field organizers monthly salaries that ranged from $70 to $100 per month, still the stipend barely covered expenses, if they were frugal.[62] As in most things, Paul attempted to transfer imposed frugality into an advantage to be harvested. Organizers were cautioned by her to exercise conspicuous frugality, since "the more frugal you are, the greater the appeal you will make to people from whom you will have to collect money."[63]

The necessity to make do was inconvenient and the efforts to change hearts and minds was frustrating. But most organizers were not deterred and viewed the hardships as well worth the price for ultimate success. But the exhaustingly long hours and nearly impossible schedules began to take their toll. Paul herself had succumbed to exhaustion on several occasions over the course of her suffrage career. Ill health and frazzled nerves forced her into a hospital at one point early on.[64] In addition to her own health, she had to be aware of her changes, for each one lost to the campaign meant a significant diminishment of effort. Inquir-

ing about the health of one organizer, Mabel Vernon commented, "Poor Alice Paul has been fairly desperate, I hear, because so many of the organizers have failed her on account of illness."[65] For some, the stress resulted in more than just a few days of being under the weather. Edna Latimer, after six weeks in Arizona, required a complete rest in a San Francisco sanitarium.[66] Most tragically, the vivacious and energetic Inez Milholland, so much in demand as a speaker, and who suffered from pernicious anemia, ignored the warnings of her father and her husband to conserve her strength. Milholland collapsed in the middle of a speech in Los Angeles, on October 22. Rushed to a local hospital, she received repeated transfusions over the course of the next several weeks as she alternately rallied and then failed. Her death on November 25, at the age of thirty, sent shock waves through suffrage circles.[67]

Throughout the campaign, the NWP had to contend with NAWSA, which, predictably, viewed the activities of the younger suffragists as detrimental to suffrage. To be sure, NAWSA's own strategy had changed in interesting ways. Carrie Chapman Catt was a much shrewder politician than Anna Howard Shaw had been. Catt also had a far greater facility for organization and management, as well as an eye for what had to be done to secure suffrage. NAWSA's convention of 1916, held in September of that year, was significant for good reason: Woodrow Wilson was the featured speaker, thanks in large measure to Carrie Chapman Catt's efforts.

Wilson had agreed to speak to the NAWSA convention the previous August, in response to Hughes' endorsement of the federal amendment. When the President walked out on to the stage on the evening of September 8, the convention gave him a thunderous welcome. For the first time, Wilson did not overtly champion the states' rights position, although neither did he endorse federal suffragism. "I have not come to fight anybody, *but with somebody*." he declared. "We feel the tide; we rejoice in the strength of it; and we shall not quarrel in the long run as to the method of it."[68]

Not only was Wilson responding to Hughes' declaration, he was also making a bid for the votes of the former Bull Moose Progressives, Independents, and Agrarians who were disenchanted with his failure to pursue further domestic reform during the previous two years.[69] His attempts to correct the situation, beginning in 1916, included supporting several pieces of social legislation which, for a variety of reasons, he had previously rejected and failed to support. These included the

Adamson Eight-Hour Day Law, the Keating-Owen Child Labor Act, the Rural Credits Act, and a Federal Workman's Compensation Act. Woodrow Wilson was, in most cases, an astute politician. As both Governor of New Jersey and as President of the United States, Wilson demonstrated time and again a great capacity to read his constituency and articulate the issues accordingly. Extending the franchise as an act of social justice, in line with his support of other social justice measures, was a matter of political expediency.[70]

At the same time, Wilson's speech to NAWSA was also evidence of his evolving position on the suffrage issue. Wilson, a Southerner by birth, subscribed wholeheartedly to views regarding women and their proper place commonly held by most Southerners. Indeed, as a very young man, he once stated that universal suffrage lay "at the foundation of every evil in this country."[71] While he had left that notion far behind him, at least as it applied to white males, Wilson had not yet accepted women as full citizens entitled to full equal rights, by the time he was elected President. But with three daughters of his own to contend with, and with his adoption of a states' rights position as his defense when questioned by suffragists regarding the issue, Wilson had succumbed to modest changes in his own beliefs that, when coupled with his perceptions of what was politically expedient, proved beneficial for suffrage. Whatever NAWSA delegates may have felt about his reasons for appearing at the convention, they were more than pleased with his speech. Anna Howard Shaw spoke for most of them when she declared, "We have waited *so* long, Mr. President! We have dared to hope that our release might come in your Administration and that yours would be the voice to pronounce the words to bring our freedom."[72]

With the implementation of Catt's "Winning Plan," which, like the NWP strategy, focused on federal suffragism, the two organizations technically were not that far apart. Yet, NAWSA's refusal to yield any quarter to the upstart NWP prevented a cooperative working relationship from developing. Thus, while the campaign of 1916 unfolded, the ever-present animosities surfaced and often revealed the deep-seated feelings of bitterness of some NAWSA people toward the NWP. "The situation in Chicago is extremely difficult," reported Abby Scott Baker, the NWP's national press chairwoman. "The animosity of Mrs. [Ruth Hanna] McCormick is almost unbelievable. She has broken up three meetings after they had been arranged for Mrs. [Louisine] Havemeyer, and we have

reason to believe that she had [our] banners taken down in the town where she has her summer home."[73]

By election day, November 7, 1916, everyone was glad the campaign was over. Exhausted organizers waited in anticipation for the results. The race between Wilson and Hughes was one of the closest in American political history. In the last days of the campaign, some organizers detected movement away from Wilson and toward Hughes. In California, for example, the NWP organizer was told that "the street railway men are falling away [from Wilson], and the local labor leaders cannot get them back in line." The city editor of a Los Angeles daily—a Wilson supporter—expressed his fear that "it is the last swing. I am afraid the election will come on the crest of it. If it does, California will be lost to us."[74]

Suffragists notwithstanding, the war in Europe, not women's rights, weighed most heavily on the minds of Americans as they went to the polls on November 7. The election hung in the balance for some time as California slowly counted its votes. When the last vote had been counted, Wilson emerged victorious—although just barely—winning 277 electoral votes to Hughes' 254. Of the twelve suffrage states, Wilson won all but Oregon and Illinois, despite the NWP campaign. It is one of the ironies of the campaign that Wilson's narrow victory in 1916 was attributed to the women's vote—because of the peace issue. Women in California, with thirteen electoral votes and the election in the balance, voted disproportionately for Wilson, according to the *New York Times*. William Allen White observed that if women in Kansas had not voted for Wilson, "Kansas would have gone for Hughes." And analysts in Arizona, Idaho, Utah, and Washington credited women with swinging their combined eighteen electoral votes to the Democratic column.[75]

Many NWP organizers were disappointed and discouraged. They had hoped for a more obvious victory. But the campaign itself was far from a failure. Paul had stressed time and again the importance of "spread[ing] abroad the impression of a very active campaign on the part of women against Democrats."[76] The response of both the Republicans and the Democrats demonstrated the success of this strategy. The Republicans tried to capitalize on the NWP campaign; the Democrats tried to put a damper on it. Both parties attempted to win over women voters, and the Democrats, in particular, mounted a major effort toward this end.[77]

Then, too, Illinois, which did go for Hughes, was the only one of the twelve suffrage states where women's votes were counted separately from men's votes. In that state, Hughes won 52.6 percent of the overall vote. Women voters went for the Republican candidate by 55.3 percent, while only 49.9 percent of the male voters voted for Hughes.[78] In Illinois, it appears that women did indeed register a protest vote against Wilson.

Regardless of which party won in 1916, the NWP could not lose. As the *Wichita* [Kansas] *Eagle* observed, "When the Congress next meets, no matter whether Wilson or Hughes is elected, the women of the nation are going to have a powerful argument for national woman suffrage."[79] A *Ventura* [California] *Free Press* editorial noted that "the universal opinion of political leaders of all parties is that no new political party ever before made such a remarkable showing in a presidential campaign as has the National Woman's Party."[80] The Democrats, asserted the *New Republic,* owed their victory to women voters. "Yet but for women suffrage, to which he tepidly assents, Mr. Wilson would not have been continued in the White House. The balance of power, so far as Congress is concerned, and so far as rival parties are concerned, is conceivably in women's hands."[81]

Alice Paul had no intention of allowing the Democrats to forget to whom they owed their victory. Not that they were likely to forget. Vance C. McCormick, the chairman of the Democratic National Committee, in his own postelection analysis, noted the advisability of attending to the party's weak spots before the elections of 1918. "Our weakest spot is the suffrage situation," McCormick confided to a fellow committeeman. "We must get rid of the suffrage amendment before 1918 if we want to control the next Congress."[82] As the *San Francisco Examiner* noted, suffrage had ceased to be a "western vagary. Nothing that has 2,000,000 votes is ever vague to the politicians."[83]

Notes

1. In 1912, Democrat Key Pittman won the Nevada race with 7,942 votes (39.8 percent), over Republican candidate W. A. Massey, with 7,853 votes (39.3 percent); a switch of 45 votes would have produced a different winner, *Congressional Quarterly's Guide to U.S. Elections,* p. 493.

2. Alice Paul, quoted in Irwin, *Up Hill with Banners Flying,* pp. 152-154.

3. The card index is contained in the NWP Papers; on Maud Younger, see "Maud Younger," *Notable American Women,* III, pp. 699-700; Maud Younger, "The Diary of an Amateur Waitress: An Industrial Problem from the Worker's Point of View," *McClure's Magazine,* XXVII (March 1907), pp. 543-552, and XXVIII (April 1907),

pp. 665-677; "Taking Orders: A Day as a Waitress in a San Francisco Restaurant," *Sunset Magazine* XXI (October 1908), pp. 518-522; and "Revelations of a Woman Lobbyist," *McCall's,* XLX (September, October, and November 1919), passim.

4. Irwin, *Up Hill with Banners Flying,* pp. 134-144.

5. Report of the National Advisory Council, December 1916, NWP Papers; see also, Alice Paul to Mrs. Lucius Cuthbert, April 14, 1916, NWP Papers.

6. Lucy Burns to Alice Park Locke, March 25, 1916, Alice Park Locke Papers, Hunington Library.

7. Margery Ross to Joy Webster, April 8, 1916, NWP Papers; see also, Harriot Stanton Blatch to W. H. Gates, February 25, 1916; Alice Paul to Harriot Stanton Blatch, March 1916; Harriot Stanton Blatch to Alice Paul, March 7, March 15, and March 17, 1916, all in NWP Papers.

8. Ella Reigel to Joy Webster, April 26, 1916, NWP Papers.

9. Ella Reigel to Joy Webster, April 29, 1916, NWP Papers.

10. Olive H. Hasbrook to Joy Webster, April 28, 1916; Margery Ross to Joy Webster, June 1916; Ella Reigel to Joy Webster, April 13 and 29, 1916; Harriot Stanton Blatch, Speech to Audience in Salem, Oregon, May 10, 1916; Annette McCrea to Alden Thomas, May 15, 1916; and Ella Reigel to Joy Webster, May 3, 1916, all in NWP Papers.

11. Report of the Proceedings of the National Woman's Party Convention, June 5-7, 1916, NWP Papers.

12. Constitution of the National Woman's Party, NWP Papers.

13. Report of the Proceedings of the National Woman's Party Convention, June 5-7, 1916, NWP Papers. Paul remained chairwoman of the Congressional Union as well.

14. *New York World,* June 7 and 8, 1916.

15. Report of the Proceedings of the National Woman's Party Convention, June 5-7, 1916, NWP Papers; *New York World,* June 8, 1916; Irwin, *Up Hill with Banners Flying,* p. 161.

16. Charles A. Beard, "Third Party Functions," *The Suffragists,* IV (November 25, 1916), p. 6.

17. *Campaign Text-Book 1916,* NWP Papers.

18. Arthur S. Link and William M. Leary, Jr., "The Election of 1916," in Arthur Schlesinger, et al., eds., *The History of American Presidential Elections 1789-1968,* III (1917), pp. 2245-2270.

19. *New York Times,* June 17, 1916; see also, *History of Woman Suffrage,* V, pp. 712-715.

20. *New York Times,* June 17, 1916.

21. For a discussion of the various party planks, from the perspective of the NWP, see *The Suffragist,* V: June 17, 1916 (Republican platform); July 1, 1916 (Democratic platform); July 8, 1916 (Progressive platform); July 22, 1916 (Socialist platform); and July 29, 1916 (Prohibitionist platform).

22. Alice Paul to Mabel Vernon, April 20, 1916, Mabel Vernon Papers, Bancroft Library, University of California at Berkeley.

23. Alice Paul to Mabel Vernon, April 20, 1916, Mabel Vernon Papers.

24. *New Republic,* VI (November 21, 1914), p. 4.

25. Ibid., IX (November 18, 1916), p. 59.

26. Charles A. Beard to Carrie Chapman Catt, August 5, 1916, NWP Papers.

27. Speech delivered at Salem, Oregon by Mrs. Harriot Stanton Blatch, May 10, 1916, NWP Papers; Paul Interview, pp. 154-155; Vernon Interview, pp. 191-192.

28. Paul Interview, pp. 155-156.

29. Alice Paul to Harriot Stanton Blatch, July 7, 1917, NWP Papers; Anne Martin to Abby Scott Baker, August 10, 1916, Martin Papers; Paul Interview, pp. 155-156; Ella Reigel to Joy Webster, June 29, 1916, and Anne Martin to Margaret Whittemore, July 22, 1916, both in NWP Papers.

30. Vernon Interview, pp. 191-192.

31. *New York Times,* August 1, 1916.

32. Alice Paul to Mrs. Lucius Cuthbert, August 23, 1916, NWP Papers.

33. Woodrow Wilson to Mrs. E. P. Davis, August 5, 1916, Wilson Papers.

34. Anne Martin to Natalie Gray, July 7, 1916, NWP Papers.

35. Alice Paul to Mrs. Robert Morton, July 5, 1916, NWP Papers.

36. Resolutions Adopted by the National Woman's Party, August 11, 1916; *Campaign Text-Book 1916,* both in NWP Papers; see also Alice Paul to Mrs. Lucius Cuthbert, August 23, 1916, NWP Papers.

37. *Campaign Text-Book 1916.* NWP Papers. Mabel Vernon was Alice Paul's first paid organizer. Vernon had graduated Swarthmore a year ahead of Paul, but the two did not really know each other until the suffrage period. Paul had been apprised of Vernon's varied talents by a mutual friend shortly after the Congressional Union was organized. She invited Vernon to Washington and asked the Baltimore native how much she would need to live on; Vernon, then a schoolteacher, estimated she could get along on $70 a month, Paul guaranteed that amount and the bargain was struck. Neither was ever sorry. A month before the Colorado Springs meeting, during Fourth of July ceremonies in Washington, Vernon achieved national notoriety as the woman who had to be forceably removed from Woodrow Wilson's reviewing stand when she proceeded to heckle the President for his refusal to take up the suffrage issue. The idea was Paul's, but the adventuresome Vernon readily agreed to it. Paul managed to secure platform tickets for Wilson's speech. At appropriate moments during the speech, Vernon called out loudly and clearly, "Mr. President, what will you do for suffrage?" Wilson ignored the question, but after several similar interruptions, Secret Service Agents escorted Vernon off the stage, asking as they went out, "What makes you act that way?" Paul remained on stage, impassively observing the scene. Later, recalling the Secret Service agents' question to friends, one of them asked Vernon, "Why didn't you say, 'She does!'", referring to Paul. See, for example,

the *Washington Post* and the *New York Times,* July 5, 1916. Vernon Interview, pp. 61-62, 141-142; and, "Mabel Vernon," *Notable American Women,* IV, pp. 711-712.

38. "Inez Milholland Boissevain," *Notable American Women,* I, pp. 188-190; Paul Interview, pp. 170-173, 339-340, 496; Vernon Interview, pp. 19-21, 64-65; Irwin, *Up Hill with Banners Flying,* pp. 98, 160, 177; Stevens, *Jailed for Freedom,* pp. 48-60.

39. The term "second generation" was Mabel Vernon's description of the new NWP organizers. Vernon referred to those women who were with the Congressional Union from the very beginning as the first generation. Those who came into the organization after 1914 were the second generation, and a third generation, according to Vernon, came in after 1916. Vernon Interview, pp. 141-158.

40. Stevens, *Jailed for Freedom,* Appendix D, pp. 354-371; Vernon Interview, pp. 141-158; Reyher Interview, pp. 33-45.

41. The membership of the Congressional Union and National Woman's Party probably never constituted more than five per cent of the nation's suffragists. At the numerical height of its success, the NWP enrolled fewer than 50,000 members, whereas NAWSA's membership numbered in the hundreds of thousands. The difference was that the NWP members were almost always active and a significant number sacrificed jobs and personal lives to work full-time for the cause. Thus, their relatively small numbers were extremely significant in terms of productivity and influence. Paul Interview, pp. 327-329; Vernon Interview, pp. 190-191.

42. Irwin, *Up Hill with Banners Flying,* pp. 178-179; *New York Times,* October 23, 1916.

43. Iris Calderhead to Anne Martin, October 25, 1916, Martin Papers.

44. Alice Paul to Mrs. Lucius Cuthbert, August 23, 1916, NWP Papers; Alice Paul to Organizers, September 20, 1916, and Alice Paul to Mrs. Stevenson, September 20, 1916, both in Martin Papers; *The Suffragist,* IV (August 19, 1916), p. 6.

45. W. Y. Morgan to John S. Simmons, September 27, 1916, Martin Papers.

46. Abby Scott Baker to Anne Martin, September 21, 1916, Martin Papers; see also, Helen Bonnifield to Mabel Vernon, November 12, 1916, Vernon Papers.

47. Philip S. Triplett to Mabel Vernon, September 30, 1916, NWP Papers.

48. Doris Stevens to Alice Paul, September 20, 1916, NWP Papers. Stevens analysis proved to be accurate, as both the events of the time and later historical analysis demonstrated. See Link and Leary, "The Election of 1916," p. 2257.

49. Alice Paul to Doris Stevens, September 25, 1916, NWP Papers.

50. Anne Martin to Alice Paul, October 3, 1916, Martin Papers.

51. Anne Martin to Alice Paul, September 30, 1916, Martin Papers.

52. Abby Scott Baker to Anne Martin, September 29, 1916, Martin Papers.

53. *Campaign Text-Book 1916*, NWP Papers.

54. Cook, *Crystal Eastman On Women and Revolution*, pp. 15-20, 241-247.

55. Edith Barringer to Anne Martin, September 23, 1916, Martin Papers.

56. Mrs. J. E. Drennan to Alva Belmont, September 27, 1916; Nannie T. Daniels to Alva Belmont, September 28, 1916; Emma Haley Flanagan to Alva Belmont, September 30, 1916, and, Jessie Earnshaw to Alva Belmont, October 1, 1916, all in NWP Papers.

57. Helen Heffernon to Mabel Vernon, October 20, 1916, Vernon Papers.

58. Abby Scott Baker to Mabel Vernon, September 26, 1916, Vernon Papers; see also, H. V. Castle to Mabel Vernon, October 28, 1916, and Mabel Davis to Mabel Vernon, October 17, 1916, all in Vernon Papers.

59. Margaret Fay Whittemore to Mabel Vernon, September 28, 1916, Vernon Papers.

60. Clara Louise Rowe to Joy Webster, May 21, 1916, NWP Papers.

61. Irwin, *Up Hill with Banners Flying*, p. 183.

62. Report of the Treasury Department of the 1916 Campaign, NWP Papers.

63. Alice Paul to Alice Henkle, September 3, 1916, NWP Papers; Vivian Pierce to Joy Webster, September 21, and September 24, 1916; and Elsie Hill to Joy Webster, September 27, 1916, NWP Papers.

64. Paul Interview, pp. 104, 108-109; Vernon Interview, pp. 37-38.

65. Mabel Vernon to Doris Stevens, October 14, 1916, Vernon Papers.

66. C. F. Clark to Mabel Vernon, September 30, 1916 and October 8, 1916; and, Mabel Vernon to Maud Younger, October 6, 1916, all in Vernon Papers; Gertrude Crocker to Lucy Burns, October 18, 1916, Martin Papers.

67. Alice Park Locke to Anne Martin, November 17, 1916, Martin Papers. A glance at Inez Milholland's itinerary reveals that her speaking schedule was as exhausting as that of any of the candidates and, in retrospect, much too demanding given her physical impairment. After leaving New York on October 4, Milholland was scheduled to speak in forty-three different cities in Wyoming, Idaho, Montana, Oregon, Washington, Utah, Nevada, Arizona, California, Kansas, and Illinois, all in less than one month. Revised Itinerary of Inez Milholland, n.d. (1916), NWP Papers.

68. Baker and Dodd, eds., *The Public Papers of Woodrow Wilson*, IV, pp. 297-300.

69. Bull Moose Progressives were members of the Republican Party who refused to support William Howard Taft in the election of 1912. Bull Moose Progressives, instead, cast their lot with Theodore Roosevelt. This split in the Republican Party is generally credited with throwing the election to Woodrow Wilson.

70. Lunardini and Knock, "Woodrow Wilson and Woman Suffrage: A New Look," *Political Science Quarterly* XCV (Winter 1980/81), pp. 670-671; see also, Arthur S. Link, *Wilson: Campaigns for Progressivism and Peace 1916-1917*, Princeton: Princeton University Press (1965), passim; and Link, *Woodrow Wilson and the Progressive Era 1910-1917*, New York: Harper Torchbooks (1963), passim.

71. Diary entry, June 19, 1876, *The Papers of Woodrow Wilson*, 36 vols., Arthur S. Link et al., eds., III, p. 143.

72. Catt and Shuler, *Woman Suffrage and Politics*, p. 260.

73. Abby Scott Baker to Anne Martin, September 29, 1916, Martin Papers.

74. Beulah Amidon to Anne Martin, November 1, 1916, Martin Papers.

75. *New York Times*, November 10 and 12, 1916; *Literary Digest*, November 18, 1916, pp. 1312-1316; *New Republic*, November 25, 1916, pp. 86-87; see also, Link, *Wilson, Campaigns For Progressivism and Peace*, p. 161 fn.; and, Catt and Shuler, *Woman Suffrage and Politics*, pp. 264-265.

76. See, for example, Alice Paul to Organizers, September 20, 1916; Alice Paul to Mrs. Stevenson, September 20, 1916; and Alice Paul to Organizers, n.d. (ca. October 1916), all in Martin Papers.

77. See, for example, Elizabeth Bass, Chairwoman of the Democratic National Committee's Woman's Bureau, to "Dear Madam," September 18, 1916, NWP Papers; and Harriet E. Vittum, Director of Woman's Work, Republican National Committee, to Anne Martin, September 22, 1916, Martin Papers.

78. *Congressional Quarterly's Guide to U.S. Elections*, Election of 1916: Presidential Results by State; see also Gilson Gardner, "The Work of the Woman's Party," *The Suffragist*, IV (November 25, 1916), p. 4.

79. Quoted in *The Suffragist*, IV (November 25, 1916), p. 8.

80. Ibid.

81. *New Republic*, IX (November 25, 1916), pp. 85-86; see also similar excerpts from the *San Francisco Examiner*, *Wichita Eagle*, *Utica* [New York] *Dispatch*, *Flagstaff* [Arizona] *Sun*, and the *Oroville* [California] *Mercury*, all quoted in *The Suffragist*, IV (November 25, 1916), pp. 4-8.

82. Vance C. McCormick, quoted in Irwin, *Up Hill with Banners Flying*, p. 183.

83. Quoted in *The Suffragist*, IV (November 25, 1916), p. 8.

ELLEN CAROL DUBOIS (ESSAY DATE 1987)

SOURCE: DuBois, Ellen Carol. "Working Women, Class Relations, and Suffrage Militance: Harriot Stanton Blatch and the New York Woman Suffrage Movement, 1894-1909." In, pp. 176-209. New York: New York University Press, 1998.

In the following essay, DuBois discusses Blatch's ideas and suffrage work in the context of the politics of the Progressive Era.

More than any other period in American reform history, the Progressive Era eludes interpretation. It seems marked by widespread concern for social justice and by extraordinary elitism, by democratization and by increasing social control. The challenge posed to historians is to understand how Progressivism could simultaneously represent gains for the masses and more power for the classes. The traditional way to approach the period has been to study the discrete social programs reformers so energetically pushed in those years, from the abolition of child labor to the Americanization of the immigrants. Recently, historians' emphasis has shifted to politics, where it will probably remain for a time. Historians have begun to recognize that the rules of political life, the nature of American "democracy," were fundamentally reformulated beginning in the Progressive Era, and that such political change shaped the ultimate impact of particular social reforms.

Where were women in all this? The new focus on politics requires a reinterpretation of women's role in Progressivism. As the field of women's history has grown, the importance of women in the Progressive Era has gained notice, but there remains a tendency to concentrate on their roles with respect to social reform. Modern scholarship on the Progressive Era thus retains a separate spheres flavor; women are concerned with social and moral issues, but the world of politics is male. Nowhere is this clearer than in the tendency to minimize, even to omit, the woman suffrage movement from the general literature on the Progressive Era.[1]

Scholarship on woman suffrage is beginning to grow in detail and analytic sophistication, but it has yet to be fully integrated into overviews of the period.[2] Histories that include woman suffrage usually do so in passing, listing it with other constitutional alterations in the electoral process such as the popular election of senators, the initiative, and the referendum. But woman suffrage was a mass movement, and that fact is rarely noticed. Precisely because it was a mass political movement—perhaps the first modern one—woman suffrage may well illuminate Progressive-Era politics, especially the class dynamics underlying their reformulation. When the woman suffrage movement is given its due, we may begin to understand the process by which democratic hope turned into mass political alienation, which is the history of modern American politics.

To illuminate the origin and nature of the woman suffrage movement in the Progressive Era I will examine the politics of Harriot Stanton Blatch. Blatch was the daughter of Elizabeth Cady Stanton, the founding mother of political feminism. Beginning in the early twentieth century, she was a leader in her own right, initially in New York, later nationally. As early as 1903, when politics was still considered something that disreputable men did, like smoking tobacco, Blatch proclaimed: "There are born politicians just as there are born artists, writers, painters. I confess that I should be a politician, that I am not interested in machine politics, but that the devotion to the public cause . . . rather than the individual, appeals to me."[3]

Just as her zest for politics marked Blatch as a new kind of suffragist, so did her efforts to fuse women of different classes into a revitalized suffrage movement. Blatch's emphasis on class was by no means unique; she shared it with other women reformers of her generation. Many historians have treated the theme of class by labeling the organized women's reform movement in the early twentieth century "middle-class." By contrast, I have tried to keep open the question of the class character of women's reform in the Progressive Era by rigorously avoiding the term. Characterizing the early twentieth-century suffrage movement as "middle-class" obscures its most striking element, the new interest in the vote among women at both ends of the class structure. Furthermore, it tends to homogenize the movement. The very term "middle-class" is contradictory, alternatively characterized as people who are not poor, and people who work for a living. By contrast, I have emphasized distinctions between classes and organized my analysis around the relations between them.

No doubt there is some distortion in this framework, particularly for suffragists who worked in occupations like teaching. But there is far greater distortion in using the term "middle-class" to describe women like Blatch or Carrie Chapman Catt or Jane Addams. For example, it makes more sense to characterize an unmarried woman with an independent income who was not under financial compulsion to work for her living as "elite," rather than "middle-class." The question is not just one of social stratification, but of the place of women in a whole system of class relations. For these new style suffragists, as for contemporary feminists who write about them, the complex relationship between paid labor, marital status, and women's place in the class structure was a fundamental puzzle. The concept of "middle-class" emerged among early twentieth-century reformers, but may ultimately prove more useful in describing a set of relations *between* classes that was coming into being in those years, than in designating a segment of the social structure.

Blatch, examined as a political strategist and a critic of class relations, is important less as a unique figure than as a representative leader, through whose career the historical forces transforming twentieth-century suffragism can be traced. The scope of her leadership offers clues to the larger movement: She was one of the first to open up suffrage campaigns to working-class women, even as she worked closely with wealthy and influential upper-class women; she pioneered militant street tactics and backroom political lobbying at the same time. Blatch's political evolution reveals close ties between other stirrings among American women in the Progressive Era and the rejuvenated suffrage movement. Many of her ideas paralleled Charlotte Perkins Gilman's influential reformulation of women's emancipation in economic terms. Many of Blatch's innovations as a suffragist drew on her prior experience in the Women's Trade Union League. Overall, Blatch's activities suggest that early twentieth-century changes in the American suffrage movement, often traced to the example of militant British suffragettes, had deep, indigenous roots. Among them were the growth of trade unionism among working-class women and professionalism among the elite, changing relations between these classes, and the growing involvement of women of all sorts in political reform.

The suffrage revival began in New York in 1893-1894, as part of a general political reform movement. In the 1890s New York's political reformers were largely upper-class men concerned about political "corruption," which they blamed partly on city Democratic machines and the bosses who ran them, partly on the masses of voting men, ignorant, immigrant, and ripe for political manipulation. Their concern about political corruption and about the consequences of uncontrolled political democracy became the focus of New York's 1894 constitutional convention, which addressed itself largely to "governmental procedures: the rules for filling offices, locating authority and organizing the different branches."[4]

The New York woman suffrage movement, led by Susan B. Anthony, recognized a great opportunity in the constitutional convention of 1894. Focusing on political corruption, Anthony and her allies argued that women were the political reformers' best allies. For while men were already voters and vulnerable to the ethic of partisan loyalty—indeed a man without a party affiliation in the 1890s was damned close to un-

sexed—everyone knew that women were naturally nonpartisan. Enfranchising women was therefore the solution to the power of party bosses. Suffragists began by trying to get women elected to the constitutional convention itself. Failing this, they worked to convince the convention delegates to include woman suffrage among the proposed amendments.[5]

Anthony planned a house-to-house canvass to collect signatures on a mammoth woman suffrage petition. For the $50,000 she wanted to fund this effort, she approached wealthy women in New York City, including physician Mary Putnam Jacobi, society leader Catherine Palmer (Mrs. Robert) Abbe, social reformer Josephine Shaw Lowell, and philanthropist Olivia (Mrs. Russell) Sage. Several of them were already associated with efforts for the amelioration of working-class women, notably in the recently formed Consumers' League, and Anthony had reason to think they might be ready to advocate woman suffrage.[6]

The elite women were interested in woman suffrage, but they had their own ideas about how to work for it. Instead of funding Anthony's campaign, they formed their own organization. At parlor meetings in the homes of wealthy women, they tried to strike a genteel note, emphasizing that enfranchisement would *not* take women out of their proper sphere and would *not* increase the political power of the lower classes. Eighty-year-old Elizabeth Stanton, observing the campaign from her armchair, thought that "men and women of the conservative stamp of the Sages can aid us greatly at this stage of our movement."[7]

Why did wealthy women first take an active and prominent part in the suffrage movement in the 1890s? In part they shared the perspective of men of their class that the influence of the wealthy in government had to be strengthened; they believed that with the vote they could increase the political power of their class. In a representative argument before the constitutional convention, Jacobi proposed woman suffrage as a response to "the shifting of political power from privileged classes to the masses of men." The disfranchisement of women contributed to this shift because it made all women, "no matter how well born, how well educated, how intelligent, how rich, how serviceable to the State," the political inferiors of all men, "no matter how base-born, how poverty stricken, how ignorant, how vicious, how brutal." Olivia Sage presented woman suffrage as an antidote to the growing and dangerous "idleness" of elite women, who had forgotten their responsibility to set the moral tone for society.[8]

Yet, the new elite converts also supported woman suffrage on the grounds of changes taking place in women's status, especially within their own class. Jacobi argued that the educational advancement of elite women "and the new activities into which they have been led by it—in the work of charities, in the professions, and in the direction of public education—naturally and logically tend toward the same result, their political equality." She argued that elite women, who had aided the community through organized charity and benevolent activities, should have the same "opportunity to serve the State nobly." Sage was willing to advocate woman suffrage because of women's recent "strides . . . in the acquirement of business methods, in the management of their affairs, in the effective interest they have evinced in civic affairs."[9]

Suffragists like Jacobi and Sage characteristically conflated their class perspective with the role they saw for themselves as women, contending for political leadership not so much on the grounds of their wealth, as of their womanliness. Women, they argued, had the characteristics needed in politics—benevolence, morality, selflessness, and industry; conveniently, they believed that elite women most fully embodied these virtues. Indeed, they liked to believe that women like themselves were elite *because* they were virtuous, not because they were wealthy. The confusion of class and gender coincided with a more general elite ideology that identified the fundamental division in American society not between rich and poor, but between industrious and idle, virtuous and vicious, community-minded and selfish. On these grounds Sage found the purposeless leisure of wealthy women dangerous to the body politic. She believed firmly that the elite, women included, should provide moral—and ultimately political—leadership, but it was important to her that they earn the right to lead.[10]

The problem for elite suffragists was that woman suffrage meant the enfranchisement of working-class, as well as elite, women. Jacobi described a prominent woman who "had interested herself nobly and effectively in public affairs, . . . but preferred not to claim the right [of suffrage] for herself, lest its concession entail the enfranchisement of ignorant and irresponsible women." An elite antisuffrage organization committed to such views was active in the 1894 campaign as well, led by women of the same class,

with many of the same beliefs, as the prosuffrage movement. As Stanton wrote, "The fashionable women are about equally divided between two camps." The antis included prominent society figures Abby Hamlin (Mrs. Lyman) Abbott and Josephine Jewell (Mrs. Arthur) Dodge, as well as Annie Nathan Meyer, founder of Barnard College and member of the Consumers' League. Like the elite suffragists, upper-class antis wanted to insure greater elite influence in politics; but they argued that woman suffrage would decrease elite influence, rather than enhance it.[11]

Elite suffragists' willingness to support woman suffrage rested on their confidence that their class would provide political leadership for all women once they had the vote. Because they expected working-class women to defer to them, they believed that class relations among women would be more cooperative and less antagonistic than among men. Elite women, Jacobi argued before the 1894 convention, would "so guide ignorant women voters that they could be made to counterbalance, when necessary, the votes of ignorant and interested men." Such suffragists assumed that working-class women were too weak, timid, and disorganized to make their own demands. Since early in the nineteenth century, elite women had claimed social and religious authority on the grounds of their responsibility for the women and children of the poor. They had begun to adapt this tradition to the new conditions of an industrial age, notably in the Consumers' League, formed in response to the pleas of women wage earners for improvement in their working conditions. In fact, elite antis also asserted that they spoke for working-class women, but they contended that working-class women neither needed nor wanted to vote.[12]

From an exclusively elite perspective, the antisuffrage argument was more consistent than the prosuffrage one; woman suffrage undoubtedly meant greater political democracy, which the political reform movement of the 1890s most fundamentally feared. Elite suffragists found themselves organizing their own arguments around weak refutations of the antis' objections.[13] The ideological weakness had political implications. Woman suffrage got no serious hearing in the constitutional convention, and the 1894 constitutional revisions designed to "clean up government" ignored women's plea for political equality.

The episode revealed dilemmas, especially with respect to class relations among women, that a successful suffrage movement would have to address. Elite women had begun to aspire to political roles that led them to support woman suffrage, and the resources they commanded would be crucial to the future success of suffrage efforts. But their attraction to woman suffrage rested on a portrait of working-class women and a system of class relations that had become problematic to a modern industrial society. Could elite women sponsor the entrance of working-class women into politics without risking their influence over them, and perhaps their position of leadership? Might not working-class women assume a newly active, politically autonomous role? The tradition of class relations among women had to be transformed before a thriving and modern woman suffrage movement could be built. Harriot Stanton Blatch had the combination of suffrage convictions and class awareness to lead New York suffragists through that transition.

The 1894 campaign, which confronted suffragists with the issue of class, also drew Blatch actively into the American woman suffrage movement. She had come back from England, where she had lived for many years, to receive a master's degree from Vassar College for her study of the English rural poor. A powerful orator, she was "immediately pressed into service . . . speaking every day," at parlor suffrage meetings, often to replace her aged mother.[14] Like her mother, Blatch was comfortable in upper-class circles; she had married into a wealthy British family. She generally shared the elite perspective of the campaign, assuming that "educated women" would lead their sex. But she disliked the implication that politics could ever become too democratic and, virtually alone among the suffragists, criticized all "those little anti-republican things I hear so often here in America, this talk of the quality of votes." And while other elite suffragists discussed working-class women as domestic servants and shop clerks, Blatch understood the centrality of industrial workers, although her knowledge of them was still primarily academic.[15]

Blatch's disagreements with the elite suffrage framework were highlighted a few months after the constitutional convention in an extraordinary public debate with her mother. In the *Woman's Journal*, Stanton urged that the suffrage movement incorporate an educational restriction into its demand, to respond to "the greatest block in the way of woman's enfranchisement . . . the fear of the 'ignorant vote' being doubled." Her justification for this position, so at odds with the principles of a lifetime, was that the enfranchisement of "educated women" best supplied "the imperative need at the time . . . woman's influence in public life." From England, Blatch wrote a powerful dissent. Challenging the authority of her venerated mother was a dramatic act that—perhaps deliberately—marked the end of her political daughterhood. She defended both the need and the capacity of the working class to engage in democratic politics. On important questions, "for example . . . the housing of the poor," their opinion was more informed than that of the elite. She also argued that since "the conditions of the poor are so much harder . . . every working man needs the suffrage more than I do." And finally, she insisted on the claims of a group her mother had ignored, working women.[16]

The debate between mother and daughter elegantly symbolizes the degree to which class threatened the continued vitality of the republican tradition of suffragism. Partly because of her participation in the British Fabian movement, Blatch was able to adapt the republican faith to modern class relations, while Stanton was not. As a Fabian, Blatch had gained an appreciation for the political intelligence and power of the working class very rare among elite reformers in the U.S. When she insisted that the spirit of democracy was more alive in England than in the U.S., she was undoubtedly thinking of the development of a working-class political movement there.[17]

Over the next few years, Blatch explored basic assumptions of the woman suffrage faith she had inherited, in the context of modern class relations. In the process, like other women reformers of her era, such as Charlotte Perkins Gilman, Florence Kelley, Jane Addams, and numerous settlement house residents and supporters of organized labor, she focused on the relation of women and work. She emphasized the productive labor that women performed, both as it contributed to the larger social good and as it created the conditions of freedom and equality for women themselves. Women had always worked, she insisted. The new factor was the shift of women's work from the home to the factory and the office, and from the status of unpaid to paid labor. Sometimes she stressed that women's unpaid domestic labor made an important contribution to society; at other times she stressed that such unpaid work was not valued, but always she emphasized the historical development that was taking women's labor out of the home and into the commercial economy. The question for modern society was not whether women should work, but under what conditions, and with what consequences for their own lives.[18]

Although Blatch was troubled by the wages and working conditions of the laboring poor, her emphasis on work as a means to emancipation led her to regard wage-earning women less as victims to be succored, than as exemplars to their sex. She vigorously denied that women ideally hovered somewhere above the world of work. She had no respect for the "handful of rich women who have no employment other than organizing servants, social functions and charities." Upper-class women, she believed, should also "work," should make an individualized contribution to the public good, and where possible should have the value of their labor recognized by being paid for it.[19] As a member of the first generation of college-educated women, she believed that education and professional achievement, rather than wealth and refinement, fitted a woman for social leadership.

Turning away from nineteenth-century definitions of the unity of women that emphasized their place in the home, their motherhood, and their exclusion from the economy, and emphasizing instead the unity that productive work provided for all women, Blatch rewrote feminism in its essentially modern form, around work. She tended to see women's work, including homemaking and child rearing, as a mammoth portion of the world's productive labor, which women collectively accomplished. Thus she retained the concept of "women's work" for the sex as a whole, while vigorously discarding it on the individual level, explicitly challenging the notion that all women had the same tastes and talents.[20]

Her approach to "women's work" led Blatch to believe that the interconnection of women's labor fundamentally shaped relations among them. Here were the most critical aspects of her thought. Much as she admired professional women, she insisted that they recognize the degree to which their success rested on the labor of other women, who cared for their homes and their children. "Whatever merit [their homes] possess," Blatch wrote, "is largely due to the fact that the actress when on the stage, the doctor when by her patient's side, the writer when at her desk, has a Bridget to do the homebuilding for her." The problem was that the professional woman's labor brought her so much more freedom than the housemaid's labor brought her. "Side by side with the marked improvement in the condition of the well-to-do or educated woman," Blatch observed, "our century shows little or no progress in the condition of the woman of the people." Like her friend Gilman, Blatch urged that professional standards of work—good pay, an emphasis on expertise, the assumption of a lifelong career—be extended to the nurserymaid and the dressmaker, as well as to the lawyer and the journalist. Until such time, the "movement for the emancipation of women [would] remain . . . a well-dressed movement."[21]

But professional training and better wages alone would not give labor an emancipatory power in the lives of working-class women. Blatch recognized the core of the problem of women's work, especially for working-class women: "How can the duties of mother and wage earner be reconciled?" She believed that wage-earning women had the same desire as professional women to continue to enjoy careers and independence after marriage. "It may be perverse in lowly wage earners to show individuality as if they were rich," Blatch wrote, "but apparently we shall have to accept the fact that all women do not prefer domestic work to all other kinds." But the problem of balancing a career and a homelife was "insoluble—under present conditions—for the women of the people." "The pivotal question for women," she wrote, "is how to organize their work as home-builders and race-builders, how to get that work paid for not in so called protection, but in the currency of the state."[22]

As the female labor force grew in the late nineteenth century, so did the number of married women workers and demands that they be driven from the labor force. The suffrage movement had traditionally avoided the conflict between work and motherhood by pinning the demand for economic equality on the existence of unmarried women, who had no men to support them.[23] Blatch confronted the problem of work and motherhood more directly. In a 1905 article, she drew from the utopian ideas of William Morris to recommend that married women work in small, worker-owned manufacturing shops where they could have more control over their hours and could bring their children with them. Elsewhere, she argued that the workplace should be reorganized around women's needs, rather than assume the male worker's standards, but she did not specify what that would mean. She never solved the riddle of work and children for women—nor have we—but she knew that the solution could not be to force women to choose between the two nor to banish mothers from the labor force.[24]

Blatch's vision of women in industrial society was democratic—all must work and all must be recognized and rewarded for their work—but it was not an egalitarian approach nor one that recognized most working women's material concerns. According to Blatch, women worked for psychological and ethical reasons, as much as for monetary ones. "As human beings we must have work," she wrote; "we rust out if we have not an opportunity to function on something." She emphasized the common promises and problems work raised in women's lives, not the differences in how they worked, how much individual choice they had, and especially in how much they were paid. She was relatively unconcerned with the way work enabled women to earn their livings. No doubt, her own experience partially explains this. As a young woman fresh out of college in the 1870s, she had dared to imagine that her desire for meaningful work and a role in the world need not deprive her of marriage and motherhood, and it did not. Despite her marriage, the birth of two children, and the death of one, she never interrupted her political and intellectual labors. But she also never earned her own living, depending instead on the income from her husband's family's business. In later years, she joked about the fact that she was the only "parasite" in the organization of self-supporting women she headed.[25]

But the contradictions in her analysis of the problem of work and women reflected more than her personal situation. There were two problems of work and women: the long-standing exploitation of laboring women of the working classes and the newly expanding place of paid labor in the lives of all women in bourgeois society. While the two processes were not the same, they were related, and women thinkers and activists of the Progressive period struggled to understand how. As more women worked for pay and outside of the home, how would the meaning of "womanhood" change? What would be the difference between "woman" and "man" when as many women as men were paid workers? And what would be the class differences between women if all of them worked? Indeed, would there be any difference between the classes at all, once the woman of leisure no longer existed? Virtually all the efforts to link the gender and class problems of work for woman were incomplete. If Blatch's analysis of work, like Gilman's, shorted the role of class, others' analyses, for instance Florence Kelley's, underplayed what work meant for women as a sex.

Blatch rethought the principles of political equality in the light of her emphasis on women's work. At an 1898 congressional hearing, Blatch hailed "the most convincing argument upon which our future claims must rest—the growing recognition of the economic value of the work of women."[26] Whereas her mother had based her suffragism on the nineteenth-century argument for natural rights and on the individual, Blatch based hers on women's economic contribution and their significance as a group.

The contradictions in Blatch's approach to women and work also emerged in her attempts to link work and the vote. On the one hand, she approached women's political rights as she did their economic emancipation, democratically: Just as all sorts of women must work, all needed the vote. Wealthy women needed the vote because they were taxpayers and had the right to see that their money was not squandered; women industrial workers needed it because their jobs and factories were subject to laws, which they had the right to shape. On the other hand, she recognized the strategic centrality of the enormous class of industrial workers, whose economic role was so important and whose political power was potentially so great. "It is the women of the industrial class," she explained, "the wage-earners, reckoned by the hundreds of thousands, . . . the women whose work has been submitted to a money test, who have been the means of bringing about the altered attitude of public opinion toward woman's work in every sphere of life."[27]

Blatch returned to New York for several extended visits after 1894, and she moved back for good in 1902. She had two purposes. Elizabeth Stanton was dying, and Blatch had come to be with her. Blatch also intended to take a leading role in the New York City suffrage movement. On her deathbed in 1902, Stanton asked Anthony to aid Blatch. However, hampered by Anthony's determination to keep control of the movement, Blatch was not able to make her bid for suffrage leadership until Anthony died, four years later.[28]

Meanwhile, Blatch was excited by other reform efforts, which were beginning to provide the resources for a new kind of suffrage movement. During the first years of the twentieth century two movements contributed to Blatch's political education—a broadened, less socially exclusive campaign against political corruption and a democratized movement for the welfare of working women. By 1907, her combined experience in these two movements enabled her to put her ideas about women and work into practice within the suffrage movement itself.

Women had become more active in the campaign against political corruption after 1894. In New York City, Josephine Shaw Lowell and Mary

Putnam Jacobi formed the Woman's Municipal League, which concentrated on educating the public about corruption, in particular the links between the police and organized prostitution. Women were conspicuous in the reform campaigns of Seth Low, who was elected mayor in 1901.[29]

By the early 1900s, moreover, the spirit of political reform in New York City had spread beyond the elite. A left wing of the political reform movement had developed that charged that "Wall Street" was more responsible for political corruption than "the Bowery." Women were active in this wing, and there were women's political organizations with links to the Democratic party and the labor movement, a Women's Henry George Society, and a female wing of William Randolph Hearst's Independence League. The non-elite women in these groups were as politically enthusiastic as the members of the Woman's Municipal League, and considerably less ambivalent about enlarging the electorate. Many of them strongly supported woman suffrage. Beginning in 1905, a group of them organized an Equal Rights League to sponsor mock polling places for women to register their political opinions on election day.[30]

Through the 1900s Blatch dutifully attended suffrage meetings, and without much excitement advocated the municipal suffrage for propertied women favored by the New York movement's leaders after their 1894 defeat. Like many other politically minded women, however, she found her enthusiasm caught by the movement for municipal political reform. She supported Low for mayor in 1901 and believed that his victory demonstrated "how strong woman's power really was when it was aroused." By 1903 she suggested to the National American Woman Suffrage Association (NAWSA) that it set aside agitation for the vote, so that "the women of the organization should use it for one year, nationally and locally, to pursue and punish corruption in politics." She supported the increasing attention given to "the laboring man" in reform political coalitions, but she pointedly observed that "the working woman was never considered."[31]

However, working-class women were emerging as active factors in other women's reform organizations. The crucial arena for this development was the Women's Trade Union League (WTUL), formed in 1903 by a coalition of working-class and elite women to draw wage-earning women into trade unions. The New York chapter was formed in 1905, and Blatch was one of the first elite women to join. The WTUL represented a significant move away from the tradition of elite, ameliorative sisterhood at work in the 1894 campaign for woman suffrage. Like the Consumers' League, it had been formed in response to the request of women wage earners for aid from elite women, but it was an organization of both classes working together. Blatch had never been attracted to the strictly ameliorative tradition of women's reform, and the shift toward a partnership of upper-class and working-class women paralleled her own thinking about the relation between the classes and the role of work in women's lives. She and other elite women in the WTUL found themselves laboring not for working-class women, but with them, and toward a goal of forming unions that did not merely "uplift" working-class women, but empowered them. Instead of being working-class women's protectors, they were their "allies." Instead of speaking on behalf of poor women, they began to hear them speak for themselves. Within the organization wage earners were frequently in conflict with allies. Nonetheless, the league provided them an arena to articulate a working-class feminism related to, but distinct from, that of elite women.[32]

Although prominent as a suffragist, Blatch participated in the WTUL on its own terms, rather than as a colonizer for suffrage. She and two other members assigned to the millinery trade conducted investigations into conditions and organized mass meetings to interest women workers in unions. She sat on the Executive Council from 1906 through 1909 and was often called on to stand in for President Mary Dreier. Her academic knowledge of "the industrial woman" was replaced by direct knowledge of wage-earning women and their working conditions. She was impressed with what she saw of trade unionism, especially its unrelenting "militance." Perhaps most important, she developed working relations with politically sophisticated working-class women, notably Leonora O'Reilly and Rose Schneiderman. Increasingly she believed that the organized power of labor and the enfranchisement of women were closely allied.[33]

Working-class feminists in the league were drawn to ideas like Blatch's—to conceptions of dignity and equality for women in the workplace and to the ethic of self-support and lifelong independence; they wanted to upgrade the condition of wage-earning women so that they, too, could enjoy personal independence on the basis of their labor. On the one hand, they understood why most working-class women would want to leave their hateful jobs upon marriage; on the other, they knew that women as a group, if not the individual worker, were a permanent factor in the modern labor force. Mary Kenney O'Sullivan of Boston, one of the league's founders, believed that "self support" was a goal for working-class women, but that only trade unions would give the masses of working women the "courage, independence, and self respect" they needed to improve their conditions. She expected "women of opportunity" to help in organizing women workers, because they "owed much to workers who give them a large part of what they have and enjoy," and because "the time has passed when women of opportunity can be self respecting and work *for* others."[34]

Initially, the demand for the vote was less important to such working-class feminists than to the allies. Still, as they began to participate in the organized women's movement on a more equal basis, wage-earning women began to receive serious attention within the woman suffrage movement as well. Beginning about 1905, advocates of trade unionism and the vote for women linked the demands. At the 1906 suffrage convention WTUL member Gertrude Barnum pointed out that "our hope as suffragists lies with these strong working women." Kelley and Addams wrote about the working woman's need for the vote to improve her own conditions. In New York, Blatch called on the established suffrage societies to recognize the importance of the vote to wage-earning women and the importance of wage-earning women to winning the vote. When she realized that existing groups could not adapt to the new challenges, she moved to form her own society.[35]

In January 1907, Blatch declared the formation of a new suffrage organization, the Equality League of Self-Supporting Women. The *New York Times* reported that the two hundred women present at the first meeting included "doctors, lawyers, milliners and shirtmakers."[36] Blatch's decision to establish a suffrage organization that emphasized female "self-support"—lifelong economic independence—grew out of her ideas about work as the basis of women's claim on the state, the leadership role she envisioned for educated professionals, and her discovery of the power and political capacity of trade-union women. The Equality League provided the medium for introducing a new and aggressive style of activism into the suffrage movement—a version of the "militance" Blatch admired among trade unionists.

Initially, Blatch envisioned the Equality League of Self-Supporting Women as the political wing of the Women's Trade Union League. All the industrial workers she recruited were WTUL activists, including O'Reilly, the Equality League's first vice-president, and Schneiderman, its most popular speaker. To welcome working-class women, the Equality League virtually abolished membership fees; the policy had the added advantage of allowing Blatch to claim every woman who ever attended a league meeting in her estimate of its membership. She also claimed the members of the several trade unions affiliated with the Equality League, such as the bookbinders, overall makers, and cap makers, so that when she went before the New York legislature to demand the vote, she could say that the Equality League represented thousands of wage-earning women.[37]

Blatch wanted the Equality League to connect industrial workers, not with "club women" (her phrase), but with educated, professional workers, who should, she thought, replace benevolent ladies as the leaders of their sex. Such professionals—college educated and often women pioneers in their professions—formed the bulk of the Equality League's active membership. Many were lawyers, for instance Ida Rauh, Helen Hoy, Madeleine Doty, Jessie Ashley, Adelma Burd, and Bertha Rembaugh. Others were social welfare workers, for instance the Equality League's treasurer, Kate Claghorn, a tenement housing inspector and the highest paid female employee of the New York City government. Blatch's own daughter, Nora, the first woman graduate civil engineer in the United States, worked in the New York City Department of Public Works. Many of these women had inherited incomes and did not work out of economic need, but out of a desire to give serious, public substance to their lives and to make an impact on society. Many of them expressed the determination to maintain economic independence after they married.[38]

Although Blatch brought together trade-union women and college-educated professionals in the Equality League, there were tensions between the classes. The first correspondence between O'Reilly and Barnard graduate Caroline Lexow was full of class suspicion and mutual recrimination. More generally, there were real differences in how and why the two classes of working women demanded the vote. Trade-union feminists wanted the vote so that women industrial workers would have power over the labor laws that directly affected their working lives. Many of the college-educated self-supporters were the designers and administrators of this labor legislation. Several of them were, or aspired to be, government employees, and political power affected their jobs through party patronage. The occupation that might have bridged the differences was teaching. As in other cities, women teachers in New York organized for greater power and equal pay. The Equality League frequently offered aid, but the New York teachers' leaders were relatively conservative and kept their distance from the suffrage movement.[39]

Blatch's special contribution was her understanding of the bonds and common interests uniting industrial and professional women workers. The industrial women admired the professional ethic, if not the striving careerism, of the educated working women, and the professionals admired the matter-of-fact way wage-earning women went out to work. The fate of the professional woman was closely tied to that of the industrial worker; the cultural regard in which all working women were held affected both. Blatch dramatized that tie when she was refused service at a restaurant because she was unescorted by a man (that is, because she was eating with a woman). The management claimed that its policy aimed to protect "respectable" women, like Blatch, from "objectionable" women, like the common woman worker who went about on her own, whose morals were therefore questionable. Blatch rejected the division between respectable women and working women, pointing out that "there are five million women earning their livelihood in this country, and it seems strange that feudal customs should still exist here."[40]

The dilemma of economically dependent married women was crucial to the future of both classes of working women. Blatch believed that if work was to free women, they could not leave it for dependence on men in marriage. The professional and working-class members of the Equality League shared this belief, one of the distinguishing convictions of their new approach to suffragism. In 1908 Blatch and Mary Dreier chaired a debate about the housewife, sponsored by the WTUL and attended by many Equality League members. Charlotte Perkins Gilman took the Equality League position, that the unemployed wife was a "parasite" on her husband, and that all women, married as well as unmarried, should work, "like every other self-respecting being." Anna Howard Shaw argued that women's domestic labor was valuable, even if unpaid, and that the husband was dependent on his wife. A large audience attended, and although they "warmly applauded" Gilman, they preferred Shaw's sentimental construction of the economics of marriage.[41]

A month after the Equality League was formed, Blatch arranged for trade-union women to testify before the New York legislature on behalf of woman suffrage, the first working-class women ever to do so. The New York Woman Suffrage Association was still concentrating on the limited, property-based form of municipal suffrage; in lethargic testimony its leaders admitted that they had "no new arguments to present." Everyone at the hearing agreed that the antis had the better of the argument. The Equality League testimony the next day was in sharp contrast. Clara Silver and Mary Duffy, WTUL activists and organizers in the garment industry, supported full suffrage for all New York women. The very presence of these women before the legislature, and their dignity and intelligence, countered the antis' dire predictions about enfranchising the unfit. Both linked suffrage to their trade-union efforts: While they struggled for equality in unions and in industry, "the state" undermined them, by teaching the lesson of female inferiority to male unionists and bosses. "To be left out by the State just sets up a prejudice against us," Silver explained. "Bosses think and women come to think themselves that they don't count for so much as men."[42]

The formation of the Equality League and its appearance before the New York legislature awakened enthusiasm. Lillie Devereux Blake, whose own suffrage group had tried "one whole Winter . . . to [interest] the working women" but found that they were "so overworked and so poor that they can do little for us," congratulated Blatch on her apparent success. Helen Marot, organizing secretary for the New York WTUL, praised the Equality League for "realizing the increasing necessity of including working women in the suffrage movement." Blatch, O'Reilly, and Schneiderman were the star speakers at the 1907 New York suffrage convention. "We realize that probably it will not be the educated workers, the college women, the men's association for equal suffrage, but the people who are fighting for industrial freedom who will be our vital force at the finish," proclaimed the newsletter of the NAWSA.[43]

The unique class character of the Equality League encouraged the development of a new style of agitation, more radical than anything practiced in the suffrage movement since Elizabeth Stanton's prime. The immediate source of the change was the Women's Social and Political Union of England (WSPU), led by Blatch's comrade from her Fabian days, Emmeline Pankhurst. Members of the WSPU were just beginning to be arrested for their suffrage protests. At the end of the Equality League's first year, Blatch invited one of the first WSPU prisoners, Anne Cobden-Sanderson, daughter of Richard Cobden, to the United States to tell about her experiences, scoring a coup for the Equality League. By emphasizing Cobden-Sanderson's connection with the British Labour Party and distributing free platform tickets to tradeunion leaders, Blatch was able to get an overflow crowd at Cooper Union, Manhattan's labor temple, two-thirds of them men, many of them trade unionists.[44]

The Equality League's meeting for Cobden-Sanderson offered American audiences their first account of the new radicalism of English suffragists, or as they were beginning to be called, suffragettes. Cobden-Sanderson emphasized the suffragettes' working-class origins. She attributed the revival of the British suffrage movement to Lancashire factory workers; the heroic figure in her account was the working-class suffragette Annie Kenney, while Christabel Pankhurst, later canonized as the Joan of Arc of British militance, went unnamed. After women factory workers were arrested for trying to see the prime minister, Cobden-Sanderson and other privileged women, who felt they "had not so much to lose as [the workers] had," decided to join them and get arrested. She spent almost two months in jail, living the life of a common prisoner and coming to a new awareness of the poor and suffering women she saw there. Her simple but moving account conveyed the transcendent impact of the experience.[45]

Cobden-Sanderson's visit to New York catalyzed a great outburst of suffrage energy; in its wake, Blatch and a handful of other new leaders introduced the WSPU tactics into the American movement, and the word "suffragette" became as common in New York as in London. The "militants" became an increasingly distinct wing of the movement in New York and other American cities. But it would be too simple to say that the British example caused the new, more militant phase in the American movement. The developments that were broadening the class basis and the outlook of American suffragism had prepared American women to respond to the heroism of the British militants.[46]

The development of militance in the American suffrage movement was marked by new aggressive tactics practiced by the WSPU, especially open-air meetings and outdoor parades. At this stage in the development of British militance, American suffragists generally admired the heroism of the WSPU martyrs. Therefore, although the press emphasized dissent within the suffrage movement—it always organized its coverage of suffrage around female rivalries of some sort—the new militant activities were well received throughout the movement. And, conversely, even the most daring American suffragettes believed in an American exceptionalism that made it unnecessary to contemplate going to prison, to suffer as did the British militants.[47]

Despite Blatch's later claims, she did not actually introduce the new tactics in New York City. The first open-air meetings were organized immediately after the Cobden-Sanderson visit by a group called the American Suffragettes. Initiated by Bettina Borrman Wells, a visiting member of the WSPU, most of the American Suffragettes' membership came from the Equal Rights League, the left-wing municipal reform group that had organized mock polling places in New York since 1905. Feminist egalitarians with radical cultural leanings, its members were actresses, artists, writers, teachers, and social welfare workers—less wealthy versions of the professional self-supporters in the Equality League. Their local leader was a librarian, Maud Malone, whose role in encouraging new suffrage tactics was almost as important as, although less recognized than, Blatch's own.[48]

The American Suffragettes held their first open-air meeting in Madison Square on New Year's Eve, 1907. After that they met in the open at least once a week. Six weeks later, they announced they would hold New York's first all-woman parade. Denied a police permit, they determined to march anyway. The twenty-three women in the "parade" were many times outnumbered by the onlookers, mostly working-class men. In a public school to which they adjourned to make speeches, the American Suffragettes told a sympathetic audience that "the woman who works is the underdog of the world"; thus she needed the vote to defend herself. Socialists and working women rose from the floor to support them. Two years later the Equality League organized a much more successful suffrage parade in New York. Several hundred suffragettes, organized by occupation, marched from Fifty-ninth Street to Union Square. O'Reilly, the featured speaker, made "a tearful plea on behalf of the working girl that drew the first big demonstration of applause from the street crowd."[49]

Perhaps because the American Suffragettes were so active in New York City, Blatch held the Equality League's first open-air meetings in May 1908 upstate. Accompanied by Maud Malone, she organized an inventive "trolley car campaign" between Syracuse and Albany, using the interurban trolleys to go from town to town. The audiences expressed the complex class character of the suffrage movement at that moment. In Syracuse Blatch had her wealthy friend Dora Hazard arrange a meeting among the workers at her husband's factory. She also held a successful outdoor meeting in Troy, home of the Laundry Workers' Union, one of the oldest and most militant independent women's trade unions in the country. Albany was an antisuffrage stronghold, and its mayor tried to prevent the meeting, but Blatch outwitted him. The highlight of the tour was in Poughkeepsie, where Blatch and Inez Milholland, then a student at Vassar College, organized a legendary meeting. Since Vassar's male president forbade any woman suffrage activities on college grounds, Blatch and Milholland defiantly announced they would meet students in a cemetery. Gilman, who was extremely popular among college women, spoke, but it was the passionate trade-union feminist Schneiderman who was the star.[50]

Blatch believed that the first function of militant tactics was to gain much-needed publicity for the movement. The mainstream press had long ignored suffrage activities. If an occasional meeting was reported, it was usually buried in a small back-page article, focusing on the absurdity and incompetence of women's efforts to organize a political campaign. Gilded Age suffragists themselves accepted the Victorian convention that respectable women did not court public attention. The Equality League's emphasis on the importance of paid labor for women of all classes struck at the heart of that convention. Blatch understood "the value of publicity or rather the harm of the lack of it." She encouraged open-air meetings and trolley car campaigns because they generated much publicity, which no longer held the conventional horror for her followers.[51]

Militant tactics broke through the "press boycott" by violating standards of respectable femininity, making the cause newsworthy, and embracing the subsequent ridicule and attention. "We . . . believe in standing on street corners and fighting our way to recognition, forcing the men to think about us," an American Suffragette manifesto proclaimed. "We glory . . . that we are theatrical." The militant pursuit of publicity was an instant success: Newspaper coverage increased immediately; by 1908 even the sneering *New York Times* reported regularly on suffrage. The more

outrageous or controversial the event, the more prominent the coverage. Blatch was often pictured and quoted.[52]

The new methods had a second function: they intensified women's commitment to the movement. Militants expected that overstepping the boundary of respectability would etch suffrage beliefs on women's souls, beyond retraction or modification. Blatch caught the psychology of this process. "Society has taught women self sacrifice and now this force is to be drawn upon in the arduous campaign for their own emancipation," she wrote. "The new methods of agitation, in that they are difficult and disagreeable, lay hold of the imagination and devotion of women, wherein lies the strength of the new appeal, the certainty of victory." Borrman Wells spoke of the "divine spirit of self-sacrifice," which underlay the suffragette's transgressions against respectability and was the source of the "true inwardness of the movement."[53]

If suffrage militants had a general goal beyond getting the vote, it was to challenge existing standards of femininity. "We must eliminate that abominable word ladylike from our vocabularies," Borrman Wells proclaimed. "We must get out and fight." The new definition of femininity the militants were evolving drew, on the one hand, on traditionally male behaviors, like aggression, fighting, provocation, and rebelliousness. Blatch was particularly drawn to the "virile" world of politics, which she characterized as a male "sport" she was sure she could master. On the other hand, they undertook a spirited defense of female sexuality, denying that it need be forfeited by women who participated vigorously in public life. "Women are no longer to be considered little tootsey wootseys who have nothing to do but look pretty," suffragette Lydia Commander declared. "They are determined to take an active part in the community and look pretty too." A member of a slightly older generation, Blatch never adopted the modern sexual ethic of the new woman, but she constantly emphasized the fact that women had distinct concerns that had to be accommodated in politics and industry. These two notes—the difference of the sexes and the repressed ability of women for manly activities—existed side by side in the thought of all the suffrage insurgents.[54]

The militant methods, taking suffrage out of the parlors and into the streets, indicated the new significance of working-class women in several ways. Blatch pointed out that the new methods—open-air meetings, newspaper publicity—suited a movement whose members had little money and therefore could not afford to rent halls or publish a newspaper. As a style of protest, "militance" was an import from the labor movement; WTUL organizers had been speaking from street corners for several years. And disrespect for the standards of ladylike respectability showed at least an impatience with rigid standards of class distinction, at most the influence of class-conscious wage-earning women.[55]

Working-class feminists were eager to speak from the militants' platform, as were many Socialists. A Socialist cadre, Dr. Anna Mercy, organized a branch of the American Suffragettes on the Lower East Side, which issued the first suffrage leaflets ever published in Yiddish. Militants also prepared propaganda in German and Italian and, in general, pursued working-class audiences. "Our relation to the State will be determined by the vote of the average man," Blatch asserted. "None but the converted . . . will come to us. We must seek on the highways the unconverted."[56]

However, it would be a mistake to confuse the suffragettes' radicalism with the radicalism of a working-class movement. The ultimate goal of the suffragettes was not a single-class movement, but a universal one, "the union of women of all shades of political thought and of all ranks of society on the single issue of their political enfranchisement." While the Equality League's 1907 hearing before the state legislature highlighted trade-union suffragists, at the 1908 hearing the league also featured elite speakers, in effect deemphasizing the working-class perspective.[57] Militants could neither repudiate the Socialist support they were attracting, and alienate working-class women, nor associate too closely with Socialists, and lose access to the wealthy. Blatch—who actually became a Socialist after the suffrage was won—would not arrange for the Socialist party leader Morris Hillquit to join other prosuffrage speakers at the 1908 legislative hearing. Similarly, the American Suffragettes allowed individual Socialists on their platform but barred Socialist propaganda. Speaking for Socialist women who found the "idea of a 'radical' suffrage movement . . . very alluring," Josephine Conger Kaneko admitted that the suffragettes left her confused.[58]

Moreover, the militant challenge to femininity and the emphasis on publicity introduced a distinctly elite bias; a society matron on an open-air platform made page one while a working girl did not, because society women were obliged by conventions and could outrage by flouting them. In their very desire to redefine femininity, the militants were anxious to stake their claim to it, and it was upper-class women who determined femininity. In Elizabeth Robin's drama about the rise of militance in the British suffrage movement, *The Convert,* the heroine of the title was a beautiful aristocratic woman who became radical when she realized the emptiness of her ladylike existence and the contempt for women obscured by gentlemen's chivalrous gestures. The Equality League brought *The Convert* to New York in 1908 as its first large fund-raising effort; working-class women, as well as elite women, made up the audience. Malone was one of the few militants to recognize and to protest against excessive solicitousness for the elite convert. She resigned from the American Suffragettes when she concluded that they had become interested in attracting "a well-dressed crowd, not the rabble."[59]

Blatch's perspective and associations had always been fundamentally elite. The most well connected of the new militant leaders, she played a major role in bringing the new suffrage propaganda to the attention of upper-class women. She presided over street meetings in fashionable neighborhoods, where reporters commented on the "smart" crowds and described the speakers' outfits in society-page detail. Blatch's first important ally from the Four Hundred was Katherine Duer Mackay, wife of the founder of the International Telephone and Telegraph Company and a famous society beauty. Mackay's suffragism was very ladylike, but other members of her set who followed her into the movement were more drawn to militance: Alva Belmont, a veritable mistress of flamboyance, began her suffrage career as Mackay's protégé. The elitist subtext of militance was a minor theme in 1908 and 1909. But by 1910 becoming a suffragette was proving "fashionable," and upper-class women began to identify with the new suffrage style in significant numbers. By the time suffragette militance became a national movement, its working-class origins and trade-union associations had been submerged, and it was in the hands of women of wealth.[60]

From the beginning, though, class was the contradiction at the suffrage movement's heart. In the campaign of 1894, elite women began to pursue more power for themselves by advocating the suffrage in the name of all women. When Cobden-Sanderson spoke for the Equality League at Cooper Union in 1907, she criticized "idle women of wealth" as the enemies of woman suffrage, and she was wildly applauded. But what did her charge mean? Were all rich women under indictment, or only those who stayed aloof from social responsibility and political activism? Were the militants calling for working-class leadership of the suffrage movement or for cultural changes in bourgeois definitions of womanhood? This ambiguity paralleled the mixed meanings in Blatch's emphasis on working women; it coincided with an implicit tension between the older, elite women's reform traditions and the newer, trade-union politics they had helped to usher in; and it was related to a lurking confusion about whether feminism's object was the superfluity of wealthy women or the exploitation of the poor. It would continue to plague suffragism in its final decade, and feminism afterward, into our own time.

Notes

1. A good overview of political history in the Progressive Era can be found in Arthur S. Link and Richard L. Mc-Cormick, *Progressivism* (Arlington Heights, Ill., 1983), 26-66. The "separate spheres" framework of Progressive-Era historiography has been identified and challenged by Paula Baker, "The Domestication of Politics: Women and American Political Society, 1780-1920," *American Historical Review,* 89 (June 1984), esp. 639-47; and by Kathryn Kish Sklar, "Hull House in the 1890s: A Community of Women Reformers," *Signs,* 10 (Summer 1985), 658-77; Kathryn Kish Sklar, "Florence Kelley and the Integration of 'Women's Sphere' into American Politics, 1890-1921," paper delivered at the annual meeting of the Organization of American Historians, New York, April 1986 (in Sklar's possession).

2. Steven M. Buechler, *The Transformation of the Woman Suffrage Movement: The Case of Illinois, 1850-1920* (New Brunswick, 1986); Mari Jo Buhle and Paul Buhle, eds., *The Concise History of Woman Suffrage: Selections from the Classic Work of Stanton, Anthony, Gage and Harper* (Urbana, 1978); Carole Nichols, *Votes and More for Women: Suffrage and After in Connecticut* (New York, 1983); Anne F. Scott and Andrew Scott, eds., *One Half the People* (Philadelphia, 1975); and Sharon Strom, "Leadership and Tactics in the American Woman Suffrage Movement: A New Perspective from Massachusetts," *Journal of American History,* 52 (Sept. 1975), 296-315.

3. "Mrs. Blatch's Address," clipping, 1903, Women's Club of Orange, N.J., Scrapbooks, IV (New Jersey Historical Society, Trenton). Thanks to Gail Malmgreen for this citation.

4. Richard L. McCormick, *From Realignment to Reform: Political Change in New York State, 1893-1910* (Ithaca, 1979), 53. An excellent account of the political reform movement in the 1890s in New York City can be found in David C. Hammack, *Power and Society: Greater New York at the Turn of the Century* (New York, 1982).

5. Susan B. Anthony and Ida Husted Harper, eds., *The History of Woman Suffrage,* vol. IV: *1883-1900* (Rochester, 1902), 847-52; New York State Woman Suffrage Party, *Record of the New York Campaign of 1894* (New York, 1895); Ida Husted Harper, ed., *The Life and Work of Susan B.* Anthony (3 vols., Indianapolis, 1898-1908), II, 758-76, esp. 759.

6. Mary Putnam Jacobi, "Report of the 'Volunteer Committee' in New York City," in *Record of the New York Campaign,* 217-20; Maud Nathan, *The Story of an Epoch-making Movement* (Garden City, 1926); William Rhinelander Stewart, ed., *The Philanthropic Work of Josephine Shaw Lowell* (New York, 1926), 334-56.

7. *New York Times,* April 14, 1894, 2; ibid., April 15, 1894, 5. Mrs. Robert (Catherine) Abbe's suffrage scrapbooks provide extensive documentation of the New York suffrage movement, beginning with this campaign. Mrs. Robert Abbe Collection (Manuscript Division, New York Public Library). Theodore Stanton and Harriot Stanton Blatch, eds., *Elizabeth Cady Stanton as Revealed in Her Letters, Diary, and Reminiscences* (2 vols., New York, 1922), II, 299.

8. Mary Putnam Jacobi, "Address Delivered at the New York City Hearing," in *Record of the New York Campaign,* 17-26; Olivia Slocum Sage, "Opportunities and Responsibilities of Leisured Women," *North American Review,* 181 (Nov. 1905), 712-21.

9. Ibid.

10. Ibid

11. Jacobi, "Report of the 'Volunteer Committee,'" 217; Stanton and Blatch, eds., *Elizabeth Cady Stanton,* II, 305; *New York Times,* May 3, 1894, 9. Abby Hamlin Abbott and Josephine Jewell Dodge were both Brooklyn residents; the division between suffragists and antis reflected a conflict between the elites of Manhattan and Brooklyn over the 1894 referendum to consolidate the two cities into Greater New York. See Hammack, *Power and Society,* 209.

12. Jacobi, "Address Delivered at the New York City Hearing," 22; *New York Times,* April 12, 1894, 5. "The woman in charge of the [anti] protest . . . told a reporter . . . that her own dressmaker has secured about forty signatories to the protest among working women." Ibid., May 8, 1894, 1.

13. *Woman's Journal,* May 12, 1894, 147.

14. Ibid., May 19, 1894. The study, patterned after Charles Booth and Mary Booth's investigation of the London poor, on which Blatch worked, was published as Harriot Stanton Blatch, "Another View of Village Life," *Westminster Review,* 140 (Sept. 1893), 318-24.

15. Stanton and Blatch, eds., *Elizabeth Cady Stanton,* II, 304; unidentified clipping, April 25, 1894, Scrapbook XX, Susan B. Anthony Collection (Manuscript Division, Library of Congress); *New York Times,* April 25, 1894, 5; ibid., May 3, 1894, 9; *New York Sun,* April 15, 1894, n.p.

16. *Woman's Journal,* Nov. 3, 1894, 348-49; ibid., Dec. 22, 1894, 402; ibid., Jan. 5, 1895, 1. Blatch wrote that her mother's position "pained" her but there is no evidence of any personal conflict between them at this time. Ibid., Dec. 22, 1894, 402.

17. Harriot Stanton Blatch and Alma Lutz, *Challenging Years: The Memoirs of Harriot Stanton Blatch* (New York 1940), 77. *Woman's Journal,* Jan. 18, 1896, 18.

18. *Woman's Journal,* May 12, 1900, 146-47. Along with Blatch and Charlotte Perkins Gilman, Florence Kelley and Jane Addams were the most important figures to focus on women and class. See Charlotte Perkins Gilman, *Women and Economics: A Study of the Economic Relation between Men and Women as a Factor in Social*

Evolution (Boston, 1898); Florence Kelley, *Woman Suffrage: Its Relation to Working Women and Children* (Warren, Ohio, 1906); Florence Kelley, "Women and Social Legislation in the United States," *Annals of the American Academy of Political and Social Science,* 56 (Nov. 1914), 62-71; Jane Addams, *Newer Ideals of Peace* (New York, 1907); and Jane Addams, *Twenty Years at Hull House* (New York, 1910). Some of the other women reformers who wrote on women and work early in the century were Rheta Childe Dorr, *What Eight Million Women Want* (Boston, 1910); Lillian Wald, "Organization among Working Women," *Annals of the American Academy of Political and Social Science,* 27 (May 1906), 638-45; and Anna Garlin Spencer, *Woman's Share in Social Culture* (New York, 1913).

19. Harriot Stanton Blatch, "Specialization of Function in Women," *Gunton's Magazine,* 10 (May 1896), 349-56, esp. 350.

20. Ibid.

21. Ibid., 354-55; see also Blatch's comments at a 1904 suffrage meeting in New York, *Woman's Journal,* Dec. 31, 1904, 423.

22. Blatch, "Specialization of Function in Women," 350, 353.

23. See, for example, the response of the New York City Woman Suffrage League to a proposal before the American Federation of Labor to ban women from all nondomestic employment. *New York Times,* Dec. 23, 1898, 7.

24. Harriot Stanton Blatch, "Weaving in a Westchester Farmhouse," *International Studio,* 26 (Oct. 1905), 102-5; *Woman's Journal,* Jan. 21, 1905; ibid., Dec. 31, 1904, 423.

25. Blatch, "Weaving in a Westchester Farmhouse," 104; Blatch and Lutz, *Challenging Years,* 70-86; Rhoda Barney Jenkins interview by Ellen Carol DuBois, June 10, 1982 (in Ellen Carol DuBois's possession); Ellen DuBois, "'Spanning Two Centuries': The Autobiography of Nora Stanton Barney," *History Workshop,* no. 22 (Fall 1986), 131-52. esp. 149.

26. Anthony and Harper, eds., *History of Woman Suffrage,* IV, 311.

27. "Mrs. Blatch's Address," Women's Club of Orange, N.J., Scrapbooks; Anthony and Harper, eds., *History of Woman Suffrage,* IV, 311.

28. Harriot Stanton Blatch to Susan B. Anthony, Sept. 26, 1902, in *Epistolary Autobiography,* Theodore Stanton Collection (Douglass College Library, Rutgers University, New Brunswick, N.J.).

29. Oswald Garrison Villard, "Women in New York Municipal Campaign," *Woman's Journal,* March 8, 1902, 78-79.

30. *New York Times,* Jan. 14, 1901, 7. The Gertrude Colles Collection (New York State Library, Albany) is particularly rich in evidence of the less elite, more radical side of female political reform in these years. On the mock voting organized by the Equal Rights League, see *Woman's Journal,* Dec. 28, 1905, and *New York Times,* Nov. 7, 1906, 9.

31. Anthony and Harper, eds., *History of Woman Suffrage,* IV, 861; Ida Husted Harper, ed., *History of Woman Suffrage,* vol. VI: *1900-1920* (New York, 1922), 454; *New York Times,* March 2, 1902, 8; *Woman's Tribune,* April 25, 1903, 49. After Blatch had become an acknowledged leader of the New York suffrage movement, the coworker who, she felt, most shared her political perspective was Caroline Lexow, daughter of the man who had conducted the original investigation of police corruption in New York in 1894. See Blatch and Lutz, *Challenging Years,* 120-21; and Isabelle K. Savelle, *Ladies' Lib: How Rockland Women Got the Vote* (Nyack, N.Y., 1979).

32. Minutes, March 29, 1906, reel 1, New York Women's Trade Union League Papers (New York State Labor Library, New York). On the WTUL, see Nancy Schrom Dye, *As Equals and as Sisters: Feminism, the Labor Movement, and the Women's Trade Union League of New York* (Columbia, 1980); and Meredith Tax, *The Rising of the Women: Feminist Solidarity and Class Conflict, 1880-1917* (New York, 1980), 95-124.

33. Dye, *As Equals and as Sisters,* 63; Minutes, April 26, Aug. 23, 1906, New York Women's Trade Union League Papers; *New York Times,* April 11, 1907, 8.

34. Mary Kenney O'Sullivan, "The Need of Organization among Working Women (1905)," Margaret Dreier Robins Papers (University of Florida Library, Gainesville); Sarah Eisenstein, *Give Us Bread but Give Us Roses: Working Women's Consciousness in the United States, 1890 to the First World War* (London, 1983), 146-50.

35. *Woman's Journal,* March 17, 1906, 43; Kelley, *Woman Suffrage;* Jane Addams, "Utilization of Women in Government," in *Jane Addams: A Centennial Reader* (New York, 1960), 116-18; *Woman's Journal,* Dec. 31, 1904, 423; "Mrs. Blatch's Address," Women's Club of Orange, N.J., Scrapbooks. There was a lengthy discussion of working women's need for the vote, including a speech by Rose Schneiderman, at the 1907 New York State Woman Suffrage Association convention. See Minute Book, 1907-10, New York State Woman Suffrage Association (Butler Library, Columbia University, New York). The WTUL identified woman suffrage as one of its goals by 1907. Dye, *As Equals and as Sisters,* 123.

36. *New York Times,* Jan. 3, 1907, 6; *Woman's Journal,* Jan. 12, 1907, 8.

37. *Progress,* June 1907. Carrie Chapman Catt to Millicent Garrett Fawcett, Oct. 19, 1909, container 5, Papers of Carrie Chapman Catt (Manuscript Division, Library of Congress).

38. *Woman's Journal,* Aug. 17, 1907, 129. On Nora Blatch (who later called herself Nora Stanton Barney), see DuBois, "'Spanning Two Centuries,'" 131-52. Those self-supporters who, I believe, had independent incomes include Nora Blatch, Caroline Lexow, Lavinia Dock, Ida Rauh, Gertrude Barnum, Elizabeth Finnegan, and Alice Clark. See, for example, on Nora Blatch, ibid., and on Dock, see *Notable American Women: The Modern Period,* ed. Sicherman et al. (Cambridge, 1980), 195-98.

39. Caroline Lexow to Leonora O'Reilly, Jan. 3, 1908, reel 4, Leonora O'Reilly Papers (Schlesinger Library, Radcliffe College, Cambridge, Mass.); O'Reilly to Lexow, Jan. 5, 1908, ibid.; Robert Doherty, "Tempest on the Hudson: The Struggle for Equal Pay for Equal Work in the New York City Public Schools, 1907-1911," *Harvard Educational Quarterly,* 19 (Winter 1979), 413-39.

The role of teachers in the twentieth-century suffrage movement is a promising area for research. For information on teachers' organizations in the Buffalo, New York, suffrage movement, I am indebted to Eve S. Faber, Swarthmore College, "Suffrage in Buffalo, 1898-1913" (unpublished paper in DuBois's possession).

40. *New York Times,* June 6, 1907, 1.

41. On self-support for women after marriage, see *New York World,* July 26, 1908, 3; and Lydia Kingsmill Commander, "The Self Supporting Woman and the Family," *American Journal of Sociology,* 14 (March 1909), 752-57. On the debate, see *New York Times,* Jan. 7, 1909, 9.

42. *New York Times,* Feb. 6, 1907, 6. Harriot Stanton Blatch, ed., *Two Speeches by Industrial Women* (New York, 1907), 8. The Equality League's bill authorized a voters' referendum on an amendment to the New York constitution, to remove the word "male" from the state's suffrage provisions, thus enfranchising New York women. Since the U.S. Constitution vests power to determine the electorate with the states, the aim was to win full suffrage in federal, as well as state, elections for New York women. With minor alterations, the measure finally passed, but in 1915 New York voters refused to enfranchise the women of their state; a second referendum in 1917 was successful. See Blatch and Lutz, *Challenging Years,* 156-238.

43. *Woman's Tribune,* Feb. 9, 1907, 12; Minutes, April 27, 1909, New York Women's Trade Union League Papers; *Progress,* Nov. 1908.

44. Blatch and Lutz, *Challenging* Years, 100-101; *Progress,* Jan. 1908, p. 1.

45. *Woman's Journal,* Dec. 28, 1907, 205, 206-7.

46. By 1908, there was a racehorse named "suffragette." *New York Evening Telegram,* Sept. 16, 1908. Blatch noted that once she left England in the late 1890s, she and Emmeline Pankhurst did not communicate until 1907, after they had both taken their respective countries' suffrage movements in newly militant directions. Blatch to Christabel Pankhurst, in Christabel Pankhurst, *Unshackled: How We Won the Vote* (London, 1959), 30.

47. The first American arrests were not until 1917. For American suffragists' early response to the WSPU, see the *Woman's Journal,* May 30, 1908, 87. Even Carrie Chapman Catt praised the British militants at first. *Woman's Journal,* Dec. 12, 1908, 199. For an example of divisive coverage by the mainstream press, see "Suffragist or Suffragette," *New York Times,* Feb. 29, 1908, 6.

48. On Bettina Borrman Wells, see A. J. R., ed., *Suffrage Annual and Women's Who's Who* (London, 1913), 390. Thanks to David Doughan of the Fawcett Library for this reference. The best sources on the Equal Rights League are the Gertrude Colles Collection and *The American Suffragette,* which the group published from 1909 through 1911. See also Winifred Harper Cooley, "Suffragists and 'Suffragettes,'" *World To-Day,* 15 (Oct. 1908), 1066-71; and Elinor Lerner, "Jewish Involvement in the New York City Woman Suffrage Movement," *American Jewish History,* 70 (June 1981), 444-45. The American Suffragettes found a predecessor and benefactor in seventy-five-year-old Lady Cook, formerly Tennessee Claflin, in 1909 the wife of a titled Englishman. "Our Cook Day," *American Suffragette,* 1 (Nov. 1909), 1.

49. On the first open-air meeting, see *New York Times,* Jan. 1, 1908, 16. On the parade, see ibid., Feb. 17, 1908, 7; there is also an account in Dorr, *What Eighty Million Women Want,* 298-99; *New York Evening Journal,* May 21, 1910.

50. Equality League of Self-Supporting Women, *Report for Year 1908-1909* (New York, 1909), 2; Blatch and Lutz, *Challenging Years,* 107-9. On Vassar, see also *New York American,* June 10, 1908.

51. Harriot Stanton Blatch, "Radical Move in Two Years," clipping, Nov. 8, 1908, suffrage scrapbooks, Abbe Collection. Blatch "starred" in a prosuffrage movie, *What Eighty Million Women Want,* produced in 1912. Kay Sloan, "Sexual Warfare in the Silent Cinema: Comedies and Melodramas of Woman Suffragism," *American Quarterly,* 33 (Fall 1981), 412-36. She was also very interested in the propaganda possibilities of commercial radio, according to Lee de Forest, a pioneer of the industry, who was briefly married to her daughter. Lee de Forest, *Father of Radio: The Autobiography of Lee de Forest* (Chicago, 1950), 248-49.

52. Mary Tyng, "Self Denial Week," *American Suffragette,* 1 (Aug. 1909); *New York Herald,* Dec. 19, 1908.

53. Blatch, "Radical Move in Two Years"; Mrs. B. Borrman Wells, "The Militant Movement for Woman Suffrage," *Independent,* April 23, 1908, 901-3.

54. "Suffragettes Bar Word 'Ladylike,'" clipping, Jan. 13, 1909, suffrage scrapbooks, Abbe Collection; Blatch and Lutz, *Challenging Years,* 91-242; *New York Herald,* March 8, 1908. On militants' views of femininity and sexuality, see also "National Suffrage Convention," *American Suffragette,* 2 (March 1910), 3.

55. Blatch and Lutz, *Challenging Years,* 107; Dye, *As Equals and as Sisters,* 47.

56. *Woman's Journal,* May 30, 1908, 87; Blatch, "Radical Move in Two Years."

57. Borrman Wells, "Militant Movement for Woman Suffrage," 901; *Woman's Journal,* Feb. 29, 1908, 34.

58. *New York Times,* Feb. 11, 1908, 6; [Josephine C. Kaneko], "To Join, or Not to Join," *Socialist Woman,* 1 (May 1908), 6.

59. On *The Convert,* see Equality League, *Report for 1908-1909,* 4; Jane Marcus, "Introduction," in *The Convert* (London, 1980), v-xvi; *New York Call,* Dec. 9, 1908, 6; and Minutes, Dec. 22, 1908, New York Women's Trade Union League Papers. Maud Malone also charged the American Suffragettes with discrimination against Socialists and Bettina Borrman Wells with personal ambition. For her letter of resignation, see *New York Times,* March 27, 1908, 4.

60. *New York Times,* May 14, 1909, 5. On Mackay and her Equal Franchise Society, see *New York Times,* Feb. 21, 1909, part 5, 2. On Blatch's relation to Mackay, see Blatch and Lutz, *Challenging Years,* 118. "As for the suffrage movement, it is actually fashionable now," wrote militant Inez Haynes, who very much approved of the development. "All kinds of society people are taking it up." Inez Haynes to Maud Wood Park, Dec. 2, 1910, reel 11, National American Woman Suffrage Association Papers (Manuscript Division, Library of Congress). Gertrude Foster Brown, another wealthy woman recruited by Blatch, wrote her own history of the New York suffrage movement in which she virtu-

ally ignored the role of working-class women. Gertrude Foster Brown, "On Account of Sex," Gertrude Foster Brown Papers, Sophia Smith Collection (Smith College, Northampton, Mass.).

WOMEN AND THE LAW

MARY FRANCES BERRY (ESSAY DATE 1986)

SOURCE: Berry, Mary Frances. "Gaining Woman Suffrage: The Nineteenth Amendment." In *Why ERA Failed: Politics, Women's Rights, and the Amending Process of the Constitution,* pp. 30-44. Bloomington, Ind.: Indiana University Press, 1986.

In the following essay, Berry traces the progress of legislation regarding women's suffrage from the Seneca Falls Convention of 1848 to the ratification of the nineteenth amendment to the Untied States Constitution in 1930.

In the struggle to gain consensus for a woman suffrage amendment, supporters had on their side a powerful tradition of representative government, based on the consent of the governed, as old as the Declaration of Independence and the founding of the Nation. But they were also opposing another powerful tradition in conflict with it, concerning appropriate roles for women. That tradition exhibited variations in different regions of the country, but it was essentially the view that, because women were intellectually inferior, morally superior, in need of protection, and dependent on men, they had no place in the disorderly world of politics. The potency of this tradition made demonstrating the necessity for woman suffrage a difficult matter. Furthermore, divisions among suffrage supporters over tactics and strategy helped to delay progress. As in the case of the income tax and the Fourteenth Amendment a negative Supreme Court decision helped to engender support. But proponents needed seventy-two years, from the first introduction of the proposal at Seneca Falls in 1848, to gain the consensus required for successful ratification of the Nineteenth Amendment.

Some women had the right to vote in the colonies, until colonial legislatures repealed it. New Jersey, in 1776, permitted women who were over age twenty-one, who had at least fifty pounds worth of property and who were at least one-year residents to vote. But the provision was repealed in 1806. The national Constitution of 1789 permitted participation in federal elections only by those who were permitted to vote in elections for "the most numerous branch" of each state's legislature. Therefore, so long as state laws did not extend the suffrage to women, they could not vote in federal elections. Some women continued to seek political rights, and, determined to gain more practical and legal control over their own lives, organized a strong movement in the late antebellum period.[1]

Women in the women's rights movement insisted on control over their own wages and property, joint guardianship over children, and improved inheritance rights when they were widowed. But the right to vote, the most controversial demand in the Seneca Falls Declaration of 1848 (drawn up by Elizabeth Cady Stanton, Lucretia Mott, and others, as the first public protest against the treatment of women as inferior), gradually gained a central place in the struggle. Although mostly relevant to the propertied classes, women had more success (through a series of married women's property acts) in the enactment of legislation to achieve their economic than political demands in the nineteenth century. By the time of Reconstruction, with the enactment of the franchise for freedmen, women still could not vote. Critics of woman suffrage, including many women, continued to believe that the public participation of women in politics on an equal basis would change woman's role as wife and mother, as well as her intellectual status, and would lead to demands for sexual equality in the home. Such a change, they asserted, would operate to the detriment of family stability and the welfare of children.[2]

The leaders of the women's rights movement were abolitionists and women's groups worked assiduously, through the National Women's Loyal League (organized by Elizabeth Cady Stanton and Susan B. Anthony), for a constitutional amendment outlawing slavery. In its incipient stages, the movement was greatly influenced by strategies and ideas developed in the anti-slavery struggle. Women could work for abolition as an expression of Christian charity, and religious work had long been accepted as an appropriate extension of the home for their sex. But once slavery was abolished in the Thirteenth Amendment, they began to focus more particularly on suffrage. They believed that when blacks gained the right of political participation, women would be included.

Many blacks asked for economic rights, including land for the freedmen, as a fundamental basis for assuring freedom and equality; but the most important black leader, Frederick Douglass, and his adherents preferred to emphasize political rights, which could be used to gain and protect economic opportunity. Suffragists were divided when it became clear that women would not be enfranchised along with black men. Black women such as Frances Ellen Harper, and white women such as Julia Ward Howe and Lucy Stone, were willing to delay suffrage for women and support suffrage for black men if they could not achieve both. Sojourner Truth took the opposite view, joining Stanton and Anthony in opposing suffrage for black men only. Some Republican political leaders saw black suffrage as a less controversial and expensive response to the freedmen than acceding to their demands for economic benefits. Furthermore, some party leaders believed black suffrage would be the linchpin that would ensure Republican party political power. Because of the urgency of insuring the enactment of black male suffrage, the Republicans did not want to jeopardize their efforts by proposing the more controversial idea of woman suffrage. Much to the consternation of some women's rightists, they were left out of the Fourteenth and Fifteenth amendments.[3]

Consequently, instead of seeing black suffrage as a real, yet unenforced response to black demands for equality—the quest for land having been rejected—some suffragists saw the exclusion of women's rights solely as an abandonment of their interests. Angered at the lack of Republican support, these women turned to some of the worst elements in the Democratic party for support. Anthony and Stanton joined forces with George Train, a wealthy anti-black Democrat who financed a newspaper for them, to appeal for the franchise for white women in order to counter the effect of black male voting, which, they claimed, could lead to black supremacy. Stanton, arguing against the Fifteenth Amendment, stated that it was wrong to elevate an ignorant and politically irresponsible class of men over the heads of women of wealth and culture, whose fitness for citizenship was obvious. She asserted, in behalf of a woman suffrage amendment

> If you do not wish the lower orders of Chinese, African, German, and Irish, with their low ideas of womanhood to make laws for you and your daughters . . . to dictate not only the civil, but moral codes by which you shall be governed, awake to the danger of your present position and demand that women, too, shall be represented in the government.

These appeals to prejudice by white women leaders were unfortunate. They undermined the moral force of their demand for suffrage, based on the highest purpose of broad representation in a political democracy. Furthermore, the posture taken helped to identify the women's movement as an upper middle-class white women's movement, and as essentially racist, although some black women ardently supported women's suffrage.[4]

Facing the exclusion of women from the Fourteenth and Fifteenth amendments, the suffragists needed a well organized campaign to achieve their objective. This was particularly the case since many women had to be persuaded that the idea would not prove detrimental to families by challenging women's traditional place in the home. But instead of reconciling their differences, they formed two separate organizations. The National Woman Suffrage Association, for women only, was organized with Stanton as its president in 1869; and the leaders of the New England Association (who supported suffrage for black men as a temporary expedient) formed the American Woman Suffrage Association a few weeks later, with Republicans and abolitionists as major supporters, and Henry Ward Beecher as president. Both organizations were designed to achieve woman suffrage, but the Stanton group decided to include all women's rights issues, while the Beecher group focused only on the suffrage.[5]

Whatever contributions to a development of women's rights consciousness these organizations made, divided and fighting among themselves, they did not gain inclusion of women's suffrage in the Constitution. In 1866, Senator Edgar A. Cowen, Republican of Pennsylvania, had tried to amend a bill to give the vote to blacks in the District of Columbia, to provide woman suffrage, but failed by a 9-37 vote. In 1868, Republican Senator Samuel C. Pomeroy of Kansas presented a proposed suffrage bill to the Senate, and Indiana Congressman George W. Julian presented a joint resolution on the subject to both houses in 1869. Both proposals died without a vote being taken. Twelve resolutions to extend suffrage to women were introduced between 1875 and 1888 in the Congress. Usually they were reported back to the committee to which they had been referred, with extended reports from the majority and the minority. In 1878, Senator A. A. Sargent of California, a friend of Susan B. Anthony's, introduced into the Senate the Anthony amendment, which is the text of the Nineteenth Amendment as finally passed by Congress. After hearings, Sargent's proposal was reported adversely back to committee. In 1887, a women's suffrage amendment gained a vote on the Senate floor, but lost 34-16. Twenty-two of the opposing senators were from the South. In 1888, Mason of Illinois unsuccessfully attempted to give "widows and spinsters" the right to vote, on the rationale that they had no male voter to represent their interests.[6]

In the National Association, President Stanton's support of Victoria Woodhull, which she regarded as consistent with women's rights, did not help the movement. Woodhull, a charismatic, clairvoyant stockbroker and courtesan, and a vocal supporter of woman suffrage, appeared on the scene in 1871. She publicly avowed "free love," and made charges leading to a titillating scandal and lawsuit, alleging sexual misconduct against the first president of the American Suffrage Association, Henry Ward Beecher, and the wife of reform editor Theodore Tilton, both of whom were Beecher's parishioners. Although Beecher was acquitted, identification of the movement with the taint of immorality impeded further progress and further divided the two suffrage organizations.[7]

Gradually, however, age, maturity, judgment, persistent agitation, and organization enabled the suffragists to regain some lost ground. Anthony orchestrated helpful publicity from time to time. For example, arrested for voting, along with three of her sisters and twelve other Rochester women in the presidential election of 1872, she was found guilty and fined $100, which she never paid. The judge did not order her arrested because his Republican supporters did not want further publicity about the issue. In addition, he did not want her to be in a position to appeal the case to a higher court. The Grant administration quietly pardoned all sixteen women and the election inspectors who let them vote. In addition, her organization continued to hold national meetings every year in Washington, thus gaining some political support. The Anthony amendment was repeatedly introduced in Congress and reported out of committee until 1896, but consistently met failure.[8]

In the meantime, the Supreme Court made it clear that nothing but an amendment would give women the suffrage. Francis Minor, a St. Louis lawyer, sued for his wife's right to vote, based on the Fourteenth Amendment's clause that no state shall abridge the privileges and immunities of citizens of the United States. His wife was president of the Missouri Woman Suffrage Association. In 1875, the Supreme Court, in *Minor* v. *Happersett,* ruled that this clause did not apply to state laws preventing women from voting.[9]

Undaunted by the Court's decision, and with Stanton hoping it would help their argument that they needed a constitutional amendment, the two organizations continued the long weary battle of trying to gain the suffrage. The National Association focused on a federal constitutional amendment, while the American Association tried to gain suffrage state by state. But they made little progress in persuading the public that female voting was necessary, or that, in the alternative, denying the right was an egregious violation of democratic rights that needed remedying.[10]

In the late nineteenth century, the women's movement gradually began to recognize the need to heal its divisions before a major push for woman suffrage could be made throughout the country. The divisions did not seem to make much sense anyway. Suffragists outside the East, where the great battles over the Fourteenth and Fifteenth amendments had taken place, found the continued separation between the National and American Associations irrational. Little progress was being made on the issues relative to marriage, divorce and family in Stanton's agenda. There were more professional writers and women of independent means in the movement, and, during a period of social turmoil, of strikes and radical labor organizations, both organizations had become more focused on suffrage alone. In the absence of any basic disagreement, the daughter of Lucy Stone, Alice Stone Blackwell, and the leaders of the Women's Christian Temperance Union worked to bring the National and American Associations together.[11]

The merger was accomplished in 1890 with Stanton as president of the new organization, the National American Woman Suffrage Association. However, geographic schisms still emerged at every convention over strategy, tactics, and timing on such issues as whether to proceed state by state, or to go all-out for a federal amendment. Stanton also continued to stray from the suffrage-only focus; for example, when she published *The Woman's Bible* in 1895, a work with which the Association disavowed any connection. When Anthony succeeded Stanton after two years, she was better able to minimize the disputes. In 1900, Anthony chose as her successor Carrie Chapman Catt, who had been a very effective chairwoman of the Association's organization committee from 1895 to 1900. Catt served for four years, until, some historians believe, she was forced to resign by New Yorkers and southerners who objected to her support of Anthony's federal amendment after the organization had adopted a policy of proceeding state by state. Others cite her growing involvement in the international suffrage movement. Ann Shaw, who succeeded Catt but was not as good an organizer, let the state organizations follow their own instincts; the movement grew weaker. Southern women continued to argue that sectional and state prejudices had to be addressed, They believed that otherwise not enough state support to create a federal amendment could be generated. The Association acknowledged their point of view by announcing the principle of states' rights in the 1903 convention. State affiliates could use whatever approach they deemed necessary in campaigning for woman suffrage. This left southern members free to express their racism and northern members free to tolerate it, in a movement supposedly devoted to political rights for all.[12]

The consensus the suffrage supporters needed for their cause came faster in the West where a confluence of forces brought women the vote in Wyoming, Colorado, Utah, and Idaho. In Wyoming a peculiar combination of circumstances worked to achieve the first territorial adoption of woman suffrage in 1869. Esther Morris embraced suffragism at a lecture by Susan B. Anthony, which she attended after losing an inheritance because she was a female instead of a male heir. In South Pass, Wyoming, she began converting others to the cause of suffrage at private social occasions while preparing for the town's first election campaign. South Pass, the largest community in Wyoming, with 6,000 votes, had the largest number of women. Both candidates in South Pass endorsed woman suffrage, fearing the loss of some male votes through the influence of women. One of the candidates who was elected, whose wife was a suffragist, favored the idea and came to believe the cause was just. He thought she deserved the ballot since black males had been given the right to vote. His suffrage bill, introduced into the new legislature, passed. The governor of Wyoming, who was from Salem, Ohio (where he had attended a women's rights meeting) and was married to a suffragist, signed the bill into law. The legislature thought that giving women the vote would signal the kind of social stability that would attract good publicity and settlers to the new territory. By the time eastern antisuffragist arguments began to penetrate the area, it was too late to reopen the question. The result of female voting did little to change political events in Wyoming, despite the hopes of suffragists and the fears of antisuffragists. In addition, the peculiar circumstances of its passage in Wyoming could not be counted on to bring suffrage elsewhere. When Wyoming was admitted as a state in 1890, it was only after a heated debate in the Congress over whether admitting a suffrage state would encourage the granting of voting rights elsewhere. The Wyoming legislature prevailed when they made it clear that they would not give up women's suffrage as the price of admission to the Union.[13]

In Utah, where there were as many women as men, the elders of the Mormon church decided to give suffrage willingly to women. They believed the congressional criticism of polygamy in the territory would be deflected by letting women vote, who would thereby affirm their own belief in plural marriage. Therefore, women in Utah were given the vote in 1870. Stanton and Anthony welcomed the women into the National Association, but the American Suffrage Association rejected them because of their endorsement of polygamy. The Mormon strategy backfired when Congress, in 1877, reinforced the outlawing of polygamy, and took the vote away from Mormon women because of their complicity with the policy. But after Wyoming was admitted to the Union, with congressional acceptance of woman suffrage, the Mormon church gave up plural marriages, and in 1896 Utah was admitted to the Union, whereupon the state gave women the right to vote.[14]

While the Utah dispute was before the Congress, Colorado enacted suffrage. With the radical Populist party controlling the legislature, the state gave women the suffrage with male majority support in a referendum endorsing it. Historians have speculated about why Colorado acted as it did. Some assert that the difficult geography, climate and pioneer existence made the inhabitants radical in their approach to any issue. Others argue that the people in the many small towns, voting against the saloons and corporate interests, expected women to purify politics. Little, however, that could be called purification occurred.[15]

In 1896, Idaho, where populism also held sway during economic hard times, enacted woman suffrage. As a mass democratic movement, populism supported the extension of suffrage and women's participation in politics. Carrie Catt, who led the campaign in Colorado, was again at the forefront in Idaho. William Jennings Bryan carried the state in the 1896 election at which suffrage was enacted. At the same time, in Kansas, woman suffrage was rejected (according to Susan B. Anthony) because the Republicans and Whisky Democrats thought the women's vote would keep the state dry. The basis for this fear is unclear, because in none of the early four suffrage states did Prohibition become law before the Prohibition amendment. However, in California, the pro-liquor vote in the large cities did combine to defeat woman suffrage in 1896. For the next fourteen years, not one additional state gave women the vote, despite the organizational efforts of the National American Suffrage Association.[16]

Many of the women who were involved in the suffrage movement were prohibitionists, but the Prohibition issue could hurt or help the cause depending on local circumstances. The prohibitionist strategy of drying up the towns and rural areas by local options made the cities fear the women's vote, because many still believed women would vote dry. The Woman's Christian Temperance Union, founded in 1874 while the women's suffrage groups were divided, was extremely successful. It had many more members than the Associations. Frances Willard, the second president of the Temperance Union, was converted by Anthony and became an ardent suffragist, leading the organization gradually to support the suffrage efforts. Willard preached temperance, suffrage, and child labor protection, in the context of the acceptable female interest in strengthening the family. It was a "home protection" movement. After Willard's death in 1898, however, the Temperance Union reverted to focusing entirely on the dry cause.[17]

The dry cause continued to make faster progress than the suffrage movement, using local option and state laws. The South presented a special problem for the suffragists. The drys had great success there, but southerners did not permit black men to vote and were not about to endorse female voting with its implications for affecting the traditional role of women and its enfranchisement of black women. Women in the South worked for the drys in the interest of home and family, but did not mount a woman suffrage campaign. Some suffragists argued that the success of their cause was delayed by the liquor issue until after Prohibition was enacted. But the leading reformers in the Women's Christian Temperance Union who came from the upper middle class, gradually became more interested in suffrage than Prohibition. Being a suffragist became more fashionable than being involved in Prohibition activities, especially in the cities. By 1916, more women reformers belonged to the suffrage cause than to the Temperance Union. In fact, the controversy over liquor may have been beneficial, because many women had their first education as reformers in the Prohibition movement before moving on to the suffrage cause.[18]

After Stanton died in 1902 and Anthony in 1906, new leaders and issues came into prominence in the suffrage cause. Like Prohibition, progressivism helped the cause also. The emphasis in the Progressive movement on ending corrupt politics provided a reinforced rationale for including women voters, that is, as a means of purifying politics by insuring decisions that would protect the home and family. Women's clubs proliferated, and women's support for reforms (even when they could not vote) was a major force in the successes of the Progressive period. Their involvement helped to achieve enough support to enact woman suffrage in Washington, California, Oregon, Arizona, Nevada, Montana, and Kansas between 1910 and 1914.[19]

The votes for suffrage came from declining small towns, educated urban and suburban middle-class voters, and some of the working men in cities who saw the vote as a means for their wives and daughters to protect themselves. By the 1912 presidential election, two of the four candidates, Theodore Roosevelt and Eugene Debs, supported women's suffrage. Roosevelt, the Bull Moose candidate that year, had long supported feminist causes. His Harvard senior dissertation was entitled, "The Practicability of Equalizing Men and Women Before the Law." He did not publicly support suffrage, however, until he became the Progressive candidate on a platform supporting votes for women. Large numbers of women who could vote in some western states by 1912, voted for him, but they did not vote en bloc for his candidacy.[20]

New directions and new leaders emerged to advance the suffrage cause. The daughter of Elizabeth Stanton, Harriet Blatch, returned to New York after twenty years in England where she had experienced the militant suffrage tactics of the women there. She preached that the movement must broaden its base from the middle-class reformers and become more dramatically militant. She set up her own political union in 1907 to incorporate college students, factory workers, and union organizers. Then the wealthy Alva Belmont decided to give support to the suffrage cause on the condition that she be accorded power in it, offering the National American Association permanent headquarters in New York. But westerners and southerners did not welcome her involvement. When these women led their organizations to support their vice-president, Jane Addams, in endorsing Theodore Roosevelt in the 1912 election (even though the group was supposed to be non-partisan), Belmont withdrew her support. She joined the Congressional Union and its successor, the Woman's party, which she supported for many years.[21]

When Alice Paul and Lucy Burns, who had experienced incarceration and hunger strikes with British suffragettes, set up the Congressional Union in 1913 to focus solely on gaining a federal constitutional amendment by more militant tactics, another strong element had to be taken into account. Alice Paul had been named chairman of the congressional committee of the National American Association at its December 1912 convention. As committee chairman she organized a suffrage parade of 5,000 women in March 1913, just before Woodrow Wilson's inauguration. The women were mobbed and insulted, generating new publicity for the voting rights cause. Thereafter, she angered southerners by proposing that western Democratic women voters be asked to vote Republican to frighten Wilson and the Democrats into voting a suffrage amendment out of Congress. She was expelled for violating the National's bipartisanship policy, and for being too assiduous in working for a federal amendment. She and Burns established the Congressional Union and began attracting suffragists from the National. In 1917, Harriet Blatch's and Alice Paul's organizations merged to form the National Woman's party, which soon became very successful with its straightforward support of a federal amendment.[22]

At this juncture, some women began to seek a states' rights constitutional amendment for woman suffrage. Kate Gordon, the Louisiana president of the Southern States Woman Suffrage Conference, and a member of the National Board of the National American Woman Suffrage Association from 1901-1910, saw it as a way for the Democratic party to support women's rights. She began promoting the idea in the early 1900's, repeating the now familiar arguments that enfranchising white women was a way to maintain white supremacy in the South. The proposal acknowledged that the South had moved from violence and intimidation to more sophisticated means of preventing black men from voting. The states' rights amendment strategy could permit southern states to grant suffrage to women, but to institute literacy tests and other procedural barriers used against black men, to keep black women from voting. The approach failed to gain broad support because, at about the same time, blacks started attacking the procedural barriers as violations of the Fifteenth Amendment. More importantly, many of the southern legislators had been

ON THE SUBJECT OF...

JANE ADDAMS (1860-1935)
Born in Cedarville, Illinois, Jane Addams is remembered as an influential social activist and feminist icon; she was the most prominent member of a notable group of female social reformers who were active during the first half of the twentieth century. Foremost among her many accomplishments was the creation of Hull House in Chicago. Staff from this settlement provided social services to the urban poor and successfully advocated for a number of social and industrial reforms. An ardent pacifist, Addams was Chair of The Woman's Peace Party, President of the International Congress of Women, and helped found the Women's International League for Peace and Freedom. She became the second woman to receive the Nobel Peace Prize in 1931, in recognition of her lifelong efforts to end war, aid humanity, and promote peace. In the presentation speech for the Prize, which was made in Addams's absence (she was too ill to attend the ceremony), Professor Halvdan Koht declared: "In honoring Jane Addams, we also render homage to the work which women can do for peace and human brotherhood." Addams also supported women's suffrage, Prohibition, and was a founding member of the American Civil Liberties Union (ACLU). Her writings include the widely read, autobiographical *Twenty Years at Hull House* (1910).

Koht, Halvdan. In *Nobel Lectures. Peace,* by Frederick W. Haberman. Vol. 2, pp. 125-35. Amsterdam: Elsevier, 1972.

using states' rights arguments only as a smokescreen. Actually, they thought voting for women was inappropriate. Furthermore, many northern suffragists were committed to a national amendment approach as the simplest strategy possible.

But the states' rights arguments did not go away. By 1914, some leading suffragists persuaded the Association to support a substitute amendment. Named for Democratic Senator John F. Shafroth of Colorado and Congressman A. Mitchell

Palmer of Pennsylvania, it provided that if more than 8 percent of the legal voters in a state petitioned for a referendum, and in the referendum a majority voting on the issue voted favorably, women in the states could be enfranchised. The Association endorsed the proposal on the ground that congressmen would probably vote for it, even if they opposed suffrage, in order to give the local people a chance to express their wishes. Also, initiatives and referenda had become important progressive reforms accepted by both parties. In addition, as more states adopted suffrage they could be added to the list of those which would support the national Susan B. Anthony amendment. But almost as soon as the Association endorsed Shafroth-Palmer, a storm of opposition arose over the idea of conducting campaigns in each state for something less than the Anthony amendment, and the endorsement was dropped.[23]

Meanwhile, in 1915, Carrie Chapman Catt resumed the presidency of the National American Association. She increased membership from 100,000 to two million in two years. She cooperated with Alice Paul, but also kept up ties with Woodrow Wilson as she tried to get him to support women's suffrage. She was a seasoned political operator who understood that the militancy of the Woman's party offered a good counter pressure as she moved in a less threatening, more conciliatory fashion.[24]

In 1914, Alice Paul had tried to punish the Democrats for opposing suffrage by enlisting western women to vote against them in the midterm elections. She was not as successful as she had hoped, but when fewer Democrats than expected won, the Democrats in the House moved the suffrage amendment to the floor. However, the proposal was defeated, falling seventy-eight votes short of the two-thirds majority needed for passage.[25]

The election of 1916 tested the non-partisan policy of the National American Association against the Woman's party policy of supporting whatever party seemed more committed to suffrage. Because Wilson supported his party's platform of women's suffrage through state action instead of a national amendment, the Woman's party campaigned against him. Hughes ran on a Republican platform supporting a federal amendment, but Wilson won the election, although narrowly, with ten of the twelve states in which women could vote supporting him. As a result, members of Congress did not have to feel threatened by the female vote.[26]

In the face of such adversity, both the Association and the Woman's party renewed their efforts. By the time World War I was declared in 1917, antiwar sentiment had become a significant element within the women's reform movement, clouding the suffragists' efforts. Women reformers such as Jane Addams and Florence Kelley were confirmed pacifists. Carrie Chapman Catt was personally opposed to American intervention in the war because of her pacifism, but the Association pledged support for the war effort. In fact, many women diverted their efforts from suffrage to war work, including joining the Red Cross and selling bonds. This patriotic posture helped in carrying New York state for suffrage in 1917, by dislodging the notion that women would vote for peace and not support the war. The suffrage cause was also helped by petitions, signed by over a million New York women asking for the vote, which disproved the notion that women did not want it. In the same year Rhode Island, Michigan, and Nebraska gave women the right to vote in presidential elections. By this time, a sufficient number of congressmen were from states in which women had the vote to generate enough consensus for passage in Congress of the Anthony amendment.[27]

During the war, women put on military uniforms, drilled, and worked in non-traditional occupations as streetcar conductors, mechanics, bricklayers, electricians, and armament factory workers. Wilson still hesitated to support a suffrage amendment, but Catt knew she needed him to get the southern states to ratify. She made it clear that she would leave him unpressured to determine when he would declare his endorsement. The National Woman's party, however, continued to picket the White House, heckled Wilson, and harassed the Senate. About a hundred women were arrested and went on a hunger strike, during which they were forcibly fed like the English suffragists, all with great publicity. Catt kept informing Wilson ahead of time about demonstrations, relying on him to value her confidence and to come around eventually to the cause. The Republicans in the House decided to embarrass the Democrats by supporting the amendment. It passed by just one vote beyond a two-thirds majority. Although Wilson then declared his support, the Democrats were still split, as mostly southerners voted against it. In the Senate, after the amendment failed by two votes to obtain two-thirds, Wilson asked the Senate to vote for it as a war measure, to make the world safe for democracy. But he still could not gain a sufficient number of Democratic votes.[28]

In 1918, the Republicans gained control of the incoming Congress in the off-year elections. The Association joined the Woman's party in campaigning against four anti-suffrage senators, two of whom were defeated. Seeing the handwriting on the wall, the Democratic leadership tried to pass the amendment in the lame duck session so as not to be blamed for its lack of success, but failed by one vote in the Senate. In the new Congress it passed in the House by a 3-1 voting margin, and in the Senate by two-thirds, with the South still in opposition. The southern Democrats voted negatively because they did not fear retribution at the polls; and they felt their constituents supported their efforts to keep black women, along with black men, from the polls, and to keep women out of the political arena. However, with the groundwork already laid in the states, ratification came rapidly. Northeastern state voters, fearful of adding immigrant women to those immigrant men whose vote they believed was influenced by political bosses, and the South with its traditional attitudes toward women, remained obdurate. All of the western states and most of the remaining northern ones ratified, until there were thirty-five. Finally, Tennessee ratified, bringing the number to thirty-six. During the ratification process, Catt insisted that women would not be the captives of any party. She cited the example of her work with Wilson and with the Republicans to gain suffrage. She asserted that she did not want women to be tied to one party, as blacks had been tied to the Republicans. Nor did she want them to alienate the Democrats. Once victory was won, Catt followed through on her assertions. She arranged to have the final victory convention of the Association become the first meeting of the nonpartisan League of Women Voters.[29]

Unrelenting, though unsuccessful, the anti-suffrage American Constitutional League, in April 1920, began filing lawsuits to keep the amendment from going into effect. The Maryland League for State Defense challenged the amendment by bringing suit against the registration of two Baltimore women for the 1920 election. They argued that the constitutional guarantee, that no state's equal representation in the Senate would be changed without the state's consent, had been violated. They asserted that the basis of election of senators had been determined by thirty-six other states, without Maryland's consent, making the amendment illegal; but the Baltimore Court of Appeals dismissed the suit. Another suit, filed

Photograph of the headquarters of the National League of Women Voters.

in the U.S. Supreme Court in 1921 by the same group and advancing similar claims, was also dismissed. Insulated from charges of illegality, it remained to be seen what women would do with their vote.[30]

One harbinger of future difficulties in the struggle for women's equality came from the identification of the suffrage cause as a white women's movement. When Susan B. Anthony asked ardent women's rights supporter Frederick Douglass not to speak at the Association's convention in 1894 in Atlanta, Georgia, for fear of offending southern sensibilities, she irritated large numbers of blacks. At the suffrage march organized by the National American Woman Suffrage Association and Alice Paul's Congressional Union in 1913 in Washington, the day before Wilson's inauguration, Ida Wells-Barnett, a black leader of the Illinois Alpha Suffrage Club, was told not to march with the Chicago contingent, but to stay at the rear so as not to disturb southern women. Wells-Barnett defied the leaders by stepping into line between two Chicago white women and proceeding along the line of march.[31]

These were only examples of a general pattern of insensitivity or anti-black bias, whether for expediency or otherwise, on the part of suffragist leaders. They achieved their objectives while exhibiting their prejudices, but the Nineteenth Amendment meant suffrage largely for white women until the Voting Rights Act of 1965 was passed. In fact, the white supremacy arguments for woman suffrage had little positive effect in the South. Most of the southern state legislatures voted against ratification of the Nineteenth Amendment.[32]

The consensus required to gain the Nineteenth Amendment evolved only with great difficulty. In the face of opposition or lukewarm support from many women, the movement's leaders abandoned the strategy of emphasizing that women needed to act as individuals, and that suffrage would make far-reaching changes in women's roles in society. Instead, the reformers pointed to the lack of change in the roles of women, men, and children in the western states in which women could vote, and the continuing male economic control in the society, as an argument to gain consensus. In doing so they effected a reconciliation between two apparently conflicting traditions and undermined many of the arguments of suffrage opponents. They also argued that expanding the suffrage to women would fulfill the American tradition of representative government without negative effects, and with the positive influence of validating the existing political system. Because the amendment was largely self-enforcing, proponents did not have to worry that if women voted to make substantive changes in society they would face repeal as had the Prohibition supporters. Once there were enough suffrage states to make female voters a significant factor in presidential elections, candidates for that office had to take a position on the issue. Congressmen and senators in the suffrage states also had to pay attention to the women's desire for a federal constitutional amendment. The attention paid to states' rights and the race issue to placate the South was largely wasted.

Many southern state legislators simply opposed changing the traditional role of women to include political participation and used the other issues as camouflage when dealing with suffragists. In the final stages of the struggle, the militant and direct action tactics of the National Woman's party gave additional credibility to the moderate reform efforts of the Association. As in the case of the symbolic Prohibition amendment, state-based consensus helped to develop a national consensus, which was aided by the exigencies of war in which women gave patriotic supportive services.

Judging from the history of the woman suffrage battle, gaining effective state amendments to be used as a base from which to draw states to ratify a controversial federal amendment would be a workable strategy. Also, supporters could accept militant tactics, such as hunger strikes and direct action, in an attempt to gain ratification,

following Catt's example. They could draw attention to their less-militant behavior in the cause, while understanding that direct action carried out persistently over a long period of time can help to create the climate necessary for ratification.

Following ratification of the Nineteenth Amendment, as women's votes continued to be undifferentiated from men's, no immediate far-reaching changes occurred in women's roles. But in the 1920s women who had become suffragists in order to promote progressive social causes, and others who had focused on the vote as an end in itself, participated in a wide variety of causes, including maternal and child health, consumer legislation, making government more efficient and less corrupt, jury service, and conservation. They also became involved in the unsuccessful movement to gain a constitutional amendment to outlaw the use of child labor. Others in the National Woman's party transferred their single-issue focus, now that suffrage was gained, to an effort to gain an equal rights amendment.

Notes

1. Andrew Sinclair, *The Emancipation of the American Woman* (New York: Harper & Row, 1965), pp. 30-32; Eleanor Flexner, *Century of Struggle: The Woman's Rights Movement in the United States* (Cambridge: Harvard University Press, 1959, 1972), pp. 143-44.

2. Sinclair, *Emancipation,* pp. 84-90; Leo Kanowitz, *Women and the Law: The Unfinished Revolution* (Albuquerque: University of New Mexico Press, 1969), pp. 35-41; David Morgan, *Suffragists and Democrats: The Politics of Woman Suffrage in America* (East Lansing: Michigan State University Press, 1972), p. 41; Carl Degler, *At Odds: Women and the Family in America from the Revolution to the Present* (New York: Oxford University Press, 1980), pp. 342-50; Flexner, *Century of Struggle,* pp. 71-77.

3. Ellen DuBois, *Feminism and Suffrage: The Emergence of an Independent Women's Movement in America* (Ithaca, NY: Cornell University Press, 1978), pp. 53-64; Flexner, *Century of Struggle,* pp. 110-11, 144-45; Mary Frances Berry, *Military Necessity and Civil Rights Policy: Black Citizenship and the Constitution, 1861-1868* (Port Washington, NY: Kennikat Press, 1977), pp. 92-95.

4. Aileen S. Kraditor, *Ideas of the Woman Suffrage Movement, 1890-1920* (New York: Columbia University Press, 1965), pp. 131, 172, 213; Flexner, *Century of Struggle,* p. 220; DuBois, *Feminism and Suffrage,* p. 178. On racism in the suffrage movement generally, see Paula Giddings, *When and Where I Enter: The Impact of Black Women on Race and Sex in America* (New York: Morrow Co., 1984), pp. 119-31, 159-70; Angela Y. Davis, *Women, Race, and Class* (New York: Random House, 1981), pp. 109-26; Rosalyn Terborg-Penn, "Afro-Americans in the Struggle for Woman Suffrage" (Ph.D. dissertation, Howard University, 1977).

5. DuBois, *Feminism and Suffrage,* pp. 164-75; Flexner, *Century of Struggle,* pp. 152-53.

6. Flexner, *Century of Struggle*, pp. 148-49, 174-75; Herman Ames, *The Proposed Amendments to the Constitution of the United States during the First Century of Its History,* Annual Report of the American Historical Association (1896), vol. II (Washington, D.C.: Government Printing office, 1897), pp. 237-38.

7. William O'Neill, *Everyone Was Brave: The Rise and Fall of Feminism in America* (Chicago: Quadrangle Books, 1969), pp. 25-31; Flexner, *Century of Struggle*, p. 154; Sinclair, *Emancipation*, pp. 191-93.

8. Sinclair, *Emancipation*, pp. 193-95; Flexner, *Century of Struggle*, pp. 167-69, 175; Elisabeth Griffin, *In Her Own Right: The Life of Elizabeth Cady Stanton* (New York: Oxford University Press, 1983), p. 154.

9. Sinclair, *Emancipation*, p. 195; *Minor v. Happersett,* 21 Wallace 162 (1875); Flexner, *Century of Struggle*, pp. 168-70.

10. Sinclair, *Emancipation*, pp. 172-73.

11. Sinclair, *Emancipation*, pp. 293-94; Flexner, *Century of Struggle*, pp. 216-20; Kraditor, *Ideas of the Woman Suffrage Movement*, p. 4.

12. Flexner, *Century of Struggle*, pp. 221, 237-39, 249; Kraditor, *Ideas of the Woman Suffrage Movement*, pp. 163-66.

13. Sinclair, *Emancipation*, pp. 208-12; Flexner, *Century of Struggle*, pp. 177-78; Miriam Chapman, "The Story of Woman Suffrage in Wyoming, 1869-1890" (MA thesis, University of Wyoming, 1952); Julie R. Jeffrey, *Frontier Women: The Trans-Mississippi West, 1840-1880* (New York: Hill and Wang, 1979), pp. 190-93; Glenda Riley, *Women and Indians on the Frontier, 1825-1915* (Albuquerque: University of New Mexico Press, 1984), p. 13.

14. Flexner, *Century of Struggle*, pp. 162-63, 212-15; Jeffrey, *Frontier Women*, p. 190.

15. Sinclair, *Emancipation*, pp. 216-17; Flexner, *Century of Struggle*, pp. 222-23.

16. Flexner, *Century of Struggle*, pp. 222-24, 217-19.

17. Sinclair, *Emancipation*, pp. 222-23; Flexner, *Century of Struggle*, pp. 181-85; Janet Giele, "Social Change in the Woman Suffrage Movement, 1890-1920" (Ph.D. dissertation, Columbia University, 1962).

18. Sinclair, *Emancipation*, pp. 223-28; Flexner, *Century of Struggle*, pp. 185-86; Kraditor, *Ideas of the Woman Suffrage Movement*, pp. 162-83; David Morgan, *Suffragists and Democrats*, pp. 158-66.

19. Sinclair, *Emancipation*, pp. 227, 229; Lauren Kessler, "A Siege of the Citadels: Search for a Public Forum for the Ideas of Oregon Woman Suffrage," 84 *Oregon Historical Quarterly* (1983): 117-49; Flexner, *Century of Struggle*, pp. 151-53; O'Neill, *Everyone Was Brave*, pp. 18-24, 33-38; Kraditor, *Ideas of the Woman Suffrage Movement*, pp. 110-31.

20. Sinclair, *Emancipation*, pp. 324-26; Flexner, *Century of Struggle*, pp. 249, 262.

21. Flexner, *Century of Struggle*, pp. 221, 237-39, 249; Kraditor, *Ideas of the Woman Suffrage Movement*, pp. 163, 166.

   Flexner, *Century of Struggle*, pp. 298-302, 249-52; 258-59.

22. Flexner, *Century of Struggle*, pp. 302-303, 263-64; Susan D. Becker, *The Origins of the Equal Rights Amendment: American Feminism Between the Wars* (Westport, CT: Greenwood Press, 1981), pp. 44-48.

23. Flexner, *Century of Struggle*, pp. 267-74; Morgan, *Suffragists and Democrats*, pp. 92-95.

24. Flexner, *Century of Struggle*, p. 303.

25. Sinclair, *Emancipation*, pp. 303-304, 326; Flexner, *Century of Struggle*, p. 269.

26. Sinclair, *Emancipation*, pp. 328-30; Flexner, *Century of Struggle*, pp. 276-77.

27. Sinclair, *Emancipation*, p. 331; Flexner, *Century of Struggle*, pp. 305-15.

28. Sinclair, *Emancipation*, pp. 331-34; Flexner, *Century of Struggle*, pp. 278-79, 288-290; Sidney Roderick Bland, "Techniques of Persuasion: The National Woman's Party and Woman Suffrage, 1913-1919" (Ph.D. dissertation, George Washington University, 1977).

29. Sinclair, *Emancipation*, pp. 331-39; Flexner, *Century of Struggle*, pp. 291-93; Lemons, *The Woman Citizen: Social Feminism in the 1920's* (Urbana: University of Illinois Press, 1973), p. 29; Flexner, *Century of Struggle*, pp. 240, 242, 311-13.

30. *Leser v. Garnett,* 258 U.S. 130 (1922); William L. Marbury, "The 19th Amendment and After," 7 *University of Virginia Law Review* (October 1920): 1-29.

31. Rosalyn Terborg-Penn, "Discrimination Against Afro-American Women in the Woman's Movement, 1830-1920," in Sharon Harley and Rosalyn Terborg-Penn, eds., *The Afro-American Woman: Struggles and Images* (Port Washington, NY: Kennikat Press, 1978), pp. 17-28; Paula Giddings, *When and Where I Enter: The Impact of Black Women on Race and Sex in America* (New York: Morrow Co., 1984), pp. 127-28; Nancy Cott, "Feminist Politics in the 1920's: The National Woman Party," 71 *Journal of American History* (1984): 50-54; Kraditor, *Ideas of the Woman Suffrage Movement*, p. 213; Rosalyn Terborg-Penn, "Discontented Black Feminists: Prelude and Postscripts to the Nineteenth Amendment," in Lois Scharf and Jan M. Jackson, eds., *Decades of Discontent: The Women's Movement, 1920-1940* (Westport, CT: Greenwood Press, 1983).

32. Virginia, North Carolina, South Carolina, Georgia, Alabama, Louisiana, Mississippi, and Florida ratified neither the Nineteenth Amendment nor ERA. Maryland and Delaware did not ratify the Nineteenth Amendment, but did ratify ERA.

NANCY F. COTT (ESSAY DATE 1990)

SOURCE: Cott, Nancy F. "Historical Perspectives: The Equal Rights Amendment Conflict in the 1920s." In *Conflicts in Feminism*, edited by Marianne Hirsch and Evelyn Fox Keller, pp. 44-59. New York: Routledge, 1990.

In the following essay, Cott discusses the perceived conflict of interest between equal rights for women and gender-based protective legislation in the aftermath of the ratification the nineteenth amendment.

Campaigning for ratification of the Equal Rights Amendment during the 1970s, feminists who found it painful to be opposed by other groups of women were often unaware that the first proposal of that amendment in the 1920s had caused a bitter split between women's groups claiming, on both sides, to represent women's interests. The 1920s conflict itself echoed some earlier ideological and tactical controversies. One central strategic question for the women's rights movement in the late nineteenth century had concerned alliances: should proponents of "the cause of woman" ally with advocates for the rights for freed slaves, with temperance workers, or labor reformers, or a political party, or none of them? At various times different women leaders felt passionately for and against such alliances, not agreeing on what they meant for the breadth of the women's movement and for the priority assigned to women's issues.[1] The 1920s contest over the equal rights amendment reiterated that debate insofar as the National Women's Party, which proposed the ERA, took a "single-issue" approach, and the opposing women's organizations were committed to maintaining multiple alliances. But in even more striking ways than it recapitulated nineteenth-century struggles the 1920s equal rights conflict also predicted lines of fracture of the later twentieth-century women's movement. The advantages or compromises involved in "multi-issue" organizing are matters of contemporary concern, of course. Perhaps more important, the 1920s debate brought into sharp focus (and left for us generations later to resolve) the question whether "equal rights"—a concept adopted, after all, from the male political tradition—matched women's needs. The initial conflict between women over the ERA set the goal of enabling women to have the same opportunities and situations as men *against* the goal of enabling women freely to be different from men without adverse consequences. As never before in nineteenth-century controversies, these two were seen as competing, even mutually exclusive alternatives.

The equal rights amendment was proposed as a legal or civic innovation but the intrafeminist controversy it caused focused on the economic arena. Indeed, the connection between economic and political subordination in women's relation to men has been central in women's rights advocacy since the latter part of the nineteenth century. In the Western political tradition, women were historically excluded from political initiatives because they were defined as dependent—like children and slaves—and their dependence was read as fundamentally economic. Nineteenth-century advocates, along with the vote, claimed woman's "right to labor," by which they meant the right for women to have their labor recognized, and diversified. They emphasized that women, as human individuals no less than men, had the right and need to use their talents to serve society and themselves and to gain fair compensation. Influential voices such as Charlotte Perkins Gilman's at the turn of the century stressed not only women's service but the necessity and warrant for women's economic independence. Gilman argued simultaneously that social evolution made women's move "from fireside to factory" inevitable, and also that the move ought to be spurred by conscious renovation of outworn tradition.

By the 1910s suffragists linked political and economic rights, and connected the vote with economic leverage, whether appealing to industrial workers, career women, or housewives. They insisted on women's economic independence in principle and defense of wage-earning women in fact. Since the vast majority of wage-earning women were paid too little to become economically independent, however, the two commitments were not identical and might in practice be entirely at odds.[2] The purpose to validate women's existing economic roles might openly conflict with the purpose to throw open economic horizons for women to declare their own self-definition. These tensions introduced by the feminist and suffrage agitation of the 1910s flashed into controversy over the equal rights amendment in the 1920s.

The ERA was the baby of the National Women's Party, yet not its brainchild alone. As early as 1914, a shortlived N.Y.C. group called the Feminist Alliance had suggested a constitutional amendment barring sex discrimination of all sorts. Like the later NWP, the Feminist Alliance was dominated by highly educated and ambitious women in the arts and professions, women who believed that "equal rights" were their due while they also aimed to rejuvenate and reorient thinking about "rights" around female rather than only male definition. Some members of the Feminist Alliance surely joined the NWP, which emerged as the agent of militant and political action during the final decade of the suffrage campaign.[3]

A small group (engaging perhaps five percent of all suffragists), the NWP grew from the Congressional Union founded by Alice Paul and Lucy Burns in 1913 to work on the federal rather than the state-by-state route to woman suffrage. Through the 'teens it came to stand for partisan tactics (opposing all Democrats because the Democratic administration had not passed woman suffrage) and for flamboyant, symbolic, publicity-generating actions—large parades, pickets in front of the White House, placards in the Congress, hunger-striking in jail, and more. It gained much of its energy from leftwing radical women who were attracted to its wholesale condemnation of gender inequality and to its tactical adaptations from the labor movement; at the same time, its imperious tendency to work from the top down attracted crucial financial and moral support from some very rich women. When the much larger group, the National American Woman Suffrage Association, moved its focus to a constitutional amendment in 1916, that was due in no little part (although certainly not solely), to the impact of the NWP. Yet while imitating its aim, NAWSA's leaders always hated and resented the NWP for the way it had horned in on the same pro-suffrage turf while scorning the NAWSA's traditional nonpartisan, educative strategy. These resentments festered into deep and longlasting personal conflicts between leaders of the two groups.

Just after the 19th Amendment was ratified in August of 1930, the NWP began planning a large convention at which its members would decide whether to continue as a group and, if so, what to work for. The convention, held six months later and tightly orchestrated by chairman Alice Paul, brushed aside all other suggestions and endorsed an ongoing program to "remove all remaining forms of the subjection of women," by means of the elimination of sex discrimination in law.[4] At the outset, NWP leaders seemed unaware that this program of "equal rights" would be much thornier to define and implement than "equal suffrage" had been. They began surveying state legal codes, conferring with lawyers, and drafting numerous versions of equal rights legislation and amendments at the state and federal levels.

Yet the "clean sweep" of such an approach immediately raised a problem: would it invalidate sex-based labor legislation—the laws regulating women's hours, wages, and conditions of work—that women trade unionists and reformers had worked to establish over the past thirty years? The doctrine of "liberty of contract" between employer and employed had ruled court interpretations of labor legislation in the early twentieth century, stymying state regulation of the wages and hours of male workers. State regulation for women workers, espoused and furthered by many women in the NWP, had been made possible only by differentiating female from male wage-earners on

the basis of physiology and reproductive functions. Now members of the NWP had to grapple with the question whether such legislation was sex "discrimination," hampering women workers in the labor market. Initially, there was a great deal of sentiment within the NWP, even voiced by Alice Paul herself, that efforts at equal rights legislation should not impair existing sex-based protective labor legislation. However, there was also contrary opinion, which Paul increasingly heeded; by late November 1921 she had come to believe firmly that "enacting labor laws along sex lines is erecting another handicap for women in the economic struggle." Some NWP affiliates were still trying to draft an amendment that would preserve special labor legislation, nonetheless, and continued to introduce equal rights bills with "safeguards" in some states through the following spring.[5]

Meanwhile women leaders in other organizations were becoming nervous and distrustful of the NWP's intentions. Led by the League of Women Voters (successor to the NAWSA), major women's organizations in 1920 formed a national lobbying group called the Women's Joint Congressional Committee. The LWV was interested in eliminating sex discrimination in the law, but more immediately concerned with the extension of sex-based labor legislation. Moreover, the LWV had inherited NAWSA's hostility to Alice Paul. The first president of the LWV, Maud Wood Park, still smarted from the discomfiture that NWP picketing tactics had caused her when she headed the NAWSA's Congressional Committee from 1916 to 1920.[6] Other leading groups in the Women's Joint Congressional Committee were no less suspicious of the NWP. The National Women's Trade Union League since the mid-1910s had concentrated its efforts on labor legislation to protect women workers. Florence Kelley, director of the National Consumers' League, had been part of the inner circle of the NWP during the suffrage campaign, but on the question of protective labor laws her priorities diverged. She had spent three decades trying to get state regulation of workers' hours and conditions, and was not about to abandon the gains achieved for women.[7]

In December 1921, at Kelley's behest, Paul and three other NWP members met for discussion with her and leaders of the League of Women Voters, the National Women's Trade Union League, the Woman's Christian Temperance Union, and the General Federation of Women's Clubs. All the latter objected to the new constitutional amendment now formulated by the NWP: "No political, civil or legal disabilities or inequalities on account of sex, or on account of marriage unless applying alike to both sexes, shall exist within the United States or any place subject to their jurisdiction." Paul gave away no ground, and all left feeling that compromise was unlikely. Each side already thought the other intransigent, though in fact debate was still going on within the NWP.[8]

By mid-1922 the National Consumers' League, the LWV, and the Women's Trade Union League went on record opposing "blanket" equal rights bills, as the NWP formulations at both state and federal levels were called. About the same time, the tide turned in the NWP. The top leadership accepted as definitive the views of Gail Laughlin, a lawyer from Maine, who contended that sex-based labor legislation was not a lamented loss but a positive harm. "If women can be segregated as a class for special legislation," she warned, "the same classification can be used for special restrictions along any other line which may, at any time, appeal to the caprice or prejudice of our legislatures." In her opinion, if "protective" laws affecting women were not abolished and prohibited, "the advancement of women in business and industry will be stopped and women relegated to the lowest, worst paid labor."[9] Since NWP lobbyists working at the state level were making little headway, a federal constitutional amendment appeared all the more appealing. In November 1923, at a grand conference staged in Seneca Falls, New York, commemorating the seventy-fifth anniversary of Elizabeth Cady Stanton's Declaration of Sentiments, the NWP announced new language: "Men and women shall have equal rights throughout the United States and every place subject to its jurisdiction." The constitutional amendment was introduced into Congress on December 10, 1923.[10]

In the NWP view, this was the logical sequel to the 19th Amendment. There were so many different sex discriminations in state codes and legal practices—in family law, labor law, jury privileges, contract rights—that only a constitutional amendment seemed effective to remove them. The NWP took the language of liberal individualism, enshrined the catch-phrase of "equal rights," to express its feminism. As Alice Paul saw it, what women as a gender group shared was their subordination and inequality to men as a whole; the legal structure most clearly expressed this subordination and inequality, and therefore was the logical point of attack. The NWP construed this agenda as "purely feminist," that is, appealing to women as women, uniting women around a

concern common to them regardless of the other ways in which they might differ. Indeed, at its founding postsuffrage convention the NWP leadership purposely bypassed issues it saw as less "pure," including birth control, the defense of black women's voting rights in the South, and pacifism, which were predictably controversial among women themselves.

The NWP posited that women could and would perceive self-interest in "purely" gender terms. Faced by female opponents, its leaders imagined a fictive or abstract unity among women rather than attempt to encompass women's real diversity. They separated the proposal of equal rights from other social and political issues and effects. Although the campaign for equal rights was initiated in a vision of inclusiveness—envisioned as a stand that all women could take—it devolved into a practice of exclusiveness. The NWP's "appeal for conscious sex loyalty" (as a member once put it) went out to members of the sex who could subordinate identifications and loyalties of class, ethnicity, race, religion, politics, or whatever else to a "pure" sense of themselves as women differentiated from men. That meant principally women privileged by the dominant culture in every way except that they were female.[11]

In tandem with its lobbying for an equal rights amendment, the NWP presented its opposition to sex-based labor legislation as a positive program of "industrial equality." It championed women wage-earners who complained of "protective" legislation as restrictive, such as printers, railroad conductors, or waitresses hampered by hours limitation, or cleaning women fired and replaced by men after the passage of minimum-wage laws. Only a handful of working-class women rose to support for the ERA, however.[12] Mary Anderson, former factory worker herself and since 1919 the director of the U.S. Women's Bureau which was founded to guide and assist women workers, threw her weight into the fight against the amendment. Male trade unionists—namely leaders of the American Federation of Labor—also voiced immediate opposition to the NWP aims, appearing at the very first U.S. Senate subcommittee hearings on the equal rights amendment. Male unionists or class-conscious workers in this period put their faith in collective bargaining and did not seek labor legislation for themselves, but endorsed it for women and child workers. This differentiation derived partly from male workers' belief in women's physical weakness and veneration of women's "place" in the home, partly from presumptions about women workers being difficult to organize, and also from the aim to keep women from competing for men's jobs. Male unionists tended to view wage-earning women first as women—potential or actual wives and mothers—and only secondarily as workers. For differing reasons women and men in the labor movement converged in their support of sex-based legislation: women because they saw special protection necessary to defend their stake in industry and in union organizations, limited as it was; men to hold at bay women's demands for equal entry into male-controlled union jobs and organizations.[13]

The arguments against the equal rights amendment offered by trade unionists and by such women's organizations as the League of Women Voters overlapped. They assumed that an equal rights amendment would invalidate sex-based labor laws or, at least, destine them for protracted argument in the courts, where judges had shown hostility to any state regulation of employer prerogatives. They insisted that the greatest good for the greatest number was served by protective labor laws. If sex-based legislation hampered some—as the NWP claimed, and could be shown true, for instance, in the case of women linotypists, who needed to work at night—then the proper tactic was to exempt some occupations, not to eliminate protective laws whole. They feared that state welfare legislation in place, such as widows' pensions, would also be at risk. They contended that a constitutional amendment was too undiscriminating an instrument: objectionable sex discriminations such as those concerning jury duty, inheritance rights, nationality, or child custody would be more efficiently and accurately eliminated by specific bills for specific instances. Sometimes, opponents claimed that the ERA took an unnecessarily federal approach, overriding states' rights, although here they were hardly consistent for many of them were at the same time advocating a constitutional amendment to prohibit child labor.

Against the ERA, spokeswomen cited evidence that wage-earning women wanted and valued labor legislation and that male workers, too, benefitted from limits on women's hours in factories where men and women worked at interdependent tasks. Before hours were legally limited, "we were 'free' and 'equal' to work long hours for starvation wages, or free to leave the job and starve!" WTUL leader Pauline Newman bitterly recalled. Dr. Alice Hamilton, pioneer of industrial medicine, saw the NWP as maintaining "a purely negative program, . . . holding down in their present condi-

tion of industrial slavery hundreds of thousands of women without doing anything to alleviate their lot."[14] Trade-unionist and Women's Bureau colleagues attacked the NWP's vision as callously class-biased, the thoughtless outlook of rich women, at best relevant to the experience of exceptional skilled workers or professionals. They regularly accused the NWP of being the unwitting tool (at best) or the paid servant of rapacious employers, although no proof of the latter was ever brought forward. They heard in the NWP program the voice of the ruling class, and denounced the equal rights amendment as "class" legislation, by and for the bourgeoisie.[15]

Indeed, at the Women's Bureau Conference on Women in Industry in 1926, the NWP's opposition to sex-based labor legislation was echoed by the President of the National Association of Manufacturers, who declared that the "handful" of women in industry could take care of themselves, and were not served by legislative "poultices." In this controversy, the positions also lent themselves to, and inevitably were colored by, male "allies" whose principal concerns dealt less with women's economic or legal protection or advancement than political priorities of their own. At the same conference the U.S. Secretary of Labor appointed by President Coolidge took the side of sex-based protective legislation, proclaiming that "the place fixed for women by God and Nature is a great place," and "wherever we see women at work we must see them in terms of motherhood." What he saw as the great danger of the age was the "increasing loss of the distinction between manliness and true femininity."[16]

Often, ERA opponents who supported sex-based labor legislation—including civic-minded middle-class women, social welfare reformers, government officials, and trade union men—appeared more concerned with working women's motherhood than with economic justice. "Women who are wage earners, with one job in the factory and another in the home have little time and energy left to carry on the fight to better their economic status. They need the help of other women and they need labor laws," announced Mary Anderson. Dr. Hamilton declared that "the great inarticulate body of working women . . . are largely helpless, . . . [and] have very special needs which unaided they cannot attain. . . ."[17] Where NWP advocates saw before their eyes women who were eager and robust, supporters of protective legislation saw women overburdened and vulnerable. The former claimed that protective laws penalized the strong; the latter claimed that the

ERA would sacrifice the weak. The NWP looked at women as individuals, and wanted to dislodge gender differentiation from the labor market. Their opponents looked at women as members of families—daughters, wives, mothers, and widows with family responsibilities—and believed that the promise of "mere equality" did not sufficiently take those relationships into account. The one side tacitly positing the independent professional woman as the paradigm, the other presuming the doubly-burdened mother in industry or service; neither side distinguished nor addressed directly the situation of the fastest-growing sector of employed women, in white-collar jobs. At least half of the female labor force—those in manufacturing and in domestic and personal service—worked in taxing, menial jobs with long hours, unpleasant and often unhealthy conditions, very low pay, and rare opportunities for advancement. But in overall pattern women's employment was leaving these sectors and swelling in clerical, managerial, sales, and professional areas. In 1900, women in white-collar work constituted under 18 percent of all women employed. But by 1920 that proportion had doubled, and by 1930 was 44 percent.[18]

The relation of sex-based legislation to women workers' welfare was more ambiguous and complicated than either side acknowledged. Such laws immediately benefitted far larger numbers of employed women than they hindered, but the laws also had a negative impact on women's overall economic opportunities, both immediately and in the long term. Sex segregation of the labor market was a very significant factor. In industries monopolizing women workers, where wages, conditions, and hours were more likely to be substandard, protective legislation helped to bring things up to standard. It was in more desirable crafts and trades more unusual for women workers, where skill levels and pay were likely to be higher—that is, where women needed to enter in order to improve their earnings and economic advancement—that sex-based protective legislation held women back. There, as a contemporary inquiry into the issue said, "the practice of enacting laws covering women alone appears to discourage their employment, and therefore fosters the prejudice against them." The segregation of women into low-paid, dead-end jobs that made protective laws for women workers necessary, was thus abetted by the legislation itself.[19]

By 1925, all but four states limited working women's hours; eighteen states prescribed rest periods and meal hours; sixteen states prohibited night work in certain occupations; and thirteen had minimum wage regulations. Such regulation was passed not only because it served women workers, but also because employers, especially large corporate employers, began to see benefits in its stabilization of the labor market and control of unscrupulous competition. Although the National Association of Manufacturers, fixed on "liberty of contract," remained opposed, large employers of women accepted sex-based labor legislation on reasoning about "protection of the race," or could see advantages for themselves in it, or both. A vice-president of Filene's, a large department store in Boston, for instance, approved laws regulating the hours, wages, and conditions of women employees because "economies have been effected by the reduction of labor turnover; by reduction of the number of days lost through illness and accidents; and by increase in the efficiency of the working force as well as in the efficiency of management." He appreciated the legislation's maintaining standards as to hours, wages, and working conditions "throughout industry as a *whole,* thus preventing selfish interests from indulging in unfair competition by the exploitation of women. . . ."[20]

While the anti-ERA side was right in the utilitarian contention that protective laws meant the greatest good to the greatest number of women workers (at least in the short run), the pro-ERA side was also right that such laws hampered women's scope in the labor market and sustained the assumption that employment advantage was not of primary concern to women. Those who advocated sex-based laws were looking at the labor market as it was, trying to protect women in it, but thereby contributing to the perpetuation of existing inequalities. They envisaged wage-earning women as veritable beasts of burden. That group portrait supplanted the prior feminist image of wage-earning women as a vanguard of independent female personalities, as equal producers of the world's wealth. Its advocates did not see that their conception of women's needs helped to confirm women's second-class position in the economy. On the other hand, the ERA advocate who opposed sex-based "protections" were envisioning the labor market as it might be, trying to insure women the widest opportunities in that imagined arena, and thereby blinking at existing exploitation. They did not admit to the vulnerabilities that sex-based legislation addressed, while they overestimated what legal equality might do to unchain women from the economic stranglehold of the domestic stereotype.

Women on both sides of the controversy, however, saw themselves as legatees of suffragism and feminism, intending to defend the value of women's economic roles, to prevent economic exploitation of women, and to open the doors to economic opportunity. A struggle over the very word feminism, which the NWP had embraced, became part of the controversy. For "us even to use the word feminist," contended Women's Trade Union League leader Ethel Smith, "is to invite from the extremists a challenge to our authenticity." Detractors in the WTUL and Women's Bureau called the NWP "ultra" or "extreme" feminists. Mary Anderson considered herself "a good feminist" but objected that "over-articulate theorists were attempting to solve the working women's problems on a purely feministic basis with the working women's own voice far less adequately heard." Her own type of feminist was moderate and practical, Anderson declared; the others, putting the "woman question" above all other questions, were extreme and abstract. The bitterness was compounded by a conflict of personalities and tactics dragged on from the suffrage years. Opponents of the ERA, deeply resenting having to oppose something called equal rights, maligned the NWP as "pernicious," women who "discard[ed] all ethics and fair play," an "insane crowd" who espoused "a kind of hysterical feminism with a slogan for a program."[21] Their critiques fostered public perception of feminism as a sectarian and impracticable doctrine unrelated to real life and blind to injustices besides sex inequality. By the end of the 1920s women outside the NWP rarely made efforts to reclaim the term feminist for themselves, and the meaning of the term was depleted.

Forced into theorizing by this controversy, not prepared as philosophers or legal theorists, spokeswomen on either side in the 1920s were grappling with definitions of women's rights as compared to men's that neither the legal nor economic system was designed to accommodate. The question whether equality required women to have the same rights as men, or different rights, could not be answered without delving into definitions. Did "equality" pertain to opportunity, treatment, or outcome?[22] Should "difference" be construed to mean separation, discrimination, protection, privilege—or assault on the very standard that the male was the human norm?[23]

Opponents of the ERA believed that sex-based legislation was necessary because of women's biological and social roles as mothers. They claimed that "The inherent differences are perma-

nent. Women will always need many laws different from those needed by men"; "Women as such, whether or not they are mothers present or prospective, will always need protective legislation"; "The working mother is handicapped by her own nature."[24] Their approach stressed maternal nature and inclination as well as conditioning, and implied that the sexual division of labor was eternal.

The NWP's approach, on the other hand, presupposed that women's differentiation from men in the law and the labor market was a particular, social-historical, and not necessary or inevitable construction. The sexual division of labor arose from archaic custom, enshrined in employer and employee attitudes and written in the law. The NWP approach assumed that wives and mothers as well as unencumbered women would want and should have open access to jobs and professions. NWP proponents imagined that the sexual division of labor (in the family and the marketplace) would change, if women would secure the same rights as men and have free access to wage-earning. Their view made a fragile potential into a necessary fact. They assumed that women's wage-earning would, by its very existence, challenge the sexual division of labor, and that it would provide the means for women's economic independence—although neither of these tenets was necessarily being realized.

Wage-earning women's experience in the 1910s and 1920s, as documented by the Women's Bureau, showed that the sexual division of labor was budged only very selectively and marginally by women's gainful employment. Most women's wages did not bring them economic independence; women earned as part of a plan for family support (as men did, though that was rarely stressed). Contrary to the NWP's feminist visions, in those places in the nation where the highest proportions of wives and mothers worked for pay, the sexual division of labor was most oppressively in place. To every child growing up in the region of Southern textile and tobacco mills, where wives and mothers worked more "jobs" at home and in the factory than any other age or status group—and earned less—the sexual division of labor appeared no less prescriptive and burdensome than it had before women earned wages.[25]

Critiques of the NWP and its ERA as "abstract" or "extreme" or "fanatical" represented the gap between feminist tenets and harsh social reality as an oversight of the NWP, a failure to adjust their sights. Even more sympathetic critics, such as one Southern academic, asked rhetorically, "Do the feminists see in the tired and haggard faces of young waitresses, who spend seventy hours a week of hard work in exchange for a few dollars to pay for food and clothing, a deceptive mask of the noble spirit within?" She answered herself, "Surely it is not an increasing army of jaded girls and spent women that pours every day from factory and shop that the leaders of the feminist movement seek. But the call for women to make all labor their province can mean nothing more. They would free women from the rule of men only to make them greater slaves to the machines of industry."[26] Indeed, the exploitation of female service and industrial workers at "cheap" wages cruelly parodied the feminist notion that gainful employment represented an assertion of independence (just as the wifely duties required of a secretary parodied the feminist expectation that wage-earning would challenge the sexual division of labor and reopen definitions of femininity). What such critics were observing was the distance between the potential for women's wage-earning to challenge the sexual division of labor, and the social facts of gender and class hierarchy that clamped down on that challenge.

Defenders of sex-based protective legislation, trying to acknowledge women's unique reproductive endowments and social obligations, were grappling with problems so difficult they would still be present more than half a century later. Their immediate resolution was to portray women's "difference" in merely customary terms. "Average American women prefer to make a home for husbands and children to anything else," Mary Anderson asserted in defense of her position. "They would rather fulfill this normal function than go into the business world."[27] Keeping alive a critique of the class division of wealth, protective legislation advocates lost sight of the need to challenge the very sexual division of labor that was the root of women's "handicap" or "helplessness." As compared to the NWP's emphasis on the historical and social construction of gender roles, advocates of sex-based protective legislation echoed customary public opinion in proposing that motherhood and wage-earning should be mutually exclusive. They easily found allies among such social conservatives as the National Council of Catholic Women, whose representatives testified against the ERA because it "seriously menaced . . . the unity of the home and family life" and contravened the "essential differences in rights and duties" of the two sexes which were the "result of natural law." Edging into plain disapproval of mothers of young children who

earned, protective legislation supporters became more prescriptive, less flexible, than wage-earning mothers themselves, for whom cash recognition of their labor was very welcome. "Why should not a married woman work [for pay], if a single one does?" demanded a mill worker who came to the Southern Summer School for Women Workers. "What would men think if they were told that a married man should not work? If we women would not be so submissive and take everything for granted, if we would awake and stand up for our rights, this world would be a better place to live in, at least it would be better for the women. . . ."[28]

The onset of the Depression in many ways worsened the ERA controversy, for the one side thought protective legislation all the more crucial when need drove women to take any jobs available, and the other side argued that protective legislation prevented women from competing for what jobs there were. In the 1930s it became clear that the labor movement's and League of Women Voters' opposition to the equal rights amendment ran deeper than concern for sex-based legislation as an "entering wedge." The Fair Labor Standards Act of 1938 mandated wages and hours regulation for all workers, and the U.S. Supreme Court upheld it in 1941; but the labor movement and the LWV still opposed the ERA. Other major women's organizations, however—most importantly the National Federation of Business and Professional Women's Clubs and the General Federation of Women's Clubs—and the national platforms of both the Republican and the Democratic Party endorsed the ERA by 1944.[29]

We generally learn "winners'" history—not the history of lost causes. If the ERA passed by Congress in 1972 had achieved ratification by 1982, perhaps historians of women would read the trajectory of the women's movement from 1923 to the present as a steady upward curve, and award the NWP unqualified original insight. The failure of the ERA this time around (on new, but not unrelated grounds) compels us to see the longer history of equal rights in its true complexity.[30] The ERA battle of the 1920s seared into memory the fact of warring outlooks among women while it illustrated the inevitable intermeshing of women's legal and political rights with their economic situations. If the controversy testified to the difficulty of protecting women in the economic arena while opening opportunities to them, even more fundamentally the debate brought into question the NWP's premise that the articulation of sex discrimination—or the call for equal rights—would arouse all women to mobilize as a group. What kind of a group were women, when their occupational and social and other loyalties were varied, when not all women viewed "women's" interests, or what constituted sex "discrimination," the same way? The ideological dimensions of that problem cross-cut both class consciousness and gender identity. The debate's intensity, both then and now, measured how fundamental was the re-vision needed if policies and practices of economic and civic life deriving from a male norm were to give full scope to women—and to women of all sorts.

Notes

1. A good introduction to the issue of alliances in the 19th-century women's movement, and an essential text on the mid-19th-century split is Ellen Carol Dubois, *Feminism and Suffrage: The Emergence of an Independent Women's Movement, 1848-1869* (Ithaca, N.Y.: Cornell, 1978).

2. See Leslie Woodcock Tentler, *Wage-Earning Women: Industrial Work and Family Life in the U.S., 1900-1930* (N.Y.: Oxford, 1979), chapter 1, on industrially employed women's wages, keyed below subsistence.

3. On feminists in the final decade of the suffrage campaign, see Nancy F. Cott, *The Grounding of Modern Feminism* (New Haven: Yale, 1987), 23-66.

4. For more detailed discussion of the February 1921 convention, see Nancy F. Cott, "Feminist Politics in the 1920s: The National Women's Party," *Journal of American History*, 71:1 (June 1984).

5. Paul to Jane Norman Smith, Nov. 29, 1921, folder 110, J. N. Smith Coll., Schlesinger Library (hereafter SL). See NWP correspondence of Feb.-Mar. 1921 in the microfilm collection, "The National Woman's Party, 1913-1974" (Microfilm Corp. of America), reels #5-7 (hereafter NWP with reel#), and Cott, *Grounding*, 66-74, 120-25, for more detail.

   In Wisconsin, prominent NWP suffragist Mabel Raef Putnam put together a coalition which successfully lobbied through the first state equal rights bill early in 1921. This legislation granted women the same rights and privileges as men *except for* "the special protection and privileges which they now enjoy for the general welfare." See Edwin E. Witte, "History and Purposes of the Wisconsin Equal Rights Law," typescript, Dec. 1929, Mabel Raef Putnam Collection, SL; and Peter Geidel, "The National Women's Party and the Origins of the Equal Rights Amendment" (M.A. thesis, Columbia University, 1977), chapter 3.

6. Maud Wood Park, *Front Door Lobby*, ed. Edna Stantial (Boston: Beacon, 1960), 23.

7. Historians' treatments of women's organizations' differing views on the ERA in the 1920s include William N. O'Neill, *Everyone Was Brave* (Chicago: Quadrangle, 1969), 274-94; J. Stanley Lemons, *The Woman Citizen: Social Feminism in the 1920s* (Urbana: Univ. of Illinois, 1973), 184-99; William Chafe, *The American Woman: Her Changing Social, Economic and Political Roles* (N.Y.: Oxford, 1972), 112-32; Sheila M. Rothman, *Woman's Proper Place: A History of Changing Ideals and Practices,*

1870 to the Present (N.Y.: Basic, 1978), 153-65; Susan Becker, *Origins of the Equal Rights Amendment: American Feminism between the Wars* (Westport, Conn.: Greenwood, 1981), 121-51; Alice Kessler-Harris, *Out to Work: A History of Wage-Earning Women in the U.S.* (N.Y.: Oxford, 1982), 194-95, 205-12; Judith Sealander, *As Minority Becomes Majority* (Westport, Conn.: Greenwood, 1983). Fuller documentation of my reading of both sides can be found in Cott, *Grounding*, 122-29 and accompanying notes.

8. "Conference on So-called 'Equal Rights' Amendment Proposed by the National Women's Party Dec. 4, 1921," ts. NWTUL Papers, microfilm reel 2; "Conference Held December 4, 1921," ts., NWP #116; Kelley to Hill, Mar. 23, 1921, NWP #7; Ethel Smith to Members and Friends, Dec. 12, 1921, folder 378, Consumers League of Massachusetts Collection, SL.

9. NWP National Council minutes, Dec. 17, 1921, Feb. 14, 1922, Apr. 11, 1922, NWP #114. To the NWP inner circle Laughlin's point was borne out by a 1923 ruling in Wisconsin, where, despite the Equal Rights Bill, the attorney-general declined to strike down a 1905 law which prohibited women from being employed in the state legislature. He likened the prohibition to an hours-limitation law, because legislative service required "very long and often unreasonable hours." Alice Paul read his decision as "an extremely effective argument against" drafting equal rights bills with exemptions for sex-based protective legislation. Anita L. Pollitzer to Mrs. Jane Norman Smith, Jan. 5, 1922, folder 110, and Paul to Jane Norman Smith, Feb. 20, 1923, folder 111, Smith Coll.

10. National Council Minutes, June 19, 1923, NWP #114. Before 1923 the ERA went through scores of drafts, recorded in part F, NWP #116. Versions akin to the suffrage amendment—e.g. "Equal rights with men shall not be denied to women or abridged on account of sex or marriage . . ."—were considered in 1922, but not until 1943 was the amendment introduced into Congress in the form "Equality of rights under the law shall not be denied or abridged by the U.S. or by any state on account of sex," modeled on the 19th Amendment, which in turn was modeled on the 15th Amendment.

11. Quotation from Edith Houghton Hooker, Editor's Note, *Equal Rights* (the NWP monthly publication), Dec. 22, 1928, p. 365. See *Grounding*, 75-82.

12. The two most seen on NWP platforms were Josephine Casey, a former ILGWU organizer, suffrage activist, later a bookbinder, and Mary Murray, a Brooklyn Railway employee who had resigned from her union in 1920 to protest its acceptance of laws prohibiting night work for women.

13. Kessler-Harris, *Out to Work*, 200-05, and "Problems of Coalition-Building: Women and Trade Unions in the 1920s," in *Women, Work and Protest*, ed. Ruth Milkman (Boston: Routledge and Kegan Paul, 1985), esp. 132.

14. Pauline Newman, ts. debate with Heywood Broun, c. 1931, folder 130, Pauline Newman Coll., SL; Alice Hamilton to Alice Paul, May 7, 1926, folder 19, Alice Hamilton Coll., SL. More extensive documentation of the debate can be found in the notes in *Grounding*, 325-26.

15. Kessler-Harris, *Out to Work,* 189-94, reveals ambivalent assessments of labor legislation by ordinary wage-earning women.

16. Printed release from the National Association of Manufacturers, "Defend American Womanhood by Protecting their Homes, Edgerton Tells Women in Industry," Jan. 19, 1926, in folder 1118, and ts. speech by James Davis, U.S. Sec. of Labor, Jan. 18, 1926, in folder 1117, Box 71, Mary Van Kleeck Coll., Sophia Smith Collection, Smith College.

17. Mary Anderson, "Shall There Be Labor Laws for Women? Yes," *Good Housekeeping,* Sept. 1925, 16 (reprint, June 1927), folder 60, Mary Anderson Coll., SL; Alice Hamilton, "The Blanket Amendment—A Debate," *Forum,* 72 (Aug. 1924), 156.

18. See Oppenheimer, *Female Labor Force,* 3, 149; Lois Scharf, *To Work and to Wed* (Westport, Conn., 1981) 15-16; Winifred Wandersee, *Women's Work, and Family Values, 1920-1940* (Cambridge, Harvard, 1981) 85, 89.

19. Elizabeth F. Baker, "At the Crossroads in the Legal Protection of Women in Industry," *Annals of the American Academy of Political and Social Science,* 143 (May 1929), 277. Summary of protective legislation in 1925 in Edward Clark Lukens, "Shall Women Throw Away their Advantages," reprint from the *Amer. Bar Assoc. Journal,* Oct. 1925, folder 744, SL.

Recently historians have stressed the regressive potential of sex-based protective laws. See Rothman, *Woman's Proper Place,* 162-64; Nancy Schrom Dye, *As Equals and as Sisters: Feminism, Unionism and the Women's Trade Union League of New York* (Columbia, Missouri: Univ. of Missouri; 1980), 159-60; Olive Banks, *Faces of Feminism: A Study of Feminism as a Social Movement* (N.Y.: St. Martin's, 1981), 115; Judith A. Baer, *The Chains of Protection: The Judicial Response to Women's Labor Legislation* (Westport, Conn.: 1978), and Kessler-Harris, *Out to Work,* esp. 212.

20. T. K. Cory to Mary Wiggins, Nov. 10, 1922, folder 378, Consumer's League of Mass. Coll., SL. See n. 16, above.

21. Ethel M. Smith, "What is Sex Equality and What Are the Feminists Trying to Accomplish," *Century Monthly Magazine,* 118 (May 1929), 96; Mary Anderson, "Shall There Be Labor Laws for Women? Yes"; Alice Stone Blackwell to Carrie Chapman Catt, May 16, 1927, Catt Papers (Library of Congress), microfilm reel 2; Mary Anderson to Mrs. [Margaret Dreier] Robins, Feb. 4, 1926, folder 67, Mary Anderson Coll., SL; Mary Anderson, *Woman at Work: The Autobiography of Mary Anderson as told to Mary N. Winslow* (Minneapolis: Univ. of Minnesota, 1951), 168.

22. There is a valuable discussion of differing meanings for "equality" between the sexes in Jean Bethke Elshtain, "The Feminist Movement and the Question of Equality," *Polity* 7 (Summer 1975), 452-77.

23. This is, of course, the set of issues that has preoccupied feminist lawyers in the 1980s. For a sense of the recent debate, see, e.g., Wendy Williams, "The Equality Crisis: Some Reflections on Culture, Courts, and Feminism" *Women's Rights Law Reporter,* 7:3 (Spring 1982), 175-200; Nadine Taub, "Will Equality Require More than Assimilation, Accommodation or Separation from the Existing Social Structure?" *Rutgers Law Review,* 37 (1985), 825-44; Lucinda Finley, "Transcending Equality Theory: A Way Out of the Maternity and the Workplace Debate," *Columbia Law Review,* 86:6 (Oct.

1986), 1118-82; and Joan Willams, "Deconstructing Gender," *Michigan Law Review,* 87:4 (Feb. 1989), 797-845.

24. Florence Kelley, "Shall Women Be Equal before the Law?" (debate with Elsie Hill), *Nation,* 114 (Apr. 12, 1922), 421; NLWV pamphlet [1922], 10, in folder 744, Woman's Rights Collection, SL; Alice Hamilton, "The Blanket Amendment—A Debate," *Forum,* 72 (Aug. 1924), 156; Florence Kelley, "The New Woman's Party," *Survey,* 47 (Mar. 5, 1921), 828.

25. Dolores Janiewski, *Sisterhood Denied: Race, Gender and Class in a New South Community* (Phila.: Temple, 1985), 30-32, 127-50; Table 26 (134) shows less than 40% of Durham women above age 12 engaged only in unpaid housework.

26. Guion G. Johnson, "Feminism and the Economic Independence of Woman," *Journal of Social Forces,* 3 (May 4, 1925), 615; cf. Tentler, *Wage-Earning Women,* esp. 25, 45-46, and Wandersee, *Women's Work,* on motivations and psychological results of women's wage-earning.

27. Mary Anderson quoted in unidentified newspaper clipping, Nov. 25, 1925, in folder 349, Bureau of Vocational Information Collection, SL. Cf. Ethel Smith's objection that the NWP's feminism required that "men and women must have exactly the same things, and be treated in all respects as if they were alike," as distinguished from her own view that "men and women must each have the things best suited to their respective needs, which are not all the time, nor in all things, alike." Ethel M. Smith, "What Is Sex Equality . . . ?," 96.

28. National Council of Catholic Women testimony at U.S. Congress (House of Representatives) subcommittee of Committee on the Judiciary, hearings, 1925, quoted in Robin Whittemore, "Equality vs. Protection: Debate on the Equal Rights Amendment, 1923-1937" (M.A. thesis, Boston Univ., 1981), 19; mill worker quoted in Mary Frederickson, "The Southern Summer School for Women Workers," *Southern Exposure,* 4 (Winter 1977), 73. See also Maurine Greenwald, "Working-Class Feminism and the Family Wage Ideal: The Seattle Debate on Married Women's Right to Work, 1914-1920," *Journal of American History,* 76:1 (June 1989), 118-49.

29. For the history of the NWP in the 1930s and 1940s see Becker, *Origins of the Equal Rights Amendment.* On the initiatives of the National Federation of Business and Professional Women's Clubs and other groups to forward the equal rights amendment, see Lemons, *Woman Citizen,* 202-04, and the papers of Lena Madesin Phillips and Florence Kitchelt at SL.

30. Jane L. Mansbridge's astute analysis, *Why We Lost the ERA* (Chicago: Univ. of Chicago, 1986) is essential reading on the failed 1970s campaign for ratification.

FURTHER READING

Criticism

Becker, Susan D. *The Origins of the Equal Rights Amendment: American Feminism between the Wars,* Westport, Conn.: Greenwood Press, 1981, 300 p.

Examines the various efforts of feminist organizations to bring about legal changes for women between the two wars.

Buechler, Steven M. *The Concise History of Woman Suffrage: Selections from the Classic Work of Stanton, Anthony, Gage, and Harper,* Urbana: University of Illinois Press, 1978, 468 p.

Introduces and presents writings of several representatives of the suffrage movement.

————. *The Transformation of the Woman Suffrage Movement: The Case of Illinois, 1850-1920,* New Brunswick, N.J.: Rutgers University Press, 1986, 258 p.

Examines the history of the suffrage movement in Illinois for the light it sheds on the national movement.

Burt, Elizabeth V. "The Ideology, Rhetoric, and Organizational Structure of a Countermovement Publication: The Remonstrance, 1890-1920." *Journalism & Mass Communication Quarterly* 75, no. 1 (spring 1998): 69-83.

Analyzes the style and ideology of this anti-suffrage journal.

Cott, Nancy F. *The Grounding of Modern Feminism,* New Haven, Conn.: Yale University Press, 1987, 372 p.

Explores the theoretical and practical underpinnings of modern feminism, including ideas on suffrage.

Crawford, ed., Elizabeth. *The Women's Suffrage Movement: A Reference Guide,* London, England: UCL Press, 1999, 785 p.

Research and bibliographic guide.

Eustance, Claire Joan Ryan, and Laura Ugolini, eds. *A Suffrage Reader: Charting Directions in British Suffrage History,* London and New York, England and N.Y.: Leicester University Press, 2000, 214 p.

Collection of recent essays on issues related to the history of suffrage.

Flexner, Eleanor. *Century of Struggle: The Women's Rights Movement in the United States,* Cambridge, Mass.: Harvard University Press, 1975, 405 p.

Provides history of women's rights and suffrage.

Frost, Elizabeth and Kathryn Cullen-DuPont. *Women's Suffrage in America: An Eyewitness History,* New York: Facts on File, 1992, 452 p.

Overview of the suffrage movement from 1800 to 1920, incorporating many primary source documents.

Hannam, June Mitzi Auchterlonie, and Katherine Holden. *The International Encyclopedia of Women's Suffrage,* Santa Barbara, Cal.: ABC-CLIO, 2000, 380 p.

Comprehensive reference source for the suffrage movement.

Harris, Barbara and JoAnn K. McNamara, eds. *Women and the Structure of Society: Selected Research from the Fifth Berkshire Conference on the History of Women,* Durham, N.C.: Duke University Press, 1984, 305 p.

Collection of essays on the history of suffrage, focusing on women working within and changing social structures.

Harrison, Patricia Greenwood. *Connecting Links: The British and American Woman Suffrage Movement,* Westport, Conn.: Greenwood Press, 2000, 281 p.

Discusses connections between and parallel events in the British and American suffrage movements.

Irwin, Inez Hayes. *The Story of Alice Paul and the National Women's Party,* Fairfax, Va.: Denlinger's Publishers, Ltd., 1964, 512 p.

Biography of Alice Paul written by a colleague from the suffrage movement.

Howard, Angela and Sasha Ranae Adams Tarrant, eds. *Opposition to the Women's Movement in the United States, 1848-1929,* New York: Garland, 1997, 379 p.

Collection of essays and primary sources on the opposition to the suffrage movement.

Joannou, Maroula and June Purvis, eds. *The Women's Suffrage Movement: New Feminist Perspectives,* Manchester, England: Manchester University Press, 1998, 227 p.

Collection of recent essays on suffrage.

Jorgensen-Earp, ed., Cheryl R. *Speeches and Trials of the Militant Suffragettes,* Madison and Teaneck, N.J.: Fairleigh Dickinson University Press, 1999, 399 p.

Anthology of speeches and trial documents related to various members of the suffrage movement.

Klasko, George and Margaret G. Klosko, eds. *The Struggle for Women's Rights: Theoretical and Historical Sources,* Upper Saddle River, N.J.: Prentice Hall, 1999, 285 p.

Collection of sources relating to suffrage.

Kraditor, Aileen S. *Ideas of the Woman Suffrage Movement 1890-1923,* New York, N.Y.: Columbia University Press, 1965, 313 p.

Discusses the theoretical, philosophical, political, and social ideas of the suffrage movement.

Law, Cheryl. *Suffrage and Power: The Women's Movement 1918-1925,* London, England: I. B. Tauris, 1997, 260 p.

Examines feminism and suffrage in relation to power shifts in society.

Marshall, Susan E. *Splintered Sisterhood: Gender and Class in the Campaign against Woman Suffrage,* Madison: University of Wisconsin Press, 1997, 347 p.

Explores the handling of gender and class by the suffrage movement.

McKenzie, Midge. *Shoulder to Shoulder,* New York: Knopf, 1975, 338 p.

Popular historical overview of the suffrage movement.

Milford, Wendy. "Socialist-Feminist Criticism: A Case Study, Women's Suffrage and Literature, 1906-14." In *Re-Reading English,* edited by Peter Widdowson, pp. 179-92. London, England: Methuen, 1982.

Examines Elizabeth Robins's novel The Convert *and the work of the Women Writers Suffrage League.*

Neuman, Nancy M., ed. *A Voice of Our Own: Leading American Women Celebrate the Right to Vote,* San Francisco, Cal.: Jossey-Bass Publishers, 1996, 265 p.

Collection of essays on women's right to vote by such figures as Rosalynn Carter, Betty Ford, Bernardine Healy, Donna Shalala, Hillary Rodham Clinton, and Condoleezza Rice.

Pugh, Martin. *The March of Women: A Revisionist Analysis of the Campaign for Women's Suffrage 1866-1914,* Oxford, England: Oxford University Press, 2000, 303 p.

History of the progress of suffrage in England, noting influences on the movement.

Purvis, June and Sandra Stanley Holton, eds. *Votes for Women,* London, England: Routledge, 2000, 297 p.

Collection of new essays on various aspects of the suffrage movement.

Shulman, Alix. *To the Barricades: The Anarchist Life of Emma Goldman,* New York: Thomas Y. Crowell Company, 1971, 255 p.

Biography of the noted anarchist reformer and feminist.

Terborg-Penn, Rosalyn. *African American Women in the Struggle for the Vote, 1850-1920,* Bloomington: Indiana University Press, 1998, 192 p.

Explores the treatment of race by the suffrage movement as well the role played by African American women in the campaign for women's right to vote.

Ticknor, Lisa. *The Spectacle of Woman: Imagery of the Suffrage Campaign, 1907-1914,* Chicago, Ill.: University of Chicago Press, 1988, 334 p.

Examines how suffragists used visual imagery to emphasize and promote their ideas during public gatherings and in the press.

Van Voris, Jacqueline. *Carrie Chapman Catt: A Public Life,* New York: The Feminist Press, 1987, 307 p.

Biography of Carrie Chapman Catt focusing on her political work.

Ware, Susan. *Modern American Women: A Documentary History,* second edition, Boston, Mass.: McGraw-Hill, 2002, 468 p.

Contains several chapters on aspects of suffrage through the winning of the vote.

WOMEN'S LITERATURE FROM 1900 TO 1960

The early decades of the twentieth century were filled with dramatic turmoil and change within United States and abroad, all of which impacted the nascent feminist movement. Two world wars, rapid industrialization, urbanization, and a depression placed enormous stress on traditional social structures and domestic relationships, from the workplace to the family. In fact, more women entered the professional workforce during the first two decades of the century than at any other time in history. Though American women were granted suffrage in 1920, these were difficult times for the feminist movement. The issue of suffrage had united many women around a common cause, but once women gained the right to vote, the movement suffered from conflict and lack of formal organization. The militant nature of many suffragists also caused the movement to lose momentum in mainstream society, and for many years feminists were viewed as an extremist minority.

Despite the success of the suffrage movement and the great influx of women into the workplace before and during World War II, a resurgence of traditional attitudes concerning the home and family would come to define the postwar period. As many feminists argue, the wars served to both empower and suppress women, whose newfound freedom and independence during the world wars was almost immediately ceded to a newly reestablished sense of patriarchy. Women who had sup-

ported the war effort through their labor returned home and were once again relegated to domestic duties and secondary status. Such restricted gender roles, exemplified by the conformity and traditionalism of the 1950s, continued to limit the opportunities and experiences of women until the rebirth of the feminist movement during the late 1960s and 1970s.

Amid such conflicts and evolving gender roles, the first half of the twentieth century witnessed a flourishing in the literary arts and the development of new media such as radio, film, and, by the late 1940s, television. American drama in particular reached a high point in the 1920s, with dramatists Eugene O'Neill, Elmer Rice, and Maxwell Anderson writing many of their best works during this decade. Meanwhile, poets such as Amy Lowell, H. D., and Sara Teasdale elaborated upon the prewar modernism pioneered by T. S. Eliot, W. B. Yeats, Wallace Stevens, and Ezra Pound. By the late 1950s, however, celebrated poets such as Sylvia Plath and Anne Sexton would lead a turn away from formal detachment toward a more emotion-laden subjectivity in confessionalism. During the first half of the twentieth century many male and female authors also turned to the novel to sketch and satirize the materialism and anomie of the modern condition. Important novelists of the period include Theodore Dreiser, F. Scott Fitzgerald, and Ernest Hemingway, along with well-known female novelists Edith Wharton, Katherine Anne Porter, and Gertrude Stein, whose experimentalism defied classification.

A growing number of women writers from diverse racial and ethnic backgrounds also emerged during this time. Drawing upon their varied experiences as Asians, Africans, and Native Americans, many of these female writers addressed issues of gender and ethnic identity from new and compelling perspectives. Together, such women provided insight into the lives of women in general and the often denigrated minority populations of which they were a part. In particular, African-American writers came to prominence as part of the literary and artistic movement known as the Harlem Renaissance, which reached its peak during the 1920s and 1930s. This movement provided opportunities for many African-American women writers, including Zora Neale Hurston, Nella Larsen, and Jessie Redmon Fauset, to address issues of race and gender in their works. Such writers also gained appreciation for their declaration of cultural independence and their contribution to the development of an indigenous American language and literature.

While women writers and artists participated in the thriving arts and literary movements during these years, many of them struggled deeply as creators. The world wars had a profound effect on the generation of writers that witnessed them, particularly women who bore the brunt of the social and cultural changes that resulted from these conflicts. Caught between their own aspirations as writers and artists, but confronted with a reality that provided little in terms of equal opportunity or rights, many female authors felt frustrated during these years. In addition, female literary achievement was largely downplayed in academic institutions due to the negative backlash against the suffragists and, more broadly, because of a patronizing and dismissive view of female intellectuals among male cultural elites.

Contemporary critic Elaine Showalter has drawn attention to the conflict, repression, and even decline suffered by many women writers during the early twentieth century. According to Showalter and other scholars, the years following the end of World War I were difficult for female novelists and poets in particular, who were regarded as writers of little substance. Yearning to write about serious issues facing their times but pushed to the periphery, poets such as Teasdale, H. D., Lowell, and Edna St. Vincent Millay were unable to find suitable literary models in past female poets. Additionally, the notion of poetry as an art form that transcends personal and emotional experience, a view expounded by male poets such as Eliot and Pound, led many female poets to feel that their work was being marginalized. Faced with stiff reaction against the type of personal and lyrical poetry many of them wanted to write, Millay and others found it increasingly difficult to continue writing. Some female writers curtailed their creative work and turned their energies to political causes instead, using alternate means such as journalism and reporting to express their opinions. Some writers found ways to incorporate political activism in their fiction and established a model for women writers of the 1960s and beyond.

REPRESENTATIVE WORKS

Jane Addams
Twenty Years at Hull House (essays) 1910

Simone de Beauvoir
L'invitée [*She Came to Stay*] (novel) 1943

Le deuxième sexe. 2 vols. [*The Second Sex*] (nonfiction) 1949

Tous les hommes sont mortels [*All Men Are Mortal*] (novel) 1946

Gwendolyn Bennett
"To a Dark Girl" (poem) 1923

"Fantasy" (poem) 1927

Elizabeth Bishop
"Roosters" (poem) 1946

Louise Bogan
The Blue Estuaries (poetry) 1923

Body of this Death (poetry) 1923

Sleeping Fury (poetry) 1937

Elizabeth Bowen
The House in Paris (novel) 1935

"The Demon Lover" (short story) 1945

Kay Boyle
American Citizen Naturalized in Leadville, Colorado (poetry) 1944

"Winter Night" (poem) 1946

Gwendolyn Brooks
A Street in Bronzeville (poetry) 1945

Annie Allen (poetry) 1949

Pearl S. Buck
The Good Earth (novel) 1931

Willa Cather
My Ántonia (novel) 1918

One of Ours (novel) 1922

Death Comes for the Archbishop (novel) 1927

Not under Forty (essays) 1936

Kate Chopin
The Awakening (novella) 1906

Rachel Crothers
The Three of Us (play) 1906

A Man's World (play) 1909

When Ladies Meet (play) 1932

Susan and God (play) 1937

Isak Dinesen
Seven Gothic Tales (short stories) 1934

Den Afrikanse Farm [*Out of Africa*] (autobiographical novel) 1937

Hilda Doolittle (H. D.)
Tribute to the Angels (poetry) 1945

"May 1943" (poem) 1950

Helen in Egypt (poetry and prose) 1961

Jessie Redmon Fauset
There is Confusion (novel) 1924

Plum Bun (novel) 1928

The Chinaberry Tree (novel) 1931

Zona Gale
Mothers to Men (short stories) 1911

Miss Lulu Bett (novel; also adapted as play) 1920

Charlotte Perkins Gilman
"The Yellow Wallpaper" (novella) 1892

Women and Economics (nonfiction) 1898

Something to Vote For (play) 1911

Herland (novel) 1915

Susan Glaspell
Suppressed Desires (play) 1915

Trifles (play) 1916

Bernice (play) 1919

Alison's House (play) 1930

Shirley Graham
It's Morning (play) 1940

Angelina Weld Grimké
Rachel (play) 1916

Lillian Hellman
The Children's Hour (play) 1934

Days to Come (play) 1936

The Little Foxes (play) 1939

Watch on the Rhine (play) 1941

Elizabeth Jane Howard
The Long View (novel) 1956

Zora Neale Hurston
"How It Feels to Be Colored Me" (essay) 1928

Mules and Men (folklore) 1935

Their Eyes Were Watching God (novel) 1937

Dust Tracks on a Road (autobiography) 1942

Georgia Douglas Johnson
Safe (play) 1929

Nella Larsen
Quicksand (novel) 1928

Passing (novel) 1929

Doris Lessing
Martha Quest (novel) 1952

Amy Lowell
A Dome of Many-Coloured Glass (poetry) 1912

Pictures of the Floating World (poetry) 1919

Ballads for Sale (poetry) 1927

Edna St. Vincent Millay
A Few Figs from Thistles (poetry) 1920

Make Bright the Arrows: 1940 Notebook (poetry) 1940

Murder of Lidice (ballad) 1942

Margaret Mitchell
Gone with the Wind (novel) 1936

Marianne Moore
Poems (poetry) 1924; also published as *Observations*, 1924

"In Distrust of Merits" (poem) 1943

Predilections (essays and criticism) 1955

Mollie Panter-Downes
One Fine Day (novel) 1946

Sylvia Plath
The Colossus (poetry) 1960

Katherine Anne Porter
The Ship of Fools (novel) 1927

Adrienne Rich
Change of World (poetry) 1951

The Diamond Cutters, and Other Poems (poetry) 1955

Muriel Rukeyser
Wake Island (poetry) 1942

Letter to the Front (poem) 1944

Edith Sitwell
Lullaby (poetry) 1942

Serenade: Any Man to Any Woman (poetry) 1942

Gertrude Stein
Tender Buttons: Objects, Food, Rooms (poetry) 1914

The Autobiography of Alice B. Toklas (memoir) 1933

Elizabeth Taylor
At Mrs. Lippincote's (novel) 1945

Sara Teasdale
Helen of Troy, and Other Poems (poetry) 1911

Rivers to the Sea (poetry) 1915

A Country House (poetry) 1932

Edith Wharton
House of Mirth (novel) 1905

Tales of Men and Ghosts (short stories) 1910

Ethan Frome (novella) 1911

The Age of Innocence (novel) 1920

Virginia Woolf
Mrs. Dalloway (novel) 1925

A Room of One's Own (essay) 1929

Three Guineas (essay) 1938

Elinor Wylie
Nets to Catch the Wind (poetry) 1921

"Jewelled Bindings" (essay) 1923

PRIMARY SOURCES

AMY LOWELL (POEM DATE 1914)

SOURCE: Lowell, Amy. "The Captured Goddess." In *Sword Blades and Poppy Seed*. New York: Macmillan, 1914.

In the following poem, the narrator evokes a figure of divinity and mystical experience through descriptions of flowers, colors, and stones, but then withdraws in shock as the goddess figure is bound by men and offered for sale in the marketplace.

"THE CAPTURED GODDESS"

Over the housetops
Above the rotating chimney-pots,
I have seen a shiver of amethyst,
And blue and cinnamon have flickered
A moment,
At the far end of a dusty street.

Through sheeted rain
Has come a lustre of crimson,
And I have watched moonbeams
Hushed by a film of palest green.

It was her wings,
Goddess!
Who stepped over the clouds,
And laid her rainbow feathers
Aslant on the currents of the air.

I followed her for long,
With gazing eyes and stumbling feet.
I cared not where she led me,
My eyes were full of colours:
Saffrons, rubies, the yellows of beryls,
And the indigo-blue of quartz;
Flights of rose, layers of chrysoprase,
Points of orange, spirals of vermilion,
The spotted gold of tiger-lily petals,
The loud pink of bursting hydrangeas.
I followed,
And watched for the flashing of her wings.

In the city I found her,
The narrow-streeted city.
In the market-place I came upon her,
Bound and trembling.
Her fluted wings were fastened to her sides with
    cords,
She was naked and cold,
For that day the wind blew
Without sunshine.

Men chaffered for her,
They bargained in silver and gold,
In copper, in wheat,
And called their bids across the market-place.

The Goddess wept.
Hiding my face I fled,
And the grey wind hissed behind me,
Along the narrow streets.

SARA TEASDALE (POEM DATE 1919)

SOURCE: Teasdale, Sara. "If Death Is Kind." In *Flame and Shadow*. New York: Macmillan, 1920.

In the following poem, originally written in 1919, the speaker ruminates on the subject of death and the afterlife.

Perhaps if Death is kind, and there can be
    returning,
    We will come back to earth some fragrant
    night,

And take these lanes to find the sea, and bend-
　　ing
Breathe the same honeysuckle, low and white.

We will come down at night to these resounding
　　beaches
And the long gentle thunder of the sea,
Here for a single hour in the wide starlight
We shall be happy, for the dead are free.

LOUISE BOGAN (POEM DATE FEBRUARY 1922)

SOURCE: Bogan, Louise. "Women." *The Blue Estuaries: Poems 1923-1968,* New York: Farrar, Straus and Giroux, 1968.

The following is a well-known poem by author Louise Bogan originally published in 1922.

"WOMEN"

Women have no wilderness in them,
They are provident instead,
Content in the tight hot cell of their hearts
To eat dusty bread.

They do not see cattle cropping red winter grass,
They do not hear
Snow water going down under culverts
Shallow and clear.

They wait, when they should turn to journeys,
They stiffen, when they should bend.
They use against themselves that benevolence
To which no man is friend.

They cannot think of so many crops to a field
Or of clean wood cleft by an axe.
Their love is an eager meaninglessness
Too tense, or too lax.

They hear in every whisper that speaks to them
A shout and a cry.
As like as not, when they take life over their
　　door-sills
They should let it go by.

MARIA CHONA (ESSAY DATE 1936)

SOURCE: Chona, Maria. "The Autobiography of a Papago Woman," edited by Ruth Underhill. *Memoirs of the American Anthropological Association* 46 (1936): 36-7.

Chona was born in Mesquite Root, a Papago village in the Spanish province of Upper Pimeria, now Arizona. Daughter to Con Quien, a village governor, Chona was a noted basketweaver and medicine woman, and possessed extensive knowledge of tribal affairs, customs, and traditions. The following excerpt is from chapter six in her autobiographical account of her life.

VI

My father said to me: "Look, my girl. We are going to marry you, over at that house."

ON THE SUBJECT OF...

ISAK DINESEN (1885-1962)

Born Karen Christentze Dinesen in 1885 in Rungsted, Denmark, Isak Dinesen was an author acclaimed for her poetic prose style, complex characters, and intricate plots. She is best known for *Seven Gothic Tales* (1934)—a collection of short stories written in a romantic style and employing fantasy to explore aristocratic sensibilities and values—and the autobiographical novel *Den afrikanske farm* (1937; *Out of Africa*). Dinesen studied English at Oxford University and painting at the Royal Academies in Copenhagen, Paris, and Rome. Following her marriage to Baron Bror Blixen-Finecke in 1914, Dinesen moved to East Africa as the owner and manager of a coffee plantation near present-day Nairobi, Kenya. After the death of her lover Denys Finch-Hatton and the eventual sale of her farm in 1931, Dinesen returned to Denmark. *Out of Africa* presents Dinesen's experiences as a British East African coffee plantation owner, her relationship with the Africans who lived and worked on and around her plantation, her divorce from Blixen, her affair with Finch-Hatton, and the ultimate failure of her coffee enterprise. Dinesen became a founding member of the Danish Academy in 1960 and died in Rungsted in 1962. Dinesen's views on feminism and women's issues are related in her posthumously-published works, such as *Breve fra Afrika 1914-31* (1978; *Letters from Africa: 1914-1931*), a collection of her correspondence, and *Daguerreotypes, and Other Essays* (1979).

He did not say the boy's name out of modesty, just motioned with his lips eastward down the valley. The place he meant was Where the Water Whirls Around, where I went with my clay jars every time our pond went dry. I knew every house there and the people in them. I knew who the marriageable young man was. It was the medicine man's son. I had never spoken to him; I had never spoken to any young men except relatives and of course we do not marry relatives. But my breasts

ON THE SUBJECT OF...

AMY LOWELL (1874-1925)

Amy Lowell is remembered for her forceful theorizing on poetics, her eccentric, outspoken personality, and her iconoclastic approach to poetic form. Although she was Ezra Pound's successor as chief advocate of Imagism—a movement that stressed clarity and succinctness in presenting the poetic image—Lowell is herself generally categorized as a minor, though versatile, poet, whose work displays occasional bursts of brilliance. Influenced in both style and theme by her studies of Far Eastern verse, she also sought to liberate poetry from the strictures of meter, using as her vehicles free verse, polyphonic prose, and haiku. Lowell was born in 1874 into the socially prominent, affluent Lowell family of Boston, Massachusetts. In later years, the proper, conservative values Lowell acquired in her youth clashed with her naturally independent and domineering personality, creating an unresolved conflict that is reflected in her life and work. In her late twenties Lowell decided to become a poet. In 1913 she met Pound and immediately embraced Imagism, a style she first employed in her collection *Sword Blades and Poppy Seed* (1914). With this widely acclaimed work, Lowell moved to the forefront of American poetry, a position from which she lent support to other writers, among them D. H. Lawrence. During the next decade, she wrote several books of criticism and over six hundred poems, edited three Imagist anthologies, and became a popular speaker at American universities. Accompanying Lowell during her last years was Ada Russell, a former actress who became Lowell's secretary, close friend and inspiration for several love poems. Lowell died in 1925, shortly after completing *John Keats,* a biography of the poet whom she saw as her greatest influence. *What's O'Clock,* a collection of what is viewed as the best of Lowell's late work, was posthumously published and awarded the Pulitzer Prize for poetry in 1926.

were getting large, now. That is how we know when a girl should marry. "They ought to be used for something," we say.

So my father and mother had been consulting. It must have been when I was asleep at night for I had not heard them. They had decided on a man to ask and then my father had sent my mother to tell my aunts and uncles about it. They all approved. They had not told the boy yet. That is done last of all. But of course no man would refuse, even if he already had a first wife. It would not be polite.

My father went on talking to me in a low voice. That is how our people always talk to their children, so low and quiet the child thinks he is dreaming it. But he never forgets.

"We want you to behave yourself as we have always taught you to. Stay there in the right way. Don't wait for your mother-in-law to tell you what to do. Get up early, find wheat, grind flour. If you can't make tortillas, have flour ready for her to make them. You stay right there and make your home there. It has been here, but now you belong there. Stay home, don't run around. Do your work, carry the wood, cook something, whatever there is. Any work you see, you do it.

"Don't go off to people's houses and walk around and gossip. Gossip may spoil a good home. That husband of yours, listen to him. Don't talk when he's talking, for he is like a chief to you. Don't beg him to take you with him here and there, but if he wants you to go, go whether you feel like it or not. Don't one day get mad at your mother-in-law or father-in-law. Don't think you can get mad and run home. A day will come when your husband will want to visit us and will bring you. Now that's your home and if good luck is with you, you will grow old and die there. This is the way it is. Now I'm going over to tell the boy's father and mother."

So my father went to those peoples' house, down Where the Water Whirls Around.

"Your son is industrious and I have an industrious daughter. Shall we marry them?"

No one can say anything but yes to such a question. If they really thought the girl was lazy and bad, they would try to be away from home. But they were very distant relatives and, of course, someone had told them what was being talked about. They said: "Very well."

My father told them: "I'm going to see that my daughter behaves herself. You watch her, too, and make sure that she follows my training." They said: "That is what we feel about our son. We have talked to him long enough; he should know his duty. See that he follows it and so will we."

So they sent the boy to our house so that in my first nights with a man I could have my mother near. Before he came, my mother said: "If he wants anything, don't be afraid of him. That's why we are having you marry."

But I was very much afraid. I did not go and hide in the granary basket, the way one of my friends did. That was Rustling Leaves, but she was being married to an old medicine man who had her three sisters as wives already. My husband was a boy, not much older than I and he had no other wives. Only, when I thought of him, fear ran through me like a snake. He used to come to our house after dark, because it would not be modest for him to sit and eat with our family by daylight. And when morning stood up he went away. That's how I was married.

OVERVIEWS

ELAINE SHOWALTER (ESSAY DATE 1991)

SOURCE: Showalter, Elaine. "The Other Lost Generation." In *Sister's Choice: Tradition and Change in American Women's Writing*, pp. 104-26. Oxford: Clarendon Press, 1991.

In the following essay, Showalter discusses the difficulties faced by women writers in the 1920s and 1930s, notably postwar hostility toward the women's movement, negative reactions against women in academia, and the secondary domestic and social roles relegated to women that marginalized female artists.

'I never was a member of a "lost generation,"' the poet Louise Bogan wrote to her friend Morton Zabel in the 1930s, trying to account for the problems she was facing in her career.[1] Bogan meant that she had not belonged to the famous group of literary pilgrims who fled the United States in disillusionment after World War I, to cultivate their Muse in London or Montparnasse. Yet in another, and more important sense, Bogan and her female contemporaries *were* members of a generation lost to literary history and to each other. For—despite the presence of Edith Wharton, Gertrude Stein, Katherine Anne Porter, and other women—the post-war literary movement that we have come to call the Lost Generation was in fact a community of men. In the 1920s, according to the critic John Aldridge, 'the young men came to Paris. With their wives and children,

cats and typewriters, they settled in flats and studios along the Left Bank and in the Latin Quarter.'[2] Functional and anonymous as typewriters to male literary historians, the wives of the expatriates were none the less often ambitious writers themselves. Their marginalization, moreover, paralleled the dilemma of other American women writers who stayed at home. While the 'lost generation' of Ernest Hemingway and F. Scott Fitzgerald became literary legend, another generation of American women writers suffered a period of conflict, repression, and decline.

For the literary women who came of age in the 1920s, the post-war hostility to women's aspirations, the shift from the feminist to the flapper as the womanly ideal, and especially the reaction against the feminine voice in American literature in the colleges and the professional associations made this decade extraordinarily and perhaps uniquely difficult. American society's expectations of modern womanhood were strikingly at odds with its image of artistic achievement. Women writers who had established their careers in the earlier part of the century found themselves out of touch with the new ideals; as Willa Cather would later remember, 'the world broke in two in 1922 or thereabouts;'[3] and for many women of her older generation it was impossible to cross the divide.

In order to understand the problems of American women writers in the 1920s and 1930s, we must also look at what was happening to American women generally during this period. First we need to look at the feminist crash of the 1920s—the unexpected disintegration of the women's movement after the passage of the Nineteenth Amendment. The 1920s were feminism's awkward age. The political coalitions of the suffrage campaign had dissolved into bitter and warring factions. While the suffragists had prophesied that an enfranchised female electorate would bring sweeping social reform to the United States, they were grievously disappointed when women did not press *en masse* for an end to war, prostitution, and poverty. To many feminists, moreover, Democratic and Republican party politics seemed crude, boorish, and mundane after the heightened utopian rhetoric and ennobling sense of sisterly mission conferred by suffrage activism. By the mid-1920s, it was widely acknowledged that the women's vote had failed to materialize. Women did not seem able to deliver a united vote that would give them power at the polls; instead they voted like their fathers and husbands, or simply stayed at home. Even one of the new female politicians, Democratic committeewoman Emily Newell Blair, acknowledged that the ballot had not brought women either power or political solidarity: 'I know of no woman today who has any influence or political power because she is a woman. I know of no woman who has a following of other women. I know of no politician who is afraid of the woman vote on any question under the sun.'[4]

As articles began to appear in the popular press on the 'failure' of women's suffrage, there were also signs of failure and disillusion on the personal level. The feminism of an earlier generation had been forged in the intense personal relationships of women's culture. Many female intellectuals and activists of the pre-war generation—women like Jane Addams or Sarah Orne Jewett—had been raised to believe that women were the purer sex, blessed with little sexual appetite. The novelist Mary Austin recalled in 1927 that in her youth 'nobody, positively *nobody*, had yet suggested that women are passionately endowed even as men are.'[5] Many ambitious women had forgone marriage and satisfied their emotional needs in intimate friendships with other women, or in communal female living in women's colleges or settlement houses. What they sacrificed in sexual passion they made up for in independence and the freedom to devote all their creative energies to their work.

But 'modern' women read Freud and struggled to liberate themselves from outmoded sexual inhibitions. The heroine of the Jazz Age became the flapper, with her bobbed hair, short skirts, bathtub gin, and easy kisses. The feminism of the suffragettes seemed irrelevant or dated to the young women of the 1920s, who had been exposed to the messages of psychoanalysis, advertising, and Hollywood. The women's colleges that had been the avant-garde for the previous generation felt the shock wave of major changes in the 1920s. No longer intellectual sanctuaries where bright girls were initiated into intense female communities, they became sites of struggle over regulations and restrictions about heterosexual mixing. Even Bryn Mawr, the last holdout, offered tea dances by 1929 and allowed Princeton students to play the men's parts in student plays. The rituals and traditions that had united women students as a group withered away as students demanded more personal freedom and interaction with men. Ambitious women of the 1920s expected that they could have careers of their own, without surrendering the traditional feminine experiences of romance, marriage, and motherhood. 'By the time

I grew up,' Lillian Hellman recalled, 'the fight for the emancipation of women, their rights under the law, in the office, in bed, was stale stuff. My generation didn't think much about the place or the problems of women.'[6]

But these fantasies of lives that successfully balanced love and work were premature in a society where the husband's role was unexamined and unaltered, where wives were still expected to serve their men and their families, where in fact women's reproductive, marital, legal, and vocational rights were few. Encountering the real tensions between their writing and their personal lives led to disillusionment for women of Hellman's generation. Older feminists too felt bitter and betrayed. The younger generation did not seem to recognize their sacrifice or wish to emulate it. For a pioneer of women's higher education like Wellesley's Vida Scudder, the 1920s were 'the bleakest years of her life.'[7]

While this shift in female attitudes towards personal achievement caused anxiety and conflict for women planning literary careers in the 1920s and 1930s, hostility towards female authorship and feminine values in academia and the literary establishment further stigmatized women's writing. A country taking new pride in its cultural heritage after the war saw only weakness and sentimentality in the contribution women had made to our national literature. In the years following the war, women writers were gradually eliminated from the canon of American literature as it was anthologized, criticized, and taught.

We can see the signs of this devaluation of women's writing as public honors for a few celebrated token figures were accompanied by mockery of women readers and writers in private literary correspondence and exclusion of women's literature from serious critical consideration. Although Willa Cather received an honorary degree from Princeton in 1931—the first woman to be so honored—her critical reputation, like that of her contemporary Edith Wharton, diminished. Both women were scorned by critics of the 1930s as decorous relics of a bygone age. While at the beginning of his career Fitzgerald acknowledged the influence of such important novelists as Cather and Wharton, he also complained that the American novel was being emasculated by female conventionality and propriety. Yet there was little tolerance for female unconventionality, originality, and impropriety from the very men who lamented the dictatorship of feminine prudery. Hemingway, for example, learned what he needed from Gertrude Stein, but could not imagine her being part of his literary circle. 'There is not much future in men being friends with great women,' he wrote in his memoir of Paris, *A Moveable Feast* (published posthumously in 1964), 'and there is usually even less future with truly ambitious women writers.'

Perhaps the worst casualties of the inter-war period were the women poets. The image of the woman poet, or 'poetess,' as she might still be called, was much more stereotyped and limiting than that of the novelist. The popular image of the American 'female lyrist' was that of a 'sweet singer' with three names, a pretty, youthful creature who wrote about love and renunciation, in a song as spontaneous, untaught, and artless as the lark's. After the war, however, American women poets needed to search for precursors who could define the shape of a serious woman poet's career as she matured and grew in artistry, range, and technique. Some, like Sara Teasdale, Edna St Vincent Millay, and H. D. (Hilda Doolittle), looked to Sappho, the Greek lyricist whose work existed only in fragments; and indeed reinvented her to provide a poetic matrilineage for themselves. Many turned to the English poets Elizabeth Barrett Browning and Christina Rossetti. Others welcomed the rediscovery of a uniquely American female poetic voice, heralding the critical revival of Emily Dickinson in the late 1920s. Amy Lowell championed Dickinson's poetic genius and praised her unorthodox meters and rhymes during a period when mainstream critics regarded her work as eccentric, and her place in American literary history as inconspicuous. Genevieve Taggard's biography of Dickinson in 1931 was one of the first written outside of the poet's family circle, and Taggard was editing a collection of Dickinson's poems and letters when she died.

Yet none of these precursors seemed wholly satisfying either in their personal lives or in their poetic careers. Amy Lowell's poem 'The Sisters' (1925) summarized her generation's sense of marginality and eccentricity:

> Taking us by and large, we're a queer lot
> We women who write poetry. And when you
> think
> How few of us there've been, it's queerer still.

Reviewing the work of her 'older sisters' in poetry—Sappho ('a leaping fire'), Barrett Browning ('squeezed in stiff conventions'), and Dickinson ('she hung her womanhood upon a bough')—Lowell regretfully concludes that none offers her a model for the kind of poetry she wants to write:

> Goodbye, my sisters, all of you are great,
> And all of you are marvellously strange,

And none of you has any word for me.
I cannot write like you.

American women poets like Lowell were particularly troubled by the advent of a modernist poetic aesthetic. Before the war, there had been a place for the female poet in American culture, albeit a limited and sentimental one. But T. S. Eliot and Ezra Pound, among others, proclaimed the need for a severe poetry that transcended personal experience and emotion—precisely the modes in which women lyric poets had been encouraged to specialize. Serious, or 'major,' poetry, Eliot, Pound, and their disciples argued, was intellectual, impersonal, experimental, and concrete. Furthermore, they believed, women were by nature emotional creatures who could inspire major poems but lacked the genius to produce them. As John Crowe Ransom declared in an essay entitled 'The Poet as Woman' (1936), 'A woman lives for love . . . safer as a biological organism, she remains fixed in her famous attitudes, and is indifferent to intellectuality.' Even laudatory reviews of particular women poets frequently included derisory generalizations about the deficiencies of women's poetry as a genre; Theodore Roethke, for example, provided a lengthy catalogue of 'charges most frequently levelled against poetry by women': 'lack of range—in subject matter and emotional tone—and lack of a sense of humor . . . the embroidering of trivial themes; a concern with the mere surfaces of life . . . lyric or religious posturing . . . lamenting the lot of the woman; caterwauling, writing the same poem about fifty times, and so on.'[8]

Even when women produced feminine versions of modernism, reimagining myths, for example, from female perspectives (such as Bogan's 'Cassandra' and 'Medusa', Millay's 'An Ancient Gesture,' describing Penelope, and H. D.'s 'Eurydice'), as James Joyce and T. S. Eliot had modernized the myths of Ulysses and the Grail, their experiments were ignored or misunderstood. As they attempted to forge a new tradition for themselves against this patronizing aesthetic, American women poets struggled with the conflict between their ambitions to create and their internalized obligations to behave as beautiful and selfless Muses for men. This conflict can be seen as the common thread in a number of otherwise disparate poetic careers.

Sara Teasdale was one of the most famous female poets of her era. Yet she had been raised to believe in the romantic feminine myth of love as woman's whole experience, and she could never allow herself to acknowledge a primary commitment to art. 'Art can never mean to a woman what it means to a man,' she reassured an admirer. 'Love means that.' Believing that 'a woman ought not to write . . . it is indelicate and unbecoming,' Teasdale sought to curb her poetic ambitions, as she also repressed her sexual energies. Her early poems were wistful love lyrics that corresponded to her sense of feminine delicacy and decorum. When Teasdale married in 1914, her businessman-husband boasted that 'she has put the duties of her womanhood (motherhood and wifehood) above *any* art and would I believe rather be the fond mother of a child than the author of the most glorious poem in the language.' A rejected suitor, the Populist poet Vachel Lindsay, foresaw a new role for Teasdale in which her 'woman heart' would express itself in verse that was both maternal and modest in scope: 'You ought to make yourself the little mother of the whole United States,' he enthusiastically suggested.

Yet marriage did not bring the ecstasies that she had anticipated, or the motherly role men envisioned for her. Only a few years later, Teasdale had an abortion, unable to imagine maternity and poetic creativity as other than antagonistic roles. In the 1920s she retreated into isolation and psychosomatic illness, as her poetry took up themes of frustration and suffering. As a young woman, Teasdale had believed that the woman who wished to be a poet should 'imitate the female birds, who are silent—or, if she sings, no one ought to hear her music until she is dead.' In 1933, convinced that her lyrics had become unfashionable, but unable to develop a new and strong poetic voice, she took her own life.[9]

Another strategy for American women poets of the period seeking to reconcile femininity and creativity was the celebration of the miniature and the decorative, in exquisitely crafted sonnets and lyrics. Elinor Wylie, for example, specialized in images of whiteness, crystal, ice, glass, porcelain, and jewels. Unlike that of Teasdale, Wylie's life had been full of scandal, including adultery, divorce, and the desertion of her son. The precision of her poetic forms and the chilliness of her imagery helped Wylie defend herself against charges of overwrought feminine emotionalism and sexual promiscuity. Her most famous poems, such as 'Velvet Shoes,' about walking in the snow, and a series of sonnets about winter landscapes, established her persona as a daughter of the Puritans devoted to austerity, silence, and self-denial. In such books as *Nets to Catch the Wind* (1921) and in her essay 'Jewelled Bindings' (1923), Wylie presented her view of the lyric poem as a 'small jeweled receptacle' in two or three well-polished stanzas. The image associated the female lyric with the female body itself, especially since Wylie was celebrated for her silver gowns, dresses like a kind of metallic armor, in which her slender body reminded Van Wyck Brooks of 'some creature living in an iridescent shell.'[10]

The themes of reticence, confinement, and silence so prominent in the work and personae of Teasdale and Wylie can be seen as the dominant ones of the modernist women poets; and we can understand them as in part a response to anxieties about female creativity. In the Imagism of 'H. D.' and the elipses of Marianne Moore, subjective elements were made ambiguous or obscure. Moore's difficult and allusive poems withheld any hint of a self behind the text; the critic Hugh Kenner's remark that Moore was a 'poet of erasures' for whom deletion 'was a kind of creative act' suggests that the aesthetic of reticence demanded vigilant self-control.[11] Léonie Adams and Louise Bogan also chose a severely impersonal poetry, dissociating themselves from what they saw as the sentimental excess of much women's writing. Bogan was outspoken about her contempt for a female tradition in poetry, although she did not recognize the self-hatred behind her stance. Rejecting a proposal to edit an anthology of women's verse in 1935, she wrote that 'the thought of corresponding with a lot of female songbirds made me acutely ill. It is hard enough to bear with my own lyric side.'[12]

Yet these cautious choices also seemed to restrict the poets to minor status. Writing about Marianne Moore in the *Literary History of the United States* (1948), for example, a critic remarked that 'she is feminine in a very rewarding sense, in that she makes no effort to be major.' While Moore's self-effacement might seem rewarding in contrast to the bawling ambition of her male contemporaries, this is a revealing statement about the way in which femininity and minority status were linked in the critical mind. For many women poets of the period, feeling '*very* minor,' as Bogan noted, was a painful reminder of their dilemma. At the same time that Bogan pursued her austere credo of withdrawing 'her own personality from her productions,' she envied male poets their scope, ambition, variety, and freedom to express personality.

Often Bogan's sense of creative inhibition was expressed in physical images of size and weight. In a review of Edna St Vincent Millay's poetry, Bogan noted that 'women who have produced an impressively bulky body of work are few.' Just as she lamented the absence of a female precursor with a substantial body of work, Bogan longed to write 'fat words in fat poems,' like her friend Theodore Roethke, instead of the spare, chiseled, even anorexic verses she could allow herself.[13]

At the beginning of her career, Edna St Vincent Millay showed promise of becoming the most daring and successful presence in her generation of women poets. After her widely publicized youthful debut in 1912, when her poem 'Renascence' won a prize sponsored by a poetry society, Millay became as notorious for her love affairs as for her art. Her first book, *A Few Figs from Thistles* (1920), established her as a bold voice for the New Woman. Such flippant lines as these from 'First Fig'—'My candle burns at both ends; / It will not last the night; But ah, my foes, and oh, my friends— / It gives a lovely light!'—suggested that Millay would insist upon the kind of sexual freedom and emotional independence that had always been the prerogative of men. Raised by a strong mother in a family of loving and talented sisters, and a student at Vassar during the height of the suffrage movement, Millay became a passionate lifelong feminist. Unlike some of her contemporaries, she took pride in the achievements of other women. 'Isn't it wonderful how the lady poets are coming along?' she wrote in delight after reading Louise Bogan.[14] Millay dedicated her powerful sonnet-sequence *Fatal Interview* to the memory of Elinor Wylie, and even in unsuccessful poems like 'Menses' she made a daring attempt to explore taboo female sexual experience and bring it into the realm of acceptable poetic subjects.

Yet Millay, too, suffered from the period's critical resistance to the first-person lyric as a serious art form. Working with such traditional poetic genres as the ballad, lyric, and sonnet, she was patronized by critics favoring formal and linguistic experimentation. In the 1930s, as she sought to incorporate her political interests into her writing, she disappointed an audience that expected her to remain a romantic laureate. Like Teasdale, she suffered a series of breakdowns as her popularity waned.

Millay was not the only woman poet of this generation who found it increasingly difficult to create as she grew older. Many seemed to run out of suitably 'impersonal' subjects, and were finally silenced by years of self-censorship. Léonie Adams, having published two widely praised volumes of 'metaphysical' poetry in the 1920s, virtually stopped writing by 1933. Louise Bogan simply could not imagine a woman poet who survived as

an artist when youth, beauty, and romance were past: 'Has there ever *been* an old lady poet?' she sadly inquired.[15] Between 1941 and 1968, Bogan wrote only ten poems and was frequently hospitalized for depression.

One way to resist the label of 'minor woman lyricist' was to write poems reflecting the political struggles of the Great Depression. Genevieve Taggard began her career with *For Eager Lovers* (1922), a book of poems about love, courtship, and pregnancy that reminded reviewers of Teasdale and Millay. Yet Taggard, a socialist and radical who had written for *The Masses* and who was active in left-wing organizations and writers' groups, became impatient with this limited cultural role. 'I have refused to write out of a decorative impulse,' she explained, 'because I conceive it to be the dead end of much feminine talent.' Neither could she accept the impersonal mask of the modernist aesthetic. Acknowledging the importance of Eliot as a poet, she none the less sharply criticized his elitist politics, his anti-Semitism, and his contempt for women.[16] Believing that the most personal lyric could reveal the feelings of a whole community, Taggard used the form to write about the experience of the working class, in collections that critics promptly denounced as mere propaganda.

Ironically, women poets like Taggard and Millay who turned to politics in the 1930s as a way of establishing their strength and universality found themselves condemned by yet another set of double sexual and literary standards. As the historian Elinor Langer has noted, 'the radical movement of the 1930s was a male preserve.'[17] Like other left-wing groups, the Communist Party of America welcomed women into its ranks but elevated few to leadership and presented few as candidates for public office. Leftist groups saw feminist issues as not only potentially divisive but also as less important than the struggle of the working class. Women's roles and needs were subordinated to those of workers, and women organizers were expected to sacrifice personal ambitions, family, and children for the good of the party. Political work—picketing, demonstrating, writing, and distributing party leaflets and tracts—demanded enormous commitments of women's time and energy.

Moreover, as the historians Alice Kessler-Harris and Paul Lauter have pointed out, 'The cultural apparatus of the Left in the thirties was, if anything, more firmly masculist than its political institutions.'[18] Women were only token members of left-wing cultural and literary organizations such as the John Reed Clubs, and they were also underrepresented on the editorial boards and pages of radical journals: six women were listed among fifty-five editors and writers on the masthead of *The New Masses*. At the *Partisan Review*, also, male editors expected women to be frivolous, less than intellectually and politically serious. Mary McCarthy recalled that when she started writing for the *Partisan Review* she was given the job of drama critic because 'I was a sort of gay, good-time girl from their point of view. . . . They thought the theater was of absolutely no consequence.'[19]

Finally, the literary and aesthetic values of the Left favored male writers, male protagonists, and masculine themes. In 'Go Left, Young Writers,' an editorial for *The New Masses* in 1929, Michael Gold described the advent of a new kind of American writer, 'a wild youth of about twenty-two, the son of working-class parents, who himself works in the lumber camps, coal mines, and steel mills, harvest fields and mountain camps of America.' The vogue of this tough-guy artist implicitly cast doubt on the more private or domestic subject matter of women's fiction, even though for men, too, the lumberjack role was often a pose. In addition, the insistence that left-wing art should focus on economic oppression and the workplace created special problems for women. Only 25 percent of all women, and less than 15 percent of married women, worked outside the home during the 1930s; and few of these worked in the coal mines or steel mills. Once more women's special experiences were devalued or ignored.

What were the effects of political involvement for women writing during the 1930s? Despite their difficulties, some women felt nourished and inspired by the urgency of the issues before them and by the excitement of sharing revolutionary goals with male and female comrades. They found encouragement, communion, and fellowship in left-wing organizations. For the novelist Meridel Le Sueur, for example, the 1930s were a period of satisfying literary productivity and of 'nourishing' associations with political men and working women. From her point of view, the decade was 'a good time to be a woman writer, or any kind of writer.'[20] Like other politically active women in the decade, such as Josephine Herbst, Martha Gellhorn, Tillie Olsen, and Mary Heaton Vorse, Le Sueur developed new forms of reportage, combining journalism with a committed personal voice that made the work a precursor of the 'nonfiction novel' of the 1970s. Her best-known essays are

outspoken, colloquial, graphic vignettes of female experience during the Depression. 'Women Are Hungry' (1934) describes the special anguish of women on the breadlines:

> The women looking for jobs or bumming on the road, or that you see waiting for a hand-out from the charities, are already mental cases as well as physical ones. A man can always get drunk or talk to other men, no matter how broken he is in body and spirit; but a woman, ten to one, will starve alone in a hall bedroom until she is thrown out, and then she will sleep alone in some alley until she is picked up.

Yet there were other women on the Left trying to write about gender as well as class, who were isolated from each other, and who had no support either from women's groups or Communist Party networks. Furthermore, as Le Sueur admitted, the party demanded a particular style of writing from its members and had little tolerance for other literary forms. Most Marxist literary critics were hostile to the formal and linguistic experiments of modernist writers such as James Joyce, D. H. Lawrence, and Virginia Woolf; they dismissed such aesthetic preoccupations with language as bourgeois or decadent. Instead they advocated 'proletarian realism,' the theory that literature should describe and celebrate the lives, struggles, and triumphs of working-class people under capitalism. Literary innovation was to take the form of recording the language and dialect of the working class, or the 'folk,' extending reportage and documentary into a narrative form.

But even Le Sueur had been profoundly influenced by Lawrence, whose writing about sexuality helped her overcome the puritanism of her Midwest upbringing and gave her a model for some of her lyrical short stories of the 1920s about female sexuality and pregnancy. Such subjects, however, were taboo among left-wing critics in the 1930s, as were the styles and subjectivities of women's writing. When left-wing women writers moved away from the permitted subjects to discuss private female experiences, their work was harshly condemned by radical male critics. Whittaker Chambers rebuked Le Sueur for the 'defeatist attitude' of her essays about women, and other reviewers disparaged her fictional efforts to describe women's feelings and their sexuality. Le Sueur struggled during the decade to purge her fiction of what she called its 'narcissistic' elements; but later she ruefully recalled that the Communist Party tried 'to beat the lyrical and emotional out of women.'[21]

We can see the effects of this pressure on the development of her writing during the period. In her early work, Le Sueur had been drawn to explorations of women's awakening sexual consciousness in the tradition of Kate Chopin's *The Awakening* and Edith Wharton's *Summer,* and to almost mythic projections of the cycle of separation from the mother, reproduction, and death. 'Persephone' is a haunting allegory about a young girl's abduction from her mother, a Demeter-figure identified with nature and fertility. In subsequent stories such as 'Wind' and 'Annunciation,' Le Sueur described female rites of passage, including sexual initiation and pregnancy. Yet her major fictional work of the 1930s, a novella called *The Girl* (1936), which describes a community of women from different backgrounds who help each other to survive the Depression, was rejected by her publisher and remained unpublished until 1971.

Tillie Olsen has written in her book *Silences* (1978) about the periods of creative paralysis that beset writers and especially women writers, listing among the causes the moments when 'political involvement takes priority.' Olsen's own experiences in the 1930s are a case in point. Coming from a socialist immigrant background in Nebraska, Olsen grew up aware of the suffering of women and the poor, and familiar with both a radical and a feminist literary tradition. She had read the work of Rebecca Harding Davis, Willa Cather, Olive Schreiner, and Agnes Smedley, as well as that of John Dos Passos and Langston Hughes. When she joined the Young Communist League as a talented young writer in 1931, Olsen was assigned to a series of political tasks in the Midwest, including organizing women in factories and writing skits and plays for the Communist Party. During these years, too, she was working at a series of low-paid jobs and taking care of two daughters. For Olsen, 'it was not a time that my writing self could be first.'[22] Her writing self, indeed, had to be postponed until many years later, and in some sense it has never been fully recovered; a prizewinning book of short stories, *Tell Me a Riddle* (1961), and an unfinished novel, *Yonnondio* (1974), are fragments of a career that was damaged by long deferral.

Yonnondio, like *The Girl,* was begun in the 1930s and only published forty years later. Like Le Sueur's book, it is about the struggle for survival: a family moving from mining to tenant farming and finally to the slaughterhouses and packing plants of Omaha. Yet the novel has a strong subjective and experimental quality. It is the story of the daughter, Mazie, an autobiographical heroine who, in Olsen's original plan, was to have become a writer, and her mother Anna. But Olsen was never able to finish the book. In the tradition of feminist writers like Olive Schreiner, she wanted a place for the lyric, the personal, the mythic, and the fantastic. But her immersion in the aesthetic of proletarian realism made it difficult for her to develop the psychological elements of her story— the wrenchingly intense mother-daughter bond, the conflicts of sexual desire and feminine respectability, and the power struggles of marriage. These had to be suppressed in favor of a more impersonal account of the struggle between workers and bosses. Olsen was silenced by her internal conflicts as well as by the external pressures of family and work.

Josephine Herbst was another significant novelist on the Left whose work was both nourished and distorted by the formulas of the 1930s. While Herbst was never an active feminist, her life and career were shaped by her profound feelings about other women. Her mother's stories first stimulated her imagination and made her want to become a writer; in the early 1920s her favorite sister's death after an abortion was a never-to-be-forgotten blow. Although Herbst was married to the left-wing writer John Herrmann, she also had two profound love affairs with women. Deep friendships with other women writers, especially Katherine Anne Porter and Genevieve Taggard, gave her a stronger base in a female literary community than Olsen or Le Sueur had enjoyed. Herbst's political radicalism was also an important part of her life, although at many times she recognized that she was being marginalized or used as a token woman.

For Herbst's fictional development, however, the times were mixed. In 1920 she had an affair with Maxwell Anderson, then a married young reporter; when she became pregnant, he insisted on an abortion. The bitter novel she finished in 1922, 'Unmarried,' was never published. In a trilogy of novels based on her family's history in America, Herbst later tried to avoid the 'constricted "I"' deplored by Marxist critics and to submerge autobiography in an epic story of American society. But the documentary devices and the mixture of social consciousness and personal narrative that worked for male writers like Dos Passos struck readers as less significant when the central protagonists were women. Herbst's reputation declined, and although she worked for many years on a memoir of her life in the 1920s and 1930s, when she died it was found unfinished.[23]

Another neglected writer of the 1930s was Tess Slesinger. The daughter of a cultured and prosperous Jewish family, Slesinger studied writing at Swarthmore and Columbia. In 1928 she married Herbert Solow, assistant editor of the *Menorah Journal,* and through him met many of the young left-wing New York intellectuals of the period. The couple were divorced in 1932, and Slesinger drew on this experience for her only novel, *The Unpossessed* (1934). Like Le Sueur and Olsen, Slesinger was drawn to the literary experiments of the modernist writers, and her novel was strongly influenced in its style and narrative technique by Katherine Mansfield and Virginia Woolf; its stream-of-consciousness technique is especially akin to Woolf's *Mrs. Dalloway* (1925). Slesinger uses two heroines to represent the modern woman of the 1930s: Margaret Flinders, the working woman married to a Marxist intellectual, and Elizabeth Leonard, a boyish art student, who has bohemian love affairs and reads *Ulysses.* Through her account of the founding of a left-wing journal, Slesinger satirizes the sexism of the literary Left. One intellectual leader proclaims that 'the point about a woman . . . is her womb'; and the women heroines wonder how to reconcile their desires for marriage and motherhood with their intelligence and their political ideals. In the bitter concluding section, 'Missis Flinders,' Margaret is made to have an abortion by her husband Miles, who fears that becoming parents would make them soft and bourgeois. The death of their child is clearly a signal of the death of their marriage, and perhaps also of their political movement. Slesinger ends with a despairing image of Margaret's barrenness and emotional sexlessness: 'She had stripped and revealed herself not as a woman at all, but as a creature who would not be a woman and could not be a man.' Published independently of the book, 'Missis Flinders' was one of the first stories about abortion to appear in an American magazine.

But Slesinger's insistence that personal relationships as well as political ones needed to be revolutionized was lost on her male contemporaries. While the mainstream press generally praised her book, the work offended male radical critics, such as Philip Rahv, who complained in the *Partisan Review* that it lacked 'a disciplined orientation for radicalized intellectuals;' Joseph Freeman in the *Daily Worker* called it 'bourgeois and reactionary.' In the late 1930s, Slesinger went to Hollywood as a film writer and became active in the Screen Writers' Guild. Her last, unfinished novel, left in fragments when she died of cancer in 1944, was a study of Hollywood written from the perspective of the film industry's workers, rather than its tycoons or stars.[24]

The frustration, fragmentation, and silencing that plagued women poets and novelists generally during the 1920s and 1930s were especially acute for black women writers, who struggled not only with personal conflicts but also with racism and with pressures to conform to the aesthetic ideals of the Harlem Renaissance. As in the Left, the cultural theory and practice of the Harlem Renaissance was strongly male-dominated. Influential critics of the period, such as Alain Locke in *The New Negro* (1925), argued that the black writer should strive for positive expressions of black culture and for racial uplift, as well as for pure art. In the 1930s, when some leading black intellectuals such as Richard Wright joined the Communist Party, they argued that the black artist had a primary responsibility to portray racial oppression and struggle. Women were expected to provide loving maternal nurturance for the new movement and its artists, not to lead it. The novelist Dorothy West recalled how in 1926 she joined a literary group in Harlem, but because she was 'young and a girl . . . they never asked me to say anything.' The highly educated and sophisticated women writers who participated in the movement often felt estranged from the working-class black community whose experiences they were expected to represent. Insulted by racist stereotypes of the black woman as erotic and primitive, they also felt hampered by family and religious pressures to deny their sexuality.

One of the most gifted women of the group the Harlem Renaissance called the 'ultra-respectables' was the novelist Jessie Redmon Fauset. Educated at Cornell, where she was elected to Phi Beta Kappa, Fauset went on to graduate study at the University of Pennsylvania and the Sorbonne. From 1919 to 1926 she was the literary editor of the NAACP journal *The Crisis.* Fauset's male contemporaries admired her intelligence and culture, especially in her conventionally feminine role as the mentor or 'midwife' for young black writers. Langston Hughes recalled her parties for the black intelligentsia in which conversations about literature sometimes took place in French. Claude McKay praised her for being 'as prim and dainty as a primrose.' But her refined hyperfemininity affronted those fighting oppression or defending the folk sources of black consciousness. Fauset's novels were as deeply concerned with problems of female sexual identity as with racial conflict; they show how race and gender together create permutations of power and powerlessness. Yet her romantic plots were mocked as 'sophomoric, trivial and dull,' or as 'vapidly genteel, lace-curtain romances.' Even McKay called her novels 'fastidious and precious,' and to critics of the Harlem Renaissance, Fauset is sometimes described as the 'Rear Guard.'

Fauset's own relationship to her literary community, however, was more critical and innovative than these condescending terms would suggest. On the one hand, she deplored the cult of primitivism and the limits that white publishers set on the portrayal of blacks in fiction. Most publishers, she wrote in protest, 'persist in finding only certain types of Negroes interesting and if an author presents a variant they fear that the public either won't believe in it or won't stand for it.' Indeed, Fauset's first novel, *There Is Confusion* (1924), was rejected by publishers because it contained 'no description of Harlem dives, no race riot, no picturesque abject poverty.' 'White readers just don't expect Negroes to be like this,' her publishers complained.[25]

On the other hand, Fauset's portraits of black middle-class women, struggling with sexual politics as well as with racial tensions, challenged the stereotypes of black male readers. Fauset's most important novel, *Plum Bun* (1929), uses a contrast between two sisters, the light-skinned Angela and the dark Virginia, to dramatize the temptations of 'passing' for her gifted black women. For Fauset, the theme of 'passing' has a double meaning; it refers both to the racial conflicts of the mulatto who can enter the white world and to the divided sensibility of the woman artist who must conceal or sacrifice her vision in response to social definitions of femininity. As one character in the novel remarks, 'God doesn't like women.' Each sister represents an aspect of Fauset's own identity. Through the vivid Jinny, a teacher in Harlem, she describes the intellectual world of the Harlem Renaissance and its male idols, like the spellbinding theorist Van Meier. Through the gifted artist Angela, who studies in New York and Paris, Fauset shows the steady subversion of female talent by myths of romance and domesticity. Whether she is courted by the cynical white playboy Roger or the idealistic black painter Anthony, Angela fears that she will risk losing love and security if she appears strong or insists on putting her art first; to be beloved and feminine she must be 'dependent, fragile . . . to the point of ineptitude.' In marrying Anthony, she determines to make his happi-

ness her career: 'At the cost of every ambition which she had ever known she would make him happy. After the manner of most men his work would probably be the greatest thing in the world to him. And he should be the greatest thing in the world to her.'

Similar themes of female sexuality and frustrated ambition are explored in the remarkable novels of Nella Larsen. The daughter of a Danish mother and a West Indian father, Larsen studied at Fisk University and the University of Copenhagen, and trained as a nurse in New York. Later she became a librarian. Her literary career was brief and intense. On the basis of her two novels, *Quicksand* (1928) and *Passing* (1929), she was offered a Guggenheim Fellowship for creative writing in 1930—the first black woman to be so honored. But Larsen never finished another book. After her return from Europe, as she dissolved her marriage to a prominent black physicist, her career ended in silence and obscurity.

We may look for the clues to Larsen's unhappy career in the tensions of her two novels about cultivated women of mixed parentage trying to find a place for themselves in the Harlem art world, in white society, or in the black rural South. In *Quicksand*, the mulatto heroine Helga Crane is intellectual and cosmopolitan, but she feels alienated and alone wherever she goes. At the black Southern college where she teaches English, she is repelled by the caution of her black colleagues and by their self-denying emphasis on racial uplift. In Harlem, she is both intrigued by the glamor and imagination of black society and irritated by its obsession with race. Yet when she goes to live with relatives in Denmark, Helga misses the company of other blacks, experiencing a belated sense of racial identity she had not even known she possessed. Resisting marriage, moreover, she is tormented by the intensity of sexual desires that are unacceptable in all her social worlds. Larsen imagines a grim resolution to Helga's dilemma; wandering into a black revivalist prayer meeting in New York, she finds a release for her stifled emotions in the Bacchic frenzy of worship and song. 'In the confusion of seductive repentance,' she marries the evangelical preacher and goes to live with him in Alabama, a marriage that sentences her to permanent imprisonment in childbearing and poverty. Although she is gifted with intelligence and beauty, Helga seems doomed by both her sexuality and her race.

The most important and productive woman writer of the Harlem Renaissance, Zora Neale Hurston, experienced similar conflicts in her life, but managed to transcend them in her work. Raised in the all-black community of Eatonville, Florida, where her father was the mayor, Hurston grew up with the direct experience of rural Southern society that writers like Fauset and Larsen from the urban Northeast had missed. In 1925, however, having begun to establish a reputation in Harlem as one of the most talented and irreverent young writers, Hurston won a scholarship to Barnard College, where she was the only black student. Trained as an anthropologist by Franz Boas, and subsidized by a wealthy white patron of black writers whom she called 'Godmother,' Hurston returned to the South with the eyes of an observer, and with the methods of a social scientist rather than an artist. The tall tales of her childhood had been redefined as 'folklore,' and her task was to collect and analyze them. Yet Hurston kept her aesthetic identity intact; she survived both the pressure of the academic community to distance herself from black culture and the pressure of the white literary community to romanticize it. The books she wrote in the 1930s—most notably *Mules and Men* (1935), *Their Eyes Were Watching God* (1937), and *Moses: Man of the Mountain* (1939)—are memorable for what Hurston called 'a Negro way of saying,' a subtle, pungent, and original style that draws force from the black vernacular but is carefully crafted and influenced by literary models as well. However, Hurston's determination to write from inside black culture and to withstand fashionable issues of racial tension or oppression ('I do not belong to the sobbing school of Negrohood,' she wrote in 'How It Feels to Be Colored Me') antagonized her male contemporaries. Richard Wright, Sterling A. Brown, and Ralph Ellison accused her of pandering to a white audience and attacked her use of dialect humor as 'minstrel technique.' Like Fauset and Larsen, Hurston had to make her way as an independent and strong female artist in the face of male opposition.

Hurston's finest book, *Their Eyes Were Watching God,* blends several traditions of American writing. In technique, it is a modernist novel that incorporates surreal elements into its realism, and that alternates between the sophisticated verbal range of an omniscient narrator and a more intimate folk idiom that represents the consciousness of the heroine, Janey. Hurston's use of dialect, folklore, and a mulatto heroine roots her in the Afro-American literary tradition as well. But the novel is primarily the story of a woman's evolution from loneliness to independence. In what it includes and what it leaves out, it demonstrates

Hurston's commitment to traditions of female narrative. Unlike her predecessors in the 1920s, Hurston was not afraid to make female sexuality a central theme in her fiction. Janey's growth to personal maturity is reflected by the sexual as well as emotional terms of her three marriages, which represent three stages of her inner development. Married at sixteen to an older man for whom she feels no desire and who would turn her into a 'mule' (one who carries a burden passed by white men to black men to black women), she bolts. Her second marriage, to the domineering and possessive Joe Starks, becomes a power struggle that ends with her silencing and subordination. After Joe's death, Janey chooses Tea Cake, a younger man, who insists that she 'partakes wid everything,' that she share both his work and his play. Tender and affectionate, Tea Cake teaches her to fish and to shoot; he cooks for her and encourages her to tell stories with the men. Yet at the end of the novel, after Tea Cake has been bitten by a rabid dog, Janey is forced to shoot him.

Why does Hurston arrange her plot so that her heroine is forced to destroy a loving and egalitarian hero, if not because her heroine's survival meant more to her than romantic love? Having learned how to speak and to work, Janey must end on her own, free to make her own way in the world. Hurston's strong resistance to saddling her heroine with domestic burdens, however idealized, is made clear by the fact that despite three marriages, in two of which sex plays an important role, Janey has no children; in fact, the novel seems deliberately constructed to make us look away from this striking omission, to make us ignore such a lapse in its realism. In *Quicksand*, Helga Crane ends up pregnant and immobilized with her fifth child; in *Their Eyes Were Watching God,* Janey remains unencumbered and so is free to realize her dreams.

The 1930s did not end happily for American women writers. Within the academic institutions of American literature, women were increasingly marginalized. In 1935, the first edition of a standard college textbook, *Major American Writers,* included no women at all. Even the great bestsellers of the decade, such as Pearl Buck's *The Good Earth* (1931) and Margaret Mitchell's *Gone with the Wind* (1936), were taken as confirmations of women's talent for a popular literature that could never compete with male art. During the last years of her life, Zora Neale Hurston moved from job to job, forgotten and neglected. When she died in 1960, she was living in a welfare home, working as a maid. Her grave was unmarked.

Yet despite all the difficulties and defeats, American women writers in the 1920s and 1930s produced an important body of work that has finally become influential, as we begin to incorporate it into a three-dimensional understanding of American literary history. Although the feminist movement waned during these decades, many strong women writers resisted the pressures to abandon their own visions and voices. In every genre—poetry, the short story, the novel—women writers between the wars advanced the honest exploration of female experiences and female lives. Moreover, many revised the aesthetic techniques and narrative strategies of their male contemporaries, in order to record uniquely female perspectives. As the feminist critics Sandra Gilbert and Susan Gubar have noted, the sonnet sequences of Wylie and Millay expressed female sexual desires within a genre traditionally devoted to the expression of male desire.[26] The more experimental poets of the period—Gertrude Stein, H. D., Marianne Moore—contested the linguistic, syntactical, and thematic conventions of what Stein called 'patriarchal poetry.' Women novelists on the Left infused the stiff formulas of proletarian realism with psychological nuance and lyric force. And the women writers of the Harlem Renaissance insisted on telling their own stories despite neglect, condescension, or critical abuse.

Ultimately, the value of the literature of the past has to be measured in terms of its continued impact on readers, writers, and critics. No book is ever lost as long as there are new generations of readers to enjoy it, new generations of writers to be stimulated by it, new generations of critics to reveal its fuller meanings. By this standard, women writers between the wars have already established their place in our literary tradition. Ignored or misunderstood in their own day, they often died in disappointment. Several of their most ambitious books were left incomplete. But their achievement has survived, making them significant precursors of the world in which we live as well as the one in which we read and write. Like the contemporary renaissance in American women's poetry and fiction, the development of a female tradition of political writing has been founded upon the work of women writers of the 1920s and 1930s. Perhaps the fate of Zora Neale Hurston, in many ways the most painfully 'lost' member of a lost generation, can serve as an example for all. When Hurston died, her books were out of print; histories of Afro-American writing ignored or disparaged her work; aspiring young writers studied American literature without even encountering her name. But today she is recognized not only as a gifted black woman writer but also as what the novelist Alice Walker, who made a pilgrimage in the 1970s to put a headstone on Hurston's grave, called 'a genius of the South.' For Walker and for many of the leading women writers, black and white, of the 1980s, *Their Eyes Were Watching God* has become one of the most important books in a literary tradition that continues to inspire them and to enable their work. As we continue to enlarge that tradition, the lost generation of American women's writing may offer further surprises and riches. We must not let it become lost again.

Notes

1. Louise Bogan to Morton Zabel, cited in Elizabeth Frank, *Louise Bogan: A Portrait* (New York: Knopf, 1985), 33.

2. John Aldridge, *After the Lost Generation* (New York: Noonday Press, 1958), 13.

3. See Hermione Lee, *Willa Cather: Double Lives* (New York: Pantheon, 1989), 183.

4. Emily Newell Blair, cited in William H. Chafe, *The American Woman: Her Changing Social, Economic, and Political Role* (New York: Oxford University Press, 1972), 30.

5. Mary Austin, 'The Forward Turn,' *The Nation,* 20 July 1927, 58.

6. Lillian Hellman, *An Unfinished Woman* (New York: Bantam, 1970), 29.

7. Helen L. Horowitz, *Alma Mater: Design and Experience in the Women's Colleges* (New York: Knopf, 1984), 287-8.

8. Theodore Roethke, 'The Poetry of Louise Bogan,' *Selected Prose of Theodore Roethke,* ed. Ralph J. Mills, Jr. (Seattle: University of Washington Press, 1965), 133-4.

9. See William Drake, *Sara Teasdale: Woman and Poet* (San Francisco: Harper & Row, 1979).

10. See Stanley Olson, *Elinor Wylie: A Biography* (New York: Dial Press, 1978).

11. Hugh Kenner, 'More than a Bolus of Idiosyncracies,' *New York Times Book Review,* 17 July 1977, 14.

12. *What the Woman Lived: Selected Letters of Louise Bogan, 1920-1970,* ed. Ruth Limmer (New York: Harcourt Brace Jovanovich, 1973), 86.

13. Frank, *Louise Bogan,* 77.

14. *The Letters of Edna St. Vincent Millay,* ed. Allan Ross Macdougal (New York: Harper, 1952), 173.

15. Katha Pollitt, 'Sleeping Fury,' *The Yale Review* (Summer 1985), 600.

16. See Hortense Flexner King, 'Genevieve Taggard, 1894-1948,' *Sarah Lawrence College Alumnae Magazine,* 14 (Fall 1948), 12; and Genevieve Taggard, 'Children of the Hollow Men,' *Christian Register Unitarian,* 125 (Nov. 1946), 441-2.

17. Elinor Langer, *Josephine Herbst: The Story She Could Never Tell* (Boston: Little, Brown & Co., 1984), 120.

18. Alice Kessler-Harris and Paul Lauter, 'Introduction,' to Tess Slesinger, *The Unpossessed* (New York: Feminist Press, 1984), xi. I am very much indebted to this essay for background material on the Left and fiction in the 1930s.

19. Mary McCarthy, interviewed by Elisabeth Sifton in *Women Writers at Work: The Paris Review Interviews* (New York: Viking Penguin, 1989), 183.

20. Elaine Hedges, 'Introduction,' to Meridel Le Sueur, *Ripening: Selected Work, 1927-1980* (Old Westbury, NY: Feminist Press, 1982), 15. See also Robert Shaffer, 'Women and the Communist Party, USA,' *Socialist Review*, 99 (May-June 1979), 73-118.

21. Hedges, 'Introduction,' 8-11.

22. Deborah Rosenfelt, 'From the Thirties: Tillie Olsen and the Radical Tradition,' *Feminist Studies*, 7 (Fall 1981), 383.

23. See Elinor Langer, 'Afterword,' to Josephine Herbst, *Rope of Gold* (Old Westbury, NY: Feminist Press, 1984), 441.

24. See Janet Sharistanian, 'Afterword,' to Tess Slesinger, *The Unpossessed*, 370-1.

25. See Deborah E. McDowell, 'Introduction,' to Jessie Redmon Fauset, *Plum Bun* (London: Pandora Press, 1985), ix-xxiv.

26. Sandra M. Gilbert and Susan Gubar, *The Norton Anthology of Literature by Women* (New York: W. W. Norton, 1985), 1241-2.

JEANNE LARSEN (ESSAY DATE 1993)

Larsen, Jeanne. "Lowell, Teasdale, Wylie, Millay, and Bogan." In *The Columbia History of American Poetry*, edited by Jay Parini, pp. 203-32. New York: Columbia University Press, 1993.

In the following excerpt, Larsen examines the careers of such early-twentieth century poets as Amy Lowell and Sara Teasdale, examining how their writings relate to those of other writers including Louise Bogan, Hilda Doolittle, Adelaide Crapsey, Genevieve Taggard, and others.

Passionate expression of emotion, revelation of personal sensibility, apparent delicacy overlaying sensuality and self-assertion, musicality created by diction and cadence, a vigorous grace of form: these qualities are characteristic of much work by a succession of American women poets. This tradition reached a peak in the second and third decades of the twentieth century, when such poets as Sara Teasdale (1884-1933), Elinor Wylie (1885-1928), and Edna St. Vincent Millay (1892-1950) enjoyed popular favor, flourishing careers, and critical praise.

The reasons for the broad appeal of their musical and moving poems are apparent on first read-ing. The fascinating complexities beneath polished surfaces are not. Through the 1940s American students continued to read poems by these women; some of their work maintained a quiet popularity in the years that followed. Yet by mid-century all three—like other successful female poets of their era—had fallen into critical disregard.

A new assessment of such disregard, and of the poetry itself, has begun. Understanding the value of these poets' work, and the reasons behind the changing estimations of that value, restores to us a fuller picture of a vital era in American poetry. It can also offer us a new avenue into work by other American poets, including not only Amy Lowell (1874-1925) and Louise Bogan (1897-1970) but also such neglected writers as Adelaide Crapsey (1878-1914), Anne Spencer (1882-1975), Georgia Douglas Johnson (1886-1966), Genevieve Taggard (1894-1948), Eunice Tietjens (1884-1944), and H. D. (Hilda Doolittle, 1886-1961).

For half a century Teasdale, Wylie, and Millay have generally been ignored or treated as embarrassing mistakes in vulgar taste. Lowell is often presented as an interesting, somewhat comic, figure in literary sociology, but hardly someone to be taken seriously as a poet. Bogan earned respect for her work as a critic as well as prizes for her poetry, yet all too frequently she too has been passed over or short-changed or praised in terms that distort her poetic achievement.

What has caused this? A study of anthologies of twentieth-century verse suggests that the changes in critical appraisal do have some correlation with the gender of the poets—and of those who do the selecting. Important anthologies edited by women and published in multiple editions from the mid-teens to the mid-thirties (such as Margery Gordon and Marie B. King's *Verse of Our Day*, or Harriet Monroe and Alice Crobin Henderson's *The New Poetry*, or Jesse Belle Rittenhouse's three collections of "modern verse") contain much greater ratios of female poets to male than do present-day anthologies, edited by men, that cover the same period.

But gender alone does not explain the situation. Some poetry by women was accorded a place in the canon. The marvelously dry, and ostensibly self-deprecatory, syllabic verse of Marianne Moore (1887-1972) evidently did not threaten critics in the antifeminist period in American literary scholarship that took hold during the thirties and gained strength after World War II. Even Louise Bogan, whose work derived creative energy from her complex (and sometimes inhibiting) relationship with the female lyrical tradition, was rather one-sidedly praised by her friend Theodore Roethke for freedom from the "embroidering," "lyric . . . posturing," "lamenting the lot of the woman," and "caterwauling" of other women poets. An appearance of neutered chastity, of restraint in language and content was, it seems, acceptable in ways that stirring self-expression and musicality were not.

Consciously avant-garde female poets of the early twentieth century have been neglected too, but for different reasons than more lyrical writers. In the poetry of Gertrude Stein (1874-1946), Mina Loy (1882-1966), and Laura Riding Jackson (1901-1991) the reader finds difficult experimental language, conspicuous erudition, and profound displays of intellectual force. Loy explored epistemological, metaphysical, and aesthetic issues, rejecting traditional concepts of femininity through a rigorous and unsentimental analysis of female experience and consciousness in patriarchial culture; Stein and Riding Jackson did the same through brilliant complexities of thought and linguistic innovation. Their avant-garde qualities deprived the three of a broad popular audience, but at least they could not belittled in terms suggesting a shallow girlishness.

Yet just as the sly subversions and covert sexuality of Moore's poetry have recently been brought to light, so the value of Stein's, Loy's, and Riding Jackson's work is overcoming critical evasion and sloth. No longer can the poetry of early twentieth-century American women be limited to one or two representatives accorded a quiet niche within an androcentric hierarchy, if the work seems inhibited rather than passionate, if it does not boldly claim a place in the grand traditions of English lyric or philosophical verse, if it eschews heightened sound and assertive rhythms, and if it does not call attention to such disruptive phenomena as female artistic creativity and female desire. Recent critical and biographical studies such as Jean Gould's and Richard Benvenuto's on Lowell, William Drake's and Carol Schoen's on Teasdale, Judith Farr's on Wylie, and a growing body of work on Millay and Bogan reveal the increasing interest in some of these women and their work.

The foundations for the current reassessment were, in fact, laid in 1923, just as the golden years were drawing toward an end. In her essay "Two Generations in American Poetry," Amy Lowell tells us that from the late nineteenth century through the first decade of the next American readers of poetry found themselves in "a world of sweet appreciation . . . of caged warblers, which species of gentle music-makers solaced it monthly from the pages of the *Century* or the *Atlantic Monthly*. "Then, as life in the United States changed, a poetic revolt began. ("Prosperity is the mother of art," writes the pragmatic Lowell, "no matter how odd such an idea may seem.")

So far, the story is a familiar one, though other critics have found more of interest than Lowell did in such turn-of-the-century lyric poets as Lizette Woodworth Reese (1856-1935) and Louise Imogen Guiney (1861-1920). But observe how Lowell describes the work of the new generation, the generation of Carl Sandburg, Robert Frost, H. D. and other Imagists, Edgar Lee Masters, and (though she does not mention him by name) of Ezra Pound: "this new poetry, whether written by men or women, was in essence masculine, virile, very much alive. Where the nineties had warbled, it was prone to shout."

Observe, too, how she describes the literary generation that followed, a breathtaking ten years later. Of the younger poets, the ones "doing the better work" she calls the Lyrists. She praises their skill in versification, and declares expression of emotion to be their "chief stock in trade." The best of them, she tells us, are Elinor Wylie and Edna St. Vincent Millay: "It is, indeed, a feminine movement, and remains such even in the work of its men."

Readers today may find themselves troubled by Lowell's unexamined images of shouting, virile masculinity and musical, emotional femininity, even though the poet-critic was quick to describe Wylie as "one of the most intellectual" of American poets. Yet in understanding the poets and the poetry of the United States from the mid-1910s through the 1930s—as in understanding the history of their changing critical reception—considerations of sexual difference and gender politics are inescapable. Recent scholars, including Sandra M. Gilbert and Susan Gubar, Emily Stipes Watts, Cheryl Walker, Elaine Showalter, William Drake, Jean Gould, Alicia Suskin Ostriker, Gillian Hanscombe and Virginia L. Smyers, and Bonnie Kime Scott have followed Lowell's lead in investigating the various powerful effects of gender on the lives and art of literary women of that era.

One such effect may indeed be "warmth of feeling" or "poetic intensity." In 1951 Louise Bogan stated in her history of twentieth-century American poetry that the line of this quality "moves on unbroken" from the nineteenth century to the twentieth, in the poetry of women.

And despite the disdain she had professed in 1935 for the work of "female songbirds" and her "own lyric side," Bogan here shows the shift in attitudes that was to continue through her later years. She argues that restoration of emotional energy to American poetry was grounded in "womanly attributes," was made possible through the liberating social changes effected by feminists, and was "accomplished almost entirely by women poets through methods which proved to be as strong as they seemed delicate."

Those strong and delicately realized methods of their craft, that "poetic intensity," the "line of feeling" running through the work of Lowell, Teasdale, Wylie, Millay, and Bogan herself, commends them to us. They (as well as H. D. and their other poetic sisters and daughters) have had to come to terms with—to don or drape anew-the mantle of their nineteenth-century heritage of female lyricism. Most often, they have done so to very good effect.

Eclectic and wide-ranging in her art, Amy Lowell is usually discussed in terms other than her relationship to the female lyrical tradition. But, in fact, she wrote beautifully of personal passions, and her work is a record of stimulating and successful experimentation with the music of finely wrought words.

Despite the self-doubts engendered in her as a girl who did not fit the standard image of female beauty, when she came into her own in her thirties Lowell took herself quite seriously as an artist and as a Professional. She was also generous in her support of other writers, male as well as female, writing in new voices and new modes, In a successful power stuggle with Ezra Pound she advocated a collaborative—rather than his authoritarian—approach to the editing of the second Imagist anthology. In all of this she drew on the nineteenth-century tradition of professional women writers, on a conventionally masculine assertiveness, and on the conventionally feminine ability to connect with others. This same range of traits is evident when she places herself in literary history.

In her long poem "The Sisters," Lowell constructs for herself a literary ancestry that makes evident the complex relationships of women writers in her day to their foremothers. The poem begins by explaining the relative scarcity of women poets: it is a result of the great demands of motherhood and the other "every-day concerns" of women's lives. Here the poet breaks with the many Victorian writers who celebrated female self-sacrifice and a circumscribed domesticity.

Naming Sappho, Elizabeth Barrett Browning, and Emily Dickinson as her "older sisters," Lowell explores their greatness, the differences among them, and "how extraordinarily unlike / Each is to me." Perhaps, in the way of poets, she protests her uniqueness a bit too much, but this is hardly surprising in a time when "we women who write poetry" were considered "a queer lot." The nineteenth-century female lyricists are left out altogether, and Barrett Browning is chided for her failure to write "beyond the movement of pentameters." Dickinson is most highly praised, especially for her "range of mind." But when Lowell commends Sappho for her impassioned amatory poems and "her loveliness of words," the younger writer praises the very qualities that distinguished those of her contemporaries she dubbed the Lyrists.

Lowell's covert affinities with other earlier literary women are made clearer in her perceptive and subversive book-length poem, *A Critical Fable*, published anonymously in 1922. In this witty, antimisogynist description of the contemporary poetic scene (which sent the American literary world into a buzz of curiosity, outrage, and sly delight), she again gives Dickinson top marks, citing her as the one nineteenth-century American poet-male or female—she can "sincerely admire." But the poem's narrator remains open to a variety of poetic styles, assuring us that current literary taste gives "no prominence / To rhyme or the lack of it."

Here, Lowell jocularly describes herself and her work as "electrical . . . prismatic . . . outrageous . . . erratic / And jarring to some, but to others ecstatic," an innovator and champion of the bold new generation. Yet she admits "there's always a heart / Hid away in her poems for the seeking; impassioned, / Beneath silver surfaces cunningly fashioned." Recognizing this is essential to a complete picture of this poet of many voices and modes.

Those carefully made poems of Lowell's express her belief in the fundamental relationship of poetry and music, a belief that, despite the formal innovations of much of her poetry, clearly links her to the lyrical tradition. In 1919 she gave a lecture at Harvard (famous in part for being the first ever given by a woman at that proud institution) entitled "Some Musical Analogies in Modern Poetry." The preface to Lowell's breakthrough second book, *Sword Blades and Poppy Seed*

(1914), advocates an alternative name for vers libre: "unrhymed cadence," a term that draws deliberately on musicology's vocabulary for expressive rhythmic phrasing. "Merely chopping prose lines into lengths does not produce cadence," Lowell writes; "it is constructed upon mathematical and absolute laws of balance and time." This position not only defended free verse against those who criticized it as impoverished or anarchistic, it also allowed her to publish poems in the new mode alongside sonnets and other metrical poems with varied rhyme schemes—as well as experiments in "polyphonic prose," the intense interweaving of vowels, consonants, and accentual patterns that she liked to compare to the many voices of an orchestra.

The groundwork for her careful attention to effects of sound must have been laid by the formal poetry of the nineteenth-century "music-makers" Lowell heard as a child. She grew up listening to the much-admired light verse of her famous cousin James Russell Lowell, and to what her father chose to read aloud: the songlike poems written (often by women) for children, and selections from Longfellow or Frances Ridley Havergal's Morning Bells. (Amy Lowell's biographer, S. Foster Damon, describes this anthology as "abominable"—presumably because it contained the sentimental rhymed and metrical verse so popular at the time.)

In a 1917 essay entitled "Poetry as Spoken Art" we learn something of why Lowell did so well at public readings of her work: "Poetry is as much an art to be heard as is music," she writes, and gives very good advice on how to read all kinds of poems aloud. The essay describes the essential linkage of sound and feeling that every lyric poem enacts. It is the "musical quality" of poetry "which differentiates it from prose, and it is this musical quality which bears in it the stress of emotion without which no true poetry can exist."

The last six poems in Lowell's Pulitzer Prize-winning book What's O'Clock (which she completed shortly before her death in 1925), exemplify how Lowell found in the sonnet a form still vital, still capable of containing and shaping that "stress of emotion." The sequence is addressed to Eleonora Duse, the acclaimed actress who more than twenty years before had set young Amy afire with the idea of making art from words; it explores themes of beauty's endurance and power to inspire. As suits passionate poems written to this demanding form, metaphors of molding, carving, mirroring, stamping, and lenses made of "twisted glass" mingle with those evoking the heat and

dazzle of intense responses to the actress and her art. The second poem of the six announces its musical nature by declaring itself "a letter or a poem—the words are set / To either tune." It then describes the poet (or, in a brilliant ambiguity, the poem itself) as a drop of sealing wax "impressed" with "a fret of workmanship." The result is "like melted ice"—frozen, "precise / And brittle"; nonetheless, the sonnet suggests, having been so formed, it may show images of great, even divine, power. And of course, such well-made poems enabled the poet to express quite openly her feelings for the one she so admired.

Despite the emotional repression advocated by the androcentric Modernist aesthetic, Lowell's work demonstrates that her self-description in A Critical Fable is indeed accurate. One indication is her many striking images of sexuality. Some of these are not gender-marked, or include a phrase, such as "supple-limbed youth" in "White and Green" (1914), that steers the reader toward assuming heterosexual desire. One of her best-known poems, the free-verse dramatic monologue "Patterns" (1916) presents female sexuality as "softness . . . pink and silver" hidden away, waiting to be released by a "heavy-booted," stumbling male lover. Like earlier female writers of the so-called Erotic school such as Ella Wheeler Wilcox (1850-1919), Lowell here objects to the suppression of womanly desire: "passion / Wars against the stiff brocade," against "each button, hook, and lace" of the persona's proper attire.

The poet sometimes—as in the relatively early poems "Clear, with Light Variable Winds," "The Basket," and "The Shadow"—adopted a male point of view when celebrating an idealized female beauty. Over time Lowell increasingly used explicit images of lesbian eroticism; many of her love poems were inspired by her longtime companion, Ada Dwyer Russell. For example, in "Aubade" (written in 1913, about a year and a half after Lowell met Russell, and published after Russell began sharing her home in 1914), the poet writes:

> As I would free the white almond from the green
>   husk
> So would I strip your trappings off,
> Beloved.
> And fingering the smooth and polished kernel
> I should see that in my hands glittered a gem
>   beyond counting.

The 1919 Pictures of the Floating World is rich with such images. "The Weather-Cock Points South" describes parting the "leaves" of the beloved, "The smaller ones, / Pleasant to the touch, veined with purple; / The glazed inner leaves," until "you stood up like a white flower." In "A Decade," Lowell writes: "When you came, you were like red wine and honey, / And the taste of you burnt my mouth with its sweetness."

Lowell broke with the previous century by writing, as in these examples, both more far more explicitly and in the Imagist mode. But at the same time she was carrying on the feminine tradition of ardent love poems. The same held true when she helped enrich twentieth-century American poetry by drawing on the literary heritage of China and Japan. *Fir-Flower Tablets,* the 1921 anthology of renditions of Chinese verse that Lowell produced in conjunction with her old schoolmate, Florence Wheelock Ayscough, acknowledges a distant foremother: its title translates the name of the fine sheets of paper made by the most successful woman poet of Chinese poetry's golden age, Xue Tao, whose best-known work includes superlative amatory verse. Lowell's search for new forms led her to write English haiku. But despite its title and its debt to Japanese models, the late sequence "Twenty-Four Hokku on a Modern Theme" reminds the reader once again of poems by nineteenth-century American women, as its lucid images mingle sorrow, self-abnegation, and self-pity with moving declarations of adoration.

The variety of form, tone, and voice within the full range of Amy Lowell's work makes her impossible to pigeonhole with a single convenient label such as Imagist. She strove to learn from many poets and to forge a new aesthetic for a new age. She also strove to write each poem in whatever manner best suited it; often that manner was rooted in the lyrical and passionate poetry of the immediate past.

Sara Teasdale is sometimes taken to be Amy Lowell's opposite: an unrebellious daughter to nineteenth-century poets in the traditional feminine mode, a sentimental songbird warbling on in the new century. Indeed, in *A Critical Fable,* Lowell underlines the negative implications of that metaphor, describing Teasdale as "a little green linnet / Hung up in a cage," and faults her for a range limited to one tone, "the reflex amatorial." Yet Lowell is quick to observe that Teasdale's "poetry succeeds, in spite of fragility, / Because of her very remarkable agility." This "dainty erotic" is characterized as a skillful seducer of her audience, who reveals to the careful reader "a primitive passion so nicely refined," then slips away, thus preserving her essential autonomy. Although Lowell pokes at bit of fun at "Our love-poet, *par*

excellence," she also places Teasdale squarely in a line of descent from Lowell's own poetic foremothers, Sappho and Elizabeth Barrett Browning—only "Our Sara is bolder" than the latter, "and feels quite at ease / As herself."

If Lowell's relationship to the female lyric tradition is stronger than most of her critics would have us see, Teasdale's is more complex. Teasdale's work is charged with a deceptive air of spontaneity; it shines with a deceptively clear gloss. But—as her notebooks and letters reveal—the art and effort were in fact considerable. And the poems themselves remind us that the caged bird's song is not always a simple one.

Teasdale achieved striking, subtle effects from metrical variations and from the use of varied line-length. But in the early years of her poetic maturity she tuned her ear to the cadences of vers libre, and learned from the new way of writing a great deal about word choice and the power of the image. From then on she occasionally chose to use a musically adept free verse.

Whatever the form, her lyrics focused on the expression—and examination—of human feeling. In a 1919 essay she states, "The poem is written to free the poet from an emotional burden." Teasdale lived and wrote in a time of enormous social change, and her poetry draws into question notions of the previous era about what was proper in women's lives—especially, emotional lives—and women's art.

In her own life, deftly though she managed it, that questioning was costly. Her biographers show that it was also unconscious or quickly repressed, as Teasdale clung to appearances of the old order in the day of the New Woman. At age twenty-four, living in her parents' home, she professed impatience with women who chose self-realization over self-sacrifice, off-handedly citing the heroine of Ibsen's *A Doll's House.* But even in her earliest collection of poems, Teasdale writes to an exalted ideal lover, "I bid you awake at dawn and discover / I have gone my way and left you free." For all that this departure is said to be a "gift" that breaks the speaker's heart, the slam of the door as Nora leaves the doll's house in search of her own freedom seems to echo—contradictory and poignant—between these lines.

Certainly Teasdale's description of the changing times into which the nineteenth-century British poet Christina Rossetti had been born tells us something about both women: "Such changes are a strain on the individual called upon to undergo them. We cannot live through one of the crucial acts of the drama of civilization without paying for the privilege." Teasdale's often painful relations with men—her tendency toward love relationships unrequited on one side or the other, and her evasive marriag—show something of how she paid.

Teasdale defended sincere, direct self-expression as essential to true poetry—and hid herself behind a variety of complex, conflicting speakers who suggest a complex, conflicted self. "The finest utterance of women's hopes has been on love," she wrote in the introduction for *The Answering Voice* (1917; revised edition, 1928), her anthology of love poems by women. Again and again the speaker of her poems is "crying after love" ("Spring Night," 1915), in lyrics that appear intensely personal. Teasdale's first two books in particular (*Sonnets to Duse and Other Poems,* published privately in 1907, and *Helen of Troy and Other Poems,* 1911) contain many brief, skillful expressions of love-longing. Sometimes a poem appears to accept the limitations assigned to women, as in "The Wanderer":

> But what to me are north and south,
> And what the lure of many lands,
> Since you have leaned to catch my hands
> And lay a kiss upon my mouth.

But often passion remains unrealized: "Loves come to-night to all the rest / But not to me." ("But Not to Me").

Even the early poems, however, reveal underlying tensions between sexuality and the chastity required by Victorian morality. The very female image of the "velvet rose" in "A Maiden" evokes an intense, frustrated physical desire:

> And since I am a maiden
> My love will never know
> That I could kiss him with a mouth
> More red than roses blow.

The poem "Union Square" points out the cost of traditional feminine modesty, causing a sensation when *Helen of Troy* was published. Though the poem's speaker claims to feel it is "well" that the man she loves "never leaned to hear / The words my heart was calling," she cries out with envy of the streetwalkers who are able (in a naively glorified picture of a sex-worker's life) to "ask for love," as she may not.

A sharp irony is also at work in "The Kiss," with its interrogation of the same romanticized notions she appears to express uncritically elsewhere. After the speaker receives the kiss she hoped for, she becomes "like a stricken bird / That cannot reach the south." What causes this wounding that prevents fulfillment? "His kiss was not so wonderful / as all the dreams I had," we are told—and are left to wonder whether the hurt comes from the lover's inadequacy or from the idealization of romantic love as a woman's one source of happiness. Indeed, the poem leaves open the question of whether the "dreams" were dreams of a romance no real man could live up to or other dreams (like those of "The Wanderer," who in fact had "loved the green, bright north, / And . . . the cold, sweet sea") that must now be given up.

Many poems in *Rivers to the Sea* (1915) posit the conflict between romance and self quite distinctly. "I Am Not Yours" is sometimes read as an example of the desire women were expected to have, to be "lost" in love. In fact, the poem quite subversively asserts an individuality that continues despite that well-learned longing: "Yet I am I, who long to be / Lost as a light is lost in light."

The title of another poem casts the struggle in disguised terms, "New Love and Old." But the true tension emerges at the end, when the love now set aside is asked, "Shall I be faithless to myself / Or to you?" The answer to this dilemma could be almost flippant, in a tone more usually associated with Millay, or even Dorothy Parker (1893-1967); in "Song," a lover is given distinct demands:

> You must love me gladly
> Soul and body too,
> Or else find a new love,
> And good-bye to you.

Sometimes, in a more conventional manner, the resolution to the conflict between vulnerability and independence lies in death, as in the beautiful lyric, "I Shall Not Care."

Teasdale's career was to explore this crucial tension many times, moving more and more often to the side of the self. "The Crystal Gazer" (in *Dark of the Moon,* 1926) expresses the intent to "take my scattered selves and make them one." And the first poem in the same book, "On the Sussex Downs," locates the source of poetic creativity quite clearly: "It was not you, though you were near. . . . It was myself that sang in me."

The final section of *Flame and Shadow* (1920) is titled "Songs for Myself." Although its first poem, "The Tree," begins, "Oh to be free of myself," and although those following pick up the growing themes of age, disillusionment, and mortality, "Song Making" tells us that the poet "'had to take my own cries / And thread them into a song"—even though "the debt is terrible /

That must be paid." Teasdale never stopped making a personal and passionate art, however painful the process.

One alternative to the "terrible" price of self-awareness achieved through self-expression is silence, an alternative many women have chosen. Teasdale examines this cultural expectation in a number of poems. In "From the Sea" (1915), a woman addresses a man she adores, saying, "praise me for this, / That in some strange way I was strong enough / To keep my love unuttered." Yet her first knowledge of her unattainable beloved came from the speaking-out of poetry: "all my singing had prefigured you."' "Night Song at Amalfi" (1915) more distinctly undermines the ideal of feminine reticence:

> Oh, I could give him weeping,
> Or I could give him song—
> But how can I give silence
> My whole life long?

"What Do I Care" (1920) seems, however, to repudiate the effort to assert individuality through the lyrical expression of emotion. Yet it does not choose self-effacement, it speaks of the greater strength of the mind, which is "a flint and a fire . . . proud and strong," while the poet's songs are only "a fragrance" and "do not show me at all": the last line states, "It is my heart that makes my songs, not I." But of course, in a rich and thought-provoking paradox, all this is set forth in the form of a song.

The idea of silence did attract Teasdale. She wrote (in "Those Who Love," 1926) of romantic heroines like Guinevere and Iseult, "Those who love the most, / Do not talk of their love." Even her Sappho asserts (in Teasdale's 1915 poem "Sappho") that she seeks at her life's end autonomy in a rest from making poetry: "I will not be a reed to hold the sound / Of whatsoever breath the gods may blow, / Turning my torment into music for them." Again, the reader discovers a paradox, for of course this refusal is expressed in seven pages of powerful blank verse. And what the world knows of Sappho it knows from her poetry. An earlier poem to the Greek poet's daughter, "Cleis" (1911), reminds us that Cleis, too, was preserved in a poem. Teasdale knew the same would be true of her; "Refuge" (1917) is but one of many houses "made of shining words, to be / My fragile immortality."

Teasdale continued to consider, in poetry, the value of keeping still. By 1926, when *Dark of the Moon* was published, Teasdale could write, "I have less need now than when I was young / To share

myself with every comer / Or shape my thoughts into words with my tongue" ("The Solitary"). In her last book, *Strange Victory* (1933), Teasdale was to assert in one poem ("Age") that silence is appropriate to "the sad wisdom of age."

Teasdale's poetry ultimately subverted nineteenth-century ideas of feminine fulfillment in romantic love. The young dreamer of the early poems came to learn that "the heart asks more than life can give" ("Moonlight," 1920). A few years later she advised, "Take love when love is given, / But never think to find it / A sure escape from sorrow" ("Day's Ending," 1926). Yet in the book she finished shortly before her death, *Strange Victory,* Teasdale indicates that some sort of comfort is possible. "Last Prelude" suggests that the longed-for release from painful separateness that romantic love did not provide could come in the upward rush of "melody," in poetic inspiration. And in "Secret Treasure" the poet declares the value both of lyrical art and of autonomy within the mind, telling us that even when no poems took shape in actual words, she found "unencumbered loveliness" in "a hidden music in my brain."

* * *

For Louise Bogan, the resolution of what her society defined as a dissonant combination, "woman" and "poet," was not so easy. Her strategies for psychological survival and aesthetic success included a discriminating use of restrictions in the form and content of her poetry. She found in intellectual and verbal rigor a way to assert her artistic gifts, one that conveys a transformed version of the inhibition often required of female poets. The results included compelling, tightly disciplined poems on the disturbing topic of womanly emotionality—metrical and free-verse lyrics that display an unsurpassed sense of the music of the English language.

Biographers point out that Bogan's observations of her parents' turbulent relationships and her mother's extramarital affairs must have taught her early on to distrust unrestrained emotions. Yet young Louise also associated her mother with beauty, talent, and vitality. As late as 1962, in a lecture that carries forward her growing pride in the artistic achievements of women, Bogan counsels that women writers "must not lie . . . whine . . . attitudinize . . . theatricalize . . . nor coarsen their truths." She particularly denounced both "the role of the femme fatale" and "little girlishness."

Bogan's striving for a controlled impersonality—untainted by stock feminine poses or sentimental excess—was, of course, grounded in more than the circumstances of her childhood, two difficult marriages, or the painful love affairs of her early twenties. It was a carefully developed aesthetic position, an aspect of male Modernist doctrine that she assimilated and bent to her own purposes. Although the volume of Bogan's work was reduced by her self-imposed limitations, her critical principles enabled her to make enduring art.

Born almost a quarter-century after Lowell, Bogan reached maturity not with, but slightly after, a major feminist efflorescence in politics and literature. In the fall of 1923, when her first volume of poetry appeared, she was featured in *Vanity Fair* as one of the youngest "Distinguished American Women Poets Who Have Made the Lyric Verse Written by Women in America More Interesting Than That of Men." But her association there with Lowell, Millay, Teasdale, Wylie, and other literary woman was a far more positive thing than it came to be for critics in subsequent decades.

The reassertion of dominance by male Modernists (and their critical followers) analyzed by Gilbert and Gubar in *No Man's Land* had much to do with the revolt against the self-expressive poetry of the female lyricists. A similar anxiety may have brought about Bogan's insistence on women's limitations. Perhaps she described herself when she said in 1962, "The blows dealt women by social and religious change were real, and in certain times and places definitely maiming." Her next sentence seems to pick its way through territory mined with psychological peril, asserting that woman is "not the opposite or the 'equal' (or the rival) of man, but man's complement." And women's art, she felt, must accord with what she saw as women's nature.

As Bogan's place in the canon of modern poetry grows more secure, it is important not to forget the effect upon her work of the female lyricist tradition about which she felt such ambivalence. When musical verse with the appearance at least of direct and simple self-expression went out of style during the 1930s, she dissociated herself (in the words of a 1938 essay quoted by Jaqueline Ridgeway) from its potential excesses of "bathos" and "limpness" of form even as she reminded her readers of the "high tension" at work in the best such poems. She also hinted at the role of gender

in fashion's swing, noting the "ridicule" and "contempt" being directed toward "Female lyric grief."

In her late teens Bogan read Teasdale, Guiney, Reese, and other women skilled at expressing feeling tempered by highly polished forms—and learned much from them. Yet she needed to differentiate herself. The poem "My Voice Not Being Proud," in her first book (*Body of this Death,* 1923), claims a poetic voice not "like a strong woman's, that cries / Imperiously aloud." The intricate rhyme scheme of the poem reins in every end-word but the headstrong "cries." In fact, however, the voice is certainly strong, and quietly proud.

Like Teasdale and Millay, moreover, Bogan develops the heritage of nineteenth-century women's poetry by voicing a critique of romantic love. In "Knowledge" (1923) she echoes the previous era's association of love and death in terms of present-day disillusionment: "passion warms little / of flesh in the mould." "The Changed Woman" (1923) "relearns" the nineteenth-century lesson that ardor brings wounds—and the twentieth-century lesson that "the wound heals over." But, we're told, this woman will ultimately yield again to the "unwise, heady" and seductive force "ever denied and driven"; readers are invited to reexamine the title with all the skepticism of the new age. "Girl's Song" (1929) similarly unites with the familiar theme of springtime love-sorrow, a modern worldly awareness that "another maiden" will fall for the faithless lover.

Bogan's poetry makes clear the price for women of the old myths of romance—and the new myths of her own Greenwich Village experiments in free love. She expresses compassion for those who have lived by both versions of vulnerability to the passions, even as she wryly reproves their foolishness. "Chanson Un Peu Naive" (1923) releases a radiant scattershot of ironies, aimed at the female experience of sex, at those who intend to escape the near-death it brings (physically, in orgasm or childbirth, as well as emotionally, in betrayal), at those who believe lovers' lies even while they utter them, at those like the young Millay who make the "pretty boast" of liberation, at those who fail to recognize that pain's warning signal may make it one's truest friend, and at those—including of course herself—who fashion poetry from all this.

Nevertheless, formal verse seemed necessary to Bogan to handle risky emotions. A 1948 letter states that the "burden of feeling" (the phrase echoes Teasdale's 1919 essay) is best taken up "instantly" by a practiced poetic technique (Bogan's emphasis). In "Single Sonnet" (*Sleeping Fury,* 1937) the poet calls on the "heroic mold" of the poem's structure to "take up, as it were lead or gold / The burden." Feeling is described as a "dreadful mass" that cannot be lifted from its torpor without "Staunch meter"; Ridgeway notes that the typescript of the poem indicates it was written at Cromwell Hall, the sanitarium where Bogan received treatment in 1931.

Bogan's early poem, "Sub Contra" (1923), expresses the tension between upwelling emotion and its containment in poetry. The title suggests that a lyric begins in resonant tones almost beneath the threshold of hearing, building from delicate tremors to "one note rage can understand." The poet invokes sounds rooted in the heart, which rouse the mind—as well as craft, which brings what is "riven" into the harmony of a chord. The poem, however, snaps shut with a warning against excess control. The final rhymed iambic tetrameter couplet plays off against the previous loosely cadenced stresses and subtle echoings (the preceding rhymes have run *abcdefcedbaf*) as it calls for freedom from rigidity—"for every passions sake."

Thus Bogan carries on her argument against the overwrought thrill her poetic mothers were accused of and against the neurotic deadening of sensibility of the backlash. The formal poem without "life" provided by feeling is a lackluster thing, like an artificial "Homunculus" (1937). The homunculus-poem, not engendered in ardent procreation but constructed in a learned alchemist's fleshless flask, "lacks . . . Some kernel of hot endeavor," a hazardous but essential source of bodily—perhaps specifically female—energy. In her pivotal 1947 essay "The Heart and the Lyre" Bogan wrote of the "impoverishment" that would result from an abandonment by women of emotionality "because of contemporary pressures or mistaken self-consciousness." Written after years of analysis and introspection, one of Bogan's rare last poems ("Little Lobelia's Song," 1968) was to recognize a further danger of repression: how speechless rage at abandonment sours into sleeplessness, depression, and tears.

Dangerous though it may seem, then, Bogan joins her foremothers in declaring passion essential to poetry. And she too found an empowerment in the making of verbal music. The title of her "Song for a Slight Voice" (*Dark Summer,* 1929) alludes ironically to the notion of an unassertive songstress, but the speaker warns:

If ever I render back your heart
So long to me delight and plunder,
It will be bound with the firm strings
That men have built the viol under.

Clearly, the singer, and the energetic rhythms of her song, have considerable ability to control.

Music, born of the emotions and needed as protection from the hurt they can bring, is in Bogan's view something as greatly to be desired as sexual release. "Musician" (*Poems and New Poems,* 1941) uses the rhyme scheme of a modified Shakespearean sonnet on short lines individually modulated to embody meaning through rhythm. An erotic yearning charges the descriptions of the music-maker's hands. But the much-desired plucking of strings—like the relief of poetic inspiration—has been long delayed. In light of the artistic silences of Bogan's later years these warnings seem prophetic.

Studies by Elizabeth Frank and Gloria Bowles, among others, have recently joined the volumes edited by Martha Collins and Ruth Limmer in elucidating Bogan's life and work. Many aspects of her art have received critical notice—her remarkable use of myth, her compelling explorations of the unconscious, her deep concern with mutability and the human condition, her relation to the Romantic as well as the Symbolist and High Modernist aesthetics. Yet no one aspect seems more essential to our understanding of that art than its grounding in the body: the body that pulses, hears, and sings. "The Alchemist" (1923) speaks of how flesh "still / Passionate" and oddly "unmysterious," outlasts all efforts of will and mind to refine it away. "You may have all things from me," a woman says to a lover in "Fifteenth Farewell" (1923), "save my breath." The first of these two intricately crafted Petrarchan sonnets finds in that "slight life in my throat . . . / . . . Close to my plunging blood," the inbreathing and outflow from which the lyric poem is born. This very physical thing is stronger than heart's pain or the rift between emotions and intellect, the divided "breast and mind."

Bogan seemed intensely aware that her body was a female one. Frustrated when her work was treated by critics in round-up reviews of recent books by women, she struggled with assimilated misogynist attitudes of her times. In a letter written two months before her fortieth birthday the only woman she lists among the nine examples of "oddly assorted authors" she read in her formative years is the British lyric poet Alice Meynell (1847-1922), although in fact there were a number of others. She describes "what I did and what I felt" then as "*sui generis.*" Yet unique though she was, she came to know her parentage—her mothers and her fathers both. Bogan spoke human truths that transcend the channels formed by gender, but she spoke with a profound awareness of gender's molding force on the experience and the expression of those truths.

Further Reading

Bogan, Louise. *Achievement in American Poetry, 1900-1950.* Chicago: Henry Regnery, 1951.

———. *The Blue Estuaries: Poems, 1923-1968.* New York: Farrar, Straus and Giroux, 1968.

Drake, William. *The First Wave: Women Poets in America, 1915-1945.* New York: Macmillan, 1987.

Lowell, Amy. *Complete Poetical Works of Amy Lowell.* Boston: Houghton Mifflin, 1955.

Millay, Edna St. Vincent. *Collected Poems.* Ed. Norma Millay. New York: Harper and Row, 1956.

Teasdale, Sara. *The Collected Poems of Sara Teasdale.* New York: Macmillan, 1937.

Walker, Cheryl. *Masks Outrageous and Austere: Culture, Psyche, and Persona in Modern American Women Poets.* Bloomington: Indiana University Press, 1991.

———. *The Nightingale's Burden: Women Poets and American Culture Before 1900.* Bloomington: Indiana University Press, 1982.

Watts, Emily Stipes. *The Poetry of American Women from 1632 to 1945.* Austin: University of Texas Press, 1977.

Wylie, Elinor. *Collected Poems of Elinor Wylie.* New York: Knopf, 1932.

———. *Last Poems of Elinor Wylie.* New York: Knopf, 1943.

IMPACT OF THE WORLD WARS

PHYLLIS LASSNER (ESSAY DATE SUMMER 1990)

SOURCE: Lassner, Phyllis. "The Quiet Revolution: World War II and the English Domestic Novel." *Mosaic* 23, no. 3 (summer 1990): 86-100.

In the following essay, Lassner studies the impact of World War II on female British authors, contending that these writers used the conventions of the domestic novel as a filter for their experiences during the war through which they questioned both the domestic and political ideology of war and society.

In her 1982 poem entitled "Picture From the Blitz," Lois Clark commemorated the British women who suffered the loss of their homes while holding down the home front during World War II:

After all these years
I can still close my eyes and see
her sitting there,
in her big armchair,
grotesque under an open sky,
framed by the jagged lines of her broken house.

The English domestic novel similarly survived the Battle of Britain, but its import was equally altered forever by the image of a woman who may have nowhere to go when her home is destroyed. Such a change, however, was not merely the result of physical destruction and dislocation; it also had much to do with the way the war on the home front exposed the relationship between the patriarchal ideologies which informed such novels and the sexual politics which conditioned women's daily lives.

As much recent scholarship has shown, both World Wars I and II had deep and lasting effects on women's lives and consciousnesses. Despite disagreement about whether women's wartime experiences were empowering or dehumanizing, feminist scholars maintain that both wars were conducted by societies "organised on aggressively competitive principles" and that whether women were pacifists or complicit with the patriarchy, this was a "wartime state" (Tylee 200). To collapse the significance of both wars, however, is to overlook an important difference.

At a time when World War II was brought home by "the terrifying whine, of Messerschmitts 110 and 109" (Lister 403), many British women writers recognized that this war was not "only one of a sequence of wars" (Gubar "My Rifle" 228). Indeed, noting that it was "easy enough" to see continuities between the horrors of World Wars I and II, Storm Jameson argued that a terrible singularity pertained to "the cruelties the Nazis practice on Poles, Czechs, Jews, in the name of racial purity and on their own countrymen in the name of order" (*Journey* 95-96). Recalling how easy it was to be a pacifist in World War I and between the wars, she now reconsiders the cost of saving "the human mind and spirit," and concludes that she cannot, "with the pacifists, cry: Submit, submit. The price was too high; the smell from the concentration camps, from cells where men tortured men, from trains crammed to suffocation with human cattle, choked the words back into my throat" (*Journey* 6).

In their agony over the targeted destruction of their own homes and families and concern for Nazism's victims outside Britain, many British women writers reconsidered their politics about home and nation. As Catherine Reilly has noted,

ON THE SUBJECT OF...

INDIRA GANDHI (1917-1984)

One of the world's most powerful women, the late Indian prime minister Indira Gandhi dominated her country's politics for almost two decades before her assassination in 1984. Gandhi owed her start in public life to her illustrious father, Jawaharlal Nehru, India's beloved independence leader and first prime minister, but she quickly proved to be an adroit politician in her own right. Gandhi built a charismatic relationship with the Indian masses in a strongly male-dominant culture and consistently confounded her political opponents, most notably when she regained power with a landslide victory in the 1980 elections after being ousted from office three years earlier by voters opposed to her authoritarian form of government. Gandhi was criticized during her career for lacking a consistent political ideology or clear vision of India's future, but even her detractors acknowledged her achievements in strengthening India as a regional power and keeping her country's chronic religious, ethnic, and separatist tensions in check. Tragically, however, Gandhi's firm response to communal violence ended with her assassination at the hands of Sikh religious extremists avenging her government's assault on a Sikh holy place being used as a terrorist headquarters. Gandhi's life has inspired dozens of biographies, and she wrote her autobiography, *My Truth/ Indira Gandhi* (1981), in addition to numerous collections of political speeches.

"the disillusionment engendered" by World War I changed into "a calm acceptance of what had to be done" (*Chaos* xxii). Despite the death of 60,000 civilians in the 1941 Winter Blitz, personal testimony reveals that "the vast majority of British women wanted no truck with pacifism" (Costello 211). As Angus Calder notes, men and women from different political and economic sectors felt that there was "some purpose in this for almost everyone" (57). Thus Stevie Smith felt justified in railing against the "dream darkness" and "dotty idealismus" of "pan Germanism and Naziism"

even while she deplored a history of British imperialism (*Over the Frontier* 258, *Me Again* 174). In her review of Vera Brittain's *England's Hour*, Smith shares Brittain's empathy for victims on both sides of the war, but she is also enraged at Brittain's failure to recognize that the stubborn heroism of a civilian population is a necessary "military weapon" against the German hope to demoralize the British people and make them capitulate (*Me Again* 176).

Like Stevie Smith, other British women writers have also viewed World War II as a very different experience from the war which was to end all wars. These novels not only address women's unequal status in their own homes; they also challenge the patriarchal state which demands that they cope with food shortages, relocations and deaths for a war effort which also classifies them as "immobile" (Minns 10). In addition, they also share the fear and rage at the ubiquity of Hitler's war expressed by Virginia Woolf, who invokes his name for every mention of "tyranny, the insane love of power" ("Thoughts" 155). Because these women felt that Hitler could not be stopped and their loved ones saved except in a total war, they felt empowered to play an active role and to exercise their own definition of humanity.

Thus these writers were empowered not by the death of men in the battlefield, as Gilbert and Gubar claim (*Land* 1:67, 2:262), but by their own debates and formation of their own grounds for participating in the war. Instead of complying with men's reasons for war, they formed their own reasons out of their own agonizing experiences. They supported the war effort, not to salvage a pre-war illusion of stability or, as Nancy Huston claims, to produce sons to die valiantly (119), but to be able to have their children join them in redefining home and homeland. Jameson felt that "on what [women] think . . . depends the future of this land, the future of all the children in it. Let no one tell you what to think. Think for yourself" ("Courage" 15). As a result of thinking for themselves, they were "fighting in the front-line trenches . . . for the first time in the world" (Bloom 33). By filtering their experience and understanding of World War II through the conventions of domestic novels, they questioned the political ideology of war and its relation to domestic ideology.

At first reading, such novels seem to make a simple substitution to accommodate the war-time situation: the familiar upper-middle-class household is transported to temporary quarters in provincial towns where husbands are attached to

Indira Gandhi, Prime Minister of India, a renowned world leader, and writer of political essays.

military installations. Yet the nostalgia in each of these novels is overlaid with an ambivalence which becomes a political statement as persistent in its call for change as Virginia Woolf's *Three Guineas,* Storm Jameson's moral fables, and Stevie Smith's nightmare vision.

What happens in these revisionary domestic novels is that in the face of a war on the home front, melancholy yields to a yearning for change, a development which has a revolutionary aspect because it occurs in "the class" that Elizabeth Bowen observed, "in England changes least of all." Her novel of the 1930s, *The House in Paris,* shows how this world had withstood "the Boer War, the [Great] War and other fatigues and disasters [with] so many opportunities to behave well" (70). The gentle satire in this statement points to a conservatism which fits quite comfortably into the form of the domestic novel. Its model is the irony which drives the novels of Jane Austen. Set within an ideology which "glorified the values of family and home," the ironic twist shows a tempered resistance to "duty, self-sacrifice, and endurance" (Fryckstedt 9). Despite British losses in World War I and economic disaster, the inter-war period was

a time of rebuilding a society which still believed it had a shaping role in the world and at home.

With the bombing of the home front, however, gentle satire could no longer hold the center of the domestic novel. The onslaught of World War II destroyed forever the unquestioned assumption that the family home was an inviolate sanctuary preserving universally held values. Death and evacuation forced women to confront disturbances in domestic life which earlier could be managed with humor. As Jane Lewis and others have observed, without the stability secured by an empire still conceived to be viable, the roles of housewife and hostess became noticeably frustrating and constraining (116).

Against this background, domestic fiction is challenged in new ways. Its ideology is exposed as a powerful and negative force in women's lives through a questioning of the idea that a "powerful and rewarding sense of community . . . and continuity" are "necessary values of the nation in wartime" (Featherstone 156). These values are shown to have had the effect of coercing women into believing that it was best for them to retain their roles as "angels of the hearth" in order to preserve the domestic sanctuary for which their men were sacrificing their lives. Although domestic fiction had inculcated and perpetuated these values even in the quietest times, it took the war to expose the propagandist nature of the genre—to suggest that the message of the domestic novel was no different than that produced by the Ministry of Information. In their revision of domestic plots, women writers discovered that representing the Blitz and evacuation also required the challenging of the old ideologies which assumed that women were "passive, weak and 'naturally' inferior" (Lewis 135). As such, these novels reveal the anxieties behind what Bowen called the "unconscious sereneness" of "living and letting live" (70).

. . . . .

Of the four novels I wish to discuss, *The Long View* by Elizabeth Jane Howard (1956) is the most radical in form. It dissects a marriage spanning the years 1926-50 by beginning at the moment of its breakup and working backward to the first meeting of Antonia and Conrad Fleming. The novel's startling retrospective plotting dramatizes a view of history as determined and depressing. Written years after the war, the novel suggests that women are necessary and exploited during war but barely relevant afterward. At the same time, however, the perspective created by the narrative structure shows a persistent resistance on the part of these women.

The Long View incorporates the social changes of its time span in the consciousness of Antonia, but because we see her awareness emerging at the beginning of the novel—at the moment when it may be too late to change the direction of her life—we share her entrapment. We are forced to watch her fated development without hope of any literary or social surprises. When it begins, in 1950, the novel depicts a woman's futile efforts to discover and sustain what little sense of self she has grafted from her upper-middle-class life. Looking ahead to her next twenty-five years, she realizes that she has had no "violent facile conviction to support her . . . no god-like creature brimming with objective love and wisdom to whom she could turn" (34-35). This melancholy view of a woman caught in the stasis which her world takes for stability becomes a challenge to the reader. As we review her life for the past twenty-five years, we also review the social and literary forces which seemed, in the twenties, to promise women self-determination. In the narrative space of Antonia's life, we see how these promises left women wiser

but still trapped in domestic space. For the contemporary reader, from the perspective of new promises for women's liberation and of new feminist perspectives on women's writing, Howard's novel is a sobering experience.

The Long View shows the interaction of social and literary experiment with women's psychological, social and literary imprisonment in domestic scenes of the fifties. When the novel begins, the Flemings' marriage has reached the end of a protracted stalemate. When the novel ends by retrospectively returning to 1926, we are thus aware of the doomed nature of Antonia's youthful innocence and open-ended dreams of self-definition. This long and critical retrospective view shows how the curious mixture of idealism and cynicism of the twenties created a bind for female character: whatever highs and lows the world endured, the fates of women in the domestic novel remained bound to the care and feeding of family establishments.

In the time warp of *The Long View,* all emotional and social modulations are dramatized in terms of domestic conflict. The opening scene, wherein Antonia Fleming views her dinner party as "the kind of unoriginal thought expected of her" (9), makes it clear that the domestic power which enabled Mrs. Ramsey and Mrs. Dalloway to create a moment of harmony has atrophied. Over the long and disastrous course of the Flemings' marriage, woman's domain functions not only as a battleground, but as the sacred fount on which women are worshiped and discarded. They cannot but fulfill and disappoint male fantasies of ageless and infinitely fascinating grace and beauty while they serve as the emotional and social barometer of the hearth. The following exchange between Antonia and her first disappointed and disappointing lover prefigures the categorical distinctions in which a patriarchal ideology has caged the female. When he asserts, "Domestic creatures never have any choice, you see—not like the wild ones," she questions whether it is possible to "divide people up like that," into "Wild, or domestic" (313). Only during World War II, an episode at the formal and thematic center of the novel, is there a possibility for Antonia to define her own responsibilities and thus other categories for female experience.

The second part of the novel, "1942," opens with a domestic scene turned inside out. Harboring various evacuated mothers and children as well as convalescent soldiers, the upper-middle-class home is shell-shocked. One mother, Mrs. Fawcett, is disenfranchised at another angel's hearth and seems reduced to a parody of a general without a war. "With a kind of expert wildness," she appears to have lost her sanity, her sense of self, as she is forced to give up her own home and become an object in another woman's imprisoning space (72). The repetition of "wildness" to indicate choice is clearly ironic here. As a term which connotes a romantic dream of the free and noble savage, "wildness" typically champions men's yearning for self-discovery but marks women with comparable dreams as deviant. Mrs. Fawcett's wildness, however, like the "unaccountable" Land Girl doing farm work at the Flemings' country house who "exuded sex," represents a rebellion against all the upper-middle-class arrangements of power and order as they originate in the home (73). When Mrs. Fawcett quarrels with the Land Girl and shows her contempt for gentility and cleanliness, she expresses a rage which undoes all the propaganda and myths about the "national characteristic of being magnificent in a crisis" (72).

Another woman billeted with Antonia reverses Mrs. Fawcett's disorder: "Dorothy lived a life dominated by Hitler" and by her wish for his assassination. Within her obsession, however, is a cautionary vision: an omnipotent Hitler whose "fiendish ingenuity" threatens to control Britain (72). Mrs. Fawcett's sense of geo-political disaster inspires Antonia to recognize the oppression within her own home. Driven by her husband's patriarchal imperatives, Antonia develops her own vision through a new sense of community which the historian Eric Taylor calls "the strange sisterhood of war" (34). Like the crazy-quilt mix of women who relocate together in Sylvia Townsend Warner's story "Sweethearts and Wives," it is through the "feminine unreason" of the other women in Howard's novel that Antonia begins to sense her own "frostbitten mind," paralyzed from domestic responsibility (76, 73).

The war mobilizes Antonia's sense of herself by forcing her to enact her desires. She expresses her intense love for her children by keeping them in England against her husband's wishes and she disturbs his compulsive designs for living by taking in evacuees and wounded. When her husband comes home on leave, Antonia turns his accusations of her weak-mindedness against him. At the very moment that she acknowledges his injunction not to "identify [her]self" with the war, she suddenly recognizes that she has betrayed his expectations and discovered her own: "The notion . . . that perhaps *he* could not really choose the part she played for him, occurred to balance

their uneven intimacy" (84). Making her "political unconscious" conscious (Marcus 58), Antonia speaks and acts in opposition to a husband/commander who has tired of her precisely because she has so completely fulfilled his desire for her and has therefore become for him, "ineffective and improvident" (78). When she makes no move to learn to cook, and even as she succumbs to her husband's embrace, Antonia comes to terms with her own desire and her own vision of this war. Her actions relieve "the selfish private panic" which defined the "frivolous inconsequent dream" of her pre-war life (76).

At this pivotal moment in her marriage, however, with internal and world war threatening her every movement, Antonia sacrifices a sustained enactment of her desires to a futile hope for continuity. The end of the novel retrospectively brings this futility full circle. At a party, Antonia meets the man who is to become her husband. The scene is evocative of popular romance; on the last step of a staircase, a nameless man speaks gently, pronouncing her fate: "'This isn't the end: it may very well be the beginning': and picked up her hand again as though it was a piece of essential equipment without which neither of them could begin to move from the end of the staircase" (352). Like the myths inscribed in "The Sleeping Beauty" or "Snow White," rescue by the prince is predicted by the form.

Howard's tale, however, like her circular staircase, curls back to a beginning which signifies that the prince's rescue, the "beginning" of his tale, is not a journey to happily ever after. If Antonia makes her own destiny by offering her hand, the backward movement of the novel shows how the mixed messages of her traditional background make this inevitable. Even as the wartime experience fostered women's independence, by 1950, when this novel begins, it is clear, as Karen Anderson points out, that the war also "generated confusion, insecurity, and anxiety," out of which grew an "ambivalence" which is no more surprising than "the attempt to reconcile conflicting values and behavior with the strident certitudes of the postwar 'feminine mystique'" (111).

. . . . .

Women's entrapment in the domestic myths legitimized by World War II also forms the center of Betty Miller's novel, *On the Side of the Angels* (1945). In this work the Carmichael family relocates to a house in a provincial town where the husband serves as medical officer at an army installation. The contrast between the "family life" established among the officer corps and what takes place in the family home provides the method by which Miller creates a scathing critique of the social morality of the English upper middle class and the domestic novel.

War, in *On the Side of the Angels,* is both an experience and the subject of debate for the two central female characters. Typical of the English novel, two sisters (Claudia and Honor) represent different responses to the dislocations which are exposed at the heart of the English middle-class society. In a "state of perpetual civil war," Claudia is a portrait of ambivalence (99). She is "irritated" by "all this male pirouetting" and by her older married sister's "complacency, accepting everything" (18). Yet despite the fact that she is a teacher of history, its lessons are lost on her when she is seduced into a romance starring a tall, dark commando, the enigmatic Neil Herriot. Claudia searches for her own point of view between two traditional tales which inscribe the constraint of women. Engaged to Andrew, a young man with a weak heart, she is expected to become part of his tradition-bound family home, but in her vision of it as "the future," she is already "opposed" to the "cherished" past" of "the temperate life at Honeybourne" (23, 72). Although some critics have argued that Miller supports Andrew's attitudes, actually the novel charts Claudia's unsteady course between two positions: Andrew's eloquent arguments about universal emotions becoming war when projected outward and the life or death rhetoric of her impostor commando, Herriot (Cooper, Munich & Squier 17). At the end, Claudia joins Andrew to temper their equally romantic if opposed views of war. This alliance between a man with a damaged heart and a woman who is a "potential source of unrest" reflects a feeling of "affectionate irony" toward the future of their nation (40, 238).

Claudia and her sister struggle against men's stories about war. Unlike Claudia, however, Honor rarely speaks openly for herself, living only in the expectation that she will embroider herself into the texture of a man's world. In the split society of home and army, the home is expected to function like a garage, a place where broken men come to be mended. Miller, however, unearths a conflict between the interests of domestic and army life in the scene where Colin Carmichael, out walking with his Colonel, is "humiliated" by his wife's (Honor's) unexpected presence: "A male world, without loyalties outside the rigid artifact of military life" confronts the housewife's "complacent challenge" (38-39). Burning with shame,

Honor becomes aware of her dishonor: her "femininity . . . the slipshod contours, of all that was inchoate, ununiformed about her: that which was capable of giving offense . . . to the men before her" (39).

Even categorical distinctions between "domestic" and "wild," between woman as "anarchy" or as mother can be dispensed with here, for the woman does not count; the object of male desire lies well outside the confines of the kitchen garden (72). As Colin vies with Herriot, the imposter, for the Colonel's attentions, it is clear that the family home is only a breeding station for male bonding. Miller shows that what World War II really provided was basically a morally and psychologically justifiable outlet for the reification of a patriarchal society. Nurtured by the family home but free of its constraints, men thrive in the games of war. As Simon Featherstone observes, the community of men who "protect 'the sleeping English hills and fields and homesteads' . . . is represented as and for England . . . for a single purpose. The action of gathering together transforms the village community into the 'wartime community', with the effect that traditional values are preserved and even heightened by a new singularity of social and hence national purpose" (156).

Miller's novel shows the casualties of that national purpose and women's redefinition of it. Like Virginia Woolf's angel, Honor is "free" to help herself to scraps "once everyone else was served" (205). She cannot, however, follow Woolf's call in *Three Guineas* to join a Society of Outsiders. Miller's Honor is in the double bind of wanting to preserve her life with her children while suffering the deprivation it affords. Whereas Woolf declared, "As a woman, I have no country. As a woman I want no country. As a woman my country is the whole world" (103), Honor's slogan might be, "As a woman I want a country. As a woman my country is the home front."

Honor's performance on the home front, however, is not as compliant as her sister claims, for her "lethargy and benevolence alike, seemed to sanction a certain fertile disorder" (119). Drawn in opposition to Andrew's mother, who "by instinct of class preservation" stands for old values in old domestic novels, Honor disrupts the house she rents from the conservative couple who preserve themselves by moving to a hotel (70). As Honor recognizes the cost of her servitude, she begins to imagine what her country might be like, to feel her husband's absence as "something positive: a leaden weight from the oppression of which she did not know how to escape" (205). At the end of the novel, when Colin calls to say he will be having supper with his Colonel, the narrative focus turns to a child's lead soldier, a "tiny Guardsman, faceless, shouldering resolutely his damaged rifle" (237).

The differing positions of Claudia and Honor intersect with the experience of the war in an incident at the heart of the novel, the shooting down of an enemy plane. As the townspeople bury the German pilot, the only reaction given expression is that of the Carmichael's nursemaid: "Edith, who knew no values, who, solitary, had nothing to lose or gain by the betrayal of her emotions . . . unguardedly expressed, the very ecstasy of love itself" (161). When Colin accuses her of feeling that "the enemy is really her ally," that she has displaced the hate she must feel for "us all," he exposes the unbridgeable gulf between his experience of war and that of the women. Relying on old categories of them and us, his analysis guarantees that women, like the enemy, are "the other."

The empathy expressed by Edith is similar to that expressed by Margaret Kennedy in her memoir of wartime domestic life, *Where Stands a Winged Sentry*. Her fears for her children's lives and future led her to recognize the uniqueness of World War II: "We discovered unsuspected passions and loyalties. We realised which things we valued most"; "Surely," Kennedy continues, "[i]t must . . . be all right to pray that both England and Germany may be delivered from the Nazis" (22). The values Kennedy openly expresses are the same as those which Colin is incapable of reading in Edith or in Honor. These are the values which Honor embodies at the end of the novel, alone, wanting to and having to protect her baby, but representing as well, an empathetic commitment to a relationship which defines family and homeland in opposition to her husband. Susan Suleiman sees such an opposing force as figured in terms of "the mother's body . . . a place of disorder and extreme singularity in relation to the collective order of culture" (368). In this sense, Honor's "absent and rapt" oneness with her baby is not in the service of patriarchal war but, in its expression of love and empathy, in opposition to it (238). According to Suleiman, the mother's body must also be "the link between nature and culture, and as such must play a conserving role" (368). Because the mothers in these domestic novels are confronted with a war on the home front, they

are conserving only what they need in order to imagine a culture based on a mother's empathy.

. . . . .

Elizabeth Taylor's *At Mrs Lippincote's* is another testament to the way definitions of home and homeland are feminized in these wartime domestic novels. The protagonists, Julia and Roddy Davenant, have moved to a rented house in a provincial town near his army base with their son Oliver. Like Honor, Julia discovers through the dislocation of war that the home front is besieged by irreconcilable differences in the couple's expectations of each other and of marriage and family purpose. Like Colin Carmichael, Roddy finds the camaraderie of army life more congenial than family intimacy. Like Honor, Julia "leaves disorder" in her wake and is challenged by the different vision of another woman relative, Roddy's cousin Eleanor (6).

As in Miller's novel, in *At Mrs Lippincote's* the contiguous communities of home and army are seen to reflect an uneasy alliance, a cold war which questions the purpose of a nation. Through the expression of power and patriotism represented by army life, women are shown to be manipulated into believing that they must repress their needs for individuation and submit to the higher purpose of protecting the nation.

At Mrs Lippincote's is structured as a process of Julia awakening to her individuality by testing herself against women's traditional roles. A wife and mother, she has "no life of her own, all she could hope for would be a bit of Roddy's—" (20). Moreover, she is responsible for weaning her son from the intimacy they share and grooming him for the higher purposes of the world she cannot enter: "Could [Julia] have taken for granted a few of those generalizations invented by men and largely acquiesced in by women (that women live by their hearts, men by their heads, that love is woman's whole existence and especially that sons should respect their fathers), she would have eased her own life and other people's." Julia's lot is therefore not an easy one because she makes a revolutionary discovery, that "I love myself" (26).

One way Taylor dramatizes Julia's development is by having her read earlier women's novels. In order to assess the governing conventions of her life, Julia must become a critical reader, reinterpreting the conventions of romance and realist fiction. At first, Julia passively responds to *Jane Eyre* as romance. Feeling oppressed and in need of rescue, she identifies the Wing Commander who befriends her as Mr. Rochester. Only when she decides to leave her house for a walk by

ON THE SUBJECT OF...

THE LITTLE REVIEW

Launched by Margaret Anderson in 1914, the *Little Review* was a monthly avant-garde magazine of literature and the arts. Anderson founded the magazine to "reach people with ideas" and to "offer the best conversation the world has to offer." The magazine was successful, making literary history with almost every issue, publishing the new, the provocative, and the untried, including work by writers Sherwood Anderson, Ernest Hemingway, T. S. Eliot, Ezra Pound, William Carlos Williams, Gertrude Stein, and Jean Cocteau. Anderson, an ardent feminist, also used the *Little Review* to espouse the cause, by publishing or reviewing the works of Olive Shreiner, Emma Goldman, and other feminists of the early twentieth century.

The most familiar and noteworthy achievement of the *Little Review* was its serialization, beginning in 1918 with James Joyce's *Ulysses*. Declared obscene, four issues of the *Little Review* in which Joyce's work appeared were burned by the United States Postal Service, and Anderson and her associate editor, Jane Heap, were convicted of obscenity charges. The magazine became a quarterly in 1921, the year of the obscenity charges, and appeared at irregular intervals thereafter. Anderson moved the magazine to Paris in the early 1920s and by 1929, faced with continual financial struggles and weary of the magazine, allowed its demise.

herself does she recognize the potentially transformative aspects of Bronte's text. Thus when she and the Wing Commander compare recipes from favorite novels, Julia is able to express her preference for the boeuf en daube from *To the Lighthouse*, a text which he finds too modern. Similarly just as she comes to see the tropes of rescue tales as self-imprisoning, so she later rejects the moral of Flaubert's realist fable: "I never wanted to be a Madame Bovary. That way for ever—literature teaches us as much, if life doesn't—lies disillusion and destruction. I would rather be a good mother, a fairly good wife, and at peace" (204). Such an alternative, however is equally self-defeating.

As Nancy Armstrong has observed, Taylor's novel suggests that domestic fiction is a successful form of those chapbooks that prescribe the formation of female character according to traditional codes of conduct. Domestic fiction appeals to women readers in a self-justifying way: it inscribes a romance that conforms to beliefs women have internalized about needing "to be brave and competent, look their best and stand by—or possibly behind—their men. Family life must be held together . . ." (Waller & Vaughan-Rees 13). In wartime, the message is as loud and clear as a poster proclaiming "*Your* courage / *Your* cheerfulness / *Your* resolution / WILL BRING US VICTORY" or the Queen's tribute to women's "readiness to serve . . . the State in a work of great value" (Minns 11, 28). Such propaganda turns out to be just as deadly as either accepting or rejecting Madame Bovary's romantic fantasies and interpreting Jane Eyre's quest for selfhood as a rescue by Mr. Rochester. As she corrects her reading, Julia forms a consciousness which heals what Gilbert and Gubar describe as the split personality imagined by woman writers as a saving grace (*Madwoman* 16). At the same time that she rejects the Wing Commander's copy of *Wuthering Heights* as the gift of "an incurable sentimentalist," she also tears up all her letters from Roddy (206). The "borrowed hearth" has shown her that to be its angel, accepting "the little rules" which are supposed to keep the nation safe, has been like "skat-[ing] on thin ice" (214, 105, 213).

Julia's growing opposition to Roddy parallels her antipathy toward his cousin Eleanor. A romantic who would like to see Lord Byron in the sickly Mr. Aldridge, Eleanor's odyssey comes to a dead end. Despite her view of Mr. Aldridge's communist cell as courageous and interdependent, Eleanor finds herself "bored" and "depressed" with its "courage" and "interlaced" lives. Likewise, her idealization of Roddy as "always braver and nobler" leads to devaluing herself and feeling "shut away in [the] air-tight compartments" of his home (126, 123). Frustrated finally by the failure of her romantic vision, she explodes. Like the evacuees in *The Long View*, and like the war itself, her rage exposes the emotional isolation of middle-class women. Projecting her anger onto her sister-in-law, Eleanor accuses Julia of being responsible for Roddy's infidelities, but in so doing, she forces Julia to express her own anger, which she had denied for the sake of stability.

Julia's refusal to acquiesce to "the little rules" which unify the life of a house signals the breakdown of the power of domestic ideology (105).

Seeing through the myths of home and hearth gives her the critical language to dissect the romantic legends which keep women in their separate sphere. Written at the end of the war, the novel marks an important rupture in an ideology which had assumed immense power over women's lives. Jane Lewis describes the contradictory message involved here for middle-class women: having won more mobility, legal freedom and increased expectations of sexual pleasure by World War II, they had also to yield to "staunchly defended strict separation of spheres" (135-36). As in Miller's novel, however, the maternal sphere here is also a saving grace. Only Julia can save her son from the lingering illness which, like the war, he inherits from his father. If it turns out that Oliver is not "good at games," that is, his father's war games, it is because of his mother's tutelage (31).

If Julia, like Honor and Antonia, cannot begin to imagine alternatives for herself outside the domestic sphere, it is because in a total war these women are able to rebel enough to recognize a newly developed sense of themselves, but not enough to threaten the fabric of a nation that they would like to save for their children. In their unhappiness and self-recognition, the war also assumes a different meaning for these women. It is no longer about global domination, but about the sharing of power which begins in the family home.

· · · · ·

One Fine Day (1946) by Mollie Panter-Downes presents the English domestic scene in the form of a bittersweet elegy to values which had to be disturbed. The war cannot be viewed as a passing disruption, but as the external correlative of a society endangered from within. As Stephen and Laura Marshall try to adjust to their different expectations when he returns from the war, the assumptions which kept them mutually dependent before are exposed as anomalies. The props supporting a privileged society tumble when women, like the servant class, are shown to share an awakening self-consciousness about a need for self-definition. They discover life outside the "domestic chalk line." Panter-Downes uses a wealth of domestic detail to inscribe women's experience of stifling sameness "bound to the tyranny of [the] house" (45). In contrast with its now undomesticated, wild garden and with Barrow Down to which Laura briefly escapes, the house is shown to be crumbling as a result of husband and wife being at odds with its imperatives.

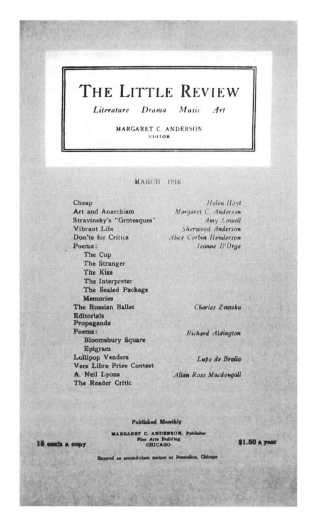

Table of contents page for *The Little Review,* March 1916.

The post-war period of *One Fine Day* reels from the battles of domestic life exposed by the war. The rationing which shapes English life after the war becomes a metaphor for the emptiness Laura feels in attempting to rebuild a sense of stability and continuity in her home. Like *The Long View, One Fine Day* looks backward and forward, but just as it follows a sequential line from past to future, it is also more optimistic. In 1946, shortly after the end of the war, there is much to look forward to. Yet despite the exclamation that Laura "was feeling so extremely happy" (184), Panter-Downes clearly has reservations: nowhere in this novel is there a sign that women will have more than "dead food" to nourish their sense of a life outside the family domain (65). Just as Laura's daughter is named Victoria, the traditions of the past have not been destroyed by the war, but "could be seen here as something living which did not stop abruptly, but went on, stretching out to the present, on into the future" (110). Unlike the satiric domestic scenes in Evelyn Waugh's *Put Out More Flags,* these novels see nothing funny about the role of tradition in women's lives on the home front. Panter-Downes sees tradition as a pressure on women to keep "The British Empire [which] seemed to have contracted into the modest white house" from turning to "dust and ashes" (73, 182).

Yet the potential for change is embedded in Laura's character. Just as she never learns how to dust, so she possesses a nature always in conflict with domesticity. Like Antonia's recognition of her own desires, Honor's affirmation of mother love, and Julia's critical reading, Laura is envisioned as a woman contained in her own becoming.

. . . . .

All four novels present ambivalence as a first step toward the possibilities for change in English domestic society. Basically this ambivalence takes the form of juxtaposing mothers who recognize their exploitation but adhere quietly to their family responsibilities with "wild women" and those who explode in protest. Yet, ambivalence is also portrayed in the mothers themselves, who at each novel's end are seen managing their domestic duties, but whose sense of a blunted self is abetted by the urgent need to save their children from the very real horrors that Audrey Beecham images in her poem, "Eichmann":

> incense of Belsen is stench in the nostrils of
> heaven
> Ashes of Ravensbruck idly drift over the air
> Lightly touch down in the teacups of innocent
> parties
> Dusting with grey the blondest of teenage-dyed
> hair.

Far from being indicative of passive maternal impulses, the concern in these novels with the victims of war is a sign of "subjectivity, agency, or initiative" (Greene 8).

In these novels mothers act on several fronts at once. They hold down the home front in order to protect their children, but like Honor, they also protest the war by redefining domestic priorities as a commitment to an interdependent love which they hope will reshape the core of their nation: "It was as if the focus of peace that was Honor with the child at her breast, deepening, permeated the whole house: as if from her body there radiated a beneficent influence which . . . was detected by senses that were incapable at the same time of recognizing its source" (232). This is not a "mother who is overly invested in her child, powerless in the world," the figure whom contemporary feminists worry about (Greene 8). This is a woman whose definition of family and nation represents both an alternative to war and her own reasons for holding down the home front. Rosamond Lehmann's story, "When the Waters Came," dramatizes the way motherhood provides initiative to reimagine a nation's fate. Imagining the flood epic as a domestic tale of World War II casts a woman in the role of transforming natural and political disaster into a vision of regeneration. When the earth thaws after an ice storm which deadens the earth, a mother saves her drowning daughter and, in so doing, saves her world.

Thus instead of being an anti-liberationist factor, "the physical and emotional experience of motherhood and of maternal love" becomes the means whereby women realize that they have been exploited by a patriarchal order which must be reimagined in order to save what they value (Suleiman 370). In her agony over the war, Margaret Kennedy embeds political protest in an expression of maternal love: "The future of all these children, of all the children in the world perhaps, is in the balance. . . . There has never been any moment quite like this before in the whole of history . . . and we have no power, *no power,* to save them from a most hideous fate. We can only wait for tomorrow" (104). To wait may seem passive and compliant, but as a position which holds the ground supporting the lives of children, it holds fast against internal as well as external dangers.

Ambivalent and complex, the women in these novels interrogate what feminist critics point to as "the essentialist assumptions" of the conventional war text (Cooper 15). In their redefinitions of the home front, they can not be reduced to either apolitical nurturing figures or politically compliant victims of culture. These women struggle to distinguish their idea of home and family from that which they inherited or married. They represent the reconstruction of female character in the course of an historical crisis their writers recognized as threatening to the lives of women and their children, both of whom are the keys to change.

Works Cited

Anderson, Karen. *Wartime Women: Sex Roles, Family Relations and the Status of Women During World War II.* Westport, CT: Greenwood, 1981.

Armstrong, Nancy. *Desire and Domestic Fiction: A Political History of the Novel.* New York: Oxford UP, 1986.

Beecham, Audrey. "Eichmann." Reilly 17.

Bloom, Ursula. "Courage." *Women in Wartime: The Role of Women's Magazines 1939-1945.* Ed. Jane Waller and Michael Vaughan-Rees. London: Optima, 1987. 33.

Bowen, Elizabeth. *The House in Paris.* Harmondsworth: Penguin, 1987.

Calder, Angus. *The People's War: Britain 1939-45.* London: Cape, 1969.

Clark, Lois, "Picture From the Blitz." Reilly 27.

Cooper, Helen, Adrienne Munich, and Susan Squier. "Arms and the Woman: The Con[tra]ception of the War Text." *Arms and the Woman: War, Gender, and Literary Representation.* Ed. Helen Cooper et al. Chapel Hill: U of North Carolina P, 1989. 9-24.

Costello, John. *Love, Sex and War: Changing Values 1939-45.* London: Collins, 1985.

Featherstone, Simon. "The Nation as Pastoral in British Literature of the Second World War." *Journal of European Studies* 26 (1986):155-68.

Florence, Mary Sargant, Catherine Marshal, C. K. Ogden. *Militarism Versus Feminism: Writings On Women and War.* Ed. Margaret Kamester and Jo Vallacott. London: Virago, 1987.

Fryckstedt, Monica C. "Defining the Domestic Genre: English Women Novelists of the 1850's." *Tulsa Studies in Women's Literature* 6 (1987): 9-25.

Gilbert, Sandra M., and Susan Gubar. *The Madwoman in the Attic: The Woman Writer and the Nineteenth-Century Literary Imagination.* New Haven: Yale UP, 1979.

———. *No Man's Land: The Place of the Woman Writer in the Twentieth Century.* 2 vols. New Haven: Yale UP, 1988, 1989.

Gubar, Susan. 'This Is My Rifle, This Is My Gun: World War II and the Blitz on Women.' *Behind the Lines: Gender and The Two World Wars.* Ed. Margaret Randolph Higonnet et al. New Haven: Yale UP, 1987. 227-59.

Greene, Gayle. "Family Plots." *The Woman's Review of Books* 7 (1990): 8-9.

Howard, Elizabeth. *The Long View.* London: The Reprint Society, 1957.

Huston, Nancy. "The Matrix of War: Mothers and Heroes." *The Female Body in Western Culture.* Ed. Susan R. Suleiman. Cambridge: Harvard UP, 1986. 119-36.

Jameson, Storm. "In Courage Keep Your Heart." Waller and Vaughan-Rees 14-15.

———. *Journey From the North II.* London: Virago, 1984.

Kennedy, Margaret. *Where Stands a Winged Sentry.* New Haven: Yale UP, 1941.

Lehmann, Rosamond. "When the Waters Came." *Wave Me Goodbye: Stories of the Second World War.* Ed. Anne Boston. London: Virago, 1988. 1-5.

Lewis, Jane. *Women in England 1870-1950: Sexual Divisions and Social Change.* Bloomington: Indiana UP, 1984.

Lister, Elizabeth. "Goering and Beethoven." *The Listener* 18 Sept. 1941: 403.

Marcus, Jane. "The Asylums of Antaeus. Women, War and Madness: Is There a Feminist Fetishism?" *The Difference Within: Feminism and Critical Theory.* Ed. Elizabeth Meese and Alice Parker. Philadelphia: Benjamins, 1989. 49-84.

Miller, Betty. *On The Side of The Angels.* New York: Penguin, 1986.

Minns, Raynes. *Bombers & Mash: The Domestic Front 1939-45.* London: Virago, 1980.

Panter-Downes, Mollie. *One Fine Day.* New York: Penguin, 1986.

Reilly, Catherine. *Chaos of the Night: Women's Poetry and Verse of the Second World War.* London: Virago, 1984.

Smith, Stevie. *Me Again: Uncollected Writings.* Ed. Jack Barbera and William McBrien. New York: Vintage, 1983.

———. *Over the Frontier.* New York: Pinnacle, 1982.

Suleiman, Susan Rubin. "Writing and Motherhood." *The (M)other Tongue: Essays in Feminist Psychoanalytic Interpretation.* Ed. Shirley Nelson Garner, Claire Kahane, and Madelon Sprengnether. Ithaca: Cornell UP, 1985. 352-77.

Taylor, Elizabeth. *At Mrs Lippincote's.* London: Davies, 1945.

Taylor, Eric. *Women Who Went to War: 1938-46.* London: Hale, 1988.

Townsend, Colin, and Eileen Townsend. *War Wives: A Second World War Anthology.* London: Grafton, 1989.

Tylee, Claire M. "'Maleness Run Riot'—The Great War and Women's Resistance to Militarism." *Women's Studies International Forum* 11 (1988):199-210.

Waller, Jane, and Michael Vaughan-Rees. *Women in Wartime: The Role of Women's Magazines 1939-1945.* London: Optima, 1987.

Woolf, Virginia. *Three Guineas.* New York: Harcourt, 1966.

———. "Thoughts On Peace In An Air Raid." *The Death of the Moth and other Essays.* London: Hogarth, 1942. 154-57.

SANDRA M. GILBERT AND SUSAN GUBAR (ESSAY DATE 1994)

SOURCE: Gilbert, Sandra M., and Susan Gubar. "Charred Skirts and Deathmask: World War II and the Blitz on Women." In *No Man's Land: The Place of the Woman Writer in the Twentieth Century,* pp. 211-65. New Haven, Conn.: Yale University Press, 1994.

In the following essay, Gilbert and Gubar contend that while World War I provided a huge impetus to women writers, World War II, in contrast, was perceived by many as a revival of patriarchal values. Gilbert and Gubar examine the impact of both wars on women's writing and social positions, arguing that women's literary responses to World War II are poignant records of hopelessness in the face of confusion about sex roles and social expectations.

There is too much fathering going on just now and there is no doubt about it fathers are depressing. Everybody nowadays is a father, there is father Mussolini and father Hitler and father Roosevelt and father Stalin and father Lewis and father Blum and father Franco is just commencing now and there are ever so many more ready to be one.

—Gertrude Stein

The War she endured was different.

—H. D.

The place I am getting to, why are there these
    obstacles—

The body of this woman,
Charred skirts and deathmask
Mourned by religious figures, by garlanded
    children.
And now detonations—
Thunder and guns.

                —Sylvia Plath

After H. D. had followed the swastikas chalked on the Vienna pavement directly to Freud's door, she realized that in analysis she would have to conceal her dread of war because of her Jewish Professor's vulnerability, but her fear of militarism was let loose during the London blitz. Enduring "the full apocryphal terror of fire and brimstone," she learned to "switch" her mind into the "dimension out of time" that she presents as a *"haven/ heaven"* in *Trilogy* (*CP* 543). Yet she remained "sick to death of tensions and tiredness and distress and distorted values and the high pitched level and the fortitude" demanded by nearly a hundred days of bombing.[1] And her later texts about the Second World War grew increasingly pessimistic about the war's impact on the relationship between the sexes. From *Helen in Egypt* (begun 1952) to *Thorn Thicket* (composed 1960), H. D.'s poems and prose examined the claim Helen makes about her sister that "the War she endured was different"—different from the First World War and from the war experienced by men—because, as this memoirist put it about herself, "the War was my husband."[2] As if generalizing about what it might mean to live in an erotic partnership with destruction, H. D.'s companion, Bryher, declared, "The First War had opened a few doors but . . . the Second slammed many of them shut."[3]

Although, as Bryher's comment suggests and as we argued in *Sexchanges,* the Great War became a crux that elicited gloom about masculine paralysis from many literary men while exciting glee about female mobility in many literary women, World War II functioned differently in the literary imagination of both sexes. Writing in occupied France, Gertrude Stein contrasted the freedom she had attained in the First World War with her subsequent sense of disaster: "You begin a thing in one war and you lose it in the next war. From war to war."[4] Stein's 1937 protest against too much fathering, which we have used as our first epigraph here, represents the reactions of many of her female contemporaries who also experienced in World War II a resurgence of patriarchal politics. Her sentiments were echoed by the heroine of Doris Lessing's *Martha Quest* (1952) who fears about the Second World War that "this new war was in some way necessary to punish her."[5] Although many literary women enlisted in intel-

ligence, propaganda, and refugee work, they often intimated that what had been gained in the earlier conflict was lost in the later.

Elizabeth Bowen's short story "The Demon Lover" (1945), read as a ghost story exploring the impact of the two wars on the relationship between the sexes, dramatizes the ways in which World War II destroyed women's traditional sphere—the domestic world of the home—and unleashed male hostility against women. When Mrs. Drover, the central character, returns to her bombed townhouse, she finds a mysterious letter from a fiancé who had been reported missing in the Great War. This letter from the dead is a reversal of the usual trope in which the envelope encloses news of death. She stealthily escapes from her damaged house to avoid the man, for he had "never been kind" to her. But when she enters a waiting taxi, she discovers that he is its driver, and he sweeps her screaming "into the hinterland of deserted streets."[6] Although Mrs. Drover had been effectively freed from an unsatisfying relationship by the Great War, her suffering during World War II seems to represent a return of the repressed. Haunted by guilt, Bowen's central character appears to suffer a punishment related to her survival after the disappearance of her fiancé in World War I.

From the forties on—that is, from the wartime writing of Virginia Woolf, Elizabeth Bishop, Edith Sitwell, Kay Boyle, Gwendolyn Brooks, and Carson McCullers to the postwar work of H. D., Harriet Arnow, Muriel Spark, and Doris Lessing—a surprising number of poems, stories, and novels by women focused on the vulnerability of female characters alienated from or threatened by their so-called defenders. More striking than, say, Stein's attacks on fathers Hitler and Mussolini were such women's critiques of the forces fighting for father Roosevelt and father Churchill. During the same period in which Pearl S. Buck argued that "psychologically and emotionally, war sets women back both in man's mind and in their own,"[7] a number of literary women presented not only fascist but also Allied militarism as a logical extension of misogyny. Why did the contemporaries of women from Bryher and Stein to Lessing perceive the Second World War as a threat to the second sex?

According to Stein, World War I was "a nice war, a real war, a regular war," while "certainly nobody no not anybody thinks this war is a war to end war."[8] Her remark points to one of the major differences between the two world wars, for World War *II* was only one of a sequence of wars. As a repetition, the Second World War was perceived by both sexes with much less idealism than had accompanied the beginning of the Great War, which haunted their memories. For men, and in particular for literary men, the earlier war marked a historical and imaginative watershed: "Never such innocence again," Philip Larkin explained in his poem "MCMXIV" (1960). Directly addressing "a conscript of 1940," Herbert Read recalled about the last group of soldiers, "We went where you are going, into the rain and the mud," and warned the next generation of combatants, "We think we gave in vain. The world was not renewed." Keith Douglas, demoralized by a repetition of warfare that proved the futility of the brilliant protest poetry of the Great War, hopelessly concluded about Isaac Rosenberg's earlier "Break of Day in the Trenches," "Rosenberg I only repeat what you were saying." In addition, even those literary men who, in C. Day Lewis's words, wrote war poetry to "defend the bad against the worse," suffered from the feeling of belatedness explained by Stephen Spender's remark that the poetry against "fascism had already been written . . . during the Spanish war."[9]

For women, and in particular for feminists like Ray Strachey and Vera Brittain, women's economic decline during the interwar years generated skepticism about government propaganda which encouraged female mobilization. Of course women were urged to join the war effort as, say, WACS (Women's Auxiliary Corps) or Wrens (Women's Royal Naval Service) or as Rosie the Riveters in the factories. By the early forties, the female labor force in Britain and the United States had expanded by over 40 percent, approximately three-quarters of it consisting of married women. Mrs. Laughton Matthews, the director of the Wrens, almost echoed triumphant female responses to the earlier war in her claim, "This war has exploded so many of the old theories about women."[10] Yet a number of recruitment posters had to be taken out of circulation when protests were lodged against the glamour they cast over dangerous, difficult jobs, while other come-ons presented war work as a necessary but only temporary departure from women's more important homemaking and childrearing responsibilities: "Some jubilant day mother *will* stay home again, doing the job she likes best—making a home for you and daddy," the Adel Precision Products ad promises about its pencil-factory workers.[11]

As auxiliary units, ruled by the military but not legally within it, many English and American women's corps received no insurance, no benefits, and no ranks equivalent to those of men. Not

ON THE SUBJECT OF...

ELIZABETH BOWEN (1899-1973)

Noted for her subtle, evocative novels and short stories, Elizabeth Bowen is compared with such novelists of sensibility as Jane Austen, Henry James, and Virginia Woolf. Bowen was born on June 7, 1899, in Dublin, Ireland. After her father was hospitalized with mental illness and her mother died from cancer in 1912, she was sent to boarding school in Kent, England, and later to the London Council School of Art, which she left after two terms in 1919. It was during this period, when she was living on her own in London, that Bowen began to write seriously. Her first short story collection, *Encounters,* was published in 1923. By 1929 she had published two more volumes of short stories and two novels, establishing a rate of production she maintained much of her life. During the 1930s Bowen began to associate with Woolf and the Bloomsbury circle in London. Her experiences living and working as an air-raid warden in the besieged city during World War II inspired what many critics consider her finest short story collection, *The Demon Lover* (1945), which explores war's insidious effects on the human psyche. She is perhaps best known for her novel *The Death of the Heart* (1938), and critics point to that phrase as an apt summation of Bowen's recurrent theme: the inevitable disillusionment inherent in human relationships, particularly as innocent characters make the painful passage to experience. Critics praise Bowen for her descriptive, finely pitched style, and they often compare her with Katherine Mansfield for her extreme sensitivity to perceptions of light, atmosphere, color, and sound. Like Mansfield, Bowen is considered expert at presenting the emotional dynamics of a situation and then swiftly illuminating their significance.

surprisingly, too, soon after the war women's military organizations were characterized as an "expression of free-flowing penis-envy"; they represented, it was thought, "the masculinity complex institutionalized, pure and simple."[12] Mrs. Matthews was prescient, if powerless, when she added to her assertion that "facts have shown that women can do anything" the proviso that "we must see that [female recruits] are not disappointed as they were in many ways after the last war." In spite of the economic freedom gained by, say, the subjects of the film *Rosie the Riveter,* women might have interpreted War Department brochures explaining that "a woman worker . . . is a substitute—like plastics instead of metal" to mean that, as a substitute, the female war worker was to be exchanged as soon as possible for the real thing. Even the most celebratory books about the female war effort concluded with the conciliatory proclamation, "The majority of girls are looking forward to running homes of their own, not to running a man's job." Understandably, then, Margaret Mead complained about the "continuous harping on the theme: 'Will the women be willing to return to the home?'" a question "repeated over and over again . . . by those to whose interest it will be to discharge women workers, regardless of whether they are wives, widows, or spinsters, as soon as the war is over." And one year after the war, three million American women, as well as over a million British women, were laid off or left their wartime jobs.[13]

But if the women who entered the labor force and the services paradoxically faced a heightened rhetoric about women's proper place in the home, both men and women knew that, as an adumbration of a third World War or even a fourth, the Second World War could never be considered a "Great" war. Indeed, if World War II had any singularity, it was as the first *total war,* waged by all against all. The whole female population, not just the women serving in the air and armed forces, was no longer insulated from the brutality of the battlefield. As Paul Fussell has observed, "The Second World War, total and global as it was, killed worldwide more civilian men, women, and children than soldiers, sailors, and airmen."[14]

Although during the 1914-18 conflict many women were protected by the sharp demarcation between the safety of the home front and the fighting in no man's land, during World War II civilians throughout Europe were affected by bombings, air raids, blackouts, evacuation, rationing, geographical dislocation, housing and food shortages, or enemy occupation. For this reason, literary men and women shared a common abhorrence of assaults that seemed virtually apocalyptic: while Dylan Thomas's "A Refusal to Mourn the Death, by Fire, of a Child in London" (1945)

lamented, "Deep with the first dead lies London's daughter," Edith Sitwell envisioned humanity crucified and "blind as the nineteen hundred and forty nails / Upon the Cross."[15] Concentration camps, trajectory guns, long range rockets, "strategic" raids, military mistakes, firebombings, and atomic bombs closed the gap between home and war front, displaying the vulnerability of women and the domestic sphere.

Even as technology rendered civilians more vulnerable, it made possible a kind of depersonalization that insulated crews in large bombers and transport aircraft from the reality of destruction: "When those on earth / Die, there is not even a sound," a flyer admits in James Dickey's poem "The Firebombing" (1964), which recalls Dickey's own experiences, and he therefore becomes "enthralled" by "aesthetic contemplation" of the destruction he has created. "You only see the first plume and first fall," John Ciardi's pilot observes in "Take-Off over Kansas" (1947), so "you think, 'It was not human after all.'"[16] The irrationality as well as the deprivation of military life combined with the increased destructive capabilities of the machinery of war to fill many men with dread, although Robert Graves has pointed out that a larger proportion of the military was occupied with civilian-oriented duties than ever before and John Press has argued that some soldiers "enjoying, albeit with a twinge of guilt, the green pastures of Kenya, the pleasures of Egypt, or the imperial grandeur of India might reflect that they were a great deal safer and more comfortable than people in the cities and towns of Britain."[17]

But of course the airplane and zeppelin that Yeats envisioned pitching "like King Billy bomb-balls in / Until the town lies beaten flat" destroyed countless men trapped inside fox holes, submarines, and bombers.[18] One of the most moving American war poems—Randall Jarrell's "The Death of the Ball Turret Gunner" (1945)—dramatizes the terrible vulnerability of the man operating machine guns set into the plexiglass belly of a B-17 or B-24 bomber; speaking from death's kingdom, Jarrell's airman first finds himself awakened by flak, then, "When I died they washed me out of the turret with a hose."[19] Many servicemen suffered not only from the guilt and anesthetization Dickey and Ciardi describe but also from the miseries of combat, imprisonment, and dislocation depicted in Jarrell's verse.

No longer encased in the static but symbolically resonant trenches of no man's land, soldiers participated in a mobile war that was broadcast on radios and filmed in movies. For, as Paul Fussell has observed, "Compared to all previous wars, the Second was uniquely the Publicity War."[20] From the perspective of both men and women, media coverage brought the war home, as if to illustrate the expansion of the "theater" of war from the battlefield to the home front, and espionage played a much more prominent role in the Second World War than it had in the First: the enemy was potentially anyone anywhere. World War II therefore ended the possibility of a separate sphere for women; it seemed less a generational conflict between fathers and sons than a road to universal apocalypse, or so the firebombing of Dresden and the atomic bombing of Hiroshima and Nagasaki demonstrated. In fact, the only separate sphere created was in the ghettos and camps where Jews were segregated into male and female barracks as part of a process that led to total depersonalization and death. That the enemy had also defined itself in explicitly masculinist terms meant that women were inexorably involved in the ideological debates that distinguished World War II from the nationalist struggles of the Great War. Because fascism in Germany and Italy evolved as a reaction against the emasculation associated with World War I and the Depression, the fascist "father" regarded his leadership as a sexual mastery over the feminized masses.

The potentially infinite sequentiality of world wars, the technological advances in destructive capability, the obliteration of a safe home front, the extensive media coverage, the genocide, and the ideological threat of fascism: all these horrified men and women both. Yet many literary women also felt victimized by men who were presumably on their own side. Certainly feminist polemicists, as well as women novelists and poets, mourned the suffering of their male contemporaries. But in spite of (or perhaps because of) the sense of grief and alienation literary men recorded, literary women also feared that male vulnerability in wartime would result in hostility toward or violence against women. While total warfare called into question any stark dichotomizing of home and combat fronts, the two most persistent images of women in literature written by men—the whore and "the girl he left behind"—tended to place women in a realm of their own even as these character types were often judged by highly conventional norms of compliancy or loyalty on the one hand and indifference or betrayal on the other. Not only did the whore and "the girl he left behind" tend to blur into each other; they both also modulated between masculine desire (for a refuge from battle) and masculine dismay (at the

insufficiency of that refuge). As we shall see, then, even those men who were distressed by the hypertrophied masculinity spawned by the crisis of war often attempted to cope with their fear of emasculation by reconstructing a sexual mythology of separate spheres.

Literary women's responses to World War II, frequently an articulation of dread, have long gone unheard because we have failed to realize that they were grappling with ideologies that reified gender arrangements as rigidly as they had been demarcated in the Victorian period but in a newly sexualized way. Far more explicit about the connection between heterosexuality and masculine bonding than the literature produced during the Great War, the works of literary women and men record mutual hopelessness about the confusion of sex with death that was turning men into demon lovers and women into their willing victims. Indeed, for those literary women who reacted to the "thunder and guns" as Sylvia Plath did in the sixties, World War II marked the demise of a dream of Herland that had shaped earlier feminist fantasies and the rise of a recognition that within the no man's land of history all that subsisted behind the fictionalized mythologies of femininity were the "charred skirts and death-mask" of the dead woman, a nowoman.

. . . . .

Elizabeth Bishop's "Roosters" (1946) is scathing in its denunciation of war as a battle cry of virility, and it reads like a brilliant gloss on two questions posed in a letter by Virgina Woolf: "Musn't our next task be the emancipation of man?" and "How can we alter the crest and the spur of the fighting cock?"[21] Bishop's answers, like those of many of her aesthetic compatriots, remain gloomily equivocal about the possibility that women will be able to disentangle definitions of manhood from warfare. "Roosters" uses the image of the fighting cock to link masculinity with militarism in a trope exploited by feminist polemicists and women artists; it also uncovers the association of guns and virility in the texts of literary men who were equally concerned that a battle of the sexes threatened to turn the war into a virtual blitz on women.

"Roosters" begins by satirizing militarism as a masculinism that awakens the sleeping speaker "in the gun-metal blue dark."[22] With their "protruding chests / in green-gold medals, dressed," Bishop's cocks arise "with horrible insistence," screaming their "uncontrolled, traditional cries." Gloating and floating over "our beds" and "our churches," they screech a refrain—"This is where I live!" or "Get up! Stop dreaming!"—that wakes "us here" to "unwanted love, conceit and war" (36). Bishop's fowls are endowed with an "excrescence" which "makes a most virile presence," and they therefore seem physically programmed for violence: "The crown of red / set on your little head / is charged with all your fighting blood" (37). Given Bishop's pun on the word *cock*, her roosters imply that militarism must be understood as stupid, biological cruelty motivating a senseless but inexorable masculine territorial imperative. The cockpit of a plane is here represented as the site of ceaseless cockfights and the cocked firearm is simply an "excrescence." Yet the whole world is terrorized, for "making sallies / from all the muddy alleys," the roosters mark out "maps like Rand McNally's" (36).

To be sure, after crowing as "poor Peter" weeps at his betrayal of Christ, one of Bishop's roosters reappears during what appears to be a turn in the poem as a chanticleer whose spurs are composed of Peter's tears, suggesting that "'deny, deny, deny' / is not all the roosters cry" (38). Yet Bishop's poem does not solve the problem of escalating hatred through a simple affirmation of Christian love. Although Peter's forgiveness, like the sun that rises at the end of "Roosters," has caused a number of critics to view its development as a redemptive "mov[e] from a country morning to the morning of Christianity," there is a disturbing similarity in the language used to describe the kamikaze cocks falling from midair ("Down comes a first flame-feather") and that used to delineate Peter's treacherous "falling, beneath the flares."[23] Equally sardonic are the rhymes of the poem ("sallies," "alleys," "McNally's" or "guess," "bless," "forgiveness") as well as the speaker's judgment that "St. Peter's sin / was worse than that of Magdalen / whose sin was of the flesh alone" (37).

In addition, the poet's question "How could the night have come to grief?" is ambiguous. For while it might suggest self-criticism on the part of the speaker (how could I have thought that the night would come to grief?), it also can be read as sad acknowledgement (how terrible that the night did come to grief). Finally, the dawn in the last verse stanza—

The sun climbs in,
following "to see the end,"
faithful as enemy, or friend—

is equivocal (was Peter an "enemy, or friend"? the "end" of the night's destruction or the "end" of life as the speaker had known it?), and the rising sun (during the war associated with Japan) succeeds only in making the cocks *almost* inau-

dible" (39; emphasis ours). The poet therefore implies that the songs they have sung, which have "flung" them in "dung," subsist even in "those cock-a-doodles" said to "bless."

An attack not only on male aggression but also on male mythologies of heroism, "Roosters" further deflates the rhetoric of unwanted love, conceit, and war by demonstrating how the fighting cocks, who turn the world into a barnyard, transform wives into hens who lead lives "of being courted and despised":

Cries galore
come from the water-closet door,
from the dropping-plastered henhouse floor,

where in the blue blur
their rustling wives admire,
the roosters brace their cruel feet and glare

with stupid eyes
while from their beaks there rise
the uncontrolled, traditional cries.

[35]

Either the rustling wives admire the cruel feet and stupid eyes of the crowing cocks or the hens lie dead "with open, bloody eyes" while the cocks' "metallic feathers oxidize." To the extent that the poem articulates Bishop's sense that in wartime women can only watch and wait or die, it poses a question—"Roosters, what are you projecting?" (36)—that informed the responses of a number of Bishop's contemporaries who depicted women "courted and despised" as whores, wives, and mothers. But a critique of the trope of militarism as masculinism that the roosters were projecting emerged even before the outbreak of the war in feminist polemics that assumed women were in a privileged situation from which to oppose fascism as the extreme but logical conclusion of masculine domination.

According to Mary Beard, the Nazis, who were trained "in isolation from women," consisted of "battalions of bachelors" and, borrowing a title from Hemingway, she argued that these "'men without women'" constituted "a menace to the liberties of women."[24] For Winifred Holtby, fascist ideology, which evolved as a reaction against the Continental women's movement and which curtailed women's new-won freedoms in Germany and Italy, effectively removed women from the work force and denied them any right but the right to produce and sacrifice the next generation of sons. Identifying D. H. Lawrence's doctrine in *Aaron's Rod* (that "men must submit to the greater soul in a man for their guidance; and women must submit to the positive power-soul in man for their being") with Goering's glamorization of leadership in *Germany Reborn* ("From the first moment that I met and heard [Hitler] I belonged to him body and soul"), Holtby protested in 1935, "But a world of hero-worshippers is a world in which women are doomed to subordination."[25] Similarly, in *Three Guineas* (1938), Woolf declared that dictators always insist it is the "essence of manhood to fight," and she therefore speculated that the fascist states might be able to reveal "to the younger generation at least the need for emancipation from the old conception of virility" (186, 187).

Katherine Burdekin's 1937 dystopia, *Swastika Night* (which Daphne Patai views as a major influence on George Orwell's *1984*), analyzes fascism as male domination: her novel presents Europe after seven centuries of Nazi hegemony as a feudal state in which a "Reduction of Women" program has arrogated women to the submissive, physical function of breeding and restricted them to ghettos while Nazi rulers bond in homosexual attachments and legalize their rights to rape women and remove all male children over one year of age from their mothers.[26] The inauguration of Hitler's new society occurs in a scene that connects the triumph of fascism with the fateful emergence of a misogyny so lethal it does not merely "reduce" women; it mutilates and destroys them. A lonely, last holdout encounters the body of a naked young woman on a roadside, a mangled body which convinces him of the impossibility of public dissent: "The hair had all been pulled out, leaving nothing but a ghastly red skull-cap of blood. The body was covered with innumerable stabs and cuts that looked as if they had been made with a penknife. The nipples had been cut off" (84).

Although this victim was murdered because she had scorned the idea that women should be "animals and ugly and completely submissive" (82), those who survive acknowledge that "it was beneath the dignity of a German man to have to risk rejection by a mere woman": "*all* women [are] at [men's] will like the women of a conquered nation" (81). Therefore, under the masculinism that is fascism in Burdekin's work, women, living "according to an imposed pattern" that legislates sexual exploitation and inculcates self-hatred, are "not women at all": "The human values of this world are masculine. There are no feminine values because there are no women" (107-08).[27]

Of course, Allied propaganda, like Archibald Macleish's *Fall of the City* (1938) and Edna St. Vincent Millay's *Murder of Lidice* (1942), often relied on the idea that fascism directly threatened women: both texts use grief-stricken or dead women to measure the effects of German aggression. During the war, a series of posters graphically presented the enemy as the man who would rape and murder "our" women. Whether the woman was portrayed as an Aryan-looking mom about to be caught in the clutches of hands resembling claws, or a ravaged corpse lying amid the ruins of a landscape obliterated by the huge face of Adolf Hitler, or a naked prey draped over the shoulder of a predatory Japanese soldier, the female functions as bounty: both the bountiful fertility that must be saved and the booty that constitutes the spoils of war [. . .]. Not only could the madonna and child of "Keep These Hands Off!" be torn apart from each other by the grasping fingers, but the woman could be penetrated, as she is in both "This Is the Enemy" posters, by stake, gun, or (given the disheveled and nude figures) the magnified, bestialized masculinity of the German and Japanese enemy.

Identification of fascism with masculinism, as well as women's past noncombatant status, initially led women writers to assume that, as Muriel Rukeyser put it, while "all the strong agonized men" who "wear the hard clothes of war" found it difficult "to remember" why they are fighting, "women and poets see the truth arrive," and they "believe and resist forever."[28] Rukeyser's "Letter to the Front" (1944) goes on to explain that the woman poet speaks for "labor, women, Jews, / Reds, Negroes," a claim comparable to Marianne Moore's vow in "In Distrust of Merits" (1943) that "'we'll / never hate black, white, red, yellow, Jew, / Gentile, Untouchable'" (*CP* 137). Yet the passion for U.S. involvement in a "good" war and the patriotism of "Letter to the Front" are shadowed by Rukeyser's alienation from the forces fighting fascism, her intimation that female lives were being threatened by Allied, as well as Axis, forces.

Although Rukeyser was emphatic in her belief that the war must be won "in love and fighting," in the "Home thoughts from home" included in "Letter to the Front" she admits that "a man fights to win a war, / To hang on to what is his," be it "his own birth" or "his own whore," and she documents the sense of unreality experienced by women who become a symbol of peace:

> We hold belief. You fight and are maimed and
>   mad.
> We believe, though all you want be bed with one
> Whose mouth is bread and wine, whose flesh is
>   home.
>
> [239]

The poet admits, "We are that home you dream across a war"; yet when she hears "the singing of the lives of women" at the end of the poem, she confronts not a mouth of "bread and wine," a flesh that "is home," but instead "the sorrow of the loin," the "sad dreams of the belly, of the lip, / Of the deep warm breast," for "all sorrows have their place in flesh, / All flesh will with its sorrow die." Although she believes "it is time for the true grace of women" to emerge and free "a new myth among the male / Steep landscapes," she can only imagine resistance and regeneration in negative terms, and specifically in terms of a new form of humanity evolving "not as traditional man" (243).

Rukeyser's conviction that returning soldiers at the war's end would desire a sacramental consummation with women but would encounter a home battle waged against "labor, women, Jews, / Reds, Negroes" helps explain why many women, in spite of their loathing of fascism, felt suspicious of the forces fighting fascism. Indeed, a 1941 essay by Lillian E. Smith and Paula Snelling speculated, "If man dared to thrust into the open his unending secret enmity against woman, there might be less of nation warring with nation; less need for him to merge his longing for superiority into a great mass-lust for power, less need for him to find outlet for his hate." In addition, because, as Smith and Snelling pointed out, "home has no wall around it that will protect it from aerial bombs" and because women were moving toward what Rukeyser called "a wider giving" (217), they confronted the possibility of losing the security and the privileges, as well as the privations, of their traditional domestic sphere.[29]

As Vera Brittain observed, "Modern war struck more fiercely than ever before at those things which meant life to the majority of women—children, homes, education, healing."[30] At the same time, the historical exclusion of women from the military was dramatically challenged by the first draft of unmarried women into the British Armed Forces; according to Winifred Holtby, the technological nature of warfare meant that there was "no reason why, if wars are to be fought at all, women should not be subject to conscription, service and death on the same terms as men."[31] No wonder, then, that the future of feminism itself seemed vexed to some of its most ardent advocates. Woolf's metaphorical ignition in *Three Guineas* of the "vicious and corrupt word" *feminism*, a parodic enactment of Nazi book burning, is the most ironic sign of her frustration at the alternatives available to women, for she cannot burn the words *Tyrant* and *Dictator*, which "are not yet obsolete" (101-02).

While Woolf implies that she looks forward to a time when the word *feminism* will no longer be needed, Gertrude Stein dramatizes her even more intense hopelessness about women's cultural situation. In *The Mother of Us All* (1946), Stein portrays first a disgusted and later an exhausted Susan B. Anthony, who laments the fact that men will not give women the vote and attributes male recalcitrance to male anxiety: "They fear women, they fear each other, they fear their neighbor, they fear other countries and then they hearten themselves in their fear by crowding together and following each other, . . . they are brutes, like animals who stampede, and so they have written the name male into the United States constitution, because they are afraid of black men because they are afraid of women, because they are afraid afraid. Men are afraid." Significantly, however, Stein's suffragist does not look forward to the time when women will win the vote, "because having the vote they will become like men, they will be afraid, having the vote will make them afraid."[32] That the vote is finally won after Anthony is dead and reified into a statue turns the play into an elegy for the spirit of feminism.

"Dispersed are we," Miss La Trobe's gramophone scratches out at the end of *Between the Acts* (196), the play-within-the-novel Woolf wrote just before the war and, as Louise Bernikow has noted, the female modernist community was dispersed by World War II.[33] By the end of the forties the generation of feminist-modernists associated with Stein and Woolf had died or, as in the case of the Paris expatriates, scattered. The bombing of England meant, moreover, that British women of letters lived through substantially different experiences of war than did North American, Australian, and South African literary women. Paradoxically, however, precisely the sense of vulnerability which resulted from the disintegration of women's interwar communities and which is anticipated in Stein's portrait of Anthony's long life of strife produced a brilliant literary tradition that amplifies the battle cries of both sexes. Less concerned with military maneuvers than are the texts of their male contemporaries, many wartime works by women reiterate Burdekin's dread that the war constituted a specifically sexual warfare directed against women.

In Woolf's view, women who attempt to "compensate the man for the loss of his gun" must free not only Nazi but also English airmen "from the machine" ("Thoughts on Peace in an

Air Raid" [1940], *DM* 156). Yet in her last work, *Between the Acts* (1941), she is hardly confident about this project. For while the novel includes a play by Miss La Trobe that pointedly leaves the British army out of English history, militarism is obliquely represented as a threat to women when Woolf's heroine Isa broods on a *Times* article about the gang rape of a nameless, naive girl by troopers. As if to dramatize the narrative consequences of Bishop's insights into unwanted love, conceit, and war and Woolf's point that English and Nazi militarists must be liberated from their ethos of aggression, in *The Heat of the Day* (1948) Elizabeth Bowen's heroine Stella Rodney, who works during the blitz in "an organisation better called Y.X.D., in secret, exacting, not unimportant work," is horrified to realize that she cannot disentangle the identities of her lover, an Axis spy, and his antagonist, his Allied pursuer.[34] Just as her lover, Robert Kelvey, has kept Stella ignorant of his Nazi connections, so his antagonist, Robert Harrison, has proposed to collude in Kelvey's treason in exchange for Stella's sexual compliance. Besides using these male doubles to analyze the commonality of Axis and Allied "intelligence," Bowen further explores World War II as a menacing backlash against the sexual repercussions of the Great War.

Kelvey turned to Nazism after he was first raised in a "man-eating house" (288) dominated by women and then sent to Dunkirk where he received a wound he associates with his emasculated father. Seeking "to be a man in secret" (314), Kelvey illustrates Bowen's thesis that the attraction to fascism is inextricably related to what she calls a "fiction of dominance" (289). As in "The Demon Lover," in *The Heat of the Day* Bowen's central character becomes convinced that "the fateful course of her fatalistic century seemed more and more her own" (147). Like the heroine of Stevie Smith's *Over the Frontier* (1938) who comes to believe that "all holders of privilege" are "ruthless and cruel in their tenure," Stella attains a Woolfian consciousness into her own vulnerable status as an outsider.[35]

In a further elaboration of the war's brutal effect on women, Edith Sitwell's "Lullaby" (1942) presents a nightmarish reversal of Darwinian evolution in which a baboon replaces a dead mother to sing a song of devolution: "And down on all fours shouldst thou crawl," the ape cautions the child who inhabits a world of dry sockets and steel birds, "For thus from no height canst thou fall."[36] The only maternal message of perseverance possible in Sitwell's sterile environment

consists of "the discordant cry" of the poem's refrain, "Do, do, do, do," which emphasizes that the endearing "du, du" of traditional lullabies is now a stuttered warning that there is nothing to "do" but return to the dust of the ape's sunless world. Similarly, although in "Letter to the Front" Rukeyser sought an image of innocence to imagine the promise of a future after the war—"You little children, come down out of your mothers" (241)—she believed that "the sad-faced / Inexorable armies and the falling plane" transformed the prophetic woman poet she sought to be into "a childless goddess of fertility" (227).

But Sitwell's tellingly titled "Serenade: Any Man to Any Woman" (1942) is more explicit in attributing linguistic casualties to the brutality Woolf's Isa reads about in the newspaper. For what "any" man says to "any" woman is comparable to the deadly invitation issued by Bowen's demon lover. The cannoneer-speaker of "Serenade" identifies his beloved with a cannon ("Dark angel who are clear and straight / As cannon shining in the air") and woos the woman (who "can never see what dead men know!") by asking her to "die with me and be my love."[37] The ironic reversal of Marlowe's "Come live with me, and be my love" implies that the "universal Flood" of wartime destruction is composed of female, as well as male, "blood." Intoxicated less by love than by death, any man in battle, Sitwell suggests, will sing a demonic serenade of annihilation. Her dramatic monologue thus functions as a meditation on the commingling of eroticism and warfare—of weapon, phallus, and girl—that caused H. D. to view the war as her husband, that shaped Bishop's satiric portrait of fighting "cocks," and that, we will see, became quite common in literature written by men. A shared consternation about what Bishop called the "excrescence" of "virile presence" transformed American and British women's letters *to* the front into letters *from* the front. And, as Rukeyser knew, "When the cemeteries are military objectives / and love's downward drawing at the heart, . . . every letter bears the stamp of death" (250).

. . . . .

The confusion of love and death, sex and murder, girl and cannon evident in Sitwell's "Serenade" finds a parallel in the chant used to teach marines how to name their instruments correctly: "This is my rifle, / This is my gun, / This is for fighting, / This is for fun." Oddly, though, the metaphorical association of gun with penis sometimes modulated into an identification of gun with female; in *Battle Cry* (1953) Leon Uris's squat sergeant patiently explains this lesson, as he hands out rifles: "'You've got yourselves a new girl now. Forget that broad back home! This girl is the most faithful, truest woman in the world if you give her a fair shake. She won't sleep with no swab jockies the minute your back is turned. Keep her clean and she'll save your life.'" Similarly, a poem entitled "Cannoneer's Lady" (1943), by Lieutenant Morris Earle, contrasts a man's love of woman with his passion for "a howitzer [which] goes to the heart of a man": "In the retch and recoil," he explains, "The cannoneer, loving her, cared for her more / The moment this turbulent outburst began."[38]

With retrospective clarity, a number of male poets—John Ciardi and Lincoln Kirstein, for example—protested the ways military life ritualized masculinity so that, in the words of the historian John Costello, "Soldiers . . . came to regard their weapons as extensions of their virility."[39] While manuals given to U.S. army infantrymen proffered the advice "your rifle, like your girlfriend, has habits for which you must allow," Ciardi satirized "the sex of war":

> The health of captains is the sex of war:
> the pump of sperm built in their polished thighs
> powers all their blood; the dead, like paid-off
>   whores,
> sleep through the mornings where the captains
>   rise.

For Kirstein, the soldier who "feels his courage stir" in a whorehouse "can manage five-minutes' stiff routine / as skillfully as grease a jeep or service other mild machine. // Slips off his brakes; gives her the gas." Kirstein's title—"Snatch" (1964)—ironically conflates his soldiers' efforts to "snatch" pleasure on a furlough with the female "snatch" which is as depersonalized as a jeep or any other "mild machine."[40]

Many photographs of "our boys over there" reinforced the fused images of sex and death that so disturbed men and women of letters. Pinups, barely clothed or naked, adorned bunks and tanks named after women, and posters and drawings of movie stars and models jokingly represented what the men were fighting for [. . .]. With more frontal nudity than in any earlier war, the female figures painted on planes add resonance to the eerily incoherent "US Army Flyer's Lament" which included the refrain "I wish all girls were like B-24's / And I were a pilot, I'd make them all whores."[41] Indeed, when pinups were used to teach camouflage techniques and map reading to new recruits, the targets of desire and destruction became identical. Glossing this phenomenon, Ivor

Roberts-Jones, a poet who served as an artillery lieutenant, viewed the bombardment pattern produced by "the guns shout[ing] in the narrow valleys" as "little . . . shifts, like a girl arranging her dress, / At the start of the party waiting for the young men."[42]

Perhaps in consequence of all this, World War II marked an increase in the use of the word *fuck* to mean not only intercourse but also assault or exploitation. As Fussell has pointed out, numerous memoirs of veterans record their mechanized sexual experiences of "wall jobs" and "knee tremblers," but one Canadian soldier's reticence captures both the violence and the surrealism of swarms of whores "servicing" the forces: "I won't describe the scenes or the sounds of Hyde Park or Green Park at dusk and after dark. . . . You can just imagine, a vast *battlefield* of sex" (emphasis ours).[43] As Elaine Tyler May explains in her history of the cold-war era, "female sexuality continued to represent a destructive and disruptive force" after the war, perhaps most dramatically when a photograph of Rita Hayworth was attached to the hydrogen bomb dropped on the Bikini Islands and when the name "bikini" was chosen by its designer to establish the swimsuit's explosive effect.[44]

As the texts of Ciardi and Kirstein demonstrate, however, many war works produced by literary men protest, as do those by Bishop, Woolf, and Sitwell, against the excrescence of a hypertrophied virility, thereby agreeing with Cyril Connolly, the editor of *Horizon,* that the "lack [of] patriotic poetry" was a "healthy sign" of "the decline of the aggressive instinct."[45] Ciardi's captains engage in "the sex of war" only to awake among "the dead, like paid-off whores"; Kirstein's soldiers, who "service" whores, are themselves depersonalized in the "stiff routine" of giving "gas." The confusion between gun and penis led literary psychologists of warfare to examine the war as an assault on or a perversion of male sexuality: Lincoln Kirstein's terrified soldier turns to masturbation only to discover that the "big load" of the Jerries' "steel-turned tubes . . . splashes my small load"; John Hersey's *War Lover* (1959) becomes a sadist "when he gets in bed," a female character explains, because "he makes hate—attacks, rapes, milks his gland; and thinks that makes him a man."[46]

According to one critic, men of letters set out to prove "how war stripped man of his manhood, reflected his absurdity and capacity for evil."[47] The mutilated and tormented heroes of novelists from Norman Mailer and George Orwell to those later writers like Joseph Heller and Thomas Pynchon, who resemble the no-men of, say, Wilfred Owen and D. H. Lawrence, enabled some of these authors to engage in a critique of traditional masculinity, at least in part in response to an Axis ideology which associated the male with aggression. Conscious of the impersonality of technologically advanced warfare, literary men extended the point made by their precursors during the Great War, namely that combat could no longer be used as a test of individual heroism or as a masculine initiation ritual. Their most telling lesson of war, after their unmasking of what W. H. Auden called the "lie of Authority," was therefore not far removed from Auden's injunction, "We must love one another or die."

But, just as Auden rewrote this line to read "We must love one another and die,"[48] many men of letters mourned the insufficiency of women and bemoaned the inefficacy of love, responding to the related problems of emasculation (the no-man) and ritualized hypermasculinization (the he-man) by emphasizing the different spheres inhabited by the two sexes. The prostitute became an index of new sexual explicitness, playing a crucial role in commodifying female eroticism. Viewed sardonically, as in Kirstein's serviced "mild machines," or metaphorically, as in Ciardi's "dead, like paid-off whores," the whore functions as an emblem sometimes of temporary relief from warfare, sometimes of warfare itself. As the only available erotic object, the whore can offer sanctuary to the soldier because, in Richard Wilbur's words, her "much touched flesh" furnishes the opportunity to "gently seize" with hands that otherwise "kill all things." Just as frequently, however, exotic Eurasian, Italian, French, and African prostitutes are the proverbial solution to the problem of a "rusty load" that is described in the war song "Lydia of Libya" (1943): "Why are the armies of the world / Fighting for that desert land?" They fight for "Lydia of Libya, / The lady with the lacy lingerie," who has "passed all her courses" in "harem school" and therefore "devastates our forces." Often, too, as in Keith Douglas's "Cairo Jag" (1943), the soldier has to decide between getting drunk or "cut[ting] myself a piece of cake, / a pasty Syrian with a few words of English / or the Turk who says she is a princess."[49]

But of course the rest and recreation furnished by the whore is only a temporary reprieve from the horror of battle: although "Odysseus saw the sirens" as charming, "with snub breasts and little neat posteriors," John Manifold's pilot-Odysseus forgets them when faced with the more portentous reality of "alarming / Weather report, his mutineers in irons, / The radio failing." A poem entitled simply "War" (1943) exploits Homeric allusion to contrast men's vulnerability in war with women's safety: "Innocence, hired to kill, / Lies pitilessly dead. / Stone and bone lie still. / Helen turns in bed." So many of the younger generation of novelists equated "a man of war" with "a man of whore" that, like Vance Bourjaily's heroes, they often considered penicillin a far more important scientific achievement than radar, rocketry, or the atom bomb, an understandable judgment considering that the most traumatic war zone depicted in Bourjaily's *Confessions of a Spent Youth* (1960) is the bathroom of a hospital in which men infected with gonorrhea and syphilis stand, "each with a tortured penis in his hand." The hostility implicit in these scenes erupts in Melvin Tolson's "The Furlough" (1944), a poem that describes how a soldier gazes upon the "silken loveliness" of "a passion-flower of joy and pain / On the golden bed I came back to possess": "I choked her just a little, and she is dead. / A furlough is an escalator to delight / Her beauty gathers rot on the golden bed."[50]

"On the golden bed I came *back* to possess": Tolson's poem implies that the war, by rupturing relationships between the sexes, fostered insecurity and anger in men. Similarly, in "A Woman's a Two-Face" (1943), the "Dear John" letter composed by a female correspondent who claims to be busy causes the soldier-reader to think, "You must be busy, and / I wonder who's the guy."[51] Axis propaganda sought to aggravate such jealousy by producing leaflets to divide Allied fighting men over the ownership of women. Japanese posters, obscene in their racism, informed Australians away "philandering" in Africa that the English were cuckolding them back home and German posters instructed French fighting men that British servicemen were enjoying security and sex behind the lines. But Allied propaganda also spoke directly about and to servicemen's fear of their women's betrayal. Posters enjoining silence as a protection against spies implied that women's talk would kill fighting men. The female spy, a femme fatale or vamp whose charms endanger national security, was sinister in her silence, for her allure could penetrate the security needed to keep the fighting forces safe [. . .].

In the verse and the posters of the period, the most intense hatred of women surfaces in those poems that identify the "boys" as victims of a war that is the whore personified. George Barker's "To Any Member of My Generation" (1944) identifies the war as a dance "in what we hoped was life"; yet, "Who was it in our arms but the whores of death / Whom we have found in our beds today, today?" In "Careless Love" (1944) Stanley Kunitz returns to the gun/girl analogy to analyze the erotic relationship between young soldiers and the "dark beauty" of the guns that comfort them, "for what / This nymphomaniac enjoys / Inexhaustibly is boys." Similarly, just as Karl Shapiro identifies boot camp with "Virginia," a female state that is sickened "with a dry disease," whose sun rises "like a very tired whore" beckoning soldiers to death, Charles Causley exclaims,

> O war is a casual mistress
> And the world is her double bed.
> She has few charms in her mechanised arms
> But you wake up and find yourself dead.[52]

As in World War I, women were presented as posing the threat of contamination, for they could infect fighting men with syphilis. "She may look clean—but . . ." warned captions on posters featuring disarmingly healthy looking girls.[53] The danger of female pollution is used in a 1938 Pulitzer prize winning cartoon against U.S. involvement in the war that personifies the war itself as a syphilitic whore. And in a famous British poster, feminine accoutrements (both the veiled hat and its vaginal flower) grace a skull that would lure soldiers to dissolution and death [. . .]. Thus, when Thomas Pynchon's novel *V.* (1961) redefines the "V for Victory" in terms of the vulgarity, the void, and the vagina of a sinister, syphilitic Lady V, he may be sardonically referring to the phrase "Victory-girl," which was used throughout the war years as a euphemism for "whore."[54] In fact, victory was pictured as a triumphant undressing of the female in the most popular cartoon strip in England: the nubile cartoon character Jane, who was dubbed "Britain's Secret Weapon" and relished by the troops reading the *Daily Mirror,* finally lost all her clothes on V-E day.[55]

Interpreted from this perspective, it seems resonant that the figures shown under the caption "This Is the Enemy" [in Allied propaganda posters] are females linked pictorially, almost pornographically, to the villainous, foreign masters of war. As Fussell has explained about the perspective of combatants, "Civilians were different, more like 'foreigners,' indeed rather like the enemy."[56] At the conclusion of *The Naked and the Dead* (1948), Norman Mailer meditates on the female civilian as enemy when, in an effort to foster camaraderie, one major "jazz[es] up the map-reading class by having a full-size color photograph of Betty Grable in a bathing suit, with

a co-ordinate grid system laid over it." Thomas Pynchon echoes this scene at the beginning of *Gravity's Rainbow* (1973), a novel set during World War II, with Slothrop's map of London, which is sprinkled with stars, a firmament of "Carolines, Marias, Annes, Susans, Elizabeths," each marking the place where he has had an affair and each becoming visible a few days before bomb sites of V-2 rockets mysteriously appear.[57]

If the pinup was a "bomb shell," if the gun was a "girl," then the disturbing conflation of sex and death that some men described as a perversion of masculinity, some as its triumph, was often experienced by women as an attack. Perhaps the pinned-up bomb shells who became the targets of men's desire explain why military women continually confronted sexual assaults at the camps they called "Wolf Swamps" from men who jokingly translated WAAF (Women's Auxiliary Air Force) as "Women All Fuck." Even female soldiers and workers, publicly encouraged to keep up their "FQ" (feminine quotient), were displayed in quasi-pornographic nudity in magazines. And in 1940 a chorus line in London's Garrison Theatre wore and then stripped WAAF uniforms.[58] Besides slander campaigns that pictured female combatants as sexually promiscuous or contaminated with venereal disease, WASP (Women's Air Service Pilots Association) pilots were physically endangered by hostile male colleagues: when women pilots tested planes to be sent to the front, their safety was threatened by mechanical failures which were the result of sabotage—or so they suspected when traces of sugar (sure to stop an engine in seconds) were found in the gas tank of one WASP plane.[59]

. . . . .

That the images and stereotypes of popular culture affected women poets is apparent from the critical reaction to war poems by Edna St. Vincent Millay, Muriel Rukeyser, H. D., and Marianne Moore. After publishing her polemical volume *Make Bright the Arrows* (1940), Millay endorsed the view of her critics that she had committed "prostitution"; in the wake of the appearance of her pro-war *Wake Island* (1942), Rukeyser was condemned for "promiscuity" and labeled a "Poster Girl"; H. D. was attacked for patching together "religious scraps" in *Tribute to the Angels* (1945), a "quilt" she was said to use "to warm" herself; and Moore's "In Distrust of Merits"—although frequently praised and anthologized—was attacked by her admirer Randall Jarrell, who wished that in this case she had taken "her individuals with their scrupulous virtues and shown them smashed willy-nilly, tortured, prostituted, driven crazy—and not for a while but forever."[60]

H. D.'s old-fashioned quilt and Moore's scrupulous virtues suggest that women were thought to be out of touch with the harsh realities of battle: these caricatured descriptions emanated from an image just as prevalent as (but purportedly the antithesis of) that of the whore. Although endowed with a fidelity that presumably differentiated her from the prostitute, the girl he left behind could, of course, shade into the prostitute. For notwithstanding her faithfulness, the girlfriend, wife, or mother—who symbolizes why men fight, the desirable peace they sought to secure—may also represent a refuge not forthcoming. In addition this character, like the whore, reinforced the notion that women—and thus women writers—remained behind or outside the actual war effort and therefore deprived of the inside experience necessary to express the realities of worldwide combat. Like Bishop's hens in "Roosters," women not "courted and despised" as whores were "courted and despised" as witnesses of male suffering.

The spectatorship shared by literary women living outside Europe was shaped by their alienation from the sons, brothers, lovers, and husbands away at the fronts. In Bishop's language, the separation between the battling cocks and the wives in the henhouse precludes communication, for the women left behind feel hopelessly divided from the men they seek to address. Precisely this estrangement is expressed in Babette Deutsch's "For a Young Soldier" (1944), in which the poet can penetrate neither the subjectivity of the soldier ("Do you dream of what lies behind you / Or ahead?") nor the meaning of the war itself ("How can a woman scale this wall, this war?"). In "To My Son" (1944), therefore, Deutsch admits that the war inducts the soldier into a different language ("How shall we talk / To you who must learn the language / Spelled on the fields in famine, in blood on the sidewalk?"), an idiom that ensures the impotence of the mother: "I cannot hide you now, / Or shelter you ever, / Or give you a guide through hell."[61]

As Susan Schweik has explained, the predominance of the letter form in World War II literature signals the distance between the sexes, a distance that produced the image of the girl he left behind and that is brilliantly captured by a gruesome *Life* magazine photograph in which a woman writes a thank-you note to her boyfriend for the autographed Japanese skull he has sent her [. . .].[62] The comfort, security, and normalcy of the female

ON THE SUBJECT OF...

MURIEL RUKEYSER (1913-1980)

While much of Muriel Rukeyser's poetry is marked by intense emotion—outrage over social injustices and hope for overcoming them—she is also known for poems about technology and more personal issues, such as motherhood, sexuality, the poetic process, and death. Born in New York City, Rukeyser attended Vassar College, where she co-founded and edited the *Student Review,* an undergraduate literary magazine that protested the policies of the *Vassar Review.* As an undergraduate at Vassar, Rukeyser was awarded the Yale Younger Poets Prize for her first poetry collection, *Theory of Flight* (1935). While working at the *Student Review,* Rukeyser covered the 1932 Scottsboro trial in Alabama in which nine African American youths were accused of raping two white girls. She based her poem, "The Trial," on this experience. Rukeyser supported the Spanish Loyalists during the Spanish Civil war, and was jailed in Washington, D.C., for protesting the Vietnam War. From 1975 to 1976, when she was in her early sixties and in frail health, Rukeyser served as president of the American Center for PEN, an organization that supports writers' rights worldwide. During her presidency, she traveled to South Korea to voice her opposition to the death sentence of poet Kim Chi-Ha. This experience served as the basis of one of her last poems, "The Gates." Though she never identified herself overtly in her writing as a lesbian, many of her poems explore lesbian sexuality and society's resistance to it, and in the primary relationships in the latter part of her life, women played a significant role. Poems like "Despisals" explicitly identify the "despised" in society, including homosexuals, and expose the fear that perpetuates oppression.

writer "left behind" contrast sharply with the skull, a gruesome memento signaling the impossibility of her comprehending the horror "over there." The shocking juxtaposition between the female figure's complacencies—her elegant hairdo, her jewelry, her expensive suit, her fingernail polish—and the gift of the (autographed) skull symbolizes the resentment many departing servicemen felt about the girl he left behind. One soldierpoet, indefinitely separated from his wife, exclaims, "Your peace is bought with mine, and I am paid in full, and well, / If but the echo of your laughter reaches me in hell." Feelings of estrangement were also inscribed on war memorials: "For your tomorrow / We gave our today."[63]

In spite of the critique of masculine dominance articulated by many male writers, then, a curious unreality permeates positive images of women, who are often viewed as solacing outsiders or resented beneficiaries of male suffering. Whether she is the silent recipient of "V letters" or a photographed face peeping out of the pockets of dead men, the good wife, mother, or mistress in the literature of the Second World War is marked by her absence from the scene of battle which is the scene of the writing. Even in Karl Shapiro's loving poem "V-Letter" (1944), for example, the speaker cherishes the fair face of his beloved "because you wait" and because "you are my home and in your spacious love / I dream to march as under flaring flags."[64] While Shapiro believes his "love is whole / Whether I live or fail," the dead German soldier in Keith Douglas's poem *Vergissmeinnicht* (1943) is not saved by his talisman, an autographed picture which is "dishonoured" now that the combatant sprawls in the sun, decaying next to what Douglas sardonically calls "hard and good" equipment. As the only witness who might weep to see "the lover and killer . . . mingled" and mangled, the photographed female is a repository of precisely the humane values which the soldier must repress in wartime.[65]

Although a number of writers express the soldier's guilty sense that his innocent beloved would never accept the person he has had to become under the brutal and brutalizing circumstances of combat, many writers express the soldier's anger at the safety or the infidelity of the girl back home.[66] Besides being potentially unfaithful and fatefully ignorant, the girl he left behind could endanger the lives of fighting men as effectively as the vamp-spy. A host of posters suggest that even well-meaning female civilians pose a security threat: a Finnish poster, for example, presents women's lips locked up, while English cartoons and posters picture gossips as irresponsible and naive in their garrulity [. . .].

Under the pressure of such emotions, many men felt, in the words of the narrator of Leon Uris's *Battle Cry*, that there were just two kinds of women, "The ones who waited and the ones who didn't."[67] "Brotherhood of Men" (1949), Richard Eberhart's poem about the defense of Corregidor, expresses male nostalgia for the "ones who waited" and specifically for a lost female world of fertility or faithfulness: Eberhart's embattled recruits, vampires "drinking the blood of victims" in a hellish fight, are only prevented from surrendering by a vision of "mother in the midst of terror: / 'Persevere. Persevere. Persevere. Persevere.'" The epitome of what Eberhart calls "faith beyond reason," the mother represents humanistic values at odds with the dehumanizing technology of death, much as she does to James Jones's Robert E. Lee Prewitt, who is torn between a vow to his dying mother—that he "wont never hurt nobody unless its absolute a must"—and "the jism cord" that connects him to the army.[68]

George Orwell's *1984* (1949), a novel that contrasts the brutality of "Big Brother" with the hero's remembrances of the altruism of his mother, is imbued with nostalgia for a fantasy prewar world, specifically a world in which his mother tried to protect him even at the cost of her own and his sister's life. What Winston Smith must learn in Room 101, however, is that he can neither have the mother nor kill the father: indeed, when he is brainwashed to "see" five fingers where there are four, he submits to the power of his persecutor and specifically to the state's phallus, the invisible but potent symbol of authority that no single man possesses. Physically and psychologically beaten, Winston—"the last man"—relinquishes the oceanic unity he had with his mother for the perpetual warring of an Oceania ruled by Big Brother. Even though Winston's mother is elegized as a victim of the war, she is also a mother not good enough to protect her son from the vengeance of his big brothers.[69]

Orwell's dystopia reflects the anger with which many male writers, encased in what they call "the womb of war" or "the steel cocoon," articulated eerie parallels between the biological mother and the military to suggest, as John Ciardi later put it, that "the womb of woman is the kit of war." In Jarrell's "The Death of the Ball Turret Gunner," the mother has sent her son to war: "From my mother's sleep I fell into the State," declares the airman "hunched" upside down in the "belly" of the ball turret from which he is virtually aborted: "When I died they washed me out of the turret with a hose."[70] The bomber carrier as grotesque uterus reached its culmination at the end of the war when the plane over Hiroshima, the "Enola Gay," was named for the pilot's mother, and the plutonium and uranium bombs were referred to as "Fat Man" and "Little Boy." The mother who has given her son over to the state has exchanged her birth-giving function for a death-dealing one.

As guilty as Jarrell's mother is the wife of his "Gunner" (1945), for here the soldier sent away from his wife and his cat confronts his death wondering bitterly, "Has my wife a pension of so many mice? / Did the medals go home to my cat?"[71] As survivors, wives and pets—presumably interchangeable—are the beneficiaries of men's suffering and their security therefore appears sinister. Similarly, in "On Embarkation" (1945), by Alun Lewis, sobbing women on railroad platforms are "thinking of children, pensions, looks that fade, / The slow forgetfulness that strips the mind"; and in Lewis's "Christmas Holiday" (1942), when the war begins, "The fat wife comfortably sleeping / Sighs and licks her lips and smiles."[72]

No less quick than Orwell to perceive totalitarianism as a Big Brother controlling the military complex of any and all sides of the war, literary women did not react with Orwell's nostalgia for a prewar world of feminine renunciation and constancy. On the contrary, whether they examine female vulnerability in wartime, as do British and expatriate survivors of the blitz, or analyze their estrangement from the war, as do Americans geographically removed from warfare, they elaborate Bishop's belief that militarism reduces women "courted and despised" to death or spectatorship. In the face of a newly eroticized but highly traditional sexual division of labor, women writers wondered over the survival possibilities of the women in the "left behind" who could neither join forces with nor do battle against the men on their own side.

. . . . .

Analyzing the contradictions between the ideology of separate spheres embedded in so much war literature and women's increased participation in public history, many women of letters resemble Muriel Rukeyser in her effort to get "beyond the men of letters, / Of business and of death" (217-18). The new explicitness apparent in depictions of the whore and the girl he left behind, as well as the slippage between these two types, helps explain the sense of dread that pervades women's texts. Certainly the (mythologized) dichotomy between battle and home front, upon which such stereotypes depend, fostered feelings of loneliness, guilt, and anxiety about the ways the war divided the sexes, heightening sex antagonism.

Both in prose and poetry Kay Boyle examined the dangers confronted by the girl he left behind and in particular the sexual onslaughts that threatened to turn her into a whore. The physically free women in Kay Boyle's stories face the violence of sex-starved men as well as the images such men construct as a retaliation against the women they are presumably fighting to preserve but that they are really preserving themselves to fight. The American soldiers on a train carrying war brides in "Army of Occupation" (1947), for example, assault a female journalist with rowdy advances and drunken marriage proposals. In such stories as "Men" (1941) and "Defeat" (1941), moreover, Boyle's female characters either become symbols of home (for prisoners of war whose fantasies threaten to erupt into rape) or images of defeat (for French soldiers who would rather blame the Nazi occupation of their village on women dancing with the enemy than face their own army's failures).[73]

Boyle's long poem *American Citizen Naturalized in Leadville, Colorado* (1944), which focuses on the same linguistic casualties suffered by the characters left behind in Sitwell's and Deutsch's works, describes the inadequacy of both the absurd "G.I. talk" that war brides appropriate and the "alphabet of sorcery" that women in bereavement use. While the war brides jabber in a tongue foreign to them ("'Sweating out three weeks of maneuvers, or sweating the week-end pass, / Or sweating him out night after night,' they'll say, sweet-tongued as thrushes"), the "women in bereavement" look for solace to a seer who resembles no one so much as T. S. Eliot's Madame Sosostris and end up sounding like Eliot's neurasthenic Belladonna as they nervously ask, "What do you see now? . . . Do you see?" *American Citizen* describes the "polka of war brides"—the "mazurka" of women left to collect checks and await furloughs—as a ghastly *"pas seul"*:

> This is the waltz
> Of the wives whose men are in khaki. Their faces are painted
> As flawless as children's, their hearts each the flame of a candle
> That his breath can extinguish at will.[74]

While many women wrote about the rhythm of military leaves, partings, and letters to express their loneliness, others found distant lovers and husbands drained of reality. According to Margaret Mead, "Just as the man in the cartoon is pictured as looking at his rifle and saying, 'I've given you the best years of my life,' so the young women of the 1940s look at the pictures on their dressing tables, the service pins on their lapels, realizing the years which have been dedicated to absence, to breathless hope and to gnawing fear, and to a break in experience."[75] If the man who went away seemed as insubstantial to literary women as the girl he left behind did to literary men, women of letters often articulated feelings of guilt not unrelated to the resentment at female survival expressed by men of letters. That such anxieties about survival were inevitable is made clear by a poem Eleanor Roosevelt was said to have carried with her at all times for spiritual guidance, a prayer composed by Sir William Stephenson, the Canadian in charge of British intelligence operations in the United States: "As long as there be war / I then must / Ask and answer / Am I worth dying for?"[76]

Popular verse written by and about English ambulance drivers, farmers, nurses, and civil defense workers insisted that women were not left behind, but it lacks the note of exhilaration frequently resounding in comparable texts written by women during the Great War. "I'm only a wartime working girl" begins one song chanted by factory workers trying to confound the monotony of long hours of production:

> The machine shop makes me deaf,
> I have no prospects after the war
> And my young man is in the RAF.[77]

Instead of exulting in the formation of a Herland when men at the front are replaced by women in factories, post offices, and statehouses, not a few female writers moaned that England had become a "Monstrous Regiment" of women: "What host of women everywhere I see!" Alice Coats exclaims, adding "I'm sick to death of them—and they of me." Sexual deprivation, boredom, and self-revulsion, not emancipation, characterize what she experiences:

> The newsboy and the boy who drives the
>   plough:
> Postman and milkman—all are ladies now.
> Doctors and engineers—yes, even these—
> Poets and politicians, all are shes.
> (The very beasts that in the meadows browse
> Are ewes and mares, heifers and hens and
>   cows. . . .)
> All, doubtless, worthy to a great degree;
> But oh, how boring! Yes, including me.[78]

Besides suffering a "blankness" associated with the dehumanization of military service, war workers become war victims in Stevie Smith's "Who

Shot Eugenie?" (1950). As Karen Schneider has pointed out, this poem "expresses Smith's concern that the sanctioned violence of war all too insidiously infects one's consciousness and fatally poisons relations with others, even those whom we do not consider enemies." For, at the conclusion of an account of two female "campaigners," the speaker discovers her dead friend "shot, with a bullet through her head. / Yet every chamber in her revolver was full to plenty / And only in my own is there one that is empty." What Smith depicts as the surrealistic contagion of violence escalates into a sense of unreality in literature about and pictures of the bombing of England.[79]

In magazines and newspapers, photographs depicted women and children as the predominant civilian casualties of enemy blitzes, while pictures of Allied planes dropping bombs over both the Asian and the European fronts tended to represent transcendent Allied power without regard to the dismemberment or death of victims. Although a number of World War II photos of nurses, machinists, ammunition workers, and fire fighters testify to the same exhilarating sense of female camaraderie evident in World War I pictures, what is different are the images of women nearly buried alive by bombs, almost as if they were in fox holes, framed by landscapes of crumbled houses [. . .]. Within urban settings in which gas, electricity, telephone, transportation, food, water, and even houses were drastically reduced or disappeared altogether, the drudgery and danger of making do were accompanied by a bizarre sense of unreality.

After the months of the "phony war," in which enemy bombers failed to appear in the skies over England, scarcity measures—widely publicized by the government—encouraged women to retain a pretense of normal life through inventive substitutions. Defamiliarization of the home was thereby accompanied by a widespread impersonation of femininity: not only were women encouraged to produce fatless pastries and mock stews and to draw the seams of make-believe stockings on their legs; a Lewis Carrollesque Board of Trade announcement urged civilians to effect a series of metamorphoses which may have implied that, far from being "left behind," they were engaged in battles against the enemy on the home front:

> Golf Balls become Gas Masks;
> Mattresses become Life Jackets;
> Saucepans become Steel Helmets;
> Combs become Eyeshields.[80]

Those children who were not labeled like packages for deportation from the bombed cities to the safer countryside were photographed clutching symbols of a childhood made virtually impossible by the war. Those who were evacuated to foster homes often suffered intense homesickness, or so a poignant story by Sylvia Townsend Warner suggests. "Noah's Ark" (1943) describes the estrangement of two young evacuees who find the lambs and flowers of the countryside tame in comparison with their recollections of the monkeys, serpents, jaguars, crocodiles, and wolves in the city zoo. Indeed, the children take refuge from memories of "corpses . . . heaped up where the old coffee-stall used to be" by lovingly recounting stories about the zoo, "as though wild beasts were meat and drink, home and mother" to them. Even that recourse is taken away at the end of the tale when they are given a newspaper notice: *Owing to the continuance of blitz bombing the authorities of the Plymouth Zoo have caused all the dangerous animals to be destroyed.*[81]

While Warner's children grieve that there is no Noah's Ark to save the animals in the zoo from the falling rain of bombs, in H. D.'s elegy on the death of a fire-girl (female fire fighter), "May 1943" (1950), the vitality of newly arrived American soldiers contrasts sharply with the fatigue of beleaguered citizens on the home front who have themselves been reduced to an animal state:

> We've slithered so long in the rain, prowled like
>   cats in the dark,
> like owls in the black-out,
> look at us—anaemic, good-natured,
> for a rat in the gutter's a rat in the gutter,
> consider our fellowship,
> look at each one of us,
> we've grown alike, slithering,
> slipping along with fish-baskets,
> grey faces, fish-faces, frog gait,
> we slop, we hop.
>
> [CP 496]

H. D.'s denizens of the home front resemble the no-men in the trenches of World War I: slithering in the blackout, anemic but aware of fellowship in suffering, encased in a gutter of mud like rats, as wet as frogs or fish.

Because of their greater proximity to (or engagement in) warfare, the literature composed by British and expatriate American women caused them to emphasize the deaths of women, which Bishop viewed as the alternative to spectatorship. But for a number of American women writers, the widening gulf between men and the women they left behind also led to a loss of communication between the sexes and to female suffering, as Gwendolyn Brooks's verse in *A Street in Bronzeville* (1945) and *Annie Allen* (1949) most tellingly records. The voices of her "Gay Chaps at the Bar"

express their hostility toward the girls left behind—sweethearts, unfaithful correspondents—not only at a literal bar but also at the color bar which is sustained by the forces presumably representing democracy.

Brooks's elliptical sonnet sequence about the disillusionment experienced by black veterans uses male speakers whose traumatic experiences of a violent enemy and a racist army have effectively alienated them from the women to whom they return. According to the soldier-speaker of "looking," the women left behind "have no word" with which to leave the soldier: "'Good-by!' is brutal, and 'come back!' the raw / Insistence of an idle desperation." For the veteran-speaker of "mentors," the girl to whom he returns—even if she is "fragrant as the flower she wears"—must be abandoned at the "remotest whisper" of the "reproving ghosts" who haunt him, for his "best allegiances are to the dead."[82] A number of the other "soldier sonnets" in "Gay Chaps at the Bar" display the hostility of returning veterans estranged by their war experiences from the women to whom they return and effectively mentored by the dead men they have had to leave behind.

The speaker of "piano after war," for example, knows that although he may watch and listen to a female pianist whose "fingers, / Cleverly ringed, declining to clever pink, / Beg glory from the willing keys," his pleasure will be interrupted by "a multiplying cry" issuing from "bitter dead men who will never / Attend a gentle maker of musical joy." In the final couplet, his bond to his buried comrades separates him from the woman and her artistry, even as it condemns him to a frigid life-in-death: "Then my thawed eye will go again to ice. / And stone will shove the softness from my face" (52). The male personae of two other poems—"love note I: surely" and "love note II: flags"—send hate mail to women. Doubting the fidelity of the girl he left behind, the first speaker mocks her language of empty promises ("Surely your word would pop as insolent / As always: 'Why, of course I love you, dear'"), concluding that the "wounds and death" of war pale in comparison to the wound she has inflicted, for "I doubt all. You. Or a violet" (57). The second speaker, conflating the flag and the female, contrasts his own "power crumpled and wan" with the "pretty glory," "merry / Softness," and "pert exuberance" of the national emblem and the woman who symbolize what he fights for and whose vitality seems sinister in light of his suffering (58).

Thus the poems of "Gay Chaps at the Bar" evoke "the color bar, justice, and the 'bar' between life and death," as noted by D. H. Melhem; they also, however, speak about the bar that the impotent, hostile veteran sets between himself and the girl he left behind.[83] Traumatized by the color bar, Brooks's gay chaps are horrified by a military establishment so racist that black combatants wonder about the government's white leaders, "Am I clean enough to kill for them?" and respond to that humiliating question by retaliating against women. As Harry B. Shaw has shown, the predicament Brooks's soldiers confront is the irony that "they are fighting the white man more than he was fighting the enemy."[84] What did it mean to the black soldier that he faced the contradiction of fighting for and within a system that denied him full humanity? According to Brooks, this tension would catapult him into rage against women, or so her poem "Negro Hero" implies. The speaker here, based on a mess attendant who won the Navy Cross at Pearl Harbor, confronts the irony that he guards what the white man loves and projects his rage by imagining the United States as a murderous white woman: "Their white-gowned democracy was my fair lady. / With her knife lying cold, straight, in the softness of her sweet-flowing sleeve" (33). While the embittered "Negro Hero" sneers at his own allegiance to this "fair lady," Brooks's mock heroic "Anniad" suggests that black male resentment instilled by racism and war effectively destroys black women.

The heroine of Brooks's stylistically dense verse epic is left by a lover she idolizes, the "man of tan" (84), not only when he goes off to war but also when he returns: "Soldier bare and chilly then / Wants his power back again" (87). Hunting for an antidote to his "impotence" with a succession of whores, and specifically with "a maple banshee" who is more exotic and less dark than Annie, he discovers how "woman fits for recompense" (88). "Wench, whiskey and tail-end / Of your overseas disease / Rot and rout" him (91), sending him back to Annie to be nursed. Brooks's first description of Annie—"Think of sweet and chocolate / Left to folly or to fate" (83)—contrasts sharply with her last portrait: "Think of almost thoroughly / Derelict and dim and done" (93). Indeed, because the actors in "The Anniad"'s plot are presented without voices of their own, the reader is left with an unmediated series of images of sexual disease which contrast sharply with the heroic ideals implicitly evoked through allusions to *The Iliad* and *The Aeneid*.

. . . . .

In the same years that Brooks wrote about the ways the war united soldiers, living and dead,

while dividing them from women, such dissimilar artists as Wallace Stevens and Carson McCullers brooded on the same subject. Taken together, their meditations suggest that, even under the duress of suffering, the war functioned to consecrate bonds between men in a manner which isolated women. Stevens returned in one section of *Esthetique du Mal* (1944) to his earlier vision of brotherhood in "Sunday Morning" (1915)—"Supple and turbulent, a ring of men"—to compose a hymn to the fallen "soldier of time" that envisions a redemptive brotherhood set against the survival and separateness of a mysterious, even malevolent, female:

> The shadows of his fellows ring him round
> In the high night, the summer breathes for them
> Its fragrance, a heavy somnolence, and for him,
> For the soldier of time, it breathes a summer
>   sleep.
>
> In which his wound is good because life was.
> No part of him was ever part of death.
> A woman smoothes her forehead with her hand
> And the soldier of time lies calm beneath that
>   stroke.

Stevens—who asked in "Examination of the Hero in a Time of War" (1942), "Unless we believe in the hero, what is there / To believe?"—came to see the poet in wartime as a hero whose masculinity is mysteriously doubled, for "the poetry of war . . . constitutes a participating in the heroic" and the hero "arrives at the man-man as he wanted."[85]

But the shadows of fellows ringed round, the man-man in the military, constitute precisely the problem of McCullers's *Member of the Wedding* (1946), a text that analyzes mysteriously doubled masculinity by examining its heroine's inability to participate in the heroic and, by extension, its author's inability to write a work about war. McCullers's youthful heroine, Frankie Addams, who "wanted to be a boy and go to the war as a Marine," envies her older brother, who has joined the army to see the world, for "soldiers in the army can say we."[86] Within the claustrophobic heat of the kitchen she shares with the black housekeeper Berenice and her six-year-old cousin, John Henry, the war seems like just one more club that excludes Frankie, who "was not afraid of Germans or bombs or Japanese. She was afraid because in the war they would not include her and because the world seemed somehow separate from herself" (21).

Equally afraid that her only true community is composed of freaks, the tomboy Frankie gives herself a new name—F. Jasmine Addams—and believes that she can become a member of the war by becoming a member of her brother's wedding. But after Berenice tells a story about a black boy who "changed his nature and his sex," and John Henry asks, "How did that boy change into a girl?" Frankie, who is fond of exclaiming "Boyoman! Manoboy!" finds out what it means to change from a boy into a girl. She meets a soldier near the sign that reads "Prophylactic Military" and discovers that their conversation "would not join": the soldier talked "a kind of double-talk that, try as she would, she could not follow" (67).

Without a member of her own, Frankie learns that she cannot become a member of the war/wedding but must instead defend herself against the warriors. When the soldier finally takes her upstairs to his room at the Blue Moon Hotel and tries to get her to "quit this stalling" (130), she bites his tongue and brings a glass pitcher down on his head. But even Frankie's rebelliousness is relinquished after her brother and his wife reject her. First she admits that "she must find somebody, anybody that she could join with"—"she might as well ask the soldier to marry with her" (146)—and then she is accosted by "the Law," labeled "Royal Addams's daughter," and reclaimed by her father.[87] That Frankie's last act is watching the painful death of John Henry foreshadows the terrible induction into femininity McCullers would later explore in "The Ballad of the Sad Café," for John Henry has sworn not to tell anyone that Frankie "brained" a "crazy man": "If I tell I hope God will sew up my mouth and sew down my eyes and cut off my ears with the scissors" (132). The meningitis from which he suffers does sew up his mouth, eyes, and ears, just as his death signifies the demise of Frankie's childhood boy-self.

Significantly, McCullers's newly feminized heroine is fair game for a nameless draftee who is as vulnerable and isolated as she is. But *The Member of the Wedding* further analyzes the dynamics of dominance when Frankie's first act upon discovering that she cannot become a member of her brother's wedding is to call Berenice a "nigger" (135), for through Berenice's utopian vision of a peaceful world where there would be "no killed Jews and no hurt colored people" (92), *The Member of the Wedding* makes an implicit claim that Zora Neale Hurston articulates in *Dust Tracks on a Road* (1942)—namely that Hitler's criminal actions in Europe subjected Europeans to the injustices that had been inflicted on American blacks for centuries (339-42). Admittedly contro-

versial, this point is also established by Ann Petry in *The Street* (1946), when Lutie Johnson's black employer and ultimate assailant, Boots Smith, declares that "the people in the government hate Germans, but they hate me worse," adding, "They're only doing the same thing in Europe that's been done in this country since the time it started."[88]

The prostitution of Brooks's Annie as well as the attempted rapes of McCullers's Frankie and Petry's Lutie represent women's anxiety about even the most embattled of men, an anxiety attributed by McCullers to the war effectively wedding men to men. In a poem about a lover away fighting in the Spanish Civil War, Rukeyser identifies his presence on the battlefield with her own abandonment:

> I know how you recognized our war, and ran
> To it as a runner to his eager wedding
> Or our immediate love.
>
> [230]

"Wedding" himself to the war, Rukeyser's beloved has effectively widowed her. Whereas civilians were barraged with the injunction to buy "bonds," men in the forces and those who wrote about them found little if anything in which to believe except the unity or camaraderie men achieved by virtue of the holy bonds they established within the military.

To begin with, whether male characters are turned into guilty voyeurs of their own maneuvers or corpses decaying during enemy onslaughts, their authors record a hopeless sense of emasculation. From Orwell's broken "last man" to Jarrell's aborted airman, male characters are made to realize that the gun always wins in its competition with the penis. Many enlisted men recorded their alienation from the aggression of warfare as a rejection of their commanders: Howard Nemerov, for example, begins his remembrance about the air war "Hate Hitler? No, I spared him hardly a thought. / But Corporal Irmin, first, and later on / The O.C. (Flying), Wing Commander Briggs, / And the station C.O. Group Captain Ormery— / Now there were men were objects fit to hate."[89] And just as many soldiers, alienated from their superior officers, turned toward their comrades, finding in what Richard Eberhart praised as the brotherhood of man men fit to love as well as a fitting way to love men.

Perhaps the finest novel written about the war, Norman Mailer's *The Naked and the Dead*, illustrates how even those writers engaged in criticizing the identification of the gun and the penis paradoxically reify the female to rectify the relationships between men. General Cummings, a Faustian fascist with repressed homosexual tendencies, derives joy solely from power and specifically from the "phallus-shell that rides through a shining vagina of steel," a fantasy Mailer is presumably ridiculing. Significantly, however, Cummings's obsession with coming is the result of the overprotectiveness of his mother and the bitchiness of his wife. In a telling parallel his working-class double, Croft, is sexually aroused by a machine gun because his wife has been unfaithful to him. Although Mailer's fictional surrogate, Captain Hearn, seeks an alternative to Cummings and Croft's dream of a "League of Omnipotent Men," he eventually discovers that what he needs most is "control and not mating." Finally, then, Mailer's novel confirms Cummings's creed, namely that "the average man always sees himself in relation to other men as either inferior or superior. Women play no part in it. They're an index, a yardstick among other gauges, by which to measure superiority."[90]

The female characters, whether dead, disloyal, or frigid wives; randy girlfriends; or raunchy whores, play no part in the action except as "gauges" located in the "Time Machine" sections that return us to civilian life before the war. Even love, which saves men from the "lie of Authority" and serves as an alternative to Cummings's philosophy of the will to power, is a love between men: when Ridges and Goldstein bear the burden of Wilson's syphilitic body back to the beach at the end of the novel, Wilson becomes their "heart." The brotherhood of Ridges, Goldstein, and Wilson resembles the camaraderie between men described in Joseph Heller's novel about World War II *Catch-22* (1962), where Yossarian is mystically linked to his dying comrade, Snowden. Peter Aichinger's claim that "the appeal to the team spirit is perhaps the only positive motivation mentioned in the novels of World War II" is similarly borne out in *From Here to Eternity* (1951), where James Jones presents two characters (Prewitt and Warden) moving from the here and now of poker, drinking, whoring, and brawling to a fraternity that causes both men to reject their mistresses in order to wed themselves to the military.[91]

Trying to capture the apocalyptic dynamic of war in a poem included in his 1943 essay "Looking Back on the Spanish War," Orwell fixes on its eroticism when he describes the ecstasy of shaking an Italian soldier's hand: "To meet within the sound of guns, / But oh! what peace I knew then / In gazing on his battered face / Purer than any woman's!"[92] Similarly, after describing a prison camp in which "those [who] survived best were feminine," Eberhart claims that "we were at our peak when in the depths," sustained by "visions of brotherhood when we were broken."[93] Although a homoerotic love for "pals" enabled the characters of World War I authors to achieve a union "passing the love of women," as Ford Maddox Ford put it, their descriptions of comradeship are usually more overtly sensual than those of their successors. For the medicalizing of homosexuality in the intervening years had made such homoerotic expressiveness either a crime or a symptom of sickness.[94]

Oddly enough, the morbidification of homosexuality by the medical establishment also contributed to the eroticization of women. In the one arena, the popular "soldier shows"—which enabled men who were gay to subvert antihomosexual policies by wearing dresses, makeup, and wigs and using double entendre to express themselves covertly—the scripts and characters remained blatantly heterosexual, even heterosexist. Soldiers in *This Is the Army* and *Stars and Gripes* performed in chorus lines decked out in WAC uniforms, singing "With a Gun on His Shoulder or a Girl on His Arm, You Can Tell He's a Yankee Doodle Dandy," while male illusionists and caricaturists played the roles of pinups and strippers, bombshells and broads: Marlene Dietrich, Carmen Miranda, Mae West, and Gypsy Rose Lee. Allan Bérubé's account of such shows stresses the encoded freedom homosexuals achieved through government sponsored drag performances that enabled them to "display their camp sensibilities"; fear of exposure, humiliation, and discharge, however, led gay men to camouflage themselves in aggressively heterosexual roles. Similarly, while the buddy system, which encouraged comrades to pair up together and which issued in popular songs like "My Buddy," may have enabled gay lovers to live and work together, as Bérubé claims, it also spawned a fear in men who were sleeping and suffering together that, unless they demonstrated desire for women, they would be forced to confess to a "sick addiction" and be confined to a "psych" ward.[95]

The bonding of what Stevens called the man-man, depicted in war novels as an index of the enlisted man's alienation from his commander, is presumed to be redemptive only when its eroticism does not become explicitly sexual, and it is therefore almost always set against male homosexuality, which is usually diagnosed as a psychotic response to the violence of battle. Worse than being labeled a whore is being called a queer or a fairy, for homosexuals are typically presented in World War II literature as guiltridden, pathologically violent, or suicidal. In the effort to differentiate what, in another context, Eve Kosofsky Sedgwick has called "homosocial desire" from homosexuality, both the girl he left behind and the whore play crucial roles, for—as the imagined object of male desire and as the body that links men to men—they ratify men as heterosexual.[96]

Confronting the boredom of "weary hours of waiting," rather than the "dramatic thunder" of military engagement, the soldiers in Timothy Corsellis's poem "What I Never Saw" (1940) sit "together as we sat at peace / Bound by no ideal of service / But by a common interest in pornography and a desire to outdrink one another."[97] While sailors in Bentz Plagemann's *The Steel Cocoon* (1958) object to "the whole mess that made [them] need women" and while they lament that "you never know until the last minute whether you're going to get in or not," often admitting "I just want to get my gun," such sentiments prove that the "satisfying relationship" between men and boys on the ship is "merely a normal expression of the capacity, or even the need, of all men for the love of one another."[98] When pilots, infantry soldiers, sailors, hospital inmates, and prisoners of war become "buddies" or "mates" in World War II fiction, they are united by their love for each other and defended from the charge of deviancy, which such love could provoke, by their scorn for homosexuals and by the credo that "men like to get their guns off."[99]

Understandably, then, many heroines in women's fiction about the war experienced it as a big brotherhood from which they were excluded. Cut off from communication with men, the wife in Dorothy Parker's "The Lovely Leave" (1944) realizes that her husband has found in the service "companionships no—no—wife can ever give [him]," and his leave proves to her that her husband has taken leave of her and virtually married his companions in the military.[100] Far from bequeathing security, women's status as outsiders left behind helped create the suspicion that male bonding in the military would effectively replace domestic bonds and make "left behind" women even more vulnerable. Therefore, in *The Children of Violence* series (1952-69), Doris Lessing analyzes the pregnant Martha Quest's realization that her husband's enlistment satisfies a lifelong hunger

for fraternity that excludes her: "It seemed that his whole life had led without his knowing it to the climax of being with those men, his fellows, his friends, parts of himself, in real fighting, real living, real experience at last." Like Parker's heroine, Martha understands not only that "she was married to one of the boys; he would always, all his life, be one of the boys" but also that "the condition of being a woman in wartime . . . was that one should love not a man, but a man in relation to other men."[101] Thus, Lessing examines the dynamics bequeathed by what Stevens called the heroic arrival at "the man-man" and what McCullers considered the "wedding" of the "members" of the war.

. . . . .

After Lessing's Martha Quest learns to "love not a man, but a man in relation to other men," why does she experience the "dangerous and attractive . . . intoxication of war"? And why does Lessing's later *The Golden Notebook* (1962) include a novel written by a woman horrified that her work records the "feverish illicit excitement of wartime"?[102] While literary women from Woolf to Brooks and McCullers protested against militarism as masculinism—worried about a new sexual explicitness that fused the figures of the girl left behind with the whore—and analyzed the homosocial bonding of soldiers or veterans, some of their postwar successors recorded a more intense sense of devastation, for their characters masochistically embrace a constellation of oppressive forces about which they feel helpless. Because, as Keith Douglas explained in *"Vergissmeinnicht,"* during the war "the lover and the killer are mingled / who had one body and one heart," some female characters end up fatally in love with the killer. Like Elizabeth Bowen's Stella in *The Heat of the Day*, they may decide that "from the point of view of nothing more than the heart any action was enemy action now" (142).

Enemy action, in light of the feeling expressed by H. D. that the war was her husband, has less to do with militarism as a masculine problem and more with the sadomasochism instilled in male-female relationships shaped by what Lessing later called "the feverish illicit excitement of wartime." As if to elaborate upon that "intoxication" and sexual abuse, H. D.'s *Helen in Egypt* (1961) revises Homer's *Iliad* to focus on a character reared in an atmosphere contaminated by sexual violence: Helen, the daughter of Leda, who was raped by Zeus, has been abducted both by Theseus, who stole her away when she was a young maiden, and by Paris, who took her away from her husband. While *Helen in Egypt,* like *Trilogy,* suggests to some readers that the crisis of global war might enable both men and women to liberate themselves from a destructive sex antagonism that reflects and affects warfare, we will argue that it is significantly more pessimistic than the earlier epic.

Meditating on a question comparable to the one that Simone Weil had raised in her essay "The *Iliad,* Poem of Might" (1940-41)—"What does Helen matter to Ulysses?"—H. D.'s epic recalls Weil's answer: "Troy and Helen matter to the Greeks only as the causes of their shedding so much blood and tears; it is in making oneself master that one finds one is the master of horrible memories."[103] Like the Helen of Stevie Smith's "I had a dream . . ." (1962), who does not know "which of the Helen legends I was,"[104] H. D.'s heroine, the so-called cause of the Trojan War, attempts to extricate herself from the guilt which she has internalized, to disentangle Helen on the Egyptian beach from Helen on the ramparts at Troy. Implicitly revising not only Euripides' play *Helen in Egypt* and Stesichorus of Sicily's *Pallinode* but also Marlowe's, Goethe's, and Yeats's Helens, as well as Pound's Odysseus, H. D.'s verse passages are each prefaced by a prose narrative, one of which explains that "the Greeks and the Trojans alike fought for an illusion" created out of their need to "blame someone" (15).

What does Helen matter to Pound or to other mythologists of warfare, H. D. seems to ask. First, according to *Helen in Egypt,* the Greeks and the Trojans appear indistinguishable to the woman whose face launched a thousand ships: "so they fought, forgetting women, / hero to hero, sworn brother and lover, / and cursing Helen through eternity" (4). Second, the female is denounced as the cause of war. When Helen meets the wounded Achilles on the Egyptian beach, he attacks her ("for you were the ships burnt"), calls her a "witch" (16), and tries to strangle her. In addition, militarism is directly associated with male bonding: "the Command," which links past to present, becomes Achilles' "father, my brother, / my lover, my God"; it is an "ironring, unbreakable," "the hierarchy," that promises men, "You shall control the world" (61, 51-52). And finally, the role women play in war is a sacrificial one: not only is Helen punished for the fighting, but she is haunted by Iphigenia, who was told she was going to wed Achilles, when in reality she was to be sacrificed to the gods in return for fair winds; by Cassandra, who was captured as a slave and raped by the foreign lord Agamemnon; by Clytemnestra, who could only strike back at her husband, Agamemnon, with "the Will-to-Power" (97) and therefore was herself doomed; and by Polyxena, Paris's sister, who was "slain to propitiate a ghost," Achilles (218).

What Helen thinks concerning her sister Clytemnestra—that "the War she endured was different" (99)—is true of herself as well. This difference is at first portrayed through Helen's status as a "phantom" in a "timeless time" (39, 40) that is constantly shifting in a phantasmagoric way. Although in her letters H. D. claimed that the time of the blitz was "very exciting" and that her mind "had switched, as it were, into another dimension," the "dimension out of time" (137) that Helen inhabits seems to turn her into a troubled shadow of herself.[105] What Vera Brittain suggests in her novel *Account Rendered* (1945)—namely that "after this [Second World] War many civilians, both men and women, would develop symptoms of a type hitherto mainly confined to men in the Forces"—is true of Helen, who exhibits the amnesia and anesthetization associated with battle fatigue.[106] Also, like *Account Rendered,* which portrays the recurrence of shell shock in a veteran of World War I who almost hypnotically murders his wife at the onset of the blitz, *Helen in Egypt* analyzes the femicidal impulses of its veteran, Achilles.

In *Account Rendered,* the repentant suffering of the hero and his expiation lead to rebirth: "Redeemed from egoism and fear he was indeed a new man, mentally and spiritually born again" (290). A number of critics have argued that H. D.'s Achilles evolves in a similar pattern, moving from his anger at the mother who forgot to give him immortality to his murderous assault on Helen to a redemptive process that turns him into "the New Mortal." According to this reading, to which most interpreters of the poem subscribe, H. D. agrees with Virginia Woolf that the war, by revealing "the need for emancipation from the old conception of virility" (*TG* 187), could liberate the male sex from aggression.[107] More troubling, however, is H. D.'s insistence throughout *Helen in Egypt* that women are destined to desire men whose repudiation of the mother and hatred of women are strongest. During the primal scene on the beach, when Achilles assaults her, Helen's response is notably erotic:

> *O Thetis, O sea-mother,*
> I prayed,
> as he clutched my throat

with his fingers' remorseless steel,
let me go out, let me forget,
let me be lost . . .

O Thetis, O sea-mother,
I prayed under his cloak,
let me remember, let me remember,
forever, this Star in the night.

[17; ellipses H. D.'s]

Later, dissenting from the advice of Theseus, the Freud figure, Helen answers affirmatively the question posed by the entire poem: "Does Zeus decree that, forever, / Love should be born of War?" (32). Fully convinced of the identity of "La Mort, L'Amour," she remembers "the hands that ringed my throat // and no moment's doubt, / this is Love, this is Death, / this is my last Lover" (268).

That Helen's desire for Achilles is a courtship with annihilation is confirmed by the identification of Achilles with "Dis, Hades" (199) and of Helen with "Kore, Persephone" (195). *La Mort,* entangled with *L'Amour,* turns the "wheel" or "circle" that weds the woman to the warrior. As one prose gloss explains, Helen remains "almost ready for this sacrifice—at least, for the immolation of herself before this greatest love of Achilles" (245). Indeed, she remains intoxicated by recollections of the attack on the beach, associating Achilles' desire with his rage and her fate with that of Iphigenia sacrificed at Aulis: "We stare and stare / over the smouldering embers," she recalls, "till I felt the touch / of his fingers' remorseless steel . . . / *for I have promised another / white throat to a goddess, / but not to our lady of Aulis*" (269-70; ellipses H. D.'s). Mesmerized by the idea that "what she invoked" may "destroy her," Helen as Circe or witch feels herself encircled by a snarling, prowling Achilles and brought back to the painful but desirous memory of "the touch / of his fingers' remorseless steel." Whereas Woolf called on women to "compensate the man for the loss of his gun," H. D.'s heroine seems to offer herself as a sacrificial compensation to the wounded veteran, Achilles.

H. D.'s flirtation with masochism is apparent not only in her depiction of Helen's adoration of Achilles but also in the later sequence *Vale Ave* (1957), which expresses the poet's own reverence for "the Master of the Air, the Air Marshal," Sir Hugh Dowding, who was commander of the Royal Air Force fighter pilots during the Battle of Britain and one of the possible models for Achilles.[108] In a scene in *Vale Ave* almost verging on the pornographic, H. D. describes how she responds with "agony" to "his hands grasp[ing] my bare thighs

. . . that would tear open, tear apart" and "his commanding knees keep[ing] my knees locked": "my own hands clutch and tear, // and my lips part, as he releases me, and my famished mouth opens // and knows his hunger and his power" (47). Finally admitting her own subjugation not only to his "virility" but also to his spiritual primacy in deciphering the mysteries of transcendent truths—"Hugh was right, 'no woman / should explore these devious rites'"—the poet seems to relinquish the authority of the word and its mystical rituals to "the Air Lord and his pride" (57). Her last vision of their union—"he turned to attack her, crowned" (68)—captures not only the violence of his desire but her desire for violent violation.

Similarly, in *Helen in Egypt,* Helen illustrates H. D.'s belief that women are bound to be enthralled not by Paris, the lover, but by Achilles, the warrior, whose impassioned grief over his loss of omniscience—his rage against his mother—will perpetually threaten to obliterate Helen, a script that illuminates H. D.'s feeling that she was married to the war. Like Simone Weil, then, H. D. implies that when women experience a capacity to love in the midst of the brutality of warfare, "this love could only be for the master. Every other way is barred to the gift of loving."[109] The "remorseless steel" of Achilles' fingers ringing Helen's throat resembles nothing so much as the unbreakable "iron-ring" of the military "Command," an echo that enables H. D. to meditate on the enmeshed terms *eros* and *eris, L'Amour* and *La Mort,* even as it forecasts Sylvia Plath's "Every woman adores a Fascist / the boot in the face, the brute / Brute heart of a brute like you" ("Daddy," *PCP* 223).

The sadomasochistic love battle H. D. presents through Helen and Achilles surfaces in the relationships between the passengers who are journeying toward war on Katherine Anne Porter's *Ship of Fools* (1962). One of her female characters is haunted by a vision of a murderous struggle in which a man and woman "swayed and staggered together in a strange embrace, as if they supported each other; but in the man's raised hand was a long knife, and the woman's breast and stomach were pierced. The blood ran down her body and over her thighs, her skirts were sticking to her legs with her own blood. She was beating him on the head with a jagged stone, and his features were veiled in rivulets of blood." This anonymous woman, clinging to her mate in "rage and hatred," serves as a prototype for a number of the women on board the *Vera*: the two whores who enjoy being beaten by their pimps, for example, or the imprisoned Condesa who asks to be injected and sent into a drugged sleep by a physician-admirer.[110] Just as disturbingly, in the section of *The Golden Notebook* devoted to World War II, Doris Lessing describes a series of sadomasochistic relationships that prove to her protagonist Anna Wulf "how many women like to be bullied," while in Lessing's *Four-Gated City* (1969) Martha Quest's lover Jack, who had been wounded as a mine-sweeper during the war, eventually salves his haunting sense of mortality by becoming a sadistic pimp who initiates young girls into what he teaches them to consider degrading sexual acts. For H. D.'s, Porter's, and Lessing's characters, all half in love with death, "the secret ugly frightening pulse of war itself" is, in the words of Anna Wulf, the "delicious intoxication" in "the death that we all wanted, for each other and for ourselves."[111]

. . . . .

Although many critics have read *Helen in Egypt* as a joyous excavation of the maternal principle, Helen's isolation in a ring of supple and turbulent men like Achilles, Paris, and Theseus can be said to symbolize the breakdown of the female community. Without her daughter, her mother, and her sister, Helen is a phantom, a shadow, reduced by the war to a no-woman. Significantly, then, the only mother-goddess in the poem is a mother-in-law, who welcomes an epithalamion in "timeless time" which resembles nothing so much as the *liebestod* of Edith Sitwell's "Serenade." In this respect, H. D.'s late works typify the ways women writers of the fifties and sixties use the occasion of World War II to deliberate not only on the vulnerability of its survivors but also on the disintegration of the dream of Herland.

From Stein's worry about women becoming as afraid as men to Boyle's image of the mazurka of women as a pas seul and Brooks's isolated Annie, the writings of literary women brooded on the breakdown of a feminist dream of women's commonality.[112] From the fifties on, however, literary women as different as Harriet Arnow, Djuna Barnes, Paule Marshall, Muriel Spark, and Jean Rhys developed one of the insights found in *Helen in Egypt*, namely the ways in which the war divided women from one another and instilled various forms of self-division. Survival guilt, shell shock, the fragility of the home, postwar economic declines, sexual violence: all undermined or discredited the dream of Herland celebrated by earlier feminist writers. Three otherwise quite dissimilar works—Arnow's *The Dollmaker* (1954), Bar-

nes's *The Antiphon* (1958), and Marshall's *Brown Girl, Brownstones* (1959)—suggest that the war inducted mothers into a public world that was hostile to their children. Assimilation or adjustment becomes a major theme in these books, one that dramatizes the tragic consequences for mothers complicitous in systems dangerous to their daughters' survival.

Fierce conflicts between mothers and daughters, the inadequacy of the family as a survival mechanism for children, and the threats posed to female artistry are examined in sociological and religious terms by *The Dollmaker*. "How shall we sing the Lord's song in a strange land?" Arnow's heroine wonders after she has been dislocated by the war, and Arnow implies that, exiled from Herland and repatriated inside a dollhouse, the female artist can only become a dollmaker.[113] To the extent that *The Dollmaker* describes the divisions between women and the impossibility of female artistry through a critique of the theory that the Second World War liberated women by catapulting them in unprecedented numbers into the labor market, it prefigures the use of the war as a metaphor in Barnes's and Marshall's works.

In *The Dollmaker* Gertie Nevels saves the money she gains from a brother, Henley, who was killed in the war, to buy "a place of her own," adjoining her father's property. While her husband, Clovis, is away, working in the Detroit war industry, she muses: "Almost every day she would see her father. His land touched her land—her land, *her* land" (134). At first, therefore, Gertie believes that "the war and Henley's death had been a plan to help set her and her children free so that she might live and be beholden to no man, not even to Clovis" (139). Yet, although she plans to stay in Kentucky, planting crops and tracing the war routes of absent husbands for women left behind, Gertie is converted by her mother's Pauline doctrine that wives should "be in subjection unto your husbands" (141) and goes to join Clovis in Detroit. Effectively expelled from the Edenic fields of Kentucky, she lands in the dark satanic mills of Detroit, where natural rhythms are supplanted by the work shifts at the steel factories. Instead of homemade food, furniture, and books, an "Icy Heart" refrigerator dominates her tiny kitchen, while radios, movies, and educators spout a fallen language that is almost incomprehensible to Gertie, who must learn to understand what words like *hillbilly, kike, spic, commie,* and—most important—*adjustment* mean.

That Gertie has lost not only her own land but a dream of Herland is made clear through the fates of her neighbors, her children, and her art. Living among women who work in the war industry, Gertie watches her neighbors juggling paid (industrial) and unpaid (childcare) work and driven to drugs or drink to ease their sense of fragmentation. Although she herself stays at home, thereby escaping the fate of a woman who is "squashed to death in her press" (317), Gertie also feels oppressed, especially by her new dependency on her wage-earning husband: "Here everything, even to the kindling wood, came from Clovis" (338). In addition, she observes her children variously respond to the adjustment that is required of them at school. Given her own ambivalence, she hardly knows whether it is better for them to rebel openly and return home, as her oldest son does, or to conform aggressively, as her oldest daughter does. Worse still, Gertie witnesses the destruction of her most gifted child, Cassy, who is literally split in two by a railroad train that amputates her legs.

Early in the novel Cassy, who has created an imaginary friend named Callie Lou, identifies her with a huge piece of cherry wood that Gertie is in the process of whittling. Gertie is at first unsure whether the figure in the wood is "the laughing Christ with hair long and black like Callie Lou's" or "the Judas she had pitied giving back the silver" (127), but she relinquishes her artistry after her daughter's death. Striking with an ax until "the wood cried out," she splits the image to provide herself with the material she needs to produce the machine-made crosses and painted dolls that sell in Detroit. Gertie discovers that her Christlike self-sacrifice of her land was satanically self-subverting, for her renunciation of her own land has effectively turned her into a dollmaker who consigns her children to a culture perpetually at war. By the end of the novel the war has ended, but violent battles against unionization have begun. While her racist neighbors are celebrating the dropping of the atomic bomb ("Now, I figger them Japs around u atom bomb is kinda like them bugs"), a woman with a wounded husband articulates the general realization of the wives: "I don't guess a woman can ever find a job, now" (494, 495).

More oblique but just as bleak in its depiction of the war as a defeat of women, Barnes's autobiographical closet drama *The Antiphon* takes place in 1939, inside a bomb-damaged ancestral mansion. In a setting littered with battered statues (including a dummy in a British soldier's uniform), an actress-writer attends a family reunion that evokes T. S. Eliot's play of that name. This gathering mourns a primal rape scene, for Barnes's

heroine, Miranda, remembers how her father persuaded her to submit sexually to an old Cockney traveler. Looking into a dollhouse, Miranda is haunted not only by her father, a "Devil" with "a raping-hook," but also by her mother, "a *madam* by submission"; both parents had "made / Of that doll's *abattoir* a babe's *bordel*."[114] To the horror of the victim of incest, the collusion of parents has prostituted the child. The ruin of the war becomes the site for the ruin of her life, first, when her brothers attempt to murder her along with her mother and then at the end of the play, when the mother and daughter who had been divided in life exchange costumes and embrace each other in a suicidal union that leaves two entrepreneurial brothers in charge of a world at war. Only the convoluted conceits of Jacobean drama can express the despair Barnes's Miranda experiences not in a brave new world but in the old world of the dollhouse, which is associated with the sexual exploitation of the father and the complicity of the mother.

Like *The Dollmaker* and *The Antiphon, Brown Girl, Brownstones* deals with the war as a symbolic assimilation of the mother into a system injurious to her daughter. In Marshall's Brooklyn community of West Indian immigrants, the mother who works in the war industry appears alien and destructive to her children. As if enlarging upon Adrienne Rich's dictum that "the price of external assimilation is internal division,"[115] Marshall implies that the mother who functions as a socializing agent for a hostile society is a war victim who perpetuates war. *Brown Girl, Brownstones*'s Silla Boyce becomes a drudge as she works in the war factories during the night shift and in her kitchen during the days, while her husband, Deighton, idly dreams about the piece of land he has inherited in Barbados. Not only does the "formidable force" of "the mother," as Silla is usually called, "match that of the machines" producing shells, but she also exerts her will by usurping her husband's authority.[116] Specifically, behind his back she writes in his name to Barbados and sells his land in order to gain the money she needs to buy a house in Brooklyn. The forgeries are a fitting symbol of Silla's inability to find security except by conforming to a ruthless ethic of competition and by denying both her love for her husband and her own identity.

As indebted to the images of Eliot's poetry as is Barnes's play, this novel presents Deighton—"a hollow man" (116)—seeking his own obliteration by joining a religious cult in which he relinquishes adult responsibility to a "Father Peace," who teaches that "the word *mother* is a filthy word" (168). Then, after "the mother" has him deported as an illegal alien, he takes a suicidal leap from the boat returning him to Barbados and thereby attains a virtually mythic "death by water." The earlier section of the novel entitled "The War" describes the war between this couple, a series of battles which Deighton loses, to the horror of their daughter Selina, who is revolted by the way in which her father is "unmanned" and who fights "the mother," whom she calls "Hitler." Like Brooks, Hurston, and Petry, Marshall explicitly views World War II as, in Silla's words, "another white-man war" (65). But by the end of the novel Silla herself has destroyed the female community in her own home: not only has her daughter left, but the white and black roomers who befriended Selina in her growing up have been expelled by the force of "the mother's" will.

Muriel Spark and Jean Rhys, writing later, identify the war with morally impoverished communities composed not of women but of aging girls, girls as catty as the bitchy characters in Clare Boothe's satiric *The Women* (1936). Framed by V-E and V-J day celebrations, Spark's *Girls of Slender Means* (1963) is set in one of the cheap hostels "which had flourished since the emancipation of women had called for them"; however, its inhabitants—who worship "Poise" and produce fake fan letters to literary men so as to sell handwritten responses—are characterized as superficial and solipsistic.[117] When an undetonated bomb explodes in the garden and destroys the hostel, the girls who survive are those who are the most metaphysically and physically slender. Similarly, Jean Rhys's short story "The Insect World" (1976) describes the competition between "old girls" worn down by fly bombs, shortages, rationing, and overwork. Rhys's heroine, who "hated most women," suffers from a nightmare that she has been infected by a noxious, infected insect world that symbolizes her sense of the home front.[118]

But although both Rhys and Spark analyze the inadequacies of women's values and relationships, they also dramatize female vulnerability. Rhys's heroine finds herself shocked by marginalia penciled in a book by its earlier owner, markings as sinister as the tropical insects described within the volume: on one page, "He had written 'Women are an unspeakable abomination' with such force that the pencil had driven through the paper," a sentence that fills her with terror at "the hidden horror . . . that was responsible for all the other horrors" (352). Even more malevolent, amid the joyous crowds commemorating V-J day in the

London rally that concludes Spark's *Girls of Slender Means,* a young sailor quietly slips a knife between the ribs of the girl at his side. For both Rhys and Spark, the war marks the fall of Herland, the rise of a misogynist Hisland, into which women are assimilated at the cost of their lives. Toni Morrison's *Sula* (1973), if read as a historical novel, also identifies the war years with the destruction of women and their relationships. *Sula* begins with a portrait of Shadrack, a shell-shocked veteran of World War I, and dates the rift in the friendship between Sula and Nell in 1939 and the death of Sula—whose last name is "Peace"—in 1940, one year before a large proportion of the people in their town go down to death on the annual holiday Shadrack has set aside as "National Suicide Day."

That the no man's land of World War I was followed by the no woman's land of World War II made total war an apt image of contemporary women writers' anxiety about their authority and authorship. Meditating on her personal poetic development, Jane Cooper explained that "by 1951 the war had begun to seem like a mask, something to write through in order to express a desolation that had become personal," and she went on to quote one of her poems from that period:

> Guilt, war, disease—pillars of violence
> To keep a roof of symbols over my head.
> Still the rain soaks my bed
> Whenever the wind blows, riddling innocence.[119]

While Cooper echoes Edith Sitwell's "Still Falls the Rain" to record her sense of the hopeless inadequacy of her linguistic shelters, Wanda Coleman, in a poem entitled "No Woman's Land" (1979), presents herself as occupied enemy territory:

> they trample on my sensitivity
> goose-step thru streets of my affection
> line me up before the firing squad of insecurity,
>   shoot me down
>
> when the smoke clears
> my corpse interred
> they sing my praises in a hymn.

Although she concludes the poem with a defiant exclamation—"no white flag of truce / no surrender"—Coleman uses the death mask of the Second World War to protest against a blitz on herself and on "Woman's Land."[120]

Less metaphorically and more historically grounded in the war, the fates of the representative female characters in Marge Piercy's novel *Gone to Soldiers* (1987) delineate the damage done to women forced to imitate feminine or masculine roles after the war to escape the horror of no-womanhood. A female war correspondent, traumatized by the atrocities she has witnessed on the European front, returns to a career of romance writing for women's magazines and to an ex-husband she had previously hated because "he had not valued their marriage enough to preserve it."[121] Another woman, a WASP/flyer put out of commission by the cessation of war, can only continue to pilot planes by wearing men's clothes and passing as a man, a ploy that also enables her to withstand homosexual baiting. A laid-off factory worker, whose Marine lover has been subjected to the murderous brutality of Japanese island combat, finds herself nursing "a man who killed and killed and who weeps about it" (743). Because the dislocation and destruction of the war demonstrated the vulnerability of the family, Piercy implies, perhaps only a reconstruction of strikingly traditional gender roles could salve anxieties about national and personal security, or so the historian Elaine Tyler May has also speculated.[122]

But of course atomic bombs and concentration camps put into question the future of the whole human race, rendering all sex roles strikingly fictive. For two newly married intelligence officers in *Gone to Soldiers,* the "something new" that occurred at Hiroshima resembles nothing so much as a "void. A force that turns people from breathing flesh into an image on stone, like a photograph," that presages the "future . . . [as] a plain of ashes, of sand turned to glass, flesh vaporized, time itself burned up" (755-56). Piercy's Jewish heroine is more personally threatened: she is starved and overworked, undressed and beaten, shaved and numbered in Birkenau, and eventually becomes disabused of her fantasy that she can survive by "imagin[ing] that her body was hidden inside an imitation body. The men could only see the imitation rubber body, but she was the bones hidden inside that they could not see or touch" (626).

. . . . .

Encased in her "charred skirts and death-mask," the speaker of Plath's "Getting There" (1962) reacts to a boxcar of "legs, arms piled outside / The tent of unending cries— / A hospital of dolls" with the vision of a reborn but inarticulate self arising "pure as a baby" out of the "black car of Lethe" (*PCP* 249). Both Plath's sense of herself as a displaced person and her belief that the only utterance available to her is a language

of lamentation reflect the elegiac tone that accompanies the crowing of Bishop's cocks, the brooding of Brooks's veterans, the "G.I. talk" of Boyle's war brides, Sitwell's "discordant" lullabies and serenades, the incomprehensible "double-talk" of McCullers's soldier, H. D.'s liebestod, Gertie Nevel's crying wood, and Marshall's and Spark's female forgeries, all signs not only of women's psychological but also of their linguistic sense of loss. As Burdekin's *Swastika Night* had predicted, that loss was related to the "Reduction of Women" to no-women: hens, whores, battered corpses, ghosts, dolls, dollmakers, and aging girls.

Perhaps so many literary women mourned their aesthetic impotence and questioned the viability of female community because of pressures exerted by the war which issued in divisions between, say, black and white, Asian and Caucasian, or Jewish and gentile women, a number of whom found ample cause to blame each other for failures of moral and material support. As we have seen, McCullers, Brooks, and Petry criticized Allied propaganda not only by uncovering the "we" of the war as white and male but also by suggesting that it posed different problems for women of different colors even as it set them at odds. But in writings about the Holocaust and about Japanese-American internment camps, women seemed intent on explaining why women should beware women.

After the revelation of the atrocities in the concentration camps, Jewish writers like Muriel Rukeyser as well as gentiles from Katherine Anne Porter to Sylvia Plath felt that, to quote Plath, "I think I may well be a Jew" ("Daddy," *PCP* 153).[123] Because so many literary women viewed fascist ideology as a form of masculinism, because they suffered militarism as an assault, because they were imbued with the guilt of victimization, and because they saw themselves caught in a threatening assimilation process, not a few of them identified the vulnerability of women with the extermination of the Jews; but even as they examined the metaphorical relationship between womanhood and Jewishness, they confronted the immorality of the analogy.

Such an imaginative equation, of course, has a long history, going back to Margaret Fuller and Olive Schreiner, who observed that prejudice against Jews was a consequence of the same self-certifying mythology that enslaved blacks and women.[124] At the same time, femininity and Jewishness had been conflated in anti-Semitic texts like Otto Weininger's *Sex and Character* (1903), which claimed that "Judaism is saturated with femininity. . . . The most manly Jew is more feminine than the least manly Aryan." Similarly, Hitler, in his efforts to limit German women to traditionally nurturing roles (*Kinder, Kirche, Küche*), promulgated the idea that "the emancipation of women" was the product of the "Jewish mind."[125] An early literary protest against genocide written by a Christian woman, Ada Jackson's *Behold the Jew* (1943) eschews silence in the face of outrage— "If I keep silence all these things / are done of me and in my name, / and mine the guilt of bludgeonings / and massacres"—even as it indicts its readers: "While you read they die."[126] Adumbrating subsequent literary meditations on the Holocaust, Jackson addresses the unnegotiable gulf between Jewish sufferers ("they die") and female as well as male observers ("you read").

For the Jewish observer, of course, the Holocaust demands a witness. Like Rukeyser's "To Be a Jew in the Twentieth Century," a sonnet in "Letter to the Front," later works by writers as different as Adrienne Rich, Irena Klepfisz, Susan Fromberg Schaeffer, Norma Rosen, Cynthia Ozick, and Lore Segal describe Jewishness as a tragic double bind, a gift it is fatal to refuse or accept:

> If you refuse,
> Wishing to be invisible, you choose
> Death of the spirit, the stone insanity.
> Accepting, take full life. Full agonies:
> Your evening deep in labyrinthine blood
> Of those who resist, fail, and resist; and God
> Reduced to a hostage among hostages.
>
> [139]

Besides producing a body of literature dedicated to exploring what it means to be a Jew in the twentieth century and to remembering what Rukeyser described as "Full agonies," identification with Jewish suffering may help explain why the first important works produced by the so-called second wave of feminism relied on a comparison between women and Jews. In *The Second Sex* (1949), Simone de Beauvoir introduced her analysis of the construction of the feminine by deflating stereotypes of "the Jewish character" and "the eternal feminine," reminding her readers that the "Jewish problem" and the "woman problem" are not made by Jews or women. Betty Friedan, considering the housewife in the home and the prisoner in a concentration camp, alluded to Bruno Bettelheim's work on the "zombies" who inhabited Nazi camps. Friedan's *Feminine Mystique* (1963) argued that "the comfortable concentration camp that American women have walked into, or have been talked into by others, is . . . a frame of reference that denies woman's adult human identity."[127]

Significant as the comparison of the concentration camp to the housewife's space was for Friedan, however, for obvious reasons she found it necessary to conclude her discussion by explaining, "The suburban house is not a German concentration camp, nor are American housewives on their way to the gas chamber" (309). Her reservations about the analogy hint at the discomfort it could also produce in non-Jewish women. When Elizabeth Bishop wrote a poem which locates a "Jew in a newspaper hat" and the anti-Semite Ezra Pound in a madhouse, her adjectives for the poet demote him from "tragic" and "honored" to "cranky" and "wretched" not because, as one critic claims, "his simple nobility is smothered by the weakness, fragility, and insipidity of the other inmates" but because his delusions are no less pathetic than theirs. Bishop's title—"Visits to St. Elizabeths" (1950)—alludes to the hospital that housed Pound and she regulates her verse through the nonsensical, indeed cannibalistic, rhythms of "The House that Jack Built" to imply that the suffering of both poet and Jew is contained within an insane structure that even she, an Elizabeth herself, may not be able to escape.[128] From Marianne Moore to Stevie Smith, literary women explored their hatred of anti-Semitism but also their consciousness that, like Moore, they were "not competent" to promise never to hate black, white, red, yellow, Jew or their awareness of what Stevie Smith called the "final treachery of the smug goy."[129] At the same time, a number of women writers responded to the Holocaust by demonstrating that women were as guilty as men of evading their responsibilities for a previously unimaginable evil. Both Kay Boyle's "Winter Night" (1946) and Flannery O'Connor's "The Displaced Person" (1955), for example, use the ethical issues raised by the Holocaust to criticize the naïveté and jingoism of American women.

In "Winter Night," a survivor is driven to relive with the American child for whom she is babysitting a maternal role she played for a motherless girl in the camps. Besides alluding to the impossibility of communicating the terror of the European camps to Americans, the story hints at the survivor's continued entrapment in an experience that breeds grief and rage, for the Jewish babysitter has cause to resent gentile mothers not only ignorant but somehow luckier than she.[130] "The Displaced Person," which represents Catholic rather than Jewish victims of the Holocaust, more scathingly condemns American women as responsible for the destruction of displaced people. Locating her story on the farm of Mrs. McIntyre, O'Connor shows why Mrs. McIntyre and her hired workers, Mr. and Mrs. Shortley, effectively collude in the murder of a Catholic immigrant who has fled "the ovens and the boxcars" of his native Poland. Ironically, what horrifies them about Mr. Guizac is his effort to rescue his niece from rooms "piled high with bodies of dead people all in a heap, their arms and legs tangled together," by marrying her to a black worker on the farm. Because Mrs. McIntyre and Mrs. Shortley are motivated by precisely the idea of "wise blood" that led to the laws against miscegenation in Europe, they deserve the punishment they receive when they are themselves turned into displaced people.[131]

As distrustful of female merits as O'Connor, Doris Lessing's heroine in *Four-Gated City* confronts what she calls "the self-hater" by coming to terms with the fact that *I am 'The Germans are the mirror and catalyst of Europe' and also: 'Dirty Hun, Filthy Nazi.'*[132] In the context of the Holocaust, literary women necessarily confronted the guilt they shared with the rest of the world. Paradoxically, however, the very failure of the metaphorical equation of woman and Jew as well as guilt about its use foregrounded the difficulty of articulating female experiences in anything but borrowed terms. Such an aesthetic problem propels not only the grotesque stories of Boyle and O'Connor but also the very different ironies of, say, Sylvia Plath, for whom the Holocaust became a key metaphor.

Just as the Holocaust clearly called into question the savage nature of Western (and Western women's) culture, the internment of Japanese Americans was experienced as such a catastrophe that its literature only began appearing several decades after the fact. A retrospective poem entitled "To the Lady" (1976) by the Nisei writer Mitsuye Yamada best exemplifies the distrust and rage that resulted from divisions between women set in place by the prison camps. The lady of the title had asked, "Why did the Japanese Americans let / the government put them in those camps without protest?" and the speaker of the poem answers in two bitter stanzas. First, she ironically enumerates the extravagant lengths to which she herself should have gone—"should've bombed a bank / should've tried self-immolation / should've holed myself up in a / woodframe house / and let you watch me / burn up on the six o'clock news"—and then she sarcastically predicts, "YOU would've / come to my aid in shining armor / laid yourself across the railroad track / marched on Washington." The poem concludes with both

women's failure—"we didn't draw the line"—a failure that has effectively put them on two different sides: "YOU let'm / I let'm / All are punished."[133]

The "we" which the war turns into an antagonistic "YOU" and "I" in Yamada's poem has been split as definitively as it is in Ada Jackson's warning "While you read they die." Like their male contemporaries, many literary women believed that World War II marked the end of an age of innocence. Meditating on childhood's end, Muriel Spark's story "The First Year of My Life" (1975) uses the uncanny intelligence of a baby born at the end of World War I to express the author's disillusionment with modernity. Only after hearing former Prime Minister Asquith's claim that since the Great War "'All things have become new'" does this infant smile the knowing grimace of the damned.[134] Preternaturally old before her time, Spark's cynical child foresees that the promised "new" of the post-World War I generation might lead to a recycling of the past in what Lessing called the nightmare repetition of history she herself portrayed in her aptly named *Children of Violence* novels. After the Second World War, women of letters joined many of their male contemporaries in expressing despair at the nightmare repetitions of bankrupt sexual scenarios. Significantly, however, just as the assault on masculinity during World War I produced many of the strongest works associated with male modernism, so the blitz on women during World War II contributed to the formation of a female literary tradition which mourns the demise of the dream of Herland even as it documents female artistic survival behind a mask, a survival achieved only with the rictus of a grin set in place.

Notes

Epigraphs: Stein, *Everybody's Autobiography* (1937; New York: Vintage, 1973), 133; H. D., *Helen in Egypt* (New York: New Directions, 1974), 99. Further references will to be this edition, and page numbers will appear in the text; Plath, "Getting There" (1962), in *The Collected Poems,* ed. Ted Hughes (New York: Harper and Row, 1981), 249. Further references to Plath's poems will be to this edition, and page numbers will appear in the text after the abbreviation *PCP* where necessary.

1. H. D., *The Gift* (New York: New Directions, 1982), 135-37.

2. See our discussion of this passage from the unpublished "The Thorn Thicket" (Collection of American Literature, Beinecke Rare Book and Manuscript Library,

Yale University) in Gilbert and Gubar, *No Man's Land: The Place of the Woman Writer in the Twentieth Century,* vol. 2: *Sexchanges* (New Haven: Yale University Press, 1989), 308.

3. Bryher, *The Days of Mars: A Memoir, 1940-1946* (New York: Harcourt Brace Jovanovich, 1972), 120.

4. Stein, *Wars I Have Seen* (London: Batsford, 1945), 122; see the chapter "Soldier's Heart" in our *Sexchanges,* 258-323.

5. Lessing, *Martha Quest* (1952; New York: New American Library, 1970), 26.

6. Bowen, "The Demon Lover," *The Collected Stories of Elizabeth Bowen* (New York: Random House, 1982), 661-66. Further references to Bowen's stories will be to this edition, and page numbers will appear in the text.

7. Buck, *Of Men and Women* (New York: John Day, 1941), 155.

8. Stein, *Wars I Have Seen,* 49-50.

9. Vernon Scannell makes this point in *Not without Glory: Poets of the Second World War* (London: Woburn Press, 1976), 17-18. See also Chester E. Eisinger, *Fiction of the Forties* (Chicago: University of Chicago Press, 1963), 23-24. Larkin, "MCMXIV," *The Whitsun Weddings* (London: Faber, 1964), 28; Read, "To a Conscript of 1940," *Collected Poems* (New York: Horizon, 1966), 152 (see also Vance Bourjaily, *Confessions of a Spent Youth* [New York: Dial, 1960], whose hero enters World War II haunted by the poetry of the earlier war); Douglas, "Desert Flowers," in *The Terrible Rain: The War Poets 1939-1945,* ed. Brian Gardner (London: Methuen, 1983), 109; Lewis, "Where Are the War Poets?" (1943) *Poems of C. Day Lewis 1925-1972,* ed. Ian Parsons (London: Cape-Hogarth, 1977), 138; Spender's remarks are quoted in the *Norton Anthology of English Literature,* vol. 2, ed. M. H. Abrams et al. (New York: Norton, 1986), 2320.

10. Matthews, quoted in Margaret Goldsmith, *Women at War* (London: Lindasay Brummond, n.d.), 98. For statistics on female employment, see William Chafe, *The American Woman: Her Changing Social, Economic, and Political Roles, 1920-1970* (New York: Oxford University Press, 1972). A number of historians have questioned Chafe's view that an upsurge of paid employment of married women during World War II led to the later women's liberation movement. The most recent to do so is D'Ann Campbell in *Women at War with America* (Cambridge: Harvard University Press, 1984). Vera Brittain describes her generation's skepticism in *Lady into Woman: A History of Women from Victoria to Elizabeth II* (New York: Macmillan, 1953), 188 and 198.

11. Maureen Honey discusses the Adel ad in *Creating Rosie the Riveter* (Amherst: University of Massachusetts Press, 1984), 84. John Costello focuses on the advertisements of cosmetic companies, which argued that lipstick symbolizes what soldiers are fighting for, "the precious right of women to be feminine and lovely" (*Love, Sex and War: Changing Values 1939-45* [London: Pan, 1986], pl. 63 and 64).

12. Women's uniforms and status are discussed in Jack Cassin-Scott and Angus McBride, *Women at War: 1939-45* (London: Osprey, 1980), 15-18; "expression of free-flowing penis-envy": see Ferdinand Lundberg and Marynia F. Farnham, *Modern Woman, The Lost Sex* (New York: Harper, 1947), 214-215, 353-54.

13. Matthews, quoted in Goldsmith, *Women at War,* 98; War Department brochure, quoted by Eleanor F. Straub, "Women in the Civilian Labor Force," in *Clio Was A Woman: Studies in the History of American Women,* ed. Mabel E. Deutsch and Virginia C. Purdy (Washington, D.C.: Howard University Press, 1980), 218; "majority of girls": see Peggy Scott, *They Made Invasion Possible* (London: Hutchinson, 1944), 8; Mead, "The Women in the War," in *While You Were Gone: A Report on Wartime Life in the United States,* ed. Jack Goodman (New York: Simon and Schuster, 1946), 278; Costello, *Love, Sex and War,* 361.

14. Fussell, *Wartime: Understanding and Behavior in the Second World War* (New York: Oxford University Press, 1989), 132.

15. For background on the general cultural effects of war conditions, see Alan Sinfield, *Literature, Politics, and Culture in Postwar Britain* (Berkeley: University of California Press, 1989), 6-22; Thomas, "A Refusal to Mourn the Death, by Fire, of a Child in London," in *The War Poets: An Anthology of the War Poetry of the 20th Century,* ed. Oscar Williams (New York: John Day, 1945), 32; Sitwell, "Still Falls the Rain" (1942), *The Collected Poems* (New York: Macmillan, 1957), 272.

16. Dickey, "The Firebombing" (1946), *Buckdancer's Choice* (Middletown, Conn.: Wesleyan University Press, 1964), 17; Ciardi, "Take-Off Over Kansas," *Other Skies* (Boston: Little, Brown, 1947), 21-22.

17. Graves, quoted in Ian Hamilton's introduction to *The Poetry of War, 1939-45,* ed. Ian Hamilton (London: Alan Ross, 1965), 3; Press, "Poets of World War II," in *British Writers,* ed. Ian Scott-Kilvert, vol. 7 (New York: Scribner's, 1978), 421-50. Fussell quotes William Manchester's assessment that "all who wore uniforms are called veterans, but more than 90 per cent of them are as uninformed about the killing zones as those on the home front" as well as statistics that the United States Army, which grew in 1943 by two million men, contained only about 365,000 in combat units and an even smaller number in rifle companies (*Wartime* 283).

18. Yeats, "Lapis Lazuli" (1938), *The Collected Poems of W. B. Yeats* (New York: Macmillan, 1956), 292.

19. Jarrell, "The Death of the Ball Turret Gunner" (1945), *The Complete Poems* (New York: Farrar, Straus, and Giroux, 1969), 144.

20. Fussell, *Wartime,* 153.

21. Woolf, *Leave the Letters Till We're Dead: The Letters of Virginia Woolf,* vol. 6: *1936-41,* ed. Nigel Nicolson, with Joanne Trautmann (London: Hogarth, 1980), 379.

22. Bishop, "Roosters" (1946), *The Complete Poems 1927-1979* (New York: New Directions, 1971), 35. Further references will be to this edition, and page numbers will appear in the text.

23. "Mov[e] from a country morning": see William Spiegelman, "Natural Heroism," in *Modern Critical Views: Elizabeth Bishop,* ed. Harold Bloom (New York: Chelsea House, 1985), 99-100; see also Anne R. Newman, "Elizabeth Bishop's 'Roosters,'" in ibid., 117.

24. Beard, *On Understanding Women* (1931), excerpted in *Mary Ritter Beard: A Sourcebook,* ed. Ann J. Lane (New York: Schocken, 1977), 144.

25. Holtby, *Women and a Changing Civilization* (1935; Chicago: Academy Chicago, 1978), 159-60.

26. Burdekin, *Swastika Night* (Old Westbury, N.Y.: Feminist Press, 1985). In her introduction, Patai distinguishes the consciousness of "gender ideology" in Burdekin's text with its absence in *1984* (xiii-xiv). Further references will be to this edition, and page numbers will appear in the text.

27. Carson McCullers more elliptically hints at the relation between masculinism and fascism when a heroine is baffled by two words—*Pussy* and *Mussolini* scrawled on a neighborhood wall: see *The Heart Is a Lonely Hunter* (1940; New York: Bantam, 1953), 31.

28. Rukeyser, "Letter to the Front" (1944), *The Collected Poems* (New York: McGraw-Hill, 1982), 235. Further references to Rukeyser's works will be to this edition, and page numbers will appear in the text.

29. Smith and Snelling, "Man Born of Woman," *North Georgia Review* 6:1-4 (1941): 10, 17.

30. Brittain, *Lady into Woman*, 198.

31. Holtby, *Women and a Changing Civilization*, 166.

32. Stein, *The Mother of Us All* (1946), in *Gertrude Stein: Last Operas and Plays*, ed. Carl Van Vechten (New York: Vintage, 1975), 80-81.

33. Bernikow, *Among Women* (New York: Harmony, 1980), 190-92.

34. Bowen, *The Heat of the Day* (1948; New York: Knopf, 1949), 24-25. Further references will be to this edition, and page numbers will appear in the text.

35. Smith, *Over the Frontier* (1938; London: Virago, 1980), 271.

36. Sitwell, "Lullaby," *Collected Poems*, 274-75.

37. Sitwell, "Serenade: Any Man to Any Woman," *Collected Poems*, 276.

38. Uris, *Battle Cry* (1953; New York: Bantam, 1982), 48; Earle, "Cannoneer's Lady," in *Reveille: War Poems by Members of Our Armed Forces*, ed. Daniel Henderson, John Kieran, and Grantland Rice (New York: Barnes, 1943), 31.

39. Costello, *Love, Sex and War*, 120.

40. Ciardi, "The Health of Captains" (1955), *As If: Poems New and Selected* (New Brunswick, N.J.: Rutgers University Press, 1955), 13; Kirstein, "Snatch," *Rhymes of a PFC* (1964; Boston: David R. Godine, 1981), 128. For the slippage between *puellis* (girls) and *duellis* (battles), see Henry Reed's "Lessons of the War: Naming of Parts," *A Map of Verona and Other Poems* (New York: Reynal and Hitchcock, 1947), 27-29.

41. Quoted in Costello, *Love, Sex and War*, 123.

42. Roberts-Jones, "Battalion H.Q. Burma," in *Poems from India by the Members of the Forces*, ed. R. N. Currey and R. V. Gibson (London: Oxford University Press, 1946), 125.

43. *"Fuck"*: see Karen Lee Schneider, "Altered Stories, Altered States: British Women Writing the Second World War" (Ph.D. diss., Indiana University, 1991), 7-8; "I won't describe": see Fussell, *Wartime*, 109.

44. May, *Homeward Bound: American Families in the Cold War Era* (New York: Basic, 1988), 110-11.

45. Connolly, "Comment," *Horizon* 3 (1941): 5.

46. Kirstein, "Load" (1964), *Rhymes of a PFC*, 152; Hersey, *The War Lover* (New York: Knopf, 1959), 387.

47. Don Jaffe, "Poets in the Inferno: Civilians, C.O.'s and Combatants," in *The Forties: Fiction, Poetry, Drama*, ed. Warren French (Deland, Fla.: Everett/Edwards, 1969), 36.

48. Auden, "September 1, 1939" (1939), in *The English Auden*, ed. Edward Mendelson (London: Faber, 1977), 245. Mendelson argues in *Early Auden* (London: Faber, 1981) that "social revolution" is a "male preserve" for Auden and Isherwood, who present an avid warmonger in *The Dog Beneath the Skin* as a mother who has lost her sons in battle (276).

49. Wilbur, "Place Pigalle," *The Beautiful Changes* (New York: Harcourt Brace, 1947), 12; Major Fred B. Shaw, Jr., "Lydia of Libya," in *Reveille*, 217; Douglas, "Cairo Jag" (1943), in *Complete Poems*, ed. Desmond Graham (Oxford: Oxford University Press, 1978), 97. Also see Bernard Gutteridge, "Sunday Promenade: Antisirane," originally published in *Traveller's Eve* (1947) and reprinted in *Old Damson-Face: Poems 1934-1974* (London: London Magazine Editions, 1975), 43.

50. Manifold, "The Sirens," in *War Poets*, 191; Patric Dickinson, "War," in *Reveille*, 241; Bourjaily, *Confessions of a Spent Youth*, 345 (also see the cartoons of Sgt. George Baker that show servicemen afraid to shake hands with women after army sex education courses, reprinted in James Jones, *World War II* [New York: Grosset and Dunlap, 1975], 55. Fussell describes American movies with names like *Good Girls Have VD Too*, as well as British slogans like the one used in Egypt: "Remember, flies spread disease. Keep yours shut!" [*Wartime*, 108]); Tolson, "The Furlough," *Rendezvous with America* (New York: Dodd, Mead, 1944), 23-24. (Because Tolson is black, his femicidal text is especially interesting in the context of Gwendolyn Brooks's poetry about black male femicidal rage. See the discussion later in this chapter.)

51. Corporal John Readey, "A Woman's a Two-Face," in *Reveille*, 215. In this regard, the proliferation of popular songs on infidelity is pertinent: "Don't Sit under the Apple Tree with Anyone Else but Me," "Paper Doll," and "Somebody Else Is Taking My Place," for example.

52. Barker, "To Any Member of My Generation," in *War Poets*, 321; Kunitz, "Careless Love," in ibid., 166; Shapiro, "Conscription Camp" (1941) *Collected Poems, 1940-1978*, (New York: Random House, 1978), 47-48; Causley, "A Ballad for Katharine of Aragon" (1951), *Collected Poems, 1951-1975* (London: Macmillan, 1975), 14.

53. May, *Homeward Bound*, 70.

54. Pynchon, *V.* (New York: Lippincott, 1963), 318.

55. Mary Cadogan and Patricia Craig, *Women and Children First: The Fiction of Two World Wars* (London: Gollancz, 1978), 173.

56. Fussell, *Wartime*, 116.

57. Mailer, *The Naked and the Dead* (1948; New York: Holt, Rinehart and Winston, 1981), 721; Pynchon, *Gravity's Rainbow* (New York: Bantam, 1974), 21.

58. Cynthia Enloe, *Does Khaki Become You? The Militarisation of Women's Lives* (London: Pluto, 1983), 2. In *Love, Sex and War*, Costello mentions that members of the WAAF were also referred to as "Pilots' Cockpits" in

British slang and he quotes one WAAF member who recalled that "soldiers often tried to rape us" (79-80); Robert Hewison, *Under Siege: Literary Life in London, 1939-45* (London: Weidenfeld and Nicolson, 1977), 25.

59. Sally Van Wagenen Keil, *Those Wonderful Women in Their Flying Machines: The Unknown Heroines of World War II* (New York: Rawson, Wade, 1979), 197, 202, 212. D'Ann Campbell quotes Virginia Gildersleeve explaining, "If the Navy could possibly have used dogs or ducks or monkeys" instead of women, certain admirals would have preferred them (*Women at War with America*), 37.

60. For Millay, see discussion in Chapter 2; on Rukeyser, see "Grandeur and Misery of a Poster Girl," *Partisan Review* 10:5 (1943): 472-73; on Moore, see Randall Jarrell, "Poetry in War and Peace," *Kipling, Auden & Co.* (New York: Farrar, Straus, and Giroux, 1980), 129-30; on H. D., see Jarrell, "*Tribute to the Angels* by H. D.," ibid., 135.

61. Deutsch, "For a Young Soldier" and "To My Son," *Take Them, Stranger* (New York: Henry Holt, 1944), 58-59.

62. Schweik, *A Gulf So Deeply Cut: American Women Poets and the second World War* (Madison: University of Wisconsin Press, 1991), 85-109. See the discussion of this picture in Fussell, *Thank God for the Atom Bomb and Other Essays* (New York: Summit, 1988), 49. Although he believes the *Life* photo and caption are "without a trace of irony or outrage," Fussell does not examine what its effect might be on the female viewer.

63. David Geraint Jones, "The Light of Day," in *Terrible Rain*, 154 (see also Gervase Stewart's "Poem" in ibid., 149); inscription on the memorial at Kohima, quoted in ibid., 161.

64. Shapiro, "V-Letter" (1944), *Collected Poems*, 87-88.

65. Douglas, *"Vergissmeinnicht"* (1943), *Complete Poems*, 111.

66. "There's the girl I 'left behind,'" the speaker of "Nebraska Gunner at Bataan" (1943) exclaims, "I wonder, would she love me yet / If she could watch me grimly kill," and so he wants to "keep her safe back there": see Corporal Richard F. Ferguson in *Reveille*, 71.

67. Uris, *Battle Cry*, 2.

68. Eberhart, "Brotherhood of Men," *Collected Poems, 1930-1976* (New York: Oxford University Press, 1976), 101; Jones, *From Here to Eternity* (New York: Scribner's, 1951), 16. Consider, also, A. A. Milne's war verse: "I march along and march along and ask myself each day: / If I should go and lose the war, then what will Mother say? / The Sergeant will be cross and red, the Captain cross and pink / But all I ever ask myself is, What will Mother think?" ("Song for a Soldier," *Behind the Lines* [New York: Dutton, 1940], 31).

69. Orwell, *1984* (1949; New York: New American Library, 1981), 81, 206, 222. Daphne Patai also argues that "Orwell assails Big Brother's domination but never notices that he is the perfect embodiment of hypertrophied masculinity" (*The Orwell Mystique: A Study of Male Ideology* [Amherst: University of Massachusetts Press, 1984], 251).

70. Ciardi, "Health of Captains," 13; Jarrell, "Death of the Ball Turret Gunner," 144. See the similar imagery in

Ciardi, "Two Songs for a Gunner" (1951), *As If*, 24; Oscar Williams, "The Man in that Airplane," in *War Poets*, 443.

71. Jarrell, "Gunner" (1945), *Complete Poems*, 204.

72. Lewis, "On Embarkation" (1945) and "Christmas Holiday" (1942), *Selected Poetry and Prose* (London: Allen and Unwin, 1966), 84, 99.

73. Boyle, "Army of Occupation" (1947), "Men" (1941), and "Defeat" (1941), *50 Stories* (New York: Penguin, 1980), 439-53, 275-87, and 294-304.

74. Boyle, *American Citizen Naturalized in Leadville, Colorado* (New York: Simon and Schuster, 1944), 6, 11, 12, 6, 7.

75. Mead, "Women in the War," 125.

76. See Ursula Vaughan Williams, "Penelope" (1948), Juliette de Bairacli-Levy, "Threnode for Young Soldiers Killed in Action" (1947), and Rachael Bates, "The Infinite Debt" (1947), in *Chaos of the Night: Women's Poetry and Verse of the Second World War*, ed. Catherine Reilly (London: Virago, 1984), 125, 8, and 27, as well as the war fiction composed by Elizabeth Taylor, Betty Miller, and Elizabeth Jane Howard; "as long as there be war": see Fussell, *Wartime*, 168.

77. Quoted in Ranes Minns, *Bombers and Mash: The Domestic Front 1939-1945* (London: Virago, 1980), 37.

78. Coats, "The 'Monstrous Regiment'" (1950), in *Chaos of the Night*, 29-30.

79. Schneider, "Altered Stories, Altered States," 117; Smith, "Who Shot Eugenie?" *Harold's Leap* (1950), *The Collected Poems of Stevie Smith* (London: Allen Lane, 1975), 292-93. See also Sylvia Lynd, "The Searchlights" (1945), Catherine Brewster Toosey, "Colour Symphony" (1941), and Margery Lawrence, "Garden in the Sky" (1950), in *Chaos of the Night*, 81, 121, and 74.

80. Quoted in Minns, *Bombers and Mash*, 33.

81. Warner, "Noah's Ark," *A Garland of Straw: Twenty-Eight Stories by Sylvia Townsend Warner* (New York: Viking, 1943), 97, 100, 104. In this volume, also see "The Trumpet Shall Sound" and "From Above," both about the impact of the blitz on women (68-79 and 189-96).

82. Brooks, "Gay Chaps at the Bar" (1945), *The World of Gwendolyn Brooks* (New York: Harper and Row, 1971), 51, 53. Further references to Brooks's poems will be to this edition, and page numbers will appear in the text.

83. Melhem, *Gwendolyn Brooks: Poetry and the Heroic Voice* (Lexington: University Press of Kentucky, 1987), 42.

84. Shaw, *Gwendolyn Brooks* (Boston: Twayne, 1980), 62.

85. Stevens, "Sunday Morning" (1915), "How red the rose that is the soldier's wound" (sect. 6 of *Esthetique du Mal* [1942]), "Examination of the Hero in a Time of War" (1942), and "[Prose statement on the poetry of war]" (1942), in *The Palm at the End of the Mind: Selected Poems and a Play by Wallace Stevens*, ed. Holly Stevens (New York: Archon, 1984) 7, 256-57, 201, 205, and 206. Also see "Dutch Graves in Bucks County," in ibid., 236-39.

86. McCullers, *The Member of the Wedding* (New York: Bantam, 1981), 39, 127. Further references will be to this edition, and page numbers will appear in the text.

87. In respect to its elaboration of a father-daughter model of heterosexuality, *Member of the Wedding* resembles Edith Wharton's *Summer*. See our *Sexchanges*, 155-56.

88. Petry, *The Street* (New York: Pyramid, 1961), 162. Jean Bethke Elshtain quotes a black domestic who took a high-paying factory job: "Hitler was the one that got us out of the white folks' kitchen" (*Women and War* [New York: Basic, 1987)], 190). Fussell points out that until well into the war, Red Cross workers segregated the blood plasma of blacks from that of whites (*Thank God for the Atom Bomb*), 141. One of the most insightful journalists during the forties, Rebecca Stiles Taylor, wrote columns about women, mobilization, and the war effort that emphasize the special vulnerability and resiliency of black women: see *The Chicago Defender*, 1939-44.

89. Nemerov, "IFF," *War Stories: Poems about Long Ago and Now* (Chicago: University of Chicago Press, 1987), 29.

90. Mailer, *Naked and the Dead*, 568, 580, 322.

91. Ibid., 672; Aichinger, *The American Soldier in Fiction, 1880-1963: A History of Attitudes Toward Warfare and the Military Establishment* (Ames: Iowa State University Press, 1976), 41. In the film version of *From Here to Eternity*, Deborah Kerr sadly tells Bert Lancaster that he has married the military.

92. Orwell, "Looking Back on the Spanish War" (1943), *A Collection of Essays by George Orwell* (New York: Doubleday, 1954), 214.

93. Eberhart, "Brotherhood of Men," 103, 105.

94. Ford, quoted in our *Sexchanges*, 301. The homoerotic overtones of works by Wilfred Owen, Herbert Read, and Ford contrast with the aggressively heterosexual context established in the literature of World War II.

95. Bérubé, *Coming Out under Fire: The History of Gay Men and Women in World War Two* (New York: Penguin, 1991), 97, 188-89.

96. The best discussion of the violently destructive, suicidal homosexual in the literature of World War II is in Peter G. Jones, *War and the Novelist* (Columbia: University of Missouri Press, 1976), 113-61; Eve Kosofsky Sedgwick, *Between Men: English Literature and Male Homosocial Desire* (New York: Columbia University Press, 1985).

97. Corsellis, "What I Never Saw" (1940), in *Terrible Rain*, 71.

98. Plagemann, *The Steel Cocoon* (New York: Viking, 1958), 63-64, 20.

99. Jones, *From Here to Eternity*, 643.

100. Parker, "The Lovely Leave," *The Portable Dorothy Parker* (New York: Penguin, 1944, 1977), 17. Hannah Lees's *Till the Boys Come Home* (New York: Harper, 1944) is reviewed by Diana Trilling and praised for depicting the boredom of wives left by men eager for an adventure together during the war: see *Reviewing the Forties* (New York: Harcourt Brace Jovanovich, 1978), 101.

101. Lessing, *A Proper Marriage* (1952; New York: New American Library, 1970), 238. See also Olivia Manning, *The Levant Trilogy* (London: Penguin, 1983), 154-56 and 197, and Robert K. Morris, "Olivia Manning's *Fortunes of War*: Breakdown in the Balkans, Love and Death in the Levant," in *British Novelists Since 1900*, ed. Jack I. Biles (New York: AMS Press, 1987), 247.

102. Lessing, *Proper Marriage*, 238; Lessing, *The Golden Notebook* (New York: Bantam, 1979), 63.

103. Weil, "The *Iliad*, Poem of Might" (1940-41), in *The Simone Weil Reader*, ed. George A. Panichas (New York: David McKay, 1977), 171.

104. Smith, "I had a dream . . . ," *Collected Poems*, 421-23.

105. H. D., *Gift*, 133-37.

106. Brittain, *Account Rendered* (London: Virago, 1982), 214. Further references will be to this edition, and page numbers will appear in the text.

107. We are here presenting an alternative to the more optimistic readings of *Helen in Egypt* offered by Susan Stanford Friedman in "Creating a Women's Mythology," in *Signets: Reading H. D.*, ed. Susan Stanford Friedman and Rachel Blau DuPlessis (Madison: University of Wisconsin Press, 1990), 373-405, and Cheryl Walker, *Masks Outrageous and Austere* (Bloomington: Indiana University Press, 1991), 128-30.

108. H. D., *Vale Ave* (1957), in *New Directions in Prose and Poetry 44*, ed. J. Laughlin (New York: New Directions, 1982), 18-68. Further references will be to this edition, and page numbers will appear in the text.

109. Weil, "*Iliad*, Poem of Might," 158, 159.

110. Porter, *Ship of Fools* (Boston: Atlantic-Little, Brown, 1962), 144.

111. Lessing, *Golden Notebook*, 98, 153.

112. See Elizabeth Bowen, "The Happy Autumn Fields," *Collected Stories*, 671-85, for a tale that presents the daydreams of a woman in a bombed house, visions that link her to a Victorian (female) world of love and ritual that is as beyond renovation as the house.

113. Arnow, *The Dollmaker* (New York: Avon, 1972), 151. Further references will be to this edition, and page numbers will appear in the text.

114. Barnes, *The Antiphon* (London: Faber, 1958), 94-95.

115. Rich, "The Eye of the Outsider: The Poetry of Elizabeth Bishop," *Boston Review* 8:2 (1983): 16.

116. Marshall, *Brown Girl, Brownstones* (Old Westbury, N.Y.: Feminist Press, 1981), 100. Further references will be to this edition, and page numbers will appear in the text.

117. Spark, *The Girls of Slender Means* (New York: Knopf, 1963), 27-28. In *The Prime of Miss Jean Brodie* (New York: Laurel, 1980), Spark's heroine is described as "a born Fascist" (150 and 153).

118. Rhys, "The Insect World" (1976), *The Collected Short Stories* (New York: Norton, 1987), 356. Further references will appear in the text.

119. Cooper, "Nothing Has Been Used in the Manufacture of This Poetry that Could Have Been Used in the Manufacture of Bread" (1974), *Scaffolding: New and Selected Poems* (London: Anvil, 1984), 35.

120. Coleman, "No Woman's Land," *Mad Dog Black Lady* (Santa Barbara, Calif.: Black Sparrow, 1979), 26.

121. Piercy, *Gone to Soldiers* (New York: Fawcett Crest, 1988), 318. Further references will be to this edition, and page numbers will appear in the text.

122. See May, *Homeward Bound*, 58-91.

123. For a similar point, see Porter, *Ship of Fools*: When La Condesa states her belief that to be a German is "an incurable malady . . . as hopeless as being a Jew," her lover replies, "Or a woman" (236).

124. See Margaret Fuller, *Woman in the Nineteenth Century* (1845; Columbia: University of South Carolina Press, 1980), 30. On Schreiner, see *An Olive Schreiner Reader,* ed. Carol Barash (London: Pandora, 1987), 202-03 and 248.

125. Weininger, *Sex and Character* (London: William Heinemann, [1906]), 306; Hitler, quoted and discussed in Susan Griffin, *Pornography and Silence* (New York: Harper, 1981), 172.

126. Jackson, *Behold the Jew* (New York: Macmillan, 1944), 21, 22. See also Schweik, *Gulf So Deeply Cut,* 17-22.

127. De Beauvoir, *The Second Sex,* trans. and ed. H. M. Parshley (New York: Bantam, 1961), xxiii; Friedan, *The Feminine Mystique* (New York: Dell, 1983), 308. Further references will be to this edition, and page numbers will appear in the text.

128. "His simple nobility": see Spiegelman, "Natural Heroism," 98; Bishop, "Visits to St. Elizabeths" (1950), *Complete Poems,* 133-35.

129. Smith, *Over the Frontier,* 158.

130. Boyle, "Winter Night" (1946), *50 Stories,* 606.

131. O'Connor, "The Displaced Person" (1955) *The Complete Stories of Flannery O'Connor* (New York: Farrar, Straus, and Giroux, 1971), 196.

132. Lessing, *The Four-Gated City* (New York: Knopf, 1969), 516. See also Denise Levertov, "During the Eichmann Trial" (1961), *Poems: 1960-1967* (New York: New Directions, 1983), 65, as well as the final poem in *The Sorrow Dance.*

133. Yamada, "To the Lady," *Camp Notes and Other Poems* (San Lorenzo, Calif.: shameless hussy press, 1976), n.p. See Susan Schweik's more extended discussion of Nisei women poets, *Gulf So Deeply Cut,* 173-212, and Hisaye Yamamoto, *Seventeen Syllables and Other Stories* (Albany, N.Y.: Kitchen Table, Women of Labor Press, 1988). On government policies to fingerprint and intern Italian-American "enemy aliens," see Concetta Doucette, "Fingerprinting Children Is Not New," *Italian Americana* 10:1 (1991): 79-82, and Stephen Fox, *The Unknown Internment: An Oral History of the Relocation of Italian Americans during World War II* (Boston: Twayne, 1990).

134. Spark, "The First Year of My Life" (1975), *The Stories of Muriel Spark* (New York: Dutton, 1985), 268.

WOMEN AND THE DRAMATIC TRADITION

CYNTHIA SUTHERLAND (ESSAY DATE SEPTEMBER 1978)

Sutherland, Cynthia. "American Women Playwrights as Mediators of the 'Woman Problem.'" *Modern Drama* 21 (September 1978): 319-36.

In the following essay, Sutherland examines a withdrawal from more strident portrayals of feminist concerns in plays of the 1920s, including Zona Gale's Miss Lulu Bett.

Ibsen's Nora shut the door of her "doll's house" in 1879. Among the generation of American women born in the 1870's and 1880's, Zona Gale, Zoe Akins, and Susan Glaspell all won Pulitzer Prizes. Rachel Crothers, the successful dramatist who wrote more than three dozen plays, characterized her own work as "a sort of Comédie Humaine de la Femme." In an interview in 1931 she said: "With few exceptions, every one of my plays has been a social attitude toward women at the moment I wrote it . . . I [do not] go out stalking the footsteps of women's progress. It is something that comes to me subconsciously. I may say that I sense the trend even before I have hearsay or direct knowledge of it." During a period in which most American play-wrights confined their work to representations of the middle class, these women were distinctive because they created principal roles for female characters whose rhetoric thinly veiled a sense of uneasiness with what Eva Figes and others more recently have called "patriarchal attitudes."

Such capitulation to public opinion evident in the modification of the ending by a writer who had supported the Woman's Peace Union, the Woman's Peace Party (Wisconsin), Jane Addams and the Hull-House workers and who later helped to write the Wisconsin Equal Rights Law, has considerable significance.

By the turn of the century, the mostly "abolitionist" women who had originated the battle for suffrage in the 1840s and 1850s were either dead or retired, and a new generation of leaders was attempting to expand popular support through the use of muted political rhetoric which intentionally avoided controversy. The majority of women resisted arguments advocating changes in sex roles on the grounds that their inherent femininity would be diminished and their homes threatened. In the *Ladies' Home Journal,* Jane Addams argued benignly that a woman who wanted to "keep on with her old business of caring for her house and rearing her children" ought to "have some conscience in regard to public affairs lying outside her immediate household." The conciliatory strategy of feminist leaders like Addams and Carrie Chapman Catt exalted the family, motherhood, and domestic values, minimized conflicts between self-realization and inhibiting social conditions, and often disregarded the arguments of radical feminists who insisted that only basic alterations in the organization of the family and sexual relationships could effect substantive changes in women's lives.

For many members of audiences, political issues continued to be dissociated from personal lives in which an equator divided the world of human activity marking "homemaking" and "breadwinning" as hemispheres. In 1924, a study of a fairly large group of young girls indicated that a substantial number planned to choose marriage over a "career" and that few had developed alternative goals. Asked to "name the four heroines in history or fiction whom [they] would most like to resemble," only two of 347 chose women identified chiefly or even at all with feminist causes. They elected, rather, to live vicariously through husbands and children, accepting the traditional sex-role differentiation in which "instrumental/task functions are assigned to males, and expressive/social functions to females."

Glaspell, Akins, Gale, and Crothers chronicled the increasingly noticeable effects of free love, trial marriage, the "double standard," career, divorce, and war on women's lives. Public rhetoric generally subsumed private sexual rhetoric in the theatre during this period, and dramatic discourse tended to mediate conflicting views of women's "legitimate" place in society more often than it intensified dispute. Although the sector of life subtended by domesticity was being steadily decreased by technological and economic developments in the early years of the century, feminist leaders, artists, and housewives shared the common inability to suggest an alternative social structure through which discontent might be alleviated. To the extent that female characters on the stage accepted the traditional sex role, a diminished state of consciousness manifested itself in language that avoided strong or forceful statements, evinced conformity, consisted of euphemism and question-begging, and celebrated the processes which safely domesticated erotic pleasure. As contemporary critics, we tend to be disappointed by portrayals of women who cannot express, much less resolve, their problems. Yet, here, precisely, I believe, is the reason for the popular success and the "critical" failure of many of these plays. The spectacle of dramatic characters conducing themselves in the ironic guise of people only half aware of conflicts between individuation and primary sex role has usually been interpreted as trivial, the result of mediocre artistry, rather than what it is—the theatrical encoding of a "genderlect," or to put it another way, a language that reflects the internalizing by members of society of a particular system of sex differentiation and values.

However, during the period before the thirty-sixth state ratified the Nineteenth Amendment in 1920, a significant number of plays did present exceptionally articulate female artists as figures incarnating the dilemma of people torn by the conflicting demands of sex role and career. *In A Man's World* (National Theatre, Washington, D.C., October 18, 1909), Rachel Crothers's protagonist Frank Ware is a novelist who oversees a club for girls who "need another chance." She has published anonymously a defense of women's rights which even her friends—themselves painters, writers, and musicians—agree is much too good to have been written by a woman. After accidentally discovering that her fiancé, Malcolm Gaskell, has fathered her adopted seven-year-old son (the deserted mother had been her friend and died in childbirth), she renounces him. Avoiding a facile reconciliation, Crothers chose rather to stress Frank's abhorrence of her lover's complacent refusal to acknowledge responsibility for the deplorable consequences of his own sexual license. In the final curtain scene, their relationship is abruptly severed:

> FRANK. Oh, I want to forgive you . . . tell me you know it was wrong—that you'd give your life to make it right. Say that you know this thing is a crime.
>
> GASKELL. No! Don't try to hold me to account by a standard that doesn't exist. Don't measure me by your theories. If you love me you'll stand on that and forget everything else.
>
> FRANK. I can't. I can't.

In *He and She* (Poughkeepsie, 1911), Crothers again explored the dilemma of a woman who must decide between sex role and career, in this instance, motherhood or sculpting. Ann Herford surrenders the commission she has won in a national competition to her husband, Tom, who has been openly skeptical that his wife could do "anything for a scheme as big" as the project required for the contest. When he wins only the second prize, his ego is badly shaken, and he retrenches to the familiar rhetorical stance of chief breadwinner. Reconciliation comes only after Ann abandons her prize in response to the needs of her teenage daughter. Crothers, although she shows a woman conceding final "victory" to her primary sex role, allows her character to voice bitterness and disappointment:

> TOM . . . you've not only beaten me—you've won over the biggest men in the field—with your own brain and your own hands; in a fair, fine Hard fight . . . there'll be times when you[ll] eat your heart out to be at work on it—when the artist in you will *yell* to be let out.

ANN. I know . . . And I'll hate you because you're doing it—and I'll hate myself because I gave it up—and I'll almost—hate—her . . . my heart has almost burst with pride—not so much that *I* had done it—but for all women . . . then the door opened—and Millicent [their daughter] came in. There isn't any choice Tom—she's part of my body—part of my soul.

Ann's uneasy capitulation to the obligations of motherhood is carefully orchestrated by the simplistic attitudes of two women who are in love with her husband's close friend, a partially carica-tured "male chauvinist" hard-liner; one woman accepts a promotion in her job rather than toler-ate what she views as his suffocating demands, the other chases him because she believes that "all the brains a woman's got [are]—to make a home—to bring up children—and to keep a man's love." That Tom and Ann might exchange roles, he taking over as parent temporarily while she carves her frieze, is outside the realm of dramatic choice, because, in Crothers's dialectical structure, the men and women are shown to be incapable of conceiving this as an alternative. General expectations that a shift towards a more egalitar-ian society would lead to personal and social enfranchisement in the progressive era as middle-class women moved in the direction of greater self-consciousness are clearly undercut in the end-ings of Crothers's plays.

A vastly more imaginative if less independent playwright, Susan Glaspell both directed and acted in her own plays. From 1913 until 1922, she worked with the Provincetown Players. A sound-ing board for new ideas, the Provincetown group produced plays that sometimes spoofed feminist excesses, yet usually respected the seriousness of the "movement's" political aims. In *Suppressed De-sires* (Wharf Theatre, Provincetown, Summer, 1915), Glaspell ridiculed a woman who nearly wrecks her marriage by testing psychoanalytic theories on her sister and husband, and in *Close the Book* (Playwright's Theatre, 1917), she poked fun at a liberated girl who naively insists, *"Hand on heart,"* that she is "not respectable." In *Woman's Honor* (Playwright's Theatre, 1918), she presents a satiric sketch of the effects of the "double stan-dard." A young man accused of murder refuses to provide himself with an alibi by identifying his married mistress. He is beleaguered by a bevy of volunteers, each of whom wants to sacrifice her own "honor" to save him by claiming that *she* has been the anonymous lover. The women are comic types with predictable opinions about female honor: "The Shielded One," "The Motherly One," "The Silly One," "The Mercenary One," and

"The Scornful One." The last of these expresses her resentment of society's definition of "woman's honor": "Did it ever strike you as funny that woman's honor is only about one thing, and that man's honor is about everything but that thing?" With amusing logic, she tells the prisoner that since "woman's honor means woman's virtue," the lady for whom he "propose[s] to die has no virtue." Caught in the midst of chatter, he resigns himself: "Oh, *hell, I'll plead guilty,*" rather than be faced by another speechifying female.

But in her most famous play, *Trifles* (Wharf Theatre, Province-town, Summer, 1916), Glaspell began to explore seriously the more violent psychological aspects of women trapped in love-less marriages. Minnie Wright has strangled her husband. The wives of the sheriff and a neighbor have come to her home to collect a few things to make her more comfortable in jail. As their husbands search for evidence that would provide a motive, the women discover among Minnie's "trifles" a canary's carcass and decide to defy the law by concealing it, guessing that her husband "wrung—its neck . . . Wright wouldn't like the bird—a thing that sang—She used to sing. He killed that, too." The neighbor expresses her regret: "I might have known [Minnie] needed help! I know how things can be—for women . . . We live close together and we live far apart. We all go through the same things—it's all just a differ-ent kind of the same thing." As they leave, the women explain to the men who have ridiculed Minnie's "trifles" that she was going to "knot" her quilt, a subdued, ironic, and grisly reminder of the manner in which a stifled wife has enacted her desperate retaliation. In the theatre of the next decade, the motifs of the caged bird and the lost singing voice were to become the hallmarks of numerous "domesticated" women who aban-doned careers.

In *Trifles,* Glaspell had negotiated that por-trayal of a woman's violent repudiation of her husband's narrow notion of sex role by removing her from the sight of the audience (a technique she later was to repeat in *Bernice and Allison's House*). But the play in which she confronted most vehemently the sex-role imprisonment of women is *The Verge,* first performed by the Playwright's Theatre in its last season (November 14, 1921). Claire Archer rejects her daughter and murders her lover. Her insane passion to breed a fresh botanical species which she calls "Breath of Life," one which may be "less beautiful—less sound— than the plants from which [it] diverged," ex-presses her radical rejection of biological and cultural inheritance—she is identified as the "flower of New England . . . what came of men who made the laws that made . . . [the] culture." She has divorced a "stick-in-the-mud artist and married—[a] man of flight," who she has hoped will "smash something," but who also has turned out to be baldly conventional. The son who had shared her vision of transcendence is dead. Driven by frustration and disappointment, in a terrifying scene, she strikes her daughter across the face with the roots of an "Edge Vine," believing that both the girl and the plant are incurable conformists. Her words echo horribly those of familiar mythic murderesses: "To think that object ever moved in my belly and sucked my breast." When the lover who has rejected her frenetic sexual advances returns because he wants to keep her "safe" from harm, she strangles him as a "gift" to the plant, choosing to break "life to pieces in the struggle" to cast free from traditional sex role. A demented Demeter, Claire has been mesmerized by an apocalyptic vision: "Plants . . . explode their species—because something in them knows they've gone as far as they can go. Something in them knows they're shut in. So [they] go mad—that life may not be imprisoned. Break themselves up—into crazy things—into lesser things, and from the pieces—may come one sliver of life with vitality to find the future. How beautiful. How brave. Glaspell's representation of a failed Goddess-Mother was treated respectfully by reviewers in England, but in this country it was largely misunderstood or ignored.

Written a year earlier, another study of a woman's plight, Zona Gale's *Miss Lulu Bett,* opened at the Belmont Theatre on December 27, 1920 and subsequently won the Pulitzer Prize. Like Rachel Crothers and Susan Glaspell, Zona Gale had come to New York from the Midwest and was sympathetic to feminist causes despite her mother's caveat to shun radical politics and women's groups—"I would let that mess of women alone!" she had advised her daughter. The novel on which Gale had based her play had been immediately successful, and in eight days, she had hastily, though with considerable dramatic skill, adapted it for production. Even though *Miss Lulu Bett* did not present a threatening subject (for "old maids" were commonly seen not as electing spinsterhood but as having had it thrust upon them by faithless lovers or deprivation), strong critical pressure influenced Gale to alter the last act, in which, like Ibsen's Nora, Lulu walks out of the house in which she has been a virtual servant to become an independent woman. Gale rewrote

the last act so that it conformed more closely to her popular novel, which concluded with Lulu comfortably established as a respectable wife. This story of a drab but resourceful and dry-witted woman—whom Fannie Hurst called a "shining star" reflected in "greasy reality"—ran for 186 performances. Such capitulation to public opinion evident in the modification of the ending by a writer who had supported the Woman's Peace Union, the Woman's Peace Party (Wisconsin), Jane Addams and the Hull-House workers and who later helped to write the Wisconsin Equal Rights Law, has considerable significance. It anticipated the new style of mediation used by playwrights who continued to dramatize aspects of the "woman problem" in the 1920's.

After World War I and the extension of the franchise, the momentum towards fully equal status for women slowed considerably. One of Rachel Crothers's characters sees herself as an exception to what was to become an increasingly regressive trend: "I haven't slipped back one inch since the war. Most women who sort of rose to something then have slumped into themselves again, but I've gone *on.* My life gets much fuller and wider all the time. There's no room for men. Why, *why* should I give up my own personal life—or let it be changed in the slightest degree for a man?" But the woman who speaks these somewhat fatuous lines will, during the course of the dramatic action, reveal her disingenuousness by seducing a member of the British upper class so that her "personal life" and career are, in fact, exchanged for marriage.

Statistics on employment indicate that the percentage of females in the total labor force had decreased from 20.9 in 1910 to 20.4 in 1920. Among women, the proportion of the total college enrollment dropped—three of every four new professionals chose traditionally female-dominated fields, and the number of doctors decreased by nearly one-third. Female architects and lawyers continued at less than three percent, and attendance at professional schools increased only slightly. When members of Pruette's test group were questioned, only thirty-two percent indicated that they would like to be successful *themselves* in "some chosen work"; the remainder opted for success "through" husband and family. The choice between marriage and career continued to be polarized; and the divorce rate rose steadily. By 1929, Suzanne la Follette was to comment that "the traditional relations of the sexes is far from being reversed in this country, [but] . . . has shifted away enough to cause alarm among those to whom it seems the right and inevitable relation *because* it is conventional." Many of the changes affecting women's lives were seen as detrimental to their femininity. George Jean Nathan opined that ". . . women more and more have ceased to be the figures of man's illusion and more and more have become superficially indistinguishable from man himself in his less illusory moments. In sport, in business, in drinking, in politics, in sexual freedom, in conversation, in sophistication and even in dress, women have come closer and closer to men's level and, with the coming, the purple allure of distance has vamoosed." The plays of this period characterize masculine responses that range from reactionary to adjustive but are rarely innovative. Crothers spoofs (or does she?) a gentleman's overreaction to a woman who aggressively courts him: ". . . it seems to be awfully important . . . nowadays to be a woman . . . I'm not criticizing. Men *are* totally unnecessary, I s'pose, except for breeding purposes. And we go on taking ourselves for granted in the same old relationships with women. Stupid of us, isn't it?"

Early in the 1920s, the struggle against social oppression had shifted towards a rebellion against convention in which the manipulation of style was both means and end. The flapper was sometimes a flamboyant flouter, as Zelda Fitzgerald's life apparently proved, but she generally strayed only temporarily from acceptable patterns of conduct, because her values were essentially the same as those of her parents. Cocktail in one hand and cigarette in the other, she made an avocational pretense of "rebellion" that was quite compatible with middle-class wisdom, as she mimicked the demands of earlier feminists for sexual equality.

The plays that Crothers wrote in the 1920's signal her own ambivalence toward the contrived stance of young women whose gold-plated philosophy was an amalgam of "free-thinking" writers like Ellen Key, Mona Cairn, Havelock and Edith Ellis. Like Congreve's Millamant, they were choosing to "dwindle into a wife" rather than persevere in a search for practical alternatives. Crothers's formulaic plot for flappers continued to have the staple elements described by Clara Claibourne Park in her study of the young women in Shakespeare's comedies: "Invent a girl of charm and intellect; allow her ego a brief premarital flourishing; make clear that it is soon to subside into voluntarily-assumed subordination; make sure that it is mediated by love." But Crothers's perspective is ironic, because she juxtaposes romantic

courtship and the harsh antagonisms that often grow between marriage, partners. The plays she wrote during these years strongly emphasized deteriorating sexual relationships over a period of time, thus undermining the power of the traditional plot to sustain communal custom through ritual reenactment, In *Mary the Third* (Thirty-ninth Street Theatre, February 5, 1925), the playwright presented three generations of women in the throes of choosing mates. The grandmother, Mary the First, traps a mate with flirtation in 1870; the mother, Mary the Second, yields to the proposal of her most vigorous but most unsuitable lover in 1897. These two women are seen as mere anachronisms by Mary the Third, in 1923, who fecklessly flaunts convention by insisting that she will choose her mate only after going off to the country on an experimental trip with two men and another woman to "live naturally and freely for two weeks—doing a thing we know in the bottom of our souls is *right,* and knowing perfectly well the whole town is going to explode with horror." However, after only a few hours, Mary rationalizes her own lack of persistence, deciding to be "magnanimous" to the "deep prejudices" of her parents. She returns home. Fearful of being scolded, she and her brother hide and are horrified when they accidentally overhear their parents in a fight (reminiscent of Strindberg and foreshadowing Albee) that shaves off the thin skin concealing the bleeding tissue of their marriage. They hear their father tell their mother: "I'm flabbergasted at you. You seem to have lost what sense you did have. . . . I can't count on you. You aren't *there*. Sometimes I think you aren't the woman I married at all," and their mother's even more devastating reply: "And sometimes I think you're a man I *couldn't* have married. Sometimes I loathe everything you think and say and do. When you grind out that old stuff I could *shriek*. I can't breathe in the same room with you. The very sound of your voice drives me insane. When you tell me how right you are—I could strike you." The fate of the marriage of Mary the Third has left unresolved at the conclusion. Even though Mary the Second is seen her mother's agonized entrapment and recognized its partial basis in her inability to earn an independent income, the daughter herself yields to the pressures of convention and enters marriage knowing just as little about her future husband as her grandmother and mother had known of theirs. Self-deceived, she has only partly digested the teachings of those writers who had argued for new kinds of marriages: ". . . you *ought* to be able to [make your own living] . . . I shall have my own money. I'll *make* it. I shall live with a man because I love him and only as long as I love him. I shall be able to take care of myself *and* my children if necessary. Anything else gives the man a horrible advantage, of course. It makes the woman a kept woman." Significantly, Mary has rejected an intelligent suitor who has warned her that "unless we change the entire attitude of men and women towards each other—there won't be any marriage in the future" and disregarded the fact that she is as ill-trained to support herself as her mother had been.

Crothers's plays signal changes in the treatment of the "woman problem" in the theatre during the twenties. The dialectic between the "new woman" and her "old-fashioned" relatives increasingly undercut conventional comic endings as reconciliation with older patterns became a hollow act. In a series of skillfully constructed one-act plays, Crothers continued her mordant comment by creating the character of a successful but shallow politician, Nancy Marshall, whose words expose a growing "tokenism" in the feminist views of many of her contemporaries:

> We women must be considerate of each other. If I am nominated I'm going to be awfully strong for that . . . Men have made a mess of it—that's all. The idea that there aren't enough houses in New York to go 'round. What nonsense! . . . All those awful people with money who never had any before in their lives ought not to be allowed to crowd other people out. It's Bolshevism—just Bolshevism . . . And not enough school teachers to go 'round . . . People ought simply to be made to teach school, whether they want to or not . . . I can't teach school. God knows I'd be glad to— and just show them if my hands weren't so full now of—I'm going to have awful circles under my eyes from standing so long.

She contrasts her own knowledge of the nuances of political style with her female opponent's corpulent presence on the hustings: "She is so unpopular I should think she'd withdraw from sheer embarassment . . . she is so unattractive. That's why the men have put her up . . . they're not afraid of her because they *know* she'll never get anywhere." The sheer vacuousness of Nancy Marshall's political views elicits the response from her best friend that "Between you and her I'd vote for the best man going," and comes into sharp relief when compared to the comment of Mary Dewson, director of women's work for the Democratic party, after the election of 1932: ". . . we did not make the old-fashioned plea that our candidate was charming, . . . we appealed to the intelligence of the country's women."

In a one-act sequel, after the same friends calls her an "old maid," Nancy Marshall suddenly comprehends the real "importance of being a woman" and hastily puts on a proper gown for the purpose of attracting a proposal of marriage. The customary import of the courtship scene is compromised, because the gentleman of her choice has been rejected, in an earlier scene, by Patti Pitt, a young woman who sees herself as public property (she is an entertainer!), but who actually has meant it when she said "It's power, . . . I've got it and mustn't throw it away . . . Any woman can get married, but I have something more important to do" (*The Importance of Being a Woman*). The satiric treatment of both women by Crothers indicates that she was sensitive to the processes of rationalization used by women confronted by the choice between career and marriage, and had identified in those who opted for the latter an erosion of energy that was to continue to perpetuate, for a number of years in the theatre, the prominence of the "feminine mystique."

In the 1930's, Clare Boothe's satire, *The Women* (Ethel Barrymore Theatre, December 26, 1936), slashed at materialistic Park Avenue matrons, but also reflected an underside of the cultural milieu as female characters turned increasingly to divorces, affairs, and sometimes to temporary careers. In a late play by Crothers, *When Ladies Meet* (Royale Theatre, October 6, 1932), the scenario of the struggle of female characters for economic and moral independence receives less emphasis than the failing and futile relationships all the women have with the men. Mary, a writer, and Claire, a wife, are both in love with the latter's philandering husband. Mary has continued to reject the persistent courtship of good-natured Jimmie, a friend who puts women "in pigeon holes and tab[s] them—[according to] a *man's* idea of women." Jimmie shrewdly arranges a meeting of mistress and wife at a mutual friend's country house. The play's title is drawn from a remarkable scene that occurs "when ladies meet" to discuss the fictional case in Mary's novel in which a mistress tells her lover's wife that she wants to live for a year with him on a trial basis. Claire's comments on the verisimilitude of Mary's novel barely conceal her response to her own situation:

> I suppose *any* married woman thinks the other woman ought to know enough not to believe a married man, if he's making love to her . . . I happen to be married to a man who can no more help attracting women than he can help breathing. And of course each one thinks she is the love of his life and that he is going to divorce me. But he

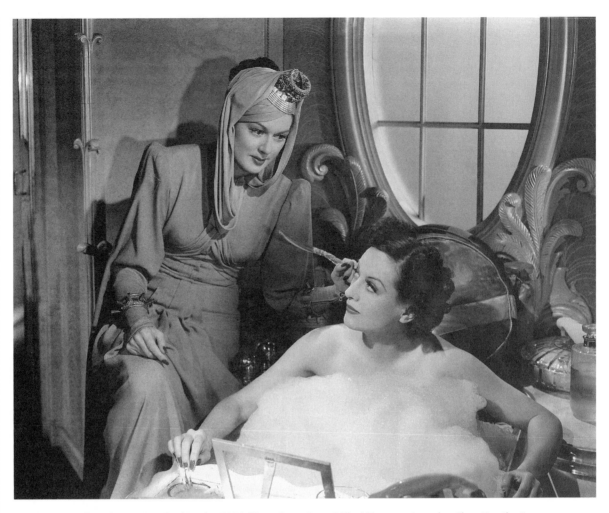

Rosalind Russell and Joan Crawford in the 1939 film adaptation of *The Women* written by Clare Boothe Luce.

doesn't seem to . . . I can always tell when an affair is waning. He turns back to the old comfortable institution of marriage as naturally as a baby turns to the warm bottle . . . I'd say [to the mistress] *of course* something *new* is interesting. Of *course* I look the same old way—and sound the same old way—and eat the same old way and walk the same old way—*and so will you*—after a while. I'd say *of course* I can understand his loving you—but are *you prepared to stand up to the job of loving him?* Most of the things you find so irresistible in him are terribly hard to live with. You must love him so abjectly that you're glad to play second fiddle just to keep the music going for *him.*

When her husband unexpectedly blunders into the room, fiction become's reality—true to Claire's prediction—he begs to return, but she rejects him with a newly discovered decisiveness: "You can't conceive that I *could* stop loving you. It happened in just one second—I think-when I saw what you'd done to [Mary] . . . I'm not going *home—now—or ever.*" Mary will continue to write and to live alone. The theme of the emotional

consequences of both disintegrating marriages and the pursuit of careers had been introduced earlier in the play by their hostess, who diagnoses women's restlessness as due to a far-reaching lack of fulfillment in either institution . . . "Men mean a great deal more to women than women do to men . . . I don't care *what* strong women—like Mary tell you about loving their work and their *freedom*—it's all *slush.* Women *have got to be loved.* That's why they're breaking out so . . . They daring to have lovers—good women—because they just *can't stand being alone.*"

Crothers had managed to write, on the average, a play a year since 1904. The incipient thirty-year-long quietism in feminist activities produced by apathy, factionalism, and personal loneliness is evident in the uneasy resignation of her later female characters. The playwright's response to a reporter, in 1941, revealed her final alienation from feminist causes and repeated her earlier assertion that her plays had mirrored, *mutatis mutan-*

dis, the social evolution of sex roles: "What a picayune, self-conscious side all this woman business has to it . . . I've been told that my plays are a long procession reflecting the changing attitudes of the world toward women. If they are, that was completely unconscious on my part. Any change like that, that gets on to the stage, has already happened in life. Even the most vulgar things, that people object to with so much excitement, wouldn't be in the theatre at all if they hadn't already become a part of life."

In 1931, the Pulitzer Prize was given to Susan Glaspell, the first woman to win it in a decade. In *Alison's House* (Civic Repertory Theatre, December 1, 1930), her last play, she again returned to the dramatic techniques she had used during her years with the Provincetown a decade earlier. Zoe Akins won the Prize, in 1935, for *The Old Maid* (Empire Theatre, January 7, 1935) but her skillful dramatic adaptation (like Edith Wharton's novelette published eleven years earlier) is set back in time. Both prize-winning plays safely distanced controversial feminist issues by presenting women tethered by Edwardian proprieties rather than more immediately recognizable topical restraints. It is possibly worth pointing out that the plays for which American women have won Pulitzer Prizes deal essentially with the "old maid" figure in whom the threat of sex-role conflict is "neutralized," as did the near-winner, Lillian Hellman's *The Children's Hour* (Maxine Elliott Theatre, November 20, 1934), which dealt with the cruel ostracism of suspected lesbians.

The efforts of women to understand and determine their own lives, their failure to develop effective strategies for the realization of personal gratification, their continuing attachment to the perimeters of capitalism were portrayed by Glaspell, Gale, Crothers, and Akins less as a passionate subjugation than as the restless sojourn of half-articulate captives in a land that seemed alien to them. Marriage continued to be the first choice and a career the second of most women, as their enrollment percentage in colleges continued to drop steadily from 40.3 in 1930 to 30.2 in 1950. In the theatre, divorcees and professional women continued to be perceived as "threats" to the institution of marriage, because they personified women's fulfillment through chosen alternative social roles. Not until the late 1950s would public attention again focus on the issues probed so searchingly by this generation of playwrights. Certainly, isolated expressions of "feminist" theatre, like Sophie Treadwell's *Machinal* (Plymouth Theatre, September 7, 1928), had

continued, but they were generally short-lived, and for a quarter of a century, there was no reappearance of the serious concern with the "woman problem" that had characterized the work of America's women playwrights from the Midwest.

My comments have been limited to plays written by middle-class women who bring to issue kinship rules and incest taboos in which primary sex role determines generic restrictions for dramatic action. A thoroughgoing analysis would have included, among others, the ordinary females and heteroclites created by Clare Kummer, Rose Pastor Stokes, Alice Gerstenberg, Alice Brown, Sophie Treadwell, Rita Wellman, Neith Boyce, Lula Vollmer, Maurine Watkins, Charlotte Perkins Gillman, and Julie Herne. Nor have I mentioned Edward Sheldon, George Middleton, Bayard Veiller, Sidney Howard, George Kelly, Eugene O'Neill, and S. N. Behrman, who were remarkably sensitive to the predicaments of female characters and deserve to be reevaluated in this light.

As theatre historians and critics, we must now attempt to refine our working lexicon. Beyond female roles dictated by kinship structures (e.g. wife, mother, daughter, sister, bride, mother-in-law, widow, grandmother), there exist other roles which are more or less independent (e.g., coquette, ingénue, soubrette, career woman, servant, shaman, witch, bawd, whore) as well as interdependent roles (e.g., the other woman, mulatto). Only by developing descriptive categories with some historical precision can we hope to account for both formulaic successes and changes in dramatic modes. A more accurate vocabulary for female "dramatis personae" could help us to understand the interrelationships between the theatre and evolving social milieus in this and other periods.

SALLY BURKE (ESSAY DATE 1996)

SOURCE: Burke, Sally. "The Woman Question Onstage." In *American Feminist Playwrights: A Critical History,* pp. 29-64. New York: Twayne, 1996.

In the following essay, Burke provides an overview of drama written by women during the suffrage era and the early years of feminism, focusing on the works of such authors as Charlotte Perkins Gilman, Rachel Crothers, and Susan Glaspell.

The Woman Question was an umbrella phrase coined during the nineteenth century to cover a multitude of questions. For some, it signaled a desire for honest debate; for others, it functioned as a code phrase whose purpose was to answer the "Question" by proving woman's inferiority. The Woman Question carried ramifications in politics,

Colette, a renowned early twentieth-century French writer.

terms of economics, authority, and even comfort in woman remaining subservient and who called on the construct of female inferiority to preserve the status quo, attempting to use the quality of her "womanliness" itself, however vaguely defined, to limit a woman's activity. Proponents of this philosophy ranked African Americans, women, and children as inferior to the white male; both skull and brain size were measured to "prove" quantitatively woman's lesser mental capability. Also argued was woman's functional inferiority, a tenet that led to the trumpeting of woman's presumed inability to deal with scientific and abstract data. Furthermore, even physicians raised alarms about the effects that the rigors of higher education would have on her reproductive system.

Questions of woman's role and nature continued to influence the view of women in an evolving American society; in the June 1914 issue of *Forum,* playwright and critic Florence Kiper stated: "Every play produced on the American stage, with perhaps a few negligible exceptions, has its say on the feminist question." Feminist playwrights confronted political, personal, and social issues both through and beyond the domestic sphere as they interrogated societal values and illuminated age-old conflicts in dramas dealing with suffrage, women's rights, and the New Woman.

From Seneca Falls to Suffrage

In the aftermath of the Revolution, as the public arena open to men expanded while woman's work became increasingly confining and as male enfranchisement broadened, women in ever greater numbers perceived their exclusion from suffrage as untenable. Later, as they organized, gathered signatures on antislavery petitions, and risked wrath and ridicule for speaking in public against slavery, these white, mostly middle-class women began to sense an analogy between parts of the slaves' plight and their own. They, too, were possessions. They were deprived of wage and property rights and even of the guardianship of their children; they were forbidden to vote. That even among male abolitionists they were not always welcome was strikingly apparent when the American women delegates to the 1840 World Anti-Slavery Convention in London were forced to sit in the balcony merely because of their gender. There delegate Lucretia Mott met Elizabeth Cady Stanton. As the women discussed the meaning of their exclusion, seeds were sown that grew into the Seneca Falls Women's Rights Convention of 1848.

the arts, religion, philosophy, economics, science, and the broader area of social relationships. Many and varied questions were raised. For instance, is woman man's property? Is she entitled to property in her own right? To higher education? May she control her sexuality through contraception? What effect does her employment have on the capitalist system and on the family? And of increasing importance, should women vote? How great a fear of women actually exercising power through the ballot does resistance to women suffrage illustrate?

Formal statements of the Question took shape in the second quarter of the nineteenth century. Margaret Fuller's *Woman in the Nineteenth Century* (1845) envisions a future of limitless potential for women, looking forward to the emergence of a "female Newton," for example; Fuller decries the sexual double standard and calls for economic "self-dependence" for women. To those who doubt woman's ability to take part in the affairs of government, she offers the actress and the Quaker preacher as examples of females versed in public expression.

Taking a different position were the patriarchy and its supporters, who had a vested interest in

ON THE SUBJECT OF...

COLETTE (1873-1954)

Sidonie-Gabrielle Colette, better known as Colette, was an important figure in early twentieth-century French literature. Her impressive series of novels, stories, plays, and newspaper articles include chronicles of backstage life in turn-of-the-century music halls, novels of love and betrayal from the early 1900s through World War II, and nostalgic reminiscences of her childhood. All of Colette's works are marked by sensitive descriptions of nature, sexual frankness, and a flair for the theatrical. She was widely acclaimed as a popular novelist and was considered one of the best women writers of her day. Elected to Belgium's Royal Academy of French Language and Literature in 1935, Colette was the first woman to serve as president of France's prestigious literary jury, the Goncourt Academy, and the first woman to attain the rank of Grand Officer of the Legion of Honor. While not overtly treating or advancing the feminist movements of the late nineteenth or twentieth centuries, Colette's varied works of fiction allow for both coquetry and independence, as well as fidelity and sexual adventure among women.

In 1893 Colette married Henry Gauthier-Villars, better known as Willy. Her life for the next thirteen years in Paris was was filled with disillusion, for Willy, a music critic and entrepreneur, was reportedly a ruthless, scheming, publicity seeker. Colette became unhappy during her early marriage to Willy, and for a long period she was seriously ill with an unexplained malady. It was soon after her recovery that Willy suggested to her that she write down some of the stories about her childhood, and add some salacious details—which she obediently did. At first Willy put them aside, but he later decided that he had made a mistake and printed them under his own name. Thus was the first of the Claudine series, *Claudine à l'eacute;cole* (1900; translated as *Claudine at School,* 1930), born; thus too did Sidonie Gabrielle Willy become Colette the writer. The book sold forty thousand copies in the first few months, and a long writing career followed, including such sequels as *Claudine à Paris* (*Claudine in Paris,* 1901), *Claudine en ménage* (*Claudine Married,* 1902).

The convention itself, now a landmark in the history of women's rights, was called by Stanton in her hometown and attended by 250 women and men. Here was adopted a document variously known as the Declaration of Principles, the Declaration of Rights, and the Declaration of Sentiments. This last title speaks volumes about the socialization of women. Written by Stanton, the declaration was modeled on the Declaration of Independence and held that "the history of mankind is a history of repeated injuries and usurpations on the part of man toward woman, having in direct object the establishment of an absolute tyranny over her." But the title Declaration of Sentiments reveals how completely women had accepted the male view of them as creatures of feeling. The instrument itself, however, insisted on woman's "immediate admission to all the rights and privileges which belong to them as citizens of the United States." The accompanying resolutions included one calling for woman suffrage; more than 70 years were to pass before women would be enfranchised. On 26 August 1920, the Nineteenth Amendment became law. Today the Women's Rights National Historical Park stands on the convention site. A memorial in the form of a water wall, 9 feet tall and 120 feet long, engraved with the text of the Declaration of Sentiments, was completed in 1993.

The Suffrage Dramas; or, Parlor Plays in Peoria

Mercy Warren used drama to urge a revolution against a foreign tyranny; her spiritual daughters employed it to expose domestic tyranny. Warren also cast a searching eye on the dominion men held over women; the suffragist playwrights focused on the injustice done a citizenry deprived of its natural rights because of gender.

Many of the earliest dramas dealing with suffrage, such as *The Spirit of '76,* were against it. Of those plays supporting the cause, quite a few originated as "parlor" dramas, brief, amateurish works utilizing small casts and the props readily found in the average middle-class household; others were closet dramas intended for a reading audience only. The popularity of the parlor play represents a compromise between America's Puritan conscience, still uneasy about theater, and its historical love of the dramatic. Like the young Anna Cora Mowatt, who entertained family and friends with private performances, large numbers of middle-class Americans staged parlor plays. Collections of such plays were published, and popular women's magazines sometimes included plays among their articles.[1] Suffragists used circuses, pageants, picketing, and parades as street theater to win support for their cause. The suffrage parlor plays themselves, first performed in private homes or published in feminist journals, and later performed at suffragist meetings, became such popular vehicles for propaganda and fund-raising that in the later days of the struggle for the vote their venues became rented commercial theaters and fashionable hotels. Students at the women's colleges also presented the plays on their campuses. The male gaze is obvious in the work of a *New York Times* journalist reporting on the 16 December 1910 presentation of *How They Won the Vote* at Barnard. While his only remark on the play was that it had a cast of 10 characters, he did not neglect to notice that "There were no pretty girls selling tickets at the door, as there usually are at Barnard plays."

Suffragists writing for this noncommercial theater argued many different positions. In fact, there are suffragist plays situated in liberal, material, and radical/cultural positions, and several combinations thereof. The liberals argued from an Enlightenment natural rights philosophy; cultural suffragists, on the other hand, contended that the government needed women because of their very difference from men.

The ancestors of these playwrights had, of course, perceived some of the same problems. Warren and Rowson, though predating Mowatt, are the more feminist, Warren through her inference in *The Group* that society could benefit from the patriarchy listening to the women it preferred to silence, and Rowson through both the Utopian vision of Fetnah and the outspokenness of Rebecca. When suffragists began writing and producing plays, they, like Warren and Rowson, offered a feminist solution to inequity, proposing that the ballot would bring justice.

A cultural feminist position is evident in *Something to Vote For* (1911) by Charlotte Perkins Gil-

man, a social theorist, novelist, short-story writer, and journalist. Oriented toward a materialist position in such works as her famous *Women and Economics* (1898), *The Home: Its Work and Influence* (1903), *Human Work* (1904), and *Man Made World: Our Androcentric Culture* (1911), Gilman takes a different stance in her drama. Addressing women who feel they are well represented at the polls by their influence on the men in their lives, Gilman asks them to examine their womanly concerns and realize that they, more sensitive to human needs than are men, do indeed have reason to vote.

In *Something to Vote For* the antisuffrage members of the wealthy widow Carroll's women's club are set against the suffragist Dr. Strong, the symbolically named female physician who is to speak at the meeting. The closed minds of the club women are illustrated in their bylaws, which preclude discussion of woman suffrage. In this restriction, Gilman mirrors the constitutions of many actual clubs whose members felt that such discussion would be divisive. When Dr. Strong presents the Pure Milk Bill as an issue that appeals to the "motherheart and housekeeping sense of every woman" and that is "sure to make every woman want to vote," the women respond with cries of "No" and hisses.

Dr. Strong is to test milk from the plant of Mr. Billings, head of the Milk Trust and lobbyist against the bill. Before the meeting, she speaks with a milk inspector about the role bad milk plays in the high infant mortality rate. Saying, "I really believe that if mothers ran the milk business they would not be willing to poison other women's babies to make money for their own," she plots to switch the good milk Billings has brought to the meeting for the contaminated product he sells in poor neighborhoods. The doctor and the inspector expose the impure milk and Billing's greed. Shocked by the dirt in the milk, Mrs. Carroll proclaims: "Now we see what our 'influence' amounts to! Rich or poor, we are all helpless together unless we wake up to the danger and protect ourselves. That's what the ballot is for, ladies—to protect our homes! To protect our children! To protect the children of the poor! I'm willing to vote now! I'm glad to vote now! I've got something to vote for! Friends, sisters, all who are in favor of women suffrage and pure milk say Aye!" The play ends with a chorus of "Aye! Aye!"

While suffrage dramas may not have actually played in Peoria, Catherine Waugh McCulloch's *Bridget's Sisters, or, The Legal Status of Illinois Women* (1911) is set in Illinois. Setting her drama in 1868 to show the relevance of past and present abuse, lawyer McCulloch examines women's lack of legal status through Bridget O'Flannigan, a washerwoman who not only must hide her wages from her abusive, alcoholic husband but who has those wages attached to pay his bar bill. Bridget symbolizes all working married women subject to economic and personal exploitation. The courtroom scene highlights patriarchal arrogance. Not only does Patrick O'Flannigan assert that the bar owner "will find I am the only one who owns Bridget and her wages," but the owner admits he ignored Bridget's pleas not to sell liquor to her husband because Pat "is the head of the family and is the best judge whether he wants to drink." With the women who employ Bridget gathered in the courtroom, the play becomes something of a lecture. The laws of coverture, separate estate, and curtsey are discussed as a prelude to the judge's decision that "a wife's wages absolutely belong to her husband." Asking rhetorically why women have not risen to right such "wrongs," he suggests as reasons for female docility the facts that each woman thinks she's alone, that male domination has broken the spirit of most women, and that many women do not care about "sister women's sufferings." A debate among the women follows; woman's lack of human, moral, and civil rights is explained, culminating in a citation of the dismissal of rape charges because the rapist's orphaned 10-year-old victim was, incredible as this may seem to modern sensibilities, past the age of consent under then-current Illinois law. Brought to unity, the women decide to form an Equal Suffrage Association.

As dramas, these and others of the subgenre tend to be simplistic and didactic. Many roles are caricatures. Several make deprecating use of Irish and black servants, reminding us of the many suffragists who were greatly incensed that immigrant and black men were granted the franchise before native-born white women. Several, in their attempts to overcome the cliché of the feminist as a mannishly clad, cigar-smoking harridan, offer the old chestnuts of love and marriage as rewards to the right-thinking suffragist. As propaganda, however, the plays were successful as these feminist suffragist playwrights, working in the tradition of Warren and Rowson and imagining solutions to the Woman Question, seized the power of the pen and the stage and the passion of the current moment to dramatize their political points.

Drama and Society at the Turn of the Century and Beyond

With no little irony, the authors of the 1848 Declaration of Sentiments had resolved "[that] the objection of indelicacy which is so often brought against woman when she addresses a public audience, comes with a very ill-grace from those who encourage, by their attendance, her appearance on the stage, in the concert, or in feats of the circus." By the last decade of the nineteenth century, the coalition of feminists and suffragist playwrights, of dowagers, matrons, and debutantes appearing onstage, had done much to augment the aura of respectability brought to the theater by actors and playwrights such as Rowson and Mowatt.

In 1917, the inclusion of drama as a Pulitzer Prize category marked another milestone in its approach to respectability; the award went to Jesse Lynch Williams's *Why Marry?* Four years later, in 1921, the prize was awarded to a woman for the first time, going to Zona Gale for the dramatization of her novel *Miss Lulu Bett*. Women also were prime movers in the little theater movement, a burgeoning of smaller theaters that grew out of the exploitation of actors and playwrights by the Broadway syndicates. Called variously amateur, nonprofit, and civic, little theaters arose in many major cities in the United States. Philanthropists Alice and Irene Lewisohn presided over the metamorphosis of the Henry Street Settlement House theater into the Neighborhood Playhouse in 1915. That same year, Susan Glaspell helped found the Provincetown Players.

The rise of realism also influenced the stage; dramatists such as William Dean Howells and James A. Herne brought realism in staging, character, plot, and theme to the theater. In 1913 Alice Gerstenberg dramatized the conflict of the id and ego in *Overtones* by splitting her two female characters into projections of each psychological state. Each character was portrayed by two actors, one presenting the social self, the other her alter ego, who voiced the thoughts the social self dared not. Gerstenberg became the first American to present the dramatization of the subconscious mind onstage; by introducing expressionistic devices to the American stage she added the exploration of psychological realism to the dramatist's arsenal. Furthermore, male and female playwrights both began to focus on social issues.

Despite strides made by women in life and in the theater, negative images of them in both areas appeared regularly onstage. Eugene Walter's *The*

Easiest Way (1908) combined both, presenting the theater as the site of vice and the central character, a female actor, as corrupt. Fear of the New Woman appears in several works. William Vaughn Moody's *The Faith Healer* (1910) and Clyde Fitch's *The City* (1909) present images of women ostensibly harmed by the new freedoms gained through the women's movement.

The oddest of all the images of women on-stage was strange primarily because of its medium, not its message. Geraldine Maschio notes that female impersonators first appeared in American minstrel shows in the 1840s and reached the height of their popularity at the turn of the century. "Created and enacted by men, female impersonation attempted to prescribe and control the behavior of women by offering a three-dimensional image of the feminine ideal. That this image was created by a man meant that, as with other prescriptions, it carried the weight of authority."[2] What better image of the male gaze come to life than a male-created, male-enacted portrayal of the ideal female, the true object of desire? The impersonators were praised for being "more womanly in . . . by-play and mannerisms than the most charming female imaginable, [and] creat[ing] . . . an ideal to which all obedient women aspired"; the belief in supremacy of the white male as creator is reflected in a reviewer's comment that "just as a white man makes the best stage Negro, so a man gives a more photographic interpretation of femininity than the average woman" (Maschio, 45, 46).

The New Woman

Contrary to these images was the New Woman herself. Like the varied questions that led society to try to apprehend her, she was not one but several. She was the social reformer in the settlement house, the factory worker, the telephone operator, the flapper, the stenographer. She was all those women learning to openly question authority that neither included nor heeded her. She was the woman ridiculed for trying to achieve anything on her own in an era that called on middle-class white women merely to exist, to be rather than to do. Knowing also the unequal treatment she was liable to under the law, she joined the National Woman's Party to urge enactment in 1923 of an equal rights amendment, which stated that "men and women shall have equal rights throughout the United States and every place subject to its jurisdiction." She enjoyed the freedom of new courtship patterns made possible by the automobile and the telephone; she feared being left an old maid. She was, in short, all the

women celebrated and feared, castigated and feted under the title New Woman—and she was the woman whose unfair treatment, predicated on her sex, lay at the heart of many of the plays in which American feminist playwrights confronted the Woman Question.

From Broadway to Provincetown: Rachel Crothers and Susan Glaspell

Rachel Crothers and Susan Glaspell brought the New Woman to the American stage. Crothers was one of the most successful Broadway dramatists of the first quarter of the twentieth century. Glaspell cofounded the Provincetown Players, a company devoted to innovation in American drama, and wrote many of the company's most successful plays. From the Great White Way of Broadway to the fishing shacks and dunes of Cape Cod, these two playwrights played major roles in the advancement of American dramatic art.

RACHEL CROTHERS: THE TROUBLE WITH GENDER

Rachel Crothers (1870[3]-1958) was a force to be reckoned with in theater for more than three decades. Herself the daughter of a New Woman—her mother began her medical studies after the age of 40—Crothers brought to the stage more New Women than any dramatist of her era. Among these women are muckraking activist/author Frank Ware of *A Man's World* (1909); journalist Ruth Creel and sculptor Ann Herford of *He and She* (1911); and novelist Mary Howard of *When Ladies Meet* (1932).

In 1891 she studied at the New England School of Dramatic Instruction. On graduating in 1892 she returned to Illinois, but her desire to be part of the theater was unquenched. In 1896 she enrolled at the Stanhope-Wheatcroft School of Acting in New York, where she spent one term as a student and four years as an instructor. The opportunities to write plays for her students, to direct these plays, and to design the costumes, sets, and props were, as she noted "of inestimable value because the doors of the theater are very tightly closed to women in the work of directing and staging plays" (Gottlieb, 18).

Although he begins by stating that "there are not many finer records in the American theatre than that achieved by Rachel Crothers," Burns Mantle calls her "America's first *lady* [emphasis added] dramatist" in his 1938 *Contemporary American Playwrights,* illustrating that the same double standards Crothers resisted in her dramas were alive in theater. This pigeonholing by sex was undoubtedly influenced by the virulent prejudice against women other than as actors at the turn of century. As Doris Abramson remarks: "[I]nterviews with and articles about 'lady playwrights' were often placed on the society page."[4] Critic George Jean Nathan frequently referred to women playwrights as "girls." Walter Pritchard Eaton, while somewhat less sexist, still made man the measure. In his 1910 review of *A Man's World,* he finds the play "just misses the masculinity of structure and the inevitableness of episode necessary to make it dramatic literature" (Abramson, 57).

Crothers represents and celebrates the New Woman. Beginning with her earliest plays, she exposes the fictions about women created by the patriarchy to reinforce its paradigms of womanhood,[5] as she illustrates the arbitrariness of socialization by gender and the concomitant cost for women and society in the unfulfilled human potential for work, love, or both. Aware of the difficulty of resisting such socialization, Crothers portrays many women who are unable or unwilling to pay that price, choosing instead to submit themselves to the "rules" of a patriarchal society. Some critics feel that in the middle years of her career Crothers herself may have bowed to her audience's inability to overcome its patriarchal prejudices and that her dramas from this period somehow impugn her feminist credentials. Yet Crothers was as "woman conscious" in her drama as she was in her life. She told Djuna Barnes during an interview for the May 1931 issue of *Theater Guild* magazine that "For a woman, it is best to look to women for help; women are more daring, they are glad to take the most extraordinary chances." She added: "I think I should have been longer about my destiny if I had to battle with men alone."

In 1931 Crothers told Henry Albert Phillips: "With few exceptions every one of my plays has been a social attitude toward women at the moment I wrote it . . . I [do not] go out stalking the footsteps of women's progress. It is something that comes to me subconsciously. I may say that I sense the trend even before I have hearsay or direct knowledge of it."[6] Whether her perceptions were subconscious or not, Crothers dramatized such human—not exclusively women's—issues as the need for meaningful work and the ensuing conflicts for some women between marriage (and sometimes motherhood) and career; the problems inherent in assuming that double standards were "natural"; the resistance and resentment encountered by assertive, successful women; and the loneliness that might impel a single woman into an unsatisfying marriage. In a 13 February 1912 interview with the *Boston Evening Transcript,*

Crothers said that she chose women as her central characters because "women are in themselves more dramatic than men, more changing and a more significant note of the hour in which they live. If you want to see the signs of the times, watch women. Their evolution is the most important thing in modern life."

The tension between woman's increasing awareness of herself as a human being and man's desire to maintain the status quo is illustrated in her plays. In several the male lead refers to his counterpart as "little girl," evincing a desire to keep her dependent on him. From *The Three of Us* (1906) through *When Ladies Meet* (1932), the males in more than a dozen of Crothers's major dramas, including *A Man's World* and *He and She,* express the desire to "take care of" the females, even as Crothers makes it apparent through the accomplishments of these women that they need no caretakers. Many are over 30—Crothers prided herself on creating plays wherein the protagonist was not a 17-year-old ingenue. The male desire to protect actually masks the patriarchal privilege within middle-class marriage whereby a woman traded her youth, beauty, and sexuality for economic dependence on a man. Many of Crothers's plays question the assumptions about male and female grounded in generalizations about gender that inevitably work to secure the comfort and reinforce the power of the patriarchy. Crothers's feminism is visible in her plays, and, despite claims to the contrary by some late-twentieth-century critics, with no subversion of the texts, for most of those texts themselves subvert the patriarchal social order.[7]

Crothers's earliest works were brief one-act dramas written for her students. In two, *Criss-Cross* (1899) and *The Rector* (1902), New Women protagonists confront society's unfairness to women. Crothers's protagonist may have either career or marriage; she evidences artistic or personal competence only at the price of losing the man she loves.

With *The Three of Us* (1906), her first Broadway drama, Crothers began to probe the societal conventions that impede women's self-determination. Concepts such as the basis of woman's honor and the double standard are closely questioned, yet Crothers's critics fault her for her protagonist's choosing to "adopt" the patriarchal code rather than abandon her brother. As Judith L. Stephens explains, Progressive Era politics, the dramatic conventions of the time, and "the prevailing belief in women's moral superiority exert[ed] a strong influence in determining the bounds within which the meaning of gender was constructed and negotiated in Progressive era drama."[8] Thus, "Progressive era plays reinforced such gender ideology by their moralistic nature and conventional structure even as they incorporated ideas intended to effect 'progress for women'" (Stephens, 292). While Crothers did not always openly transgress these principles of drama and sexual politics, she managed to subvert several tenets of male-female relationships deemed "natural" in her era.

Rhy MacChesney, the nonconformist protagonist of *The Three of Us,* "is forceful and fearless as a young Amazon, with the courage of belief in herself—the audacity and innocence of youth which has never known anything but freedom—the lovableness of a big nature and sunniness of an undying sense of humor. What she wears is very far from the fashion, but has charm and individuality and leaves her as free and unconscious of her strength and beauty as an animal." Just as her unconventional dress announces freedom from slavery to fashion, her search through an old trunk for "a dress of mother's" to wear to a party and her catching the keys to that trunk "like a boy" signal Crothers's refusal to valorize traditional signs of gender.

Believing herself free to do as she wishes, Rhy resists the idea that she has seriously compromised herself by coming to a man's home alone at night and that she has no alternative but to become his mistress. Shocked at the extent to which she is a prisoner of gender, she angrily responds: "It's true, then—all women must be afraid. I haven't believed it. I've thought we could do anything that was *right* in *itself.* I *still* think it! A good woman hasn't anything to be afraid of. Nothing can make a thing wrong that really is right. I'm not afraid of the *world*—it's *you*—*you* who can't understand. That this *could* have happened to me—to me!" Her belief that only Berresford, a villain, would presume to judge on appearances is dispelled when Townley, her sweetheart, enters, assumes she *has* dishonored herself, and tells her: "You shan't leave here till you say you'll marry this man. Don't you care anything for your honor and your good name?" As the men joust over who'll defend her tarnished honor, Rhy breaks in: "Don't you dare speak to me of my honor and my good name! Don't you dare to say you'll 'take care of it.' My honor! Do you think it's in your hands? It's my own and I'll take care of it and of everyone who *belongs* to me. I don't need you—either of you. 'Love—protection—trust!' Why I have to fight you both. Don't talk to me about whom I'm going to marry. That's a very little thing. Something else comes first!"

Rhy realized that her brother Clem had sold information that Berresford used to discredit Townley; Clem is the "something else [that] comes first." Despite her telling him that he sold his self respect quite cheaply for Berresford's $500, Clem remains defiant until she tells him she went alone to Berresford's and was discovered there by Townley. For her brother's benefit, she "sobs unrestrainedly," telling Clem: "I've got *you* to take care of me." After Rhy reclaims Clem, she and Townley are reconciled when she asks him to believe in the power of her love. The curtain falls as Rhy says, "We must make a good man of [Clem]. I have you to help me."

Although the play falls within the scope of the Progressive Era dramas described by Stephens, with Rhy making the self-sacrificing, moral decision and the men recouping positions of power, not everyone was oblivious to the challenges posed to conventional notions of woman and goodness. Mary Carolyn Davis wrote in the 1 June 1918 issue of the *Nation*—some 12 years after the play's premiere—that it "gave the deathblow to the cherished theatrical convention that a woman's honor must be fatally injured because she happens to be alone in a room with a man after sundown."[9] Surely some in the audience also recognized in the final line a comment on the social construction of manhood. Many reviewers, however, did respond within the range described by Stephens. In the 3 June 1907 edition of the *Chicago News,* the writer praises Rhy because she is "not the emancipating trumpeter of noisy deeds for femininity, but the holy woman of the great resplendent life of throbbing motherhood"! It would appear that for this writer the madonna/feminist dichotomy is more threatening than that of the madonna/whore, a division used by the patriarchy from time immemorial to classify women.

Continuing her scrutiny of the unfairness of a male-dominated world, Crothers anatomized the power of the patriarchy through its manifestations in the double standard in *A Man's World* (1909), a social problem drama that concerns the relationship between Frank Ware, feminist and novelist, and Malcolm Gaskell, a reporter, as it is affected by their attitudes toward the double standard. Frank, raised by her writer father "to see—to know—to touch all kinds of life" discerned very early the limitations put on women: "[t]he more I knew—the more I thought women had the worst of it." While living in Paris, Frank and her father take in a young, unmarried, pregnant woman whom Frank sees "suffer the tortures of hell through her disgrace." When the woman dies giving birth, Frank adopts the baby boy, whom she names Kiddie. Years later, after falling in love with Gaskell, she discovers he is Kiddie's father. When Gaskell, who had abandoned Kiddie's mother without knowing of her pregnancy, learns of his paternity, he claims male prerogative and refuses to acknowledge he's done anything wrong; Frank, therefore, rejects him. Crothers, like most feminists of the era, argues not for more sexual freedom for women but for a single standard of abstinence and fidelity for both sexes.

Branching from this issue are such related topics as the power of love, woman's need for economic independence, the value of work, and the pain of loneliness. Frank, an active and engaging character who is described in her initial appearance as "strong, free, unafraid, with the glowing charm of a woman at the height of her development," is also the primary focus of the debates about these concerns. One of Crothers's superior women, Frank is, through her name, announced as forthright. She is a successful novelist who centers her work around social problems concerning women. Frank's economic independence is an expression of Crothers's materialist feminism; Frank is "free" because her privileged background, education, and talent have enabled her to earn her way, and she recognizes that social conditions that are condoned, even sanctioned, by the patriarchy are responsible for the plights of the women of the Lower East Side about whom she writes.

In her novels, Frank exposes the conditions underlying the poverty, prostitution, and social decay of the slums. Because of her subject matter, the strength of her style, and her "male" name, early reviewers assumed Frank was a man: "*The Beaten Path* is the strongest thing that Frank Ware has ever done. Her first work attracted wide attention when we thought Frank Ware was a man, but now that we know she is a woman we are more than ever impressed by the strength and scope of her work. . . . Her great cry is for women—to make them better by making them freer." Such a "cry" flies in the face of the patriarchal system that seeks to make women virtuous by making them prisoners of the code that so dismayed Rhy. Frank's "friends," no less skeptical of woman's talent, wonder where and how she gets her material and think that a man must be helping her. During one conversation, her male friends also speculate about whether Kiddie is Frank's biological child and wonder why, if he is not, she refuses to divulge his parentage.

Zeroing in on the sexual double standard, Crothers effects a stunning reversal of the situation presented in *The Three of Us*. Rather than dramatizing the plight of a woman who is convicted of immorality on the basis of mere appearances, she presents a man who absolves himself from responsibility for his actions because of his gender. Gaskell, whom Frank agrees to marry while blinded by love for her idealized vision of him, is actually an arrogant, unpleasant character. Crothers makes the true Gaskell very unattractive as she illustrates both his callousness and his conviction of male superiority. Of Frank's book, he says: "You haven't got at the social evil in the real sense. You couldn't tackle that. It's too big for you. . . . You don't get *at* the thing. You keep banging away about woman—woman and what she could do for herself if she would. Why—this is a man's world. Women'll never change anything." Turning then to her activities with the girls' club she sponsors, he declares that she is wasting her time with these lower-class girls whom he sees as promiscuous. In this, Gaskell represents the patriarchal view that once a girl is "ruined" there's no redeeming her. (The "ruiner" is, of course, free from any censure.) This attitude also underlies his urgent desire to know about Kiddie's background; he arrogantly informs Frank: "I'm a man. You're a woman. I love you. I have the right to know your life."

Gaskell's assumption of privilege—like that of all the men, fictional or real, who have subscribed to this view of woman—has a long history. The sexual double standard has been in force for thousands of years. Men often assigned a lower level of sexual desire to women, and then went to great lengths legally and socially to ensure that their myth, necessary to what they saw as the orderly functioning of society, was maintained. Crothers has Gaskell, albeit unknowingly, admit as much when in a marvel of circular logic he proclaims: "Man sets the standard for woman. He knows that she's better than he is and he demands that she be—and if she isn't she got to suffer for it. That's the whole business in a nutshell—and you know it." Not only does he claim to speak for all men, Gaskell is also quite open about his view of woman's role in life. He avers: "Women are only meant to be loved—and men have got to take care of them. That's the whole business."

When revealed as Kiddie's father, he is unrepentant. He insists that nothing has changed and that the separation Frank now perceives between them is based only on her ideas, which are, of course, inconsequential: "[S]ince the beginning of time one thing has been accepted for a man and another for a woman. Why on earth do you beat your head against a stone wall? Why do you try to put up your ideals against the facts?" When Frank will not accept the "facts," he enlists the patriarchy's version of the natural order: "You're a woman. I'm a man. We don't live under the same laws. It was never meant to be. Nature, nature made men different."

Despite Frank's rejection of his argument about the essence of male and female and his recourse to nature, Gaskell insists she not "hold [him] to account by a standard that does not exist." Frank learns that he is not the man she imagined him to be, not the "fine and honest man" her culture encouraged her to lean on. He is not even a man who, to save their relationship, would do the minimum she asks and admit he'd been wrong. Thus, in the only ending possible, Frank remains true to her feminist values and the lovers part.

The play's characters are varied and vivid, the dialogue crisp and convincing, and the tension satisfying. This is not a preachy polemic but a logical working out of the incompatibility of Frank's liberal feminism and Gaskell's inflexible belief in women's inferiority as encoded in the double standard. In the June 1914 issue of *Forum,* Florence Kiper called the play "honest [and] well built drama, interesting to feminists not only because of its exposition of a modern sex-problem, but also because it is written by a woman—one who does not attempt to imitate the masculine viewpoint, but who sees the feminine experience through the feminine temperament." Eaton, in the review previously cited, could not resist sneering as he reported that Frank "has a little theory—women do get such theories tenaciously into their heads nowadays—that she does not care to have to forgive the man she loves for any unsavory episodes connected with 'the living of a man's life!'" Not only is the sneer inappropriate; Eaton is clearly wrong. Frank was ready to forgive Gaskell's past if he would only admit he had been wrong.

A Man's World provoked such a stir that Augustus Thomas responded to it with his dramatic defense of the double standard, *As a Man Thinks* (1911). Here Dr. Seelig, countering the argument in which his wife makes a direct reference to Crothers—"And that woman dramatist with her play was right. It is a man's world"—proclaims, "There is a double standard of morality because upon the golden basis of women's virtue rests the welfare of the world." The sophistry behind Thomas's argument is worthy of a Malcolm Gaskell.

The secondary theme of *A Man's World,* woman's talent and her right to employ it, becomes the focus in *He and She.* Taken on tour in hopes of securing a Broadway run, the play premiered in Poughkeepsie, New York; rechristened *The Herfords,* it opened in Boston in 1912, but did not make it to Broadway until 1920, at which time the original title was restored and Crothers played the lead. In 1980, playwright Emily Mann directed a revival.

The play concerns the apparently egalitarian marriage of Ann and Tom Herford, two successful sculptors. Tom is completing his entry in a design competition for a building frieze. Ann, having second thoughts about Tom's design, develops one that she wishes him to submit instead. When he refuses, she enters the competition. Ann wins the commission, and the egalitarian spirit of the marriage begins—on Tom's part—to erode. As various family members and friends debate woman's role as mother, worker, and artist, the situation seems to defy resolution until the Herfords' daughter Millicent presents herself as needing her mother's attention. Ann decides that Millicent needs her more than she herself needs her art and asks Tom to execute her design.

The issue of women and work is raised almost with the curtain. Keith, Tom's assistant, asks him: "Have you ever been sorry that Mrs. Herford is a sculptor—instead of just your wife?" Keith's word choice is interesting; the "just" implies that Ann would be something less than she is were she "just" Tom's wife, while the "sorry" infers that there is something less than desirable about a wife who is "more" than just a wife. Keith is engaged to journalist Ruth Creel, who will marry him if he lets her keep working. He wonders how she can keep doing all that has made her so successful and tend a house too. He protests that Ruth, unlike Ann, who works in her studio at home, is "tied down to office hours and it's slavery." He never questions the fact that his ideal of having "a girl by my own fireside to live for me alone" would make her both a slave and a house prisoner. Keith claims to be quite liberal: "I'm strong for women doing anything they want to do—in general—But when it's the girl you love and want to marry it's different."

Tom, mildly amused, tells him that his attitude about working women in the abstract should not differ from his attitude about a particular working woman, but Keith cannot see beyond the fact that "[t]he world [read men] has got to have homes to live in and who's going to make 'em if the women don't do it?" When Tom mentions the excellence of Ruth's mind, Keith responds: "Oh, mind be damned. I want a wife." Later he asks Tom's sister Daisy, who is secretly in love with him, whether she sees anything wrong in "wanting a girl to give up hard, slavish work and let him take care of her." The difficulty of many household tasks is elided in Keith's question; for him it is simply invisible. The audience may realize who is really being taken care of; Keith never will. The basis of Keith's argument is his detestation of the fact that women who work do not need men to survive. As he sees it: "The minute a woman makes enough to buy the clothes on her back, she thinks she and God Almighty are running the earth and men are just little insects crawling around." Keith protests the fact that woman's economic independence saps his power to decree what she will do; Crothers introduces these issues as part of the subplot because this seeming caricature is voicing emotions that Tom will experience.

When Ann wins the competition, Tom shows himself caught in the patriarchal mind-set; although act 1 ends with an egalitarian handshake as Tom welcomes Ann to the competition, in act 2 Crothers shows him to be brother to Keith. They first learn that Tom has come in second; Ann consoles him. Shortly, they learn that Ann has won. Tom seems to handle the news well. Yet minutes later he is asking her what *she* will do with their 16-year-old daughter that summer and telling her that he will not touch any of her commission money. He accuses her of letting her ambition run amok, then, sounding like Malcolm Gaskell, tells her: "You're a woman and I'm a man. You're not free in the same way. If you won't stop because I ask it—I say you *must* . . . I demand it. I say you've *got* to."

Tom is no different from Keith. He feels his manhood threatened by Ann's ability to earn the $100,000 commission and fears her economic success will lessen her interest in her roles as wife, mother, and mistress of the house. At bottom, he too wants "a girl by [his] own fireside to live for [him] alone." Ann and Ruth, on the other hand, speak of the need for economic independence, and Ann tells her father that a woman's ability to make a living can mitigate any blow.

Keith and Tom are figurative sons of Ann's father, the quintessential patriarch Dr. Remington. He is, in Ann's word, "mid-Victorian" in his at-

titude at best and medieval at worst. A doctor, as representative of the patriarchy, is a frequent character in the drama of this era. In James Herne's *Margaret Fleming* (1890), Dr. Larkin validates Margaret's decision to raise her husband's illegitimate child and to allow Philip back into their home by saying, "[T]his world needs just such women as you"; in *As a Man Thinks,* Dr. Seelig valorizes both the double standard and woman's supposedly superior moral nature. Dr. Remington literally is the patriarch; he issues commands to both the women and the younger men. One of his comments—"And here's that pretty little Ruth thing—knowing so much it makes my head ache"—dehumanizes Ruth and demeans her intelligence, and his words to Tom—"[I]f you don't look out you'll be so mixed up you'll be upstairs keeping house and Ann will be downstairs keeping shop"—clearly indicate his position on woman's place. He assumes that human rights are man's to dispense and explains that women must not exercise their rights: "the more women make good—the more they come into the vital machinery of running the world, the more they complicate their own lives and the more tragedies they lay up for themselves." Claiming recourse to "natural" law, he adds, "The development of women hasn't changed the laws of creation . . . [for] no matter how far she goes she doesn't change the fundamental laws of her own—. . . mechanism." She must choose between the "two sides of her own nature." His biological determinism is debunked by Ruth's and Ann's love for their work, by their success, and by the fact that the men are those who decree that women must choose.

Selecting motherhood as possibly the strongest weapon in his arsenal, he claims that sitting "by her own fireside with children on her knee . . . [is] the only thing in the game that's worth a cent—anyway." Besides ignoring the millions of women who are not of his sociocultural milieu, his argument fails to account for Ruth, who is uninterested in rearing children. The argument falls short in his daughter's case also. Her only child, a selfish daughter who literally pulls Ann away from her work, is at 16 well beyond sitting on her mother's knee.

That Remington, despite his pose of egalitarian benevolence, finds women inferior becomes obvious when he chastises Ann for humiliating Tom. He tells her that Tom has suffered "a blow tonight that no man on earth could stand," that is, being beaten by a *woman*. Later, perhaps advising him to trade a physical blow for a metaphoric one, when Tom says he doesn't give orders to Ann, Remington responds: "The devil you don't. She'd like it. A woman—a dog and a walnut tree—the more you beat 'em the better they be."

Crothers exposes the fear, jealousy, and selfishness underlying the patriarchal order as Ann challenges her father with these words: "You've *never* thought I had any right to work—never believed in my ability, now that I've proved I have some—Why can't you acknowledge it?" In fact, both Ann's husband and her father acknowledge her ability, but not to her. Before he knows the outcome of the contest, Tom tells Keith: "The men judging this *know*. I'd trust them with anything. The fellows who lose will have no kick coming on that score." Remington reminds Tom about Ann's having offered her design to him: "[S]he laid her genius at your feet once and she'd do it again." Even recognizing her genius, he is willing to see it subjugated to her gender; her success bothers him so much that he says he'd rather see her happy as a woman than as an artist, once again refusing to see that, for Ann, the two are inextricably bound, and once again concealing the fact that the choice he would have her make is dictated by his preference, not by woman's "dual" nature.

Because the patriarchy as embodied by the three men will brook no alternative to its ownership of women and children—even though all the men try to veil this ownership by romanticizing, rationalizing, and spiritualizing it—the three adult women must respond to its dictates. Daisy subscribes to the philosophy that a couple cannot be happy unless the man dominates. Although she labels Daisy's emotional restatement of the law of coverture something from the dark ages, Ruth literally disappears from the drama after Remington declares the primacy of motherhood. Ann is left, many critics claim, to effect a compromise with Tom. But Crothers did not write of a compromise; she detailed a sacrifice. Learning that Millicent has become engaged to the chauffeur at her boarding school,[10] Ann succumbs to the pressure to take care of her child and asks Tom to execute her design. Giving up her art, Ann reverts to the gender role prescribed by her father, her era, and her class. What has Tom given? He says he will not let her sacrifice herself for their daughter and warns her that surrendering the commission will cause anguish to the artist in her, but he speaks only after Ann has made her decision. She has sacrificed her art, the work that brought her personal fulfillment and a way of illustrating the talents and capabilities of women. Her last line: "Put out the light," signifies the extinguishing of

her inner light of inspiration for the sake of a selfish child who will soon leave home.

Because its conclusion highlights this sacrifice, *He and She* is decidedly more feminist than is usually recognized. Ann bows to the patriarchal vision of what makes woman valuable and lovable: her ability to serve, to submit, to sacrifice. The ending illuminates the wastefulness of her action, for by concluding her drama in darkness Crothers shows that the opposite of Ann's healthy self-interest (branded selfishness by the men) is a bleak self-*less*-ness.

That Ann's sacrifice was most likely undertaken in vain was not lost on the contemporary audience. Alexander Woollcott saw clearly that Crothers was roiling the waters, not calming them. In the *New York Times* of 13 February 1920, he deemed the play a tragedy: "for something fine and strong dies in the last act. It is the hope, the ambition and all the future work of a genius—deliberately slain in order that the 'she' of *He And She* may be able to play more attentively and more whole-heartedly what she is *driven* [emphasis added] to regard as her more important role—that of wife and mother." In the 25 May 1980 *New York Times*, Jean Ashton remarked: "*He And She,* like Miss Crothers's other plays, is a descriptive, not a prescriptive work. Far from accepting this or any of her comedies as anti-feminist, Miss Crothers noted simply that the freedom women had achieved in the early years of the 20th century was tenuous and deceptive. Men still made the rules; women who broke them did so at tremendous cost."

While the 1920 version of *He and She* is decidedly feminist, the decade of the 1920s saw the paradox of women who had secured the right of suffrage and gained access to higher education retreating from social activism and returning to the home. This resurgence of domesticity—an effect of backlash against woman's progress that has recurred with disheartening regularity throughout the history of the woman's movement—finds its way into Crothers's drama, but even when she began to create social comedies rather than deal with social problems, gender issues were never absent from her work.

Although *Susan and God* (1937), the last of Crothers's produced plays, was named the most outstanding play of the season by the Theater Club, it is little more than a satire of the Oxford movement, and its protagonist, Susan Trexler, genuinely unlikable. *When Ladies Meet,* coming five years earlier, is the capstone of Crothers's career in dealing with the evolution of the modern woman. Its protagonist, 32-year-old Mary Howard, is a successful novelist who cares what women of her *"own kind"* think of her work; Mary, despite her success, feels incomplete without a man in her life. Her emotions lead her to contemplate an affair with her married publisher, Rogers Woodruff. Her inclination is prefigured in her latest novel, which centers around such an affair. Woodruff, described as having "an irresistible charm for women," is a romanticized idol for Mary; she cannot see, behind his charismatic mask, the clichéd character who tries to persuade her to become his lover with the oldest of lines: "If you [loved me] you wouldn't hesitate one second. . . . If you loved me—like that—you'd take me." Mary agrees to go with him to Bridget Drake's country place, but Jimmie, who himself loves Mary, shows up with Woodruff's wife, Claire, in tow, having first made sure Woodruff is called away on business.

Neither woman knows of the other's relationship to Woodruff. They like each other almost immediately, and they discuss Mary's books. Claire declares Mary's earlier novel *Alice* "astonishingly true, from a girl's standpoint"; Mary thinks that she's preparing "something *new* and *honest*—from a woman's standpoint." When she asks Claire her opinion of the situation in the novel, her prospective lover's wife reminds her that the other woman "ought to know enough not to believe a married man—if he's making love to her"—and that the wife might not be as much of a "dub" as the novel's protagonist believes her to be. Once the three members of this triangle come together, Woodruff tries to keep up the pretense that he and Mary are at Bridget's merely to work.

Seeing Mary's pain at his rejection enables Claire to see her own. Realizing she, too, has been creating a fiction based on the false premises that her husband can't help attracting women and that his infidelities mean little when he returns home to her, she no longer wants him. Admiring each other, the women can no longer pretend that the wife is a dub and the potential mistress a slut; recognizing each other, they see through him. Rejecting a man-centered existence that merely staves off loneliness, these superior women mature, and this is Crothers's point: when ladies meet in an atmosphere of confidence and trust, they become women, women deserving a better partner than Rogers Woodruff.

In this late play as in Crothers's first works, women decide to forgo love with a particular man, but there is a notable difference. In the earlier plays, the superior woman yields her interest in the male to another, perhaps weaker, woman in an action indicative of the "noble" self-sacrifice held up to women as ideal in this particular mythic mode of womanhood. Now, instead of silent suffering and surrender, the women undergo a course of self-discovery that allows them to realize the unworthiness of the man who lies to them both.

Crothers brought the New Woman—strong, talented, and intelligent—onstage; many of her woman-centered dramas focus on the social problems that arise when woman's human rights conflict with the patriarchal order. Considering that she wrote at a time when for the majority of her audience the overriding question of a woman's life drama concerned who, and sometimes whether, she would marry, Crothers's creation of at least one strongly feminist play in each of the last four decades of her career—*The Three of Us* (1906) and *A Man's World* (1909); the reworking of *The Herfords* (1912) as *He and She* (1920), and *When Ladies Meet* (1932)—is remarkable. Even her social comedies respond to issues raised by the Woman Question. She pursued these issues in a manner calculated to challenge the limitations placed on women by the patriarchal system, chronicling, for example, the folly of man's obsessive concern with woman's body as the repository of *his* honor. Crothers allows audiences to see the arguments about woman's place in society from a woman's perspective, both her own and those of her characters, some of whom mature from their romantic dependence on man as the imagined vehicle of fulfillment to achieve both a sense of self and freedom from the male ego's limited perception of her.

Dramatically, her work is important in the history of the development of serious social comedy in America. Crothers's early plays show her rapidly increasing command of structural and stylistic techniques. Her bright, witty, yet realistic dialogue ranks with the best of its era. Her central focus, which is the Woman Question, gives the Crothers canon a unified purpose. Often criticized as a "formula" playwright or a sentimentalist, Crothers instead presented dramas that dealt with real-life questions. The tragedy she illuminated, as Woollcott noted, was that of women "driven" into choices that sap the power and creativity of one-half of humankind.

ON THE SUBJECT OF...

SUSAN GLASPELL (1876-1948)

Susan Glaspell is best known for her role as co-founder of the influential theatre group the Provincetown Players; she also earned acclaim for her dramatic works and fiction published during the first half of the twentieth century. Glaspell was born in 1876 in Davenport, Iowa. She earned a doctorate at Drake University in nearby Des Moines in 1899, and became a reporter for both the *Des Moines Daily News* and the *Des Moines Capital.* By 1901, Glaspell was also publishing regularly in various magazines aimed at female readers. In 1910 began a romantic relationship with George Cram Cook; Cook and his wife divorced within a few years and Glaspell moved with him to New York City. The couple married in 1913, and in 1915 they co-founded the Provincetown Players, which was designed to produce the works of promising new American playwrights. Most prominent among the writers drawn to the Provincetown Players was Eugene O'Neill; however, Glaspell also proved an accomplished playwright; in 1916 Provincetown Players staged her first one-act drama, *Trifles,* which is generally considered Glaspell's masterpiece, and which she later adapted into the short story "A Jury of Her Peers," the title story of a 1927 collection. Glaspell and Cook moved to Greece, where Cook died in 1922. Glaspell married Norman Matson, a writer, in 1925; the couple divorced in 1931. In 1930 Glaspell enjoyed her greatest literary success with the play *Alison's House,* in which a dead poet's relatives confront their feelings about love. Glaspell was awarded a Pulitzer Prize for this work, which was the last play she ever wrote. She published several novels, including *Ambrose Holt and Family* (1931), *The Morning is Near Us* (1939), and *Judd Rankin's Daughter* (1945), before her death in Provincetown in 1948.

SUSAN GLASPELL: NEW WAYS OF IMAGING WOMEN ONSTAGE

Susan Glaspell (1876-1948), who helped transform American drama through her connection with the Provincetown Players and who created new ways of representing women onstage, began writing early, publishing short stories in such magazines as *Youth's Companion.* Upon graduation from Drake University in Davenport, Iowa, she became a reporter for the Des Moines *Daily News.* In 1901 she returned to Davenport to devote full time to her fiction, publishing two or three stories each year; in 1920 she published *Plays,* a collection of her dramas.

In 1913 Glaspell married George Cram Cook. Whatever else marriage brought Glaspell, its most significant aspect for American drama was her becoming, with Cook, a founder of the Provincetown Players. Founded in a fishing shack on a pier in Provincetown, Massachusetts, and devoted to producing only original plays by American playwrights, the theater counted among its contributors Edna St. Vincent Millay, Theodore Dreiser, and Djuna Barnes, but none so important to transforming American theater as Eugene O'Neill and Glaspell herself. When her first play, *Suppressed Desires,* cowritten with Cook, was rejected by the Washington Square Players, she and Cook presented it in their apartment; in the summer of 1915 they again performed it. Although the players were not formally organized until 1916, the season that introduced Glaspell's *Trifles,* the preceding summer may truly be counted as the birth date of this remarkable theater.

Encouraged by the attendance and by favorable reviews given their summer seasons, the group moved to New York in the winter of 1916. They named themselves the Provincetown Players and, as O'Neill suggested, called their playhouse The Playwrights' Theatre, a move that underscored the primacy of the playwright in their enterprise. They also decided "that active members must either write, act, produce, or donate labor."[11] This dictum provided a showcase for the other talents of Glaspell. In addition to providing more plays for the theater than any playwright except O'Neill, she directed some of her own plays and acted in *Suppressed Desires, Trifles, The People* (1917), *Close the Book* (1917), *Woman's Honor* (1918), *The Outside* (1918), *Bernice* (1919), and *The Inheritors* (1921), for all of which, with the exception of *Suppressed Desires,* she was the sole author. She not only spoofed Freudian analysis in *Suppressed Desires* and satirized the male vision of woman in *Woman's Honor,* she also illustrated the difficulty of truly representing woman onstage in *Trifles, Bernice,* and *Alison's House* (1930). In both *The Outside* and *The Verge* (1922), she dealt with woman's struggle with a malecentered language while at the same time she demonstrated her facility as an expressionist. Almost all of the plays deal with the problems women encounter in attempting, against the strong current of patriarchal authority, to forge identities of their own.

In *Trifles, Bernice,* and *Alison's House,* Glaspell constructs dramas around women who never appear onstage; paradoxically, the presence of these characters is strongly felt. In this device lies a striking achievement: she brings the absent women onstage diegetically, while at the same time their absence serves as a commentary on the manner in which the patriarchy has deprived women of their substance. That these women appear only through the words of others speaks to the constructed nature of womanhood itself.

Trifles, Glaspell's first play as sole author, was loosely based on a murder trial she covered for the Des Moines *Daily News.*[12] In her reverential biography of Cook, Glaspell explains that he had announced a play of hers for production and refused to accept that she had none:

> So I went out on the wharf . . . and looked a long time at that bare little stage. After a time the stage became a kitchen—a kitchen there all by itself. I saw just where the stove was, the table, and the steps going upstairs. Then the door at the back opened, and people all bundled up came in—two or three men, I wasn't sure which, but sure enough about the two women, who hung back, reluctant to enter that kitchen. . . . Whenever I got stuck, I would run across the street to the old wharf, sit in that leaning little theater under which the sea sounded, until the play was ready to continue.[13]

The social conditions pertaining to the plot of *Trifles* were set forth by Charlotte Perkins Gilman in *The Man-Made World, or Our Androcentric Culture:* Women have no standing; in the "proprietary family" of the patriarchy, their purpose is "first and foremost [as] a means of pleasure to [man]." Furthermore, family relationships are arranged "from the masculine viewpoint. . . . From this same viewpoint . . . comes the requirement that the woman shall serve the man." Accordingly, "[t]he dominant male, holding his woman as property . . . has hedged them in with restrictions of a thousand sorts," which ensure that "she cannot develop humanly, as he has, through social contact, social service, true social life."[14] These attitudes and restrictions cripple the lives of all three women presented in the play.

Ostensibly a murder mystery, the play deals on its surface with the attempt of Sheriff Peters, County Attorney Henderson, and Mr. Hale, a neighbor, to discover evidence relating to the murder of John Wright, whose wife, Minnie, has been jailed for the crime. Mrs. Peters has come to gather some personal belongings for Minnie, and Mrs. Hale to keep Mrs. Peters company. While the men inspect the bedroom in which Mr. Wright was strangled and search the barn for clues, the women uncover—and cover up—both the motive for the crime and the physical evidence thereof.

The play opens on an empty stage; the kitchen, gloomy and cluttered, offers the audience its first glimpse into the Wrights' lives. The set is a mute message, later elaborated in the women's dialogue. Shortly, the door opens; as the characters enter Glaspell offers another wordless message, this one concerning hierarchy. First to enter is the middle-aged sheriff, next the young county attorney, then Hale, followed by the women. The sheriff and the county attorney function as the ultimate emblem of the patriarchy: the law. Hale, not privileged by a connection to the law, as a man takes precedence over the women. The men immediately stride to the stove for warmth while the women, fearful and nervous, "stand close together near the door." Their action presages the warmth of sisterly community, which they will shortly discover.

The men's priorities are obvious; Glaspell indicates that the sheriff steps "away from the stove . . . as if to mark the beginning of official business." They allow nothing they deem extraneous to enter even the periphery of their consciousness. The lack of sensitivity among the men becomes apparent early. When they discover that, as Minnie had feared, the cold in the house had broken her jars of preserves, the sheriff is incredulous: "Well, can you beat the women! Held for murder and worrying about her preserves." Stating a central theme, Hale adds: "Well, women are used to worrying about trifles." Their smug scoffing heightens Glaspell's bipolar irony: "trifles" such as food and housekeeping are basic to the preservation of life itself, and it is the males' ignorance of such details that causes them to overlook the key to the crime itself.

Declaring there to be "[n]othing here but kitchen things," the sheriff leads the men upstairs to examine the murder scene, leaving the women—who had "move[d] a little closer together"—free to move about the kitchen. Years of habit lead them to begin cleaning the unkempt room. As they work, they speak of John Wright. Adding to the faded wallpaper, the uncurtained windows, and Hale's comment about his unwillingness to share the cost of a party-line telephone as evidence of Wright's niggardliness, Mrs. Hale declares: "Wright was close. I think maybe that's why she kept so much to herself. She didn't even belong to the Ladies' Aid. I suppose she felt she couldn't do her part, and then you don't enjoy things when you feel shabby." Her husband's miserliness had cut Minnie off from community, both in person and by telephone. Even in her own home she had no voice, for Hale had noted that he "didn't know as what his wife wanted made much difference to John."

The women who eventually become silent champions of Minnie do not identify themselves as her friends. Mrs. Peters had not met her before she was jailed; Mrs. Hale has known her 20 years, but had not visited in more than a year. They do not, therefore, take her part because of personal bias; rather, they come to see themselves and Minnie as Everywoman, imprisoned by patriarchal convention. The literally imprisoned Minnie, absent from the stage and thereby silent, reminds us of Warren's Sylvia, present in *The Group* only through the dialogue of the men who have arrogated to themselves her voice, a character who, "silent, mourns her fate." Minnie's absence also echoes the social position of a woman after marriage: as the law of coverture made clear, and as Crothers's Daisy approvingly reiterates in *He and She*, marriage erases a woman's identity. Significantly, Mrs. Hale refuses to accept this negation and persists in referring to her as Minnie Foster, not as Minnie Wright.

Glaspell's implicit criticism of the philosophy of separate spheres becomes obvious as the men, counting the women unable to recognize clues, leave them behind in the woman's world of the kitchen. Assuming that nothing merits their attention in this "preserve" of trifles, the men move upstairs. As the audience hears their footsteps on the floor above, Glaspell indulges in an aural pun: physically, the men are literally over the heads of the women—a reminder also of man's position as head of the household—while figuratively, the facts of the case go over the men's heads.

The women find the quilt Minnie had been working, one square of which is marked by erratic stitching quite different from the rest. Without stopping to wonder why, Mrs. Hale resews the square. This direct, but as yet unknowing, action echoes her earlier remarks uttered in Minnie's defense; when the county attorney said Minnie wasn't "much of a housekeeper," Mrs. Hale said in a "stiff" reply: "There's a great deal of work to be done on a farm." And when she says that "[m]en's hands aren't always as clean as they might be"

and that she "didn't think a place'd be any cheerfuller for John Wright's being in it," she points out men's failings. Now she and Mrs. Peters speculate about the tension underlying the irregular stitching. As she had earlier moved closer to Mrs. Peters, Mrs. Hale now moves closer to Minnie. She wishes she had visited more often, for she knows how difficult it must have been to live isolated and childless with John Wright, "a hard man. . . . Like a raw wind that gets to the bone."

Discovering the bird cage with its door hanging from one hinge, then the bird with its neck wrung, she decides that Wright killed both Minnie's singing spirit and the bird, so moves to conceal this evidence. Mrs. Hale criticizes the investigators for "sneaking" around Minnie's house: "Locking her up in town and trying to get her own house to turn against her!" Mrs. Peters, as the wife of the sheriff, counsels, "[T]he law is the law." Yet remembrance moves her. Seeing the dead bird, she recalls her own enraged response in childhood to the boy who "took a hatchet . . . before my eyes" to her pet kitten, and remembers the eerie stillness that enveloped her homestead when her two-year-old son, then her only child, had died. Still, even then she persists: "The law has got to punish a crime, Mrs. Hale"; Mrs. Hale declares that her own failure to visit "was a crime! Who's going to punish that?" From this perspective it is but a small step to the third crime—John Wright's spiritual and emotional, if not physical, abuse of his wife—and to the guilt the patriarchy must bear for its dirty hands, for its enforcement of the traditions and codes that led to Minnie's despair. Here one finds the three Everywomen, the wife, the wife of the law, and the murderer, all imprisoned in the patriarchal order; here one begins to appreciate Glaspell's further ironies. The symbolically named Minnie, small and insignificant, has risen against this system, but so far has succeeded only in exchanging one prison for another. But Glaspell is not done; the surname *Wright* also brims with irony: that John could be Mr. Right and that Minnie's rights were violated so severely that she thereby had a right to kill her husband.

The women, resisting for once the gender discrimination that imprisons them, tacitly agree to conceal the evidence; they rebel against abstract justice and act through sympathy and empathy. Glaspell suggests, in the manner of the cultural feminists, that a woman's law, which takes into account not just the deed but also the circumstances and context in which the deed is performed, is superior to the law of the patriarchy.

The final line of the play reverberates with this principle as Mrs. Hale, who had initially been abashed by the men's laughter at her question about whether Minnie had intended to quilt or knot the squares of her quilt, later lets Mrs. Peters say: "We think she was going to—knot it," then ends the play by standing center stage, her hand over the pocket that conceals the dead bird, and announcing for Mrs. Peters, for Minnie, for herself, for every woman: "We call it—knot it, Mr. Henderson." This splendid line laces together the image of John Wright with the noose knotted elaborately around his neck and the women's refusal, albeit one they cannot voice without endangering themselves, to be coopted yet again by the male system.

Trifles is the most frequently anthologized one-act play by an American woman; it is often praised as a paradigm of play construction. Overtly and inherently dramatic while at the same time subtle, economical, and understated, the play's form replicates its action in both its departure from the male dramatic traditions of through line—with its rising action, climax, and falling action—and linear exposition and in its lack of resolution. Glaspell must have realized it would be dishonest to resolve a conflict that remains, sadly, unresolved.

Alison's House won Glaspell the 1931 Pulitzer Prize, an award that brought the Pulitzer jury the disapproval of most critics and reviewers; the play was equally unpopular with audiences, running only 41 performances. Conventional in style and structure, the play even conforms to the neoclassic unities, taking place in fewer than 24 hours and utilizing two rooms of the same home as its set. It is notable, however, for being the third in Glaspell's trilogy of dramas focusing on a woman who never appears and for challenging a patriarchal system that cares more about preserving appearances and the status quo than about humanity.

Centered on Emily Dickinson surrogate Alison Stanhope, the play concerns the discovery, 18 years after her death, of poems that chronicle Alison's affair with a married man. As her surviving family prepares to move Agatha, who served as her sister's caretaker, from the old homestead, which is to be sold, they argue over whether the poems should be destroyed or published.

Glaspell resolves the conflict in favor of the new century. The poems will be published, a "letter to the world," which will allow it to perceive the human Alison, not some spirit treading the ether in virginal white. All will know "the story she never told. She has written it, as it never was written before. The love that never died—loneliness that never died—anguish and beauty of her love!" In *He and She*, Ann Herford regrets not executing her frieze because it would have been a gift for women, who could have looked at its strength and beauty and said: "A woman did that." In *Alison's House*, that gift is given; women will have the strength and beauty of Alison's work: "Because Alison said it—for women."

Saying it for women is Glaspell's concern in two of her more experimental dramas, *The Outside* and *The Verge*. In these works, women's attempts to speak for themselves illustrate the pitfalls inherent in allowing oneself to be defined by a male-devised, gender-centered grammar. The fixity of form basic in such a language contrasts with the flux of nature as, in both these plays, the forces of life contend with those of death.

The Outside begins with a scene that functions as envoi and emblem. Into a lifesaving station now converted into a private home, two men carry a drowning victim. Mrs. Patrick enters and demands that they leave: "You have no right here. This isn't the lifesaving station any more. Just because it used to be—I don't see why you should think—This is my house! And—I want my house to myself!" As she speaks, one of the men "put[s] his head through the door. One arm of the [victim] is raised and the hand reaches through the doorway." Thus the prologue shows death invading Mrs. Patrick's house, just as, on the dunes around the house, the sands encroach on and smother the scrub growth vying for survival on a set that marks Glaspell's move from realism to symbolism and expressionism. Mrs. Patrick bought the house with her husband as a summer place. Subsequently, he left her, and she retreated to this buried house. She appears to enjoy watching the sand engulf the scant life forms on the dunes and fears "Spring—coming through the storm to take me—take me to hurt me." She fears being bruised into life again, and this fear underlies her repeated comment: "I must have my house to myself!"

Seeking someone who "doesn't say an unnecessary word," she hired as her housekeeper Allie Mayo, "a bleak woman" with "that peculiar intensity of twisted things which grow in unfavoring places." Once a young woman teased by her husband for her loquaciousness, Allie, struck by the inanity of the remarks her friends offer when her husband disappears while on a whaling trip, retreats into silence. Through Allie, Glaspell introduces the thematic and structural problem of the play: what to do with and about words when, as inadequate as we know them to be, they are yet all that we have. She handles the issue imitatively, by allowing the halting dialogue of the play to illustrate its own meaning.

As Mrs. Patrick leaves the house, angry at the men for having left the corpse behind, Allie calls out: "Wait." Mrs. Patrick is "held," "arrested," by the unaccustomed sound of Allie's voice. Allie goes on "in a slow, labored way—slow monotonous, as if snowed in by silent years." Her voice falls to a whisper; she labors, rocking back and forth, to give birth to words "not spoken but breathed from pain." Because she assumes Mrs. Patrick's husband has died, Allie tells her own story to illustrate that withdrawal is "not the way." Shocked by Mrs. Patrick's revelation and hurt by her reminder that she'd been told Allie did not "say an unnecessary word," Allie insists that her words are vital. In a mutually stumbling syntax, the women debate their positions. As Glaspell makes obvious, their mistakes lie in investing too much of themselves in their marriages; the symbolic burial they have been undergoing in the dunes repeats their earlier act of burying their own identities in those of their husbands. They must strive now to find words to express themselves, for those selves have only an embryonic existence. Clearly, a command of the idiom of self demands the possession of a sense of self; until woman forges that identity she will struggle in a language that identifies her as the other.

Claire Archer, protagonist of *The Verge*, attempts to save her own life by subjugating herself in marriages to two unimaginative men, but each disappoints her. Now three men—her husband, her friend the philosopher, and her lover the artist, the triumvirate of Harry, Tom, and Dick, who among them cannot come close to understanding her—cause her much impatience as she anxiously awaits the flowering of Breath of Life, a new form of plant life she has created.

This most expressionist of Glaspell's dramas opens in Claire's greenhouse, which is more laboratory than nursery. A shaft of light emitted through an open trapdoor in the floor illuminates a strange plant with a "twisted stem"; frosty "patterns" are visible on the greenhouse glass, a violent "wind . . . makes patterns of sound," and "At the back grows a strange vine. It is arresting rather than beautiful. The leaves of this vine are not the form that leaves have been. They are at once repellent and significant." The ominous mood, sight, and sound dissipate as the dialogue begins. Because Claire has diverted the heat from the house into her greenhouse/laboratory, Harry has come to eat his breakfast in comfort; soon Dick follows. The talk is that of a comedy of manners; as Harry mildly berates Claire for being a poor hostess, Claire tries to persuade Harry to try his egg without salt, and Tom, finding himself locked out, fires a revolver to gain the attention of those inside the glass house. Yet beneath the surface move the roots of another drama, which twists around the conventional comedy. To Dick, Harry says that creating something unsettles a woman. Disturbed because Claire has dared to reach beyond the usual, Harry questions her state of mind, but his real unease arises because she is breaking the bonds of womanhood and presuming to arrogate to herself the male roles of creator and scientist. When he tells Dick, "I'd like to have Charlie Emmons see her—he's fixed up a lot of people shot to pieces in the war," Glaspell's allusion to the war between the sexes is obvious. This reference is especially relevant in light of the research of Judith Lewis Herman, who in *Trauma and Recovery* asserts, "There is a war between the sexes. . . . Hysteria is the combat neurosis of the sex war."[15] Here, too, arises the question of whether Claire is "on edge," that is, in a liminal stage, willing to risk going mad so life itself need not be imprisoned. Or is she on the edge of sanity, driven there by pressures to conform to her "womanly" role?

In the name Claire Archer, Glaspell suggests both clarity of vision and the ability to bridge, to create by spanning and mixing various forms. But behind this "flower of New England" lies the history of her ancestors, "the men who made the laws that made New England." Yearning to break out of this mold, just as her plants sometimes go beyond their species and "go mad—that sanity mayn't lock them in," Claire seeks escape from the prison of the patriarchy, seldom better envisaged than it is here, as the set form, the hardened heritage of the "saints" of Puritanism who inflicted such dehumanizing laws and customs on women.

Claire is distracted; as she holds vigil for Breath of Life, her daughter, Elizabeth, who has spent most of her life in boarding schools and school vacations with Claire's sister Adelaide, arrives. As one who wishes to slip the bounds of forms, Claire is a most unlikely mother for Elizabeth, who at 17 is a mature conformist. While Claire wards off the embrace of this stranger, Elizabeth confides her wish to help her "produce a new and better kind of plant." Claire, haltingly reaching for the right words, tells her: "These plants—(*beginning flounderingly*) Perhaps they are less beautiful—less sound—than the plants from which they diverged. But they have found—otherness." She indicates the strange vine at the back of the greenhouse as one that had "crept a little way into—what wasn't." But the Edge Vine has now reverted to its original form, so Claire asks Dick to destroy it. Elizabeth declares it is wrong of Claire to play God just to change, not to improve, plants. Suddenly, Claire perceives in Elizabeth her Puritan ancestors; she uproots the Edge Vine and but for Harry's wresting it from her would strike Elizabeth with this traitor plant. Claire's estrangement resounds through her words: "To think that object ever moved my belly and sucked my breasts." Terrible as these words are, nothing less would so blatantly demonstrate Claire's commitment to what she calls "outness" and "otherness" and her refusal to be seduced by what she sees as her creations.

Act 2 opens in the late afternoon of the following day. That Claire has not been liberated by rejecting her creations is obvious; she appears alone in "a tower which is thought to be round but that does not complete the circle. The back is curved, then jagged lines break from that, and the front is a queer bulging window-. . . . The whole structure is as if given a twist by some terrific force—like something wrong." This obvious phallic symbol being both erose and under pressure suggests the "terrific force" may be Claire's own struggle to break out of the patriarchal prison, but the stage directions also emphasize her continuing confinement; she is "seen through the huge ominous window as if shut into the tower." The glass of the greenhouse repeats itself in the window, and both, by promoting a sense of distance, comment on the difficulty of representing women within traditional dramatic forms—as does the play's structure, which twice veers from comedy of manners to *drame*. The coercion to conform continues. Personifying conformity and femininity as defined by the male, Adelaide berates Claire, calling her experiments nonsensical. She prescribes a "cure": Claire must be a mother to her daughter and so cease to be unnatural, and she must become a consumer, not a creator: "Go to Paris and get yourself some awfully good-looking clothes."

But Claire is not Ann Herford, who can sublimate her own needs for those of a grown child. She calls out for Tom, her philosopher, and sends the others away. Earlier Claire had difficulty articulating what her work meant; now she searches for the words with which to ask Tom to pursue their relationship beyond the platonic, to express something that's "not shut up in saying." Although Claire suggests they might find "radiance," Tom refuses; she persists and once again the play breaks form as her words become poetry:

> I want to be;
> Do not want to make a rose or make a
>   poem—
> Want to lie upon the earth and know.
>   . . . . .
> But scratch a little dirt and make a flower;
> Scratch a bit of brain—something like a poem.

The conflicting sentiments here mirror Claire's conflicted state. The patriarchy tells her that as a woman she should "be," not do, yet her own consciousness pushes her "to make a flower / . . . [or] something like a poem." Rejected by Tom, Claire turns to her present lover, Dick. By now overwhelmed, she desires to disappear: "Anything—everything—that will let me be nothing!"

In act 3 the scene is again the greenhouse, where Harry pursues Dick with a revolver as the play careens toward farce. When Harry claims he wishes to show Claire "I've enough of the man in me to—" Claire tells him he is being ridiculous. In a stage direction charged with double meaning, Claire appropriates the phallic weapon—"taking the revolver from the hand she has shocked to limpness"—puts it out of sight, and becomes again the detached seeker of "outness" and "otherness" as she points to the men and says: "One—two—three. You-love-me. But why do you bring [your quarrel] out here?" Her attention belongs now to Breath of Life, which, unlike the Edge Vine, has gone on: "it is—out." Moving again into poetry, she speaks, even in her victory, with disillusionment:

> Out?
> You have been brought in.
> A thousand years from now, when you are but a
>   form too
>   long repeated
> Perhaps the madness that gave you birth will
>   burst again,
> And from the prison that is you will leap pent
>   queerness
> To make a form that hasn't been—
> To make a person new.
> And this we call creation.
> Go away!

Dick and Harry leave, but Tom, perceiving this Nietzschean overreacher to be on the verge of insanity, offers to keep her "from fartherness—from harm—safe." Claire, aghast that the person who might "be a gate" instead "fill[s] the place," places her hands around his throat, choking off his breath. As the others, alerted by the crash of breaking glass, rush in, Glaspell notes that "she has taken a step forward, past them all." The drama ends as Claire the creator sings "Nearer My God to Thee," not in subservience to the supreme patriarch but in acknowledgment of her own god-like potential.

Glaspell is not, of course, sanctioning murder; the act must be read symbolically. Only by daring to break the confines of the patriarchy, confines that may come disguised as the love that wishes to keep one "safe," can women imagine and create new ways of being. The daring with which the playwright approaches her topic matches the boldness with which she employs expressionist techniques to achieve a spectacularly effective enwrapment of style, subject, structure, symbol, image, and theme.

Unfortunately, the success of the Provincetown Theatre, of which Glaspell's plays were so large a part, was, to Cook, the sign of a spiritual failure; in 1922 he deemed the theater a mediocrity. He and Glaspell left for Greece. By the time Glaspell returned to America following Cook's death, the Provincetown had undergone changes in management and philosophy. The conventional comedy *The Comic Artist* (1928), on which she collaborated with her second husband, Norman Matson, was produced in London, the almost equally conventional *Alison's House* at the Civic Repertory Theatre. After these, Glaspell wrote no more plays. Perhaps she was wounded by the critics' outcry against *Alison's House* receiving the Pulitzer, but it is more likely she realized that while she was away she had quite literally lost her stage.

American theater owes a great debt to Susan Glaspell, whose dramatic talents as playwright, actor, and director exploded on the stage of the Provincetown Players along with Minnie Wright's preserves. The aftershocks continue today, for she dared envision and bring to life onstage her own New Women. These women experience their own anagnorsis, challenging and rejecting male-defined norms, including such concepts as woman's honor, abstract justice, and the male's right to dominate and control, while they move toward the formation of female community.

Dramatically, her innovations were challenging. The economy of stagecraft manifested in most of her settings, perhaps initially dictated by the scant resources of the group, became in time a symbolism that resounded throughout each drama. Her use of the absent woman demonstrated how an offstage story can be used onstage.

Finally, she used language itself in a new way—a way that continues to be misunderstood. C. W. E. Bigsby speaks about her "natural reticence,"[16] an evaluation not far removed from Isaac Goldberg's comments, in 1922, about her being "reticent, laconic." Goldberg notes that Glaspell is "largely the playwright of woman's selfhood," and he realizes that "this acute consciousness of self . . . begins with a mere sense of sexual differentiation."[17] Acute as his perception is, he is unable, as apparently is Bigsby, to realize that Glaspell is not imbuing her characters with any "natural reticence" of her own; rather, she works toward verisimilitude. Woman, even the rebellious woman, having been so long denied a voice in determining her own destiny, would initially be able to exercise a newfound voice only haltingly; her stammer arises from sexist oppression, from silencing. While Glaspell did not create a woman's discourse, she demonstrated the inadequacy of man's for her New Woman.

Twentieth-Century Feminist Foremothers

Rachel Crothers and Susan Glaspell were major forces in early-twentieth-century American drama. As a voice for the New Woman, Crothers explored feminist issues in a manner that marks her a worthy successor to Warren and Rowson; in her comedies she is a more than worthy successor to Mowatt. Glaspell, long held in O'Neill's shadow, is beginning, finally, to be recognized as a major force in reshaping the drama that brought American theater into the twentieth century. She, as much as O'Neill, pioneered a symbolic and expressionist drama on the stage. She deserves to be more widely known and to be known as much more than the author of *Trifles*, excellent as that play is.

Notes

1. A selection of suffrage plays has been complied by Bettina Friedl in *On to Victory: Propaganda Plays of the Woman Suffrage Movement* (Boston: Northeastern University Press, 1987).

2. Geraldine Maschio, "A Prescription for Femininity: Male Interpretation of the Feminine Ideal at the Turn of the Century," *Women and Performance: A Journal of Feminist Theory* 4, no. 1 (1988-89): 43; hereafter cited in the text as Maschio.

3. In *Notable Women in American Theatre: A Biographical Dictionary*, ed. Alice Robinson et al. (New York: Greenwood Press, 1989), 185, Liz Fugate gives 1870 as the birth date for Crothers appearing in the 1880 U.S. Census, but she notes that dates of 1871 and 1878 are also cited frequently; this volume is hereafter cited in the text as *Notable Women*. Lois Gottlieb gives the 1878

date in *Rachel Crothers* (Boston: Twayne Publishers, 1979), 1; hereafter cited in the text as Gottlieb. The 1870 date solves the apparent problem presented by the 14-year-old high school graduate going on her own to drama school in Boston.

4. Doris Abramson, "Rachel Crothers: Broadway Feminist," *Modern American Drama: The Female Canon,* ed. June Schlueter (Rutherford, N.J.: Fairleigh Dickinson University Press, 1990), 59; hereafter cited in the text as Abramson.

5. Mourning the debunking of these patriarchal constructions, George Jean Nathan in "Clinical Notes," *American Mercury* 19 (1930): 242, observed that "women have more and more ceased to be figures of man's illusion and more and more have become superficially indistinguishable from man himself in his less illusory moments. In sports, in business, in drinking, in politics, in sexual freedom, in conversation, in sophistication and even in dress, women have come closer and closer to men's level and, with the coming, the purple allure of distance has vamoosed."

6. Quoted by Cynthia Sutherland, "American Women Playwrights as Mediators of the 'Woman Problem,'" *Modern Drama* 21 (September 1978): 319; hereafter cited in the text as Sutherland.

7. It is true, however, that in several of her later plays Crothers opts for the traditional "happy" ending of marriage—or remarriage—for her protagonist.

8. Judith L. Stephens, "Gender Ideology and Dramatic Convention in Progressive Era Plays," *Performing Feminisms: Feminist Critical Theory and Theatre,* ed. Sue-Ellen Case (Baltimore: Johns Hopkins University Press, 1990), 286; hereafter cited in the text as Stephens.

9. Unfortunately, such was not the case. Crothers uses this very situation of a type of "sunshine morality" as the pivot of the plot of *Nice People* (1921), and the same kind of thinking that condemns Rhy in *The Three of Us* still leads critics of rape victims to ask: "What was she doing out at that hour?"

10. Ann may be responding more to a class issue than to her child's (assumed) needs. She asks Millicent: "Do you want to disgrace us? How any child of mine could even speak—even speak to such a—. Oh, the disappointment. Where's your pride?"

11. Helen Deutsch and Stella Hanau. *The Provincetown: A Story of the Theatre* (New York: Farrar and Rinehart, 1931), 16.

12. "'Murder, She Wrote': The Genesis of Susan Glaspell's *Trifles,*" Linda Ben-Zvi's insightful study of the relationship between Glaspell's news reporting and the creation of Trifles, appears in *Theatre Journal* 44 (May 1992): 141-62.

13. Susan Glaspell, *The Road to the Temple* (New York: Frederick Stokes, 1927), 255-56; hereafter cited in the text as *Road.*

14. Charlotte Perkins Gilman, *Man Made World: Our Androcentric Culture* (1911; reprint, New York: Johnson Reprint, 1971), 32, 35, 38, and 39.

15. Judith Lewis Herman, *Trauma and Recovery* (New York: Basic Books, 1992), 32.

16. C. W. E. Bigsby, *A Critical Introduction to Twentieth-Century American Drama, 1900-1940* (Cambridge: Cambridge University Press, 1982), 27.

17. Isaac Goldberg, *The Drama of Transition: Native and Exotic Playcraft* (Cincinnati: Stewart Kidd Company, 1922), 472-74.

PATRICIA R. SCHROEDER (ESSAY DATE 1996)

SOURCE: Schroeder, Patricia R. "Remembering the Disremembered: Feminist Realists of the Harlem Renaissance." In *Realism and the American Dramatic Tradition,* edited by William W. Demastes, pp. 91-106. Tuscaloosa: University of Alabama Press, 1996.

In the following essay, Schroeder discusses the work of African-American women playwrights during the Harlem Renaissance, pointing out that this was one of the first opportunities for such writers to present a realistic view of female African-American experience, focusing on such issues as gender roles in the African-American community, the impact of poverty, and reproductive freedom.

When Angelina Weld Grimké's realist play *Rachel* was first produced by the NAACP's Drama Committee in 1916, it became something of a cause célèbre in the African-American theatrical community. The program notes from the 1916 production, which proclaim the play as "the first attempt to use the stage for race propaganda"[1] provoked what one recent critic has called a "cultural war . . . [fought] over accurate depictions of the African-American community."[2] Central to this conflict over representation, which affected both female and male theatre practitioners and became one of the defining motifs of the Harlem Renaissance,[3] were the competing aesthetic theories of W. E. B. Du Bois and Alain Locke.[4]

For Du Bois, all art was propaganda. Defining a "Negro theatre" that would be centered in African-American experience and written by African Americans, Du Bois espoused "race" or "propaganda" plays that would depict racial discrimination realistically, demonstrate its detrimental consequences on worthy black Americans, and so prove to white audiences that African Americans deserved a chance at material success and social equality.[5] The other camp, led by Alain Locke, vehemently disagreed with this agenda, arguing that individual expression—art for its own sake—was the only appropriate goal of creative endeavor.[6] Together with Montgomery Gregory, and in direct reaction to the 1916 production of *Rachel,* Locke resigned from the NAACP Drama Committee and began to develop the alternative dramatic form that would become the hallmark of his soon-to-be-formed Howard Players: the folk play.[7] Focusing on the everyday experiences, customs, beliefs, traditions, music, and language of ordinary black people without emphasizing racial oppression, the folk plays of the 1920s were, in effect, an African-American-centered celebration of daily life in black communities, written primarily for black audiences.

Despite the heated controversy between these two intellectual leaders and the editorial barbs they launched at each other through the competing literary journals, *The Crisis* and *Opportunity,* Du Bois's propaganda plays and Locke's folk dramas shared some largely unrecognized common goals, not the least of which is a common reliance on stage realism. While class differences remained an issue (with Du Bois favoring genteel characters of bourgeois aspirations and Locke promoting working-class folk in their own milieu),[8] both critics saw the black-centered theatre as a place where the prevailing stage stereotypes of African Americans (the demeaning legacy of minstrel shows) could be replaced by representations of human beings. And since both Du Bois and Locke demanded accurate stage portrayals of the African Americans they knew offstage, both obviously accepted the mimetic power of theatre to mirror reality in an unmediated way. For playwrights of this era, before poststructuralism undermined our faith in realism's mimetic capabilities, stage realism, by approximating as closely as possible the life experienced in African-American communities, could vividly protest the oppression of its members (in propaganda plays) and also commemorate black culture (in folk plays).

Working within this dynamic African-American theatrical community of the period were a large number of women playwrights,[9] who faced all the racial tensions and aesthetic conflicts of their male counterparts, with the additional problems of depicting the largely effaced black female experience and of combating degrading sexual stereotypes as well as racial ones. This problem of stereotypical representation was an especially complex one for African-American women of the era. Both in popular culture and in literary and theatrical texts of the period, black women were routinely depicted as either stolid matriarchs or wanton whores, with "no equitable variations in between."[10] In a poignant 1925 essay on then current images of black women, Elise Johnson McDougald explained the psychological damage done to women who could not help but absorb the false but ubiquitous representations of them: "Even in New York, the general attitude of mind causes the Negro woman serious difficulty. She is conscious that what is left of chivalry is not directed at her. She realizes that the ideas of

beauty, built up in the fine arts, have excluded her almost entirely. Instead, the grotesque Aunt Jemimas of the streetcar advertisements, proclaim only an ability to serve, without grace or loveliness. Nor does the drama catch her finest spirit. She is most often used to provoke the mirthless laugh of ridicule; or to portray feminine viciousness or vulgarity not peculiar to Negroes. This is the shadow over her."[11] Given this cultural climate, both on and off the stage, it is clear that replacing stereotypical images of African-American women would be of paramount importance to these female playwrights. Realism, with its ability to present coherent and developing characters who are shaped by and respond to their environments, offered these dramatists a built-in opportunity to assert the creativity and humanity of black women.

While stereotypes of mammy and whore dominated representations of black women, the reality of African-American women's lives before the twentieth century had been all but erased from American history. There are, of course, multiple reasons for such oversight, ranging from poor record keeping by slave owners to a widespread politics of silence among black women determined to protect their privacy and middle-class status. Given this secrecy and silence surrounding African-American women's shared and individual histories, writing plays to reconstruct their lives was both challenging and important. As Barbara Christian has pointed out, the concept of remembering and reevaluating the past "could not be at the center of a narrative's [or a play's] revisioning of history until the obvious fact that African-Americans did have a history and culture was firmly established in American society";[12] without such factual background information, writers would lack the details necessary to impart authenticity to their works and audiences would lack a context in which to read or view. For these women playwrights of the Harlem Renaissance, therefore, a crucial first step in claiming the stage for a black feminist vision was to discover and depict the historical and cultural facts that black women had repressed or to which they had been denied access.

For this task, like the tasks of depicting oppression and overturning stereotypes, African-American women playwrights turned to realism. While their numerous plays dramatize subjects as varied as lynching, poor treatment of black war veterans, gender roles within the black community, and the debilitating effects of poverty, the explicitly feminist issues of reproductive freedom and motherhood appear repeatedly in their works, and will form the focal point for my analysis of their plays. For even within the confines of this one narrow topic, examples abound of black female playwrights turning to realism to protest racial discrimination, to correct degrading stereotypes, and to reclaim something of African-American women's unrecorded history.

An early and obvious example of such a play is Grimké's *Rachel,* which, as we saw above, sparked the furor over dramatic aesthetics that would become one defining element of the Harlem Renaissance. A clear-cut example of the propaganda play that Du Bois espoused, this realist drama takes place behind the fourth wall of the Loving family parlor. The Lovings are a respectable, middle-class family consisting of a mother, a son Tom, and a daughter Rachel. The title character is an ebullient teenager when we first meet her, devoted to her family and her education. Her dominant characteristics are a love for children (especially "the little black and brown babies") and a fervent desire someday to marry and raise a large family of her own.[13] As she matures into a young woman in the second and third acts, however, she learns that her father and an elder brother were killed by a lynch mob, and she suffers when her young adopted son is physically and verbally abused by a gang of white boys. Traumatized by this violent racism, Rachel refuses the marriage proposal of the man she loves, vowing never to marry and bring more black children into the world to be blighted by racial abuse.

In commenting on her motives for writing this play—which some contemporary reviewers saw as advocating genocide[14]—Grimké defines white women as her target audience and motherhood as the hook by which she would enlist their support in black women's causes: "If anything can make all women sisters underneath their skins, it is motherhood. If then I could make the white women of this country see, feel, understand just what effect their prejudice and the prejudice of their fathers, brothers, husbands, sons were having on the souls of the colored mothers everywhere and upon the mothers that are to be, a great power to affect public opinion would be set free and the battle would be half won."[15]

Motherhood is certainly a key issue of the play, and, in fact, a number of critics have complained that Grimké overloaded the play with excessive sentimentality on this topic. These commentators criticize Rachel's frequent effusions about babies and motherhood and the flowery language in which she habitually discusses them.[16]

Given Grimké's goal of enlisting white women in black women's causes, however, I am inclined to agree with Judith Stephens, who sees Grimké as *intervening* in the cultural code the play ostensibly espouses. Stephens writes: "In *Rachel,* Angelina Grimké threw the image of idealized motherhood back at white women in an attempt to make them see what meaning this so-called 'revered institution' might hold for black women. . . . In writing *Rachel,* Grimké used the sentimental language of the [era's] dominant gender ideology, which idealized motherhood, but the play does not support or concede to that ideology. Instead, it breaks dominant gender ideology by raising the issue of race and asking white women to consider what black mothers must face."[17]

Despite Grimké's avowed interest in engaging a white female audience, a number of recent critics have asserted, probably correctly, that she also sought a black audience "that needed to see an image of its members . . . as they wished themselves to be."[18] In order to protest the unfair treatment of blacks in a white-dominated society, Grimké consciously created characters to represent (in her words) "the best type of colored people."[19] These characters are middle-class paragons, conscientious about family, work, school, and upward mobility; they speak proper English; in short, they are clear-cut examples of the genteel models advocated by Du Bois.

Grimké's probable interest in engaging two audiences—a white one that needed to be shown the conditions of oppression and a black one that needed to see positive stage images of itself—led her on both counts to employ the conventions of realism. In a letter written about *Rachel,* Grimké mentions reading the realist plays of Henrik Ibsen and the naturalist dramas of August Strindberg and Gerhart Hauptmann.[20] Not surprisingly, she imported a number of their dramatic conventions into her own play. In addition to the fourth-wall set and developing characters already mentioned, Grimké structured her play according to a realistic causal logic: stories from the past and incidents occurring in the present combine to form an unbreakable chain of events that restricts Rachel's options and leads inexorably to her rejection of motherhood.

While partaking perhaps of more sentimentality and melodrama than current taste will accept as credible, Grimké's realist play did have a lasting impact on the black women playwrights who followed her. While "the stark realism and political nature" of *Rachel* startled many of Grimké's male contemporaries,[21] and while the debate over whether writing should be political or simply artistic continued to rage, *Rachel* defined playwriting as a powerful ideological tool for other black women playwrights of the Harlem Renaissance who followed Grimké's lead.

Grimké's influence on other playwrights can be seen as early as 1919, just three years after the original production of *Rachel*, when her close friend Mary P. Burrill published a realist, pro-birth control play in Margaret Sanger's *Birth Control Review*. Unlike Grimké, Burrill created characters who are neither genteel nor upwardly mobile. Instead, they are poor rural women trapped in an endless cycle of childbearing and poverty. What Burrill's *They That Sit in Darkness* shares with *Rachel*, however, is an interest in documenting the anguish of African-American motherhood, a protest agenda, and a realist dramatic form.

Like *Rachel, They That Sit in Darkness* employs the fourth-wall convention, depicting one of the two rooms in the Jasper family's overcrowded rural shack. The action concerns two women: Malinda Jasper, who is the mother of ten children, and her seventeen-year-old daughter Lindy, who is preparing to leave for Tuskegee Institute on a grant. Using a sort of documentary realism, the play depicts the typical events of a day in this mother and daughter's lives. The stark and dingy setting, Malinda's and Lindy's weariness as they struggle over a washtub and with the many unruly younger children, the lack of milk for the baby and food for the others, and Malinda's apparent weakness (she has recently delivered her tenth baby) all vividly illustrate the destitution under which the family suffers and counteract the notion prevalent in the era (and lingering into our own) that poverty is somehow deserved or can be overcome by a willingness to work.

The climax of the play comes with the entrance of Elizabeth Shaw, a white visiting nurse, who arrives to check on Malinda's heart condition. Their brief conversation about birth control is central to the play. When Nurse Shaw naively counsels Malinda to avoid hard work and future pregnancies, the following dialogue ensues:

MRS. JASPER: But whut kin Ah do—de chillern come!

MISS SHAW: You must be careful.

MRS. JASPER: *Be keerful!* Dat's all you nurses say! . . . Ah been keerful all Ah knows how but whut's it got me—ten chillern, eight living an' two daid! You gotta be telling me sumpin' bettertn dat, Mis' Liz'beth!

MISS SHAW (FERVENTLY): I wish to God it were lawful for me to do so! My heart goes out to you people that sit in darkness, having, year after year, children you are physi-

cally too weak to bring into the world— children that you are unable not only to educate but even to clothe and feed. Malinda, when I took my oath as a nurse, I swore to abide by the laws of the State, and the law forbids my telling you what you have a right to know![22]

This brief exchange manifests many of the conflicts of the play. The contrast in the two women's dialects, for instance, illustrates realistically the differences in class and education that accompany their difference in race. Further, Miss Shaw believes in the letter of the law; she has accepted the privileges her race, education, job, and access to information have afforded her, and will not violate this power structure to help Malinda control her reproductive destiny or her life. The fact that the state prevents health care professionals from providing information that would save women's lives—and that even Miss Shaw thinks they have a right to know—underscores the complex network of unseen authorities that conspire to maintain the darkness of impoverished lives.

The plot, like that of *Rachel*, is structured according to a realistic causality. Miss Shaw's refusal to share information with Malinda leads inevitably to Malinda's death. That the cycle will be endlessly repeated as long as birth control information is withheld is abundantly clear through Lindy's fate. Realizing that she cannot attend college as planned, Lindy relinquishes her dream of improving the family's condition and takes her mother's place as caretaker to the other children.

Burrill was also clearly attempting to refute racist and sexist images in her portrayal of the Jasper women, who defy the traditional stereotypes of black women. Malinda and Lindy are neither stoic maternal figures nor promiscuous whores. Furthermore, they are not passive victims, but actively seek ways out of their entrapment: Malinda wants birth control information and Lindy wants an education. In these two characters, Burrill has created positive images of black women who seek to change their lives; their inability to overcome their victimization is clearly portrayed as society's fault, not theirs.[23] Burrill emphasizes this point in her starkly naturalistic set, which illustrates the power of environment (both physical and social) to control destinies. With its realistic dialogue, naturalistic set, and the inevitable causality that leads to Malinda's death and the loss of Lindy's single opportunity, the play depends upon techniques of stage realism to denounce the law's enforcement of poverty and ignorance that, like the people they enchain, endlessly reproduce themselves. *They That Sit in Darkness* illustrates the strategic use of realism as a form of social criticism, as a way of documenting what is in order to suggest what should be.

Other women of the Harlem Renaissance followed the leads of Grimké and Burrill in writing propaganda plays about current issues like lynching and suffrage. Another group, however, chose to focus on African-American women of the past, writing history plays and dramatic recreations of the lost voices of their female ancestors. Both male and female playwrights of the period took this mission of recovering lost stories seriously and wrote dramas about the achievements of African-American historical figures, presenting them from an African-American viewpoint. Randolph Edmonds's *Nat Turner* (1935), May Miller's *Harriet Tubman* (1935), and Langston Hughes's *Emperor of Haiti* (1936) are all prominent examples of this genre.

Several women playwrights, however, wrote realist plays to reclaim African-American women's history in a general way, by depicting the conditions of those women about whom specific facts are unknown, unrecorded, or simply repressed as unspeakable. In several striking cases, African-American women playwrights turned to a story that, as Toni Morrison comments in her novel *Beloved,* "was not a story to pass on."[24] I refer to the story recounted in *Beloved* and depicted in several plays of the era, that of a mother's killing her child to protect it from a life of racial or sexual abuse.

Georgia Douglas Johnson's 1929 play, *Safe,* exemplifies this genre. Set in a small southern town in 1893, *Safe* presents a double action. Onstage, the plot centers on Liza Pettigrew, happily married and about to give birth to her first child. Offstage, although discussed by the characters and in part overheard by the audience, an angry mob lynches seventeen-year-old Sam, a polite neighbor boy, for slapping the face of a white man who had first struck him. These two events fuse when Sam is heard outside screaming for his mother and Liza's baby is born, identified as a son, and strangled by his distraught mother to keep him (in her words) "safe from the lynchers."[25]

As this summary reveals, *Safe* inherited both its protest agenda and its realist method from *Rachel* and *They That Sit in Darkness. Safe* further illustrates the mutually influential relationship between public issues (the lynching) and private tensions (Liza's maternal fears). Because this double plot skillfully interweaves the political and

the personal in a causal chain, the play defines lynching as "*both* a violent crime *and* a pervasive influence in daily life."[26] By bringing the chilling results of lynching into the Pettigrews' peaceful living room, Johnson protested the way racial violence hovered menacingly over even the joyful aspects of African-American domestic life—including the birth of a baby who (unlike Malinda's children) is eagerly awaited.

In addition to the anti-lynch message of this propaganda play, however, Johnson clearly illustrates the way motherhood was intertwined with racial oppression for African-American women. In explaining this connection, scholar Kathy Perkins has written that certain issues of the era "could only be expressed by a black woman. Neither the white nor the black male playwright could express the intense pain and fear a black woman experienced concerning her children—wondering, for instance, if the child she carried for nine months would be sold into slavery, or be a son who might one day be lynched."[27] While I hesitate to endorse the seeming essentialism of Perkins's statement (which implies that the conditions of African-American motherhood are unimaginable to others), within *Safe* Liza's despair does identify motherhood as something unique and terrible for black women of this historical period, a condition that reveals the inseparability of race, gender, and historical context in defining feminist issues.

As Perkins's comment above further suggests, this conflict within African-American motherhood is a particularly distressing legacy of slavery. When a child could be sold at an owner's whim, when a slave woman's behavior could be coerced by threats to her child, when a child was the result of rape, or when a child's inevitable slave status would only perpetuate the institution of slavery, motherhood became a profoundly vexed issue.[28] As a result, an emotionally overwrought mother might actually view infanticide as an act of love and protection, as Liza in *Safe* evidently did when faced with a lynch mob. Moving beyond the era of lynching, deeper into the historical past, playwright Shirley Graham explored the connections between motherhood, slavery, and infanticide in her powerful 1940 drama, *It's Morning.*[29]

Information about actual historical cases of infanticide among slaves is difficult to obtain. While historians like Eugene Genovese claim that slave abortions and infanticide were not a problem for slave owners because "the slaves . . . loved their children too much to do away with them,"[30] oral histories and court records suggest that the infanticide committed by Margaret Garner, the historical slave woman on whom Toni Morrison loosely based her protagonist Sethe in *Beloved,* was not unique.[31] While the handful of documented cases of slave infanticide certainly does not indicate a general trend, surviving slave narratives suggest that those mothers who killed their children acted out of love, motivated by "an understanding of the living death that awaited their children under slavery."[32]

But child killing may simply have been the most extreme example of a widespread, and of course undocumented, female slave resistance to the institution of slavery. Using actions ranging from sexual abstinence to abortion networks to infanticide, these women rejected "their vital economic function as breeders," an opposition with major political and economic implications for the slave owners.[33] After slavery was abolished, a politics of silence arose among black women regarding their past rebellious actions and their own sexuality, a "culture of dissemblance" designed for self-protection.[34] Events like infanticide, then, routinely left out of formal histories and seen in African-American oral tradition as "not a story to pass on," would clearly be of interest to a playwright bent on recovering African-American women's lost history.

Graham's *It's Morning,* the most obvious example of this genre, is set in a slave cabin on the last day of December, 1862.[35] Cissie, a slave mother, has just received word that her vivacious fourteen-year-old daughter, Millie, has been sold to a lascivious creditor. In response to Cissie's grief, Grannie Lou, the oldest slave on the plantation, recounts two stories to the group of slaves gathered in Cissie's cabin. First, she tells them that Cissie was once as lighthearted as her daughter, until an overseer vowed to break her will and did so with repeated rapes. Second, she narrates the tale of a queenly slave woman from Africa, noted for her strength in cutting down cane stalks, who lined up her three sons to watch the sunrise and beheaded them from behind—with one swoop of her cane knife—to prevent their being sold down river. Cissie overhears this last story and, at dawn on the next day (New Year's Day), kills Millie with a cane knife. The play ends with Cissie's proffering Millie's limp body to the horrified Yankee boy who arrives too late with the news that slavery has been abolished, suggesting that the sunrise framing him in the doorway, symbol of a new day dawning for the freed slaves, will never obliterate the ghastly atrocities on which slavery was built.

Despite this rather melodramatic symbolism at the end, the play, like *Rachel* and *They That Sit in Darkness,* depends on techniques of dramatic realism to counteract stereotypes. While Cissie's action can be seen as a mercy killing designed to spare Millie the life of degradation that Cissie herself has suffered, murdering her own child as a safeguard against sexual abuse effectively undermines Cissie's status as either nurturing mammy or loose woman. In recreating slave life onstage, however, Graham's realism serves another end, one distinct in both purpose and technique from that used by Grimké and Burrill twenty years earlier or by Johnson in her version of the Medea story. Instead of depicting present conditions to protest them, Graham's play dramatizes a past that has been suppressed. To accomplish this recreation of the forgotten past, Graham fused the cause-and-effect logic, realistic setting, and upstanding characters typical of propaganda plays with the dialect, oral stories, and music that characterize folk plays. Because of this innovative embedding of African rhythms and culture within a traditional Aristotelian structure, Elizabeth Brown-Guillory has described *It's Morning* as "a major breakthrough in African-American drama."[36]

Graham's attention to representing African-American slave culture faithfully is apparent from the beginning of the playtext. In the opening stage directions, the playwright comments that the diverse dialects in *It's Morning* are intentionally not uniform, but are meant to reflect the various African languages from which slave dialects evolved as well as the changes in pitch and volume that African Americans use to indicate changes in meaning. And by employing realism's linear causality, Graham elucidates the tragic and long-lasting consequences of sexual abuse, which range in this play from spiritual damage to murder.

Yet because of the folk elements incorporated into this conventionally realistic framework, the play offers some hope for cultural survival beyond that suggested by the rising sun of the conclusion. By depicting oral history in action, *It's Morning* makes explicit the importance of keeping the past alive through storytelling. Both Cissie's past and the legend of the noble African woman are communicated to the slave women and to the audience through Grannie Lou's unofficial history, a spoken tale. Despite their lack of formal documentation, Grannie's remembered truths are powerful: they explain Cissie's motives for killing Millie and provide a model (complete with choice of weapon) for the murder. To be sure, without Grannie Lou's oral history Cissie might never have taken her tragic action. However, in the context of the play, Grannie Lou's story emphasizes the heroism of the African mother and suggests the defiance and pride of black people who must use drastic measures to resist their enslavement. Furthermore, without such oral histories and without plays like this one, women like Cissie would be in the same straights as those Morrison described for her character Beloved: "Disremembered and unaccounted for, she cannot be lost because no one is looking for her" (p. 274). Combining a realistic structure with elements of folk drama, Graham could record some of the content of African-American oral history, embody its interactive form, document its authority, and restore voice to long-silenced African-American women.

Arguing convincingly about realism's inherent theoretical limitations, materialist feminists Judith Newton and Deborah Rosenfelt have stated that "literature and cultural production [do not] 'reflect' history in a simple mimetic moment. Since we live within myths and narratives about history, there can in fact be no reflections of it. Literature, rather, draws upon various ideological productions of history or discourses about history to make its own production."[37] Given the widely accepted poststructuralist mistrust of realism's claim to record offstage reality faithfully and objectively, this critique of mimetic representational strategies is hard to quarrel with. But when viewed in the context of the interlocking factors of race, gender, and social oppression faced by the female playwrights of the Harlem Renaissance era, realism was clearly a valuable instrument for protesting conditions as they were and for recording and acknowledging alternative versions of history. In fact, what these early black feminists did was exactly what Newton and Rosenfelt espouse: they questioned the established "productions of history" and replaced them with their own "discourses about history," borrowing realism's referential power to document abuse, to dispute degrading stereotypes, and to resurrect and preserve a facet of herstory that had been disremembered and unaccounted for. Arguing against the use of inherited conventions like realism for African-American feminists, Audre Lorde has stated that the master's tools will never dismantle the master's house.[38] These pioneering African-American realists, however, saw a sledgehammer lying in the master's yard and used it to their advantage. In so doing, they created in American drama a tradition unique to African-American

women and left a legacy that we residents of the postmodern cosmos would do well not to disremember.

Notes

1. Cited in Robert J. Fehrenbach, "An Early Twentieth-Century Problem Play of Life in Black America: Angelina Grimké's *Rachel*," in *Wild Women in the Whirlwind: Afra-American Culture and the Contemporary Literary Renaissance*, ed. Joanne M. Braxton and Andree Nicola McLaughlin (New Brunswick: Rutgers UP, 1990), pp. 89-106, at 91.

2. Wahneema Lubiano, "But Compared to What? Reading Realism, Representation, and Essentialism in *School Daze, Do the Right Thing*, and the Spike Lee Discourse," *Black American Literature Forum* 25 (1991): 263.

3. It is difficult to define the Harlem Renaissance (or the New Negro Renaissance, or the Negro Renaissance) with any precision, since both the name of this African-American aesthetic movement and the exact dates of its influence are currently under debate. "Harlem Renaissance" is the most familiar title, but scholars like Katana Hall (*Reclaiming the Legacy: An Afracentric Analysis of Selected Plays by African American Wimmin Playwrights, 1916-1930*, Ph.D. diss., Bowling Green State University, 1990) have correctly pointed out that this term devalues the contributions of such artists as Alain Locke and Georgia Douglas Johnson, who, like many other writers of the time, lived and worked outside New York (p. 28). Other critics challenge the dates usually assigned, which are based on the end of World War I in 1919 and the stock market crash in 1929. Abraham Chapman, for instance, contends that certain defining elements of Harlem Renaissance literature were recognizable as early as the mid-1910s in Claude McKay's poetry ("The Harlem Renaissance in Literary History," *CLA Journal* 11 [Sept. 1967]: 44-45), while several other scholars suggest extending the endpoint to coincide with the Harlem riots in 1935 or even into the civil rights era of the 1960s. For overviews of these controversies see Nathan Irvin Huggins, "Introduction," *Voices from the Harlem Renaissance* (New York: Oxford UP, 1976), pp. 3-10; Jay Plum, "Rose McClendon and the Black Units of the Federal Theatre Project: A Lost Contribution," *Theatre Survey* 33 (Nov. 1992): 144-53; and Cary D. Wintz, *Black Culture and the Harlem Renaissance* (Houston: Rice UP, 1988), p. 13.

Whatever the exact title and duration of this Renaissance, the decade of the 1920s saw the emergence of an African-American dramatic tradition that extended beyond the '20s and Harlem and to which both women and men contributed.

4. For a comprehensive overview of the Du Bois/Locke debate, see Samuel A. Hay, *African American Theatre* (Cambridge: Cambridge UP, 1994). This volume contains a discussion of Hay's work and the Du Bois/Locke debate in Bergesen and Demastes's essay on Baraka and August Wilson.

5. W. E. B. Du Bois, "Krigwa Little Theatre Movement," *The Crisis* 32 (1926): 134-36.

6. See Locke's comments about propaganda plays as cited in Huggins, *Voices from the Harlem Renaissance*, esp. pp. 312-13.

7. For details of Locke's reaction, see Leslie Catherine Sanders, *The Development of Black Theatre in America: From Shadows to Selves* (Baton Rouge: Louisiana State UP, 1988), p. 23.

8. The class bias of Du Bois's position has been well explained by Rebecca T. Cureau, "Toward an Aesthetic of Black/Folk Expression," in *Alain Locke: Reflections on a Modern Renaissance Man*, ed. Russell J. Linneman, pp. 77-90 (Baton Rouge: Louisiana State UP, 1982).

9. In 1987 Nellie McKay estimated that during the Harlem Renaissance eleven black women published twenty-one plays as compared to only a half-dozen black male playwrights; see "'What Were They Saying?': Black Women Playwrights of the Harlem Renaissance," in *The Harlem Renaissance Re-examined*, ed. Victor A. Kramer (New York: AMS Press, 1987), pp. 129-46. However, McKay's estimate has already been shown to be low, especially given the controversy over the ending date of the Renaissance; see Kathy Perkins, ed., *Black Female Playwrights: An Anthology of Plays Before 1950* (Bloomington: Indiana UP, 1989), p. 1. Furthermore, McKay's estimate does not include the many black women's plays that were performed in community schools, auditoriums, and churches, but never published; see her "Black Theater and Drama in the 1920s: Years of Growing Pains," *Massachusetts Review* (Winter 1987): 615-26.

10. Cynthia Belgrave, quoted in Elizabeth Brown-Guillory, *Their Place on Stage: Black Women Playwrights in America* (New York: Praeger, 1988), p. 107. For further examination of these and other persistent literary stereotypes of black women, see Barbara Christian, *Black Women Novelists: The Development of a Tradition, 1892-1976* (Westport, Conn.: Greenwood Press, 1980), pp. 10-19.

11. Elise Johnson McDougald, "The Task of Negro Womanhood," in *The New Negro: An Interpretation*, ed. Alain Locke (1925; rpt. New York: Arno, 1968), p. 370.

12. Barbara Christian, "'Somebody Forgot to Tell Somebody Something': African-American Women's Historical Novels," in *Wild Women in the Whirlwind*, p. 333.

13. Angelina Weld Grimké, *Rachel*, in *Black Theater, U.S.A.: Forty-five Plays by Black Americans, 1847-1974*, ed. James V. Hatch (New York: Free Press, 1974), p. 143.

14. See Gloria T. Hull, *Color, Sex, and Poetry: Three Women Writers of the Harlem Renaissance* (Bloomington: Indiana UP, 1987), p. 121, for a summary of these reviews.

15. Qtd. in Jeanne-Marie A. Miller, "Angelina Weld Grimké: Playwright and Poet," *CLA Journal* 21 (June 1978): 517.

16. See, for example, Hatch, ed., *Black Theater, U.S.A.*, p. 138; Fehrenbach, "Problem Play," p. 97; and Hull's summary of this response in *Color, Sex, and Poetry*, pp. 121-23.

17. Judith L. Stephens, "The Anti-Lynch Play: Toward an Interracial Feminist Dialogue in Theatre," *Journal of American Drama and Theatre* 2.3 (1990): 62.

18. Hatch, ed., *Black Theater. U.S.A.*, p. 137; see also Hull, *Color, Sex, and Poetry*, pp. 117-18.

19. Quoted in Miller, "Angelina Weld Grimké," p. 515.

20. In Fehrenbach, "Problem Play," pp. 95-96.

21. Freda L. Scott, "Black Drama and the Harlem Renaissance," *Theatre Journal* 37.4 (Dec. 1985): 429.

22. Mary P. Burrill, *They That Sit in Darkness*, in Perkins, ed., *Black Female Playwrights*, pp. 71-72.

23. McKay, "What Were They Saying," pp. 138-39.

24. Toni Morrison, *Beloved* (New York: Knopf, 1987), p. 274. Subsequent references are cited in the text.

25. Georgia Douglas Johnson, *Safe* (1929), in *Wines in the Wilderness: Plays by African American Women from the Harlem Renaissance to the Present*, ed. Elizabeth Brown-Guillory (Westport, Conn.: Greenwood Press, 1990), p. 32.

26. Judith L. Stephens, "Anti-Lynch Plays by African American Women: Race, Gender, and Social Protest in American Drama," *African American Review* 26 (Summer 1992): 332.

27. Perkins, ed., *Black Female Playwrights*, p. 2.

28. Darlene Hine and Kate Wittenstein, "Female Slave Resistance: The Economics of Sex," in *The Black Woman Cross-Culturally*, ed. Filomina Chioma Steady (Cambridge, Mass.: Schenkman, 1981), pp. 295-96.

29. While the Harlem Renaissance is usually seen as ending before 1940 (the date of Graham's play), she herself was involved in the artistic endeavors of the period and later married W. E. B. Du Bois. Furthermore, as my third note explains, the endpoint of the Harlem Renaissance is open to debate. More to the point of this chapter, *It's Morning* clearly inherited its dramatic conventions and thematic imperatives from Grimké and other writers of the Renaissance years, so I decided to include it in this discussion of feminist realists of the Harlem Renaissance.

30. Eugene Genovese, *Roll, Jordan, Roll: The World the Slaves Made* (New York: Random House, 1972), p. 497.

31. Raymond M. and Alice H. Bauer, for instance, quote five examples of documented slave infanticides in "Day to Day Resistance to Slavery," *Journal of Negro History* 27 (Oct. 1942): 388-419, as does Deborah Gray White in *Ar'n't I a Woman?: Female Slaves in the Plantation South* (New York: Norton, 1985), with little apparent overlap between the two sets of cases. For the details of documented cases of slave infanticide in the United States, see Bauer and Bauer, "Day to Day Resistance," pp. 416-18; Hine and Wittenstein, "Female Slave Resistance," pp. 291-95; B. A. Botkin, ed., *Lay My Burden Down: A Folk History of Slavery* (Athens: U of Georgia P, 1989 rpt. of 1945 edition), p. 54; Gerda Lerner, ed., *Black Women in White America: A Documentary History* (New York: Random House, 1973), pp. 38, 61-62; and White, *Ar'n't I a Woman?* pp. 87-89.

32. Hine and Wittenstein, "Female Slave Resistance," p. 295.

33. Hine and Wittenstein, "Female Slave Resistance," p. 296.

34. Darlene Clark Hine, "Rape and the Inner Lives of Black Women in the Middle West: Preliminary Thoughts on the Culture of Dissemblance," *Signs* 14 (Summer 1989): 915.

35. Throughout this discussion, I refer to the version of *It's Morning* printed in Perkins's anthology *Black Female Playwrights* and housed (according to Perkins's bibliography) in the Fisk University Library special collection, Nashville, Tenn. A different version of the same play with the slightly different title *It's Mornin'*

appears in Elizabeth Brown-Guillory's anthology *Wines in the Wilderness*. While Brown-Guillory cites no manuscript, she evidently bases her version of the play on the 1940 Yale University Theatre production (p. 83). In the Yale version, the story line, many of the characters, and many of the speeches are identical to those in the Fisk version. However, the Yale version dramatizes two things that occur offstage in the version under discussion: the visit of the slave owner, Mrs. Tilden, to Cissie's cabin, and the New Year's party Cissie gives so that Millie may enjoy one final day of happiness.

36. Brown-Guillory, *Wines in the Wilderness*, p. 82. Her comment on the play refers to the Yale version rather than to the one under discussion. However, since her statement refers to elements common to both plays (like Grannie Lou's status as voodoo woman and Graham's use of music), it is equally relevant to the version under discussion.

37. Judith Newton and Deborah Rosenfelt, "Introduction: Toward a Materialist-Feminist Criticism," in *Feminist Criticism and Social Change: Sex, Class, and Race in Literature and Culture*, ed. Newton and Rosenfelt (New York: Methuen, 1985), p. xxiii.

38. Audre Lorde, "The Master's Tools Will Never Dismantle the Master's House," in *This Bridge Called My Back: Writings by Radical Women of Color*, ed. Cherríe Moraga and Gloria Anzaldúa, pp. 98-101 (New York: Kitchen Table Press, 1981).

ASIAN AMERICAN INFLUENCES

NING YU (ESSAY DATE FALL 1996)

SOURCE: Yu, Ning. "Fanny Fern and Sui Sin Far: The Beginning of an Asian American Voice." *Women and Language* 19, no. 2 (fall 1996): 44-47.

In the following essay, Yu compares the work of Sui Sin Far with Fanny Fern, noting that Fern provided a model upon which Sui Sin Far developed her literary voice and critique of racism, establishing a female literary tradition followed by subsequent Asian American artists such as Maxine Hong Kingston and Judy Syfer.

The lack of a role model, as Alice Walker points out, "is an occupational hazard for the artist, simply because models in art, in behavior, in growth of spirit and intellect—even if rejected—enrich and enlarge one's view of existence" (4). The first Chinese American fiction writer, Edith Maude Eaton, or Sui Sin Far, had to cope with this "hazard" when she started her literary career near the turn of the century. Born in 1865 to an English father and a Chinese mother, Edith Maude Eaton grew up in an era notorious for its "violent anti-Chinese sentiment and legally sanctioned discriminatory policies" (Falvey, backcover). Taking "tremendous pride" in her Chinese heritage (Ammons 107), Eaton early decided to "write

wrongs in order to right them" (Ling 32), defying "the stereotype of the passive, impassive, fragile, inscrutable 'Oriental,'" and refusing to "take on the identity assigned her by racist whites" (Ammons 107). Anticipating "her spiritual great grand-daughter Maxine Hong Kingston by three-quarters of a century, she creates herself as a fighter" (Ammons 107). As the first Chinese American "woman warrior," Eaton had to address both the racial injustice she and her people suffered daily and the bias and misunderstanding she faced as an independent young woman struggling against two equally male dominant, though otherwise different, cultures. Yet such an ideal double voice was not available to her, and the voice of Chinese Americans, male or female, was rather effectively silenced by the hegemonic white male culture.

The only American text written by someone of Chinese descent before Eaton, Lee Yan Phou's *When I Was a Boy in China*, describes "Chinese sports, games, food, clothing, folk tales, and ceremonies" (Kim 25) but does not address Chinese American situations. As one of the dozen elite students sent by the Chinese government to the U. S. for a Western education, Lee knew nothing about the ordinary Chinese American's life on the margin. Neither Lee's life nor his book could help a young female from a poor mixed race family find her position in literary arenas of late-nineteenth-century America.

However, unable to find a model in her own race, Eaton searched among contemporary authors of her own gender for a voice that could be adopted and adapted for her own purpose; she found it in Sara Payson Willis Parton, or Fanny Fern, a pioneer woman author who "advocated and practiced—both in her life and in her writing—individualism for women" (Warren 306). Fanny Fern was already a household name before her major work *Ruth Hall* was published in 1854. According to Nancy A. Walker, Fanny Fern was "the most widely reprinted and most highly paid newspaper columnist of the 1850s" (1). Nathaniel Hawthorne used to dismiss his contemporary popular women authors as the "damned mob of scribbling women," but he modified his harsh criticism after reading *Ruth Hall*. He confessed in a letter to his publisher:

> In my last, I recollect, I bestowed some vituperation on female authors. I have since been reading "Ruth Hall"; and I must say I enjoyed it a good deal. The woman writes as if the devil was in her; and that is the only condition under which a woman ever writes anything worth reading.
>
> (I, 78)

ON THE SUBJECT OF...

DJUNA BARNES (1892-1982)

Born in 1892 in Cornwall-on-Hudson, New York, Barnes began writing at an early age to support her mother and three brothers. She contributed frequently to New York City newspapers and to such magazines as *Smart Set* and *Vanity Fair*. After nearly two decades of publishing poetry, fiction, and drawings, Barnes published her landmark novel, *Nightwood*, in 1936. Both the form and the content of *Nightwood* were informed by her years, first among the bohemian writers in Greenwich Village and, after 1920, among the expatriate artists living in Paris. Barnes and many of her peers, including James Joyce, Gertrude Stein, and Ezra Pound, have made the period famous for their radical experimentation with language and literary convention. The expatriate community also offered an open-mindedness about sexuality unavailable in the United States; a large number of the women publicly identified as lesbian or bisexual, and many of the men were gay. Barnes's own sexuality, as well as her frank and, at the time, ground-breaking, portrayal of homosexuality in her works has informed much of the critical assessment of her writing. After publishing *Nightwood*, Barnes experienced a series of personal crises, including failed relationships, financial difficulties, and alcoholism. She moved into a small apartment in New York's Greenwich Village, where she remained secluded for the rest of her life. Barnes continued to write, but not prolifically, and it took her years to complete her obscure verse drama, *The Antiphon* (1958).

Indeed, Fanny Fern expanded the genre of "domestic novel" beyond the closure of "marriage plot," claimed her "own language as a precondition of autonomy, and thus made a "major contribution of American fiction" (Walker 62). She is a major figure in her "own historical moment" and today's "reevaluation of women's literary history" (Walker 40). It is small wonder that young Eaton should choose Fanny Fern as a role model when embarking on her literary endeavor.

The affinity between Eaton and Parton is too striking for one not to assume that Eaton deliberately emulated Parton: like Parton's flowery pen name, Fanny Fern, Eaton's pseudonym, Sui Sin Far, is also derived from a plant; it is a transliteration of the Chinese word for narcissus (literally, "water immortal flower").[1] Moreover, Parton's first collection of essays is entitled *Fern Leaves from Fanny's Portfolio*, while Eaton's autobiographical essay is called "Leaves from the Mental Portfolio of an Eurasian." Although in her *Between Worlds* Professor Amy Ling anticipates me in noticing the similarity between the two "flowery" titles, the focus of her book requires her to refrain from discussing the affinity between the two in any length or depth. I wish to argue in this paper that from a major voice among America's early feminist writers, Sui Sin Far, the first Asian American fiction writer, has adapted stylistic tactics that literary women use to negotiate a space for their own voices within an oppressive and hegemonic patriarchal discourse.

Feminist critics have identified two major tactics in women's writing. Sometimes women authors would declare open warfare on the dominant discourse and choose "to assume the symbolic armor, to name the law and to attack it using the same law" (Jardine 231). Sometimes they would "engage in guerrilla tactics," using irony, indirection and understatement "to vitiate the assertions in the text" (Cheung 80). Both ploys can be found in Fanny Fern's writing. For instance, in her "Hints to Young Wives," Fanny Fern launches a frontal attack on the conventional code of behavior imposed on a married woman. She begins the essay with a sketch of a young wife trying hard to live up to the expectations of the patriarchal ideology that has been taught to her as the "gospel truth" (224). The young woman stands at the front door to welcome her husband home after work, and she "chases round after the boot-jack; warms his slippers and puts 'em on" because she "imagines that's the way to preserve his affection" (224). At this moment Fanny Fern the narrator steps in with a sharp comment: "Preserve a fiddlestick! The consequence is, he's sick of the sight of her . . ." (224). Fanny Fern winds up her short piece with an episode from her own life. Like the imaginary young wife in the sketch, Fanny Fern was once also such a "[p]oor little innocent fool" who one day, while obediently mending her husband's coat despite "a crucifying headache," found in the pocket a love-letter from her husband to her dress-maker. Then she told herself, and by extension to the imaginary young wife and all the married women who read her works, "'*F-a-n-n-y F-e-r-n! If you—are—ever—such—a—confounded fool again'—and I wasn't.*" Here Fanny Fern is at once identifying and subverting the dominant discourse by adopting an authoritative voice to challenge the authority of the patriarchal ideology. Fanny Fern first singles out the rationale that a husband's affection should be preserved, and then she shows that the affection between husband and wife is mutual and the forced submissiveness of the wife spoils the husband and destroys rather than preserves the affection.

Such a frontal attack can be found in Sui Sin Far's autobiographical essay as well. Although Sui Sin Far is known for her satire on the gender bias practiced in both American and Chinese cultures, the following example demonstrates her skillful adaptation of Fanny Fern's direct tactics in an attack against racist prejudice. Working as a stenographer near one of the five Great Lakes at the turn of the century, she tried to avoid revealing her racial background "in a Middle West town" where people held "strong prejudices against [her] mother's countrymen" (905). Yet, one day, at a dinner party including her new employer, landlady and a few other white colleagues, the following conversation ensued:

> My employer shakes his rugged head. "Somehow or other," says he, "I cannot reconcile myself to the thought that the Chinese are humans like ourselves. They may have immortal souls, but their faces seem to be so utterly devoid of expression that I cannot help but doubt."
>
> "Souls," echoes the town clerk. "Their bodies are enough for me. A Chinaman is, in my eyes, more repulsive than a nigger."
>
> "They always give me such a creepy feeling," puts in the young girl with a laugh.
>
> "I wouldn't have one in my house," declares my landlady.
>
> (905)

At this juncture, Eaton's employer noticed her silence and asked her opinion about the issue. Eaton courageously confronted the prejudice against her race: "Mr. K., the Chinese people may have no souls, no expression on their faces, be altogether beyond the pale of civilization, but whatever they are, I want you to understand that I am—I am a Chinese" (906). Here Eaton uses her opponents' "law" against that "law" itself. Judging from Eaton's facial features her employer included her into the "us" in his attack of the

Chinese as the "other," yet by revealing her racial background Eaton exposed the senselessness of the physical, psychological and spiritual distinctions the white man drew between the "us" and "other." Professor Amy Ling has accurately summed up Sui Sin Far's frontal attack on racism as "sincere and earnest, straightforward, and purposeful [with a mission] to right wrongs by writing them" (*Between Worlds* 32). I venture to suggest here that the sincere and earnest frontal attack against social wrongs is a traditional and powerful weapon of the American writing women.

Another weapon that Fanny Fern and Sui Sin Far shared is irony. Fanny Fern uses irony and indirection, or what Cheung calls the "guerrilla tactics," in "A Chapter on Literary Women" to satirize Colonel Van Zandt's male chauvinist prejudice against women. The female narrator (probably Fern) feigns surprise when she first hears of the Colonel's plan to search for a wife, and then points out the conflict between such a plan and the Colonel's "central" position in the patriarchal world:

> Want a wife, do you? I don't see but your buttons, and strings, and straps, are all tip-top. Your laundress attends to your wardrobe, your *hotel de maitre* to your appetite, you've nice snug quarters at the——House, plenty of 'fine fellows' to drop in upon you, and what in the name of the gods do you want of a 'wife?'
>
> (*Fern Leaves* 178)

At the first glance, the woman narrator seems to embrace and reinforce the centrality of the male by assigning the wife, or any woman, the servile roles of the cook, the seamstress, the laundress and housemaid. Yet she sets up this male-centered world picture only to subvert it through the Colonel's own words. His response to her questions reveals that his central position in the domestic world is self-claimed and the true source for his need to centralize the male self is, ironically, intellectual inferiority:

> I should desire my wife's thoughts and feelings to centre in me,—to be content in the little kingdom where I reign supreme,—to have the capacity to appreciate me, but not brilliancy enough to outshine me, or to attract 'outsiders'.
>
> (*Fern Leaves* 178)

Colonel Van Zandt's celebration of the male's central position in the little domestic kingdom as well as the larger outside world is based on suppressing the woman, forcing her "to be content" so that he could "reign supreme," to be modest so that she wouldn't "outshine" him, to be isolated so that the outsiders couldn't see her innate superiority.

Sui Sin Far is equally skillful in her use of ironic satire. In "Mrs. Spring Fragrance," the titular story of her collected works, Sui Sin Far also satirizes the false superiority that male-dominant culture assigns to man. Writing to her husband at home in Seattle while she is visiting San Francisco, Jade Spring Fragrance begins her letter in an exaggerated tone that seems to conform to but actually undermines the male-centered culture: "GREAT AND HONORED MAN,—Greeting from your plum blossom, who is desirous of hiding herself from the sun of your presence for a week of seven days more." She winds up the letter in equally inflated formality: "I continue for ten thousand times ten thousand years Your ever loving and obedient woman, Jade." (*Mrs. Spring Fragrance* 6). The letter's ironic tone is made clear by the context in which it is written. Through out the story Jade Spring Fragrance is presented as superior to her husband in intelligence, language skills, literary imagination, artistic taste, cultural sophistication and social understanding and involvement. Yet in the letter she is playing the role of a submissive wife who basks in the superior male sunshine of her husband. Although a man of gentle heart, Mr. Spring Fragrance is slow-witted if not plainly dumb. He derives his value as a literary figure from his wife and through out the story he is referred to as Mr. Spring Fragrance (Spring Fragrance is a typical first name for a Chinese girl but an unlikely last name for a man) rather than Mr. Sing Yook, which is his "business name." It is also worth noting that in the letter, the "loving obedient" woman simply informs her "GREAT AND HONORED MAN," but does not ask for his permission, as the cultural code requires and the formality of the letter suggests, that she is going to stay in San Francisco for another week.

However, Sui Sin Far improves rather than slavishly imitates Fanny Fern's irony. To meet the challenge of defending both women and Chinese Americans, Sui Sin Far gives her irony a double-edge so that it undercuts not only the male-chauvinist fantasy but also the white supremacist hypocrisy, furnishing her heroine with an effective weapon to expose some Americans' self-righteous claim that America is China's protector. Mrs. Spring Fragrance tells her husband in the same letter about her first encounter with one of China's "protectors" in San Francisco:

> Mrs. Samuel Smith, an American lady, known to my cousin, asked for my accompaniment to a magniloquent lecture the other evening. The subject was "America, the Protector of China!" It was most exhilarating, and the effect of so much expression of benevolence leads me to beg of you

to forget to remember that the barber charges you one dollar for a shave while he humbly submits to the American man a bill of fifteen cents. And murmur no more because your honored elder brother, on a visit to this country, is detained under the roof-tree of this great Government instead of under your own humble roof. Console him with the reflection that he is protected under the wing of the Eagle, the Emblem of Liberty. What is the loss of ten hundred years or ten thousand times ten dollars compared with the happiness of knowing oneself so securely sheltered? all of this I have learned from Mrs. Samuel Smith, who is as brilliant and great of mind as one of your own superior sex.

(7)

Sui Sin Far's contrastive use of exaggeration ("magniloquent," "most exhilarating," "the loss of ten hundred years or ten thousand times ten dollars") and understatement ("forget to remember," "murmur no more") reveals the wide gap between the harsh reality in Chinese American life and the white supremacist fantasy of America as a godlike protector of China. Like the centrality of Fern's Colonel Van Zandt, America's role of China's protector is self-claimed. The source of both evils is the same inflated ego whose rampant growth depends on putting down others to claim a false superiority. Both edges of Sui Sin Far's ironic dagger meet to form a sharp point: "[A]ll this I learned from Mrs. Samuel Smith, who is as brilliant and great of mind as one of your own superior sex."

At an early stage of her literary career, Sui Sin Far was able to develop a double voice that challenges both racism and male dominance. Her double voice is necessitated by her dual identity as minority and woman. She is a cultural exile, someone "who is capable of invoking or experiencing two realities simultaneously" (Shih 66). As a woman, Sui Sin Far has access to a rich legacy from the sisterhood of women authors who write wrongs to right wrongs; as a minority woman, she has the opportunity and the need to use women's tactics in a new field, where she gives women's irony an added edge. Because of her creative use of women author's tradition in the field of Asian American literature, Sui Sin Far's voice of strong frontal attack and tone of feminist irony are echoed not only in Maxine Hong Kingston's "On Discovery" but also in Judy Syfer's "I Want a Wife."

Notes

1. Amy Ling translated *Sui Sin Far* as "water fragrance flower." But the Chinese character *xian*, or *sin* in Eaton's transliteration, means "immortal," while the Chinese word for "fragrance" is *xiang*. For Professor

Ling's translation of Eaton's pseudonym see *Between Worlds: Women Writers of Chinese Ancestry*, New York: Pergamon Press, 1990; 41.

References

Ammons, Elizabeth. "Audacious Words: Sui Sin Far's *Mrs. Spring Fragrance*." *Conflicting Stories: American Women Writers at the Turn of the Century*. By Ammons. New York: Oxford University Press, 1991, 105-20.

Cheung, King-kok. *Articulate Silences: Hisaye Yamamoto, Maxine Hong Kingston, Joy Kogawa*. Ithaca, New York: Cornell University Press, 1993.

Fern, Fanny (Sara Willis Parton). *Ruth Hall and Other Writings*. Joyce W. Warren ed. New Brunswick, NJ: Rutgers University Press, 1986.

Hawthorne, Nathaniel. *Letters to William Ticknor, 1851-1869*. C. E. Frazer-Clark, Jr. ed., 2 vols. Newark, NJ: Carteret Book Club, Inc., 1972.

Jardine, Alice. "Pre-texts for the Transatlantic Feminist." *Yale French Studies* 62 (1981): 220-36.

Ling, Amy. *Between Worlds: Women Writers of Chinese Ancestry*. New York: Pergamon Press, 1990.

Shih, Shu-mei. "Exile and Intertextuality in Maxine Hong Kingston's *China Men*." In James Whitlark and Wendell Aycock eds.. *The Literature of Emigration and Exile*. Lubbock, Texas: Texas Tech University Press, 1994; 65-77.

Sui Sin Far. *Mrs. Spring Fragrance*. Catherine Falvey ed. Albany: New College and University, Inc., 1994.

———. "Leaves from the Portfolio of an Eurasian." In Paul Lauter et al. eds. *The Health Anthology of American Literature* (second edition) Vol. 2. Lexington, MA: D. C. Heath and Company, 1994, 901-910.

Syfer, Judy. "I Want a Wife." *Ms*. December 1971.

Walker, Alice. *In Search of Our Mothers' Gardens: Womanist Prose*. New York: Harcourt Brace Jovanovich, 1983.

Walker, Nancy A. *Fanny Fern*. New York: Twayne Publisher, 1993.

Warren Joyce W. *Fanny Fern: An Independent Woman*. New Brunswick, NJ: Rutgers Univ. Press, 1992.

FURTHER READING

Criticism

Abramson, Doris. "Rachel Crothers: Broadway Feminist." *Modern American Drama: The Female Canon* (1990): 55-65.

Discussion of Crothers as a feminist playwright.

Bair, Deirdre. "Simone de Beauvoir: Politics, Language, and Feminist Identity." *Yale French Studies*, no. 72: 149-62.

Examines Beauvoir's views on political action in the context of her philosophy and views on feminist theory.

Barbeito, Patricia Felisa. "'Making Generations' in Jacobs, Larsen, and Hurston: A Genealogy of Black Women's Writing." *American Literature* 70, no. 2 (June 1998): 365-96.

Theorizes that the lineage of black women's writing places an immense significance on the procreative nature of the black female body, and that this image shapes the work of Harriet Jacobs, Nella Larsen, and Zora Neale Hurston in very distinct ways.

Calder, Jenni. "World War and Women—Advance and Retreat." In *War and the Cultural Construction of Identities in Britain*, edited by Barbara Korte and Ralf Schneider, pp. 163-82. Amsterdam, Netherlands: Rodopi, 1994.

Offers a brief history of women during the world wars, noting the ways in which each war redefined notions of femininity and the challenges faced by women.

Flores, Yolanda. Introduction to *The Drama of Gender: Feminist Theatre by Women of the Americas*, pp. 1-20. New York: Peter Lang, 2000.

Studies interactions between female playwrights and the development of theater and feminist literary theory in the works of women writers of the Americas, noting the literary and historical context of Latina and African-American women playwrights.

Gubar, Susan. "'This Is My Rifle, This Is My Gun': World War II and the Blitz on Women." In *Behind the Lines: Gender and the Two World Wars*, edited by Margaret Randoph Higonnet, Jane Jenson, Sonya Michel, and Margaret Collins Weitz, pp. 227-59. New Haven, Conn.: Yale University Press, 1987.

Contends that the literature written by women during World War II had more to do with sexual antagonism directed toward women rather than with the war itself, as reflected in female literary works that depict the ruin of their lives and communities during this time.

Hebble, Susan Morrison. "Women Writers of the Harlem Renaissance." In *The History of Southern Women's Literature*, edited by Carolyn Perry and Mary Louise Weaks, pp. 298-308. Baton Rouge: Louisiana State University Press, 2002.

Provides an overview of women writers associated with the Harlem Renaissance, theorizing that the movement's focus on race and racial identity actually served to suppress issues of gender and sexism in the work of African-American female writers.

Higonnet, Margaret R. "Realism: A Feminist Perspective." In *The Powers of Narration*, edited by Gerald Gillespie and André Lorant, pp. 267-75. Tokyo, Japan: International Comparative Literature Association, 1991.

Argues that nineteenth-century female writers such as George Sand have been wrongly excluded from literary realist classifications, and that Sand's writings exemplify the ways in which women authors use and deviate from the conventions of literary realism to create a unique female perspective.

Hull, Gloria T. *Color, Sex, and Poetry: Three Women Writers of the Harlem Renaissance*. Bloomington, Ind.: Indiana University Press, 1987, 240 p.

Includes essays on the subjects of race, gender, and poetry during the Harlem Renaissance, with detailed discussion of works by Alice Dunbar-Nelson, Angelina Weld Grimké, and Georgia Douglas Johnson.

Keyssar, Helen. "Rites and Responsibilities: The Drama of Black American Women." In *Feminine Focus: The New Women Playwrights*, edited by Enoch Brater, pp. 226-40. New York: Oxford University Press, 1989.

Offers analysis of Angelina Weld Grimké's Rachel, *including discussion of the play's diverse range of opinions and views, including the celebratory.*

Lesinska, Zofia P. *Perspectives of Four Women Writers on the Second World War: Gertrude Stein, Janet Flanner, Kay Boyle, and Rebecca West.* New York: Peter Lang, 2002, 189 p.

A study of various lesser-known texts by female authors that respond to World War II and its accompanying political turmoil.

Lucky, Crystal J. "Black Women Writers of the Harlem Renaissance." In *Challenging Boundaries: Gender and Periodization,* edited by Joyce W. Warren and Margaret Dickie, pp. 91-106. Athens: University of Georgia Press, 2000.

A comparative analysis of women writers during the Harlem Renaissance, calling for a reevaluation of their works in the context of gender studies.

Marcus, Laura. "Virginia Woolf and the Hogarth Press." In *Modernist Writers and the Marketplace,* edited by Ian R. Willison, Warwick Gould, and Warren Chernaik, pp. 124-50. New York: Macmillan, 1996.

A brief overview of Woolf's history with the Hogarth Press, stressing her concern with experimental freedom and reaching a sympathetic readership.

Noe, Marcia. "The New Woman in the Plays of Susan Glaspell." In *Staging a Cultural Paradigm: The Political and the Personal in American Drama,* edited by Barbara Ozieblo and Miriam López-Rodríguez, pp. 149-62. Brussels, Belgium: Peter Lang, 2002.

Studies the figure of the "new woman" in the plays written by Glaspell between 1914 and 1922.

Oles, Carol Hilda Raz. "The Feminist Literary Movement." In *Poetry after Modernism,* edited by Robert McDowell, pp. 1-36. Brownsville, Oreg.: Story Line Press, 1998.

Survey of feminist poetry from the 1960s and 1970s, including the works of Adrienne Rich, Sylvia Plath, Nikki Giovanni, Audre Lorde, and Alice Walker.

St. Germain, Amos. "The Flowering of Mass Society: An Historical Overview of the 1920s." In *Dancing Fools and Weary Blues: The Great Escape of the Twenties,* edited by Lawrence R. Broer and John D. Walther, pp. 13-44. Bowling Green, Ohio: Bowling Green State University Press, 1990.

Provides a social, historical, and cultural overview of life in the United States during the 1920s.

Schroeder, Patricia B. "Realism and Feminism in the Progressive Era." In *The Cambridge Companion to American Women Playwrights,* edited by Brenda Murphy, pp. 31-46. New York: Cambridge University Press, 1999.

Argues that many feminist playwrights in the Progressive Era used stage realism to highlight feminist issues, in contrast to the prevailing critical and academic view that realism on the stage was fundamentally incompatible with feminist interests.

Schofield, Mary Anne. "Underground Lives: Women's Personal Narratives, 1939-45." In *Literature and Exile,* edited by David Bevan, pp. 121-48. Amsterdam, Netherlands: Rodopi, 1990.

Maintains that personal narratives are fundamental in gaining an understanding of feminist theory since they present and are grounded in the real-life experiences of women writers.

Schweik, Susan. *A Gulf So Deeply Cut: American Women Poets and the Second World War.* Madison, Wis.: University of Wisconsin Press, 1991, 385 p.

Collection of essays on notable women poets writing during and about World War II. Includes detailed analysis of Muriel Rukeyser's Letter to the Front *and works by Gwendolyn Brooks, H. D., Elizabeth Bishop, and others.*

Schweizer, Bernard. *Rebecca West: Heroism, Rebellion, and the Female Epic.* Westport, Ct.: Greenwood Press, 2002, 160 p.

Comprehensive appraisal of West's writings, drawing attention the epic quality of her works.

Susag, Dorothea M. "Zitkala-Sa (Gertrude Simmons Bonnin): A Power(full) Literary Voice." *Studies in American Indian Literature* 5, no. 4 (winter 1993): 3-24.

Analysis of three autobiographical essays by Zitkala-Sa published in the Atlantic Monthly *in 1900, noting that these works reveal a powerful feminine and ethnic point of view.*

Tylee, Claire M. "'Despised and Rejected': Censorship and Women's Pacifist Novels of the First World War, 1916-18." In *The Great War and Women's Consciousness: Images of Militarism and Womanhood in Women's Writings, 1914-64,* pp. 103-29. New York: Macmillan, 1990.

Survey of war literature in England during World War I, noting that many novels written during this period avoided the subject of war altogether, while others were censored because of their pessimism about the conflict.

Wall, Cheryl A. *Women of the Harlem Renaissance.* Bloomington, Ind.: Indiana University Press, 1995, 246 p.

Includes essays on the Harlem Renaissance in general, as well as specific articles focusing on the works of Jessie Redmon Fauset, Nella Larsen, and Zora Neale Hurston, and a bibliography of writings by women writers during the Harlem Renaissance.

Williams, Deborah Lindsay. "Sisterhood and Literary Authority in *The House of Mirth, My Ántonia,* and *Miss Lulu Bett.*" In *Not In Sisterhood: Edith Wharton, Willa Cather, Zona Gale, and the Politics of Female Authorship,* pp. 87-123. New York: Palgrave, 2001.

Places Edith Wharton, Willa Cather, and Zona Gale in the political and intellectual context of their times and offers analysis of Wharton's The House of Mirth, *Cather's* My Ántonia, *and Gale's* Miss Lulu Bett, *which are presented as breakthrough achievements in establishing all three authors as significant literary figures.*

Yogi, Stan. "Rebels and Heroines: Subversive Narratives in the Stories of Wakako Yamauchi and Hisaye Yamamoto." In *Reading the Literatures of Asian America,* edited by Shirley Geok-lin Lim and Amy Ling, pp. 131-50. Philadelphia, Penn.: Temple University Press, 1992.

Offers analysis of several short stories by Wakako Yamauchi and Hisaye Yamamoto that evoke the struggles of Japanese immigrant women who chafe against the strict codes of Issei family and culture.

THE FEMINIST MOVEMENT IN THE 20TH CENTURY

The feminist movement in the United States and abroad was a social and political movement that sought to establish equality for women. The movement transformed the lives of many individual women and exerted a profound effect upon American society throughout the twentieth century. During the first two decades of the century, women's groups in the United States worked together to win women's suffrage, culminating in the ratification of a constitutional amendment in 1920 that guaranteed women the right the vote. During the later twentieth century, women's groups would again band together, this time to formulate and advocate for the Equal Rights Amendment (ERA). Though this proposed constitutional amendment ultimately failed to gain approval in the late 1970s, it became a rallying point for diverse women's groups and drew national attention to the feminist cause.

The period between 1917 and the early 1960s was marked by two world wars and a subsequent economic boom that brought many American women into the workplace, initially to provide labor during the war, and then to help achieve and maintain a new higher standard of living enjoyed by many middle-class families. However, as women joined the workforce they became increasingly aware of their unequal economic and social status. Women who were homemakers, many with college educations, began to articulate their lack of personal fulfillment—what Betty Friedan in her enormously influential *The Feminine Mystique* (1963) called "the problem that has no name."

Other events in the United States, notably the civil rights movement, contributed to the rise of the feminist movement. During the early 1960s, the civil rights movement gathered momentum, aided by new anti-racist legislation, and reached a major goal in 1964 with the passage of the Civil Rights Act. Many feminists interpreted the ban on racial discrimination, established by the Civil Rights Act, to apply to gender discrimination as well. The student movement was also at its height in the 1960s, leading many younger citizens to question traditional social values and to protest against American military involvement in Vietnam. Feminist groups followed the example set by these movements, adopting the techniques of consciousness raising, protests, demonstrations, and political lobbying in order to further their own agenda.

The founding of the National Organization for Women (NOW) in 1966 marked the formation of an official group to represent and campaign for women's concerns. Leaders such as Friedan, Bella Abzug, Shirley Chisholm, and Gloria Steinem pressured politicians to become aware of women's concerns and to work on legislation that would improve the quality of women's lives. At the same time, many other organizations emerged to deal with feminist causes, including the National Abortion and Reproductive Rights Action League, National Displaced Homemakers, the battered women's movement, the Women's Equity Action League, Women Organized for Employment, and Women Office Workers. In the early 1970s feminist leaders also established a detailed program of proposed political and legal reforms, and in 1975 the National Women's Agenda was presented to President Gerald Ford, all state governors, and all members of Congress. In 1977, feminists organized a National Women's Conference in Houston, where they drafted an action plan that included twenty-six resolutions; the plan was subsequently distributed to government officials to remind them of their responsibility to female constituents. NOW and the newly organized National Women's Political Caucus worked to influence politicians and legislators while continuing their effort to keep women's issues prominent in the media.

During the 1980s, American society was colored by an increasingly conservative political climate and the feminist movement experienced a backlash within their ranks and from anti-feminist detractors. Feminism had always been criticized for being a predominantly white, upperclass movement and for its failure to adequately understand and represent the concerns of poor, African-American, and Hispanic women. The movement had already splintered in the 1970s along the lines of liberal feminists, who focused on the rights of women as individuals; radical feminists, who aligned themselves with revolutionary groups, viewing women as a disenfranchised class of citizens; and lesbians, who had been very much a part of the early feminist movement, but now found more in common with the gay liberation movement. Legislative gains achieved in the 1970s—notably Congress's passing of the ERA amendment and key judicial decisions, chief among them *Roe* v. *Wade*, which guaranteed women's reproductive rights—were under attack by conservative and religious antiabortion coalitions and an organized anti-ERA effort led by Phyllis Schlafly. Some state legislatures backtracked under pressure, overturning or diluting court decisions made in the previous decade. President Ronald Reagan also made his opposition to the ERA public. Due to a combination of political and social factors, the amendment failed to pass in the individual states. In addition, some women who had subscribed to the tenets of the feminist movement now voiced their displeasure at being negatively labeled anti-male and expressed regret at the loss of personal security that traditional women's roles offer. Their concerns echoed in the neoconservative writings of authors such as Naomi Wolf, Susan Faludi, and Camille Paglia.

Nevertheless, feminists pressed on, maintaining pressure on legislators to address women's issues such as reproductive rights, pay equity, affirmative action, sexual harassment, and the handling of rape victims in the courts. In retrospect, the early 1960s has been termed the "first wave" of the feminist movement, and the activists of the 1970s and 1980s have been called the "second wave." In the 1990s there emerged a "third wave" of feminists, still concerned with many of the same problems as their predecessors, but now wishing to work from within the political and legal establishments rather than criticizing them from the outside. This mostly younger generation of feminists would also stress the need to broaden the scope of feminism, emphasizing global networking, human rights, worldwide economic justice, and issues pertaining to race, gender, and class.

REPRESENTATIVE WORKS

Bella Abzug
Bella! Ms. Abzug Goes to Washington (nonfiction) 1972

Paula Gunn Allen
The Sacred Hoop: Recovering the Feminine in American Indian Tradition (essays) 1986

Cherríe Moraga and Gloria Anzaldúa
This Bridge Called My Back: Writings by Radical Women of Color [editors] (anthology) 1981

Ti-Grace Atkinson
Amazon Odyssey (nonfiction) 1974

Boston Women's Health Book Collective
Our Bodies, Ourselves (nonfiction) 1973

Susan Brownmiller
Against Our Will: Men, Women, and Rape (nonfiction) 1975

In Our Time: A Memoir of a Revolution (autobiography) 1999

Shirley Chisholm
Unbought and Unbossed (autobiography) 1970

Andrea Dworkin
Pornography: Men Possessing Women (nonfiction) 1981

Susan Faludi
Backlash: The Undeclared War against American Women (nonfiction) 1991

Betty Friedan
The Feminine Mystique (nonfiction) 1963

It Changed My Life: Writings on the Women's Movement (nonfiction) 1976

The Second Stage (nonfiction) 1981

Carol Gilligan
In a Different Voice: Psychological Theory and Women's Development (nonfiction) 1982

Germaine Greer
The Female Eunuch (nonfiction) 1970

Lucy Lippard
The Pink Glass Swan: Selected Essays on Feminist Art (criticism) 1995

Catharine A. MacKinnon
Feminism Unmodified: Discourses on Life and Law (nonfiction) 1987

Kate Millett
Sexual Politics (nonfiction) 1970

Robin Morgan
off our backs [founder, with others] (periodical) 1970-

Sisterhood Is Powerful [editor] (anthology) 1970

Letty Cottin Pogrebin, Gloria Steinem, and Robin Morgan
Ms. [founders, with others] (periodical) 1972-

Camille Paglia
Sexual Personae: Art and Decadence from Nefertiti to Emily Dickinson (criticism) 1990

Gloria Steinem
Outrageous Acts and Everyday Rebellions (essays) 1983

Susan Ware
Modern American Women: A Documentary History [editor] (anthology) 1969; revised edition, 2002

Naomi Wolf
The Beauty Myth (nonfiction) 1990

Fire with Fire (nonfiction) 1993

NATIONAL ORGANIZATION FOR WOMEN (N.O.W.) STATEMENT OF PURPOSE (ESSAY DATE 1966)

SOURCE: National Organization for Women (N.O.W.) Statement of Purpose. 1966.

In the following statement of purpose, the founding members of N.O.W. outline their goals, emphasizing that the organization will be the voice of women seeking equality in employment, education, politics, and under the law.

We, men and women, who hereby constitute ourselves as the National Organization for Women, believe that the time has come for a new movement toward true equality for all women in America, and toward a fully equal partnership of the sexes, as part of the world-wide revolution of human rights now taking place within and beyond our national borders.

The purpose of NOW is to take action to bring women into full participation in the mainstream of American society now, exercising all the privileges and responsibilities thereof in truly equal partnership with men.

We believe the time has come to move beyond the abstract argument, discussion and symposia over the status and special nature of women which has raged in America in recent years; the time has come to confront, with concrete action, the conditions that now prevent women from enjoying the equality of opportunity and freedom of which is their right, as individual Americans, and as human beings.

NOW is dedicated to the proposition that women, first and foremost, are human beings, who, like all other people in our society, must have the chance to develop their fullest human potential. We believe that women can achieve such equality only by accepting to the full the challenges and responsibilities they share with all other people in our society, as part of the decision-making mainstream of American political, economic and social life.

We organize to initiate or support action, nationally, or in any part of this nation, by individuals or organizations, to break through the silken curtain of prejudice and discrimination against women in government, industry, the professions, the churches, the political parties, the judiciary, the labor unions, in education, science, medicine, law, religion and every other field of importance in American society. Enormous changes taking place in our society make it both possible and urgently necessary to advance the unfinished revolution of women toward true equality, now. With a life span lengthened to nearly 75 years it is no longer either necessary or possible for women to devote the greater part of their lives to child-rearing; yet childbearing and rearing which continues to be a most important part of most women's lives—still is used to justify barring women from equal professional and economic participation and advance.

Today's technology has reduced most of the productive chores which women once performed in the home and in mass-production industries based upon routine unskilled labor. This same technology has virtually eliminated the quality of muscular strength as a criterion for filling most jobs, while intensifying American industry's need for creative intelligence. In view of this new industrial revolution created by automation in the mid-twentieth century, women can and must participate in old and new fields of society in full equality—or become permanent outsiders.

Despite all the talk about the status of American women in recent years, the actual position of women in the United States has declined, and is declining, to an alarming degree throughout the 1950's and '60s. Although 46.4% of all American women between the ages of 18 and 65 now work outside the home, the overwhelming majority—75%—are in routine clerical, sales, or factory jobs, or they are household workers, cleaning women, hospital attendants. About two-thirds of Negro women workers are in the lowest paid service occupations. Working women are becoming increasingly—not less—concentrated on the bottom of the job ladder. As a consequence full-time women workers today earn on the average only 60% of what men earn, and that wage gap has been increasing over the past twenty-five years in every major industry group. In 1964, of all women with a yearly income, 89% earned under $5,000 a year; half of all full-time year round women workers earned less than $3,690; only 1.4% of full-time year round women workers had an annual income of $10,000 or more.

Further, with higher education increasingly essential in today's society, too few women are entering and finishing college or going on to graduate or professional school. Today, women earn only one in three of the B.A.'s and M.A.'s granted, and one in ten of the Ph.D.'s.

In all the professions considered of importance to society, and in the executive ranks of industry and government, women are losing ground. Where they are present it is only a token handful. Women comprise less than 1% of federal judges; less than 4% of all lawyers; 7% of doctors. Yet women represent 51% of the U.S. population. And, increasingly men are replacing women in the top positions in secondary and elementary schools, in social work, and in libraries—once thought to be women's fields,

Official pronouncements of the advance in the status of women hide not only the reality of this dangerous decline, but the fact that nothing is being done to stop it. The excellent reports of the President's Commission on the Status of Women and of the State Commissions have not been fully implemented. Such Commissions have power only to advise. They have no power to enforce their recommendations; nor have they the freedom to organize American women and men to press for action on them. The reports of these commissions have, however created a basis upon which it is now possible to build.

Discrimination in employment on the basis of sex is now prohibited by federal law, in Title VII of the Civil Rights Act of 1964. But although nearly one-third of the cases brought before the Equal Employment Opportunity Commission during the first year dealt with sex discrimination and the proportion is increasing dramatically, the Commission has not made clear its intention to enforce the law with the same seriousness on behalf of women as of other victims of discrimination. Many of these cases were Negro women, who are the victims of the double discrimination of race and sex. Until now, too few women's organizations and official spokesmen have been willing to speak out against these dangers facing women. Too many women have been restrained by the fear of being called "feminist."

There is no civil rights movement to speak for women, as there has been for Negroes and other victims of discrimination. The National Organization for Women must therefore begin to speak.

We believe that the power of American law, and the protection guaranteed by the U. S. Constitution to the civil rights of all individuals, must be effectively applied and enforced to isolate and remove patterns of sex discrimination, to ensure equality of opportunity in employment and education, and equality of civil and political rights and responsibilities on behalf of women, as well as for Negroes and other deprived groups.

TONI MORRISON (ESSAY DATE 1971)

SOURCE: Morrison, Toni. "What the Black Woman Thinks about Women's Lib." In *Public Women, Public Words: A Documentary History of American Feminism*, edited by Dawn Keetley and John Pettegrew, pp. 71-7. Madison, Wis.: Madison House, 1997.

In the following essay, originally published in 1971, Morrison suggests that black women's low participation in the predominantly white women's liberation movement reflects black women's distrust of white people in general, but at the same time acknowledges that this attitude is slowly beginning to change.

They were always there. Whenever you wanted to do something simple, natural and inoffensive. Like drink water, sit down, go to the bathroom or buy a bus ticket to Charlotte, N.C. Those classifying signs that told you who you were, what to do. More than those abrupt and discourteous signs one gets used to in this country—the door that says "Push," the towel dispenser that says "Press," the traffic light that says "No"—these signs were not just arrogant, they were malevolent: "White Only," "Colored Only," or perhaps just "Colored," permanently carved into the granite over a drinking fountain. But there was one set of signs that was not malevolent; it was, in fact, rather reassuring in its accuracy and fine distinctions: the pair that said "White Ladies" and "Colored Women."

The difference between white and black females seemed to me an eminently satisfactory one. White females were *ladies,* said the sign maker, worthy of respect. And the quality that made ladyhood worthy? Softness, helplessness and modesty—which I interpreted as a willingness to let others do their labor and their thinking. Colored females, on the other hand, were *women*—unworthy of respect because they were tough, capable, independent and immodest. Now, it appears, there is a consensus that those anonymous sign makers were right all along, for there is no such thing as Ladies' Liberation. Even the word "lady" is anathema to feminists. They insist upon the "woman" label as a declaration of their rejection of all that softness, helplessness and modesty, for they see them as characteristics which served only to secure their bondage to men.

Significant as that shift in semantics is, obvious as its relationship to the black-woman concept is, it has not been followed by any immediate comradery between black and white women, nor has it precipitated any rush of black women into the various chapters of NOW. It is the *Weltanschauung* of black women that is responsible for their apparent indifference to Women's Lib, and in order to discover the nature of this view of oneself in the world, one must look very closely at the black woman herself—a difficult, inevitably doomed proposition, for if anything is true of black women, it is how consistently they have (deliberately, I suspect) defied classification.

It may not even be possible to look at those militant young girls with lids lowered in dreams of guns, those middle-class socialites with 150 pairs of shoes, those wispy girl junkies who have always been older than water, those beautiful Muslim women with their bound hair and flawless skin, those television personalities who think chic is virtue and happiness a good coiffure, those sly old women in the country with their ancient love of Jesus—and still talk about The Black Woman. It is a dangerous misconception, for it encourages lump thinking. And we are so accustomed to that in our laboratories that it seems only natural to confront all human situations, direct all human discourse, in the same way. Those who adhere to the scientific method and draw general conclusions from "representative" sampling are chagrined by the suggestion that there is any other way to arrive at truth, for they like their truth in tidy sentences that begin with "all."

In the initial confrontation with a stranger, it is never "Who are you?" but "Take me to your leader." And it is this mode of thought which has made black-white relationships in this country so hopeless. There is a horror of dealing with people one by one, each as he appears. There is safety and manageability in dealing with the leader—no matter how large or diverse the leader's constituency may be. Such generalizing may be all right for plant analysis, superb for locating carcinogens in mice, and it used to be all right as a method for dealing with schools and politics. But no one would deny that it is rapidly losing effectiveness in both those areas—precisely because it involves classifying human beings and anticipating their behavior. So it is with some trepidation that anyone should undertake to generalize about still another group. Yet something in that order is legitimate, not only because unity among minorities is a political necessity, but because, at some point, one wants to get on with the differences.

What do black women feel about Women's Lib? Distrust. It is white, therefore, suspect. In spite of the fact that liberating movements in the black world have been catalysts for white feminism, too many movements and organizations have made deliberate overtures to enroll blacks and have ended up by rolling them. They don't want to be used again to help somebody gain power—a power that is carefully kept out of their hands. They look at white women and see them as the enemy—for they know that racism is not confined to white men, and that there are more white women than men in this country, and that 53 percent of the population sustained an eloquent silence during times of greatest stress. The faces of those white women hovering behind that black girl at the Little Rock school in 1957 do not soon leave the retina of the mind.

When she was interviewed by Nikki Giovanni last May in *Essence* magazine, Ida Lewis, the former editor-in-chief of *Essence,* was asked why black women were not more involved in Women's Lib, and she replied: "The Women's Liberation Movement is basically a family quarrel between white women and white men. And on general principles, it's not good to get involved in family disputes. Outsiders always get shafted when the dust settles. On the other hand, I must support some of the goals [equal pay, child-care centers, etc.]. . . . But if we speak of a liberation movement, as a black woman I view my role from a black perspective—the role of black women is to continue the struggle in concert with black men for the liberation and self-determination of blacks. White power was not created to protect and preserve us as women. Nor can we view ourselves as simply American women. We are black women, and as such we must deal effectively in the black community."

To which Miss Giovanni sighed: "Well, I'm glad you didn't come out of that Women's Lib or black-man bag as if they were the alternatives." . . .

Miss Lewis: "Suppose the Lib movement succeeds. It will follow, since white power is the order of the day, that white women will be the first hired, which will still leave black men and women outside." . . .

It is an interesting exchange, Miss Lewis expressing suspicion and identifying closely with black men, Miss Giovanni suggesting that the two are not necessarily mutually exclusive.

But there is not only the question of color, there is the question of the color of experience. Black women are not convinced that Women's Lib serves their best interest or that it can cope with the uniqueness of their experience, which is itself an alienating factor. The early image of Women's Lib was of an élitist organization made up of upper-middle-class women with the concerns of that class (the percentage of women in professional fields, etc.) and not paying much attention to the problems of most black women, which are not in getting into the labor force but in being upgraded in it, not in getting into medical school but in getting adult education, not in how to exercise freedom from the "head of the house" but in how to *be* head of the household.

Black women are different from white women because they view themselves differently and lead a different kind of life. Describing this difference is the objective of several black women writers and scholars. But even without this newly surfacing analysis, we can gain some understanding of the black woman's world by examining archetypes. The archetypes created by women about themselves are rare, and even those few that do exist may be the result of a female mind completely controlled by male-type thinking. No matter. The most unflattering stereotypes that male minds have concocted about black women contain, under the stupidity and the hostility, the sweet smell of truth.

Look, for example, at Geraldine and Sapphire—Geraldine, that campy character in Flip Wilson's comic repertory, and Sapphire, the wife of Kingfish in the Amos and Andy radio and TV series. Unlike Nefertiti, an archetype that black women have appropriated for themselves, Geraldine and Sapphire are the comic creations of men. Nefertiti, the romantic black queen with the enviable neck, is particularly appealing to young black women, mainly because she existed (and there are few admirable heroines in our culture), was a great beauty and is remote enough to be worshiped. There is a lot of talk about Sojourner Truth, the freed slave who preached emancipation and women's rights, but there is a desperate love for Nefertiti, simply because she was so pretty.

I suppose at bottom we are all beautiful queens, but for the moment it is perhaps just as well to remain useful women. One wonders if Nefertiti could have lasted 10 minutes in a welfare office, in a Mississippi gas station, at a Parent Association meeting or on the church congregation's Stewardess Board No. 2. And since black women have to endure, that romanticism seems a needless *cul de sac,* an opiate that appears to make life livable if not serene but eventually must separate us from reality. I maintain that black women are already O.K. O.K. with our short necks, O.K. with our callused hands. O.K. with our tired feet and paper bags on the Long Island Rail Road. O.K. O.K. O.K.

As for Geraldine, her particular horror lies in her essential accuracy. Like any stereotype she is a gross distortion of reality and as such highly offensive to many black women and endearing to many whites. A single set of characteristics provokes both hatred and affection. Geraldine is defensive, cunning, sexy, egocentric and transvestite. But that's not all she is. A shift in semantics and we find the accuracy: for defensive read survivalist; for cunning read clever; for sexy read a natural unembarrassed acceptance of her sexuality; for egocentric read keen awareness of individuality; for transvestite (man in woman's dress) read a masculine strength beneath the accouterments of glamour.

Geraldine is offensive to many blacks precisely because the virtues of black women are construed in her portrait as vices. The strengths are portrayed as weaknesses—hilarious weaknesses. Yet one senses even in the laughter some awe and respect. Interestingly enough, Geraldine is absolutely faithful to one man, Killer, whom one day we may also see as caricature.

Sapphire, a name of opprobrium black men use for the nagging black wife, is also important, for in that marriage, disastrous as it was, Sapphire worked, fussed, worked and fussed, but (and this is crucial) Kingfish did whatever he pleased. Whatever. Whether he was free or irresponsible, anarchist or victim depends on your point of view. Contrary to the black-woman-as-emasculator theory, we see, even in these unflattering caricatures, the very opposite of a henpecked husband and emasculating wife—a wife who never did, and never could, manipulate her man. Which brings us to the third reason for the suspicion black women have of Women's Lib: the serious one of the relationship between black women and black men.

There are strong similarities in the way black and white men treat women, and strong similarities in the way women of both races react. But the relationship is different in a very special way.

For years in this country there was no one for black men to vent their rage on except for black women. And for years black women accepted that rage—even regarded that acceptance as their unpleasant duty. But in doing so, they frequently kicked back, and they seem never to have become the "true slave" that white women see in their own history. True, the black woman did the housework, the drudgery; true, she reared the children, often alone, but she did all of that while occupying a place on the job market, a place her mate could not get or which his pride would not let him accept. And she had nothing to fall back on: not maleness, not whiteness, not ladyhood, not anything. And out of the profound desolation of her reality she may very well have invented herself.

If she was a sexual object in the eyes of the men, that was their doing. Sex was *one* of her dimensions. It had to be just one, for life required many other things of her, and it is difficult to be regarded solely as a sex object when the burden of field and fire is on your shoulders. She could cultivate her sexuality but dared not be obsessed by it. Other people may have been obsessed by it, but the circumstances of her life did not permit her to dwell on it or survive by means of its exploitation.

So she combined being a responsible person with being a female—and as a person she felt free to confront not only the world at large (the rent man, the doctor and the rest of the marketplace) but her man as well. She fought him and nagged him—but know that you don't fight what you don't respect. (If you don't respect your man, you manipulate him, the way some parents treat children and the way white women treat their men—if they can get away with it or if they do not acquiesce entirely.) And even so, the black man was calling most of the shots—in the home or out of it. The black woman's "bad" relationships with him were often the result of his inability to deal with a competent and complete personality and her refusal to be anything less than that. The saving of the relationship lay in her unwillingness to feel free when her man was not free.

In a way black women have known something of the freedom white women are now beginning to crave. But oddly, freedom is only sweet when it is won. When it is forced, it is called responsibility. The black woman's needs shrank to the level of her responsibility; her man's expanded in proportion to the obstacles that prevented him from assuming his. White women, on the other hand, have had too little responsibility, white men too much. It's a wonder the sexes of either race even speak to each other.

As if that were not enough, there is also the growing rage of black women over unions of black men and white women. At one time, such unions were rare enough to be amusing or tolerated. The white woman moved with the black man into a black neighborhood, and everybody tried to deal with it. Chances are the white woman who married a black man liked it that way, for she had already made some statement about her relationship with her own race by marrying him. So there were no frictions. If a white woman had a child out of wedlock by a black man, the child was deposited with the black community, or grouped with the black orphans, which is certainly one of the reasons why lists of black foundling children are so long. (Another reason is the willingness of black women to have their children instead of aborting and to keep them, whatever the inconvenience.)

But now, with all the declarations of independence, one of the black man's ways of defining it is to broaden his spectrum of female choices, and one consequence of his new pride is the increased attraction white women feel for him. Clearly there are more and more of these unions, for there is clearly more anger about it (talking black and sleeping white is a cliché) among black women. The explanations for this anger are frequently the easy ones: there are too few eligible men, for wars continue to shoot them up; the black woman who complains is one who would be eliminated from a contest with any good-looking woman—the complaint simply reveals her inadequacy to get a man; it is a simple case of tribal sour grapes with a dash of politics thrown in.

But no one seems to have examined this anger in the light of what black women understand about themselves. These easy explanations are obviously male. They overlook the fact that the hostility comes from both popular beauties and happily married black women. There is something else in this anger, and I think it lies in the fact that black women have always considered themselves superior to white women. Not racially superior, just superior in terms of their ability to function healthily in the world.

Black women have been able to envy white women (their looks, their easy life, the attention they seem to get from their men); they could fear them (for the economic control they have had over black women's lives) and even love them (as mammies and domestic workers can); but black women have found it impossible to respect white women. I mean they never had what black men have had for white men—a feeling of awe at their accomplishments. Black women have no abiding admiration of white women as competent, complete people. Whether vying with them for the few professional slots available to women in general, or moving their dirt from one place to another, they regarded them as willful children,

pretty children, mean children, ugly children, but never as real adults capable of handling the real problems of the world.

White women were ignorant of the facts of life—perhaps by choice, perhaps with the assistance of men, but ignorant anyway. They were totally dependent on marriage or male support (emotionally or economically). They confronted their sexuality with furtiveness, complete abandon or repression. Those who could afford it, gave over the management of the house and the rearing of children to others. (It is a source of amusement even now to black women to listen to feminists talk of liberation while somebody's nice black grandmother shoulders the daily responsibility of child rearing and floor mopping and the liberated one comes home to examine the housekeeping, correct it, and be entertained by the children. If Women's Lib needs those grandmothers to thrive, it has a serious flaw.) The one great disservice black women are guilty of (albeit not by choice) is that they are the means by which white women can escape the responsibilities of womanhood and remain children all the way to the grave.

It is this view of themselves and of white women that makes the preference of a black man for a white woman quite a crawful. The black women regard his choice as an inferior one. Over and over again one hears one question from them: "But why, when they marry white women, do they pick the raggletail ones, the silly, the giddy, the stupid, the flat nobodies of the race? Why no real women?" The answer, of course, is obvious. What would such a man who preferred white women do with a real woman? And would a white woman who is looking for black exotica ever be a complete woman?

Obviously there are black and white couples who love each other as people, and marry each other that way. (I can think of two such.) But there is so often a note of apology (if the woman is black) or bravado (if the man is) in such unions, which would hardly be necessary if the union was something other than a political effort to integrate one's emotions and therefore, symbolically, the world. And if all the black partner has to be is black and exotic, why not?

This feeling of superiority contributes to the reluctance of black women to embrace Women's Lib. That and the very important fact that black men are formidably opposed to their involvement in it—and for the most part the women understand their fears. In The Amsterdam News, an editor, while deploring the conditions of black political organizations, warns his readers of the consequences: "White politicians have already organized. And their organizers are even attempting to co-opt Black women into their organizational structure, which may well place Black women against Black men, that is, if the struggle for women's liberation is viewed by Black women as being above the struggle for Black liberation."

The consensus among blacks is that their first liberation has not been realized; unspoken is the conviction of black men that any more aggressiveness and "freedom" for black women would be intolerable, not to say counterevolutionary.

There is also a contention among some black women that Women's Lib is nothing more than an attempt on the part of whites to become black without the responsibilities of being black. Certainly some of the demands of liberationists seem to rack up as our thing: common-law marriage (shacking); children out of wedlock, which is even fashionable now if you are a member of the Jet Set (if you are poor and black it is still a crime); families without men; right to work; sexual freedom, and an assumption that a woman is equal to a man.

Now we have come full circle: the morality of the welfare mother has become the avant-garde morality of the land. There is a good deal of irony in all of this. About a year ago in the *Village Voice* there was a very interesting exchange of letters. Cecil Brown was explaining to a young black woman the "reasons" for the black man's interest in white girls: a good deal about image, psychic needs and what not. The young girl answered in a rather poignant way to this effect: yes, she said, I suppose, again, we black women have to wait, wait for the brother to get himself together—be enduring, understanding, and, yes, she thought they could do it again . . . but, in the meantime, what do we tell the children?

This woman who spoke so gently in those letters of the fate of the children may soon discover that the waiting period is over. The softness, the "she knows how to treat me" (meaning she knows how to be a cooperative slave) that black men may be looking for in white women is fading from view. If Women's Lib *is* about breaking the habit of genuflection, if it *is* about controlling one's own destiny, *is* about female independence in economic, personal and political ways, if it is indeed about working hard to become a person, knowing that one has to work hard at becoming anything, *Man* or *Woman*—and it succeeds—then we may

have a nation of white Geraldines and white Sapphires, and what on earth is Kingfish gonna do then?

The winds are changing, and when they blow, new things move. The liberation movement has moved from shrieks to shape. It is focusing itself, becoming a hard-headed power base, as the National Women's Political Caucus in Washington attested last month. Representative Shirley Chisholm was radiant: "Collectively we've come together, not as a Women's Lib group, but as a women's political movement." Fannie Lou Hamer, the Mississippi civil-rights leader, was there. Beulah Sanders, chairman of New York's Citywide Coordinating Committee of Welfare Groups, was there. They see, perhaps, something real: women talking about human rights rather than sexual rights—something other than a family quarrel, and the air is shivery with possibilities.

ROE V. WADE (LEGAL DECISION DATE 1973)

SOURCE: *Roe v. Wade,* 1973.

In the following excerpt from the landmark legal decision regarding Roe v. Wade, *the United States Supreme Court upholds women's unconditional right to have an abortion—a right that had been denied them since the late 1800s.*

The principal thrust of appellant's attack on the Texas statutes is that they improperly invade a right, said to be possessed by the pregnant woman, to choose to terminate her pregnancy. Appellant would discover this right in the concept of personal "liberty" embodied in the Fourteenth Amendment's Due Process Clause; or in personal, marital, familial, and sexual privacy said to be protected by the Bill of Rights . . . ; or among those rights reserved to the people by the Ninth Amendment. . . . Before addressing this claim, we feel it desirable briefly to survey, in several aspects, the history of abortion, for such insight as that history may afford us, and then to examine the state purposes and interests behind the criminal abortion laws.

It perhaps is not generally appreciated that the restrictive criminal abortion laws in effect in a majority of States today are of relatively recent vintage. Those laws, generally proscribing abortion or its attempt at any time during pregnancy except when necessary to preserve the pregnant woman's life, are not of ancient or even of common-law origin. Instead, they derive from statutory changes effected, for the most part, in the latter half of the 19th century. . . .

ON THE SUBJECT OF...

GERMAINE GREER (1939-)
A controversial feminist critic and scholar, Germaine Greer emerged as a maverick spokesperson for the women's movement with the publication of *The Female Eunuch* (1970). This international best seller, distinguished for its frank, iconoclastic discussion of female anatomy, sexuality, and irreverence toward mainstream feminist views, established Greer as a compelling public intellectual and celebrity. In *The Female Eunuch*, Greer rails against the social and psychological oppression of women in modern society, encouraging women to reclaim their independence and vitality, or "woman energy" by eschewing monogamy, heterosexual marriage, and traditional child-rearing. Greer advocates open relationships, sexual freedom, and communal parenting as an antidote to female passivity, repressed desire, and debilitating dependence on men for security and the false promises of romantic love. In subsequent books, such as *Sex and Destiny* (1984), *The Change* (1991), and *The Whole Woman* (1999), Greer similarly combines scholarly analysis, personal observation, and high rhetoric to provide thought-provoking commentaries on the social status of women in contemporary society. Greer was born near Melbourne, Australia, in 1939. She earned a B.A. from the University of Melbourne in 1959, an M.A. at the University of Sydney in 1961, and in 1964 won a Commonwealth scholarship to study at Newnham College, Cambridge University, in England, where she earned a Ph.D. in 1967. Greer subsequently taught English at the University of Warwick in England from 1967 to 1973, during which time she was involved in the theater, appeared on television shows, and contributed a column to the London *Sunday Times*. Greer also entered the circles of rock stars and the British counterculture during the late 1960s, contributed to the underground magazine *Oz*, and cofounded *Suck*, a radical pornographic magazine in whose pages nude photographs of Greer once appeared.

[At] the time of the adoption of our Constitution, and throughout the major portion of the 19th century, abortion was viewed with less disfavor than under most American statutes currently in effect. Phrasing it another way, a woman enjoyed a substantially broader right to terminate a pregnancy than she does in most States today. At least with respect to the early stage of pregnancy. . . .

Three reasons have been advanced to explain historically the enactment of criminal abortion laws in the 19th century and to justify their continued existence.

It has been argued occasionally that these laws were the product of a Victorian social concern to discourage illicit sexual conduct. Texas, however, does not advance this justification in the present case, and it appears that no court or commentator has taken the argument seriously. The appellants and amici contend, moreover, that this is not a proper state purpose at all and suggest that, if it were, the Texas statutes are overbroad in protecting it since the law fails to distinguish between married and unwed mothers.

A second reason is concerned with abortion as a medical procedure. When most criminal abortion laws were first enacted, the procedure was a hazardous one for the woman. This was particularly true prior to the development of antisepsis. Antiseptic techniques, of course, were based on discoveries by [British surgeon Joseph] Lister, [French microbiologist Louis] Pasteur, and others first announced in 1867, but were not generally accepted and employed until about the turn of the century. Abortion mortality was high. . . . Thus, it has been argued that a State's real concern in enacting a criminal abortion law was to protect the pregnant woman, that is, to restrain her from submitting to a procedure that placed her life in serious jeopardy.

Modern medical techniques have altered this situation. Appellants and various amici refer to medical data indicating that abortion in early pregnancy, that is, prior to the end of the first trimester, although not without its risk, is now relatively safe. Mortality rates for women undergoing early abortions, where the procedure is legal, appear to be as low as or lower than the rates for normal childbirth. Consequently, any interest of the State in protecting the woman from an inherently hazardous procedure, except when it would be equally dangerous for her to forgo it, has largely disappeared. Of course, important state interests in the areas of health and medical standards do remain. The State has a legitimate interest in seeing to it that abortion, like any other medical procedure, is performed under circumstances that insure maximum safety for the patient. . . . Moreover, the risk to the woman increases as her pregnancy continues. Thus, the State retains a definite interest in protecting the woman's own health and safety when an abortion is proposed at a late stage of pregnancy.

The third reason is the State's interest—some phrase it in terms of duty—in protecting prenatal life. Some of the argument for this justification rests on the theory that a new human life is present from the moment of conception. The State's interest and general obligation to protect life then extends, it is argued, to prenatal life. Only when the life of the pregnant mother herself is at stake, balanced against the life she carries within her, should the interest of the embryo or fetus not prevail. Logically, of course, a legitimate state interest in this area need not stand or fall on acceptance of the belief that life begins at conception or at some other point prior to live birth. In assessing the State's interest, recognition may be given to the less rigid claim that as long as at least potential life is involved, the State may assert interests beyond the protection of the pregnant woman alone.

Parties challenging state abortion laws have sharply disputed in some courts the contention that a purpose of these laws, when enacted, was to protect prenatal life. Pointing to the absence of legislative history to support the contention, they claim that most state laws were designed solely to protect the woman. Because medical advances have lessened this concern, at least with respect to abortion in early pregnancy, they argue that with respect to such abortions the law can no longer be justified by any state interest. There is some scholarly support for this view of original purpose. . . .

It is with these interests, and the weight to be attached to them, that this case is concerned.

The Constitution does not explicitly mention any right of privacy. In a line of decisions, however, . . . the Court has recognized that a right of personal privacy, or a guarantee of certain areas or zones of privacy, does exist under the Constitution. . . .

This right of privacy, whether it be founded in the Fourteenth Amendment's concept of personal liberty and restrictions upon state action, as we feel it is, or . . . in the Ninth Amendment's reservation of rights to the people, is broad enough to encompass a woman's decision whether or not to terminate her pregnancy. . . . We, therefore, conclude that the right of personal privacy includes the abortion decision, but that this right is not unqualified and must be considered against important state interests in regulation. . . .

The appellee and certain amici argue that the fetus is a "person" within the language and meaning of the Fourteenth Amendment. In support of this, they outline at length and in detail the well-known facts of fetal development. . . . The Constitution does not define "person" in so many words. . . . But in nearly all . . . instances, the use of the word is such that it has application only postnatally. None indicates, with any assurance, that it has any possible prenatal application. . . . In short, the unborn have never been recognized in the law as persons in the whole sense.

In view of all this, we do not agree that, by adopting one theory of life, Texas may override the rights of the pregnant woman that are at stake. We repeat, however, that the State does have an important and legitimate interest in preserving and protecting the health of the pregnant woman . . . and that it has still another important and legitimate interest in protecting the potentiality of human life. These interests are separate and distinct. Each grows in substantiality as the woman approaches term and, at a point during pregnancy, each becomes "compelling."

With respect to the State's important and legitimate interest in the health of the mother, the "compelling" point, in the light of present medical knowledge, is at approximately the end of the first trimester. This is so because of the now-established medical fact . . . that until the end of the first trimester mortality in abortion may be less than mortality in normal childbirth. . . . It follows that, from and after this point, a State may regulate the abortion procedure to the extent that the regulation reasonably relates to the preservation and protection of maternal health. . . . This means, on the other hand, that for the period of pregnancy prior to this "compelling" point, the attending physician, in consultation with his patient, is free to determine, without regulation by the State, that, in his medical judgment, the patient's pregnancy should be terminated. . . .

With respect to the State's important and legitimate interest in potential life, the "compelling" point is at viability. This is so because the fetus then presumably has the capability of meaningful life outside the mother's womb. State

An estimated 5,000 people marching in protest outside the Minnesota Capitol in protest of the Supreme Court's January 22, 1973 decision in the *Roe v. Wade* case.

regulation protective of fetal life after viability thus has both logical and biological justifications. If the State is interested in protecting fetal life after viability, it may go so far as to proscribe abortion during that period, except when it is necessary to preserve the life or health of the mother. . . .

Our conclusion . . . means, of course, that the Texas abortion statutes, as a unit, must fall. (Justice Blackmun, delivering the opinion of the United States Supreme Court as documented in *Supreme Court Reporter*, Volume 93)

KATE MILLETT (ESSAY DATE 1998)

SOURCE: Millett, Kate. "How Many Lives Are Here. . . ." In *The Feminist Memoir Project: Voices from Women's Liberation*, edited by Rachel DuPlessis and Ann Snitow, pp. 493-95. New York: Three Rivers Press, 1998.

In the following essay, Millett recounts the urgency, excitement, and liberating sense of purpose and solidarity experienced by women involved in the feminist movement during the 1960s.

How many lives are here, since for every woman who tells her story in feminism in this ground-breaking collection, there are a thousand others, ten thousand others. For these "representative lives" are only one sampling of a great historical wave. It came at us full tide and from all sides and swept our lives into action, sudden meaning, a transforming vitality, a consuming energy that is still unspent.

History broke over a generation of women who were changed utterly and in the process changed their own times, a change still going on around the world, change still hardly reckoned yet, a chain reaction that will set still others in motion. And it begins with such small steps: a pamphlet, an evening between friends, a challenge at a meeting, then a demonstration, then a network of consciousness-raising groups. It begins with an atmosphere arising out of the great example of the struggle for black civil rights and with the passage of a civil rights law that, virtually by accident, empowered women as well, and thus opened a path. It also began because of a disastrous and unpopular war and resistance to that war by a left whose male chauvinism became insupportable. Yet another path opened. And there was always the example of our foremothers once we could see our way back to them and see ourselves as another wave of the longest revolution. Women came together from different political directions and backgrounds, formal and informal groupings, in neighborhoods or places of study. They explored and agreed, disputed and disagreed, analyzed and synthesized, proclaimed and pronounced and denounced and roughed out a style and an agenda of goals we are still hotly pursuing.

Women's Liberation became an explosion. The women in this collection were on the front line of this movement and felt its first energy, that explosive moment. Feminism became enormous and took on issue after issue: wages led to law and then to health; sexual self-definition led to abortion and then to lesbian rights; the image of women led to advertising and textbooks or toys and war. As you read, you can see a historical phenomenon like this begin with afternoons among "a gang of four" friends positing an autonomous left feminism in Naomi Weisstein's Chicago apartment, which would lead to the Chicago Women's Liberation Union, which sprouted a school and women's studies, a speakers bureau and child care and even a rock band whose triumphs and failures seem a metaphor for the times.

"Every day someone else became a lesbian," Amy Kesselman muses, remembering this time of discovery and change. Out of whirls of activity and experiment came genuine service and solid achievement. The stories here are stories of risk taking: Anselma Dell'Olio's vital immigrant past and her brave forays into feminist theater, Barbara Epstein's thoughtful ambivalence in the face of communism. There was fun in the Lavender Menace "zap," impudence and daring and humor. There was daring in the Chicago "Jane" project that performed eleven thousand abortions before legalization. There is pain in Roxanne Dunbar's stories of rape, even in a rapist's conviction in court: suspended sentence and a two hundred dollar fine. There is another pain in Weisstein's and in Jo Freeman's and other accounts of "trashing," doctrinaire attacks on women by other women, and there is a fine courage in Dell'Olio's denunciation of it as "Divisiveness and Self-Destruction."

There is movement building here, the nervy excitement of meetings and organizations, the march of groups in cities: Bread and Roses, Radical Women, WITCH, Redstockings, the Sisterhood of Black Single Mothers and the Woman's Survival Space, women's peace camps, the Herstory Archives. A woman's law movement came into being, a woman's health movement. The romance of politics was always an inner struggle, as Vivian Gornick reminds us, a battle with the self for discipline and strength, or for class or racial or ethnic identity, as Priscilla Long and Meredith Tax, Barbara Omolade, Michele Wallace, Lourdes Benería, and Shirley Geok-lin Lim demonstrate. Or for autonomy within marriage or recognition for relationship, as Alix Kates Shulman and Joan Nestle work it out from different poles of origin. The turmoil of the very self in transformation while it tries to transform the culture around it. It has not changed enough, nor have we. The divisions of class and race beset us still. This being America, the role of black feminism must become pivotal, crucial, the linchpin securing the wheel itself, if U.S. feminism would be liberatory to feminism worldwide. And though we come together across class, class divides us still. As it was meant to do, and means to do still in an increasingly ruthless capitalism, the so-called "global economy" presenting itself as iron necessity. The stakes get bigger, tougher.

"What I'd like to convey"—Rosalyn Baxandall fills in the essential—"what I think has been neglected in the books and articles about the women's liberation movement—is the joy we felt. We were, we believed, poised on the trembling edge of a transformation. . . . There was a yeastiness in the air that made us cocky and strong. Sure there were splits and backbiting among us, but there was also fun and great times. For me the women's liberation movement was love at first sight."

Really, after all, this is a love story: love for ideas that had come alive in political action and possibility, love for a vision of freedom and for the camaraderie that brought that liberation into being. We called it sisterhood. It was euphoric and over the top, excessive and insufficient all at once. There were terrible shortcomings in how this movement faced differences in race and class, which are slowly being redeemed. There were downs and depressions, times when support fell through and community failed: Jo Freeman and Carol Hanisch give powerful and moving testimony here. There is an emptiness afterwards and a slightly elegiac tone at the end of a great many of these pieces.

ON THE SUBJECT OF...

PHYLLIS SCHLAFLY (1924-)

Dubbed the "Gloria Steinem of the Right," Phyllis Schlafly represented conservative American women in the 1970s who feared and rejected the women's liberation movement. Born in St. Louis in 1924, Schlafly was educated at Washington University and Radcliffe College, worked briefly as a congressional aide, and married a wealthy Illinois lawyer in 1949. Although a self-described housewife and mother of six, she ran for Congress three times, wrote and published several books on conservative issues, worked as a radio commentator, and was editor of the *Phyllis Schlafly Newsletter*. By organizing and operating the Stop ERA lobby as well as the Eagle Forum, she aroused enough opposition to prevent ratification of the Equal Rights Amendment to the Constitution. Schlafly's campaign, and her testimony against the amendment in more than thirty state legislatures, helped convince voters and legislators the ERA was a threat to American values, the family, and traditional sex roles. After the defeat of the ERA, Schlafly's Eagle Forum waged a national campaign against the women's liberation movement, whose leaders Schlafly asserted were fanatics, leading American women on a misguided quest to resolve their personal problems and identity crises through legal and political reform. In *The Power of the Positive Woman* (1977), *The Power of the Christian Woman* (1981), and most recently *Feminist Fantasies* (2003), Schlafly denounces feminism, and encourages women to find creative, intellectual, and spiritual fulfillment in marriage and motherhood, dedication to God, and by embracing the differences between the sexes. Schlafly's first book, *A Choice Not an Echo* (1964), championing Senator Barry M. Goldwater for the Republican presidential nomination, sold over 3 million copies and helped Goldwater to secure his party's nomination. With a retired military man, Admiral Chester Ward, Schlafly coauthored several books on the subjects of national defense policy and nuclear strategy, including *The Gravediggers* (1964), *Strike from Space* (1965), *The Betrayers* (1968), and *Kissinger on the Couch* (1975).

The social transformation that has come about since, the gradual unfolding and extension of feminism into every corner of our lives and into so many societies worldwide, had its kernel as well as its parallel in accounts like these, lives like these. And it goes on. The "click" of recognition and resolve will continue among other women now, younger, or distant, or yet to come.

OVERVIEWS

MYRA MARX FERREE AND BETH B. HESS (ESSAY DATE 1994)

SOURCE: Ferree, Myra Marx, and Beth B. Hess. "Two Steps Forward, One Step Back: Defending Gains, 1983-92." In *Controversy and Coalition: The New Feminist Movement across Three Decades of Change*, rev. ed., pp. 159-93. New York: Twayne, 1994.

In the following essay, Ferree and Hess explore key developments affecting the women's movement between 1983 and 1992, noting changes in strategy used to preserve gains in the areas of reproductive rights, employment law, and political life.

With the election of Ronald Reagan in 1980, the national political agenda shifted markedly toward the Right. In the following decade, under both Presidents Reagan and Bush, many fronts on which feminist gains had been realized in the 1970s came under direct attack. Outspoken antifeminists were appointed to the judiciary and placed in charge of civil rights enforcement; social programs benefiting poor women were cut or abandoned; and reproductive choice was openly opposed. For the New Feminist Movement, the major challenges of the 1980s included maintaining public approval for positions that a popular president and the federal government no longer supported; resisting efforts to reframe feminist concerns in hostile language; and defending feminist organizations and their members from direct, sometimes violent, attack.

In this chapter, we argue that the hostile climate in which the New Feminist Movement existed in this period led to major changes in organization, strategy, and emphasis. We call this decade one of "defensive consolidation" because much of the movement's efforts were directed at defending feminist perspectives and programs, and because such efforts required more extensive consolidation among feminist organizations regardless of their specific form of feminist perspective (radical, socialist, liberal, or career) or organizational strategy (educational/political, direct action/self-help, or cultural/entrepreneurial). Much of this consolidation occurred along substantive lines. That is, whereas in previous decades one could more easily speak of "the" women's movement, there now appeared to be many specific movements—the battered women's movement, the reproductive rights movement, the antirape movement, the pay equity movement, to name just a few—and these specialized movements drew on the organizational strengths and individual skills of feminists in a variety of social locations to effect progress on specific issues.

For example, the battered women's movement came to include the following: openly feminist public officials and legislators working on this issue; managers, employees, board members, and volunteers at community-based shelters; people who turned out for demonstrations or wrote checks or letters of support for programs; community activists and educators; supportive law enforcement personnel and lawyers. The variety of their efforts meant that laws were passed, implemented, and monitored for effectiveness; programs were funded and staffed; public consciousness was raised. Thus, the movement that consolidated around a specific issue—ending woman battering—engaged an enormous variety of feminist activists at all levels from grassroots to federal with strategies that ranged from institutional to confrontational.

Because this was already the third decade of the active mobilization of the New Feminist Movement, it is appropriate to speak of it as a *mature* movement. Maturity does not imply that the movement has ceased to grow or develop, but rather that many of the early organizations were now institutionalized, that is, they had developed regular patterns of interaction with individuals and groups in their environment. In contrast to previous decades, the movement's energies were at this time less directed to founding new groups (organizational proliferation) than to accomplishing unfinished goals. Many activists had a base of experience in a variety of feminist organizations on which they could draw for both good ideas and bad examples. Some of the organizational problems facing the movement in this decade included recruiting new generations of activists into existing organizations and passing on the lessons learned in the 1960s and 1970s.

In the first section of this chapter, we examine three specific struggles waged by feminist organizations in this period of defensive consolidation: reproductive rights, sexual violence, and economic justice. These issues dominated the political agenda of the 1980s, and each issue posed both serious threats and new opportunities for mobilization. The second section looks at how changes in the political environment affected recruitment among young women, and how the defensive demands of the period shaped the organizations and strategies of the movement.

Old Problems, New Issues

Gains made in previous decades combined with the resistance to change by the New Right and the federal government placed feminists in the position of having to defend what they thought they had already won. In many cases, this led to a broadening and deepening of alliances, but it also made feminism more of a reactive movement—that is, one that responded to threats rather than setting its own agenda for the future (proactive). These threats came in a variety of forms. Each of the three issues considered in this section posed different types of dangers in equally varied arenas. The battle over reproductive rights has been waged largely in the courts and on the streets; the struggle over sexual violence has been carried out largely in the media; and the conflict over economic priorities has been played out primarily in state and federal legislatures.

REPRODUCTIVE RIGHTS

In the Courts

As we saw in chapter 6, by the early 1980s, the abortion issue had been radically transformed by the mobilization of anti-choice constituencies at both the grassroots and the national level, supported by the White House and many friendly state governments of both parties. The initiative now passed to those seeking to limit severely or totally ban abortion, placing reproductive rights activists on the defensive. Feminists could no longer rely on a protective Supreme Court, as justices supporting *Roe* v. *Wade* were replaced by justices selected precisely for their antiabortion views. By the late 1980s, a majority of the Court was ready to undermine the premises of *Roe,* if not overturn it completely. Three major decisions between 1989 and 1991 eroded women's right to reproductive choice and spurred reactive mobilization among feminists.

In *Webster* v. *Reproductive Health Services* (1989), the Court left standing a Missouri statute that barred public hospitals and employees from performing abortions, required physicians to test for fetal viability, and stated that human life "begins at conception." In effect, the Court invited other states to enact ever more restrictive legislation. Many states, mostly in the South, but also Pennsylvania, Utah, and the Territory of Guam, responded immediately with laws that raised obstacles for women and health-care providers, including the mandate of a twenty-four- or forty-eight-hour waiting period after the woman was informed about fetal development and the requirements that a minor secure permission from one—or even both—parents and that a married woman inform her husband.

The first of these increasingly restrictive state statutes reached the Supreme Court in the case of *Planned Parenthood of Southeastern Pennsylvania* v. *Casey,* decided in July 1992. A bare majority of justices upheld the basic right of a woman to control her reproductive life but nonetheless left standing virtually all of the Pennsylvania law. The Court also enunciated a new standard by which to judge the constitutionality of similar statutes: whether the restrictions constitute an "undue burden" on the woman. The practical outcome will be a wide disparity among the states in the availability of legal abortion, depending in part on how effectively feminists mobilize in each state to resist these laws in the future.

The Reagan and Bush administrations also issued regulations that subverted the intent of laws they were charged with carrying out. One such rule barred workers in family planning clinics receiving federal funds from even mentioning abortion as a possible option for their clients. In *Rust* v. *Sullivan* (1991), the Supreme Court upheld this regulation, declaring that the government had no obligation to "support" speech of which it disapproved. Despite the decision's implications for free speech in all areas of public life, its practical effect was limited, since this regulation was rescinded in early 1993 by newly elected President Clinton. Clinton also reversed policies that banned abortion in military hospitals, denied Medicaid funding for abortions for poor women, and barred approval of the abortifacient drug RU486, although Congress has the power to restore such barriers.

Clinton's first appointment to the Supreme Court, Ruth Bader Ginsberg, reflected a commitment to reproductive rights that may guide lower-level judicial appointments as well. But because it will take many appointments to reverse the conservative tilt of the federal judiciary, pro-choice advocates have shifted their attention back to Congress in order to seek protection of reproductive rights. In 1991, a Freedom of Choice Act was introduced by 32 Senators and 132 Representatives but had made only halting progress toward enactment by early 1994. NOW and some feminist legislators withdrew their support from the bill when limitations on abortion funding were added, since this would mean fewer reproductive rights for poor women than for the middle class.

On the Streets

Antiabortion forces have not depended solely on the courts or the federal administration to achieve their goals. Demonstrations and protests at hospitals, clinics, and physicians' offices escalated throughout the 1980s, so effectively harassing providers that most hospitals and doctors no longer perform the procedure. By the end of the 1980s, only 10 percent of all abortions were performed in hospitals, compared to almost half in 1974. This was originally considered a positive trend by feminists who favored the more client-centered and less expensive treatment offered in free-standing clinics. However, as the practice of abortion became isolated from the medical mainstream and localized in the hands of a few providers in separated facilities, antiabortionists were able to concentrate their attacks on these small and relatively unprotected sites (Beam and Paul 1992). At the same time, medical schools and residency programs stopped training students in the techniques of safe abortion. As a consequence, in the United States today, abortion services are not available in 80 percent of counties, especially in the Rocky Mountain states and in the South (Henshaw 1991; Lewin 1992).

The aggressive confrontational mode of the antiabortion movement began in 1984 with the first "Action for Life" training conferences, which evolved in 1987 into an organization called Operation Rescue (OR), under the leadership of Randall Terry and Joseph Scheidler. Operation Rescue employs coercion and intimidation to close clinics, harass health-care personnel, and deter women from seeking abortions, as vividly illustrated by its 1988 "siege" of family planning facilities in Atlanta, Georgia, during the Democratic National Convention.

A typical OR performance includes obstructing clinic entrances with a human chain of protesters (often locked to doors and to each other), laying down (or telling their children to lay down) in front of cars, aggressively confronting clinic clients and personnel with threats and moral condemnation, and resisting arrest by going limp and refusing to give their names. Despite obvious differences between some of these tactics and the nonviolent protests of the Civil Rights movement, antiabortion protesters have successfully framed their actions as borrowed from this tradition. Other protesters may follow clients or providers to their homes, threaten their families, make harassing phone calls at all hours, and throw bricks through their windows.

In the five years between 1987 and 1992, there were over five hundred blockades at hundreds of clinics around the country. Other, more violent actions over the decade included 390 cases of criminal vandalism, dozens of burglaries, physical assaults on providers and patients, and hundreds of fires, bombs, and noxious gas attacks (National Abortion Federation 1992). Physicians who provide abortion in their private practice have also been harassed at their homes as well as at their offices. Even before the 1993 murder of Dr. David Gunn, one of the few physicians serving family planning clinics in Florida, fewer and fewer doctors were willing to perform the procedure. As anti-choice violence escalated, so did the cost of insurance and security, forcing some clinics out of business and other providers to decide that this was too risky and unpleasant a way to practice medicine (Hyde 1994; Simonds 1994). The result is that the availability of legal, safe abortion has been substantially curtailed. By 1991, only 7 percent of rural counties had even one abortion provider (Beam and Paul 1992).

The successes of the anti-choice mobilization activated all sectors of the women's movement to defend clinics and their clients. An alliance was also forged between feminists and the family planning network, despite the latter's initial concerns about their public image and tax status (Staggenborg 1991). The National Abortion and Reproductive Rights Action League (NARAL) and Planned Parenthood are now strongly allied with NOW and the women's policy network, and feminist organizations at all levels have placed the defense of reproductive rights at the top of their agenda, diverting valuable resources from proactive fights on other issues.

At the local level, feminists have responded creatively and energetically to Operation Rescue by training crisis intervention teams to defend clinics and to provide protective escorts for clients. These countertactics have proven successful in turning back OR assaults in many cities, but once the immediate crisis is over and the national media have left the scene, lower-level harassment continues day after day, week after week (Simonds 1994). Involvement in ongoing clinic defense have thus become an important form of feminist

activism. New defensive organizations have sprung to life, such as Students Organizing Students, founded after the *Webster* decision and already counting 150 campus chapters in 1991 (Kamen 1991).

Conclusion

In the twenty years since *Roe,* regardless of national administration, public opinion has steadily favored the pro-choice position (see chapter 4). Such support is not without its nuances and ambiguities. While endorsing a general right to choose, many Americans make distinctions among the reasons women have for terminating a pregnancy. Although 80 to 95 percent favor the right to a legal abortion in cases of rape, incest, fetal deformity, or threat to the mother's life or health, only about half support legal abortions for reasons such as being poor, unmarried, or not wishing to have another child. However, 43 percent feel that a woman should have the right to choose under any circumstance, compared to under 20 percent who would deny abortion in all cases. Polls also indicate that most Americans do not support the obstruction of family planning clinics, nor do they wish to see *Roe* v. *Wade* overturned (Schmittroth 1991). In fact, pro-choice organizations received a record number of contributions in the months immediately following the *Webster* decision, and membership in NARAL doubled (to 400,000).

At the same time that most Americans support woman's right to legal abortion, many also express strong personal reservations. In her reanalysis of national survey data, Scott (1989) found women are more likely than men to express moral reservations but equally likely to endorse the legal right. While individuals may be ambivalent, the public debate has become polarized. Feminist scholars' efforts to hear women's voices and represent their complex decision-making processes (e.g., Ginsburg 1989; Gilligan 1982) are drowned out by the anger and violence of the confrontation. Thus the simple need to defend choice rather than a proactive and inclusive vision of reproductive rights (e.g., Petchesky 1984; Rothman 1989) has dominated women's movement politics in this decade.

SEXUAL VIOLENCE

While the struggle over reproductive rights has often been physical, the battle between feminists and the New Right over sexual violence has been a war of words. Both sides are actively engaged in contesting the media's framing of the issue. One significant achievement of feminist organizations in the 1970s was the building of a substantial consensus in the United States that women ought to be able to walk the streets in safety and to feel secure in their homes and workplaces. Over the past decade, feminists have offered new labels, arguments, and strategies addressing various behaviors on the continuum of sexual violence: workplace harassment, physical abuse in the home, rape, and incest. At the same time, the antifeminist backlash has attempted to trivialize these issues with claims that date rape is a myth and that women are "whining" about outcomes that they have either invited or imagined (e.g., Roiphe 1993). Debates over whether women or men are to blame for the undeniable prevalence of sexual violence have intensified, and the feminist attempt to build a consensus that would hold men accountable for their actions now seems in danger of slipping away.

Sexual Harassment

This term covers a wide range of behaviors that were viewed as the inevitable result of "natural sexual attraction" until the late 1970s. Even though "sex discrimination" as a broad category was outlawed by the Civil Rights Act of 1963, it took almost two decades for sexual harassment to be reframed as an actionable form of unlawful discrimination.

The first cases claiming that workplace demands for sexual favors constituted sex discrimination were filed by African-American women in the late 1970s (MacKinnon 1987, 60-65). In 1980, the EEOC ruled that harassment on the basis of sex was a violation of the Civil Rights Act. Among the actions so defined were unwelcome sexual advances and requests for sexual favors; other verbal and physical conduct when submission is either explicitly or implicitly made a condition of employment or the basis of employment decisions; conduct that interferes with an individual's work performance and creates an intimidating, hostile, or offensive working environment (Seals, Jenkins and Manale 1992). In 1986, the Supreme Court affirmed the illegality of sexual harassment in *Meritor Savings Bank* v. *Vinson*.

Although the language of the statute is gender neutral, the great majority of the victims are women for several reasons: women are still perceived as legitimate targets for male attention and aggression; harassment is part of the "normal" working conditions of many sex-typed jobs such as waitressing and nursing; male co-workers can use sexual harassment to defend their turf from women trying to enter male sex-typed jobs; men

are more likely than women to be in supervisory positions with the power to harass subordinates (Martin 1989).

Most feminist attention has been directed toward raising awareness of the issue in the courts and among victims. The well-publicized confirmation hearings of Clarence Thomas as Justice of the Supreme Court in 1991 greatly raised consciousness on the issue, but the hearings also revealed the obstacles to bringing a successful sexual harassment suit. Anita Hill, a law professor who had worked for Thomas both at the Education Department and when he directed the EEOC, charged that he had created a hostile environment and engaged in unwelcome sexual conversations. Her claims were ridiculed and her character and sanity attacked. According to public opinion polls, the hearings initially left women as well as men more convinced by Thomas's denial than by Hill's testimony. However, as the television images faded, opinion dramatically reversed, with a majority in 1992 believing Hill (Gallup October 1991 and December 1992). In effect, the hearings were a national consciousness-raising session on sexual harassment, demonstrating how sexist assumptions affect a woman's credibility and how she is treated by authorities, as well as the personal costs and political significance of speaking out (Morrison 1992).

Anita Hill was blamed for not reporting the behavior of her boss at the time it happened (when it was not clear the courts would treat it as illegal), but her response was more typical than not. A survey of federal government employees found that 42 percent of the women (but only 14 percent of the men) said they had been sexually harassed, yet only 5 percent took any kind of formal action (Tangri, Burt, and Johnson 1982). Similarly, a national poll in 1991 found that four out of ten women had experienced unwanted sexual advances at their workplace, but only 4 percent reported the incident (Kolbert 1991). Use of legal remedies is inhibited by cumbersome reporting procedures as well as a lack of clear-cut penalties (Seal Jenkins, and Manale 1992), a situation that feminists are attempting to remedy through their unions and state legislatures. At the urging of the women's policy network in Washington, the Civil Rights Restoration Act of 1991 included explicit penalties for sexual harassment, but they were relatively mild compared to penalties for other infractions.

Feminist organizing on college campuses in the 1980s has focused on sexual harassment, with the goals of raising consciousness among actual and potential victims and changing administrative codes and penalties. One study of college women found that 30 percent had experienced sexual harassment from at least one male instructor during their undergraduate years (Dziech and Weiner 1984). Peer harassment in college is also common, ranging from acts such as loudly "rating" the attractiveness of women passers-by to physical attacks (Paludi and Barickman 1991). Because the courts have held that the absence of a specific antiharassment policy implicitly condones such behavior, institutions of higher learning are attempting to define standards of inappropriate conduct. For example, in 1993, after much controversy, the University of Virginia instituted a policy forbidding instructors to have any sexual contact with students under their supervision.

The general public and school authorities often view sexual harassment and assault as somehow caused by the woman or girl. "Boys will be boys" and "she must have asked for it" are still common responses (American Association of University Women 1992), as was evident in reactions to well-publicized sexual attacks on schoolmates by young men in New York, New Jersey, and California in the early 1990s. Given the pressures not to report such incidents, most feminists believe that these practices are far more widespread than the few highly visible cases suggest—that is, that these are not the extreme or unusual events that the public and press have assumed, but everyday reality for young women.

In another well-publicized case, the 1991 convention of an organization of U.S. Navy fliers known as the Tailhook Association, several hundred officers assaulted more than eighty women. Although previous conventions were characterized by similar levels of sexual violence, this one came to public notice when one of the women, a naval officer herself, reported the incident to her superiors who in turn began an investigation. By this time, thanks to years of feminist organizing in the military, investigative procedures and penalties were in place that made it possible for the officer to seek redress; still, top Navy personnel attempted to hush up the scandal and excuse the perpetrators.

While there can be little doubt that the well-publicized Hill-Thomas hearings and the Tailhook Association orgy raised public awareness of the pervasiveness of the problem, they also stimulated backlash. Antifeminists claim that statutes and policies against sexual harassment violate freedom of speech; that what women perceive as sexual advances or a hostile environment are merely men doing "what comes naturally," and if women are offended by it, they should stay out of the places where it occurs; and that men are now so afraid of being falsely accused that their rights are being violated. Yet the feminist definition of sexual harassment seems to be holding up against this attempt to reframe the issue.

In the Democratic primary elections of 1992, unexpected victories were won by half a dozen candidates whose campaign was largely based on reaction to the Hill-Thomas hearings, and several of these candidates went on to win national office. Sixty-two percent of the public agrees that if more women had been in the Senate, the Hill-Thomas hearings would have been conducted very differently. As MacKinnon concludes, "if the question is whether a law designed from women's standpoint and administered through this legal system can do anything for women—which always seems to me a good question—this experience (with sexual harassment cases) so far gives a qualified and limited yes" (1993, 146).

Domestic Violence

The women's movement of the 1970s defined violence against children and wives (and partners in unmarried unions) as battering, a form of illegitimate and illegal abuse, and provided alternatives such as shelters for women attempting to flee such attacks. Prior to that point, domestic violence had been largely veiled by the curtain of privacy drawn around the nuclear family. Breaking through this shield of secrecy was a difficult task, and it is still far from complete. Many Americans continue to support a man's right to coerce obedience or sexual compliance from his wife, and because women are expected to keep the peace within the home, wives are often blamed (and blame themselves) when men erupt in anger. Although gender-neutral language has become customary in speaking about the problem, much of the violence is clearly predicated on gender-specific expectations of authority and submission.

This has not prevented an ongoing debate over the prevalence and gender distribution of violent acts in the home. The most commonly used estimates of the frequency of assault come from the National Family Violence Surveys of 1975 and 1985 and suggest that 16 percent of all couples (married or not) experience at least one episode of violence a year. These data are widely criticized, however, because they indicate that men are as likely as women to be assaulted, information that antifeminists have seized upon to minimize the extent of wife-beating as a social problem. Feminists point out that even if both strike out, it is the wife who is more likely to be seriously injured, and she is typically responding defensively to a history of spousal violence (Brush 1990; Kurz 1989; Yllo and Bograd 1988). Department of Justice data show that women are three times as likely as men to be violently assaulted by someone with whom they are intimate (Harlow 1991), and that between 22 and 35 percent of women treated in hospital emergency rooms are victims of ongoing abuse (National Coalition against Domestic Violence 1991).

In the 1980s, feminist organizations began to devote more attention to the problems of women who actively defend themselves against further assaults. Not fitting the stereotype of the passive and innocent victim, such women often end up in prison for their attempted self-defense. One television docudrama, "The Burning Bed," did much to raise consciousness of this issue. Focusing on the actual case of a long-term battering victim who finally killed her husband while he slept, the dramatization may have helped the general public to grasp a point that was being raised by feminist legal scholars: under a "reasonable woman" standard of self-defense, women in constant fear of their lives are not acting with excessive force when they strike back, even against a disarmed or sleeping man (Smith 1993). Not all juries have accepted this defense, but the feminist reframing of the issue has persuaded several governors to commute the sentences of women who killed their batterers. Although there is evidence that the presence of resources for battered women—shelters, hotlines, legal aid—reduces the likelihood of killing an abusive partner (Browne and Williams 1993), such resources are neither universally available nor sufficient to stop the abuse. The numerous cases in which ex-husbands or ex-boyfriends have killed former wives or girlfriends after years of stalking and harassing them, often when protection orders issued by the courts barred them from contacting the victim, indicate the depth of the problem.

In sum, despite adopting the less political language of "domestic violence" in the 1980s, feminists have continued to frame issues of battering in ways that make men's responsibility for these assaults understood. Although women are still far from secure from assault by family members, feminist organizations have developed consciousness of the problem and of a woman's right to self-defense when society fails to protect her.

Rape and Sexual Abuse

Against the force of custom and renewed efforts by antifeminists to define sexual assault as a harmless game, feminists have continued to frame sexual assault, even between intimates and family members, as a crime. Victim blaming assumed new dimensions in the 1980s, as attention has shifted from assaults by strangers in dark alleys (the stereotypical but much less common case) to attacks by acquaintances, friends, and even fathers. The issues of incest and date rape that have become prominent in the 1980s evoked a conservative response aimed at discrediting the victims by suggesting that adult survivors of incest are victims of "false memory syndrome," and that women who are raped in dating situations are "asking for it" (Estrich 1993).

In all rape trials, including those with celebrity defendants such as William Kennedy Smith or Mike Tyson, the jury's verdict still largely depends on whether the victim is successfully presented as a naive innocent or as a sexually experienced woman, as well as how threatening the alleged perpetrator looks to the jurors. Press coverage plays on these themes, and there are additional biases based on the race of both victim and defendant. The media sensationalize the rare instances when a white woman is raped by a nonwhite man, giving support to the popular myth of the minority rapist and obscuring the reality that most women are raped by men of their own race and class. Conversely, the media's tendency to ignore rapes, even serial rape-murders, of women of color creates the illusion that these women are not victims (Benedict 1992; Hall 1983).

The press often stereotypes rapists in terms of class, race, and ethnicity instead of focusing on the gender violence of the crime. In the 1980s, several well-publicized rape cases made this particularly evident. Coverage of a 1983 gang rape in New Bedford, Massachusetts, (dramatized in the movie, *The Accused*), denigrating the Portuguese-American rapists on the basis on their ethnicity, succeeded in mobilizing their ethnic community to defend the men (and blame the Portuguese-American victim). Similarly, the institutionalized racism of the mainstream press in the Central Park Jogger case led to their portraying the African-American teenagers as wild animals and blaming the perpetrators' brutality on their family structure, social class, and the ghetto culture, while ignoring the similarities to cases of gang rape by white men and boys. The African-American press responded by redefining the boys as innocents being lynched (Chancer 1987; Benedict 1992). In both cases, race and ethnicity diverted the media from covering the basic issue of sexual violence.

Press treatment of victims continues to discourage women from reporting rapes. In the 1980s, the policy of not printing the name of rape victims (unless another paper has done so first) came into question, with some feminists arguing that anonymity perpetuated the idea that rape was shameful and others claiming that it merely acknowledged the fact that the coverage was often demeaning and shaming. Silence about rape continues to create uncertainty about its prevalence. In 1991, the Department of Health and Human Services funded a broad-based survey of American women in which respondents were asked about both attempted and completed rapes in the past year and at any time in their lives. Extrapolating to all American women, their estimate is that 680,000 women were victims of forcible rape each year, over 12 percent had been sexually assaulted at some time, and that 60 percent of sexual assaults occur in childhood (National Victim Center 1992).

Other data confirm the frequency of sexual assault in American families. For example, a survey of sixth- through twelfth-graders in a middle-class Los Angeles school district found that nearly 20 percent of the girls had experienced an unwanted sexual encounter, almost all involving an older relative or family friend (Erikson and Rapkin 1991). Antifeminists cast doubt on the credibility of children's accounts but also refuse to believe adult survivors, returning to Freud's claim that such numbers must represent fantasy and false memory rather than real experiences.

The most extensive debate has been generated by feminist attention to acquaintance rape in general and date rape on campus in particular. As more young women define sexual encounters that included force or threats as being rape, antifeminists blame the women's movement for having changed the rules of the game—for having imposed a "politically correct" sexuality that takes the "natural" excitement and risk out of dating (Paglia 1990; Gibbs 1991; Roiphe 1993). Camille Paglia, an academic favored by conservative intellectuals, has used the media effectively to propound her view that men do indeed suffer blue balls and only a naive or stupid woman would allow herself to be raped. Women college students are apparently not persuaded; many have organized in their collective defense (from using bathroom graffiti to identify potential rapists to

holding demonstrations demanding harsher penalties than the college administration had imposed). Along with improved lighting and locks, educational programs for male students about what "no" means are being provided on many campuses, usually through the college's women's center or committee on the status of women. The infrastructure of feminist organization created on many campuses in the 1970s is responding vigorously to the challenge of date rape in the 1980s.

Conclusion

Patricia Smith (1993), a noted legal scholar, concludes that in all three crimes of sexual violence—harassment, battering, and rape—great social change and legal progress for women has been seen, but that the pervasiveness of these abusive practices attests to the continuing sexism of society. Police and prosecutors, judges and juries, reflect the attitudes of the general public and continue to minimize the harms done to women. Changes in the law achieved in this decade are only a small part of a broader social challenge to norms legitimating male violence and male domination that will surely take many decades to accomplish.

ECONOMIC JUSTICE

The Republican administrations of the 1980s cut back social services and reduced the real income of welfare recipients and low-wage workers while providing massive tax cuts and transfer payments for businesses and wealthy Americans on the theory that the benefits of elite investment would "trickle down" to create prosperity for all. Vast military expenditures created both a short-term economic boom and a quadrupling of the federal debt but failed to trickle down to women, then as now on the bottom of the economic ladder. Instead, the gap between rich and poor widened, and many women's basic economic survival was placed at risk (Amott 1993). Conflict between feminists and the New Right on this issue played out primarily in the legislative arena, where social policy is set, and where the recession brought on by the national economic policy in the 1980s greatly reduced revenues available for social programs.

Affirmative Action

Despite the gains made by women professionals and college graduates in the 1970s in entering high-prestige male-dominated occupations (see chapter 1), almost half of the female labor force, especially women of color, remains concentrated in the low-paying service sector. Comparing the median incomes of year-round full-time workers in 1991, women earned 74¢ for every dollar earned by a man (up from 60¢ in 1979), but a good proportion of the decline in the size of the wage gap was due to a fall in men's wages rather than a rise in women's incomes. Studies continue to indicate that sex and race discrimination play a major role in income inequality (Baron and Newman 1990; England 1992).

Such discrimination had been the target of civil rights legislation and executive action in the 1960s, which sought to redress the effects of decades of preferential hiring of white males. Executive Order 11375, issued in 1967 under President Lyndon Johnson, required that companies receiving federal contracts take positive steps ("affirmative action") to recruit and train women and minority men, to set goals and timetables for compliance, and to demonstrate that they were making good-faith efforts to meet these objectives. Affirmative action policy does *not* require setting quotas for hiring, nor does it mandate preferential treatment of unqualified or less qualified candidates. That most Americans are misinformed about these points is due in part to media carelessness and in part to an intentional effort by conservative politicians to win votes from working-class white men by playing on their anxieties about unemployment and job competition.

The media failed to distinguish "affirmative action" from "affirmative relief," which is a court judgment that finds that a particular employer has actively discriminated and orders a remedy in the form of accelerated hiring or promotion of the affected category of workers. In carrying out affirmative relief, a judge may set a quota and timetable to remedy a past pattern of illegal actions, just as back-pay awards are made to offset the effects of salary discrimination. Between media misrepresentation and conscious efforts by conservative groups and politicians to depict all affirmative action as "reverse discrimination," the continuation of patterns of discrimination against women and minority men has not been seriously challenged for over a decade.

Throughout the 1980s, not only did the Justice Department withdraw from even minimal enforcement of equal opportunity statutes, but it argued successfully before the Supreme Court that more of the burden of proof should fall on the *victims* of discrimination. Evidence of a pattern of disadvantage was no longer enough to shift to employers the burden to provide proof of a nondiscriminatory cause for the pattern; plaintiffs had to show evidence of "malicious intent." Such evidence of a frame of mind is extremely difficult to find, especially since most employers today know better than to put their discriminatory thoughts into writing.

In addition, in the *Grove City* case, the Court ruled that higher education institutions receiving federal funding could discriminate in programs other than the specific one being funded; for example, the chemistry department was free to indulge in discrimination if only the financial aid office got federal money. Presidents Reagan and Bush personally campaigned against affirmative action, referring to employment targets as "quotas" and remedies for past discrimination as "reverse discrimination" against whites, and suggesting it was difficult to find more than a few "qualified" white women or persons of color.

In response to these attacks, the women's policy network joined with other civil rights groups to press for an act of Congress reaffirming the original intent and interpretation of the 1963 Civil Rights Act. After civil rights and feminist organizations spent several years energetically lobbying for it, the Civil Rights Restoration Act passed Congress, only to be vetoed by President Bush. Although Bush eventually signed a much diluted version of the law in 1991, the final version was so weak on remedies for gender discrimination that many women's organizations withdrew their support for it.

At this writing the stance of the Clinton administration is still unclear, but twelve years of failure to enforce equal opportunity policies already jeopardizes the labor force gains women made in previous decades. Discrimination cases are harder to win, and more costly to bring. Regulatory mechanisms have been dismantled, and incentives for true affirmative action are virtually nonexistent. Although the backlash movement would like to blame feminists for women's economic struggles, feminists are committed to convincing the general public that the remedy for their problems in the workplace is more equality, not less.

Pay Equity/Comparable Worth

Because of sex segregation, women and men rarely hold the same jobs, and the work historically done by women is paid much less on average than that performed by men. The concept of pay equity, or comparable worth, is based on the principle that people who do jobs that (1) require a similar level of skill and effort, (2) take place under similar working conditions, and (3) involve a similar level of responsibility should receive similar paychecks. The 1980s saw major battles, primarily in the public (government) sector, to reevaluate all jobs and set wage scales based not on the historic gender of the occupation but on its comparable worth to the employer (Steinberg 1987; Acker 1989). By the end of the decade, many state governments had made adjustments in their wage-setting policies, and a number of local governments were engaged in conducting comparable worth studies or had already implemented some pay equity proposals. The outcome was typically a compromise among unions, employing agencies, feminist lobbies, and state legislatures that stopped well short of full equity but nonetheless established the principle of cross-gender comparison and improved wages for employees in female-dominated jobs (Acker 1989; Evans and Nelson 1989). By mobilizing union women in particular, the pay equity movement highlighted the relation between gender and class and raised feminist consciousness among working-class women (Blum 1991). Although elite women have been important sponsors of comparable-worth legislation, their interests lead them to try to limit the cost of settlements, to advocate technocratic rather than democratic decision processes, and to defend managerial control over wage-setting (Acker 1989; Blum 1991).

Not only has the pay equity issue enhanced the potential for working-class feminism that the career feminism of earlier decades slighted, but it has encouraged cross-class alliances among feminists and others concerned with economic justice. For example, the National Committee on Pay Equity (NCPE), a lobbying and information clearinghouse, is a coalition of religious, labor, civil rights, legal, professional, and women's organizations in the United States and Canada. Other new groups include the Women's Economic Agenda Project in California, the Women's Agenda in Pennsylvania, and the Women's Lobbyist Fund in Montana. These organizations held their first national conference in 1987. With Clinton's election in 1992, one Washington lobbyist noted that "the faxes are flying" among women's groups that are trying to formulate a national agenda on economic justice for women, with pay equity as a crucial element.

The backlash movement has attacked comparable worth in the same ringing tones it applied to the ERA and reproductive rights; Clarence Thomas, while still head of the EEOC, called it "the looniest idea since loony tunes." But these denunciations do not appear to have found much resonance among the general public, where strong majorities favor some sort of pay equity measures (National Committee on Pay Equity 1992).

Family Policies and Poverty

Beginning in the late 1970s, feminists concerned with economic justice directed attention to the fact that the majority of Americans living in poverty were women and children, and this phenomenon came to be termed "the feminization of poverty" (Pearce 1978). They highlighted several causes of women's impoverishment, such as divorce, low wages, and declining opportunities for blue-collar jobs.

Studies in this decade showed how often divorce drove even middle-class women to welfare for a few years, and how the lack of alimony and minimal levels of child support left single mothers penniless (Weitzman 1985; Sugarman and Hill 1990). Judges had been quick to turn the feminist claim that women should be economically independent into a myth that women actually were financially self-sufficient and so required only the most modest levels of transitional support.

Feminist responses included organizing displaced homemakers—midlife women divorced after a long period of full-time homemaking and child rearing. The National Displaced Homemaker Network coordinated efforts by similar networks on the state level to direct funds for job training to centers for displaced homemakers (e.g., twelve such centers were operating in 1992 in Connecticut alone). To date, very little federal support has been forthcoming, although some states have imposed a fee on marriage licenses to pay the costs of programs for battered women and displaced homemakers, a formal recognition of the risks women face in conventional marriage.

Another response to the poverty of women and children was to seek more energetic enforcement of court-ordered child-support payments from absent fathers. However, the means that state legislatures have used to implement such programs have often led to invasion of the privacy of divorced or unmarried women and to defining women in terms of economic dependence on some man. These policies also do very little to raise the standard of living of most single mothers. In some states welfare benefits are cut by the amount collected from absent fathers. Feminist opinion is increasingly divided on the merits of even lobbying state legislatures to experiment with such programs.

But many women are poor even if they are not divorced or out of the labor force, and this is particularly true for women of color. Many women have critiqued the "feminization of poverty" concept, arguing that women of color had always been poor, and that neither marriage nor a job was a reliable route out of poverty. Men of color also have low wages and high unemployment, and the jobs available to women of color themselves often pay such low wages that even year-round full-time work (itself hard to find) is inadequate to bring a family out of poverty. In 1992, a full-time job at just above the minimum wage provided an annual pretax income of less than $10,000. Feminists have thus joined a wider coalition arguing for a higher minimum wage, an earned income tax credit, universal health insurance, and an expanded Headstart program for preschoolers as practical steps to bring many women out of poverty and to reduce its effects on their children (Bergman 1986).

Conclusions

The framing of economic justice as a feminist issue grew throughout the 1980s. The need to defend reproductive rights is, however, a competing concern, and the drive for gender equality in the workplace is also increasingly presented as a "family issue" rather than one of feminism (Spalter-Roth and Schreiber 1994). Most feminist organizations see poverty as a women's issue, and many activists have targeted women's poverty as their primary focus in legislative lobbying (Boles 1991). Although those career feminists who had a narrow vision of economic opportunity were able uncritically to applaud gains made by a small number of professional and managerial women, most feminists found much to criticize in the limited opportunities and growing poverty of a large segment of the female population. The national administration in the 1980s was so apparently indifferent to the needs of real families and real children, while trumpeting support for "family values" and "unborn children," that many feminists made defeating these politicians a major goal. The change of administration in 1993 was thus most welcome, but the achievement of actual changes in policy remains a challenge for the coming decade.

Political Strategies and Dilemmas

Although feminist organizations were put on the defensive by the backlash movement, issues such as reproductive rights, equal opportunity, violence against women, and the welfare of the family increasingly came to be the main lines of political and cultural conflict (Freeman 1993). Both the high salience of feminist issues and the reactive position of feminist organizations played a major role in shaping the nature of the women's movement in this decade.

In this section, we look at how the "culture war" over feminism has shaped public perceptions of the movement and particularly the orientations and activism of young women. We see it especially manifest in what we call "the myth of the postfeminist generation." We then turn to an analysis of the defensive transformations of organizations and the continuation of proactive strategies throughout this decade.

THE MYTH OF THE POSTFEMINIST GENERATION

As we saw in chapter 4, about 30-40 percent of all Americans now define themselves as "feminist," a historically impressive percentage. Nonetheless, critics have rushed to proclaim (yet again) the "death" of feminism and the advent of a "postfeminist generation" (e.g., Bolotin 1982). This new generation is described as (1) disillusioned with what they perceive to be the feminist promise of "having it all"—a fulfilling career, a happy marriage, and accomplished children—and (2) worried that to be labeled "feminist" is also to be seen as "unfeminine." In the late 1980s, news magazines and advertisers hailed the dawn of a postfeminist era characterized by a return to conventional patterns of marriage and domesticity. This conclusion was based largely on anecdotal evidence and wishful thinking; the public opinion data reviewed in chapter 4 show instead a continuing trend toward more feminist opinions and higher levels of self-identification with feminism. Susan Faludi argues that this presentation of feminism as passé or dangerous was a part of a media backlash (1991), but there are a number of additional reasons why the image of feminism was changing in this decade.

One change is the baseline for comparison: in the late 1960s and early 1970s, journalists assumed feminists were wild-eyed fanatics with whom few if any women would identify; whereas in the late 1980s and early 1990s, many media pundits seemed puzzled that not all women were feminists. The label "feminist" was still felt to be somewhat risky, implying a person who was angry and "shrill," but the disavowal of feminism also seemed dangerously behind the times, suggesting a lack of awareness of discrimination and/or a repudiation of equality as a goal (Kamen 1991).

ON THE SUBJECT OF...

SUSAN FALUDI (1959-)

The backlash is at once sophisticated and banal, deceptively 'progressive' and proudly backward. It deploys both the 'new' findings of 'scientific research' and the dime-store moralism of yesteryear; it turns into media sound bites both the glib pronouncements of pop-psych trend-watchers and the frenzied rhetoric of New Right preachers. The backlash has succeeded in framing virtually the whole issue of women's rights in its own language. Just as Reaganism shifted political discourse far to the right and demonized liberalism, so the backlash convinced the public that women's 'liberation' was the true contemporary American scourge—the source of an endless laundry list of personal, social, and economic problems.

Faludi, Susan. "Introduction: Blame it on Feminism." In *Backlash: The Undeclared War Against American Women*, 1991. Reprint, p. xviii. New York: Anchor Books/Doubleday, 1992.

Susan Faludi was hailed as the leader of a new generation of feminists with the release of her debut book, *Backlash: The Undeclared War Against American Women* (1991), which received the National Book Critics Circle Award for general nonfiction. In 1991 she won both the Pulitzer Prize and a John Hancock Award for Excellence in Business and Financial Journalism for "The Reckoning," an exposé about the 1986 leveraged buyout of Safeway Stores, which appeared on the front page of the *Wall Street Journal* on May 16, 1990. Faludi's best-seller, *Backlash,* grew out of a sensational 1986 *Newsweek* cover story about the bleak prospects for single, professional women in America. Faludi maintains that the *Newsweek* article is just one of many insidious media creations that prey upon the fears and insecurities of liberated women, and argues that the gains toward equality earned by the women's movement in the 1960s and 1970s were systematically eroded in the 1980s. She singles out the regressive influence of advertising, the film industry, politicians, academics, the religious right, the men's movement, the news media, and conservative "pro-family" organizations whose resistance to social change has undermined women's independence. Faludi concludes that the gains made by the women's movement are fragile and easily lost; however, through a unified and concerted effort, and armed with a healthy skepticism toward the media, the rights won can be preserved and extended.

Somehow, the ideal seemed to shift to being "feminist" (in the sense of being enlightened about and emancipated from past forms of subordination) but not "a feminist" (in the sense of being angry about continuing inequality). As Stacey (1989) documents, many of the assumptions of feminism have passed into the common wisdom; the life that even conventional young women expect to live today is not that of their mothers or foremothers.

A second change is in the visibility of criticism of the movement by academic women, both feminist and not. The media were quick to publicize economist Sylvia Hewlett's (1986) charges that the New Feminist Movement was to blame for the failure of American institutions to correct the conditions that disadvantage and impoverish single mothers. More recently, the media has celebrated the deeply misogynist views of art historian Camille Paglia (1990). Paglia, who has been warmly welcomed into the conservative establishment and funded by its foundations, claims that male domination, including sexual assault, is natural, necessary, and secretly desired by women. Also, blaming women and the feminist movement for women's failure to achieve full equality has become commonplace among journalists.

As Faludi (1991) also documents, motion pictures and television programs began to portray unmarried women with professional careers as homicidally dangerous while celebrating what the media claimed was a "trend" toward well-paid professional women throwing over their careers for full-time motherhood. Although individuals can always be found to exemplify a purported "phenomenon," there is no statistical evidence for such a general tendency. Biased and uncritical reporting of the supposedly low probability of marriage for unmarried women in their thirties or the high level of infertility of women who defer childbearing, and of a myriad of other dangers of careerism undoubtedly affected how younger women thought about their future.

Such a negative view of feminism in the media was, of course, nothing new: solemn proclamations of the editors' wishful thinking that the movement was dead date back to 1971 (*Ms.* "No Comment" 1982). But if young women were actually rejecting feminism, where did all the enrollments in women's studies courses come from? One conservative response was to label the trend toward more inclusive curricula on college campuses as a conspiracy of "political correctness," in which faculty pressured or mandated enrollment in "intellectually shallow" courses (Bloom 1987; D'Souza 1991). It was evident to these critics that there could be no intellectual merit in courses focusing on women, ethnic minorities, or others whose works had been traditionally excluded from the conventional curriculum.

Ironically, it was the newcomers, such as women's studies programs, who were declared to be intolerant, ideological storm troopers, imposing their perspective on the university's "impartial" and "apolitical" decisions about who and what should be studied. The backlash refrain was to label women's studies and ethnic studies programs "victim studies," mocking the oppression and exclusion these groups had endured. These intellectual attacks spilled over into an increasingly intolerant and nasty mood on campuses toward people of color, feminists, lesbians, and gays. Physical attacks and campus hate crimes increased.

In this climate, it hardly seems surprising that many college women are hesitant to express their feminist views in class or in peer groups (Schneider 1988; Kamen 1991). However, attitude change among college women and men has also gone less deep than many feminists expected. College women continue to expect their husbands to earn more than they do (even while saying they believe in equal pay for women and men); they still expect to compromise only their own careers in order to raise children (even while they endorse shared child rearing in principle); and they expect to be supported by a man's income for some portion of their life (even though they assert the value of economic independence for women) (Machung 1989).

Some observers see parallels between the resistance to feminism in the early part of this century and the claim that young women are less feminist today, and argue that the women's movement is once again "in abeyance" (Taylor and Whittier 1993). Although feminism was expressed in a strong and well-organized social movement in the 1920s, its organizational strength withered in the following decades. Few young women born in the 1920s or 1930s were exposed to feminism as a coherent or comprehensive perspective. Observers soon noted that the average age of women identified as feminists was relatively high and rising. Feminism was perceived as something "old-fashioned" and feminists as out of touch with modern "emancipated" women and the new realities of expanding opportunities and more egalitarian marriages.

This pattern led Alice Rossi (1982) to suggest that feminist accomplishments are achieved in a repeating, two-phase multigeneration process. The first generation, chafing at the limitations clearly imposed on them as women, struggles for structural change. The modest changes they achieve are part of the social environment of women of the second generation, who are able to explore opportunities and experience freedoms that are still new and perceived as remarkable progress. The third generation then takes such accomplishments for granted but again experiences the limits and restrictions that remain and, chafing against these boundaries, becomes another first generation mobilizing for change.

Rossi argues that changes on the structural level are not sufficient for lasting progress; only when changes are assimilated into women's everyday life can the need for further changes be known. Her argument is based both on the historical record and on the theoretical premise that feminist demands arise from women's daily experiences and that without such resonance, feminist claims will fail to awake a supportive response. When change is rapid, however, "generations" could be very short.

From a different perspective, Gloria Steinem (1983) argues that the apparent conservatism of some young women ten years ago was a reflection of their stage in the life course. Unlike men, for whom youth can be the period of radical experimentation ultimately tempered by the responsibilities of work and family, women are more likely to be radicalized by age. It is misleading to extrapolate a universal pattern from the male model, because it is women's direct experience of marriage, motherhood, employment, divorce, and aging itself that underscore the difficulties of being female and transform conventional women into feminists. The status of women—and their rewards for accepting the male-defined criteria of value—may be highest when they are young. As Carolyn

Heilbrun (1988) has also argued, women may only realize their radical disagreement with the status quo as they discover themselves living a life for which they never had models and no longer seek others' approval. The women who seemed conservative a decade ago may have already been radicalized by the events of their lives.

Does this add up to an authentic "postfeminism" in the current generation? Although antifeminist opinions are more evident in the media, the attitudes of young women remain just as feminist as their mothers' views (see chapter 4). Moreover, the increasing numbers of young women in established feminist organizations, as well as a proliferation of new organizations focused on mobilizing the younger generation of feminists, suggest that the complacency of the late 1970s has already been replaced by an urgency and anxiety to defend gains already won. Many established feminist groups have "young feminist" networks (e.g., NOW's Young Feminist Conference and the Center for Women's Policy Studies' Feminist Futures Project). Some of the organizations founded by and for this younger generation have contributed to the revival of grassroots, confrontational feminist politics in the later part of this decade (Kamen 1991). Other young feminists are seeking academic degrees that will enable them to pursue a career in feminist law or community work or education, as seen in the continuing expansion of women's studies-inspired graduate programs in fields as diverse as public policy and theology. Young feminist professionals in Washington have organized their own Women's Information Network (WIN) for both career networking and political support (Kamen 1991). Women's studies is also a means by which activists can pass on the organizational lessons they have learned from their past decades of experience to the women—regardless of their ages—who have not shared that history.

A major challenge facing the feminist movement in the 1990s is moving from the reactive stance of the 1980s to a more proactive vision of the future. If that vision is to find resonance, it will need to incorporate the concerns of women born after the New Feminist Movement had already mobilized and made its mark. Rather than "postfeminists," this cohort could be appropriately called "second-generation feminists." Some call themselves the "Third Wave" (Manegold 1992). Their lives are not as restricted as their mothers', but they face an abundance of challenges and obstacles to achieving political and social equality and self-determination. The perspectives and is-

ON THE SUBJECT OF...

GLORIA STEINEM (1934-)

In my first days of activism, I thought I would do this ("this" being feminism) for a few years and then return to my real life (what my "real life" might be, I did not know). Partly, that was a naïve belief that injustice only had to be pointed out in order to be cured. Partly, it was a simple lack of courage.

But like so many others now and in movements past, I've learned that this is not just something we care about for a year or two or three. We are in it for life—and for our lives. Not even the spiral of history is needed to show the distance traveled. We have only to look back at the less complete people we ourselves used to be.

Steinem, Gloria. "Far from the Opposite Shore." In *Outrageous Acts and Everyday Rebellions*, pp. 361-62. New York: Holt, Rinehart and Winston, 1983.

Gloria Steinem is known as one of the most vocal and influential leaders in the American feminist movement. Born in Toledo, Ohio, Steinem earned scholarships and fellowships to several universities, and spent her graduate school years in India, where she became socially and politically active in fighting injustice. She returned to the United States in the 1960s, worked as a freelance reporter, and helped found *Ms.* in 1972, the first national magazine operated by women for the advancement of women's causes. Some of Steinem's works are collected in *Outrageous Acts and Everyday Rebellions* (1983), an anthology that ranges from her early, notorious "I Was a Playboy Bunny" exposé, to the later, more feminist theory-based articles she contributed to *Ms.*, including the comical yet incisive "If Men Could Menstruate." Although some critics and activists have faulted Steinem for representing only the more pleasant, nonthreatening elements of the feminist perspective in her writing, she has received popular and critical acclaim for her evocative, entertaining prose style, investigative reporting abilities, for working to raise both women's consciousness and their self-esteem, and for making feminist issues both accessible and familiar to the public.

sues of the second-generation feminists who become activists will play a major role in shaping the agenda and priorities of feminism in the coming years; the hard-won lessons of inclusiveness and diversity are part of the legacy on which they will have to build (Pfister 1993).

DEFENSIVE ADAPTATIONS AND ORGANIZATIONAL MATURITY

The reactive, defensive stance feminists adopted in the 1980s also had organizational consequences for the movement. First, the hostile political climate encouraged the development of broad coalitions, since allies were necessary to prevent erosion of significant employment and reproductive rights. Second, when all were under attack, differences among varieties of feminism became far less significant and similarities more important, so that ideological conflicts declined sharply. Because the New Right was trying to make feminism an unspeakable "*F*-word," variations in feminist identity became less defining of individuals or organizations than ever before (Heilbrun 1988). Indeed, varieties of visions for the future are primarily important for proactive movements; when feminist priorities are centered on defending gains already won, such visions are increasingly irrelevant. As Hyde (1994) points out, ideology does play a part in defensive movements by suggesting a preferred strategy and providing a network of past allies to mobilize against attacks; in the struggle to survive, some feminist organizations she studied became more conservative and professional, and others became more embedded in broad political resistance movements.

But to a greater extent than ever before, in the early 1990s there was a single feminist community, characterized by strategic cooperation of direct action/self-help, political/educational, and cultural/entrepreneurial groups in activist networks organized to target specific issues such as women's health, battering, or reproductive rights (Boles 1991). The proliferation of feminist organizations in the 1970s reached a stage in the 1980s in which institutionalization and long-term survival rather than growth dominated the agenda, a stage of movement maturity. Part of the price of this necessary institutionalization was specialization— that is, the increasing autonomy of "submovements" with specialized concerns such as the battered women's movement, the antirape movement, the pro-choice movement, or the women's health movement (Tierney 1982; Matthews 1994; Morgen 1994; Staggenborg 1991).

In fact, these different "submovements" had by the 1980s established unique sets of relationships—whether hostile, supportive, or mixed— with the funding agencies, foundations, and local communities with which they routinely dealt. They also competed for the scarce resources available from the government, and for the time, energy and commitment of individual feminists. Over the 1980s, involvement with specialized submovements became increasingly important in defining the identity of feminist organizations and activists. Gelb (1989) shows how the American form of politics (weak parties and a strong lobbying system) encouraged this development; whereas Boles (1991) argues that the emergence of broad coalitions at local, state, and federal levels also reflects the principle of federalism embodied in the American system. Much policymaking important to women is not centralized but requires coordinated efforts at all levels to be effective.

We further argue that the hostility toward feminism expressed by the national administration in the 1980s encouraged an organizational shift toward state-level, coalition politics. As we saw in the previous chapter, the original focus of feminist organizations was on grassroots direct action and women's community building at the local level, or on bureaucratic organizations lobbying for political gains on the national level. In the 1970s, the long, bruising struggle over the ERA gave birth to a third level of organization— namely, in the individual states, since the amendment needed ratification by state legislatures (Mathews and DeHart 1990; Berry 1986). As the federal climate became increasingly chilly in the 1980s, feminists turned more of their attention to the state legislatures to defend gains and pursue goals other than the ERA.

By 1989, feminists in forty states had created ongoing and diversified coalitions to address women's issues; one of the first such networks, the Wisconsin Women's Network (founded in 1979) is supported by sixty-seven dues-paying member organizations and over a thousand individual members and has two paid staffers and over a dozen policy task forces (Boles 1991, 46). In several states, such coalitions produced policies and laws that expanded women's rights well beyond the national baseline, although in others, feminists simply struggled to resist increasingly punitive and restrictive laws. The variation between states in feminist strategies and successes is a topic that requires further research.

Supporters of the Equal Rights Amendment march in Washington, D.C. on August 26, 1977.

Within each submovement, state-level coalitions connected direct action service providers with each other and with politicians, administrators, and educators concerned with each specific issue (Boles 1991). Because states are relatively small, their emergent women's policy networks depended heavily on the local direct action groups and feminist cultural community, as well as on formally organized political groups (Taylor and Whittier 1993). By 1990, there were over two hundred local-level commissions on the status of women, which Boles describes as "quite similar to the small groups of the radical branch of the women's movement, but with a difference: much of their activity now is undertaken in cooperation with governmental bureaucracies" (1991, 47). Thus, boundaries also blurred between self-help groups, political organizations, and individual entrepreneurs and professionals.

At the same time, it became increasingly clear that feminist commitment was not for a brief battle, but for a lifetime of struggle. Change would not come easily or soon. Mature feminist organizations were faced with the challenge of making sustaining a career in feminism possible, both emotionally and financially (Daniels 1991; Whittier 1994; Remington 1990). In the face of an increasingly angry and violent countermovement,

abetted by the inaction of federal and many local authorities, problems of emotional burnout were heightened (Simonds 1994). Great financial strains were created by the federal government's efforts to take funding away from women's health centers (Hyde 1994). Individual activists needed not only adequate income but also interpersonal support and opportunities for personal growth in their work—requirements that not all feminist organizations could meet (Morgen 1994; Remington 1990). Nonetheless, the women's community forged by cultural/entrepreneurial groups in the previous decades had become strong enough to sustain the commitment of those engaged in direct action/self-help and political/educational activities in the 1980s (Taylor and Rupp 1993). Lesbian feminists have always played a major role in maintaining this community, and their efforts were increasingly central to many feminist organizations (Whittier 1994).

PROACTIVE FEMINIST MOBILIZATIONS

The wide reach and increasingly integrated structure of mature feminist submovements defensively addressing issues high on the public agenda should not conceal feminist mobilization in other areas. Although when under attack from the Right, organizations' success could often be measured by sheer survival, the New Feminist Movement also developed strategies for change. Some of the feminist initiatives that bore fruit in the 1980s and early 1990s were the result of decades of earlier mobilization; others represented a return to styles of feminist activism that were more characteristic of earlier decades. We look here at three types of proactive feminist politics: unobtrusive mobilization within institutions, electoral politics, and the new grassroots direct action groups that formed in this decade.

Unobtrusive Mobilization

As examples of what she calls unobtrusive mobilization within institutions, Mary Katzenstein (1990) examines the development of feminist consciousness, organization, and strategy in two improbable contexts: the U.S. military and the Roman Catholic Church. Although both institutions are large, bureaucratic, strongly hierarchical and male-dominated, they nonetheless experienced substantial internal feminist activism that indelibly changed their structure and practices. Such unobtrusive mobilizations occurred in other institutions as well; we also look briefly at the judiciary and academia.

In the case of the military, the introduction of the All Volunteer Force (AVF) in 1973, with its competitive wages and career opportunities, brought an influx of female recruits. In the first few years, the expansion in women's numbers and rights was dramatic: the percentage of women serving in the armed forces tripled between 1972 and 1976; ROTC and the service academies were opened to women; mandatory dismissal for pregnancy was ended; and dependents' benefits were extended to their families. By 1980 the backlash began to be felt, as military leaders announced a need to "pause" in recruitment efforts and reassess the role of women (Stiehm 1989). Although women increased from 2 percent of the military in 1972 to 11 percent in 1992, this increase represented less than the increase projected in the 1970s. The coordinating body for women's affairs, the Defense Advisory Commission on Women in the Service (DACOWITS), began to exert pressure on the separate services to remove obstacles to women's rising through the ranks, most particularly the rules barring them from direct combat. The gains made, as evidenced by the greater visibility of women in the Panama and Desert Storm campaigns, further convinced the public that women can and do serve with distinction in all roles opened to them. Lobbying by women overturned the congressional prohibition on women in combat, and in 1993 the Clinton administration shifted the burden of proof to the military to demonstrate why a particular job should be closed to women and dropped most restrictions on women in aerial and naval combat roles.

DACOWITS has also focused on developing enforceable procedures for responding to cases of sexual harassment; when the Navy's own procedures were not followed, the assaults at the Tailhook convention became a public scandal. The integration of women in military roles also opened up a broader discussion of military values, sexuality, and gender stereotyping. "Witchhunts" directed against women—accusing them of being lesbians and threatening them with dishonorable discharges—had often been used to punish women for counterstereotypical behavior or for refusing men's sexual advances. Such accusations increasingly invoked an active defense from women's organizations such as WEAL and raised consciousness about the damaging effects of antihomosexuality policies on both men and women in the military, fostering a wider debate on sexuality and the double standard (Stiehm 1989).

In the Roman Catholic Church, women's extremely limited access to formal positions of leadership encouraged Catholic feminists to concentrate on changing the way women think about hierarchy and status (Katzenstein 1994). For some, the answer lies in "woman-church," small nonhierarchical groups of women reclaiming the church as a house-based community of believers (Ruether 1986; Farrell 1991). The long-term decline in the number of men in holy orders opened up some ceremonial and administrative church roles to women at the parish level, but the more profound change has come as both nuns and laywomen have rethought conventional answers to why the church is so male-dominated. Debates over inclusive language have led feminists to discuss more inclusive practices and to speak out strongly on issues of social justice. In some cases, this outspokenness has led to a visible split with the male hierarchy, which often places a higher priority on antiabortion activities than on ministering to the poor (Katzenstein 1994).

In the judiciary, change is evident as over half the states have at least one female justice on their highest court, and in Minnesota women constitute a majority on the state supreme court. Both as individuals and as members of the caucus of women on state court benches, these judges have spurred nearly every state to conduct a serious review of practices in the courtroom and in the law that constitute gender bias. Training programs have been set up in many states to help male judges become more aware of ways in which they may be discriminating against lawyers who appear before them, plaintiffs and defendants in the cases they hear, jurors they empanel, and staff they employ (Gender Bias Task Force Reports from Connecticut, New Jersey, Maryland, and New York are good examples). Moreover, law schools have gone beyond merely admitting more women to recognizing the importance of feminist issues in the law. Between 1986 and 1992, the number of law school courses focusing on women has grown from 30 to 145, and nine law schools (including Harvard, Yale, and Chicago) publish journals devoted to feminist jurisprudence (*About Women on Campus* 1993, 9).

In academia, there is probably no discipline, from accounting to zoology, that has not been affected by unobtrusive mobilization over the past two decades. It is projected that by 1995, 40 percent of all doctorates will be awarded to women, compared to 14 percent in 1970 (U.S. Bureau of the Census 1993, 172). With the increased representation of women in all fields of study, feminist caucuses and task forces in many disciplines have actively directed attention to gaps in knowledge, the gendered nature of course content, and the chilly classroom climate for future generations of scholars.

Feminist caucuses and task forces are also concerned with the status of women within the profession as a whole. Although in 1992 women constituted 27 percent of America's higher education faculty, they remain clustered disproportionately in lower ranks, less prestigious institutions, and in stereotypically feminine fields. Furthermore, the research topics pursued by feminist scholars are not typically those that receive the highest rewards in their discipline, where the "canon" of worth is still monopolized by a predominantly upper-middle-class, heterosexual white male elite. This can be seen in publishing patterns in sociology, for example, where female scholars and gender issues remain marginalized, though less so than in the past (Grant and Ward 1991; Ferree and Hall 1990).

The feminist struggle within academia, therefore, is not just over jobs and promotions, though these basic needs have been difficult enough to attain. The financial costs and personal difficulties of bringing a sex discrimination suit, the veil of secrecy around much academic decision-making, the falsification of records, and the lack of administrative accountability have often made pursuit of job equity an exercise in futility (Theodore

1986; Pleck 1990). But the challenges to women in academia also include gaining greater control over standards of evaluation of scholarship, input into decisions about curricula and requirements, and better conditions for professional development for both faculty and students.

In conclusion, we can see that there has been a mobilization of feminist pressure groups and caucuses within a variety of institutions. The focus of such groups has not been restricted to achieving the personal advancement of their members alone, as some observers of career feminist initiatives in the early 1970s would have predicted. In many diverse institutional contexts, feminist mobilization has also challenged the standards and practices of parent organizations in fundamental ways.

Electoral Politics

The 1980s backlash mobilized a feminist response at both national and state levels, which included an increase in the number of women running for political office. The heightening of gender consciousness in the general public and the salience of specific issues such as sexual harassment and reproductive choice also increased the chances of electoral success among women candidates in the early 1990s. Funding, traditionally a problem for women candidates, grew substantially when the Hill-Thomas hearings starkly illustrated the overwhelming control of men in congressional committees. Organizations raising money for pro-choice women candidates in 1992 reported record donations. EMILY's List, founded in 1985 to support pro-choice Democratic women, was a major contributor to some campaigns. By 1993, women constituted 20 percent of all state legislators, 11 percent of the members of the U.S. House of Representatives, and 7 percent of the Senate—still not impressive numbers, but a substantial increase from 1971, when women constituted a mere 5 percent of state legislators and fewer than 3 percent of members of Congress.

The 1980s saw the emergence and spread of a gender gap in voting behavior; women were significantly more supportive of Democratic candidates than were men. Beginning in the presidential election of 1980s, in which women were 6-9 percent less likely to vote for Ronald Reagan, the gap grew throughout the decade, reflecting women's negative experiences with Reagan-era policies. Thus in 1988, most men saw their fortunes as improving (52 percent), while most women did not (56 percent reported that their lives were getting worse or staying the same). Reagan's appointments were also more male-dominated than the previous administration's: whereas 15 percent of President Carter's appointments to the federal bench were women, the proportion of women among Reagan's appointments fell by half, to 8 percent. Top policymaking appointments show a similar pattern: 18 percent were women under Carter, 12 percent under Reagan, and a slightly lower percentage under Bush (Tillet and Krafchek 1991). The early appointments by President Clinton show a sharp reversal: There are highly visible women in top posts in the Departments of Justice, Commerce, and Environmental Protection, as well as Health and Human Services.

The increasing importance of women in politics reflects in part their growing strength as voters. Before the reemergence of feminism, women had voted at a significantly lower rate than men, but by 1980 women matched and then exceeded the turnout of their male peers. Because adult women outnumber men, women voters hold the key to electoral success: In the 1992 election, women accounted for 54 percent of all voters. Women's priorities on average differ from those of men; women are more interested in heath, education, welfare, and the link between work and family, and they are less concerned than men about national defense, taxes, and foreign affairs. The voting strength of women as a constituency surely played a role in the passage of the Family and Medical Leave Act of 1993, for example, which Clinton signed after two years of Bush vetoes. The lobbying for this law was led by the Council of Presidents, a coordinating body for the heads of forty-nine different Washington-based women's organizations, first founded in 1985. Passing this law is thus a significant long-term proactive victory for the movement.

The 1992 election also tripled the number of women in the Senate. Women's share of the House rose to forty-seven seats, a tiny percentage, but nearly twice the share held in 1990. At state and local levels women also ran well, capturing twenty-one major state offices and increasing their representation in state legislatures from 18 to 23 percent in just one year. Many of these candidates had shaped their campaigns to highlight issues raised by the New Feminist Movement; several anti-choice referenda were also defeated at the state level.

Not only has a crucial corner been turned, so that the presence of a woman candidate is no longer a novelty in itself, but the increasing visibility of women as a voting constituency has brought salience to some previously ignored issues. Although not all women elected to office are feminists, and not all politicians will support a more woman-centered agenda, there are now certain key prerequisites in place for feminist political influence to grow over the next decade. The parental leave bill enacted in 1993 was only the first item on the Council of Presidents' Women's Agenda, which includes issues such as childcare, health care, pay equity and reproductive rights.

Grassroots Direct-Action

In addition to electoral victories and mobilization within institutions, the New Feminist Movement also made gains in the 1980s at the local level, producing new forms of direct action at the grass roots that often engaged young activists. To an extent that surprised the media pundits who are so eager to declare the death of feminism, radical direct action groups actually increased in this decade. The Women's Action Coalition (WAC), formed in January 1992 in New York City, was soon followed by similar groups in Minneapolis, Houston, Toronto, Los Angeles, and other cities. As one member put it, "Anita Hill was our founding member. . . . [T]he catalyst in large part was seeing an all-white-male Senate Judiciary Committee grilling a black man and a black woman. There was this feeling of 'I'm going to take it to the streets. I'm angry'" (Saltpeter, cited in Hoban 1992). A "Guide to Direct Action Groups," published in *Harper's Bazaar,* brought an avalanche of letters from women throughout the country who were looking for a way to express their outrage over the Hill-Thomas hearings and anxious to found local chapters (Sheppard 1992).

Composed primarily of women in their twenties and early thirties, WAC has turned media attention to issues as diverse as nonpayment of child support in the United States and the widespread rape of Muslim women in Bosnia. WAC tactics include street theater, demonstrations, and other public protests reminiscent of the zap actions of the 1960s. New York's WAC has its own Drum Corps for marches, and a snappy logo—an eye, with the slogan "WAC is watching. We will take action." In the words of one activist, "We are oppressed but we are not going to be victimized" (Murray, in Hoban 1992). WAC has targeted family law courts for protests on Mother's Day, challenged Operation Rescue in front of abortion clinics, marched in front of court-houses where rape cases are being tried, demonstrated in front of museums that do not show women artists, and held regular vigils in front of the United Nations to protest the systematic use of rape as a terrorist tactic in the former Yugoslavia (Hoban 1992; Manegold 1992).

Although WAC is the most visible sign of the "new" grassroots energy of feminism, it is not the only one. WHAM, the Women's Health Action Mobilization was formed in 1989, taking its inspiration for street protests from the demonstrations staged by the radical AIDS protest group ACT-UP. Within a year, WHAM had a mailing list of three thousand names and held dozens of local meetings on issues from herbal medicine to abortion rights. Most of the members are under age thirty, and many are willing to risk arrest for their cause (Manegold 1992). Guerrilla Girls, founded in New York in 1985, calls itself "the conscience of the art world" and uses anonymous hit-and-run tactics to highlight sexist practices in museums, advertising, and media in general. Their posters, stickers, and street theater (in which they don gorilla masks and leather jackets) are aimed at art shows that virtually exclude women artists (Withers 1988). Direct actions, such as Take Back the Night marches, which were first held in San Francisco in 1978, spread to working-class communities such as Waukegan, Illinois, where four hundred people turned out for the 1990 march organized by their local coordinating council against sexual assault (Kamen 1991, 299). Such marches are virtually institutionalized on many campuses.

Other local direct actions may not be coordinated by an ongoing group but spring from the desire to protest specific actions dramatically. For example, Taylor and Whittier (1992b) report on a group of feminists in Ohio who sent pig testicles through the mail to a judge who had said that a four-year-old rape victim was "a promiscuous young lady." Other dramatic forms of public protest are also invented. For example, in Arizona, after charges of acquaintance rape against a basketball player were dropped, women protesters were arrested for outlining their bodies on the sidewalk in chalk with the slogan "rape is not a sport" (*About Women on Campus* 1993).

Third Wave is a new organization of "twenty-something" African-American and white feminists that has attempted to bridge the gap between spontaneous local protest actions, ongoing direct action groups, and more conventional forms of political action. Drawing on the language of the Civil Rights movement, Third Wave sponsored "Freedom Summer '92," a voter registration drive for pro-choice young people (Manegold 1992).

Similar goals characterize the Fund for a Feminist Majority (FFM), founded by former NOW President Eleanor Smeal, and attracting a less age-specific membership. FFM provided an alternative to NOW when NOW's own leadership seemed to be abandoning the electoral arena in the mid-1980s. Both Third Wave and FFM—and increasingly, NOW—are committed to combining the "insider" strategies of lobbying and voting with the "outsider" tactics of taking to the streets.

Conclusions

In this chapter we have examined the issues and organizational changes that characterized feminist activism in the period of defensive consolidation. During the openly hostile administrations of Presidents Reagan and Bush, the feminist agenda was dominated by struggles to preserve reproductive choice, to combat sexual violence, and to protect poor women from some of the worst economic consequences of "trickle-down" economics. Despite a sense of shared adversity and some limited successes in broad coalition building, the major thrust of this period was specialization, that is, organizing around specific issues. Feminists of very different perspectives and organizational affiliations were able to unite around particular policy concerns, raising funds and activating networks toward this goal, creating a vast web of submovements. In some ways, opposition strengthened the movement, creating a need for state organization and shattering some young women's complacency about gains already won. But constant defense took a toll as well, both in individual burnout and organizational collapse.

Unobtrusive mobilizations within many institutions changed organizational practices and challenged conventional thinking on many issues. Increased victories in electoral politics in the 1990s and a rebirth of direct action tactics at the grass roots provided the foundation for further mobilization in the coming decade. The new burst of energy and activism from second-generation feminists suggests that they are already defining their own agenda for the future of feminism. In the final chapter, we survey the accomplishments and unfinished agenda of the past three decades.

Bibliography

About Women on Campus. 1993. Students protest against failure to handle rape issues. *National Association for Women in Education* 2 (spring): 1.

Acker, J. 1989. *Doing comparable worth: gender, class and pay equity.* Philadelphia: Temple University Press.

American Association of University Women. 1992. *How schools shortchange girls: The A.A.U.W. Report.* New York: AAUP Educational Foundation.

Amott, T. L. 1993. *Caught in the crisis: Women and the U.S. economy today.* New York: Monthly Review Press.

Baron, J. N., and A. E. Newman. 1990. For what it's worth: Organizations, occupations, and the value of work done by women and nonwhites. *American Sociological Review* 55: 155-75.

Beam, C., and D. Paul. 1992. A question of access: Is abortion really still legal? *Sojourner* 18 (September): 17-18.

Benedict, H. 1992. *Virgin or vamp: How the press covers sex crimes.* New York: Oxford University Press.

Bergmann, Barbara. 1986. *The economic emergence of women.* New York: Basic Books.

Berry, M. F. 1986. *Why ERA failed.* Bloomington: Indiana University Press.

Bloom, A. 1987. *The closing of the American mind.* New York: Simon & Schuster.

Blum, L. 1991. *Between feminism and labor: The significance of the comparable worth movement.* Berkeley: University of California Press.

Boles, J. 1991. Form follows function: the evolution of feminist strategies. *The Annals of the American Academy of Political and Social Science* (May): 38-49.

Bolotin, S. 1982. Voices from the postfeminist generation. *New York Times Magazine,* 26 October, 29ff.

Browne, A., and K. Williams. 1993. Gender, intimacy and lethal violence: Trends from 1976 through 1987. *Gender & Society* 7, no. 1: 78-98.

Brush L. D. 1990. Violent acts and injurious outcomes in married couples. *Gender & Society* 4: 56-67.

Chancer, L. 1987. New Bedford Massachusetts: March 6, 1983 to March 22, 1984: The before and after of a group rape. *Gender & Society* 1, no. 3: 239-61.

Daniels, A. K. 1991. Careers in feminism. *Gender & Society* 5: 583-607.

D'Souza, D. 1991. *Illiberal education: The politics of race and sex on campus.* New York: The Free Press.

Dzeich, B. and L. Weiner 1984. *The lecherous professor.* Boston: Beacon Press.

England, P. 1992. *Comparable worth: Theories and evidence.* New York: Aldine de Gruyter.

Erickson, P. I., and A. J. Rapkin. 1991. Unwanted sexual experiences among middle and high school youth. *Journal of Adolescent Health* 12: 319.

Estrich, S. 1993. Rape. In *Feminist jurisprudence,* edited by P. Smith. New York: Oxford.

Evans, S., and B. J. Nelson. 1989. *Wage justice: Comparable worth and the paradox of technocratic reform.* Chicago: University of Chicago Press.

Faludi, S. 1991. *Backlash: The undeclared war against American women.* New York: Crown.

Farrell, S. 1991. It's our church too: Women's position in the Catholic church today. In *The social construction of gender,* edited by J. Lorber and S. Farrell, 228-54. Newbury Park, Calif.: Sage.

Ferree, M. M., and E. J. Hall. 1990. Visual images of American society: Gender and race in introductory sociology textbooks. *Gender & Society* 4, no. 4: 500-33.

Freeman, J. 1993. Feminism vs. Family Values: Women at the 1992 Democratic and Republican Conventions. *PS* 26 (March): 21-28.

Gallup Organization. 1991. Report of poll conducted 14 October for CNN and archived at the Roper Center. Storrs, Conn.: University of Connecticut.

Gallup Organization. 1992. Report of poll conducted 1-3 October for CNN and archived at the Roper Center. Storrs, Conn.: University of Connecticut.

Gelb, J. 1989. *Feminism and politics: A comparative perspective.* Berkeley: University of California Press.

Gibbs, N. 1991. When is it rape? *Time,* 3 June, 48-55.

Gilligan, C. 1982. *In a different voice.* Cambridge: Harvard University Press.

Ginsburg, F. 1989. *Contested lives.* Berkeley: University of California Press.

Grant, L., and K. B. Ward. 1991. Gender and publishing in sociology. *Gender & Society* 5: 207-23.

Hall, J. D. 1983. The mind that burns in each body: Women, rape, and racial violence. In *The powers of desire,* edited by A. Snitow, C. Stansell, and S. Thompson. New York: Monthly Review Press.

Harlow, C. W. 1991. *Female victims of violent crime.* U.S. Bureau of Justice Statistics, NJC-126826: January.

Heilbrun, C. 1988. *Writing a woman's life.* New York: Norton.

Hewlett, S. A. 1986. *A lesser life: The myth of women's liberation in America.* New York: Warner.

Hoban, P. 1992. Big WAC Attack. *New York,* 3 August, 30-35.

Hyde, C. 1994. Feminist social movement organizations survive the new right. In *Feminist organizations: Harvest of the new women's movement,* edited by M. M. Ferree and P. Y. Martin. Philadelphia: Temple University Press.

Kamen, P. 1991. *Feminist fatale.* New York: Donald Fine.

Katzenstein, M. F. 1990. Feminism within American institutions: Unobtrusive mobilization in the 1980's. *Signs* 16, no. 1: 27-54.

———. 1994. Discursive politics and feminist activism in the Catholic Church. In *Feminist organizations: Harvest of the new women's movement,* edited by M. M. Ferree and P. Y. Martin. Philadelphia: Temple University Press.

Kolbert, E. 1991. Sexual harassment at work is pervasive, survey suggests. *New York Times,* 11 October, 1ff.

Kurz, D. 1989. Social science perspectives on wife abuse: Current debates and future directions. *Gender & Society* 3: 489-505.

Machung, A. 1989. Talking career, thinking job: Gender differences in career and family expectations of Berkeley seniors. *Feminist Studies* 15, no. 1 (spring): 35-58.

MacKinnon, C. 1987. *Feminism unmodified: Discourses on life and law.* Cambridge: Harvard University Press.

Manegold, C. 1992. No more nice girls: In angry droves, radical feminists just want to have impact. *New York Times,* 12 July.

Martin, S. E. 1989. Sexual harassment: The link joining gender stratification, sexuality and women's status. In *Women: A feminist perspective*, 3d ed., edited by Jo Freeman. Palo Alto, Calif.: Mayfield.

Mathews, D. G., and J. S. DeHart. 1990. *Sex, gender, and the politics of ERA: A state and the nation*. New York: Oxford University Press.

Matthews, N. 1994. Feminist clashes with the state: The case of state-funded rape crisis centers. In *Feminist organizations: Harvest of the new women's movement*, edited by M. M. Ferree and P. Y. Martin. Philadelphia: Temple University Press.

Morgen, S. 1994. It was the best of times, it was the worst of times: Emotional discourse in the work cultures of feminist health clinics. In *Feminist organizations: Harvest of the new women's movement*, edited by M. M. Ferree and P. Y. Martin. Philadelphia: Temple University Press.

Morrison, T. 1992. *Race-ing justice, en-gender-ing power*. New York: Pantheon.

National Coalition against Domestic Violence. 1991. Letter to members. Washington, D.C.

National Committee on Pay Equity. 1992. *Newsnotes*. Washington, D.C.: NCPE.

National Victim Center. 1992. *National women's study*. Washington, D.C.

Paglia, C. 1990. *Sexual personae: Art and decadence from Nefertiti to Emily Dickinson*. New Haven, Conn.: Yale University Press.

Paludi, M., and R. Barickman. 1991. *Academic and workplace sexual harassment: A resource manual*. Albany: SUNY Press.

Pearce, D. 1978. The feminization of poverty: Women, work and welfare. *Urban and Social Change Review* (February): 1-17.

Petchesky, R. 1984. *Abortion and woman's choice: The state, sexuality and reproductive freedom*. Boston, Mass.: Northeastern University Press.

Pfister, B. 1993. Building the next feminism: Facing the questions of equity and inclusion in the 1990s. *Democratic Left* 21, no. 2: 14-17.

Pleck, E. 1990. The unfulfilled promise: Women and academe. *Sociological Forum* 5:517-24.

Remington, J. 1990. *The need to thrive: Women's organizations in the Twin Cities*. St. Paul: Minnesota Women's Press.

Roiphe, K. 1993. Rape hype betrays feminism: Date rape's other victim. *New York Times Magazine*, 13 June, 26ff.

Rossi, A. 1982. *Feminists in politics: A panel analysis of the first national women's conference*. New York: Academic Press.

Rothman, B. K. 1982. In *Labor: Women and power in the birthplace*. New York: W. W. Norton.

Ruether, R. 1986. *Women-Church: Theology and practice*. San Francisco: Harper & Row.

Schmittroth, L. 1991. *Statistical record of women worldwide*. Detroit: Gale Research.

Schneider, B. 1988. Political generations in the contemporary women's movement. *Sociological Inquiry* 58, 1 (winter): 4-21.

Schreiber, R., and R. Spalter-Roth. 1994. Outsider issues and insider tactics: Strategic tensions in the women's policy network in the 1980s. In *Feminist organizations: Harvest of the new women's movement*, edited by M. M. Ferree and P. Y. Martin. Philadelphia: Temple University Press.

Scott, J. 1989. Conflicting beliefs about abortion: Legal approval and moral doubts. *Social Psychological Quarterly* 52: 319-26.

Seals, B., P. Jenkins, and J. Manale. 1992. Sexual harassment. Paper presented at midyear meeting of Sociologists for Women in Society.

Sheppard, N. 1992. *WAC Talk*. "Women talk to WAC" Undated Supplement.

Simonds, W. 1994. Feminism on the job: Ideology and practice in an abortion clinic. In *Feminist organizations: Harvest of the new women's movement*, edited by M. M. Ferree and P. Y. Martin. Philadelphia: Temple University Press.

Smith, P. 1993. *Feminist jurisprudence*. New York: Oxford.

Spalter-Roth, R., and R. Schreiber. 1994. Outsider issues and insider tactics: Strategic tensions in the women's policy network in the 1980s. In *Feminist organizations: Harvest of the new women's movement*, edited by M. M. Ferree and P. Y. Martin. Philadelphia: Temple University Press.

Staggenborg, S. 1991. *The Pro-Choice movement*. New York: Oxford University Press.

Steinberg, R. 1987. Radical challenges in a liberal world: The mixed success of comparable worth. *Gender & Society* 1, no. 4: 466-75.

Steinem, G. 1983. An appeal to young women. Address to NWPC Annual Meeting, San Antonio, spring, 1983, cited in *Comment*, 14 no. 2.

Stiehm, J. 1982. Women, men, and military service: Is protection necessarily a racket? In *Women, power, and policy* edited by E. Boneparth, 282-93. New York: Pergamon.

————. 1989. *Arms and the enlisted woman*. Philadelphia: Temple University Press.

Sugarman, S. D., and H. Hill, eds. 1990. *Divorce reform at the crossroads*. New Haven, Conn.: Yale University Press.

Tangri, S., Burt, M., and Johnson, L., 1982. Sexual harassment at work: Three explanatory models. *Journal of Social Issues* 38, no. 4: 33-54.

Taylor, V., and L. Rupp. 1993. Women's culture and lesbian feminist activism: A reconsideration of cultural feminism. *Signs* 19, no. 1: 32-61.

Taylor, V., and N. Whittier. 1992a. Theoretical approaches to social movement culture: The culture of the women's movement. Paper presented at the Workshop on Culture and Social Movements, June 18-20, San Diego.

————. 1993. The new feminist movement. In *Feminist frontiers III*, edited by L. Richardson and V. Taylor. New York: McGraw-Hill.

Theodore, A. 1986. *The campus troublemakers: Academic women in protest*. Houston, Tex: Cap and Gown Press.

Tierney, K. 1982. The battered women's movement and the creation of the wife-beating problem. *Social Problems* 29: 207-20.

Tillet, R., and D. Krafchek, 1991. Factsheet on women's political progress. *National Women's Political Caucus.*

U.S. Bureau of the Census. 1993. Educational attainment in the U.S. 1992. *Current Population Reports*, P-20, no. 462 (July).

Weitzman, L. J. 1985. *The divorce revolution: The unexpected social and economic consequences for women and children in America.* New York: The Free Press.

Whittier, N. 1994. Turning it over: Personnel change in the Columbus Ohio women's movement 1969-1984. In *Feminist organizations: Harvest of the new women's movement*, edited by M. M. Ferree and P. Y. Martin. Philadelphia: Temple University Press.

Withers, J. 1988. Art essay: The guerrilla girls. *Feminist Studies* 14, no. 2: 284-300.

Yllo, K., and M. Bograd, eds. 1988. *Feminist perspectives on wife abuse.* Newbury Park, Calif.: Sage.

ALICE ECHOLS (ESSAY DATE 1997)

SOURCE: Echols, Alice. "Nothing Distant about It: Women's Liberation and Sixties Radicalism." In *Women Transforming Politics: An Alternative Reader*, edited by Cathy J. Cohen, Kathleen B. Jones, and Joan C. Tronto, pp. 456-76. New York: New York University Press, 1997.

In the following essay, Echols points out how the ideology and methodology of 1960s political radicals, especially their linking of the personal and the political, directly supported and served as a model for the women's liberation movement.

On 7 September 1968 the sixties came to the Miss America Pageant when one hundred women's liberationists descended on Atlantic City to protest the pageant's promotion of physical attractiveness and charm as the primary measures of women's worth. Carrying signs that declared, "Miss America Is a Big Falsie," "Miss America Sells It," and "Up against the Wall, Miss America," they formed a picket line on the boardwalk, sang anti-Miss America songs in three-part harmony, and performed guerrilla theater. The activists crowned a live sheep Miss America and paraded it on the boardwalk to parody the way the contestants, and, by extension, all women, "are appraised and judged like animals at a county fair." They tried to convince women in the crowd that the tyranny of beauty was but one of the many ways that women's bodies were colonized. By announcing beforehand that they would not speak to male reporters (or to any man for that matter), they challenged the sexual division of labor that consigned women reporters to the "soft" stories and male reporters to the "hard" news stories. Newspaper editors who wanted to cover the protest were thus forced to pull their female reporters from the society pages to do so.[1]

The protesters set up a "Freedom Trash Can" and filled it with various "instruments of torture"—high-heeled shoes, bras, girdles, hair curlers, false eyelashes, typing books, and representative copies of *Cosmopolitan, Playboy,* and *Ladies' Home Journal.* They had wanted to burn the contents of the Freedom Trash Can but were prevented from doing so by a city ordinance that prohibited bonfires on the boardwalk. However, word had been leaked to the press that the protest would include a symbolic bra-burning, and, as a consequence, reporters were everywhere.[2] Although they burned no bras that day on the boardwalk, the image of the bra-burning, militant feminist remains part of our popular mythology about the women's liberation movement.

The activists also managed to make their presence felt inside the auditorium during that night's live broadcast of the pageant. Pageant officials must have known that they were in for a long night when early in the evening one protester sprayed Toni Home Permanent Spray (one of the pageant's sponsors) at the mayor's booth. She was charged with disorderly conduct and "emanating a noxious odor," an irony that women's liberationists understandably savored. The more spectacular action occurred later that night. As the outgoing Miss America read her farewell speech, four women unfurled a banner that read, "Women's Liberation," and all sixteen protesters shouted "Freedom for Women," and "No More Miss America" before security guards could eject them. The television audience heard the commotion and could see it register on Miss America's face as she stumbled through the remainder of her speech. But the program's producer prevented the cameramen from covering the cause of Miss America's consternation.[3] The television audience did not remain in the dark for long, because Monday's newspapers described the protest in some detail. As the first major demonstration of the fledgling women's liberation movement, it had been designed to make a big splash, and after Monday morning no one could doubt that it had.

In its wit, passion, and irreverence, not to mention its expansive formulation of politics (to include the politics of beauty, no less!), the Miss America protest resembled other sixties demonstrations. Just as women's liberationists used a sheep to make a statement about conventional femininity, so had the Yippies a week earlier lampooned the political process by nominating a pig, Pegasus, for the presidency at the Democratic National Convention.[4] Although Atlantic City witnessed none of the violence that had occurred in Chicago, the protest generated plenty of hostility among the six hundred or so onlookers who gathered on the boardwalk. Judging from their response, this new thing, "women's liberation," was about as popular as the antiwar movement. The protesters were jeered, harassed, and called "commies" and "man-haters." One man suggested that it "would be a lot more useful" if the protesters threw themselves, and not their bras, girdles, and makeup, into the trash can.[5]

Nothing—not even the verbal abuse they encountered on the boardwalk—could diminish the euphoria women's liberationists felt as they started to mobilize around their own, rather than other people's, oppression. Ann Snitow speaks for many when she recalls that in contrast to her involvement in the larger, male-dominated protest Movement,[6] where she had felt sort of "blank and peripheral," women's liberation was like "an ecstasy of discussion." Precisely because it was about one's own life, "there was," she claims, "nothing distant about it."[7] Robin Morgan has contended that the Miss America protest "announced our existence to the world."[8] That is only a slight exaggeration, for as a consequence of the protest, women's liberation achieved the status of a movement both to its participants and to the media; as such, the Miss America demonstration represents an important moment in the history of the sixties.[9]

Although the women's liberation movement began to take shape only toward the end of the decade, it was a paradigmatically sixties movement. It is not just that many early women's liberation activists had prior involvements in other sixties movements, although that was certainly true, as has been ably documented by Sara Evans.[10] And it is not just that, of all the sixties movements, the women's liberation movement alone carried on and extended into the 1970s that decade's political radicalism and rethinking of fundamental social organization, although that is true as well. Rather, it is also that the larger, male-dominated protest Movement, despite its considerable sexism, provided much of the intellectual foundation and cultural orientation for the women's liberation movement. Indeed, many of the broad themes of the women's liberation movement—especially its concern with revitalizing the democratic process and reformulating "politics" to include the personal—were refined and recast versions of ideas and approaches already present in the New Left and the black freedom movement.

Moreover, like other sixties radicals, women's liberationists were responding at least in part to particular features of the postwar landscape. For

instance, both the New Left and the women's liberation movement can be understood as part of a gendered generational revolt against the ultra-domesticity of that aberrant decade, the 1950s. The white radicals who participated in these movements were in flight from the nuclear family and the domesticated versions of masculinity and femininity that prevailed in postwar America. Sixties radicals, white and black, were also responding to the hegemonic position of liberalism and its promotion of government expansion both at home and abroad—the welfare/warfare state. Although sixties radicals came to define themselves in opposition to liberalism, their relation to liberalism was nonetheless complicated and ambivalent. They saw in big government not only a way of achieving greater economic and social justice, but also the possibility of an increasingly well managed society and an ever more remote government.

In this chapter I will attempt to evaluate some of the more important features of sixties radicalism by focusing on the specific example of the women's liberation movement. I am motivated by the problematic ways "the sixties" has come to be scripted in our culture. If conservative "slash and burn" accounts of the period indict sixties radicals for everything from crime and drug use to single motherhood, they at least heap guilt fairly equally on antiwar, black civil rights, and feminist activists alike. By contrast, progressive reconstructions, while considerably more positive in their assessments of the period, tend to present the sixties as if women were almost completely outside the world of radical politics. Although my accounting of the sixties is in some respects critical, I nonetheless believe that there was much in sixties radicalism that was original and hopeful, including its challenge to established authority and expertise, its commitment to refashioning democracy and "politics," and its interrogation of such naturalized categories as gender and race.

Women's discontent with their place in America in the sixties was, of course, produced by a broad range of causes. Crucial in reigniting feminist consciousness in the sixties was the unprecedented number of women (especially married white women) being drawn into the paid labor force, as the service sector of the economy expanded and rising consumer aspirations fueled the desire of many families for a second income.[11] As Alice Kessler-Harris has pointed out, "homes and cars, refrigerators and washing machines, telephones and multiple televisions required higher incomes." So did providing a college education for one's children. These new patterns of consumption were made possible in large part through the emergence of the two-income family as wives increasingly "sought to aid their husbands in the quest for the good life." By 1960, 30.5 percent of all wives worked for wages.[12] Women's growing participation in the labor force also reflected larger structural shifts in the U.S. economy. Sara Evans has argued that the "reestablishment of labor force segregation following World War II ironically reserved for women a large proportion of the new jobs created in the fifties due to the fact that the fastest growing sector of the economy was no longer industry but services."[13] Women's increasing labor force participation was facilitated as well by the growing number of women graduating from college and by the introduction of the birth control pill in 1960.

Despite the fact that women's "place" was increasingly in the paid workforce (or perhaps because of it), ideas about women's proper role in American society were quite conventional throughout the 1950s and the early 1960s, held there by a resurgent ideology of domesticity— what Betty Friedan called the "feminine mystique." But, as Jane De Hart-Mathews has observed, "the bad fit was there: the unfairness of unequal pay for the same work, the low value placed on jobs women performed, the double burden of housework and wage work."[14] By the mid-1960s at least some American women felt that the contradiction between the realities of paid work and higher education on the one hand and the still pervasive ideology of domesticity on the other had become irreconcilable.

Without the presence of other oppositional movements, however, the women's liberation movement may not have developed at all as an organized force for social change. It certainly would have developed along vastly different lines. The climate of protest encouraged women, even those not directly involved in the black movement and the New Left, to question conventional gender arrangements. Moreover, many of the women who helped form the women's liberation movement had been involved as well in the male-dominated Movement. If the larger Movement was typically indifferent, or worse, hostile to women's liberation, it was nonetheless through their experiences in that Movement that the young and predominantly white and middle-class women who initially formed the women's liberation movement became politicized. The relationship between women's liberation and the larger Movement was at its core paradoxical. If the Movement was a site of sexism, it also provided white women a space in which they could develop political skills and self-confidence, a space in which they could violate the injunction against female self-assertion.[15] Most important, it gave them no small part of the intellectual ammunition—the language and the ideas—with which to fight their own oppression.

Sixties radicals struggled to reformulate politics and power. Their struggle confounded many who lived through the sixties as well as those trying to make sense of the period some thirty years later. One of the most striking characteristics of sixties radicals was their ever-expanding opposition to liberalism. Radicals' theoretical disavowal of liberalism developed gradually and in large part in response to liberals' specific defaults—their failure to repudiate the segregationists at the 1964 Democratic National Convention, their lack of vigor in pressing for greater federal intervention in support of civil rights workers, and their readiness (with few exceptions) to support President Lyndon B. Johnson's escalation of the Vietnam War. But initially some radicals had argued that the Movement should acknowledge that liberalism was not monolithic but contained two discernible strands—"corporate" and "humanist" liberalism. For instance, in 1965 Carl Oglesby, an early leader of the Students for a Democratic Society (SDS), contrasted *corporate liberals,* whose identification with the system made them "illiberal liberals," with *humanist liberals,* who he hoped might yet see that "it is this movement with which their own best hopes are most in tune."[16]

By 1967 radicals were no longer making the distinction between humanist and corporate liberals that they once had. This represented an important political shift for early new leftists in particular who once had felt an affinity of sorts with liberalism.[17] Black radicals were the first to decisively reject liberalism, and their move had an enormous impact on white radicals. With the ascendancy of black power many black militants maintained that liberalism was intrinsically paternalistic, and that black liberation required that the struggle be free of white involvement. This was elaborated by white radicals, who soon developed the argument that authentic radicalism involved organizing around one's own oppression rather than becoming involved, as a "liberal" would, in someone else's struggle for freedom. For instance, in 1967 Gregory Calvert, another SDS leader, argued that the "student movement has to develop an image of its own revolution . . . instead of believing that you're a revolutionary

ON THE SUBJECT OF...

BETTY FRIEDAN (1921-)

Born in Peoria, Illinois, Friedan graduated *summa cum laude* from Smith College in 1942. Faced with the necessity of sacrificing marriage and motherhood in pursuit of an academic career, she turned down the research fellowship she was offered, began working as a reporter in New York City, and was married in 1947. Fired from her job after requesting a second maternity leave, Friedan became a freelance writer for women's magazines. She interviewed housewives about their lives, and this research formed the basis of *The Feminine Mystique* (1963). In this best-selling work, Friedan argued that "feminine mystique," the belief that women gained fulfillment only from marriage and motherhood, is responsible for the boredom, fatigue, and dissatisfaction that has pervaded the lives of many American women. *The Feminine Mystique* has been credited with revitalizing interest in the women's movement. In 1966 Friedan cofounded the National Organization for Women (NOW) and served as its president until 1970. Under her guidance, NOW lob-bied for the legalization of abortion, the passage of the Equal Rights Amendment, and the equal treatment of women in the workplace. Friedan, however, came into frequent conflict with radical feminists over the issue of lesbianism as a political stance, which she opposed on the grounds that it alienated mainstream women and men sympathetic to the movement. Political infighting between Friedan and such prominent activists as Gloria Steinem and Bella Abzug disrupted the 1973 National Women's Political Caucus, and Friedan later indirectly accused them of manipulating the balloting to prevent the participation of her supporters. Friedan discussed this controversy and chronicled her early involvement with the women's movement in *It Changed My Life: Writings on the Women's Movement* (1976). In *The Second Stage* (1981), Friedan discussed the emergence of the Superwoman myth—the image of the woman who effortlessly juggles her career, marriage, and children—, or as Friedan dubbed it, the "feminist mystique." Friedan warned that the Superwoman image, as unrealistic as the perfect housewife image from the 1960s, could have lasting negative effects on the women's movement.

---

because you're related to Fidel's struggle, Stokely's struggle, always someone else's struggle."[18] Black radicals were also the first to conclude that nothing short of revolution—certainly not Johnson's Great Society programs and a few pieces of civil rights legislation—could undo racism. As leftist journalist Andrew Kopkind remembered it, the rhetoric of revolution proved impossible for white new leftists to resist. "With black revolution raging in America and world revolution directed against America, it was hardly possible for white radicals to think themselves anything less than revolutionaries."[19]

Radicals' repudiation of liberalism also grew out of their fear that liberalism could "co-opt" and thereby contain dissent. Thus, in 1965 when President Johnson concluded a nationally televised speech on civil rights by proclaiming, "And we *shall* overcome," radicals saw in this nothing more than a calculated move to appropriate Movement rhetoric in order to blunt protest. By contrast, more established civil rights leaders reportedly cheered the president on, believing that his declaration constituted a significant "affirmation of the movement."[20] Liberalism, then, was seen as both compromised and compromising. In this, young radicals were influenced by Herbert Marcuse, who emphasized the system's ability to reproduce itself through its recuperation of dissent.[21]

Just as radicals' critique of materialism developed in the context of relative economic abundance, so did their critique of liberalism develop at a time of liberalism's greatest political strength. The idea that conservativism might supplant liberalism at some point in the near future was simply unimaginable to them. (To be fair, this view was not entirely unreasonable given

Johnson's trouncing of Barry Goldwater in the 1964 presidential election.)

This was just one of many things that distinguished new leftists from old leftists, who, having lived through McCarthyism, were far more concerned about the possibility of a conservative resurgence. For if sixties radicals grew worlds apart from liberals, they often found themselves in conflict with old leftists as well. In general, new leftists rejected the economism and virulent anticommunism of the non-communist Old Left. In contrast to old leftists, whose target was "class-based economic oppression," new leftists (at least before 1969, when some new leftists did embrace dogmatic versions of Marxism) focused on "how late capitalist society creates mechanisms of psychological and cultural domination over *everyone*."[22] For young radicals the problem went beyond capitalism and included not only the alienation engendered by mass society, but also other systems of hierarchy based on race, gender, and age. Indeed, they were often more influenced by existentialists like Camus or social critics like C. Wright Mills and Herbert Marcuse, both of whom doubted the working class's potential for radical action, than by Marx or Lenin. For instance, SDS president Paul Potter contended that it would be "through the experience of the middle class and the anesthetic of bureaucracy and mass society that the vision and program of participatory democracy will come."[23] This rejection of what Mills dubbed the "labor metaphysic" had everything to do with the different circumstances radicals confronted in the sixties. As Arthur Miller observed, "The radical of the thirties came out of a system that had stopped and the important job was to organize new production relations which would start it up again. The sixties radical opened his eyes to a system pouring its junk over everybody, or nearly everybody, and the problem was to stop just that, to escape being overwhelmed by a mindless, goalless flood which marooned each individual on his little island of commodities."[24]

If sixties radicals initially rejected orthodox and economistic versions of Marxism, many did (especially over time) appropriate, expand, and recast Marxist categories in an effort to understand the experiences of oppressed and marginalized groups. Thus exponents of what was termed "new working-class theory" claimed that people with technical, clerical, and professional jobs should be seen as constituting a new sector of the working class, better educated than the traditional working class, but working class nonetheless. According to this view, students were not members of the privileged middle class, but rather "trainees" for the new working class. And many women's liberationists (even radical feminists who rejected Marxist theorizing about women's condition) often tried to use Marxist methodology to understand women's oppression. For example, Shulamith Firestone argued that just as the elimination of "economic classes" would require the revolt of the proletariat and their seizure of the means of production, so would the elimination of "sexual classes" require women's revolt and their "seizure of control of reproduction."[25]

If young radicals often assumed an arrogant stance toward those remnants of the Old Left that survived the 1950s, they were by the late 1960s unambiguously contemptuous of liberals. Women's liberationists shared new leftists' and black radicals' rejection of liberalism, and, as a consequence, they often went to great lengths to distinguish themselves from the liberal feminists of the National Organization for Women (NOW). (In fact, their disillusionment with liberalism was more thorough during the early stages of their movement building than had been the case for either new leftists or civil rights activists because they had lived through the earlier betrayals around the Vietnam War and civil rights. Moreover, male radicals' frequent denunciations of women's liberation as "bourgeois" encouraged women's liberationists to distance themselves from NOW.) NOW had been formed in 1966 to push the federal government to enforce the provisions of the 1964 Civil Rights Act outlawing sex discrimination—a paradigmatic liberal agenda focused on public access and the prohibition of employment discrimination. To women's liberation activists, NOW's integrationist, access-oriented approach ignored the racial and class inequities that were the very foundation of the "mainstream" that NOW was dedicated to integrating. In the introduction to the 1970 bestseller *Sisterhood Is Powerful,* Robin Morgan declared that "NOW is essentially an organization that wants reforms [in the] second-class citizenship of women—and this is where it differs drastically from the rest of the Women's Liberation Movement."[26] In *The Dialectic of Sex,* Shulamith Firestone described NOW's political stance as "untenable even in terms of immediate political gains" and deemed it "more a leftover of the old feminism rather than a model of the new."[27] Radical feminist Ti-Grace Atkinson went even further, characterizing many in NOW as only wanting "women to have the same opportunity to be oppressors, too."[28]

Women's liberationists also took issue with liberal feminists' formulation of women's problem as their exclusion from the public sphere. Younger activists argued instead that women's exclusion from public life was inextricable from their subordination in the family and would persist until this larger issue was addressed. For instance, Firestone claimed that the solution to women's oppression was not inclusion in the mainstream, but rather the eradication of the biological family, which was the "tapeworm of exploitation."[29]

Of course, younger activists' alienation from NOW was often more than matched by NOW members' disaffection from them. Many liberal feminists were appalled (at least initially) by women's liberationists' politicization of personal life. NOW founder Betty Friedan frequently railed against women's liberationists for waging a "bedroom war" that diverted women from the real struggle of integrating the public sphere.[30]

Women's liberationists believed that they had embarked on a much more ambitious project— the virtual remaking of the world—and that theirs was the real struggle.[31] Nothing short of radically transforming society was sufficient to deal with what they were discovering: that gender inequality was embedded in everyday life. In 1970 Shulamith Firestone observed that "sex-class is so deep as to be invisible."[32] The pervasiveness of gender inequality and gender's status as a naturalized category demonstrated to women's liberationists the inadequacy of NOW's legislative and judicial remedies and the necessity of thoroughgoing social transformation. Thus, whereas liberal feminists talked of ending sex discrimination, women's liberationists called for nothing less than the destruction of capitalism and patriarchy. As defined by feminists, patriarchy, in contrast to sex discrimination, defied reform. For example, Adrienne Rich contended, "Patriarchy is the power of the fathers: a familialsocial, ideological, political system in which men—by force, direct pressure, or through ritual, tradition, law and language, customs, etiquette, education, and the division of labor, determine what part women shall or shall not play, and in which the female is subsumed under the male."[33]

Women's liberationists typically indicted capitalism as well. Ellen Willis, for instance, maintained that "the American system consists of two interdependent but distinct parts—the capitalist state, and the patriarchal family." Willis argued that capitalism succeeded in exploiting women as cheap labor and consumers "primarily by taking

NOW president Betty Friedan marching in celebration of the fiftieth anniversary of the passing of the Nineteenth Amendment in New York, August 26, 1970.

advantage of women's subordinate position in the family and our historical domination by man."[34]

Central to the revisionary project of the women's liberation movement was the desire to render gender meaningless, to explode it as a significant category. In the movement's view, both masculinity and femininity represented not timeless essences, but rather "patriarchal" constructs. (Of course, even as the movement sought to deconstruct gender, it was, paradoxically, as many have noted, trying to mobilize women precisely on the basis of their gender.)[35] This explains in part the significance abortion rights held for women's liberationists, who believed that until abortion was descriminalized, biology would remain women's destiny, thus foreclosing the possibility of women's self-determination."[36]

Indeed, the women's liberation movement made women's bodies the site of political contestation. The "colonized" status of women's bodies became the focus of much movement activism. The discourse of colonization originated in Third

World national liberation movements but, in an act of First World appropriation, was taken up by black radicals who claimed that African Americans constituted an "internal colony" in the United States. Radical women trying to persuade the larger Movement of the legitimacy of their cause soon followed suit by deploying the discourse to expose women's subordinate position in relation to men. This appropriation represented an important move and one characteristic of radicalism in the *late* 1960s, that is, the borrowing of conceptual frameworks and discourses from other movements to comprehend the situation of oppressed groups in the United States—with mixed results at best. In fact, women's liberationists challenged not only tyrannical beauty standards, but also violence against women, women's sexual alienation, the compulsory character of heterosexuality and its organization around male pleasure (inscribed in the privileging of the vaginal over clitoral orgasm), the health hazards associated with the birth control pill, the definition of contraception as women's responsibility, and, of course, women's lack of reproductive control. They also challenged the sexual division of labor in the home, employment discrimination, and the absence of quality child care facilities. Finally, women's liberationists recognized the power of language to shape culture.

The totalism of their vision would have been difficult to translate into a concrete reform package, even had they been interested in doing so. But electoral politics and the legislative and judicial reforms that engaged the energies of liberal feminists did little to animate most women's liberationists. Like other sixties radicals, they were instead taken with the idea of developing forms that would prefigure the utopian community of the imagined future.[37] Anxious to avoid the "manipulated consent" that they believed characterized American politics, sixties radicals struggled to develop alternatives to hierarchy and centralized decision making.[38] They spoke often of creating "participatory democracy" in an effort to maximize individual participation and equalize power. Their attempts to build a "democracy of individual participation" often confounded outsiders, who found Movement meetings exhausting and tedious affairs.[39] But to those radicals who craved political engagement, "freedom" was, as one radical group enthused, "an endless meeting."[40] According to Gregory Calvert, participatory democracy appealed to the "deep anti-authoritarianism of the new generation in addition to offering them the immediate concretization of the values of openness, honesty, and

community in human relationships."[41] Women's liberationists, still smarting from their firsthand discovery that the larger Movement's much-stated commitment to egalitarianism did not apply equally to all, often took extraordinary measures to try to ensure egalitarianism. They employed a variety of measures in an effort to equalize power, including consensus decision making, rotating chairs, and the sharing of both creative and routine movement work.

Fundamental to this "prefigurative politics," as sociologist Wini Breines terms it, was the commitment to develop counterinstitutions that would anticipate the desired society of the future.[42] Staughton Lynd, director of the Mississippi Freedom Schools and a prominent new leftist, likened sixties radicals to the Wobblies (labor radicals of the early twentieth century) in their commitment to building "the new society within the shell of the old."[43] According to two early SDSers, "What we are working for is far more than changes in the structure of society and its institutions or the people who are now making the decisions. . . . The stress should rather be on wrenching people out of the system both physically and spiritually."[44]

Radicals believed that alternative institutions would not only satisfy needs unmet by the present system, but also, perhaps, by dramatizing the failures of the system, radicalize those not served by it but currently outside the Movement. Tom Hayden proposed that radicals "build our own free institutions—community organizations, newspapers, coffeehouses—at points of strain within the system where human needs are denied. These institutions become centers of identity, points of contact, building blocks of a new society from which we confront the system more intensely."[45]

Among the earliest and best known of such efforts were the Mississippi Freedom Democratic Party and the accompanying Freedom Schools formed during Freedom Summer of 1964. In the aftermath of that summer's Democratic National Convention, Bob Moses [Parris] of the Student Nonviolent Coordinating Committee (SNCC) even suggested that the Movement abandon its efforts to integrate the Democratic Party and try instead to establish its own state government in Mississippi. And as early as 1966 SNCC's Atlanta Project called on blacks to "form our own institutions, credit unions, co-ops, political parties."[46] This came to be the preferred strategy as the sixties progressed and disillusionment with traditional politics grew. Rather than working from within the system, new leftists and black radicals instead formed alternative political parties, media, schools, universities, and assemblies of oppressed and unrepresented people.

Women's liberationists elaborated on this idea, creating an amazing panoply of counterinstitutions. In the years before the 1973 Supreme Court decision decriminalizing abortion, feminists established abortion referral services in most cities of any size. Women's liberationists in Chicago even operated an underground abortion clinic, "Jane," where they performed about one hundred abortions each week.[47] By the mid-1970s most big cities had a low-cost feminist health clinic, a rape crisis center, and a feminist bookstore. In Detroit, after "a long struggle to translate feminism into federalese," two women succeeded in convincing the National Credit Union Administration that feminism was a legitimate "field" from which to draw credit union members. Within three years of its founding in 1973, the Detroit credit union could claim assets of almost one million dollars. Feminists in other cities soon followed suit. Women's liberation activists in Washington, D.C., formed Olivia Records, the first women's record company, which by 1978 was supporting a paid staff of fourteen and producing four records a year.[48] By the mid-1970s there existed in most cities of any size a politicized feminist counterculture, or a "women's community."

The popularity of alternative institutions was that at least in part they seemed to hold out the promise of political effectiveness without cooptation. Writing in 1969, Amiri Baraka (formerly LeRoi Jones), a black nationalist and accomplished poet, maintained, "But you must have the cultural revolution. . . . We cannot fight a war, an actual physical war with the forces of evil just because we are angry. We can begin to build. We must build black institutions . . . all based on a value system that is beneficial to black people."[49]

Jennifer Woodul, one of the founders of Olivia Records, argued that ventures like Olivia represented a move toward gaining "economic power" for women. "We feel it's useless to advocate more and more 'political action' if some of it doesn't result in the permanent material improvement of the lives of women."[50] Robin Morgan termed feminist counterinstitutions "concrete moves toward self-determination and power."[51] The situation, it turned out, was much more complicated. Women involved in nonprofit feminist institutions such as rape crisis centers and shelters for battered women found that their need for state or private funding sometimes militated against adherence to feminist principles.

Feminist businesses, by contrast, discovered that while they were rarely the objects of cooptation, the problem of recuperation remained. In many cases the founders of these institutions became the victims of their own success, as mainstream presses, recording companies, credit unions, and banks encroached on a market they had originally discovered and tapped.[52] For instance, by the end of the 1970s Olivia was forced to reduce its staff almost by half and to scuttle its collective structure.[53] Today k. d. lang, Tracy Chapman, Michelle Shocked, and Sinead O'Connor are among those androgynous women singers enjoying great commercial success, but on major labels. Although Olivia helped lay the groundwork for their achievements, it finds its records, as Arlene Stein has observed, "languishing in the 'women's music' section in the rear [of the record store] if they're there at all."[54]

The move toward building counterinstitutions was part of a larger strategy to develop new societies "within the shell of the old," but this shift sometimes had unintended consequences. While feminist counterinstitutions were originally conceived as part of a culture of resistance, over time they often became more absorbed in sustaining themselves than in confronting male supremacy, especially as their services were duplicated by mainstream businesses. In the early years of the women's liberation movement this alternative feminist culture did provide the sort of "free space" women needed to confront sexism. But as it was further elaborated in the mid-1970s, it ironically often came to promote insularity instead—becoming, as Adrienne Rich has observed, "a place of emigration, an end in itself," where patriarchy was evaded rather than confronted.[55] In practice, feminist communities were small, self-contained subcultures that proved hard to penetrate, especially to newcomers unaccustomed to their norms and conventions. The shift in favor of alternative communities may have sometimes impeded efforts at outreach for the women's liberationists, new leftists, and black radicals who attempted it.

On a related issue, the larger protest Movement's great pessimism about reform—the tendency to interpret every success a defeat resulting in the Movement's further recuperation (what Robin Morgan called "futilitarianism")—may have encouraged a too-global rejection of reform among sixties radicals. For instance, some women's liberation groups actually opposed the Equal Rights Amendment (ERA) when NOW revived it. In September 1970 a New York-based group, The Feminists, denounced the ERA and advised femi-

ON THE SUBJECT OF...

SHIRLEY CHISOLM (1924-)

In 1968 Shirley Anita St. Hill Chisolm became, in her words, "the first American citizen to be elected to Congress in spite of the double drawbacks of being female and having skin darkened by melanin." She also became the first African American woman to seek the presidential nomination of a major political party in 1972. Born in Brooklyn, New York, Chisolm spent most of her childhood living with her grandparents in Barbados. She returned to New York to complete high school, and earned a bachelor's degree in 1946 and a master's degree in 1952. Chisolm worked as an early childhood educator, and went on to serve as a child care center director and education consultant to the New York City Bureau of Child Welfare before being elected to the New York State Assembly in 1964. During her career as an assembly-woman (1964-1968) and later as a member of the U.S. House of Representatives (1968-1983), Chisolm was a vocal proponent of funding for child care services, equal rights for women, labor and minimum wage reform, educational issues, ending poverty, and advancing civil rights. In one of her first addresses to the U.S. House of Representatives, on May 21, 1969, Chisolm introduced the Equal Rights Amendment, and declared: "As a black person, I am no stranger to race prejudice. But the truth is that in the political world I have been far oftener discriminated against because I am a woman than because I am black." In 1984 Chisolm was elected the first chairperson of the National Political Congress of Black Women; she now holds the title Chair Emeritus.

Chisolm, Shirley. In *Unbought and Unbossed,* p. xi. Boston: Houghton Mifflin, 1970.

Chisolm, Shirley. In "Address to the United States House of Representatives: Washington, DC: May 21, 1969." Congressional Record, Extension of Remarks, E4165-6. Women's Liberation Movement: An On-line Archival Collection, Special Collections Library, Duke University, http://scriptorium.lib.duke.edu/wlm/equal/ (30 March 2004).

nists against "squandering invaluable time and energy on it."[56] A delegation of Washington, D.C., women's liberationists invited to appear before the senate subcommittee considering the ERA testified, "We are aware that the system will try to appease us with their [*sic*] paper offerings. We will not be appeased. Our demands can only be met by a total transformation of society which you cannot legislate, you cannot co-opt, you cannot *control*."[57] In *The Dialectic of Sex,* Firestone went so far as to dismiss child care centers as attempts to "buy women off" because they "ease the immediate pressure without asking why the pressure is on *women*."[58]

Similarly, many SDS leaders opposed the National Conference for New Politics (NCNP), an abortive attempt to form a national progressive organization oriented around electoral politics and to launch an antiwar presidential ticket headed by Martin Luther King, Jr., and Benjamin Spock. Immediately following NCNP's first and only convention, in 1967, the SDS paper *New Left Notes* published two front-page articles criticizing NCNP organizers. One writer contended that "people who recognize the political process as perverted will not seek change through the institutions that process has created."[59] The failure of sixties radicals to distinguish between reform and reformism meant that while they defined the issues, they often did little to develop policy initiatives around those issues.[60] Moreover, the preoccupation of women's liberationists with questions of internal democracy (fueled in part by their desire to succeed where the men had failed) sometimes had the effect of focusing attention away from the larger struggle in an effort to create the perfect movement. As feminist activist Frances Chapman points out, women's liberation was "like a generator that got things going, cut out and left it to the larger reform engine which made a lot of mistakes."[61] In eschewing traditional politics rather than entering them skeptically, women's liberationists, like other sixties radicals, may have lost an opportunity to foster critical debate in the larger arena.

If young radicals eschewed the world of conventional politics, they nonetheless had a profound impact on it, especially by redefining what is understood as "political." Although the women's liberation movement popularized the slogan "the personal is political," the idea that there is a political dimension to personal life was first embraced by early SDSers who had encountered it in the writings of C. Wright Mills.[62] Rebelling against a social order whose public and private spheres were highly differentiated, new leftists called for a reintegration of the personal with the political. They reconceptualized apparently personal problems—specifically their alienation from a campus cultural milieu characterized by sororities and fraternities, husband and wife hunting, sports, and careerism, and the powerlessness they felt as college students without a voice in campus governance or curriculum—as political problems. Thus SDS's founding Port Huron Statement of 1962 suggested that for an American New Left to succeed, it would have to "give form to . . . feelings of helplessness and indifference, so that people may see the political, social, and economic sources of their private troubles and organize to change society."[63] Theirs was a far more expansive formulation of politics than what prevailed in the Old Left, even among the more renegade remnants that had survived into the early sixties.[64] Power was conceptualized as relational and by no means reducible to electoral politics.

By expanding political discourse to include personal relations, new leftists unintentionally paved the way for women's liberationists to develop critiques of the family, marriage, and the construction of sexuality. (Of course, nonfeminist critiques of the family and sexual repressiveness were hardly in short supply in the 1950s and 1960s, as evidenced by *Rebel without a Cause, Catcher in the Rye,* and Paul Goodman's *Growing Up Absurd,* to mention but a few.) Women's liberationists developed an understanding of power's capillarylike nature, which in some respects anticipated those being formulated by Michel Foucault and other poststructuralists.[65] Power was conceptualized as occupying multiple sites and as lodging everywhere, even in those private places assumed to be the most removed from or impervious to politics—the home and, more particularly, the bedroom.

The belief of sixties radicals that the personal is political also suggested to them its converse—that the political is personal. Young radicals typically felt it was not enough to sign leaflets or participate in a march if one returned to the safety and comfort of a middle-class existence. Politics was supposed to unsettle life and its routines, even more, to transform life. For radicals the challenge was to discover, underneath all the layers of social conditioning, the "real" self unburdened by social expectations and conventions. Thus, SNCC leader Stokely Carmichael advanced the slogan, "Every Negro is a potential black man."[66] Shulamith Firestone and Anne Koedt argued that among the "most exciting things to come out of the women's

movement so far is a new daring . . . to tear down old structures and assumptions and let real thought and feeling flow."[67] Life would not be comfortable, but who wanted comfort in the midst of so much deadening complacency? For a great many radicals, the individual became a site of political activism in the sixties. In the black freedom movement the task was very much to discover the black inside the Negro, and in the women's liberation movement it was to unlearn niceness, to challenge the taboo against female self-assertion.[68]

Sixties radicalism proved compelling to many precisely because it promised to transform life. Politics was not about the subordination of self to some larger political cause; instead, it was the path to self-fulfillment. This ultimately was the power of sixties radicalism. As Stanley Aronowitz notes, sixties radicalism was in large measure about "infus[ing] life with a secular spiritual and moral content" and "fill[ing] the quotidian with personal meaning and purpose."[69] But "the personal is political" was one of those ideas whose rhetorical power seemed to sometimes work against or undermine its explication. It could encourage a solipsistic preoccupation with self-transformation. As new leftist Richard Flacks presciently observed in 1965, this kind of politics could lead to "a search for personally satisfying modes of life while abandoning the possibility of helping others to change theirs."[70] Thus the idea that "politics is how you live your life, not who you vote for," as Yippie leader Jerry Rubin put it, could and did lead to a subordination of politics to lifestyle.[71] If the idea led some to confuse personal liberation with political struggle, it led others to embrace an asceticism that sacrificed personal needs and desires to political imperatives. Some women's liberation activists followed this course, interpreting the idea that the personal is political to mean that one's personal life should conform to some abstract standard of political correctness. At first this tendency was mitigated by the founders' insistence that there were no personal solutions, only collective solutions, to women's oppression. Over time, however, one's self-presentation, marital status, and sexual preference frequently came to determine one's standing or ranking in the movement. The most notorious example of this involved the New York radical group The Feminists, who established a quota to limit the number of married women in the group.[72] Policies such as these prompted Barbara Ehrenreich to question "a feminism which talks about universal sisterhood, but is horrified by women who wear spiked heels or call their friends 'girls.'"[73] At the same time, what was personally satisfying was sometimes upheld as politically correct. In the end, both the women's liberation movement and the larger protest Movement suffered, as the idea that the personal is political was often interpreted in such a way as to make questions of lifestyle absolutely central.

The social movements of the sixties signaled the beginning of what has come to be known as "identity politics," the idea that politics is rooted in identity.[74] Although some New Left groups by the late 1960s did come to endorse an orthodox Marxism whereby class was privileged, class was not the pivotal category for these new social movements.[75] (Even those New Left groups that reverted to the "labor metaphysic" lacked meaningful working-class participation.) Rather, race, ethnicity, gender, sexual preference, and youth were the salient categories for most sixties activists. In the women's liberation movement, what was termed "consciousness-raising" was the tool used to develop women's group identity.

As women's liberationists started to organize a movement, they confronted American women who identified unambiguously as women, but who typically had little of what Nancy Cott would call "we-ness," or "some level of identification with 'the group called women.'"[76] Moreover, both the pervasiveness of gender inequality and the cultural understanding of gender as a natural rather than a social construct made it difficult to cultivate a critical consciousness about gender even among women. To engender this sense of sisterhood or "we-ness," women's liberationists developed consciousness-raising, a practice involving "the political reinterpretation of personal life."[77] According to its principal architects, its purpose was to "awaken the latent consciousness that . . . all women have about our oppression." In talking about their personal experiences, it was argued, women would come to understand that what they had believed were personal problems were, in fact, "social problems that must become social issues and fought together rather than with personal solutions."[78]

Reportedly, New York women's liberationist Kathie Sarachild was the person who coined the term *consciousness-raising*. However, the technique originated in other social movements. As Sarachild wrote in 1973, those who promoted consciousness-raising "were applying to women and to ourselves as women's liberation organizers the practice a number of us had learned in the civil rights movement in the South in the early 1960's."[79] There they had seen that the sharing of personal problems, grievances, and aspirations— "telling it like it is"—could be a radicalizing experience. Moreover, for some women's liberationists consciousness-raising was a way to avoid the tendency of some members of the movement to try to fit women within existing (and often Marxist) theoretical paradigms. By circumventing the "experts" on women and going to women themselves, they would be able to not only construct a theory of women's oppression but formulate strategy as well. Thus women's liberationists struggled to find the commonalities in women's experiences in order to formulate generalizations about women's oppression.

Consciousness-raising was enormously successful in exposing the insidiousness of sexism and in engendering a sense of identity and solidarity among the largely white, middle-class women who participated in "c-r" groups. By the early 1970s even NOW, whose founder Betty Friedan had initially derided consciousness-raising as so much "navel-gazing," began sponsoring c-r groups.[80] But the effort to transcend the particular was both the strength and the weakness of consciousness-raising. If it encouraged women to locate the common denominators in their lives, it inhibited discussion of women's considerable differences. Despite the particularities of white, middle-class women's experiences, theirs became the basis for feminist theorizing about women's oppression. In a more general sense the identity politics informing consciousness-raising tended to privilege experience in certain problematic ways. It was too often assumed that there existed a kind of core experience, initially articulated as "women's experience." Black and white radicals (the latter in relation to youth) made a similar move as well. When Stokely Carmichael called on blacks to develop an "ideology which speaks to our blackness," he, like other black nationalists, suggested that there was somehow an essential and authentic "blackness."

With the assertion of difference within the women's movement in the 1980s, the notion that women constitute a unitary category has been problematized. As a consequence, women's experiences have become ever more discretely defined, as in "the black female experience," "the Jewish female experience," or "the Chicana lesbian experience." But, as Audre Lorde has argued, there remains a way in which, even with greater and greater specificity, the particular is never fully captured.[81] Instead, despite the pluralization of the subject within feminism, identities are often still

Photograph of Betty Friedan (top row, standing in center) with other feminists including Yoko Ono (seated, 2nd row, center), gathering in Friedan's home on June 7, 1973.

imagined as monolithic. Finally, the very premise of identity politics—that identity is the basis of politics—has sometimes shut down possibilities for communication, as identities are seen as necessarily either conferring or foreclosing critical consciousness. Kobena Mercer, a British film critic, has criticized the rhetorical strategies of "authenticity and authentication" that tend to characterize identity politics. He has observed, "if I preface a point by saying something like, 'as a black gay man, I feel marginalized by your discourse,' it makes a valid point but in such a way that preempts critical dialogue because such a response could be inferred as a criticism not of what I say but of what or who I am. The problem is replicated in the familiar cop-out clause, 'as a middle-class, white, heterosexual male, what can I say?'"[82]

The problem is that the mere assertion of identity becomes in a very real sense irrefutable. Identity is presented as not only stable and fixed, but also insurmountable. While identity politics gives the oppressed the moral authority to speak (perhaps a dubious ground from which to speak), it can, ironically, absolve those belonging to dominant groups from having to engage in a criti-

cal dialogue. In some sense, then, identity politics can unintentionally reinforce Other-ness. Finally, as the antifeminist backlash and the emergence of the New Right should demonstrate, there is nothing inherently progressive about identity. It can be, and has been, mobilized for reactionary as well as for radical purposes.[83] For example, the participation of so many women in the antiabortion movement reveals just how problematic the reduction of politics to identity can be.

Accounts of sixties radicalism usually cite its role in bringing about the dismantling of Jim Crow and disfranchisement, the withdrawal of U.S. troops from Vietnam, and greater gender equality. However, equally important, if less frequently noted, was its challenge to politics as usual. Sixties radicals succeeded both in reformulating politics, even mainstream politics, to include personal life, and in challenging the notion that elites alone have the wisdom and expertise to control the political process. For a moment, people who by virtue of their color, age, and gender were far from the sites of formal power became politically engaged, became agents of change.

Given the internal contradictions and short-comings of sixties radicalism, the repressiveness of the federal government in the late 1960s and early 1970s, and changing economic conditions in the United States, it is not surprising that the movements built by radicals in the sixties either no longer exist or do so only in attenuated form. Activists in the women's liberation movement, however, helped bring about a fundamental realignment of gender roles in this country through outrageous protests, tough-minded polemics, and an "ecstasy of discussion." Indeed, those of us who came of age in the days before the resurgence of feminism know that the world today, while hardly a feminist utopia, is nonetheless a far different, and in many respects a far fairer, world than what we confronted in 1967.

Notes

1. See Carol Hanisch, "A Critique of the Miss America Protest," in *Notes from the Second Year: Women's Liberation,* ed. Shulamith Firestone and Anne Koedt (New York: Radical Feminism, 1970), 87; and Judith Duffet, "Atlantic City Is a Town with Class—They Raise Your Morals While They Judge Your Ass," *Voice of the Women's Liberation Movement* 1, no. 3 (October 1968). The protesters also criticized the pageant's narrow formulation of beauty, especially its racist equation of beauty with whiteness. They emphasized that in its forty-seven-year history, the pageant had never crowned a black woman Miss America. That weekend the first Black Miss America Pageant was held in Atlantic City.

2. See Lindsy Van Gelder, "Bra Burners Plan Protest," *New York Post,* 4 September 1968, which appeared three days before the protest. The *New York Times* article by Charlotte Curtis quoted Robin Morgan as having said about the mayor of Atlantic City, "He was worried about our burning things. He said the boardwalk had already been burned out once this year. We told him we wouldn't do anything dangerous—just a symbolic bra-burning." Curtis, "Miss America Pageant Is Picketed by 100 Women," *New York Times,* 8 September 1968.

3. See Jack Gould's column in the *New York Times,* 9 September 1968.

4. The Yippies were a small group of leftists who, in contrast to most of the Left, had enthusiastically embraced the growing counterculture. For a fascinating account of the 1968 convention, see David Farber, *Chicago '68* (Chicago: University of Chicago Press, 1988).

5. Curtis, "Miss America Pageant."

6. For the sake of convenience, I will use the term *Movement* to describe the overlapping protest movements of the sixties—the black freedom movement, the student movement, the antiwar movement, and the more selfconsciously political New Left. I will refer to the women's liberation movement as the *movement;* here I use the lower case simply to avoid confusion.

7. Snitow, interview by author, New York, 14 June 1984. Here one can get a sense of the disjuncture in experiences between white and black women; presumably, black women had not felt the same sense of distance about their civil rights activism.

8. Robin Morgan, *Going Too Far: The Personal Chronicle of a Feminist* (New York: Random House, 1978), 62.

9. Yet virtually all the recently published books on the sixties either slight or ignore the protest. This omission is emblematic of a larger problem, the failure of authors to integrate women's liberation into their reconstruction of that period. Indeed, most of these books have replicated the position of women in the larger, male-dominated protest Movement—that is, the women's liberation movement is relegated to the margins of the narrative. Such marginalization has been exacerbated as well by the many feminist recollections of the sixties that demonize the Movement and present women's liberation as its antithesis. Sixties books that textually subordinate the women's liberation movement include James Miller, *Democracy Is in the Streets: From Port Huron to the Siege of Chicago* (New York: Simon and Schuster, 1987); Tom Hayden, *Reunion: A Memoir* (New York: Random House, 1988); Todd Gitlin, *The Sixties: Years of Hope, Days of Rage* (New York: Bantam, 1987); and Nancy Zaroulis and Gerald Sullivan, *Who Spoke Up? American Protest against the War in Vietnam* (Garden City, NY: Doubleday, 1984). A notable exception is Stewart Burns, *Social Movements of the 1960's: Searching for Democracy* (Boston: Twayne, 1990).

10. Sara Evans, *Personal Politics: The Roots of Women's Liberation in the Civil Rights Movement and the New Left* (New York: Vintage Books, 1979).

11. Sara Evans has argued that in their attempt to combine work inside and outside the family, educated, middle-class, married white women of the 1950s were following the path pioneered by black women. See Evans, *Born for Liberty: A History of Women in America* (New York: Free Press, 1989), 253-54. As Jacqueline Jones and others have demonstrated, black women have a "long history of combining paid labor with domestic obligations." According to Jones, in 1950 one-third of all married black women were in the labor force, compared to one-quarter of all married women in the general population. One study cited by Jones "concluded that black mothers of school-aged children were more likely to work than their white counterparts, though part-time positions in the declining field of domestic service inhibited growth in their rates of labor force participation." Jones, *Labor of Love, Labor of Sorrow: Black Women, Work, and the Family, from Slavery to the Present* (New York: Vintage Books, 1986), 269.

12. Alice Kessler-Harris, *Out to Work: A History of Wage-Earning Women in the United States* (New York: Oxford University Press, 1982), 302.

13. Evans, *Born for Liberty,* 252.

14. Jane De Hart-Mathews, "The New Feminism and the Dynamics of Social Change," in *Women's America: Refocusing the Past,* 2d ed., ed. Linda Kerber and Jane De Hart-Mathews (New York: Oxford University Press, 1987), 445.

15. I think that this was an experience specific to white women. The problem of diffidence seems to have been, if not unique to white women, then especially

acute for them. This is not to say that issues of gender were unimportant to black women activists in the sixties, but that gender seemed less primary and pressing an issue than race. However, much more research is needed in this area. It could be that the black women's noninvolvement in women's liberation had as much, if not more, to do with the movement's racism than any prioritizing of race.

16. Carl Oglesby, "Trapped in a System," reprinted as "Liberalism and the Corporate State," in *The New Radicals: A Report with Documents,* ed. Paul Jacobs and Saul Landau (New York: Vintage Books, 1966), 266. For a useful discussion of the New Left's relationship to liberalism, see Gitlin, *The Sixties,* 127-92.

17. See Howard Brick, "Inventing Post-Industrial Society: Liberal and Radical Social Theory in the 1960's" (paper delivered at the 1990 American Studies Association Conference). In September 1963 the electoral politics faction of SDS had even succeeded in getting the group to adopt the slogan "Part of the Way with LBJ." Johnson's official campaign slogan was "All the Way with LBJ." See Gitlin, *The Sixties,* 180.

18. Gregory Calvert, interview, *Movement* 3, no. 2 (1967): 6.

19. Andrew Kopkind, "Looking Backward: The Sixties and the Movement," *Ramparts* 11, no. 8 (February 1973): 32.

20. That evening seven million people watched Johnson's speech to Congress announcing voting rights legislation. According to C. T. Vivian, "a tear ran down" Martin Luther King's cheek as Johnson finished his speech. Juan Williams, *Eyes on the Prize: America's Civil Rights Years, 1954-65* (New York: Penguin, 1988), 278.

21. Elinor Langer discusses the ways Marcuse's notion of repressive tolerance was used by the Movement. See her wonderful essay, "Notes for Next Time," *Working Papers for a New Society* 1, no. 3 (fall 1973): 48-83.

22. Ellen Kay Trimberger, "Women in the Old and New Left: The Evolution of a Politics of Personal Life," *Feminist Studies* 5, no. 3 (fall 1979): 442.

23. Potter quoted from Miller, *Democracy Is in the Streets,* 196.

24. Miller quoted from Gitlin, *The Sixties,* 9. Although the broad outlines of Miller's argument are correct, some recent scholarship on 1930s radicalism suggests that it was considerably more varied and less narrowly economistic than has been previously acknowledged. For example, recent books by Paula Rabinowitz and Robin Kelley demonstrate that some radicals in this period understood the salience of such categories as gender and race. See Paula Rabinowitz, *Labor and Desire: Women's Revolutionary Fiction in Depression America* (Chapel Hill: University of North Carolina Press, 1991); Robin Kelley, *Hammer and Hoe: Alabama Communists during the Great Depression* (Chapel Hill: University of North Carolina Press, 1990).

25. Shulamith Firestone, *The Dialectic of Sex: The Case for Feminist Revolution,* rev. ed. (New York: Bantam Books, 1971), 10-11.

26. Robin Morgan, in *Sisterhood Is Powerful,* ed. Morgan (New York: Vintage Books, 1970), xxii.

27. Firestone, *The Dialectic of Sex,* 33. For a very useful history of women's rights activism (as opposed to wom-

en's liberation) in the postwar years, see Cynthia Harrison, *On Account of Sex: The Politics of Women's Issues, 1945-68* (Berkeley: University of California Press, 1988).

28. Ti-Grace Atkinson, *Amazon Odyssey* (New York: Link Books, 1974), 10. In contrast to other founders of early radical feminist groups, Atkinson came to radicalism through her involvement in the New York City chapter of NOW, admittedly the most radical of all NOW chapters. Atkinson made this remark in October 1968 after having failed badly in her attempt to radically democratize the New York chapter of NOW. Upon losing the vote she immediately resigned her position as the chapter's president and went on to establish The Feminists, a radical feminist group.

29. Firestone, *The Dialectic of Sex,* 12.

30. Betty Friedan, *It Changed My Life: Writings on the Women's Movement* (New York: Random House, 1976), 153. Friedan was antagonistic to radical feminism from the beginning and rarely missed an opportunity to denounce the man-hating and sex warfare that she claimed it advocated. Her declamations against "sexual politics" began at least as early as January 1969.

31. Due to limitations of space and the focus of this chapter, I do not discuss the many differences among women's liberationists, most crucially, the conflicts between "radical feminists" and "politicos" over the relationship between the women's liberation movement and the larger Movement and the role of capitalism in maintaining women's oppression. This is taken up at length in Alice Echols, *Daring to Be Bad: Radical Feminism in America, 1967-75* (Minneapolis: University of Minnesota Press, 1989).

32. Firestone, *The Dialectic of Sex,* 1. It is the opening line of her book.

33. Adrienne Rich quoted from Hester Eisenstein, *Contemporary Feminist Thought* (Boston: G. K. Hall, 1983), 5.

34. Ellen Willis, "Sequel: Letter to a Critic," in *Notes from the Second Year,* ed. Firestone and Koedt, 57.

35. See Ann Snitow, "Gender Diary," *Dissent,* spring 1989, 205-24; Carole Vance, "Social Construction Theory: Problems in the History of Sexuality," in *Homosexuality, Which Homosexuality?* ed. Anja van Kooten Niekark and Theo van der Maer (Amsterdam: An Dekken/ Schorer, 1989).

36. Ellen Willis discusses the centrality of abortion to the women's liberation movement in the foreword to *Daring to Be Bad.* For the young, mostly white middle-class women who were attracted to women's liberation, the issue was forced reproduction. But for women of color, the issue was as often forced sterilization, and women's liberationists would tackle that issue as well.

37. Stanley Aronowitz, "When the New Left Was New," in *The Sixties without Apology,* ed. Sohnya Sayres, Anders Stephanson, Stanley Aronowitz, and Fredric Jameson (Minneapolis: University of Minnesota Press, 1984), 32.

38. C. Wright Mills quoted from Miller, *Democracy Is in the Streets,* 86.

39. The phrase is from SDS's founding statement, "The Port Huron Statement," which is reprinted in full as an appendix to Miller's book, *Democracy Is in the Streets,*

333. For instance, Irving Howe, an influential member of the Old Left who attended a couple of SDS meetings, called them "interminable and structureless sessions." Howe, "The Decade That Failed," *New York Times Magazine,* 19 September 1982, 78.

40. The statement appeared in a pamphlet produced by the Economic Research and Action Project of SDS. Miller quotes it in *Democracy Is in the Streets,* 215.

41. Gregory Calvert, "Participatory Democracy, Collective Leadership, and Political Responsibility," *New Left Notes,* 2, no. 45 (18 December 1967): 1.

42. See Breines's summary of prefigurative politics in *Community and Organization in the New Left, 1962-68* (New York: Praeger, 1982), 1-8.

43. Staughton Lynd, "The Movement: A New Beginning," *Liberation* 14, no. 2 (May 1969).

44. Pat Hansen and Ken McEldowney, "A Statement of Values," *New Left Notes,* 1, no. 42 (November 1966): 5.

45. Tom Hayden, "Democracy Is . . . in the Streets," *Rat* 1, no. 15 (23 August-5 September 1968): 5.

46. The Atlanta Project's position paper has been reprinted as "SNCC Speaks for Itself," in *The Sixties Papers: Documents of a Rebellious Decade,* ed. Judith Clavir Albert and Stewart Albert (New York: Praeger, 1984), 122. However, the title assigned it by the Alberts is misleading because at the time it was written in the spring of 1966, it did not reflect majority opinion in SNCC.

47. Rosalind Petchesky, *Abortion and Woman's Choice: The State, Sexuality, and Reproductive Freedom* (New York: Longman Press, 1984), 128.

48. Michelle Kort, "Sisterhood Is Profitable," *Mother Jones,* July 1983, 44.

49. Amiri Imanu Baraka, "A Black Value System," *Black Scholar,* November 1969.

50. Jennifer Woodul, "What's This about Feminist Businesses?" *off our backs* 6, no. 4 (June 1976): 24-26.

51. Robin Morgan, "Rights of Passage," *Ms.,* September 1975, 99.

52. For a fascinating case study of this as it relates to women's music, see Arlene Stein, "Androgyny Goes Pop," *Out/Look* 3, no. 3 (spring 1991): 26-33.

53. Kort, "Sisterhood Is Profitable," 44.

54. Stein, "Androgyny Goes Pop," 30.

55. Adrienne Rich, "Living the Revolution," *Women's Review of Books* 3, no. 12 (September 1986): 1, 3-4.

56. Quoted from Jane Mansbridge, *Why We Lost the ERA* (Chicago: University of Chicago Press, 1986), 266.

57. "Women's Liberation Testimony," *off our backs* 1, no. 5 (May 1970): 7.

58. Firestone, *The Dialectic of Sex,* 206.

59. Steve Halliwell, "Personal Liberation and Social Change," *New Left Notes,* 2, no. 30 (4 September 1967): 1; see also Rennie Davis and Staughton Lynd, "On NCNP," *New Left Notes* 2, no. 30. (4 September 1967): 1.

60. See Charlotte Bunch, "The Reform Tool Kit," *Quest* 1, no. 1 (summer 1974).

61. Frances Chapman, interview by author, New York, 30 May 1984. Here Chapman was speaking of the radical feminist wing of the women's liberation movement, but it applies as well to women's liberation activists.

62. For more on the prefigurative, personal politics of the sixties, see Breines, *Community and Organization in the New Left*; Miller, *Democracy Is in the Streets*; and Aronowitz, "When the New Left Was New."

63. Quoted from Miller, *Democracy Is in the Streets,* 374.

64. Although individual social critics such as C. Wright Mills influenced the thinking of new leftists, the noncommunist Left of the 1950s and early 1960s remained economistic and anticommunist. Indeed, the fact that the board of the League for Industrial Democracy—the parent organization of SDS in SDS's early years—ignored the values section of the Port Huron Statement suggests the disjuncture between old and new leftists. For another view stressing the continuities between the Old and the New Left, see Maurice Isserman, *If I Had a Hammer . . . The Death of the Old Left and the Birth of the New Left* (New York: Basic Books, 1987).

65. See Judith Newton, "Historicisms New and Old: 'Charles Dickens' Meets Marxism, Feminism, and West Coast Foucault," *Feminist Studies* 16, no. 3 (fall 1990): 464. In their assumption that power has a source and that it emanates from patriarchy, women's liberationists part company with Foucauldian approaches that reject large-scale paradigms of domination.

66. Carmichael quoted from Clayborne Carson, *In Struggle: SNCC and the Black Awakening of the 1960's* (Cambridge: Harvard University Press, 1981), 282.

67. Firestone and Koedt, "Editorial," in *Notes from the Second Year,* ed. Firestone and Koedt.

68. However, the reclamation of blackness was often articulated in a sexist fashion, as in Stokely Carmichael's 1968 declaration, "Every Negro is a potential black man." See Carmichael, "A Declaration of War," in *The New Left: A Documentary History,* ed. Teodori Massimo (Indianapolis: Bobbs-Merrill, 1969), 277.

69. Aronowitz, "When the New Left Was New," 18.

70. Richard Flacks, "Some Problems, Issues, Proposals," in *The New Radicals,* ed. Jacobs and Landau, 168. This was a working paper intended for the June 1965 convention of SDS.

71. Excerpts from Jerry Rubin's book, *Do It,* appeared in *Rat* 2, no. 26 (26 January-9 February 1970).

72. "The Feminists: A Political Organization to Annihilate Sex Roles," in *Notes from the Second Year,* ed. Firestone and Koedt, 117.

73. Ehrenreich quoted from Carol Ann Douglas, "Second Sex 30 Years Later," *off our backs* 9, no. 11 (December 1979): 26.

74. The term *identity politics* was, I think, first used by black and Chicana feminists. See Diana Fuss, *Essentially Speaking: Feminism, Nature, and Difference* (New York: Routledge, 1989), 99.

75. Jeffrey Weeks locates the origins of identity politics in the post-1968 political flux. He argues that "identity politics can be seen as part of the unfinished business of the 1960's, challenging traditionalist hierarchies of

power and the old, all-encompassing social and political identities associated, for example, with class and occupation." Perhaps Weeks situates this in the post-1968 period, because class held greater significance for many British new leftists than it did for their American counterparts. Weeks, "Sexuality and (Post) Modernity" (unpublished paper).

76. Nancy Cott, *The Grounding of Modern Feminism* (New Haven: Yale University Press, 1987), 5.

77. Amy Kesselman, interview by author, New York, 2 May 1984.

78. "The New York Consciousness Awakening Women's Liberation Group" (handout from the Lake Villa Conference, November 1968).

79. Kathie Sarachild, "Consciousness-Raising: A Radical Weapon," in *Feminist Revolution,* ed. Redstockings (New Paltz, NY: Redstockings, 1975), 132.

80. Betty Friedan, *It Changed My Life* (New York: Norton, 1985), 101.

81. Audre Lorde, *Zami: A New Spelling of My Name* (Freedom, CA: Crossing Press, 1982), 226.

82. Lorraine Kenney, "Traveling Theory: The Cultural Politics of Race and Representation: An Interview with Kobena Mercer," *Afterimage,* September 1990, 9.

83. Mercer makes this point as well in Kenney, "Traveling Theory," 9.

CHARLOTTE BUNCH (ESSAY DATE 2001)

SOURCE: Bunch, Charlotte. "Women's Human Rights: The Challenges of Global Feminism and Diversity." In *Feminist Locations: Global and Local, Theory and Practice,* edited by Marianne DeKoven, pp. 129-46. New Brunswick, N.J.: Rutgers University Press, 2001.

In the following essay, Bunch discusses some aspects of global feminism, including networking among organizations in various countries, the struggle for human rights, and the notion of equality in relation to diversity.

I want to start with a story from the first African Women's Leadership Institute that I attended in Uganda (February 1997) because it illustrates issues I want to discuss and conveys the sense of possibility that I feel about what I call global feminism. While the term *global feminism* is problematic, it still has resonance for many as a way of describing the growth of feminism(s) around the world over the past two decades. The African Women's Leadership Institute was organized by four young women from different countries in Africa who had attended the global leadership institutes sponsored by the Center for Women's Global Leadership each year and who have been active in the Global Campaign for Women's Human Rights.

They brought twenty-five women, ages twenty-five to forty, from eighteen countries in Africa for three weeks of intensive training in a program that was explicitly dealing with feminism and leadership for the twenty-first century. The fact that over three hundred women applied to spend three weeks there speaks volumes about both the growth of feminism in the region and the seriousness of women's commitments to it. The participants were diverse in terms of country, ethnic identity, and class. Some worked in the public sector in politics and government; many came from nongovernmental organizations (NGOs) and grass-roots women's projects; and a few worked in private corporations or in universities. Their backgrounds were diverse as were their issues of primary concern. Yet as so often happens in events like this, there was also a commonality in the stories that they told about the discrimination and violence that they faced as women that brought them together in spite of their differences.

In one of the opening lectures, Patricia Mc-Fadden, a feminist theorist from Swaziland, wove together the themes of feminism in Africa with analysis of colonialism and the ways in which Western patriarchy had imposed itself on the continent. At the same time, she talked about how this should not blind women to the indigenous forms of patriarchy that they also had to confront. She ended her analysis of the intersection of race, class, gender, and sexuality in Africa with a participatory exercise in which she asked women to list on the board names that feminists get called in their country. A multitude of words spewed forth from bra burners to unfeminine to promiscuous to frigid to lesbian to Western/white-identified to women who can't get a man to women who want to be a man to women who are ugly to women who read too much (and "lose contact with their roots") to the "know-alls" and even "Beijing Women," referring to the Fourth World Conference on Women held in Beijing in 1995. Even though these names were expressed in various local languages often reflecting particular cultural concepts, the same accusations that women have experienced in other parts of the world kept appearing on the list. It reminded me that one of the universalities of the feminist struggle is the commonality of our opposition.

McFadden also asked participants to say why they do or don't call themselves feminists. Many replied that before they came to the institute, they didn't or weren't sure whether to call themselves a feminist for various reasons. But many added that after this lecture they would do so because now they understood that was who they were and how the term had been used against women. It was a transforming process that I have seen happen in different ways and arenas around the world. Yet it is still powerful to see how demystifying this word and understanding the way in which it has been used against women enables many to recognize its political nature and reinforces their ability to stand up to those who put women down.

Women's Global Networking

The struggle to reclaim and broaden feminism is central to working for women's human rights. Someone once asked if we say "women's human rights" because it's easier for people to accept than feminism. The intention of this movement has not been to avoid the word feminism, but rather to take feminist analysis into the arena of human rights and use it to make women's claims more indisputable by defining them as human rights. By applying feminist concepts and gender analysis to human rights theory and practice, we seek to transform a major body of work and its related institutions that have enormous influence, both practically and theoretically, in the world, and make them more inclusive of women's lives and experiences. Looking at human rights from a gender-conscious point of view has already begun to challenge the limited parameters of what was previously defined as human rights and opened new avenues of government accountability to women.

The growth of women's movements around the world since the 1970s and the United Nations Decade for Women (1975-1985) with its world conferences on women provided the context and background for the movement for women's human rights to emerge in the 1990s. The four UN world conferences on women held from 1975 to 1995 became places where women at the regional and global levels got to know one another and to exchange information, ideas, and strategies. While there have been many other women's international events where such exchange took place as well, the UN conferences played a particularly important role because they provided resources for and a legitimacy to what women were doing that was critical to many women's ability to participate. This global feminist discussion has often been rocky with important contentious debates, but it also has enabled networks and groups of women to see where they share common goals and can build linkages across differences. The irony is that the United Nations certainly never intended to facilitate global feminist networking, but it has helped to create the conditions and sometimes the context from which many women have developed a greater understanding of one another and found ways to work together.

When I speak of the "global" in global feminism, I do not see it in opposition to the "local." This is one of those false dualisms that we must transcend. The greatest strength of women's movements in every region of the world, including the United States, is in the wide diversity of particularized local activity that women do. Most of what feminism has achieved in the last three decades has been through fairly small, specific, local organizations or projects of a million different sorts. These are often competing and debating with one another how to describe various women's experiences and what changes women should seek. In this process, women have developed their own analyses of the reality of women in their particular setting and built strategies responsive to their own specific struggles. It is the richness of this very particularized and local experience that makes it possible to imagine global networking that is reflective of women's diversity. Through the process of development by each specific group of women of their own priority issues and identities the feminist discourse has remained vital and evolved over time. This attention to diversity should also provide the basis for creating more inclusive strategies and visions for the future. These diverse, local, and particularized women's movements are the ground upon which any global activity must build and where it must always return to check out its viability.

Nevertheless, over the past decade, many women have come to feel that working in thousands of small separate projects is not enough. The changes feminists seek demand addressing global forces that are affecting so much of local life today. More women are understanding that their particularized concerns and projects cannot be viewed in isolation from this larger context. For example, the global economy is transforming the conditions of women's work both in the paid economy and at home; organizing in this sector must take this into account. Feminist analysis of the global economy is growing as women examine how their lives are affected by trends like the privatization policies that go by many different names: structural adjustment in the third world, the downsizing of employees and services in the United States, and ending the service sector and job guarantees in Eastern Europe.

Global culture and media also have significant impacts on women's lives and on our efforts to organize. To take an example from that list of things that feminists in Africa get called, one stereotype that has been created by the media and spread through global culture is feminists as "bra burners." Even though, as Patricia McFadden pointed out, the bra was a Western invention with no roots in African culture, nonetheless, feminists there get accused of being Western because they're "bra burners." Some of the women at the African Institute asked, "Where did this term come from?" In the ensuing discussion it was noted that media-created stereotypes spread rapidly from continent to continent. Further, even men who otherwise oppose each other politically will often eagerly use the same media-generated concepts when it comes to what's wrong with feminists.

One of the most damaging and persistent stereotypes used by men everywhere and reinforced by the media is to say that feminism is only Western (white) and middle class (bourgeois). Many feminist leaders and groups have certainly made mistakes and taken actions that reflected these biases, and this must be continuously challenged as we work to create concepts and strategies that are inclusive of women's diversity. However, the continual litany that this is what feminism is and who defines it is a profound insult to the millions of diverse women worldwide, including in the United States, whose ideas and lives have given shape to feminism not only in the past few decades but also over centuries. There have been vibrant feminist movements in many countries of Asia, Africa, and Latin America at various points during this century and certainly since the 1970s. Yet, the media systematically neglects reporting on them and usually focuses only on the terrible problems women there face—if it notices them at all. Thus, the feminisms and movements of women in the rest of the world remain unknown to most. Similarly, there is not one Western feminism but rather quite a diverse range of feminisms expressed by different groups of women living in Western countries. Yet most of these faces of feminism are rarely if ever acknowledged in the media. Thus, even to speak of global feminism requires reclaiming the term *feminism* and recognizing how distortions of it have been systematically used to exacerbate differences among women.

Perhaps the greatest challenge feminists face locally is that at the same time a global phenomenon is on the rise of different kinds of fundamentalisms and backlash, both religious and secular. Religious fundamentalism—whether Christian, Muslim, Hindu, Jewish, or Buddhist—and secular fundamentalism like nationalism in the former Yugoslavia, all force women to identify with the particular narrow identity of their group and to disavow "the other." Most of these fundamentalisms also demand that women be the carriers of the cultural purity of their particular group. When women are identified with culture—as reproducers and bearers of tradition—their freedom is usually circumscribed by the male leaders of their group, and they are often also used as the front line against feminism. The ability of competing fundamentalisms to unite as a global force against feminists was made clear at the Women's Conference in Beijing when right-wing Republican U.S. congressmen were in agreement with the Vatican, the Islamic mullahs, and the secular Chinese Communist government in their opposition to the inclusion of gender, sexuality, and reproductive rights in the Platform for Action.

Growing recognition of the global forces affecting women's lives has fueled women's efforts at global networking during the 1990s—including within the women's human rights movement. And this is where the UN world conferences have come to play a key role. Prior to the World Conference on Women in Nairobi in 1985, most of what went on in the name of global feminism or international women's work was information sharing or solidarity work supporting another group's needs. But the global networking that has emerged in the nineties goes beyond solidarity—though that continues to be important—to a more integrated understanding of the connection between what's happening in one country and another. Thus, not only do women care about what's happening to other women in Afghanistan or Rwanda, but also we understand that the advance of fundamentalism anywhere has implications for its growth in other countries and the instability and violence of armed conflicts spill over many borders. Feminists of course still need to act out of solidarity but also to understand that events in diverse parts of the world affect each other. Global networks that have the capacity to respond with a greater international effort can thus strengthen local work.

Understanding the need for more global connections among women gained considerable ground at the time of the third UN World Conference on Women in Nairobi. In 1975, at the first UN World Conference on Women in Mexico City, the debates were generally divided along the lines of the three prevailing UN blocs and the slogan for the UN Decade symbolized this: "Equality, Development, and Peace." These terms reflected what was understood as central to the "woman question" in each of the three blocs. Thus, Equality was seen primarily as a feminist issue coming from Western industrialized countries; Peace was included at the request of the Eastern Socialist bloc; and Development was perceived as key to the improvement of women's lives in third-world countries. At the end of the decade conference in Nairobi by contrast, many women had rejected this division into separate areas and were calling for an understanding of the intersection of these issues. The seeds of several future global networks were sown in Nairobi. One of the groups leading in this effort was DAWN—Development Alternatives with Women for a New Era—a group of women from the South who worked together to produce a book for Nairobi that was a feminist analysis of development and international capitalism and their impact on women. To respond to the challenges posed by the global economy, they called for strategies that crossed North and South lines, with leadership from Southern feminists. They saw no hope of achieving the kind of changes women sought nationally without building alliances that moved both South-South and North-South. Alliances like these played a key role in beginning to shift the discussion of development in the international community to take greater account of women and gender analysis.

The UN world conferences in the 1990s became the occasion for many of these nascent networks to emerge in a more public arena. Women were already sharing strategies and information around development, health, the environment, violence, et cetera. What the world conferences provided was an opportunity to make more visible women's experiences and to showcase feminist/gender-aware perspectives on major global issues. Throughout the eighties many women had been involved in significant efforts to redefine development, and witnessed how the United Nations and some other development agencies began to reflect some of women's concerns in what came to be called human development, a concept that went beyond the prevailing economic development theories. Similar work to redefine society's major paradigms became the focus of women's global networking around the UN world conferences: The Earth Summit on the Environment in Rio in 1992; the World Conference on Human Rights in Vienna in 1993; the International Conference on Population and Development in Cairo in 1994; the World Summit for Social Development in Copenhagen in 1995; the World Conference on Women in Beijing in 1995; the Habitat World Conference on Human Settlement in Istanbul in 1996; and the World Food Summit in Rome in 1997.

Feminist analysis and practice moved into these global public spaces as women brought work done on issues concerning violence, reproductive rights, pay equity, women's political participation, et cetera, to the agendas of the world conferences. The women demonstrated what a gender analysis means in terms of global public policy. While there were of course many differences and debates among women about what should be done at the conferences and how to define a gendered approach, these were generally political differences, not ones based primarily on identity and geography. Women found themselves agreeing with some of the women from different countries and as often disagreeing with some of the women from their own identity groups. While women drew on the insights gained in identity politics, they also recognized the need to move beyond that in order to create a global political force.

These global networks are still emerging, but their experience points to the possibility of organizing that builds on the specificity that women have developed around particular identities and takes account of diversity but also creates a broader political analysis from that place. This is an effort to take the best of identity politics and its grounding in the particulars of differences according to race, class, sexuality, nationality, and other factors and move from that knowledge toward a common political analysis of the larger forces at work. It assumes that diverse experiences can help build broader strategies and more effective next steps. An example of how this works can be seen in the women's human rights movement that has grown out of this impetus for global feminist networking.

The international movement for women's human rights crystallized around the second United Nations World Conference on Human Rights held in Vienna in 1993. It emerged in response to numerous concerns and reflected women's collaborative efforts in diverse contexts. In particular, many women in different regions believed that the issues they were organizing against—especially various forms of gender-based violence such as battery, rape, female genital mutilation, female infanticide, or trafficking—were human rights crises that were not being taken seriously as human rights violations. Thus, despite the many differences among the women organizing for the Vienna conference, women were able to articulate, develop, and act upon a common agenda that took as its focal point the issue of gender-based violence against women.

One of the major expressions of this movement at the international level has been the Global Campaign for Women's Human Rights—a loose coalition of groups and individuals worldwide formed in preparation for the Vienna conference. Several organizations and regional networks worked together to launch the Global Campaign, and they used networking as a primary mode of mobilizing women. This coalition pursued a number of diverse strategies and advanced various issues under the broad umbrella of demanding that women be put on the agenda in Vienna and that violence against women be recognized as a human rights violation. Having gained recognition of women's rights as human rights in Vienna, the Global Campaign then coordinated a series of actions that included workshops, strategic planning meetings, human rights caucuses, and hearings on women's human rights at the International Conference on Population and Development in Cairo, the World Summit for Social Development in Copenhagen, and the Fourth World Conference on Women in Beijing.

Since these conferences, one of the ongoing tasks of the Global Campaign for Women's Human Rights has been pushing for implementation of the various UN world conference commitments to women. Activists have coordinated efforts globally to lobby the various human rights mechanisms of the UN to fulfill their commitment to the full integration of gender concerns and awareness into their work. Similarly, much effort has gone into working with regional and national bodies, both governmental and nongovernmental, for the full incorporation of gender consciousness and women's human rights into their agendas. In 1998, the Global Campaign utilized this same method of networking in putting forth several broad themes under the slogan Celebrate and Demand Women's Human Rights. This effort sought to bring women's perspectives into commemorations of the fiftieth anniversary of the Universal Declaration of Human Rights at the global level and to encourage diverse but coordinated expressions of this theme locally.

Another ongoing initiative of the women's human rights movement that embodies this approach is the "16 Days of Activism against Gender Violence," an international campaign which links November 25 (International Day against Violence against Women) to December 10 (International Human Rights Day). The 16 Days Campaign aims to provide a global umbrella for local activities that promote public awareness about gender-based violence as a human rights concern and that seek specific commitments to women's human rights at all levels. Groups participating in the campaign select their own particularized objectives and determine their own local activities, but all are done with a sense of being part of this larger global focus.

The driving force of these campaigns has been commitment to action-oriented networking and to building linkages among women across multiple boundaries including class, race, ethnicity, religion, and sexual orientation, both within local and national-level communities and across geopolitical divides. In these activities, the women's human rights movement has utilized human rights approaches to strengthen local mobilization efforts and to advance local objectives, while at the same time linking them to a larger international movement with broad common goals. It has thus incorporated a wide range of particularized women's issues into an overall international framework for action and change.

Why Human Rights?

One of the first questions that the women's human rights movement has had to address is why feminists should use the human rights concepts and framework for our concerns at all? The limitations in the origins of modern human rights practice are real: it's Western, it's male, it's individualistic, its emphasis has been on political and not economic rights. However, looking beyond its origins to the particular movements for change in the twentieth century that have taken up this concept, we see that the idea that all people have fundamental human rights has become one of the most powerful concepts that disenfranchised groups have used to legitimize their struggles. In the anticolonial independence movements in Asia and Africa, in struggles against dictatorships in Latin America, in movements for the rights of the indigenous, in the African American movement in the United States, human rights language has given voice to claims to be included in the human community as equal citizens. As each group that has been excluded from mainstream power and political discourse stakes their claim to human rights, the term and the practice that derives from it has also been revitalized and expanded in its meaning—taking it further from those limited origins and closer to the ideal of universal human rights for all. The whole body of human rights literature as well as the UN treaties and mechanisms to enforce them established in the last fifty years has had to change and grow as each group has laid out its claims.

Women are following this historical precedent in demanding full recognition of our humanity and posing challenges that are already beginning to transform human rights concepts and practice to be more responsive to women's lives. Human rights language creates a space in which different accounts of women's lives and new ways of demanding change can be developed. Women from many different countries have used it to articulate diverse demands in relation to a broad array of issues. Human rights also provide overarching principles to frame visions of justice for women without dictating the precise content of those visions. As an ethical concept, human rights speak to values and principles that are not tied to any one religion and can be useful to feminists in answering conservative or fundamentalist attacks.

Human rights is a powerful term that transforms the discussion from being about something that is a good idea to that which ought to be the birthright of every person. Thus it provides a powerful vocabulary for naming gender-based violations and impediments to the exercise of women's full equality and citizenship that legitimizes the demand that these be taken seriously. For many women, it has been empowering to realize that abuses they endure or have endured such as rape, battery, forced marriage, or bodily mutilations are recognized as violations of their humanity. Further, by interpreting abuses of women as human rights violations, women gain greater access to the large body of international and regional human rights treaties, covenants, and agreements that make up international human rights law and practice.

Human rights is as close as we have in the world today to an agreement about what is crucial to human dignity. It is at the center of debates over what every person should have the right to and what no person or state should be able to violate. The Universal Declaration of Human Rights adopted by all the governments in the United Nations in 1948 remains the core document for human rights deliberations. It defines human rights as universal, inalienable, and indivisible. All of these defining characteristics are important for women.

The idea of human rights as *inalienable* means that no one can voluntarily abdicate her/his human rights since those are rights which we have by virtue of being human. This also means that

no person or group can deprive another individual of her/his human rights. Thus, for example, debts incurred by migrant workers or by women caught up in sex-trafficking can never justify indentured servitude (slavery), or the deprivation of food, of freedom of movement, or of compensation. Human rights cannot be sold, ransomed, or forfeited for any reason. In theory, then, these are not rights which a country gives or can take away from anyone since they inhere in each person. Further, if governments do deprive citizens of these rights or fail to protect them, they are in violation of their obligation as a state to promote and protect their citizens' rights.

The *universality* of human rights means that human rights should apply to every single person equally, for everyone is equal in simply being human. While such an interpretation of universality may seem simple, this egalitarian premise has a radical edge that makes it one of the most challenged issues in human rights. By invoking the universality of human rights, women have demanded the incorporation of women- and gender-aware perspectives into all of the ideas and institutions that are already committed to the promotion and protection of human rights. Further, universality challenges the contention that the human rights of women (or any group) can be limited by religious or culturally specific definitions of their role.

It is important to note that the concept of universality in human rights does not mean that everyone is or should be the same, but rather that all are equal in their rights by virtue of their humanity. Further, it demands that these rights not be culturally circumscribed and denied to any one group of humans. Of course interpretations of human rights are not static but represent what the prevailing forces in the human community decide are the fundamentals of what is acceptable for the treatment of people. The question then is, who decides what are these agreed-upon human rights? Women are demanding both an end to the double standard of who has human rights and, perhaps even more important, the right to be engaged in their ongoing definition and interpretation. In cultures where there is debate about whether the concept of human rights is being imposed from the outside, women have argued that the concept of universality means that they have the right to be part of those deciding how to interpret human rights principles in their context and that their interpretation must apply equally to men and women.

The *indivisibility* of human rights means that none of the rights that are considered to be fundamental is supposed to be seen as more important than any of the others and that they are interrelated. Moreover, since human rights encompass civil, political, social, economic, and cultural facets of human existence, the indivisibility premise highlights that the ability of people to live their lives in dignity and to exercise their human rights fully depends on the recognition that these aspects are interdependent. The fact that human rights are indivisible is important for women, since their civil and political rights historically have been compromised by their economic status, by social and cultural limitations placed on their activities, and by the ever-present threat of violence that often constitutes an insurmountable obstacle to women's participation in public and political life.

Indivisibility also challenges the historic Western bias in favor of civil and political rights over social and economic rights. Many people in the United States don't even realize that the Universal Declaration of Human Rights includes social and economic rights. However, many groups throughout the world have spent a great deal of time working on how to demand and realize rights to things like development, housing, and employment. Women's human rights activists have rejected a human rights hierarchy which places either political and civil rights or socioeconomic rights as primary. Instead, women have charged that political stability cannot be realized unless women's social and economic rights are also addressed; that sustainable development is impossible without the simultaneous respect for, and incorporation into the policy process of women's cultural and social roles in the daily reproduction of life; and that social equity cannot be generated without economic justice and women's participation in all levels of political decision making.

While indivisibility has not yet been realized in human rights practice, it reinforces what feminists have called intersectionality or the interrelatedness of factors like race, class, age, gender, and sexuality. A person's rights or experience of violation cannot often be divided out according to one of these factors alone, for how one experiences each of these is affected by the others. The everyday reality of this principle was reiterated in most of the testimonies presented in the hearings and tribunals organized by the Global Campaign for Women's Human Rights at the UN world conferences. As women told the story of how they were violated in one area of their lives such as domestic violence, it was evident how this was exacerbated by other factors such as race or their lack of economic or political rights in other areas. Further, indivisibility of human rights reminds us that human rights are not for some while others can be left on the margins. As long as the rights of some are denied—whether on the basis of race, gender, culture, sexual orientation, or other factors—the human rights of all are undermined.

These basic concepts reflect the ideals of human rights while the considerable body of human rights standards, treaties and mechanisms that have evolved over the past fifty years are intended to translate those ideals into reality. These are particularly useful to establishing governmental accountability for protecting and promoting the human rights of women. While governments may not fulfill these obligations, most claim to care about human rights and are sensitive to both internal and external pressure to live up to the treaties they have signed. These have sometimes provided the basis for legal challenges to national law. For example, a woman in Botswana sued her government for the right to give her children her own nationality under the terms of the Convention on the Elimination of All Forms of Discrimination against Women (CEDAW). She won her suit on the grounds that this was sex discrimination that violated CEDAW, which her country had ratified. Since a number of countries do not allow women to pass on their nationality to their children, who must take that of the father, her victory had implications beyond Botswana.

In the effort to bring the issue of rape and forced pregnancy in war and conflict onto the international human rights agenda, women have successfully utilized human rights arenas such as the Vienna World Conference on Human Rights and mechanisms such as the International Criminal Tribunals for the former Yugoslavia and Rwanda. The United Nations is currently engaged in setting up an international criminal court, which can have a significant impact on how such crimes against women are pursued in the future. They are debating the terms of the court: what will be the definition of war crimes? Will rape, sexual slavery, forced pregnancy, and other violations of women be war crimes and under what conditions? Will crimes against women outside of warfare be included in the jurisdiction of an international criminal court? Will individuals be able to bring crimes before the international court, or will it only be governments who can do so? The decisions made now will determine what kind of access women will have to this international justice system in the future. Women's human rights activists from all regions of the world have operated for several years as an ongoing international group called the Women's Caucus for Gender Justice in the International Criminal Court to inject a gender perspective and to influence such decisions from the inception of the court rather than having to add gender later on, as women must do in so many of the existing human rights bodies.

There are a number of other treaties, standards, and mechanisms that the United Nations and regional organizations have developed for realizing human rights which women are now seeking to address from a gender-conscious perspective. But for people in the United States, we face a particular problem because our government claims to be a big defender of human rights internationally yet has refused to ratify many human rights treaties. It has refused to do so precisely because it is afraid that people in this country will use them to address abuses of human rights within the United States. The Convention on the Elimination of All Forms of Discrimination against Women, for example, is much more progressive than anything in the U.S. Constitution, even than the ERA, which was defeated. There are a number of provisions in the Convention on the Rights of the Child as well that cover human rights in the family that have been useful to women elsewhere, but the U.S. Government is the only industrialized country that has ratified neither of these treaties. The United States has also refused to ratify the Covenant on Social, Economic, and Cultural Rights, because it might become the basis for challenging economic policies here. Indeed, some welfare rights organizations are now doing just that—utilizing human rights principles and covenants to challenge U.S. welfare policy.

One of the most important future potential uses of human rights is to be the basis for establishing standards by which international financial institutions and multinational corporations can be held accountable for the impact of their policies. In the trend toward privatization in recent years, many governments find themselves relatively helpless in the face of violations by multinational corporations or in relation to the World Trade Organization. The question is, do we as a human community believe there should be checks on these transnational forces? Some people are beginning to look at whether the human rights system can be utilized to establish standards of what is expected from the private sector in the world today. Women's human rights advocates must be present from the beginning of this important exploration or once more, gender-aware perspectives on the responsibilities of global economic forces and the rights of women workers may be left out.

Another demonstration of the power of talking about women's rights as human rights could be seen at the Fourth World Conference on Women in Beijing as women articulated the various issues of the agenda as questions of the human right to education, to political participation, to health care, to a life free of violence, et cetera. Many governments became nervous and began to talk about how the conference must not "create any new rights." However, the expanding interpretation of human rights principles from the perspective of previously excluded groups like women always brings with it the articulation of "new"— that is, not previously recognized—rights. The clearest example of this for women has been the rapid acceptance in the nineties of violence against women as a violation of human rights; the greatest resistance to this expansion has been the reluctance of many to recognize sexual rights as human rights. Further, it was clear in Beijing that many governments recognized that women's increasing use of human rights language implied a greater demand for government accountability to the promises that were being made. Identifying these issues as human rights does not automatically provide ways of holding governments accountable, but it does open wider the doors of the human rights system for women to take steps toward more effective measures for such accountability.

Summary

The success and extent of women's human rights networking globally is all the more significant in light of critiques that suggest that the effort to find a common articulation of women's concerns or a common basis for women's organizing is seriously flawed. Some argue that to do so is to universalize the category of woman and to impose a limited agenda on all women on the basis of the experience of some women—usually white, middle class, and living in the north. Given the ways in which geography, ethnicity, race, culture, sexuality, class, and tradition shape what it means to be a woman and the specificities of local and national politics, it is important not to conceive of women or the women's movement as singular and coherent entities. Nevertheless, the experience of the women's human rights movement suggests that a global feminism driven by international feminist networking is also possible. Such networking does not require homogeneity of experience or perspective, or even ongoing consensus across a range of issues. Rather it can be built around acknowledging diversity while also finding common moments at the intersection of diverse paths.

Even as women have worked to recognize, admit, and incorporate diverse perspectives in their thinking and work, they have also struggled to create alliances and to work together in solidarity across differences in the face of conservative and fundamentalist backlashes against feminism occurring in many parts of both the North and the South. Through an understanding of the exercise of power as global and interconnected (that is, universally experienced, though different in its effects) universal human rights can be seen as a system of accountability required by the way power is exercised. In this way, the idea of universal human rights serves as a regulative principle which informs the articulation of women's local demands and strengthens their resistance to abuses of power.

When local women's groups use human rights thinking and practice, especially in the context of international networking, they actively demonstrate the complementary links between universal ideals and local struggles for justice. The Global Campaigns for Women's Human Rights can be seen as one example of the kind of mobilization that is necessary to translate international human rights standards into local social and political practice. Although it is difficult to find a common framework through which to analyze women's lives and organize for change without falling into the trap of false universalization, the international movement for women's human rights has consciously strived to challenge the idea that we must choose between universality and particularity. The movement began with the central operating principle that its concepts and activities should be developed through a process of networking with women who work and organize at the local, national, and international levels in all regions of the world. Similar types of networking have been taken up as a method of organizing by tens of thousands of women from all over the world, and they have successfully linked together women from diverse backgrounds to work on common projects.

The experiences that women gained in networking nationally, regionally, and internationally around the UN world conferences have provided the basis of trust for many to now seek to work on common and diverse projects in collaboration and solidarity on a regular basis. As this work gets translated into local and global expressions, the ability of women's networking to provide a model for affirming the universality of human rights while respecting the diversity of our particular experiences will grow. This can then lead us to take more effective action on behalf of all human rights in a time when the need for common action globally based on ethical principles is greatly needed.

Notes

This essay is based on "Women's Rights Are Human Rights: Discourses of Universality and Particularlity," a presentation given as part of the Thinking about Women Series at the Institute for Research on Women at Rutgers University in 1997.

I would like to acknowledge in particular the collaboration of Samantha Frost and Niamh Reilly in the development of some of these ideas for an earlier essay.

FEMINIST LEGAL BATTLES

GINETTE CASTRO (ESSAY DATE 1984)

SOURCE: Castro, Ginette. "Feminism and the Law." In *American Feminism: A Contemporary History,* translated by Elizabeth Loverde-Bagwell, pp. 199-222. New York: New York University Press, 1990.

In the following essay, originally published in French in 1984, Castro details the political goals of the women's movement, including the struggle to pass the Equal Rights Amendment and efforts to ensure equality for women in the workplace.

The Program

About 1973, the liberal branch of the Women's movement began trying to establish a detailed program. This new orientation seems to us to have been a realistic adjustment to take account of two factors. First, some basis for action appeared necessary in order to enable the movement to move forward coherently and to use its energy constructively toward external goals instead of wasting it in internal quarrels. Second, it was essential to build as broad a base as possible to unify women, particularly so as to make available to the struggle the resources of nonfeminist women's organizations that had been alienated from the movement by shock actions or outrageous declarations, and

ON THE SUBJECT OF...

BELLA ABZUG (1920-1998)

"We are bringing women into politics to change the nature of politics, to change the vision, to change the institutions. Women are not wedded to the policies of the past. We didn't craft them. They didn't let us."

Abzug, Bella. "Plenary Speech, Fourth World Conference on Women. September 12, 1995, Beijing, People's Republic of China." *Gifts of Speech at Sweet Briar College* (online) <http://gos.sbc.edu/a/abzug.html>.

Sporting her trademark floppy hats, attorney, activist, congresswoman, and author Bella Abzug was outspoken in her efforts to bring awareness to women's issues, to defend her clients against Senator Joseph McCarthy's investigation into alleged communist activities, to end the war in Vietnam, to advocate civil rights, and to impeach President Richard M. Nixon following the Watergate scandal. Born July 24, 1920, in New York City, Abzug began her career as an attorney, being admitted to the Bar of New York State in 1947. She worked as a private practice attorney from 1947 to 1970. In 1961 she served as legislative director of the Women's Strike for Peace, a position she held until 1970 when she became the first Jewish woman elected to Congress. She served in the House of Representatives from 1970 until 1976. On her first day in Congress in 1971, Abzug introduced a resolution calling for the withdrawal of all troops from Indochina, and in 1975 she introduced the first bill addressing civil rights for gays and lesbians. Abzug became an assistant whip to House Speaker Thomas "Tip" O'Neill, Jr., and coauthored legislation concerning privacy acts and the freedom of information act. Abzug served as co-chair of President Jimmy Carter's National Advisory Committee on Women from 1978 to 1979, and assisted and founded a number of women's advocacy groups, including Women-USA, Women's Foreign Policy Council, Women's Environmental and Development Organization, and the National Women's Political Caucus. Abzug's published works include *Bella! Ms. Abzug Goes to Washington* (1972) and *Gender Gap: Bella Abzug's Guide to Political Power for American Women* (1984; coauthored with Mim Kelber).

that could weigh heavily in determining the outcome of the battle. The development of a platform for reform would reveal how much common interest there was between feminist and nonfeminist women's organizations. Moreover, the inclusion of a wide range of proposals in this platform would have another advantage: every woman, from radical militant to nonfeminist, and every organization, from political caucus to labor union, could find something in it to support.

The first formal program platform developed by the new feminist movement in the United States was the *National Women's Agenda,* presented on 2 December 1975 to President Gerald Ford, the governors of the fifty states, and members of Congress. It had been signed by ninety women's organizations, who recognized in the preamble the priority of their common interest in every sector and at every level of American society, while affirming their continuing desire for pluralism in their purposes and points of view. The platform covered eleven headings for bold and substantial reforms.

The second platform was developed at the National Women's Conference held in Houston in November 1977. It, too, corresponded to a pragmatic spirit of coalition: "We must agree when we can, disagree when we have to, but never lose sight of our overall objectives."[1]

Adopted within the framework of a conference financed by federal funds, the Houston action plan was duly made official on 17 August 1978 by the publication of a 308-page report, *The Spirit of Houston,* and the nomination of a National Advisory Committee for Women, cochaired by Bella Abzug and Carmen Delgado Votaw. The committee's assignment under the Department of Labor was to advise the president and Congress with a view toward gradual execution of the plan. This official recognition corresponded to the will of the Houston delegates, as expressed in Resolution 26 of the platform, and translated their desire to make the government face up to its responsibilities and recognize women's issues as a national concern.

The Houston action plan contains twenty-six resolutions, three of which have been widely publicized because of the bitter divisions they have provoked among women and the doubt that has reigned over their adoption. We are speaking of the Equal Rights Amendment, the right to the voluntary interruption of pregnancy, and freedom of choice in sexual preference. With deliberate regularity, each of the twenty-six resolutions is introduced in the platform by a time-honored phrase placing the issue in the hands of legislators at the federal or state level, either demanding the establishment of permanent structures (as in the case of all the resolutions on violence), recommending new legislation (supporting child care centers and opposing discrimination against pregnant working women), or demanding enforcement of existing laws.

Political Power

RELATIONS WITH THE POWER STRUCTURE

Having obtained official recognition of their demands, the feminists who believed in reforming the existing system particularly favored one method of action over others: political pressure on government agencies, the president, or Congress. A powerful feminist lobby developed, of which the leading voices were the National Women's Political Caucus (NWPC), the Women's Lobby, Inc., founded by Carol Burris and Flora Crater, and the National Organization for Women (NOW).

Political pressure from liberal feminists was considerably increased in the 1976 presidential election campaign. The NWPC had formed a Democratic Task Force in 1974 and a Republican Task Force in 1975, which participated in the state party caucuses and the national party conventions. In 1976, Republican women had obtained their party's support for the Equal Rights Amendment, although not a declaration in favor of the 1973 Supreme Court decision legalizing abortion; however, they suffered a dual setback in 1980 when President-elect Ronald Reagan and the New Right vowed firm opposition to both abortion and the ERA. Democratic feminists, who were much more numerous in the NWPC than Republicans, no doubt because most women in Congress were Democrats, had no difficulty in persuading their party to support the ERA. More delicate were their negotiations that led the Democratic party to approve the Supreme Court decision allowing the voluntary interruption of pregnancy. Needless to say, the sexual preference plank of the feminist platform was rejected out of hand by both Democrats and Republicans.

Although the women of the NWPC were close to the traditional parties and had entrée to the inner circles of national politics, the same could not be said of NOW. Some of its officers, Karen de Crow and Artie Scott, were asked by the NWPC Republican Task Force to leave Kansas City, where the 1976 Republican party convention was being held, for fear that their mere presence might suffice to jeopardize the negotiations for adoption of the ERA in the party platform. Similarly, the evening reception to which NOW invited delegates to the Democratic convention was ostentatiously snubbed by many of them, while the one given by the NWPC was a huge success. In the eyes of politicians, NOW was a frighteningly militant organization, incarnating their worst nightmares of feminism. We see this factor as both positive and necessary, in that NOW's independence from traditional politics enabled it to retain its uniqueness as a feminist organization, and was the only way to guarantee the support of the radical minority of feminists, whose presence in the ranks was, we believe, the best guarantee against the movement's being co-opted. By the end of the 1970s, NOW had lost its aura of middle-class respectability, and was even perceived as belonging to the radical Left, as Elinor Langer[2] points out. In any case, it was a force to be reckoned with; if we can take the word of Gloria Steinem, it was collecting more money than even the Democratic party.

The 1976 presidential campaign also saw the appearance in the liberal feminist press of political profiles of the candidates according to their positions on women's issues. *Ms.,* for instance, measured the views of five presidential hopefuls and forty congressional candidates. The NWPC, after having passed feminist judgment in 1976 on the respective positions of presidential candidates Ford and Carter, came back to the charge in the 1978 congressional elections and devoted five pages of the *Women's Political Times* to the voting records of all the members of the House of Representatives on sixteen feminist bills submitted in the intervening two years, scoring them from 0 to 100. The practice was continued in subsequent elections.

In the lead-up to Ronald Reagan's election, it appears, therefore, that liberal feminists were gambling on the strength of the women's vote, counting feminists and nonfeminists. However, this would not be a block vote resulting from any specifically feminine characteristic, but rather would be a reflection of women's new political awareness and participation, inspired by feminists of the androgynous approach. Militants were cheered in this gamble by the results of a 1980 Harris poll showing that significantly more women intended to vote, as well as a twenty-point difference between male and female voters among supporters of Ronald Reagan in the 1980 presidential campaign. The gender gap was born, and it

Gloria Steinem (1934-) poses with a cover of *Ms.* magazine depicting a pregnant President Jimmy Carter in front of the White House, c. 1977.

continued to make headlines in all the publications of the Women's movement. Gloria Steinem and her staff at *Ms.* even devoted the magazine's cover to it in March 1984, inviting readers to participate in a new Harris poll on their intention to vote and their views for or against the reelection of Ronald Reagan. As another publication subsequently reported, "the 1984 election results showed the same gender gap that had first appeared in 1980. Women were still 8% more likely to vote Democratic than men. But because the gap did not increase, the press coverage gave the impression that it had disappeared."[3]

Only time will tell whether the new factor of the women's vote will have a durable existence as such in a still sexually polarized society, or whether it is a temporary phenomenon, as a personally directed reaction against a president who, after campaigning on his opposition to the ERA, blamed rising unemployment on the increased number of women in the labor market and did everything possible to overturn the 1973 Supreme Court ruling permitting abortion. In August 1983, American women's antipathy for Ronald Reagan was intensified when Barbara Honnegger resigned from her position in charge of women's affairs at the Department of Justice, denouncing the hypocrisy of the "demagogue" in the White House who publicly claimed to oppose sexual discrimination but privately had blocked Honnegger's report on a hundred discriminatory statutes.

GETTING INVOLVED IN THE POLITICAL POWER STRUCTURE

The Ninety-eighth Congress of the United States, elected in November 1982, counted only twenty-four women. Granted, thanks to a theatrical gesture from President Reagan, a woman, Sandra Day O'Connor, had finally been appointed to the Supreme Court; granted, the U.S. ambassador to the United Nations (Jeanne Kirkpatrick) and the secretary of transportation (Elizabeth Dole) were women; but, important though they were, these promotions remained exceptions to the rule and ought not to mask the dramatic underrepresentation of women in American politics.

In 1976, according to figures gathered in the bicentennial year by the National Women's Education Fund, in the course of two centuries of American history, the Senate had seated only 11 women in contrast to 1,715 men, and the House of Representatives, 87 women against 9,521 men. In the same period, only 5 women had held cabinet posts, and none had ever sat on the Supreme Court.

These statistics were scrupulously published by the *Women's Political Times,* demonstrating that the NWPC was actively aware of this underrepresentation of women. Faced with the reluctance of lawmakers to enact legislation responding to feminist demands, the NWPC, in keeping with the philosophy of liberal feminists, presented itself as a lobbying organization whose purpose was to build a "national feminist network." This expression used by Mildred Jeffrey, then president of the NWPC, seems to have been calling for a counterpart to the "old boy network." Congresswoman Barbara Nikulski (Democrat from Maryland) parodied the way in which key posts were assigned: "You know," she said, "Pete Preppy looks through his yearbook, calls up Mike Macho and says 'Got anyone good for State?' 'Sure,' answers Mike, 'try Tom Terrifico.'"[4]

Clearly, the NWPC's main concern has been effectiveness. A program of feminist demands already has existed for more than a decade; its execution depends upon bringing more women into political life. The introduction of women, in the NWPC's view, should be done according to the traditional rules of the political game, and within the two-party system. The NWPC has never foreseen a third-party effort; this stance was reiterated in 1989 when the NWPC resisted NOW's call for one. Therefore, the first level of action by NWPC militants has been to gain more representation by women at the national Democratic and Republican party conventions. Their work has met with partial success, since in 1980, the goal of equal sexual representation among delegates was attained among Democrats, but not among Republicans.[5]

The NWPC itself also has held national conventions. The one held in San Antonio in July 1983 attracted a number of candidates for the Democratic nomination. "I am a feminist," Walter Mondale was not afraid to declare, but his proposals on women's issues, like those of the other candidates, were rather vague. The NWPC strengthened its efforts to promote the election of more women by making financial contributions to their campaigns, knowing full well that money is the overriding problem of all candidates.

But what precisely has become of feminism among women candidates and women elected to office? In the light of ten sample candidacies followed by the NWPC in 1976, it appeared that even if the candidates were known to hold feminist views, they never campaigned solely on feminist issues. Some even restrained their ardor when appearing in heartland areas. The position of those already elected is obviously more comfortable. Several interesting initiatives and successes can be signaled here. First, there are the results obtained in the Ninety-third and Ninety-fourth Congresses. The passage of the landmark Equal Credit Opportunity Act, forbidding sexual discrimination in the granting of credit, was due to the work of Margaret Heckler, Leonor Sullivan, and Bella Abzug. Minimum wage legislation was extended to domestic workers thanks to the initiative of Shirley Chisholm, and the military academies were opened to women on a bill introduced by Patricia Schroeder. The honors, again, are due to a woman, Martha Keys, for the measure grant-

ing a 20 percent tax deduction to low-income families for expenses related to child care. During the Ninety-fifth Congress, for the first time in the history of the United States, fifteen of the eighteen congresswomen formed a bipartisan women's committee to transcend party differences and to join forces, whenever possible, on issues concerning women. The committee agreed to meet every Tuesday and invite various cabinet members to discuss their policies, particularly regarding the hiring and promotion of women.

The NWPC congratulated itself for another initiative, presenting it as a good illustration of the feminist network in operation, as a chain of solidarity linking elected women to their women constituents. In one of the first examples of this networking, the NWPC president Mildred Jeffrey testified, in January 1978, before the congressional committee charged with studying proposed amendments to the Humphrey-Hawkins Full Employment Act, and made several suggestions for modifying the bill. Some days later, Barbara Mikulski took up the relay, and introduced in Congress a number of measures proposed by the NWPC. On 9 March 1978, two of these measures were enacted by the legislators: increased child care facilities for single mothers, and greater representation of women and ethnic minorities on the consulting committees proposed by the Full Employment and Balanced Growth Act, in proportion to their members in the labor force.

Again, the rule of equal representation, dear to liberal feminists, has been at work in the ultimate illustration of how feminist networking has enabled women to gain access to power. According to the NWPC, the federal agencies which, under President Jimmy Carter, were directed by women—Patricia Robert Harris at Housing and Urban Development, Juanita Kreps at Commerce, Eleanor Holmes Norton at the EEOC, and Grace Olivarez at the Community Services Administration—recruited as many women staff members as men.

The picture darkened considerably under President Ronald Reagan. Sandra Day O'Connor appeared little disposed to support feminist claims, as witness her dissenting vote in June 1983 when the Supreme Court reasserted the right of American women to the voluntary interruption of pregnancy. As for Elizabeth Dole, in an interview granted to Judith Mann soon after taking office as secretary of transportation, she was content to repeat President Reagan's statements on sexual discrimination, without lending any support to the Equal Rights Amendment.

The Constitutional Battle and the Struggle against the Antifeminist Backlash

THE EQUAL RIGHTS AMENDMENT

At the start of the 1980s the liberal forces of the Women's movement were still fighting for the same cause that the National Women's party had been championing since the end of World War I: the Equal Rights Amendment. This had become the primary objective of the egalitarian feminists, and they threw all their resources into this battle. This factor contributed to the general impression that the liberal wing had taken over the Women's movement at the expense of the radical influence, an impression that was reinforced by the forming of coalitions around the egalitarian battle plan.

The reasons for such crystallizations are obvious. Although militants recognized that the Equal Rights Amendment alone could not eradicate sexist prejudices from individuals or the society, they nevertheless believed that an amendment to the Constitution was the only possible remedy to destroy the underlying prejudice of the fundamental law of the land. The soundness of their argument cannot be denied, if we recall the government interpretation, in the case of women army doctors in World War II claiming equal pay, that the accepted constitutional meaning of the term *person* did not include the female sex. It was all the more frustrating and humiliating for American feminists, in the best-organized women's rights movement in the world, to be facing defeat, after more than half a century of combat, for lack of three ratifying votes. In 1980, in fact, thirty-five states had ratified the amendment, thirty-three having done so in the three years following the historic vote of Congress in 1972 passing the ERA. But after 1975, only two further ratifications had been scored, and in three states, legislatures that had already voted ratification now voted in favor of rescinding their previous votes, although the constitutionality of this rescission was doubtful. Not surprisingly, the strongest opposition came from the South. The same nine southern states that had earlier refused to ratify the amendment granting women the vote now refused to ratify the one granting sexual equality. The taste of defeat was all the more bitter in that numerous surveys had shown that, with little variation, there was a constant majority of public support for the ERA. When President Reagan took office, this majority even rose sharply from 58 to 63 percent.

How, then, can we explain the ERA's successive failures to be ratified, either through legislative votes, as in North Carolina and Florida, or by local referendum for the adoption of a home-grown ERA modifying the state constitution, as in New Jersey and New York? Feminist analysts have decided that the main reason lies in their previous underestimation of the opposition. It had been naive of them to believe that their only opponents were sincere but misguided housewives. In the analysis of the NWPC, NOW, and the editors of *Ms.*, the ERA's real adversaries have been the organized political forces of the extreme Right. Of the women who have made careers out of urging other women not to have careers but to stay home and vote against sexual equality, the most notorious include the following: Phyllis Schlafly, an outspoken ultraconservative and head of the National Stop ERA Movement; Helen Andelin, author of *The Secret Power of Femininity* and founder of the Femininity Forum, under whose banner the California anti-ERA forces were assembled; Maureen Startup, also from California, who organized a convention for that state's annulment of its previous ratification of the ERA; Annette Stern, a "home executive" in her own preferred term, leader of the New York group most hostile to the ERA, Operation Wake Up, and founder of WUNDER.[6] According to feminist sources, the funding for these groups has come, partially or entirely, from openly racist organizations like the John Birch Society, from anti-Communist groups like the Cardinal Mindszenty Foundation, or from bastions of traditionalism like the American Legion and the Daughters of the American Revolution. Powerful opposition has also come from the direction of organized religion, led by the Baptist, Mormon, and Catholic churches. Last but far from least, the economic implications of equality must not be overlooked. As the NOW leaders observed, big business has been visible by its absence from the coalitions supporting passage of the Equal Rights Amendment. The hostility of the world of high finance is definitive proof of early feminist successes. Court-ordered retroactive correction of sexual discrimination has cost big companies a lot of money: $100 million for AT& T, for example, and $75 million for Sears. But these sums are minuscule in comparison with the real amounts involved, according to the estimate of a private economist consulted by Elinor Langer:

> If, in 1970, women who worked had earned the same amount per hour as men who worked, it would have cost employers an additional $96 billion in payroll alone. . . . If women had earned the same as men and worked the same number of hours, the addition to the payroll would have been $303 billion.[7]

More recent figures from the Labor Department show that in 1988, women made up 44.8

percent of the U.S. labor force, and that in the 1990s, they will fill 60 percent of new jobs, so that by the year 2000, women will account for about half of the work force.

It is understandable what worry this can cause in powerful and recalcitrant business sectors, such as insurance companies, for example, which furthermore are well represented in state legislatures, according to a NOW study of the Illinois state senate.

In state legislatures called to vote for or against the federal amendment, therefore, it has been easy for multinational companies to defend their special interests. The ERA has become a political hot potato, and this, say the feminist analysts, is the second reason for its defeat. The vote of Florida legislators on the ERA, for example, as the local press objectively reports, was not really for or against sexual equality; instead, the ERA vote was used by them as a bargaining chip for unrelated political transactions, some negotiating to retain their chairmanship of a committee, others wanting to put an obstacle in the path of a political adversary favorable to the amendment. As the editorial writer of the *Women's Political Times* bluntly put it, "They're playing political football with our issue."[8]

Naturally, this sport has been concealed behind a smokescreen. When speaking publicly, opponents of the ERA have found pretexts in the language of the amendment itself, with scare talk about the institutionalization of public toilets in common to both sexes, homosexual marriages, and the military draft for women, all scaremongering images which they evoked as representative of the Women's movement itself, and as the logical outcome of passage of the ERA. Now we confront the third reason for the ERA's failure, in the view of feminist analysts: the negative image that many women have of feminists, stereotyped as ruthlessly ambitious career women with hearts of steel under their elegant business suits, or else as bare-breasted, bisexual flaming revolutionaries. Trying to understand the crushing defeat suffered by the ERA in New York, Lindsy Van Gelder interviewed four women whose interests and opinions coincided with the spirit of the ERA, but who nonetheless had voted against it in a referendum simply because they had wanted to censure the Women's movement for the image it gave of itself, and had refused to give the movement their vote of confidence.[9]

Here we reencounter the same old problem of credibility, which has always undermined feminist

efforts. The problem is all the more serious in that it creates opposition to feminism in certain categories of women themselves, particularly housewives and low-income wage earners. While some opposition comes from groups that defend their special interests by pretending to believe that the concept of a politically organized women's rights movement is fundamentally unsound and unnecessary, housewives and low-income women are sincere in rejecting the ERA out of fear for their own security. Feminists engaged in reform face a double challenge: on the one hand, to convince women that their action is worthwhile and that the stereotypes are false; on the other hand, to expose the intrigues of power and money interests hiding behind the skirts of Phyllis Schlafly and her troops.

To meet this challenge, feminists recognized early the need to come out of isolation and form alliances. They saw that well-chosen allies could bring much-needed credibility to their image; this would signify the creation of a united front, as opponents had done in the National Stop ERA Movement. For this reason, as soon as the anti-ERA backlash effect began to appear, a policy of coalition emerged among feminists, beginning in about 1975, of which the first fruit was the *US National Women's Agenda*. A broad coalition for the ERA was created in the following year: ERAmerica, which, from its founding, brought together more than a hundred diverse organizations, including women's clubs, religious groups, labor unions, and civic bodies, all denouncing the sexual discrimination that afflicted American women and proclaiming the legitimacy of the amendment through which they were seeking their place in the Constitution. This coalition, which opened a new era in feminist militancy, did not come about solely through the will of feminists; it seems to have resulted from a growing awareness among all sorts of liberal organizations of the real implications of opposition to the ERA, thus confirming what feminists had been alleging about the true identity of the special interest groups opposing it. In fact, it began to appear more and more evident that the extreme Right was using the ERA as a political "litmus test," as a victory on this issue could be the prelude to other conservative offensives against, for example, arms reduction, consumer protection, and labor union demands. According to the *Women's Political Times,* key liberal leaders held an important strategy meeting in Washington from 17 to 19 April 1978 to devise common ways of countering the new upsurge of strength on the extreme

Right.[10] They decided to establish a permanent regional structure to facilitate communication with each other. But even more important, it seems to me, was the dialogue opened in the late 1970s between feminists and labor union leaders, ending more than a century of mutual suspicion. New relationships of reciprocity developed: in exchange for labor union support for the ERA, the NWPC committed itself to support labor and social legislation such as the Humphrey-Hawkins Full Employment Act and the Labor Law Reform Bill. I think it is important to mention this agreement, since it rested on a basis of equality and mutual respect. By this I mean that there was no trace of paternalism in this labor union support, and this fact, expressing united struggle for a common cause, is the great advance achieved by the new feminism of the 1960s and 1970s over the protofeminism of the postwar years.

This cooperation with others seems to us to have opened a new era for militant feminism in more than one way. It has not only brought feminism out of isolation, but also drawn it out of a defensive posture. Too often, in fact, feminists have been content to spend their time denying the half-truths spread by Phyllis Schlafly about public toilets, homosexual marriages, and the draft. Regarding public toilets common to both sexes, for example, feminists have recalled that the Supreme Court has already recognized a constitutional right to personal privacy in intimate matters in the 1965 case *Griswold v. Connecticut*. The legalization of homosexual marriages would not be discriminatory if it applied to both sexes. On the draft, feminists have proposed that both men and women should be exempt if they have children under eighteen years of age. But in the new era of cooperation, starting in the late 1970s, feminists began a positive approach to demonstrate the benefits of the Equal Rights Amendment to those most frightened by it: housewives. In the case of divorce, they began emphasizing, the elimination of inequality before the law would mean that housewives would be guaranteed the right to compensation for services rendered, instead of uncertain and humiliating alimony payments. Widows whose husbands had died without leaving a will would automatically be entitled to receive their husbands' pensions, instead of having to fight a costly legal battle to do so. The ERA would eliminate an existing tax inequality, in which the estates of widows but not widowers were subject to inheritance taxes. Every housewife would have the same access to credit as her husband, which was not yet the case, in spite of the Equal Opportunity Credit Act.

This return to the offensive was marked by renewed vigor in NOW, 100,000 members strong after gaining new adherents at the Houston conference. The oldest organization in new feminism started off on a new footing in February 1978, with a solemn proclamation of a state of emergency for the Equal Rights Amendment, excluding any possibility of failure. "We have passed the point of no return,"[11] they said, in announcing a new, two-level strategy: state and federal. At the state level, they would mount a campaign in every state that had not yet ratified the ERA. At the federal level, they would lobby Congress to obtain an extension of the deadline for ratification, originally set at 30 March 1979.

The boldest scheme devised by NOW was a boycott of the states whose legislatures had voted against ratification. All liberal organizations were urged not to hold any meetings or conventions in the fifteen recalcitrant states.[12] The boycott results were encouraging for feminists, since 380 organizations of all types heard the appeal. The NOW initiative cost many cities dearly, hitting where it hurt. Miami Beach lost $9 million following the cancellation of convention reservations by the American Library Association, the National Organization of Religious Women, and the National Education Association. Chicago lost $15 million in similar circumstances. The attorney general of the state of Missouri, estimating the lost business to Kansas City and Saint Louis at $18 million, filed a suit against NOW for violation of the antitrust laws. Similar legal action was brought by the state of Nevada and by a travel agency in New Orleans. Recalling that the antitrust laws were aimed at business activities in restraint of trade, NOW retorted that a boycott was not a business activity, and that in any case, independent organizations were free to opt for or against the boycott. Further, NOW filed a countersuit for defamation, claiming $20 million from each of the accusing states. An initial success was gained when a federal district court in Missouri recognized that a boycott is a legitimate form of political expression.

The National Organization for Women outshone itself with another initiative: the demand for extension of the original seven-year deadline for ratification of the ERA. Credit is due to NOW for the legal research regarding the constitutionality of the extension measure. Investigations revealed that no clause in the Constitution imposes a time limit for ratification; this practice began only with the Eighteenth Amendment.

They also argued that although a time limit was mentioned in the preamble to the ERA, there was none in the text of the amendment itself; furthermore, since this time limit had been set by Congress, then Congress had the authority to modify it. Having done its homework, the feminist lobby threw all its weight into the battle and carried off a new success, since the extension of the deadline was voted in by a comfortable majority of 233 to 189 in the House of Representatives, and by 60 to 39 in the Senate. As recalled by the countdown kept by the *National NOW Times,* a new date was set for sexual equality: 30 June 1982.

This proved to be a vain effort, alas, because under fire from the New Right, the new deadline expired without the Equal Rights Amendment being ratified by any other state. With regard to the Constitution, the new feminist militants had suffered the same setback as the post-World War II ERA activists; that is, although they were uncontestably better organized and better supported, with a majority in numerous public opinion polls, they were still far from escaping from the trap of combat by proxy. In July 1982, immediately after expiration of the deadline, the Equal Rights Amendment was introduced anew to Congress, but American women would have to await the pleasure of the chairmen of the House and Senate Judiciary Committees for the ERA to be inscribed again on the legislative calendar. A vote did take place in the House of Representatives in November 1983, but the amendment failed, six votes short of the required two-thirds majority, with the Democrats dividing 225-38 in favor and the Republicans opposing it 109-53.[13]

VOLUNTARY INTERRUPTION OF PREGNANCY

On 22 January 1973, in the case of *Roe v. Wade,* the Supreme Court, ruling for the first time on the issue of abortion, rendered a decision in favor of its legality in the United States. This historic decision immediately aroused an army of dissenters. The forces opposing a woman's right to choose the voluntary interruption of pregnancy have been, by and large, the same as those fighting the Equal Rights Amendment. On each anniversary of the Supreme Court ruling, in contrast to the symbolic funeral rites feminists used to hold for women who had died from the butchery of illegal backstreet abortions, now the antichoice forces, calling themselves partisans of the "right to life," began organizing emotional demonstrations in front of the Capitol Building and elsewhere. Thousands of children from Catholic and fundamentalist Protestant schools, let out of lessons for the occasion, were paraded, waving red roses symbolizing the children who will never be born. The Catholic church is believed to have invested huge sums annually in the campaign to overturn the Supreme Court decision, and there has also been a faction of resistance in the medical professions. Opposition has been focused in the National Right-to-Life Committee, established in the 1970s. The most fanatical foes of abortion have frequently had recourse to violence against family planning centers and feminist clinics. A more insidious and more dangerous strategy, from the feminist point of view, has been the attempt to outlaw abortion entirely through a constitutional amendment. In spring 1977, only four years after *Roe v. Wade,* the *Women's Political Times* announced that seventy members of Congress had already offered such constitutional amendments. Feminist ranks were worried, recognizing that there was a serious risk of returning to the days of dangerous illegal abortions that existed before 1973; in 1977, with those days still fresh in mind, the journalist Roberta Brandes Gratz summarized the case in a thought-provoking article entitled "Never Again! Never Again?" She cited Koryne Horbal, a member of the National Abortion Rights Action League (NARAL), who reproached feminists for being too soft and yielding on this question: "women's groups have not made it clear to liberal Congressmen and state legislators that abortion is a non-negotiable issue."[14]

It was essential to communicate to liberal male politicians that they could not dodge an uncomfortable situation by giving their support to women on other controversial issues in exchange for defection on the thornier question of abortion.

In early 1983, after Senator Jesse Helms had tried in vain to push through a constitutional amendment asserting that human life begins at conception, his colleague Orrin Hatch attempted to open debate on another amendment that would give state legislatures or Congress the right to outlaw abortion. In 1983, and again in 1986, the Supreme Court reaffirmed the right of American women to voluntary interruption of pregnancy, but opposition only increased. Just before the end of President Reagan's second term, his administration filled a friend-of-the court brief with the Supreme Court, asking it to overturn its 1973 *Roe v. Wade* decision. The Court, fortified by conservative members named by President Reagan, agreed to review the case of *Webster v. Reproductive Health Services,* in what many viewed as the most serious challenge to the legality of abortion since 1973. The case came before the

Supreme Court in April 1989, and to show their support for *Roe v. Wade,* feminists rallied in one of the largest political demonstrations ever held in Washington, rivaling others that have marked historic turning points, such as the 1963 march for civil rights. Working together through the coordination of the Fund for the Feminist Majority under President Ellie Smeal, feminists drew an estimated 300,000 women from all over the United States, in contrast to only a few hundred antichoice advocates who marched in opposition. "It's a turning point," said Ellie Smeal. "It's a totally new ball game. It's given us the confidence that we are the majority."

The Supreme Court's decision, in July 1989, considerably reduced American women's abortion rights, confirming several essential clauses of a restrictive Missouri law. By five votes to four, the Court held constitutional the provision forbidding public funding for the voluntary interruption of pregnancy. Therefore, the decision left the states free not to finance abortions. Also, contrary to the 1973 ruling in *Roe v. Wade,* the July 1989 decision allowed tests on the viability of the foetus at twenty weeks after conception. In addition, the Court under Chief Justice Rehnquist judged constitutional the preamble to the Missouri law which declared that "life begins at conception." Admittedly, the justices said that this declaration did not necessarily have concrete applications on the right to abortion; nevertheless, they let stand Missouri's definition of conception as the moment of fertilization. Finally, the Court reversed itself on one of the fundamental bases of its 1973 ruling, which gave women an absolute right to abortion during the first trimester (three months) of pregnancy without state intervention in their privacy; henceforth, following *Webster,* the states can intervene from the first trimester.

Consequently, the abortion debate now will be focused at the state level. Instead of a uniform law for the whole country, each state will have its own abortion laws. American women who have the means to pay for an abortion will travel to the so-called liberal states, but the new restrictions will dramatically strike poor women, as well as the youngest and those least informed. Pro-choice advocates fear a return to risky illegal abortions.

In the three months following the *Webster* decision, the Supreme Court agreed to review other abortion-related cases: Ohio and Minnesota laws involving the constitutionality of parental-notification rules for minors, and an Illinois statute requiring abortions to be performed in strictly licensed clinics. The Pennsylvania legisla-

ture was about to pass new severely restrictive legislation that appeared destined to be challenged in the Supreme Court, and other collisions seemed likely.

The decision in *Webster v. Reproductive Health Services* galvanized American public opinion and political attention. It not only gave a jolt to the Women's movement, but seemed to arouse pro-choice advocates far beyond the ranks of already convinced feminists. In a story headed, "Can Pro-Choicers Prevail?," *Time* magazine reported on 14 August 1989 that since the Court had agreed to review the case, NOW and NARAL had each gained 50,000 new members. Three months after the decision, when President George Bush vetoed legislation that would have provided federal funding of abortions for women who were the victims of rape or incest, the House only failed by a narrow margin to override the veto. The president's stance, which was seen as allowing abortion rights to women of means and denying them to all others, was widely criticized by members of his own party as politically damaging. Representative Bill Green, Republican, of New York, said, "Mr. Bush may have stumbled on the one issue that could cost him the election in 1992."

The Feminist Struggle and Women at Work

In keeping with Resolution 10 of the Houston platform, and in keeping with the importance assigned by egalitarian feminists to women's rights in the workplace and their systematic attacks on sexual discrimination, numerous initiatives have aimed at combating sexually discriminatory practices and at improving women's lot in employment. The observer could even conclude that the fierce fighting for the Equal Rights Amendment is primarily motivated by the desire to obtain equality for women in hiring, salaries and job responsibilities. This is the basis on which all the previously mentioned professional associations operate, considering that women are not "stealing men's jobs," but that an enormous majority of them are working out of economic necessity. In 1981, they represented 43 percent of the total national active labor force (including full-time and part-time work), and of these, roughly 45 percent were single, widowed, separated, or divorced, while about 25 percent were married to men earning less than $10,000 per year. In 1988, the figure for working women in the national active labor force had risen to 44.8 percent, and among young women, it was much higher. The Labor Department estimated two-thirds of married women aged 20 to 34 were working, and that by the end of the century, women would represent roughly half the American labor force. According to the feminist philosophy of survival, work, for a great many women, is a necessity, the only way to escape social determinism.

LEGAL ACTION

The preferred form of legal action has been to file a court suit pleading for application of existing legislation, specifically, the legislation known as Title VII of the 1964 Civil Rights Act. It must be said that the author of the sexual clause of this act had considerably underestimated its importance. Feminists and women plaintiffs influenced by feminism have, in fact, invoked Title VII not only regarding injustices in hiring, salary, or promotion, but also for any matter concerned with sexual harassment. Numerous feminist advice centers[15] were set up in the 1970s to provide information about the legal procedures to follow in such cases. Numerous such suits have been filed and won under Title VII; in one of the first examples, Diane Williams, an employee at the Department of Justice, received $16,000 in back pay for having been fired after refusing to give in to the sexual advances of her boss.

Feminist militancy in the workplace has favored court action, and particularly, class action suits. As a new embodiment of "sisterhood," this form of protest appears above all as the collective response of women to their common oppression. It was born, in the most spontaneous way, among women in journalism. On 16 March 1970, forty-six women employed by *Newsweek* filed a suit with the Equal Employment Opportunity Commission (EEOC) claiming that the magazine was practicing sexual discrimination by restricting them to tasks of research and compilation; *Newsweek* at that time had only one female editor for fifty-one male editors, twelve female reporters for sixty-four male reporters and thirty-four female researchers for only one male researcher. An agreement was signed, on the symbolic date of 26 August 1970, stating a declaration of good intentions on the part of the employer and establishing a women's committee charged with seeing that the management carried out its promises. Two months after the *Newsweek* initiative, 147 women employees of Time Incorporated undertook similar action, for the same reasons. The accord reached in the Time suit stipulated that all jobs in the company should be henceforth open to all qualified persons, regardless of sex, and that compliance would be supervised by the Human Rights Division of the State of New York.

The class action suit for sexual discrimination took on a new dimension when filed by a group whose common interests were outside the job field. It became a collective summons to a class of officials issued by an organized class of feminists. This was the interesting procedure followed by the Women's Equity Action League (WEAL) regarding discrimination in higher education.

Before it is possible to enter battle in the name of the law, there has to be a law covering the issue; in this case, the law concerned private or public institutions of higher education receiving federal funds. Now, although Title VII of the 1964 Civil Rights Act included sexual discrimination, this title does not mention education. However, Title VI of the same act applies to all institutions receiving federal funds, therefore including teaching institutions, but does not include the clause on sexual discrimination. Thus, a gap existed in the law as it stood, and it needed to be remedied. WEAL did research to dig up an appropriate precedent, and found executive order 11246 of 24 September 1965, amended by executive order 11375 of 13 October 1967, which forbade sexual discrimination in federal employment and applied to all contractors and subcontractors with the federal government.

On 31 January 1970, WEAL filed its first class action suit, summoning the federal administration to apply this executive order to all university establishments bound by contracts with the federal government. Several hundred suits were filed by the same and other organizations within the Women's movement against institutions of higher learning, the first target being the University of Maryland. Feminist pressure was also exercised on Congress, through Edith Green, Democratic congresswoman from Oregon, who in February 1970 submitted four bills aimed at eliminating all sexual discrimination in teaching institutions. Under pressure from two directions, in the euphoric year of 1972, which also saw the passage by Congress of the Equal Rights Amendment, the Ninety-Second Congress adopted Title IX of the Amendments to the Federal Education Act stipulating that:

> No person in the United States shall, on the basis of sex, be excluded from participation in, be denied the benefits of, or be subjected to discrimination under any educational program or activity receiving Federal financial assistance.[16]

Now it was a matter of getting the law enforced. This was the second grand offensive of WEAL, launched when the Department of Health, Education, and Welfare published some alarming statistics: HEW revealed, in fact, that of 3,472 university-level institutions, nearly two-thirds had either not returned the proper forms certifying their conformance with the antidiscriminatory legislation, or had falsified their declarations. In spite of this, no institution had been penalized. WEAL's response was immediate and dramatic. The group filed suit against the secretary of health, education, and welfare for administrative negligence in the matter of sexual discrimination. The suit was granted a favorable outcome by the courts, which ordered further investigations in seventeen states. A settlement was reached in 1978 between the parties, in which the secretary undertook to investigate respect for civil rights in schools and universities, and to recruit 898 staff members, to be assigned to an HEW subagency, the Office of Civil Rights; by this recruitment, HEW was to make up for its delay in examining 3,000 discrimination complaints that had been lying unattended, and to do so by 30 September 1979.

These figures belied a new myth circulating in the 1970s on university campuses alleging reverse sexual discrimination; rumors were heard of women being hired and promoted just because they were women. In 1978, representation of women on the faculties of America's ten most prestigious universities was stagnating at 15 percent, after having declined between 1971 and 1974, and overall, only 8 percent of these women had reached the peak of the academic pyramid. However, by 1981, according to data presented by Catharine Stimpson at a colloquium in Toulouse, France,[17] 35 percent of all U.S. college and university teachers were women.

Another major initiative undertaken by WEAL in this second offensive concerned sexual discrimination in the retirement schemes that applied in most universities. Until 1978, in fact, it was customary in the United States for women to pay higher retirement contributions than men for an equal or lower pension, on the theory that women live longer than men. However, 84 percent of men and women have equal longevity. In other words, all women were penalized because a minority of them live longer. This was the basis of a class action suit filed by WEAL against more than 2,000 university establishments whose retirement funds were administered by the Teacher's Insurance and Annuity Association. In July 1983, the Supreme Court affirmed the lower court's 1978 decision which ended the regime of higher retirement contributions for women, proclaiming the principle of equal retirement pensions for equal contributions. However, this decision had no retroactive effect.

FROM FEMINIST LAW STUDENT TO FEMINIST LAWYER

Feminists' interest in legal action has been shown by a massive influx of women enrolling in law schools. In 1970, for example, women represented only 10 percent of first-year law students; in 1980, they made up a quarter of the beginning enrollment. By 1989, 40 percent of the law students in the United States were women. Pursuing law studies has been seen as a political act in the cause of women's rights, and figured among the militant activities listed by one of my radical feminist correspondents. As early as 1973, Judith Hole and Ellen Levine reported the words of a woman jurist who said that every law school in the country was harboring a group of militant feminists. If anyone wonders about the political motivation that might drive an increasing number of young women toward this sector of the university, it seems obvious that their choice is the result of a primary commitment to the feminist movement and their awareness that women need to know how to use the laws or reform them for their own benefit. In any case, the Women's Liberation movement has always needed lawyers.

The first action by feminist law students consisted of transforming women' rights issues into a new branch of legal studies. Their objective was to gain acceptance in the law schools of an emerging academic discipline, to be called women's rights law. Their argument was that numerous sexist laws remained on the books in many states, and that lawsuits for sexual discrimination were on the increase; these factors provided substantial material for debate and for fascinating research. Furthermore, it was important that graduating classes of women lawyers should be trained in these areas to prevent this lucrative market being entirely taken over by men. The mission of eradicating sexism from the patriarchal legal system could only be incumbent upon women of goodwill.

The first success in this matter was the appearance of specific courses on women and the law, such as the one taught by the feminist jurist Diane Schulder at the University of Pennsylvania, beginning in 1969. The following year, similar courses were started at Yale, Georgetown, and George Washington University, focusing on sexism in state laws and analyzing Supreme court decisions concerning the status of women. The year 1971 saw the birth of the first periodical aimed at jurists specializing in women's rights law: the *Women's Rights Law Reporter*.

Actions by women law students had early echoes in the legal professions. The Law Women's Caucus of the faculty of the University of Chicago Law School filed a suit with the EEOC in February 1970 against the university's placement office, which offered its services to notoriously sexist law firms. Under pressure from the EEOC, the law school promised to ostracize any firm guilty of sexual discrimination. Similar decisions were taken by the law schools of the University of California at Berkeley and the University of Michigan.

At the professional level, feminist lawyers naturally took up the relay. Here again, they resorted to class action suits. In March 1971, the Legal Task Force of the Professional Women's Caucus filed a class suit against all law schools receiving federal funds, for sexual discrimination in the recruitment of law students. The action was based on statistics published by the Committee on Women in Legal Education formed by the Association of American Law Schools, indicating that between 1966 and 1970, the number of women law students had only increased by an average of 3 percent, and in the same period, a third of the law schools had seen their percentage of women students decline.

Following the same reasoning that inspired women to study law, feminist lawyers have put their skills at the service of the cause of women's rights. Nonprofit groups and associations were formed. Human Rights for Women, for example, was born in 1968. This tax-exempt foundation, created with a generous donation from Alice Paul, one of the leading suffragists, specialized in the documentation or even financing of sexual discrimination lawsuits. Landmark suits aided by this foundation include the 1969 cases of *Bowe et al. v. Colgate Palmolive* and *Mengelhock v. State of California*.[18] In the same spirit, but on a larger scale, radical feminists of the Chicago Women's Liberation Union established a legal clinic where, every Wednesday night, legal advisers came to give counseling to women wishing to pursue legal action to defend their rights.

By 1989, women lawyers made up 20 percent of their profession and were boldly challenging the status quo. From 30 March to 2 April 1989, over 1,300 women attended the Twentieth Women and the Law Conference held in Oakland, California, on the theme "In the Courtroom and in the Community: Twenty Years of Feminist Struggle." There were more than a hundred workshops, covering a broad range of issues in criminal law, education, economic empowerment, employment, feminist jurisprudence, family law, housing, health, immigration, international law, sex, violence, and women in prison. The workshop called Unpacking Violence against Women focused on a feminist theoretical basis for activism against violence against women; its closing speaker was Catharine A. MacKinnon, one of the leading feminist scholars of jurisprudence, best-known for pioneering the theoretical work behind establishing sexual harassment as a form of sex discrimination and for drafting an antipornography ordinance with Andrea Dworkin.

FROM SUPPORT GROUP TO UNION?

Feminist legal action has also been undertaken by office workers, and this is interesting from another point of view: it shows the emergence of permanent workers' defense structures in an employment sector that is overwhelmingly female (80.1 percent of office workers are women). By 1984, a grid of mutual-interest groups covering this enormous force of working women was well established. In the feminist surge of the 1970s, some twenty or more such associations were organized, usually at the city level. The most well known have been Union WAGE in Berkeley, Women Organized for Employment (WOE) in San Francisco, Women Employed (WE) in Chicago, Women Office Workers (WOW) in New York, and 9 to 5 in Boston. The financial resources of these groups have come from dues paid by the members, grants given by various nonprofit organizations, conferences, lectures, and other initiatives. On the morning of 16 July 1977, when I met members of the group 9 to 5, they were busily engaged in a book sale, selling such feminist works as Jean Tepperman's *Not Servants, Not Machines: Office Workers Speak Out,* at the foot of Massachusetts Avenue in Cambridge.

For the day of the national secretaries' strike in 1974, Women Employed and 9 to 5 jointly published a Secretary's Bill of Rights, which first proclaimed the human dignity of secretaries, and went on to address the social legislation covering them. As a member of 9 to 5 told us, clerical workers were asking not only for their rights on the job, but also wanted the consideration of being treated as human beings. To achieve this goal, different groups have pursued two types of strategy. One consists of putting pressure on government agencies to enforce the law; thus, the group 9 to 5 filed lawsuits against banks, insurance companies, and publishing firms in Boston, in order that the official order for "affirmative action" should not be just vain words. The second strategy consists of organizing workers at the workplace. In this case, the aim is to make them aware of the political dimension of their position as workers in relation to management, and to train them in activist techniques enabling them to use their power, organize meetings, and manage protest activities.

Although these groups have won some legal battles against an insurance company here or there, their successes remain fragmentary. According to a pamphlet published in 1979 by the Women's Work Project,[19] the condition of office workers had even deteriorated in the previous twenty or thirty years, particularly in the matter of salaries. A woman office worker who, in 1956, received 72 percent of the salary of her male colleagues, only received 60 percent of a man's salary in 1975. Inevitably the question arose, as asked by Jean Tepperman in 1976 and repeated by Wendy Stevens in 1979:[20] don't we need a union of women office workers? The idea quickly spread among those concerned. The group 9 to 5, which formerly had viewed the idea unfavorably, now began to think that women were ready to try this. In fact, thanks to the activities of the organization mentioned above, many women office workers have acquired experience in activism and public speaking, enabling them to play a role at the highest levels of labor unions, and perhaps to amend existing unions so that feminism is not entirely absorbed by unionism. It seems certain that only a national organization, bringing together women office workers in a united front, would permit these new talents to have sufficient impact to make a real change in the working conditions for women in this employment sector and to protect their jobs. A new menace is cited by the Women's Work Project pamphlet, that is, the accelerated pace of office automation, which they claim is being used by big banking corporations as a convenient way of ridding themselves of the growing demands of their employees.

In the employment sector, as in the civil rights field, a policy of unity is needed. We have seen the first fruits of the struggle, and we can say that this experimentation with a strategy of coalition is the most significant evolution in feminism in recent years. This new orientation recalls that followed by nineteenth-century feminism in its earliest phase, when the cause of women was linked with that of the black slaves in a common struggle for rights. Do twentieth-century feminists run the risk of being the big losers in this policy of coali-

tion, as their sisters were in 1865? I think a negative answer can be given to this question, since the political contexts appear to me to be quite different. In the 1860s, the black question was the crucial issue, and the women's question had been raised, in some ways, as a side issue. In contrast, if we consider the virulence of the antifeminist backlash in the 1980s, it appears that the women's question, even if it does not make the headlines every day, has been perceived as the primordial issue today in the field of civil rights. Nevertheless, this assessment does not imply a relaxation of vigilance.

Notes

1. "Houston: A Reaffirmation for NWPC," editorial, *Women's Political Times* 2, no. 4 (Winter 1977): 2.

2. Elinor Langer, "Why Big Business Is Trying to Defeat the ERA: The Economic Implications of Equality," *Ms.* 4, no. 1 (May 1976): 106.

3. Jo Freeman, "Women at the 1988 Democratic Convention," *Off Our Backs* (October 1988): 5.

4. "Mr. President, Thank You, But," editorial, *Women's Political Times* 2, no. 1 (Winter 1977): 2.

5. Yet, the requirement for equal division by sex does not apply to superdelegates (members of Congress and governors) whose presence "still tips the balance in favor of males. The 1984 Democratic party convention had 50 more men than women delegates, and in 1988, there were over a hundred more men." *Off Our Backs* (October 1988): 4.

6. Women United to Defend Existing Rights.

7. Langer, "Why Big Business," 102.

8. "ERA Down the Wire," *Women's Political Times,* 2, no. 2 (Spring 1977): 2.

9. Lindsy Van Gelder, "The 400,000 Voter Misunderstanding," *Ms.* 4, no. 9 (March 1976): 67.

10. Diane Fitzgerald, "Liberal Leaders Plan Counter to Right," *Women's Political Times* 3, no. 2 (Summer 1978): 5.

The participants were Gloria Steinem for *Ms.*; Mildred Jeffrey for the NWPC; Ellie Smeal for NOW; Ben Albert and Victor Kramber for the AFL-CIO; Carl Wagner for the American Federation of State, County, and Municipal Employees; Jim Farner for the Coalition of American Public Employees; the Democratic senator from New Hampshire, Thomas J. McIntyre; Russ Hemenway for the National Committee for an Effective Congress; Joyce Hamlin for the United Methodist church; Carol Costin for Network, and Wes McCuun, a researcher who had specialized for sixteen years in studying right-wing political activities.

11. National Organization for Women, "Declaration of a State of Emergency," March 1978.

12. The NOW boycott was aimed at Alabama, Arizona, Arkansas, Florida, Georgia, Illinois, Louisiana, Mississippi, Missouri, Nevada, North Carolina, Oklahoma, South Carolina, Utah, and Virginia.

13. Berry, *Why ERA Failed,* 106.

14. Cited by Roberta Brandes Gratz in "Never Again! Never Again?" *Ms.* 6, no. 1 (July 1977): 54.

15. Among these were the Alliance against Sexual Coercion, in Cambridge, Massachusetts, and the Working Women United Institute, in New York.

16. U.S. Department of Labor, *Handbook on Women Workers,* Bulletin 297 (Washington, D.C.: U.S. Government Printing Office, 1975), 300.

17. "Femmes, féminisme et recherches," colloquium held in Toulouse, France, 17, 18, and 19 December 1982.

18. These two cases concerned so-called protective legislation, claiming that such laws actually imposed a handicap on women by their provisions forbidding women to lift certain weights and to work overtime.

19. The Women's Work Project, *Women Organizing the Office* (Washington, D.C.: Women in Distribution, 1979).

20. Tepperman, *Not Servants, Not Machines,* 92. Wendy Stevens, "Women Organizing the Office," *Off Our Backs* 9, no. 4 (April 1979): 10.

MARY FRANCES BERRY (ESSAY DATE 1986)

SOURCE: Berry, Mary Frances. "Legal Developments in the Courts and in the States: The Brooding Omnipresence of ERA." In *Why ERA Failed: Politics, Women's Rights, and the Amending Process of the Constitution,* pp. 86-100. Bloomington, Ind.: Indiana University Press, 1986.

In the following essay, Berry charts the progress of Equal Rights Amendment ratification in various states, noting that pro-women judicial decisions actually detracted from the perceived need for the Equal Rights Amendment.

Despite its failure, the campaign for ERA's ratification stimulated significant alteration in the legal status of women. Brown, Emerson, Falk, and Freedmen in the influential 1971 *Yale Law Review* article widely used in the congressional debates preceding the passage of ERA, predicted that "any present hope for large-scale change can hardly be deemed realistic" if one relied on the courts to guarantee equality for women under the Fourteenth Amendment. Although it is true that courts did not guarantee equality, between 1972 and 1982 the Supreme Court gradually broadened protection for women under the Fourteenth Amendment equal protection clause. The Court also interpreted broadly the provisions of the 1963 amendment to the Fair Labor Standards Act requiring equal pay for equal work between men and women, and Title VII of the Civil Rights Act of 1964 outlawing sex discrimination by employers of more than fifteen persons. In addition to Supreme Court action, several states adopted state ERA's during the same period, although some had been adopted previously. However, little guidance as to whether ERA would be ratified could be gained from the existence of a state ERA without analyzing its uses by a state's courts and legislature.[1]

In 1971 while the ERA was before the Congress, the Supreme Court had upheld an Idaho woman's claim that a state court's appointment of her estranged husband as administrator of her deceased child's estate under state law which favored men as administrators, violated the equal protection clause of the Fourteenth Amendment.[2] In 1973, the Court found a federal law distinguishing between women and men unconstitutional as a violation of equal protection implicit in the Fifth Amendment. The law automatically made dependents of male military personnel eligible for a basic subsistence allowance but made dependents of female military personnel prove actual dependency.[3] The Court also declared unconstitutional under the Fourteenth Amendment a Utah law that required divorced fathers to support their sons to age twenty-one but their daughters only to age eighteen;[4] an Oklahoma law that permitted the sale of beer to women at age eighteen but to men only at age twenty-one;[5] and a Louisiana law that excluded women from jury duty unless they were volunteers.[6]

In the employment area, in 1971 the Court decided that refusing to hire women, but not men, with preschool age children violated Title VII of the Civil Rights Act of 1964.[7] Also the Court found that paying women day workers less, as a minimum wage, than men night shift workers when both performed the same tasks, violated the Equal Pay Act of 1963.[8] The Court also decided that an Alabama law that stipulated minimum height and weight requirements for prison guards illegally excluded women from these jobs in violation of Title VII of the Civil Rights Act of 1964.[9]

In addition, the Supreme Court decided that states could not force women to take maternity leave at a specific time, but that employers could deny disability benefits to women undergoing normal pregnancy.[10] Congress responded by enacting the Pregnancy Discrimination Act of 1978 to make clear that the benefits should be provided.[11] The Court also found that Social Security programs could not provide benefits to widows that they did not give to widowers.[12] The overall effect of these decisions was to provide for more equal treatment between women and men under the law.

After ERA had been voted out of the Congress and was in the state ratification process in 1978,

Your body is a battleground

1989 illustration by Barbara Kruger depicting a woman's body as a focus of political and social conflict.

erty tax in 1974 and a federal law that gave women reserve officers a longer period than men in which to seek promotion gained approval.[15] Also, the Court upheld a state law charging a male with statutory rape for having sex with a female under eighteen but not a woman who had sex with a male under age eighteen.[16] In short, the Court still recognized certain differences between men and women and indicated a clear ideological position permitting the recognition of these differences in law.

The Court also refused to accept the doctrine that practices which appear to be neutral, but which have a disproportionate negative impact on one sex only, should be subjected to "strict scrutiny" and struck down on the basis of disparate impact. For example, in 1979, the Court refused to reject a Massachusetts veterans' preference law that resulted in the total exclusion of women from the upper echelons of the state civil service. The Court rationalized that the law seemed to treat all veterans equally, even though women had less opportunity to be veterans, given the restricted opportunities for military service, so to gain preferences.[17] If the proponents of ERA still believed that the protections the Court refused to give were necessary in these cases, they still needed an ERA. In 1973, Justice Powell specifically mentioned the absence of an ERA as a reason *not* to treat sex classification as "suspect," saying that ratification would "resolve the substance of this precise question." Essentially, the Court asserted that women who wanted ERA did not need ERA because they had the Fourteenth Amendment; but they were also being told they could not have "strict scrutiny" under the Fourteenth Amendment unless they did have ERA.[18]

The legality of abortion as an option for pregnant women was affirmed by the Court during this same period, but the decision did not keep opponents from arguing throughout the ratification campaign that an ERA would enshrine abortion as a constitutional right. Proponents, many of whom favored legal abortion, found themselves having to argue the issue with legislators and opponents who either did not understand the legal irrelevancy or pretended they did not. Phyllis Schlafly in her *Reports* and public appearances constantly linked the amendment to abortion. In heavily Catholic Illinois the argument was particularly effective.[19]

The Supreme Court, in *Roe* v. *Wade* in 1973, struck down a Texas law that made abortion a criminal offense, on the grounds that the law violated a woman's constitutional right of privacy

the Supreme Court decided a number of cases which took a less expansive view of women's legal equality. One decision announced that Title VII prohibits an employer from requiring women to make larger contributions in order to get the same monthly pensions as men.[13] But the Court refused to accept the doctrine that government classification by gender must be regarded as inherently suspect, requiring a state to prove a compelling interest to pass the challenged law because there was no other way to achieve a necessary result. This doctrine, which lawyers refer to as "strict scrutiny," requires such a standard when race classification is enacted into law. However, the Court did go so far as to move beyond the previously used "rational basis" test, which required only that the legislation be reasonable, not arbitrary, and have a fair and substantial relation to the object of the legislation. The Court majority adopted a "modified rational basis" test. This test required that the classification "must serve important governmental objectives and must be substantially related to the achievement of those objectives." The importance of these doctrines is that they define how much a person who challenged the law in question had to prove and what arguments were acceptable in defense.[14]

The Court's refusal to adopt a "strict scrutiny" test permitted it to uphold a number of laws that would have been declared unconstitutional if they had involved discrimination by race. In 1975, a state law exempting widows from a special prop-

under the Fourteenth Amendment. Justice Blackmun's majority opinion stated that in the first and second trimester of pregnancy a woman had the right, with her physician, to choose, and the state's power was subordinate to their decision. In the third trimester the state could prohibit abortion, but not if it was needed to save the life or health of the mother. In *Doe* v. *Bolton* in 1973, the Court used the same doctrine to void a Georgia law that made abortion criminal and had unnecessary medical exceptions.[20]

The Court upheld, however, the right of states to refuse to pay the cost of non-therapeutic abortions. In *Maher* v. *Doe* in 1977, the Court decided that it was not a denial of equal protection of the laws for Connecticut to deny public funding for Medicaid recipients' abortions. In *Harris* v. *McRae,* the Court upheld a federal law enacted in 1976, called the Hyde amendment, in response to *Roe* v. *Wade,* that prohibited Medicaid funding for abortions that were not medically necessary. Essentially, women had a right to abortion, but funding for health care for poor women could not be used for their abortions. In 1983, in a series of cases, the Court reaffirmed *Roe* v. *Wade* and its progeny. Efforts continued in the Congress to gain a constitutional amendment to outlaw abortion, and opponents of the Equal Rights Amendment continued to argue that it would permit abortion, although abortion was already permitted. They also argued ERA would change the Court's posture on funding of abortions for poor women. However, the Court in *Harris* v. *McRae* decided that the protection of a right from governmental interference did not imply governmental responsibility to pay for the right involved. Nothing in the opinion decided that an equal rights for women amendment would convert a non-right to payment into a right to payment. But this fact did not dampen the discussions of abortion in the ratification campaigns.[21]

Opponents also continued to argue that an ERA would legalize homosexual marriages, despite court decisions to the contrary. In *Baker* v. *Nelson,* the Supreme Court of Minnesota in 1971 decided that the right to marry without regard to sex is not a fundamental right compelled by the federal Constitution. No reported cases had been decided differently. In the hearings on the Equal Rights Amendment in the Congress the issue was raised again and again, although the proponents of the amendment affirmed the view of the cases that prohibiting discrimination on the basis of sex did not mean or imply prohibiting discrimination on the basis of sexual preference. In other words, if a state decided to legalize marriages between men and men, it would be required to legalize marriages between women and women, or vice versa. But otherwise the amendment would have no effect on legalizing sexual preference. What was overlooked continuously in the interjection of such issues as abortion and homosexuality into the debates, was the fact that the Equal Rights Amendment, like the equal protection clause of the Fourteenth Amendment, had nothing to do with private conduct but covered only actions by government.[22]

Although opponents kept raising it as an argument against ERA, the issue of women and the draft was settled by the Supreme Court in 1981. Essentially, with or without the Equal Rights Amendment, Congress could decide under its powers to make rules concerning the military—either to draft women or not. Congress could also, with or without an ERA, assign women to combat and other tasks, so long as they based assignments on individual abilities to perform and not on the fact that a person was a woman or a man. Even with ERA, the Congress would be required to do no more or less.[23]

In addition to the statutes and case law on women's rights in the courts, several states passed equal rights amendments and laws during the unsuccessful struggle to ratify ERA. However, three of the states (Illinois, Virginia, and Utah) that did not ratify ERA had state provisions in their own constitutions. Nine of the states that ratified ERA (Colorado, Hawaii, Maryland, Massachusetts, New Hampshire, New Mexico, Pennsylvania, Texas, and Washington) had provisions that read the same or about the same as the federal provision. They prohibited the states from abridging equality of rights on account of sex.

Illinois, which did not ratify ERA, had adopted a new constitution in 1970 which included in the Bill of Rights an equal rights provision which states: "The equal protection of the laws shall not be denied or abridged on account of sex by the state or its units of local government and school districts."

A closer look at the Illinois experience supports the view that the arguments made by federal ERA opponents in that state, as in others with equal rights amendments, could be made validly only about matters under federal control, such as military service. This was because any issues involving state action were already controlled by the state ERA. Phyllis Schlafly, who began her anti-ERA campaign in Illinois only because Alton, Illinois was her home, said she supported Illinois's state ERA. She viewed it, as did Senator Sam J. Ervin, Jr., of North Carolina, as permitting fair and reasonable distinctions on the basis of gender, unlike the federal ERA which uses "equality of rights" language. This argument is specious because the Illinois ERA was interpreted by that state's supreme court in *People* v. *Ellis* to make sex a "suspect" classification, and, therefore, subjected sex-based distinctions to "strict scrutiny" and not to a test of fairness or reasonableness.[24]

In Illinois family law on custody issues, the best interest of the child continued to be the operable theory with no presumption that the mother had a superior custody right. In *Marcus* v. *Marcus* in 1975, the appellate court stated that: "The fact that a mother is fit is only one facet of the situation, and, standing for itself, it does not authorize a denial of custody to the father, when this appears necessary because of other considerations."[25] But the courts held that the state ERA permits, in some cases, the presumption that custody of children of tender age be given to the mother, as one of several factors considered flexibly in determining child custody cases.[26] In *Atkinson* v. *Atkinson* in 1980, the Illinois appellate court found that despite the state ERA, a trial court could consider the sex of the children as one factor in custody cases.[27]

On the issue of marriage licenses, Illinois adopted strict equality of treatment for males and females. In *Phelps* v. *Bing* in 1974, the Illinois Supreme Court invalidated a state law that provided different age limits by gender. The law had provided that a female could obtain a marriage license without parental consent at age eighteen, with parental consent at sixteen, and at fifteen by court order; while a male had to be twenty-one to marry without parental consent, eighteen to marry with consent, and sixteen to marry by court order.[28]

On married women's names, the attorney general of Illinois issued an opinion in February 1974, that because of ERA women could keep and use their own names just as men did. In addition, in a 1976 case the Illinois Supreme Court held that the doctrine of "interspousal immunity," barring personal injury suits between spouses, did not violate the state ERA because its provisions apply equally to men and women.[29]

In athletics, the state appellate court found in *Petrie* v. *Illinois High School Association* that the Illinois ERA did not prohibit a state high school athletic conference from refusing to permit boys to play on the all-girl volleyball team when there was no compelling state interest in fostering interscholastic athletic competition. The dissent objected that this result was an example of attempting to protect females because they are classified as weak and inferior. The court did not decide what would happen if there were both boys' and girls' volleyball teams and either a boy or girl was prohibited from choosing to try out for either.[30]

When Karren O'Connor, an exceptionally talented eleven-year-old female basketball player, was refused a try-out on the boys' team, she attempted to gain an injunction against the policy under the Fourteenth Amendment, the Fifth Amendment, and the state ERA. The lower court granted an injunction. However, she lost in the appellate court which found the trial court had analyzed the federal claim without using the "rational basis" standard, which required only that the law be substantially related to a legitimate governmental interest. The appellate court, citing *Petrie*, discounted the claim under the Illinois ERA. The U.S. Supreme Court denied an appeal. The case was sent back for a trial on the merits.[31]

Consistently using the "strict scrutiny" standard in analyzing its Equal Rights Amendment regarding pensions, the state upheld the equal rights of dependent husbands and wives to receive accidental death benefits under the state retirement system. Also, in *People* v. *Ellis,* Illinois courts invalidated a juvenile justice provision for differential treatment if girls were under eighteen or if boys were under seventeen. Using "strict scrutiny" as the standard again, the court decided the same age had to be used for both.[32]

In two kinds of cases, males accused of criminal behavior attempted to use the ERA to gain acquittal. The physical difference that permits women, but not men, to become pregnant helped to decide the issues. A father lost an appeal of his incest conviction based on the fact that a mother who committed incest with a son received a lesser penalty by statute than a father who committed incest with a daughter. The court analyzed the case based on the identification of the culprit, deciding that the probability of pregnancy of the person on whom the incest was inflicted justified a harsher penalty.[33] In 1974 the appellate court held that the state rape statute, under which only men could be convicted of the crime, was not made unconstitutional by virtue of the ERA. The court found that even under the "strict scrutiny" test there was a compelling state interest in seeing to it that men did not rape women who could become pregnant. However, the court noted that a woman could be guilty of rape of a woman, as an accessory, an aider, or abettor of the male rapist.[34]

A similar result was reached in a 1979 case when a man objected to the revocation of his prohibition from a conviction for pandering, on the grounds that the statute which made it a crime to compel a woman, but not a man, to become a prostitute was unconstitutional. The court held that the man could not challenge the law because men and women alike could be convicted of the crime of enticing a female to be a prostitute. Furthermore, the court stated, he would have lost because even under "strict scrutiny" the state could show a compelling interest in protecting women, who could become pregnant, from prostitution while choosing not to protect men.[35]

In another case in 1979, the court decided that a statute which prohibited a person of one sex from performing a massage on an individual of the other sex was unconstitutional under the state ERA. The state could not, under the "strict scrutiny" doctrine, show that the classification was necessary to prevent obscene conduct. The court asserted that either sex could engage in obscene conduct and if the state's objective was to outlaw such behavior, the law did not need to discriminate on the basis of sex.[36]

While ERA was before the states for ratification, the Illinois courts in general had held that the state's ERA did not invalidate laws based on biological differences between women and men. "Strict scrutiny" had been uniformly applied, but so long as similarly situated males and females were treated identically, there was no issue of classification based on sex. In addition, the state ERA was held to operate prospectively, so that any conduct that occurred before its adoption could not be challenged under its provisions.

In addition to court cases, the Illinois state legislature amended provisions of the state code to bring them into conformity with the state ERA. Such matters as discrimination in credit cards, admission to public schools, physical education classes, and interscholastic athletics were all the subject of statutory changes. In addition, the legislature in July 1980 enacted a broad Human Rights Act barring discrimination between women and men in employment, real estate transactions, access to financial credit, and public accommodations.[37]

In sum, in Illinois under the state ERA everything that could be done under state constitutional control which could equalize the status of men and women was being done. But Illinois had one of the most protracted struggles, led by Phyllis Schlafly and based on fears about matters controlled by the national government, to prevent the ratification of the federal ERA. Other than the strategy of attempting to obtain the election of proratification legislators, the proponents of ERA in Illinois needed to find ways to persuade more legislators and their constituents that issues beyond state control, such as military service and abortion, would also be resolved under a federal ERA in ways that would not be harmful to men, women, children, or families. They did not make the case in time for ratification to occur.

In Utah, one of the three states with state ERAs that did not ratify the Equal Rights Amendment, women's rights had come early. The Mormon church supported woman suffrage in territorial days, but since there were as many women as men in the new state, they would have voted it down. At the same time and for the same reasons, to blunt arguments that women were treated unfairly under polygamy, the state constitution of 1896 stated: "The rights of citizens of the State of Utah to vote and hold office shall not be denied or abridged on account of sex. Both male and female citizens of the State shall enjoy equally all civil, political, and religious rights and privileges."[38]

The provision, unlike the federal ERA, covers public and private conduct. But in 1933 the same constitution expressly authorized the establishment of a minimum wage for women and children only.[39] It also prohibited children under fourteen and women from working in underground mines, until 1980 when the clause excluding women was abolished.[40]

During the period of the ratification struggle, in addition to the clear evidence in the constitution itself that the rights granted women were purposefully limited, the Utah Supreme Court never invalidated a statute based on ERA. Routinely, consistent with their understanding that the state ERA served a narrow political purpose at the time and was really a sham, the state's highest court used a "rational basis" test, requiring only that legislation be reasonable and related to the legislative purpose in cases brought under the state ERA. By emphasizing traditional husband-wife relations and biological factors, the court reduced the state ERA to a nullity. In family law cases, the Utah court continued to assert that women should care for and have custody of children, especially in their earliest years.[41] It upheld different ages of majority for men and women only to be reversed by the U.S. Supreme Court.[42] It also upheld gender distinctions in state laws covering wills, based on the duty of the husband to support the wife.[43] Furthermore, in employment cases, the Utah Supreme Court rejected a female police officer's argument that paying her less than male police officers performing the same work and with the same degree of competency violated the state ERA. The court took into account not only seniority, but other "factors."[44]

The Utah Supreme Court also rejected a pregnant woman's claim that a law declaring a pregnant individual ineligible for unemployment insurance for twelve weeks prior to and six weeks after childbirth was illegal under the state ERA. The woman was involuntarily separated for reasons unrelated to pregnancy and wanted to collect unemployment compensation. The court accepted that view on the grounds that it would be equally applicable to men, if they could become pregnant, and stated, "What she should do is work for the repeal of the biological law of nature. . . . In the matter of pregnancy there is no way to find equality between men and women." The U.S. Supreme Court vacated the judgment, holding that the conclusive presumption that all women could not work at any job when pregnant violated the due process clause of the Fourteenth Amendment.[45]

In addition to the Utah court's disdain for the ERA, the state legislature undertook no comprehensive statutory review to gender neutralize the state code. Essentially, in Utah opponents of ERA could make all of the same arguments about the impact on families, employment, and the like that could be made in states that did not have ERAs, since their own state ERA was well understood as purposely having little impact. They could, in addition, raise the same issues raised in Illinois concerning abortion and military service.

Virginia, the third state with an ERA in its constitution that did not ratify the federal ERA, provides another instructive example of the barriers to ratification. The state provision in the due process clause of the constitution states: "The right to be free from any governmental discrimination upon the basis of religious conviction, race, color, sex, or national origin shall not be abridged, except that mere separation of the sexes shall not be considered discrimination."[46]

Two differences from the proposed federal ERA were obvious: sex was in the same category, with the same legal rules to be applied, as other dis-

crimination, and unlike the Utah ERA, private conduct was not covered; second, unlike the federal amendment and all other state ERAs, Virginia's provision expressly states that "mere separation of the sexes" is not a violation. This language, apparently directed at "unisex" toilets and prisons, could, of course, reduce the general effect of the ERA on the grounds that any classification is merely permissible separation of the sexes.[47]

Furthermore, the Virginia Supreme Court adopted a "rational basis" standard for analyzing cases under the state ERA, even though race and sex discrimination are both forbidden in its language. It can be argued that the court should have adopted a "strict scrutiny" standard, since under a U.S. Supreme Court analysis, such cases require such a standard. It could also be argued that the court should have used a "modified rational basis" standard requiring more justification, as the U.S. Supreme Court has since 1976 in sex discrimination cases. But it had done neither.[48] The Virginia Supreme Court, in deciding a 1973 case challenging its use of the "rational basis" test in upholding the statute's sex-based classification, decided that the state ERA is "no broader than the Equal Protection Clause of the Fourteenth Amendment . . . where a statute is based on a reasonable classification that bears a rational relationship to the objective of the state . . . there is no impermissible discrimination under the Constitution of Virginia."[49] The result is that in Virginia courts women have a harder time winning a case under the state ERA than they would under the equal protection clause of the Fourteenth Amendment.

Before the defeat of the federal ERA, the Virginia legislature had acted to eliminate some instances of sex bias in the state code. Spouses were required to support each other and their children. There was no legal bar to support and maintenance for a husband when he was dependent. Women and men had the same grounds for annulment and divorce, and strong fair credit and housing provisions and prohibitions against sex discrimination in automobile insurance had been enacted. However, the husband was still presumed to be the owner of all real property that his wife possessed during the marriage, unless the woman could introduce facts to prove the husband gave up the ownership. Only women could be rape victims and only men perpetrators of rape and seduction. Illegitimate children could inherit from their mothers in all circumstances, but from their intestate fathers only if the father had taken a series of elaborate steps to establish paternity.[50]

In general, Virginia's ERA had less effect on the legal rights of women than use of the Fourteenth Amendment equal protection clause by itself would have had. Statutes that could be declared illegal under the state ERA remained in force, and court decisions limited the amendment's impact. Essentially, opponents of the federal ERA could still make arguments about threats to the traditional understanding of women's roles in Virginia alongside arguments about the possible impact on military service and abortion.

Alaska's ERA, passed in 1972, covered private and public conduct. The state courts used the same standards for deciding ERA claims as those utilized by the federal courts in Fourteenth Amendment sex discrimination cases. This means that women in Alaska had more protection against discrimination than women in Virginia, but less than those in Illinois. Alaska had a number of antidiscrimination laws on the books before the state ERA, but the state legislature made substantial modifications in the state code to make it gender neutral. The greatest gain for women in the state under the federal ERA would be to require the use of a "strict scrutiny" standard, which would require proof that a challenged law was based on a compelling state interest to reach a necessary goal that could be reached in no other way.[51]

In Colorado's 1972 state ERA, the courts had persistently used "closest judicial scrutiny" for deciding claims, including the provision of different treatment reasonably related and genuinely based on physical characteristics unique to one sex. This result accorded with the practice in Illinois and followed closely the analysis in the legislative history of the federal Equal Rights Amendment. The legislature also undertook a general review of the statutes to make them gender neutral after the state ERA was enacted.[52]

Also in 1972, Hawaii added an equal rights amendment to its constitution. The state supreme court did not determine the proper standard for review, but upheld a rule requiring female, but not male, visitors to an all-male prison to wear brassieres. A rule it found to survive both the "substantially related" and "strict scrutiny" tests. In every session since 1972 the state legislature acted to revise the code and constitution to bring them into conformity with the state ERA.[53]

Connecticut's ERA, dating from 1974, covers private and public conduct. At the time of the federal ratification effort, the supreme court, like the one in Hawaii, left open the possibility that it would use the "strict scrutiny" test. The state already had several antidiscrimination laws on the books before 1974, and because the legislature quickly changed numerous state laws to make them gender neutral, there was virtually no litigation in Connecticut.[54]

Maryland's ERA of 1972, like the one in Utah, also covers private conduct. The legislature and the courts were assiduous in enforcing an absolute standard even higher than "strict scrutiny" to make the ERA a viable tool for striking down discrimination. A challenged law had to be absolutely necessary to reach an essential state legislative goal. In 1977 in *Rand* v. *Rand,* the state's highest court asserted that sex could not be a factor in determining the parental child support obligation which had previously been attributed to fathers.[55]

Massachusetts's 1976 ERA, like those in Utah and Maryland, also covers private conduct. The state legislature enacted a series of bills to create gender neutrality in the law. Furthermore, state courts required a standard even more rigid than strict scrutiny, what seemed at times to be an absolute ban on sex-based classifications.[56]

The Montana 1972 ERA also applies to state and private actions. The legislature made substantial modifications in the state code to bring equality of treatment to women and men. However, the state's supreme court persisted in using the less rigid test elaborated by the U.S. Supreme Court in sex discrimination cases and had not used "strict scrutiny" as a standard.[57]

New Hampshire's 1974 ERA covers state action only. There had been only one case as of 1982, and in it the court did not decide the standard of review to be used. In this case, *Buckner* v. *Buckner,* the court decided that to permit alimony for a wife but not a husband violated the state ERA. The legislature partially reformed the state code, but several provisions remained, such as maximum hours provisions for women and the amount of night work they could do, different minimum ages for marriage for males and females, and sex-based language to define separate property and liability for spousal debts. Considering the inactivity in the state, it could have been argued during the ratification period that greater impact could be had under a federal ERA.[58]

New Mexico's ERA of 1973 which covers both private and state action on its face, was assumed by the state's attorney general to cover only state action. The courts did not articulate the standard of review to be used. The state attorney general asserted that, based on the history of the federal amendment, absolute prohibition or strict scrutiny must be the standard. After a systematic study undertaken upon the ratification of the state ERA, the legislature revised the state laws, changing twenty-six statutes and two constitutional amendments in the 1973 session. The state still, however, had a maximum hours of work for women law and one which made it justifiable homicide for a husband to kill someone in order to prevent an unlawful action against his wife. No similar defense existed for wives who were defending their husbands.[59]

Pennsylvania's ERA of 1971 led to far-reaching changes in legislation and in court decisions in which an almost absolute standard of review was used. The language of the amendment is substantially similar to that of the proposed federal amendment except that it does not have a state action requirement. It was used to require an equal right of support for both sexes, to give married women and men the right to use their own names, to equalize grounds for divorce for both partners, to gender neutralize alimony, to allocate child support according to each parent's ability to pay, to recognize a wife's contribution as homemaker in distributing property upon divorce, and to invalidate the minimum height requirement for police officers. In addition, the Pennsylvania legislature undertook a massive review of the statutes. Indeed, Pennsylvania had been making maximum use of the ERA and had no reason not to ratify the federal amendment.[60]

Texas's 1972 ERA also covers private conduct, but the courts held that it required governmental involvement. The courts held that sex is a suspect classification that requires "strict scrutiny," but there was no comprehensive review of state laws. However, some legislation was passed including making spousal support and child support gender neutral, granting that both parents can be natural guardians of their minor children, and guaranteeing that credits and loans must be extended without regard to sex.[61]

Washington's 1972 ERA was interpreted as an absolute prohibition against classification based on gender except where unique physical characteristics permit differential treatment or affirmative action is required. The state supreme court in 1975 said that by ratifying the amendment citizens "intended to do more than what was already contained in the otherwise governing constitutional provisions, Federal and state, by which discrimination based on sex was permissible under the rational relationship and strict scrutiny tests."

Also, an omnibus bill was passed in the legislature in 1973 to implement review of the state's code to bring it into compliance with ERA.[62]

Wyoming's ERA dates from 1890, but there was an express provision preventing women from working in mines that was not repealed until 1980. The language of the state provisions lent themselves to a weaker standard than "strict scrutiny," although few cases had been brought and the courts had not articulated a clear standard. There was no general legislative review movement by 1982 and some sex-based statutes remained unchallenged in the code, including seats and rest periods for women workers only and no work for female children in many occupations during certain hours.[63]

Unlike the states without ERAs, in which such matters as the husband's responsibility for providing financial support for the family might still be controversial, the states with effective state ERAs had less cause for disputes over whether ERA should be ratified. Illinois, Washington, Texas, Pennsylvania, New Mexico, Maryland, Massachusetts, Connecticut, Hawaii, and Colorado had practically no reason; and Montana, New Hampshire, and Wyoming had little reason not to ratify ERA based on the existence of strong ERA implementation possibilities in their states. Virginia and Utah had every reason to oppose the federal ERA since their own ERAs had been enforced narrowly. In states with broad ERA enforcement, refusal to support a federal ERA had to be focused on issues beyond state control, such as the draft or federal funding for abortion. Some states that passed state ERAs contemporaneous with the federal ERA debated most of the same issues at the same time which indicates that within their borders a broad consensus existed not only for immediate approval of the federal ERA, but to take positive action within the state. In those states the federal action served to stimulate state responses. The states with no ERAs or narrow ERAs, or a pattern of nonimplementation when challenges were brought, would naturally not be favorably disposed toward a federal ERA that might necessitate substantial changes in traditional roles. The proponents should have expected Utah and Virginia not to ratify. The Illinois case was more surprising, but after the quick organization of the opponents, a difficult struggle could have been predicted.

The attempt to gain ratification of a federal ERA did affect the path of legal developments in the courts and in the states. Some state ERAs predate the 1972 passage of the federal amendment in Congress, and some have come after. But the existence or nonexistence of a state ERA without an analysis of its uses offered little guidance as to whether a federal amendment would be ratified by the state's legislature.

During the latter stages of the federal amendment ratification campaign, the Supreme Court continued to decide cases providing greater women's equality without reaching the "strict scrutiny" standard that a federal ERA could impose. But the more the Court tended toward expanding equality, the less force arguments for a federal amendment had. Indeed, the absence of a state ERA, or the nonenforcement of an existing one with a negative pattern of Supreme Court decisions, provided a better case for the approval of a federal ERA than legal developments tending toward greater equality. Patterns of enhanced legal protection made the case harder rather than easier to make. Proponents of ERA needed to hope for more negative decisions and state inaction, while opponents benefited from the persistence of a positive pattern. Vigorous implementation of state ERAs and court decisions tending toward more equality only helped to undermine any sense of urgency and to build consensus against ratification. On the other hand, negative implementation and court action could have helped engender a perception of necessity required to build consensus for ERA's approval.

Notes

1. Barbara A. Brown et al., "The Equal Rights Amendment: A Constitutional Basis for Equal Rights," 80 *Yale Law Journal* (1971): 871.

2. *Reed* v. *Reed*, 404 U.S. 71 (1971).

3. *Frontiero* v. *Richardson*, 411 U.S. 677 (1973).

4. *Stanton* v. *Stanton*, 421 U.S. 7 (1975).

5. *Craig* v. *Boren*, 429 U.S. 190, 197 (1976).

6. *Taylor* v. *Louisiana*, 419 U.S. 522 (1975).

7. *Phillips* v. *Martin-Marietta Co.*, 400 U.S. 542 (1971).

8. *Corning Glass Works* v. *Brennan*, 417 U.S. 188 (1974).

9. *Dothard* v. *Rawlinson*, 433 U.S. 321 (1977).

10. *Cleveland Board of Education* v. *LeFleur*, 414 U.S. 632 (1974).

11. *Geduldig* v. *Aiello*, 417 U.S. 484 (1974).

12. *Weinberger* v. *Wiesenfeld*, 420 U.S. 636 (1975); *Califano* v. *Goldfarb*, 430 U.S. 199 (1977).

13. *Los Angeles Dept. of Water & Power* v. *Manhart*, 435 U.S. 702 (1978).

14. *Craig* v. *Boren*, 429 U.S. 190, 197 (1976); *Califano* v. *Webster*, 430 U.S. 313, 316-317 (1977).

15. *Kahn* v. *Shevin*, 416 U.S. 351 (1974); *Schlesinger* v. *Ballard*, 419 U.S. 498 (1980).

16. *Rostker* v. *Goldberg*, 453 U.S. 498 (1975).

17. *Personnel Administrator* v. *Feeney*, 442 U.S. 256 (1979).

18. *Frontiero* v. *Richardson*, 411 U.S. 677 (1973).

19. Janet K. Boles, *The Politics of the Equal Rights Amendment: Conflict and the Decision Process* (New York: Longman, 1979), pp. 107-108.

20. *Roe* v. *Wade*, 410 U.S. 113 (1973); *Doe* v. *Bolton*, 410 U.S. 179 (1973).

21. *Maher* v. *Roe*, 432 U.S. 464 (1977); *Roe* v. *Wade*, 410 U.S. 113 (1973); *Harris* v. *McRae*, 448 U.S. 297 (1980). Schlafly insists that ERA proponents must ensure the impossibility of a reversal of *Harris* v. *McRae* if they ever want an equal rights amendment. The only way they could do that would be to add specific language to the text of ERA to prohibit absolutely any reversal. "Why Congress Must Amend the ERA," *The Phyllis Schlafly Report*, November 1983.

22. *Baker* v. *Nelson*, 191 N.W. 2d 185 (1971). Again Schlafly put the "burden of proof" on opponents to prohibit absolutely any legislation of sexual preference by putting explicit language in ERA. "Why Congress Must Amend the ERA," *The Phyllis Schlafly Report*, November 1983.

23. *Rostker* v. *Goldberg*, 453 U.S. 57 (1980). Citing legal analyses written before *Rostker* was decided, Schlafly asserts that ERA would "make unconstitutional the male-only draft registration law plus the laws exempting women from military combat" without explaining that under *Rostker* the Congress can include women now if it should decide to do so without ERA. "Why Congress Must Amend the ERA," *The Phyllis Schlafly Report*, November 1983.

24. *People* v. *Ellis*, 57 Ill. 2d 127; 311 N.E. 2d 98 (1974). On state ERAs, see generally, ERA Impact Project, a joint project of the NOW Legal Defense and Education Fund and the Women's Law Project (1982) and Dawn Marie Driscoll and Barbara J. Rouse, "Through a Glass Darkly: A Look at State Equal Rights Amendments," 12 *Suffolk Law Review* (Fall 1978): 1282, 1300. Carol Felsenthal, *The Biography of Phyllis Schlafly, The Sweetheart of the Silent Majority* (Chicago: Regnery Gateway, 1982; originally published by Doubleday, 1981), p. 305.

25. *Marcus* v. *Marcus*, 24 Ill. App. 3d 401, 407 (1975); 320 N.E. 2d 581.

26. *Randolph* v. *Dean*, 27 Ill. App. 3d 913; 327 N.E. 2d 473.

27. *Atkinson* v. *Atkinson*, 402 N.E. 2d 831; 82 Ill. App. 3d 617.

28. *Phelps* v. *Bing*, 316 N.E. 775 (1974); 58 Ill. 2d 32.

29. *Steffo* v. *Stanley* 39 Ill. App. 3d 915, 350 N.E. 2d 886 (1976); *Tyrken* v. *Tyrken*, 63 Ill. App. 3d 199; 379 N.E. 2d 804 (1978).

30. *Petrie* v. *Illinois High School Association*, 75 Ill. App. 3d 980, 394 N.E. 2d 855 (1979).

31. *O'Connor* v. *Board of Education*, 645 F.2d 578; 454 U.S. 1085 (1981), *cert. denied*.

32. *People* v. *Ellis*, 57 Ill. 2d 127; 311 N.E. 2d 98 (1974); Illinois Attorney General Opinion in No. S-979 (October 23, 1975) at 9-10.

33. *People* v. *Boyer,* 63 Ill. 2d 433; 349 N.E. 2d 50 (1976); *People* v. *Yocum,* 66 Ill. 2d 211; 361 N.E. 2d 1369 (1977); 431 U.S. 941, *cert. denied.*

34. *People* v. *Medrano,* 24 Ill. App. 3d 429; 321 N.E. 2d 97 (1974).

35. *People* v. *Sherrod,* 50 Ill. App. 3d 552; 365 N.E. 2d 993 (1979).

36. *Wheeler* v. *City of Rockford,* 69 Ill. App. 3d 220; 387 N.E. 2d 358 (1979).

37. Smith-Hurd Illinois Annotated Statutes, Ch. 121-1/2, Sec. 385.1; Ch. 95, Sec. 301, *et seq.;* Ch. 122, Sec. 27-1; 34-18 (Supp. 1980); Ch. 68, Sec. 1-101, *et seq.* (Supp. 1980).

38. Utah Constitution, Art. 4, Sec. 1 (1896).

39. Utah Constitution, Art. 16, Sec. 8 (1933).

40. Utah Constitution, Art. 16, Sec. 3 (1980).

41. *Cox* v. *Cox,* 532 P.2d 994 (1975).

42. *Stanton* v. *Stanton,* 517 P.2d 1010 (1974). But see *Stanton* v. *Stanton,* 421 U.S. 7 (1975), also 522 P.2d 112 (1976), and 429 U.S. 59 (1977), "per curiam".

43. *In re Estate of Armstrong,* 440 P.2d 881 (1968).

44. *Kopp* v. *Salt Lake City,* 506 P.2d 809 (1973).

45. *Turner* v. *Department of Employment Security,* 531 P.2d 870 (1975); 423 U.S. 44 (1975), "per curiam".

46. Virginia Constitution, Art. 1, Sec. 11 (1971).

47. Driscoll and Rouse, "Through a Glass Darkly," pp. 1282, 1300.

48. *Craig* v. *Boren,* 429 U.S. 190 (1976).

49. *Archer and Johnson* v. *Mayes,* 213 Va. 633; 194 S.E.2d 707 (1973) at 708.

50. Virginia Code, Sec. 20-61 (Replacement Vol. 1977); Virginia Code, Sec. 20-91 (Replacement Vol. 1975); Virginia Code, Sec. 59.1-21.19 (Cumulative Supplement, 1980), Sec. 36-90 (Replacement Vol. 1976), Virginia Code, Sec. 38.1-381.5 (Cumulative Supplement, 1980); Virginia Code, Sec.55-47.1 (Replacement Vol. 1980), sec. 18.2-61 (Replacement Vol. 1976), Sec. 64.1-5.1-5.2 (Replacement Vol. 1980).

51. *Plas* v. *State,* 598 P.2d 966 (1979); Alaska Constitution, Art. 1, Sec. 3 (1972); Alaska Statutes of 1962, Sec. 23.10.155 (Michie 1972 Pamphlet), Sec. 1.5511e 205 (Michie 1980 Cumulative Supplement), Sec. 18.80.210, 230; Alaska Statutes 18.80.220, 240, 250 (Michie 1974 Pamphlet).

52. Colorado Constitution, Art. II, Sec. 29 (1972); Colorado Revised Statutes 1973, 86-110, *et seq.,* 31-30.601 *et seq.* (1978 Cumulative Supplement); Colorado Revised Statutes 24-34-402, 24-34-502, 24-34-602, 5-1-109, 24-50-141 (1983 Replacement Volume); *People* v. *Salinas,* 551 P.2d 703 (1976); *People* v. *Green,* 514 P.2d 769 (1973).

53. *Holdman* v. *Olim,* 581 P.2d 1164 (1978); Sherry Broder and Beverly Wee, "Hawaii's Equal Rights Amendment: Its Impact on Athletic Opportunities and Competition for Women," 2 *Hawaii Law Review* 97, 111 (Winter 1979).

54. Connecticut Constitution, Art. I, Sec. 20 (1974); Connecticut General Statutes, 4-61. t-w; 31-12-19; 53-35;

Connecticut General Statutes, 36-436 *et seq.* (1979 Rev.), 46b-40 *et seq.* (1979 Rev.), 53a-65; *Page* v. *Welfare Commissioner,* 365 A.2d 1118 (1976).

55. Maryland Constitution, Art. 46 (1972); *Kline* v. *Ansell,* 414 A.2d 929 (1980); *Rand* v. *Rand,* 280 Md. 508, 374 A.2d 900 (1977); Maryland Code, Art. 72A, Sec. 1 (Cumulative Supplement, 1977); Maryland Code, Art. 49B, Sec. 16(a) (1979 Replacement Volume), Art. 100, Sec. 55A, 55B. Maryland Code, (Replacement Volume 1979), Art. 493, 19a; Art. 100, 82e, 11(b)(9), (c)(1) and (2); Art. 100, 21(b); Art. 48A, 354F, 477J.

56. Massachusetts Constitution, Part I, Art. I (1976); *Commonwealth* v. *King,* 372 N.E.2d 196 (Mass. Sup. Jud. 1977). Massachusetts General Legislative Acts, Ch. 208, Sec. 34; Ch. 273, Sec. 3c 208, Sec. 12, 13, 20, 20A; Ch. 188, Sec. 1, 3, 4, 6, 7, 8; Ch. 30, Sec. 2628; Ch. 121 B, Sec. 1, 3, 4; Ch. 117, Sec. 3; Ch. 118, Sec. 3; Ch. 208, Sec. 1; Ch. 273, Sec. 1, 15; Ch. 272, Sec. 7; Ch. 15, Sec. 1A, 1E, 20A; Ch. 17, Sec. 14; Ch. 19, Sec. 15; Ch. 23A, Sec. 4; Ch. 122, Sec. 2; Ch. 272, Sec. 1, *et seq.;* Ch. 209, Sec. 1.

57. Montana Constitution, Art. II, Sec. 4 (1973); *State* v. *Craig,* 545 P.2d 649 (1976). Revised Code of Montana, 10-301-10-310 (1947), 23-3027; 75-8704; 83-3-3 (1947) and repealing 36-102 (1947); Montana Code Annotated, 40-2-102; 40-4-203; 40-4-204; 40-4-212; 45-5-503; 49-2-306, 49-3; 39-7-203 (1979).

58. New Hampshire Constitution, Part I, Art. II (1974); *Buckner* v. *Buckner,* 415 A.2d 871 (1980). New Hampshire Revised Statutes Annotated, Sec. 275.15, 275.17; 457.4; 460:1; 460.3; 458.7 (VIII); 458.7(XI); (Replacement Vol. 1977) 458.7 (XIII); 458.7 (XII); 164-A:1(II).

59. *Schaab* v. *Schaab,* 531 P.2d 954 (1974) and *Futrell* v. *Ahrens,* 540 P.2d 214 (1975); New Mexico Constitution, Art. II, Sec. 18 (1973); Attorney General Opinion No. 75-75 at 196 (12/24/75), No. 95-16 at 59 (2/21/75); New Mexico Statutes Annotated, Sec. 40-1-5, 4-1, 4-7, 3-7, 3-13, 3-8, 3-9, 3-12 (1978); New Mexico Statutes Annotated, 40-A-9-21, Sec. 30-2-7 (1978).

The Code review was published in seven law review articles: Leo Kanowitz, "The New Mexico Equal Rights Amendment: Introduction and Overview," 3 *New Mexico Law Review* 1 (January 1973); Anne K. Bingaman, "The Effects of an Equal Rights Amendment on the New Mexico System of Community Property: Problems of Characterization, Management, and Control", 3 *New Mexico Law Review* 11 (January 1973); Willis H. Ellis, "Equal Rights and the Debt Provisions of New Mexico Community Property Law", 3 *New Mexico Law Review* 57 (January 1973); Kendall O. Schlenker, "Tax Implications of the Equal Rights Amendment," 3 *New Mexico Law Review* 69 (January 1973); Joseph Goldberg and Mariclaire Hale, "The Equal Rights Amendment and the Administration of Income Assistance Programs in New Mexico," 3 *New Mexico Law Review* 84 (January 1973); Charles Daniels, "The Impact of the Equal Rights Amendment on the New Mexico Criminal Code," 3 *New Mexico Law Review* 106 (January 1973); Jennie D. Behles and Daniel J. Behles, "Equal Rights in Divorce and Separation," 3 *New Mexico Law Review* 118 (January 1973).

60. Pennsylvania Constitution, Art. I, Sec. 28 (1971); see, for example, *Commonwealth* v. *Butler,* 328 A.2d 851, 458 Pa. 289, and Margaret K. Krasik, "Comment: A Review of the Implementation of the Pennsylvania

Equal Rights Amendment," 14 *Duquesne Law Rev.* 683 (1976); *Henderson* v. *Henderson*, 458 Pa. 97, 101; 327 A.2d 60, 62 (1974) "per curiam."

61. Texas Constitution, Art. 1, Sec. 3a (1972); *Mercer* v. *Board of Trustees*, 538 S.W.2d 201 (Texas Cir. App. 1976); Texas Family Code Annotated, Sec. 4.02 and 12.011 (Vernon, 1975), Sections 4.02, 3.59 (Vernon Supplement 1980); Texas Penal Code Annotated, Sec. 25.05 (Vernon, 1974); Texas Probate Code Annotated, Sec. 109(a), 271 (Vernon, 1980).

62. Washington Constitution, Art. 31, Sec. 1 (1972); *Darrin* v. *Gould,* 540 P.2d 885 (1975), 85 Wash. 2d 859, at 889; *Marchioro* v. *Chaney*, 582 P.2d 487, 491 (1978).

63. Wyoming Constitution, Art. 1, Sec. 2, 3, Art. VI, Sec. 1 (1890); Wyoming Statutes, Title 276-101(b), 102 (1977), Title 27-6-106 (1977).

WENDY KAMINER (ESSAY DATE 1993)

SOURCE: Kaminer, Wendy. "Feminism's Identity Crisis." In *Public Women, Public Words: A Documentary History of American Feminism,* edited by Dawn Keetley and John Pettegrew, pp. 458-67. Madison, Wis.: Madison House, 1997.

In the following essay, first published in 1993, Kaminer charts the evolution of feminist ideas through popular culture and the media in the 1990s, noting a persistent ambivalence toward the role of women in society.

My favorite political moment of the 1960s was a Black Panther rally in a quadrangle of Smith College on a luxuriant spring day. Ramboesque in berets and ammunition belts, several young black males exhorted hundreds of young white females to contribute money to Bobby Seale's defense fund. I stood at the back of the crowd watching yarn ties on blonde pony-tails bobbing up and down while the daughters of CEOs nodded in agreement with the Panthers' attack on the ruling class.

It was all so girlish—or boyish, depending on your point of view. Whatever revolution was fomenting posed no apparent threat to gender roles. Still, women who were not particularly sensitive to chauvinism in the counterculture or the typical fraternity planned to attend graduate or professional school and pursue careers that would have been practically unthinkable for them ten years earlier. Feminism was altering their lives as much as draft avoidance was altering the lives of their male counterparts.

Today, three decades of feminism and one Year of the Woman later, a majority of American women agree that feminism has altered their lives for the better. In general, polls conducted over the past three years indicate strong majority support for feminist ideals. But the same polls suggest that a majority of women hesitate to associate themselves with the movement. As Karlyn Keene, a resident fellow at the American Enterprise Institute, has observed, more than three quarters of American women support efforts to "strengthen and change women's status in society," yet only a minority, a third at most, identify themselves as feminists.

Many feminists take comfort in these polls, inferring substantial public support for economic and political equality, and dismissing women's wariness of the feminist label as a mere image problem (attributed to unfair media portrayals of feminists as a strident minority of frustrated women). But the polls may also adumbrate unarticulated ambivalence about feminist ideals, particularly with respect to private life. If widespread support for some measure of equality reflects the way women see, or wish to see, society, their unwillingness to identify with feminism reflects the way they see themselves, or wish to be seen by others.

To the extent that it challenges discrimination and the political exclusion of women, feminism is relatively easy for many women to embrace. It appeals to fundamental notions of fairness; it suggests that social structures must change but that individuals, particularly women, may remain the same. For many women, feminism is simply a matter of mommy-tracking, making sure that institutions accommodate women's familial roles, which are presumed to be essentially immutable. But to the extent that feminism questions those roles and the underlying assumptions about sexuality, it requires profound individual change as well, posing an unsettling challenge that well-adjusted people instinctively avoid. Why question norms of sex and character to which you've more or less successfully adapted?

Of course, the social and individual changes demanded by feminism are not exactly divisible. Of course, the expansion of women's professional roles and political power affects women's personality development. Still, many people manage to separate who they are in the workplace from who they are in bed, which is why feminism generates so much cognitive dissonance. As it addresses and internalizes this dissonance and women's anxiety about the label "feminism," as it embarks on a "third wave," the feminist movement today may suffer less from a mere image problem than from a major identity crisis.

It's difficult, of course, to generalize about how millions of American women imagine feminism and what role it plays in their lives. All one can say with certitude is that different women define and relate to feminism differently. The rest—much of this essay—is speculation, informed by conversations with editors of women's magazines (among the most reliable speculators about what women want), polling data, and ten years of experience studying feminist issues.

Resistance to the Label

Robin Morgan, the editor in chief of *Ms.,* and Ellen Levine, the editor in chief of *Redbook,* two veterans of women's magazines and feminism, offer different views of feminism's appeal, each of which seem true, in the context of their different constituencies. Morgan sees a resurgent feminist movement and points to the formation of new feminist groups on campus and intensified grass-roots activity by women addressing a range of issues, from domestic violence to economic revitalization. Ellen Levine, however, believes that for the middle-class family women who read *Redbook* (the average reader is a thirty-nine-year-old wage-earning mother), feminism is "a non-issue." She says, "They don't think about it; they don't talk about it." They may not even be familiar with the feminist term of art "glass ceiling," which feminists believe has passed into the vernacular. And they seem not to be particularly interested in politics. The surest way not to sell *Redbook* is to put a woman politician on the cover: the January, 1993, issue of *Good Housekeeping,* with Hillary Clinton on the cover, did poorly at the newsstands, according to Levine.

Editors at more upscale magazines—*Mirabella, Harper's Bazaar,* and *Glamour*—are more upbeat about their readers' interest in feminism, or at least their identification with feminist perspectives. Gay Bryant, *Mirabella'*s editor in chief, says, "We assume our readers are feminists with a small 'f.' We think of them as strong, independent, smart women; we think of them as pro-woman, although not all of them would define themselves as feminists politically." Betsy Carter, the executive editor of *Harper's Bazaar,* suggests that feminism has been assimilated into the culture of the magazine: "Feminism is a word that has been so absorbed in our consciousness that I don't isolate it. Asking me if I believe in feminism is like asking me if I believe in integration." Carter says, however, that women tend to be interested in the same stories that interest men: "Except for subjects like fly-fishing, it's hard to label something a man's story or a woman's story." In fact, she adds, "it seems almost obsolete to talk about women's magazines." Carter, a former editor at *Esquire,* recalls that *Esquire'*s readership was 40 percent female, which indicated to her that "women weren't getting what they needed from the women's magazines."

Ruth Whitney, the editor in chief of *Glamour,* might disagree. She points out that *Glamour* runs monthly editorials with a decidedly "feminist" voice that infuses the magazine. *Glamour* readers may or may not call themselves feminists, she says, but "I would call *Glamour* a mainstream feminist magazine, in its editorials, features, fashions, and consumerism." *Glamour* is also a pro-choice magazine; as Whitney stresses, it has long published pro-choice articles—more than any other mainstream women's magazine, according to her. And it is a magazine for which women seem to constitute the norm: "We use the pronoun 'she' when referring to a doctor, lawyer, whomever, and that does not go unnoticed by our readers."

Some women will dispute one underlying implication of Betsy Carter's remarks—that feminism involves assimilation, the merger of male and female spheres of interest. Some will dispute any claims to feminism by any magazine that features fashion. But whether *Ms.* readers would call *Harper's Bazaar, Mirabella,* and *Glamour* feminist magazines, or magazines with feminist perspectives, their readers apparently do, if Betsy Carter, Gay Bryant, and Ruth Whitney know their audiences.

Perhaps the confident feminist self-image of these up-scale magazines, as distinct from the cautious exploration of women's issues in the middle-class *Redbook,* confirms a canard about feminism—that it is the province of upper-income urban professional women. But *Ms.* is neither up-scale nor fashionable, and it's much too earnest to be sophisticated. Feminism—or, at least, support for feminist ideals—is not simply a matter of class, or even race.

Susan McHenry, a senior editor at *Working Woman* and the former executive editor of *Emerge,* a new magazine for middle-class African-Americans, senses in African-American women readers "universal embrace of women's rights and the notion that the women's movement has been helpful." Embrace of the women's movement, however, is equivocal. "If you start talking about the women's movement, you hear a lot about what we believe and what white women believe."

For many black women, devoting time and energy to feminist causes or feminist groups may simply not be a priority. Black women "feel both racism and sexism," McHenry believes, but they consider the fight for racial justice their primary responsibility and assume that white women will pay primary attention to gender issues. Leslie Adamson, the executive secretary to the president of Radcliffe College, offers a different explanation. She doesn't, in fact, "feel" sexism and racism equally: "Sex discrimination makes me indignant. Racial discrimination makes me enraged." Adamson is sympathetic to feminism and says that she has always "had a feminist mind." Still, she does not feel particularly oppressed as a woman. "I can remember only two instances of sex discrimination in my life," she says. "Once when I was in the sixth grade and wanted to take shop and they made me take home economics; once when I visited my husband's relatives in Trinidad and they wouldn't let me talk about politics. Racism has always affected me on a regular basis." Cynthia Bell, the communications director for Greater Southeast Healthcare System in Washington, D.C., offers a similar observation: "It wasn't until I graduated from college that I encountered sexual discrimination. I remember racial discrimination from the time I remember being myself."

Black women who share feminist ideals but associate feminism with white women sometimes prefer to talk about "womanism," a term endorsed by such diverse characters as Alice Walker (who is credited with coining it) and William Safire. Susan McHenry prefers to avoid using the term "women's movement" and talks instead about "women moving." She identifies with women "who are getting things done, regardless of what they call themselves." But unease with the term "feminism" has been a persistent concern in the feminist movement, whether the unease is attributed to racial divisions or to residual resistance to feminist ideals. It is, in fact, a complicated historical phenomenon that reflects feminism's successes as well as its failures.

"The Less Tainted Half"

That feminism has the power to expand women's aspirations and improve their lives without enlisting them as card-carrying feminists is a tribute to its strength as a social movement. Feminism is not dependent on ideological purity (indeed, it has always been a mixture of conflicting ideologies) or any formal organizational structure. In the nineteenth century feminism drew upon countless unaffiliated voluntary associations of women devoted to social reform or self-improvement. Late-twentieth-century feminism has similarly drawn upon consciousness-raising groups, professional associations, community-action groups, and the increased work-force participation of middle-class women, wrought partly by economic forces and a revolution in birth control. Throughout its 150-year history feminism has insinuated itself into the culture as women have sought to improve their status and increase their participation in the world outside the home. If women are moving in a generally feminist direction—toward greater rights and a fairer apportionment of social responsibilities—does it matter what they call themselves?

In the nineteenth century many, maybe most, women who took part in the feminist movement saw themselves as paragons of femininity. The great historic irony of feminism is that the supposed feminine virtues that justified keeping women at home—sexual purity, compassion, and a talent for nurturance—eventually justified their release from the home as well. Women were "the less tainted half of the race," Frances Willard, the president of the National Woman's Christian Temperance Union, declared, and thus were the moral guardians of society.

But in the long run, identifying feminism with femininity offered women limited liberation. The feminine weaknesses that were presumed to accompany feminine virtues justified the two-tier labor force that kept women out of executive positions and political office and out of arduous, high-paying manual-labor jobs (although women were never considered too weak to scrub floors). By using femininity as their passport to the public sphere, women came to be typecast in traditional feminine roles that they are still playing and arguing about today. Are women naturally better suited to parenting than men? Are men naturally better suited to waging war? Are women naturally more cooperative and compassionate, more emotive and less analytic, than men?

A great many American women (and men) still seem to answer these questions in the affirmative, as evidenced by public resistance to drafting women and the private reluctance of women to assign, and men to assume, equal responsibility for child care. Feminism, however, is popularly deemed to represent an opposing belief that men and women are equally capable of raising children and equally capable of waging war. Thus feminism represents, in the popular view, a rejection of femininity.

Feminists have long fought for day-care and family-leave programs, but they still tend to be blamed for the work-family conundrums. Thirty-nine percent of women recently surveyed by *Redbook* said that feminism had made it "harder" for women to balance work and family life. Thirty-two percent said that feminism made "no difference" to women's balancing act. This may reflect a failure of feminists to make child care an absolutely clear priority. It may also reflect the association of feminism with upper-income women like Zoë Baird, who can solve their child-care problems with relative ease. But, as Zoë Baird discovered, Americans are still ambivalent about women's roles within and outside the home.

Feminism and the careerism it entails are commonly regarded as a zero-sum game not just for women and men but for women and children as well, Ellen Levine believes: wage-earning mothers still tend to feel guilty about not being with their children and to worry that "the more women get ahead professionally, the more children will fall back." Their guilt does not seem to be assuaged by any number of studies showing that the children of wage-earning mothers fare as well as the children of full-time homemakers, Levine adds. It seems to dissipate only as children grow up and prosper.

Feminists who dismiss these worries as backlash risk trivializing the inevitable stresses confronting wage-earning mothers (even those with decent day care). Feminists who respond to these worries by suggesting that husbands should be more like wives and mothers are likely to be considered blind or hostile to presumptively natural sex differences that are still believed to underlie traditional gender roles.

To the extent that it advocates a revolution in gender roles, feminism also comes as a reproach to women who lived out the tradition, especially those who lived it out unhappily. Robin Morgan says, "A woman who's been unhappily married for forty years and complains constantly to her friends, saying 'I've got to get out of this,' might stand up on a talk show and say feminism is destroying the family."

The Wages of Equality

Ambivalence about equality sometimes seems to plague the feminist movement almost as much today as it did ten years ago, when it defeated the Equal Rights Amendment. Worth noting is that in the legal arena feminism has met with less success than the civil-rights movement. The power of the civil-rights movement in the 1960s was the power to demonstrate the gap between American ideals

of racial equality and the American reality for African-Americans. We've never had the same professed belief in sexual equality: federal equal-employment law has always treated racial discrimination more severely than sex discrimination, and so has the Supreme Court. The Court has not extended to women the same constitutional protection it has extended to racial minorities, because a majority of justices have never rejected the notion that some degree of sex discrimination is only natural.

The widespread belief in equality demonstrated by polls is a belief in equality up to a point—the point where women are drafted and men change diapers. After thirty years of the contemporary women's movement, equal-rights feminism is still considered essentially abnormal. Ellen Levine notes that middle-class family women sometimes associate feminism with lesbianism, which has yet to gain middle-class respectability. Homophobia is not entirely respectable either, however, so it may not be expressed directly in polls or conversations; but it has always been a subtext of popular resistance to feminism. Feminists have alternately been accused of hating men and of wanting to be just like them.

There's some evidence that the fear of feminism as a threat to female sexuality may be lessening: 77 percent of women recently surveyed by *Redbook* answered "yes" to the question "Can a woman be both feminine and a feminist?" But they were answering a question in the abstract. When women talk about why they don't identify with feminists, they often talk about not wanting to lose their femininity. To the extent that an underlying belief in feminine virtues limits women to feminine roles, as it did a hundred years ago, this rejection of the feminist label is a rejection of full equality. In the long run, it matters what women call themselves.

Or does it? Ironically, many self-proclaimed feminists today express some of the same ambivalence about changing gender roles as the "I'm not a feminist, but . . ." women (". . . but I believe in equal opportunity or family leave or reproductive choice"). The popular image of feminism as a more or less unified quest for androgynous equality, promoted by the feminists' nemesis Camille Paglia, is at least ten years out of date.

The Comforts of Gilliganism

Central to the dominant strain of feminism today is the belief, articulated by the psychologist Carol Gilligan, that women share a different voice and different moral sensibilities. Gilligan's work—notably *In a Different Voice* (1982)—has been effectively attacked by other feminist scholars, but criticisms of it have not been widely disseminated, and it has passed with ease into the vernacular. In a modern-day version of Victorian True Womanhood, feminists and also some anti-feminists pay tribute to women's superior nurturing and relational skills and their "general ethic of caring." Sometimes feminists add parenthetically that differences between men and women may well be attributable to culture, not nature. But the qualification is moot. Believers in gender difference tend not to focus on changing the cultural environment to free men and women from stereotypes, as equal-rights feminists did twenty years ago; instead they celebrate the feminine virtues.

It was probably inevitable that the female solidarity at the base of the feminist movement would foster female chauvinism. All men are jerks, I might agree on occasion, over a bottle of wine. But that's an attitude, not an analysis, and only a small minority of separatist feminists turn it into an ideology. Gilliganism addresses the anxiety that is provoked by that attitude—the anxiety about compromising their sexuality which many feminists share with nonfeminists.

Much as they dislike admitting it, feminists generally harbor or have harbored categorical anger toward men. Some would say that such anger is simply an initial stage in the development of a feminist consciousness, but it is also an organizing tool and a fact of life for many women who believe they live in a sexist world. And whether or not it is laced with anger, feminism demands fundamental changes in relations between the sexes and the willingness of feminists to feel like unnatural women and be treated as such. For heterosexual women, feminism can come at a cost. Carol Gilligan's work valorizing women's separate emotional sphere helped make it possible for feminists to be angry at men and challenge their hegemony without feeling unwomanly. Nancy Rosenblum, a professor of political science at Brown University, says that Gilliganism resolved the conflict for women between feminism and femininity by "de-eroticizing it." Different-voice ideology locates female sexuality in maternity, as did Victorian visions of the angel in the house. In its simplest form, the idealization of motherhood reduces popular feminism to the notion that women are nicer than men.

Women are also widely presumed to be less warlike than men. "Women bring love; that's our role," one woman explained at a feminist rally against the GulfWar which I attended; it seemed less like a rally than a revival meeting. Women shared their need "to connect" and "do relational work." They recalled Jane Addams, the women's peace movement between the two world wars, and the Ban the Bomb marches of thirty years ago. They suggested that pacifism was as natural to women as childbirth, and were barely disconcerted by the presence of women soldiers in the Gulf. Military women were likely to be considered self-hating or male-identified or the hapless victims of a racist, classist economy, not self-determined women with minds and voices all their own. The war was generally regarded as an allegory of male supremacy; the patriarch Bush was the moral equivalent of the patriarch Saddam Hussein. If only men would listen to women, peace, like a chador, would enfold us.

In part, the trouble with True Womanhood is its tendency to substitute sentimentality for thought. Constance Buchanan, an associate dean of the Harvard Divinity School, observes that feminists who believe women will exercise authority differently often haven't done the hard work of figuring out how they will exercise authority at all. "Many feminists have an almost magical vision of institutional change," Buchanan says. "They've focused on gaining access but haven't considered the scale and complexity of modern institutions, which will not necessarily change simply by virtue of their presence."

Feminists who claim that women will "make a difference" do, in fact, often argue their case simply by pointing to the occasional female manager who works by consensus, paying little attention to hierarchy and much attention to her employees' feelings—assuming that such women more accurately represent their sex than women who favor unilateral decision-making and tend not to nurture employees. In other words, different-voice feminists often assume their conclusions: the many women whose characters and behavior contradict traditional models of gender difference (Margaret Thatcher is the most frequently cited example) are invariably dismissed as male-identified. . . .

Feminism Succumbs to Femininity

The feminist drive for equal rights was supposed to have been revitalized last year, and it's true that women were politically activated and made significant political gains. It's clear that women are moving, but in what direction? What is the women's movement all about?

Vying for power today are poststructural feminists (dominant in academia in recent years), political feminists (office-holders and lobbyists), different-voice feminists, separatist feminists (a small minority), pacifist feminists, lesbian feminists, careerist feminists, liberal feminists (who tend also to be political feminists), anti-porn feminists, eco-feminists, and womanists. These are not, of course, mutually exclusive categories, and this is hardly an exhaustive list. New Age feminists and goddess workshoppers widen the array of alternative truths. And the newest category of feminism, personal-development feminism, led nominally by Gloria Steinem, puts a popular feminist spin on deadeningly familiar messages about recovering from addiction and abuse, liberating one's inner child, and restoring one's self-esteem.

The marriage of feminism and the phenomenally popular recovery movement is arguably the most disturbing (and potentially influential) development in the feminist movement today. It's based partly on a shared concern about child abuse, nominally a left-wing analogue to right-wing anxiety about the family. There's an emerging alliance of anti-pornography and anti-violence feminists with therapists who diagnose and treat child abuse, including "ritual abuse" and "Satanism" (often said to be linked to pornography). Feminism is at risk of being implicated in the unsavory business of hypnotizing suspected victims of abuse to help them "retrieve" their buried childhood memories. Gloria Steinem has blithely praised the important work of therapists in this field without even a nod to the potential for, well, abuse when unhappy, suggestible people who are angry at their parents are exposed to suggestive hypnotic techniques designed to uncover their histories of victimization.

But the involvement of some feminists in the memory-retrieval industry is only one manifestation of a broader ideological threat posed to feminism by the recovery movement. Recovery, with its absurdly broad definitions of addiction and abuse, encourages people to feel fragile and helpless. Parental insensitivity is classed as child abuse, along with parental violence, because all suffering is said to be equal (meaning entirely subjective); but that's appropriate only if all people are so terribly weak that a cross word inevitably has the destructive force of a blow. Put very simply, women need a feminist movement that makes them feel strong.

Enlisting people in a struggle for liberation without exaggerating the ways in which they're oppressed is a challenge for any civil-rights movement. It's a particularly daunting one for feminists, who are still arguing among themselves about whether women are oppressed more by nature or by culture. For some feminists, strengthening women is a matter of alerting them to their natural vulnerabilities.

There has always been a strain of feminism that presents women as frail and naturally victimized. As it was a hundred years ago, feminist victimism is today most clearly expressed in sexuality debates—about pornography, prostitution, rape, and sexual harassment. Today sexual violence is a unifying focal point for women who do and women who do not call themselves feminists: 84 percent of women surveyed by *Redbook* considered "fighting violence against women" to be "very important." (Eighty-two percent rated workplace equality and 54 percent rated abortion rights as very important.) Given this pervasive, overriding concern about violence and our persistent failure to address it effectively, victimism is likely to become an important organizing tool for feminism in the 1990s.

Feminist discussions of sexual offenses often share with the recovery movement the notion that, again, there are no objective measures of suffering: all suffering is said to be equal, in the apparent belief that all women are weak. Wage-earning women testify to being "disabled" by sexist remarks in the workplace. College women testify to the trauma of being fondled by their dates. The term "date rape," like the term "addiction," no longer has much literal, objective meaning. It tends to be used figuratively, as a metaphor signifying that all heterosexual encounters are inherently abusive of women. The belief that in a male-dominated culture that has "normalized" rape, "yes" can never really mean "yes" has been popularized by the anti-pornography feminists Andrea Dworkin and Catharine MacKinnon. (Dworkin devoted an entire book to the contention that intercourse is essentially a euphemism for rape.) But only five years ago Dworkin and MacKinnon were leaders of a feminist fringe. Today, owning partly to the excesses of multiculturalism and the exaltation of victimization, they're leaders in the feminist mainstream.

Why is feminism helping to make women feel so vulnerable? Why do some young women on Ivy League campuses, among the most privileged people on the globe, feel oppressed? Why does feminist victimology seem so much more pervasive among middle- and upper-class whites than among lower-income women, and girls, of color?

Questions like these need to be aired by feminists. But in some feminism circles it is heresy to suggest that there are degrees of suffering and oppression, which need to be kept in perspective. It is heresy to suggest that being raped by your date may not be as traumatic or terrifying as being raped by a stranger who breaks into your bedroom in the middle of the night. It is heresy to suggest that a woman who has to listen to her colleagues tell stupid sexist jokes has a lesser grievance than a woman who is physically accosted by her supervisor. It is heresy, in general, to question the testimony of self-proclaimed victims of date rape or harassment, as it is heresy in a twelve-step group to question claims of abuse. All claims of suffering are sacred and presumed to be absolutely true. It is a primary article of faith among many feminists that women don't lie about rape, ever; they lack the dishonesty gene. Some may call this feminism, but it looks more like femininity to me.

Blind faith in women's pervasive victimization also looks a little like religion. "Contemporary feminism is a new kind of religion," Camille Paglia complains, overstating her case with panache. But if her metaphor begs to be qualified, it offers a nugget of truth. Feminists choose among competing denominations with varying degrees of passion, and belief; what is gospel to one feminist is a working hypothesis to another. Still, like every other ideology and "ism"—from feudalism to capitalism to communism to Freudianism—feminism is for some a revelation. Insights into the dynamics of sexual violence are turned into a metaphysic. Like people in recovery who see addiction lurking in all our desires, innumerable feminists see men's oppression of women in all our personal and social relations. Sometimes the pristine earnestness of this theology is unrelenting. Feminism lacks a sense of black humor.

Of course, the emerging orthodoxy about victimization does not infect all or even most feminist sexuality debates. Of course, many feminists harbor heretical thoughts about lesser forms of sexual misconduct. But few want to be vilified for trivializing sexual violence and collaborating in the abuse of women.

The Enemy Within
The example of Camille Paglia is instructive. She is generally considered by feminists to be practically pro-rape, because she has offered this advice to young women: don't get drunk at fraternity parties, don't accompany boys to their rooms, realize that sexual freedom entails sexual risks, and take some responsibility for your behav-

ior. As Paglia says, this might once have been called common sense (it's what some of our mothers told us); today it's called blaming the victim.

Paglia is right: it ought to be possible to condemn date rape without glorifying the notion that women are helpless to avoid it. But not everyone can risk dissent. A prominent feminist journalist who expressed misgivings to me about the iconization of Anita Hill chooses not to be identified. Yet Anita Hill is a questionable candidate for feminist sainthood, because she was, after all, working for Clarence Thomas voluntarily, apparently assisting him in what feminists and other civil-rights activists have condemned as the deliberate nonenforcement of federal equal-employment laws. Was she too helpless to know better? Feminists are not supposed to ask.

It is, however, not simply undue caution or peer pressure that squelches dissent among feminists. Many are genuinely ambivalent about choosing sides in sexuality debates. It is facile, in the context of the AIDS epidemic, to dismiss concern about date rape as "hysteria." And it takes hubris (not an unmitigated fault) to suggest that some claims of victimization are exaggerated, when many are true. The victimization of women as a class by discriminatory laws and customs, and a collective failure to take sexual violence seriously, are historical reality. Even today women are being assaulted and killed by their husbands and boyfriends with terrifying regularity. When some feminists overdramatize minor acts of sexual misconduct or dogmatically insist that we must always believe the woman, it is sometimes hard to blame them, given the historical presumption that women lie about rape routinely, that wife abuse is a marital squabble, that date rape and marital rape are not real rape, and that sexual harassment is cute.

Feminists need critics like Paglia who are not afraid to be injudicious. Paglia's critiques of feminism are, however, flawed by her limited knowledge of feminist theory. She doesn't even realize what she has in common with feminists she disdains—notably Carol Gilligan and the attorney and anti-pornography activist Catharine MacKinnon. Both Paglia and MacKinnon suggest that sexual relations are inextricably bound up with power relations; both promote a vison of male sexuality as naturally violent and cruel. But while Paglia celebrates sexual danger, MacKinnon wants to legislate even the thought of it away. Both Paglia and Gilligan offer idealized notions of femininity. But Gilligan celebrates gender stereotypes while Paglia celebrates sex archetypes. Paglia also offers a refreshingly tough, erotic vison of female sexuality to counteract the pious maternalism of *In a Different Voice*.

To the extent that there's a debate between Paglia and the feminist movement, it's not a particularly thoughtful one, partly because it's occurring at second hand, in the media. There are thoughtful feminist debates being conducted in academia, but they're not widely heard. Paglia is highly critical of feminist academics who don't publish in the mainstream; but people have a right to choose their venues, and besides, access to the mainstream press is not easily won. Still, their relative isolation is a problem for feminist scholars who want to influence public policy. To reach a general audience they have to depend on journalists to draw upon and sometimes appropriate their work.

In the end feminism, like other social movements, is dependent on the vagaries of the marketplace. It's not that women perceive feminism just the way *Time* and *Newsweek* present it to them. They have direct access only to the kind and quantity of feminist speech deemed marketable. Today the concept of a feminist movement is considered to have commercial viability once again. The challenge now is to make public debates about feminist issues as informed as they are intense.

THIRD-WAVE FEMINISM

LISA MARIA HOGELAND (ESSAY DATE SPRING 2001)

SOURCE: Hogeland, Lisa Maria. "Against Generational Thinking, or, Some Things That 'Third Wave' Feminism Isn't." *Women's Studies in Communication* 24, no. 1 (spring 2001): 107-21.

In the following essay, Hogeland explores disagreements between older feminists and third-wave feminists, asserting that their differences are political, not generational.

In the 1980s and 1990s, feminists began to worry about "the next generation" of feminism. In 1983, *Ms.* Magazine published a "Special Issue on Young Feminists," and the first of the several books and anthologies asserting a "third wave" of U.S. feminism uniquely the province of young women appeared in 1991 (Kamen, 1991; Wolf, 1993; Findlen, 1995; Walker, 1995; Heywood & Drake, 1997; Baumgardner & Richards 2000). In this essay, I offer two stories about my own history with generational rhetoric in order to illuminate some of the ways that it can be inflam-

matory and divisive. More importantly, as I will argue, the rhetoric of generational differences in feminism works to mask real political differences—fundamental differences in our visions of feminism's tasks and accomplishments. Given the uneven successes of the movement, the unevenness of change in women's lives and circumstances, the unevenness of change in institutions, such fundamental differences are inevitable. Feminists are differently situated in relation to what feminist movement has (and has not) accomplished, and *generation* is perhaps the least powerful explanatory factor for our different situations.

I want to locate these different visions of feminism not in relation to generation, then, or in relation to the naïve vision of the history of feminist movement that names young women's feminism a distinct and separate "wave," but rather in relation to the most important and undertheorized issue in contemporary feminism: the relationship between consciousness and social change. I trace three understandings of that relationship in early second wave feminism, locating them in feminist work on the practice of consciousness raising (CR). I then explore the distinct political meanings of CR in each of these understandings: CR as recruitment device for a mass movement, CR as personal transformation, and CR as a mid-point between theory and action. Each of these points to a distinct vision of feminist movement, and these contrasting visions are the real political differences in feminism.

Each of the three kinds of feminism I identify has been claimed as the province of a particular feminist "generation." Mass-movement feminism has been claimed both as a specific hunger on the part of young(er) women, and as a kind of feminist orthodoxy against which young(er) women rebel. Personal-transformation feminism has been claimed both as the particular vantage point of old(er) feminists, and as a struggle specific to a later generation of feminists. Theory-building/zap-action feminism has been claimed for grrrl/girl feminism, though such a claim obscures its stylistic similarity (at least) to such second-wave activities as the 1968 Miss America Pageant demonstration and Redstockings' disruptions of the New York abortion hearings in 1969. There is, I argue, nothing specifically generational about any of these feminisms; they are political stances with particular histories in the movement. They may be differently nuanced for women of various age groups, historical experiences, and geographical or institutional locations—but these differences in nuance do not add up to generational difference, not least because the nuances themselves are so uneven. The effect of using claims of generational difference to stand in for political difference is to reify ageism in the movement—on both sides of a putative generational divide. Here, then, are some things that "third wave" feminism isn't.

Generational Stories, Political Theories

Both of my stories about generational rhetoric in feminism involve *Ms.* Magazine. In April 1983, during my first year of graduate school, *Ms.* (not then at its best as a feminist magazine) published a "Special Issue on Young Feminists." The women interviewed and discussed were largely my age, early twenties, and nearly all were in college or graduate school.[1] The general tone of the issue was how much feminism had accomplished to make the writers' lives better and freer, and how much they felt able to take for granted some kinds of feminist gains.

My life did not feel to me so settled, and reading these accounts of "my" generation of feminists infuriated me. I was particularly outraged by one young woman's account of her relationship with her woman Chaucer professor at Yale, far too cozily for my tastes describing how feminism had made it possible for "us" to study such Dead White Men as Chaucer (Wolf, 1983). My knee jerked: I had only a few years before been thrown out of the office of my Chaucer professor at Stanford, because I suggested to him that his telling rape jokes in lecture did not help me to learn about the Wife of Bath. Feminists of "my" generation were done with this kind of struggle, the writer seemed to me to be asserting, and I most assuredly was not done. In any case, I wrote—and *Ms.* printed—a very cranky letter insisting that "we" were not done with the issues of an earlier generation. Interestingly, the young woman happily reading Dead White Men was Naomi Wolf.

In 1994, I published an essay called "Fear of Feminism" in the new *Ms.*, describing some of the reasons I saw that young women did not identify themselves as feminists (Hogeland, 1994). I wrote about the difficulties of being a radical in a conservative political climate, the institutional opposition to feminist movement, and the burden for young women in particular of our culture's overreliance on romance as an arena for the self. I thought I had implied—and I had certainly meant to imply—that young women today who do identify as feminists and do feminist work, do so

under very difficult conditions, conditions in some ways more difficult than for women of "my" generation.

The letter-writers to *Ms.* read the essay quite differently. They were insulted by my arguing that feminism for them was tricky and dangerous, just as I had been insulted more than a decade earlier by the magazine's suggestion that feminism was easy for women my age. More importantly, the letter writers felt that I was criticizing them for not being "feminist enough" by comparison to "my" generation—and, implicitly, that I was using a certain kind of age privilege to denigrate their experience. Some of the writers clearly thought I was old enough to have been a pioneering second-waver, overstating both our age difference and my age-related feminist authority.[2] A similar misidentification occurred in Jennifer Baumgardner and Amy Richards's response to a 2000 review of their "third wave" book, *Manifesta,* in *The Nation;* "I am their cultural contemporary," rather than "an unreconstructed second waver," Michelle Jensen insists in reply (Jensen, 2001, p. 2).

What these stories suggest—aside from my nice personal lesson about karma—is that generational thinking pushes emotional buttons, the more so for young and younger women, who are too often described and too infrequently given voice in accounts of "their" generation (a failing to which I confess: "Fear of Feminism" is about young women, but does not give them voice). Generational thinking is always unspeakably generalizing: one reason we react so vehemently to accounts of "our" generation is that changes in feminist ideas, and the social, political, and institutional impact of feminism itself have been so uneven. No account can be sufficiently inclusive, and to feel ourselves excluded from or marginalized within "our" generation causes pain.[3]

More importantly, the unevenness of whatever changes we might identify in feminism or in its effects suggests that generational thinking may not be at all useful in accounting for real political differences in feminism. These differences are more usefully accounted for by getting to the heart of them—and the heart of these differences is, I believe, in the different ways we see the relationship between consciousness and change, between individuals and social movements. We have in feminism radically different understandings of how change happens, of what constitutes social change, and thus of the goals and purposes of feminism itself. But these differences are not generational: they are political and theoretical,

ON THE SUBJECT OF...

NAOMI WOLF (1962-)

A provocative author and commentator on women's issues, Naomi Wolf emerged as one of the most powerful new voices of American feminism during the early 1990s. Though often at odds with the beliefs and issues that structured the nascent feminist movement of the 1960s and 1970s, Wolf has developed pointed criticisms regarding the culturally dominant notions of beauty, power, sexuality, and motherhood, which she feels continue to prevent women from gaining full equality with men at all levels of society. Wolf offers extended considerations of each of these themes in several best-selling books, including *The Beauty Myth* (1990), *Fire with Fire* (1993), *Promiscuities* (1997), and *Misconceptions* (2001). Born in San Francisco, California, Wolf grew up in the city's Haight-Ashbury district, the center of the social and sexual revolutions of the 1960s and early 1970s. She graduated from Yale University in 1984, received a Rhodes scholarship, and pursued graduate studies at New College, Oxford University. Her first book, *The Beauty Myth*, is based on research she initially conducted for her dissertation at Oxford. Following the popular success of this work, Wolf left Oxford and returned to the United States, continuing to research and write about feminist issues. *The Beauty Myth* examines the use of traditional ideas about beauty as a political weapon against women's claims for equality. Tracing ideas of feminine beauty throughout the centuries, Wolf argues that obsessive and unrealistic expectations of beauty help men defend their power by encouraging women to destroy themselves physically, draining their psychological and emotional energy and thereby slowly eroding the initial gains of feminism. Wolf encourages women to seek other images of female beauty in places such as women's films, novels, and art, and suggests that younger women draw upon the work of second-wave feminists to form an intergenerational alliance to advocate for alternative notions of beauty that are more faithful to the needs of feminine desires and the female body.

and they have roots in second-wave theories and practices of consciousness raising (CR).

To trace out these understandings, I will lay out an abbreviated and rather schematic account of the history of CR in the late 1960s and early 1970s. In the early years of Women's Liberation, the place, purpose, and function of CR was hotly contested. There are three different conceptions of CR that stand in for three different kinds of politics:

1. CR as recruitment strategy: in which CR is a point of entry into a politics based on a mass movement;

2. CR as personal transformation: in which personal life is a critical site for social change;

3. CR as theory-building: in which CR helps a particular group of women focus on a specific problem they will address, turning from theory to activism based on implementing the insights gained from CR.

In an early, complex theorization of CR, Kathie Sarachild included all of these processes: the CR group was to assemble and interrogate women's experience, to train its members to start other groups, to unlearn strategies of submission to patriarchy, and to shift its focus at the close of CR to a specific political activity.[4] In *The Politics of Women's Liberation,* Jo Freeman argued that CR groups were logical places from which to publish feminist material, to found feminist institutions such as rape crisis centers, and to begin study groups (Freeman, 1975, pp. 118-19). As the decade wore on, and especially as CR was taken up as a practice by thousands of women who came into Women's Liberation with no previous experience in radical politics, a different kind of CR practice emerged. Anita Shreve describes the practice of her group, "The rules were simple: Each woman could speak for as long as she liked. When she was finished, no one could comment or criticize" (Shreve, 1989, p. 21; see also pp. 44-46).[5] This version of CR, called "soft" CR by Claudia Dreifus and others, turned the interrogation of women's experience into the simple affirmation of it (Williams, 1975). "Soft" CR was the version forwarded by the guides to CR put out by Los Angeles NOW in 1974 (Ann, 1974; Gosier, Gardel, and Alrich, 1974), and by *Ms.* in 1975 (Redstockings, 1975; Willis, 1978). Over the course of the 1970s, CR became less theoretical as a practice and less directly connected to Movement recruitment, and the three different understandings of the practice became increasingly separable.

Each of these visions of CR accompanies a specific theory of social change, as I argue below. I use the vague term "accompanies" quite deliberately, because chicken-and-egging the question of whether one's theory of social change derives from or constructs one's vision of CR is, for me, a non-issue; how we see CR and how we understand social change are mutually constitutive.

CR as Recruitment Strategy

Mass-movement feminism has conventionally been understood as liberal feminism, but its politics are more complicated than a simple liberal/radical divide can address. Mass-movement feminism is a politics of numbers, of media pressure, of persuasion and rhetoric. The strategy of organizing massive numbers of women (and perhaps men) need not assume that institutions are democratic, but only that they are responsive to pressure, especially the pressure of numbers. Mass actions can serve as recruitment events and as radicalizing experiences for women who participate in them; alternatively, they may simply be fun. Most feminists of whatever persuasion have participated in such actions as a strategy at some time, but not all feminists believe such actions to be the centerpiece of feminist political work.

There is in fact considerable debate in contemporary feminism about the importance and efficacy of mass-action, mass-movement politics, just as there was in the 1970s. In a 1976 article in *off our backs,* for example, Brooke Williams and Hannah Darby critiqued the rhetoric of recruitment that justified the emergence of feminist-oriented businesses; such businesses recruited women into the movement for what purpose? they asked, because in their thinking, simply increasing the number of women who identified with the Movement without attending to real political education and specific political goals and analyses was an insufficient, even misguided, strategy.

More recently, we can see the call for a mass-movement feminism in works such as Naomi Wolf's *Fire with Fire,* which argues that feminists should eliminate their focus on divisive issues like abortion, the better to mobilize a majoritarian mass movement. "A feminism worthy of its name," Wolf argues, "will fit every woman, and every man who cares about women, comfortably"; rather than "a specific agenda," she suggests, feminism should constitute itself as "a conviction of female worth" so that the movement need not be "of the minority, by the minority" (Wolf, 1993, pp. 132, 126). As Bonnie J. Dow points out in critiquing Wolf's position, "Some aspects of feminist ideology—antiracism, antihomophobia, commitment to economic justice for women of all classes—are perceived by many women as against their interests. Such women may be very committed to improving their own lives, but that does not make them feminists" (Dow, 1996, pp. 216-17; see also pp. 212-13). Individual women's self-interest may not be identical with feminist politics, as Dow suggests, and it is not entirely clear what a mass movement "for women" might mean without a more focused political agenda.

Another way of seeing this debate over the efficacy of mass-movement oriented feminism, and one that returns us to its relationship to CR, is to see it in terms of ways that feminists understand mass-media coverage of feminist issues. In *Fire with Fire,* Wolf argues that "the balance of power around gender changed, possibly forever" because of the Thomas - Hill hearings; women watched the white guys in ties on the Judiciary Committee "not get it," and went into the 1992 elections looking for "retaliation" (Wolf, 1993, pp. 5-6). Of course, if we are willing to accept the election of Bill Clinton as a crucial political achievement of feminist movement, then Wolf's account of the "genderquake" might be accurate (though let's not forget that Thomas was confirmed; that Clinton was, at best, a mixed bag for feminists; and that George W. Bush promises to appoint more justices just like Thomas).

As Dow and I have argued elsewhere, media coverage of feminist issues such as sexual harassment and domestic violence does not constitute CR. Instead, media coverage promotes a certain level of basic awareness of feminist issues—and may, as in the case of the Thomas - Hill hearings, motivate large numbers of women to move toward feminist organizations—but it may also do so without attending directly to feminist analyses. Such media coverage means, we argue, "that surprising numbers of women know the nuclear family can be a dangerous place for women, that the second shift is unfair to women, that beauty standards are oppressive to women, that divorce is the fast track to poverty for women, and that U.S. society does nothing to facilitate women's combining waged work with childrearing" (Dow and Hogeland, 1997, p. 13). But media coverage of feminist issues rarely addresses the politics of such knowledge, presenting instead a view of the world as a dangerous place for individual women to negotiate individually—or with the right partner. Knowledge may not always equal power, just as putting large numbers of bodies in one place may not always equal change.

CR as Personal Transformation

The politics of personal transformation depends ultimately on a model of social change as a slow, even generational, process, based on a kind of "ripple effect": personal changes affect individuals, who in turn affect other individuals. At some point (somehow), there will be a critical mass of small changes, that will lead to (or will constitute) large-scale social change. In many instances, such a personal-transformation approach to feminism has tended to be anti-materialist (feminist therapy, feminist spirituality), though we can see more materialist versions of it in "consumer feminisms"—in consumer boycotts most notably, where individual acts of (non)consumption add up to large-scale political action. The danger, of course, of such a comparison lies in the ways that consumer boycotts can turn over into consuming feminism-as-lifestyle. That is, "consumer feminism" too easily creates a temptation to substitute buying stuff for political action. How we spend our money is certainly about politics (politically conditioned, like self-esteem—what we might think of as para-political), and can be an important political strategy, especially in the forms of targeted non-consumption and targeted small-business support. But the tendency to see all spending decisions as political is too easily cooptable by advertisers and others into the belief that "lifestyle" decisions are politics (Radner, 1994; S. J. Douglas, 1994; and Goldman, Heath, & Smith, 1991).

The view that politics are based in personal transformations is often theorized sequentially: personal change precedes political change; change yourself first, and then change the world. At base, such a theory of social change is sentimental—think of Harriet Beecher Stowe's "Concluding Remarks" to *Uncle Tom's Cabin,* where she suggests that her readers have two important powers for change: "There is one thing that every individual can do,—they can see to it they *feel right*" and "you can pray!" (Stowe, 1852, pp. 624 -25, emphases original). Jane Tompkins's important chapter on *Uncle Tom's Cabin* in her *Sensational Designs* (1985) establishes ways this model of social change has historically been associated with women. In many respects, the critical-mass theory of social change is simply a more modern version of earlier understandings of women's influence, replacing the civic morality women were supposed to inculcate in husbands and sons with a kind of civic feminism. If such nineteenth-century notions of women's influence constituted a kind of domestic feminism, we might understand the parallel late-twentieth-century notions as feminism domesticated.

To be fair, though, the problem of belief is central here: if you believe in Stowe's vision of social-change-through-prayer (which is to say, if you believe in a deity Who, when sufficiently entreated, will intervene in systems of domination), then prayer (or its equivalent practices) is the logical political response to your theory of how the world works. If you don't believe in social change *ex machina* or in the *deus* behind it, this vision of how change happens is likely to be the more frustrating because its religious underpinnings can be so difficult to tease out.

CR as personal transformation necessarily prioritizes those aspects of patriarchy that are attributable to men's sexism (and women's internalized sexism), rather than to the structures of institutions. An unfortunate by-product of this understanding of social change, and one we can see writ large in the US political landscape, is that it establishes hypocrisy as a worse fault than inaction. If we must purge ourselves of sexism before we can combat it in the social or political arenas, then action can always be postponed until we ourselves are somehow liberated—as if individual liberation were possible inside oppressive social structures. As Naomi Wolf put in *Fire with Fire,* "Feminism means freedom, and freedom must exist inside our own heads before it can exist anywhere else" (1993, p. 120). In practice, this vision entails CR that leads to more CR, based on a notion of human perfectibility (which is, of course, unattainable), and ultimately on notions of political "purity" (a religious, not a political concept). Because of the hypocrisy question, this vision of social change also mires us in lifestyle litmus tests (how can you be a feminist if you eat meat? wear make-up?), and a notion of feminism-as-identity, rather than feminism as practice. Let me be clear: I do believe that personal transformations are politically relevant, just as they are politically (and historically) conditioned. But *the personal is political* was meant to argue that politics construct our lives at home, as a way of breaking the public/private barrier in our theorizing—it was never meant to argue that our lives at home were our politics. (see Dow, 1996, pp. 209-212).

Implicitly or explicitly, personal transformation theories of social change tend to rely on metaphors of organic-changes-over-time, which makes them particularly amenable to generational rhetoric. Both old(er) and young(er) feminists have laid claim to personal transformation as their uniquely available mode—old(er) feminists have claimed it as a specific reward for having lived through feminist political struggle, and young(er) feminists have claimed it as their specific legacy from previous generations of struggle.[6] There is nothing generational about the politics of personal transformation: it's an understanding of how social change works that dates back to the first wave of US feminism, a consistent thread in feminist movement today, and a political stance within the movement.

CR as Theory-Building

The politics of theory-building sets out CR as a practice that enables feminists to find a specific target for feminist activity, a specific point of intervention into that amorphous thing called patriarchy. It is not "freedom" the group discovers or creates in the CR process, but some shared and particular oppression. In this model, the CR group uses its experience of CR to move toward a strategy for resistance, an agenda for action, and possibly toward the creation of a feminist institution.

These CR-based interventions need not be on the scale of the 1970 Women's Strike for Equality March on 5th Avenue, nor the 1992 abortion rights march on Washington. They tend, instead, to be either small-group theatrics or institutionally-oriented. The 1968 Miss America Pageant demonstration and the 1969 Redstockings disruption of the New York abortion hearings exemplify the former tendency ("No More Miss America!" 1970, pp. 586-88; Echols, 1989, pp. 140-43), as do the organizing strategies of Lesbian Avengers (Schulman, 1994). CR groups based in universities exemplify the latter tendency, as they have sometimes moved to found or support Women's Studies programs, to encourage the hiring of women faculty members, to combat sexism in its various forms on campus, and to engage in coalition work with other groups.

Theory-building CR in the 1970s is perhaps best exemplified by the Combahee River Collective, whose 1977 "A Black Feminist Statement" has played an important role in making the intersections of race, class, and sexuality, as well as gender, central to feminist analyses. The Collective describes some of the insights generated from its CR practices, and draws links between these insights, the group's political engagements, and its politico-theoretical stances on issues such as separatism. The Collective's manifesto, one of the most important contributions to feminist theory in the latter part of the decade, charts the group's movement through a broad range of activities: it operated as a study group, did CR, held retreats, met with other groups, and was, in 1977, on the verge of compiling a collection of Black feminist writing.

Theory-building CR is the basis for some kinds of feminist service-provision, and for the creation of feminist-alternative institutions. Feminist service-provision—rape-crisis centers, battered women's shelters, and the like—was designed not only to respond to women's needs in ways patriarchal institutions could (or would) not, but also to provide homes for feminist political analyses of these issues.[7] As these institutions became "professionalized"—often in concert with their receiving funding from local, state, or federal governments—a different kind of struggle and a different kind of analysis emerged. As is also the case in Women's Studies programs, for instance, feminist service-provision organizations struggle with questions of the extent to which their analyses and, indeed, their missions, can be compromised by their relationships to funding sources, certification processes, institutional locations, and so forth. Both the founding of these institutions and their continuation depend on feminist theorizing about strategies for intervening in patriarchy.

Accounts of CR in contemporary feminism that ignore its theory-building component work to disconnect CR from its foundational importance to many important feminist practices. Theory-building is by no means a specific practice of the early second wave, as anyone who reads young(er) women's zines can testify. Setting theory as the mid-point between personal experience and political action is not generational or generation-specific; it is, rather, a specific understanding of social change and a specific political stance in the movement.

Conclusions

One of the claims some young(er) feminists make to generational specificity is in the style of post-punk, DIY (Do It Yourself), youth-culture grounded rock music, zines, and political activity (see, e.g., Klein, 1997). The in-your-face activist style of Riot Grrrls and other young(er) feminists is, however, neither unique nor specific to a younger generation of feminists; it bears, in fact, quite marked similarities to some early second-wave activities. But young(er) feminists too often simply don't know much about the zap-actions, the mimeographed flyers, the materiality of early second-wave protest. Too, we can see a stylistic similarity in the rhetorical and discursive strategies of (some of) the essays collected in Barbara Findlen's *Listen Up* and in *Sisterhood Is Powerful*; think of the struggle for intimacy between writer and reader, the studied informality, the sense of urgency—these are not generationally different.

My point here is not that young(er) feminists have nothing new to say—quite the contrary, in fact—but rather that notions of generational rupture or divides work effectively to prevent us from seeing the powerful persistence of political beliefs, of specific women's issues, and of strategies for change. And, of course, if we cannot see what persists, neither can we see what is new. Young(er) and old(er) feminists have much to say to each other about their specific historical locations, about the effects of ageism on their efforts, about how women's experiences in patriarchy differ because of age. But the false belief that political differences are generational differences make these and other crucial conversations impossible.

That we can see young(er) and old(er) feminists claiming each of my three analyses of how social change works as specifically available to their generation evidences something important about contemporary feminist movement. First, the construction of putative generational divide is easier than confronting real political difference, real disagreements about the goals of feminist movement, real divides among different ways we see the world. Second, it is easier to construct these differences as generational because of the persistence of ageism, and, more benignly, simple age-stratification, in and outside of feminist movement. Our friendship networks are rarely integrated by age, and too often form the core of our sense of feminist identity and practice; our issues rarely assemble us in truly multi-generational movement or organizations. Our sense of "our" generation is too often too simply our friendship network, our institutional location, our geographic situation, our own lives and the lives of a few other folks significant to us.

This age stratification is further overdetermined by ways that the history of second-wave feminism is little taught and poorly understood, even in Women's Studies. It's become a truism that the second wave was racist, for instance, no matter that such a blanket argument writes out of our history the enormous and important contributions of women of color in the 1970s. A more nuanced view must account for both what women of color did in the decade and for the necessary critiques of movement racism (King, 1994, p. 13).

Likewise, it's become a truism that second-wave feminism enshrined middle-class women's experience as universal, which allows us to ignore the stunning numbers of working-class women enmeshed in educational upward mobility who were central to feminist movement in the decade (see Rosen, 1995, pp. 325-26). The absolutism of both these views reinforces young(er) feminists' sense of themselves and their politics as distinct from earlier feminist movement, and from old(er) feminists as well; to explore continuities would be to admit to racism and classism, and, in some sense, the refusal of such continuities may serve to work for white feminists as a kind of inoculation against confronting the persistence of these forces.[8]

If our daily lives, our political practices, and our sense of history all work to reconfirm our too-easy sense of generational divide, it is perhaps the less surprising that feminists manage not to engage in serious and sustained debates about political differences. Attributing our differences to generation rather than to politics sets us firmly into psychologized thinking, and into versions of mother/daughter relations—somehow, we are never sisters who might have things to teach each other across our differences and despite our rivalries. We neither agree to disagree nor do we disagree; instead, we agree to evade. We foreclose the real conversations feminists must have about politics, conversations that could help us clarify our positions, conversations that could help us work more effectively both together and separately.

Notes

1. The interviews included two men, the sons of Alix Kates Shulman and Audre Lorde, and two non-student activists (Van Gelder, 1983); the four essayists included a woman who described her college experience and two who identify themselves in their author notes by their educational affiliations. The notable exception in the issue is the article by a working-class woman, Deborah Branscum, whose essay concludes by calling for feminists to organize in and transform the labor movement. In the context of essays and mini-interviews by students at and graduates of institutions such as Yale, Vassar, Smith, and University of California at Santa Barbara, Branscum's essay on union organizing is clearly intended to remind us that not all young women are as privileged as these; because it is the sole exception, I'm not sure that it succeeded in doing so.

2. One letter writer responded: "please understand that my generation is incredibly thankful for your courage, and recognizes that we would never be where we are without you" (Kaplan, 1995, p. 8). I don't think so: my pioneering second wave feminist activity was in 1971, when I circulated a petition at my elementary school to force the dress code to include trousers for

girls. It wasn't exactly Redstockings. Naomi Wolf and I are roughly the same age, and certainly the same "generation" in any demographic reckoning, yet at this moment in *Ms.*, I was clearly being identified as a second-waver, and Wolf (whose spending-money-as-feminism strategies were invoked by Kaplan) was as clearly being identified as a third-waver.

3. Clearly, the category "generation" has enormous affective power, even when its explanatory power is limited. This power derives in no small part from the relentless "generationalizing" strategies of mass media and advertising, which identify us by generation (and generation-as-style looms large here) in order to construct us as consumers.

4. See the abbreviated version of her outline as Robin Morgan (1970, pp. xxvi-xxviii) describes it for a sense of the broad range of activities a CR group was supposed to undertake. Sarachild's outline is remarkable precisely for its inclusiveness and tough-mindedness: in the group as she outlines it, individual narratives are crossquestioned, resistances confronted, feminist theory studied and written, organizers trained, and CR actions planned. Sarachild's version is, I suggest, CR in its ideal state, rather than CR as it was most often practiced.

5. Shreve's book, *Women Together, Women Alone: The Legacy of the Consciousness-Raising Movement* describes CR as specifically important to white, middle-class, suburban women who never otherwise joined the Movement: the CR that emphasized personal transformation and de-emphasized social change was particularly well-suited for such women. Shreve's analysis, though, is highly colored by her sense that CR was a phenomenon separable from the women's movement, indeed, a parallel movement unto itself.

6. By the late 1970s, this position was being asserted in *Ms.*, as Susan Dworkin's (1978) and Lynne Sharon Schwartz's (1978, p. 41) reviews of *Some Do* and *Burning Questions* (respectively) asserted what they saw as the movement's shift to "a quieter, more individualized search for fulfillment" in contrast to the novels' more activist-oriented visions of feminism. At the other end of the generational spectrum, one might pick up the special issue of *Lighthouse*, the Radcliffe women's magazine, devoted to "Feminism—A Personal Perspective" (many thanks to Cally Waite for sending it to me). The writers in *Lighthouse* describe their particular brand of feminism, "personal feminism," as "characterized by individuals in all parts of the world who are slowly incorporating equality into their particular world views" (Crapo, 1996, p. 4). Such a "personal feminism," moreover, is specifically designed to help people see "more readily" that "feminism [is] a movement which is productive rather than threatening" (Funk, 1996, p. 22). Both "generations" of writers are holding out for a kind of feminism that is non-confrontational and non-ideological—a thoroughly depoliticized feminism, in effect.

7. Carol Ann Douglas (in Douglas, E. B., and Dejanikus, 1976, p. 23) argues that "providing support for [women in difficulties] is a political message" that there are alternatives to patriarchy. This is an argument that has largely disappeared from U.S. feminism, as feminist service provision has become so thoroughly professionalized; indeed, Baumgardner and Richards (2000, p. 296) make quite the opposite argument in their very smart discussion of volunteering

vs. activism, arguing that feminist women volunteers "often execute work the government should be funding" in the guise of political activism.

8. Patricia Hill Collins suggested the term "inoculation" to me in a somewhat different context. For old(er) white feminists, the inoculative gesture may take the form of "I used to be a racist but now I know better" apologia; see DuCille (1994, pp. 612-17), for a brilliant critique of this gesture.

References

Ann. (1974, July). NOW: a new perspective? *off our backs*, 9.

Baumgardner, J. and A. Richards. (2000). *Manifesta: Young women, feminism, and the future*. New York: Farrar, Straus and Giroux.

Branscum, D. (1983, April). Young feminists III. *Ms.*, 46, 89.

Combahee River Collective. (1977, 1983). A black feminist statement. C. Moraga and G. Anzaldúa, Eds. *This bridge called my back: Writings by radical women of color*, 2nd ed. (pp. 210-218). New York: Kitchen Table.

Crapo, A. (1996, Jan.). Reflections on feminism: The role we ask it to play. *Lighthouse* 6, 3-5.

Douglas, C. A., E. B., and T. Dejanikus. (1976, Sept.). how feminist is therapy? *off our backs*, 2-3, 22-23.

Douglas, S. J. (1994). *Where the girls are: Growing up female with the mass media*. New York: Times.

Dow, B. J. (1996). *Prime-time feminism: Television, media culture, and the women's movement since 1970*. Philadelphia: U of Pennsylvania.

Dow, B. J., and L. M. Hogeland. (1997, Winter). When feminism meets the press, our real politics get lost. *On The Issues*, 12-13.

Dreifus, C. J. (1973). *Women's fate: Raps from a feminist consciousness-raising group*. New York: Bantam.

duCille, A. (1994, Spring). The occult of true black womanhood: Critical demeanor and black feminist studies. *Signs* 19, 3: 591-629.

Dworkin, S. (1978, Dec.). Sex and excess, rev. of *Some do* by Jane DeLynn. *Ms.*, 38, 41.

Echols, A. (1989). *Daring to be bad: Radical feminism in America, 1967-1975*. Minneapolis: U of Minnesota.

Findlen, B., Ed. (1995). *Listen up: Voices from the next feminist generation*. Seattle: Seal.

Freeman, J. (1975). *The politics of women's liberation*. New York: Longman.

Funk, C. (1996, Jan.). Personal feminism: Thoughts on the individual nature of feminism. *Lighthouse* 6, 2: 21-22.

Goldman, R., D. Heath, and S. L. Smith. (1991). Commodity feminism. *Critical Studies in Mass Communication* 8: 333-51.

Gosier, D., L. N. Gardel, and A. Aldrich. (1974, Dec.). now or never. *off our backs*, 23.

Heywood, L. and J. Drake, Eds. (1997). *Third wave agenda: Being feminist, doing feminism*. Minneapolis: U of Minnesota.

Hogeland, L. M. (1994, Nov/Dec.). Fear of feminism. *Ms.*, 18-21.

Hornaday, A. (1983, April). Young feminists II. *Ms.*, 45-6.

Jensen, M. (2001, 22 Jan.). Jensen replies. *The Nation,* 2.

Joreen [J. Freeman]. (1973). The tyranny of structureless-ness. A. Koedt, E. Levine, and A. Rapone, Eds. *Radical feminism* (pp. 285-99). New York: Quadrangle.

Kamen, P. (1991). *Feminist fatale.* New York: Fine.

Kaplan, J. S. (1995, March/April). Letter. *Ms.*, 8.

King, K. (1994). *Theory in its feminist travels: Conversations in U.S. women's movements.* Bloomington: Indiana U.

Klein, M. (1997). Duality and redefinition: Young feminism and the alternative music community. L. Heywood and J. Drake, Eds., *Third wave agenda: Being feminist, doing feminism* (pp. 207-225). Minneapolis, U Minnesota.

Morgan, R. (1970). Introduction: The women's revolution. R. Morgan, Ed., *Sisterhood is powerful: An anthology of writings from the women's liberation movement* (pp. xv-xlvi) New York: Vintage.

Radner, H. (1994). *Shopping around: feminine culture and the pursuit of pleasure.* New York: Routledge.

Redstockings. (1975, July). Ms. *off our backs,* 28-33.

Rosen, R. (1995). The female generation gap: Daughters of the fifties and the origins of contemporary American feminism. L. K. Kerber, A. Kessler-Harris, and K. K. Sklar, Eds., *U.S. history as women's history: New feminist essays* (pp. 313-34). Chapel Hill: U of North Carolina.

Schulman, S. (1994). *My American history: Lesbian and gay life during the Reagan/Bush years.* New York, Routledge.

Shreve, A. (1989). *Women together, women alone: The legacy of the consciousness-raising movement.* New York: Viking.

Schwartz, L. S. (1978, March). How foolish I was, how mellow I've become, rev. of *Burning Questions* by A. K. Shulman. *Ms.*, 40-41.

Stowe, H. B. *Uncle Tom's cabin.* 1852; rpt. New York: Penguin, n.d.

Tomkins, J. (1985). *Sensational designs: The cultural work of American fiction, 1790-1860.* New York: Oxford.

Van Gelder, L. (1983, April). Grown-up children of feminist mothers—what they think of it all. *Ms.*, 44-5, 90.

Walker, R., Ed. (1995). *To be real: Telling the truth and changing the face of feminism.* New York: Anchor.

Williams, B. (1975, Jan.). Rev. of *Women's fate: Raps from a feminist consciousness-raising group* by C. Dreifus. *off our backs,* 18.

Williams, B., and H. Darby. (1976, March). business vs. revolution. *off our backs,* 28.

Willis, E. (1978). The conservatism of *Ms.* Redstockings, Eds., *Feminist revolution,* 2nd ed. (pp. 170-71). New York: Random House.

Wolf, N. (1993). *Fire with fire: The new female power and how to use it.* New York: Fawcett.

Wolf, N. (1983, April). Young feminists IV. *Ms.*, 46, 89-90.

FURTHER READING

Criticism

Chadwick, Whitney. "In and Out of the Mainstream." In *Women, Art, and Society,* pp. 297-346. London: Thames and Hudson, 1991.

Traces developments in the world of fine art as they relate to women from World War II onward.

Chafe, William H. "The Road to Equality 1962-Today." In *No Small Courage: A History of Women in the United States,* edited by Nancy F. Cott, pp. 529-86. New York: Oxford University Press, 2000.

Detailed analysis of the social and historical factors that contributed to the rise of the women's movement in the 1960s and beyond.

Davis, Angela. *Woman, Race, and Class.* New York: Random House, 1981, 271 p.

Comments on aspects of race and class in a critique of the feminist movement.

Davis, Flora. "The Founding of NOW." In *Moving the Mountain: The Women's Movement in America since 1960,* pp. 49-68. New York: Simon & Schuster, 1991.

Examination of the social, economic, and cultural factors that provided a fertile ground for the founding of the National Organization for Women in 1966 and its chief legal victories during the next several years.

De Hart, Jane Sherron. "Rights and Representation: Women, Politics, and Power in the Contemporary United States." In *U.S. History* as *Women's History,* edited by Linda K. Kerber, Alice Kessler-Harris, and Kathryn Kish Sklar, pp. 214-42. Chapel Hill: University of North Carolina Press, 1995.

Discusses aspects of women's involvement in politics during the 1980s and 1990s.

De Hart, Jane Sherron, and Donald Mathews. "The Cultural Politics of the ERA's Defeat." In *Feminist Frontiers II: Rethinking Sex, Gender, and Society,* edited by Laurel Richardson and Verta Taylor, pp. 458-63. New York: McGraw-Hill, 1989.

Explores the social and cultural factors that contributed to the failed campaign to ratify the Equal Rights Amendment.

Echols, Alice. *Daring to Be Bad: Radical Feminism in America 1967-1975.* Minneapolis: University of Minnesota Press, 1989, 416 p.

Discusses the historical and social conditions that led to the emergence of radical feminism in the 1960s.

Friedan, Betty. "The Problem That Has No Name." In *The Feminine Mystique,* pp. 15-32. New York: W. W. Norton, 1963.

The first chapter of her influential work The Feminine Mystique, *Friedan identifies the underlying feelings of dissatisfaction and unhappiness experienced by American women in the early 1960s.*

Freedman, Estelle B. *No Turning back: The History of Feminism and the Future of Women.* New York: Ballantine Books, 2002, 446 p.

Survey of the history of the women's movement.

Freeman, Jo. *The Politics of Women's Liberation.* New York: David McKay, 1975, 268 p.

An in-depth study of the legal and political issues stemming from the feminist movement in the 1960s and 1970s.

Gelb, Joyce. "Feminism in Government: Advocacy and Policy-Making." In *Feminism and Politics: A Comparative Perspective,* pp. 90-136. Berkeley: University of California Press, 1989.

Examines legislature related to women in the United States and Great Britain.

Gelb, Joyce, and Marian Lief Palley. *Women and Public Policies.* 2nd ed. Charlottesville: University of Virginia Press, 1996, 268 p.

Explores feminist responses to the U.S. political and judicial system, focusing on Title IX and reproductive issues.

Ginsburg, Faye. *Contested Lives: The Abortion Debate in the American Community.* 2nd ed. Berkeley: University of California Press, 1998, 337 p.

Outlines the course of the debate regarding women's reproductive rights in the second half of the twentieth century.

Harrison, Cynthia. *On Account of Sex: The Politics of Women's Issues, 1945-1968.* Berkeley: University of California Press, 1988, 337 p.

Detailed exploration of the main political and legal issues in the early phase of the feminist movement.

Hartmann, Susan M. *From Margin to Mainstream: American Women and Politics Since 1960.* New York: Knopf, 1989, 218 p.

A history of feminist political involvement, legal battles, and changes in the workplace.

Hazou, Winnie. *The Social and Legal Status of Women: A Global Perspective.* New York: Praeger, 1990, 222 p.

Comments on women in relation to family, law, and employment, focusing on the United States and its connection to global trends.

Heywood, Leslie, and Jennifer Drake, eds. *Third Wave Agenda: Being Feminist, Doing Feminism.* Minneapolis: University of Minnesota Press, 1997, 268 p.

Detailed discussion of the characteristics, representation, and activism of third-wave feminists.

Hirsch, Marianne, and Evelyn Fox Keller, eds. *Conflicts in Feminism.* New York: Routledge, 1990, 397 p.

Collection of essays on historical, social, and literary aspects of feminism.

Kerber, Linda K., and Jane Sherron De Hart. *Women's America: Refocusing the Past.* 3rd ed. New York: Oxford University Press, 1991, 588 p.

Anthology of primary writings of the feminist movement, with commentary by the editors.

Kolodny, Annette. "The Lady's Nor for Spurning: Kate Millett and the Critics." *Contemporary Literature* 17, no. 4 (1976): 541-62.

Uses reviews of Kate Millett's Flying *as a starting point for discussing criticism by and about women's writing.*

Linden-Ward, Blanche, and Carol Hurd Green. *Changing the Future: American Women in the 1960s.* New York: Twayne, 1992, 585 p.

Examines changes in legislation, employment, and social trends that affected the lives of women in the 1960s.

Luker, Kristin. *Abortion and the Politics of Motherhood.* Berkeley: University of California Press, 1984, 324 p.

Surveys the legal, political, and social issues involved in the fight for women's reproductive rights.

Mansbridge, Jane. *Why We Lost the ERA.* Chicago: University of Chicago Press, 1986, 327 p.

Examines the progress of the Equal Rights Amendment and the reasons for its failure to be ratified.

Riddle, John M. *Eve's Herbs: A History of Contraception and Abortion in the West.* Cambridge, Mass.: Harvard University Press, 1997, 341 p.

Explores the history, social implications, and legal ramifications of contraception in the West, with emphasis on the last few decades of the twentieth century.

Rosen, Ruth. *The World Split Open: How the Modern Women's Movement Changed America.* New York: Viking, 2000, 446 p.

Traces social changes brought about by the women's movement from the 1950s through the 1980s backlash and beyond.

Roszak, Betty, and Theodore Roszak, eds. *Masculine/Feminine: Readings in Sexual Mythology and the Liberation of Women.* New York: Harper Colophon Books, 1969, 316 p.

Wide-ranging collection of primary sources and contemporary commentaries on "the man problem," male involvement in feminism, and the growth of feminist militancy.

Scanlon, Jennifer, ed. *Significant Contemporary American Feminists: A Biographical Sourcebook.* Westport, Conn.: Greenwood Press, 1991, 361 p.

Biographical reference work on figures in the women's movement.

Schacht, Steven P., and Doris W. Ewing, eds. *Feminism and Men: Reconstructing Gender Relations.* New York: New York University Press, 1998, 310 p.

Collection of essays focusing on gender politics and possible roles for men in the feminist movement.

Smith, Barbara. "For All My Sisters, Especially Beverly and Demita." In *Toward a Black Feminist Criticism,* pp. 1-17. Freedom, Ca.: Out & Out Books, 1977.

One of the first formal essays outlining a theory of black feminist criticism. Smith deplores the lack of a space for black feminist writers in mainstream publications, and explores the connections between politics, artistry, race, and gender issues as they pertain to black women authors.

Vacker, Barry. "Skyscrapers, Supermodels, and Strange Attractors: Ayn Rand, Naomi Wolf, and the Third Wave Aesthos." In *Feminist Interpretations of Ayn Rand,* edited by Mimi Reisel Gladstein and Chris Matthew Sciabarra, pp. 115-56. University Park: Pennsylvania State University Press, 1999.

Explores interrelationships between architecture, fashion, and philosophy and their connection to artistic ideals and the aesthetic principles of third-wave feminism.

OTHER SOURCES FROM GALE:

Additional coverage of the Feminist Movement is contained in the following sources published by the Gale Group: *Contemporary Literary Criticism,* Vols. 65, 76, 180.

WOMEN'S LITERATURE FROM 1960 TO THE PRESENT

In several lectures she gave during the 1930s and later, writer Virginia Woolf reflected upon the challenge she and her fellow female artists faced at the beginning of the century—Woolf noted that although women had been writing for centuries, the subjects they had written about and even the style in which they wrote was often dictated not by their own creative vision, but by standards imposed upon women by society in general. Advances in women's issues, such as the right to vote, the fight for reproductive rights, and the opportunities women gained during the first half of the century in the arena of work outside the home were major developments. Despite these changes, women artists during these years continued to feel restricted by imposed standards of creativity. It would take, notes Elaine Showalter in numerous essays detailing the growth and development of women's writing in the twentieth century, several decades before women would completely break the mold of respectability under which they felt compelled to write. Fuelled by the feminist movement of the early twentieth century, many women authors began to explore new modes of expression, focusing increasingly on issues that were central to their existence as women and as artists. By the end of the 1950s and the beginning of the 1960s, with the rise of the second wave feminist movement, women artists began expanding their repertoire of creative expression to openly include, and even celebrate their power and experiences as

women. Works such as Betty Friedan's *The Feminine Mystique* (1963), Sylvia Plath's *The Bell Jar* (1971), and others by authors like Germaine Greer, Gloria Steinem, and Marilyn French all helped to awaken the feminine consciousness, paving the way for later writers to explore the reality of women's experience in their writings openly and freely. Works of literature by women authors during the 1960s and later thus began to focus increasingly on women's viewpoints, with issues such as race and gender, sexuality, and personal freedom taking center stage. Additionally, these years also witnessed the emergence of feminist literary theorists, many of whom set about redefining the canon, arguing for inclusion of women writers who had been marginalized by mainstream academia in the past. The latter half of the twentieth century also provided fertile ground for growing recognition of women writers of color. Lesbian literature has also flourished, and women have openly explored concerns about sexuality, sexual orientation, politics, and other gender issues in their works.

Prior to the mid-1960s, women writers who ventured beyond the established feminine stereotypes were regularly characterized as "outcasts," denounced as vulgar or, in the case of Simone de Beauvoir, even "frigid." Nonetheless, many of them persisted in exploring new ways of expression, and poets such as Adrienne Rich, Audre Lorde, and others continued to write works articulating the struggle they faced as authors who could choose to "write badly and be patronized or to write well and be attacked," according to Showalter. Another aspect of this struggle to gain respect as independent artists was the fight between women who felt compelled to "transcend" their femininity, opting to write as androgynous artists—Woolf chief among them—and others, including Erica Jong, who felt strongly that unless women could find the means to express themselves openly and clearly, they might as well not write at all. Eventually, many women writers in the 1960s and later broke through the stereotypical and restrictive paradigm of female authorship, creating and publishing works that abounded in an open celebration and exploration of issues that were central to women's existence, including sexuality. By the 1990s, critical and academic opinion had shifted, and works such as Eve Ensler's *The Vagina Monologues,* which deals directly with women's physical and emotional experiences, were hailed as both innovative and literary.

A similar, yet different path to progress marks the writing of women authors of color, who eventually gained critical recognition for their efforts as chroniclers of their cultures, races, and gender. Although there were numerous black female authors writing during the early part of the century, especially during the heyday of the Harlem Renaissance, black feminist authors's exploration of both race and gender issues in their writing kept them outside the American feminist discourse that was dominated by either black male activists or white feminists. Scholars have also pointed to the fact that while works such as Friedan's *The Feminine Mystique* did much to draw attention to the emerging feminine consciousness, they did not address the needs and issues significant to women of color. Further, the narrative strategies used by such pioneering black authors such as Zora Neale Hurston, whose works focused primarily on the private and domestic domain, were, until the 1970s and 1980s, dismissed by both white feminists and black male intellectuals because of the perception that their focus was too limited and narrow. Later critical opinion, however, has reevaluated the writing style and strategies used by many female authors of color to recognize that the personal narrative is a powerful and uniquely expressive mode of extrapolating and commenting upon the state of the world inhabited by these writers. Asian writers have used these strategies particularly well to counter stereotyped images of their own culture and gender. In several anthologies published in the late-twentieth

century, including *Aiiieeeee!!* Asian writers, both male and female have attempted to create new images of Asian American literature. Asian women writers have been faulted for creating what are perceived as unrealistic portrayals of Asian American culture, especially images of the Asian woman as powerful and dominant, often seen in the works of such writers as Maxine Hong Kingston and Amy Tan. Mitsuye Yamada has addressed this conflict in her writing, arguing for a cohesive creative vision and the space to express it.

Modern women's writing continues to explore new genres and means of expression, and women writers today participate fully in both the creative and scholarly process. Women's studies, feminist literary theory, and women's mode of writing and expressing are now established areas of academic environments, and women are exacting continued and growing control over their own literary and social spheres.

REPRESENTATIVE WORKS

Denise Chávez
The Last of the Menu Girls (short stories) 1986

Face of an Angel (novel) 1994

Alice Childress
Florence (play) 1949

Wedding Band: A Love/Hate Story in Black and White (play) 1966

Wine in the Wilderness (play) 1969

A Hero Ain't Nothin' But a Sandwich (novel) 1973

Frank Chin
Aiiieeeee!: An Anthology of Asian American Writers [editor, with others] (anthology) 1974

Hélène Cixous
Dedans [*Inside*] (novel) 1969

La Jeune née [with Catherine Clément; *The Newly Born Woman*] (essays) 1975

Annie Dillard
Pilgrim at Tinker Creek (essays) 1976

Holy the Firm (essays) 1977

Teaching a Stone to Talk (essays) 1982

Chitra Banerjee Divakaruni
Arranged Marriage (short stories) 1995

The Mistress of Spices (novel) 1997

Rosalyn Drexler
The Line of Least Existence and Other Plays (plays) 1967

The Cosmopolitan Girl (novel) 1974

Buchi Emecheta
Second Class Citizen (novel) 1974

The Bride Price (novel) 1976

Maria Irene Fornes
The Widow (play) 1961

Fefu and Her Friends (play) 1977

The Conduct of Life (play) 1985

Rebecca Gilman
The Land of Little Horses (play) 1992

The Glory of Living (play) 2001

Joy Harjo
She Had Some Horses (poetry) 1983

In Mad Love and War (poetry) 1990

The Woman Who Fell from the Sky (poetry) 1994

Beth Henley
Crimes of the Heart (play) 1979

The Debutante Ball (play) 1985

Gish Jen
Mona in the Promised Land (novel) 1996

Who's Irish?: And Other Stories (short stories) 1999

Erica Jong
Fruits & Vegetables (poetry) 1971

Fear of Flying (novel) 1973

Half-Lives (poetry) 1973

Any Woman's Blues (novel) 1990

Sappho's Leap (novel) 2003

Adrienne Kennedy
Funnyhouse of a Negro (play) 1962

A Movie Star Has to Star in Black and White (play) 1976

People Who Led to My Plays (autobiography) 1987

Maxine Hong Kingston
The Woman Warrior: Memoirs of a Girlhood among Ghosts (novel) 1976

China Men (nonfiction) 1980

Joy Kogawa
Obasan (novel) 1981

The Rain Ascends (novel) 1995

Audre Lorde
The Black Unicorn (poetry) 1978

Zami: A New Spelling of My Name (memoir) 1982

Anchee Min
Red Azalea (memoir) 1994

Katherine (novel) 1995

Toni Morrison
The Bluest Eye (novel) 1970

Sula (novel) 1973

Song of Solomon (novel) 1977

Beloved (novel) 1987

Bharati Mukherjee
The Tiger's Daughter (novel) 1972

The Middleman and Other Stories (short stories) 1988

The Holder of the World (short stories) 1993

Rochelle Owens
Futz (play) 1965

Chucky's Hunch (play) 1981

Sylvia Plath
The Bell Jar (novel) 1963

Ariel (poetry) 1965

Katherine Anne Porter
The Collected Stories of Katherine Anne Porter (short stories) 1965

Adrienne Rich
The Dream of a Common Language: Poems, 1974-1977 (poetry) 1978

An Atlas of the Difficult World: Poems, 1988-1991 (poetry) 1991

Dark Fields of the Republic: Poems 1991-1995 (poetry) 1995

Wendy Rose
Bone Dance: New and Selected Poems, 1965-1993 (poetry) 1994

Ntozake Shange
for colored girls who have considered suicide / when the rainbow is enuf: A Choreopoem (play) 1975

Boogie Woogie Landscapes (play) 1979

Mary Tallmountain
There is no Word for Goodbye (poetry) 1981

Amy Tan

The Joy Luck Club (novel) 1989

The Hundred Secret Senses (novel) 1995

The Bonesetter's Daughter (novel) 2001

Megan Terry

*Calm Down Mother: A Transformation Play for Three
     Women* (play) 1965

Viet Rock: A Folk War Movie (musical) 1966

Approaching Simone (play) 1970

Alice Walker

You Can't Keep a Good Woman Down (short stories)
     1981

The Color Purple (novel) 1982

Mitsuye Yamada

Camp Notes and Other Poems (poetry) 1976

Hisaye Yamamoto

Seventeen Syllables and Other Stories (short stories)
     1988

PRIMARY SOURCES

DENISE LEVERTOV (POEM DATE 1967)

SOURCE: Levertov, Denise. "Hypocrite Women." In
Poems, 1960-67. New Directions, 1967.

*The following poem by Levertov was composed in 1967,
and like many of the poet's other works, it focuses on issues of female self-definition and the complex nature of
femininity.*

"HYPOCRITE WOMEN"

Hypocrite women, how seldom we speak
of our own doubts, while dubiously
we mother man in his doubt!

And if at Mill Valley perched in the trees
the sweet rain drifting through western air
a white sweating bull of a poet told us

our cunts are ugly—why didn't we
admit we have thought so too? (And
what shame? They are not for the eye!)

No, they are dark and wrinkled and hairy,
caves of the Moon . . .   And when a
dark humming fills us, a

coldness towards life,
we are too much women to
own to such unwomanliness.

Whorishly with the psychopomp
we play and plead—and say
nothing of this later.   And our dreams,

with what frivolity we have pared them
like toenails, clipped them like ends of
split hair.

GERMAINE GREER (ESSAY DATE MAY 1970)

SOURCE: Greer, Germaine. "The Politics of Female
Sexuality, *Oz*, May 1970." In *The Madwoman's Under-
clothes: Essays in Occasional Writings,* pp. 36-7. New
York: Atlantic Monthly Press, 1986.

*In the following excerpt, originally published in 1970,
Greer reflects on the nature of female sexuality, arguing
for acceptance of the female sexual organs by women
themselves.*

From Female Energy Oz, for which I was guest editor.

One of the chief mechanisms in the suppression of female humanity is the obliteration of
female sexuality. Historically the process can be
traced in the change in the iconography of
women. In the Middle Ages women were characterized as lustful, allies of the devil weaning men
from God and noble intellectual pursuits; woman-
hatred had a virtue which is lacking from more
recent forms of stereotyping in that it allowed the
women energy, diabolical energy, but energy
nevertheless. The rise of the Protestant commercial classes brought with it a change in the
characterization of women: they became chaste
guardians of their husbands' honour, emblems of
prestige and possession. The historical process can
be observed in microcosm in the growing up of
every female child. From an unknown quantity as
an infant human being, she passes through a
sexual phase, which the Freudians describe as
masculine; her pre-adolescent sexuality is explained as an infantile stage of penis envy, which
ought, if due process is observed, to dwindle into
the passivity of the mature woman. From subject,
she declines into object, and her status as toy for
man's delectation is indefatigably illustrated in
the popular imagery of sexual intercourse, the missionary position, big boobs, suspender belts and
all the paraphernalia of pornography.

In order that women might become sex objects rather than sexual people, sex itself was

devalued. Instead of extending through all forms of communication into the 'highest pinnacle of the human spirit' (Nietzsche) it became 'a momentary itch' (Amis). Women lost spirit and were made flesh. Desire was localized in the male genital, the visible doodle, the tag of flesh that could become as hard as a fist. The interpretation of souls and bodies became the pummelling of one lump of meat by a harder lump of meat. Sexuality became as masculine a virtue as packing a good left. No one thought to object that in the sexual battle the bigger and stronger picked upon the smaller and weaker. Women like asses were made to bear. If the softer flesh was further tenderized by pummelling, the tremulous dangling thing in which the male located his sex was safe from any threat, except the anxiety which was the unavoidable result of having invested male sexuality in a lump of meat in the first place. In his efforts to allay his anxiety that his tassel might not turn into a fist when required, that it might be smaller than the man-next-door's, the male forbade comparison to his woman. From her he extracted fidelity. Fast vehicles, bombs, male bonding were called into service to allay his persistent phallic anxiety. Women lost interest in all of it, the competitive sports, the war game, the games of darts with the boys.

JAMAICA KINCAID (SHORT STORY DATE 26 JUNE 1978)

SOURCE: Kincaid, Jamaica. "Girl." In *At the Bottom of the River*, pp. 3-5. Farrar, Straus, and Giroux, Inc., 1979.

The following story, "Girl," was the first short story to be published by Kincaid. It appeared in the June 26, 1978 edition of The New Yorker, *and was eventually reissued in Kincaid's award-winning short story collection* At the Bottom of the River (1979).

Wash the white clothes on Monday and put them on the stone heap; wash the color clothes on Tuesday and put them on the clothesline to dry; don't walk barehead in the hot sun; cook pumpkin fritters in very hot sweet oil; soak your little cloths right after you take them off; when buying cotton to make yourself a nice blouse, be sure that it doesn't have gum on it, because that way it won't hold up well after a wash; soak salt fish overnight before you cook it; is it true that you sing benna in Sunday school?; always eat your food in such a way that it won't turn someone else's stomach; on Sundays try to walk like a lady and not like the slut you are so bent on becom-

ON THE SUBJECT OF...

ERICA JONG (1942-)

"If 'woman writer' ceases to be a polite but negative label, it will be due in great measure to the efforts of Erica Jong."

Reardon, Joan. "'Fear of Flying': Developing the Feminist Novel." *International Journal of Women's Studies* 1, no. 3 (May-June 1978): 306-20.

Best known for her novel *Fear of Flying* (1973), Erica Jong has received both popular and critical recognition for her frank, satirical treatment of sexuality in her works. Born in 1942, Jong grew up on the Upper West Side of New York City. She graduated from Barnard College in 1963, earned an M.A. in English literature at Columbia University in 1965, and in 1966 married Allan Jong, a Chinese-American psychiatrist. The Jongs moved to Heidelberg, Germany, where Allan served in the military until 1969, and Erica taught at the University of Maryland Overseas Division. It was while living in Germany that Jong departed from writing poetry in the formal style of William Butler Yeats, W. H. Auden, and Dylan Thomas, and began developing her own distinctive approach to treating the human condition. In her works Jong presents observations on such topics as aging, love, sex, feminism, and death, and while her treatment of these topics is often serious, her tone is largely life-affirming and humorous. It was with her poetry collection *Fruits and Vegetables* (1971) that Jong first gained critical attention, but it was with the publication of *Fear of Flying* that she received popular notice. The novel, which traces the life of Isadora Wing, a writer who travels extensively and seeks spiritual, emotional, and physical fulfillment in various relationships with men, has been characterized as a *bildungsroman* in the tradition of Henry Miller's *Tropic of Cancer*, and James Joyce's *Odyssey*.

ing; don't sing benna in Sunday school; you mustn't speak to wharf-rat boys, not even to give directions; don't eat fruits on the street—flies will follow you; *but I don't sing benna on Sundays at all and never in Sunday school*; this is how to sew on a button; this is how to make a buttonhole for the button you have just sewed on; this is how to hem a dress when you see the hem coming down and so to prevent yourself from looking like the slut I know you are so bent on becoming; this is how you iron your father's khaki shirt so that it doesn't have a crease; this is how you iron your father's khaki pants so they don't have a crease; this is how you grow okra—far from the house, because okra tree harbors red ants; when you are growing dasheen, make sure it gets plenty of water or else it makes your throat itch when you are eating it; this is how you sweep a corner; this is how you sweep a whole house; this is how you sweep a yard; this is how you smile to someone you don't like too much; this is how you smile to someone you don't like at all; this is how you smile to someone you like completely; this is how you set a table for tea; this is how you set a table for dinner; this is how you set a table for dinner with an important guest; this is how you set a table for lunch; this is how you set a table for breakfast; this is how to behave in the presence of men who don't know you very well, and this way they won't recognize immediately the slut I have warned you against becoming; be sure to wash every day, even if it is with your own spit; don't squat down to play marbles—you are not a boy, you know; don't pick people's flowers—you might catch something; don't throw stones at blackbirds, because it might not be a blackbird at all; this is how to make a bread pudding; this is how to make doukona, this is how to make pepper pot; this is how to make a good medicine for a cold; this is how to make a good medicine to throw away a child before it even becomes a child; this is how to catch a fish; this is how to throw back a fish you don't like, and that way something bad won't fall on you; this is how to bully a man; this is how a man bullies you; this is how to love a man, and if this doesn't work there are other ways, and if they don't work don't feel too bad about giving up; this is how to spit up in the air if you feel like it, and this is how to move quick so that it doesn't fall on you; this is how to make ends meet; always squeeze bread to make sure it's fresh; *but what if the baker won't let me feel the bread?*; you mean to say that after all you are really going to be the kind of woman who the baker won't let near the bread?

AUDRE LORDE (POEM DATE 1978)

SOURCE: Lorde, Audre. "From the House of Yemanjá." In *The Black Unicorn.* Crossing Press, 1978.

In the following poem, Lorde, who described herself as "a black lesbian feminist writer poet," uses a Western Nigerian legend about the goddess of the oceans to reflect upon the role of a mother.

"FROM THE HOUSE OF YEMANJÁ"[1]

My mother had two faces and a frying pot
where she cooked up her daughters
into girls
before she fixed our dinner.
My mother had two faces
and a broken pot
where she hid out a perfect daughter
who was not me
I am the sun and moon and forever hungry
for her eyes.

I bear two women upon my back
one dark and rich and hidden
in the ivory hungers of the other
mother
pale as a witch
yet steady and familiar
brings me bread and terror
in my sleep
her breasts are huge exciting anchors
in the midnight storm.

All this has been
before
in my mother's bed
time has no sense
I have no brothers
and my sisters are cruel.

Mother I need
mother I need
mother I need your blackness now
as the august earth needs rain.

I am
the sun and moon and forever hungry
the sharpened edge
where day and night shall meet
and not be
one.

Note

1. Mother of the other *Orisha* [goddesses and gods of the Yoruba people of Western Nigeria], Yemanjá is also the goddess of oceans. Rivers are said to flow from her breasts. One legend has it that a son tried to rape her. She fled until she collapsed, and from her breasts, the rivers flowed. Another legend says that a husband insulted Yemanjá's long breasts, and when she fled with her pots he knocked her down. From her breasts flowed the rivers, and from her body then sprang forth

all the other *Orisha*. River-smooth stones are Yeman-
já's symbol, and the sea is sacred to her followers.
Those who please her are blessed with many children
[Lorde's note].

LESLIE MARMON SILKO (SHORT STORY DATE 1981)

SOURCE: Silko, Leslie Marmon. "Yellow Woman." In
Storyteller, pp. 54-62. New York: Seaver Books, 1981.

*A Native American from Laguna Pueblo, Silko often
retells legends derived from the oral folklore traditions of
her own people. The following excerpt, from the short
story* Yellow Woman, *is an example of Silko's use of
these traditions in her own writing.*

I

My thigh clung to his with dampness, and I
watched the sun rising up through the tamaracks
and willows. The small brown water birds came to
the river and hopped across the mud, leaving
brown scratches in the alkali-white crust. They
bathed in the river silently. I could hear the water,
almost at our feet where the narrow fast channel
bubbled and washed green ragged moss and fern
leaves. I looked at him beside me, rolled in the
red blanket on the white river sand. I cleaned the
sand out of the cracks between my toes, squinting
because the sun was above the willow trees. I
looked at him for the last time, sleeping on the
white river sand.

I felt hungry and followed the river south the
way we had come the afternoon before, following
our footprints that were already blurred by lizard
tracks and bug trails. The horses were still lying
down, and the black one whinnied when he saw
me but he did not get up—maybe it was because
the corral was made out of thick cedar branches
and the horses had not yet felt the sun like I had.
I tried to look beyond the pale red mesas to the
pueblo. I knew it was there, even if I could not see
it, on the sandrock hill above the river, the same
river that moved past me now and had reflected
the moon last night.

The horse felt warm underneath me. He shook
his head and pawed the sand. The bay whinnied
and leaned against the gate trying to follow, and I
remembered him asleep in the red blanket beside
the river. I slid off the horse and tied him close to
the other horse. I walked north with the river
again, and the white sand broke loose in footprints
over footprints.

"Wake up."

He moved in the blanket and turned his face
to me with his eyes still closed. I knelt down to
touch him.

"I'm leaving."

He smiled now, eyes still closed. "You are coming with me, remember?" He sat up now with his
bare dark chest and belly in the sun.

"Where?"

"To my place."

"And will I come back?"

He pulled his pants on. I walked away from him, feeling him behind me and smelling the willows.

"Yellow Woman," he said.

I turned to face him. "Who are you?" I asked.

He laughed and knelt on the low, sandy bank, washing his face in the river. "Last night you guessed my name, and you knew why I had come."

I stared past him at the shallow moving water and tried to remember the night, but I could only see the moon in the water and remember his warmth around me.

"But I only said that you were him and that I was Yellow Woman—I'm not really her—I have my own name and I come from the pueblo on the other side of the mesa. Your name is Silva and you are a stranger I met by the river yesterday afternoon."

He laughed softly. "What happened yesterday has nothing to do with what you will do today, Yellow Woman."

"I know—that's what I'm saying—the old stories about the ka'tsina spirit and Yellow Woman can't mean us."

My old grandpa liked to tell those stories best. There is one about Badger and Coyote who went hunting and were gone all day, and when the sun was going down they found a house. There was a girl living there alone, and she had light hair and eyes and she told them that they could sleep with her. Coyote wanted to be with her all night so he sent Badger into a prairie-dog hole, telling him he thought he saw something in it. As soon as Badger crawled in, Coyote blocked up the entrance with rocks and hurried back to Yellow Woman.

"Come here," he said gently.

He touched my neck and I moved close to him to feel his breathing and to hear his heart. I was wondering if Yellow Woman had known who she was—if she knew that she would become part of the stories. Maybe she'd had another name that her husband and relatives called her so that only the ka'tsina from the north and the storytellers would know her as Yellow Woman. But I didn't go on; I felt him all around me, pushing me down into the white river sand.

Yellow Woman went away with the spirit from the north and lived with him and his relatives.

She was gone for a long time, but then one day she came back and she brought twin boys.

"Do you know the story?"

"What story?" He smiled and pulled me close to him as he said this. I was afraid lying there on the red blanket. All I could know was the way he felt, warm, damp, his body beside me. This is the way it happens in the stories, I was thinking, with no thought beyond the moment she meets the ka'tsina spirit and they go.

"I don't have to go. What they tell in stories was real only then, back in time immemorial, like they say."

He stood up and pointed at my clothes tangled in the blanket. "Let's go," he said.

I walked beside him, breathing hard because he walked fast, his hand around my wrist. I had stopped trying to pull away from him, because his hand felt cool and the sun was high, drying the river bed into alkali. I will see someone, eventually I will see someone, and then I will be certain that he is only a man—some man from nearby—and I will be sure that I am not Yellow Woman. Because she is from out of time past and I live now and I've been to school and there are highways and pickup trucks that Yellow Woman never saw.

It was an easy ride north on horseback. I watched the change from the cottonwood trees along the river to the junipers that brushed past us in the foothills, and finally there were only piñons, and when I looked up at the rim of the mountain plateau I could see pine trees growing on the edge. Once I stopped to look down, but the pale sandstone had disappeared and the river was gone and the dark lava hills were all around. He touched my hand, not speaking, but always singing softly a mountain song and looking into my eyes.

I felt hungry and wondered what they were doing at home now—my mother, my grandmother, my husband, and the baby. Cooking breakfast, saying "Where did she go?—maybe kidnapped," and Al going to the tribal police with the details: "She went walking along the river."

The house was made with black lava rock and red mud. It was high above the spreading miles of arroyos and long mesas. I smelled a mountain smell of pitch and buck brush. I stood there beside the black horse, looking down on the small, dim country we had passed, and I shivered.

"Yellow Woman, come inside where it's warm."

II

He lit a fire in the stove. It was an old stove with a round belly and an enamel coffeepot on top. There was only the stove, some faded Navajo blankets, and a bedroll and cardboard box. The floor was made of smooth adobe plaster, and there was one small window facing east. He pointed at the box.

"There's some potatoes and the frying pan." He sat on the floor with his arms around his knees pulling them close to his chest and he watched me fry the potatoes, I didn't mind him watching me because he was always watching me—he had been watching me since I came upon him sitting on the river bank trimming leaves from a willow twig with his knife. We ate from the pan and he wiped the grease from his fingers on his Levis.

"Have you brought women here before?" He smiled and kept chewing, so I said, "Do you always use the same tricks?"

"What tricks?" He looked at me like he didn't understand.

"The story about being a ka'tsina from the mountains. The story about Yellow Woman."

Silva was silent; his face was calm.

"I don't believe it. Those stories couldn't happen now," I said.

He shook his head and said softly, "But someday they will talk about us, and they will say, 'Those two lived long ago when things like that happened.'"

He stood up and went out. I ate the rest of the potatoes and thought about things—about the noise the stove was making and the sound of the mountain wind outside. I remembered yesterday and the day before, and then I went outside.

I walked past the corral to the edge where the narrow trail cut through the black rim rock. I was standing in the sky with nothing around me but the wind that came down from the blue mountain peak behind me. I could see faint mountain images in the distance miles across the vast spread of mesas and valleys and plains. I wondered who was over there to feel the mountain wind on those sheer blue edges—who walks on the pine needles in those blue mountains.

"Can you see the pueblo?" Silva was standing behind me.

I shook my head. "We're too far away."

"From here I can see the world." He stepped out on the edge. "The Navajo reservation begins over there." He pointed to the east. "The Pueblo boundaries are over here." He looked below us to the south, where the narrow trail seemed to come from. "The Texans have their ranches over there, starting with that valley, the Concho Valley. The Mexicans run some cattle over there too."

"Do you ever work for them?"

"I steal from them," Silva answered. The sun was dropping behind us and shadows were filling the land below. I turned away from the edge that dropped forever into the valleys below.

"I'm cold," I said; "I'm going inside." I started wondering about this man who could speak the Pueblo language so well but who lived on a mountain and rustled cattle. I decided that this man Silva must be Navajo, because Pueblo men didn't do things like that.

"You must be a Navajo."

Silva shook his head gently. "Little Yellow Woman," he said, "you never give up, do you? I have told you who I am. The Navajo people know me, too." He knelt down and unrolled the bedroll and spread the extra blankets out on a piece of canvas. The sun was down, and the only light in the house came from outside—the dim orange light from sundown.

I stood there and waited for him to crawl under the blankets.

"What are you waiting for?" he said, and I lay down beside him. He undressed me slowly like the night before beside the river—kissing my face gently and running his hands up and down my belly and legs. He took off my pants and then he laughed.

"Why are you laughing?"

"You are breathing so hard."

I pulled away from him and turned my back to him.

He pulled me around and pinned me down with his arms and chest. "You don't understand, do you, little Yellow Woman? You will do what I want."

And again he was all around me with his skin slippery against mine, and I was afraid because I understood that his strength could hurt me. I lay underneath him and I knew that he could destroy me. But later, while he slept beside me, I touched his face and I had a feeling—the kind of feeling for him that overcame me that morning along the river. I kissed him on the forehead and he reached out for me.

When I woke up in the morning he was gone. It gave me a strange feeling because for a long time I sat there on the blankets and looked around the little house for some object of his—some proof that he had been there or maybe that he was coming back. Only the blankets and the cardboard box remained. The .30-30 that had been leaning in the corner was gone, and so was the knife I had used the night before. He was gone, and I had my chance to go now. But first I had to eat, because I knew it would be a long walk home.

I found some dried apricots in the cardboard box, and I sat down on a rock at the edge of the plateau rim. There was no wind and the sun warmed me. I was surrounded by silence. I drowsed with apricots in my mouth, and I didn't believe that there were highways or railroads or cattle to steal.

When I woke up, I stared down at my feet in the black mountain dirt. Little black ants were swarming over the pine needles around my foot. They must have smelled the apricots. I thought about my family far below me. They would be wondering about me, because this had never happened to me before. The tribal police would file a report. But if old Grandpa weren't dead he would tell them what happened—he would laugh and say, "Stolen by a ka'tsina, a mountain spirit. She'll come home—they usually do." There are enough of them to handle things. My mother and grandmother will raise the baby like they raised me. Al will find someone else, and they will go on like before, except that there will be a story about the day I disappeared while I was walking along the river. Silva had come for me; he said he had. I did not decide to go. I just went. Moonflowers blossom in the sand hills before dawn, just as I followed him. That's what I was thinking as I wandered along the trail through the pine trees.

It was noon when I got back. When I saw the stone house I remembered that I had meant to go home. But that didn't seem important any more, maybe because there were little blue flowers growing in the meadow behind the stone house and the gray squirrels were playing in the pines next to the house. The horses were standing in the corral, and there was a beef carcass hanging on the shady side of a big pine in front of the house. Flies buzzed around the clotted blood that hung from the carcass. Silva was washing his hands in a bucket full of water. He must have heard me coming because he spoke to me without turning to face me.

"I've been waiting for you."

"I went walking in the big pine trees."

I looked into the bucket full of bloody water with brown-and-white animal hairs floating in it. Silva stood there letting his hands drip, examining me intently.

"Are you coming with me?"

"Where?" I asked him.

"To sell the meat in Marquez."

"If you're sure it's O.K."

"I wouldn't ask you if it wasn't," he answered.

He sloshed the water around in the bucket before he dumped it out and set the bucket upside down near the door. I followed him to the corral and watched him saddle the horses. Even beside the horses he looked tall, and I asked him again if he wasn't Navajo. He didn't say anything; he just shook his head and kept cinching up the saddle.

"But Navajos are tall."

"Get on the horse," he said, "and let's go."

The last thing he did before we started down the steep trail was to grab the .30-30 from the corner. He slid the rifle into the scabbard that hung from his saddle.

"Do they ever try to catch you?" I asked.

"They don't know who I am."

"Then why did you bring the rifle?"

"Because we are going to Marquez where the Mexicans live."

III

The trail leveled out on a narrow ridge that was steep on both sides like an animal spine. On one side I could see where the trail went around the rocky gray hills and disappeared into the southeast where the pale sandrock mesas stood in the distance near my home. On the other side was a trail that went west, and as I looked far into the distance I thought I saw the little town. But Silva said no, that I was looking in the wrong place, that I just thought I saw houses. After that I quit looking off into the distance; it was hot and the wildflowers were closing up their deep-yellow petals. Only the waxy cactus flowers bloomed in the bright sun, and I saw every color that a cactus blossom can be; the white ones and the red ones were still buds, but the purple and the yellow were blossoms, open full and the most beautiful of all.

Silva saw him before I did. The white man was riding a big gray horse, coming up the trail toward us. He was traveling fast and the gray horse's feet sent rocks rolling off the trail into the dry tumbleweeds. Silva motioned for me to stop and we watched the white man. He didn't see us right away, but finally his horse whinnied at our horses and he stopped. He looked at us briefly before he loped the gray horse across the three hundred yards that separated us. He stopped his horse in front of Silva, and his young fat face was shadowed by the brim of his hat. He didn't look mad, but his small, pale eyes moved from the blood-soaked gunny sacks hanging from my saddle to Silva's face and then back to my face.

"Where did you get the fresh meat?" the white man asked.

"I've been hunting," Silva said, and when he shifted his weight in the saddle the leather creaked.

"The hell you have, Indian. You've been rustling cattle. We've been looking for the thief for a long time."

The rancher was fat, and sweat began to soak through his white cowboy shirt and the wet cloth stuck to the thick rolls of belly fat. He almost seemed to be panting from the exertion of talking, and he smelled rancid, maybe because Silva scared him.

Silva turned to me and smiled. "Go back up the mountain, Yellow Woman."

The white man got angry when he heard Silva speak in a language he couldn't understand. "Don't try anything, Indian. Just keep riding to Marquez. We'll call the state police from there."

The rancher must have been unarmed because he was very frightened and if he had a gun he would have pulled it out then. I turned my horse around and the rancher yelled, "Stop!" I looked at Silva for an instant and there was something ancient and dark—something I could feel in my stomach—in his eyes, and when I glanced at his hand I saw his finger on the trigger of the .30-30 that was still in the saddle scabbard. I slapped my horse across the flank and the sacks of raw meat swung against my knees as the horse leaped up the trail. It was hard to keep my balance, and once I thought I felt the saddle slipping backward; it was because of this that I could not look back.

I didn't stop until I reached the ridge where the trail forked. The horse was breathing deep gasps and there was a dark film of sweat on its neck. I looked down in the direction I had come from, but I couldn't see the place. I waited. The wind came up and pushed warm air past me. I looked up at the sky, pale blue and full of thin clouds and fading vapor trails left by jets.

I think four shots were fired—I remember hearing four hollow explosions that reminded me of deer hunting. There could have been more shots after that, but I couldn't have heard them because my horse was running again and the loose rocks were making too much noise as they scattered around his feet.

Horses have a hard time running downhill, but I went that way instead of uphill to the mountain because I thought it was safer. I felt better with the horse running southeast past the round gray hills that were covered with cedar trees and black lava rock. When I got to the plain in the distance I could see the dark green patches of tamaracks that grew along the river; and beyond the river I could see the beginning of the pale sandrock mesas. I stopped the horse and looked back to see if anyone was coming; then I got off the horse and turned the horse around, wondering if it would go back to its corral under the pines on the mountain. It looked back at me for a moment and then plucked a mouthful of green tumbleweeds before it trotted back up the trail with its ears pointed forward, carrying its head daintily to one side to avoid stepping on the dragging reins. When the horse disappeared over the last hill, the gunny sacks full of meat were still swinging and bouncing.

IV

I walked toward the river on a wood-hauler's road that I knew would eventually lead to the paved road. I was thinking about waiting beside the road for someone to drive by, but by the time I got to the pavement I had decided it wasn't very far to walk if I followed the river back the way Silva and I had come.

The river water tasted good, and I sat in the shade under a cluster of silvery willows. I thought about Silva, and I felt sad at leaving him; still, there was something strange about him, and I tried to figure it out all the way back home.

I came back to the place on the river bank where he had been sitting the first time I saw him. The green willow leaves that he had trimmed from the branch were still lying there, wilted in the sand. I saw the leaves and I wanted to go back to him—to kiss him and to touch him—but the mountains were too far away now. And I told myself, because I believe it, he will come back sometime and be waiting again by the river.

English author Angela Carter (1940-1992).

I followed the path up from the river into the village. The sun was getting low, and I could smell supper cooking when I got to the screen door of my house. I could hear their voices inside—my mother was telling my grandmother how to fix the Jell-O and my husband, Al, was playing with the baby. I decided to tell them that some Navajo had kidnapped me, but I was sorry that old Grandpa wasn't alive to hear my story because it was the Yellow Woman stories he liked to tell best.

BHARATI MUKHERJEE (SHORT STORY DATE 1988)

SOURCE: Mukherjee, Bharati. "The Management of Grief." In *The Middleman and Other Stories.* Canada: Penguin Books, 1988.

Born in India, Mukherjee, who now resides in Canada, writes stories that often reflect on issues significant to people who have migrated from one culture to another. In the following excerpt, Mukherjee captures the tragic consequences of an airline crash on a set of neighbors and friends as they struggle to cope with their loss.

Four days later, I find Kusum squatting on a rock overlooking a bay in Ireland. It isn't a big rock, but it juts sharply out over water. This is as close as we'll ever get to them. June breezes balloon out her sari and unpin her knee-length hair.

She has the bewildered look of a sea creature whom the tides have stranded.

It's been one hundred hours since Kusum came stumbling and screaming across my lawn. Waiting around the hospital, we've heard many stories. The police, the diplomats, they tell us things thinking that we're strong, that knowledge is helpful to the grieving, and maybe it is. Some, I know, prefer ignorance, or their own versions. The plane broke into two, they say. Unconsciousness was instantaneous. No one suffered. My boys must have just finished their breakfasts. They loved eating on planes, they loved the smallness of plates, knives, and forks. Last year they saved the airline salt and pepper shakers. Half an hour more and they would have made it to Heathrow.

Kusum says that we can't escape our fate. She says that all those people—our husbands, my boys, her girl with the nightingale voice, all those Hindus, Christians, Sikhs, Muslims, Parsis, and atheists on that plane—were fated to die together off this beautiful bay. She learned this from a swami in Toronto.

I have my Valium.

Six of us "relatives"—two widows and four widowers—choose to spend the day today by the waters instead of sitting in a hospital room and scanning photographs of the dead. That's what they call us now: relatives. I've looked through twenty-seven photos in two days. They're very kind to us, the Irish are very understanding. Sometimes understanding means freeing a tourist bus for this trip to the bay, so we can pretend to spy our loved ones through the glassiness of waves or in sun-speckled cloud shapes.

I could die here, too, and be content.

"What is that, out there?" She's standing and flapping her hands and for a moment I see a head shape bobbing in the waves. She's standing in the water, I, on the boulder. The tide is low, and a round, black, head-sized rock has just risen from the waves. She returns, her sari end dripping and ruined and her face is a twisted remnant of hope, the way mine was a hundred hours ago, still laughing but inwardly knowing that nothing but the ultimate tragedy could bring two women together at six o'clock on a Sunday morning. I watch her face sag into blankness.

"That water felt warm, Shaila," she says at length.

"You can't," I say. "We have to wait for our turn to come."

I haven't eaten in four days, haven't brushed my teeth.

"I know," she says. "I tell myself I have no right to grieve. They are in a better place than we are. My swami says I should be thrilled for them. My swami says depression is a sign of our selfishness."

Maybe I'm selfish. Selfishly I break away from Kusum and run, sandals slapping against stones, to the water's edge. What if my boys aren't lying pinned under the debris? What if they aren't stuck a mile below that innocent blue chop? What if, given the strong currents. . . .

Now I've ruined my sari, one of my best. Kusum has joined me, knee-deep in water that feels to me like a swimming pool. I could settle in the water, and my husband would take my hand and the boys would slap water in my face just to see me scream.

"Do you remember what good swimmers my boys were, Kusum?"

"I saw the medals," she says.

One of the widowers, Dr. Ranganathan from Montreal, walks out to us, carrying his shoes in one hand. He's an electrical engineer. Someone at the hotel mentioned his work is famous around the world, something about the place where physics and electricity come together. He has lost a huge family, something indescribable. "With some luck," Dr. Ranganathan suggests to me, "a good swimmer could make it safely to some island. It is quite possible that there may be many, many microscopic islets scattered around."

"You're not just saying that?" I tell Dr. Ranganathan about Vinod, my elder son. Last year he took diving as well.

"It's a parent's duty to hope," he says. "It is foolish to rule out possibilities that have not been tested. I myself have not surrendered hope."

Kusum is sobbing once again. "Dear lady," he says, laying his free hand on her arm, and she calms down.

"Vinod is how old?" he asks me. He's very careful, as we all are. *Is,* not was.

"Fourteen. Yesterday he was fourteen. His father and uncle were going to take him down to the Taj and give him a big birthday party. I couldn't go with them because I couldn't get two weeks off from my stupid job in June." I process bills for a travel agent. June is a big travel month.

Dr. Ranganathan whips the pockets of his suit jacket inside out. Squashed roses, in darkening

ON THE SUBJECT OF...

ANGELA CARTER (1940-1992)

Angela Carter's career spanned less than three decades but covered many genres, including novels, short stories, screenplays, and nonfiction. Her writing is noted for its vivid prose, Gothic settings, eroticism, violence, use of fantasy and fairy tales, and surrealism that combine to form dream worlds influenced by Freudian theory and futuristic fiction. Two of her best known novels are *Shadow Dance* (1966) and *Magic Toyshop* (1967). As an essayist, Carter's most influential work is *The Sadeian Woman and the Ideology of Pornography* (1979), an exploration of the Marquis de Sade's depiction of women and their modern-day counterparts. As an editor and translator, she produced several collections of fairy tales, and as a fiction writer, she wrote fairy tales that were mired in her own theories of sexual dominance and violence. Carter won many awards for her writing, including the James Tait Black Memorial Award for her novel *Nights at the Circus* (1984). By the time of her death from cancer in 1992, Carter was hailed as one of Britain's foremost writers.

shades of pink, float on the water. He tore the roses off creepers in somebody's garden. He didn't ask anyone if he could pluck the roses, but now there's been an article about it in the local papers. When you see an Indian person, it says, please give him or her flowers.

"A strong youth of fourteen," he says, "can very likely pull to safety a younger one."

My sons, though four years apart, were very close. Vinod wouldn't let Mithun drown. *Electrical engineering,* I think, foolishly perhaps: this man knows important secrets of the universe, things closed to me. Relief spins me lightheaded. No wonder my boys' photographs haven't turned up in the gallery of photos of the recovered dead. "Such pretty roses," I say.

"My wife loved pink roses. Every Friday I had to bring a bunch home. I used to say, Why? After twenty odd years of marriage you're still needing proof positive of my love?" He has identified his wife and three of his children. Then others from Montreal, the lucky ones, intact families with no survivors. He chuckles as he wades back to shore. Then he swings around to ask me a question. "Mrs. Bhave, you are wanting to throw in some roses for your loved ones? I have two big ones left."

But I have other things to float: Vinod's pocket calculator; a half-painted model B-52 for my Mithun. They'd want them on their island. And for my husband? For him I let fall into the calm, glassy waters a poem I wrote in the hospital yesterday. Finally he'll know my feelings for him.

"Don't tumble, the rocks are slippery," Dr. Ranganathan cautions. He holds out a hand for me to grab.

Then it's time to get back on the bus, time to rush back to our waiting posts on hospital benches. . . .

EVE ENSLER (PLAY DATE 1998)

SOURCE: Ensler, Eve. "I Was Twelve. My Mother Slapped Me." In *The Vagina Monologues: The V-Day Edition*, pp. 35-8. New York: Villard, 2001.

The following excerpt is from Eve Ensler's The Vagina Monologues, *originally published in 1998. The work has also been enacted by various performers on stage, including Ensler, and is viewed as both an exploration and celebration of women's unique experiences and identity.*

I was Twelve. My Mother Slapped me.

Second grade, seven years old, my brother was talking about periods. I didn't like the way he was laughing.

I went to my mother. "What's a period?" I said. "It's punctuation," she said. "You put it at the end of a sentence."

My father brought me a card: "To my little girl who isn't so little anymore."

I was terrified. My mother showed me the thick sanitary napkins. I was to bring the used ones to the can under the kitchen sink.

I remember being one of the last. I was thirteen.

We all wanted it to come.

I was so afraid. I started putting the used pads in brown paper bags in the dark storage places under the roof.

Eighth grade. My mother said, "Oh, that's nice."

In junior high—brown drips before it came. Coincided with a little hair under my arms, which grew unevenly: one armpit had hair, the other didn't.

I was sixteen, sort of scared.

My mother gave me codeine. We had bunk beds. I went down and lay there. My mother was so uncomfortable.

One night, I came home late and snuck into bed without turning on any lights. My mother had found the used pads and put them between the sheets of my bed.

I was twelve years old, still in my underpants. Hadn't gotten dressed. Looked down on the staircase. There it was.

Looked down and I saw blood.

Seventh grade; my mother sort of noticed my underwear. Then she gave me plastic diapers.

My mom was very warm—"Let's get you a pad."

My friend Marcia, they celebrated when she got hers. They had dinner for her.

We all wanted our period.

We all wanted it *now*.

Thirteen years old. It was before Kotex. Had to watch your dress. I was black and poor. Blood on the back of my dress in church. Didn't show, but I was guilty.

I was ten and a half. No preparation. Brown gunk on my underpants.

She showed me how to put in a tampon. Only got in halfway.

I associated my period with inexplicable phenomena.

My mother told me I had to use a rag. My mother said no to tampons. You couldn't put anything in your sugar dish.

Wore wads of cotton. Told my mother. She gave me Elizabeth Taylor paper dolls.

Fifteen years old. My mother said, "Mazel tov." She slapped me in the face. Didn't know if it was a good thing or a bad thing.

My period, like cake mix before it's baked. Indians sat on moss for five days. Wish I were Native American.

I was fifteen and I'd been hoping to get it. I was tall and I kept growing.

When I saw white girls in the gym with tampons, I thought they were bad girls.

Saw little red drops on the pink tiles. I said, "Yeah."

My mom was glad for me.

Used OB and liked putting my fingers up there.

Eleven years old, wearing white pants. Blood started to come out.

SUSAN BROWNMILLER (ESSAY DATE 1999)

SOURCE: Brownmiller, Susan. "Feminist Author." In *In Our Time: Memoir of a Revolution*, pp. 251-53. New York: The Dial Press, 1999.

In the following excerpt, Brownmiller recalls experiences she had with the media regarding the publication of Against Our Will, *her groundbreaking book about rape and its consequences.*

I have to admit that my abilities as a media communicator were imperfect. I lacked a certain humility and betrayed too much impatience, interpreted as arrogance, before a live studio audience. The person who brought me down on *The Phil Donahue Show* was Eldridge Cleaver, a very adept communicator indeed.[1] Cleaver's unabashed confession in *Soul on Ice* that he had vented his rage against white men by raping white women, practicing first on black women to develop his confidence, had made him an obvious feminist target. Naturally I had given him what-for in *Against Our Will*. Even Angela Davis in her radio program was not about to defend Eldridge Cleaver, who had become anathema to black radicals during his exile for many acts having nothing to do with rape. Cleaver had undergone a strange transformation in Algiers and Paris after he'd been thrown out of the Black Panther Party by the Huey Newton faction. In place of "Power to the People," he began promoting codpiece trousers of his own design as a masculine identity statement. (Cleaver's spiritual conversion took root and flowered after his unsuccessful foray into men's fashion.) Returning to the States to square away some earlier criminal charges, the former Panther volunteered to reporters that he had been tremendously affected by *Against Our Will*. Quick as a flash, the Donahue producers arranged a two-part program for Cleaver and me, inviting the La Leche League of Green Bay, Wisconsin, to fill the studio seats.

"Uh-oh, white women in polyester, they're your people," Cleaver muttered as we took our places on the *Donahue* set. Neither of us figured that the militant breast-feeders might be more suspicious of a radical feminist than of a former Black Panther wanting to recant about rape. Things started off well enough. I asked Cleaver to apologize to black women. He did. Then I asked him to apologize to white women. He did that as well. Penitence was an unaccustomed role for the irrepressible showman. Midway through the program the old Eldridge of the street smarts reasserted himself. He started playing to the crowd.

"Aww, you know what those young girls are like," he teased with a big grin. "There's a word for it—I can't say it here but I know you all know it. C., uh, T." The audience tittered. I tried to bring them back. Sensing his advantage, Cleaver leaped from his chair. "Damn, woman, you won't let a man speak!"

Cheers and applause. It was all over for me. The La Lechers went for the kill. "Have *you* been raped? What makes *you* an expert?" one of them taunted.

We had a postmortem after the show. Donahue was devastated. His producers were devastated. I was devastated. So, curiously enough, was Eldridge Cleaver. As he packed his suit into a garment bag for his next public appearance, he looked at me gravely and said, "Don't make the mistake I made. Don't get too far ahead of the people."

By late 1976, a moment in time when *Against Our Will* was reaching bookstores in its paperback edition and I was meeting Cleaver on *Donahue*, four hundred rape crisis centers were in place around the country.[2] Few of the centers, however, bore more than a faint resemblance to the original radical feminist model run by a volunteer collective of movement women. Professional social workers and psychologists had moved into the field, and even in cities where they hadn't, most of the centers had applied for and received federal funding, either through the LEAA (Law Enforcement Assistance Administration) or the NIMH (National Institute of Mental Health). The newly available public monies, a tribute to the antirape movement's success, acted to turn the centers into pure service and counseling organizations with paid staffs and conventional structures. With amazing speed, the rape crisis centers became *part* of the system, not a radical political force in opposition to the system. I witnessed the evolution firsthand while I was on the road with my book.

Changes in the law took place just as swiftly. In one year, 1975, thirty states overhauled their rape laws to make them more equitable to victims. Between 1970, when the feminist movement first

ON THE SUBJECT OF...

GRACE PALEY (1922-)

Over four decades Paley has published only forty-five short stories, but these works place her at the forefront of American short story writers. The world of Paley's fiction is intensely local and socially conscious, centering primarily upon a few blocks in Manhattan's Greenwich Village where she lived, raised her children, and participated in various political movements, organizations, and demonstrations during the 1960s and 1970s. Paley's fiction vividly chronicles aspects of female experience in the United States from approximately 1950 to 1989. Paley was named the first official New York State writer in 1989. Her 1994 *The Collected Stories* was a National Book Award nominee and Pulitzer Prize finalist. As adolescents Paley's parents had participated in the Socialist movement in Russia and were imprisoned for these activities. When freed, they fled to the United States with their family, living in the Bronx and working at menial jobs so that Paley's father could attend medical school. Her father became a physician in the neighborhood and conducted his practice from their home. To her family's dismay, Paley neither completed a college degree nor embarked on any kind of professional career. She attended college briefly, married Jess Paley at age nineteen, and relocated to Greenwich Village. She had two children with Paley and spent her time as a mother, housewife, occasional clerical worker, and emerging political activist, before she quietly began writing in the early 1950s. Her first story collection, *The Little Disturbances of Man* (1959) garnered such critical acclaim that Paley was offered a teaching post at Columbia University, followed by a Guggenheim fellowship in fiction in 1961 and two grants, one from the National Council on the Arts and another from the National Institute of Arts and Letters, in 1970. In the years between her publications, Paley has received numerous honors and has been active in various movements and organizations, including playing an instrumental role in the establishment of a women's committee within PEN.

started to talk about rape, and 1979, when the militance had receded, every state in the union went through a serious reevaluation of its rape codes and made significant adjustments.[3] Hospital procedures and police attitudes were transformed as well. The revolution in thinking about rape was profound. I am very proud to have been part of it, along with thousands of others who did not write best-selling books. . . .

Notes

1. Eldridge Cleaver on *Donahue*: The programs were broadcast in Oct. 1976.

2. Four hundred rape crisis centers: Janet C. Gornick and David S. Meyer, "Changing Political Opportunity: The Anti-Rape Movement and Public Policy," *Journal of Policy History*, Vol. 10, No. 4, 1998.

3. Changes in state laws: Gornick and Meyer.

OVERVIEWS

ELAINE SHOWALTER (ESSAY DATE 1973)

SOURCE: Showalter, Elaine. "Killing the Angel in the House: The Autonomy of Women Writers." *Antioch Review* 32, no. 3 (1973): 339-53.

In the following essay, Showalter reflects on the growth of writing from a feminist perspective, focusing on women's issues and emotional expression in women's writing in the twentieth century, briefly discussing the works of various authors, including Virginia Woolf, Mary McCarthy, Sylvia Plath, Erica Jong, and Elizabeth Sargent.

Killing the Angel in the House was part of the occupation of a woman writer.

—Virginia Woolf

In a paper called "Professions for Women," read to the Women's Service League in 1931, Virginia Woolf recalled two crises of her professional life: fighting off the spectre of Victorian respectability she ironically named the Angel in the House (after the self-sacrificing heroine of Coventry Patmore's popular verse-novel); and struggling to find the courage to "tell the truth about my own experiences as a body." In the first battle she thought she had won; the second, she thought no woman had ever won. The two battles are, of course, part of the same continuous war for artistic autonomy which women writers have fought since they first picked up the pen.

Woolf visualized the oppressive phantom as a graceful young woman, the spirit of Victorian womanhood, who hovered over her as she wrote, and whispered, "Be sympathetic, be tender; flatter; deceive; use all the arts and wiles of our sex. Never let anybody guess that you have a mind of your own. Above all, be pure." Yet this exemplary female had always been a male ideal rather than a living woman. This jealous guardian, forbidding wrath or wit or independence, sounds very much, in fact, like an agent of Leslie Stephen, Virginia Woolf's father, who alternately encouraged her to write, and insisted on her adherence to strict standards of womanly conduct. With his death in 1904, she was freed both from the requirements of keeping his house, and from the need to please him. She recognized that either of these demands would have destroyed her art; in her diary many years later she noted: "His life would have entirely ended mine. What would have happened? No writing, no books;—inconceivable. . . ." She felt that her imagination was liberated by his death, and also that she had managed to kill the Angel in the House.

Yet she knew that within her lay a rich hoard of feminine experience, locked and inaccessible; remembering herself as a young girl, she said in "Professions for Women":

> . . . she had thought of something, something about the body, about the passions, which it was unfitting for her as a woman to say. Men, her reason told her, would be shocked. The consciousness of what men will say of a woman who speaks the truth about her passions had roused her from her artist's state of unconsciousness. . . . For though men sensibly allow themselves great freedom in these respects, I doubt that they realize or control the extreme severity with which they condemn such freedom in women.

As this statement suggests, Virginia Woolf consciously refrained from writing about her own sexuality. The absence of sex in her writings may be explained away, or defended, or even made a virtue, as a sign of her lofty standards of health, normalcy, and refinement; but her reticence is in fact a renunciation. In her novels, sexual passion becomes a masculine property, comprehended by women in moments of empathy rather than experience, as in *Mrs. Dalloway* when Clarissa kisses Sally Sewall and experiences with brief intensity what men feel. Like other male properties—power, hierarchy, aggression, and anger—passion, we feel, is one Virginia Woolf is happy to renounce.

Nagged by the shade of her father, and conscious of the power of male disapproval, Virginia Woolf developed a literary theory which had the effect of neutralizing her own conflict between the desire to present a woman's whole experience, and the fear of such revelation. It is a theory of the androgynous mind and spirit; a fusion of masculine and feminine elements, calm, stable, subtle, unimpeded by consciousness of sex or individuality. She meant it to be a luminous and fulfilling symbol, but like most highly principled utopian projections, her vision of the serene androgynous imagination lacks zest and vigor. Whatever else one may say of androgyny, it represents an escape from the confrontation with femininity.

In her own novels, Woolf often presents the female sensibility as the polar opposite of the male—a duality which has much in common with D. H. Lawrence. The artist, embodied in Woolf herself, transcends the polarity represented by characters such as Mr. and Mrs. Ramsay in *To the Lighthouse*: male reason, intellect, force, and sterility versus female emotion, lyricism, love, and fecundity. If Lily Briscoe, the painter who represents the author, rejects both of these extremes for the sake of her art, she nonetheless creates the strong impression that the art of the woman—motherhood exemplified by Mrs. Ramsay—is the truer dedication.

When Woolf looked at her sister-writers she readily perceived how their circumstances as women had made them weak; she was not as quick to see where they had been made strong. In the name of androgyny, she pities the excesses of women who worked closer to the core of female consciousness, and in particular she pities and regrets their rage. Writing of Charlotte Brontë in *A Room of One's Own*, Woolf notes, ". . . we constantly feel an acidity which is the result of oppression, a burned suffering smoldering beneath her passion, a rancour which contracts these books, splendid as they are, with a spasm of pain."

If only Brontë could have transcended that anger, that bitter consciousness of oppression, Woolf thinks, she would have been a better writer. Yet it is precisely that bitter consciousness which informs Charlotte Brontë's books with the authority of experience. Although the stereotype of the woman writer is still diminutive, the reality of the feminine tradition in English and American literature is quite different. As Ellen Moers points out in an important article which appeared in *Harper's* in 1963, the authentic line from which women writers trace their descent is one of protest, innovation, and confrontation. As Moers says,

> Writing self-consciously as a woman, the Victorian woman of genius thought relatively little of her special female sensibility, but a good deal of a social fact: that women were an oppressed majority. "You may try, but you can never imagine,"

says a gifted woman in one of George Eliot's novels, "what it is to have a man's force of genius in you, and yet to suffer the slavery of being a girl." To be a woman of genius, brought up from earliest childhood with the sense of being a freak and a misfit, and with the experience of being inhibited and denied, provided a readymade insight into something of how it felt to be a Yorkshire millhand, a ranting Methodist—or a Negro slave.

Women's anger can be rendered obliquely. Other aspects of female experience, however, are unthinkable, unspeakable, or unprintable. The Angel in the House commands that their existence should be avoided, denied, or suppressed. Woolf chose avoidance, and in her work, at least, she succeeded. Other women writers manifest more ambivalence; they struggle to keep in touch with "taboo" but significant psychic levels of feeling and energy, and simultaneously search for covert, risk-free ways to present these feelings. The conflicts can be extensive and creatively exhausting, draining off energies which could go into art.

The Mask of Madness

The battle to stay alive, to fight for one's emotional independence against the smothering embrace of the Angel, is fought repeatedly in women's literature. An early and neglected example, one of the most brilliant, is Charlotte Perkins Gilman's short story, "The Yellow Wallpaper." Published in 1892, the story is the narrative of the mental breakdown of a young mother undergoing a "rest cure" (like the one Gilman herself endured at the hands of Dr. S. Weir Mitchell); and it is electric with the repressed anger of the woman who knows that she is being destroyed in the name of love and concern. As she tells her story—one of virtual imprisonment, enforced solitude and inertia, prescribed by her doctor-husband—the reader gradually understands that she does not love her husband, nor appreciate his care. Rather, she is seething with frustration and resentment at his power to confine, control, and trivialize her. In her detested bedroom, she fancies she sees a woman in the pattern of the yellow wallpaper—a woman who shakes the walls with her efforts to escape, who circles the room endlessly on her hands and knees, looking for the way out, who is "all the time trying to climb through. But nobody could climb through the pattern—it strangles so. . . ." The woman, of course, is herself, trying to break out of her life; but she can do so only by being mad. In the story's terrifying conclusion, she locks herself in her room, systematically ripping the paper off the walls. In the role of madness, she can express her aggressions

against her husband; and when at last he breaks into the room, and faints in shock at the sight of her, there is a triumph in her narrative. Yet she is truly mad; she has defeated him only by destroying herself.

It is rather disturbing to encounter in this story a description of the cure Virginia Woolf repeatedly underwent for neurasthenia (probably manic-depression): darkened rooms, rich food, bed rest, and no writing. As Leonard Woolf describes it in *Beginning Again,* Virginia's illness came from activity and vanished with inertia:

> If Virginia lived a quiet vegetative life, eating well, going to bed early, and not tiring herself mentally or physically, she remained perfectly well. But if she tired herself in any way, if she was subjected to any severe physical, mental, or emotional strain, symptoms at once appeared which in the ordinary person are negligible and transient, but with her were serious danger signals. The first symptoms were a peculiar "headache" low down at the back of the head, insomnia, and a tendency for the thoughts to race. If she went to bed and lay doing nothing in the darkened room, drinking large quantities of milk and eating well, the symptoms would slowly disappear and in a week or ten days she would be well again.

If she resisted at this stage, a crisis was sure to follow, and on four occasions led to a serious breakdown.

As in her own life extreme vivacity, activity, and excitement were the signals of mania presaging a depressive episode, so in her novels unchecked consciousness is always alarming. Women particularly do not indulge themselves in it. Yet, according to Prof. Nancy Bazin, Woolf seems to have related the emotions of the manic state to the female mode of perception, and particularly to her mother. Androgyny represents a perilous balance between the female mania and the male depression; but Woolf recognized the more intense state as richly fertile: ". . . these curious intervals in life—I've had many—are the most fruitful artistically—one becomes fertilized—think of my madness at Hogarth—and all the little illnesses. . . ."

Clarissa Dalloway exemplifies the self-restraint of many of Woolf's heroines. She, more than the others, has extinguished as much as possible all the excitement of her inner life: her male double, Septimus Smith, lives out the intense possibilities which Woolf saw as dangerous. His suicide is both an exorcism and a warning to Clarissa, who returns to the chaste and sanitary room where she sleeps alone on a narrow white cot and lulls herself with historical narratives. For Clarissa, for

Charlotte Gilman's heroine, and for many of their sisters in literature, a room of one's own is a prison as well as a sanctuary. Psychologically enfeebled by their conditioning, they dare not defy society to do and say what they want; they struggle in a vague way to be let out of their rooms, but never understand that by this time the doors are locked from the inside.

The frequency with which one encounters madness in the heroines and in the lives of women writers seems to suggest that for them it is a form of genuine self-expression, sometimes the only one possible. As R. D. Laing's research into the genesis of schizophrenia has shown, madness may indeed be divinest sense, a way of maintaining the self in the face of baffling and contradictory reality. On the simplest level, madness offers a woman a socially acceptable excuse for expressing anger and hostility; and, conversely, the expression of these "unfeminine" feelings may be construed as signs of madness. Gilman's heroine has to behave in accordance with the role of the madwoman before she can confront her husband. Madness hath its privileges, one of which is honesty.

The mask of madness appears with sad regularity in women's books to the present day. In Sylvia Plath's *The Bell Jar*, for example, Esther Greenwood's total rejection of the feminine role is acted out before the curtain of the asylum, a curtain behind which the author can slip when her audience appears too shocked. If crazy Esther Greenwood is disgusted by childbirth, bored by men, unimpressed by male nudity ("turkey neck and turkey gizzards"), Sylvia Plath can claim to be a normal mother and housewife, and describe the novel to her own mother as "a potboiler." Mrs. Plath's horrified commentary on the novel—"as this book stands by itself, it represents the basest ingratitude"—is a sample of the pressures faced by women writers, the double bind of the demands of personal loyalty and the urgency of artistic truth.

However comprehensible or brilliantly appropriate madness appears as a response to the woman artist's existential dilemma, it is neither a dynamic nor a liberated response, but a ruse. And as ruses go, it is a very costly one. It would be cheaper to kill the Angel in the House.

II

Actually, writing is an ideal profession for women. You don't have to go to an office, you don't have to be away with half your mind on your household . . . wondering if it rains, did you close the windows? And for the woman who is tied down to her home, writing is a wonderful emotional release, to say nothing of the extra income it can bring.
—Faith Baldwin, ad for the Famous Writers School

If a woman is tied down to her home, one asks, what will be the emotions she needs to release in her writing? And what will she write about, besides these emotions and her fantasies of escape? The answer to the first question is that she will feel a large measure of anger, frustration, and resentment. The answer to the second is that she will have to write about what happens in that household, what she sees through those windows. In *Lolita*, Vladimir Nabokov tells an anecdote of a monkey in the Jardin des Plantes given an easel and brushes; the creature's first painting showed the bars of its cage. It sometimes seems that women's experience is as restricted and as foolish; women internalize literary values as well as other kinds, and their own vision often strikes them as dull and small.

Women critics have agreed with men that women writers are often timid, conservative, and conventional. In her review of *The Second Sex*, Elizabeth Hardwick quotes approvingly de Beauvoir's strictures on artistic women: "Narcissism and feelings of inferiority are, according to Simone de Beauvoir, the demons of literary women. Women want to please, 'but the writer of originality, unless dead, is always shocking, scandalous; novelty disturbs and repels.'"

Women, it is argued, never go anywhere or do anything; they have less experience to write about than men. But with so little opportunity for experience, so little space in which to channel psychic energy, women, as the ad from the Famous Writers School so shrewdly recognizes, *need* writing as an escape-valve for their desperate need for self-expression.

The dilemma of the woman writer in the second half of the twentieth century—struggling against convention to tell her own truth, and faced with male critics' contempt for it, and female critics' suspicion of it—is dramatized in the case of Mary McCarthy and *The Group*. Published in 1963, *The Group* is a subversive novel about women's roles and marriage, a deliberate exposure of the fantasy of the educated American woman's freedom. As McCarthy described it, the novel is about the failure of the idea of "progress in the feminine sphere." Nothing—not education, not politics, not technology, not sex—can jolt these somnolent young women, these sleeping beauties, from their Vassar tower, into dynamic growth. They are empty at the core, because they have never been free to experience themselves without the screen of male authority: cook books, sex books, child-rearing books, merge in their minds with their Vassar lectures, as infallible guides to the conduct of life.

In 1963 this message—McCarthy even makes the happiest woman in the book a lesbian—was not one America wished to recognize. While the book became a best-seller because of its allegedly sexy passages (sex from the woman's point of view seemed especially titillating and risqué) and because women readers responded to its underlying anger and accuracy, the male intellectuals hastened to attack this "trivial lady-writer's book" (Norman Podhoretz). John W. Aldridge thunderously banished McCarthy from the intellectual kingdom in an essay entitled "Princess Among the Trolls." Now, he announced triumphantly, the masquerade was over. She was no great thinker; she gave herself airs; she felt superior to men; in fact, she hated men. *The Group,* according to Aldridge, was a kind of wish fulfillment for her, enabling her to act out her self-deluding fantasies of intellectual dominance. "It is probably not surprising," he says wearily, "that Miss McCarthy's militant egotism should ultimately take the form of militant feminism and find its most satisfactory expression in the sexual contest between the brute male and the morally and intellectually superior female."

Norman Mailer, as one might guess, went wild. In a long essay called "The Case Against McCarthy," he ranted against the detail of *The Group,* seeing in it what he calls the "profound materiality of women." In a classical Freudian analysis of his own metaphors and obsessions, Mailer describes this detail as the "cold lava of anality, which becomes the truest part of her group, her glop, her impacted mass." With sensitive critics like these, and best-sellerdom to boot, *The Group* virtually destroyed Mary McCarthy's literary and intellectual reputation. By the time Hollywood got hold of it, Pauline Kael reports in "The Making of *The Group,*" McCarthy herself was regarded as "poison . . . she's competitive"; the book was interpreted as proof that higher education made women aggressive and neurotic.

Yet there is great irony in McCarthy's fall as a "militant feminist," for the chorus of women's voices in her fiction creates a veritable symphony of female self-hatred. McCarthy is only merciless with her own sex; it is to the women in her narratives that she directs her most relentless mockery. In her famous short story "The Man in the Brooks

Brothers Shirt," the Babbitty man on the train emerges with considerable dignity and integrity, despite his crude middleclass tastes; it is the autobiographical arty heroine who is stripped of all self-respect and pretension. Similarly, in *The Group,* the female characters internalize all their aggressions against men. John Aldridge managed to find Amazons triumphant, but in truth, Kay, Noreen, Priss, and the rest pour their anger and frustration into bitchiness with each other, self-doubt, self-sacrifice, depression, madness, and suicide. They do not confront their men, much less defeat them.

Pauline Kael was more perceptive when she said that McCarthy's satire was an effort to protect herself against the horrible image of the castrating woman by "betraying other women. And of course women who are good writers succeed in betrayal but fail to save themselves." Since *The Group,* we have heard no more about women from McCarthy. Her subsequent books, a report from Vietnam, and a recent novel, *Birds of America,* narrated by an expatriate college boy obsessed with ecology, have found more favor.

It takes courage to hold out, for most women writers defying the stereotypes come in for much more abuse than McCarthy. The Brontës were called "outcasts from their sex"; Elizabeth Barrett Browning pronounced "coarse"; Kate Chopin's *The Awakening* banned as moral poison; Simone de Beauvoir denounced as frigid; Kate Millett proclaimed a pervert. In her remarkable long poem, "Snapshots of a Daughter-in-Law," Adrienne Rich describes the choices women have—to write badly and be patronized or to write well and be attacked [. . .].

Standing in the shadow of Virginia Woolf, women writers were encouraged to be androgynous, to transcend consciousness of their sex, certainly not to write about it. The highest praise a woman writer could expect was to be absolved from being a "woman writer." As Erica Jong writes in "Bitter Pills for the Dark Ladies":

> The ultimate praise is always a question of nots:
> viz. not like a woman
> viz. "certainly not another 'poetess'"
> meaning
> she got a cunt but she don't talk funny
> & he's a nigger but he don't smell funny
> & the only good poetess is a dead.

In 1963 the spirit of rebellion and passion in women writers seemed so extinct that Ellen Moers sadly predicted "no reason to believe that English and American literary women, as a group or as a sex, will ever again make the kind of gesture—and the splash—that they made in the nineteenth and twentieth centuries." Yet 1962-63 saw the publication of *The Feminine Mystique, The Group, The Bell Jar,* and *The Golden Notebook.* And suddenly women were once again intent on exploring their own experience. Now a new generation of angry young women, great-granddaughters of the Brontës, is speaking in language which will not go gentle. No more arts and wiles, no more fun and games. Today women writers are involved in a fierce encounter with the physical and sexual and social facts of their lives and, given women's experience, the encounter is bound to be bloody.

III

Higgledy-piggledy
Dorothy Richardson
Wrote a huge book with her
Delicate muse.
Where (though I hate to seem
Uncomplimentary)
Nothing much happens and
Nobody screws.

        —John Hollander, *Double Dactylics*

Once the penis has been introduced into
the poem, the poet lets herself down
until she is sitting on the muse
with her legs outside him. He need
not make any motions at all.

        —Erica Jong, "Arse Poetica"

Today we are in a female Renaissance, a new Golden Age of women writers, an era of eros and anger. And if the new women writers defy male critics on paper and to their faces, they also create problems for their sisters. Used to the soothing myths of their sex's greater "spirituality" and "purity," many women find it profoundly disturbing to encounter expressions of female rage and eroticism, and particularly to find reflected in contemporary literature some of their own most deeply concealed doubts, beliefs, and feelings.

One form the new consciousness takes is role-reversal; the woman beats the man at his own game. Elizabeth Sargent's blunt and lusty poem, "A Sailor At Midnight," for example, reverses the roles of the hunter and the prey in a one-night stand. The woman picks up a sailor, and alarms him because their intercourse makes her bleed:

A sort of dread
Struck him. "What are you anyway," he
    whispered.
  "Are you a virgin?"
"No, I'm a poet," I said. "Fuck me again."

Women students of mine respond with mingled envy and suspicion to Sargent's directness. The woman's intellectual superiority, her

sexual imperiousness, and her exuberant (or exhibitionistic?) obscenity are presented here with a self-confidence which contrasts forcefully with Mary McCarthy's lady on the train. Sargent's woman can really claim to be "myn owene womman, wel at ese"; and modern women find it hard to identify with self-possession.

Even more troubling than Sargent's poetry is Denise Levertov's "Hypocrite Women," which challenges the numbness women induce as an evasion of sexual and spiritual commitment, and the self-hatred which such denials engender:

Hypocrite women, how seldom we speak
of our own doubts, while dubiously
we mother man in his doubt!

And if at Mill Valley perched in the trees
the sweet rain drifting through western air
a white sweating bull of a poet told us

our cunts are ugly—why didn't we
admit we have thought so too? (And
what shame? They are not for the eye!)

No, they are dark and wrinkled and hairy,
caves of the Moon. . . . And when a
dark humming fills us, a

coldness towards life
we are too much women to
own to such unwomanliness.

Whorishly with the psychopomp
we play and plead—and say
nothing of this later. And our dreams,

With what frivolity we have pared them
like toenails, clipped them like ends of
split hair.

This is a subtler confrontation with the Angel, one which accepts a male view of female sexuality, and seems to use it to berate women. But Levertov is using the familiar details of physical maintenance, the constant paring and pruning of women's daily existence, to suggest the excision of female sexual consciousness.

Physical sexuality is a central theme of much of women's writing at the present, and while it is not the whole of womanhood, it is vital; it must be faced. "The blood jet is poetry," Sylvia Plath wrote. For women it is not the blood of war and wounds, but of nature. And the taboos are still strong, surrounding menstruation, for example, "that terrible female vulgarity of blood," as Mary McCarthy calls it. Even strong men seem to fear it; Norman Mailer owns himself beaten by Germaine Greer's challenge to women on the menstrual mythos: "If you think you are emancipated, you might consider the idea of tasting your own menstrual blood—if it makes you sick, you've a long way to go, baby."

Earlier women writers, if they mentioned menstruation at all, emphasized its shamefulness; in Katherine Anne Porter's *Noon Wine,* the Southern belles make themselves sick with home remedies designed to postpone menses before a ball, lest the young men suspect and be disgusted. In Carson McCullers' *The Member of the Wedding,* the trauma of menarche is clearly a part of Frankie's suffering; yet it is never mentioned. Recently, however, women are beginning to defy the taboos, to accept and describe the quality of this recurrent experience, its cultural ramifications, and its effect on women's self-image. In *Such Good Friends,* Lois Gould hilariously describes the modern female ritual of learning to use Tampax; while the heroine crouches in the bathroom, half afraid she has no vagina, her friends call out encouraging instructions. Menstruation also figures in women's pornographic writing, although it is conspicuously absent from male pornographers' fantasies; it does not stop Diane di Prima from joining an orgy with Kerouac and Ginsberg, which she relates in her *Memoirs of a Beatnik.*

Helpless Bodies; Free Wills

When they talk about their "experiences as bodies," the new women writers are anything but sentimental. As Alicia Ostriker writes in her long poem about pregnancy, "Once More Out of Darkness," which opposes an image of regeneration to the (male) images of our century as a wasteland, and of woman as a quagmire.

> What I have said and
> What I will say is female
> Not feminine
>   Yes I said yes
> Not analytical not romantic
>   But the book of practical facts.

The central experience of Joan Didion's *Play It As It Lays* is the heroine's abortion. Reduced to quintessential femaleness, Maria experiences herself as nothing. In herself, without the sheltering identity of her director-husband, she does not exist except as a body. The abortionist's sadism ("'Hear that scraping, Maria?' the doctor said. 'That should be the sound of music to you . . . don't scream, Maria, there are people next door . . .'") is not much different from the shrill brutality of the actor who finds out, after he has mistreated her, that she is married to a powerful man: "'Just hold on, cunt . . . *You never told me who you were.*'" Her life, its whole meaning, is literally in the careless hands of men; the abortion is only one event in her destruction.

Similarly, accounts of childbirth often emphasize the control and usurpation of female experience by men. The woman is most helpless when she should be most strong. In Sylvia Plath's *The Bell Jar,* childbirth is a clear symbol of the female condition; the woman becomes an object, deprived of will and stupefied, the utter opposite of the joyous creator, the poet. She is at the mercy of nature, science, and men, made passively to accept the narcotics that will further enslave her, since they make her forget the pain and thus condemn her to relive it. Esther has been taken to see a delivery by her medical-student beau, whom she perceives as threatening and even sinister in his omnivorous claims on her life. The prospective mother is a grotesque captive: "She seemed to have nothing but an enormous spider-fat stomach and two ugly little spindly legs propped in the high stirrups, and all the time the baby was being born she never stopped making this inhuman whooing noise." She has been drugged. Sylvia Plath rejects with horror the loss of consciousness and control, the manipulation of the woman's life by male expertise, the numbing of the woman's spirit to the pain which represents her only chance of free will:

> I thought it sounded just like the sort of drug a man would invent. Here was a woman in terrible pain, obviously feeling every bit of it or she wouldn't groan like that, and she would go straight home and start another baby, because the drug would make her forget how bad the pain had been, when all the time, in some secret part of her, that long, blind, doorless and windowless corridor of pain was waiting to open up and shut her in again.

Even when the experience of childbirth is serene and dignified, as in Margaret Drabble's *The Waterfall,* it has troubling aspects. Drabble's heroine Jane is alone, in a cold house, tended by a midwife who has anxiously concentrated all the sources of heat in one room. Again the isolated room becomes a symbol of female experience. Still it is not childbirth, but a prosaic and particularly contemporary aspect of femaleness—a blood clot from birth control pills—which finally brings Jane into possession of herself:

> The price that modern woman must pay for love. In the past, in old novels, the price of love was death, a price which virtuous women paid in childbirth, and the wicked, like Nana, with the pox. Nowadays it is paid in thrombosis or neurosis: one can take one's pick . . . I am glad I cannot swallow pills with impunity. I prefer to suffer, I think.

There is a great deal of anger in some of these books. Virginia Woolf might not have approved of their rancor, nor of their insistent femaleness, but I think she would have envied their author's freedom. Amazingly, Virginia Woolf and James Joyce lived identical life spans: 1882-1941. Yet how much he could think and say which she was forbidden! Today women writers are no longer willing to be silent about themselves, like Karl Shapiro's poets, "no belly and no bowels, only consonants and vowels." Good-bye to all that, writes Robin Morgan in a violent declaration of independence:

> . . . we are rising, powerful in our unclean bodies; bright glowing mad in our inferior brains; wild hair flying, wild eyes staring, wild voices keening; undaunted by blood we who hemorrhage every twenty-eight days; laughing at our own beauty we who have lost our sense of humor; mourning for all each precious one of us might have been in this one living-time place had she not been born a woman. . . ."

If few women feel this rage, even fewer can still pretend not to hear it expressed.

Beyond androgyny, women have a lot to say.

SALLY BURKE (ESSAY DATE 1996)

SOURCE: Burke, Sally. "The Second Wave: A Multiplicity of Concerns." In *American Feminist Playwrights: A Critical History*, pp. 139-90. New York: Twayne Publishers, 1996.

In the following excerpt, Burke provides a brief history of the second-wave feminist movement, as well as examines the growth and writings of many feminist playwrights during the 1960s to the mid-1990s, including Alice Childress, Megan Terry, Adrienne Kennedy, Rosalyn Drexler, and others.

Under the veneer of 1950s complacency, a new consciousness simmered among women. Buoyed by a self-confidence developed when many managed homes and jobs during World War II, women who had apparently accepted the retreat from feminism and careers ordained by the return of the men did not forget that their earlier success had proven there was no "natural" gendering of labor into men's and women's work. Like their foremothers who underwent change during America's earlier wars, these women incubated ideas that formed the basis of the second wave of the women's movement. Of course, women's absence from most history, written as it is by men, concealed their common cause with Abigail Adams, the abolitionists, the suffragists, even their mothers or grandmothers who might have had similar experiences during World War I.

Feminists have been forced by this absence to keep reinventing the wheel, that is, a feminist consciousness, defined by Gerda Lerner as: "(1) . . . the awareness of women that they belong to a subordinate group and that, as members of such a group, they have suffered wrongs; (2) the recognition that their condition of subordination is not natural, but societally determined; (3) the development of a sense of sisterhood; (4) the autonomous definition by women of their goals and strategies for changing their condition; and (5) the development of an alternate vision of the future."[1] Since the late 1960s, feminist theorists have labored to ensure that, despite conservative backlash, the principles of sexual equality and the history of the struggle to bring about that equality are not again eclipsed, that women will retain possession of feminist consciousness and a usable past.

The second wave of the women's movement concerned itself with multiple issues. Under the banner of equal rights, women worked to effect equality between the sexes in such areas as education, employment, wages, the family, child rearing, and government. As their precursors in the first wave had learned to organize in the abolitionist movement, many women of the second wave received their education in the Civil Rights movement, recognizing that sex, as well as color, led to a denial of rights. Equally important to the reawakening of American feminist consciousness was the 1963 publication of Betty Friedan's *The Feminine Mystique*. While much of what Friedan articulated had been said before, her focus on "the problem without a name" helped women realize that they were not alone, that others felt imprisoned by a society that circumscribed their lives according to their biology. Some perceived that the "problem" was social, not personal, and thus began the journey to women's realizations that "the personal is the political" and that the solution to the "problem" is political.

In 1961, President Kennedy established the Commission on the Status of Women. Its 1963 report demonstrated that women were victims of discrimination and recommended action in education and counseling, home, community, employment and labor standards, social security for widows, paid maternity leave, and equality under the law. The recommendations, while startling to many, asked for far less than women would soon demand for themselves. Women who had worked on state and national commissions grew weary of rhetoric followed by inaction. In 1968, at the third National Conference of State Commissions on the Status of Women, several delegates attempted to submit a resolution demanding that laws against discrimination be enforced; when they were told that the conference would accept no resolutions, they perceived the need for organization. This was the genesis of NOW, the National Organization for Women, formed "[t]o take action to bring women into full participation in the mainstream of American society NOW, exercising all the privileges and responsibilities thereof in truly equal partnership with men."

The women of the 1960s and 1970s, like their foremothers in the suffrage and temperance movements, paraded to protest inequality and used street theater to attract media attention. For example, "At the 1968 Miss America pageant," a group of radical young women "crowned a live sheep, tossed objects of female torture—girdles, bras, curlers, issues of the *Ladies Home Journal*—into a 'freedom trashcan,' and auctioned off an effigy: 'Gentlemen, I offer you the 1969 model. She's better every year. She walks. She talks. She smiles on cue. *And* she does housework.'"[2] While demonstrations called attention to the widespread perception of women as sex objects, women continued working in other areas. In 1970 NOW filed discrimination complaints with the Office of Federal Contract Compliance against 1,300 corporations; by 1971, the Women's Equity Action League had filed discrimination complaints against more than 250 academic institutions. Women confirmed, with statistical evidence, that their educations had been damaged by gender stereotyping. To countervail such damages, women lobbied for legislation outlawing sex discrimination in public schools and most colleges, which Congress passed in 1972.

The resurgent feminism of the 1960s and 1970s also challenged patriarchal privilege within families. As inexpensive oral contraceptives became available, birth rates fell; women, with and without children, employed outside the home gained some economic independence and no longer felt constrained to remain in unhappy or abusive marriages. Also, the age at marriage rose for women and more women remained single altogether.

By 1980, more than half the women in two-parent families were employed outside the home. New models for families came into being as males were urged to become active participants in child rearing. In the 1976 edition of *Baby and Child Care,* Dr. Benjamin Spock declared the father's responsibility to be as great as the mother's. In the 1980s and 1990s, new definitions of family arose: the "molded families" of second marriages, the two

parents of the same-sex families of gay or lesbian partners, the single-parent family, and other variations of the so-called "ideal." By the mid-1990s, some states were extending health care and other benefits to unmarried domestic partners. By 1991, according to the U.S. Census, men with wives employed outside the home were the primary caregivers for 20 percent of children age five and younger. The Family Leave Act of 1993 guaranteed leave for childbirth or family illness to wife or husband. Clearly, feminism had had an impact.

Praxis: Transforming Stage and Society

The playwrights of the second wave sought to transform both the stage itself and the society it reflected. In the 1960s, off-Broadway revues, regional theaters, and newly created feminist theaters began producing plays by women in large numbers. These works were characterized by significant structural and thematic innovations. The playwrights melded the comic with the serious, blended musical and conventional theater, combined individual and social themes, and frequently replaced the traditional plot utilizing climax, recognition, and through-line with circular or contiguous structures and scenes of transformation. Gender roles were blurred, inverted, or abolished, and many dramas resisted closure. Emulating Alice Gerstenberg, Susan Glaspell, and Sophie Treadwell, feminist dramatists began using expressionistic techniques to portray the female psyche, to dramatize and explore women's oppression and the uniqueness of their fragmented lives. Others discovered ways to dramatize woman's reawakened feminist consciousness. These playwrights sought, through a praxis of the stage, to transform actor, audience, and world by using drama to promote women's awareness of their situation and to assist them in imagining alternatives to their oppression. These playwrights desired not only to dramatize women's experiences but also to change the conditions of their lives.

Agents of Change

When asked by the *New York Times* on 20 May 1973, "Where are the Women Playwrights?" Rosalyn Drexler replied, "They are deployed about the city waiting to make their move. They have already learned how to take apart and put together their typewriters in a matter of minutes, and how to keep them clean and well lubricated. At a signal . . . all women playwrights will shoot the vapids and proceed to a secret rendezvous where a secret store of explosive topics is waiting to be used.

Joan Allen, Joanne Camp, Anne Lange and Cynthia Nixon, in a scene from *The Heidi Chronicles* by Wendy Wasserstein.

With proper handling, each sentence will find its mark." Her tongue-in-cheek metaphor holds seeds of truth. The feminist playwrights who had left or been turned away by the commercial theater had found homes in the cafés and studio theaters of off- and off-off-Broadway, in regional and feminist theaters. Yet except by scholars who began analyzing feminist drama in the mid-1970s, these playwrights were largely ignored. Even though seven women dramatists won Obies (the Obie Award was established by the *Village Voice* in 1956 to honor excellence in off-Broadway drama) between 1958 and 1978, the 10 plays included in Ross Wetzsteon's *The Obie Winners: The Best of Off Broadway* are by male playwrights. Ignoring Pulitzer Prize winners *Crimes of the Heart* (Beth Henley, 1981), *'night, Mother* (Marsha Norman, 1983), and *The Heidi Chronicles* (Wendy Wasserstein, 1989), *Time* selected plays by male dramatists only for its January 1990 best-of-the-decade issue.

To combat such ignorance and indifference, women have formed alliances designed to make it known that, in Julia Miles's words, women playwrights "exist, they are talented, and they are ready to enter the mainstream theatre."[3] In 1978, partly in reaction to learning that only 7 percent of the playwrights produced in funded nonprofit theaters from 1969 to 1975 were women, Miles founded the Women's Project at the American Place Theatre in New York. While Miles identifies neither herself nor the Women's Project as specifically feminist, the Women's Project has produced works by Maria Irene Fornes, Emily Mann, and many other feminist playwrights. By 1985, with a membership of approximately 200 playwrights and directors, the Women's Project had reviewed more than 4,000 scripts and presented 150 rehearsed readings. By 1994, it had produced 70 plays and published 5 anthologies. While its now 400 members have received numerous fellowships and grants, in her mission statement artistic director Miles says, "We measure our success by the increased courage and energy women are bringing to the stage. . . . A more tangible measure is the increase in the numbers of women working in the theatre from approximately 6 percent to 7 percent for playwrights and directors [in 1978] to three times that number [in 1994]." Other organizations that have promoted women playwrights include the Women's Program of the American Theatre

Author Alice Childress (1920-1994), American playwright.

Association, the Women and Theatre Program, Women's Interart Theatre, the Women's Theatre Council, and the Committee for Women of the Dramatists Guild. In 1989, the First International Women Playwrights Festival and Conference was held in Buffalo, New York; the third met in July 1994 in Australia.

Negative images of women continued to predominate onstage. The vacuous but castrating Mommy of Edward Albee's *The American Dream* (1961) is an appropriate ancestor to the male-devouring Martha of his *Who's Afraid of Virginia Woolf?* (1962). The white Lula of Amiri Baraka's *Dutchman* (1964) uses her sexuality to lure, en-snare, demean, and murder Clay. Women are presented as marginal creatures by David Mamet, Sam Shepard, David Rabe, and Israel Horovitz. Even as diegetic characters, women are debased by Mamet's males. In *American Buffalo* (1975), Teach labels Ruthie a "vicious dyke" who has "not one loyal bone" in her body. Shepard's female characters are beaten to insensibility (*A Lie of the Mind*, 1985) and raped (*The Tooth of Crime*, 1972), while in Rabe's *Goose and Tomtom* (1981) Lulu is tied up, blindfolded, hung in a closet and periodi-cally raped by Tomtom, who says, "I love to bang 'em, man. They got the plumbing, you know what I mean." As Susan Smith Harris concludes, "The

very fact of the commercial success of these three writers points to a domination of a patriarchal, phallocentric theater system."[4] Horovitz's Margy Burke, the title character of *The Widow's Blind Date* (1989), is gang-raped by men whose motives range from desiring to take her virginity to punishing her for being a whore, but who blame her for their crime. Countering such images and stereotypes by resisting the identities they posit and thus recover-ing womanhood is one task of the feminist play-wright.

The vanguard of the feminist playwrights of the second wave actually preceded the onset of the women's movement in the 1970s. Writing in the early 1960s with wit, insight, courage, and determination, playwrights such as Megan Terry, Myrna Lamb, Adrienne Kennedy, Rochelle Owens, and Rosalyn Drexler produced works in a flower-ing that was anticipated in the plays of their fore-mothers. Inspired by both the Civil Rights and anti-Vietnam War movements, these pioneers used the stage to illustrate that the violence of rape, inequality, and the assumed inferiority of women were human, as well as women's, issues. To experience the transition from being the other to being the center was the heady experience these playwrights offered female audiences.

Alice Childress: From the 1940s to Tomorrow

In April 1994, the New WORLD Theater at the University of Massachusetts produced *Florence* in tribute to Alice Childress (1920-94), whose career spanned six decades, from the original staging of *Florence* in 1949 to the 1994 production. Born in South Carolina, Childress moved to Harlem where she was raised by her grandmother; she left high school in her junior year to earn her living. At 19 she helped found the American Negro Theatre and worked there as a playwright, actor, and director for 12 years. She credits her grandmother with exposing her to art, encouraging her to write, and taking her to the Salem Church where, at Wednes-day night testimonials, she learned to be a writer. "[P]eople, mostly women, used to get up and tell their troubles to everybody," she recalled. "I couldn't wait for person after person to tell her story. . . . That's where I got my writing inspira-tion."[5]

Her *Gold through the Trees* (1952) was the first play by a black woman to be professionally produced. *Trouble in Mind* (1955) won the first Obie Award for the best original off-Broadway play. Asked about the "firsts" attached to her name, Childress commented: "I never was ever

ON THE SUBJECT OF...

ALICE CHILDRESS (1920-1994)

Alice Childress is considered a pivotal yet critically neglected figure in contemporary black American literature. Because she wrote about such topics as miscegenation and teenage drug abuse, some of Childress's works have been banned from schools and libraries in various regions. In her dramas as well as in her novels for children and adults, Childress drew upon her own experiences and created relatively commonplace protagonists. Childress was born in Charleston, South Carolina, but grew up in Harlem in New York City. She was raised primarily by her grandmother, who was an early influence on her writing, and inspired her to write about everyday events. Childress attended high school for two years but left before graduation. She held several jobs while acting as a member of the American Negro Theatre in Harlem; as part of the company, she performed in *A Midsummer-Night's Dream* and other works. Childress was also in the original cast of *Anna Lucasta* on Broadway, but found acting unful-

filling. She began to write dramas, later attributing this decision in part to her grandmother. In 1949 Childress's first play, *Florence,* was staged, and the critical praise it received launched Childress's career. With *Gold through the Trees* (1952), she became the first black woman to have a play professionally produced on the American stage, and with *Trouble in Mind* (1955), a play about a group of actors rehearsing *Chaos in Belleville,* a fictional drama with an anti-lynching message, she became the first woman to win an Obie Award for best original off-Broadway play. By far her best-known work, *A Hero Ain't Nothin' but a Sandwich* (1973), is the story of thirteen-year-old Benjie Johnson's emerging addiction to heroin. The work was highly controversial and is the subject of the majority of critical attention to Childress's works. Despite overwhelming praise for its realistic treatment of a sensitive issue, several school districts banned *Hero,* apparently on the grounds that the theme of the work was inappropriate for young readers. Childress encountered similar resistance to her plays; for instance, the state of Alabama refused to air *Wine in the Wilderness* (1969), when it was produced for television that same year.

interested in being the first woman to do anything. I always felt that I should be the 50th or the 100th. Women were kept out of everything. [Being first] almost made it sound like other women were not quite right enough or accomplished enough, especially when I hear 'the first Black woman.' When people are shut out of something for so long, it seems ironic when there's so much going on about 'the first'" (Brown-Guillory 1987, 68). Childress viewed race as the dominant factor in her life and work: "Being a woman adds difficulty to self expression, but being Black is the larger factor of struggle against the odds. Black men and women have particular problems above and beyond the average, in any field of endeavor."[6] She also decried "people who say, 'I'm not a *black* playwright, I'm a playwright who *happens* to be black.' Like they're some goddamned accident! You know? Happenstance. I am a woman and I am black. . . . The person who

says, 'I'm not a woman playwright,' or 'I'm not black, I'm a writer who happens to be black,' et cetera, is deluding herself."[7] Her dramas address the difficulties of the struggle against racism and sexism, legacies of a white patriarchy that doubly oppresses black women. Rather than concern herself with a genteel middle class, Childress wrote, as did Georgia Douglas Johnson and Mary Burrill, of the lower economic class. . . .

Megan Terry: "Mother of American Feminist Drama"

Named the "Mother of American Feminist Drama" by Helene Keyssar (Keyssar, 53), Megan Terry (born 1932) has written more than 60 plays, been translated into every major language, and produced internationally. Born in Seattle, Terry began working with the Seattle Repertory Playhouse at 14; artistic director Florence James's technique of having the actors write biographies of what their characters were doing offstage, was, Terry says, "one of the things that got me into writing."[8] In 1966, she held a writer-in-residence fellowship at the Yale School of Drama. She has taught theater and given seminars in playwriting across the country.

Moving to New York in 1956, she worked in several theaters and in 1963 joined Joseph Chaikin at the Open Theatre, where she served as playwright-in-residence and ran the playwrights' workshop. Eight of her dramas were produced there, the most notable being *Viet Rock: A Folk War Movie* (1966). In the early 1970s she began working with the Omaha Magic Theatre, and in 1974 moved to Omaha and became playwright-in-residence, performer, composer, designer, and photographer. Her book, *Right Brain Vacation Photos—New Plays and Production Photographs, 1972-1992,* highlights the production of 25 of her works as well as dramas by Rosalyn Drexler, Rochelle Owens, and Maria Irene Fornes. Since its founding in 1968, the Omaha Magic Theatre, "which typically mocks and demystifies patriarchal sites and practices,"[9] has produced more than 100 plays and musicals.

According to Jill Dolan, "Many contemporary feminist theatre makers, such as Megan Terry . . . , left the experimental theatres to form their own groups when their invisibility in the male forums was articulated by the American women's liberation movement."[10] Terry, who acknowledges that "the women's movement enabled me to leave New York and give up that whole careerism business—the man's world of career stuff," defines feminist drama as "[a]nything that gives women confidence, shows them to themselves, helps them to begin to analyze whether it's a positive or negative image" (Jenkins, 329). Her dramas confront sexism, gender roles, the repression and oppression of women, and sexist language with the intent of disrupting what the patriarchy claims as the natural order. As a teacher, Terry acquaints her students with feminist dramatists: "I taught Emily Mann's *Still Life.* . . . My students were *outraged* that they'd never heard of this play, nor the work of Maria Irene Fornes, nor Roz Drexler, Rochelle Owens, Adrienne Kennedy, . . . Ntozake Shange, . . . Tina Howe. They knew none of these people, and they were getting their master's degrees!" (Betsko and Koening, 385).

Common to many feminist dramatists is "the strategy of transformation" (Keyssar, xiii); Terry is often credited with introducing it onstage. Transformation itself is variously defined as a training technique for actors, a means of dramatizing the instability of character, a disruption of the conventions of realist theater and the status quo that those conventions support, thus a means of "throw[ing] the spectator's focus onto society and the way it maintains oppressive roles and attitudes" (Savran, 241). Transformation is thus seen as a means of "inspir[ing] and assert[ing] the possibility for change" that can bring about "transformation of the self and the world" (Keyssar, xiv). Strindberg's expressionism may be an influence; in the preface to *A Dream Play* (1902), Strindberg wrote, "Anything may happen, anything seems possible and probable. . . . The characters split, double, multiply, vanish, solidify, blur, clarify." Strindberg's influence is discernible in Terry's remark, "I was more crazy about Strindberg and Ionesco and Sartre" than about other modern Europeans (Savran, 245). In Terry's transformations, too, anything may change and, "These changes occur swiftly and *almost without transition,* until the audience's dependence upon any fixed reality is called into question. A member of our audience once said that these continual metamorphoses left him feeling 'stationless,' which is precisely the point."[11]

Transformation in feminist drama also has roots in women's psychology and life experience. Julia Kristeva, Hélène Cixous, and Luce Irigaray all write of the fluidity of woman's experience and find her reality to be other than the binary thinking characteristic of phallic logic.[12] That her time is so open to interruption is reflected in the abrupt changes of character, scene, and event found in transformational drama. Action frequently proceeds not in a linear manner but by contiguity, a principle described by feminist theorists as a nearness that creates a work "constantly in the process of weaving itself, at the same time ceaselessly embracing words and yet casting them off to avoid becoming fixed, immobilized."[13] Terry works in the tradition of Glaspell, who also eschewed linear development. Claire's intent in *The Verge* in dealing with her plant forms applies equally well to feminist playwrights' experiments with dramatic structure: "I want to break it up! If it were all in pieces, we'd be . . . shocked to aliveness. . . . There'd been strange new comings together—mad new comings together."

Terry's first transformational drama, *Calm Down Mother,* was produced in 1965. The play, written because "there were no parts for women" (Savran, 253), is often cited as the first truly feminist American drama. Its three characters, identified only as Woman One, Woman Two, and Woman Three, are variously parts of a plant form;

two delicatessen clerks and a customer; a woman filled with anger; a writer; two friends and the dying mother of one; nursing-home patients; a subway door; call girls; sides of a triangle; a mother and her daughters; and three amused gentlewomen. As the play begins, the plant splits and from it emerges Margaret Fuller, who asserts that she knows who she is because, "My father addressed me not as a plaything, but as a living mind." The transformations that follow expose the ills resulting from the institutionalized sexism of American society. The writer, for example, thinks, "Maybe if I keep talking and writing . . . I won't seem so small, at least not so small to me." A woman who has just escaped an "impossible marriage" is questioned about restraining orders. Women as victims of society's stress on them as sexual beings appear in the nursing-home patients whose nurse signals their superfluity—"Your cream's all gone. Time for the heap"—and in the young woman pressured by priests into abandoning birth control. Her sister, who refuses to "sit there in the church every Sunday, kneeling and mumbling and believing all that crap that those men tell you," is disowned by her mother, herself a victim of patriarchal religion. As the play ends, the three at once confirm and confront the idea that anatomy is destiny as they progress from proclaiming, "The eggies in our beggies [sic] are enough," to turning their backs on the audience in its representation of sexist society and asking, in unison, "ARE THEY?" Although beaten down by sexist assumptions, woman's mind and spirit as initially represented by Margaret Fuller rise to resist being apprehended merely as a medium for reproduction.

Terry's best-known play, *Viet Rock: A Folk War Movie,* "was translated into every major language and was proclaimed in every major, and many minor, cities all over the world" (Betsko and Koening, 382). Terry directed the play, which has the distinction of being both the first rock musical ever staged—featuring such songs as "The Viet Rock" and "War Au Go Go"—and the first to deal with the Vietnam War.[14] . . .

Maria Irene Fornes: From the Absurd to the Oppressed

Maria Irene Fornes's career began with *The Widow* (1961). In 1982 she was awarded an Obie for sustained achievement in the theater; her total of seven Obies is unique among women in the theater. Born in Cuba in 1930, Fornes emigrated to America in 1945. She studied painting, spending some time in Paris, where she was profoundly

moved by Roger Blin's 1954 production of Samuel Beckett's *Waiting for Godot.* In a memorial tribute, she remarked, "I more than just admire Beckett. He had a personal impact on me; he provided me with a new vision. . . . I was illuminated by it."[15]

The author of more than 30 plays, Fornes also teaches playwriting, designs scenery and costumes, and, like Crothers, Sophie Treadwell, Hellman, and Terry, directs her own plays. She also directs the INTAR Hispanic Playwrights-in-Residence Laboratory. A founding member of New York Theater Strategy, she served as president, fundraiser, production coordinator, bookkeeper, and secretary; this work interfered with her playwriting for six years, a drought that ended with the production of *Fefu and Her Friends* (1977).

Fornes identifies herself as a feminist: "To be a feminist I think means that you follow a political process that has a development and you are part of the development and you adhere to it. I am a feminist in that I am very concerned and I suffer when women are treated in a discriminatory manner because I am a woman."[16] Furthermore, Fornes invites "the audience to view the underside of patriarchal culture through women's eyes. . . . Fornes's mirror reflects disturbing images of patriarchy in general and of male behavior in particular."[17]

Returning full-time to writing and directing with *Fefu and Her Friends,* she examined women and their roles, investing her dramas with sympathy, empathy, and compassion. *Fefu* brought her Obies for writing and direction. The plot of this challenging drama centers on eight women who meet at Fefu's home to plan a fund-raising event. Although it is 1935, these women, untouched by the Great Depression, seem at first comfortable and self-sufficient in this domestic setting that functions as a concretization of woman's sphere. Although the play's action stretches from noon through the evening, Fefu's husband, Phillip, remains outside, seen by some of the women but not the audience. Fefu tells her friends that Phillip "married me to have a constant reminder of how loathsome women are," and begins to reveal the pernicious effects of the patriarchal control that looms just outside, keeping woman both nervous and in her place. Her metaphor of the stone in damp soil illuminates the state of male/female relationships: "that which is exposed to the exterior . . . is smooth and dry and clean. That which is not . . . [the] underneath, is slimy and filled with fungus and crawling with worms. It is another life that is parallel to the one we manifest. It's there. The way worms are underneath the stone. If you don't recognize it . . . [*whispering*] it eats you." The arrival of Julia, confined to a wheelchair by a surreal hunting accident in which she was not hit by a bullet but fell anyway, underscores the manner in which patriarchal control devours both body and spirit. . . .

Adrienne Kennedy: "A Growth of Images"

Adrienne Kennedy (born 1931) was raised in a racially mixed suburb of Cleveland. Her parents were active in the black community. Attending racially and ethnically mixed schools, Kennedy did not experience the sting of racism until she attended Ohio State University, where she encountered overt racial hatred from the women in her dormitory. "The white students on campus did not socialize nor interact in any fashion with black students. This experience made an indelible mark on her sensibility and engendered anger and hatred for racism which would find compelling expression in her plays."[18] Kennedy is best known for her complex, enigmatic dramas, which have been translated into several languages and have been produced in Paris, London, and Rome.

The Great Lakes Theater Festival staged her first full production in Cleveland when it held the first Adrienne Kennedy Festival in 1992, during which the play it had commissioned, *The Ohio State Murders*, received its world premiere. Calling her writing "a growth of images," Kennedy stated, "Autobiographical work is the only thing that interests me. . . . I see my writings as being an outlet for inner, psychological confusion and questions stemming from childhood."[19] If self is the subject of her expressionistic, surrealistic dramas, sui generis but also in the tradition of Marita Bonner's *The Purple Flower*, Glaspell's *The Verge*, and Treadwell's *Machinal*, that self is infinite, containing woman, man, god, and beast; it is also a template for the experience of the African American woman. As epilogue to her autobiography, *People Who Led to My Plays* (1987), Kennedy writes, "My plays are meant to be states of mind" (*People*, n.p.). An avant-gardist, she fashions her poetic dramas through arresting verbal and visual imagery. Like Terry, she changes scenes at a rapid pace. Her characters often split into several selves and her drama's form is often equally fragmented. She writes in a non-Western, circular time and may utilize sets simultaneously or superimpose them one upon the other. From herself as subject,

Kennedy spins a thread that winds through her oeuvre, connecting the plays through shared characters and themes.

Kennedy frequently speaks of the women of her family—mother, aunt, and grandmother—as heroes and inspiration. bell hooks, discussing Kennedy's feminism, comments that "there is an emergent perspective on women's identity . . . that can be read as linked to a growing political concern in the fifties and sixties with female identity—with women's efforts to come to voice—to establish a writer's identity, and this concern is there in Kennedy's work."[20] hooks also celebrates Kennedy's autobiography for "[d]ocument[ing] . . . the harsh nuances and textures that characterize [black women's] relationships to many white women" (183), something that Beah Richards and Childress also document. In a comment foreshadowing reaction to Anita Hill's testimony before the 1991 Senate Judiciary Committee hearings on Clarence Thomas's nomination to the Supreme Court, Susan E. Meigs wrote that Kennedy's "characters represent the community of women, largely excluded from the political mechanisms of black protest, who are nonetheless expected to sacrifice gender issues for racial concerns."[21] For Kennedy, as for Childress, "the history of race . . . is the predominant question of my existence."[22] Significantly, Kennedy identifies Childress as a "great inspiration" (Betsko and Koening, 257). She also credits Lorraine Hansberry's success as inspiring: "I had abandoned playwriting . . . because I thought there was no hope; but with LH's success, I felt reawakened" (*People*, 109).

Funnyhouse of a Negro (1964) was written while Kennedy was in Ghana accompanying her husband on a research trip. If Tommy in Childress's *Wine in the Wilderness* is, in Bill's word, "together"—sure of herself, knowing who she is—Kennedy's Sarah is her polar opposite. In the multicultural chaos of *Funnyhouse*, Sarah fragments into four selves: the Duchess of Hapsburg, Queen Victoria Regina, Jesus, and Patrice Lumumba. Daughter of a woman who "looked like a white woman" and a father who is "the darkest one of us all," Sarah isolates herself in her room. Surrounded by artifacts of the dominant white culture, she writes poetry imitative of Edith Sitwell and has what she describes as her "vile . . . nigger" dream of herself and her white friends living "in rooms with European antiques, photographs of Roman ruins, pianos and oriental carpets." Although she "long[s] to become even a more pallid Negro" than she is, she cannot prevent her father, whom she characterizes as the "wild black beast" who raped her mother, from knocking on her door and begging "forgiveness for . . . being black." All of Sarah's selves speak of the black man as their father; all intend to kill him or believe they have already done so.

Describing the various sets as "my rooms," Sarah tells why she fantasizes about the Hapsburg chamber, the room in Victoria's castle, the hotel where she imagines killing her father, and the jungle; they are "the places myselves exist in." But, she adds, "I know no places. That is, I cannot believe in places. To believe in places is to know hope and to know the emotion of hope is to know beauty. It links us across a horizon and connects us to the world. I find there are no places only my funnyhouse." A culture that insists on identities established on the basis of either/or offers no room for the mulatto, for one who is both and thereby more. Sarah, who begins the play "faceless . . . with a hangman's rope about her neck," ends by hanging herself. She appears to be one more tragic mulatto, like the character cited by Mrs. Carter in *Florence*, killing herself because she is not white. Kennedy, however, does not wish to promulgate this white myth any more than did Childress. Sarah's death, announced from the outset by the noose, becomes a call for the creation of new spaces, for the accommodation of new identities beyond the prison of white patriarchy's binaries.

In *A Movie Star Has to Star in Black and White* (1976), Kennedy continues to deal with representation and transformation. Clara, identified as a playwright and quoting lines she "wrote" for Kennedy's second drama, *The Owl Answers* (1965), keeps vigil at the bedside of her comatose brother while she works through problems in her marriage by projecting herself into scenes from the movies *Now Voyager, Viva Zapata,* and *A Place in the Sun*. The drama testifies to Kennedy's lifelong fascination with film, film stars, and fame, yet it also graphically presents the conundrum of the representation of minorities. Clara's life is the subject and she narrates her own drama, but in a unique manner. She is present in the reenactment of the films, sitting in the boat behind the actor playing Shelley Winters in the scene from *A Place in the Sun,* for example. But Clara, who "plays a bit part" in this story of her life, does not speak. The movie images speak for her, delivering not lines from the movies but from Clara's story. Although Kennedy's protagonist remains sub-

sumed by the white majority, she is neither killed nor, as in *The Owl*, transformed into a nonhuman being, and thus moves closer to speaking for herself.

With *The Alexander Plays,* a quartet centered on the character Suzanne Alexander, a writer, Kennedy continued her "autobiography." No longer strained through white masks or voices, Suzanne Alexander speaks for herself. The first play, *She Talks to Beethoven* (1989), is set in Ghana; as she anxiously awaits the arrival of her husband who vanished two days earlier, Suzanne reads from a diary that has been written on Beethoven, the subject of her current project. So strong is Beethoven's presence for her that he appears; they converse about creativity and fame, and she discovers messages from her missing husband in the notebooks the deaf composer used for communication. When David returns, Suzanne asks if he sent Beethoven; in a voice not unlike Beethoven's, David replies, "I knew he would console you while I was absent," marking the interconnectedness of love, creativity, and art. Parts 3 and 4 of Kennedy's quartet, *The Film Club* (1992) and *The Dramatic Circle* (1992), deal with David's later disappearance; the first is Suzanne's monologue, the second its dramatization.

The most important of the four plays, *The Ohio State Murders,* premiered at the Great Lake's Festival's Adrienne Kennedy Festival in 1992. Beginning as a monologue in which Suzanne rehearses the talk she is to give on the genesis of the violent imagery in her work, the play enlarges into a restaging of Suzanne's memories of her undergraduate days. Kennedy's own pain at the prejudice she experienced living in a dormitory is searingly present in Suzanne's story. More shocking is the tale of the betrayal of this gifted young woman enrolled at the university in an era when minorities had to qualify to become English majors by taking "trial courses." The rage that imploded to split Kennedy's earlier protagonists as they turned inward is directed outward at a patriarchy that employs its privileged status to flatter, seduce, abandon, and murder. Declaring Suzanne's work "brilliant," white professor Robert Hampton seduces her. When she becomes pregnant, he insists he could not be responsible. Later he kidnaps and kills one of her infant twins; several months later, posing as a researcher, he imprisons the baby sitter, murders his second daughter, and kills himself. . . .

Rosalyn Drexler: The Art of Experimentation

Like Kennedy, Rosalyn Drexler (born 1926) is an experimental writer, a classification she also ascribes to life: "Life is experimental because it is changing from moment to moment, and you're never quite sure of the result, but you know something is happening and you are going in an organic direction. Only death is non-experimental. There's nothing more to work with."[23] Drexler gave herself much to work with in a life that includes work as playwright, novelist, singer, painter, wrestler, masseuse, waitress, playground director, and sculptor. Her experience as a wrestler, for example, informs the plot of *Delicate Feelings* (1984). Drexler won Obies for her first play, *Home Movies* (1964), for *The Writer's Opera* (1979), and for three one-act plays, collectively titled *Transients Welcome* (1984). Puns, double entendre, literary allusions, and non sequitur abound in her work. She acknowledges Ionesco as another self (Lamont 1993, viii); several critics also detect the zaniness of the Marx Brothers in her dramas. Her works have been identified as theater of the ridiculous, absurd, collage, and farce; she describes them as "inside out . . . things that most characters only think are given voice and spoken in my work," and feels she has experienced discrimination "because of the kind of noncommercial work [she does]" (Betsko and Koening, 132 and 129). Rosette Lamont calls her destabilization of discourse a "semiotics of instability," within which she deconstructs the "naturalness" of male/female relationships in which the woman is presented as always already inferior. Instead, "Woman as the desiring subject is central to most of her work"[24] She also exposes the tactics of the patriarchy; in *She Who Was He* (1976), Thutmose, Queen Hatshepsut's husband, arranges her murder, "then attempts to erase her name from history, has servants chipping away at obelisks raised in her honor, removes her name from scroll and tomb" (Betsko and Koening, 130).

Raunchiness and humor mark *Home Movies*. In what might be seen as a twentieth-century version of *Fashion*, Mrs. Verdun holds calling hours in her bedroom for guests who include homosexual poet Peter Peterouter, the sneering, stuttering intellectual Charles Arduit, the sly priest Father Shenanagan, Sister Thalia, and John the Truckdriver. Peter, acknowledging his homosexuality, also claims that an encounter in a gymnasium with the missing "well hung" patriarch left him "covered with the rash." Mr. Verdun arrives home literally encased in a large wooden closet delivered by John. He then "breaks his way out of the closet [and] prances around." He tells Mrs. Verdun, "My hormones are in top form" and, singing a sado-masochistic song, they go behind the curtain. In Drexler's hands, the portrait of the controlling patriarch becomes one of the first comic portrayals of bisexuality on the American stage.

The Bed Was Full (1964) was staged in 1983 by the Omaha Magic Theatre, which also presented *Room 17C* (1983), *The Line of Least Existence* (1987), and *The Heart That Eats Itself* (1988). *The Bed Was Full* parodies farce. A wife suspected of infidelity is pursued by a paranoid detective as people literally fall from overhead ramps into bed. In the midst of the absurdity, Drexler limns a male-dominated society in which violence imperils woman's attempts at self-determination, as is illustrated by the model Kali being kidnapped at gunpoint by Joel, who desires her as his model and muse.

In *Occupational Hazard,* the 1992 version of *The Heart That Eats Itself* (1988), Drexler contemplates the nature of art and artist. She calls this adaptation of Kafka's "A Hunger Artist," "a portrait of the artist as suicide" (Lamont 1993, x). Using the play as a vehicle for social critique, Drexler adds a flashback scene illustrating the sexual harassment of Emma by the Official of the Review Board of the Accident Compensation Authority, the agency for which the Artist works before leaving to pursue his calling. As she shoves the Official away and chokes him with her legs he feels only pleasure, then forces her to take money, with the threat, "And remember, mum's the word. Your future depends on it." . . .

Rochelle Owens: "Challenging the Categories"

Asked about the dramatist's function, Rochelle Owens (born 1936) responded, "To improve the well-being of the human psyche by revealing the multitudinous levels of human experience. To get rid of the false, dangerous and sanctimonious images the society inevitably is fixated on. To inspire and generate the possibility of authentic awareness of the sacred obligation of being alive."[25] This advocate of theater as praxis was born in Brooklyn, where she attended public schools, and later studied at the New School for Social Research. A sponsor of the Women's Interart Center, Owens also helped establish the theater arts magazines *Scripts* and *Performance,* served on the advisory board of *Performing Arts Journal,* and taught drama at the University of Oklahoma.

She calls her early work "protofeminist [in] structure and dynamics. Protofeminist because it preceded the wave of political and sociological consciousness of the late seventies. Many women were writing incredible plays which pointed up a warped, sexist reality. . . . I think our work, beyond being avant-garde (that means getting rid of old structures, finding new meaning and creating new forms) also had an aware sensibility of the paradox and the inherent—almost genetic—cellular injustice between the sexes" (Betsko and Koening, 346). As one of several women playwrights responding to the question, "Where Are the Women Playwrights?" in the 20 May 1973 issue of the *New York Times,* Owens noted that while many women were writing for the theater, few were being produced, adding, "[T]hat sad fact is just a part of the general cultural attitude toward the female—women viewed in a particular framework are made invisible and totally ignored . . . [a woman who] dares to write [a] play . . . must have guts of steel and great forbearance to transcend the devious undermining, the negative expectations, and a mountain of other assaults on her sensibilities." In a later interview, she remembers being reviewed as "a housewife who writes plays." Such blatant sexism is among the subjects of her dramas, as are power, bestiality, scapegoating, love, murder, and theater itself—all part of her strategy of "challenging the established categories of theater" (Betsko and Koening, 344, 347).

Owens's *Futz* (1961), ostensibly a tale of bestiality concerning Cy Futz's passion for his pig, Amanda, proves to be a tale of scapegoating and misogyny when viewed under a feminist lens. Futz lives far from town and carries on his porcine amours in the privacy of his barn; to observe this "Satan" at his "abominations" with the pig he calls his "wife," the townfolk must go to his farm. As Cy protests, "I wasn't near people. They came to me and looked under my trousers all the way up to their dirty hearts. They murdered my *own* life." The women in the play, having suffered years of being branded sluts and bitches, agree that "no woman is good" and acquiesce in their own oppression. In the 10 February 1968 *New Yorker,* Edith Oliver called *Futz* "a witty, harsh, fanciful, and touching dramatic poem," but, like other critics, overlooked its feminism. In a 1978 interview, Owens stated, "When *Futz* and my other plays were first produced, there was absolutely no feminist perspective on the part of the critics and intellectuals who had either read or seen my work. Thus, these plays were often seen as a cry for freedom for males. You see, the women were invis-ible. There were women in the plays obviously. The women's story was there. But the critics didn't see it. They all had blinders on. That's why feminism is so important."[26] In 1967 *Futz* won Obies for writing, directing, and acting. . . .

Myrna Lamb: "One Ultimate Revolution"

In her introduction to *The Mod Donna and Scyklon Z: Plays of Women's Liberation* (1971), Myrna Lamb (born 1935) writes: "There are many valid revolutions which we must support. . . . And there is one ultimate revolution which encompasses them all, and that is the liberation of the female of the species."[27] Lamb feels the feminist movement has enabled women to see "themselves differently . . . as potential artists, not merely cooks and bottle-washers"; she wants her drama to effect social change and is "very hurt when people interpret [her] work as purely personal and psychological and don't see the political . . . substructure."[28] She helped found the New Feminist Repertory Theatre, which in 1969 premiered three of her one-act dramas—*But What Have You Done for Me Lately?* and *The Serving Girl and the Lady,* and *In The Shadow of the Crematoria*—an event that Honor Moore describes as a "breakthrough in feminist theatre" (Moore, 499).

In *But What Have You Done for Me Lately?* a male lawmaker implanted with a pregnant uterus offers to the female physician who performed the implant all the reasons why the fetus must be aborted. She counters each protest by echoing the responses made by the patriarchy as it exerts control over women's bodies in the name of religion or humanity; recalling her own unwanted pregnancy, she disparages "righteous male chauvinists of both sexes who identif[y] with the little clumps of cells and g[i]ve them precedence over the former owners of the host bodies." To the Man's protestations, the physician responds, "If one plea is valid, then they might all be. So you must learn to accept society's interest in the preservation of the fetus, within you, within all in your condition." She informs him that as a legislator he killed women, careers, spirits, love, and self-respect. Finally, she agrees to take his case before a board "composed of many women, all of whom have suffered in some way from the laws you so ardently supported." The board decides, "[o]ut of compassion for the potential child and regarding qualities of personality and not sex that make you a potentially unfit mother, . . . that the pregnancy is to be terminated." Written, Lamb admits, as a polemic, *But What Have You Done For Me Lately?* is a powerful statement of woman's right to self-determination.

While other playwrights of the second wave wrote plays that were feminist in philosophy, orientation, and subject matter and utilized anti-realist structure and techniques such as transformation and nonlinear time schemes, held by many to be essential to feminist drama, Lamb made feminism itself her topic in *The Mod Donna: A Space-age Musical Soap Opera with Breaks for Commercials* (1970). On the surface a tale of mate swapping that satirizes the "new morality" of the 1970s, *The Mod Donna* incorporates issues of class status and capitalism into its plea for women's liberation. *The Mod Donna* intersperses choric songs and "commercials" dramatizing the dilemmas of women's everyday lives into the narrative of the capitalist "boss couple," Chris and her husband, Jeff, and the underling couple Donna and Charlie. Lamb details in the commercials and songs the ways in which women are bombarded with such messages as "Be desirable," and "Food is love / . . . So pick up that trusty kitchen tool." In the main plot, Chris, fearing her marriage going stale, has Jeff bring Donna, wife of Charlie, general manager at Jeff's business, into their home and their marriage. Chris convinces Jeff he needs a child to validate his manhood, persuades Donna to bear that child, then decides her marriage has been revitalized and tells the pregnant Donna that she is no longer needed. When Donna refuses to leave, Chris gives Charlie pictures of Donna performing various sex acts with Jeff. Inflamed, Charlie, refusing even to recognize the role Jeff, his employer and master in the capitalist system, plays in Donna's seduction, wields a blunt instrument in what the stage directions call a "symbolic execution" of Donna, a graphic illustration of the manner in which capitalism seizes on women as scapegoats and consumes not only their labor but the women themselves. As the drama ends, the chorus sings of "Our true need / LIBERATION." . . .

Jane Chambers: Dramatizing Lesbian Desire

The best-known plays of Jane Chambers (1937-83) bring onstage the representation of the lesbian and of lesbian desire, not by an outsider—as is the case in Hellman's *The Children's Hour*—but by a member of the community. Born in South Carolina, Chambers studied acting at the Pasadena Playhouse in California. Her dramas have been produced off-Broadway as well as in regional and community theaters and on television.

Chambers was playwright-in-residence for The Glines, a New York Theater established in 1976 by producer John Glines to present drama about the gay life experience. In 1982 the Fund for Human Dignity presented her with its annual award, which honors those who by "their work or by the example of their lives, have made a major contribution to public understanding and acceptance of lesbians and gay men." Chambers was instrumental in fighting what Karla Jay described in the 29 May 1979 *Boston Phoenix* as the oppression arising from "having other people tell your story." In 1984, the Women and Theatre Program of the American Theatre Association (now the Association for Theatre in Higher Education) established the Jane Chambers Playwriting Award for plays written by a woman from a feminist perspective, with a majority of women's roles.

Chambers wrote *A Late Snow* (1974) as a screenplay but was told by her agent, "Nobody's going to buy a movie script about lesbians." To her protest that the successful Broadway play of 1968 about gay men, *The Boys in the Band,* was being filmed, he countered, "Fags are funny, dykes are gloomy."[29] In 1974, when it was produced at Playwrights Horizons, several women refused to read for a role as a lesbian; two who were cast quit—one the night before the play opened (Hoffman, xi). The play presents five women stranded by a snowstorm. Before the storm, Quincey, Ellie's lover, comes to the cabin to install a Dutch cupboard, purchased from Ellie's former lover Pat, as a present celebrating Quincey and Ellie's first anniversary. While Pat helps Quincey move the cupboard into the cabin, Ellie, a college professor, returns from the out-of-town conference she's been attending, bringing with her, Margo, a famous writer. Later, the college roommate Ellie loved unrequitedly arrives. . . .

Martha Boesing: A Radical Voice

An eminent voice in feminist theater, Martha Boesing (born 1936) was the founder, artistic director, and playwright-in-residence of Minneapolis's At the Foot of the Mountain theater from 1974 to 1984; her work has been described as among "the most ambitious and innovative . . . in terms of both form and content."[30] Boesing received her bachelor of arts degree in English from Connecticut College, where her first play, *Accent on Fools,* was produced in 1956. She began doctoral work in theater at the University of Minnesota but left to begin her career with the Minneapolis Repertory Theatre. Actor, director, librettist, designer, and manager, in 1986 Boesing played the title role in At the Foot of the Mountain's *Fefu and Her Friends,* a production directed by Fornes. Her dramas have been presented across American and in Canada, Great Britain, Berlin, and Australia.

Lynne Greeley describes Boesing's dramas as falling into three categories: historic collages in which "Boesing quote[s] the original words of historical figures from documents, such as speeches and biographies, around which the characters [are] built"; collaborative pieces created with the companies by which they were staged; and those dramas of which she is the sole author.[31] In 36 plays and librettos, Boesing deploys her feminist consciousness over issues such as: the threat of nuclear destruction; deep ecology; addictions of various kinds—food, sex, love, and money, as well as chemicals; American involvement in Central America; the effects of Columbus's voyages to the New World; and the Great Depression, always with an eye toward exposing the oppressions of a society erected on patriarchal values and always celebrating the role of feminist consciousness in re-forming both the theater and the world.

In *River Journal* (1975), a modern morality play with music, Boesing works in the tradition of dramatizing the fragmented self, established by Alice Gerstenberg in *Overtones* and continued by Kennedy in *Funnyhouse of a Negro* and *The Owl Answers* and Marsha Norman in *Getting Out.* Here the fragmenting force is patriarchal marriage, analyzed as forcing women to repress their true selves and—to satisfy their husbands—become both flirtatious coquettes and self-sacrificing mother figures. Because this phenomenon is widespread and might be seen by the audience as "natural," Boesing calls for a production incorporating masks, costumes recalling school plays or pageants, and ritual. . . .

Emily Mann: The Theater of Testimony—Society on Trial

Born in Boston in 1952, Emily Mann was raised in Chicago. She attended the University of Chicago Laboratory High School, where she worked on several plays, including Megan Terry's *Viet Rock* and, at 16, directed her first play. As a freshman at Harvard University, she wrote her first play, then from her sophomore year on devoted herself to directing. A Bush Fellowship took her to the University of Minnesota/Guthrie Theatre program, in which she earned a master of fine arts degree in 1976. At the Brooklyn Academy of Music Theatre Company, she directed Crothers's *He and She.* In July 1990 she became artistic director of the McCarter Theater. In the 13 January 1991 *New York Times,* she told Hilary De Vries she was interested in creating a multicultural theater, because, "There are invisible racial and economic barriers that I want to break down. I want to create a theater of different American voices." In addition to Obies for playwriting and directing, Mann received the 1983 Rosamund Gilder Award for "outstanding creative achievement in the theater." She credits "Megan Terry, Irene Fornes, Rosalyn Drexler, Rochelle Owens, and Ntozake Shange [with] revolutioniz[ing] the theater in the seventies. These women radicalized our perception of and our consciousness about theater" (Betsko and Koening, 282).

Called fugues, compositions for voices, documentary drama, and theater of testimony, Mann's plays—combining monologue, dialogue, music, film, and slides and deriving from personal interviews, trial transcripts, and news accounts, both print and electronic—are truly innovative. Her works are not docudramas for she does not offer dramatic reenactment; instead, she distills material from real life in her dramatic retort, working an alchemy of deconstruction. Her work "forces the spectator to confront his or her own attitudes and beliefs and, without offering a facile solution, encourages reevaluation of deeply troubling issues" (Savran, 146). Although Mann is sometimes reluctant to be labeled a feminist, her plays and her philosophy proclaim her feminism. The form of her drama is nonlinear; she puts women in the subject position and eschews dramatizing violence, because "I did not want to perpetuate the myth that violence is sexy, I did not want to be a party to it . . . it's not sexy, and it's not fun. It's rare to see violence between men and women onstage or in film which is not somehow erotic. I want to break down those clichés" (Betsko and Koening, 285). Whether the violence concerns the Holocaust, Vietnam, domestic abuse, or murder, the deed is reported; as in classical Greek drama, the audience sees effects, not enactment. Mann's moral philosophy is also feminist in its insistence on personal responsibility: "I think anything you put on a stage is a great responsibility because you have the power to move and change. . . . You've got to take complete responsibility for both the statements you make and the effect you have on a crowd" (Savran, 158).

Annulla, An Autobiography (1986), which originated as *Annulla Allen: Autobiography of a Survivor* (1974), Mann's first drama, premiered at the Guthrie in a production she directed in 1977. It derives from interviews Mann conducted with the aunt of a friend when she and the friend were traveling in Europe. In the play, Annulla, living in London at the age of 74, delivers a monologue about her life's progress from an affluent, indulged childhood, through having her husband imprisoned in Dachau while she remained free by posing as an Aryan, to working as a domestic servant when she escapes to London. The play is framed by the voice of a 32-year-old American woman, an obvious Mann surrogate. Annulla, who has "seen firsthand men's barbarism taken to his [*sic*] extreme with Hitler," is writing a play, *The Matriarchs,* based on her theory that, "If there were a global matriarchy . . . there would be no more of this evil. *I have all the answers in my play!*" A cultural feminist who believes that mother love "is the most powerful response in the world of a positive kind" and that "No woman who has ever loved her child could be a Stalin or a Hitler," Annulla leaves no space for women who are not mothers and ignores her destructive relationship with her own mother.

In *Still Life,* Mann revisits the issues of violence and feminism. In 1981, the play won Mann Obies for playwriting and direction. The play distills 140 hours of interviews with people she met in Minneapolis. Its staging is simple: the three characters, a man, his mistress, and his wife, sit at a table facing the audience, to whom they address their monologues; they seldom seem aware of each other. (Although the play is drawn from life, this style of presentation is markedly similar to that of Samuel Beckett's *Play,* and Mann does name Beckett as an influence on her work.) Mark, a Vietnam veteran brutalized by the war, has "brought the war home," terrorizing his wife, Cheryl, who says, "Mark wants to kill me." Yet Nadine, the mistress, sees him as the gentlest man she's ever known. Their testimony puts America itself on trial, exposing the interstices between expectations and reality. Mark, whose "biggest question of all my life was / How would I act under combat? / That would be who I was as a man," presents "courage" in combat as proof of manhood, an idea as ancient as warfare itself. Nadine sees herself as a feminist, and while she justly points out that keeping a house and raising children involve "a tremendous amount of work / that in our society is not measurable," she can also speak unironically about women being given "permission" to

drive and has no qualms about her affair with another woman's husband. Mann's critique of patriarchal marriage is reminiscent of Boesing's *River Journal.*

As she did in *Still Life,* Mann uses the audience as a jury in *Execution of Justice,* a drama constructed around the trial of Dan White, former city supervisor, for the murders of San Francisco mayor George Moscone and Harvey Milk, the first openly gay city supervisor. The play was cowinner of the Actors Theatre of Louisville's 1983 Great American Play Contest. Mann combines film and television footage, the trial transcript, and personal interviews in this dramatization of the tensions within Dan White and between conservative and liberal factions in the city; in the process, she spotlights media excesses. She also adds the testimony of those she names the "uncalled witnesses," a chorus that includes a city policeman, a gay rights activist, friends of White, Moscone, and Milk, and a young mother. As Mann's title implies, the workings of the system itself were on trial in this case and, ultimately, Justice herself was executed. White, whom the defense depicted as an all-American boy debilitated by family worries and his consumption of junk food—his lawyers conceived the now infamous "Twinkie defense"—was found guilty of only voluntary manslaughter. While the Young Mother asks, "What are we teaching our sons?" White is given the maximum sentence: seven years and eight months.

Mann is a playwright concerned with moral problems and social justice, who uses documentary material in a nonlinear, nonrealistic manner. Despite Fornes's insistence that the dramas are "not theatre literature. It may be serious and subtle work, but it's not a play" (Savran, 65), Mann has moved theater in new directions by using documentary materials to denaturalize many of the assumptions of a patriarchal society and by confronting her audiences with the difficult decisions that her plays refuse to make for them. Indeed, Emily Mann herself is the most compelling witness in her "theater of testimony."

Ntozake Shange: Loving the "god" Within

Ntozake Shange, born in 1948 in Trenton, New Jersey, to Elois Williams, a psychiatric social worker, and Paul T. Williams, a physician, was named Paulette for her father, who had wanted a boy. The family moved to St. Louis when she was eight; there she was bused to a German-American school, where she experienced the bitterness of racism. At home, Shange met W. E. B. Du Bois, Josephine Baker, Miles Davis, Paul Robeson, and César Chávez. At eighteen she entered Barnard College, majoring in American studies; at 19, after separating from her lawstudent husband, she made the first of several suicide attempts. Nevertheless, she earned a bachelor's degree with honors in 1970. Moving to California, she renounced her "slave name" in 1971 and became *Ntozake* (she who comes with her own things) *Shange* (who walks like a lion). She earned a master's degree in American studies from the University of Southern California, Los Angeles, and began teaching women's studies and African American studies at Sonoma State. She describes the courses she taught as being "inextricably bound to the development of my sense of the world, myself, and women's language" and as "root[ing] me to an articulated female heritage and imperative."[32]

Shange regrets the fact that most plays by black men focus on their battles with white men, and celebrates drama by black women because it does not "continually focus all of our attention on the Other. Our attention [is] in our community."[33] To focus this attention, Shange employs her own orthography. She seldom uses capital letters; employs ampersands, virgules, abbreviations, phonetic spellings, and black dialect; and generally eschews commas and apostrophes. Her language signifies her resistance to the King's English, about which she comments, "i cant count the number of times i have viscerally wanted to attack deform or maim the language that i waz taught to hate myself in / the language that perpetuates the notions that cause pain to every black child as he/she learns to speak of the world & the 'self.'"[34]

As a feminist, Shange insists on the linkage of the personal and the political: "I think the dangerous mistake that women make is to assume the personal is not political. When I make a personal statement, it is to me a political statement" (Betsko and Koening, 370). Interviewed for the 7 May 1989 *New York Times,* she spoke of the place of gender in her writing: "I'm a playwright. But I'm a woman first. I am not a generic playwright. I am a woman playwright. And I would hope that my choice of words and my choice of characters and situations reflect my experience as a woman on the planet. I don't have anything that I can add to the masculine perception of the world. What I can add has to be from what I've experienced. And my perceptions and my syntax, my colloquialism, my preoccupations are founded in race and gender." According to Shange, black

women, to be represented at all, must themselves do the writing.[35] Shange saw the necessity for black women to "move our theater into the drama of our lives" (Foreword, ix), which she accomplishes partly by legitimating female desire in "writing about adolescent girls and young women. . . . And one of the reasons I try to investigate girls from different backgrounds and girls with different senses of success is because I want to make sure that we all know that none of our desires are illegitimate."[36] In form, Shange's drama is feminist and nonlinear, incorporating music, character transformation, and dream sequences. It is also African and African American in its utilization of oral and musical forms found in both cultures. She has won Obies for *for colored girls* and for *Mother Courage and Her Children* (1980), her adaptation of Brecht's play.

for colored girls who have considered suicide / when the rainbow is enuf, only the second play by a black woman to be presented on Broadway (Hansberry's *A Raisin in the Sun* was the first) began its trip there at the Bacchanal, a women's bar in Berkeley, California, in 1974. In September 1976, it opened at the Booth Theater where it ran for two years. The play earned an Obie, the Outer Circle Critics Award, the Audelco (Audience Development Committee) Award for excellence in black theater, the Golden Apple Award, and Tony, Grammy, and Emmy Award nominations. Reminiscent of Marita Bonner's *The Purple Flower* in its use of music and dance, *for colored girls* in its final form consists of 20 poems that together function as a bildungsroman, chanting the coming into consciousness and community of a black Everywoman. Shange calls her drama a "choreopoem"—a term she coined to describe a drama in which the speakers dance or move while delivering their lines—which combines metered prose and jazz rhythms, and which she felt fit, somehow, between genres. . . .

Practice and Praxis

The experimental playwrights of the second wave challenged and deconstructed conventional theater practice. They replaced the through line with a circular structure, set chronological time reeling into nonlinear representation, infused music, dance, and poetry into the prosaic pattern of male-dominated dramas and identified women as desiring subjects rather than adjuncts or reflections of male characters. Moreover, they often eschewed catharsis and closure, preferring that their audiences leave the theaters both aware of, and pondering the solutions to, the oppression they have witnessed.

Notes

1. Gerda Lerner, *The Creation of Feminist Consciousness: From the Middle Ages to Eighteen-Seventy* (New York: Oxford University Press, 1993), 274.

2. Sara M. Evans, *Born for Liberty: A History of Women in America* (New York: The Free Press, 1989), 283.

3. Julia Miles, introduction to *The Women's Project: Seven New Plays by Women* (New York: Performing Arts Journal Publications and American Place Theatre, 1980), 11.

4. Susan Smith Harris, "En-gendering Violence: Twisting 'Privates' in the Public Eye," *Public Issues, Private Tensions*, ed. Matthew Roudané (New York: AMS Press, 1993), 127. Smith discusses the presentation and treatment of women in the dramas of Mamet, Shepard, and Rabe. I am indebted to her for pointing out several of these images.

5. "Alice Childress: A Pioneer Spirit: An Interview by Elizabeth Brown-Guillory," *Sage* 4, no 1 (Spring 1987): 66; hereafter cited in the text as Brown-Guillory 1987.

6. Alice Childress, "A Candle in a Gale Wind," *Black Women Writers (1950-1980): A Critical Evaluation*, ed. Mari Evans (Garden City, N.Y.: Doubleday, 1984), 115.

7. Kathleen Betsko and Rachel Koening, "Alice Childress," *Interviews with Contemporary Women Playwrights* (New York: William Morrow, 1987), 73; this volume is hereafter cited in the text as Betsko and Koening.

8. David Savran, *In Their Own Words: Contemporary American Playwrights* (New York: Theatre Communications Group, 1988), 243; hereafter cited in the text as Savran.

9. Elin Diamond, "Mimesis, Mimicry, and the 'True-Real,'" in *Acting Out: Feminist Performances*, ed. Linda Hart and Peggy Phelan (Ann Arbor: University of Michigan Press, 1993), 375; hereafter cited in the text as Diamond.

10. Jill Dolan, *The Feminist Critic as Spectator* (Ann Arbor: University of Michigan Press, 1988), 85; hereafter cited in the text as Dolan 1988.

11. Peter Feldman, "Notes for the Open Theatre Production," in *Four Plays by Megan Terry* (New York: Simon and Schuster, 1967), 201.

12. See, for example, Julia Kristeva, "Women's Time," *Signs* 7, no. 1 (Autumn 1981): 13-35; Hélène Cixous, "The Laugh of the Medusa," in *New French Feminisms: An Anthology*, ed. Elaine Marks and Isabelle de Courtivon (New York: Shocken Books, 1981), 245-64; and Luce Irigaray, "And the One Doesn't Stir without the Other," *Signs* 7, no. 1 (Autumn 1981): 60-67.

13. Luce Irigaray, "This Sex Which Is Not One," in *New French Feminisms*, 103.

14. Toby Silverman Zinman, "Search and Destroy: The Drama of the Vietnam War," *Theatre Journal* 42, no. 1 (March 1990): 5-26.

15. "Fellow Artists Remember Beckett," *Beckett Circle* 11, no. 2 (Spring 1990): 4.

16. Scott Cummings, "Seeing with Clarity: The Visions of Maria Irene Fornes," *Theatre* 17, no. 1 (1985): 55.

17. Catherine A. Schuler, "Gender Perspective and Violence in the Plays of Maria Irene Fornes and Sam Shepard," in *Modern American Drama*, 224.

18. Margaret B. Wilkerson, "Diverse Angles of Vision: Two Black Women Playwrights," *Theatre Annual* 40 (1985): 107.

19. Adrienne Kennedy, "A Growth of Images," *Drama Review* 21, no 4 (December 1977): 42.

20. bell hooks, "Critical Reflection: Adrienne Kennedy, the Writer, the Work," *Intersecting Boundaries: The Theatre of Adrienne Kennedy*, ed. Paul Bryant-Jackson and Lois More Overbeck (Minneapolis: University of Minnesota Press, 1992), 182.

21. Susan E. Meigs, "No Place but the Funnyhouse: The Struggle for Identity in Three Adrienne Kennedy Plays," in *Modern American Drama*, 173.

22. Adrienne Kennedy, Introduction to *The Dramatic Circle*, in *Moon Marked and Touched by Sun: Plays by African-American Women*, ed. Sydne Mahone (New York: Theatre Communications Group, 1994), 189.

23. Rosette C. Lamont, introduction to *Women on the Verge: 7 Avant-Garde American Plays*, ed. Rosette C. Lamont (New York: Applause, 1993); xxxvi; hereafter cited in the text as Lamont 1993a.

24. Rosette C. Lamont, "Rosalyn Drexler's Semiotics of Instability," *Theatre* 17, no. 1 (Winter 1985): 75.

25. *Playwrights, Lyricists, Composers on Theater*, ed. Otis L. Guernsey, Jr. (New York: Dodd, Mead and Co., 1974), 349.

26. C. B. Coleman, "The Androgynous Muse: An Interview with Rochelle Owens," *Theater* 20, no. 2 (Spring 1989): 21; hereafter cited in the text as Coleman.

27. Myrna Lamb, introduction to *The Mod Donna and Scyklon Z: Plays of Women's Liberation* (New York: Pathfinder Press, 1971), 28; hereafter cited in the text as Lamb.

28. Linda Thurston, "An Interview with Myrna Lamb," *Second Wave* 1 (1971): 13.

29. William M. Hoffman, Introduction to *Gay Plays: The First Collection*, ed. William M. Hoffman (New York: Avon, 1979), x; hereafter cited in the text as Hoffman.

30. Vivian M. Patraka, "Notes on Technique in Feminist Drama: *Apple Pie* and *Signs of Life*," *Women and Performance* 1, no. 2 (1984): 58.

31. Lynne Greeley, *Spirals from the Matrix: The Feminist Plays of Martha Boesing, An Analysis*. Ph.D. diss., University of Maryland, 1987, 126.

32. Ntozake Shange, introduction to *for colored girls who have considered suicide / when the rainbow is enuf* (New York: Macmillan Publishing Co., 1977), x; hereafter cited in the text as *colored girls*.

33. Neil Lester, "An Interview with Ntozake Shange," *Studies in American Drama, 1945-Present* 5 (1990): 45.

34. Ntozake Shange, "foreword/unrecovered losses/black theater traditions," *Three Pieces* (New York: Penguin, 1982), xii; hereafter cited in the text as "foreword."

35. Brenda Lyons, "Interview with Ntozake Shange," *Massachusetts Review* 28 (Winter 1987): 690; hereafter cited in the text as Lyons.

36. Ntozake Shange, introduction to *The Resurrection of the Daughter: Liliane*, in *Moon Marked*, 323; hereafter cited in the text as introduction to *Resurrection*.

WOMEN AUTHORS OF COLOR

ELLIOTT BUTLER-EVANS (ESSAY DATE 1989)

SOURCE: Butler-Evans, Elliott. "Enabling Discourse for Afro-American Women Writers." In *Race, Gender, and Desire: Narrative Strategies in the Works of Toni Cade Bambara, Toni Morrison, and Alice Walker*, pp. 37-58. Philadelphia, Penn.: Temple University Press, 1989.

In the following essay, Butler-Evans writes that the rise of Black feminist discourse took a secondary role in comparison to the issues surrounding the politics of race, however, he feels the resulting Black feminist literature is more complex than that of Black nationalist or general liberal feminist writing.

The broad-based political movement that provided the context for the Black Aesthetic did not exist for Black feminist discourse. In the 1960s, race became the overriding sign for all Black oppression. This subjection of Black feminist discourse to the politics of race had a largely negative impact on the production, distribution, and reception of literature written by Black women. Barbara Smith, addressing this issue, argued:

> The fact that a parallel Black feminist movement has been much slower in evolving cannot help but have an impact upon the situation of Black women writers and artists and explains in part why during this very same period we have been so ignored. There is no political movement to give power or support to those who want to examine Black women's experience through studying our history, literature, and culture. There is no political presence that demands a minimum level of consciousness and respect from those who write or talk about our lives. Finally, there is not a developed body of Black feminist political theory whose assumptions could be used in the study of Black women's art.[1]

It was not solely the absence of a political presence and the suppression of an alternative voice that impeded the emergence of Black feminist literature. Equally significant was Black women's relationship to the civil rights struggle and the emergent liberal white feminist movement of the 1960s and 1970s. The agenda of Black male activists dominated the political questions focused on race. Moreover, the formation of the National Organization for Women and the publication of Betty Friedan's *The Feminine Mystique*, while signifying the emerging consciousness of white feminists, significantly failed to address issues related to Black women.[2]

The ideological tensions generated by conflicts between Black women and white feminists, as well as Black males, are addressed in the Combahee River Collective statement. This treatise, prepared by a group of Black feminists, speaks to the disempowerment of Black women in both the Black liberation movement and feminist politics.

> Black feminist politics [had] an obvious connection in and for black liberation movements, particularly those of the 1960s and 1970s. Many of us were active in those movements . . . and all our lives were affected and changed by their ideology, their goals, and the tactics used to achieve their goals. It was our experience and disillusionment within these liberation movements, as well as experience on the periphery of the white male left, that led to the need to develop a politics that was antiracist, unlike those of white women, and antisexist, unlike those of Black and white men.[3]

Thus, Black feminist discourse is fraught with ideological complexities. Central to its formation is identification with and opposition to the discursive formations generated by the racial politics of Black males and the gender politics of white females. Members of the collective elaborate:

> Although we are feminists and lesbians, we feel solidarity with progressive Black men and do not advocate the fractionalization that white women who are separatists demand. Our situation as Black people necessitates that we have solidarity around the fact of race, which white women, of course, do not need to have with white men, unless it is their negative solidarity as racial oppressors. We struggle together with Black men against racism, while we also struggle with Black men about sexism.
>
> (Pp. 356-366)

The fusion of race and gender issues in Black feminist discourse results in textual production that is far more complex than that of Black nationalist or liberal feminist texts. The emergence of a specific Black feminist consciousness is at its roots akin to Lucien Goldmann's concept of genetic structuralism. Addressing the transformations characteristic of emergent consciousness, Goldmann wrote:

> All human behavior is an attempt to give a meaningful response to a particular situation and tends, therefore, to create a balance between the subject of action and the object on which it bears the environment. . . .

American novelist Gloria Naylor (1950-).

Human relations are presented as two-sided processes: destructuration of old structurations and structurations of new totalities capable of creating equilibria capable of satisfying the new demands of the social groups that are elaborating them.[4]

For Goldmann, the processes of "destructuration" and "restructuration" occur within a context in which individuals always belonged to several groups (e.g., family, nation, race), each acting on his or her consciousness to form a "unique, complex, and relatively incoherent structure." When the group comes into a consciousness of its own, however, memberships in other units tend to cancel one another out and "we are confronted with a much simpler, more coherent structure."[5]

I would argue that what emerges in Black feminist discourse in general and the narratives of Black women in particular is probably less a "simpler, more coherent structure" than a discursive formation marked by tensions and dissonance; however, Goldmann's concepts of "destructuration" and "restructuration" seem central to the production of texts generated in a political context that is both race and gender specific.

The Combahee Statement illuminates the race-gender problematic in Black feminist discourse. As self-named lesbian-feminists, the mem-

bers of the collective opposed homophobia along with racism and sexism. Racial politics, however, precluded total identification with sexual politics. Arguing that the perceived anti-male bias of the politics of lesbian separatism omits "far too much and far too many people, particularly Black men, women, and children," the Combahee women explicitly stated their opposition to, and difference from, the politics of lesbian separatism:

> We reject the stance of lesbian separatism because it is not a viable political analysis or strategy for us. We have a great deal of criticism and loathing for what men have been socialized to be in this society, what they support, how they act, and how they oppress. But we do not have the misguided notion that it is their maleness, per se . . . that makes them what they are. As Black women we find any type of biological determinism a particularly dangerous and reactionary basis upon which to build a politic. We must also question whether lesbian separatism is an adequate and progressive political analysis and strategy . . . since it so completely denies any but sexual sources of women's oppression, negating the facts of race and class.

(P. 367)

One might expect, then, that the narratives of Black women are almost always driven by ideological positions that are essentially dissonant and at times even contradictory. If we read the political text, or more accurately the historical moment of their production, we are able to identify the tensions that inform their creation.

The Reconceptualization of Feminist Discourse

Discussion of the narrative strategies employed by Black women writers properly begins with an exploration of their semiotic practices. The racial dimension of Afro-American women's fiction may be traced to Black Aesthetic discourse, but the insertion of a Black female subject requires extensive revision of that discourse. Not only the rewriting of the racial narrative but a significant reconceptualization of feminist discourse would be needed to accommodate the politics of race. The intricate restructuring of narrative priorities in the representation of experience necessary to such a revision is rather like Sandra Gilbert and Susan Gubar's description of the relationship of the woman writer to patriarchal discourse in general. Addressing the issues central to a woman's narrating her story, they write:

> Her battle . . . is not against her (male) precursor's reading of the world but against his reading of her. In order to define herself as an author she must redefine the terms of her socialization. Her

revisionary struggle, therefore, often becomes a struggle for what Adrienne Rich has called "Revision—the act of looking back, of seeing with fresh eyes, of entering an old text from a new critical direction . . . an act of survival."[6]

Gilbert and Gubar conclude by arguing that women writers "actively seek a female precursor who . . . proves by example that a revolt against patriarchal literary authority is possible."[7] Directions in Black feminist criticism in general have rediscovered Zora Neale Hurston as a female precursor. Nevertheless, one should be mindful of the dangers inherent in postulating too hastily the existence of a "tradition" of Afro-American women's narrative. Hazel Carby's recent discussion of Black feminist criticism illuminates the problems inherent in such a critical approach:

> Black feminist criticism has too frequently been reduced to an experiential relationship that exists between black women as critics and black women as writers who represent black women's reality. Theoretically, this reliance on a common, or shared, experience is essentialist and ahistorical. Following the methodologies of mainstream literary criticism and feminist literary criticism, black feminist criticism presupposes the existence of a tradition and has concentrated on establishing a narrative of that tradition. This narrative constitutes a canon from these essentialist views of experience which is then placed alongside, though unrelated to, traditional and feminist canons.[8]

Although I do not argue for the creation or construction of a Black women's narrative "tradition" that has its genesis in Hurston's fiction, or even that her work might be read as a model for Black women's writing, I do suggest that an examination of her textual strategies significantly clarifies the problems characteristic of race- and gender-specific narratives.

The Narrative Strategies of Zora Neale Hurston

Hurston wrote during the Harlem Renaissance and the Great Depression, two moments in history when Black letters were dominated by male voices, and a politicized Black male discourse focused on racial oppression. Introducing a female subject and proto-feminist discourse, Hurston focused on the deconstruction of privileged and valorized epistemologies and the substitution of alternative feminine perceptions. Whereas the dominant view favored science, Hurston praised folk wisdom. Black male narratives focused on the public arena and racial strife; Hurston stressed the private and domestic. And whereas Black male narratives addressed the struggles between an in-

ON THE SUBJECT OF...

GLORIA NAYLOR (1950-)

Known for her lyrical prose and her skillful infusion of the mythical and magical in her novels, Naylor realistically portrays the varied lives of African Americans, particularly her examinations of the dual pressures of being a minority and a woman in a Caucasian, male-oriented society. Naylor's parents were sharecroppers in Robinson, Mississippi who moved to New York City one month before Naylor was born on January 25, 1950. Naylor attended Andrew Jackson High School in Queens, New York. Upon graduation she became a Jehovah's Witness missionary for seven years, and later returned to New York in 1975 to pursue a degree in nursing at Medgar Evers College. When Naylor recognized her strong interest in literature, she transferred to Brooklyn College to study English. While studying at Brooklyn College, Naylor published her first short story, "A Life on Beekman Place," in *Essence*. She later expanded the story into her first novel, *The Women of Brewster Place* (1982), which won the American Book Award for best new novel in 1983. She received her B.A. from Brooklyn College in 1981 and her M.A. in African-American studies from Yale in 1983, the same year she was awarded a National Endowment for the Arts fellowship. One of the recurring themes explored in Naylor's work is the special bond that can exist between women, whether out of common experience or of shared history. In *The Women of Brewster Place*, Naylor chronicles the aspirations and disappointments of seven female residents of Brewster Place, a dilapidated ghetto housing project. Naylor devotes individual chapters to the lives of each of her characters, detailing the circumstances that brought the women to the neighborhood, their relationships with each other, and the devastating events that heighten the difficulty of leaving Brewster Place. As the women cope with living in a racially polarized and sexist society, they encounter abuse and indifference from their fathers, husbands, lovers, and children, and alleviate their suffering through female solidarity and nurturing.

ner Black world and an outer white world, Hurston largely restricted her explorations to the inner world of Black life.[9]

Hurston's deconstructive strategies signaled a political and cultural intervention essentially different from the dominant racial discourse of the period. Those who claimed the right to address racial issues were more or less in harmony with the position Wright articulated in "Blueprint," and the issues Hurston raised were largely discredited. The two discursive formations—Black male writers' emphasis on racial struggle and Hurston's on the private and personal—are distinguished in much the same way as Michel Foucault's "subjugated and scientific knowledges."

> By subjugated knowledges one should understand . . . a whole set of knowledges that have been disqualified as inadequate to their task or insufficiently elaborated; naive knowledges, located low down on the hierarchy, beneath the required level of cognition or scientificity. I believe that it is through the reemergence of these low ranking knowledges, these unqualified even disqualified knowledges . . . and which I would call a popular knowledge (*le savoir de gens*) though it is far from being a general commonsense knowledge, but is on the contrary a particular, local, regional knowledge, a differential knowledge incapable of unanimity and which owes its force only to the harshness with which it is opposed by everything surrounding it—that it is through the reappearance of this knowledge . . . that criticism performs its work.[10]

Hurston undermines scientific knowledge by emphasizing subjugated forms of knowledge, a strategy that is clearly evident in her approach to anthropological chores. When Hurston "does" anthropology, nothing separates the anthropologist and the subject of her inquiry; she strongly emphasizes, sometimes explicitly and other times implicitly, the relationship between the two. We observe in her work the fusion of Geertz's notion of the "experience-near" and the "experience-distant" approaches to anthropological research.[11]

In one of the first deconstructive readings of Hurston's works, Barbara Johnson addresses Hurston's "strategies and structures of problematic address" and manner of "dealing with multiple agendas and heterogeneous implied readers."[12] Arguing that Hurston alternately narrates from an "inside" and an "outside," Johnson considers a passage from *Mules and Men*:

> The shifts and reversals in this passage are multiple. Hurston begins as an outsider, a scientific narrative voice that refers to "these people" in the third person, as a group whose inner lives are difficult to penetrate. Then, suddenly, she leaps into

the picture she has just painted, including herself in a "we" that addresses a "you"—the white reader, the new implied outsider. The structure of address changes from description to direct address. From that point on it is impossible to tell whether Hurston the narrator is *describing* a strategy or *employing* one.[13]

This rather intricate narrative strategy becomes even more evident in Hurston's fiction in which the merging of at least two narrative voices produces the text's ideology. Of particular interest is the manner in which a seemingly simple realistic narrative is transformed into a statement of proto-feminist ideology. This process can be seen at work in the modes of narration in *Their Eyes Were Watching God,* generally considered to be one of the earliest statements of Black feminist ideology.

"de mule uh de world"

Their Eyes Were Watching God was produced in a period in which Afro-American fiction, indeed most writing of the time, primarily emphasized the political. In the post-Harlem Renaissance and the Great Depression period, Black writers saw the patronage system decline as a literary mode of production.[14] Wright's "Blueprint" was the earliest expression of concern for the political content of art. And perhaps the most concrete application of Wright's theory to his own works was in two of his early short stories, "Fire and Cloud" and "Bright and Morning Star," both of which focused on the fusion of the ideologies of Black nationalism and Marxism to achieve political power. Other Black writers of the period, while not necessarily Marxist in their orientation, also highlighted issues primarily related to the Black liberation struggle. Arna Bontemps's rereading and reinscription of the Gabriel Prosser slave rebellion in Virginia in 1800 resulted in the reconstruction of that event as a metaphor for the transhistorical Black quest for freedom.[15] William Attaway's novels, with their focus on the cultural dislocation resulting from the shift of the Black population from the rural South to the urban North, from an economy based on agriculture to one in which technology and industry were dominant, and from a politics based on race to one that assumed class as a central element, further contributed to the prevailing trends in fictional development among Black writers during the period.[16]

Produced within this historical and cultural milieu, Hurston's novel was significant for its radical refusal to reproduce the ideologies that informed Black cultural production of the period. *Their Eyes Were Watching God* actually undermines

Black writing of the time through its insertion of the feminine. While novels by Black males focused on racial struggles between Blacks and whites, Hurston's novel explored the personal, internal struggles between men and women in the Black community. While her male colleagues represented the heroic and antiheroic exploits of Black males, Hurston focused almost exclusively on the Black woman's quest for personal freedom. And while Black male writers generally viewed Black folklore and the folk tradition as peripheral to the major concerns of their narratives, Hurston saw them as fundamental elements, as constituting dominant existential modalities of Black life, and gave folklore a central role in her narrative.

The ideology of *Their Eyes Were Watching God* is produced through a somewhat intricate narrative process. Janie, the putative narrator, tells her story to Pheoby, who mediates between Janie's world and that of the reader, establishing external frames of references for the issues generated by the narrative. Two voices, articulated in two essentially different linguistic codes, always address the reader and the interplay of these voices produces the ideology of the text. Basil Bernstein's concepts of elaborated and restricted codes might be helpful here. Identifying linguistic codes directly with the social class of speakers, Bernstein defines the elaborated code as that of the middle-class speaker and the restricted code as that of the working class. Bernstein describes their roles:

> Elaborated codes orient their users towards universalistic meanings, whereas restricted codes orient, sensitize their users to particularistic meanings. . . . Elaborated codes are less tied to a given or local structure and thus contain the potentiality of change in principles. . . . When codes are elaborated the socialised has more access to the grounds of his own socialisation and so can enter into reflexive relationship to the social order he has taken over. Where codes are restricted, the socialised has less access to the grounds of his socialisation, and thus reflexiveness may be limited in range.[17]

Janie and her peers employ a subliterate linguistic mode largely represented by its evocation of Black speech patterns. Marked by its identification with a rural Black folk culture, it establishes the difference between its world and that of the reader. (My assumption here, of course, is that the reading public is largely middle class and white.) This code, which often depends on parable and metaphor, situates Hurston's characters in the realm of the exotic, the racially and culturally different. Thus their discourse—represented by the particular and concrete and

hermetically enclosed within a specific Black culture—allows the reader to distance himself or herself from events in the narrative. The external narrator, however, employs a code that is the same as that of the apparent reader, and through her mediations situates that discourse in another realm, bestowing upon it ideological significance. This narrative ploy can be seen in several key episodes of the novel.

Nanny, Janie's grandmother, concerned about her granddaughter's welfare and recognizing her own suffering, advances an argument for Janie's need to marry:

> Honey, de white man is de ruler of every thing as far as Ah been able tuh find out. Maybe it's some place way off in de ocean where de black man is in power, but we don't know nothin' but what we can see. So de white man throw down de load and tell de nigger man tuh pick it up. He pick it up because he have to, but he don't tote it. He hand it to his womenfolks. De nigger woman is de mule uh de world so far as Ah can see. Ah been praying for it to be different with you.[18]

The figure of the Black woman as "de mule uh de world" becomes a dialectical metaphor,[19] subsuming the major episodes and illuminating an aspect of the text's ideology. Nanny enlarges on this metaphor through her personal story when she relates her experience as a victim of sexual exploitation by her white master and recalls the rape of her daughter (Janie's mother). The metaphor, embedded within a parable, also is used to support Nanny's argument for a marriage based on property and security.

For Janie, however, the figure of the "mule" directly conflicts with her metaphors of the pear tree and the horizon. Hence the two figures represent at a colloquial level the tensions that the text seeks to resolve and the ideologies it wishes to explore. Within this context, the narrative remains within the realm of the particular: the conflict between a wise old Black woman and her naive granddaughter. There is still distance between the world of the text and that of the reader.

The external narrator transcodes that conflict, however, restating it in the linguistic framework of the reader. After inserting two rhetorical questions—"Did marriage end the cosmic loneliness of the unmated?" and "Did marriage compel love like the sun of the day?"—she undermines Nanny's position through irony. Describing Janie's impending marriage to Logan Killicks, she observes:

In the few days to live before she went to Logan Killicks and his often-mentioned sixty acres, Janie asked inside of herself and out. She went back and forth to the pear tree continuously wondering and thinking. Finally out of Nanny's talk and her own conjectures, she made a sort of comfort for herself. Yes, she would love Logan after they were married. She could see no way for it to come about, but Nanny and the old folks had said it, so it must be so. Husbands and wives always loved each other, and that was what marriage meant.

(P. 38)

Clearly what is foreshadowed here is the failure of the marriage. Even the tone in which the narrator describes Janie's entry into the marriage is ominous ("In the few days in which she had to live," and Killicks's "often-mentioned sixty acres"), and the text from that moment simply moves to illustrate that marriage does not end "the cosmic loneliness of the unmated" or "compel love like the sun of the day." Janie's desire for "things sweet wid mah marriage lak when you sit under a pear tree and think" is destined to go unfulfilled. The failure of the marriage constitutes an epiphany for Janie, but it is the narrator who intervenes to interpret the episode: "The familiar people and things had failed her so she hung over the gate and looked up the road towards way off. She knew now that marriage did not make love. Janie's first dream was dead, so she became a woman" (P. 44).

What occurs in the episodes focused on the union between Logan and Janie, then, is the demystification of marriage as a romantic institution. The mystical and sensuous world of the pear tree stands in direct contrast to the crude reality of marriage as an unromantic institution based on security and property. This ideological statement is reinforced almost entirely through the narrator's mediation, which comments on, enlarges, and interprets Janie's feelings, thereby placing them in a larger context.

The relationship of narrative stance to the production of ideology is far more complex in sections of the text that explore Janie's marriage to Joe Starks. Here the issue is the empowerment of men and the resulting suppression of women's voices. Through complex narrative strategies of irony, direct commentary, and intertextuality, Hurston reinforces the ideology of the text. The tone of this section is announced in the description of the couple on the day of their marriage:

He was very solemn and helped her to the seat beside him. With him on it, it sat like some high, ruling chair. From now on until death she was going to have flower dust and spring time sprinkled over everything. A bee for her bloom. Her old

thoughts were going to come in handy now, but new words would have to be made and said to fit them.

(Pp. 54-55)

Here the narrator's appropriation of the language and perceptions of the world of the characters encapsulates what will eventually represent the areas of major conflict between Janie and Joe. The ruling chair, representing Joe's need for power and control, will later appear recurrently in the depiction of their marriage as the symbol of male power and dominance, as well as the location from which she is totally objectified. Joe "[builds] a high chair for her to sit and overlook the world," thereby alienating her from the world of real people with whom she wishes to interact. The narrator again contextualizes Janie's position that "we ain't natural wid one 'nother" by broadening its frame of reference:

Janie soon began to feel the impact of awe and envy against her sensibilities. The wife of the mayor was not just another woman as she had supposed. She slept with authority and so was part of it in the town mind. She couldn't get but so close to most of them in spirit.

(P. 74)

In at least one point in the narrative, Hurston reintroduces irony to comment on male oppression of women. While Joe's physical abuse of Janie occurs within a particular and personal context, its presentation in the narrative expands it to reflect on the seemingly trivial events that often lead to domestic violence. Focusing on the moment when Janie withdrew from her marriage, the narrator describes the physical attack as follows:

It happened over one of those dinners that chasten all women sometimes. They plan and they fix, and they do, and then some kitchendwelling fiend slips a scrochy, soggy, tasteless mess into their pots and pans. Janie was a good cook and Joe had looked forward to his dinner as a refuge from other things. So when the bread didn't rise, and the fish wasn't quite done at the bone, and the rice was scorched, he slapped Janie until she had a ringing sound in her ears.

(P. 112)

This narrative establishes a link between Janie and Joe's specific domestic situation and the larger world in which marital discord leads to domestic violence. This linkage of the particular world of Eatonville and the world of the reader is made even more forcefully when the narrator intervenes to explain the impact of Janie's verbal triumph over Joe in the "signifying" contest. What is at issue is not only the intervention of a woman in a largely male ritual but the status of manhood itself. The narrator then interprets the encounter for the reader, placing it in a broader context and thereby connecting it with a world that is recognizable to the reader:

> Janie had robbed him of his illusion of irresistible maleness that all men cherish, which was terrible. The thing that Saul's daughter had done to David. But Janie had done worse, she had cast down his empty armor before men and they had laughed and would keep on laughing. When he paraded his possessions hereafter, they would not consider the two together.
>
> (P. 123)

The verbal exchange is then removed from its lighthearted context and, through the narrator's mediation, becomes a metaphor for large issues of the code of manliness and a direct statement of male-female relationships. Throughout those episodes of the novel that focus on the union between Janie and Joe, there is a recurrent intertextuality, a strategy in which much of the material from Hurston's other works is retextualized and appears as embedded narratives. These appearances in their new contexts give the material larger metaphorical significance. All the bawdiness of the lying sessions is reproduced here, but it assumes special significance because it represents a world of male camaraderie from which women are excluded, and the incident of the mule, taken from *Mule Bone*, the collaborative effort between Hurston and Langston Hughes,[20] becomes an extended metaphor, reinvoking Nanny's original metaphor and indirectly commenting on Janie's marital situation. The anthropological materials, commented on and illuminated by the external narrator, are reworked within the context of the novel as tropes through which the underlying ideology of the text is explored. This transcoding of materials from the restricted code to the metalanguage of elaborate codes demands that the reader confront its ideology.

The narrator's intervention is even more direct in her exploration of Janie's internal conflict, the tensions between the "inside" and the "outside." Because Janie "didn't read books," her sense of self-worth is diminished (P. 119). This direct separation between Janie and the reader justifies a narrative intervention in which the narrator interprets Janie's life for us. Still, in carefully remaining within the world of Eatonville and simultaneously taking a position outside it, the narrator mediates between text and reader. The language of the narrator, although increasingly metaphorical, is couched in the code of the reader without dramatically removing itself from the Eatonville milieu.

Hence the inside-outside dichotomy (which represents the private and public sides of Janie's life) and the image of Janie's starching and ironing her face (which represents her acting out public roles) keep the text grounded in the epistemology of the concrete material world. And as metaphorical vehicles, they enable the reader to grasp the ideological content of the text, thus reinforcing it. An example of this strategy is seen in Hurston's treatment of the encounter between Janie and Joe in the store. Joe, sensitive about his physical degeneration, attempts to ridicule and degrade Janie by disparaging her physical appearance. At the conclusion of his tirade, the narrator interprets the crowd's response:

> A big laugh started off in the store but people got to thinking and stopped. It was funny if you looked at it right quick, but it got pitiful if you thought about it awhile. It was like somebody snatched off part of a woman's clothes while she wasn't looking and the streets were crowded. Then too, Janie took the middle of the floor to talk right into Jody's face, and that was something hadn't been done before.
>
> (P. 122)

This direct address to the reader—"It was funny if you looked at it right quick, but it got pitiful if you thought about it awhile"—elicits a reexamination of the episode and the insertion of it within the broader ideological framework of the novel. An event that, unmediated, seemed like raucous humor among "primitive" Blacks, is metaphorically expanded to represent the dehumanizing of Janie. The movement from Janie in particular to a woman in general ("It was like somebody snatched off part of a woman's clothes") even more strongly demands that the incident be read as a metaphor for the degradation of all women.

The narrative strategy in the section of the novel that focuses on Janie's union with Joe, then, is always determined by the ideology of the text. Through a complex interplay between elaborate and restricted codes, the particular and often seemingly exotic is transmuted and reconstructed as a metaphor for larger issues. Here the narrative intervention is more direct than in the treatment of Janie's union with Killicks because the issues involved—the powerlessness of women and the dominance of men—are considerably more complex. While the Killicks episode simply deconstructed the mythology of marriage as a romantic institution, the Starks episode explores it as the site of women's oppression.

The third division of the text, those episodes in which the dominant focus is the union between Janie and Tea Cake, involves still more complex narrative strategies. The apparent unifying focus is the marriage itself, representing Janie's discovery of both her pear tree and horizon, and thereby evoking the ideal nonoppressive representation of marriage. Yet in this section of the novel the most radical departures from the novel's concerns are introduced. Not only does a subtext undermine the romantic depiction of marriage, but narrative boundaries collapse as political issues are inserted into the text.

On the surface, an idyllic union is constructed. Janie abandons the world of property and responsibility to embark on the carefree life promised by a union with Tea Cake. Her act marks not only an assertion of freedom but a dramatic break with her past. It becomes a total repudiation of Nanny's view, which valued "property and titles." Rejecting Nanny's position on the grounds that "Ah done live Grandma's way, now Ah means tuh live mine," Janie explains to her friend Pheoby:

> She was borned in slavery when folks, dat is black folks, didn't sit down anytime dey felt lak it. So sittin' on porches lak de white madam looked lak uh mighty fine thing tuh her. Dat's what she wanted for me—don't keer whut it cost. Git up on uh high chair and sit dere. She didn't have time tuh think whut tuh do after you got up on de stool uh do nothin'. De object wuz tuh git dere. So Ah got up on de high stool lak she told me, but Pheoby, Ah done nearly languished tuh death up dere. Ah felt like de world wuz cryin' extry and Ah ain't read de common news yet.
>
> (P. 173)

This statement of rebellion summarizes the failure of the first two marriages and signals the emergence of Janie's new consciousness. The "high chair" and "high stool" metaphors point even more specifically to the union with Starks and reemphasize for the reader the particular failures of that marriage. It projects an ideal picture of marriage in Janie's union with Tea Cake. Yet central to that union is an emphasis on an uncomplicated life marked by the couple's working together in the fields, indulging in sensual pleasures, and participating in the various rituals—parties, lying sessions—that are part of an organic Black community. Even those moments of jealousy that the couple experiences are initially represented in a light manner. In presenting this idyllic picture of marriage, however, the text glides over some of the problems with the union, seeming to move away from its own ideology.

This is evident when Tea Cake beats Janie "tuh show dem Turners who is boss." The narrator intervenes to place the incident in context from Tea Cake's point of view:

> When Mrs. Turner's brother came and she brought him over to be introduced, Tea Cake had a brainstorm. Before the week was over he had whipped Janie. Not because her behavior justified his jealousy, but it relieved that awful fear inside him. Being able to whip her reassured him in possession. No brutal beating at all. He just slapped her around a bit to show he was boss. Everybody talked about it next day in the fields. It aroused a sort of envy in both men and women.
>
> (P. 218)

The narrative perspective employed raises two important points. In the previous description of Joe Starks's slapping Janie, the narrator's tone is one of strong disapproval and the focus is clearly on Janie's response, signaling the point in her marriage when she could no longer be "petal blossom" open with Joe. The shift to Tea Cake's perspective, the trivializing of the incident in the text ("No brutal beating at all. He just slapped her around a bit to show he was boss."), and the suppression of Janie's voice result in an ideological ambiguity. The description of the community's approval and envy would indicate that Hurston is describing a culture in which violence against women was normal. Most significant is the narrator's refusal to judge the act or represent it in a manner that would make Tea Cake a villain or an unsympathetic character.

This episode might be seen as one of several in which both the narrative focus and resultant ideology of the text become less clearly delineated than they are in earlier sections of the novel. New thematic materials are introduced that signal two forms of disruption: deconstructions of the previously depicted organic black communities and the overall apparent unity of the text. While the episodes that depict the union between Tea Cake and Janie suggest a surface ideological closure and resolution, the materials in the subtext highlight dissonances and contradictions.

An example of this is seen in the representation of Mrs. Turner in the text. The introduction of the political issue of "colorism" inserts an issue peripheral to the dominant ideology of the text. Mrs. Turner's scorn for blacks, depicted at the level of caricature, is symbolic of the self-hatred that some light-complexioned blacks experience. Her rejection of everything black: "White doctors always gits mah money. Ah don't go in no nigger store tuh buy nothin' neither. Colored folks don't know nothin' bout no business" (p. 211) and her celebration of her own white features ("Look at me! Ah ain't got no flat nose and liver lips. Ah'm uh featured woman" [p. 211]) make her a figure for ridicule. The narrator, however, depicts her as a comic-tragic figure:

> Mrs. Turner, like all other believers, had built an altar to the unattainable—Caucasian characteristics for all. Her god would smite her, would hurl her from pinnacles and lose her in deserts. But she would not forsake his altars. Behind her crude words was a belief that somehow she and others through worship could attain her paradise—a heaven of straight-haired, thin-lipped, high-nose bone white seraphs.
>
> (P. 216)

The introduction of color strife within the black community serves two purposes in the text. First, it reinforces the image of Janie as both maverick and heroic figure. As a fair-complexioned black, she chooses to identify with ordinary blacks, thus manifesting what Alice Walker later describes as "racial health." This depiction of Janie resonates with Hurston's larger battle with her contemporaries in that it addresses, at least indirectly, the absurdity of denying one's racial identity and seeking total absorption into white culture. Second, it is a deconstruction and rejection of the myth of the tragic mulatta. The mulatta figure, inscribed in previous literature as the embodiment of refinement and heroism, surfaces here as both comic and pathetic.[21]

The hurricane episode introduces still another issue that seems to be extraneous to the major theme of the text: the oppressive relationship between the white world and the black world. Whereas the focus on Janie emphasized intraracial conflict, the shift to Tea Cake addresses the ideology of racism. In this section of the novel, the white world looms as a destructive and omnipresent force, which shapes Tea Cake's understanding of his survival within a racist society. Complaining to Janie about the need to try to reach the Everglades, where they are known by whites, Tea Cake argues:

> [In Palm Beach] De [blacks] de white man know is nice colored folks De ones he don't know is bad niggers. . . .
>
> Ah done watched it time and time again; each and every white man think he know all de good darkies already. He don't need tuh know no mo'. So far as he's concerned, all dem he don't know

oughta be tried and sentenced tuh six months behind de United States privy house at hard smellin'.

> (P. 255)

Only limited attention is given to this episode, but it introduces the issue of racial politics into the text. Tea Cake's encounter with whites is always depicted as degrading and dehumanizing. Through the inscription of this dehumanization and degradation, Hurston moves the text from its major focus—Janie's coming to womanhood and self-awareness—to the oppressive relationship between the Black community and the white community. Again the novel, inserting an alternative discourse, transgresses its predetermined narrative boundaries.

The major episode in which this shift in narrative focus occurs is at Janie's trial. Janie, whose guilt or innocence is to be determined by "twelve strange white men," is presented as also having to contend with the bigotry of the Black community, which would demand that she pay with her life for having killed Tea Cake in self-defense. Indicating the force of the opposition that Janie faces, the narrator represents the community as a single voice:

> Tea Cake was a good boy. He had been good to that woman. No nigger woman ain't never been treated no better. Naw suh! He worked like a dog for her and nearly killed himself saving her in the storm, then soon as he got a little fever from the water, she had took up with another man. Sent for him to come there from way off. Hanging was too good. All they wanted was a chance to testify.
>
> (P. 276)

The response replicates earlier reactions to Janie's digressions from community mores—Nanny's disapproval of Janie's rejection of Logan Killicks, the response of the Eatonville citizenry to her rebellion against Joe Starks, and her initial romantic involvement with Tea Cake. Essentially different here is the construction of the entire community as a monolothic voice, the reification and objectification of communal opposition. The intolerance of the community to women, especially Janie, who depart from its codes of acceptable conduct is thereby reinforced.

These seemingly extraneous matters—the colorism issue, the Black-white conflict, and intolerance in the community—all appear to disrupt the unity of the text, but they represent narrative ruptures generated by an attempt to structure an ideological position from both race and gender concerns. These episodes relate to problems that must be explored in any attempt to construct Black feminist discourse. As I later illustrate, at least two of the three issues are inscribed in the narratives of Morrison, Bambara, and Walker. Their fiction consists of the significant reconceptualizing, revising, and rewriting of earlier texts. Its racial content is grounded in the protonationalism of Wright's early works and the heterogeneous discourses that constitute the Black Aesthetic. Inasmuch as racial discourses construct race around the sign of the Black male, however, the Black female subject becomes the major thrust of Black women's narratives. Central to their strategy is a self-construction that begins with the realization that they are divided between two political imperatives: a politics of race that often suppresses issues of gender, and a politics of gender that marginalizes racial issues. Narrative becomes a vehicle for synthesis and the construction of a new political vision. Such a self-construction inevitably involves the search for alternative modes of narration.

Notes

1. Barbara Smith, "Toward A Black Feminist Criticism," in *But Some of Us Are Brave: Black Women's Studies*, ed. Gloria T. Hull, Patricia Bell Scott, and Barbara Smith (New York: Feminist Press, 1983), 159.

2. For a discussion of the roles assigned to Black women in the Black political movement and the white feminist movement, see Marable, *How Capitalism Underdeveloped Black America*; and Paula Giddings, *When and Where I Enter: The Impact of Black Women on Race and Sex in America* (New York: Bantam, 1985), 299-324.

3. See "The Combahee River Collective: A Black Feminist Statement," in *Capitalist Patriarchy and the Case for Socialist Feminism*, ed. Zillah R. Eisenstein (New York: Monthly Review Press, 1979), 363. Hereafter cited in the text by page number.

4. Lucien Goldmann, *Towards A Sociology of the Novel*, trans. Alan Sheridan (London: Tavistock, 1978), 156.

5. Ibid., 158.

6. Sandra M. Gilbert and Susan Gubar, *The Madwoman in the Attic: The Woman Writer and the Nineteenth-Century Literary Imagination* (New Haven: Yale University Press, 1979), 49.

7. Ibid.

8. Hazel V. Carby, *Reconstructing Womanhood: The Emergence of the Afro-American Woman Novelist* (New York: Oxford University Press, 1987), 16.

9. My concepts of "inner" and "outer" worlds are adapted from Lotman. According to Ann Shukman's reading of Lotman, "The inner/outer opposition may be variously interpreted in different cultures and different texts as 'own people/other people,' 'believers/heathens,' 'culture/barbarity.'" Of course, implicit in my reading of Hurston's works is the concept of an imaginary (i.e., created by images) inner world of Black women that posits its opposition to outer worlds of white men and women and Black men. See Ann Shukman, *Literature and Semiotics: A Study of the Writings of Yu. M. Lotman* (Amsterdam: North-Holland, 1977), 95-96.

10. Michel Foucault, *Power/Knowledge: Selected Interviews and Other Writings 1972-77*, ed. Colin Gordon and trans. Colin Gordon, Leo Marshall, John Mepham, and Kate Soper (New York: Pantheon, 1980), 82. Examining Hurston's works within this framework were first made possible by my discussions with Harryette Mullen, who viewed the lying sessions in *Mules and Men* as examples of Hurston's valorizing subjugated knowledges. I have attempted here to expand on Mullen's insight, applying it to other aspects of Hurston's narrative strategy.

11. See "From the Natives' Point of View: On the Nature of Anthropological Understanding," in Clifford Geertz, *Local Knowledge: Further Essays in Interpretive Anthropology* (New York: Basic Books, 1983), 55-70. Adapting the terms "experience-near" and "experience-distant" from the psychoanalyst Heinz Kohut, Geertz defines the former term to indicate what a person "might himself naturally and effortlessly use to define what he or his fellows see, feel, think, imagine, and so on, and which he would readily understand when applied to by others." An "experience-distant" concept is described by Geertz as one that "specialists . . . employ to forward their scientific, philosophical, or practical aims."

12. See Barbara Johnson, "Thresholds of Difference: Structures of Address in Zora Neale Hurston," *Critical Inquiry* 12, no. 1 (Autumn 1985): 278-289.

13. Ibid., 286.

14. The phrase "literary mode of production" is from Terry Eagleton, who describes it as "a unity of certain forces and social relations of literary production in a social formation." See Terry Eagleton, *Criticism and Ideology: A Study in Marxist Literary Theory* (London: Verso Press, 1982), 45.

15. See Arna Bontemps, *Black Thunder: Gabriel's Revolt: Virginia: 1800* (Boston: Beacon Press, 1968; originally published by Macmillan in 1936).

16. See William Attaway, *Let Me Breathe Thunder* (New York: Doubleday, 1939), and *Blood on the Forge* (New York: Doubleday, 1941).

17. Basil Bernstein, "Social Class, Language, and Socialisation" in *Power and Ideology in Education*, ed. Jerome Karabel and A. H. Halsey (New York: Oxford University Press, 1977).

18. Zora Neale Hurston, *Their Eyes Were Watching God* (Urbana: University of Illinois Press, 1978; originally published by Lippincott in 1937), 29. Hereafter cited in the text by page number.

19. What I have in mind here is analogous to Lacan's *point de capiton*, or "primal metaphor." For Lacan, such a signifier ends the "process of transposition (*glissement*) of 'ambulatory' signifieds in a discourse, pinning them down and producing a new signification." See Anthony Wilden, "Lacan and the Discourse of the Other," in Jacques Lacan, *Speech and Language in Psychoanalysis*, trans. Anthony Wilden (Baltimore: Johns Hopkins University Press, 1981), 274.

20. For a discussion of the controversy centered on this play and the impact it had on the personal and profes-

sional relationship of Hughes and Hurston, see Robert Hemenway, *Zora Neale Hurston: A Literary Biography* (Urbana: University of Illinois Press, 1977), 135-158.

21. For a discussion of *Eyes* as a revision of the tragic mulatta myth, see Barbara Christian, *Black Women Novelists: The Development of a Tradition, 1892-1976* (Westport, Conn.: Greenwood, 1980), 57-61.

ESTHER MIKYUNG GHYMN (ESSAY DATE 1995)

SOURCE: Ghymn, Esther Mikyung. Introduction to *Images of Asian American Women by Asian American Women Writers*, pp. 1-10. New York, N.Y.: Peter Lang, 1995.

In the following introduction to her book about Asian American women authors, Ghymn reviews the history of Asian American women's writing in English, touching on issues of race and gender as they are addressed in the works of such authors as Mitsuye Yamada, Maxine Hong Kingston, Amy Tan, and Hisaye Yamamoto.

The purpose of this study is to examine the images of Asian American women as presented by twelve prominent Asian American women writers. Almost all the well-known Asian American women writers are from the West, and they have recreated their own cultural roots in their images of Asian American women, images which now form a crucial part of Asian American literature. This study is much needed, for, as Robyn R. Warhol points out, "If women have traditionally occupied the margins, though, women of color have been doubly marginalized" (Warhol and Herndl, p. 687). Only through studies such as this one will this history of neglect be reversed.

The images of Asian American women offered by Asian American women writers can be approached in a variety of ways. In fact, more and more voices have joined the traditional critical chorus with such new strains and stresses as deconstruction, psychoanalysis, feminism, narratology, and dialogism, so much so that one wonders if we all are still hearing the same notes. As Wayne Booth points out in his *Critical Understanding*, "We can hope that new modes will be invented, but nothing is more self-destructive than the current fashion of cheering each new rocket as if it had finally given us all the light we need-and then sighing when it quickly fizzles out. All new modes will simply enter the destructive logomachy that we all deplore, unless we learn to meet them with the arts of recovery and renovation that can meanwhile be profitably applied to the modes we already have" (Booth, *Critical Understanding*, p. 40). To use a different metaphor, new theories dressed in newly invented terminology are all too often like firecrackers that explode but fall into darkness after a few bright moments. My own approach will be more traditional, as I inquire into the structural and cultural meanings implicit in literary images of Asian American women.

Asian American women have been portrayed as stereotypes in American literature for a long time. Elaine Kim of the University of California, Berkeley, and Frank Chin, playwright and critic, believe that this is due to racial and ethnic prejudice. Kim argues that "stereotypes of racial minorities are a record of prejudices; they are part of an attempt to justify various attitudes and practices. The function of stereotypes of Asians in Anglo-American literature has been to provide literary rituals through which myths of white racial supremacy might be continually reaffirmed, to the everlasting detriment of the Asian" (Kim, *Asian American Literature* p. 21). Likewise, Chin states, "The ideal racial stereotype is a low-maintenance engine of white supremacy whose efficiency increases with age, as it becomes authenticated and historically verified" (Chin, *Aiiieeeee,* p. xxvii). I do not agree that the sole cause of stereotyping is racial prejudice, however, as we all know that stereotypes are not exclusively assigned to people with different racial backgrounds. Stereotypes have always existed in literature, as in the heroes and heroines of medieval romances, the stock characters of morality tales, and even some of Dickens' characters. Stereotypes are literary tools. As Kim and Chin suggest, however, the stereotype of the Asian in Anglo-American literature is particularly troubling.

In an effort to fight their unappealing image, Asian American women have banded together to publish anthologies of their own writings. *The Forbidden Stitch* (edited by Shirley Geoklin Lim), *Making Waves* (edited by Asian Women United of California), *Home to Stay* (edited by Sylvia Watanabe and Carol Bruchac), and *This Bridge Called My Back* (edited by Cherríe Moraga and Gloria Anzaldúa) have been important vehicles for female Asian Americans to express themselves, following in the footsteps of other minority women such as black women writers who have rejected their traditional images. In the introduction to these anthologies the editor usually states something to this effect: "Contrary to the erroneous stereotype that Asian American women are passive and submissive, this anthology shows that we are not afraid to rock the boat. Making waves. This is what Asian American women have done and will continue to do" (Watanabe and Bruchac, p. xi). The new voices in these anthologies have outlined strikingly new images of Asian American women. These images are a result of how Asian American women define themselves. Asian male writers have different perceptions. For example, Frank Chin comments on "faking" by Maxine Hong Kingston and Amy Tan. The new images presented by Asian American women are not realistic enough to satisfy the male writers. Indeed, if Asian American women writers are dominant and powerful, where does this leave Asian American men? However, literature is not sociology, and the self-images presented by Asian American women need to be understood in their literary contexts.

For the Asian American woman, it has been difficult to separate issues of race and gender. According to Mitsuye Yamada, a second generation poet, "The two are not at war with one another; we shouldn't have to sign a 'loyalty oath' favoring one over the other. However, women of color are often made to feel that we must make a choice between the two" (Yamada, p. 73). In fact, issues of race and gender are both obstacles that Asian American writers have to overcome. As Amy Ling recently notes, "For women of Chinese ancestry . . . writing is not only an act of self-assertion but an act of defiance against the weight of historical and societal injunctions" (Ling, *Between Worlds* p. 1). Indeed, discrimination against Asian women has existed for centuries, and all recent writing by such women must be read against this historical fact.

It is interesting to note that there are parallel stereotypes for white women as well. Ling points out that "two main stereotypes persist for the Asian women in America; they are polar extremes, roughly parallel to the whore/madonna or the 'madwoman in the attic/angel in the house' dichotomies for white women" (Ling, *Between Worlds* p. 12). Similarly, feminist Sandra Gilbert points out, in her "Toward a Feminist Poetics," "A woman writer must examine, assimilate, and transcend the extreme images of 'angel' and 'monster' which male authors have generated for her" (Gilbert and Gubar, *The Madwoman in the Attic*, p. 17). Thus the problem of discrimination and invisibility is not limited to Asian women but is common to all women.

Various theorists have tried to define the feminine imagination. The early French feminist, Simone de Beauvoir, offers this attempt in *The Second Sex*: "I shall try to show exactly how the concept of the 'truly feminine' has been fashioned—why woman has been defined as the Other—and what have been the consequences from man's point of view" (Beauvoir, p. xxix).

Elaine Showalter, however, warns against going too far in stretching the feminist issue: "I am also uncomfortable with the notion of a 'female imagination.' The theory of a female sensibility revealing itself in an imagery and form specific to women always runs dangerously close to reiterating the familiar stereotypes" (Showalter, p. 273). I agree with Showalter. Although I understand and support the feminist's need to assert herself in society, I believe social issues and literary principles should be clearly separated and even distinguished. The idea that the female's mind has qualities inherently different from the male's is itself discriminatory. Nor do I believe that only women can create and understand women characters. Memorable characters such as Madame Bovary and Anna Karenina, among numerous others, have been created by male authors. Madame Bovary's mind has been realistically and sympathetically portrayed by Flaubert. Likewise, Anna Karenina's mind, filled with insecurities and jealousies, has been drawn compassionately but accurately by Tolstoy. Good artists are hardly limited to writing only about their own sex.

Nor do I believe that "American literature is male," as Judith Fetterley states in her "Introduction to the Politics of Literature" (Fetterley, p. 493). The images of Louisa Alcott's four sweet little women, the sensuous and suffering Scarlet O'Hara, Daisy Miller, Isabel Archer, and countless other heroines are a prominent part of American literature. People have a capacity to understand each other despite differences of race and gender. Pearl Buck's *The Good Earth*, James Michener's *Hawaii*, and James Clavell's *Shogun* are stories about foreign settings and characters, yet the American audience can still understand and enjoy these stories. If this were not true, Comparative Literature departments would have to close their doors. The degree of understanding is determined largely by a writer's skill. As Booth quotes Kant, "the understanding is universal in the sense of being shared by all human beings" (Booth, *Critical Understanding*, p. 262).

Nor should imaginative characters be manipulated to fit psychoanalytic theories. I do not agree with David Holbrook, who argues in *Images of Women in Literature*, "If we are to understand the symbolism of culture around the figure of woman, we must attend to these processes of consciousness and find new modes of understanding that will bring together the explorations of the therapists—working under a deep and grave engagement with severe problems—and the interests of the literary critic who tries to investigate the truth of human experience" (Holbrook, p. 4). This new approach seems not to enrich our understanding of human experience but rather to confuse and complicate understanding. To try to put a character on a psychiatric couch is like trying to talk to paper dolls. Art should be left alone as art. For example, Mona Lisa's simple face and gentle smile are considered by many the most beautiful in the world. Of what value would it be to ask why she is smiling or what she is thinking about? A beautiful image of a woman created by an artist and appreciated by its audience has its own validity. Fictional characters are an author's creations. The job of the psychoanalyst is to attend to real people, not fictional characters.

Almost all studies of Asian American literature have been sociologically oriented. Kim's approach is typical: "I have deliberately chosen to emphasize how the literature elucidates the social history of Asians in the U.S. within the sociohistorical and cultural contexts important to me because when these contexts are unfamiliar, the literature is likely to be misunderstood and unappreciated" (Kim, *Asian American Literature*, p. xv). It is certainly true that racial prejudice has affected the portrayal of stereotypes in literature, but I would like to add James Baldwin's comment that "Literature and sociology are not one and the same; it is impossible to discuss these as if they are." Characters in stories should not be taken out of the imaginative worlds to which they belong. Thus, when we look at the images of women in the works of Asian American writers, we should judge them in the context of the imaginative texts in which we find them. One cannot take a flower out of an impressionistic painting and describe it as a real flower. Nor can one pick a leaf from a Van Gogh painting and look at it under a microscope. The total imagery of the work should be taken into consideration. From whose vision are the characters seen as dragons, tigers, or swans? From whose window in the house of fiction should we look at the images? Are the narrators reliable or unreliable? Are the daughters really telling the mothers' stories? How does self-image affect the telling? Are there recurring images and motifs? What are the authors' basic intentions? These literary questions have been explored in examining works already established in the literary canon. They should be asked here, for to enter the literary canon all works should undergo the same literary scrutiny.

The author's careful choice of words in creating a certain image is crucial to one's overall artistic creation. As Booth says in *The Rhetoric of Fiction*, "The author makes his readers. If he makes them badly—that is, if he simply waits, in all purity, for the occasional reader whose perceptions and norms happen to match his own, then his conception must be lofty indeed if we are to forgive him for his bad craftsmanship. But if he makes them well—that is, makes them see what they have never seen before, moves them into a new order of perception and experience altogether—he finds his reward in the peers he has created" (Booth, *Rhetoric of Fiction*, p. 397). Booth's point is especially relevant here, for if an American audience is to understand stories with Asian and Asian American characters, the authors have to employ the right elements of style and structure to make the audience understand their intentions.

Embedded in different rhetorical strategies, these new images by Asian American writers constitute a crucial part of the various works. How clearly these images are communicated to the reader depends on the writer's skill and the reader's understanding. I agree with Scholes and Kellogg that "the story takes the shape its author has given it, a shape governed for us primarily by the point of view through which the characters and events are filtered" (Scholes and Kellogg, p. 275). How effectively the authors have used point of view and other narrative strategies depends on their background and skill. Kingston and Tan, born and educated in the States, have used similes and metaphors that are familiar to Americans. Dragons, tigers, stairs, and bones are used to depict and define the Asian American woman. These images suggest how recent Asian American women define themselves. Paradoxically, these same images conjure up different connotations for an Asian audience. For example, it is considered unfavorable in Asia to describe a woman as a tiger. The image of a tiger woman in Asia implies someone cunning and vicious. Different animals conjure up different associations in various cultures. To be called a pig is insulting in America, but in Korea a woman born in the year of a pig is praised for her gentle qualities. Such images and their meanings can be confusing if an Asian American writer does not consider their effect on a non-Asian reader. And the Asian American writer must keep other differences in mind as well. Even such elements as colors have to be treated with care. The color red in China means good luck. Thus brides wear a red wedding dress. But for a bride to wear a red dress in the Western literary tradition would suggest a fallen woman. To convey a certain image, then, the Asian American artist cannot present a photocopy of the Asian American world but an artistic reproduction of life shaped by his guiding principles and images.

Knowledge of different customs and body language is also important if the writer is to capture the essence of certain scenes. For example, when Hana in Uchida's *Picture Bride* notices Ya-maka, a young man staring at her "squarely," she feels horrified. The American reader might wonder why she is "horrified," as Uchida does not explain the matter. However, it is natural for Hana to feel this way because in Asian culture a man should not stare directly at another man's wife. There are numerous other nonverbal communication patterns and gestures which need to be translated to an American audience. Just as a foreigner can become confused when visiting a foreign country, a foreign character can be misunderstood by an American audience. Rich nuances and subtle gestures can be lost on this audience. As Susan Jerrolds says in "Masculinity as Excess in Vietnam Films," "Thus, while the concept of excess enables us to read individual narrative arrangements, it enables us to see as well how cultural narratives are negotiated, reformulated, and 'adopted'" (Jerrolds, p. 1007). As Jerrolds remarks, authors trying to embody cultural narratives often employ very strong stylistic devices to make their points clear.

Of course, all successful authors employ marked stylistic devices as they embody their intentions. I believe that the novels of Maxine Hong Kingston and Amy Tan are carefully crafted in just this way. In fact, Kingston once remarked to me that her next book will not only have a peaceful theme but also a peaceful style. In other words, Kingston consciously uses style to convey her meaning. Her use of ghosts in *The Woman Warrior* indicates that this work is not a realistic treatment of an Asian American girl growing up in Stockton, California, but a novel in which realism is overshadowed by fantasy. Here Kingston develops a new form of autobiography not really dependent on her own life, one in which Kingston, as Sidonie Smith points out, "reads herself into existence through the stories her culture tells about women" (Smith, p. 1058). Amy Tan's *The Joy Luck Club* is also a combination of entertaining fact and fable, and *The Kitchen God's Wife* is a morality tale whose title is taken from a Chinese fairy tale.

There is also the related issue of fidelity to (so-called) historical or cultural fact. For a critic such as Frank Chin, who considers racial heritage the most important issue, it is irritating when he sees the old legends inaccurately incorporated into Kingston's and Tan's works. Chin insists that "Kingston, Hwang, and Tan are the first writers of any race, and certainly the first writers of Asian ancestry, to so boldly fake the bestknown works from the most universally known body of Asian literature and lore in history" (Chin, *The Big Aii-ieeeee*, p. 3). It is true that Kingston and Tan have distorted Chinese legends, but I hope to show that to have presented the real legends would have distorted the essence of their imaginative works and that the primary purpose of their works is hardly to reproduce legends.

The images of Asian American women presented by writers such as Monica Sone, Mary Paik, Wakako Yamauchi, Hisaye Yamamoto, Yoshiko Uchida, Jade Snow Wong, and Kim Ronyoung are similar to the new definition of the Asian American woman as embodied in Kingston and Tan. This study examines nine novels, four autobiographies, two short stories, and a poem by these Asian American women writers. It includes a study of mothers and daughters in Kingston's *The Woman Warrior* and Tan's *The Joy Luck Club*; a study of girls growing up in California in Wong's *The Fifth Chinese Daughter*, Paik's *The Quiet Odyssey*, Uchida's *Journey to Topaz*, *Journey Home*, *A Jar of Dreams*, and *Desert Exile*, Sone's *Nisei Daughter*, and Kingston's *The Woman Warrior*; a study of wives in Uchida's *Picture Bride*, Ronyoung's *Clay Walls*, *The Woman Warrior*, and *The Kitchen God's Wife*; a study of madwomen in Yamauchi's "And the Soul Shall Dance," Yamamoto's "The Legend of Miss Sasagawara," and Kingston's portrait of Moon Orchid in *The Woman Warrior*; and a study of prostitutes and pariahs in *Thousand Pieces of Gold* by Ruthanne Lum McCunn, "All the Girls Cried" by Kathy Wong, and (once again) *The Woman Warrior*.

Kingston and Tan are the most prominent of these writers and their images are the most memorable, so I have chosen to begin with the chapter on mothers and daughters. By first examining their exemplary works, filled with new images, the other, more conventional works can be better understood and clarified. The second chapter explores how girls in various works see themselves as second generation Asian Americans. Do the girls undergo similar experiences? How are their experiences portrayed by the different writers? What are the problems of growing up Asian in America? How do the various writers let the audience understand their perceptions? The chapter on wives examines the problems these women face with their husbands, while the chapter on madwomen asks who the madwomen are and what makes them the way they are. The final chapter on prostitutes asks how these women are painted in various texts. Including the mad-women and prostitutes gives a fuller and more realistic representation of Asian American women in America for these prostitutes were the first Asian women to arrive in the States, soon to be followed by the picture brides. Brief historical background is provided to explain the social background and to allow the reader to relate the real and the image. It is also important to understand the milieu of the Asian women writers in studying their images. As Virginia Woolf says in "Women and Fiction," "It is only when we can measure the way of life and the experience of life made possible to the ordinary woman that we can account for the success or failure of the extraordinary woman as a writer" (Woolf, p. 44). Comparison to other English, French, and American women writers is occasionally made to show how Asian American women have created their images.

Thus, the purpose of this study is to examine how Asian American women are projected in many works by Asian American women. These images constitute "a portion of the essence of the meaning of the literary work, never a mere decoration" (Holman and Harmon, p. 248). Although created and clothed with various colors, the new image of a courageous Asian American woman dominates each of these works. What emerges from all these works is a new celebration of the Asian American woman. These new images of strength and virtue negate the former stereotypes of Asian American women. Thus, as I noted earlier, Asian American women have recreated their cultural roots in new images. These images are now an integral part of Asian American literature and a valuable addition to the new multicultural American literary tradition.

FEMINIST LITERARY THEORY

ANNETTE KOLODNY (ESSAY DATE 1979)

SOURCE: Kolodny, Annette. "Dancing Through the Minefield: Some Observations on the Theory, Practice, and Politics of a Feminist Literary Criticism." In *Feminisms: An Anthology of Literary Theory and Criticism*, edited by Robyn R. Warhol and Diane Price Herndl, pp. 97-116. New Brunswick, N.J.: Rutgers University Press, 1991.

In the following essay, Kolodny traces the rise and development of feminist literary critical theory in the mid-twentieth century and beyond.

Had anyone the prescience, ten years ago, to pose the question of defining a "feminist" literary criticism, she might have been told, in the wake of Mary Ellmann's *Thinking about Women*,[1] that it involved exposing the sexual stereotyping of women in both our literature and our literary criticism and, as well, demonstrating the inadequacy of established critical schools and methods to deal fairly or sensitively with works written by women. In broad outline, such a prediction would have stood well the test of time, and, in fact, Ellmann's book continues to be widely read and to point us in useful directions. What could not have been anticipated in 1969, however, was the catalyzing force of an ideology that, for many of us, helped to bridge the gap between the world as we found it and the world as we wanted it to be. For those of us who studied literature, a previously unspoken sense of exclusion from authorship, and a painfully personal distress at discovering whores, bitches, muses, and heroines dead in childbirth where we had once hoped to discover ourselves, could—for the first time—begin to be understood as more than "a set of disconnected, unrealized private emotions."[2] With a renewed courage to make public our otherwise private discontents, what had once been "felt individually as personal insecurity" came at last to be "viewed collectively as structural inconsistency"[3] within the very disciplines we studied. Following unflinchingly the full implications of Ellmann's percipient observations, and emboldened by the liberating energy of feminist ideology—in all its various forms and guises—feminist criticism very quickly moved beyond merely "expos[ing] sexism in one work of literature after another,"[4] and promised, instead, that we might at last "begin to record new choices in a new literary history."[5] So powerful was that impulse that we experienced it, along with Adrienne Rich, as much "more than a chapter in cultural history": it became, rather, "an act of survival."[6] What was at stake was not so much literature or criticism as such, but the historical, social, and ethical consequences of women's participation in, or exclusion from, either enterprise.

The pace of inquiry these last ten years has been fast and furious—especially after Kate Millett's 1970 analysis of the sexual politics of literature[7] added a note of urgency to what had earlier been Ellmann's sardonic anger—while the diversity of that inquiry easily outstripped all efforts to define feminist literary criticism as either a coherent system or a unified set of methodologies. Under its wide umbrella, everything has been

ON THE SUBJECT OF...

PAULA GUNN ALLEN (1939-)

Much of Paula Gunn Allen's work is preoccupied with her identity as a woman, mixed blood, and lesbian in Laguna and white society; a registered member of the Laguna Pueblo tribe, Allen was born in Cubero, New Mexico, in 1939. Spending her early years in Cubero, Allen was sent to a Catholic boarding school in Albuquerque at age six, and her Christian upbringing is often reflected in her writings. Allen encountered the works of Gertrude Stein in high school, and has explained that her early attempts at writing were highly influenced by the Stein. She attended various schools before earning a B.A. in English in 1966 and an M.F.A. in creative writing in 1968 from the University of Oregon. She earned a Ph.D. in American Studies and American Indian Studies from the University of New Mexico in 1975, and has since taught there and at other American universities. Allen has received numerous awards, including a National Endowment for the Arts fellowship and the 1990 Native American Prize for Literature. Focusing on themes of assimilation, self-identity, and remembrance, Allen frequently examines the quest for spiritual wholeness. Her poetry collections, including *The Blind Lion* (1974), *Shadow Country* (1982), and *Skins and Bones* (1988), often emphasize the female journey to spiritual transcendence. The search for self-actualization and an integrated self are also central to her 1983 novel, *The Woman Who Owned the Shadows*, in which the protagonist, a lesbian half blood, eventually learns to accept her sexual orientation and cultural identity rather than conform to social stereotypes. This work, which is dedicated to the Native American deity Thought Woman, additionally emphasizes the importance of storytelling in Native American culture, incorporating such diverse narrative modes as folk tales, letters, legends, dreams, and Pueblo thought singing. In her essays, including those in her popular collection *The Sacred Hoop: Recovering the Feminine in American Indian Traditions* (1986), Allen treats women's issues, the oral tradition, lesbianism, and female deities.

thrown into question: our established canons, our aesthetic criteria, our interpretative strategies, our reading habits, and, most of all, ourselves as critics and as teachers. To delineate its full scope would require nothing less than a book—a book that would be outdated even as it was being composed. For the sake of brevity, therefore, let me attempt only a summary outline.

Perhaps the most obvious success of this new scholarship has been the return to circulation of previously lost or otherwise ignored works by women writers. Following fast upon the initial success of the Feminist Press in reissuing gems such as Rebecca Harding Davis's 1861 novella, *Life in the Iron Mills,* and Charlotte Perkins Gilman's 1892 "The Yellow Wallpaper," published in 1972 and 1973, respectively,[8] commercial trade and reprint houses vied with one another in the reprinting of anthologies of lost texts and, in some cases, in the reprinting of whole series. For those of us in American literature especially, the phenomenon promised a radical reshaping of our concepts of literary history and, at the very least, a new chapter in understanding the development of women's literary traditions. So commercially successful were these reprintings, and so attuned were the reprint houses to the political attitudes of the audiences for which they were offered, that many of us found ourselves wooed to compose critical introductions, which would find in the pages of nineteenth-century domestic and sentimental fictions, some signs of either muted rebellions or overt radicalism, in anticipation of the current wave of "new feminism." In rereading with our students these previously lost works, we inevitably raised perplexing questions as to the reasons for their disappearance from the canons of "major works," and we worried over the aesthetic and critical criteria by which they had been accorded diminished status.

This increased availability of works by women writers led, of course, to an increased interest in what elements, if any, might comprise some sort of unity or connection among them. The possibility that women had developed either a unique, or at least a related tradition of their own, especially intrigued those of us who specialized in one national literature or another, or in historical periods. Nina Baym's recent *Woman's Fiction: A Guide to Novels by and about Women in America, 1820-1870*[9] demonstrates the Americanists' penchant for examining what were once the "bestsellers" of their day, the ranks of the popular fiction writers, among which women took a dominant place throughout the nineteenth century, while the feminist studies of British literature emphasized instead the wealth of women writers who have been regarded as worthy of canonization. Not so much building upon one another's work as clarifying, successively, the parameters of the questions to be posed, Sydney Janet Kaplan, Ellen Moers, Patricia Meyer Spacks, and Elaine Showalter, among many others, concentrated their energies on delineating an internally consistent "body of work" by women that might stand as a female countertradition. For Kaplan, in 1975, this entailed examining women writers' various attempts to portray feminine consciousness and self-consciousness, not as a psychological category, but as a stylistic or rhetorical device.[10] That same year, arguing essentially that literature publicizes the private, Spacks placed her consideration of a "female imagination" within social and historical frames, to conclude that, "for readily discernible historical reasons women have characteristically concerned themselves with matters more or less peripheral to male concerns," and she attributed to this fact an inevitable difference in the literary emphases and subject matters of female and male writers.[11] The next year, Moers's *Literary Women: The Great Writers* focused on the pathways of literary influence that linked the English novel in the hands of women.[12] And, finally, in 1977, Showalter took up the matter of a "female literary tradition in the English novel from the generation of the Brontës to the present day" by arguing that, because women in general constitute a kind of "subculture within the framework of a larger society," the work of women writers, in particular, would thereby demonstrate a unity of "values, conventions, experiences, and behaviors impinging on each individual" as she found her sources of "self-expression relative to a dominant [and, by implication, male] society."[13]

At the same time that women writers were being reconsidered and reread, male writers were similarly subjected to a new feminist scrutiny. The continuing result—to put ten years of difficult analysis into a single sentence—has been nothing less than an acute attentiveness to the ways in which certain power relations—usually those in which males wield various forms of influence over females—are inscribed in the texts (both literary and critical), that we have inherited, not merely as subject matter, but as the unquestioned, often unacknowledged *given* of the culture. Even more important than the new interpretations of individual texts are the probings into the consequences (for women) of the conventions that inform those texts. For example, in surveying

Kate Millet on the cover of *Time,* August 31, 1970.

selected nineteenth- and early twentieth-century British novels which employ what she calls "the two suitors convention," Jean E. Kennard sought to understand why and how the structural demands of the convention, even in the hands of women writers, inevitably work to imply "the inferiority and necessary subordination of women." Her 1978 study, *Victims of Convention,* points out that the symbolic nature of the marriage which conventionally concludes such novels "indicates the adjustment of the protagonist to society's value, a condition which is equated with her maturity." Kennard's concern, however, is with the fact that the structural demands of the form too often sacrifice precisely those "virtues of independence and individuality," or, in other words, the very "qualities we have been invited to admire in" the heroines.[14] Kennard appropriately cautions us against drawing from her work any simplistically reductive thesis about the mimetic relations between art and life. Yet her approach nonetheless suggests that what is important about a fiction is not whether it ends in a death or a marriage, but what the symbolic demands of that particular conventional ending imply about the values and beliefs of the world that engendered it.

Her work thus participates in a growing emphasis in feminist literary study on the fact of literature as a social institution, embedded not only within its own literary traditions, but also within the particular physical and mental artifacts of the society from which it comes. Adumbrating Millett's 1970 decision to anchor her "literary reflections" to a preceding analysis of the historical, social, and economic contexts of sexual politics,[15] more recent work—most notably Lillian Robinson's—begins with the premise that the process of artistic creation "consists not of ghostly happenings in the head but of a matching of the states and processes of symbolic models against the states and processes of the wider world."[16] The power relations inscribed in the form of conventions within our literary inheritance, these critics argue, reify the encodings of those same power relations in the culture at large. And the critical examination of rhetorical codes becomes, in their hands, the pursuit of ideological codes, because both embody either value systems or the dialectic of competition between value systems. More often than not, these critics also insist upon examining not only the mirroring of life in art, but also the normative impact of art on life. Addressing herself to the popular art available to working women, for example, Robinson is interested in understanding not only "the forms it uses," but, more importantly, "the myths it creates, the influence it exerts." "The way art helps people to order, interpret, mythologize, or dispose of their own experience," she declares, may be "complex and often ambiguous, but it is not impossible to define."[17]

Whether its focus be upon the material or the imaginative contexts of literary invention; single texts or entire canons; the relations between authors, genres, or historical circumstances; lost authors or well-known names, the variety and diversity of all feminist literary criticism finally coheres in its stance of almost defensive rereading. What Adrienne Rich had earlier called "revision," that is, "the act of looking back, of seeing with fresh eyes, of entering an old text from a new critical direction,"[18] took on a more actively self-protective coloration in 1978, when Judith Fetterley called upon the woman reader to learn to "resist" the sexist designs a text might make upon her—asking her to identify against herself, so to speak, by manipulating her sympathies on behalf of male heroes, but against female shrew or bitch characters.[19] Underpinning a great deal of this critical rereading has been the not-unexpected alliance between feminist literary study and feminist

studies in linguistics and language-acquisition. Tillie Olsen's commonsense observation of the danger of "perpetuating—by continued usage—entrenched, centuries-old oppressive power realities, early-on incorporated into language,"[20] has been given substantive analysis in the writings of feminists who study "language as a symbolic system closely tied to a patriarchal social structure." Taken together, their work demonstrates "the importance of language in establishing, reflecting, and maintaining an asymmetrical relationship between women and men."[21]

To consider what this implies for the fate of women who essay the craft of language is to ascertain, perhaps for the first time, the real dilemma of the poet who finds her most cherished private experience "hedged by taboos, mined with false-namings."[22] It also explains the dilemma of the male reader who, in opening the pages of a woman's book, finds himself entering a strange and unfamiliar world of symbolic significance. For if, as Nelly Furman insists, neither language use nor language acquisition are "gender-neutral," but are, instead, "imbued with our sex-inflected cultural values";[23] and if, additionally, reading is a process of "sorting out the structures of signification,"[24] in any text, then male readers who find themselves outside of and unfamiliar with the symbolic systems that constitute female experience in women's writings, will necessarily dismiss those systems as undecipherable, meaningless, or trivial. And male professors will find no reason to include such works in the canons of "major authors." At the same time, women writers, coming into a tradition of literary language and conventional forms already appropriated, for centuries, to the purposes of male expression, will be forced virtually to "wrestle" with that language in an effort "to remake it as a language adequate to our conceptual processes."[25] To all of this, feminists concerned with the politics of language and style have been acutely attentive. "Language conceals an invincible adversary," observes French critic Hélène Cixous, "because it's the language of men and their grammar."[26] But equally insistent, as in the work of Sandra M. Gilbert and Susan Gubar, has been the understanding of the need for *all* readers—male and female alike—to learn to penetrate the otherwise unfamiliar universes of symbolic action that comprise women's writings, past and present.[27]

To have attempted so many difficult questions and to have accomplished so much—even acknowledging the inevitable false starts, overlapping, and repetition—in so short a time, should certainly have secured feminist literary criticism an honored berth on that ongoing intellectual journey which we loosely term, in academia, "critical analysis." Instead of being welcomed onto the train, however, we've been forced to negotiate a minefield. The very energy and diversity of our enterprise have rendered us vulnerable to attack on the grounds that we lack both definition and coherence; while our particular attentiveness to the ways in which literature encodes and disseminates cultural value systems calls down upon us imprecations echoing those heaped upon the Marxist critics of an earlier generation. If we are scholars dedicated to rediscovering a lost body of writings by women, then our finds are questioned on aesthetic grounds. And if we are critics, determined to practice revisionist readings, it is claimed that our focus is too narrow, and our results are only distortions or, worse still, polemical misreadings.

The very vehemence of the outcry, coupled with our total dismissal in some quarters,[28] suggests not our deficiencies, however, but the potential magnitude of our challenge. For what we are asking be scrutinized are nothing less than shared cultural assumptions so deeply rooted and so long ingrained that, for the most part, our critical colleagues have ceased to recognize them as such. In other words, what is really being bewailed in the claims that we distort texts or threaten the disappearance of the great Western literary tradition itself[29] is not so much the disappearance of either text or tradition but, instead, the eclipse of that particular *form* of the text, and that particular *shape* of the canon, which previously reified male readers' sense of power and significance in the world. Analogously, by asking whether, as readers, we ought to be "really satisfied by the marriage of Dorothea Brooke to Will Ladislaw? of Shirley Keeldar to Louis Moore?" or whether, as Kennard suggests, we must reckon with the ways in which "the qualities we have been invited to admire in these heroines [have] been sacrificed to structural neatness,"[30] is to raise difficult and profoundly perplexing questions about the ethical implications of our otherwise unquestioned aesthetic pleasures. It is, after all, an imposition of high order to ask the viewer to attend to Ophelia's sufferings in a scene where, before, he'd always so comfortably kept his eye fixed firmly on Hamlet. To understand all this, then, as the real nature of the challenge we have offered and, in consequence, as the motivation for the often overt hostility we've aroused, should help us learn to negotiate the minefield, if not with grace, then with at least a clearer comprehension of its underlying patterns.

The ways in which objections to our work are usually posed, of course, serve to obscure their deeper motivations. But this may, in part, be due to our own reticence at taking full responsibility for the truly radicalizing premises that lie at the theoretical core of all we have so far accomplished. It may be time, therefore, to redirect discussion, forcing our adversaries to deal with the substantive issues and pushing ourselves into a clearer articulation of what, in fact, we are about. Up until now, I fear, we have only piecemeal dealt with the difficulties inherent in challenging the authority of established canons and then justifying the excellence of women's traditions, sometimes in accord with standards to which they have no intrinsic relation.

At the very point at which we must perforce enter the discourse—that is, claiming excellence or importance for our "finds"—all discussion has already, we discover, long ago been closed. "If Kate Chopin were *really* worth reading," an Oxford-trained colleague once assured me, "she'd have lasted—like Shakespeare"; and he then proceeded to vote against the English department's crediting a women's studies seminar I was offering in American women writers. The canon, for him, conferred excellence; Chopin's exclusion demonstrated only her lesser worth. As far as he was concerned, I could no more justify giving English department credit for the study of Chopin than I could dare publicly to question Shakespeare's genius. Through hindsight, I've now come to view that discussion as not only having posed fruitless oppositions, but also as having entirely evaded the much more profound problem lurking just beneath the surface of our disagreement. That is, that the fact of canonization puts any work beyond questions of establishing its merit and, instead, invites students to offer only increasingly more ingenious readings and interpretations, the purpose of which is to validate the greatness already imputed by canonization.

Had I only understood it for what it was then, into this circular and self-serving set of assumptions I might have interjected some statement of my right to question why *any* text is revered and my need to know what it tells us about "how we live, how we have been living, how we have been led to imagine ourselves, [and] how our language has trapped as well as liberated us."[31] The very fact of our critical training within the strictures imposed by an established canon of major works and authors, however, repeatedly deflects us from such questions. Instead, we find ourselves end-lessly responding to the *riposte* that the over-whelmingly male presence among canonical authors was only an accident of history—and never intentionally sexist—coupled with claims to the "obvious" aesthetic merit of those canonized texts. It is, as I say, a fruitless exchange, serving more to obscure than to expose the territory be-ing protected and dragging us, again and again, through the minefield.

It is my contention that current hostilities might be transformed into a true dialogue with our critics if we at last made explicit what appear, to this observer, to constitute the three crucial propositions to which our special interests inevita-bly give rise. They are, moreover, propositions which, if handled with care and intelligence, could breathe new life into now moribund areas of our profession: (1) Literary history (and with that, the historicity of literature) is a fiction; (2) insofar as we are taught how to read, what we engage are not texts but paradigms; and, finally, (3) that since the grounds upon which we assign aesthetic value to texts are never infallible, un-changeable, or universal, we must reexamine not only our aesthetics but, as well, the inherent biases and assumptions informing the critical methods which (in part) shape our aesthetic responses. For the sake of brevity, I won't attempt to offer the full arguments for each but, rather, only sufficient elaboration to demonstrate what I see as their intrinsic relation to the potential scope of and present challenge implied by feminist literary study.

1. *Literary history (and, with that, the historicity of literature) is a fiction.* To begin with, an estab-lished canon functions as a model by which to chart the continuities and discontinuities, as well as the influences upon and the interconnections between works, genres, and authors. That model we tend to forget, however, is of our own making. It will take a very different shape, and explain its inclusions and exclusions in very different ways, if the reigning critical ideology believes that new literary forms result from some kind of ongoing internal dialectic within preexisting styles and traditions or if, by contrast, the ideology declares that literary change is dependent upon societal development and thereby determined by upheav-als in the social and economic organization of the culture at large.[32] Indeed, whenever in the previ-ous century of English and American literary scholarship one alternative replaced the other, we saw dramatic alterations in canonical "wisdom."

This suggests, then, that our sense of a "liter-ary history" and, by extension, our confidence in a "historical" canon, is rooted not so much in any definitive understanding of the past, as it is in our need to call up and utilize the past on behalf of a better understanding of the present. Thus, to paraphrase David Couzens Hoy, it becomes "nec-essary to point out that the understanding of art and literature is such an essential aspect of the present's self-understanding that this self-understanding conditions what even gets taken" as comprising that artistic and literary past. To quote Hoy fully, "this continual reinterpretation of the past goes hand in hand with the continual reinterpretation by the present of itself."[33] In our own time, uncertain as to which, if any, model truly accounts for our canonical choices or ac-curately explains literary history, and pressured further by the feminists' call for some justification of the criteria by which women's writings were largely excluded from both that canon and his-tory, we suffer what Harold Bloom has called "a remarkable dimming" of "our mutual sense of canonical standards."[34]

Into this apparent impasse, feminist literary theorists implicitly introduce the observation that our choices and evaluations of current literature have the effect either of solidifying or of reshap-ing our sense of the past. The authority of any established canon, after all, is reified by our perception that current work seems to grow, almost inevitably, out of it (even in opposition or rebellion) and is called into question when what we read appears to have little or no relation to what we recognize as coming before. So, were the larger critical community to begin to seriously at-tend to the recent outpouring of fine literature by women, this would surely be accompanied by a concomitant researching of the past, by literary historians, in order to account for the present phenomenon. In that process, literary history would itself be altered: works by seventeenth-eighteenth-, or nineteenth-century women, to which we had not previously attended, might be given new importance as "precursors" or as prior influences upon present-day authors; while se-lected male writers might also be granted new prominence as figures whom the women today, or even yesterday, needed to reject. I am arguing, in other words, that the choices we make in the present inevitably alter our sense of the past that led to them.

Related to this is the feminist challenge to that patently mendacious critical fallacy that we read the "classics" in order to reconstruct the past "the way it really was," and that we read Shakespeare and Milton in order to apprehend the meanings that they intended. Short of time machines or miraculous resurrections, there is simply no way to know, precisely or surely, what "really was," what Homer intended when he sang, or Milton when he dictated. Critics more acute than I have already pointed up the impossibility of grounding a reading in the imputation of authorial intention because the further removed the author is from us, so too must be her or his systems of knowledge and belief, points of view, and structures of vision (artistic and otherwise).[35] (I omit here the difficulty of finally either proving or disproving the imputation of intentionality because, inescapably, the only appropriate authority is unavailable: deceased.) What we have really come to mean when we speak of competence in reading historical texts, therefore, is the ability to recognize literary conventions which have survived through time—so as to remain operational in the mind of the reader—and, where these are lacking, the ability to translate (or perhaps transform?) the text's ciphers into more current and recognizable shapes. But we never really reconstruct the past in its own terms. What we gain when we read the "classics," then, is neither Homer's Greece nor George Eliot's England *as they knew it* but, rather, an approximation of an already fictively imputed past made available, though our interpretive strategies, for present concerns. Only by understanding this can we put to rest that recurrent delusion that the "continuing relevance" of the classics serves as "testimony to perennial features of human experience."[36] The only "perennial feature" to which our ability to read and reread texts written in previous centuries testifies is our inventiveness—in the sense that all of literary history is a fiction which we daily recreate as we reread it. What distinguishes feminists in this regard is their desire to alter and extend what we take as historically relevant from out of that vast storehouse of our literary inheritance and, further, feminists' recognition of the storehouse for what it really is: a resource for remodeling our literary history, past, present, and future.

2. *Insofar as we are taught how to read, what we engage are not texts but paradigms.* To pursue the logical consequences of the first proposition leads, however uncomfortably, to the conclusion that we appropriate meaning from a text according to what we need (or desire) or, in other words, according to the critical assumptions or predispositions (conscious or not) that we bring to it. And we appropriate different meanings, or report different gleanings, at different times—even from the same text—according to our changed assumptions, circumstances, and requirements. This, in essence, constitutes the heart of the second proposition. For insofar as literature is itself a social institution, so, too, reading is a highly socialized—or learned—activity. What makes it so exciting, of course, is that it can be constantly relearned and refined, so as to provide either an individual or an entire reading community, over time, with infinite variations of the same text. It *can* provide that, but, I must add, too often it does not. Frequently our reading habits become fixed, so that each successive reading experience functions, in effect, normatively, with one particular kind of novel stylizing our expectations of those to follow, the stylistic devices of any favorite author (or group of authors) alerting us to the presence or absence of those devices in the works of others, and so on. "Once one has read his first poem," Murray Krieger has observed, "he turns to his second and to the others that will follow thereafter with an increasing series of preconceptions about the sort of activity in which he is indulging. In matters of literary experience, as in other experiences," Krieger concludes, "one is a virgin but once."[37]

For most readers, this is a fairly unconscious process, and not unnaturally, what we are taught to read well and with pleasure, when we are young, predisposes us to certain specific kinds of adult reading tastes. For the professional literary critic, the process may be no different, but it is at least more conscious. Graduate schools, at their best, are training grounds for competing interpretive paradigms or reading techniques: affective stylistics, structuralism, and semiotic analysis, to name only a few of the more recent entries. The delight we learn to take in the mastery of these interpretive strategies is then often mistakenly construed as our delight in reading specific texts, especially in the case of works that would otherwise be unavailable or even offensive to us. In my own graduate career, for example, with superb teachers to guide me, I learned to take great pleasure in *Paradise Lost*, even though as both a Jew and a feminist, I can subscribe neither to its theology nor to its hierarchy of sexual valuation. If, within its own terms (as I have been taught to understand them), the text manipulates my sensibilities and moves me to pleasure—as I will affirm it does—then, at least in part, that must be because, in spite of my real-world alienation from many of its basic tenets, I have been able to enter that text through interpretive strategies which allow me to displace less comfortable observations with others to which I have been taught pleasurably to attend. Though some of my teachers may have called this process "learning to read the text properly," I have now come to see it as learning to effectively manipulate the critical strategies which they taught me so well. Knowing, for example, the poem's debt to epic conventions, I am able to discover in it echoes and reworkings of both lines and situations from Virgil and Homer; placing it within the ongoing Christian debate between Good and Evil, I comprehend both the philosophic and the stylistic significance of Satan's ornate rhetoric as compared to God's majestic simplicity in Book III. But, in each case, an interpretative model, already assumed, had guided my discovery of the evidence for it.[38]

When we consider the implications of these observations for the processes of canon formation and for the assignment of aesthetic value, we find ourselves locked in a chicken-and-egg dilemma, unable easily to distinguish as primary the importance of *what* we read as opposed to *how* we have learned to read it. For, simply put, we read well, and with pleasure, what we already know how to read; and what we know how to read is to a large extent dependent upon what we have already read (works from which we've developed our expectations and learned our interpretive strategies). What we then choose to read—and, by extension, teach and thereby "canonize"—usually follows upon our previous reading. Radical breaks are tiring, demanding, uncomfortable, and sometimes wholly beyond our comprehension.

Though the argument is not usually couched in precisely these terms, a considerable segment of the most recent feminist rereadings of women writers allows the conclusion that, where those authors have dropped out of sight, the reason may be due not to any lack of merit in the work but, instead, to an incapacity of predominantly male readers to properly interpret and appreciate women's texts—due, in large part, to a lack of prior acquaintance. The fictions which women compose about the worlds they inhabit may owe a debt to prior, influential works by other women or, simply enough, to the daily experience of the writer herself or, more usually, to some combination of the two. The reader coming upon such fiction, with knowledge of neither its informing literary traditions nor its real-world contexts, will thereby find himself hard-pressed, though he may recognize the words on the page, to competently decipher its intended meanings. And this is what makes the recent studies by Spacks, Moers, Show-

alter, Gilbert and Gubar, and others so crucial. For, by attempting to delineate the connections and interrelations that make for a female literary tradition, they provide us invaluable aids for recognizing and understanding the unique literary traditions and sex-related contexts out of which women write.

The (usually male) reader who, both by experience and by reading, has never made acquaintance with those contexts—historically, the lying-in room, the parlor, the nursery, the kitchen, the laundry, and so on—will necessarily lack the capacity to fully interpret the dialogue or action embedded therein; for, as every good novelist knows, the meaning of any character's action or statement is inescapably a function of the specific situation in which it is embedded.[39] Virginia Woolf therefore quite properly anticipated the male reader's disposition to write off what he could not understand, abandoning women's writings as offering "not merely a difference of view, but a view that is weak, or trivial, or sentimental because it differs from his own." In her 1929 essay on "Women and Fiction," Woolf grappled most obviously with the ways in which male writers and male subject matter had already preempted the language of literature. Yet she was also tacitly commenting on the problem of (male) audience and conventional reading expectations when she speculated that the woman writer might well "find that she is perpetually wishing to alter the established values [in literature]—to make serious what appears insignificant to a man, and trivial what is to him important."[40] "The 'competence' necessary for understanding [a] literary message . . . depends upon a great number of codices," after all; as Cesare Segre has pointed out, to be competent, a reader must either share or at least be familiar with, "in addition to the code language . . . the codes of custom, of society, and of conceptions of the world"[41] (what Woolf meant by "values"). Males ignorant of women's "values" or conceptions of the world will necessarily, thereby, be poor readers of works that in any sense recapitulate their codes.

The problem is further exacerbated when the language of the literary text is largely dependent upon figuration. For it can be argued, as Ted Cohen has shown, that while "in general, and with some obvious qualifications . . . all literal use of language is accessible to all whose language it is . . . figurative use can be inaccessible to all but those who share information about one another's knowledge, beliefs, intentions, and attitudes."[42] There was nothing fortuitous, for example, in

Charlotte Perkins Gilman's decision to situate the progressive mental breakdown and increasing incapacity of the protagonist of "The Yellow Wallpaper" in an upstairs room that had once served as a nursery (with barred windows, no less). But the reader unacquainted with the ways in which women traditionally inhabited a household might not have taken the initial description of the setting as semantically relevant; and the progressive infantilization of the adult protagonist would thereby lose some of its symbolic implications. Analogously, the contemporary poet who declares, along with Adrienne Rich, the need for "a whole new poetry beginning here" is acknowledging that the materials available for symbolization and figuration from women's contexts will necessarily differ from those that men have traditionally utilized:

> Vision begins to happen in such a life
> as if a woman quietly walked away
> from the argument and jargon in a room
> and sitting down in the kitchen, began turning
>   in her lap
> bits of yarn, calico and velvet scraps,
>
> pulling the tenets of a life together
> with no mere will to mastery,
> only care for the many-lived, unending
> forms in which she finds herself.[43]

What, then, is the fate of the woman writer whose competent reading community is composed only of members of her own sex? And what, then, the response of the male critic who, on first looking into Virginia Woolf or Doris Lessing, finds all of the interpretative strategies at his command inadequate to a full and pleasurable deciphering of their pages? Historically, the result has been the diminished status of women's products and their consequent absence from major canons. Nowadays, however, by pointing out that the act of "interpreting language is no more sexually neutral than language use or the language system itself," feminist students of language, like Nelly Furman, help us better understand the crucial linkage between our gender and our interpretive, or reading, strategies. Insisting upon "the contribution of the . . . reader [in] the active attribution of significance to formal signifiers,"[44] Furman and others promise to shake us all—female and male alike—out of our canonized and conventional aesthetic assumptions.

3. *Since the grounds upon which we assign aesthetic value to texts are never infallible, unchangeable, or universal, we must reexamine not only our aesthetics but, as well, the inherent biases and assumptions informing the critical methods which (in part) shape our aesthetic responses.* I am, on the one hand, arguing that men will be better readers, or appreciators, of women's books when they have read more of them (as women have always been taught to become astute readers of men's texts). On the other hand, it will be noted, the emphasis of my remarks shifts the act of critical judgment from assigning aesthetic valuations to texts and directs it, instead, to ascertaining the adequacy of any interpretive paradigm to a full reading of both female and male writing. My third proposition—and, I admit, perhaps the most controversial—thus calls into question that recurrent tendency in criticism to establish norms for the evaluation of literary works when we might better serve the cause of literature by developing standards for evaluating the adequacy of our critical methods.[45] This does not mean that I wish to discard aesthetic valuation. The choice, as I see it, is not between retaining or discarding aesthetic values; rather, the choice is between having some awareness of what constitutes (at least in part) the bases of our aesthetic responses and going without such an awareness. For it is my view that insofar as aesthetic responsiveness continues to be an integral aspect of our human response system—in part spontaneous, in part learned and educated—we will inevitably develop theories to help explain, formalize, or even initiate those responses.

In challenging the adequacy of received critical opinion or the imputed excellence of established canons, feminist literary critics are essentially seeking to discover how aesthetic value is assigned in the first place, where it resides (in the text or in the reader), and, most importantly, what validity may really be claimed by our aesthetic "judgments." What ends do those judgments serve, the feminist asks; and what conceptions of the world or ideological stances do they (even if unwittingly) help to perpetuate? In so doing, she points out, among other things, that any response labeled "aesthetic" may as easily designate some immediately experienced moment or event as it may designate a species of nostalgia, a yearning for the components of a simpler past, when the world seemed known or at least understandable. Thus the value accorded an opera or a Shakespeare play may well reside in the viewer's immediate viewing pleasure, or it may reside in the play's nostalgic evocation of a once-comprehensible and ordered world. At the same time, the feminist confronts, for example, the reader who simply cannot entertain the possibility that women's worlds are symbolically rich, the reader who, like the male characters in Susan Glaspell's 1917 short story, "A Jury of Her Peers," has already assumed the innate "insignificance of kitchen things."[46] Such a reader, she knows, will prove himself unable to assign significance to fictions that attend to "kitchen things" and will, instead, judge such fictions as trivial and as aesthetically wanting. For her to take useful issue with such a reader, she must make clear that what appears to be a dispute about aesthetic merit is, in reality, a dispute about the *contexts of judgment;* and what is at issue, then, is the adequacy of the prior assumptions and reading habits brought to bear on the text. To put it bluntly: we have had enough pronouncements of aesthetic valuation for a time; it is now our task to evaluate the imputed norms and normative reading patterns that, in part, led to those pronouncements.

By and large, I think I've made my point. Only to clarify it do I add this coda: when feminists turn their attention to the works of male authors which have traditionally been accorded high aesthetic value and, where warranted, follow Olsen's advice that we assert our "right to say: this is surface, this falsifies reality, this degrades,"[47] such statements do not necessarily mean that we will end up with a diminished canon. To question the source of the aesthetic pleasures we've gained from reading Spenser, Shakespeare, Milton, and so on, does not imply that we must deny those pleasures. It means only that aesthetic response is once more invested with epistemological, ethical, and moral concerns. It means, in other words, that readings of *Paradise Lost* which analyze its complex hierarchal structures but fail to note the implications of gender within that hierarchy; or which insist upon the inherent (or even inspired) perfection of Milton's figurative language but fail to note the consequences, for Eve, of her specifically gender-marked weakness, which, like the flowers to which she attends, requires "propping up"; or which concentrate on the poem's thematic reworking of classical notions of martial and epic prowess into Christian (moral) heroism but fail to note that Eve is stylistically edited out of that process—all such readings, however useful, will no longer be deemed wholly adequate. The pleasures we had earlier learned to take in the poem will not be diminished thereby, but they will become part of an altered reading attentiveness.

These three propositions I believe to be at the theoretical core of most current feminist literary criticism, whether acknowledged as such or not. If I am correct in this, then that criticism represents more than a profoundly skeptical stance toward all other preexisting and contemporaneous schools and methods, and more than an impassioned demand that the variety and variability of women's literary expression be taken into full account, rather than written off as caprice and exception, the irregularity in an otherwise regular design. It represents that locus in literary study where, in unceasing effort, female self-consciousness turns in upon itself, attempting to grasp the deepest conditions of its own unique and multiplicitous realities, in the hope, eventually, of altering the very forms through which the culture perceives, expresses, and knows itself. For, if what the larger women's movement looks for in the future is a transformation of the structures of primarily male power which now order our society, then the feminist literary critic demands that we understand the ways in which those structures have been—and continue to be—reified by our literature and by our literary criticism. Thus, along with other "radical" critics and critical schools, though our focus remains the power of the word to both structure and mirror human experience, our overriding commitment is to a radical alteration—an improvement, we hope—in the nature of that experience.

What distinguishes our work from those similarly oriented "social consciousness" critiques, it is said, is its lack of systematic coherence. Pitted against, for example, psychoanalytic or Marxist readings, which owe a decisive share of their persuasiveness to their apparent internal consistency as a system, the aggregate of feminist literary criticism appears woefully deficient in system, and painfully lacking in program. It is, in fact, from all quarters, the most telling defect alleged against us, the most explosive threat in the minefield. And my own earlier observation that, as of 1976, feminist literary criticism appeared "more like a set of interchangeable strategies than any coherent school or shared goal orientation," has been taken by some as an indictment, by others as a statement of impatience. Neither was intended. I felt then, as I do now, that this would "prove both its strength *and* its weakness,"[48] in the sense that the apparent disarray would leave us vulnerable to the kind of objection I've just alluded to; while the fact of our diversity would finally place us securely where, all along, we should have been: camped out, on the far side of the minefield, with the other pluralists and pluralisms.

In our heart of hearts, of course, most critics are really structuralists (whether or not they accept the label) because what we are seeking are patterns (or structures) that can order and explain the otherwise inchoate; thus, we invent, or believe we discover, relational patternings in the texts we read which promise transcendence from difficulty and perplexity to clarity and coherence. But, as I've tried to argue in these pages, to the imputed "truth" or "accuracy" of these findings, the feminist must oppose the painfully obvious truism that what is attended to in a literary work, and hence what is reported about it, is often determined not so much by the work itself as by the critical technique or aesthetic criteria through which it is filtered or, rather, read and decoded. All the feminist is asserting, then, is her own equivalent right to liberate new (and perhaps different) significances from these same texts; and, at the same time, her right to choose which features of a text she takes as relevant because she is, after all, asking new and different questions of it. In the process, she claims neither definitiveness nor structural completeness for her different readings and reading systems, but only their usefulness in recognizing the particular achievements of woman-as-author and their applicability in conscientiously decoding woman-as-sign.

That these alternate foci of critical attentiveness will render alternate readings or interpretations of the same text—even among feminists—should be no cause for alarm. Such developments illustrate only the pluralist contention that, "in approaching a text of any complexity . . . the reader must choose to emphasize certain aspects which seem to him crucial" and that, "in fact, the variety of readings which we have for many works is a function of the selection of crucial aspects made by the variety of readers." Robert Scholes, from whom I've been quoting, goes so far as to assert that "there is no single 'right' reading for any complex literary work," and, following the Russian formalist school, he observes that "we do not speak of readings that are simply true or false, but of readings that are more or less rich, strategies that are more or less appropriate."[49] Because those who share the term "feminist" nonetheless practice a diversity of critical strategies, leading, in some cases, to quite different readings, we must acknowledge among ourselves that sister critics, "having chosen to tell a different story, may in their interpretation identify different aspects of the meanings conveyed by the same passage."[50]

Adopting a "pluralist" label does not mean, however, that we cease to disagree; it means only that we entertain the possibility that different readings, even of the same text, may be differently useful, even illuminating, within different contexts of inquiry. It means, in effect, that we

enter a dialectical process of examining, testing, even trying out the contexts—be they prior critical assumptions or explicitly stated ideological stances (or some combination of the two)—that led to the disparate readings. Not all will be equally acceptable to every one of us, of course, and even those prior assumptions or ideologies that are acceptable may call for further refinement and/or clarification. But, at the very least, because we will have grappled with the assumptions that led to it, we will be better able to articulate *why* we find a particular reading or interpretation adequate or inadequate. This kind of dialectical process, moreover, not only makes us more fully aware of what criticism is, and how it functions; it also gives us access to its future possibilities, making us conscious, as R. P. Blackmur put it, "of what we have done," "of what can be done next, or done again,"[51] or, I would add, of what can be done differently. To put it still another way: just because we will no longer tolerate the specifically sexist omissions and oversights of earlier critical schools and methods does not mean that, in their stead, we must establish our own "party line."

In my view, our purpose is not and should not be the formulation of any single reading method or potentially procrustean set of critical procedures nor, even less, the generation of prescriptive categories for some dreamed-of nonsexist literary canon.[52] Instead, as I see it, our task is to initiate nothing less than a playful pluralism responsive to the possibilities of multiple critical schools and methods, but captive of none, recognizing that the many tools needed for our analysis will necessarily be largely inherited and only partly of our own making. Only by employing a plurality of methods will we protect ourselves from the temptation of so oversimplifying any text—and especially those particularly offensive to us—that we render ourselves unresponsive to what Scholes has called "its various systems of meaning and their interaction."[53] Any text we deem worthy of our critical attention is usually, after all, a locus of many and varied kinds of (personal, thematic, stylistic, structural, rhetorical, etc.) relationships. So, whether we tend to treat a text as a *mimesis,* in which words are taken to be recreating or representing viable worlds; or whether we prefer to treat a text as a kind of equation of communication, in which decipherable messages are passed from writers to readers; and whether we locate meaning as inherent in the text, the act of reading, or in some collaboration between reader and text—whatever our predilection, let us not generate from it a straitjacket that limits the scope of possible analysis. Rather, let us generate an ongoing dialogue of competing potential possibilities—among feminists and, as well, between feminist and nonfeminist critics.

The difficulty of what I describe does not escape me. The very idea of pluralism seems to threaten a kind of chaos for the future of literary inquiry while, at the same time, it seems to deny the hope of establishing some basic conceptual model which can organize all data—the hope which always begins any analytical exercise. My effort here, however, has been to demonstrate the essential delusions that inform such objections: If literary inquiry has historically escaped chaos by establishing canons, then it has only substituted one mode of arbitrary action for another—and, in this case, at the expense of half the population. And if feminists openly acknowledge ourselves as pluralists, then we do not give up the search for patterns of opposition and connection—probably the basis of thinking itself; what we give up is simply the arrogance of claiming that our work is either exhaustive or definitive. (It is, after all, the identical arrogance we are asking our nonfeminist colleagues to abandon.) If this kind of pluralism appears to threaten both the present coherence of and the inherited aesthetic criteria for a canon of "greats," then, as I have earlier argued, it is precisely that threat which, alone, can free us from the prejudices, the strictures, and the blind spots of the past. In feminist hands, I would add, it is less a threat than a promise.

What unites and repeatedly invigorates feminist literary criticism, then, is neither dogma nor method but, as I have indicated earlier, an acute and impassioned *attentiveness* to the ways in which primarily male structures of power are inscribed (or encoded) within our literary inheritance; the consequences of that encoding for women—as characters, as readers, and as writers; and, with that, a shared analytic *concern* for the implications of that encoding not only for a better understanding of the past, but also for an improved reordering of the present and future as well. If that *concern* identifies feminist literary criticism as one of the many academic arms of the larger women's movement, then that *attentiveness,* within the halls of academe, poses no less a challenge for change, generating, as it does, the three propositions explored here. The critical pluralism that inevitably follows upon those three propositions, however, bears little resemblance to what Robinson has called "the greatest bourgeois theme of all, the myth of pluralism, with its consequent rejection of ideological commitment as 'too

simple' to embrace the (necessarily complex) truth."[54] Only ideological commitment could have gotten us to enter the minefield, putting in jeopardy our careers and our livelihood. Only the power of ideology to transform our conceptual worlds, and the inspiration of that ideology to liberate long-suppressed energies and emotions, can account for our willingness to take on critical tasks that, in an earlier decade, would have been "abandoned in despair or apathy."[55] The fact of differences among us proves only that, despite our shared commitments, we have nonetheless refused to shy away from complexity, preferring rather to openly disagree than to give up either intellectual honesty or hard-won insights.

Finally, I would argue, pluralism informs feminist literary inquiry not simply as a description of what already exists but, more importantly, as the only critical stance consistent with the current status of the larger women's movement. Segmented and variously focused, the different women's organizations neither espouse any single system of analysis nor, as a result, express any wholly shared, consistently articulated ideology. The ensuing loss in effective organization and political clout is a serious one, but it has not been paralyzing; in spite of our differences, we have united to *act* in areas of clear mutual concern (the push for the Equal Rights Amendment is probably the most obvious example). The trade-off, as I see it, has made possible an ongoing and educative dialectic of analysis and proferred solutions, protecting us thereby from the inviting traps of reductionism and dogma. And so long as this dialogue remains active, both our politics and our criticism will be free of dogma—but never, I hope, of feminist ideology, in all its variety. For, "whatever else ideologies may be—projections of unacknowledged fears, disguises for ulterior motives, phatic expressions of group solidarity" (and the women's movement, to date, has certainly been all of these, and more)—whatever ideologies express, they are, as Geertz astutely observes, "most distinctively, maps of problematic social reality and matrices for the creation of collective conscience." And despite the fact that "ideological advocates . . . tend as much to obscure as to clarify the true nature of the problems involved," as Geertz notes, "they at least call attention to their existence and, by polarizing issues, make continued neglect more difficult. Without Marxist attack, there would have been no labor reform; without Black Nationalists, no deliberate speed."[56] Without Seneca Falls, I would add, no enfranchisement of women, and without "consciousness raising," no feminist literary criticism nor, even less, women's studies.

Ideology, however, only truly manifests its power by ordering the *sum* of our actions.[57] If feminist criticism calls anything into question, it must be that dogeared myth of intellectual neutrality. For, what I take to be the underlying spirit, or message, of any consciously ideologically premised criticism—that is, that ideas are important *because* they determine the ways we live, or want to live, in the world—is vitiated by confining those ideas to the study, the classroom, or the pages of our books. To write chapters decrying the sexual stereotyping of women in our literature, while closing our eyes to the sexual harassment of our women students and colleagues; to display Katherine Hepburn and Rosalind Russell in our courses on "The Image of the Independent Career Women in Film," while managing not to notice the paucity of female administrators on our own campus; to study the women who helped make universal enfranchisement a political reality, while keeping silent about our activist colleagues who are denied promotion or tenure; to include segments on "Women in the Labor Movement" in our American studies or women's studies courses, while remaining willfully ignorant of the department secretary fired for her efforts to organize a clerical workers' union; to glory in the delusions of "merit," "privilege," and "status" which accompany campus life in order to insulate ourselves from the millions of women who labor in poverty—all this is not merely hypocritical; it destroys both the spirit and the meaning of what we are about. It puts us, however unwittingly, in the service of those who laid the minefield in the first place. In my view, it is a fine thing for many of us, individually, to have traversed the minefield; but that happy circumstance will only prove of lasting importance if, together, we expose it for what it is (the male fear of sharing power and significance with women) and deactivate its components, so that others, after us, may literally dance through the minefield.

Notes

"Dancing Through the Minefield" was the winner of the 1979 Florence Howe Essay Contest, which is sponsored by the Women's Caucus of the Modern Language Association.

Some sections of this essay were composed during the time made available to me by a grant from the Rockefeller Foundation, for which I am most grateful.

1. Mary Ellman, *Thinking about Women* (New York: Harcourt Brace Jovanovich, Harvest, 1968).

2. See Clifford Gertz, "Ideology as a Cultural System," in his *The Interpretation of Cultures: Selected Essays* (New York: Basic Books, 1973), p. 232.

3. Ibid., p. 204.

4. Lillian S. Robinson, "Cultural Criticism and the *Horror Vacui*," *College English* 33, no. 1 (1972); reprinted as "The Critical Task" in her *Sex, Class, and Culture* (Bloomington: Indiana University Press, 1978), p. 51.

5. Elaine Showalter, *A Literature of Their Own: British Women Novelists From Brontë to Lessing* (Princeton: Princeton University Press, 1977), p. 36.

6. Adrienne Rich, "When We Dead Awaken: Writing as Re-Vision," *College English* 34, no. 1 (October 1972); reprinted in *Adrienne Rich's Poetry*, ed. Barbara Charlesworth Gelpi and Albert Gelpi (New York: W. W. Norton Co., 1975), p. 90.

7. Kate Millett, *Sexual Politics* (Garden City, N.Y.: Doubleday and Co., 1970).

8. Rebecca Harding Davis, *Life in the Iron Mills*, originally published in *The Atlantic Monthly*, April 1861; reprinted with "A Biographical Interpretation" by Tillie Olsen (New York: Feminist Press, 1972). Charlotte Perkins Gilman, "The Yellow Wallpaper," originally published in *The New England Magazine*, May 1892; reprinted with an Afterword by Elaine R. Hedges (New York: Feminist Press, 1973).

9. Nina Baym, *Woman's Fiction: A Guide to Novels by and about Women in America, 1820-1870* (Ithaca: Cornell University Press, 1978).

10. In her *Feminine Consciousness in the Modern British Novel* (Urbana: University of Illinois Press, 1975), p. 3, Sydney Janet Kaplan explains that she is using the term "feminine consciousness" "not simply as some general attitude of women toward their own femininity, and not as something synonymous with a particular sensibility among female writers. I am concerned with it as a literary device: a method of characterization of females in fiction."

11. Patricia Meyer Spacks, *The Female Imagination* (New York: Avon Books, 1975), p. 6.

12. Ellen Moers, *Literary Women: The Great Writers* (Garden City, N.Y.: Doubleday and Co., 1976).

13. Showalter, *A Literature of Their Own*, p. 11.

14. Jean E. Kennard, *Victims of Convention* (Hamden, Conn.: Archon Books, 1978), pp. 164, 18, 14.

15. See Millett, *Sexual Politics*, pt. 3, "The Literary Reflection," pp. 235-361.

16. The phrase is Geertz's, "Ideology as a Cultural System," p. 214.

17. Lillian Robinson, "Criticism—and Self-Criticism," *College English* 36, no. 4 (1974) and "Criticism: Who Needs It?" in *The Uses of Criticism*, ed. A. P. Foulkes (Bern and Frankfurt: Lang, 1976); both reprinted in *Sex, Class, and Culture*, pp. 67, 80.

18. Rich, "When We Dead Awaken," p. 90.

19. Judith Fetterley, *The Resisting Reader: A Feminist Approach to American Fiction* (Bloomington: Indiana University Press, 1978).

20. Tillie Olsen, *Silences* (New York: Delacorte Press/ Seymour Lawrence, 1978), pp. 239-240.

21. See Cheris Kramer, Barrie Thorne, and Nancy Henley, "Perspectives on Language and Communication," Review Essay in *Signs* 3, no. 3 (Summer 1978): 646.

22. See Adrienne Rich's discussion of the difficulty in finding authentic language for her experience as a mother in her *Of Woman Born* (New York: W. W. Norton and Co., 1976), p. 15.

23. Nelly Furman, "The Study of Women and Language: Comment on Vol. 3, no. 3" in *Signs* 4, no. 1 (Autumn 1978): 184.

24. Again, my phrasing comes from Geertz, "Thick Description: Toward an Interpretive Theory of Culture" in his *Interpretation of Cultures: Selected Essays* (New York: Basic Books, 1972), p. 9.

25. Julia Penelope Stanley and Susan W. Robbins, "Toward a Feminist Aesthetic," *Chrysalis*, no. 6 (1977): 63.

26. Hélène Cixous, "The Laugh of the Medusa," trans. Keith Cohen and Paula Cohen, *Signs* 1, no. 4 (Summer 1976): 87.

27. In *The Madwoman in the Attic: The Woman Writer and the Nineteenth-Century Literary Imagination* (New Haven: Yale University Press, 1979), Sandra M. Gilbert and Susan Gubar suggest that women's writings are in some sense "palimpsestic" in that their "surface designs conceal or obscure deeper, less accessible (and less socially acceptable) levels of meaning" (p. 73). It is, in their view, an art designed "both to express and to camouflage" (p. 81).

28. Consider, for example, Paul Boyers's reductive and inaccurate generalization that "what distinguishes ordinary books and articles about women from feminist writing is the feminist insistence on asking the same questions of every work and demanding ideologically satisfactory answers to those questions as a means of evaluating it," in his "A Case Against Feminist Criticism," *Partisan Review* 43, no. 4 (1976): 602. It is partly as a result of such misconceptions that we have the paucity of feminist critics who are granted a place in English departments which otherwise pride themselves on the variety of their critical orientations.

29. Ambivalent though he is about the literary continuity that begins with Homer, Harold Bloom nonetheless somewhat ominously prophesies "that the first true break . . . will be brought about in generations to come, if the burgeoning religion of Liberated Woman spreads from its clusters of enthusiasts to dominate the West," in his *A Map of Misreading* (New York: Oxford University Press, 1975), p. 33. On p. 36, he acknowledges that while something "as violent [as] a quarrel would ensue if I expressed my judgment" on Robert Lowell and Norman Mailer, "it would lead to something more intense than quarrels if I expressed my judgment upon . . . the 'literature of Women's Liberation.'"

30. Kennard, *Victims of Convention*, p. 14.

31. Rich, "When We Dead Awaken," p. 90.

32. The first is a proposition currently expressed by some structuralists and formalist critics; the best statement of the second probably appears in Georg Lukacs, *Writer and Critic* (New York: Grosset and Dunlap, 1970), p. 119.

33. David Couzens Hoy, "Hermeneutic Circularity, Indeterminacy, and Incommensurability," *New Literary History* 10, no. 1 (Autumn 1978): 166-67.

34. Bloom, *Map of Misreading*; p. 36.

35. John Dewey offered precisely this argument in 1934 when he insisted that a work of art "is recreated every time it is esthetically experienced. . . . It is absurd to ask what an artist 'really' meant by his product: he himself would find different meanings in it at different days and hours and in different stages of his own development." Further, he explained, "It is simply an impossibility that any one today should experience the Parthenon as the devout Athenian contemporary citizen experienced it, any more than the religious statuary of the twelfth century can mean, esthetically, even to a good Catholic today just what it meant to the worshipers of the old period," in *Art as Experience* (New York: Capricorn Books, 1958), pp. 108-109.

36. Charles Altieri, "The Hermeneutics of Literary Indeterminacy: A Dissent from the New Orthodoxy," *New Literary History* 10, no. 1 (Autumn 1978): 90.

37. Murray Krieger, *Theory of Criticism: A Tradition and Its System* (Baltimore: The Johns Hopkins University Press, 1976), p. 6.

38. See Stanley E. Fish, "Normal Circumstances, Literal Language, Direct Speech Acts, the Ordinary, the Everyday, the Obvious, What Goes without Saying, and Other Special Cases," *Critical Inquiry* 4, no. 4 (Summer 1978): 627-28.

39. Ibid., p. 643.

40. Virginia Woolf, "Women and Fiction," *Granite and Rainbow: Essays* (London: Hogarth, 1958), p. 81.

41. Cesare Segre, "Narrative Structures and Literary History," *Critical Inquiry* 3, no. 2 (Winter 1976): 272-73.

42. Ted Cohen, "Metaphor and the Cultivation of Intimacy," *Critical Inquiry* 5, no. 1 (Autumn 1978): 9.

43. From Adrienne Rich's "Transcendental Etude" in her *The Dream of a Common Language: Poems 1974-1977* (New York: W. W. Norton and Co., 1978), pp. 76-77.

44. Furman, "The Study of Women and Language," p. 184.

45. "A recurrent tendency in criticism is the establishment of false norms for the evaluation of literary works," notes Robert Scholes in his *Structuralism in Literature: An Introduction* (New Haven: Yale University Press, 1974), p. 131.

46. For a full discussion of the Glaspell short story which takes this problem into account, please see my "A Map for Re-Reading: Or, Gender and the Interpretation of Literary Texts," forthcoming in a Special Issue on Narrative, *New Literary History* (1980).

47. Olsen, *Silences*, p. 45.

48. Annette Kolodny, "Literary Criticism," Review Essay in *Signs* 2, no. 2 (Winter 1976): 420.

49. Scholes, *Structuralism in Literature*, p. 144-45. These comments appear within his explication of Tzvetan Todorov's theory of reading.

50. I borrow this concise phrasing of pluralistic modesty from M. H. Abrams's "The Deconstructive Angel," *Critical Inquiry* 3, no. 3 (Spring 1977): 427. Indications

of the pluralism that was to mark feminist inquiry were to be found in the diversity of essays collected by Susan Koppelman Cornillon for her early and ground-breaking anthology, *Images of Women in Fiction: Feminist Perspectives* (Bowling Green, Ohio: Bowling Green University Popular Press, 1972).

51. R. P. Blackmur, "A Burden for Critics," *The Hudson Review* 1 (1948): 171. Blackmur, of course, was referring to the way in which criticism makes us conscious of how art functions; I use his wording here because I am arguing that that same awareness must also be focused on the critical act itself. "Consciousness," he avers, "is the way we feel the critic's burden."

52. I have earlier elaborated my objection to prescriptive categories for literature in "The Feminist as Literary Critic," Critical Response in *Critical Inquiry* 2, no. 4 (Summer 1976): 827-28.

53. Scholes, *Structuralism in Literature,* pp. 151-52.

54. Lillian Robinson, "Dwelling in Decencies: Radical Criticism and the Feminist Perspective," *College English* 32, no. 8 (May 1971); reprinted in *Sex, Class, and Culture,* p. 11.

55. "Ideology bridges the emotional gap between things as they are and as one would have them be, thus insuring the performance of roles that might otherwise be abandoned in despair or apathy," comments Geertz in "Ideology as a Cultural System," p. 205.

56. Ibid., p. 220, 205.

57. I here follow Fredric Jameson's view in *The Prison-House of Language: A Critical Account of Structuralism and Russian Formalism* (Princeton: Princeton University Press, 1974), p. 107, that: "Ideology would seem to be that grillwork of form, convention, and belief which orders our actions."

MODERN LESBIAN LITERATURE

MARY J. CARRUTHERS (ESSAY DATE SUMMER 1983)

SOURCE: Carruthers, Mary J. "The Re-Vision of the Muse: Adrienne Rich, Audre Lorde, Judy Grahn, Olga Broumas." *Hudson Review* 36, no. 2 (summer 1983): 293-322.

In the following essay, Carruthers examines four volumes of poetry in the context of what she defines as the "Lesbian poetry" movement.

The process of naming and defining is not an intellectual game, but a grasping of our experience and a key to action.

—Adrienne Rich, *On Lies, Secrets, and Silence*

This essay chiefly considers four volumes of poetry, three published in 1978 and one the previous year. They are Adrienne Rich's *The Dream of a Common Language,* Audre Lorde's *The Black Unicorn* (which includes poems published earlier in a chapbook called *Between Our Selves*), Judy Grahn's

The Work of a Common Woman (a collection of poems previously published by the Feminist Press Collective of Oakland, California), and Olga Broumas' *Beginning with O.* Among them, these volumes articulate a distinctive movement in contemporary American poetry, the definition of which is the subject of this essay. I call this movement "Lesbian poetry," because the "naming and defining" of this phrase is its central poetic preoccupation. These poets choose to deal with life at the level of metaethics—its social, psychic, and aesthetic underpinnings, which are articulable only in myth; their metaethics takes its structure from a complex poetic image of lesbian relationship.

These four poets have voices that are bold, even arrogant, in their common, urgent desire to seize the language and forge with it an instrument for articulating women. Not all women writing today write this kind of poetry, not all poets who are lesbians are Lesbian poets, nor are all Lesbian poets always lesbian. I would like very much in this essay to keep separate the realms of life and art, except where in truth they do meet, in the alchemical laboratory of language. If we insist on applying to these poets the psychoanalytical interests and expectations of Confessional poetry, we will certainly misunderstand them because we will not properly hear them.

The word *lesbian* presents in paradigm the large issues of value in language, of women's psyche and of social transformation, of alienation and apocalypse, which these poets address. Rich has defined "the lesbian in us" as "a primary intensity between women, an intensity which in the world at large [has been] trivialized, caricatured, or invested with evil." She continues:

> It is the lesbian in us who drives us to feel imaginatively, render in language, grasp, the full connection between woman and woman. It is the lesbian in us who is creative, for the dutiful daughter of the fathers in us is only a hack.
>
> (*On Lies, Secrets, and Silence*)

To think of the word *lesbian* in terms of male-excluding or man-hating is profoundly to misunderstand these poets. Their poetry does not arise directly from nor concern itself primarily with a response to men. Its energy springs rather from the perception that women together and in themselves have a power which is transformative, but that in order to recover their power women need to move psychically and through metaphor to a place beyond the well-traveled routes of patriarchy and all its institutions, especially its linguistic and rhetorical ones. That is the task of "the lesbian in us," a phrase whose meaning is a constant theme in virtually all the poems which appear in these four volumes.

In this poetry, the word *lesbian* encapsulates a myth of women together and separate from men. Broumas looks to Greek myth and especially to Sappho to seek it out, Lorde to the Yoruba Vodun of ancient Dahomey, Rich to the lives of extraordinary women about whom history has been silent or naive, and Grahn to that which is common and ordinary in all women. *Lesbian* is also the essential outsider, woman alone and integral, who is oppressed and despised by traditional society, yet thereby free to use her position to re-form and remember. She is a figure both of the satirist and the seer, a woman of integrity and power who is by nature and choice at odds with the world. *Lesbian* is also erotic connection, the primary energy of the senses which is both physical and intellectual, connecting women, a woman with herself, and women through time. Finally, *lesbian* signifies a change of relationships, radical internal transformation; it is a myth of psychic rebirth, social redemption, and apocalypse.

It is certainly true that some of the values espoused by this new myth are not new—indeed they are the values we used to call "humane." But the traditional myth-language systems which purported to incorporate them have proven unable to support them, and indeed have become actively hostile to them. Yet the solution, as these poets see it, is not the expected Modern one of revitalizing the old myths. As far as women are concerned, many myths are deservedly vitiated because they have always embodied a fundamental oppressiveness which has now fully revealed itself in violent, death-devoted modern society. Only a new myth altogether, conceived along new lines, can reclaim the world which is lost (or that which never existed but should have). That, I believe, is the artistic logic which lies behind these poets' choice of subject matter for their visionary poems.

A crucial re-vision in this new mythic system concerns the relationship of the muse to the maker of poetry. The myth of the muse is a myth which deals with the source and nature of imaginative energy. The muse traditionally is female and the poet male. He addresses her in terms of sexual rapture, desiring to be possessed in order to possess, to be ravished in order to be fruitful. The language of violent sexual encounter, of submission and dominance, describes a relationship both of possession and enslavement. She comes and goes, mysteriously; he is utterly dependent upon

her, worthless without her, yet she speaks only through him. She is wholly Other and strange, to use Simone de Beauvoir's category, a higher being in classical and Renaissance myth, an ethereally beautiful young girl in the tradition of romance. But whatever guise she assumes throughout history, the basic relationship of dominance and possession is constant between her and her poet.

In the myth of the Lesbian poets, the muse remains female. This completely changes the relationship of the poet to her poetry. Because the muse is female, she is not Other but Familiar, maternal and sororal, a well-known face in the poet's immediate community. Their relationship is not one of possession but of communal bonding. This myth seeks to recreate and remember wholeness, not through the domination of an Other which complements a gap or lack in the Self (as in Plato's egg myth, or the Oriental myth of Yin and Yang), but through a meeting of familiars which recalls a completeness that is present but forgotten or suppressed by history. Motifs and metaphors drawn from archaeology are frequent in Lesbian poetry, and the reason for this is obvious. They bespeak the recovery of a self that is deeply buried, unwritten, but recoverable as the poet, aided by a series of images embodying her muse, re-members herself in selves "who are come to make our shattered faces / whole," as Audre Lorde writes. By familiarizing the muse, Lesbian myth provides a way of seeing the poet in the woman, not as alien or monstrous, but as an aspect of her womanhood. It does not make the poetic calling any less difficult or special, but it focuses the difficulty where it really is—in the nature of her craft and individual talent, not her sex.

I will begin my particular discussion with Adrienne Rich because it is impossible not to. Adrienne Rich was an active influence in some way on all the other three writers. She has long been a friend and associate of Audre Lorde, she wrote the introduction to Judy Grahn's volume, and she is particularly acknowledged by Olga Broumas as an important poetic mother. Rich (b. 1929) has developed as a poet over a long period of time entirely within the established critical eye. As she has of late identified in her work the concerns I have called Lesbian, she has been disestablished by certain previous champions and virtually sanctified by some feminists, concurrent facts which, for all their unfairness to the poetry she actually writes, speak most eloquently for the success of her break with tradition. *The Dream of a Common Language* is probably the best introduction to the major themes and attitudes of Lesbian poetry. The poems are collected in three divisions, entitled (in order) "Power," "Twenty-One Love Poems," and "Not Somewhere Else But Here," and they constitute a complete statement pivoting on the sequence, "Twenty-One Love Poems."

The first section, "Power," is about the sources and frustrations of women's power. As she has often done before, Rich uses the life of a dead woman (Marie Curie, Elvira Shatayev) as a moral *exemplum* of woman under patriarchy, fragmented and cut off from the sources of her own power yet grasping towards it. Thus, Marie Curie "died a famous woman denying / her wounds / denying / her wounds came from the same source as her power." Her voice in these poems is meditative and homiletic, rising to a moral pitch which, while sometimes troubling to reviewers, is nothing new to American poetry. Rich would surely prefer that we think of Bradstreet and Dickinson, but I often also hear Robert Lowell in these poems.

Yet her relation to tradition, including the tradition of women, is an uneasy one. Perhaps this can best be seen in one poem in this first section, "Hunger," written for her friend, Audre Lorde. Though too long to quote in full, the following two sections [parts 1 and 3] state its essentials [. . .].

This poem, it seems to me, deliberately recalls one of the most famous of Modern poems, Yeats's "Lapis Lazuli." The Chinese scene, the contrast of intimacy and domesticity with terrors and desolation, the contrast of East and West, and of art and political life, recall strongly both the occasion of Yeats's poem and its opposition between the Western "tragic" scene and the ancient gaiety of Eastern and artistic wholeness, captured in the Chinamen carved in stone. But Rich rejects Yeats's hope in transcendence to an ultimate order, even (perhaps especially) in art. She is one of those whom Yeats dismissed as "hysterical women," identifying in her poem the reverse side of Oriental asceticism and aestheticism: starvation, indifference, suppression of the weak, a world of "hunger" and constant, violent death.

Her moral indignation rises specifically against these things as the result of oppressive patriarchy [. . .].

Her poem certainly "misreads" the terms of Yeats's poem within a post-Vietnam, American context, but in the sense developed by Harold Bloom in *A Map of Misreading*. Rich recalls Yeats in order to force us to notice the differences, particularly with regard to the nature of art. The men in

"Lapis Lazuli" see an ultimate order which underlies even tragedy, see that hunger and violence are insignificant before that order; it is the hysterical women who do not appreciate this and who insist, vainly, on trying to do something about it. Rich simply denies Yeats's suppositions. There is no order *per se* in art, suffering is not dignified, and the death of the helpless is neither indifferent nor benevolent. The comfort in Yeats's vision is illusory, and for men only. Rich's poem ends not with withdrawal into a world of fixed, aesthetic forms, but with an apocalyptic final statement of the necessity to bear a new world. The title of the last poem in this volume, "Transcendental Etude," recalls paradoxically the theme set forth in "Hunger," that transcendence comes in the embrace of daily life, and that art is nurtured within social life, to which it has obligations; it is not an alternative to society. The task of poetry, the dream of a *common* language, is epic—not romantic or "aesthetic."

Obviously, readers for whom Yeats remains the ultimate articulation of what poetry should be will be appalled by what seems to be Rich's disrespect for "art." Yeats himself, of course, was perfectly capable of moral indignation, but he was not apocalyptic; he accepted finally as inevitable both the male god and the male state, and the male art that legitimized, even while transcending, both. In starting from Yeats, Rich is claiming a privilege accorded to all young poets, that of the "anxiety of influence," to use another term from Harold Bloom. But this is no struggle of son against father for accommodation, to adjust power within an essentially unchanged structure. Just as the relationship of poet to muse is different for a woman, so is her relationship to tradition. In this instance, the woman poet accepts the role of the "hysteric," the outcast. She cannot simply make her fathers move over; she must make them, as Broumas calls them, "irrelevant." From this realization I think comes the apocalyptic conclusion of "Hunger" and the poet's daring to adopt a voice which is always uncomfortable, and these days unfashionable in the weary, self-deprecatory little rooms of some "postmodernism."

It interests me that so often in the poetry of the seventies, it is especially the Lesbian women who speak with the moral passion of seer and prophet. This is a significant new role as far as their audience is concerned. Part of the problem these women have in being heard is that they have taken to themselves an unaccustomed voice, that of epic. Aesthetic order in "Hunger" is seen as illusory, masking a crisis of humankind as cataclysmic and final as any Trojan war.

One sees this epic theme developing fully in the middle section of *The Dream of a Common Language,* but articulated in a form conventionally associated with intimate romance materials. "Twenty-One Love Poems" is modeled upon the traditional sonnet sequence, though Rich substitutes for technical sonnets poems varying between thirteen and twenty lines. They outline the story of a love affair, moving from union to estrangement, with the focus firmly upon the meditative "I" of the poet. This sequence is, as it traditionally has been, the love poetry of a conscious mind, for love is a disciplined and intelligent *social* art. It goes without saying that the lovers are women, and in her treatment of this subject lies the revolutionary nature of Rich's sequence. The world of the love affair is not "closeted," not closed off in romance; it is an epic world which shadows forth the destruction of an old order and the founding of a new. Her bold destruction of generic expectations is part of her apocalyptic theme; only in a completely new world, it suggests, can sonnets be used seriously for epic material.

From the beginning, the affair plays itself forward within a dying civilization [. . .].

It is the obligation of the poet, even in love, to "speak / to our life—this still unexcavated hole / called civilization, this act of translation, this half-world." The love affair is not an escape from the *civitas* (as it traditionally, at least since Dido, has been) but a means of redeeming it through the establishment of a new order [. . .].

This is a vision of social and moral renewal, not of orgasmic transcendence, and it indicates the precise relationship for Rich between the bonding of women and social transformation. The Lesbian love bespeaks a new moral, social order, and if it seems to have more in it of hand-holding than of *liebestod,* that is precisely why Rich can make it the basis of an epic rather than the ending of a tragedy. It is significant that the sexual consummation poem is called "Floating," and can be read at any point in the sequence. As she writes [. . .].

The love affair ends as the lover goes off "in fugue," but its legacy is a self recognized as whole and creative, together with a vision of a new social order. The act of breaking from her lover, paradoxically, by leaving her alone brings her to realize her own power and value [. . .].

She also realizes that the world in which she now lives is hostile not only to women but to bonding, *civitas,* of any sort [. . .].

Yet the apparent loneliness is really a rebirth [. . .].

That life is sustained by the dream of community, a mythic place beyond history, "not Stonehenge / simply nor any place but the mind," where the poet, alone in a "shared" solitude of dawn, "the great light," chooses to draw her magic circle, in effect beginning civilization again. It is apparent that the relationship of the magic circle to the daily life of Manhattan exists only psychically, and by a struggle "heroic in its ordinariness."

"Twenty-One Love Poems" needs the final section of the volume, "Not Somewhere Else, But Here," to fulfill its epic theme by bringing the psychic theme into a social context, as the title of the section suggests. The last poem of this final section, "Transcendental Etude," seemingly ironic in its title since the poem ends with a non-transcendent scene of daily domesticity, articulates the *civitas* which in "Twenty-One Love Poems" remains only inner and potential, a dream. "Transcendental Etude" recounts a homecoming which is also a social re-vision, a Lesbian *Odyssey* (which, together with the earlier sequences, recalls an *Aeneid* too, in the pattern of fleeing a destroyed *civitas* hostile to its household deities, resisting the temptation of mere romance, and the climactic establishment of a new *civitas* in a new place) [. . .].

At the end of this poem, Rich collapses the union of the two women lovers, muse and poet, into a single image of a woman alone in shared solitude, Penelope as Everywoman weaving the tapestry of the new poetry, the new civility [. . .].

She is a figure one has encountered before in Rich's poetry, an amalgam of those wounded heroes like Marie Curie, Elvira Shatayev, the "I" of "From an Old House in America," but in this poem she is not fractured or caged. Her world is whole and complex, uniting mind and body, society and nature, while preserving the integrity of all their forms.

The Lesbian *civitas* is a society predicated upon familiarity and likenesses, rather than oppositions. It is a world of daughters and mothers, of women in infinite variety discovering a language which celebrates their recovered energy and power. What is most troublesome in this image to the general public, of course, is its use of the lesbian bond to signify that wholeness, health, and integrity which are minimized or negated by the death-devoted sickness of male-inspired civilization. Yet the logic of this image is right, even necessary, to the task which these poets have set themselves. Poetic tradition has not given women a language in which they can readily imagine their lives with integrity and completeness. From muse to mother to mistress, women in poetry supply what is missing to men. They are the Other term in the universal dichotomy of oppositions between which the male universe swings, like Yeats's *gyres*. In rejecting the logic of opposition and the concomitant logics of dominance and submission, merging and transcendence, which so often accompany it, the Lesbian poets have created a world of likenesses by using and developing a myth at least potentially untainted by any previous tradition, because it has remained a taboo subject. In that very taboo lies their creative freedom.

Their world is also one of remnants, survivors who speak (or seek to recover) what Olga Broumas calls "the archaeology of an excised past" (*arkhé* + *logos* = "ancient speech"). Since tradition has fragmented women's lives, it has left only remnants, surviving with great difficulty and cut off from truthful speech. Hence the recurrent imagery of women as last survivors of an earlier time. Hence also the apocalyptic theme which is so strong in many of these poems. This follows logically from the perception that history has essentially excised women, except as they are related to men's lives and institutions. The belief in the need for imminent radical change in the order of things has traditionally belonged to groups who feel themselves to be permanently estranged from ordinary society. Eschatology is always radical rather than revolutionary in orientation. The distinction lies in whether one believes, as revolutionaries do, that change will occur through existing historical processes. Historical change for the revolutionary is essentially evolutionary, even when it appears abrupt. Eschatology, however, requires utter change, the end of all things as we know them, a new heaven and a new earth. It is a natural historical perspective for mystics and seers, for all those who by inclination and necessity do not vest their interest wholly in society but remain always in some way apart. The fact of her permanent estrangement is an essential ingredient of the Lesbian myth in its relationship to tradition, history, and the poetic process.

Olga Broumas (b. 1949) works more specifically than does Rich with traditional Greek myths. Yet her relationship to that tradition is radical. She deliberately strips these myths of their male-ness, producing instead an entirely female world. In so doing, she takes the stance of an "archaeologist," discovering the fragments and remnants of a lost matriarchally-inspired language which was polluted and destroyed by later Greek patriarchy. *Beginning with O* announces at once that it is revising traditional myth. In "Twelve Aspects of God," the sequence which begins the volume, Broumas makes a startling revision in the very first poem of the myth of Leda. This myth of rape, a paradigm for the brutal male dominance of women, is changed to a myth of familiar, lesbian play. Broumas accomplishes this by making the swan female. By so doing she renders "the fathers" (surely including Yeats), who have spoiled love in their myth by associating it with power, authority, and domination, useless and impotent, having no place in the completely feminized version:

> The fathers are Dresden figurines
> vestigial, anecdotal
> small sculptures shaped
> by the hands of nuns. Yours
> crimson tipped, take no part in that
> crude abnegation. Scarlet
> liturgies shake our room, amaryllis blooms
> in your upper thighs, water lily
> on mine, fervent delta
>
> the bed afloat, sheer
> linen billowing
> on the wind: Nile, Amazon, Mississippi.

History must be stripped away, as in the myth of "Io," another raped matriarch:

> One would know nothing . . .
> One would regret nothing . . .
> One would keep nothing.

In place of the fathers is "the archaeology of an excised past," a mythic place populated by ancient gods who are embodiments of feminized power (for Broumas, recalling Greek usage, has chosen to make *god* a female noun). The muses, for example, do not visit or inspire her, they *are* her and her friends:

> It's been said, we are of one mind.
> It's been said, she is happy whom
> we, of the muses, love.
>
> Spiral Mountain: the cabin
> full of our tools: guitar, tapedeck, video
> every night
>
> stars we can cast the dice by. We are
> of one mind, tuning
> our instruments to ourselves, by our triple light.

The description of an adequate myth is also the formation of a new language. Broumas, like

Rich, uses the odyssey theme, especially in "Artemis," the concluding poem of "Twelve Aspects of God":

> Let's not have tea. White wine
> eases the mind along
> the slopes
> of the faithful body, helps
>
> any memory once engraved
> on the twin
> chromosome ribbons, emerge, tentative
> from the archaeology of an excised past.
>
> I am a woman
> who understands
> the necessity of an impulse whose goal or origin
> still lie beyond me.

That goal is a language which is truthful, sensuous, and complete:

> I work
> in silver the tongue-like forms
> that curve round a throat
>
> an arm-pit, the upper
> thigh, whose significance stirs in me
> like a curviform alphabet
> that defies
>
> decoding, appears
> to consist of vowels, beginning with O, the O-
> mega, horseshoe, the cave of sound.
> What tiny fragments
> survive, mangled into our language.

Poor as they are, however, they are both the remnant and the foundation of a redemptive, apocalyptic myth:

> I am a woman committed to
> a politics
> of transliteration, the methodology
> of a mind
> stunned at the suddenly
> possible shifts of meaning—for which
> like amnesiacs
>
> in a ward on fire, we must
> find words
> or burn.

For Broumas, as for the other Lesbian poets, lesbian love provides an image of psychic and social wholeness. Her Artemis is the sensuous, sexual muse and poet of the new world. Most often of all these poets, Broumas achieves a complexly articulate eroticism without vagueness or reticence. This is her most distinctive voice. Though she acknowledges her immediate poetic maternity in Plath, Woolf, Sexton, and Rich, it is clear that her ultimate and in a sense her most direct nurturing source is Sappho. Though the erotic theme is strong in *Beginning with O*, her

most striking sequence of love-poems is a group of five, published only in a loose-leaf chapbook dated December, 1976 and called *Caritas*. She appropriated this theological word for love, she says, because she could find no other that had not been damaged by association with male sexual dominance. The poems of *Caritas* are an experiment in forging a language and myth of female sexuality:

> A woman-made language would
> have as many synonyms for pink/ light-filled/
>   holy as
> the Eskimo does
> for snow.

As much religious as erotic, these poems fuse profane and divine love, consciously exploiting the tradition of religious writing which we associate with St. Theresa of Avila and other female mystics (though its roots go back through Dante and St. Bernard of Clairvaux to *The Song of Songs*). For example, in Caritas #3 she describes her lover, who is, with the aid of a flashlight and speculum, contemplating the interior of her vagina and the cervical mouth:

> This flesh, my darling, always
> invisible like the wet
> side of stones, the hidden
> hemisphere of the moon, startles you
> with its brilliance, the little
> dome a spitting
> miniature of the Hagia Sophia
> with its circlet of openings
> to the Mediterranean Sun.

As the lover watches the "seething / of holiness . . . a tear / forms in the single eye, carmine / and catholic." It is a moment of adoration and of recognition, familiarity:

> You too, my darling, are
> folded, clean
> round a light-filled temple.

These are not just visual but tactile poems, touch and taste being two senses which do not permit distance or detachment. They are filled with tongue and fingertips:

> Imagine now
> how your fingertips throb. You follow
> the spinal valley, dipping
> its hollow core like a ladle of light
> in your ministering fingers.

The lovers' embrace is

> like a finger inside
> the tight-gummed,
> spittle-bright, atavistic
> suckle of
> a newborn's fragile-lipped
> mouth.

Love-making is a playful activity, each partner remaining throughout fully aware of self and other. There is no mystical swoon in these poems, and no "union" in the traditional sense. The speaker is always conscious and sentient. The emphasis is upon two together, not two made one—like a dance, a choric song. Thus, in Caritas #2 the speaker describes her lover's knees "dancing. Ecstatic as nuns / in their delirious habit," the orgasm "a choir / of sundial alarums." In the first poem,

> I lie
> between your sapling thighs, my tongue
> flat on your double-lips, giving
> voice, giving
> voice.

The sequence concludes:

> Laugh, lover, laugh
> with me. In that side-
> splitting reservoir, in the promised calm
> of its heaving waters, you'll
> bend, you'll see this woman's
> beautiful
> and familiar face.

Innocence, play, sentience, and familiarity are the marks of Broumas' erotic language. Her love poetry desires not *raptus,* the loss of self, but depicts union through recognition, through images of choir, dance, laughter, touch, of diverse yet familiar voices making sweet harmony. The tongue, organ of speech and consciousness, which in romantic tradition is opposite and inadequate to the desired unconscious *raptus* of sexual union, is in this new context an instrument both of sex and consciousness. In that fortunate Lesbian correspondence, Broumas lays the foundation of her myth, as these lines from the poem "Rumpelstiltskin" in *Beginning with O* demonstrate:

> Tongues
> sleepwalking in caves. Pink shells. Sturdy
> diggers. Archaeologists of the right
> the speechless zones
> of the brain.

Judy Grahn (b. 1940) is a love poet too, although her poetry is not particularly erotic. *The Work of a Common Woman* is sensual, but celebrates sweat and hard work rather than sexual play. Grahn is a "working-class poet," but she is neither a socialist-realist nor a slumming idealist. "Commonness" to her is not a new kind of exclusivity, for her "common woman" is Everywoman, that which is ordinary and common and binds women together. She is a love poet in the traditions of Whitman, Ginsberg, cummings, with more than a little bit of Gertrude Stein. Grahn

borrows many of their repetitive, incantatory techniques, but transmutes them to celebrate the energy common to women in their diverse work. An example, from "She Who":

> Carol and
> her crescent wrench
> work bench
> wooden fence
> wide stance . . .
> Carol and her
> new lands
> small hands
> big plans . . .
> Carol is another
> queer
> chickadee
> like me, but Carol does
> everything
> better
> if you let her.

Her sensualness occurs in the dance-like, ritualistic patterns of much of her poetry. She seems able to find songs or enchantments in virtually every aspect of the language of women. "She Who," a group of diverse pieces which Grahn has recorded as well as published, contains a birth chant made from the midwife's instructions during natural childbirth, a funeral rite, an exorcism of all the hateful names that men have called women, a liturgy of heroic women evoked to give energy and to heal. These rituals, designed as Grahn writes, to make "our poetry what it should be and once was: specific, scientific, valuable, of real use," are interspersed with fables and *exempla,* the whole sequence resembling a Book of Common Prayer for women. Holding it all together is the powerfully evocative, syntactically polypositional "She Who." These poems are social activities, designed to replicate in readers, especially through reading aloud, the ideal of Lesbian civility.

Her most interesting and ambitious poem is the meditation, "A Woman Is Talking to Death." Grahn has always insisted in her poems on what is factual, plain and simple. There are no obvious metaphors or myths. She has said of her early sequence, "The Common Woman": "I wanted to accentuate the strengths of their persons without being false about the facts of their lives." Of "A Woman is Talking to Death" she wrote, "This poem is as factual as I could possibly make it." The precise description of a fatal accident involving a motorcycle and an automobile on the Bay Bridge becomes an extended meditation on the futility of trying to work within a society fascinated by destruction. The poem clarifies sharply what women know of the difference between love and death; as Grahn says of it, it began "a redefinition for myself of the subject of love."

In this poem, the Lesbian "I" is ostracized, unwanted even when she tries to be conventionally helpful and socially constructive as a witness, a supporter of the police:

> that same week I looked into the mirror
> and nobody was there to testify;
> how clear, an unemployed queer woman
> makes no witness at all,
> nobody at all was there for
> those two questions: what does
> she do, and who is she married to?

Those on the inside, both predators and victims, state and citizen, are in collusion with death:

> there are as many contradictions to the game,
> as there are players.
> a woman is talking to death,
> though talk is cheap, and life takes a long time
> to make
> right. He got a cheesy lawyer
> who had him cop a plea, 15 to 20
> instead of life
> Did I say life?
>
> the arrogant young man who thought he
> owned the bridge, and fell asleep on it
> he died laughing: that's a fact.
> the driver sits out his time
> off the street somewhere,
> does he have the most vacant of
> eyes, will he die laughing?

Her exclusion, she comes to realize, is her freedom, her life in the community of women who remove themselves from death and his society:

> my lovers teeth are white geese flying above me
> my lovers muscles are rope ladders under my
> hands
> we are the river of life and the fat of the land
> death, do you tell me I cannot touch this
> woman?
> if we use each other up
> on each other
> that's a little bit less for you
> a little bit less for you, ho
> death, ho ho death.
>
> Bless this day oh cat our house
> help me not be such a mouse
> death tells the woman to stay home
> and then breaks in the window.

Society has outlawed the lesbian, "that's a fact." But so is the liberty and integrity which that fact bestows. The dead motorcyclist, the jailed driver, the indifferent police and courts, all linked in a brotherhood of death, lead the poet to remember her own collusion with "death" when,

arrested by the military authorities for being a lesbian, she was ordered to be publicly ostracized and to betray her lovers:

> When I was arrested and being thrown out
> of the military, the order went out: don't
> anybody
> speak to this woman, and for those three
> long months, almost nobody did; the dayroom,
> when
> I entered it, fell silent til I had gone; they
> were afraid, they knew the wind would blow
> them over the rail, the cops would come,
> the water would run into their lungs.
> Everything I touched
> was spoiled. They were my lovers, those
> women, but nobody had taught us to swim.
> I drowned, I took 3 or 4 others down
> when I signed the confession of what we
> had done   together.
>
> No one will ever speak to me again.

But realizing that even if she wants to be accepted, a lesbian cannot be for she is "unspeakable," her decision is to withdraw from death, being silenced becoming the occasion for a new articulateness:

> ho and ho poor death
> our lovers teeth are white geese flying above us
> our lovers muscles are rope ladders under our
> hands
> even though no women yet go down to the sea
> in ships
> except in their dreams.

Thus the poetry of love is the poetry of work, of commonness, of fact set forth in song. Grahn's latest group of poems is an unfinished sequence, "Confrontations with the Devil in the Form of Love." The devil-love is romance, the myths of required self-sacrifice, possession and submission, "the Love dog scratching / at the door of my lonesomeness, / beating her tail against the leg / of my heart," a country-and-western-style parody of woman. But need is not love:

> Don't misunderstand my hands
> for a church with a steeple
> open the fingers & out come the people;
> nor take my feet to be acres of solid brown earth,
> or anything else of infinite worth
> to you, my brawny turtledove;
> do not get me mixed up with Love.
>
> not until we have ground we call our own
> to stand on
> & weapons of our own in hand
> & some kind of friends around us
> will anyone ever call our name Love.

That place does not yet exist. What we have now is romance, "which is so much / easier and so much less / than any of us deserve."

Grahn idealizes but does not sentimentalize the Lesbian bond, because she makes us aware of the facts of aloneness, the penalties of her choice, and the tenuousness of her dream. She is also tough in rejecting the false securities and illusory paradises that romantic idealism produces. Grahn does not look to others to teach her love; her love comes with integrity. Love is a disciplined school of self-knowledge, self-valuation, learned through the world of work and fact. It is that discipline which underlies the apocalyptic dream defined in "A Woman is Talking to Death":

> only the arrogant invent a quick and meaningful
>   end
> for themselves, of their own choosing.
> everyone else knows how very slow it happens
> how the woman's existence bleeds out her years,
> how the child shoots up at ten and is arrested
>   and old
> how the man carries a murderous shell within
>   him
> and passes it on.
>
> we are the fat of the land, and
> we all have our list of casualties
>
> to my lovers I bequeath
> the rest of my life
>
> I want nothing left of me for you, ho death
> except some fertilizer
> for the next batch of us
>
> who do not hold hands with you
> who do not embrace you
> who try not to work for you
> or sacrifice themselves or trust
> or believe you, ho ignorant
> death, how do you know
> we happened to you?
>
> wherever our meat hangs on our own bones
> for our own use
> your pot is so empty
> death, ho death
> you shall be poor

Like Adrienne Rich, Audre Lorde (b. 1934) has also produced a large body of poetry over an appreciable length of time. In her recent poems, including some in *Coal,* she has come to see in the bonding of women an image both of home and of a new world. *The Black Unicorn* (an image which richly summarizes the self-image of the poet) specifically develops the image of woman-bonding as a necessary start to the end of all forms of oppression. She writes in "Between Our Selves" of the selling into slavery of her pregnant great-grandmother:

> Under the sun on the shores of Elmina
> a black man sold the woman who carried

> my grandmother in her belly
> he was paid with bright yellow coin
> that shone in the evening sun
> and in the faces of her sons and daughters.
> When I see that brother behind my eyes
> his irises are bloodless and without color
> his tongue clicks like yellow coins
> tossed up on this shore
> where we share the same corner
> of an alien and corrupted heaven
> and whenever I try to eat
> the words
> of easy blackness as salvation
> I taste the color
> of my grandmother's first betrayal.
>
> I do not believe
> our wants
> have made all our lies
> holy.

In this "alien and corrupted heaven," Lorde speaks of loneliness and homelessness, fragmentation and lies, contrasted often to a vision of a new world which is also home. The odyssey theme is Lesbian—women together can figure forth home, the lover is the bridge, as in "Bridge through My Window," from *Coal*:

> In curve scooped out and necklaced with light
> burst pearls stream down my out-stretched arms
>   to earth.
> Oh bridge my sister bless me before I sleep
> the wild air is lengthening
> and I am tried beyond strength or bearing
> over water.
>
> Love, we are both shorelines
> a left country
> where time suffices
> and the right land
> where pearls roll into earth and spring up day.
> Joined, our bodies have passage into one
> without merging
> as this slim necklace is anchored into night.
>
> And while the we conspires
> to make secret its two eyes
> we search the other shore
> for some crossing home.

The poem incorporates the prevalent image of remnant survivors in an alien country seeking to get home through their bond, which is both home, "the right land," and passage home.

In creating her version of the Lesbian myth, Lorde draws upon Dahomeian religious myths, which are matriarchal in character, and ritual, in which women figure prominently. This mythic system provides a society of women, and it operates in Lorde's poetry much as the Greek myths do in Broumas', as a remembrance, an archaeology. For example, in "125th Street and Abomey," she invokes the mother-goddess:

> Head bent, walking through snow
> I see you Seboulisa
> printed inside the back of my head
> like marks of the newly wrapped akai
> that kept my sleep fruitful in Dahomey
> and I poured on the red earth in your honor
> those ancient parts of me
> most precious and least needed
> my well-guarded past
> the energy-eating secrets
> I surrender to you as libation . . .
> give me the woman strength
> of tongue in this cold season. . . .
>
> Seboulisa mother goddess with one breast
> eaten away by worms of sorrow and loss
> see me now
> your severed daughter
> laughing our name into echo
> all the world shall remember.

Her myth is also apocalyptic, as, for example, in these lines from "The Women of Dan Dance with Swords in Their Hands to Mark the Time When They were Warriors":

> I come like a woman
> who I am
> spreading out through nights
> laughter and promise
> and dark heat
> warming whatever I touch
> that is living
> consuming
> only
> what is already dead.

More so than her white fellows, Lorde takes violence as a central, dominant theme for her poetry. Seboulisa, the Dahomeian goddess, cut off one breast so that she might fight more easily, but violence is not always seen as so productive. Lorde's poetry is haunted by the images of the "children who become junk": the heroin-drugged girl of "My Daughter the Junkie on a Train," Donald DeFreeze, ten-year-old Clifford Glover who was shot by a white cop, the teenager in the poem "Power" who succumbs to "rhetoric" and rapes and murders an 85-year-old white woman "who is somebody's mother," the women who are "stones in my heart" because "you do not value your own / self / nor me."

But violence is the prerequisite for rebirth, the apocalypse necessary to create a new earth. Lorde often uses the Lazarus figure (seen as a woman) set free by an act of violence that bears her to a new and truer being. In "Martha," a poem from *Coal*, she meditates upon a former lover nearly killed in a car accident and her long recovery:

> No one you were can come so close
> to death without dying
> into another Martha.
> I await you
> as we all await her
> fearing her honesty
> fearing
> we may neither love nor dismiss
> Martha with the dross burned away,
> fearing
> condemnation from the essential.
>
> You cannot get closer to death than this Martha
> the nearest you've come to living yourself.

It is instructive to compare this poem with Plath's "Lady Lazarus," a poem which ends with a terrible, avenging, disembodied self-image ("Out of the ash / I rise with my red hair / And I eat men like air"). Martha is more herself, more essentially embodied through violence and death than she was before: "Martha with the dross burned away." The experience of violence passes through death to peace discovered in an integrated self. It is a necessary part of healing, not merely cataclysmic but truly apocalyptic:

> The difference between poetry and rhetoric
> is being
> ready to kill
> yourself
> instead of your children.
>
> "Power"

For Lorde, as for all these Lesbian poets, the most important virtue—imaged by the female bond—is integrity: alienation and secrecy are reborn as the power of wholeness. The final poem of *The Black Unicorn*, "Solstice," expresses this process eloquently:

> My skin is tightening
> soon I shall shed it
> like a monitor lizard
> like remembered comfort
> at the new moon's rising
> I will eat the last signs of my weakness
> remove the scars of old childhood wars
> and dare to enter the forest whistling
> like a snake that has fed the chameleon
> for changes
> I shall be forever.
>
> May I never remember reasons
> for my spirit's safety
> may I never forget
> the warning of my woman's flesh
> weeping at the new moon
> may I never lose
> that terror
> that keeps me brave
> May I owe nothing
> that I cannot repay.

Yet integrity is not isolation. Because it is constructed through sharing and bonding, through seeing the selves in others, recognizing and recovering them, it leads to a truly civilized and social vision of being. Lorde, like the other three poets under discussion, never withdraws. Her African archaeology is firmly attached in Harlem, where it transforms and redeems. Because her muses are so intensely familiar and intimate (even when cloaked in the myth of a distant Dahomeian goddess), she can present her poetic faces whole, the myth and the life, the self and civility:

> Between the canyons of their mighty silences
> mother bright and father brown
> I seek my own shapes now
> for they never spoke of me
> except as theirs
> and the pieces I stumble and fall over
> I still record as proof
> that I am beautiful
> twice
> blessed with the images
> of who they were
> and who I thought them once to be
> of what I move
> toward and through
> and what I need
> to leave behind me
> most of all
> I am blessed within my selves
> who are come to make our shattered faces
> whole.
>
> "Outside"

In summary, Lesbian poetry celebrates integrity as the metaethic of civilization. Virtually all its images—those of apocalypse, exile, fragmentation, re-cognition, familiarity, and bonding—are ingredients of a vision of personal wholeness and truth. Muse, mother, lover are familiars who come together in an integrated psyche, the Lesbian magic circle. More radical than this psychic myth, however, is their social one, the ethic of Lesbian civility, especially as it links themes such as exile and odyssey with apocalypse and redemption (the influence of Mary Daly may be crucial in defining this link, though her *Gyn/Ecology* is virtually contemporaneous with the volumes discussed in this essay). The Lesbian psyche is not simply reborn or rediscovered, it is redeemed and redemptive. Lazarus (often in disguise) is an important figure for Judy Grahn in "A Woman is Talking to Death" as well as for Audre Lorde in "Martha," and Broumas' Greek deities are not merely reconstructed but transfigured. Marie Curie, the wounded heroine, is redeemed by the woman of "Transcendental Etude." Lesbian redemption is not transcendent, however; it never loses its

historical embedding in the world of "fact" so important to Judy Grahn, the world of Harlem and island of Manhattan. The epic dimension of their poetry distinguishes these four poets absolutely from their immediate "confessional" precursors, especially Plath and Sexton. Their lives and times are embodied in their work together with an apocalyptic "time-tension," the unspoken Lesbian past and the ineffable Lesbian future bearing continuously upon the present. In achieving their epic theme, the familiarization of the muse by the Lesbian poet is essential, for it is that crucial metaphoric relationship which makes the woman at home in the poet, able to create new worlds through the power of an integrated self.

CAROLYN DEVER (ESSAY DATE 1997)

SOURCE: Dever, Carolyn. "Obstructive Behavior: Dykes in the Mainstream of Feminist Theory." In *Cross-Purposes: Lesbians, Feminists, and the Limits of Alliance*, edited by Dana Heller, pp. 19-41. Bloomington, Ind.: Indiana University Press, 1997.

In the following essay, Dever argues that feminist theory has at least partly been influenced by a set of lesbian responses that have helped shape, divert, and eventually develop mainstream feminist literary theory.

The "obstructive behavior" I hope to analyze in this chapter involves the consideration of "dykes," by which I mean obstructions that impede or redirect a current or flow.[1] I want to argue that feminist theory has come into being in relation to a set of "dykes," through contact with critical obstructions that shape, divert, and otherwise help to define the mainstream. The function of these dykes is an ambiguous one; they are at once necessary and problematic, central yet diversionary. Dykes are not *of* the mainstream, but the mainstream necessarily shapes itself in response to the presence of dykes.

At its most literal level, my title should signify a concern with the tendentious shape-shifting that has characterized feminist theory, producing new and innovative theoretical concerns and applications. At another level, however, it should signify its concern with the discourse of "obstruction," with impudent behaviors and political impediments that have confronted, ideally to challenge and to change, academic feminism. At still another level, I am concerned with the discourses of sexuality in feminism, and the sense in which the issue of sexuality itself operates as a "dyke," as a shaping impediment. For colloquially, *dyke* itself signifies, sometimes rudely, sometimes not, a way of being named or self-identifying as lesbian.[2] And the question of lesbians in the mainstream of feminist criticism has been the single most powerful "dyke" in the evolution of this critical discourse.

The *Oxford English Dictionary* definition of *dyke* or *dike* (the latter is the "more conventional" spelling), depends on an interestingly redoubled sense of ambiguity. The *OED* traces the etymology of *dyke* through a series of exchanges of masculine and feminine cases, evolving, perhaps ironically, from versions of the word *dick* in the masculine to versions of the word *dyke* in the feminine, pausing only in Icelandic at the neuter. Its history of etymological indeterminacy notwithstanding, *dyke* consistently signifies a form of diversionary obstruction, whether ditch, trench, mound, embankment, or dam, though the obstruction is conceived alternately as *either* a trench or a wall: "The application thus varies between 'ditch, dug out place,' and 'mound formed by throwing up the earth,' and may include both." Under its first definition, a dyke is "an excavation narrow in proportion to its length, a long and narrow hollow dug out of the ground; a DITCH, trench, or fosse," "such a hollow dug out to hold or conduct water." Under its second, it is "an embankment, wall, causeway," and still more specifically, "'a bank formed by throwing the earth out of the ditch' (Bosworth)," or "a wall or fence. . . . The wall of a city, a fortification."

Dyke is a word that presupposes the complication, conflation, even the collapse of binary categories. Confounding notions of masculinity and femininity in the case of etymology, of structure in the architectural significance of a barrier, conflicting definitions of *dyke* exploit an ambiguity at the heart of the concept itself. In its first definition, a "narrow hollow dug out of the ground," the function of the dyke is to enable another activity, such as the holding or the conducting of water, but is essentially passive: it exists primarily not as a presence but as an absence, as negative space sculpted from the positive surface of the earth. Yet in its alternate definition, the dyke exceeds that positive surface, existing as the highly visible *surplus* of earth in fortifying relation to the populace whose existence it protects and enables; whether as a canal permitting transport from one place to another or as a protective wall impeding that transport, the well-being of its architects depends on the dyke's structural integrity. In either incarnation, the transformative capacity of the dyke remains its most powerful capital: articulating a space that is, by definition, both marginal and central, the dyke

demarcates difference, transition, liminality, and vulnerability. That vulnerability inheres in the status of the dyke as a protective structure: without the need to guard against difference, against the threat of difference to destroy, the dyke would be completely unnecessary.

A slang definition, listed below and separated from the nearly three columns of dykes in the *OED*, reads as follows: "dike, dyke . . . [Of obscure origin.] A lesbian; a masculine woman."[3] Citing as its earliest usage a 1942 entry in the *American Thesaurus of Slang*, this dyke, of obscure origin, remains distinct from the *OED*'s other dykes, yet shares with them certain implications of liminality. Not only a lesbian but also a "masculine woman," the dyke, in this definition, blurs the borderline between masculinity and femininity. In her appearance, presumably in her affective alliances, she, like her fellow dykes, marks, embodies, and deconstructs that borderline by disrupting conventional practices of self-presentation and desire. Like the other dykes, this dyke offers a limit case and a liminal space, enabling definitions of inside and outside, enabling, through her location of and as a border, binary systems of logic which exploit fixed notions of identity and identifiability.

Mainstream feminism, I want to argue, has been defined by and against its relationship to dykes, depending precisely on the dyke's function as a borderline to mark the parameters of feminist theory and practice. For twenty-five years, feminists have displayed dramatic, symptomatic forms of ambivalence to lesbians in the mainstream. At once needing and abhorring the dykes that exist at and as the shaping margins of its discourse, feminist theory has struggled to accommodate competing desires for mainstream acceptance and individual sexual diversity. Catalyzing questions about sex, sexuality, eroticism, pleasure, identity, politics, and power, the dyke in the mainstream has always been the site of contention, the source of troubling questions, both for and within feminism.

Feminist Theory in the 1970s

A Ridge, Embankment, Long Mound, or Dam, Thrown up to Resist the Encroachments of the Sea, or to Prevent Low-Lying Lands from being Flooded by Seas, Rivers, or Streams.
—Oxford English Dictionary

From the vocabulary of lesbian separatism in the 1970s through queer theory today, feminists have always engaged questions of sexuality. But although the vantage point of history often associates the early women's movement with the political enthusiasms of the Sexual Revolution, in fact, the very personal politics of sexual difference have historically marked the most dramatic fault lines among feminists. As early as 1970, at the Second Congress to Unite Women, twenty women stormed the meeting's plenary session with the words "Lavender Menace" emblazoned on their chests. Prompted to act by Betty Friedan's notorious, and perhaps apocryphal, remark that lesbians in the women's movement were a "lavender menace" who would ultimately impede cultural acceptance of feminist sympathies, the women calling themselves the "Lavender Menace" challenged conference members to confront discrimination against lesbians in the women's movement. Later renaming themselves "Radical-esbians," this group soon produced an essay titled "The Woman-Identified Woman," which argued that all sexualities exist in the service of patriarchy and that a challenge to rigid notions of sexuality must accompany feminist critiques of patriarchy. Women who fail to consider the erotic potential of other women are trapped in a patriarchal web, living their lives, setting their expectations, only in terms of their relationships to men; thus feminists fail to confront their full investment in patriarchal power until they confront the personal politics of their bedrooms. "Real" women, "feminine" women, the Radicalesbians suggest,

> are authentic, legitimate, real to the extent that we are the property of some man whose name we bear. To be a woman who belongs to no man is to be invisible, pathetic, inauthentic, unreal. He confirms his image of us—of what we have to be in order to be acceptable by him—but not our real selves; he confirms our womanhood—as he defines it, in relation to him—but cannot confirm our personhood, our own selves as absolutes. As long as we are dependent on the male culture for this definition, for this approval, we cannot be free.[4]

The Radicalesbians identify female homosexuality as a political choice. Lesbianism, within their rubric, is a political mandate more than an erotic one; the utopic vision of a lesbian-separatist community, often figured as the return of the Amazons, is frequently represented as the only plausible alternative within a radical and thoroughgoing critique of patriarchy. And indeed, this is a notion that looms large over the culture of feminist discourse to this day, for, as lesbian separatists throughout the early days of the Women's Movement insist, separatism remains a logical extreme of feminist critiques of patriarchy, a logical solution to often painfully paradoxical

attempts to live a "feminist life." As Catharine MacKinnon writes, "Feminism is the epistemology of which lesbianism is an ontology."[5]

Lesbian separatism was one of the greatest challenges to and the greatest anxieties of early feminists. Ti-Grace Atkinson presents a summary of the theory informing political lesbianism in the collection *Amazon Odyssey*: "It is the commitment of individuals to common goals, and to the death if necessary, that determines the strength of the army. . . . Lesbianism is to feminism what the Communist Party was to the trade-union movement. Tactically, any feminist should fight to the death for lesbianism because of its strategic importance."[6] Invoking metaphors ranging from the martial to the economic, Atkinson emphasizes the importance of linking feminist theory and feminist practice: "I'm enormously less interested in whom you sleep with than I am in with whom you're prepared to die."[7] Atkinson interrogates the inherently "political" nature of lesbianism, suggesting that affectional and erotic object choices themselves do not necessarily make a politics, but that lesbianism has occupied a politically significant structural position within feminism.

> Because of their particularly unique attempt at revolt, the lesbian role within the male/female class system becomes critical. Lesbianism is the "criminal" zone, what I call the "buffer" zone, between the two major classes comprising the sex class system. The "buffer" has both a unique nature and function within the system. And it is crucial that both lesbians and feminists understand the strategical significance of lesbianism to feminism.
>
> (136-37)

In Atkinson's analysis, the liminal lesbian position, the "buffer," becomes strategic turf: it is the battlefield of actual feminist practice, the space intervening between "oppressor" and "oppressed," men and women. Semantically, however, within the discursive structure of Atkinson's vision, lesbians are not women, nor are they men, feminists, oppressors, or oppressed; they exist, as dykes so often have, as the means of defining the difference between feminists and their oppressors; significantly, though, lesbians themselves manage to elude definition, categorization, political importance, even inclusion in this framework. That both "lesbians" and "feminists" must understand the crucial significance of lesbianism to feminism sacrifices lesbian interests to a larger feminist cause; nowhere are lesbians supposed to consider the significance of feminists, they are simply assumed to *be* feminists. Despite Atkinson's comment that "feminists should fight to the death for lesbians," she more frequently assumes the opposite logic: she sees lesbians as the front lines of the feminist army. Mainstream feminism for Atkinson, regardless of its radical politics, is a heterosexual movement; dykes exist merely to facilitate, protect, and maintain that mainstream. Unlike the Radicalesbians, for whom lesbianism is feminist theory in its purest form, for Atkinson, lesbianism is a means to an end, a strategic position on a much larger battleground.

Atkinson's interest in the concept of lesbianism originates in the persistence of homophobic invective against feminists: "from the outset of the Movement, most men automatically called all feminists 'lesbians.' This connection was so widespread and consistent that I began to wonder myself if maybe men didn't perceive some connection the Movement was overlooking" (135-36). Atkinson, like the Radicalesbians, wonders why feminism engenders this response: "Generally speaking, the Movement has reacted defensively to the charge of lesbianism: 'No, I'm not!' 'Yes, you are!' 'No, I'm not!' 'Prove it.' For myself I was so puzzled about the connection that I became curious. . . . Whenever the enemy keeps lobbing bombs into some area you consider unrelated to your defense, it's always worth investigating."[8] As Miriam Schneir points out in a recent discussion of the Radicalesbians, "The lesbian issue continued to generate personal and ideological splits among feminists—including among radical feminists—that sisterhood could not always surmount. Lesbians and straights both played a part in this unfortunate turn of events: Some straight feminists were afraid of being labeled dykes and wished to dissociate both the movement and themselves from lesbianism, while some lesbians claimed that lesbianism was an example of feminism in action and preached that the only true feminists were those who renounced relations with the opposite sex entirely."[9] Rather than disavow the label "dyke," Atkinson attempts to appropriate it as "buffer": within her theoretical paradigm, lesbians exist on the front line of the gender wars. The logic here is that of a speech act: the men lobbing the explosive word *dyke* succeed in labeling all practicing feminists as dykes. Atkinson assumes that those who are called dykes necessarily become dykes, whether in theory or in practice. And within her vision of feminist activism, these dykes will be sacrificed, in theory or in practice, for a mainstream feminist utopic vision.

Feminist Theory in the Early 1980s

The Application thus Varies between 'Ditch, Dug out Place,' and 'Mound Formed by Throwing up the Earth,' and may Include both.

—Oxford English Dictionary

Split between defensive responses to internalized homophobia and the political logic of separatism, feminist definitions of *lesbian* during the early 1980s are marked by a noteworthy ambivalence toward questions of sexual practice and erotic pleasure: lesbianism, when it enters into definitions of *feminism* at all, enters almost exclusively as a political ideal, undistinguished by any real erotic significance. Adrienne Rich's landmark essay "Compulsory Heterosexuality and Lesbian Existence" appeared in *Signs* in 1980. Rich's articulation of a "lesbian continuum" indicates a significant development in popular feminist attempts at self-definition. Interrogating heterosexuality as a vestigial structure of patriarchal power, Rich argues in the tradition of early political lesbians that "the denial of reality and visibility to women's passion for women, women's choice of women as allies, life companions, and community, the forcing of such relationships into dissimulation and their disintegration under intense pressure have meant an incalculable loss to the power of all women *to change the social relations of the sexes, to liberate ourselves and each other.*"[10] In the terms of Rich's argument, feminists historically have been their own worst enemies, thwarting their own political agendas through their failure to truly challenge "the social relations of the sexes." Rich suggests that homophobia informs feminists' unwillingness to ally themselves fully—politically, personally, or intellectually—with lesbians, duplicating the oppression of women more generally under patriarchal power structures and undermining the viability of all feminist theory. Recalling the Radicalesbians' argument about the need to theorize heterosexuality rigorously, not as a "natural" category but as a complex and problematic construct, Rich modifies their concluding exhortation of lesbianism as the feminist political ideal through the development of two strategic arguments.

The first, which encompasses the mission statement of Rich's essay, calls for a more comprehensive and rigorous feminist theory that takes into consideration all forms of erotic, political, and intellectual individuality; extending a critique of Dorothy Dinnerstein to feminist theory as a whole, Rich writes: "[Dinnerstein] ignores, specifically, the history of women who—as witches, *femmes seules,* marriage resisters, spinsters, autonomous widows, and/or lesbians—have managed on various levels *not* to collaborate. It is this history, precisely, from which feminists have so much to learn and on which there is overall such blanketing silence" (230). Rich's form of feminist theory would have at its center the interrogation of "compulsory heterosexuality":

> The assumption that "most women are innately heterosexual" stands as a theoretical and political stumbling block for feminism. It remains a tenable assumption partly because lesbian existence has been written out of history or catalogued under disease, partly because it has been treated as exceptional rather than intrinsic, partly because to acknowledge that for women heterosexuality may not be a "preference" at all but something that has had to be imposed, managed, organized, propagandized, and maintained by force is an immense step to take if you consider yourself freely and "innately" heterosexual. Yet the failure to examine heterosexuality as an institution is like failing to admit that the economic system called capitalism or the caste system of racism is maintained by a variety of forces, including both physical violence and false consciousness.
>
> (238-39)

Calling for a rigorous analysis of the power dynamics at stake in "compulsory heterosexuality," Rich is sharply critical of feminist unwillingness to consider the full range of sexual diversity. Her suggestion that this analysis would be anxiety-producing because feminists themselves have something at stake in the institution of heterosexuality recalls the Radicalesbians' arguments about the political inconsistencies in most attempts to combine feminist theory with a bourgeois, heterosexual life. But Rich stops short of calling for political lesbianism, insisting instead on a feminist theoretical analysis of issues previously hidden by assumptions of normative heterosexuality.

In fact, Rich's second argument represents a neat appropriation of the anxieties that inevitably seem to accompany discussions of political lesbianism. She argues, through the radical expansion of the term *lesbian,* that all feminists, in fact, all women, are already lesbians; feminist thus becomes a subset of lesbian, rather than the other way around. She explains:

> I mean the term *lesbian continuum* to include a range—through each woman's life and throughout history—of woman-identified experience, not simply the fact that a woman has had or consciously desired genital sexual experience with another woman. If we expand it to embrace many more forms of primary intensity between and among women, including the sharing of a rich in-

ner life, the bonding against male tyranny, the giving and receiving of practical and political support, if we can also hear it in such associations as *marriage resistance* and the "haggard" behavior identified by Mary Daly (obsolete meanings: "intractable," "willful," "wanton," and "unchaste," "a woman reluctant to yield to wooing"), we begin to grasp breadths of female history and psychology which have lain out of reach as a consequence of limited, mostly clinical, definitions of *lesbianism.*[11]

Rich's identification of the "lesbian continuum" is the logical yield of her interrogation of compulsory heterosexuality. She emphasizes that the deconstruction of the assumptions and dynamics informing compulsory heterosexuality will bring into view many forms of profound interconnections among women, connections that have always existed but have been obscured from view by assumptions of normative heterosexuality. In naming these relationships "lesbian," Rich accommodates and thus begins to value women's relationships with one another across a wide range of behaviors that presumably includes, but is not limited to, the erotic: "As the term lesbian has been held to limiting, clinical associations in its patriarchal definition, female friendship and comradeship have been set apart from the erotic, thus limiting the erotic itself" (240).

In addition to the notion of the "lesbian continuum" and the critique of compulsory heterosexuality, the other significant innovation of Rich's argument is its shift in the locus of activism. Identifying her task as a primarily critical one, Rich targets an audience composed principally of feminist academics. She identifies literary criticism, as well as related modes of historical and social scientific research, as central to feminist praxis and instrumental in the process of locating the lesbian continuum; literary critics and other academics possess the ability to produce a more accurate version of women's history. Significantly, however, even as Rich empowers academics within feminist activism, academics also occupy the center of her target of critique: she condemns "the virtual or total neglect of lesbian existence in a wide range of writings, including feminist scholarship" (229). By the early 1980s, literary criticism is at ground zero in what was previously a grassroots political movement, as academic work is increasingly valorized as a primary form of feminist activist intervention. Rich's focus on literary criticism constructs feminist politics as a battleground of metacriticism; the issues at stake concern not only the practicalities of feminist critique in the world at large, but also the novels of Colette, Charlotte Brontë, and Toni Morrison, and the theoretical paradigms of Mary Daly, Catharine MacKinnon, and Nancy Chodorow. Focusing on the historical period from which Rich's essay emerged, Jane Gallop, in *Around 1981: Academic Feminist Literary Theory*, argues that in the early 1980s, feminism "entered the heart of a contradiction": "It became secure and prospered in the academy while feminism as a social movement was encountering major setbacks in a climate of new conservatism. The Reagan-Bush years began; the ERA was defeated. In the American academy feminism gets more and more respect while in the larger society women cannot call themselves feminist."[12]

Underscoring Gallop's argument regarding the yawning divide between academic feminism and the lives of women "in the larger society," bell hooks, writing in 1984, sees academic discourse as part of the problem, alienating mainstream women from feminist activism. "The ability to 'translate' ideas to an audience that varies in age, sex, ethnicity, degree of literacy is a skill feminist educators need to develop. Concentration of feminist educators in universities encourages habitual use of an academic style that may make it impossible for teachers to communicate effectively with individuals who are not familiar with either academic style or jargon."[13] hooks's critique of self-conscious academic language extends from the same metacritical impulse as Rich's critical rereading of feminist texts for their prescriptions of compulsory heterosexuality. But hooks's target audience is somewhat different from Rich's; hooks sees the exclusionary language of academic feminism as part of a problematic system of oppressive power relationships relating to race, class, and gender. Far from escaping the pernicious implications of these power relations, hooks argues that feminists consistently *duplicate* them in their blindness to and exclusion of women of color and poor women. While Rich's critique focuses on assumptions of normative heterosexuality, hooks's focuses on assumptions of normative white middle-class status:

> White women who dominate feminist discourse today rarely question whether or not their perspective on women's reality is true to the lived experiences of women as a collective group. Nor are they aware of the extent to which their perspectives reflect race and class biases, although there has been a greater awareness of biases in recent years. Racism abounds in the writings of white feminists, reinforcing white supremacy and negating the possibility that women will bond politically across ethnic and racial boundaries. Past feminist refusal to draw attention to and attack racial hierarchies suppressed the link between race and class.
>
> (3)

Given hooks's useful insistence on sex, race, and class discrimination as symptoms of larger systemic problems, it is noteworthy that discrimination based on sexuality drops out of her larger structure of critique. hooks is deeply concerned that feminist theory address issues across lines of race and class, but to do so, she argues, feminism must begin to disassociate itself from its image as a movement consisting primarily of lesbians; she sees feminism as a movement dominated by dykes at the expense of diversity. hooks is sharply critical of what she perceives as the facile equation in mainstream feminism of lesbian sexuality with political correctness: "women who are not lesbians, who may or may not be in relationships with men feel that they are not 'real' feminists. This is especially true of women who may support feminism but who do not publiclly [*sic*] support lesbian rights" (151).

Unwilling to apply the same critique to homophobia that she does to racism, hooks exhorts feminists to "diversify" the public face of feminism by making clear that feminists are not necessarily lesbians or manhaters. In hooks's view, the failure of feminism to become a truly massive social movement inheres in its anxiety-producing association with nonhetero sexualities:

> My point is that feminism will never appeal to a mass-based group of women in our society who are heterosexual if they think that they will be looked down upon or seen as doing something wrong. . . . Just as feminist movement to end sexual oppression should create a social climate in which lesbians and gay men are no longer oppressed, a climate in which their sexual choices are affirmed, it should also create a climate in which heterosexual practice is freed from the constraints of heterosexism and can also be affirmed. One of the practical reasons for doing this is the recognition that the advancement of feminism as a political movement depends on the involvement of masses of women, a vast majority of whom are heterosexual. As long as feminist women (be they celibate, lesbian, heterosexual, etc.) condemn male sexuality, and by extension women who are involved sexually with men, feminist movement is undermined.
>
> (153)

The rhetoric of comprehensive, systemic analysis of power relations has shifted by this point to a more coercive rhetoric of marketing: "feminism will never appeal to a mass-based group of women in our society who are heterosexual *if* . . ." While hooks claims concern here for the discriminatory assumptions of heterosexism, nowhere else does she suggest that feminist theory pander to the comfort of the "vast majority" in exchange for a rigorous consideration of the rights and the existence of an endangered minority.

My critique of hooks's position is not a new one; in fact, the quote above is part of hooks's response to "lesbian feminist" Cheryl Clarke, who wrote an essay titled "The Failure to Transform: Homophobia in the Black Community," in which she remarks: "'Hooks delivers a backhanded slap at lesbian feminists, a considerable number of whom are black. Hooks would have done well to attack the institution of heterosexuality as it is a prime cause of black women's oppression in America.'"[14] hooks replies, "Clearly Clarke misunderstands and misinterprets my point. I made no reference to heterosexism and it is the equation of heterosexual practice with heterosexism that makes it appear that Clarke is attacking the practice itself and not only heterosexism." Clarke's point, reminiscent of Rich, that hooks should examine "the institution of heterosexuality," is revealingly translated by hooks directly into "heterosexism": it is not Clarke but hooks who makes the equation of heterosexual practice and heterosexism.[15] The question of the problematic institutional dynamics of heterosexuality is neatly subsumed under this equation; hooks's discussion continues on into a critique of feminist heterophobic impulses, in defense of "the choice women make to be heterosexual" (154). Heterosexuality, not normally seen as an endangered category, makes a strange bedfellow with the other forms of oppression and exclusion hooks treats in this text, including racial and class prejudice. hooks's heterosexuality is vulnerable, defensive, embattled, but ironically, her need to defend heterosexual practice duplicates a function of the dyke: she is eager to set up protective walls around heterosexuality, thus liberating women everywhere into the radical freedom of heterosexual object choice. In another twist of irony, hooks begins to set up dykes to defend against dykes.

hooks's logic at this point is complicated, for several reasons. In her larger argument, her desire to ensure that feminists are consistent in their critique of *any* form of compulsory sexuality, whether gay or straight, is a direct extension of powerful early feminist critiques of limiting patriarchal roles for women. However, in a book critiquing feminist marginalizations of women of color, it is strange that hooks's analysis of phobic exclusionary practices should fail to extend to her discussion of sexuality. The apparent suggestion that feminists should disassociate themselves—at least publicly—from the issue of lesbian sexuality seems linked to another paradigm of the 1970s, the antifeminist rhetoric which labeled feminists, often arbitrarily, as dykes, intimidating through the invocation of internalized homophobia.

ON THE SUBJECT OF...

BELL HOOKS (1952?-)

Born Gloria Watkins in Hopkinsville, Kentucky, bell hooks chose her great-grandmother's name as a pseudonym to honor her foremothers—she often refers to a household full of strong black women as one of her greatest influences—and uses lowercase letters to draw readers's attention away from her name and identity and focus it on her works. hooks received her B.A. from Stanford University in 1973 and her Ph.D. in English from the University of California at Santa Cruz in 1983. hooks had difficulty reconciling her small-town Southern roots with her academic life. This disparity later became a subject in her essays. In the mid-1980s, hooks became an assistant professor of Afro-American Studies and English at Yale University. Later she became a professor of English and Women's Studies at Oberlin College and then moved to City College in New York as a professor of English. In 1991 hooks earned the Before Columbus Foundation's American Book Award for *Yearning: Race, Gender, and Cultural Politics* (1990). The common theme of hooks's first two essay collections, *Ain't I a Woman: Black Women and Feminism* (1981) and *Feminist Theory: From Margin to Center* (1984), is that of black women finding a place within mainstream feminism. She explores this issue by tracing the oppression that African American women have suffered since the time of slavery, arguing that domination is at the root of racism, classism, and sexism, and that black women are at the bottom of the hierarchical struggle in the United States. In *Talking Back: Thinking Feminist, Thinking Black* (1988) hooks informs social theory and analysis with her own experience as an African American woman, demonstrating the utility of using feminist viewpoints to assess the position of African American women in American society. The focus of all of hooks's work, including *Killing Rage: Ending Racism* (1995), is to heal the divisions in American society by creating a dialogue that respects all people and leads the way to rebuilding a new society.

Instead of reading "mass-based" anxiety about lesbianism as a need for "mass-based" education about forms of prejudice as pernicious in the case of sexuality as in the case of race, hooks seems to suggest that feminists need only change the window dressing in order to appeal to a wider range of women; her feminist paradigm seems to sacrifice sexual diversity in the cause of racial diversity, while she bars altogether the possibility that lesbians of color might exist. This platform clearly—and perhaps ironically—returns to the scene of the "lavender menace," and backlash against the suggestion that the marketing of the feminist movement must occur under the aegis of "normative" sexuality.

While Barbara Smith echoes hooks's sharp criticism of white, middle-class feminist narcissism, she does not see the interests of black women and lesbians as mutually exclusive or even in competition, insisting on the importance of a feminist discourse that considers race and sexuality together: "Long before I tried to write this I realized that I was attempting something unprecedented, something dangerous, merely by writing about Black women writers from a feminist perspective and about Black lesbian writers from any perspective at all. . . . All segments of the literary world—whether establishment, progressive, Black, female, or lesbian—do not know, or at least act as if they do not know, that Black women writers and Black lesbian writers exist."[16] Jane Gallop claims, in a discussion of *The New Feminist Criticism* (the anthology in which Smith's essay is reprinted), that feminist criticism of the early and mid-1980s struggled explicitly with problems of self-definition and with issues of inclusion and exclusion.[17] Judith Roof argues that "the myriad differences among women are often reduced to the formula 'black and lesbian.' . . . I suspect that this . . . critical reliance upon black and lesbian is symptomatic of some underlying critical difficulty with multiplicity."[18] I would concur that within the discourses of feminist theory and criticism of the mid-1980s, the categories "black" and "lesbian" demarcate similar modes of "difference," both existing, in most cases, as "other than" a norm. The white, middle-class, heterosexual assumptions of that norm are made visible only through the tension produced by the defining presence of the other.

Feminist Theory in the Late 1980s

A Mass of Mineral Matter, usually Igneous Rock, Filling up a Fissure in the Original Strata, and Sometimes Rising from these like a Mound or Wall, when they have been Worn down by Denudation.

—Oxford English Dictionary

Feminist theorists became increasingly preoccupied with the discursive politics of "difference" in the years that followed these publications, to the extent that race and sexuality are equated less often. But the contentious and persistent question of dykes in the mainstream continued throughout this period to serve a uniquely definitional function for feminist theory. In the early 1980s, feminism was faced with a central division: some critics argued that feminism was all about, too much about, lesbianism and lesbian sexuality; others argued that the heterosexist bias in feminist discourse betrayed itself constantly in the marginalization and the silencing of lesbians and lesbian writers. This particular "dyke" shaped the peculiar path of feminist discourse in the second half of the 1980s.

Literary theory more generally was reinfused with the politics of activism in the mid-1980s; as the AIDS epidemic ravaged the gay male community, many critics turned to the complexities of male homoeroticism, discourses, and representation with a sense of political urgency unseen since the early days of the women's movement. Using the tools of feminist theory, literary theorists began to focus on homosexuality through the newly repoliticized discourses of masculinity. Interestingly and ironically, this development created yet another "dyke" in the world of literary criticism: while lesbians belonged to the gay rights movement and the feminist movement, suddenly they were *centrally* implicated in neither. Although questions of homosexuality were central to both feminist and gay male discourses, they were primarily about male homosexuality. Lesbians themselves existed at the discursive margins, in and as the space between these two newly prominent theoretical positions.

Through the middle years of the 1980s, the central terms of feminist literary theory underwent a significant paradigm shift, refocusing from a concern with the politics of female sex and sexuality to a theoretically broader concern with the notion of gender. As Elaine Showalter points out in the introduction to the anthology *Speaking of Gender,* which first appeared in 1989, "talking about gender means talking about both women and men." "The introduction of gender into the field of literary studies marks a new phase in feminist criticism, an investigation of the ways that all reading and writing, by men as well as by women, is marked by gender. Talking about gender, moreover, is a constant reminder of the other categories of difference, such as race and class, that structure our lives and texts, just as theorizing gender emphasizes the parallels between feminist criticism and other forms of minority discourse."[19]

The rise of gender studies over the course of the 1980s served practical as well as theoretical functions. Among other things, it opened the doors of feminist theory unambiguously to male practitioners, and as Showalter points out, presented a much more sophisticated notion of the ways in which language and power converge to shape a speaking subject, whether "male" or "female." The focus on gender served to further dismantle monolithic notions of "maleness" and "femaleness" per se, in exchange for a theory of gender as cultural construct, symptomatically reflecting larger cultural investments.

Gender theory has proved both invigorating and problematic for more conventional feminist political concerns. As Showalter notes,

> some readers . . . worry that "gender studies" could be a pallid assimilation of feminist criticism into the mainstream (or male stream) of English studies, a return to the old priorities and binary oppositions that will reinstate familiar male canons while crowding hard-won courses on women writers out of the curriculum. Others fear that talking about gender is a way for both male and female critics to avoid the political commitment of feminism. Still others raise the troubling possibility that gender will be isolated from issues of class and race.
>
> (10)

Showalter suggests that many feminists were and remain concerned that to forsake the focus on "women" in favor of a broader focus on "gender" is to retrench on feminist inroads in the academy; if there is no longer any basis for a practical concern for and with women specifically, then what is the difference, they ask, between the academy now and the academy before early feminist pioneers appeared on the horizon? The generalization outward of feminist political and theoretical interests reflects more complex notions about the ways in which structures of gender and sexuality are supported; in a poststructuralist theoretical universe which privileges indeterminacy, to talk about "women" alone is, in some sense, a return to an artificial and potentially simplistic means of categorization. Yet this artifice is belied by the materialist concerns of patriarchal class politics: the opening out of feminist theory into gender theory certainly risks the reinstitutionalization of male-centered concerns, a loss of ground in some sense, even as it represents an enriched understanding of prevailing cultural constructs.

Feminist ventures in gender theory constantly engage this ambivalence. The important linkage of feminist and gay male theories of discourse and narrative was facilitated by several prominent feminist critics, who are necessarily prompted at every turn to theorize, even to justify, the gender politics of their methodologies. For example, Eve Kosofsky Sedgwick, in the groundbreaking study *Between Men: English Literature and Male Homosocial Desire*, both avows a feminist methodology and defends her exclusive focus on male subjectivity and male homosociality. In her introduction, Sedgwick discusses "the isolation, not to mention the absolute subordination, of women, in the structural paradigm on which this study is based." She writes: "The absence of lesbianism from the book was an early and, I think, necessary decision, since my argument is structured around the distinctive relation of the male homosocial spectrum to the transmission of unequally distributed power. Nevertheless, the exclusively heterosexual perspective of the book's attention to women is seriously impoverishing in itself."[20] Profoundly feminist in its methodology, Sedgwick's rereading of Freud, Girard, and the structure of triangulated desire does not offer a deeper understanding of the place of the woman in that structure but instead demonstrates as central the vector connecting its two male subjects in a rich analysis of the male homosocial relations previously concealed by assumptions of normative heterosexuality. However, the single theoretical distinction Sedgwick makes between male and female homoeroticism is a significant one; she justifies her focus on the distinction between homosociality and homosexuality in men based on the fact that this is *more* of a distinction for men than for women:

> The diacritical opposition between the "homosocial" and the "homosexual" seems to be much less thorough and dichotomous for women, in our society, than for men. At this particular historical moment, an intelligible continuum of aims, emotions, and valuations links lesbianism with the other forms of women's attention to women: the bond of mother and daughter, for instance, the bond of sister and sister, women's friendship, "networking," and the active struggles of feminism. The continuum is crisscrossed with deep discontinuities—with much homophobia, with conflicts of race and class—but its intelligibility seems now a matter of simple common sense.
>
> (2)

Writing off the theoretical complexity, even the specific discernibility, of lesbian erotic desire as "simple common sense," Sedgwick inaugurates an era in which feminist practitioners fixate on male homoeroticism as an interesting problematic while dismissively relegating the "dyke" to the outer reaches of feminist discourse. Implicitly accepting Rich's notion of the "lesbian continuum" as theoretically exhaustive, Sedgwick ironically reinscribes the very problem Rich herself was hop-

American essayist, novelist, and poet Rita Mae Brown (1944-).

ing to dismantle. For Rich was concerned with precisely "how and why women's choice of women as passionate comrades, life partners, coworkers, lovers, community has been crushed, invalidated, forced into hiding and disguise; and . . . the virtual or total neglect of lesbian existence in a wide range of writings, including feminist scholarship." Rich concludes, in a startling prediction of a predicament redescribed a decade later: "I believe that much feminist theory and criticism is stranded on this shoal."[21]

In *The Apparitional Lesbian: Female Homosexuality and Modern Culture*, Terry Castle explores Sedgwick's resistance to or "blockage" against any form of rigorous consideration of female homosexuality:

> Lesbians, defined . . . with telling vagueness only as "women who love women," are really no different, Sedgwick seems to imply, from "women promoting the interests of other women." Their way of bonding is so "congruent" with that of other women, it turns out, that one need no longer call it homosexual. "The adjective 'homosocial' as applied to women's bonds," [Sedgwick] concludes, *"need not be pointedly dichotomized as against 'homosexual'; it can intelligibly denominate the entire continuum."* By a disarming sleight of phrase, an entire category of women—lesbians—is lost to view.[22]

Castle's objection to Sedgwick's "uncharacteristically sentimental" (71) reliance on the "continuum" metaphor begins to indicate a major problem in conventional feminist analyses of homoeroticism. Castle's critique implicitly returns to and begins to trouble Adrienne Rich's notion of the "lesbian continuum," which pointedly desexualizes lesbianism in favor of a more pan-feminist vision of meaningful engagement among women. Castle's discomfort with the "lesbian continuum" betokens a new negotiation for feminist theory: a theoretical practice that interrogates the specificity of male homoerotic desire cannot rely complacently on a notion of lesbianism that is vague, deliberately broad, and explicitly detached from any form of eroticism or desire whatsoever. Rich's argument for the "lesbian continuum" was the product of a specific historical moment and served several important functions within the discourse of feminist theory, particularly in its defusing of the term *lesbian* and its situation of feminist methodology firmly in the center of literary critical practice. However, as Castle implies, Rich's project is not the lesbian equivalent to the carefully theorized analysis of male homosociality that Sedgwick conducts in *Between Men*. Indeed, Rich's essay announces as its goal the more rigorous *inclusion* of lesbians throughout the range of academic discourses; thus Sedgwick's appropriation of Rich, in order to justify the *exclusion* of lesbians, represents a perfect, if ironic, example of the phenomenon Rich had hoped to counteract.

Pursuing the implications of Castle's argument, I would agree that feminists, working from the heritage of such broad definitions as Rich's "lesbian continuum," are quick to assume that they already fully understand "lesbianism," most conventionally as something inherently "feminist" or as something having to do with (not necessarily sexual) "female bonding." Accompanying this model are assumptions suggesting that lesbianism is only occasionally or tangentially related to sex and sexual pleasure. These assumptions are engendered in part by the history, within feminism, of a political lesbianism which constructs lesbianism as a separatist opting out of patriarchy rather than as an erotic object choice. They are also facilitated by historical conventions of female friendship and Boston marriage, which again are perceived as related more to women's mutual empathy than to mutual erotic pleasure. These assumptions suggest a dramatic historical difference in cultural perceptions of female and male homosexuality. From Gay Liberation to queer theory, analyses of male homosexuality have rarely assumed that eroticism, sexual attraction, and sex acts, covert or explicit, are marginal or irrelevant issues. Following Sedgwick's lead, feminist and queer analyses of polymorphous sexualities ironically continue to fixate on problems of *male* homoeroticism because of the perception that these relations are somehow underexplored or more complex than female homoeroticism. In turn, lesbianism is too often dismissed as either coextensive with any sort of feminist practice or completely accessible within any conventional understanding of female friendship. "What may appear 'intelligible' or 'simple common sense' to a nonlesbian critic," writes Castle, "will hardly seem quite so simple to any female reader who has ever attempted to walk down a city street holding hands with, let alone kissing or embracing another woman." She continues:

> The homosexual panic elicited by women publicly signaling their sexual interest in one another continues, alas, even "at this particular historical moment," to be just as virulent as that inspired by male homosexuality, if not more so. To obscure the fact that lesbians are women who have sex with each other—and that this is not exactly the same, in the eyes of society, as voting for women or giving them jobs—is, in essence, not to acknowledge the separate peril and pleasure of lesbian existence.

(71-72)

Explicitly detaching lesbianism from the broader concerns of feminism in general, Castle returns to Rich again, this time replacing the term that Sedgwick appropriates, "lesbian continuum," with the term that Rich uses in her title, the far more insistent and aggressive "lesbian existence." With this gesture, Castle begins to call for an analysis of female homosexuality, not homosociality, that accounts for the sexual pleasure and personal danger that accompany living as a lesbian. In response to Sedgwick's contention that male homosociality is the figure of patriarchal power, Castle suggests the insurgent potential of a theory of lesbian desire: "To theorize about female-female desire . . . is precisely to envision the taking apart of this supposedly intractable patriarchal structure. Female bonding, at least hypothetically, destabilizes the 'canonical' triangular arrangement of male desire, is an affront to it, and ultimately—in the radical form of lesbian bonding—displaces it entirely."[23]

Castle's discomfort with the feminist absorption of lesbian concerns is also reflected, some-

ON THE SUBJECT OF...

RITA MAE BROWN (1944-)

"My bitterness was reflected in the news, full of stories about people my own age raging down the streets in protest. But somehow I knew my rage wasn't their rage and they'd have run me out of their movement for being a lesbian anyway. I read somewhere too that women's groups were starting but they'd trash me just the same. . . . I wished I could get up in the morning and look at the day the way I used to when I was a child. . . . Damn, I wished the world would let me be myself."

Brown, Rita Mae. In *Rubyfruit Jungle*, 1973. Reprint, p. 246. New York: Bantam Books, 1988.

Rita Mae Brown was born in Pennsylvania and attended the University of Florida, New York University, and the New York School of Visual Arts. She became active in the feminist and lesbian rights movements in the late 1960s but left several feminist and gay rights groups, including the National Organization for Women (NOW) and Gay Liberation, when she found them intolerant of or indifferent to lesbian concerns. In 1971 she helped organize the Furies, a lesbian feminist separatist group based in Washington, D.C., and later became one of the founding editors of *Quest*, a feminist research journal. Brown chronicled her own and other lesbians' searches for a satisfactory outlet for their activism in her essay collection *A Plain Brown Rapper* (1976). Brown's first novel, *Rubyfruit Jungle* (1973), a modern, female-centered picaresque, has been compared to Mark Twain's *The Adventures of Huckleberry Finn* for its treatment of protagonist Molly Bolt, an intelligent, outspoken young woman who struggles and eventually triumphs in a society that is often hostile to her identity as a woman and a lesbian. *Rubyfruit Jungle* established Brown as a leading voice in the feminist movement and has sold over a million copies. In subsequent novels Brown has written extensively about racial and sexual issues: *Southern Discomfort* (1982) concerns a romance between a wealthy white Southern socialite and a black teenager, and *Sudden Death* (1983) depicts professional dishonesty and sexual betrayal in the world of women's tennis. Brown remains active in promoting women's political and social concerns.

what differently, however, in the initial theoretical formulation of "queer theory," which occurred in a 1991 special issues of the journal *differences* dedicated to "Lesbian and Gay Sexualities." Again, the voice behind this formulation is that of a prominent feminist, Teresa de Lauretis. In her introduction to this issue, de Lauretis notes that while gay male and lesbian discourses have evolved along basically separate paths in the past, recent critical tendencies to see them as versions of one phenomenon, "lesbian and gay" (ladies first, of course), threaten to erase the specificity of that history. She writes, "our 'differences,' such as they may be, are less represented by the discursive coupling of those two terms in the politically correct phrase 'lesbian and gay,' than they are elided by most of the contexts in which the phrase is used; that is to say, differences are implied in it but then simply taken for granted or even covered over by the word 'and.'"[24] Thus occurs the birth of "queer theory," a metacritical praxis which is "intended to mark a certain critical distance" from the formulaic and reductive phrase "lesbian and gay." "Queer theory," writes de Lauretis, "conveys a double emphasis—on the conceptual and speculative work involved in discourse production, and on the necessary critical work of deconstructing our own discourses and their constructed silences" (iv). By definition a self-interrogating methodology, conditioned by a tradition of oppression, erasure, and silence to constantly examine its own "constructed silences," queer theory is, in theory, a school of thought that is always going back to school.

De Lauretis's logic is both provocative and problematic. To replace a phrase like "lesbian and gay" with a phrase like "queer theory" is quite literally to cover over any notion of lesbian and gay difference, to subsume male and female homosexuality within the single, potentially monolithic category "queer," to depend on the self-policing integrity of queer theorists themselves to "deconstruct . . . our own discourses and their constructed silences." In its ideal form, queer theory would be a constantly self-interrogating practice, and through that self-interrogation would succeed in retaining the specificity of lesbian and gay histories while also exploring the theoretical complexity of lesbian and gay difference. However, the replacement of a tripartite term—"lesbian and gay"—with a bipartite term—"queer theory"—appears to counteract de Lauretis's desire for increased specificity. And as queer theory begins to articulate itself as a practice

distinct from feminist theory, the question of women, and particularly the question of lesbians, is persistently sidelined.

In the introduction to *Epistemology of the Closet*, Sedgwick addresses the question of a specifically lesbian-centered theoretical practice: "It seems inevitable to me that the work of defining the circumferential boundaries, vis-à-vis lesbian experience and identity, of any gay male-centered theoretical articulation can be done only from the point of view of an alternative, feminocentric theoretical space, not from the heart of the male-centered project itself."[25] Within the context of a book that is quite explicitly at "the heart of the male-centered project itself," Sedgwick's discussion of a lesbian implication to gay male theory demonstrates great ambivalence. While this introduction, like the introduction to *Between Men*, gives a nod to the urgent necessity for "feminocentric theoretical space," the place of lesbians in *Epistemology* is at best marginal. Acknowledging lesbian activists' work in the AIDS epidemic, Sedgwick writes, "The newly virulent homophobia of the 1980s, directed alike against women and men even though its medical pretext ought, if anything, logically to give a relative exemptive privilege to lesbians, reminds urgently that it is more to friends than to enemies that gay women and gay men are perceptible as distinct groups." Noting that lesbians, too, are vulnerable to AIDS, Sedgwick sees gay and AIDS activism as deeply indebted to lesbian practitioners and feminist theories:

> The contributions of lesbians to current gay and AIDS activism are weighty, not despite, but because of the intervening lessons of feminism. Feminist perspectives on medicine and health-care issues, on civil disobedience, and on the politics of class and race as well as of sexuality have been centrally enabling for the recent waves of AIDS activism. What this activism returns to the lesbians involved in it may include a more richly pluralized range of imaginings of lines of gender and sexual identification.
>
> (38-39)

Sedgwick is significantly vague about the yield of lesbian investment; that activism "*may* include a more richly pluralized range of imaginings" seems tepid consolation within a context of "virulent homophobia." Sedgwick is cautionary about the tendency of gay male discourse to "subsume" lesbian "experience and definition":

> The 'gay theory' I have been comparing with feminist theory doesn't mean exclusively gay male theory, but for the purpose of this comparison it

includes lesbian theory insofar as that (a) isn't simply coextensive with feminist theory (i.e., doesn't subsume sexuality fully under gender) and (b) doesn't a priori deny all theoretical continuity between male homosexuality and lesbianism. But, again, the extent, construction, and meaning, and especially the history of any such theoretical continuity—not to mention its consequences for practical politics—must be open to every interrogation.

(39)

Sedgwick, like de Lauretis, is always careful to argue that male and female homosexuality are very different phenomena, a useful and critical point. In fact, in this passage, as she tries to articulate a sufficiently specific and differentiated theoretical agenda for her text, Sedgwick recurs to an implicit structure of triangulation: gay male theoretical concerns, lesbian theoretical concerns, and feminist theoretical concerns are all related yet distinct entities. Once again, the "dyke" operates as the border, the literal site of connection and distinction between feminist and "gay" concerns in general. But as with all triangulated structures, as Sedgwick has demonstrated, one term is inevitably subordinated in favor of a dynamic connection between the other two. In Sedgwick's *Epistemology,* as in *Between Men,* the coincidence of feminist methodology and gay male subject matter consistently produces lesbian concerns as that third term, emerging occasionally, marginally, and principally in introductory matter. This is one example of a larger critical phenomenon in which, once again, the dyke demarcates the border of internal and external, offering a frame of reference but not a *mise en abîme.*

At the risk of the inevitable pun, I would argue that while feminist theory engendered queer theory, the two remain distinct. By now the dualism that so profoundly shaped feminist discourse at the end of the 1970s and into the early 1980s is literalized in the separate entities of feminist and queer scholarship. But what has been factored out here, oddly enough, is the specificity of lesbian discourse: caught between the feminist and the queer, the lesbian, again, occupies the problematic third position in the triangle of contemporary critical discourse. And as with the triangular structure posited in Sedgwick's early analysis, the third term is not the one that counts; the animate connection here is the one between feminists and queers, while the third, the site of literal connection and disjunction, marks the space between without signifying itself. Lesbians occupy the subordinated place of the woman in the structure of triangular desire, in which the desiring relationship is constituted between feminists and queers.

Back in 1980, in "Compulsory Heterosexuality and Lesbian Existence," Rich produced what seems today a startlingly prescient commentary. She writes, "Lesbians have historically been deprived of a political existence through 'inclusion' as female versions of male homosexuality. To equate lesbian existence with male homosexuality because each is stigmatized is to erase female reality once again."[26] Equated not only with male homosexuals but with feminism in its most generalized form, lesbians remain consistently—and paradoxically—marginalized. And as a marginalized population, dykes serve a useful function within the context of feminist and queer theories alike, acting as the border against which the mainstream can define itself. The specific location of that margin, of that "dyke," is revealing of particular, often-shifting engagements within theoretical discourses as they struggle to define themselves, their constituencies, their politics, and their activism. The dyke in the mainstream marks the space of margin and connection, offering at once a point of view that is and is not of the central flow.

Within the metaphorical structure I have explored throughout this essay, I have argued that feminist theory has consistently seen the "dyke" as marginal, protective, and contingent, as facilitating the existence of a larger whole rather than independently significant. Yet the specificity of lesbian discourses and desires has independently significant value, not only as a metacritical instrument for the analysis of a broader feminist theory, but also as an historically complex cultural phenomenon it its own right. Behind the metaphorical, architectural dyke is another dyke, a figure too often marginalized, too frequently and too vaguely appropriated within larger theoretical paradigms of sexuality and politics. For let us recall that listed below and separated from the nearly three columns of *dykes* in the *OED* is the slang definition: "dike, dyke . . . *slang.* [Of obscure origin.] A lesbian; a masculine woman."

Notes

With thanks to Kathryn Schwarz, Sarah Blake, David A. Hedrich Hirsch, and Marvin J. Taylor.

1. "Dike, dyke," *Oxford English Dictionary,* 2d ed., vol. 4, 659-60. All epigraphs that follow are excerpted from *OED* definitions of *dyke,* as cited here.

2. For a discussion of theoretical appropriations of such disparaging terms as *queer,* see Judith Butler, "Critically Queer," *Bodies That Matter,* esp. 226-30.

3. *OED*, vol. 4, 660.

4. Radicalesbians, "The Woman-Identified Woman" 166. Authorship of this essay has been attributed to Rita Mae Brown.

5. Catharine A. MacKinnon, "Feminism, Marxism, Method, and the State" 247n46.

6. Ti-Grace Atkinson, "Lesbianism and Feminism: Justice for Women as 'Unnatural,'" *Amazon Odyssey* 134, 132.

7. Ti-Grace Atkinson, "Strategy and Tactics: A Presentation of Political Lesbianism," *Amazon Odyssey* 138.

8. Atkinson, "Lesbianism and Feminism" 131.

9. Miriam Schneir, Introduction to Radicalesbians, "The Woman-Identified Woman" 161.

10. Adrienne Rich, "Compulsory Heterosexuality and Lesbian Existence" 244. Italics in original.

11. Ibid. 239. Italics in original.

12. Jane Gallop, *Around 1981* 10.

13. bell hooks, *Feminist Theory from Margin to Center* 111.

14. Quoted in hooks, *Feminist Theory* 153. hooks responds again to the emotional, if not the intellectual, implications of this issue in the essay "Censorship from Left and Right," *Outlaw Culture* 71.

15. Interestingly, hooks herself later criticizes Madonna's book *Sex* for *its* conflation of the heterosexual and the heterosexist: "Even in the realm of male homoeroticism/homosexuality, Madonna's image usurps, takes over, subordinates. Coded always in *Sex* as heterosexual, her image is the dominant expression of heterosexism. . . . In the context of *Sex*, gay culture remains irrevocably linked to a system of patriarchal control framed by a heterosexist pornographic gaze" ("Power to the Pussy," *Outlaw Culture* 16-17).

16. Barbara Smith, "Toward a Black Feminist Criticism" 168.

17. See esp. Gallop's chap. 2, "The Problem of Definition," *Around 1981*.

18. Judith Roof, *A Lure of Knowledge* 217.

19. Elaine Showalter, "Introduction: The Rise of Gender," in *Speaking of Gender* 2-3.

20. Eve Kosofsky Sedgwick, *Between Men* 18.

21. Rich, "Compulsory Heterosexuality" 229.

22. Terry Castle, *The Apparitional Lesbian* 71. Italics in original.

23. Ibid. 72. For an interesting revisionary reading of Sedgwick's paradigm of triangulated desire, see Castle's chap. 4, "Sylvia Townsend Warner and the Counterplot of Lesbian Fiction," ibid. 66-91.

24. Teresa de Lauretis, "Queer Theory: Lesbian and Gay Sexualities, an Introduction" v-vi.

25. Eve Kosofsky Sedgwick, *Epistemology of the Closet* 39.

26. Rich, "Compulsory Heterosexuality" 239.

Works Cited

Atkinson, Ti-Grace. *Amazon Odyssey: The First Collection of Writings by the Political Pioneer of the Women's Movement.* New York: Links Books, 1974, 131-89.

Butler, Judith. *Bodies That Matter: On the Discursive Limits of "Sex."* New York: Routledge, 1993.

Castle, Terry. *The Apparitional Lesbian: Female Homosexuality and Modern Culture.* New York: Columbia University Press, 1993.

de Lauretis, Teresa. "Queer Theory: Lesbian and Gay Sexualities, an Introduction." *differences* 3.2 (Summer 1991).

Gallop, Jane. *Around 1981: Academic Feminist Literary Theory.* New York: Routledge, 1992.

hooks, bell. *Feminist Theory from Margin to Center.* Boston: South End Press, 1984.

———. *Outlaw Culture: Resisting Representations.* New York: Routledge, 1994.

MacKinnon, Catharine A. "Feminism, Marxism, Method, and the State: An Agenda for Theory." In *The Signs Reader: Women, Gender, and Scholarship*, ed. Elizabeth Abel and Emily K. Abel. Chicago: University of Chicago Press, 1983, 227-56.

Oxford English Dictionary, 2d ed. Oxford: Clarendon Press, 1989.

Radicalesbians. "The Woman-Identified Woman." In *Feminism in Our Time: The Essential Writings, World War II to the Present*, ed. Miriam Schneir. New York: Vintage, 1994, 162-67.

Rich, Adrienne. "Compulsory Heterosexuality and Lesbian Existence." In *The Lesbian and Gay Studies Reader*, ed. Henry Abelove, Michèle Aina Barale, and David M. Halperin. New York: Routledge, 1993, 227-54.

Roof, Judith. *A Lure of Knowledge: Lesbian Sexuality and Theory.* New York: Columbia University Press, 1991.

Schneir, Miriam. Introduction to Radicalesbians, "The Woman-Identified Woman." In *Feminism in Our Time* 160-62.

Sedgwick, Eve Kosofsky. *Between Men: English Literature and Male Homosocial Desire.* New York: Columbia University Press, 1985.

———. *Epistemology of the Closet.* Berkeley: University of California Press, 1990.

Showalter, Elaine. "Introduction: The Rise of Gender." In *Speaking of Gender*, ed. Elaine Showalter. New York: Routledge, 1989.

Smith, Barbara. "Toward a Black Feminist Criticism." In *The New Feminist Criticism: Essays on Women, Literature, and Theory*, ed. Elaine Showalter. New York: Pantheon, 1985, 168-86.

FURTHER READING

Criticism

Abel, Elizabeth. "Black Writing, White Reading: Race and the Politics of Feminist Interpretation." In *Female Subjects in Black and White: Race, Psychoanalysis, Feminism*, edited by Elizabeth Abel, Barbara Christian, and Helene Maglen, pp. 102-31. Berkeley: University of California Press, 1997.

Contends that Toni Morrison's story "Recitatif" uses the relationship between its two protagonists to explore the operations of race in the feminine perspective.

Allen, Paula Gunn. *The Sacred Hoop: Recovering the Feminine in American Indian Traditions*. Boston, Mass.: Beacon Press, 1986, 311 p.

Anthology of essays focusing on Native American women poets.

Bonds, Diane S. "The Separative Self in Sylvia Plath's *The Bell Jar*." *Women's Studies* 18, no. 1 (1990): 49-64.

Analyzes Plath's text as a collusive dramatization of the notion of a separate and separative self.

Brügmann, Margaret. "Between the Lines: On the Essayistic Experiments of Hélène Cixous in 'The Laugh of the Medusa.'" In *The Politics of the Essay: Feminist Perspectives*, edited by Ruth-Ellen Boetcher Joeres and Elizabeth Mittman, pp. 73-86. Bloomington, Ind.: Indiana University Press, 1993.

Studies Cixous's essay as a blend of the historic, mythical, and social situation of women, one that leads the reader through a "utopian vision of possibilities."

Cheung, King-Kok. Introduction to *Words Matter: Conversations with Asian American Writers*, edited by King-Kok Cheung, pp. 1-20. Honolulu: University of Hawaii Press, 2000.

Introduces an anthology of writings by various Asian American writers who discuss the ways in which they would like their works interpreted. Also provides an overview of Asian American literature.

Chin, Frank, et al., eds. *Aiiieeeee!: An Anthology of Asian American Writers*. Washington: Howard University Press, 1974, 200 p.

Anthology of works by Asian American writers.

Christian, Barbara. "But What Do We Think We're Doing Anyway: The State of Black Feminist Criticism(s) or My Version of a Little Bit of History." In *Changing Our Own Words: Essays on Criticism, Theory, and Writing by Black Women*, edited by Cheryl A. Wall, pp. 58-74. New Brunswick, N.J.: Rutgers University Press, 1989.

Presents commentary on the lack of coverage of black women authors in feminist journals of the 1970s.

Fornes, Maria Irene, Bertha Harris, Jill Johnston, Lisa Kennedy, and Barbara Smith. "On the Beginnings of Lesbian Literature in the United States: A Symposium with Maria Irene Fornes, Bertha Harris, Jill Johnston, Lisa Kennedy, and Barbara Smith." In *Queer Representations: Reading Lives, Reading Cultures*, edited by Martin Duberman, pp. 347-55. New York, N.Y.: New York University Press, 1997.

Transcript of a symposium in which several feminist theorists discuss the rise of feminist literature and theory in the United States.

Geiger, Jeffrey. "Re-assessing the Past and Future of Feminist Film Theory." *Sexualities* 4, no. 2 (May 2001): 246-51.

Reviews three texts focusing on the development of feminist film theory.

Gilbert, Sandra M., and Susan Gubar. "Introduction: Gender, Creativity, and the Woman Poet." In *Shakespeare's Sisters: Feminist Essays on Women Poets*, edited by Sandra M. Gilbert and Susan Gubar, pp. xv-xxvi. Bloomington: Indiana University Press, 1979.

Anthology of poetry focusing on women poets, including an introduction tracing the history of the development of poetry by women.

Grice, Helena. "Asian American Women's Prose Narratives: Genre and Identity." In *Asian American Studies: Identity,*

Images, Issues Past and Present, edited by Esther Mikyung Ghymn, pp. 179-204. New York, N.Y.: Peter Lang, 2000.

Proposes that Asian American women's prose narratives offer a complex blend of various genres, including novels, autobiographies, journals, short stories, and novellas, contending that new generations of Asian American writers continue to have unique trajectories of development.

Gupton, Janet L. "'Un-ruling' the Woman: Comedy and the Plays of Beth Henley and Rebecca Gilman." In *Southern Women Playwrights: New Essays in Literary History and Criticism*, edited by Robert L. McDonald and Linda Rohrer Paige, pp. 124-38. Tuscaloosa: University of Alabama Press, 2002.

Interprets plays by Beth Henley and Rebecca Gilman as representative examples of new paths being taken by contemporary Southern female playwrights in the arena of comedy.

Hull, Gloria T., and Barbara Smith. "Introduction: The Politics of Black Women's Studies." In *All the Women Are White, All the Blacks Are Men, But Some of Us Are Brave*, edited by Gloria T. Hull, Patricia Bell Scott, and Barbara Smith, pp. i-xxxiv. Old Westbury, N.Y.: Feminist Press, 1982.

Considers the development of black women's studies programs and the politics involved.

Jain, Jasbir, and Avadhesh Kumar Singh, eds. *Indian Feminisms*. New Delhi, India: Creative Books, 2001, 231 p.

Collection of essays focusing on the development of a feminist literature in Indian writing, including overview essays on many modern Indian texts.

Kuhn, Annette. "Women's Genres: Melodrama, Soap Opera and Theory." In *Feminist Film Theory: A Reader*, edited by Sue Thornham, pp. 146-56. New York: New York University Press, 1999.

Examines theories of representation and cultural production as they pertain to television soap operas and film melodrama.

Landry, Donna. "The Word According to Moi: Politics and Feminist Literary Theory." *Criticism* 29, no. 1 (winter 1987): 119-32.

Analyzes Moi's statement that her book remains the first complete introduction to the field of feminist criticism, comparing her book to that of K. K. Ruthven's on the same subject.

McAdams, Jane. "Castings for a (New) World: The Poetry of Joy Harjo." In *Women Poets of the Americas: Toward a Pan-American Gathering*, edited by Jacqueline Vaught Brogan and Cordelia Chávez Candelaria, pp. 210-32. Notre Dame, Ind.: University of Notre Dame Press, 1999.

Argues that Harjo writes witness poetry that examines the significance of private experience in the evaluation of public issues.

Mehaffy, Marilyn, and AnaLouise Keating. "'Carrying the Message': Denise Chávez on the Politics of Chicana Becoming." *Aztlan: A Journal of Chicano Studies* 26, no. 1 (spring 2001): 127-56.

Interview with Denise Chávez, focusing on her works The Last of the Menu Girls *and* Face of An Angel.

Mulvey, Laura. "Visual Pleasure and Narrative Cinema." *Screen* 16, no. 3 (1975): 6-18.

Discusses the significance of the representation of the female form in cinema.

Oha, Obododimma. "Her Dissonant Selves: The Semiotics of Plurality and Bisexuality in Adrienne Kennedy's *Funnyhouse of a Negro*." *American Drama* 6, no. 2 (spring 1997): 67-80.

Theorizes that Funnyhouse of a Negro challenges established notions of sexual identity by broadening the scope of a single artist.

Palumbo-Liu, David. "The Politics of Memory: Remembering History in Alice Walker and Joy Kogawa." In *Memory and Cultural Politics: New Approaches to American Ethnic Literature*, edited by Amritjit Singh, Joseph T. Skerrett, Jr., Robert E. Hogan, pp. 211-26. Boston, Mass.: Northeastern University Press, 1996.

Discussion of the relationship between history, memory, and ethnic narrative in the works of Alice Walker and Joy Kogawa.

Sheridan, Susan. "From Margin to Mainstream: Situating Women's Studies." In *A Reader in Feminist Knowledge*, edited by Sneja Gunew, pp. 61-72. London, England: Routledge, 1991.

Surveys the field of women's studies, focusing on areas of feminist research and teaching as part of the academic mainstream.

Spivak, Gayatri Chakravorty. "Criticism, Feminism, and the Institution." In *The Post-Colonial Critic: Interviews, Strategies, Dialogues, Gayatri Chakravorty Spivak*, edited by Sarah Harasym, pp. 1-16. New York: Routledge, 1990.

Interview with Gayatri Spivak, a well-known cultural and literary theorist.

Uraizee, Joya. "Buchi Emecheta and the Politics of Gender." In *Black Women Writers Across Cultures: An Analysis of Their Contributions*, edited by Valentine Udoh James, James S. Etim, Melanie Marshall James, and Ambe J. Njoh, pp. 171-206. Lanham, Md.: International Scholars Publications, 2000.

Contends that Emecheta's ideology reveals itself in her work via gaps in the narrative rather than through a consistent development of people and events.

INDEXES

The main reference

Austen, Jane 1775-1817 **1:** 122, 125, 220; **2:** 104, 196, **333-384**

lists the featured author's entry in volumes 1, 2, 3, 5, or 6 of Feminism in Literature; *it also lists commentary on the featured author in other volumes of the set, which include topics associated with* Feminism in Literature. *Page references to substantial discussions of the author appear in boldface.*

The cross-references

See also AAYA 19; BRW 4; BRWC 1; BRWR 2; BYA 3; CD-BLB 1789-1832; DA; DA3; DAB; DAC; DAM MST, NOV; DLB 116; EXPN; LAIT 2; LATS 1; LMFS 1; NCLC 1, 13, 19, 33, 51, 81, 95, 119; NFS 1, 14, 18; TEA; WLC; WLIT 3; WYAS 1

list entries on the author in the following Gale biographical and literary sources:

AAL: Asian American Literature

AAYA: Authors & Artists for Young Adults

AFAW: African American Writers

AFW: African Writers

AITN: Authors in the News

AMW: American Writers

AMWR: American Writers Retrospective Supplement

AMWS: American Writers Supplement

ANW: American Nature Writers

AW: Ancient Writers

BEST: Bestsellers (quarterly, citations appear as Year: Issue number)

BG: The Beat Generation: A Gale Critical Companion

BLC: Black Literature Criticism

BLCS: Black Literature Criticism Supplement

BPFB: Beacham's Encyclopedia of Popular Fiction: Biography and Resources

BRW: British Writers

BRWS: British Writers Supplement

BW: Black Writers

BYA: Beacham's Guide to Literature for Young Adults

CA: Contemporary Authors

CAAS: Contemporary Authors Autobiography Series

CABS: Contemporary Authors Bibliographical Series

CAD: Contemporary American Dramatists

CANR: Contemporary Authors New Revision Series

CAP: Contemporary Authors Permanent Series

CBD: Contemporary British Dramatists

CCA: Contemporary Canadian Authors

CD: Contemporary Dramatists

CDALB: Concise Dictionary of American Literary Biography

CDALBS: Concise Dictionary of American Literary Biography Supplement

CDBLB: Concise Dictionary of British Literary Biography

CLC: Contemporary Literary Criticism

CLR: Children's Literature Review

CMLC: Classical and Medieval Literature Criticism

CMW: St. James Guide to Crime & Mystery Writers

CN: Contemporary Novelists

CP: Contemporary Poets

CPW: Contemporary Popular Writers

CSW: Contemporary Southern Writers

CWD: Contemporary Women Dramatists

CWP: Contemporary Women Poets

CWRI: St. James Guide to Children's Writers

CWW: Contemporary World Writers

DA: DISCovering Authors

DA3: DISCovering Authors 3.0

DAB: DISCovering Authors: British Edition

DAC: DISCovering Authors: Canadian Edition

DAM: DISCovering Authors: Modules

    DRAM: Dramatists Module; *MST:* Most-Studied Authors Module;

    MULT: Multicultural Authors Module; *NOV:* Novelists Module;

    POET: Poets Module; *POP:* Popular Fiction and Genre Authors Module

DC: Drama Criticism

DFS: Drama for Students

DLB: Dictionary of Literary Biography

DLBD: Dictionary of Literary Biography Documentary Series

DLBY: Dictionary of Literary Biography Yearbook

DNFS: Literature of Developing Nations for Students

EFS: Epics for Students

EXPN: Exploring Novels

EXPP: Exploring Poetry

EXPS: Exploring Short Stories

EW: European Writers

FANT: St. James Guide to Fantasy Writers

FW: Feminist Writers

GFL: Guide to French Literature, Beginnings to 1789, 1798 to the Present

GLL: Gay and Lesbian Literature

HGG: St. James Guide to Horror, Ghost & Gothic Writers

HLC: Hispanic Literature Criticism

HLCS: Hispanic Literature Criticism Supplement

HR: Harlem Renaissance: A Gale Critical Companion

HW: Hispanic Writers

IDFW: International Dictionary of Films and Filmmakers: Writers and Production Artists

IDTP: International Dictionary of Theatre: Playwrights

LAIT: Literature and Its Times

LAW: Latin American Writers

JRDA: Junior DISCovering Authors

LC: Literature Criticism from 1400 to 1800

MAICYA: Major Authors and Illustrators for Children and Young Adults

MAICYA: Major Authors and Illustrators for Children and Young Adults Supplement

MAWW: Modern American Women Writers

MJW: Modern Japanese Writers

MTCW: Major 20th-Century Writers

NCFS: Nonfiction Classics for Students

NCLC: Nineteenth-Century Literature Criticism

NFS: Novels for Students

NNAL: Native North American Literature

PAB: Poets: American and British

PC: Poetry Criticism

PFS: Poetry for Students

RGAL: Reference Guide to American Literature

RGEL: Reference Guide to English Literature

RGSF: Reference Guide to Short Fiction

RGWL: Reference Guide to World Literature

RHW: Twentieth-Century Romance and Historical Writers

SAAS: Something about the Author Autobiography Series

SATA: Something about the Author

SFW: St. James Guide to Science Fiction Writers

SSC: Short Story Criticism

SSFS: Short Stories for Students

TCLC: Twentieth-Century Literary Criticism

TCWW: Twentieth-Century Western Writers

WCH: Writers for Children

WLC: World Literature Criticism, 1500 to the Present

WLCS: World Literature Criticism Supplement

WLIT: World Literature and Its Times

WP: World Poets

YABC: Yesterday's Authors of Books for Children

YAW: St. James Guide to Young Adult Writers

The Author Index lists all of the authors featured in the Feminism in Literature *set. It includes references to the main author entries in volumes 1, 2, 3, 5, and 6; it also lists commentary on the featured author in other author entries and in other volumes of the set, which include topics associated with* Feminism in Literature. *Page references to author entries appear in boldface. The Author Index also includes birth and death dates, cross references between pseudonyms or name variants and actual names, and cross references to other Gale series in which the authors have appeared. A complete list of these sources is found facing the first page of the Author Index.*

A

Akhmatova, Anna 1888-1966 **5: 1–38**
　See also CA 19-20; 25-28R; CANR 35; CAP 1; CLC 11, 25, 64, 126; DA3; DAM POET; DLB 295; EW 10; EWL 3; MTCW 1, 2; PC 2, 55; RGWL 2, 3

Alcott, Louisa May 1832-1888 **2: 78, 147, 297–332**
　See also AAYA 20; AMWS 1; BPFB 1; BYA 2; CDALB 1865-1917; CLR 1, 38; DA; DA3; DAB; DAC; DAM MST, NOV; DLB 1, 42, 79, 223, 239, 242; DLBD 14; FW; JRDA; LAIT 2; MAICYA 1, 2; NCLC 6, 58, 83; NFS 12; RGAL 4; SATA 100; SSC 27; TUS; WCH; WLCWYA; YABC 1; YAW

Allende, Isabel 1942- **5: 39–64**
　See also AAYA 18; CA 125; 130; CANR 51, 74, 129; CDWLB 3; CLC 39, 57, 97, 170; CWW 2; DA3; DAM MULT, NOV; DLB 145; DNFS 1; EWL 3; FW; HLC 1; HW 1, 2; INT CA-130; LAIT 5; LAWS 1; LMFS 2; MTCW 1, 2; NCFS 1; NFS 6, 18; RGSF 2; RGWL 3; SSC 65; SSFS 11, 16; WLCS; WLIT 1

Angelou, Maya 1928- **5: 65–92**
　See also AAYA 7, 20; AMWS 4; BLC 1; BPFB 1; BW 2, 3; BYA 2; CA 65-68; CANR 19, 42, 65, 111; CDALBS; CLC 12, 35, 64, 77, 155; CLR 53; CP 7; CPW; CSW; CWP; DA; DA3; DAB; DAC; DAM MST, MULT, POET, POP; DLB 38; EWL 3; EXPN; EXPP; LAIT 4; MAICYA 2; MAICYAS 1; MAWW; MTCW 1, 2; NCFS 2; NFS 2; PC 32; PFS 2, 3; RGAL 4; SATA 49, 136; WLCS; WYA; YAW

Atwood, Margaret (Eleanor) 1939- **5: 93–124**
　See also AAYA 12, 47; AMWS 13; BEST 89:2; BPFB 1; CA 49-52; CANR 3, 24, 33, 59, 95; CLC 2, 3, 4, 8, 13, 15, 25, 44, 84, 135; CN 7; CP 7; CPW; CWP; DA; DA3; DAB; DAC; DAM MST, NOV, POET; DLB 53, 251; EWL 3; EXPN; FW; INT CANR-24; LAIT 5; MTCW 1, 2; NFS 4, 12, 13, 14; PC 8; PFS 7; RGSF 2; SATA 50; SSC 2, 46; SSFS 3, 13; TWA; WLC; WWE 1; YAW

Austen, Jane 1775-1817 **1: 122, 125, 220; 2: 104, 196, 333–384**
　See also AAYA 19; BRW 4; BRWC 1; BRWR 2; BYA 3; CD-BLB 1789-1832; DA; DA3; DAB; DAC; DAM MST, NOV; DLB 116; EXPN; LAIT 2; LATS 1; LMFS 1; NCLC 1, 13, 19, 33, 51, 81, 95, 119; NFS 1, 14, 18; TEA; WLC; WLIT 3; WYAS 1

B

Beauvoir, Simone (Lucie Ernestine Marie Bertrand) de 1908-1986 **5: 125–174**
　See also BPFB 1; CA 9-12R; 118; CANR 28, 61; CLC 1, 2, 4, 8,

F

French, Marilyn 1929- **5: 469–484**
    See also BPFB 1; CA 69-72;
    CANR 3, 31; CLC 10, 18, 60,
    177; CN 7; CPW; DAM DRAM,
    NOV, POP; FW; INT CANR-31;
    MTCW 1, 2

Fuller, Margaret 1810-1850 **3:**
    167–198
    See also AMWS 2; CDALB 1640-
    1865; DLB 1, 59, 73, 183, 223,
    239; FW; LMFS 1; NCLC 5, 50;
    SATA 25

G

Gilman, Charlotte (Anna) Perkins
    (Stetson) 1860-1935 **1:** 3–5, 314,
    325, 462–463; **5: 485–528**
    See also AMWS 11; BYA 11; CA
    106; 150; DLB 221; EXPS; FW;
    HGG; LAIT 2; MAWW; MTCW
    1; RGAL 4; RGSF 2; SFW 4;
    SSC 13, 62; SSFS 1, 18; TCLC
    9, 37, 117

H

Hansberry, Lorraine (Vivian)
    1930-1965 **6: 1–30**
    See also AAYA 25; AFAW 1, 2;
    AMWS 4; BLC 2; BW 1, 3; CA
    109; 25-28R; CABS 3; CAD;
    CANR 58; CDALB 1941-1968;
    CLC 17, 62; CWD; DA; DA3;
    DAB; DAC; DAM DRAM, MST,
    MULT; DC 2; DFS 2; DLB 7,
    38; EWL 3; FW; LAIT 4;
    MTCW 1, 2; RGAL 4; TUS

Head, Bessie 1937-1986 **6: 31–62**
    See also AFW; BLC 2; BW 2, 3;
    CA 29-32R; 119; CANR 25, 82;
    CDWLB 3; CLC 25, 67; DA3;
    DAM MULT; DLB 117, 225;
    EWL 3; EXPS; FW; MTCW 1,
    2; RGSF 2; SSC 52; SSFS 5, 13;
    WLIT 2; WWE 1

Hellman, Lillian (Florence)
    1906-1984 **6: 63–88**
    See also AAYA 47; AITN 1, 2;
    AMWS 1; CA 13-16R; 112;
    CAD; CANR 33; CLC 2, 4, 8,
    14, 18, 34, 44, 52; CWD; DA3;
    DAM DRAM; DC 1; DFS 1, 3,
    14; DLB 7, 228; DLBY 1984;
    EWL 3; FW; LAIT 3; MAWW;
    MTCW 1, 2; RGAL 4; TCLC
    119; TUS

Holley, Marietta 1836(?)-1926 **3:**
    199–220
    See also CA 118; DLB 11; TCLC
    99

Hurston, Zora Neale 1891-1960 **4:**
    31–32, 249–251, 485–492; **6:**
    89–126
    See also AAYA 15; AFAW 1, 2;
    AMWS 6; BLC 2; BW 1, 3; BYA
    12; CA 85-88; CANR 61;
    CDALBS; CLC 7, 30, 61; DA;
    DA3; DAC; DAM MST, MULT,
    NOV; DC 12; DFS 6; DLB 51,
    86; EWL 3; EXPN; EXPS; FW;
    HR 2; LAIT 3; LATS 1; LMFS 2;
    MAWW; MTCW 1, 2; NFS 3;
    RGAL 4; RGSF 2; SSC 4; SSFS
    1, 6, 11, 19; TCLC 121, 131;
    TUS; WLCS; YAW

J

Jacobs, Harriet A(nn) 1813(?)-1897
    3: 221–242
    See also AFAW 1, 2; DLB 239;
    FW; LAIT 2; NCLC 67; RGAL 4

Jewett, (Theodora) Sarah Orne
    1849-1909 **3: 243–274**
    See also AMW; AMWC 2;
    AMWR 2; CA 108; 127; CANR
    71; DLB 12, 74, 221; EXPS;
    FW; MAWW; NFS 15; RGAL 4;
    RGSF 2; SATA 15; SSC 6, 44;
    SSFS 4; TCLC 1, 22

Juana Inés de la Cruz, Sor
    1651(?)-1695 **1: 321–358**
    See also FW; HLCS 1; LAW; LC
    5; PC 24; RGWL 2, 3; WLIT 1

K

Kempe, Margery 1373(?)-1440(?) **1:**
    87, 193, 222, **359–392**
    See also DLB 146; LC 6, 56;
    RGEL 2

Kingston, Maxine (Ting Ting)
    Hong 1940- **4:** 493–496; **6:**
    127–150
    See also AAL; AAYA 8, 55;
    AMWS 5; BPFB 2; CA 69-72;
    CANR 13, 38, 74, 87, 128;
    CDALBS; CLC 12, 19, 58, 121;
    CN 7; DA3; DAM MULT, NOV;
    DLB 173, 212; DLBY 1980;
    EWL 3; FW; INT CANR-13;
    LAIT 5; MAWW; MTCW 1, 2;
    NFS 6; RGAL 4; SATA 53; SSFS
    3; WLCS

L

Lessing, Doris (May) 1919- **4:** 272,
    291, 294, 299; **6: 151–178**
    See also AFW; BRWS 1; CA
    9-12R; CAAS 14; CANR 33, 54,
    76, 122; CD 5; CDBLB 1960 to
    Present; CLC 1, 2, 3, 6, 10, 15,
    22, 40, 94, 170; CN 7; DA;
    DA3; DAB; DAC; DAM MST,
    NOV; DLB 15, 139; DLBY
    1985; EWL 3; EXPS; FW; LAIT
    4; MTCW 1, 2; RGEL 2; RGSF
    2; SFW 4; SSC 6, 61; SSFS 1,
    12; TEA; WLCS; WLIT 2, 4

M

Millay, Edna St. Vincent 1892-1950
    4: 245, 259; **6: 179–200**
    See also AMW; CA 104; 130;
    CDALB 1917-1929; DA; DA3;
    DAB; DAC; DAM MST, POET;
    DLB 45, 249; EWL 3; EXPP;
    MAWW; MTCW 1, 2; PAB; PC
    6; PFS 3, 17; RGAL 4; TCLC 4,
    49; TUS; WLCS; WP

Montagu, Mary (Pierrepont)
    Wortley 1689-1762 **1:** 116,
    118–119, 122, 193, 219–220,
    225–226, **393–422; 2:** 504, 506
    See also DLB 95, 101; LC 9, 57;
    PC 16; RGEL 2

Moore, Marianne (Craig)
    1887-1972 **4:** 244; **6: 201–232**
    See also AMW; CA 1-4R; 33-36R;
    CANR 3, 61; CDALB 1929-
    1941; CLC 1, 2, 4, 8, 10, 13,
    19, 47; DA; DA3; DAB; DAC;
    DAM MST, POET; DLB 45;
    DLBD 7; EWL 3; EXPP;
    MAWW; MTCW 1, 2; PAB; PC
    4, 49; PFS 14, 17; RGAL 4;
    SATA 20; TUS; WLCS; WP

Morrison, Toni 1931- **4:** 349–353;
    6: 233–266
    See also AAYA 1, 22; AFAW 1, 2;
    AMWC 1; AMWS 3; BLC 3;
    BPFB 2; BW 2, 3; CA 29-32R;
    CANR 27, 42, 67, 113, 124;
    CDALB 1968-1988; CLC 4, 10,
    22, 55, 81, 87, 173; CN 7;
    CPW; DA; DA3; DAB; DAC;
    DAM MST, MULT, NOV, POP;
    DLB 6, 33, 143; DLBY 1981;
    EWL 3; EXPN; FW; LAIT 2, 4;
    LATS 1; LMFS 2; MAWW;
    MTCW 1, 2; NFS 1, 6, 8, 14;
    RGAL 4; RHW; SATA 57, 144;
    SSFS 5; TUS; YAW

O

Oates, Joyce Carol 1938- **6: 267–292**

See also AAYA 15, 52; AITN 1; AMWS 2; BEST 89:2; BPFB 2; BYA 11; CA 5-8R; CANR 25, 45, 74, 113, 129; CDALB 1968-1988; CLC 1, 2, 3, 6, 9, 11, 15, 19, 33, 52, 108, 134; CN 7; CP 7; CPW; CWP; DA; DA3; DAB; DAC; DAM MST, NOV, POP; DLB 2, 5, 130; DLBY 1981; EWL 3; EXPS; FW; HGG; INT CANR-25; LAIT 4; MAWW; MTCW 1, 2; NFS 8; RGAL 4; RGSF 2; SSC 6, 70; SSFS 17; SUFW 2; TUS; WLC

P

Plath, Sylvia 1932-1963 **4: 297, 463, 466; 6: 293–328**

See also AAYA 13; AMWR 2; AMWS 1; BPFB 3; CA 19-20; CANR 34, 101; CAP 2; CDALB 1941-1968; CLC 1, 2, 3, 5, 9, 11, 14, 17, 50, 51, 62, 111; DA; DA3; DAB; DAC; DAM MST, POET; DLB 5, 6, 152; EWL 3; EXPN; EXPP; FW; LAIT 4; MAWW; MTCW 1, 2; NFS 1; PAB; PC 1, 37; PFS 1, 15; RGAL 4; SATA 96; TUS; WLC; WP; YAW

R

Rich, Adrienne (Cecile) 1929- **4: 385, 387, 511–521, 524–533; 6: 329–350**

See also AMWR 2; AMWS 1; CA 9-12R; CANR 20, 53, 74, 128; CDALBS; CLC 3, 6, 7, 11, 18, 36, 73, 76, 125; CP 7; CSW; CWP; DA3; DAM POET; DLB 5, 67; EWL 3; EXPP; FW; MAWW; MTCW 1, 2; PAB; PC 5; PFS 15; RGAL 4; WP

Rossetti, Christina (Georgina) 1830-1894 **2: 136–139; 3: 275–298**

See also AAYA 51; BRW 5; BYA 4; DA; DA3; DAB; DAC; DAM MST, POET; DLB 35, 163, 240; EXPP; LATS 1; MAICYA 1, 2; NCLC 2, 50, 66; PC 7; PFS 10, 14; RGEL 2; SATA 20; TEA; WCH; WLC

S

Sand, George 1804-1876 **3: 299–332**

See also DA; DA3; DAB; DAC; DAM MST, NOV; DLB 119, 192; EW 6; FW; GFL 1789 to the Present; NCLC 2, 42, 57; RGWL 2, 3; TWA; WLC

Sappho fl. 6th cent. B.C. **1: 423–470; 4: 243, 254, 258, 512; 5: 334–341; 6: 538**

See also CDWLB 1; CMLC 3, 67; DA3; DAM POET; DLB 176; PC 5; RGWL 2, 3; WP

Sedgwick, Catharine Maria 1789-1867 **2: 163–165; 3: 333–362**

See also DLB 1, 74, 183, 239, 243, 254; NCLC 19, 98; RGAL 4

Sexton, Anne (Harvey) 1928-1974 **6: 351–388**

See also AMWS 2; CA 1-4R; 53-56; CABS 2; CANR 3, 36; CDALB 1941-1968; CLC 2, 4, 6, 8, 10, 15, 53, 123; DA; DA3; DAB; DAC; DAM MST, POET; DLB 5, 169; EWL 3; EXPP; FW; MAWW; MTCW 1, 2; PAB; PC 2; PFS 4, 14; RGAL 4; SATA 10; TUS; WLC

Shelley, Mary Wollstonecraft (Godwin) 1797-1851 **3: 363–402**

See also AAYA 20; BPFB 3; BRW 3; BRWC 2; BRWS 3; BYA 5; CDBLB 1789-1832; DA; DA3; DAB; DAC; DAM MST, NOV; DLB 110, 116, 159, 178; EXPN; HGG; LAIT 1; LMFS 1, 2; NCLC 14, 59, 103; NFS 1; RGEL 2; SATA 29; SCFW; SFW 4; TEA; WLC; WLIT 3

Staël, Germaine de 1766-1817 **3: 403–426**

See also DLB 119, 192; EW 5; FW; GFL 1789 to the Present; NCLC 3, 91; RGWL 2, 3; TWA

Stanton, Elizabeth Cady 1815-1902 **2: 7, 59–65, 207–209, 211, 228–229, 231, 233, 235, 237–238, 240, 249–255, 259, 263, 269, 285, 287–290, 292–293; 3: 427–454**

See also CA 171; DLB 79; FW; TCLC 73

Stein, Gertrude 1874-1946 **4: 272, 278; 6: 389–432**

See also AMW; AMWC 2; CA 104; 132; CANR 108; CDALB 1917-1929; DA; DA3; DAB; DAC; DAM MST, NOV, POET; DC 19; DLB 4, 54, 86, 228; DLBD 15; EWL 3; EXPS; GLL 1; MAWW; MTCW 1, 2; NCFS

4; PC 18; RGAL 4; RGSF 2; SSC 42; SSFS 5; TCLC 1, 6, 28, 48; TUS; WLC; WP

Stowe, Harriet (Elizabeth) Beecher 1811-1896 **2: 74–75, 127, 147–150, 154–157, 159–165; 3: 455–491**

See also AAYA 53; AMWS 1; CDALB 1865-1917; DA; DA3; DAB; DAC; DAM MST, NOV; DLB 1, 12, 42, 74, 189, 239, 243; EXPN; JRDA; LAIT 2; MAICYA 1, 2; NCLC 3, 50, 133; NFS 6; RGAL 4; TUS; WLC; YABC 1

T

Tan, Amy (Ruth) 1952- **4: 493–497; 6: 433–464**

See also AAL; AAYA 9, 48; AMWS 10; BEST 89:3; BPFB 3; CA 136; CANR 54, 105; CDALBS; CLC 59, 120, 151; CN 7; CPW 1; DA3; DAM MULT, NOV, POP; DLB 173; EXPN; FW; LAIT 3, 5; MTCW 2; NFS 1, 13, 16; RGAL 4; SATA 75; SSFS 9; YAW

W

Walker, Alice (Malsenior) 1944- **6: 465–494**

See also AAYA 3, 33; AFAW 1, 2; AMWS 3; BEST 89:4; BLC 3; BPFB 3; BW 2, 3; CA 37-40R; CANR 9, 27, 49, 66, 82; CDALB 1968-1988; CLC 5, 6, 9, 19, 27, 46, 58, 103, 167; CN 7; CPW; CSW; DA; DA3; DAB; DAC; DAM MST, MULT, NOV, POET, POP; DLB 6, 33, 143; EWL 3; EXPN; EXPS; FW; INT CANR-27; LAIT 3; MAWW; MTCW 1, 2; NFS 5; PC 30; RGAL 4; RGSF 2; SATA 31; SSC 5; SSFS 2, 11; TUS; WLCS; YAW

Wharton, Edith (Newbold Jones) 1862-1937 **6: 495–534**

See also AAYA 25; AMW; AMWC 2; AMWR 1; BPFB 3; CA 104; 132; CDALB 1865-1917; DA; DA3; DAB; DAC; DAM MST, NOV; DLB 4, 9, 12, 78, 189; DLBD 13; EWL 3; EXPS; HGG; LAIT 2, 3; LATS 1; MAWW;

The Title Index alphabetically lists the titles of works written by the authors featured in volumes 1, 2, 3, 5, and 6 of Feminism in Literature *and provides page numbers or page ranges where commentary on these titles can be found. English translations of foreign titles and variations of titles are cross referenced to the title under which a work was originally published. Titles of novels, dramas, nonfiction books, and poetry, short story, or essay collections are printed in italics; individual poems, short stories, and essays are printed in body type within quotation marks; page references to illustrations appear in italic.*

A

Abahn Sabana David (Duras) **5:** 368

"The Abortion" (Sexton) **6:** 352, 365

The Absentee (Edgeworth) **3:** 99, 110–111, 125

Ada (Stein) **6:** 406

Adam Bede (Eliot) **3:** 130–132, *158*

"The Addict" (Sexton) **6:** 352

"Address: First Women's Rights Convention" (Stanton) **3:** 428–430

"Address to the Atheist" (Wheatley) **1:** 477

"An Address to the Deist" (Wheatley) **1:** 519

Adieux: A Farewell to Sartre (Beauvoir)
    See *Le céremonie des adieus: Suivi de entretiens avac Jean-Paul Sartre*

"Advancing Luna—and Ida B. Wells" (Walker) **6:** 475–476, 480–481

"African Images" (Walker) **6:** 473

"After Death" (Rossetti) **3:** 276, 282–288

The Age of Innocence (Wharton) **6:** 495–497, 506–507, 509, *520*

Agnes of Sorrento (Stowe) **3:** 456–457

Alexander's Bridge (Cather) **5:** 213–215, 247

Alias Grace (Atwood) **5:** 101–103, 105–107

"Alicia and I Talking on Edna's Steps" (Cisneros) **5:** 272

"Alicia Who Sees Mice" (Cisneros) **5:** 272

"All God's Children Need Radios" (Sexton) **6:** 353–357

All God's Children Need Traveling Shoes (Angelou) **5:** 66–76

All My Pretty Ones (Sexton) **6:** 352, 365, 367, 369, 370

"All My Pretty Ones" (Sexton) **6:** 352, 368

All Said and Done (Beauvoir)
    See *Tout compte fait*

"A Allegory on Wimmen's Rights" (Holley) (sidebar) **3:** 212

De l'Allemagne (de Staël) **3:** 405–406, 423; **4:** 403–404

"Am I a Snob?" (Woolf) **6:** 567

L'amant (Duras) **3:** 362; **5:** 359–360, 364–366, 375

L'amante anglaise (Duras) **5:** 368

"Amaranth" (H. D.) **1:** 438; **5:** 336–339

"Amé, Amo, Amaré" (Cisneros) **5:** 266

"America" (Angelou) **5:** 66

American Appetites (Oates) **6:** 275–277, 279

"Amnesiac" (Plath) **6:** 312

André (Sand) **3:** 312

"The Angel at the Grave" (Wharton) **6:** 507

"Angel of Beach Houses and Picnics" (Sexton) **6:** 384

"Angel of Fire and Genitals" (Sexton) **6:** 384

"Angels of the Love Affair" (Sexton) **6:** 383–384

"Anguiano Religious Articles Rosaries Statues . . ." (Cisneros) **5:** 258

"Anna Who Was Mad" (Sexton) **6:** 364

Anne Sexton: A Self-Portrait in Letters (Sexton) **6:** 377

secularism in **3**: 437

society reflected in literature **2**: 116–119

women Renaissance playwrights **1**: 202–218

women writers in 18th century **1**: 112–132

women writers in 19th century **2**: 99–109

World War II and women writers **4**: 261–270

English, Deirdre **2**: 67–71; **5**: 522

The English Woman's Journal (sidebar) **3**: 294

Engraving **4**: 87–88

Enlightenment **1**: 524–525; **2**: 40–42, 63

"Ennui" (Edgeworth) **3**: 94, 99, 107–110

Ensler, Eve **4**: 458–459

Enstad, Nan **4**: 94–117

"Entering the Literary Market" (Mermin) **2**: 129–140

Entre l'écriture (Cixous) **5**: 286

"Envy" (H. D.) **5**: 336–339

Ephron, Nora (sidebar) **6**: 75

"Epigram" (H. D.) **5**: 313

"An Epilogue To Mary, Queen of Scots" (Montagu) **1**: 403–404

Epistemology of the Closet (Sedgwick) **4**: 532–533

"An Epistle from a Lady in England, to a Gentleman at Avignon" (Tickell) **1**: 401–402

"Epistle from Arthur Grey, the Footman after his Condemnation for attempting a Rape" (Montagu) **1**: 403, 404

"Epistle from Mrs. Y[onge] to her Husband" (Montagu) **1**: 396–397

The Epistle of Othea to Hector (Christine). *See L'epistre d'Othéa*

"An Epistle to Lord B—t" (Montagu) **1**: 403–404

L'Epistre au dieu d'amours (Christine) **1**: 282, 283, 288; (sidebar) **1**: 290; **1**: 293–296

Epistre de la prison de vie humaine (Christine) **1**: 282, 283

L'epistre d'Othéa (Christine) **1**: 282, 304

"Epitaph for the Race of Man" (Millay) **6**: 180

Equal pay **4**: 5–7, 50, 366–367

See also Wages and salaries

Equal Rights Amendment (ERA) **4**: 408–411

abortion and **4**: 418–419

in Alaska **4**: 423

American Equal Rights Association **2**: 249–250

athletics legislation and **4**: 420

child custody legislation and **4**: 420

in Colorado **4**: 423

conflict in 1920s **4**: 224–231

Eastman, Crystal **4**: 18–19

feminist opposition to **4**: 387–388

Fourteenth Amendment and **4**: 417, 418

in Hawaii **4**: 423

in Illinois **4**: 419–421

inception **4**: 18–19

labor unions and **4**: 226–230

male criminal behavior and **4**: 420–421

march on Washington, D.C. **4**: *373*

marriage legislation and **4**: 420

in Maryland **4**: 423

in Massachusetts **4**: 423

in Montana **4**: 423

National Organization for Women **4**: 410–411

National Women's Party **4**: 18–19, 52, 224–230

in New Hampshire **4**: 423

in New Mexico **4**: 423–424

opposition to **4**: 408, 418–422

in Pennsylvania **4**: 424

race issue and **4**: 18–19

ratification of, state-by-state **4**: 417–425

in Utah **4**: 421–422

in Virginia **4**: 422–423

in Washington **4**: 424

in Wyoming **4**: 424

Equality. *See* Feminism, equality of the sexes

Equality League of Self-Supporting Women **4**: 206–207, 206–211

ERA. *See* Equal Rights Amendment

ER-America **4**: 409–410

Erdrich, Louise **5**: *433*, **433**, **433–467**

motherhood **5**: 434–436

mythology (sidebar) **5**: 452

National Book Critics Circle Award **5**: 433

principal works **5**: 434

sexuality in fiction **5**: 445–449

transformational power of female characters **5**: 443–449

women's relationships **5**: 436–443

Erdrich, Louise on **5**: 434–436

Erkkila, Betsy **1**: 482–493, 494–495; **3**: 65

"Eros" (H. D.) **1**: 438; **5**: 336–339

Eroticism

Bataille, G. **5**: 408

Beauvoir, Simone de **5**: 150–155

Broumas, Olga **4**: 516–517

Chopin, Kate **3**: 11–12

Stein, Gertrude **6**: 400–401

in Victorian era **3**: 11–12

See also Sexuality

"Der Essay als Form" (Adorno) **5**: 296–297

Essay on Irish Bulls (Edgeworth) **3**: 100–101, 104–106, 107, 111–112

An Essay on Mind, with Other Poems (Browning, E.) **2**: 467

Essay on Slavery and Abolitionism (Stowe) **3**: 475

"An Essay on the Noble Science of Self-Justification" (Edgeworth) **3**: 94, 117

L'Eté 80 (Duras) **5**: 384, 386

"The 'Eternal Eve' and 'The Newly Born Woman': Voices, Performance, and Marianne Moore's 'Marriage'" (Henderson) **6**: 224–231

Ethan Frome (Wharton) **6**: 495–497, 506–507; (sidebar) **6**: 527

domesticity in **6**: 525–528

gender roles in **6**: 527–528

narrative voice in **6**: 526

New England regionalism and **6**: 522–528

The Ethics of Ambiguity (Beauvoir). *See Pour une morale de l'ambiguité*

"Ethnic and Gender Identity in Zora Neal Hurston's *Their Eyes Were Watching God*" (Meisenhelder) **6**: 102–107

Europe, suffrage movement in **2**: 283–285; **4**: 149–158

See also specific European countries

"Eurydice" (H. D.) **5**: 327

Eva Luna (Allende) **5**: 40, 44, 46, 48–55

Evans, Mary Ann. *See* Eliot, George

Evans, Richard **4**: 148

Eve (biblical character) **1**: 58–59

Evelina; or, A Young Lady's Entrance into the World (Burney, F.) **2**: 503–505, 508–509, *517*

matriarchal power in **2**: 516–526

naming as motif **2**: 527–537

patriarchal power in **2**: 511–526

"Even now that Care" (Sidney, M.) **1**: 155–156

Evening (Akhmatova). *See Vecher*

"An Evening Praier" (Wheathill) **1**: 105

"Every Morning" (Walker) **6**: 473

"Everyday Use" (Walker) **6**: 470, 482–488

Eviction protests **4**: 43–44

Evolution, in Victorian era **2**: 414–415

Excerpt from an untitled, unpublished essay (Browning, E.) (sidebar) **2**: 477

Execution of Justice (Mann) **4**: 480

Mitchell, S. Weir and **5:** 485, 493, 511–512, 520–521
on periodicals **5:** 505
as political activist **5:** 486
principal works **5:** 487
relationship with parents **5:** 490
self-destruction of **4:** 462
sexual equality and **5:** 496–497
on sexual oppression **5:** 494–495
sexuality of **5:** 491
Stetson, Walter and **5:** 485, 490–495
Stewart, Martha and **5:** 505
suffrage and **5:** 492–493
women's culture and **6:** 520–521
Gilman, Houghton **5:** 495–496
Ginsberg, Allen **6:** 365–366
Ginsberg, Ruth Bader **4:** 360
"Girl" (Kincaid) **4:** 449–450
The Girl Strike Leader **4:** 100–101
Girls of Slender Means (Spark) **4:** 296
"Giving Birth" (Atwood) **5:** 106
Giving Up the Ghost (Moraga) **5:** 450
Glasgow, Joanne **5:** 415–416
Glaspell, Susan **4:** 306–307, 311; (sidebar) **4:** 324; **4:** 324–330, 330
"Glazed Glitter" (Stein) **6:** 414–415
Gleadle, Kathryn **2:** 53–57
"Glimpses into My Own Life and Literary Character" (Browning, E.) **2:** 469–471
The Glimpses of the Moon (Wharton) **6:** 508
Globalization
of feminism **4:** 395–403
of suffrage movement **2:** 284–285; **4:** 147–158
"Goblin Market" (Rossetti) **3:** 276, 290–295
Goblin Market, and Other Poems (Rossetti) **3:** 276, 282, 293–294
Godineau, Dominique **3:** 418
The Gods Arrive (Wharton) **6:** 496, 507
God's Mercy Surmounting Man's Cruelty (Hanson) **1:** 257–261
Godwin, William **1:** 537; (sidebar) **1:** 558
"Gold Coast's Rulers Go: Ghana Moves to Freedom" (Hansberry) **6:** 11
Goldblatt, Patricia F. **5:** 100–108
Golden, Catherine **5:** 507–519
The Golden Notebook (Lessing) **6:** 152
compared to *Play with a Tiger* **6:** 164–165, 168
feminine identity in **6:** 156–159, 162

liberation of female protagonist in **6:** 173–176
preface **6:** 153–156
women in (sidebar) **6:** 157
women's reactions to **6:** 154–155
"Golden Speech" (Elizabeth I) **1:** 188
Goldman, Emma **4:** 7–9; (sidebar) **4:** 9
Goldmann, Lucien **4:** 483–484
Goncourt Prize **5:** 375
Gone to Soldiers (Piercy) **4:** 296–297
"Good Friend" (H. D.) **5:** 327, 332–333
Good Night Willie Lee, I'll See You in The Morning (Walker) **6:** 471–472, 473
The Good Soldier: A Tale of Passion (Ford) **4:** 76–77
The Good Terrorist (Lessing) **6:** 152
Good Wives (Alcott) **2:** 298
Goodman, Susan **6:** 506
Gorsky, Susan Rubinow **2:** 112–120
"The Gospel According to Jane Eyre: The Suttee and the Seraglio" (Ward, M. C.) **2:** 420–427
Gouges, Olympe de **1:** 199–201
Government
African Americans in **4:** 40
business and **4:** 17–18
Chisolm, Shirley (sidebar) **4:** 388
against married female employees **4:** 36
women in **4:** 39, 406–407
women in judiciary **4:** 374–375
Governor General's Award **5:** 93
"The Gradual Making of *The Making of Americans*" (Stein) **6:** 429
Graham, Colin **3:** 115–119
Graham, Shirley **4:** 335–337
Grahn, Judy **4:** 517–519; **6:** 397–398
The Grandmothers (Lessing) **6:** 152
"Granite and Steel" (Moore) **6:** 212, 229
The Grass Is Singing (Lessing) **6:** 151–152
Grassroots action **4:** 376–377
Gray, Mary **6:** 374–377
Great Depression **4:** 33–36
Great Instruction (Catherine the Great) **1:** 173–175
"The Great Lawsuit. Man *versus* Men. Woman *versus* Women" (Fuller) **3:** 169–172, 174, 183
The Great Scourge and How to End It (Pankhurst, C.) **4:** 144

The Greater Inclination (Wharton) **6:** 495
Greece, ancient
classical rhetoric **1:** 459–468
political literature **1:** 20
role of Athenian women **1:** 22–23
role of Spartan women **1:** 12–14
roots of misogyny in **1:** 15–23
sacred spaces **1:** 462
sexual reproduction beliefs **1:** 17–23
women in mythology **1:** 53–56
Green, William **4:** 44
Greenfield, Susan C. **2:** 516–527
Greenwald, Elissa (sidebar) **6:** 342
Greer, Germaine (sidebar) **4:** 354; **4:** 448–449, 465–466; **5:** 410
Greg, W. R. **2:** 107
Gregory, Horace **4:** 72
Grewal, Gurleen **6:** 243–253
Grier, William S. **5:** 200
Griffin, Alice **6:** 82–86
Griffin, Susan E. **5:** 273–279
Grimké, Angelina Emily (sidebar) **2:** 249; **4:** 333–334
Grimké, Sarah Moore (sidebar) **2:** 249
Griswold v. Connecticut (1961) **4:** 58
Grogan, Susan K. **2:** 34–46
Grössinger, Christa **1:** 56–63
The Group (McCarthy) **4:** 464–465
Grubbs, Judith Evans **1:** 30–34
Grundy, Isobel **1:** 218–228, 399–406
"Guadalupe the Sex Goddess" (Cisneros) **5:** 266
Guattari, Felix **6:** 247–248
on 20th-century women writers **4:** 76–85, 271–304
on Chopin, Kate **3:** 5–30
on H. D. **5:** 337, 342
on *Jane Eyre* **2:** 405–413
misogyny of Wollestonecraft, Mary **1:** 558–569
on Sappho **1:** 432–444
on "The Yellow Wallpaper" **5:** 515
Gubar, Susan **4:** 484–485
on 20th-century women writers **4:** 76–85, 271–304
on Chopin, Kate **3:** 5–30
on *Jane Eyre* **2:** 405–413
on Sappho **1:** 432–444
on Wollenstonecraft **1:** 558–569
on "The Yellow Wallpaper" **5:** 515
Gunther-Canada, Wendy **1:** 538–550
Gustafson, Sandra M. **3:** 182
Gutwirth, Madelyn **3:** 417–418
Guy, John **1:** 167

"'Known in the Brain and Known in the Flesh': Gender, Race, and the Vulnerable Body in *Tracks*" (Tanner) **5**: 449–467
Kollwitz, Käthe **4**: 88–89
Kolodny, Annette (sidebar) **3**: 181; **4**: 497–511; **5**: 509, 513, 516, 520
Kotzebue, August von **2**: 350–352
Kraditor, Aileen **4**: 177
Krafft-Ebing, Richard von **5**: 227–228, 230–231
Kristeva, Julia **3**: 283–284; **5**: 179; **6**: 386
  on feminism **6**: 558–560
  on Oedipus **6**: 381
Krouse, Agate Nesaule **6**: 164–172
Kruger, Barbara **4**: 418
Kumin, Maxine **6**: 357–372, 358, 379
Kurtzman, Mary **6**: 314–315

L

LA (Cixous) **5**: 291
La Leche League **4**: 459
Labor practices
  factories **2**: 10–12, *11*, 34–38
  legislation and **4**: 153
  Muller v. Oregon **4**: 17–18
  regulations of 1920s **4**: 18
  See also Employment
Labor strikes **4**: 44
  California Sanitary Canning Company **4**: 45
  Chicago garment strike of 1910 **4**: 106
  Elizabethton, North Carolina **4**: 25
  in films **4**: 100–101
  of post-WW I society **4**: 15–16
  See also Labor unions
Labor unions
  1920s factories **4**: 24–25
  African American women in **4**: 46
  demonstrations (sidebar) **4**: 20
  Equal Rights Amendment and **4**: 226–230
  legislation and **4**: 44–45
  women in **4**: 44–47, 53
  See also Labor strikes
"Laborers for Liberty: 1865-1890" (Sigerman) **2**: 248–254
Lacan, Jacques **1**: 553–554, 558–559; **3**: 87
  Cixous, Hélène and **5**: 291
  psychoanalysis and **5**: 365–366
Lacey, Candida **1**: 120
Ladies' Home Journal **4**: 36
Ladies' Voices (Stein) **6**: 390

The Ladies' World **4**: 95, 96, 101–102, 108–112
"The Lady in the Pink Mustang" (Erdrich) **5**: 444
"Lady Lazarus" (Plath) **4**: 520; **6**: 294, 295, 304–306
Lady Oracle (Atwood) **5**: 94, 101, 103–107, 108; (sidebar) **5**: 114
"The Lady Who Does Her Own Work" (Stowe) **3**: 487
The Lady's New Year's Gift; or Advice to a Daughter (Halifax) **1**: 141–142
"The Lady's Resolve" (Montagu) **1**: 403
Lais (sidebar) **1**: 70
Lamb, Charles **5**: 31
Lamb, Mary Ellen **1**: 162–163
Lamb, Myrna **4**: 477–478
Lambert, Deborah G. **5**: 244–251
Lamonica, Drew **5**: 457–464
Land of the Free (Lange and Taylor) **4**: 121–122
Landlocked (Lessing) **6**: 160
Lane, Ann **5**: 501
Lange, Anne **4**: *469*
Lange, Dorothea **4**: 121–122
Langland, Elizabeth **2**: 189–190
Language
  biculturalism and **6**: 438–442
  choices of Christine de Pizan **1**: 311–317
  Cisneros, Sandra on (sidebar) **5**: 280
  cultural identity and **6**: 437–442
  in defense of women **1**: 311–317
  as female empowerment **5**: 475–476
  feminist, male readers and **4**: 500
  as political weapon **2**: 60–65
  in sentimental novels **2**: 126–129
  sexual violence and **6**: 281–290
  song in (sidebar) **5**: 293
  Stein, Gertrude and **6**: 422–430
  in Victorian literature **2**: 107
"The Language of Discretion" (Tan) **6**: 438
Lanser, Susan L. **6**: 453
Lant, Kathleen Margaret **6**: 316–318
Lanyer, Aemilia **1**: 212
"Lapus Lazuli" (Yeats) **4**: 513
Larsen, Jeanne **4**: 252–261
Larsen, Nella **4**: 249
Lascelles, Mary **2**: 338–344
Lassner, Phyllis **4**: 261–271
"The Last Asset" (Wharton) **6**: 496
The Last Man (Shelley) **3**: 364, 366–373, 397–398

The Last of the Mohicans (Cooper, J.) **3**: 354
The Last Report on the Miracles at Little No Horse (Erdrich) **5**: 434
"The Laugh of Medusa" (Cixous). *See* "Le rire de la Méduse"
"'Laughing That I May Not Weep': Mary Shelley's Short Fiction and Her Novels" (Markley) **3**: 366–373
Laurencin, Marie **4**: 89–90
Lauretis, Teresa de **3**: 189–190; **4**: 532–533; **6**: 257, 282
Lavezzo, Kathy **1**: 377–391
Law school **4**: 414–415
Lawes Resolutions of Womens Rights (anonymous) **1**: 166
Lawrence, D. H. **4**: 81–82
Lawrence, Margaret **2**: 393–399
Le Roy, Virginia **4**: 129–132
Le Sueur, Meridel **4**: 246–247
Leaflets (Rich) **6**: 330, 345
Leapor, Mary **1**: 223
Leavitt, Mary **4**: 150
Lebeden, Jean (sidebar) **3**: 466
Lecturers, importance of **2**: 46–50
Lectures in America (Stein) **6**: 390
Lederer, Katherine **6**: 77
Legacy of a Dying Mother (Bell) **1**: 253–254
"The Legacy of American Victorianism" (Douglas) **2**: 71–77
"Legal Developments in the Courts and in the States: The Brooding Omnipresence of ERA" (Berry) **4**: 417–427
"Legend of Jubal" (Eliot) **3**: 159
Legend of Jubal and Other Poems (Eliot) **3**: 159
Legend of Jubal and Other Poems, Old and New (Eliot) **3**: 159
"The Legend of Sleepy Hollow" (Irving) **2**: 157–161
Legislation
  in athletics **4**: 420
  Atkinson v. Atkinson **4**: 420
  Baker v. Nelson **4**: 419
  birth control **4**: 7–9, 35, 55–64
  Bowe et al. v. Colgate Palmolive **4**: 415
  Doe v. Bolton **4**: 419
  employment **4**: 44–45, 153
  Equal Rights Amendment **4**: 18–19, 224–231, *373*, 387–388, 408–411, 417–425
  family law **4**: 420, 421–422
  Harris v. McRae **4**: 419
  Indian Reorganization Act of 1934 **4**: 42
  last names in marriage **4**: 420
  legal status of ancient Roman women **1**: 30–33
  Maher v. Doe **4**: 419
  manus **1**: 31–32

feminism in **4:** 428–429

The Forerunner **5:** 486

Fortune **4:** 120, 122–123

Fraser's Magazine **2:** 475

Freedom **6:** 11

Freedomways **6:** 8

Freewoman **4:** 143–144

The Germ **3:** 276

Gilman, Charlotte Perkins on **5:** 505

Harper's Bazaar **4:** 125

The Keepsake **3:** 367

Ladies' Home Journal **4:** 36

The Ladies' World **4:** 95, 96, 101–102, 108–112

Life **4:** 119–120

The Lily **2:** 64

Little Review (sidebar) **4:** 268

Monthly Review **1:** 412–414, 417, 419

Ms. **4:** 405

The Nation **3:** 5

The National Citizen and Ballot Box **2:** 293

The National Era **3:** 457

New England Magazine **5:** 486, 509

The New Freewoman **4:** *143*

New Left Notes **4:** 388

New Northwest **2:** 277, **2:** 279

New York Daily Tribune **3:** 168

New York Times **4:** 36–37

New York World **4:** 189

Obliques **5:** 383

Opportunity **6:** 95

Outlook and Independent **4:** 36

Paris Review **6:** 372–375

penny press newspapers **2:** 64

Peterson's Magazine **3:** 214

photography in **4:** 119, 124–125

Revolution **2:** 251–252; (sidebar) **3:** 451

Sinister Wisdom (Rich) **6:** 337

"Le Surréalisme au service de la révolution" (journal) **5:** 382

Les temps modernes **5:** 125

Time **4:** *499*

Woman's Journal **2:** 252, 259, 311

Women's Voice **4:** 19

Perkins, Annie **5:** 191–200

Perkins, Frances **4:** 39, 42–43

Perkins, Kathy **4:** 335

Perloff, Marjorie **6:** 321–322

Perry, Ruth **1:** 114–115

Perry, Trixie **4:** 25

Persephone **3:** 82–89; **5:** 303–310

"Personalities" (Woolf, V.) **6:** 555

Persuasion (Austen) **2:** 334, 354

Peters, Phillis. *See* Wheatley, Phillis

Peterson's Magazine **3:** 214

Peticion que en forma causidica presenta al Tribunal Divino la Madre Juana Ines de la Cruz, por impetrar perdon de sus culpas (Cruz) **1:** 335–336

La petite Fadette (Sand) **3:** 300

Petite, Joseph **6:** 279–281

Les petits chevaux de Tarquinia (Duras) **5:** 360

Petrie v. Illinois High School Association **4:** 420

Pettegrew, John **1:** 146–150

"A Petticoat" (Stein) **6:** 416

Pfeiffer, Michelle **6:** *520*

"Pheasant" (Stein) **6:** 419

Phelps v. Bing (1974) **4:** 420

"The Phenomenology of Anger" (Rich) **6:** 341

The Phil Donahue Show **4:** 459

Philco **4:** 44

"Phillis Wheatley's Construction of Otherness and the Rhetoric of Performed Ideology" (Balkun) **1:** 509–521

"The Philosopher" (Brontë, E.) **2:** 433–434, 438–439

A Philosophical Enquiry into the Origins of Our Ideas of the Sublime and the Beautiful (Burke) **2:** 434

"Philosophical Satire" (Cruz). *See* "Sátira filosófica"

Philosophy

    Chinese **1:** 74–77

    exclusion of women **5:** 474

    existentialism **5:** 478–479

    Hypatia **1:** 79–83

    of Wollstonecraft, Mary **1:** 531–538

Photography

    Beals, Jesse Tarbox **4:** 117–118

    Bourke-White, Margaret **4:** 120–121

    Bubley, Esther **4:** 121

    Collins, Marjory **4:** 121

    Farm Security Administration **4:** 121–123

    fashion **4:** 123–125

    halftone printing **4:** 117, 121–122

    Johnson, Frances Benjamin **4:** 118

    Kanaga, Consuelo **4:** 118–119

    Lange, Dorothea **4:** 121–122

    of *Life* **4:** 119–120

    Migrant Mother **4:** 121–122

    Standard Oil and **4:** 123

    Standard Oil of New Jersey Photographic Project **4:** 123

Physiology of women **2:** 42–43, 178–179

"Picasso" (Stein) **6:** 417–418

Picasso, Pablo **6:** 405–407

Pictures of the Floating World (Lowell) **4:** 255–256

Piercy, Marge **4:** 296–297

Pierpont, Claudia Roth **6:** 93–102, 402–410; (sidebar) **6:** 513

Pilgrimage (Richardson, D.) **4:** 70–75

Pilkington, Laetitia **1:** 218

Pinch, Adela **2:** 481

Pinckney, Eliza Lucas **1:** 271–278

"Pity me not because the light of day" (Millay) **6:** 183

El plan infinito (Allende) **5:** 39–40

Plan of a Novel (Austen) **2:** 345

"Planetarium" (Rich) **6:** 335

Planned Parenthood **4:** 360, 361

Planned Parenthood of Southeastern Pennsylvania v. Casey (1992) **4:** 360

Plantain (Akhmatova). *See Podorozhnik*

Plath, Sylvia **4:** 297, 463, 466, 520; **6:** *293*, **293–328**

    as confessional poet **6:** 302–306

    death as theme **6:** 294

    female beauty standards **6:** 310–312

    female imagery **6:** 309–315

    femininity, objectification of **6:** 297–306

    Gothic elements in poetry **6:** 300–301

    Hughes, Ted and (sidebar) **6:** 297

    images of women **6:** 299–300

    infertility **6:** 310

    motherhood **6:** 310

    Oates, Joyce Carol on **6:** 295

    principal works **6:** 295

    prostitution as metaphor **6:** 303

    self-fulfillment (sidebar) **6:** 297

    stylistic technique **6:** 297–299

"Plath's Poems about Women" (Wagner-Martin) **6:** 309–316

Plato **1:** 19–20

Plato, Ann **2:** 143

Play It As It Lays (Didion) **4:** 466

Play with a Tiger (Lessing) **6:** 164–168, 172

Playing in the Dark: Whiteness and the Literary Imagination (Morrison) **6:** 234, 244

Plays. *See* Drama

Plays (Cavendish) **1:** 208

Plays Never Before Printed (Cavendish) **1:** 208

"Plenary Speech, Fourth World Conference on Women. September 12, 1995, Beijing, People's Republic of China" (Abzug) (sidebar) **4:** 404

Plum Bun (Fauset) **4:** 249

"The Plumet Basilisk" (Moore) **6:** 220

Podorozhnik (Akhmatova) **5:** 4, 10

"Poem 271" (Falk) **3:** 62–64